THE ENCYCLOPEDIA OF FOOTBALL

Second
Revised
Edition

THE ENCYCLOPEDIA
OF FOOTBALL

SECOND REVISED EDITION

By ROGER TREAT

A. S. BARNES & CO.
NEW YORK

TO

Peter and John Treat

FOREWORD
by
PETE ROZELLE

Commissioner of the National Football League, 1960-1961

For their efforts in producing and now revising and republishing *The Encyclopedia of Football,* which is the official encyclopedia of the National Football League, A. S. Barnes & Company deserve the thanks and congratulations of everyone associated with the National Football League.

Roger Treat, as editor, and his associates have brought forth a monumental amount of information about major league football that will be a welcome addition to the book shelves of all sports-loving Americans.

The painstaking manner in which the names of players, clubs and coaches; the history of the game, individual and team statistics and other information was collected, edited and placed in this volume is evident in each of its pages. It was truly a tremendous task.

We of the National Football League are proud of this book. It bears witness to the sound growth of the sport that had its inception in 1895. Along the way to its present position, it once numbered among its believers "Mr. Baseball," Connie Mack, who guided a professional team in 1902.

From the formation of the American Professional Football League in 1920, until today, the growth has been phenomenal. The problems of development created many failures, caused many heartbreaks, but they also served to make more determined those who saw ahead the brilliant future of professional football.

Whatever success the National Football League has had is due, in no small measure, to the wholehearted support it has received through the years from newspapermen, radio announcers and commentators, and, more recently, television announcers and commentators.

To the spectator whose passage through the turnstiles brought the wherewithal to make it possible to continue, we owe a special tribute. The fan, whose loyalty, year in and year out, has contributed his support to our teams, calls for the gratitude of all who are interested in this great game.

The Encyclopedia of Football is, in itself, a tribute to all those who have, in small or large measure, played a part in making major league football one of the nation's most popular sports.

THE PROS COME OF AGE

by **PERIAN CONERLY**
(Mrs. Charlie Conerly, *New York Giants*)

It is totally insignificant that what is generally considered the beginning of the modern era of professional football coincides with the arrival of the Conerlys on the scene. None the less, during the years 1948-61 we have seen the game grow from a stuttering stepchild into the darling of the sports world. Extensive television coverage no doubt greatly hastened its acceptance as a major sport, and today's children grow up with the game. Any sports-minded sixth grader can quote the vital statistics of every prominent player in the league. By contrast, Charlie played in the first professional game he ever saw.

To me the most heart-warming trend in the years 1948-61 concerns the enlightened attitude of the general public toward the game of professional football and more especially toward the men who play it. The man on the street is now educated to the fact that the game requires a mind as well as a body. Consequently, business firms in increasing numbers are recognizing the wisdom of adding these personable, college-educated, poised young men to their public relations staffs.

I have still another criterion for measuring this evolution of attitude. It concerns tone of voice. "Your husband plays PROFESSIONAL football?" has been the stock opening line of new acquaintances since our marriage in 1949. It remains so in 1961. But the exclamation today bears not a trace of pity.

Women are notorious for radical innovations in styles of dress, but a snapshot of rookie Conerly sporting the close-fitting leather helmet universally worn in 1948 would evoke as hearty a laugh as a picture of me wearing the ankle-trailing skirt of that year's "new look."

Needless to say, today's plastic helmets, lined with sponge rubber and fitted with webbing which acts as a shock absorber, afford far superior protection. Sponge rubber has also replaced the bulkier stuffing formerly used in the various body pads, thus lightening the player's load and allowing him increased speed and maneuverability. The use of lightweight miracle fabrics in jerseys and pants adds greatly to his comfort. The advent of practical face masks which do not impair the wearer's vision has been a boon in curtailing face injuries. Charlie comments wistfully that had such masks been available at the start of his career, his nose might possibly have retained its original shape.

Pro football has been my life, our life, and it has been good to us and to so many of our friends. It was a long road from a small high school in Mississippi to Charlie's honor day at Yankee Stadium and to my writing about football for newspapers and for this Encyclopedia. We are both grateful for the good fortune that started us on the way as well as for the busy throwing arm of my husband that kept us going.

THEIR BIG DAY—PERIAN AND CHARLES CONERLY, THRILLED BY THE CHEERS OF NEARLY 70,000 FANS, ENJOY "CONERLY DAY" AT YANKEE STADIUM, NEW YORK CITY, IN THE FALL OF 1959. THEY RECEIVED AN UNUSUALLY LARGE NUMBER OF GIFTS FROM FANS. IT WAS THIS SEASON THAT CONERLY WAS OFFICIALLY THE BEST PASSER IN THE NFL. MRS. CONERLY HAS BECOME FAMOUS AS THE AUTHOR OF FOOTBALL ARTICLES IN MANY NEWSPAPERS, INCLUDING *The New York Times*. SHE IS CONSIDERED ONE OF THE KEENEST ANALYSTS OF THE GAME.

PREFACE

"It's like a lightning-fast chess game with pawns weighing 250 pounds. I make my gambit; the defense makes the counter-play. If all my pawns, castles, knights and bishops do what they are supposed to do, my king—that's the ball carrier—goes over for a touchdown. The tiniest mistake means disaster. A guard shifts his feet and gives the play away. A halfback takes a peek at the defensive end and tells him, 'Here I come, brother, get ready.' Brains win in this league; brains and psychology."

That, to a veteran quarterback in the National Football League, is major league football, a kingdom where men of intense competitive fire play the game for pay, but would play it for free if no salary were forthcoming. They deny this, but this ancient observer, who knows them well, would bet on it.

For these men are a race apart. Football is as essential to them as breathing. Their *esprit de corps* is tremendous; their personal valor is majestic. The painful, blue-black bruises they carry from August to December, the shoulder separations, the twisted bone-joints and mangled muscles are minor annoyances to be overcome each Sunday afternoon with gallons of novocaine. The blackened eyes and lost teeth are part of the fun.

Through many seasons the writer has known these players. In the dressing rooms before and after victory and defeat; at the training camps where the All America rookie learns with dramatic suddenness that he knows very little about football; through the long train rides from coast to coast; in their homes with their wives and children; in the hospitals where they mend their broken bones. His admiration grew until it had to pour out on paper.

Thus this history.

Who were (and are) they? What did they do? Who taught them how to do it? These were the simple questions proposed by A. S. Barnes and Company, as the project started.

It was decided to begin the formal listing of statistics with the season of 1921. But the league itself kept no records until 1933. After that the material was available and the collecting of it routine. Before that was a fourteen-year void that had to be filled through excavations and research which might not have bewildered the FBI but were certainly a catastrophic experience for an amateur sleuth.

A card system was created to pick up the playing records of each man. One by one these entries were gleaned from flaky, old programs, brittle newspaper clippings, microfilms, record books and the memories of many men until nearly forty thousand individual "years played" were accumulated.

Without monumental help from many sources, this volume could never have been completed. The list of contributors follows, and if any have been shuffled aside in the confusion of ceiling-high piles of data, an apology is offered in advance.

An SOS was broadcast in all directions, endorsed by the late Commissioner Bert Bell of the NFL. The response was heart-warming. George Calhoun of Green Bay, Wisconsin, forwarded his precious, and massive, files and proved to be a true triple-threat on digging up facts which once seemed as inaccessible as the vital statistics on the population of Mars. Edward Caswell checked in from Buffalo, New York, with proof that he had been a major league football fanatic for years and years, keeping records and files of his own just for the fun of it. These two men have been the main sources of supply, the arsenals of difficult data. They are both fervent football fanatics and the writer is eternally grateful for the hours of work they have contributed to this production.

The office of the Commissioner of the National Football League has been drained of its records. Commissioner Bert Bell himself, later Commissioner "Pete" Rozelle; Joe Labrum, his assistant; the office staff, all have been loyal co-workers.

Several who were active in the league in by-gone days have contributed. Robert Haines of the old Frankford Yellowjackets; Val Ness of the Minneapolis Maroons; Ed Simandl of Orange and Newark; Ole Haugsrud of Duluth in the days of the Eskimos;

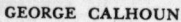
GEORGE CALHOUN   EDWARD CASWELL

Ned Kornaus of Chicago, another statistical maniac; Carroll Sollars of Mansfield, Ohio; Jim Schlemmer, Akron, Ohio, sports editor, an expert on the times when Canton, Dayton, Columbus, Hammond, Racine and Rock Island fielded their teams; Eddie Cook, once a frantic assistant in the Sports Department of the Washington *Daily News,* who found himself working once more for his old boss.

Jim Conzelman, the "Mad Genius" of the Chicago Cardinals' days of glory spearheaded by the "Dream Backfield" of a few years ago, dug into his memory of less abundant years with the Rock Island Independents, the Milwaukee Badgers, the Detroit Panthers, the Providence Steamrollers and the original Chicago (Staley) Bears, to fill in many gaps in the records. All the charter members, such as Steve Owen, Curly Lambeau, George Halas and Paddy Driscoll, who took their lumps before the days of novocaine, did their share as co-editors.

From the shadows of the early days, old players popped up to add information on themselves and teammates. Frank Lane, the frantic major league baseball trader, who was a guard for Cincinnati in 1921; Dr. George Munns (retired), who played on the same team to finance his medical education; John Bonadies of Hartford and Dr. Vincent LaCava, who managed the Hartford Blues; Joseph LaBissoniere of Hammond; Dr. Joseph Alexander of the early Giants, Rochester and Milwaukee; Rudolph Tersch of Minneapolis; Ben Friedman of Cleveland, Detroit, New York and Brooklyn; Barlow Irvin of Buffalo and Tommy Hughitt of the same team; Oliver Kraehe of the 1923 St. Louis team; Wilfrid Smith, sports editor of the Chicago *Tribune,* who played with Hammond and the Chicago Cardinals; John "Bunny" Barrett of Akron, Detroit and the Pottsville Maroons; Fred Putzier of Minneapolis; Walter Flanagan of the Rock Island years of glory, and "Mike" Wilson of the same team, now boss of NFL officials; John Lee Snoots, teammate of the fabulous Nesser brothers of Columbus Panhandle years, before the NFL was born.

Others did their share, like Homer Ruh of Columbus; Ray Witter of Rochester; Oscar "Oc" Anderson of Buffalo; Edward Hunt of the Hartford Blues; Milton Ghee of Canton and Hammond; Frank Bucher of Pottsville and Detroit; David Reese of Dayton; Gale Bullman of Columbus; Francis Matteo of Rochester, and Leo Lyons, who managed the team; Andy Nemecek of Columbus; Arda Bowser of Canton and Cleveland; Adrian Baril of Milwaukee and Minneapolis; Roman Brumm of Milwaukee and Racine; Francis Bacon of Dayton and Ken Huffine of the same team.

One of the most helpful, to whom must go special gratitude, was Jack R. Brown of the old Dayton Triangles, now athletic director of the University of Dayton, which has always turned out a fine crop of pro players; and to E. Paul "Deke" Lynch of Columbus; Aaron Hertzman of Louisville, one of the pioneers and manager of early Louisville teams; Fred Heinisch of Racine; W. Roy "Link" Lyman of the old Bears; Edward Carroll of Canton, and fans like Richard Geisler of Washington, John Crelli of Pittsburgh and Walter Farquhar of Pottsville, who like to relive the colorful, older days in the welcome letters.

The story and statistics of the All America Football Conference came by courtesy of Joe Petritz, former publicity director of Notre Dame and the AAFC. To the late Arch Ward, sports editor, and Ed Prell, major league football writer, of the Chicago *Tribune,* and to Wilfrid Smith, present sports editor, my thanks for the story of the All Star games at Chicago.

Al Ward, publicity director of the American Football League, helped keep those records straight.

The owners, publicity directors, coaches and other officials of the active clubs were harassed with inquiries, bombarded with questionnaires. They responded as nobly from the front office as their more muscular co-workers do on the playing fields.

To the registrars of more than five hundred colleges who searched their records for minor facts and reported them promptly, a salute.

Finally, for countless hours of clerical drudgery, reshuffling of lists, addressing of hundreds of envelopes, thanks to my own personal "staff": my late mother, Mrs. Esther Treat Mills; my wife, Gerda Dahl Treat, my two sons, John and Peter Treat; and to Leo McDermott, Jim Deakin, Joe Sauer, Jr., and Sue Hughes, who all contributed many hours.

Source books included: *The New Encyclopedia of Sports* by Frank Menke (A. S. Barnes, New York); *The Chicago Bears* by Howard Roberts (G. P. Putnam's Sons, New York); *My Life with the Redskins* by Corinne Griffith Marshall (A. S. Barnes, New York); *The Green Bay Packers* by Arch Ward (G. P. Putnam's Sons, New York); *Football Facts and Figures* by Dr. L. H. Baker (Farrar & Rinehart, New York); *My Greatest Day in Football* by Murray Goodman and Leonard Lewin (A. S. Barnes, New York); *The Greatest Sports Stories from the New York Times* by Allison Danzig and Peter Brandwein (A. S. Barnes, New York); *Professional Football* by Dr. William March; *Record and Rules Manual of the National Football League* from 1941 through 1961; *The National Football Guide* from 1937 through 1940; *Record Manuals of the All America Football Conference* from 1946 through 1949.

CONTENTS

CHAPTER   **PAGE**

THE ENCYCLOPEDIA OF FOOTBALL

*Second
Revised
Edition*

CHAPTER I
THE STORY OF THE GAME

THE EVOLUTION OF FOOTBALL

The celestial spirit of an unknown Dane who died in England soon after the year 1,000 A.D. may be strutting around the universe at this moment claiming that he is responsible for the game of football. He never played any version of the game as it is known today and the credit due him stems from an episode in which others used his head.

This Dane, whose name, under the circumstances, could not have been recorded for posterity, was a member of the armed forces of the "dastardly aggressor" of the moment. England was occupied by the victorious Danes, a condition which lasted from 1016 to 1042, and during that period, this unknown father of football died, and was buried on the battlefield. Time passed. The British rose again to drive the aggressors into the sea and the unknown Danish GI mouldered in his grave.

Some time later, an Englishman, digging in the old battlefield, unearthed the skull of this Dane, and, muttering about unpleasant memories of the days of the occupation, proceeded to kick the skull around the pasture. Other Englishmen joined in the fun and some youngsters, watching this new pastime, dug farther, until other Danish skulls were found. Soon, everyone in the township was kicking a skull and this sport continued until toes became more painful than the smoldering hatred of the Danes. It was not long before some minor inventive genius of the time produced the inflated bladder of a cow to take the place of the skulls, and thus the head of the unknown Dane had been used to create the embryo of football. There was a long road to travel from that pasture pastime to the passing skill of Redskin Sam Baugh, the elusive wizardry of Packer Don Hutson and the devastating black magic of T-formations. It would take nearly a thousand years to produce the lightning thrusts and bewildering deception of American Professional Football, but an ever-increasing multitude of major league fans in the United States of America is fanatically grateful that an unnamed Englishman did unearth a certain skull and did proceed to boot it for that first field goal attempt in history.

As if to set the pattern for later days, or perhaps to prove that there is nothing new, ever, anywhere, "Over-emphasis" blossomed within the first century of football history. Those who lately howled that football must be abolished to preserve the good way of life, merely parroted the words of King Henry II (1159–1189), who not only threatened banishment of the sport, but did indeed ban it forever during his reign.

The ban followed a national craze which had developed over the joys of booting the inflated bladders in contests which were a combination of soccer, vandalism and mass modified-homicide. For the "big game" of those days was played in no stadium, but around, over and through two townships. The entire population of each contestant met at a point between the towns, the bladder was tossed in the middle, and chaos broke loose. The touchdown was scored when the ball was kicked into the center of the opposing town and there were no further rules to confuse the issue. If children, gentle old ladies and valuable livestock were trampled in the process, there were no referees to step off penalties. Gardens, crops, fences and even dwellings were flattened as the valiant athletes gave it the "old college try." Nor were there any gate receipts; the fans were taking part in the game. It would have been a glorious spectacle for television with no one to dictate restrictions. The celebrations which took place in the conquered village formed a pattern for American Legion conventions of later years and King Henry soon learned that the Danish occupation had been less devastating than one season of "futballe" as it was then called.

Futballe brought on its own banishment for still another reason. National preparedness in those days required each male citizen to put in a certain number of hours of archery practice, even as his descendants would practice running into burrows to escape the weapons of the future. When King Henry found that his soldiers were too busy playing futballe to tend to their bow and arrow exercises he blew the whistle. "No more futballe," he said. "We must build our national security with such a formidable fighting force that no aggressor will dare attack."

Futballe immediately "went underground" and was played only in those communities where the big-shot hoodlums of the time were able to corrupt the local police.

This condition prevailed for the next four hundred years.

The invention of firearms bailed futballe out of official disgrace early in the sixteenth century, and James I revoked the ban at the request of thousands of sportsmen who had been playing all the time anyway, but wanted to make the game respectable. The game spread to all sections of the British Isles, and, unlike its namesake of modern times, it was a sport concerning a foot and a ball. There was no running with the ball; there was no forward passing. The previous assaults between townships were now confined to a standard-sized playing field and points were scored for driving the ball across the opponent's goal. Later refinements produced goal-posts and restrictions of the number of players. Eventually, this game became known as "Association Football" to distinguish it from other varieties. This designation was shortened to "Assoc." and, through slang, to "soccer," which it is called today.

WILBUR MOORE (35), WASHINGTON REDSKINS, SCRAPES THE CLOUDS IN A RECKLESS LEAP OVER A GREEN BAY BLOCKER TO GET AT TED FRITSCH (64), PACKER FULLBACK. GRIFFITH STADIUM, SEPTEMBER 30, 1945

In this same period, futballe drifted over into Ireland, where it was immediately condemned as a sissy game, sorely in need of a strong injection of manliness, Irish style. The denizens of Ireland added some features of their own, mainly punching with the fists. This punching was supposedly aimed at the ball with intent to propel it toward the goal-line, but it was so much more satisfying to miss the ball and punch the opponent in the head that Gaelic football, as it is played today, is still a cross between boxing and soccer with emphasis on the former. It has changed little in nearly six hundred years.

The first variation from soccer, which pointed the way to the pattern of American football, took place at Rugby College in England in 1823. During an inter-class game of soccer, a player named William Ellis, discouraged with his lack of success at kicking the ball, was inspired to pick it up in his hands and run with it, thus scoring the first touchdown in history. Ellis was temporarily disgraced by his breach of sportsmanship, but soon, more adventurous souls decided to change the rules to permit running with the ball—and thus the game of Rugby was born.

In the ranks of the Pilgrim Fathers there were plenty of soccer players. There may even have been a few soccer balls, as well as cricket equipment, on the *Mayflower* when she made her momentous trip to these shores. But, strangely enough, there is no sign that any of the early immigrants to this country were Rugby players. The game was apparently unknown, or little appreciated, until 1875, when Harvard College, feeling its muscles at soccer, and unable to find a contender among the other American colleges, challenged McGill University to come down from Montreal to play a match of football. McGill came, but, unfortunately it was a Rugby team which showed up. A compromise was reached by playing half the game under soccer rules, half under Rugby, and the American boys liked the foreign game so much that they forgot all about soccer.

The next year Harvard sold the idea of playing Rugby to Yale to start a rivalry which is still renewed annually. Six years before, Rutgers had played Princeton in a football (soccer) game, enabling these universities to lay claim to being the pioneers of intercollegiate gridiron warfare, which was to be periodically accused of over-emphasis, and also periodically forgiven by the American public which loved the game.

For many years, Yale, Harvard and Princeton, then called "The Big Three," dominated the collegiate game, with the balance of the present members of the Ivy League assuming the secondary roles. It was not until well after World War I that the public became aware that football was not the exclusive property of the Eastern seaboard.

Early All America teams were dominated by the Big Three. Occasionally a West Point player, or a member of the Carlisle Indians, would get his name on the list, but seldom.

In present times there are nearly as many "All" teams as there were players in the early days of American football. Even now these mythical line-ups seldom include the first college rookies to be selected by the major league clubs when it comes to the annual player drafts. As many big stars in the major leagues have come from such unlikely campuses as Western Michigan State, Abilene Christian, St. Anselm's, Grambling and West Louisiana Teachers as have checked in from the Big Ten and similar highly publicized collegiate leagues.

Scoring originally paid off most highly on the field goal, which counted 5 against 1 for a touchdown. As late as 1884, a safety was 1 point, a touchdown 2, a point-after-touchdown 4, and a field goal 5. Later a touchdown was awarded 5 points, the same as a field goal, with the point-after-touchdown dropping to 1 and the safety becoming 2. Finally, in 1910 the field goal was dropped to 3 points, and, in 1912 the touchdown became 6 to set up the entire scoring routine as it is today. Recently there was a movement led by Commissioner Bert Bell of the National Football League to make the touchdown equal to 7 points, to eliminate the point-after-touchdown altogether, and to provide for a sudden-death play-off in case of a tie. Bell believed that the point-after-touchdown is an unnatural sideline of football which depends too much on the skill of a few players, and that the fans deserve a decision at the end of any football game—as well as the players, owners and coaches.

The pattern of football strategy has progressed rapidly within seventy-five years from an offense which consisted mostly of "grab-it-and-run" to the intricate refinements of T-formation which can produce upward of ten thousand variations, counting individual blocking assignments, flankers, decoys and men-in-motion.

The first dramatic innovation was the so-called "flying-wedge," in which a phalanx of blocking linemen hung on to suitcase handles sewed to the pants of the man in front, and thundered down the field thus tied together with the ball carrier flitting along behind waiting for the opposition to be rolled up in a broken heap along the way.

Nate Fine Photo
STEVE BAGARUS (00), WASHINGTON REDSKINS, TAKES THE HIGH ROAD AGAINST
THE GREEN BAY PACKERS. GRIFFITH STADIUM, DECEMBER 1, 1946

This led to so many serious injuries—and deaths—and brought on such a savage game that President Teddy Roosevelt threatened to send football to Siberia if adequate safety precautions were not taken. In 1905, a gigantic Swarthmore tackle named Bob Maxwell, apparently the key-man in Swarthmore's defense, was seriously manhandled by the little gentlemen from Pennsylvania. A photograph of the bleeding Maxwell leaving the field incensed President Roosevelt and it was then that he waved the big stick at collegiate football.

The next year (1906) the forward pass was legalized in an effort to open up the game, the flying wedge was banished, and football had entered its next phase of growth.

It was not until 1913, however, that Gus Dorais (later to be coach of the Detroit Lions) and Knute Rockne, as Notre Dame players, brought the forward pass into a game with West Point and scored a sensational triumph. From that moment until the mid-1930's, the forward pass was something that a daring quarterback might demand on third down or when a game was hopelessly lost. It was a desperation measure for extreme circumstances.

And then, at little-known (at the time) Texas Christian University, there appeared a halfback named Samuel Adrian Baugh, and football, particularly the professional game, was about to make the most revolutionary change in its format to date. For Baugh, easily the most sensational passer of record, made the forward pass a routine offensive performance, a natural development of football warfare. Parenthetically, Baugh began to strike through the air at the same time that aircraft became the dominant factor of the bigger game known as "war," a fact that may have deeper meaning to deeper thinkers. This innovation led to further ramifications of football, until, in current times, roughly half of all offensive football is the forward pass.

Other changes have concerned themselves with offensive backfield formations: the single-wing, double-wing, punt, short-punt, Notre Dame box, the A and double A, and, finally and most important, the T.

The origin of the T is not entirely clear. It existed as far back as 1920, probably before that. But its devastating deception and all-around possibilities were not fully realized until George Halas, owner-coach of the Chicago Bears, and Clark Shaughnessy went to work on it in the late 1930's with the immortal Sidney Luckman as T quarterback. It was Halas who realized fully the possibilities of creating another effective blocker in the forward line by the almost too simple device of permitting the center to hand back the ball while he kept his eyes on his opponent, not looking back between his own legs. It was Halas—and Luckman—who worked out the pantomime of hand-faking that is now routine to the expert T quarterbacks. It was Halas who developed more plays now used by the other professional teams, as well as hundreds of college squads, than any other coach. Halas now claims that the Bears can call more than ten thousand different plays—and that there are still many realms in the higher strata of T-formation that he has not had time to develop as yet.

The man-in-motion, and the flankers were developed in the National Football League and their deadly possibilities have loosened up the defense so that football has become a whirlwind operation of speed combined with crushing power.

At the same time defense has been catching up with the T, and now it is almost mandatory for a professional team to have an offense which combines wing formations, short-punts, and other variations, with the T, so that the fan reaps a full menu of offensive fireworks whenever two of the major league teams tangle their talents in a showdown.

The result of this development has been higher, faster scoring. It is not unusual for a team to score more points in one game (the record of 70 is held by the Los Angeles Rams) than some teams scored in an entire season not many years ago. (The Philadelphia Eagles scored 51 points in 12 games in 1936.) Through statistical studies, training of officials and other innovations, the National Football League has speeded up its game until it now gives the fans approximately twenty more plays per game than the fastest college teams, and the average figure goes higher each season. It has also added the fifth official in the interest of better officiating and has introduced many other regulations to make its version of football the most enjoyable.

Steadily increasing attendance figures, despite the drain-off to television, radio, and the ever-present problem of bad weather in late fall, prove that major league football is the healthiest young sport in America. More and more fans are realizing each year that big league football, so far as skill and ability is concerned, bears the same relation to the college game that big league baseball does to minor league baseball.

With its rosters a listing of the finest players the thousands of colleges can produce, it is a tornado of touchdown thrills.

THE BEGINNING ERA, 1895-1920

The first professional football team to be recognized as such played in the township of Latrobe, in Westmoreland County, Pennsylvania, forty miles southeast of Pittsburgh. It was sponsored by the local YMCA. Latrobe made its artistic debut on August 31, 1895, by defeating Jeannette, another township ten miles away, by the impressive score of 12–0. For the next ten years, Latrobe fielded a powerful team which played wherever and whenever it could, for whatever cash it could get.

Dr. John Brallier, who was to become a dentist in Latrobe, is awarded the distinction of having become one of the first "confessed" professionals when he deserted the University of West Virginia team to play for Latrobe. Fielding Yost, who later denounced professional football, played for Greensburg; and "Doggie" Trenchard of Princeton, Walter Okeson of Lehigh, Walter Howard of Cornell were a few of the early college stars to join the early rampages. In 1897, the entire Lafayette backfield (Best, Barclay, Bray and Walbridge) played for Greensburg.

During the next few years, other professional teams began to appear. The city of Pittsburgh developed the Duquesne County and Athletic Club, and its rosters listed some of the finest collegiate players of the time. Arthur Poe of Princeton, "Pudge" Heffelfinger of Yale; Bemus and Hawey Pierce, the two magnificent Indians from Carlisle; G. H. Brooke and P. D. Overfield of Pennsylvania, Fred Crolius of Dartmouth, all as prominent then as the current swarms of All Americans are now, played with the Pittsburgh club.

1894   DR. JOHN BRALLIER   1934

Upper New York State followed Pennsylvania into the joys of professional football soon after the turn of the century. Teams existed in Buffalo, Syracuse, Watertown, Auburn, Corinth, Clayton, Oswego, Alexandria Bay and Ogdensburg. One of the outstanding players for Watertown and Syracuse was Phil Draper, former miracle-man back of Williams College, another great player who was born fifty years too soon to reap the gold and glory that would have been his today.

On December 28, 1902, Syracuse, with Draper, Glenn "Pop" Warner, and his brother Bill, along with the peripatetic Pierce brothers, Bemus and Hawey, played the Philadelphia Nationals to a 6–0 defeat in Madison Square Garden, New York. The officials worked in full dress, including high silk hats and white gloves. Thirty years later, the Chicago Bears defeated the Portsmouth Spartans, 9-0, indoors at Chicago Stadium. That, up to 1958, was the end of indoor football.

Also in 1902, Connie Mack organized a football team which he named the "Athletics." He put the spectacular playboy pitcher, Rube Waddell, in the line-up, much to the Rube's confusion, and claimed the championship of the world after beating Pittsburgh, which had a fullback by the name of Christy Mathewson who had once been a line-crasher at Bucknell. The Indian Pierces played for Mack—and for almost everybody else.

Starting in 1904, and lasting until 1920 when the American Professional Football Association, the father of the National Football League, was formed, Ohio was the battleground, and the nursery, for major league football. Canton, Massillon, Akron, Columbus and Dayton contained many violent and valiant men, ever ready for some periodic bloodletting against any team which cared to show up. It was at Canton that Jim Thorpe first appeared to play for many years until he finished his career with the New York Giants in 1925.

When Billy Heston, an all-time Michigan backfield ace, expressed a willingness to pick up some pocket money after finishing his college career in 1904, Canton, Massillon and Akron got themselves into a bidding auction for his services. Heston, believing he had the three teams over a barrel, lifted his demands to the point where all three rebelled and refused to hire him at any price. A year later, Heston did play one game for Canton

1902 PHILADELPHIA ATHLETICS MANAGED BY CONNIE MACK.

for a fabulous $600, was massacred on the first play by the Massillon defense and never gained another inch. He played one more game in Chicago, collected a broken leg early in the game, and that was the end of his professional career.

Charlie Moran, major league umpire of renown, was a great back for Massillon in the same era. From the Carlisle Indian school came the Pierce brothers, Bemus and Hawey, and the great players called Frank Mt. Pleasant and Albert Exendine. Later, Jim Thorpe organized an entire team of Indians, who called themselves the "Oorang Indians" and played in the NFL in 1922 and 1923, sometimes representing Marion, Ohio. Before that, Jim went through the glory, and the heartbreak, of his experiences at the 1912 Olympic games at Stockholm, where he and George Patton of West Point dominated the scene.

As time went on, Columbus and Shelby in Ohio had teams. The Columbus Pan-handles, managed by Joe Carr, who later became president of the National Football League (from 1921 until his death in 1939), had the distinction of fielding one of the strangest line-ups in football history. In 1906, seven of its eleven positions were filled by men named "Nesser." Six of these amazing players were brothers, and the seventh was Fred Nesser, the son of Ted, the oldest. None of them had ever accepted any of the offers made by many colleges. They played with many teams for many years, brother Al finally writing an end to the family saga with the Cleveland team in 1931.

In the late teens, Knute Rockne and Charles "Gus" Dorais, whose forward-passing act had recently flabbergasted a highly touted West Point team, moved into professional football. They played with so many teams, jumping from one high bidder to another, that it would be impossible to trace their careers with any degree of accuracy. It is reported that the Columbus team found itself facing Rockne in six different uniforms during one season. Dorais later became coach of the Detroit Lions from 1943 through 1947.

Men who were destined to make their fame as coaches, rather than players, appeared in the Canton-Massillon line-ups of 1919. "Tuss" McLaughry, later of Dartmouth; and the late "Jock" Sutherland and Earle "Greasy" Neale took part in those bitter struggles. Charlie Brinkley, the great Harvard drop-kicker, tried it for a while with little success. "Fido" Kempton, a tiny quarterback from Yale, joined Canton for a few games in 1921.

War must be given some credit for the birth, or at least the conception, of what is now known as the National Football League. For, in 1918, the team representing the Great Lakes Naval Training Station was chosen to play in the Rose Bowl, where it proceeded to wallop the Mare Island squad. On that Great Lakes team were the men who would mold and nurse major league football to its present prosperity. George Halas, fresh from the University of Illinois, was its brilliant end. Jim Conzelman, John "Paddy" Driscoll, Harold Erickson were in its backfield. Hugh Blacklock, a fine

CHARLIE (CHOO-CHOO) JUSTICE (22), WASHINGTON REDSKINS GREAT HALFBACK, ON THE MOVE AGAINST BALTIMORE COLTS IN 1952. CASIMIR (SLUG) WITUCKI (62) IS ABOUT TO THROW A ROAD-OPENING BLOCK FOR JUSTICE.

Bear tackle to be, was there, as were two excellent guards from Notre Dame, Jerry Jones and Emmett Keefe, who would play in the league to come.

There were many truly magnificent players in this early era of growth, many almost unknown to current fans who have been conditioned to believe that major league football "began" with the spectacular unveiling of Harold "Red" Grange in 1925. Only the name of Jim Thorpe seems to carry over from those dark days of guerrilla warfare on the fields of Pennsylvania, Ohio and upper New York, although the eyes of the old-timers will light up with a strange fire when they talk of these "good, old days" when each man either played the sixty minutes or was carried off on a stretcher. Not for them are the tactics of specialists and platoons.

Thorpe was, without doubt, a superlative back who could kick, crash or run in the open. He was a physical freak, who could, like Babe Ruth, Walter Hagen and Harry Greb, ignore all the rules in the fitness manuals and still perform at a peak efficiency beyond the reach of lesser athletes. Thorpe used an open field running technique all his own, not dodging violently, but moving with a deceptive hip-twist that seemed to make him almost impossible to drop. Jim himself explained it thus: "I gave them a leg for a second, then took it away." Another weapon Thorpe used in the early days was an illegal, and decidedly lethal, shoulder-pad which had an outer covering of sheet metal concealed under his uniform jersey. When he crashed into optimistic tacklers with this device, devastation set in. Not until he joined the New York Giants in 1925 did anyone persuade Jim that he was not allowed to carry such murderous concealed weapons onto a football field. It is generally conceded by all the deeper thinkers of the current National Football League that, if Jim Thorpe were now coming out of college, he would undoubtedly be the highest-paid rookie the league had ever known, and, perhaps, its greatest star.

All these warriors of old, many gone on to the gridirons of Valhalla, were the pioneers of America's most exciting sport. They would have played for nothing if they had to—and often did, even as "professionals." The dynamic drive of these men, joined with that of other men of similar courage and aggressiveness, made the league what it is today, and pointed the way toward the greater triumphs of the future.

STEVE VAN BUREN POWERS OVER A FALLEN REDSKIN IN A GAME BETWEEN WASHINGTON
AND PHILADELPHIA AT WASHINGTON IN 1948.

THE MODERN ERA

The actual birth of the National Football League took place during the hot afternoon of September 17, 1920, as its founders gathered in the automobile agency of Ralph Hays, in Canton, Ohio. Hays also managed the Canton Bulldogs of that year. Jim Thorpe was there, and was elected president of the new American Professional Football Association. George Halas, back from the New York Yankees baseball team which had farmed him out to St. Paul, was there, representing the Staley Starch Company of Decatur, which had named him its athletic director. Stanley Cofall, one-time Notre Dame star, then running the Massillon Tigers, was on hand to be elected vice-president. A. F. Ranney, sponsor of the Akron team, was made secretary-treasurer.

The $100,000 fee now paid by each would-be member of the NFL would have paid for no less than 1,000 franchises that hot afternoon, as they sold for $100 each. Eleven teams signed up for the season to come: Canton Bulldogs; Cleveland Indians; Dayton Triangles; Akron Professionals; Massillon Tigers; Rochester, New York; Rock Island, Illinois; Muncie, Indiana; Hammond, Indiana; the Chicago Cardinals; and the Staleys, who were to become the Chicago Bears two years later.

The league had a perilous beginning that fall with confusion abounding and starvation threatening. The less hardy were discouraged and the survivors concluded that there must be administrative, as well as artistic talent, to create healthy growth. In April of the next year, the league reorganized and elected Joe Carr, an experienced sports promoter, as its new president. It was the smartest move major league football had made to date. Carr guided the league with a wise and sure hand until his death in 1939. He was professional football's balance wheel through the stormy years of its first two decades, a fair and impartial ruler.

There was an immediate realignment of teams in that second year. Massillon, Muncie and Hammond dropped out; Green Bay, Buffalo, Detroit, Columbus and Cincinnati came in.

THE 1920 STALEY TEAM WHICH BECAME THE CHICAGO BEARS TWO YEARS LATER.

This shifting of franchises, moving to new frontiers, testing fan support in different areas, was a healthy habit the league had practiced through all its history. The NFL is continually trying for the best possible spread of its teams.

The appearance of the Green Bay Packers in 1921 was the beginning of the saga of the most fabulous football town in the world. Its population in 1920 was slightly over 31,000, but it supported its football team. Its new stadium seats about 30,000 and the SRO sign has been worn out for nearly every home game during the past forty-plus years. Its newspaper, the Green Bay *Press-Gazette*, tells about the Packers first, reports other news if it has room. Nearly 50,000 wild-eyed football maniacs make up its population today and they know more about football than any other 50,000 people on the face of the earth. Its housewives meet each Monday during the season at the Quarterback Club. The coach of the team is torn to shreds after a losing performance. Any psychopath, seeking an early death by extreme torture, can reach his goal by appearing in

Green Bay and praising any member, past or present, of that hated enemy, the Chicago Bears.

The Green Bay Packers—Curly Lambeau—and George Calhoun: through the years they have become synonymous. As a young man Curly dreamed a dream. He went to Charles Peck, an official in the Acme Packing Company of Green Bay, and explained his dream. The magnificent sum of $500—for equipment and expenses—changed hands, and the Green Bay Packers were on the way to glory. Earl Louis Lambeau would be their coach and star back. He'd get the other players somehow. They would challenge any team in the world.

Big league football was a part-time job that year. Curly's twenty-one athletes worked all day, practiced until darkness made practice impossible. They won their first ten games, beating such formidable opponents as Menominee, Marinette, Sheboygan, Racine, New London, Oshkosh, Stambaugh, and Ishpeming. They were ready to claim the championship of Wisconsin, or the whole world, until Beloit whipped them late in the season, creating 30 days of official mourning, and financial embarrassment for almost every citizen of Green Bay. But Curly Lambeau couldn't be stopped. He played until 1929, coached the Packers through 1949.

During Curly's long leadership, the Packers put Green Bay on the map as the home of rough, rugged football, boasting some of the best players in all football history. The names of Don Hutson, Lavvie Dilweg, Clark Hinkle, Cecil Isbell, August Michalske, Baby Ray and Tony Canadeo gained luster at Green Bay, to be remembered as long as football shall live. The blazing rivalry which has developed between the Packers and the Chicago Bears provides two contests each fall that combine all the explosive ingredients of an atom bomb.

The dynamo of the Packers, other than Lambeau, has been a man whose name is never printed in the programs but who has been, from the beginning, and still is, the senior adviser, the patriarchal statesman, the father confessor, the defender of the faith, the only official Monday-morning quarterback, and the historian of all things Packer. George Whitney Calhoun is his name and he is known wherever major league football has been played, from Boston to San Francisco. Even though Lambeau has moved on to other fields, Calhoun is still there, on the telegraph desk of the *Press-Gazette*, and the Packers would be lost without him.

There was a moment in the early days when the Packers came within a wink of giving up the battle because of financial problems. It was then that George Calhoun directed the move which joined together five of Green Bay's outstanding citizens in an organization which called itself the "Hungry Five" and was pledged to keep the Packers going at all costs. Their names were Earl Lambeau, Lee Joannes, Dr. W. Webber Kelly, Andy Turnbull and Gerry Clifford. They sold stock in the Packers—at $5 a share—to hundreds of Wisconsin people. They guaranteed the Packers' debts. They fought the financial warfare—always with Calhoun lurking along the sidelines, working at thankless jobs, goading the others into action, and reaping his reward in the pleasure derived from sending his hymns of Packer praise over the world in his capacity as publicity director of the team.

Occasionally, through the years, more financing has been necessary, and the Hungry Five has always produced it to make Green Bay one of the strongest franchises in the NFL. Football fans who have watched metropolitan teams play their home games before audiences too small to play craps among themselves will get a tremendous thrill by traveling to this picturesque town in upper Wisconsin on a zero day, when snowbanks line the Packers' field waist deep. There they will find a sell-out crowd rooting their heroes home. It is one of the most heart-warming pictures in the world of American sports.

For more than a decade, the National Football League, as it was renamed in 1922, battled its way along with little support from the fans and even less from some newspapers. New teams joined, dropped out; some teams moved to other cities. Players shuffled around the league, playing wherever they could find paychecks. Only the Chicago

(Staley) Bears, the Chicago Cardinals and the Green Bay Packers are left in 1959 from among those that made up the league roster under Joe Carr's leadership in 1921.

The take-off to true prosperity began in 1925, after Tim Mara had established the Giants in New York's Polo Grounds. It happened when Harold "Red" Grange, his collegiate career finished under screaming headlines, signed with the Chicago Bears. Grange was the biggest name in the country at the time. People who couldn't have named the Vice-President of the United States (by the way, who was he?) knew all about the fabulous redhead from Wheaton, Illinois. It was the flash-spark that major league football needed. His debut in Wrigley Field against the Chicago Cardinals drew 36,000 fans, all the park would hold at that time. Seven days later, 68,000 watched him play against the New York Giants in the Polo Grounds. At last the big league game was off and running after several false starts.

Grange established himself as one of the all-time greats of professional football before he retired in 1935. Just before hanging up his uniform for good, Red wrote a letter to

NEW YORK FOOT BALL GIANTS ~ CHAMPIONS ~ 1927

NEW YORK GIANTS, CHAMPIONS 1927. (NOTE THAT AL NESSER, WHO FIRST PLAYED FOR COLUMBUS IN 1906, IS HERE WITH THE GIANTS. HE PLAYED UNTIL 1931, A TOTAL OF 25 YEARS.)

Arch Ward, sports editor of the Chicago *Tribune*, containing some remarks that might be of interest to fans who may still believe that a good college team would be a match for a major league squad. It stated:

I say that a football player, after three years in college, doesn't know anything about football, Red wrote. Pro football is the difference between the New York Giants baseball team and an amateur nine. College players not only do not know how to play football, but they don't take as much interest in the game as the pros. In college you have studies to make up, lectures to attend, scholastic requirements to satisfy. In pro ball you are free from all this. You have nothing to do but eat, drink and sleep football and that is just what the boys do.

Pro football is smart. It is so smart you can rarely work the same play twice with the same results. Competition is keen. There are no set-ups in pro football. The big league player knows *football*, not just a theory or system.

In 1933, with prosperity finally peeking from around the corner where it had been hiding for five years, professional football became firmly established as a major league

RED GRANGE SIGNS HIS PROFESSIONAL CONTRACT

sport. It was in this year that the league split itself into two divisions—East and West—and thereby established a championship play-off. It also began to form an apparatus to keep official statistical records and, generally, came of age.

More than a small part of this development sprang from the agile brain of George Preston Marshall, who, with Vincent Bendix, Jay O'Brien and M. Dorland Doyle, had taken over the Boston franchise the previous year. Marshall, a dynamic and controversial gentleman, was to be the cause of many changes during the next two decades. With the help of his wife, Corinne Griffith Marshall, one-time motion-picture star, he created the greatest series of half-time entertainments ever seen in major league parks. His Redskin band of more than one hundred precision trained musicians became an annual favorite wherever it appeared. Marshall's yowling battle against the All America Football Conference was always rich with witty denunciations which delighted newspapermen and fans alike.

In 1933, Art Rooney took over the Pittsburgh franchise, while Bert Bell, later to become Commissioner, and Ludlow Wray, absorbed the old Yellowjacket Club and created the Philadelphia Eagles. Brooklyn was sold to Chris Cagle and John (Shipwreck) Kelly and Charles Bidwill bought the Chicago Cardinals. The league had received a wholesale transfusion of new, and wealthy, blood.

THE FAMED WASHINGTON REDSKINS MARCHING BAND.

With prosperity in sight, membership fees were increased to $10,000; seven years later they would go to $50,000.

Within a year, after the Chicago Bears beat the New York Giants in the first divisional play-off championship, G. A. Richards bought the Portsmouth franchise and transferred it to Detroit and Dan Topping took over the Brooklyn squad. The Cincinnati franchise was transferred to St. Louis where it died of financial malnutrition. Also in 1934, the selective draft and waiver rule was devised to absorb graduating collegians and the player limit was increased to twenty-four men. Jay Berwanger, the great University of Chicago halfback, was the first player chosen—by the Philadelphia Eagles—under the draft plan, but declined the honor and did not play major league football. In the early fall of 1934, the champion Chicago Bears were held to a scoreless tie by the College

TIM MARA OF THE NEW YORK GIANTS TURNS OVER $115,163 TO MAYOR
JAMES WALKER FOLLOWING A CHARITY GAME BETWEEN THE GIANTS AND
NOTRE DAME ALL-STARS

All-Stars in the first of an annual series sponsored at Soldier Field by the Chicago Tribune Charities.

George Marshall, convinced that Boston preferred the pattern of college football to the professional game, transferred his Redskins from Boston to Washington in 1937 and began to play to capacity crowds. The fabulous Samuel Adrian Baugh appeared from Texas Christian the same fall to start the skein of records which may always be the goal of all football passers. The same fall, the Cleveland franchise was established for Homer Marshman by league president Joseph F. Carr, who died the following spring and was replaced by Carl L. Storck.

There was more franchise juggling during the next two years. Fred J. Mandel, Jr., took over at Detroit, buying out George Richards, and Alexis Thompson bought the Pittsburgh Steeler team from Art Rooney, who, in turn, bought a half interest in the Philadelphia Eagles. The next year, 1941, Thompson transferred his entire club to Philadelphia, which Rooney and Bell vacated in order to take their franchise to Pittsburgh. At the same time, Dan Reeves and Fred Levy, Jr., bought the Cleveland franchise from Marshman to stay in Cleveland until the 1946 season (when they would move the Rams to Los Angeles, making way for the Cleveland Browns).

The league appointed its first Commissioner on March 1, 1941, naming Elmer Layden. Carl Storck resigned as president a month later and Layden was given that post also. He resigned on January 11, 1946, and Bert Bell was elected to replace him. Bell died suddenly in 1959 and was replaced by Alvin "Pete" Rozelle.

The gate receipts were climbing all through these years. The *Tribune* All-Star game at Chicago each fall was selling out to crowds of nearly ninety thousand and the championship games were playing to tremendous gatherings. More and more big-name college rookies were joining the league and it was a long road back to the days of playing for $10 per game. Public interest was rocketing, and after the fabulous Bears of 1940 devastated the Washington Redskins by 73–0 in the championship game, the deeds of the major league footballers were the top topic of conversation in sporting circles for weeks afterward. It is still accepted as gospel in football circles that the Chicago Bears of that amazing afternoon were the most lethal sports aggregation that ever appeared anywhere.

Then came Pearl Harbor and 638 National Football League members went into service in every theater of action. This wholesale departure of top-flight players weakened every team and caused the Cleveland Rams to suspend operations for the season of 1943. And, to take up the slack further, the Pittsburgh Steelers merged their squad with the Philadelphia Eagles to form a Phil-Pitt combination in 1943, then (after Phil-Pitt was dissolved) merged with the Chicago Cardinals for the 1944 season, which welcomed the return of the Cleveland Rams to active play, and also witnessed the debut of the Boston Yanks under the ownership of Ted Collins.

Collins soon learned that Boston still preferred college ball, even as George Marshall had discovered long before, and moved his team to New York as the "Bulldogs" for the 1949 season. This was a disastrous maneuver, putting three teams in the city which barely supports one properly (the New York Yankees of the All America Football Conference were operating out of Yankee Stadium that fall). The next year brought the merging of the NFL and AAFC. Topping's Yankees gave up the ghost and Collins took over at Yankee Stadium with the "New York Yanks." Some years earlier, in 1945, Topping and Collins had merged the Brooklyn franchise with the Boston club, and the next year Topping deserted to the All America, thus leaving Brooklyn open for the AAFC to put a franchise there, which Branch Rickey did. It was one of the few disasters (financial) Rickey ever brought upon himself; some games were played before fewer customers than had watched the early warfare of the Chicago Staleys nearly thirty years before.

With the war ended in 1946 and two leagues containing 18 teams in operation, the players had a financial feast for a few seasons, but it was soon apparent that the United States would not support that many major league teams. But it was growth, and the growing pains were lessened by the realization, four years later, that the big league game was solidly on the road to prosperity. New attendance records were broken each year until, in 1960 about 4,000,000 cash customers went through the gates.

The merger of the NFL and AAFC brought about a 13-team league for the 1950 season with the Baltimore Colts acting as the "swing" club, playing one game against each member team while the rest played normal schedules against divisional and traditional rivals. The Colts swung themselves into a sea of red ink and disappeared after a disastrous season in which they won one game.

A further settling down took place in 1951, with gate receipts rising all over the circuit. The championship game between the Rams and Browns, telecast from coast to coast, was, fortunately, a hair-raiser, and created thousands of new fans for the future.

At the annual meeting in January, 1952, Ted Collins sold his New York Yanks franchise back to the league, which immediately transferred it to a group of men, headed by Giles Miller of Dallas, Texas. Dallas fans were not ready to support big league football in 1952, perhaps because the team could win but one of twelve games. In 1953 the Dallas franchise was switched back to new ownership in Baltimore and started the building process which resulted in the winning of a world championship in the first over-time playoff game of history in 1958.

The spiraling success of NFL football through the 1950's led to more expansion in 1960. The Dallas Cowboys, backed by the wealth of Clinton W. Murchison Jr. and Bedford Wynne, were added to the NFL list, making an awkward 13-team schedule for that year. The Cowboys played one game with each other team in the league and had a rough season, as was to be expected. Still another franchise, the Minneapolis Vikings, was to start playing in 1961, and arrangements were under way a year ahead to provide players and management.

At the same time in 1960, still another new league, the American Football League, began operation. Teams were spotted in Boston, Buffalo, Dallas, Denver, Houston, Los Angeles, New York and Oakland, four of them in direct competition with the old NFL.

Inevitably lawsuits developed over alleged encroachment of territorial rights and other abrasive factors. Television coverage of the two leagues overlapped and brought forth more ill-feeling. Line-ups of the new league teams were, by necessity, made up of rookies and veterans of the National and Canadian leagues, and the quality of play indicated that many years must pass before it could compete with the NFL. It had already been proven by the National League's history that all famous teams had played as a unit for several seasons before they were able to jell into great teams.

As the 1961 season approached, the NFL was ready with a 14-team league with two divisions. Two more teams were being considered for the near future, with franchises to be located in new areas.

This would provide, after more than forty years of experiment and change, the ideal league situation.

It had been a long, sometimes discouraging, sometimes glorious road from the banquet table at the University of Illinois nearly fifty years before, where George Halas had heard Bop Zuppke say that it made little sense for a man to end his football career just when it was ready to begin.

The survivors from the beginning days have watched developments with fascinated wonder as they remember playing a more brutal game for what would now be considered lunch money. They have witnessed a great change in playing methods. They have seen the greatest stars of forty years come and go, a few remaining as coaches in the league, many returning to college ball to try to teach the rookies how to play the bigger game. They have learned that few All America players are ever ready for the big time until they have had a season or two of grooming.

The indomitable competitive spirit which is strong in the heart of every successful major league player battled the frightening odds through many long years to give America its most exciting game.

If these veterans took a few bows in the solitude of their souls, they had them coming.

A CHRONOLOGY
OF PROFESSIONAL FOOTBALL

(From the *Record and Rules Manual*, National Football League)

1895—First professional football game played at Latrobe, Pa., August 31, sponsored by the local YMCA. Latrobe 12, Jeannette 0.

1902—Connie Mack claimed the professional football championship of the United States for his "Philadelphia Athletics," with Rube Waddell in the line-up, after they defeated Pittsburgh, with Christy Mathewson playing, 12–6. The game was played at Pittsburgh.

First night football game at Elmira, N.Y., November 18. Philadelphia Athletics (39) vs Kanaweola A.C. (0).

First indoor football game at Madison Square Garden, December 28. Syracuse, with Glenn Warner playing guard, defeated Philadelphia Nationals, 6–0.

1905—Canton Bulldogs and Massillon Tigers organized.

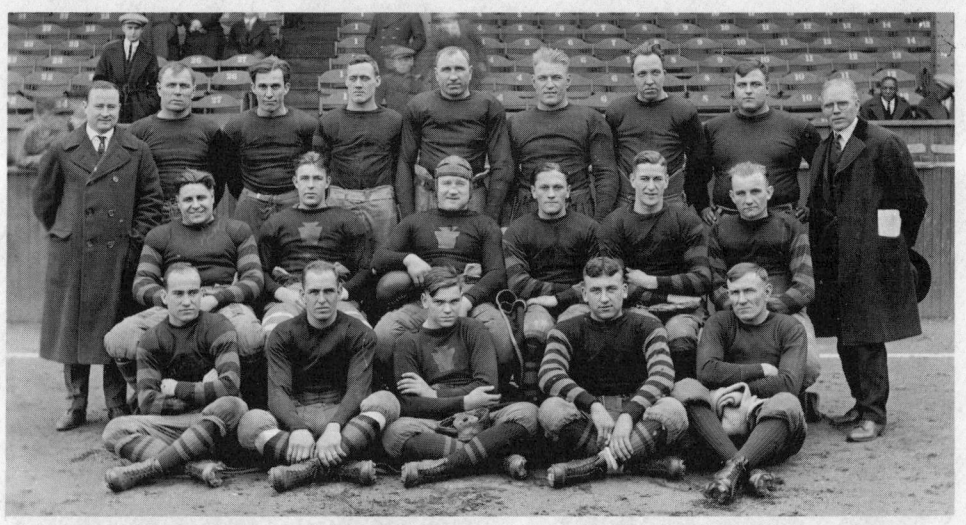

Photo by Nice

THE COLUMBUS PANHANDLES, WHO PLAYED TOGETHER BEFORE THE NATIONAL
LEAGUE WAS FORMED, THEN JOINED IT FOR SEVERAL YEARS, WERE DOMINATED
BY THE FAMOUS NESSER BROTHERS. *Front row*: BLISS, EMMETT RUH, HOPKINS,
MURTHA, JOHN NESSER: *middle row*: MULBARGER, AL NESSER, TED NESSER, GLASS-
MAN, HOMER RUH, GAULKE: *back row*: CORCORAN (TRAINER), PHIL NESSER, WOOL-
FORD, KUHNER, FRED NESSER, FRANK NESSER, WAITE, HAUCK, JOE F. CARR, MAN-
AGER AND LATER PRESIDENT OF THE NATIONAL FOOTBALL LEAGUE.

1920—American Professional Football Association formed September 17 at Canton, Ohio,
  with the following membership: Canton Bulldogs, Cleveland Indians, Dayton Tri-
  angles, Akron Professionals, Massillon Tigers, Rochester (N.Y.), Rock Island
  (Ill.), Muncie (Ind.), Staleys of Decatur (Ill.), Chicago Cardinals, and Hammond
  (Ind.).
  Jim Thorpe (Canton) elected president; Stan Cofall (Massillon), vice-president;
  A. F. Ranney (Akron), secretary and treasurer. Membership fee was set at $100.
1921—American Professional Football Association reorganized April 30 at Akron, Ohio.
  Joe F. Carr elected president; M. O'Brien (Decatur), vice-president; Carl L. Storck
  (Dayton), secretary and treasurer.
  J. E. Clair of Acme Packing Company granted franchise for Green Bay, Wisconsin,
  August 27.
1922—Franchise of George Halas for Staley A.C. transferred to Chicago and team renamed
  Chicago Bears, January 28.
  J. E. Clair turned Green Bay franchise back to league following discussion over
  alleged use of ineligible players, January 28.
  Professional football gets first eight-column newspaper headline, Chicago *Herald &*
  Examiner, January 30. It says: "Stagg Says Conference Will Break Professional
  Football Menace."
  Earl Lambeau granted franchise for Green Bay, Wis., June 24.
  Name of American Professional Football Association changed to National Football
  League.
1924—Frankford Yellow Jackets (Philadelphia) awarded franchise.
1925—Timothy J. Mara and Will Gibson granted franchise for New York for $500,
  August 1.
  James Conzelman granted franchise for Detroit, August 1.
  Harold "Red" Grange signed with Chicago Bears, November 22.

ALONZO STAGG, LEFT, WHO HAS BEEN INVOLVED IN FOOTBALL FOR GENERATIONS, GETS HIS COACH-OF-THE-YEAR TROPHY IN 1944 FROM OTTO GRAHAM, WHO CAME OUT OF NORTHWESTERN UNIVERSITY IN 1943 TO BECOME ONE OF THE GREAT QUARTERBACKS IN PRO HISTORY.

1926—Rule adopted February 6 making all players ineligible for NFL competition until they have graduated from college.

Adoption of maximum (18) and minimum (15) player limit, February 7.

Edward Butler granted franchise for Brooklyn, N.Y., July 10.

Milwaukee fined $500 on July 10 for using four high school boys against the Chicago Cardinals, and ordered to dispose of franchise within ninety days.

1927—National Football League reorganized with withdrawal of Brooklyn, Detroit and nine other clubs, July 27.

Brooklyn franchise transferred to C. C. Pyle for New York Yankees team.

1928—Detroit's application for re-instatement approved; Cleveland withdrew, August 12.

Duluth and Buffalo franchises dropped.

1929—Sale of Chicago Cardinal franchise by Chris O'Brien to Dr. David J. Jones, July 27.

C. C. Pyle surrendered Brooklyn franchise to Stapleton, Staten Island, July 27.

Pottsville (Pa.) franchise awarded to Boston syndicate, July 28.

Adoption of rule to use a fourth official, field judge, July 28.

Chicago Cardinals became first professional team to attend out-of-town training camp—at Coldwater, Mich., August 21.

1930—Player limit increased on January 25 to maximum of 20, minimum of 16.

Portsmouth franchise awarded to Harold Griffen, July 12.

Dayton franchise purchased for Brooklyn by William B. Dwyer and John Depler from Carl L. Storck, July 12.

New York Giants raised $115,163 for New York Unemployment fund by beating Notre Dame All-Stars, 21–0, December 14.

1931—Chicago Bears, Green Bay Packers and Portsmouth Spartans fined $1,000 each on July 11 for having players on their rosters who had not yet been graduated from their college classes.

1932—Inactive Boston franchise transferred to new syndicate composed of George Preston Marshall, Vincent Bendix, Jay O'Brien and M. Dorland Doyle, July 9.

Chicago Bears defeated Portsmouth Spartans, 9–0, for championship. Game played indoors at Chicago Stadium.

1933—Clipping penalty increased to 25 yards, February 25.

Goal posts returned to goal-line, February 25.

Forward passing legalized from any spot behind line of scrimmage, February 25.

Membership fee increased to $10,000, July 8.

A resolution by George P. Marshall setting up a divisional system and a championship play-off adopted, July 8.

A. J. Rooney and A. McCool awarded franchise for Pittsburgh, July 8.

Frankford Yellowjackets franchise declared forfeit and awarded to Bert Bell and Lud Wray of Philadelphia, July 9.

Chicago Cardinals franchise sold to Charles Bidwell by Dr. David J. Jones, October 24.

William Dwyer and John Depler transferred Brooklyn franchise to Christian Cagle and John Kelly, July 9.

1934—G. A. Richards purchased Portsmouth franchise and moved team to Detroit, June 30.

Chris Cagle and John Kelly transferred Brooklyn franchise to Daniel Topping, June 30.

Chicago Bears held to scoreless tie by Collegiate All-Stars in first annual All-Star game sponsored by the Chicago Tribune Charities at Soldier Field, Chicago, August 31.

Franchise of Cincinnati transferred to St. Louis, November 5.

Player selective draft and waiver rule adopted, December 10.

1935—Player limit increased to 24 men, September 4.

1936—Jay Berwanger, University of Chicago halfback, first player selected in NFL draft. Chosen by Philadelphia, February 8.

Player limit increased to 25 men, February 9.

1937—Homer Marshman granted franchise for Cleveland, February 12.

Boston franchise transferred to Washington, February 13.

1938—Player limit increased to 30 men, February 19.

1939—Kick-off out-of-bounds ruled receiving team's ball on its 45-yard line, February 11.

THE FIRST NEW YORK GIANTS TEAM OF 1925 (top) LINED UP THIS WAY: *Front row, left to right*, LYNN BOMAR, VANDERBILT; FRED PARNELL, LAFAYETTE; JOE WILLIAMS, LAFAYETTE; JOE ALEXANDER, SYRACUSE; ARTHUR CARNEY, ANNAPOLIS: CENTURY MILSTEAD, YALE; PAUL JAPPE, SYRACUSE. *Back row*, WARREN HENDRIAN, PITTSBURGH; HENRY BENKERT, RUTGERS; JACK MC BRIDE, SYRACUSE; HENRY HAINES, PENN STATE.

TWENTY-FIVE YEARS LATER (bottom)—MC BRIDE, BENKERT, ALEXANDER, CARNEY AND MILSTEAD SHOWED UP AT THE POLO GROUNDS AND LINED UP IN THE BACK ROW. THAT'S JAPPE *(third from the left in the front row)* WITH LYMAN WALBRIDGE, ED MC GINLEY AND HARRY NORDSTROM WHO MISSED THE EARLIER PICTURE BUT PLAYED ON THE SAME TEAM.

Joe F. Carr, NFL president since 1921, died at Columbus, Ohio, May 20.

Carl L. Storck named president of NFL, May 25.

1940—Detroit Lions fined $5,000 for tampering with Clyde "Bulldog" Turner, Hardin-Simmons center, drafted by the Chicago Bears, February 2.

Fred J. Mandel, Jr., purchased Detroit Lions franchise from G. A. Richards, February 10.

Membership fee increased to $50,000, April 12.

Player limit increased to 33 maximum and 22 minimum, April 12.

Clipping penalty reduced to 15 yards, April 12.

All distance penalties enforced from spot on field of play limited to half the distance to the goal, April 12.

Dennis J. Shea elected treasurer of the league, April 12.

Alexis Thompson purchased Pittsburgh Steelers franchise from Arthur J. Rooney, who then purchased half-interest in Philadelphia Eagles, December 9.

Adoption of rule prohibiting sale or trading of team's first two selections in player draft without unanimous consent of league until one playing season after player's selection.

Photo by Larry Sharkey
BALLET OF VIOLENCE—YELVERTON TITTLE LOOKS FOR SAN FRANCISCO RECEIVER IN A GAME AGAINST LOS ANGELES. THAT'S BOB GRIFFITH OF THE RAMS BEING BLOCKED OFF AT THE RIGHT.

1941—Elmer F. Layden, head coach and athletic director at Notre Dame, named Commissioner of professional football for five years, March 1.

Carl L. Storck resigned as president-secretary, April 5.

Elmer F. Layden elected president for five years, April 5.

Philadelphia franchise and club transferred to Pittsburgh and Pittsburgh franchise and club transferred to Philadelphia, April 5.

Umpire made official timer of league games, April 6.

Cleveland franchise transferred from Homer Marshman and associates to Daniel F. Reeves and Fred Levy, Jr., June 1.

1942—National Football League raised $680,384.07 for War Relief charities.

1943—Cleveland Rams, with co-owners Fred Levy and Daniel Reeves in service, granted permission to suspend operations for one season, April 6.

Free substitution rule adopted for duration, April 7.

Fred Levy transferred his stock to Daniel Reeves, April 16.

Philadelphia Eagles and Pittsburgh Steelers granted permission to merge under name of Phil-Pitt Eagles, June 13.

Ted Collins granted franchise for Boston, to become active in season of 1944, or as soon thereafter as league deems advisable, June 20.

Adoption of ten-game schedule, June 20.

Player limit reduced to 28 men for one year, August 25.

Philadelphia Eagles and Pittsburgh Steelers merger automatically dissolved on last day of season, December 5.

1944—Boston Yanks granted permission to activate franchise in season of 1944, April 19.

Cleveland Rams granted permission to resume operation in season of 1944, April 19.

Player limit of 28 reaffirmed for one year, April 20.

Free substitutions adopted for another year, April 20.

Adoption of rule assessing penalty of 5 yards for kick-offs out-of-bounds, obligating kicking team to re-kick after each offense, April 20.

Coaching from bench legalized, April 20.

Dennis J. Shea re-elected treasurer of league for three years, April 20.

Chicago Cardinals and Pittsburgh Steelers requested by league to merge for one year under the name of Card-Pitt, April 21.

Card-Pitt merger dissolved automatically on last day of season, December 3.

1945—Striking an opponent with forearm or elbow (flying elbow blocks) barred, April 9.

Inbounds spot changed from 15 to 20 yards in from side-lines for one year, April 9.

Free-substitution rule renewed for one year, April 9.

Wearing of socks in league games made mandatory, April 9.

Defensive team permitted to advance with muffed snap from center, April 9.

Brooklyn Tigers and Boston Yanks merged for one year under name of "The Yanks," April 10.

Committee named to confer with colleges on all matters pertaining to eligibility of players, April 11.

1945—By V-J Day (August 14), the National Football League's service roster for World War II, limited to men who had participated in league games, totaled 638 men, 355 of whom were commissioned, 69 decorated and 21 had lost their lives.

Pre-war player limit of 33 men restored, September 15.

National League, in special executive session at Cleveland, ratified action of Commissioner Layden in which Brooklyn's franchise was declared forfeited and all players on its active and reserve lists were assigned to Boston Yanks, December 17.

1946—Elmer F. Layden resigned as Commissioner of professional football and President of the NFL, January 11.

Bert Bell, co-owner of Pittsburgh Steelers named to succeed Layden and given three-year contract, January 11.

Substitutions limited to no more than three men at a time, January 11.

Receiving team permitted to run punts and unsuccessful field goal attempts out from behind goal-line, January 11.

Forward passes made incomplete automatically upon striking either team's goal post, January 11.

Cleveland Rams franchise and club transferred to Los Angeles, January 12.

National League entered three-year, major-minor league agreement with American Association (later renamed American League), Dixie League and Pacific Coast League, January 13.

Dan Topping announced he was abandoning Brooklyn franchise to enter a new league, December 6.

IN MEMORY OF
LT. ALBERT C. "AL" BLOZIS
110TH INFANTRY 28TH DIVISION A.E.F.
SOLDIER SCHOLAR ATHLETE
BORN JANUARY 5, 1919 GARFIELD, N.J.
KILLED IN ACTION JANUARY 31, 1945 IN FRANCE
NEW YORK FOOTBALL GIANTS 1942-43-44
GEORGETOWN COLLEGE 1939-42
WORLD CHAMPION SHOT PUTTER 1942
ERECTED 1945 BY NEW YORK FOOTBALL GIANTS

World Championship game, December 15, between Chicago Bears and New York Giants in the Polo Grounds, N.Y., drew an attendance of 58,346 and gross receipts of $282,955.25, highest in league history. Each Bear got $1,975.82; each Giant $1,295.57, a new high for players.

1947—Bert Bell's contract as Commissioner of the NFL renewed for five years, January 1. An amendment to the constitution imposing a major penalty for anyone not reporting the offer of a bribe, an attempt to fix a game or any other infraction of the rules having to do with gambling, January 1.

Addition of a fifth official, with primary duties as prescribed, to be used on the field and known as back judge—adopted January 24.

Charles W. Bidwell, owner of the Chicago Cardinals, died after brief illness, April 19. Revised use of observers by Hugh L. Ray, National Football League technical adviser, resulted in 162.1 plays per game, and all-time record. It also resulted in a new record of total yards per game—542.4.

1948—A clarification of the clipping rule, permission to use an artificial tee on the kickoff, and the equipping of all officials with whistles were among the important items passed by the Rules Committee and approved at the annual meeting, January 14. Player limit increased to 35 for the entire season.

A syndicate headed by D. Lyle Fife purchased the Detroit franchise from Fred L. Mandel, Jr., Januuary 15.

Dr. John B. "Jock" Sutherland, coach of the Pittsburgh Steelers, died on April 11 after an operation.

Hugh L. Ray, NFL technical adviser, reported that another new all-time high in plays per game had been reached in 1947 with 165.5, and that total yards had climbed to a new mark of 643.3.

1949—A syndicate headed by James P. Clark purchased the franchise of the Philadelphia Eagles from Alexis Thompson, January 15.

Bert Bell, as Commissioner-President, and Dennis Shea, as vice-president and treasurer of the NFL, appointed for ten-year terms, January 20.

Player limit of 32 adopted, January 20.

Free- substitution rule adopted for one year, January 20.

Unanimous consent of the league given for the cancellation of the Boston franchise and a new franchise award to Ted Collins in New York City under the name of the New York Bulldogs, January 21.

Hugh L. Ray, technical adviser, announced that 29 new records had been set during 1948, with 174.5 plays per game, 659 yards per game and many individual marks.

Bert Bell, Commissioner of the NFL, and Arthur Friedlund, representing the All America Football Conference, announced a merger of the two leagues. Baltimore, Cleveland and San Francisco joined the ten teams in the NFL with the balance of AAFC players placed in a pool from which they would be drafted by the 13 teams in the new organization.

1950—Free-substitution rule adopted for an indefinite time, January 23.

Upon advice of counsel and the unanimous consent of the member clubs the commissioner announced that the league would use the name National Football League, divided into National and American conferences. The American Conference to include: Chicago Cardinals, Cleveland Browns, New York Giants, Philadelphia Eagles, Pittsburgh Steelers, Washington Redskins. The National Conference: Baltimore Colts, Chicago Bears, Detroit Lions, Green Bay Packers, Los Angeles Rams, New York Yanks, San Francisco 49ers.

Carl L. Storck, secretary-treasurer of the NFL from 1921 to 1939 and president from 1939 to 1941, died in Dayton, Ohio, March 13.

A new all-time record for attendance during the regular playing season was established. A total of 1,977,556 fans witnessed the 78 games. Two play-off games drew 106,896. The championship game was attended by 29,751.

1951—The first Pro Bowl game was played, January 14, under the auspices of the Los Angeles Publishers' Association before 53,676 spectators in Los Angeles Coliseum, the American Conference All-Stars beating the National Conference All-Stars, 28–27. George P. Marshall fostered the adoption of the game by the league.

Player limit of 33 voted. A minimum of 25 men must be dressed for a championship game, January 18.

No tackle, guard or center may become eligible for a forward pass, January 18.

Baltimore Colt franchise cancelled.

Frank J. Jonet, pioneer in professional football and active with Green Bay since its inception, died at the age of 69 (August 17).

1952—The assets and franchise of the New York Yanks were purchased by the National Football League, January 19.

A new franchise was awarded the Dallas Texans after they purchased the assets of the New York Yanks from the National Football League, January 24.

The tackle eligible rule was made permanent January 18.

On pass interference on the part of the offense, the penalty shall be fifteen yards from the previous spot and not loss of down. Adopted January 18.

1953—A new franchise was awarded Baltimore and Dallas gave up after one year.

The player limit of 33 was retained.

Permanent conferences—Eastern and Western were established with Baltimore in the West and Chicago Cardinals in the East.

Jim Thorpe, the great athlete and first president of the American Professional Football Association (1920), died March 28 in Lomita, Calif.

Arthur McBride, original owner of the Cleveland Browns, sold the franchise to a syndicate headed by Dave R. Jones.

Judge Allan K. Grim of the United States District Court of the Eastern District of Pennsylvania, rendered his decision of the Anti-Trust case brought by the government against the National Football League and its members. The effect of the decision was to uphold the restrictions on telecasts into the home territory

PARKER HALL, CLEVELAND RAM HALFBACK, ABOUT TO MAKE A SUDDEN STOP AS HARRY
JACUNSKI, GREEN BAY END, FLIES OVER THE BLOCKER, CORBETT DAVIS (3), TO BRING
HIM DOWN AT STATE PARK, MILWAUKEE, IN SEPTEMBER, 1941. THAT'S BUFORD RAY,
PACKER TACKLE, ON THE GROUND BEHIND HALL.

of a club on the day that such club was playing at home (Nov. 12).

Attendance records broken again. The 72 games drew 2,164,585 spectators. In the championship play-off, each Detroit player got $2,424.10, each Cleveland man $1,654.26. A total of 134 TV outlets carried the game.

1954—Commissioner Bert Bell given a new 12 year appointment.

Offensive team ruled to have right to request dry ball when field is wet and slippery. Clock not to be stopped.

Attendance records broken again with 2,190,571 during the season.

1955—New rule to eliminate crawling by ball-carrier and lessen chance of injury through piling-on: if player touches ground with any part of body besides hands and feet while in the grasp of opponent, and, irrespective of grasp being broken, ball is declared dead immediately.

Joseph A. Donoghue elected assistant treasurer.

Attendance records continue upward with 2,521,836 and players in championship game received record high share—Cleveland, winners, got $3,508.21 each, Los Angeles losers $2,316.26. Estimated 30 million watched over 159 TV stations.

1956—Dennis J. Shea, treasurer of league since 1940 and associated since 1932, retired on pension. Austin H. Gunsel, elected treasurer.

George S. Halas, after 36 active years as player-owner-coach of Chicago Bears, retired as head coach.

Hugh L. "Shorty" Ray, technical adviser of the league from 1938 to 1952, died in his 72nd year. (Sept. 16.)

Attendance up fifth year in succession with 2,551,623. Playoff shares at record high with $3,779.19 to each winning New York player, $2,485.16 to each Chicago Bear.

1957—George Preston Marshall, owner of Washington Redskins, honored for 25 years of service to the NFL.

Anthony J. Morabito, president and co-owner of the San Francisco 49ers, died Oct. 27.

Attendance records roared up another 11% with 2,836,318 at 72 games. Players take from championship game at new high with $4,295.41 for each winning Detroit player and $2,750.30 for each losing Cleveland Brown.

1958—Bonus pick, started in 1947, eliminated.

Death took Dennis Shea, league treasurer from 1940 to his retirement in 1956; Alexander (Al) Ennis, member of the league staff; Russell W. Bogda, president of the Green Bay Packers; and Emil R. Fischer, a former president of the Packers.

1958—For the second year in succession the paid attendance record for a regular season game was broken in the Los Angeles Coliseum where the Los Angeles Rams and the Chicago Bears drew 90,833 spectators. (Nov. 2.)

The one-day paid attendance record for six championship games broken for the second time in as many years when 328,865 spectators witnessed games in Chicago (Bears), Cleveland, Los Angeles, New York, Philadelphia and Washington. (Nov. 9.)

Paid attendance for the 72 regular season games went over the three million mark for the first time in the history of the league. The record-breaking attendance for the seventh season in a row was 3,006,124 a 5.98 percent increase over 1957. The gross receipts for the championship game rose to a new record of $698,646.00. For the fourth year in succession the record for the player's share in the cham-

PHILADELPHIA EAGLE BLOCKERS ARE MAKING A CLEAN SWEEP FOR BILL BARNES WITH THE BALL IN ACTION AGAINST WASHINGTON IN SEPTEMBER, 1958.

pionship game was broken. The winning Baltimore Colts each received $4,718.77 and the losing New York Giants each $3,111.33.

Baltimore defeated New York 23 to 17 in the first use of the sudden death method of deciding a championship game. The Colts scored a touchdown after 8 minutes, 15 seconds of overtime play. (Dec. 28.)

1959—The league adopted a players benefit plan which gave insurance protection to all active players and would pay undefined monthly benefits to retired players at the age of 65. To qualify for retirement benefits a player must serve five seasons. The plan was to be financed from fees for television rights to championship games starting in 1961 and from other sources.

For the first time since 1933 no changes were made in the playing rules. (Jan. 22.) The annual selection meeting shall be held prior to the end of the season. Twenty (20) selections shall be made by each club. This is a reduction of ten from previous selection meetings. (Jan. 23.)

Timothy J. Mara, founder of the New York Giants Football Club, whose

Photo by Vic Stein & Assoc.

WILL SHERMAN, LOS ANGELES DEFENSIVE BACK, SEEMS TO HAVE SOLVED A DEFENSIVE PROBLEM WITH THIS ROUTINE. MANY TIMES DURING GAMES HE MUST HAVE WISHED THAT HE HAD HIS NET WITH HIM AS THE BALL WENT SAILING BY. HOWEVER, THE RULES COMMITTEE REFUSED TO GO ALONG.

contributions to professional football from 1925 on had much to do with the success enjoyed by the National Football League, died. (Feb. 17.)

De Bennville "Bert" Bell, Commissioner of the National Football League since 1946, died of a heart attack on October 11 at Franklin Field, where he was watching a game between Philadelphia and Pittsburgh. He was 65. Austin Gunsel was named acting Commissioner.

Attendance records broken with an increase of 4.46 percent with 3,140,409 paid spectators attending 72 games. The players' pool in the championship game between New York and Baltimore also reached a new high of $389,020.21. Each Baltimore player got $4,674.44; each New York player $3,083.27.

1960—Alvin "Pete" Rozelle, general manager of the Los Angeles Rams, was named new Commissioner of the NFL for a three-year term.

Dallas was awarded a franchise to start play during 1960 and Thomas Landry, defensive coach of the New York Giants was named the new head coach of Dallas. Three players from each club were awarded to Dallas as a basic roster.

Minneapolis-St. Paul was also awarded a new franchise to start play in 1961, and Bert Rose Jr., Los Angeles Rams publicity director, was made general manager of the new team.

The Chicago Cardinal franchise, active since the beginning of the league, was transferred to St. Louis on March 13.

The player limit, which had been maintained at 36 during the January league meeting, was raised to 38 just before league play opened to build up a backlog of experienced players for the Minneapolis team of 1961 and for others later.

1961—Player limit reduced to 36.

CHAPTER 2
THE COMMISSIONER'S OFFICE

The National Football League has been both wise and fortunate in its choice of Commissioners, and for more than 30 of its 40 years of existence, it was guided by two rare men, Joe F. Carr and Bert Bell.

Carr took control in 1921 after one year of confusion and birth pains under the presidency of Jim Thorpe, who was never more than a figurehead with publicity value. Carr ruled the league for 18 years until his death in 1939. His fearless justice and flawless faith in the future of professional football helped the league ride through its stormy adolescence until it was a strong organization ready for the tremendous race to prosperity at the end of World War II.

It was Carr who insisted in his first year of control that post-graduate football must keep faith with the colleges. He instituted the rule, always scrupulously followed, that the pro league must not negotiate with any college player until his class has graduated. Carr believed that an education was most important and that professional sports must not attempt for its own selfish reasons to disrupt the years of study.

The wisdom of this ruling was most apparent in the continued good relationships

JOE CARR, FIRST PRESIDENT OF THE NATIONAL FOOTBALL LEAGUE

between the NFL and the colleges 40 years after Carr insisted on it in 1921. By contrast, professional baseball, which has had no such interest in education, was blundering down the slide to becoming a lesser sport in 1960 while football was still climbing rapidly to the number one position on the American scene.

Carr showed his strength and courage many times during the league's formative years. In 1925 the Milwaukee team made the mistake of placing four high-school players in the line-up for a game against the Chicago Cardinals. Carr struck swiftly: Milwaukee was banished from the league; the man responsible for recruiting the players was banned from the league for life; the Cardinal owners were fined for permitting their team to take part in the game. At the same time the Pottsville Maroon team was censured for playing a game in the territory of the Frankford Yellowjackets, and the football world, in fact, the entire sports world, was applauding Joe Carr for being a Commissioner with spirit and courage.

After Carr's death in 1939, Carl L. Storck served as president until 1941, when he resigned to make way for Elmer Layden, one of the famed Four Horsemen of Notre Dame. The lull of the war years kept football operating on a restrained basis through the Storck and Layden eras, but in 1946 a new war was declared and again the NFL picked an outstanding leader to fight it. He was de Bennville "Bert" Bell, a former player, coach and owner, a man who had turned his back on his inherited life of wealth and high society, to devote all his energies to the game of football that he loved.

Bell passed his first test almost immediately. An attempt was made by New York fixers to tamper with the championship game between the Giants and the Chicago Bears in 1946. It was a moment when the integrity of pro football was at stake before public opinion, and Bell moved bravely, openly and decisively. He permitted one of the two players involved to play in the game and was rewarded by that player giving a little more than seemed possible in his performance to prove that there had never been any intention on his part of doing anything less than his best. Bell then barred both players from the league for an indefinite period.

He turned then to the "war" with the new All America Football Conference, which was shooting with its millions of dollars at the contracts of National League stars and was determined to defeat the NFL with the power of its almost unlimited funds. Four

BERT BELL

years later Bell and the NFL accepted the complete surrender of the AAFC and Bell's life contract as leader of the NFL was assured. He died at a pro football game in the fall of 1959.

The league then picked a much younger man, Alvin "Pete" Rozelle, at the time general manager of the Los Angeles Rams, and within his first year Rozelle faced a new problem, a "war" with another new league, the American Football League. The veterans who had chosen Rozelle were calm and sure that he, like Carr and Bell before him, would meet the unknown tests ahead.

A year after Bert Bell's death, Tex Maule, pro football editor of *Sports Illustrated*, wrote these words about Bert Bell, in his fine book, *THE PROS*. They seemed to say everything that those who had known Bell best would have wanted to say:

> He was a potbellied little man with a frog voice and he knew more about football than anyone. He played it and coached it and he was president of the National Football League and, a small man in a world of giants, he did very well. He died at a professional football game, and I guess that if you had asked Bert Bell the way he wanted to go, he would have said, "At a pro football game."
>
> Death came for him at a game between the Philadelphia Eagles and the Pittsburgh Steelers in 1959 and the stands were full, which must have made him very happy. As much as any one man, he was responsible for the filled stands.
>
> Bert came from a very posh Philadelphia family. They were society and politics and wealth, and Bert must have seemed a throwback to an earlier, lustier time. He went to the University of Pennsylvania and played football there, and later he coached the team. Back in the early Thirties, he bought the moribund Philadelphia Eagles and they remained moribund under his direction. Bert coached the team reasonably well, but you can't win without the horses and he didn't have horses. And he was involved in all the other myriad details of running a professional football team too. Once he stood on a downtown street corner in Philadelphia and hawked tickets to the Eagle games. He found very few takers. The nadir of his career as a pro football owner came at one game when there were more inhabitants of the press box than there were spectators in the stands.
>
> Maybe Bert's trouble was that he was ahead of his time. He was elected Commissioner of the National Football League on January 11, 1946. At the time, he was a part owner of the Pittsburgh Steelers, and more than a few of the owners thought they were electing a figurehead. Bert changed their minds in a hurry.
>
> He never took a step back from anyone, least of all the owners. In the frequent and bitter arguments between owner and owner, and owner and player, Bert was always fair. It was Bell who designed and implemented the league policy on television, which made pro football the fastest-growing professional sport in the United States. It was this little, fat and stubborn man who introduced the player draft to pro football and so equalized the teams in the league that on any Sunday the lowest team can, with a break, beat the best.
>
> None of that really makes any difference. Bert was a strong man and an intelligent one, and, above all, a fair man. You could call him at three o'clock in the morning and he would talk to you without resentment or anger, and in the last few years that took self-control because he was a sick man. His heart had begun to fail, but he overlooked that, as he overlooked anything which might have made him less of a Commissioner.
>
> I talked to him for a long time one afternoon just a couple of weeks before he died. Our conversation was interrupted by phone calls from owners and players, and in one of these calls he told an owner he was a cheapskate for trying to avoid paying an injured player.

Then he turned to me and said, "Tex, the one thing we can't forget is that this game was built and made popular by the players. We owe them everything. I don't think that any group of athletes in the world can match pro football players for honesty and character and strength."

He was, of course, right.

The Office of the Commissioner of the National Football League is the clearing house through which passes all the business of the organization. It is the keystone of the arch around which the member teams have built their own business structures.

A recital of all that the league office does would fill many pages. A brief summary of its activities will give the reader some idea of its functions as the headquarters of the league.

The Commissioner must approve every contract made between a club and a player, also all trades and sales of players. A card bearing the complete playing record of each player is kept as part of the permanent records of the league office. The eligibility of every player, according to the Constitution and By-Laws, must be proved to the Commissioner's satisfaction.

All officials, referees, umpires, field judges, back judges and linesmen are appointed by the Commissioner and assigned by him to teams of officials. For pre-season and regular season games the officiating teams are assigned to games by the Commissioner.

The Commissioner must approve all contracts for pre-season games. This involves an investigation of promoters of proposed contests, the sites of the games and other matters directly related to the games.

Every employee of every club in the league must be approved by the Commissioner. This includes not only the coaches but those responsible for management, trainers and other personnel.

The Commissioner drafts a schedule of games for each season, a task that requires several hundred hours of work.

From the Commissioner's office are sent bulletins of information to each club: the list of players signed and those being waived by teams: facts about the sale of players, which must have the Commissioner's approval before being consummated. The office compiles a reserve list of players numbering about 1,500 names and sends master questionnaires to every player whose contract is approved.

The Commissioner presides at the annual business meeting of the league. He is also the final court of appeal in any dispute between club and player. He enforces the Constitution and By-Laws of the league. He has the power to suspend and/or fine any player or executive of the league who violates the Constitution and By-Laws. The Commissioner also has sole power over the World Championship football game played each year between the winners of the Conference championships.

The Office of the Commissioner includes a treasurer, a publicity director and such assistants as the Commissioner requires for the proper conduct of his office. A technical assistant who interprets rules and keeps records of officials is a member of the Commissioner's staff.

All the statistical records of the teams and individual players are kept in the Commissioner's office. During the season these are released weekly to the press, radio and television. At the conclusion of the season the final statistics are compiled and released.

The annual *Record and Rules Manual* of the league, which contains the league's records, history, statistics, rules and other information, is edited in the office of the Commissioner.

THE OFFICIALS' SIGNALS

1

**OFFSIDE or
FREE KICK VIOLATION**
Hands on hips

ENCROACHMENT—Same signal followed by placing one hand on top of cap.

2

**CRAWLING, PUSHING
or HELPING RUNNER**
Pushing movement of hands to front with arms downward.

3

**ILLEGAL MOTION
AT SNAP**
Horizontal arc with either hand.

4

ILLEGAL FORWARD PASS
Waving hands behind back.
Intentional Grounding of Pass—Same as above followed by raised hand flung downward.

5

UNSPORTSMANLIKE CONDUCT
Arms outstretched, palms down.
(Same signal means continuing action fouls are disregarded.)

6

**INTERFERENCE WITH FAIR
CATCH or FORWARD PASS**
Pushing hands forward from shoulder with hands vertical.

7

HOLDING
Grasping of one wrist.

**ILLEGAL USE of
HANDS or ARMS**
Holding Signal followed by Interference Signal.

8

PERSONAL FOUL
Striking of One Wrist Above Head
Running into or Roughing Kicker—
 Followed by Swinging Leg
Running into Passer—
 Followed by Raised Arm Swung Forward
Tripping—
 Followed by Hooking Foot Behind Opposite Ankle
Clipping—(Below Waist)
 Followed by Striking Back of Calf with Hand
Clipping—(Above Waist)
 Followed by Striking Back of Thigh with Hand

9

**DELAY OF GAME
or EXCESS TIME-OUT**
Folded arms.

ILLEGAL FORMATION—Same signal followed by over and over rotation of forearms in front of body.

10

**TOUCHDOWN, FIELD GOAL
or SUCCESSFUL TRY**

Both arms extended above head

THE SIGNALS ON THESE PAGES ARE THOSE MORE COMMONLY USED BY THE OFFICIALS TO FACILITATE INFORMATIVE COMMUNICATION.

THE RULES COMMITTEE.

11

SAFETY

Palms together over head.

12

LOSS OF DOWN
(Follows signal for foul.)
Tapping both shoulders
with finger tips.

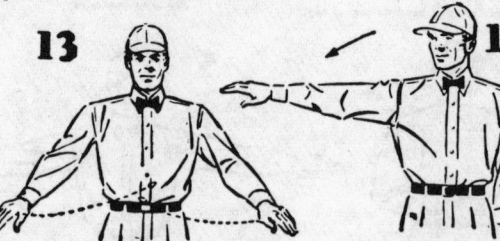

13

14

**PENALTY REFUSED, INCOM-
PLETE PASS, PLAY OVER,
or MISSED GOAL**
Sifting of hands in horizontal plane.

FIRST DOWN
Arm raised then pointed toward
defensive team's goal.

15

**DEAD BALL
or NEUTRAL ZONE
ESTABLISHED**
One arm aloft, open hand
(With fist closed — Fourth Down)

16

**NO TIME-OUT or
TIME-IN WITH WHISTLE**
Full arm circles to
simulate winding clock.

17

TIME-OUT
Hands criss-crossed over head.
TOUCHBACK
Time-Out Signal followed
by arm swung at side

K. L. Ray, Del.

NATIONAL FOOTBALL LEAGUE

PAID ATTENDANCE

	SEASON		CHAMPIONSHIP GAME
1934	492,684	(3 to 13 games)	
1935	638,178	(12 games)	
1936	816,007	(12 games)	
1937	963,039	(11 games)	
1938	937,197	(11 games)	48,120
1939	1,071,200	(11 games)	32,279
1940	1,063,025	(11 games)	36,034
1941	1,108,615	(11 games)	13,341
1942	887,920	(11 games)	36,006
1943	969,128	(10 games)	34,320
1944	1,019,649	(10 games)	46,016
1945	1,270,401	(10 games)	32,178
1946	1,732,135	(11 games)	58,346
1947	1,837,437	(12 games)	30,759
1948	1,525,243	(12 games)	36,309
1949	1,391,735	(12 games)	27,980
1950	1,977,750	(12 games–13 teams–78 games)	29,751
	(Playoffs–Cleveland–New York 30,998		
	Chicago Bears–Los Angeles 75,898)		
1951	1,913,019	(12 games)	57,522
1952	2,052,126	(12 games)	50,934
	(Playoff Detroit–Los Angeles 46,573)		
1953	2,164,585	(12 games)	54,577
1954	2,190,571	(12 games)	43,827
1955	2,521,836	(12 games)	85,693
1956	2,551,263	(12 games)	56,836
1957	2,836,318	(12 games)	55,263
	(Playoff San Francisco–Detroit 55,316)		
1958	3,006,124	(12 games)	64,185
	(Playoff New York–Cleveland 59,474)		
1959	3,314,515	(12 games)	57,545
1960	3,128,296	(12 games, 13 teams)	67,325

NATIONAL FOOTBALL LEAGUE

STANDARD PLAYERS CONTRACT

BETWEEN

....

which operates ...., and which is a member of the National
Football League, and which is hereinafter called the "Club," and ....
.... of .... hereinafter called the "Player."

In consideration of the respective promises herein the parties hereto agree as follows:

1. The term of this contract shall be from the date of execution hereof until the
first day of May following the close of the football season commencing in ....
................., subject however, to rights of prior termination as specified herein.

2. The Player agrees that during the term of this contract he will play football and
will engage in activities related to football only for the Club and as directed by the Club
according to the Constitution, By-laws, Rules and Regulations of the National Football
League, hereinafter called the "League," and of the Club, and the Club, subject to the
provisions hereof, agrees during such period to employ the Player as a skilled football
player. The Player agrees during the term of this contract to report promptly for the
Club's training seasons, to render his full time services during the training seasons and at
the Club's direction to participate in all practice sessions and in all League and other
football games scheduled by the Club.

3. For the Player's services as a skilled football player during the term of this contract,
and for his agreement not to play football or engage in activities related to football for
any other person, firm, corporation or institution during the term of this contract, and
for the option hereinafter set forth giving the Club the right to renew his contract, and
for the other undertakings of the Player herein, the Club promises to pay the Player
each football season during the term of this contract the sum of $................to be
payable as follows:

> **75% of said salary in weekly installments commencing with the first and ending
> with the last regularly scheduled League game played by the Club during such
> season and the balance of 25% of said sum at the end of said last regularly
> scheduled League game.**

In addition, the Club promises and agrees to pay the reasonable board and lodging
expenses of the Player incurred while playing for the Club in other than the Club's home
city and also to pay all proper and necessary travelling expenses of the Player and his
meals en route to and from said games.

4. The Player agrees at all times to comply with and to be bound by all the provisions
of the Constitution, By-laws, Rules and Regulations of the League and of the Club, all
of which are hereby made a part of this contract. If the Player fails to comply with said
Constitution, By-laws, Rules and Regulations the Club shall have the right to terminate
this contract or to take such other action as may be specified in said Constitution, By-laws,
Rules and Regulations, or as may be directed by the Commissioner of the League, hereinafter called the "Commissioner." The Player agrees to submit himself to the discipline
of the League and of the Club for any violation of such Constitution, By-laws, Rules and
Regulations subject however, to the right to a hearing by the Commissioner. All matters
in dispute between the Player and the Club shall be referred to the Commissioner and
his decision shall be accepted as final, complete, conclusive, binding and unappealable,

by the Player and by the Club. The Player hereby waives any and all rights of action against the Commissioner, the League, the Club or any of its members or stockholders, and against any officer of the Club or of the League arising out of or in connection with decisions of the Commissioner, except to the extent of awards made by the Commissioner to the Player. The Player hereby acknowledges that he has read said Constitution, By-laws, Rules and Regulations and that he understands their meaning.

5. The Player promises and agrees that during the term of this contract he will not play football or engage in activities related to football for any other person, firm, corporation or institution except with the prior written consent of the Club and the Commissioner, and that he will not during the term of this contract engage in any game or exhibition of baseball, basketball, hockey, wrestling, boxing or any other sport which endangers his ability to perform his services hereunder, without the prior written consent of the Club. The Player likewise promises and agrees that during the term of this contract, when, as and if he shall receive an invitation to participate in any All-Star football game which is approved by the League, he will play in said game in accordance with all the terms and conditions relating thereto, including the player compensation there in set forth, as are agreed to between the League and the Sponsor of such game.

6. The Player represents and warrants that he is and will continue to be sufficiently highly skilled in all types of football team play to play professional football of the caliber required by the League and by the Club, that he is and will continue to be in excellent physical condition, and agrees to perform his services hereunder to the complete satis-

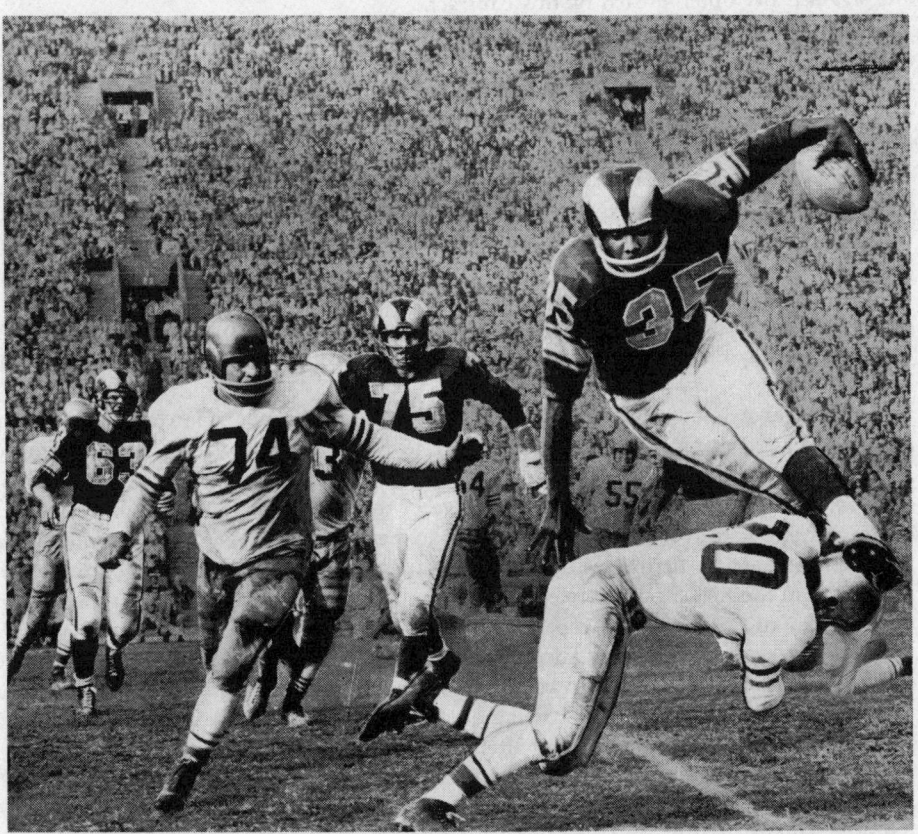

Photo by Tom Courtney
AIR STRIKE—IF YOU CAN'T GO THROUGH, GO OVER, SEEMS TO BE THE PLAN OF PAUL "TANK" YOUNGER OF THE RAMS AS HE HURDLES BILL STITS, SAN FRANCISCO DEFENSIVE BACK.

faction of the Club and its Head Coach. If in the opinion of the Head Coach the Player does not maintain himself in excellent physical condition or fails at any time during the football seasons included in the term of this contract to demonstrate sufficient skill and capacity to play professional football of the caliber required by the League and by the Club, or if in the opinion of the Head Coach the Player's work or conduct in the performance of this contract is unsatisfactory as compared with the work and conduct of other members of the Club's squad of players, the Club shall have the right to terminate this contract upon written notice to the player of such termination.

7. Upon termination of this contract the Club shall pay the Player only the balance remaining due him for travelling and board and lodging expenses and any balance remaining due him for football seasons completed prior to termination, and, if termination takes place during a football season, any balance remaining due him on that portion of his total compensation for that season as provided in paragraph 3 hereof which the number of regularly scheduled League games already played by the Club during that season bears to the total number of League games scheduled for the Club for that season.

8. The Player hereby represents that he has special, exceptional and unique knowledge, skill and ability as a football player, the loss of which cannot be estimated with any certainty and cannot be fairly or adequately compensated by damages and therefore agrees that the Club shall have the right, in addition to any other rights which the Club may possess, to enjoin him by appropriate injunction proceedings against playing football or engaging in activities related to football for any person, firm, corporation or institution and against any other breach of this contract.

9. It is mutually agreed that the Club shall have the right to sell, exchange, assign and transfer this contract and the Player's services to any other Club of the League and the Player agrees to accept such assignment and to report promptly to the assignee club and faithfully to perform and carry out this contract with the assignee club as if it had been entered into by the Player with the assignee club instead of with this Club.

10. On or before the date of expiration of this contract, the Club may, upon notice in writing to the Player, renew this contract for a further term until the first day of May following said expiration on the same terms, including rate of compensation to the Player, as are provided by this contract, except that after such renewal this contract shall not include a further option to the Club to renew the contract; the phrase 'rate of compensation' as above used shall not be understood to include bonus payments or payments of any nature whatsoever other than the precise sum set forth in paragraph '3' hereof.

11. Player acknowledges the right and power of the Commissioner of the National Football League (a) to fine and suspend, (b) to fine and suspend for life or indefinitely, and/or (c) to cancel the contract of, any player who accepts a bribe or who agrees to throw or fix a game or who, having knowledge of the same, fails to report an offered bribe or an attempt to throw or fix a game, or who bets on a game, or who is guilty of any conduct detrimental to the welfare of the National Football League or of professional football; and the Player hereby releases the Commissioner of the National Football League, individually and in his official capacity, and also the National Football League and every club and every officer, director and stockholder of the League and of every club thereof, jointly, and severally, from all claims and demands for damages and every claim and demand whatsoever he may have arising out of or in connection with the decision of said Commissioner of the National Football League in any of the aforesaid cases.

12. This agreement contains the entire agreement between the parties and there are no oral or written inducements, promises or agreements except as contained herein. This agreement shall become valid and binding upon party hereto only when, as and if it shall be approved by the Commissioner.

13. This agreement has been made under and shall be governed by the laws of the State of ....

IN WITNESS WHEREOF the Player has hereunto set his hand and seal and the Club has caused this contract to be executed by its duly authorized officer on the date set opposite their respective names.

WITNESS: ....

....   Club
                                  Date   By ....

....
                                  Date   Player

Approved ....
         Commissioner   Date   Player's Address

This Copy to be Sent to Commissioner for Approval
Return to Member Club

CHAPTER 3
THE COACHES

If one basic truth has been established in almost forty years of major league football, it is that playing experience, plus an apprenticeship of assistant coaching in the big time, is necessary before any man can become a successful coach in the National Football League. In all the years there has been but one exception to that truth, namely, Paul Brown of the Cleveland Browns. Others without these two items of experience have never ranked better than mediocre. The historic trail of the record books is strewn with the whitening bones of "brilliant" college coaches who ventured across the borders of the major league and were immediately scalped, skinned and skunked by tactics they never knew existed. They found that defenses which are air-tight in the college game are wide open to big league attack. They found veteran brain trusts licking their chops and reveling in new brands of mayhem to be practiced against outraged beginners. Many of them "resigned in mid-season"; some finished one or two years before fleeing back from whence they came.

A second basic truth has been established—that psychology, which stems from the head coach, has become the vital difference between winning and losing; that there is only a microscopic difference in playing ability between the team that wins the championship and the team which finishes in last place; that the difference is the head coach's ability to get his squad psychologically "up" for the important games.

Team spirit, when it is running near the crest in major league football, is the strongest, most devastating and unbeatable factor in any American sport. Men who can stand up and survive in this most violent contact battle must possess to high degree the qualities which produce the finest ideals of team spirit. There can be no malingering, no half-throttle courage, no playing for self alone. The head coach must blend the violent personalities of more than thirty adult males, all full of their own idiosyncrasies, into one unit. Each major league club is made up of 30 outstanding stars. There are no "bush-leaguers" around.

Mr. National Football League

GEORGE S. HALAS

George Stanley Halas, aged twenty-two, his football career finished at the University of Illinois, sat at his team's banquet in the early winter of 1917 and listened to the farewell speech of Bob Zuppke, his coach, who was complaining bitterly about certain traditional patterns of life.

"Why is it," Zup demanded, "that just when you players are beginning to know something about football after three years, I lose you—and you stop playing? It makes no sense. Football is the only sport that ends a man's career just when it should be beginning."

That remark by Bob Zuppke might well be credited with starting a series of cosmic reactions which resulted, thirty-five years later, in more than two million rabid major league football fans scrambling into National Football League parks to watch America's most thrilling sport. For the words made something click in the brain of Left End Halas, Navy-bound at the moment, but unhappy because he still had a lot of football left in his system and he didn't want it to rot there.

Halas had been an all-round athlete at Illinois, which he chose for an engineering course after graduating from Crane Tech in his native Chicago. He'd been so good at baseball that the New York Yankees wanted him as soon as the

war was over. At basketball he had sparkled, becoming team captain in his senior year. But football was his own first choice, and he had become an end instead of a halfback as he had planned, because, as Zuppke once said, "he ran so hard I was afraid he'd get killed as a halfback."

It was a happy surprise to George Halas when he reported to Great Lakes Naval Training Station to learn that the Navy was going to have football too, and that there were plenty of stars on hand to make it roll. Emmett Keefe, a guard from Notre Dame, was captain of the team. John "Paddy" Driscoll, a flashy back from Northwestern, was part of the backfield which included the versatile Jim Conzelman, Harold Erickson, Dutch Lauer and many others. Hugh Blacklock was a roadblock at tackle next to end George Halas, a neighborly pairing which was to endure long after the war was over.

Great Lakes was good enough to tie Notre Dame, to beat the Naval Academy at Annapolis, to be chosen to play in the Rose Bowl on New Year's Day, 1919, where they caused a sensation by upsetting the tremendous team from the base at Mare Island.

Halas was discharged as an ensign and soon reported to the Yankee baseball team in Florida, depressed once more because he still had lots of football left in his fuel-system and it seemed that now it must surely be over for him. He soon won a permanent job with the Yankees. Then he sustained a leg injury in a thundering slide into third base after belting one of Rube Marquard's slants through the outfield during an exhibition game. The injury sidelined him and eventually caused his release to St. Paul. He finished an impressive rookie season there and was headed back to the Yankees the next spring. But he was still restless for more football; he still remembered Bob Zuppke's remarks.

He managed to play a few football games that fall with the independent team of Hammond, Indiana, and then came the break which led the way to the Chicago Bears and the National Football League.

Mr. A. E. Staley, owner of a corn products company in Decatur, Illinois, was a sports fan who wanted his firm to be represented by teams in all possible sports. Joe "Iron Man" McGinnity managed the strong Staley baseball team. Why shouldn't George Halas, the young firebrand who would play football twenty-four hours a day if he could arrange it, be the Staley football leader?

It was all right with Halas. He worked full hours at the plant, played on its baseball team and started recruiting football players with the same acumen and fervor he still employs. When the American Professional Football Association was organized in Ralph Hays's garage at Canton, Ohio, that fall, Halas was there, ready to go with a roster of players that scared the other owners half to death. He proposed to line up with Guy Chamberlain and himself at

GUY CHAMBERLAIN   *INP*

end; Hugh Blacklock and Bert Ingwerson at tackle; Hubbard Shoemaker and Jerry Jones at guard; George Trafton, center; and the backs would be Ed "Dutch" Sternaman, Jake Lanum, Bob Koehler, Walter "Pard" Pearce and Charlie Dressen. They were the cream of the college crop. His only disappointment was the fact that Paddy Driscoll had joined the Chicago Cardinals and it would be six years before Halas could sign him to a contract.

The Staleys were indeed loaded with talent and end-coach-manager George Halas was a clever field general. They won every game until the Cardinals dumped them, 7–6. Then they came back to whip the

Cards, 10–0, to finish a glorious season.

Papa Bear was on his way.

During the ensuing three decades, Halas and his Monsters of the Midway dominated football. They won the most championships, 7; they won the most games, over 400; they scored the most points, more than 11,000; they gained the most yards, nearly 25 miles; they scored the most touchdowns, nearly 1,600; played to most fans, nearly 15,000,000. They probably made the most money. And they were definitely penalized the most.

Individually, too, they have sparkled. Their Sid Luckman holds records for most TD passes in one season (28) and in one game (7). George Halas himself holds a twenty-nine-year-old record that still stands —a 98-yard run with a recovered fumble. The entire tribe of Jim Thorpe's Oorang Indians was whooping in pursuit. He had to make the touchdown or get scalped.

The list of Bear players shines brighter than all the rest in the honor rolls of football. They have been noted for team spirit and have won many games with inferior teams because of this spirit, which originates in the explosive violence and the competitive drive of their owner-coach. Since he retired as a player in 1932 ("When they began to run over me, under me, around me and through me"), Halas has prowled the sidelines through nearly every game, except during World War II when he served in the Navy as a commander. Every cell in his body is in every play, and his spectacular rages against officiating lapses have bemused hundreds of thousands of fans.

Halas made a habit of writing "first" into the record book from the start. The Bears were the first official champions of the reorganized league in 1921 when they moved to Chicago to play that season as the Staleys and to become the Bears a year later. They were the first professional team to practice daily; the first big league team to travel coast-to-coast (the Red Grange Unveiling Tour, which started in Chicago on Thanksgiving Day, 1925, ended three months later after playing in New York, Washington, Providence, Pittsburgh, Detroit, Chicago again, Tampa, Jacksonville, Miami, New Orleans, Los Angeles, San Diego, San Francisco, Portland and Seattle). Other minor firsts were a band and a team song, and a club newspaper; and they were the first to have their games broadcast on radio, and to take movies of games for study and strategy.

Nearly every team which plays football under the banner of T-formation in 1952, whether it be professional, college or grade school, will be using plays which were first diagrammed by the Chicago Bears, which means by George Halas and his Bear-trained staff, all former Bear stars, with occasional help from the brilliant theorist, Clark Shaughnessy, now a Bear vice-president. Halas added the man-in-motion to the ineffective T of older days and made it come alive. In 1937, he bet the future of his team on the ability of an awkward young halfback named Sidney Luckman to make it work. Luckman floundered for a few weeks, but suddenly, through unbeatable determination and endless hours of practice, he got it and a new era was born in football. Halas, Luckman and the T grew to maturity together.

Luckman went on to rank himself as the smartest field general of them all. His nickname, "Mr. Quarterback," was well earned. Today George Halas will testify under oath that Sid Luckman never called a wrong play during twelve years of action; that he was always thinking so far ahead of his opponents, his teammates and everyone else, that he drove most of them crazy, including George Halas himself.

It was inevitable that someday George Halas would come up with a performance that would live forever as the mark of perfection. It happened in Griffith Stadium, Washington, D.C. on December 8, 1940, and when it was over, Steve Owen, coach of the New York Giants, which team had finished third in the Eastern division behind the Redskins, had this to say, "Now I'm glad we didn't win the Eastern championship. In fact, I'm glad we didn't finish second. Even that would have been too close to the Bears today."

For the story of that spectacle, unparalleled in football history and unlikely to be repeated, this encyclopedia will borrow from that fine book, *The Chicago Bears,* written by Howard Roberts, pro football expert of the Chicago *Daily News,* and published by G. P. Putnam's Sons, the complete story of the cold-blooded, premeditated massacre of a sorrowful group of young men known as the Washington Redskins. It was a crime committed with well-planned malice aforethought. In sixty minutes of official play, George Halas made his team do everything lethal a football team can do a little better than it has ever been done before or since, to score a staggering 73–0 humiliation over one of the strongest teams Washington has ever had —and they have had some dandies; to annihilate a team which had beaten the Bears, 7–3, only three weeks before.

It was the masterpiece of football, fashioned by George Halas. This is the way Roberts saw it:

Sunday, December 8, 1940, was a beautiful day in Washington. The sun shone brilliantly and with a warmth surprisingly pleasant for the time of year. The sky was blue and cloudless. Scarcely a breeze rippled the flags over Griffith Stadium where 36,034 people clustered in quivering anticipation as their Redskins prepared to face the Bears for the championship.

Two hours later, although the sun still shone, it was the darkest day the nation's capital would know until another Sunday, 364 days later, when Jap bombs fell on Pearl Harbor to plunge the United States into war.

The events that filled those two hours are unparalleled in sports history. They were so beyond comprehension that even those who saw them or took part in them have difficulty believing it wasn't a dream. To all but a handful of those 36,034 the dream was a nightmare, yet they left the park content. They were disappointed, certainly, but not unhappy. After all, they could tell their grandchildren that they had witnessed the impossible; that they had looked on perfection.

The Bears were perfection that day. There is no other explanation for the score that reads like a misprint in the record books: Chicago Bears 73; Washington Redskins 0.

The score itself is a story, but back of it is another one, a tale of psychology, of emotional uplift, of planning so meticulous that almost nothing was left to chance—except the fervent hope the Redskins would employ the same defense that had kept their goal line inviolate three weeks before.

Halas and his board of strategy knew from bitter experience that Washington was not a team to be taken lightly, for with Slingin' Sammy Baugh pitching passes, the Redskins were almost certain to score against the best of defenses. The trick was to keep Baugh from passing, in so far as that could be achieved. And the best way to keep Sammy from throwing touchdowns was to keep his hands off the ball as much as possible. If the Bears could control the ball throughout most of the afternoon, they might be able to outscore the enemy.

With that in mind, the faculty of Halas U. set about polishing their T until it shone. Movies of the Redskin defeat were studied over and over again. So were films of other Bear-Redskin games. From these showings and from the penciled notes in the coach's little black book were culled only the plays that had worked against Washington. These were perfected and refined; new variations were added; plays the Redskins had stopped were discarded and replaced by new ones calculated to take advantage of Ray Flaherty's defense.

The players saw the movies almost as many times as did the coaches. Every play was analyzed—why this one worked, why that one didn't, what this mistake cost, what that good block accomplished. The Bears, seeing their previous mistakes pointed out on the screen, vowed they wouldn't happen again. Morning practice on the field was followed by chalk talks, lectures, written examinations on individual assignments, more movies. Clark Shaughnessy was brought in to discuss strategy with the quarterbacks—Luckman, Masterson and Solly Sherman.

The greatest weapon Halas brought into play was psychology. The Redskins had made what Halas termed some "tactical vocal errors" after the earlier 7–3 victory, and now they were deftly turned against them. It seems that a club official with a careless disregard for the interpretation that might be placed on his words, had been quoted in the public prints as referring to the Bears by such uncomplimentary terms, as "front-runners" and a "first-half ball club." The Redskins themselves had called the Bears "crybabies" in the final minute of their earlier meeting.

When the Bears came to practice the Monday morning preceding the championship game, their eyes fell upon these disparagements of their courage and staying power plastering the walls of the clubhouse. The reaction was terrific. Mutterings grew to shouts of revenge. The boys were mad clean through. Halas kept them that way, reminding them that Washington regarded them as quitters a final time in his between-halves speech even though the score at that time was Bears 28; Washington 0.

Get one of the 1940 Bears into conversation today about that week of drill and the game itself, and you'll find him turning slightly hysterical, his voice rising in excitement and his eyes flashing.

"I've never experienced anything like it," Luckman admits with a look almost of wonder. "There was a feeling of tension in the air as though something tremendous was about to happen."

That feeling was apparent on the train en route to Washington. Ball players customarily while away train rides by playing cards or sitting around swapping stories. There is laughing, joking, wisecracks, fun. But not this time. There was no laughter, no frolicking, not a single deck of cards in sight. The Bears sat huddled in their seats, notebooks on their laps, studying.

One bit of superstition crept in, too. For luck the Bears moved from their usual Washington hotel to another, a shift Secretary Frank Halas believes entitles him to a share of credit for the momentous events that were in store.

The opening whistle unleashed a Bear attack that was concentrated fury. The kick-off sailed into the arms of Nolting, who sprinted back twenty-two yards to the twenty-four yard line. In the huddle Luckman called a "feeler," the first of four Bear offensive plays having been charted long before to test the Redskin defense. Was it the same as before? Everything depended on the answer to that question.

Kavanaugh, at left end, went 18 yards out on the flank, and the Washington right halfback followed him out. Nolting, at left half, went in motion to the right, and the Redskin backerup trailed him out. That was all Luckman wanted to see. The Washington defense was unchanged. On the play McAfee bolted between guard and tackle for eight yards.

On the next play the left end went wide again, but McAfee, the right half, went in motion to his left. Luckman, making a reverse pivot, gave the ball to Osmanski on a run to the spread side.

"Bill was really driving when I handed off that ball to him," Luckman grins. "I knew he was going someplace in a hurry."

That someplace was sixty-eight yards to a touchdown.

Here, however, is a secret never before revealed about the play—it didn't go according to plan or blueprint. Actually it called for a straight slant off tackle, but McAfee's block hadn't flattened the Redskin right end.

"George had him blocked off," says Osmanski, "but he was reaching out with his hands, and I was afraid he could grab me, so I just made a sort of dip and went out wide around end." That dip, incidentally, is now a charted play in the Bears' book.

Osmanski, who was possessed of jet-propulsion acceleration, streaked away, as Musso, pulling out from right guard to join the interference, flattened the up man in the secondary. Near the Washington thirty-five yard line Osmanski was walking a tightrope down the south sideline with Ed "Chug" Justice and Jimmy Johnston closing in on him. Osmanski saw them, but what neither he nor the two Redskins saw was George Wilson, cutting across from his position at right end, whizzing like a tornado into their path. Just as Justice set himself to tackle Osmanski, Wilson hurtled into him from the blind side with such force the impact could be felt in the stands.

"I've never seen a block like it," Halas maintains.

It knocked Justice into Johnston and both of them into a cartwheel that sent them rolling out of the field of play. Both had to be helped to their feet. As a parlay it was a knockout.

Osmanski, of course, simply kept running. As he flashed over the last white line and into the end zone with a touchdown, the big scoreboard clock showed just fifty-five seconds of playing time elapsed. Jack Manders kicked the extra point, but the parade wasn't on—not quite yet.

Max Krause, who is so much a Redskin at heart that he served as their water boy at times while he was in the Navy and too old and too busy to play football, took the next kickoff and promptly scared the Bears half to death. Straight down the field he raced for sixty-two yards before he was finally tackled on the Bear thirty-two yard line. Then came the play that turned the ball game and set the Bear adding machine in motion.

Baugh faded back and shot a long pass to Charlie Malone. The big end was in the clear with a touchdown and an almost certain tie score in his grasp—but he dropped the ball. And, as that pass trickled off his finger tips, Fate turned her back on the Redskins. Had Malone caught the ball the game might have been the nip-and-tuck, slam-bang affair a championship game is supposed to be. As it was, the Redskins never again were a factor.

No one suspected that such was the case when Bob Masterson missed a field goal attempt from the thirty-two yard line, but the handwriting soon became legible on the wall. The Bears put it there with a magnificent display of power football that swept eighty yards in seventeen plays and four first downs without the use of a pass. Luckman scored the touchdown on a sneak of about a foot under Bulldog Turner. Bob Snyder came in for Osmanski to add the point and make the score 14–0.

The Redskins, startled and shocked into desperation, tried three fruitless passes after receiving the kickoff, then were forced to punt, Luckman coming back to the Washington forty-two. Here Luckman called for almost the identical play on which Osmanski had made his great run. This time, however, Joe Maniaci was the fullback, and instead of taking the ball on a handoff, he got it on a shovel pass. Otherwise the pattern was almost identical, for

Maniaci didn't stop running until he had touchdown number three. Phil Martinovich converted, making it three different Bears to add a point after each of three scores.

Twelve minutes and forty seconds had been ticked off on the clock, and the scoreboard read: Bears 21; Redskins 0.

Still another touchdown was added before the end of the half, Kavanaugh leaping in the corner of the end zone behind Frank Filchock and Andy Farkas to catch Luckman's thirty-yard pass. Bob Snyder kicked the twenty-eighth point.

The Redskins still refused to concede defeat and came out for the second half charged with new spirit. Wee Willie Wilkin, the gigantic blond tackle, in particular, was a heroic figure until he was led off the field late in the game, crying in anger and humiliation.

But if the Redskins were fired by the half-time revival, so were the Bears. Halas' brief oration dwelt solely on the premise that Washington regarded the Bears strictly as a "first-half ball club" and "quitters."

They quickly proved this to be a myth. On the second play of the third period Baugh attempted a short pass to fullback Johnston in the flat, but Hampton Pool, the Bear end, sensed the play, batted the ball into the air, caught it, and sped fifteen yards to a touchdown. He had scored before most of the Redskins knew anything was amiss.

That was the coup de grace. The Redskins were done. You could see them wilt before your eyes as the fire and spark and spirit drained out of them like air from a punctured tire.

Three more Bear touchdowns clattered across in the third period. Nolting collected the first when he bolted through a quick-opening hole inside the Washington right tackle and scooted twenty-three yards. Two plays after the ensuing kickoff McAfee intercepted a pass by Roy Zimmerman and zigzagged thirty-four yards behind fine blocking to plant the ball in the end zone. Another Zimmerman pass boomeranged later, Turner intercepting this one and going twenty-one yards to score, aided by a furious block with which Pool removed the unhappy Zimmerman from the picture.

The fourth quarter brought more of the same as the "first-half ball club" made it seven touchdowns for the second half. Harry Clark started it with a forty-four-yard run in the course of which he powered his way right out of Filchock's tackle on the ten yard line.

The Redskins received once more, and immediately things went wrong for them again. A pass from center got away from Filchock and Turner recovered only two yards from the goal line. Famiglietti bridged this gap in one drive.

At just about this moment the public address loudspeakers boomed forth with what was probably the most ill-advised and poorly timed announcement ever made. "Those who wish to purchase season tickets for next year . . ." came the brassy voice, only to be lost in a cascade of boos and catcalls. Strangely enough those boos meant nothing for the Redskins advance sale for the '41 season had set a new record high by Christmas.

Again the Bears kicked off, and this time the Redskins held possession of the ball for only one play. The second was a pass by Filchock, and Maniaci stepped into its path, returning twenty-one yards to Washington's forty-two yard line. From there the Bears turned on the power, with Clark picking up the final yard and the last points of an historic afternoon.

Dick Plasman and Joe Stydahar added extra points from placement in this half with Maniaci getting another on a pass from Sherman. By this time the Bears didn't care much whether they kicked extra points or not, while the officials and the Washington ball club were hoping they wouldn't. Every placement kick propelled by the strong and accurate toes of the Bears, sailed into the stands and didn't return. So it was that after the last two TDs officials asked the Bears please not to kick for points. Sherman, an obliging fellow, tried passing for two points, one of which scored.

In the course of compiling this astronomical score the Bears gained 372 yards rushing to Washington's 3. But this wasn't the only unusual phase of the statistics. The Redskins, the top offensive team in the league, had been held scoreless for the first time. The Bears divided their eleven touchdowns among ten men, Clark being the only repeater. In all, sixteen Bears shared in the point production, six having a hand (or toe) in conversions. Eight Washington passes were intercepted.

The Bears never let up. So tensely were they keyed for this game that even late in the fourth period players leaving the field would whack their substitutes on the seats of their silk pants and exhort: "Pour it on. Don't let up. Pour it on." They kept on pouring their T until the cup ran over.

Superlatives fairly drooled off the typewriters of the nation's top sports writers as they reached in vain for words to describe the game. Typical of the accolades was that given a Washington newspaper by "Dutch" Bergman, then coach at Catholic University.

"I saw the perfect football team in the Bears," Bergman wrote. "I have been associated with the game as player and coach for twenty-five years, but never in that time did I ever see a team that did everything perfectly, with such flawless execution, as did the Bears in humbling the Redskins."

Phil Handler, line coach of the Chicago Cardinals, shook his head and muttered, "I've never seen anything like it and never will again."

Halas, over the radio, came up with his second masterpiece of the afternoon, this time one of understatement. "My team played a great game," he told the armchair spectators. "I think they deserved to win."

The bark of the gun ending the massacre caused some pressbox wit to remark, "George Marshall (Redskin Owner) just shot himself." The Redskin man hadn't gone to such lengths, but he was heartbroken, shamefaced, and completely at a loss to account for the holocaust.

The next day as the Bears rode triumphantly home with bruises, a championship, and a few hangovers, a Pullman passenger looked with interest at the rainbow decorating Danny Fortmann's left eye.

"My, my," he clucked sympathetically. "That's a terrible black eye you have there."

"Yes," Fortmann agreed, "but it will disappear in a day or two. Think of the Redskins—that seventy-three-to-nothing score is in the record books for all time."

George Halas, independently wealthy now, has founded a dynasty of sport. His Bears stand for quality, spirit and a dramatic ability. They are entirely his creation. The National Football League can be credited more to him than to any other man. His innovations on the T-formation dominate football in every league.

It is with restraint, rather than overenthusiasm, that the hungry Bohemian lad who listened, more than 40 years ago, to a querulous complaint by Bob Zuppke, is now called "Mr. Football" as often as he is "Papa Bear." For it was his dream alone that has grown into spectacular reality; his courage and determination that would not let it die.

BOB ZUPPKE

NATIONAL LEAGUE COACHES
(ACTIVE TEAMS)

BALTIMORE COLTS

1950   Clem F. Crowe
1953   Keith Molesworth
1954—1961   Wilbur C. Ewbank

BOSTON REDSKINS

*Franchise transferred to Washington in 1937
1932   Ludlow Wray
1933–1934   William "Lone Star" Dietz
1935   Edward Casey
1936   Ray Flaherty*

CHICAGO BEARS

*Retired October 25 to re-enter Navy
†Co-coach

1920–1929   George S. Halas
1930–1932   Ralph Jones
1933–1941   George S. Halas
1942   George S. Halas*
        Heartley Anderson†
        Luke Johnsos†
1943–1945   Heartley Anderson†
        Luke Johnsos†
1946–1955   George S. Halas
1956–1957   John L. "Paddy" Driscoll
1958–1961   George S. Halas

CHICAGO CARDINALS

(Franchise transferred to St. Louis in 1960)

*Resigned after first two games
†Co-coach

1920   Marshall Smith
1921–1922   John "Paddy" Driscoll
1923–1924   Arnold Horween
1925–1926   Norman Barry
1927   Fred Gillies
1928   Guy Chamberlain
1929–1930   Ernie Nevers
1931   Leroy Andrews*
        Ernie Nevers
1932   Jack Chevigny
1933–1934   Paul Schissler
1935–1938   Milan Creighton
1939   Ernie Nevers
1940–1942   James Conzelman
1943   Phil Handler
1944   (Merged with Pittsburgh)
1945   Phil Handler
1946–1948   James Conzelman
1949   Phil Handler†

Raymond "Buddy" Parker†
1950–1951   Earl "Curly" Lambeau
1952   Joseph Kuharich
1953–1954   Joseph Stydahar
1955–1957   Ray Richards
1958–1959   Frank Ivy

CLEVELAND BROWNS

1950–1961   Paul E. Brown

CLEVELAND RAMS

*Resigned in mid-season
†Franchise transferred to Los Angeles in 1946
1937   Hugo Bezdek
1938   Hugo Bezdek*
        Arthur Lewis
1939–1942   Earl "Dutch" Clark
1943   (Suspended operation)
1944   Aldo Donelli
1945   Adam Walsh†

DALLAS COWBOYS

1960—1961   Thomas Landry

DETROIT LIONS

(Formerly Portsmouth Spartans, 1930–33)

*Released after third game, October 4
1930–1936   George "Potsy" Clark
1937–1938   Earl "Dutch" Clark
1939   Gus Henderson
1940   George "Potsy" Clark
1941   William Edwards
1942   William Edwards*
        John Karcis
1943–1947   Charles "Gus" Dorais
1948–1950   Alvin N. "Bo" McMillin
1951–1956   Raymond "Buddy" Parker
1957–1961   George Wilson

GREEN BAY PACKERS

1921–1949   Earl "Curly" Lambeau
1950–1953   Gene Ronzani
1954–1957   Lisle W. Blackbourn
1958   Ray McLean
1959–1961   Vincent Lombardi

LOS ANGELES RAMS

(Formerly Cleveland Rams, 1937–45)

*Resigned in mid-season

1946 Adam Walsh	1939 John "Blood" McNally*
1947 Robert A. Snyder	Walter Kiesling
1948–1949 Clark Shaughnessy	1940 Walter Kiesling
1950–1951 Joe Stydahar	1941 Bert Bell†
1952–1954 Hampton Pool	Aldo Donelli‡
1955–1959 Sid Gillman	Walter Kiesling
1960–1961 Robert Waterfield	1942 Walter Kiesling
	1943 (Merged with Philadelphia)
	1944 Walter Kiesling§
	Phil Handler¶

MINNESOTA VIKINGS

1961   Norman Van Brocklin

1945   Jim Leonard
1946–1947   Dr. John B. Sutherland
1948–1951   John B. Michelosen

NEW YORK GIANTS

1925   Robert Folwell
1926   Joseph Alexander
1927–1928   Earl Potteiger
1929–1930   Leroy Andrews
1931–1953   Steve Owen
1954–1960   Jim Lee Howell
1961   Alex Sherman

1952–1953   Joseph Bach
1954   Joseph Bach‖
        Walter Kiesling
1955–1956   Walter Kiesling
1957–1961   Raymond Parker

ST. LOUIS CARDINALS

1960–1961   Frank Ivy

PHILADELPHIA EAGLES

*Merged with Pittsburgh
†Co-coaches
‡Illness after first two games

1933–1937   Ludlow Wray
1938–1940   Bert Bell
1941–1942   Earle "Greasy" Neale
1943   Earle "Greasy" Neale*
        Walter Kiesling†
1944–1950   Earle "Greasy" Neale
1951   Alvin N. "Bo" McMillin‡
        Wayne Millner
1952–1955   James W. Trimble
1956–1957   Hugh J. Devore
1958–1960   Lawrence T. "Buck" Shaw
1961—Nicholas Skorich

SAN FRANCISCO 49ers

1950–1954   Lawrence T. "Buck" Shaw
1955   Norman "Red" Strader
1956–1958   Frank Albert
1959–1961   Howard Hickey

WASHINGTON REDSKINS
(formerly Boston Redskins, 1932–36)

*Retired in 1942 to enter Navy
†Resigned November 7
‡Resigned October 18
¶Until August 22

PITTSBURGH STEELERS

*Resigned in mid-season
†Retired after 2nd game
‡Banned by Commissioner
§Merged with ChiCardinals
¶Co-coaches
‖Resigned before season opened

1933   Forrest Douds
1934   Luby DiMelio
1935–1936   Joseph Bach
1937–1938   John "Blood" McNally

1937–1942   Ray Flaherty*
1943   Arthur "Dutch" Bergman
1944–1945   Dudley DeGroot
1946–1948   A. Glenn "Turk" Edwards
1949   John E. Whelchel†
        Herman Ball
1950   Herman Ball
1951   Herman Ball‡
        Richard Todd
1952–1953   Earl "Curly" Lambeau
1954   Earl "Curly" Lambeau¶
        Joseph L. Kuharich
1955–1958   Joseph L. Kuharich
1959–1961   Michael Nixon
1961   William McPeak

"CURLY" LAMBEAU

PAUL BROWN

STEVE OWEN

JIM CONZELMAN

"BUDDY" PARKER

LAWRENCE "BUCK" SHAW

CHAPTER 4
THE PLAYERS

In more than forty years of major league football since the American Professional Football Association started to grow in 1921 a goodly number of players have galloped onto various fields to write their stories into the record books. Some have become what the sport world chooses to call "immortal"; others, often grounded by injuries, have spurted briefly through the headline sky; a few, although heavily endowed with All-American honors and glorified by collegiate publicity, have proved to be colossal failures when they really had to play football.

Many, particularly in the lean years of the 1920's, fled to professions which provided habitual eating, and disappeared into the shadows of athletic obscurity, where even their brief claims to fame are difficult to trace. In those days professional football was lucky when its line-ups, and results, were printed—even down among the goitre ads—in the papers. The names were often spelled incorrectly; the scorers of points were not even listed.

Therefore, the roster which follows in these pages is guaranteed only to 99.9% for accuracy. The confusion of similar names such as "Swede" Johnson, and the inevitable swarms of men named Smith, 55 of them to 1961, may have resulted in one man's getting credit for playing where he didn't play at all, and another's being missing, although his honorable bruises may still be painful.

The writer begs for clemency in these circumstances. He asks that any reader spotting flaws report them as calmly as possible so that future revisions of the *Encyclopedia* may make amends for these errors of fact.

The temptation to name an all-time team of stars is difficult to resist and, in the first edition of this Encyclopedia such a team, three deep in each position, was picked. This is no longer practical—if it was then—and recent public appreciation of the star defensive players complicates a selection beyond hope of solution. On the first few of the following pages, therefore, are some who brought sparkling moments to the game. Dozens of others may be equally deserving.

And so, here are the men who really wrote this book. To each one, from Wrinkle Meat to Baugh, from Abbey, Joseph to Zyntell, James, goes the editor's most sincere gratitude for memories beyond price and a deep regret that he could not have watched, from some frigid press-box, every play, of every game, that made this history.

A Gallery of
ALL STAR PLAYERS

Wide World Photo

SAMMY BAUGH

RECORDS HELD BY SAMMY BAUGH
(16 Seasons, 1937-1952)

Most passes completed	1,709
Most passes completed (one season)	210
Most passes attempted	3,016
Most passes had intercepted	205
Most yards gained on passes	22,085
Most yards gained on passes (one season)	2,938
Most touchdown passes	187
Best passing efficiency (500 or more attempts)	56.7%
Best passing efficiency (one season)	70.3%
Most punts (one game)	14
Best punting average (one season), 1940	51.4 (35 punts)
Most years active player in N. F. L.	16
Most years leading passer	6

CHAMPIONSHIP GAME RECORDS

Longest punt	85 yards
Most years participated	5
Most yards gained on passes (one game)	335

Baugh's Record Annually

	Atts.	Com.	Pct. Com.	Yds. G.	Ave. G. Com.	Td. P.	Lng. Gn.	Intrc.	Pct. Intrc.
1937	171	81	.473	1,127	13.9	7	59	14	.081
1938	128	63	.492	853	13.5	5	60	11	.086
1939	96	53	.552	518	9.7	6	*44	9	.093
1940	177	111	.627	1,367	12.3	12	*81	10	.056

1941	193	106	.549	1,236	11.6	10	55	19	.098
1942	225	132	.541	1,524	11.5	16	53	11	.049
‡1943	260	149	.573	1,953	12.9	24	72	21	.080
1944	146	82	.562	849	10.3	4	*71	8	.054
1945	182	128	†.703	1,669	13.0	11	*70	4	.022
1946	161	87	.540	1,163	13.3	8	51	17	.105
1947	†354	†210	.593	†2,938	14.0	25	74	15	.042
1948	315	185	.587	2,599	14.0	22	86	23	.073
1949	255	145	.569	1,903	13.1	18	*76	14	.055
1950	166	90	.542	1,130	12.6	10	56	11	.066
1951	154	67	.435	1,104	7.8	7	53	17	.110
1952	33	20	.606	152	12.9	2	86	1	.030
TOTAL	†3,016	†1,709	†.567	†22,085	12.9	†187	86	†205	.068

* Touchdown pass   † League record   ‡ Includes divisional playoff

DON HUTSON

RECORDS HELD BY DON HUTSON
(11 Seasons, 1935-1945)

Most passes caught—489.
Most touchdown passes caught—101.
Most yards gained catching passes—8,010.
Most points scored—825.
Most touchdowns scored—105.
Shortest touchdown pass caught—4 inches.

Season

Most touchdown passes caught—17. (Tied 1951—Elroy Hirsch, Los Angeles.)

Miscellaneous

Most years named most valuable player—2.
Most years leading pass receiver—8.
Most years leading scorer—5.
Most consecutive years leading scorer—5.
Most consecutive years leading pass receiver—5.
Most records held—14.
Most points one quarter—29.

QUARTERBACKS

SIDNEY LUCKMAN

ROBERT WATERFIELD

ROBERT LAYNE

EARL "DUTCH" CLARK

NORMAN
VAN BROCKLIN

EDWARD LeBARON

Wide World Photo
OTTO GRAHAM

THOMAS THOMPSON

CHARLES CONERLY

Nate Fine Photo
FRANK FILCHOCK

ARNOLD HERBER

YELVERTON TITTLE

QUARTERBACKS

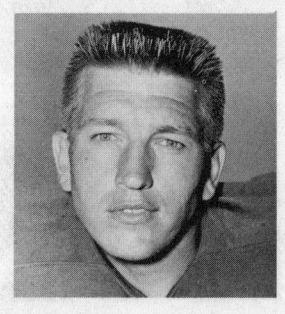

JOHN UNITAS

CECIL ISBELL

BENJAMIN FRIEDMAN

EDWARD DANOWSKI

FRANK ALBERT

TOBIN ROTE

PAUL CHRISTMAN

CLARENCE "ACE" PARKER

HENRY HOMAN

FULLBACKS

BRONKO NAGURSKI   ERNEST NEVERS   CLARKE HINKLE

ANTHONY LATONE   JOSEPH PERRY   MARLIN "PAT" HARDER

DANIEL TOWLER   WILLIAM OSMANSKI   EDWARD PRICE

THEODORE FRITSCH   MARION MOTLEY   JAMES BROWN

HALFBACKS

JAMES THORPE

HAROLD "RED" GRANGE

GEORGE McAFEE

WILLIAM DUDLEY

Wide World Photo
CLIFFORD BATTLES

EWELL DOAK WALKER

JOHN "BLOOD" McNALLY

ALPHONSE "TUFFY" LEEMANS

WILLIAM "DUB" JONES

FRANK GIFFORD

STEPHEN VAN BUREN

CHARLES TRIPPI

HALFBACKS

OLIVER MATSON

Nate Fine Photo
WILBUR MOORE

CLAUDE "BUDDY"
YOUNG

Wide World Photo
ERNEST CADDEL

HUGH McELHENNY

ANDREW FARKAS

BYRON "WHIZZER"
WHITE

WILLIAM PASCHAL

LYNN CHANDNOIS

LEONARD MOORE

HUGH GALLARNEAU

WILLIE GALIMORE

HALFBACKS

ANTHONY CANADEO

JAMES TAYLOR

KENNETH STRONG

JOHN DRISCOLL

PAUL HORNUNG

ALEX WEBSTER

JON ARNETT

RICHARD TODD

THOMAS TRACY

RAYMOND RENFRO

ROBERT
HOERNSCHEMEYER

JOHN DAVID CROW

LINEBACKERS

WILLIAM SVOBODA

JERRY SHIPKEY

THOMAS SCOTT

JOSEPH SCHMIDT

DALE DODRILL

WALTER MICHAELS.

DON PAUL

CHARLES BEDNARIK

JOSEPH MUHA

ROBERT LEE "SAM"
HUFF

CHARLES
DRAZENOVICH

WILLIAM GEORGE

GEORGE "BILL"
FORESTER

LAVERN TORGESON

JOHN CANNADY

HARLAND SVARE

NELLO FALASCHI

WAYNE ROBINSON

LESTER RICHTER

WILLIAM "ED" NEAL

JOSEPH FORTUNATO

CENTERS

MELVIN HEIN

RAYMOND WIETECHA

CLYDE TURNER

VICTOR LINDSKOG

FRANK GATSKI

CHARLES "KI" ALDRICH

Acme Photo
GEORGE TRAFTON

WILLIAM WALSH

NATHAN BARRAGER

JAMES RINGO

ALEXANDER WOJCIECHOWICZ

VINCENT BANONIS

GUARDS

GEORGE MUSSO

RILEY MATHESON

RAYMOND BRAY

JACK STROUD

LESTER BINGAMAN

FRANK KILROY

AUGUST "MIKE"
MICHALSKE

BRUNO BANDUCCI

DANIEL FORTMANN

WILLIAM WILLIS

WALTER KIESLING

LOUIS CREEKMUR

TACKLES

LEO NOMELLINI

WILBUR HENRY

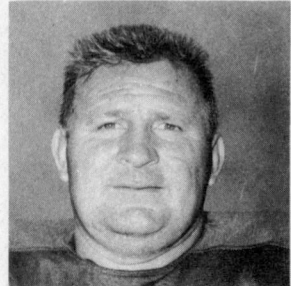
ARTHUR DONOVAN

ALBERT· GLEN
"TURK" EDWARDS

ALBERT WISTERT

ROBERT "CAL"
HUBBARD

ARNOLD
WEINMEISTER

DONALD COLO

JOSEPH STYDAHAR

FREDERICK DAVIS

ERNEST STAUTNER

ROOSEVELT BROWN

TACKLES

VICTOR SEARS

ALBERT BLOZIS

ROOSEVELT GRIER

HERBERT STEIN

EUGENE LIPSCOMB

GEORGE CONNOR

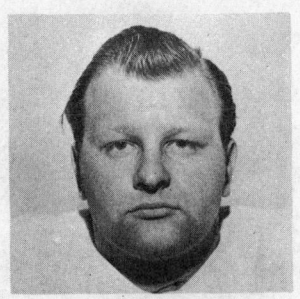

MICHAEL JARMOLUK

ROBERT ST. CLAIR

CHARLES ANE

FRANK WYDO

RICHARD
MODZELEWSKI

THURMAN McGRAW

OFFENSIVE ENDS

THOMAS FEARS

WILLIAM HOWTON

PETER PIHOS

WILLIAM WILSON

KENNETH
KAVANAUGH

HARLON HILL

ELROY HIRSCH

LUKE JOHNSOS

HUGH TAYLOR

MAC SPEEDIE

WILLIAM HEWITT

KYLE ROTE

DEFENSIVE ENDS

EUGENE BRITO

LEONARD FORD

EDWARD SPRINKLE

ANDREW ROBUSTELLI

GEORGE HALAS

NORMAN WILLEY

LaVERN DILWEG

JOSEPH TERESHINSKI

WILLIAM McPEAK

GINO MARCHETTI

WAYNE MILLNER

EDWARD CIFERS

KICKERS

LOUIS GROZA

GEORGE BLANDA

WARD CUFF

MARLIN "PAT" HARDER

ALBERT RECHICHAR

HORACE GILLOM

ROBERT WALSTON

World Wide Photo
RALPH KERCHEVAL

JOHN "JACK" MANDERS

GORDON SOLTAU

BEN AGAJANIAN

LORIS "SAM" BAKER

DEFENSIVE BACKS

THOMAS LANDRY

EMLEN TUNNELL

JOHN CHRISTIANSEN

RICHARD LANE

ROBERT YALE LARY

Wide World Photo
OTTO
SCHNELLBACHER

MARSHALL
GOLDBERG

ROBERT DILLON

JAMES DAVID

JOHN "JACK" BUTLER

WARREN LAHR

KENNETH KONZ

DEFENSIVE BACKS

JAMES PATTON   JERRY NORTON   DONALD DOLL

RUSSELL CRAFT   THOMAS BROOKSHIER   FRANCIS REAGAN

INDIVIDUAL DEPARTMENTAL CHAMPIONS

BALL CARRYING

*League Record

			Yds.	Atts.
1960	James Brown	Cleveland	1,257	215
1959	James Brown	Cleveland	1,329	290*
1958	James Brown	Cleveland	1,527*	257
1957	James Brown	Cleveland	942	202
1956	Rick Casares	Chicago Bears	1,126	234
1955	Alan Ameche	Baltimore	961	213
1954	Fletcher Perry	San Francisco	1,049	173
1953	Fletcher Perry	San Francisco	1,018	192
1952	Dan Towler	Los Angeles	894	156
1951	Edward Price	New York Giants	971	271
1950	Marion Motley	Cleveland	810	140
1949	Steven Van Buren	Philadelphia	1,146	263
1948	Steven Van Buren	Philadelphia	945	201
1947	Steven Van Buren	Philadelphia	1,008	217
1946	William Dudley	Pittsburgh	604	146
1945	Steven Van Buren	Philadelphia	832	143
1944	William Paschal	New York	737	196
1943	William Paschal	New York	572	147
1942	William Dudley	Pittsburgh	696	162
1941	Clarence Manders	Brooklyn	486	111
1940	Byron White	Detroit	514	146
1939	William Osmanski	Chicago Bears	699	121
1938	Byron White	Detroit	567	152
1937	Cliff Battles	Washington	874	216
1936	Alphonse Leemans	New York	830	206
1935	Douglas Russell	Cardinals	499	140
1934	Beattie Feathers	Chicago Bears	1,004	117
1933	Cliff Battles	Boston	737	146
1932	Robert Campiglio	Stapleton	504	104

SCORING

*League Record

			Tds.	X Pt.	FG	Total
1960	Paul Hornung	Green Bay	15	41	15	176*
1959	Paul Hornung	Green Bay	7	31	7	94
1958	James Brown	Cleveland	18	0	0	108
1957	Loras Baker	Washington	1	29	14	77
	Lou Groza	Cleveland	0	32	15	77
1956	Robert Layne	Detroit	5	33	12	99
1955	Ewell Doak Walker	Detroit	7	27	9	96
1954	Robert Walston	Philadelphia	11	36	4	114
1953	Gordon Soltau	San Francisco	6	48	10	114
1952	Gordon Soltau	San Francisco	7	34	6	94
1951	Elroy Hirsch	Los Angeles Rams	17	0	0	102
1950	Doak Walker	Detroit	11	38	8	128
1949	Marlin Harder	Cardinals	8	45	3	102
	Eugene Roberts	Giants	17	0	0	102
1948	Marlin Harder	Cardinals	6	53	7	110
1947	Marlin Harder	Cardinals	7	39	7	102
1946	Ted Fritsch	Green Bay	10	13	9	100
1945	Steven Van Buren	Philadelphia	18	2	0	110
1944	Don Hutson	Green Bay	9	31	0	85
1943	Don Hutson	Green Bay	12	36	3	117

			Tds.	X Pt.	FG	Total
1942	Don Hutson	Green Bay	17	33	1	138
1941	Don Hutson	Green Bay	12	20	0	95
1940	Don Hutson	Green Bay	7	15	0	57
1939	Andy Farkas	Washington	11	2	0	68
1938	Clark Hinkle	Green Bay	7	7	3	58
1937	Jack Manders	Chicago Bears	5	15	8	69
1936	Earl Clark	Detroit	7	19	4	73
1935	Earl Clark	Detroit	6	16	1	55
1934	Jack Manders	Chicago Bears	3	31	10	79
1933	Ken Strong	Giants	6	13	5	64
	Glenn Presnell	Portsmouth	6	10	6	64
1932	Earl Clark	Detroit	4	6	3	39

FIELD GOALS

League Record

1960	Thomas Davis	San Francisco	19
1959	George Summerall	New York	20
1958	Paige Cothren	Los Angeles	14
	Thomas Miner	Pittsburgh	
1957	Lou Groza	Cleveland	15
1956	Loras Baker	Washington	17
1955	Fred Cone	Green Bay	16
1954	Lou Groza	Cleveland	16
1953	Lou Groza	Cleveland	23*
1952	Lou Groza	Cleveland	19
1951	Robert Waterfield	Los Angeles	13*
1950	Louis Groza	Cleveland	13*
1949	John Patton	Philadelphia	9
	Robert Waterfield	Los Angeles	9
1948	John Patton	Philadelphia	8
1947	Marlin Harder	Cardinals	7
1946	Ted Fritsch	Green Bay	9
1945	Joseph Aguirre	Washington	7
1944	Kenneth Strong	New York	6
1943	Don Hutson	Green Bay	3
1942	William Daddio	Cardinals	5
1941	Clarke Hinkle	Green Bay	6
1940	Clarke Hinkle	Green Bay	9
1939	Ward Cuff	New York	7
1938	Ward Cuff	New York	5
	Ralph Kerchavel	Brooklyn	5
1937	Jack Manders	Chicago Bears	8
1936	Jack Manders	Chicago Bears	7
	Armand Niccolai	Pittsburgh	7
1935	Armand Niccolai	Pittsburgh	6
	William Smith	Cardinals	6
1934	Jack Manders	Chicago Bears	10
1933	Jack Manders	Chicago Bears	6
	Glenn Presnell	Portsmouth	6
1932	Earl Clark	Portsmouth	3

FORWARD PASSING

League Record

			Passes	Comp.	Yds.	Tds.	Inter.
1960	Milton Plum	Cleveland	250	151	2,297	21	5
1959	Charles Conerly	New York	194	113	1,706	14	4
1958	Edward LeBaron	Washington	145	79	1,365	11	10

NORMAN VAN BROCKLIN, BEST PASSER IN THE LEAGUE THREE YEARS, ENJOYS A MUDDY
SESSION AGAINST THE CHICAGO BEARS DURING A PRE-SEASON GAME IN 1958.

			Passes	Comp.	Yds.	Tds.	Inter.
1957	Thomas O'Connell	Cleveland	110	63	1,229	9	8
1956	Charles Brown	Chicago Bears	168	96	1,667	11	12
1955	Otto Graham	Cleveland	185	98	1,721	15	8
1954	Norman Van Brocklin	Los Angeles	260	139	2,637	13	21
1953	Otto Graham	Cleveland	258	167	2,722	11	9
1952	Norman Van Brocklin	Los Angeles	205	113	1,736	14	17
1951	Robert Waterfield	Los Angeles	176	88	1,566	13	10
1950	Norman Van Brocklin	Los Angeles	233	127	2,061	18	14
1949	Samuel Baugh	Washington	255	145	1,903	18	14
1948	Thomas Thompson	Philadelphia	246	141	1,965	25	11
1947	Samuel Baugh	Washington	354*	210*	2,988*	25	15
1946	Robert Waterfield	Los Angeles	251	127	1,747	18	17
1945	Samuel Baugh	Washington	182	128	1,669	11	4*
1944	Frank Filchock	Washington	147	84	1,139	13	9
1943	Samuel Baugh	Washington	239	133	1,754	23	19*
1942	Cecil Isbell	Green Bay	268	146	2,021	24	14
1941	Cecil Isbell	Green Bay	206	117	1,479	15	11
1940	Samuel Baugh	Washington	177	111	1,367	12	10
1939	Parker Hall	Cleveland	208	106	1,227	9	13
1938	Ed Danowski	New York	129	70	848	8	8
1937	Samuel Baugh	Washington	171	81	1,127	7	14
1936	Arnold Herber	Green Bay	173	77	1,239	9	13
1935	Ed Danowski	New York	113	57	795	9	9
1934	Arnold Herber	Green Bay	115	42	799	8	12
1933	Harry Newman	New York	132	53	963	8	17
1932	Arnold Herber	Green Bay	101	37	639	9	9

PASS RECEIVING

*League Record

			Caught	Yards	Tds.
1960	Raymond Berry	Baltimore	74	1,298	10
1959	Raymond Berry	Baltimore	66	959	14
1958	Raymond Berry	Baltimore	56	794	9
	Palmer Retzlaff	Philadelphia	56	766	2

RAYMOND BERRY   PALMER "PETE" RETZLAFF

			Caught	Yards	Tds.
1957	William Wilson	San Francisco	52	757	6
1956	William Wilson	San Francisco	60	889	5
1955	Peter Pihos	Philadelphia	62	864	7
1954	Peter Pihos	Philadelphia	60	872	10
	William Wilson	San Francisco	60	830	5
1953	Peter Pihos	Philadelphia	63	1,049	10
1952	Mac Speedie	Cleveland	62	911	5
1951	Elroy Hirsch	Los Angeles	66	1,495*	17*
1950	Tom Fears	Los Angeles	84*	1,116	7
1949	Tom Fears	Los Angeles	77	1,013	9
1948	Tom Fears	Los Angeles	51	698	4
1947	James Keane	Chicago Bears	64	910	10
1946	James Benton	Los Angeles	63	981	6
1945	Don Hutson	Green Bay	47	834	9
1944	Don Hutson	Green Bay	58	866	9
1943	Don Hutson	Green Bay	47	776	11
1942	Don Hutson	Green Bay	74	1,211	17*
1941	Don Hutson	Green Bay	58	738	10
1940	Don Looney	Philadelphia	58	707	4
1939	Don Hutson	Green Bay	34	846	6
1938	Gaynell Tinsley	Cardinals	41	516	1
1937	Don Hutson	Green Bay	41	552	7
1936	Don Hutson	Green Bay	34	526	9
1935	Tod Goodwin	New York	26	432	4
1934	Joseph Carter	Philadelphia	16	237	3
1933	John Kelley	Brooklyn	21	219	3
1932	Luke Johnsos	Chicago Bears	24	321	2

INTERCEPTIONS

			No.	Yards	Longest
1960	Gerald Norton	St. Louis	10	96	26
	David Baker	San Francisco	10	96	28
1959	Dean Derby	Pittsburgh	7	127	24
	Milton Davis	Baltimore	7	119	57
	Donald Shinnick	Baltimore	7	119	57
1958	James Patton	New York	11	181	42
1957	Milton Davis	Baltimore	10	219	65
	John Christiansen	Detroit	10	137	52
	John Butler	Pittsburgh	10	85	20
1956	Lindon Crow	Cardinals	11	170	42
1955	Willard Sherman	Los Angeles	11	101	36
1954	Richard Lane	Cardinals	10	181	64
1953	John Christiansen	Detroit	12	238	*92
1952	Richard Lane	Los Angeles	*14	*298	80
1951	Otto Schnellbacher	New York Giants	11	194	46
1950	Orban Sanders	New York Yanks	13	199	29
1949	Robert Nussbaumer	Cardinals	12	157	68
1948	Daniel Sandifer	Washington	13	258	54
1947	Francis Reagan	New York Giants	10	203	71
1946	William Dudley	Pittsburgh	10	242	80
1945	Leroy Zimmerman	Philadelphia	7	90	23
1944	Howard Livingston	New York Giants	9	172	40
1943	Samuel Baugh	Washington	11	112	23
1942	Clyde Turner	Chicago Bears	8	96	42
1941	Marshall Goldberg	Cardinals	7	54	16

ROBERT NUSSBAUMER

LINDON CROW

SAMUEL BAUGH

PUNTING

*League Record

	Number	Average	Longest
1960—Gerald Norton	39	45.6	62
1959—Robert Yale Lary	45	47.1	67
1958—Loris Baker	48	45.4	64
1957—Donald Chandler	60	44.6	61
1956—Norman Van Brocklin	48	43.1	72
1955—Norman Van Brocklin	60	44.6	61
1954—Patrick Brady	66	43.2	72
1953—Patrick Brady	80*	46.9	64
1952—Horace Gillom	61	45.7	73
1951—Horace Gillom	73	45.5	66
1950—Fred Morrison	57	43.3	65
1949—Michael Boyda	56	44.2	61
1948—Joseph Muha	57	47.2	82
1947—Jack Jacobs	57	43.5	74
1946—Roy McKay	64	42.7	64
1945—Roy McKay	44	41.2	73

	Number	Average	Longest
1944—Frank Sinkwich	45	41.0	73
1943—Sammy Baugh	50	45.9	81
1942—Sammy Baugh	37	46.6	74
1941—Sammy Baugh	30	48.7	75
1940—Sammy Baugh	35	51.0*	85*
1939—John Pingel			

JIM THORPE TROPHY (Most Valuable Player)

(Annual winners selected by ballot of all players in league)

1960—Norman Van Brocklin
1959—Charles Conerly
1958—James Brown
1957—John Unitas
1956—Frank Gifford
1955—Harlon Hill

BONUS PICKS

1947—Chicago Bears—Bob Fenimore (b), Oklahoma A. & M.
1948—Washington—Harry Gilmer (b), Alabama
1949—Philadelphia—Charles Bednarik (c), Pennsylvania
1950—Detroit—Leon Hart (e), Notre Dame
1951—New York Giants—Kyle Rote (b), S.M.U.
1952—Los Angeles—William Wade (b), Vanderbilt
1953—San Francisco—Harry Babcock (e), Georgia
1954—Cleveland—Bobby Garrett (b), Stanford
1955—Baltimore—George Shaw (b), Oregon
1956—Pittsburgh—Gary Glick (b), Colorado A & M
1957—Green Bay—Paul Hornung (b), Notre Dame
1958—Chicago Cardinals—King Hill (b), Rice

Bonus picks discontinued after 1958

OFFICIAL LEAGUE
MOST VALUABLE PLAYERS

(Winners of Joe F. Carr Trophy)

1938	Mel Hein	New York	center
1939	Parker Hall	Cleveland	halfback
1940	Ace Parker	Brooklyn	halfback
1941	Don Hutson	Green Bay	end
1942	Don Hutson	Green Bay	end
1943	Sid Luckman	Bears	quarterback
1944	Frank Sinkwich	Detroit	quarterback
1945	Bob Waterfield	Los Angeles	quarterback
1946	Bill Dudley	Pittsburgh	halfback

Award discontinued

WILLIAM DUDLEY

ALL-LEAGUE SELECTIONS

1931	**1932**
L.E.—Dilweg—Green Bay	L.E.—Flaherty—New York
L.T.—Hubbard—Green Bay	L.T.—Hubbard—Green Bay
L.G.—Michalske—Green Bay	L.G.—Carlson—Bears
C.—McNally—Cardinals	C.—Barrager—Green Bay
R.G.—Gibson—New York	R.G.—Kiesling—Cardinals
R.T.—Christensen—Portsmouth	R.T.—Edwards—Boston
R.E.—Badgro—New York	R.E.—Johnsos—Bears
Q.B.—Clark—Portsmouth	Q.B.—Clark—Portsmouth
L.H.—Blood—Green Bay	L.H.—Herber—Green Bay
R.H.—Grange—Bears	R.H.—Lumpkin—Portsmouth
F.B.—Nevers—Cardinals	F.B.—Nagurski—Bears

RAY FLAHERTY

1933

L.E.—Hewitt—Bears
L.T.—Hubbard—Green Bay
L.G.—Hickman—Brooklyn
C.—Hein—New York
R.G.—Kopcha—Bears
R.T.—Edwards—Boston
R.E.—Badgro—New York
Q.B.—Newman—New York
L.H.—Presnell—Portsmouth
R.H.—Battles—Boston
F.B.—Nagurski—Bears

1934

L.E.—Hewitt—Bears
L.T.—Christensen—Detroit
L.G.—Gibson—New York
C.—Hein—New York
R.G.—Kopcha—Bears
R.T.—Morgan—New York
R.E.—Badgro—New York
Q.B.—Clark—Detroit
L.H.—Feathers—Bears
R.H.—Strong—New York
F.B.—Nagurski—Bears

1935

L.E.—Smith—Cardinals
L.T.—Morgan—New York
L.G.—Kopcha—Bears
C.—Hein—New York
R.G.—Michalske—Green Bay
R.T.—Musso—Bears
R.E.—Karr—Bears
Q.B.—Clark—Detroit
L.H.—Danowski—New York
R.H.—Caddel—Detroit
F.B.—Mikaluk—Cardinals

1936

L.E.—Hewitt—Philadelphia
L.T.—Smith, E.—Green Bay
L.G.—Evans—Green Bay
C.—Hein—New York
R.G.—Emerson—Detroit
R.T.—Edwards—Boston
R.E.—Hutson—Green Bay
Q.B.—Clark—Detroit
L.H.—Battles—Boston
R.H.—Leemans—New York
F.B.—Hinkle—Green Bay

1937

L.E.—Hewitt—Philadelphia
L.T.—Stydahar—Bears
L.G.—Evans—Green Bay
C.—Hein—New York
R.G.—Musso—Bears
R.T.—Edwards—Washington
R.E.—Tinsley—Cardinals
Q.B.—Clark—Detroit
L.H.—Battles—Washington
R.H.—Baugh—Washington
F.B.—Hinkle—Green Bay

1938

L.E.—Hutson—Green Bay
L.T.—Widseth—New York
L.G.—Fortmann—Bears
C.—Hein—New York
R.G.—Letlow—Green Bay
R.T.—Stydahar—Bears
R.E.—Tinsley—Cardinals
Q.B.—Parker—Brooklyn
L.H.—Danowski—New York
R.H.—Cardwell—Detroit
F.B.—Hinkle—Green Bay

1939

L.E.—Hutson—Green Bay
L.T.—Stydahar—Bears
L.G.—Fortmann—Bears
C.—Hein—New York
R.G.—Dell Isola—New York
R.T.—Barber—Washington
R.E.—Poole—New York
Q.B.—O'Brien—Philadelphia
L.H.—Leemans—New York
R.H.—Farkas—Washington
F.B.—Osmanski, W.—Bears

1940

L.E.—Hutson—Green Bay
L.T.—Stydahar—Bears
L.G.—Fortmann—Bears
C.—Hein—New York
R.G.—Wiethe—Detroit
R.T.—Kinard—Brooklyn
R.E.—Schwartz—Brooklyn
Q.B.—Parker—Brooklyn
L.H.—Baugh—Washington
R.H.—White—Detroit
F.B.—Drake—Cleveland

1941

L.E.—Hutson—Green Bay
L.T.—Kinard, F.—Brooklyn
L.G.—Fortmann—Bears
C.—Turner—Bears
R.G.—Kuharich—Cardinals
R.T.—Wilkin—Washington
R.E.—Schwartz—Brooklyn
Q.B.—Luckman—Bears
L.H.—Isbell—Green Bay
R.H.—McAfee—Bears
F.B.—Hinkle—Green Bay

1942

L.E.—Hutson—Green Bay
L.T.—Wilkin—Washington
L.G.—Fortmann—Bears
C.—Turner—Bears
R.G.—Edwards—New York
R.T.—Artoe—Bears
R.E.—Masterson—Washington
Q.B.—Luckman—Bears
L.H.—Isbell—Green Bay
R.H.—Dudley—Pittsburgh
F.B.—Famiglietti—Bears

Official selection discontinued in 1943.

Beginning in 1943, All-League Selections have been made by the news services. A.P. —Associated Press; U.P.—United Press; I.N.S.—International News Service; U.P.I.—United Press International.)

1943

L.E.—Hutson—Green Bay (A.P., U.P.)
L.T.—Kinard, E.—Brooklyn (A.P.)
    Sears—Phil-Pitt (U.P.)
L.G.—Farman—Washington (A.P., U.P.)
C.—Turner—Chicago Bears (A.P., U.P.)
R.G.—Fortman—Chicago Bears (A.P., U.P.)
R.T.—Blozis—New York (A.P., U.P.)
R.E.—Rucinski—Cardinals (AP., U.P.)
Q.B.—Luckman—Chicago Bears (A.P., U.P.)
L.H.—Baugh—Washington (A.P., U.P.)
R.H.—Clark—Chicago Bears (A.P., U.P.)
F.B.—Canadeo—Green Bay (A.P.)
    Cuff—New York (U.P.)

1944

L.E.—Hutson—Green Bay (A.P., U.P.)
L.T.—Wistert—Philadelphia (A.P., U.P.)
L.G.—Younce—New York (A.P., U.P.)
C.—Turner—Chicago Bears (A.P., U.P.)
R.G.—Matheson—Cleveland (A.P., U.P.)
R.T.—Kinard, F.—Brooklyn (A.P.)
    Cope—New York (U.P.)
R.E.—Aguirre—Washington (A.P., U.P.)
Q.B.—Luckman—Chicago Bears (A.P.)
    Zimmerman—Philadelphia (U.P.)
L.H.—Sinkwich—Detroit (A.P., U.P.)
R.H.—Van Buren, S.—Philadelphia (A.P.)
    Cuff—New York (U.P.)
F.B.—Paschal—New York (A.P., U.P.)

1945

L.E.—Hutson—Green Bay (A.P., U.P.)
L.T.—Wistert—Philadelphia (A.P., U.P.)
L.G.—Matheson—Cleveland (A.P., U.P.)
C.—Brock—Green Bay (A.P., U.P.)
R.G.—Radovich, Detroit (A.P., U.P.)
R.T.—Cope—New York (A.P.)
    Uremovich, Detroit (U.P.)
R.E.—Benton—Cleveland (A.P.)
    Pritko—Cleveland (U.P.)
Q.B.—Waterfield—Cleveland (A.P.)
    Baugh—Washington (U.P.)
L.H.—Van Buren, S.—Phila. (A.P., U.P.)
R.H.—Bagarus—Washington (A.P.)
    Waterfield—Cleveland (U.P.)
F.B.—Westfall—Detroit (A.P.)
    Fritsch—Green Bay (U.P.)

1946
UNITED PRESS

L.E.—Benton, J.—Los Angeles
L.T.—Wistert—Philadelphia
L.G.—Lio—Philadelphia
C.—Turner—Bears
R.G.—Matheson—Los Angeles
R.T.—White—New York
R.E.—Kavanaugh—Bears
Q.B.—Waterfield—Los Angeles
L.H.—Dudley—Pittsburgh
R.H.—Filchock—New York
F.B.—Fritsch—Green Bay

WARD CUFF   LEONARD YOUNCE   FRANK COPE

1947
UNITED PRESS

L.E.—Kavanaugh—Bears
L.T.—Wistert—Philadelphia
L.G.—Younce—New York
C.—Banonis—Cardinals
R.G.—Moore, Wm.—Pittsburgh
R.T.—Davis, F.—Bears
R.E.—Kutner—Cardinals
Q.B.—Luckman—Bears
L.H.—Van Buren, S.—Philadelphia
R.H.—Baugh—Washington
F.B.—Harder—Cardinals

1948
UNITED PRESS

L.E.—Pihos—Philadelphia
L.T.—Wistert—Philadelphia
L.G.—Bray—Bears
C.—Turner—Bears
R.G.—Ramsey, G.—Cardinals
R.T.—Huffman—Los Angeles
R.E.—Kutner—Cardinals
Q.B.—Baugh—Washington
L.H.—Van Buren, S.—Philadelphia
R.H.—Trippi—Cardinals
F.B.—Harder—Cardinals

1949
UNITED PRESS
L.E.—Pihos—Philadelphia
L.T.—Sears—Philadelphia
L.G.—Bray—Bears
C.—Naumetz—Los Angeles
R.G.—Ramsey, G.—Cardinals
R.T.—Huffman—Los Angeles
R.E.—Fears—Los Angeles
Q.B.—Waterfield—Los Angeles
L.H.—Van Buren, S.—Philadelphia
R.H.—Canadeo—Green Bay
F.B.—Harder—Cardinals

1950
L.E.—Fears—Los Angeles (A.P., U.P.)
L.T.—Connor—Chicago Bears (A.P., U.P.)
L.G.—Barwegan—Bears (A.P., U.P.)
C.—Bednarik—Philadelphia (A.P.)
    Tonnemaker,—Green Bay (U.P.)
R.G.—Signaigo—New York Yanks (A.P.)
    Willis—Cleveland (U.P.)
R.T.—Weinmeister—Giants (A.P., U.P.)
R.E.—Edwards, New York Yanks (A.P.)
    Speedie—Cleveland (U.P.)
Q.B.—Lujack—Chicago Bears (A.P., U.P.)
L.H.—Walker—Detroit (A.P., U.P.)
R.H.—Geri—Pittsburgh (A.P., U.P.)
F.B.—Motley—Cleveland (A.P., U.P.)

1951
OFFENSE
Hirsch, Los Angeles (A.P., U.P.)	end
Hart, Detroit (A.P.)	end
Lavelli, Cleveland (U.P.)	end
Connor, Chicago Bears (A.P.)	tackle
Groza, Cleveland (U.P.)	tackle
Nomellini, San Francisco (A.P.)	tackle
Coulter, New York Giants (U.P.)	tackle
Creekmur, Detroit (A.P., U.P.)	guard
Barwegan, Chicago Bears (A.P., U.P.)	guard
Lindskog, Philadelphia (A.P.)	center
Gatski, Cleveland (U.P.)	center
Graham, Cleveland (A.P., U.P.)	quarterback
Walker, Detroit (A.P., U.P.)	halfback
Jones, W., Cleveland (A.P., U.P.)	halfback
Price, New York Giants (A.P.)	fullback
Towler, Los Angeles (U.P.)	fullback

DEFENSE
Brink, Los Angeles (A.P.)	end
Hart, Detroit (U.P.)	end
Ford, Cleveland (A.P., U.P.)	end
Weinmeister, New York Giants (A.P., U.P.)	tackle
DeRogatis, New York Giants (A.P.)	tackle
Connor, Chicago Bears (U.P.)	tackle
Willis, Cleveland (A.P., U.P.)	guard
Bingaman, Detroit (A.P.)	guard
Baker, New York Giants (U.P.)	guard
Bednarik, Philadelphia (A.P., U.P.)	linebacker
Younger, Los Angeles (A.P.)	linebacker
Adamle, Cleveland (U.P.)	linebacker
Schnellbacher, New York Giants (A.P., U.P.)	halfback
Shipkey, Pittsburgh (A.P.)	halfback
Lahr, Cleveland (U.P.)	halfback
Tunnell, New York Giants (A.P., U.P.)	safety

1952
OFFENSE
Box, Detroit (A.P.)	end
Speedie, Cleveland (U.P.)	end
Soltau, San Francisco (A.P., U.P.)	end
Connor, Chicago Bears (A.P.)	tackle
Groza, Cleveland (U.P.)	tackle
Nomellini, San Francisco (A.P., U.P.)	tackle
Creekmur, Detroit (A.P., U.P.)	guard
Groza, Cleveland (A.P.)	guard

Fischer, Chicago Cardinals (U.P.)   guard
Gatski, Cleveland (A.P.)   center
Walsh, Pittsburgh (U.P.)   center
Layne, Detroit (A.P.)   quarterback
Graham, Cleveland (U.P.)   quarterback
McElhenny, San Francisco (A.P., U.P.)   halfback
Towler, Los Angeles (A.P., U.P.)   halfback
Price, New York Giants (A.P., U.P.)   fullback

DEFENSE
Brink, Los Angeles (U.P.)   end
Ford, Cleveland (A.P., U.P.)   end
Pihos, Philadelphia (A.P.)   end
Weinmeister, New York Giants (A.P., U.P.)   tackle
McGraw, Detroit (A.P., U.P.)   tackle
West, Los Angeles (A.P., U.P.)   guard
Willis, Cleveland (A.P.)   guard
Bingaman, Detroit (U.P.)   guard
Bednarik, Philadelphia (A.P., U.P.)   linebacker
Shipkey, Pittsburgh (A.P.)   linebacker
Connor, Chicago Bears (U.P.)   linebacker
Christiansen, Detroit (A.P.)   halfback
Matson, Chicago Cardinals (A.P.)   halfback
Smith, R., Detroit (U.P.)   halfback
Rich, Los Angeles (U.P.)   halfback
Tunnell, New York Giants (A.P., U.P.)   safety

1953
OFFENSE
Pihos, Philadelphia (A.P., U.P.)   end
Lavelli, Cleveland (U.P.)   end
Hirsch, Los Angeles (A.P.)   end
Connor, Chicago Bears (A.P.)   tackle
Groza, Cleveland (A.P., U.P.)   tackle
Creekmur, Detroit (U.P.)   tackle
Stanfel, Detroit (A.P., U.P.)   guard
Creekmur, Detroit (A.P.)   guard
Banducci, San Francisco (U.P.)   guard
Gatski, Cleveland (A.P., U.P.)   center
Graham, Cleveland (A.P., U.P.)   quarterback
McElhenny, San Francisco (A.P., U.P.)   halfback
Walker, Detroit (A.P.)   halfback
Towler, Los Angeles (U.P.)   halfback
Perry, San Francisco (A.P., U.P.)   fullback

DEFENSE
Ford, Cleveland (A.P., U.P.)   end
Robustelli, Los Angeles (A.P.)   end
Willey, Philadelphia (U.P.)   end
Weinmeister, New York (A.P., U.P.)   tackle
Nomellini, San Francisco (A.P., U.P.)   tackle
Bingaman, Detroit (A.P., U.P.)   guard
Willis, Cleveland (A.P.)   guard
Dodrill, Pittsburgh (U.P.)   guard
Bednarik, Philadelphia (A.P.)   linebacker
Paul, Los Angeles (A.P.)   linebacker
Connor, Chicago Bears (U.P.)   linebacker
Thompson, Cleveland (U.P.)   linebacker
Keane, T., Baltimore (A.P., U.P.)   halfback
Thompson, Cleveland (A.P.)   halfback
Christiansen, Detroit (U.P.)   halfback
Gorgal, Cleveland (U.P.)   safety
Christiansen, Detroit (A.P.)   safety

1954
OFFENSE

Pihos, Philadelphia (A.P., U.P.)	end
Boyd, Los Angeles (A.P.)	end
Hill, Chicago Bears (U.P.)	end
Creekmur, Detroit (A.P., U.P.)	tackle
Groza, Cleveland (A.P., U.P.)	tackle
Stanfel, Detroit (A.P., U.P.)	guard
Banducci, San Francisco (A.P., U.P.)	guard
Walsh, Pittsburgh (A.P., U.P.)	center
Graham, Cleveland (A.P., U.P.)	quarterback
Walker, Detroit (A.P., U.P.)	halfback
Matson, Chicago Cardinals (A.P., U.P.)	halfback
Perry, San Francisco (A.P., U.P.)	fullback

DEFENSE

Ford, Cleveland (A.P., U.P.)	end
Willey, Philadelphia (A.P., U.P.)	end
Nomellini, San Francisco (A.P., U.P.)	tackle
Donovan, Baltimore (A.P., U.P.)	tackle
Bingaman, Detroit (A.P., U.P.)	guard
Dodrill, Pittsburgh (A.P.)	guard
Kilroy, Philadelphia (U.P.)	guard
Bednarik, Philadelphia (A.P., U.P.)	linebacker
Schmidt, Detroit (A.P.)	linebacker
Zatkoff, Green Bay (U.P.)	linebacker
Landry, New York (A.P., U.P.)	halfback

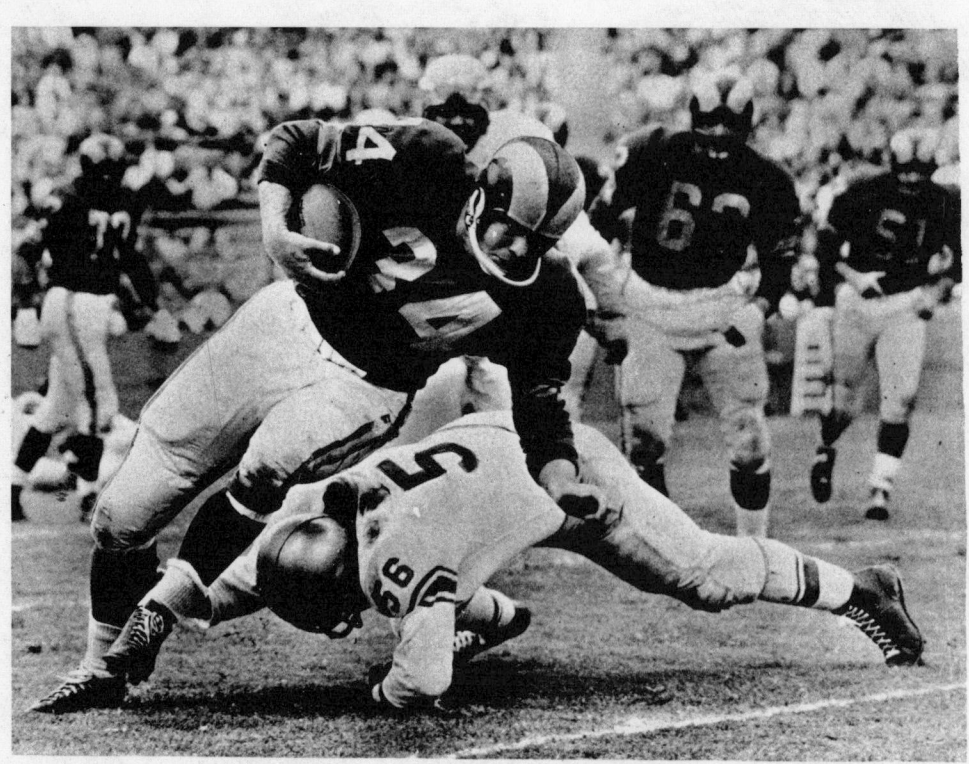

Photo by Wayne Kelly, Los Angeles Times

JOE SCHMIDT, DETROIT'S LINEBACKER, WAS AS RESPONSIBLE AS ANY OTHER FOR MAKING HEROES OUT OF DEFENSE MEN. HERE HE CUTS DOWN JOE MARCONI OF THE LOS ANGELES RAMS WITH A SLASHING TACKLE.

Dillon, Green Bay (A.P.)   halfback
David, Detroit (U.P.)   halfback
Christiansen, Detroit (A.P., U.P.)   safety

1955
OFFENSE

Hill, Chicago Bears (A.P., U.P.)   end
Wilson, San Francisco (U.P.)   end
Pihos, Philadelphia (A.P.)   end
Groza, Cleveland (A.P., U.P.)   tackle
Wightkin, Chicago Bears (A.P.)   tackle
St. Clair, San Francisco (U.P.)   tackle
Jones, Chicago Bears (A.P.)   guard
Putnam, Los Angeles (A.P.)   guard
Gibron, Cleveland (U.P.)   guard
Austin, New York (U.P.)   guard
Gatski, Cleveland (A.P., U.P.)   center
Graham, Cleveland (A.P., U.P.)   quarterback
Matson, Chicago Cardinals (A.P., U.P.)   halfback
Gifford, New York (A.P.)   halfback
Waller, Los Angeles (U.P.)   halfback
Ameche, Baltimore (A.P., U.P.)   fullback

DEFENSE

Brito, Washington (A.P., U.P.)   end
Ford, Cleveland (U.P.)   end
Robustelli, Los Angeles (A.P.)   end
Donovan, Baltimore (A.P., U.P.)   tackle
Toneff, San Francisco (A.P.)   tackle
Colo, Cleveland (U.P.)   tackle
George, Chicago Bears (A.P.)   middle guard
Dodrill, Pittsburgh (U.P.)   middle guard
Bednarik, Philadelphia (U.P.)   linebacker
Connor, Chicago Bears (U.P.)   linebacker
Zatkoff, Green Bay (A.P.)   linebacker
Schmidt, Detroit (A.P.)   linebacker
Dillon, Green Bay (A.P.)   halfback
Sherman, Los Angeles (A.P., U.P.)   halfback
Paul, Cleveland (U.P.)   halfback
Christiansen, Detroit (A.P., U.P.)   safety
Dillon, Green Bay (U.P.)   safety
Tunnell, New York (A.P.)   safety

1956
OFFENSE

Hill, Chicago Bears (A.P., U.P.)   end
Howton, Green Bay (A.P., U.P.)   end
Creekmur, Detroit (A.P., U.P.)   tackle
Brown, New York (A.P., U.P.)   tackle
Jones, Chicago Bears (A.P., U.P.)   guard
Stanfel, Washington (A.P., U.P.)   guard
Strickland, Chicago Bears (A.P.)   center
Ane, Detroit (U.P.)   center
Layne, Detroit (A.P., U.P.)   quarterback
Gifford, New York (A.P., U.P.)   halfback
Matson, Chicago Cardinals (A.P., U.P.)   halfback
Casares, Chicago Bears (A.P., U.P.)   fullback

DEFENSE

Robustelli, New York (A.P., U.P.)   end
Brito, Washington (A.P., U.P.)   end
Grier, New York (A.P., U.P.)   tackle
Donovan, Baltimore (A.P.)   tackle
Stautner, Pittsburgh (U.P.)   tackle
George, Chicago Bears (A.P., U.P.)   middle guard

Schmidt, Detroit (A.P., U.P.)	linebacker
Bednarik, Philadelphia (U.P.)	linebacker
Richter, Los Angeles (A.P.)	linebacker
Lane, Chicago Cardinals (A.P., U.P.)	halfback
Tunnell, New York (U.P.)	halfback
Christiansen, Detroit (A.P.)	halfback
Lary, Detroit (A.P.)	safety
Tunnell, New York (A.P.)	safety
Christiansen, Detroit (U.P.)	safety
Dillon, Green Bay (U.P.)	safety

1957
OFFENSE

Wilson, San Francisco (A.P., U.P.)	end
Howton, Green Bay (A.P., U.P.)	end
Brown, New York (A.P., U.P.)	tackle
Creekmur, Detroit (A.P.)	tackle
Groza, Cleveland (U.P.)	tackle
Putnam, Los Angeles (A.P., U.P.)	guard
Stanfel, Washington (A.P., U.P.)	guard
Ringo, Green Bay (A.P.)	center
Strickland, Chicago Bears (U.P.)	center
Tittle, San Francisco (A.P., U.P.)	quarterback
Gifford, New York (A.P., U.P.)	halfback
Matson, Chicago Cardinals (A.P., U.P.)	halfback
Brown, Cleveland (A.P., U.P.)	fullback

DEFENSE

Marchetti, Baltimore (A.P., U.P.)	end
Robustelli, New York (U.P.)	end
Brito, Washington (A.P.)	end
Nomellini, San Francisco (A.P., U.P.)	tackle
Donovan, Baltimore (A.P., U.P.)	tackle
Schmidt, Detroit (A.P., U.P.)	linebacker
Matuszak, San Francisco (A.P., U.P.)	linebacker
George, Chicago Bears (A.P., U.P.)	linebacker
Christiansen, Detroit (A.P.)	halfback
Dillon, Green Bay (A.P.)	halfback
Butler, Pittsburgh (U.P.)	halfback
Lary, Detroit (U.P.)	halfback
Butler, Pittsburgh (A.P.)	safety
Davis, M., Baltimore (A.P.)	safety
Dillon, Green Bay (U.P.)	safety
Christiansen, Detroit (U.P.)	safety

1958
OFFENSE

Berry, Baltimore (A.P., U.P.I.)	end
Shofner, Los Angeles (A.P., U.P.I.)	end
Brown, New York (A.P., U.P.I.)	tackle
Parker, Baltimore (A.P., U.P.I.)	tackle
Stanfel, Washington (A.P., U.P.I.)	guard
Putnam, Los Angeles (A.P., U.P.I.)	guard
Wietecha, New York (A.P., U.P.I.)	center
Unitas, Baltimore (A.P., U.P.I.)	quarterback
Moore, Baltimore (A.P., U.P.I.)	halfback
Arnett, Los Angeles (A.P., U.P.I.)	halfback
Brown, Cleveland (A.P., U.P.I.)	fullback

DEFENSE

Marchetti, Baltimore (A.P., U.P.I.)	end
Robustelli, New York (A.P.)	end
Brito, Washington (U.P.I.)	end
Lipscomb, Baltimore (A.P., U.P.I.)	tackle

Stautner, Pittsburgh (A.P., U.P.I.)	tackle
Schmidt, Detroit (A.P., U.P.I.)	linebacker
Huff, New York (A.P., U.P.I.)	linebacker
George, Chicago Bears (A.P., U.P.I.)	linebacker
Butler, Pittsburgh (A.P., U.P.I.)	halfback
Lary, Detroit (A.P., U.P.I.)	halfback
Patton, New York (A.P., U.P.I.)	safety
Dillon, Green Bay (A.P., U.P.I.)	safety

1959
OFFENSE

Berry, Baltimore (A.P., U.P.I.)	end
Shofner, Los Angeles (A.P., U.P.I.)	end
Brown, New York (A.P., U.P.I.)	tackle
Parker, Baltimore (A.P., U.P.I.)	tackle
Smith, Cleveland (A.P., U.P.I.)	guard
Jones, Chicago Bears (A.P.)	guard
Spinney, Baltimore (U.P.I.)	guard
Ringo, Green Bay (A.P., U.P.I.)	center
Unitas, Baltimore (A.P., U.P.I.)	quarterback
Gifford, New York (A.P., U.P.I.)	halfback
Moore, Baltimore (A.P.)	halfback
J. D. Smith, San Francisco (U.P.I.)	halfback
Brown, Cleveland (A.P., U.P.I.)	fullback

DEFENSE

Marchetti, Baltimore (A.P., U.P.I.)	end
Robustelli, New York (A.P., U.P.I.)	end
Lipscomb, Baltimore (A.P., U.P.I.)	tackle
Nomellini, San Francisco (A.P., U.P.I.)	tackle
Huff, New York (A.P., U.P.I.)	linebacker
George, Chicago Bears (A.P., U.P.I.)	linebacker
Schmidt, Detroit (A.P., U.P.I.)	linebacker
Woodson, San Francisco (A.P., U.P.I.)	halfback
Butler, Pittsburgh, (A.P., U.P.I.)	halfback
Derby, Pittsburgh (U.P.I.)	safety
Patton, New York (A.P., U.P.I.)	safety
Nelson, Baltimore (A.P.)	safety

1960
OFFENSE

Berry, Baltimore (A.P., U.P.I.)	end
Randle, St. Louis (A.P., U.P.I.)	end
Parker, Baltimore (A.P., U.P.I.)	tackle
Gregg, Green Bay (A.P.)	tackle
Brown, New York (U.P.I.)	tackle
Smith, Cleveland (A.P., U.P.I.)	guard
Kramer, Green Bay (A.P.)	guard
Jones, Chicago (U.P.I.)	guard
Ringo, Green Bay (A.P., U.P.I.)	center
Van Brocklin, Philadelphia (A.P., U.P.I.)	quarterback
Hornung, Green Bay (A.P., U.P.I.)	halfback
Moore, Baltimore (A.P., U.P.I.)	halfback
Brown, Cleveland (A.P., U.P.I.)	fullback

DEFENSE

Marchetti, Baltimore (A.P., U.P.I.)	end
Robustelli, New York (A.P.)	end
Atkins, Chicago (U.P.I.)	end
Jordan, Green Bay (A.P., U.P.I.)	tackle
Karras, Detroit (A.P., U.P.I.)	tackle
Bednarik, Philadelphia (A.P., U.P.I.)	linebacker
George, Chicago (A.P., U.P.I.)	linebacker
Forester, Green Bay (A.P., U.P.I.)	linebacker

Brookshier, Philadelphia (A.P., U.P.I.)	halfback
Lane, Detroit (U.P.I.)	halfback
Woodson, (A.P.)	halfback
Norton, St. Louis (A.P., U.P.I.)	safety
Patton, New York (A.P., U.P.I.)	safety

THE HELMS HALL PROFESSIONAL FOOTBALL HALL OF FAME

(The following men have been chosen by the Helms Hall board, composed of George T. Davis, Rube Samuelson, Al Santoro, Sid Ziff, Paul Zimmerman, Robert Myers, Ben Woolbert, Bill Schroeder and Paul H. Helms, Chairman.)

ALBERT, Frank—Back. San Francisco, 1946–51.

BATTLES, Clifford—Back. Boston and Washington, 1932–37.

BAUGH, Samuel—Back. Washington, 1937–52.

BEDNARIK, Charles—Center. Philadelphia, 1949–60.

BENTON, William—End. Cleveland and Los Angeles Rams and Chicago Bears, 1938–47.

BLOOD, John (McNally)—Back. Milwaukee, Green Bay, and Pittsburgh, 1925–39.

BRAY, Ray—Guard. Chicago Bears, 1939–42, 46–51 Green Bay, 1952.

CANADEO, Anthony—Back. Green Bay, 1941–52.

CARR, Joseph—First President NFL, 1921–39.

CLARK, Earl—Back. Portsmouth and Detroit, 1931–38.

DRISCOLL, John—Back. Chicago Cardinals and Bears, 1921–28.

DUDLEY, William—Back. Pittsburgh, Detroit and Washington, 1942–53.

EDWARDS, Albert Glen—Tackle. Washington, 1932–40.

FEARS, Thomas—End. Los Angeles, 1948–51.

FLAHERTY, Ray—End. New York Giants and Yankees, 1927–35.

FORTMANN, Daniel—Guard. Chicago Bears, 1936–42.

GRAHAM, Otto—Back. Cleveland, 1946–55.

GRANGE, Harold—Back. Chicago Bears and New York Yankees, 1925–35.

GROZA, Louis—Tackle. Cleveland, 1946–58.

HALAS, George—End, coach. Chicago Bears, 1921–52.

HEIN, Melvin—Center. New York Giants, 1932–45.

HENRY, Wilbur—Tackle. Canton, New York Giants and Pottsville, 1920–28.

HERBER, Arnold—Back. Green Bay and New York Giants, 1930–45.

HEWITT, William—End. Chicago Bears and Philadelphia, 1932–39, 1943.

HINKLE, Clark—Back. Green Bay, 1932–41.

HIRSCH, Elroy—Back, End. Chicago (AA-FC), 1946–48 and Los Angeles, 1948–57.

HUBBARD, Robert—Tackle. Green Bay and New York Giants, 1927–36.

HUTSON, Donald—End. Green Bay, 1935–45.

LAMBEAU, Earl—Back, coach. Green Bay, 1921–49.

LEEMANS, Alphonse—Back. New York Giants, 1936–43.

LUCKMAN, Sidney—Back. Chicago Bears, 1939–50.

LYMAN, Roy—Tackle. Canton, Cleveland and Chicago Bears, 1922–34.

McAFEE, George—Back. Chicago Bears, 1940–50.

MUSSO, George—Guard. Chicago Bears, 1933–44.

NAGURSKI, Bronko—Back. Chicago Bears, 1930–37, 1943.

NEALE, Earle—Coach. Philadelphia, 1941 –50.

NESSER, Al—Akron, 1921–25; Columbus, 1925–26; New York Giants, 1927–28; Cleveland, 1931.

NEVERS, Ernest—Back. Duluth and Chicago Cardinals, 1926–31.

OWEN, Stephen—Tackle, coach. New York Giants, 1926–52.

SHAW, Lawrence "Buck"—Coach. San Francisco, 1950–54; Philadelphia Eagles, 1958–60.

SPRINKLE, Edward—End. Chicago Bears, 1944–55.

STRONG, Kenneth—Back. Stapletons and New York Giants, 1929–47.

STYDAHAR, Joseph—Tackle, coach. Chicago Bears and Los Angeles Rams, 1936– 52.

THORPE, James—Back. Canton, Cleveland, Oorang, Rock Island, and New York Giants, 1920–26.

TITTLE, Yelverton A.—Back. Baltimore and San Francisco, 1950–60.

TRAFTON, George—Center. Chicago Bears, 1920–32.

TUNNELL, Emlen—Back. New York Giants and Green Bay, 1948–60.

TURNER, Clyde—Center. Chicago Bears, 1940–51.

VAN BROCKLIN, Norman—Back. Los Angeles and Philadelphia, 1949–60.

VAN BUREN, Steven—Back. Philadelphia, 1944–52.

WALKER, Ewell Doak—Back. Detroit, 1950–55.

WATERFIELD, Robert—Back. Cleveland and Los Angeles, 1945–52.

WOJCIECHOWICZ, Alex—Center. Detroit, 1938–46; Philadelphia, 1946–50.

CLARKE HINKLE, PACKER FULLBACK, SHOWS THE DETERMINATION WHICH MADE HIM ONE OF THE ALL-TIME PRO GREATS AS HE CARRIES THE BALL FOR A 12-YARD GAIN AGAINST THE CHICAGO BEARS IN WRIGLEY FIELD ON DECEMBER 14, 1941. HAMPTON POOLE, BEAR END, COMES IN TO CHECK HINKLE'S RUSH. THE BEARS WON 33–14.

ALL-TIME INDIVIDUAL RECORDS

BALL CARRYING

ATTEMPTS

Most Attempts

1,451 Fletcher Perry, San Francisco, 1950 –60, (eleven seasons). (Gained 7,246 yards, averaged 5.10)

1,320 Steven Van Buren, Philadelphia Eagles, 1944–1951 (eight seasons). (Gained 5,860 yards, averaged 4.4.)

1,171 Clarke Hinkle, Green Bay, 1932– 1941 (ten seasons). (Gained 3,860 yards, averaged 3.29.)

1,076 Richard Casares, Chicago Bears, 1955–60 (six seasons.) (Gained 4, 414 yards, averaged 4.1)

1,025 Anthony Canadeo, Green Bay, 1941–1944; 1946–52 (eleven seasons). (Gained 4,006 yards, averaged 4.1)

926 Alphonse Leemans, New York Giants, 1936–1943 (eight seasons). (Gained 3,117 yards, averaged 3.3.)

917 Leroy Gutowsky, Portsmouth, Detroit, Brooklyn, 1932–1939 (eight seasons). (Gained 3,278 yards, averaged 3.5.)

Most Attempts (one season)

290 James Brown, Cleveland, 1959. (Gained 1,329 yards, averaged 4.6)

271 Edward Price, New York Giants, 1951. (Gained 971 yards, averaged 3.61.)

263 Steven Van Buren, Philadelphia, 1949. (Gained 1,146 yards, averaged 4.4.)

Most Attempts (one game)

39 Harry Newman, New York Giants vs Green Bay, Nov. 11, 1934. (Gained 114 yards, averaged 2.9.)

37 James Brown, Cleveland vs Chicago Cardinals, Oct. 4, 1959. (Gained 147 yards, averaged 4.0)

35 Steven Van Buren, Philadelphia vs New York Bulldogs, Nov. 20, 1949. (Gained 174 yards, averaged 5.0.) George Grosvenor, Chicago Cardinals vs Green Bay, Dec. 6, 1936. (Gained 100 yards, averaged 2.8.)

GAINS

Total Yards Gained

7,151 in 1,415 attempts (average 5.05 yards), Fletcher Perry, San Francisco, 1950–59 (ten seasons).

5,860 in 1,320 attempts (average 4.4 yards), Steven Van Buren, Philadelphia, 1944–1951 (eight seasons).

4,197 in 960 attempts (average 4.1 yards, Anthony Canadeo, Green Bay, 1941–1944, 1946–52 (eleven seasons).

3,860 in 1,171 attempts (average 3.29 yards), Clarke Hinkle, Green Bay, 1932–1941 (ten seasons). (Note: Bronko Nagurski, Chicago Bears, credited with 4,031 yards in 872 attempts (average 4.6 yards) in nine seasons—1930–1937 and 1943—including seasons of 1930 and 1931, two years before official statistics were recorded.)

Most Yards Gained (one season)

1,527 James Brown, Cleveland, 1958

1,329 James Brown, Cleveland, 1959

1,146 Steven Van Buren, Philadelphia, 1949

1,126 Richard Casares, Chicago Bears, 1956

1,052 Anthony Canadeo, Green Bay, 1949

1,049 Fletcher Perry, San Francisco, 1954

Most Yards Gained (one game)

237 in 31 attempts, James Brown, Cleveland vs Los Angeles, Nov. 24, 1957

218 in 26 attempts, Eugene Roberts, New York Giants vs Chicago Cardinals, Nov. 12, 1950

LONGEST RUNS

Longest Run from Scrimmage

97 Andy Uram, Green Bay vs Chicago Cardinals, Oct. 8, 1939 (TD) Robert Gage, Pittsburgh vs Chicago Bears, Dec. 4, 1949 (TD)

Longest Return of Kickoff

106 Albert Carmichael, Green Bay vs Chicago Bears, Oct. 7, 1956 (TD)

105 Frank Seno, Chicago Cardinals vs New York Giants, Oct. 20, 1946 (TD)

105 Ollie Matson, Chicago Cards vs Washington, Oct. 14, 1956 (TD)

105 Abe Woodson, San Francisco vs Los Angeles, Nov. 8, 1959 (TD)

104 Claude Young, Baltimore vs Phila-
     delphia, Nov. 15, 1953 (TD)
103 Russell Craft, Philadelphia vs Los
     Angeles, Oct. 7, 1950 (TD)
103 Thomas Wilson, Los Angeles vs
     Baltimore, Nov. 25, 1956 (TD)
103 Leonard Lyles, Baltimore vs Chi-
     cago Bears, Oct. 4, 1958 (TD)
102 Douglas Russell, Chicago Cardi-
     nals vs Cincinnati, Sept. 23, 1934
     (TD)

*Longest Return with Intercepted Forward
Pass*

102 J. Robert Smith, Detroit vs Chi-
     cago Bears, Nov. 24, 1949 (TD)
100 Vern Huffman, Detroit vs Brook-
     lyn, Oct. 17, 1937 (TD)
 99 Martin Kottler, Pittsburgh vs Chi-
     cago Cardinals, Sept. 27, 1933
     (TD)
 99 Jerry Norton, Philadelphia vs New
     York Giants, Oct. 5, 1957 (TD)

Longest Return with Missed Field Goal

 99 Jerry Williams, Los Angeles vs
     Green Bay, Sept. 16, 1951 (TD)
 99 Carl Taseff, Baltimore vs Los An-
     geles, Dec. 12, 1959 (TD)

Longest Punt Return

 98 Gilbert LeFebre, Cincinnati vs
     Brooklyn, Dec. 3, 1933 (TD)
 96 William Dudley, Washington vs
     Pittsburgh, Dec. 3, 1950 (TD)
 95 Frank Bernardi, Chicago Cards vs
     Washington, Oct. 14, 1956 (TD)
 90 Andy Uram, Green Bay vs Brook-
     lyn, Oct. 12, 1941 (TD)

Longest Run with Fumble

 98 George Halas, Chicago Bears vs
     Oorang Indians, Nov. 4, 1923
     (TD)
 92 Joseph Carter, Philadelphia vs
     New York Giants, Sept. 25, 1938
     (TD)
 89 Don Paul, Cleveland vs Pitts-
     burgh, Nov. 10, 1957 (TD)
 88 Robert Pylman, Philadelphia vs
     New York Giants, Sept. 25, 1938
     (TD)

Longest Run with Intercepted Lateral Pass

 93 Richard Poillon, Washington vs
     Philadelphia, Nov. 21, 1948 (TD)

PASSING

COMPLETIONS

Most Passes Completed

1,709 Samuel Baugh, Washington, 1937–
       1952 (sixteen seasons), plus 58 in
       one Play-off and 5 Championship
       games
1,623 Robert Layne, Chicago Bears,
       1948; New York Bulldogs, 1949;
       Detroit 1950–58; Pittsburgh, 1958
       –60 (thirteen seasons), plus 46 in
       one Play-off and one Champion-
       ship game
1,553 Norman Van Brocklin, Los An-
       geles, 1949–57; Philadelphia, 1958
       –60 (twelve seasons), plus 46 in
       two Playoffs and five Champion-
       ship games
1,387 Y. A. Tittle, Baltimore, 1950; San
       Francisco 1951–60 (eleven sea-
       sons), plus 18 in one Playoff game
1,374 Charles Conerly, New York Giants,
       1948–60 (thirteen seasons), plus 33
       in three Championship games, 10
       in two Play-off games
  904 Sidney Luckman, Chicago Bears,
       1939–1950 (twelve seasons), plus
       45 in one Play-off and 5 Cham-
       pionship games
  763 Robert Waterfield, Los Angeles
       Rams, 1945–1951 (seven seasons),
       plus 46 in 4 championship games.
  732 Thomas Thompson, Pittsburgh
       1940; Philadelphia 1941–42, 1945–
       50 (nine seasons), plus 45 in one
       Play-off and 3 Championship games

Most Passes Completed (one season)

  210 Samuel Baugh, Washington, 1947
       (attempted 354)
  198 Norman Van Brocklin, Philadel-
       phia, 1958 (attempted 374)
  193 John Unitas, Baltimore, 1959 (at-
       tempted 367)
  191 Norman Van Brocklin, Philadel-
       phia, 1959 (attempted 340)
  185 Samuel Baugh, Washington, 1948
       (attempted 315)
  181 Otto Graham, Cleveland, 1952
       (attempted 364)
  181 William Wade, Los Angeles, 1958
       (attempted 341)
  180 Tobin Rote, Green Bay, 1954 (at-
       tempted 382)
  176 Y. A. Tittle, San Francisco, 1957
       (attempted 279)
  176 Sidney Luckman, Chicago Bears,
       1947 (attempted 323)
  162 Charles Conerly, New York Giants,
       1948 (attempted 299)
       John Lujack, Chicago Bears, 1949
       (Attempted 312)

Most Passes Completed (one game)

   36 Charles Conerly, New York Giants

vs Pittsburgh, Dec. 5, 1948

33 David O'Brien, Philadelphia vs Washington, Dec. 1, 1940

29 John Lujack, Chicago Bears vs New York Giants, Oct. 23, 1949

Samuel Baugh, Washington vs Los Angeles, Dec. 11, 1949

George Blanda, Chicago Bears vs Baltimore, Nov. 1, 1953

Y. A. Tittle, San Francisco vs Baltimore

28 James Hardy, Los Angeles vs Chicago Cardinals, Oct. 31, 1948

ATTEMPTS

Most Passes Attempted

3,318 Robert Layne, Chicago Bears, 1948; New York Bulldogs, 1949; Detroit, 1950–58; Pittsburgh, 1958–60 (thirteen seasons), plus 97 in

Photo by Vic Stein & Assoc.

TRAVELING MAN—LAMAR LUNDY, HUGE END FOR THE LOS ANGELES RAMS THROUGH THE 1950's, SHOWS THE TWO POWER-PLANT SHOES THAT CARRIED HIM INTO ENEMY COUNTRY. LUNDY WAS 6 FEET 7 INCHES AND ALL FOOTBALL MAN.

one Play-off and three Championship games

3,016 Samuel Baugh, Washington, 1937–1952 (sixteen seasons), plus 102 in one Play-off and 5 Championship games

2,895 Norman Van Brocklin, Los Angeles, 1949–57; Philadelphia, 1958–60 (twelve seasons), plus 75 in two Play-offs and five Championship games

2,327 Charles Conerly, New York Giants, 1948–60 (thirteen seasons), plus 23 in two Play-off games and 59 in three Championships

1,744 Sidney Luckman, Chicago Bears, 1939–1950 (twelve seasons) plus 85 in one Play-off and 5 Championship games

1,509 Robert Waterfield, Cleveland Rams, 1945; Los Angeles, 1946–1951 (seven seasons), plus 116 in one Playoff and 4 Championship games

Most Passes Attempted (one season)

382 Tobin Rote, Green Bay, 1954 (completed 180)

378 John Unitas, Baltimore, 1960 (Completed 190)

374 Norman Van Brocklin, Philadelphia, 1958 (completed 198)

367 John Unitas, Baltimore, 1959 (Completed 193)

364 Otto Graham, Cleveland 1952 (completed 181)

362 George Blanda, Chicago Bears, 1953 (completed 169)

354 Samuel Baugh, Washington, 1947 (completed 210)

344 James Finks, Pittsburgh, 1955 (completed 165)

336 Robert Layne, Detroit, 1950 (completed 152)

332 Robert Layne, Detroit, 1951 (completed 152)

Most Passes Attempted (one game)

60 David O'Brien, Philadelphia vs Washington, Dec. 1, 1940 (completed 33)

INTERCEPTIONS

Most Passes Had Intercepted

210 Robert Layne, Chicago Bears, 1948; New York Bulldogs, 1949; Detroit 1950–58; Pittsburgh, 1958–60 (thirteen seasons), plus 12 in one Play-off and three Championship games

205 Samuel Baugh, Washington, 1937–1952 (sixteen seasons) (3,016 attempts)

130 Sidney Luckman, Chicago Bears, 1939–1950 (twelve seasons)

Fewest Passes Had Intercepted (600 or more attempts)

29 Milton Plum, Cleveland, 1957–60 (four seasons)

42 Ed Danowski, New York Giants, 1934–1939, 1941 (seven seasons)

48 John Unitas, Baltimore, 1956–59 (four seasons)

Fewest Passes Had Intercepted (100 or more attempts) (one season)

3 Dwight Sloan, Detroit, 1939 (102 attempts)

4 Samuel Baugh, Washington, 1945 (182 attempts)
Paul Christman, Chicago Cardinals, 1948 (114 attempts)
Harry Gilmer, Detroit, 1955 (122 attempts)
Charles Conerly, New York, 1959 (194 attempts)
Milton Plum, Cleveland, 1960 (250 attempts)

Most Passes Had Intercepted (one game)

8 James Hardy, Chicago Cardinals vs Philadelphia, Sept. 24, 1950 (39 attempts)

7 Parker Hall, Cleveland vs Green Bay, Nov. 8, 1942 (25 attempts)
Frank Sinkwich, Detroit vs Green Bay, Oct. 24, 1943 (26 attempts)
Robert Waterfield, Los Angeles vs Green Bay, Oct. 17, 1948 (35 attempts)

Most Passes Had Intercepted (one season)

31 Sidney Luckman, Chicago Bears, 1947 (323 attempts)

25 Frank Filchock, New York Giants, 1946 (169 attempts)

27 Wilson Schwenk, Chicago Cardinals, 1942 (295 attempts)

24 Robert Waterfield, Los Angeles, 1949 (296 attempts)

Most Passes Intercepted

79 Emlen Tunnell, New York Giants, 1948–58, Green Bay, 1959–60 (1,260 yards, four touchdowns) (thirteen seasons)

Most Passes Intercepted (one season)

14 Richard Lane, Los Angeles, 1952 (298 yards, 2 touchdowns)

13   Dan Sandifer, Washington, 1948 (258 yards; 2 TD's)
Orban Sanders, New York Yanks, 1950 (199 yards)

Most Yards Returned Intercepted Passes (one season)

301   Don Doll, Detroit, 1949 (11 interceptions; 1 TD)

GAINS

Most Yards Gained on Passes

23,877   Robert Layne, Chicago Bears, 1948; New York Bulldogs, 1949; Detroit, 1950-58; Pittsburgh, 1958 –60 (thirteen seasons), plus 568 in one Play-off and 3 Championship games

23,611   Norman Van Brocklin, Los Angeles, 1949-57; Philadelphia, 1958 –60 (twelve seasons), plus 532 in 2 Play-off and 5 Championship games

22,085   Samuel Baugh, Washington, 1937– 1952 (sixteen seasons), plus 831 in one Play-off and 5 Championship games

18,854   Charles Conerly, New York Giants, 1948–60 (thirteen seasons), plus 737 in two Play-off and three Championship games

17,900   Y. A. Tittle, Baltimore, 1950; San Francisco, 1951–60 (eleven seasons), plus 248 in one Play-off game

14,683   Sidney Luckman, Chicago Bears, 1939–1950 (twelve seasons), plus 711 in one Play-off and 5 Championship games)

11,238   Robert Waterfield, Los Angeles (Cleveland) Rams, 1945–1951 (six seasons), plus 932 in one Play-off and 4 Championship games)

10,400   Thomas Thompson, Pittsburgh, 1940, Philadelphia 1941–1942, 1945–1950 (nine seasons), plus 503 yards in one Play-off and 3 Championship games

Most Yards Gained on Passes (one season)

3,099   John Unitas, Baltimore, 1960 (18 games)

2,938   Samuel Baugh, Washington, 1947 (12 games)

2,899   John Unitas, Baltimore, 1959 (12 games)

2,875   William Wade, Los Angeles, 1958 (12 games)

2,816   Otto Graham, Cleveland, 1952 (12 games)

2,722   Otto Graham, Cleveland, 1953 (12 games)

2,712   Sidney Luckman, Chicago Bears, 1947 (12 games)

2,658   John Lujack, Chicago Bears, 1947 (12 games)

2,637   Norman Van Brocklin, Los Angeles, 1954 (12 games)

2,617   Norman Van Brocklin, Philadelphia, 1959 (12 games)

2,599   Samuel Baugh, Washington, 1948 (12 games)

Most Yards Gained on Passes (one game)

554   Norman Van Brocklin, Los Angeles vs New York Yanks, Sept. 28, 1951 (27 completions)

468   John Lujack, Chicago Bears vs Chicago Cardinals, Dec. 11, 1949 (24 completions)

446   Samuel Baugh, Washington vs Boston, Oct. 31, 1948 (17 completions)

433   Sidney Luckman, Chicago Bears vs New York Giants, Nov. 14, 1943 (21 completions)

Longest Completed Pass

99   Frank Filchock, Washington, to Andy Farkas, vs Pittsburgh, Oct. 15, 1939 (includes pass and run) (TD)

98   Douglas Russell, Chicago Cardinals, to Gaynell Tinsley, vs Cleveland Rams, Nov. 27, 1938 (includes pass and run) (TD)

97   Pat Coffee, Chicago Cardinals, to Gaynell Tinsley, vs Chicago Bears, Dec. 5, 1937 (includes pass and run) (TD)

Shortest Completed Pass (for TD)

4   inches, Cecil Isbell, Green Bay, to Don Hutson, vs Cleveland, Oct. 18, 1942 (TD)

TOUCHDOWN PASSES

Most Touchdown Passes

187   Samuel Baugh, Washington, 1937– 1952 (sixteen seasons)

173   Robert Layne, Chicago Bears, 1948, New York Bulldogs, 1949; Detroit 1950–58; Pittsburgh, 1958– 59 (twelve seasons), plus one in one Play-off and 3 Championship games

173   Norman Van Brocklin, Los Angeles, 1949–57; Philadelphia, 1958– 59 (eleven seasons) plus 3 in two Play-offs and four Championship games

166   Charles Conerly, New York Giants, 1948–59 (twelve seasons), plus 4

in three Championship games

139 Sidney Luckman, Chicago Bears, 1939–1950 (twelve seasons)

96 Robert Waterfield, Los . Angeles, 1945–1951 (six seasons)

90 Thomas Thompson, Pittsburgh 1940, Philadelphia 1941–1942, 1945–1950 (nine seasons)

Most Touchdown Passes (one season)

32 John Unitas, Baltimore, 1959 (12 games

28 Sidney Luckman, Chicago Bears, 1943 (10 games)

26 Robert Layne, Detroit Lions, 1951

25 Samuel Baugh, Washington, 1947 Thomas Thompson, Philadelphia, 1948

Most Touchdown Passes (one game)

7 Sidney Luckman, Chicago Bears vs New York Giants, Nov. 14, 1943

6 Samuel Baugh, Washington vs Brooklyn, Oct. 31, 1943 Samuel Baugh, Washington vs Chicago Cardinals, Nov. 23, 1947 John Lujack, Chicago Bears vs Chicago Cardinals, Dec. 11, 1949 James Hardy, Chicago Cardinals vs Baltimore, Oct. 2, 1950

Most Consecutive Games Throwing TD Passes

47 John Unitas, Baltimore (3 in 1956, 12 in 1957, 10 in 1958, 12 in 1959, 10 in 1960 plus 3 to two Championship games

23 Cecil Isbell, Green Bay (12 in 1941, 11 in 1942)

19 Sidney Luckman, Chicago Bears (3 in 1942, 10 in 1943, 6 in 1944)

10 Samuel Baugh, Washington (2 in 1942, 8 in 1943) Samuel Baugh, Washington (10 in 1947) Charles Conerly, New York Giants (9 in 1948, one in 1949) George Ratterman, New York Yanks (10 in 1950) Robert Layne, Detroit (10 in 1951)

EFFICIENCY

Best Passing Efficiency (500 or more attempts)

57.6% Milton Plum 1957–60 (four seasons) (450 completions in 781 attempts)

56.7 Samuel Baugh, Washington, 1937–52 (16 seasons) (1,709 completions in 3,016 attempts)

55.7 Otto Graham, Cleveland, 1950–55

(six seasons) (872 completions in 1,565 attempts)

55.7 Y. A. Tittle, Baltimore, 1950; San Francisco, 1951-60 (nine seasons) (1,387 completions in 2,509 attempts)

54.1 John Unitas, Baltimore, 1956–59 (four seasons) (611 completions in 1,129 attempts)

Best Passing Efficiency (one season)

70.3% Samuel Baugh, Washington (128 completions in 182 attempts) 1945

64.7 Otto Graham, Cleveland, 1953 (167 completions in 258 attempts)

63.1 Y. A. Tittle, San Francisco, 1957 (176 completions in 279 attempts)

62.7 Samuel Baugh, Washington (111 completions in 177 attempts) 1940

61.7 Frank Filchock, Washington (55 completions in 89 attempts) 1939

60.4 Milton Plum, Cleveland (151 completions in 250 attempts) 1960

PASS RECEIVING

ALL PASSES

Most Passes Caught

489 Don Hutson, Green Bay, 1935–1945 (eleven seasons) (101 touchdowns)

407 William Wilson, San Francisco, 1951–60 (10 seasons) plus 9 in one Play-off game

400 Thomas Fears, Los Angeles, 1948–56 (nine seasons)

373 Peter Pihos, Philadelphia ,1947–55 (nine seasons)

Most Passes Caught (one season)

84 Thomas Fears, Los Angeles, 1950

77 Thomas Fears, Los Angeles, 1949 Raymond Berry, Baltimore, 1960

74 Don Hutson, Green Bay, 1942

66 Elroy Hirsch, Los Angeles, 1951 Raymond Berry, Baltimore, 1959 Robert Mann, Detroit, 1949

64 James Keane, Chicago Bears, 1947

Most Passes Caught (one game)

18 Thomas Fears, Los Angeles vs Green Bay, Dec. 3, 1950 (189 yards)

14 Don Looney, Philadelphia vs Washington, Dec. 1, 1940 (180 yards) Don Hutson, Green Bay vs New York Giants, Nov. 22, 1942 (134 yards) James Keane, Chicago Bears vs

New York Giants, Oct. 23, 1949
(193 yards)
Ralph Heywood, New York Bulldogs vs Detroit, Dec. 4, 1949 (151
yards)
13 Don Hutson, Green Bay vs Cleveland, Oct. 18, 1942 (209 yards)
12 James Benton, Los Angeles vs New
York Giants, Dec. 1, 1946 (202
yards)
Cloyce Box, Detroit vs Baltimore,
Dec. 3, 1950 (302 yards)
Ray Berry, Baltimore vs Washington, Nov. 10, 1957 (224 yards)

TOUCHDOWN PASSES

Most Touchdown Passes Received

101 Don Hutson, Green Bay, 1935–
1945 (eleven seasons)

*Most Touchdown Passes Received (one
season)*

17 Don Hutson, Green Bay, 1942
17 Elroy Hirsch, Los Angeles, 1951
15 Cloyce Box, Detroit, 1952
14 Malcolm Kutner, Chicago Cardinals, 1948
13 Kenneth Kavanaugh, Chicago
Bears, 1947

*Most Touchdown Passes Received (one
game)*

5 Robert Shaw, Chicago Cardinals
vs Baltimore, Oct. 2, 1950
4 Joseph Carter, Philadelphia vs Cincinnati, Nov. 6, 1934

Don Hutson, Green Bay vs Detroit,
Oct. 7, 1945
Robert Shaw, Los Angeles vs Wash-
ington, Dec. 11, 1949
Cloyce Box, Detroit vs Baltimore,
Dec. 3, 1950
Elroy Hirsch, Los Angeles vs New
York Yanks, Sept. 28, 1951
Harlon Hill, Chicago Bears vs San
Francisco, Oct. 31, 1954

YARDAGE GAINED

Most Yards Gained Catching Passes

8,010 Don Hutson, Green Bay, 1935–
1945 (eleven seasons)

*Most Yards Gained Catching Passes (one
season)*

1,495 Elroy Hirsch, Los Angeles, 1951
1,231 William Howton, Green Bay, 1952
1,212 Robert Boyd, Los Angeles, 1954
1,211 Don Hutson, Green Bay, 1942
1,116 Thomas Fears, Los Angeles, 1950

*Most Yards Gained Catching Passes (one
game)*

303 James Benton, Cleveland Rams vs
Detroit, Nov. 22, 1945 (10)
302 Cloyce Box, Detroit vs Baltimore,
Dec. 3, 1950 (12)
257 William Howton, Green Bay vs
Los Angeles, Oct. 21, 1956
237 Don Hutson, Green Bay vs Brooklyn, Nov. 21, 1943 (8)

Nate Fine Photo

GENERAL DWIGHT D. EISENHOWER ENJOYS A REDSKIN-NEW YORK GIANT GAME IN GRIFFITH
STADIUM, WASHINGTON, OCTOBER 28, 1945.

Wide World Photo

AL CARMICHAEL, GREEN BAY BACK, TAKES A KICKOFF SIX YARDS BEHIND HIS OWN GOAL
AND DOESN'T STOP UNTIL HE ROARS OVER THE CHICAGO BEARS GOAL LINE ON OCTOBER
7, 1956. IT WAS A NEW RECORD.

Longest Completed Pass

99 Andrew Farkas, Washington, from Frank Filchock, vs Pittsburgh, Oct. 15, 1939 (includes pass and run) (TD)

98 Gaynell Tinsley, Chicago Cardinals, from Douglas Russell, vs Cleveland Rams, Nov. 27, 1938 (includes pass and run) (TD)

97 Gaynell Tinsley, Chicago Cardinals, from Pat Coffee, vs Chicago Bears, Dec. 5, 1937 (includes pass and run) (TD)

97 Cloyce Box, Detroit from Robert Layne, vs Green Bay, Nov. 26, 1953 (includes pass and run) (TD)

Shortest Completed Pass (for touchdown)

2 inches Richard Bielski, Dallas, from Edward LeBaron, vs Washington, Oct. 9, 1960 (TD)

4 inches Don Hutson, Green Bay, from Cecil Isbell, vs Cleveland Rams, Oct. 18, 1942 (TD).

PUNTING

Most Punts (one season)

92 Howard Maley, Boston Yanks, 1947
81 Adrian Burk, Baltimore, 1950
71 Earl Girard, Green Bay, 1950
    Orban Sanders, N. Y. Yanks, 1950

Most Punts (one game)

14 Samuel Baugh, Washington vs

Philadelphia, Nov. 5, 1939
John Kinscherf, New York Giants vs Detroit, Nov. 7, 1943
George Taliaferro, N. Y. Yanks vs Los Angeles, Sept. 28, 1951

Longest Punt (Yards)

94 Wilbur Henry, Canton vs Akron, Oct. 28, 1923

88 Robert Waterfield, Los Angeles vs Green Bay, Oct. 17, 1948

86 Ralph Kercheval, Brooklyn vs Chicago Bears, Oct. 20, 1935
    Robert Waterfield, Los Angeles vs Green Bay, Oct. 5, 1947

Best Punting Average (one season)

51.4 yards, Sammy Baugh, Washington, 1942 (35 punts)

PUNT RETURNS

Most Punt Returns (one season)

38 Emlen Tunnell, New York Giants, 1953 (ret. 223 yards)

35 Woodley Lewis, Los Angeles, 1953 (ret. 267 yards)

34 Emlen Tunnell, New York Giants, 1951 (ret. 489 yards)

33 George McAfee, Chicago Bears, 1950 (ret. 284 yards)

31 Emlen Tunnell, New York Giants, 1950 (ret. 305 yards)

Most Punt Returns (one game)

7 Abisha Pritchard, Philadelphia vs

Green Bay, Nov. 29, 1942 (ret. 81 yards)

Most Punt Returns

258 Emlen Tunnell, New York Giants, 1948–58, Green Bay, 1959–60 (13 seasons) 2,206 yards, 5 touchdowns) plus 6 (11 yards) in one Play-off and two Championship games

KICKOFF RETURNS

Most Kickoff Returns and Most Yards Returned (one season)

34 Woodley Lewis, Los Angeles, 1954 (836 yards, average 24.6)

33 Albert Carmichael, Green Bay, 1956 (927 yards, average 28.1)

32 James Sears, Chicago Cardinals, 1958 (756 yards, average 23.6)

29 Edward Saenz, Washington, 1947 (797 yards, average 27.4)

28 Don Paul, Chicago Cardinals, 1950 (693 yards, average 24.8)

Most Kickoff Returns

153 Albert Carmichael, Green Bay, 1953–58 (six seasons, 3,907 yards)

141 Joseph Arenas, San Francisco, 1951–57 (seven seasons) (3,798 yards)

Most Kickoff Returns and Most Yards Returned (one game)

4 Wallace Triplett, Detroit vs Los Angeles, Oct. 29, 1950 (294 yards, average 73.6)

SCORING

POINTS

Total Points

825 Don Hutson (105 TD's, 174 extra points, 7 field goals) Green Bay 1935–1945 (eleven seasons)

742 Lou Groza, Cleveland, 1950–59 (ten seasons) (1 touchdown, 343 extra points, 131 field goals)

736 Robert Walston, Philadelphia, 1951–60 (ten seasons) (44 touchdowns, 286 extra points, 62 field goals)

644 Gordon Soltau, San Francisco, 1950–58 (nine seasons) (25 touchdowns, 284 extra points, 70 field goals)

573 Robert Waterfield, Cleveland Rams, 1945; Los Angeles Rams,

1946–52 (eight seasons) (13 touchdowns, 315 extra points, 60 field goals)

541 George Blanda, Chicago Bears, 1949–58; Baltimore, 1950 (ten seasons) (5 touchdowns, 247 extra points, 88 field goals)

534 Ewell Doak Walker, Detroit, 1950 –55 (six seasons) (34 touchdowns, 183 extra points, 49 field goals)

531 Marlin Harder, Chicago Cardinals, 1946–50; Detroit, 1951–52 (seven seasons) (38 touchdowns, 198 extra points, 35 field goals)

Most Points (one season)

176 Paul Hornung (15 TD's, 41 extra points, 15 field goals) Green Bay, 1960

138 Don Hutson (17 TD's, 33 extra points, 1 field goal) Green Bay, 1942

128 Doak Walker (11 TD's, 38 extra points, 8 field goals) Detroit, 1950

117 Don Hutson (12 TD's, 36 extra points, 3 field goals) Green Bay, 1943

114 Gordon Soltau, San Francisco, 1953 (6 touchdowns, 48 extra points, 10 field goals)
     Robert Walston, Philadelphia, 1954 (11 touchdowns, 36 extra points, 4 field goals)

110 Steven Van Buren (18 TD's, 2 extra points) Philadelphia, 1945
     Marlin Harder (6 TD's, 53 extra points, 7 field goals) Cardinals, 1948

109 John Lujack (11 TD's, 34 extra points, 3 field goals) Chicago Bears, 1950

Most Points (one game)

40 Ernest Nevers (6 TD's, 4 extra points) Chicago Cardinals vs Chicago Bears, Nov. 29, 1929

36 William Jones (6 TD's) Cleveland Browns vs Chicago Bears, Nov. 25, 1951

31 Don Hutson (4 TD's, 7 extra points) Green Bay vs Detroit, Oct. 7, 1945

30 Robert Shaw (5 TD's) Chicago Cardinals vs Baltimore, Oct. 2, 1950

27 John Driscoll (4 TD's, 3 extra points) Chicago Cardinals vs Rochester, Oct. 7, 1923

26 Gordon Soltau (3 TD's, 5 extra points, 1 field goal (San Francisco vs Los Angeles, Oct. 28, 1951

24 Don Hutson, Green Bay, 1942; Robert Shaw, Los Angeles, 1949; Cloyce Box, Detroit, 1950; Doak Walker, Detroit, 1950

TOUCHDOWNS

Most Touchdowns

105   Don Hutson, Green Bay, 1935–1945 (eleven seasons)

77   Steven Van Buren, Philadelphia, 1944–1951 (eight seasons)

63   Peter Pihos, Philadelphia, 1947–55 (9 seasons)

59   Frank Gifford, New York Giants, 1952–60 (nine seasons)

58   Hugh Taylor, Washington, 1947–54 (8 seasons)

57   Oliver Matson, Chicago Cardinals, 1952–58; Los Angeles, 1959–60 (eight seasons)

57   Fletcher Perry, San Francisco, 1950–60 (11 seasons)

55   Elroy Hirsch, Los Angeles, 1949–57 (9 seasons)

53   James Brown, Cleveland, 1957–60 (four seasons)

52   Kenneth Kavanaugh, Chicago Bears, 1940–1941, 1945–1950 (eight seasons)

50   Vern Lewellen, Green Bay, 1924–1932 (nine seasons)

49   William Wilson, San Francisco, 1951–60 (ten seasons)

48   James Benton, Cleveland Rams, 1938, 1940, 1942, 1944, 1945; Chicago Bears, 1943; Los Angeles, 1946, 1947 (nine seasons)

45   Frank Gifford, New York Giants, 1952–58 (seven seasons)

44   William Dudley, Pittsburgh, 1942, 1945, 1946; Detroit, 1947–1949; Washington, 1950–1951 (eight seasons)

42   John "Blood" McNally, Milwaukee, 1925–1927; Green Bay, 1928–1936; Pittsburgh, 1937–1939 (fifteen seasons)
      Clarke Hinkle, Green Bay, 1932–1941 (ten seasons)

Most Touchdowns (one season)

18   Steven Van Buren, Philadelphia, 1945

18   James Brown, Cleveland, 1958

17   Don Hutson, Green Bay, 1942
      Eugene Roberts, New York Giants, 1949
      Elroy Hirsch, Los Angeles, 1951

15   Malcolm Kutner, Chicago Cardinals, 1948

14   Steven Van Buren, Philadelphia, 1947

Most Touchdowns (one game)

6   Ernest Nevers, Chicago Cardinals vs Chicago Bears, Nov. 28, 1929

6   William Jones, Cleveland Browns vs Chicago Bears, Nov. 25, 1951

5   Robert Shaw, Chicago Cardinals vs Baltimore, Oct. 2. 1950

5   James Brown, Cleveland vs Baltimore, Nov. 1, 1959

FIELD GOALS

Most Field Goals

131   (Place Kicks) Lou Groza, Cleveland, 1950–59 (10 seasons)

88   (Place Kicks) George Blanda, Chicago Bears, 1949–58 (10 seasons)

Most Field Goals (one season)

23   (Place Kicks) Lou Groza, Cleveland, 1953

20   (Place Kicks) George Summerall, New York, 1959

Most Field Goals (one game)

5   Robert Waterfield (Place Kicks) Los Angeles Rams vs Detroit, Dec. 9, 1951 (17, 40, 25, 20, 39 yards)
      Ernest Nevers, Duluth vs Hartford, Nov. 28, 1926 (42, 31, 28, 26, 25 yards)

4   John Driscoll (Drop Kicks) Chicago Cardinals vs Columbus, Oct. 11, 1925 (23, 18, 50, 25 yards)
      Elbert Bloodgood (Drop Kicks) Kansas City vs Duluth, Dec. 12, 1926 (35, 32, 20, 25 yards)

4   (Place Kicks) several

Longest Field Goal
Place Kick (Yards)

56   Albert Rechichar, Baltimore vs Chicago Bears, Sept. 27, 1953

54   Glenn Presnell, Detroit vs Green Bay, Oct. 7, 1934

52   Lee Artoe, Chicago Bears vs New York Giants, Oct. 27, 1940

52   Ted Fritsch, Green Bay vs New York Yanks, Oct. 19, 1950

52   Lou Groza, Cleveland vs New York Giants, Oct. 12, 1952

52   Albert Rechichar (twice) Baltimore vs Washington, Oct. 25, 1953 and vs San Francisco, Nov. 27, 1955

52   James Martin, Detroit vs Baltimore, Oct. 23, 1960

Drop Kick (Yards)

50   John Driscoll, Chicago Cardinals vs Milwaukee, Sept. 28, 1924

50   John Driscoll, Chicago Cardinals vs Columbus, Oct. 11, 1925

50 William Henry, Canton vs Toledo, Nov. 12, 1922

EXTRA POINTS

Most Points after Touchdown

343 Lou Groza, Cleveland, 1950–59 (10 seasons)

315 Robert Waterfield, Cleveland Rams, 1945; Los Angeles Rams, 1946–1952 (8 seasons)

284 Gordon Soltau, San Francisco, 1950–58 (9 seasons)

247 George Blanda, Chicago Bears, 1949–58 (10 seasons)

174 Don Hutson, Green Bay, 1935–1945 (eleven seasons)

Most Points after Touchdown (one season)

54 Robert Waterfield, Los Angeles Rams, 1950 (missed four)

53 Marlin Harder, Chicago Cardinals, 1948 (missed none)

Most Points after Touchdown (one game)

9 Marlin Harder, Chicago Cardinals vs New York Giants, Oct. 17, 1948
Robert Waterfield, Los Angeles vs Baltimore, Oct. 22, 1950

8 Robert Snyder, Chicago Bears vs New York Giants, Nov. 14, 1943
Richard Poillon, Washington vs Boston Yanks, Oct. 31, 1948
Marlin Harder, Chicago Cardinals vs New York Bulldogs, Nov. 13, 1949

Most Consecutive Points after Touchdown

156 George Blanda, Chicago Bears, 1951–56

84 John Patton, Philadelphia (3 games in 1947, 12 in 1948, 7 in 1949)

81 Marlin Harder, Chicago Cardinals (12 games in 1948, 8 in 1949)

LENGTH OF SERVICE

MOST YEARS ACTIVE PLAYER IN LEAGUE

16 Samuel Baugh, back, Washington, 1937–52

15 John "Blood" McNally, back, Milwaukee 1925–27, Green Bay 1928–36, Pittsburgh 1937–39

15 Melvin Hein, center, New York Giants 1931–45

13 George Trafton, center, Chicago Bears 1920–32
Alex Wojciechowicz, center, Detroit 1938–45, Philadelphia 1946–50
Clyde Turner, center, Chicago Bears, 1940–52
Victor Sears, tackle, Philadelphia, 1941–53
Frank Kilroy, guard, Philadelphia, 1943–55
Emlen Tunnell, back; New York, 1948–58, Green Bay, 1959–60
Charles Conerly, back, New York, 1948–60
Robert Layne, Chicago Bears, New York Bulldogs, Detroit, Pittsburgh, 1948–60

MOST CONSECUTIVE YEARS PLAYED IN EVERY GAME

11 Sid Luckman, back, Chicago Bears 1939–49 (Record started Sept. 15, 1939, ended Oct. 16, 1949)

MOST CONSECUTIVE GAMES PLAYED

156 Emlen Tunnell, New York Giants (6 in 1948, 12 each 1949 to 1958; Green Bay 12 in 1959 and 1960; plus 2 Play-offs and 2 Championships)

MOST YEARS COACH IN NATIONAL LEAGUE

33 Earl Lambeau, Green Bay, 1921–49; Chicago Cardinals, 1950–51; Washington, 1952–54

33 George Halas, Chicago Bears, 1920–29, 1933–42, 1946–55, 1958–60

22 Stephen Owen, New York Giants, 1931–52

CHAMPIONSHIP GAME RECORDS

BALL CARRYING

Most Yards Gained

320 Steven Van Buren, Philadelphia (75 attempts; played in 3 games)

222 Otto Graham, Cleveland (47 attempts; played in 6 games)

214 Bronko Nagurski, Chicago Bears (57 attempts; played in 4 games)

206 Harry Jagade, Cleveland (30 at-

tempts; played in 3 games)

192 Elmer Angsman, Chicago Cardinals (20 attempts; played in 2 games)

178 William Osmanski, Chicago Bears (36 attempts; played in 4 games)

Most Yards Gained (one game)

196 Steven Van Buren, Philadelphia vs Los Angeles, Dec. 18, 1949 (31 attempts)

159 Elmer Angsman, Chicago Cardinals vs Philadelphia, Dec. 28, 1947 (10 attempts)

109 William Osmanski, Chicago Bears vs Washington, Dec. 8, 1940 (10 attempts)

105 James Taylor, Green Bay vs Philadelphia, Dec. 26, 1960 (24 attempts)

104 Harry Jagade, Cleveland vs Detroit, Dec. 28, 1952 (15 attempts)

102 Harry Jagade, Cleveland vs Detroit, Dec. 27, 1953 (15 attempts)

101 James Gillette, Cleveland Rams vs Washington, Dec. 16, 1945 (17 attempts)

99 Otto Graham, Cleveland Browns vs Los Angeles, Dec. 24, 1950 (12 attempts)

Longest Run from Scrimmage

70 Elmer Angsman, Chicago Cardinals (made 2 of 70 yards each) Chicago Cardinals vs Philadelphia, Dec. 28, 1947

68 William Osmanski, Chicago Bears vs Washington, Dec. 8, 1940

67 Ewell Doak Walker, Detroit vs Cleveland, Dec. 28, 1952

49 Steven Van Buren, Philadelphia vs Los Angeles, Dec. 18, 1949

FORWARD PASSING

Most Passes Completed

86 Otto Graham, Cleveland (Attempted 159; played in 6 games)

46 Robert Waterfield, Los Angeles (Attempted 95; played in 4 games)

44 John Unitas, Baltimore (attempted 69; played in 2 games)

42 Samuel Baugh, Washington (Attempted 81; played in 5 games)

41 Sidney Luckman, Chicago Bears (Attempted 76; played in 5 games)

41 Otto Graham, Cleveland Browns (Attempted 72; played in 2 games)

Most Passes Completed (one game)

27 Thomas Thompson, Philadelphia vs Chicago Cardinals, Dec. 28, 1947 (Attempted 44)

26 John Unitas, Baltimore vs New York Giants, Dec. 28, 1958 (Attempted 40)

22 Otto Graham, Cleveland Browns vs Los Angeles, Dec. 24, 1950 (Attempted 32)

20 Otto Graham, Cleveland vs Detroit, Dec. 28, 1952 (Attempted 35)

19 Otto Graham, Cleveland Browns vs Los Angeles, Dec. 23, 1951 (Attempted 40)

18 Samuel Baugh, Washington vs Chicago Bears, Dec. 12, 1937 (Attempted 33)

Robert Waterfield, Los Angeles vs Cleveland Browns, Dec. 24, 1950 (Attempted 31)

15 Sidney Luckman, Chicago Bears vs Washington, Dec. 26, 1943 (Attempted 26)

Most Passes Attempted

159 Otto Graham, Cleveland (Completed 86; played in 6 games)

95 Robert Waterfield, Cleveland and Los Angeles Rams (Completed 46 in 4 games)

81 Samuel Baugh, Washington (Completed 42 in 5 games)

76 Sidney Luckman, Chicago Bears (Completed 41 in 5 games)

Most Passes Attempted (one game)

44 Thomas Thompson, Philadelphia vs Chicago Cardinals, Dec. 28, 1947 (Completed 27)

42 Robert Layne, Detroit vs Cleveland, Dec. 26, 1954 (Completed 18)

40 John Unitas, Baltimore vs New York, Dec. 28, 1958 (Completed 26)

40 Otto Graham, Cleveland Browns vs Los Angeles, Dec. 23, 1951 (Completed 19)

35 Otto Graham, Cleveland vs Detroit, Dec. 28, 1952 (Completed 20)

33 Samuel Baugh, Washington vs Chicago Bears, Dec. 12, 1937 (Completed 18)

32 Otto Graham, Cleveland Browns vs Los Angeles, Dec. 24, 1950 (Completed 22)

31 Robert Waterfield, Los Angeles vs Cleveland Browns, Dec. 24, 1950 (Completed 18)

Most Yards Gained Passing

1,161 Otto Graham, Cleveland (86 completions; played in 6 games)

672 Robert Waterfield, Cleveland and Los Angeles Rams (46 completions in 4 games)

670 Sidney Luckman, Chicago Bears (41 completions in 5 games)

632 Samuel Baugh, Washington (42 completions in 5 games)

Most Yards Gained Passing (one game)

349   John Unitas, Baltimore vs New York Giants, Dec. 28, 1958 (26 completions)

335   Samuel Baugh, Washington vs Chicago Bears, Dec. 12, 1937 (18 completions)

312   Robert Waterfield, Los Angeles vs Cleveland Browns, Dec. 24, 1950 (18 completions)

298   Otto Graham, Cleveland Browns vs Los Angeles, Dec. 24, 1950 (22 completions)

Most Passes Had Intercepted

13   Frank Filchock, Washington and New York Giants (Played in 3 games)

12   Otto Graham, Cleveland (Played in 6 games)

9   Robert Waterfield. Cleveland and Los Angeles Rams (Played in 4 games)

8   Arnold Herber, Green Bay and New York Giants (Played in 4 games)
      Samuel Baugh, Washington (Played in 5 games)

8   Robert Layne, Detroit (Played in 3 games)

8   Norman Van Brocklin, Los Angeles and Philadelphia (Played in 5 games)

Most Passes Had Intercepted (one game)

6   Frank Filchock, New York Giants vs Chicago Bears, Dec. 15, 1946 (Attempted 26, completed 9)
      Robert Layne, Detroit vs Cleveland, Dec. 26, 1954 (Attempted 42, completed 18)
      Norman Van Brocklin, Los Angeles vs Cleveland, Dec. 26, 1955 (Attempted 25, completed 11)

5   Frank Filchock, Washington vs Chicago Bears, Dec. 8, 1940 (Attempted 13, completed 7)

4   Arnold Herber, New York Giants vs Green Bay, Dec. 17, 1944 (Attempted 22, completed 8)
      Robert Waterfield, Los Angeles vs Cleveland Browns, Dec. 24, 1950 (Attempted 31, completed 18)

3   Several

Most Touchdown Passes

10   Otto Graham, Cleveland (Played in 6 games)

7   Sidney Luckman, Chicago Bears (Played in 5 games)

6   Samuel Baugh, Washington (Played in 5 games)

4   Frank Filchock, Washington and New York Giants (Played in 3 games)
      Tobin Rote, Detroit (Played in one game)

      Charles Conerly, New York Giants (Played in 3 games)
      John Unitas, Baltimore (Played in 2 games)

3   Robert Waterfield, Cleveland and Los Angeles Rams (Played in 4 games)
      Norman Van Brocklin, Los Angeles and Philadelphia (Played in 5 games)

2   Several

Most Touchdown Passes (one game)

5   Sidney Luckman, Chicago Bears vs Washington, Dec. 26, 1943

4   Otto Graham, Cleveland Browns vs Los Angeles, Dec. 24, 1950
      Tobin Rote, Detroit vs Cleveland, Dec. 29, 1957

3   Samuel Baugh, Washington vs Chicago Bears, Dec. 12, 1937
      Otto Graham, Cleveland vs Dec. 26, 1954

2   Several

Longest Completed Pass (Yards)

82   Robert Waterfield to Glenn Davis, Los Angeles vs Cleveland Browns, Dec. 24, 1950 (TD)

78   Tobin Rote to James Doran, Detroit vs Cleveland, Dec. 29, 1957 (TD)

77   Samuel Baugh to Wayne Millner, Washington vs Chicago Bears, Dec. 12, 1937 (TD)

73   Norman Van Brocklin to Thomas Fears, Los Angeles vs Cleveland Browns, Dec. 23, 1951 (TD)

PASS RECEIVING

Most Passes Caught

24   Dante Lavelli, Cleveland (Played in 6 games)

16   Wayne Millner, Boston and Washington Redskins (Played in 4 games)
      Thomas Fears, Los Angeles (Played in 4 games)

10   James Benton, Chicago Bears and Cleveland Rams (Played in 2 games)

9   Don Hutson, Green Bay (Played in 4 games)

Most Passes Caught (one game)

12   Raymond Berry, Baltimore vs New York, Dec. 28, 1958

11   Dante Lavelli, Cleveland Browns vs Los Angeles, Dec. 24, 1950

9   Wayne Millner, Washington vs Chicago Bears, Dec. 12, 1937
      James Benton, Cleveland Rams vs Washington, Dec. 16, 1945
      Thomas Fears, Los Angeles vs Cleveland Browns, Dec. 24, 1950
      Robert Schnelker, New York vs. Baltimore, Dec. 27, 1959

8 Jack Ferrante, Philadelphia vs Chicago Cardinals, Dec. 28, 1947

Most Yards Gained

340 Dante Lavelli, Cleveland (24 receptions, played in 6 games)
313 Thomas Fears, Los Angeles (16 receptions in 4 games)
270 Wayne Millner, Washington (16 receptions in 4 games)

Most Yards Gained (one game)

178 Raymond Berry, Baltimore vs New York, Des. 28, 1958 (12 receptions)
175 Robert Schnelker, New York vs Baltimore, Dec. 27, 1959 (9 receptions)
160 Wayne Millner, Washington vs Chicago Bears, Dec. 12, 1937 (9 receptions)
146 Thomas Fears, Los Angeles vs Cleveland Browns, Dec. 23, 1951 (4 receptions)
136 Thomas Fears, Los Angeles vs Cleveland Browns, Dec. 24, 1950 (9 receptions)
131 Frank Gifford, New York Giants vs Chicago Bears, Dec. 30, 1956 (4 receptions)

Most Touchdown Passes

3 Dante Lavelli, Cleveland (Played in 6 games)
   Ray Renfro, Cleveland (Played in 5 games)
2 Several

Most Touchdown Passes (one game)

2 Several

PASSES INTERCEPTED

Most Passes Intercepted By

4 Joseph Laws, Green Bay (Played in 4 games)
   Clyde Turner, Chicago Bears (Played in 5 games)
   Kenneth Konz, Cleveland (Played in 3 games)
3 Several

Most Passes Intercepted By (one game)

3 Joseph Laws, Green Bay vs New York Giants, Dec. 17, 1944
2 Several

Most Yards Interceptions Returned

97 Don Paul, Cleveland (2 interceptions; 3 games)
76 John Sample, Baltimore (2 interceptions; 1 game)
55 Clyde Turner, Chicago Bears (4 interceptions, 5 games)
49 Dante Magnani, Chicago Bears (2 interceptions, 2 games)

48 George McAfee, Chicago Bears (3 interceptions, 3 games)
42 Sidney Luckman, Chicago Bears (3 interceptions, 5 games)
41 Garrard Ramsey, Chicago Cardinals (1 interception, 2 games)

Most Yards Interceptions Returned (one game)

76 John Sample, Baltimore vs New York, Dec. 27, 1959 (2 interceptions) (1 TD)
65 Don Paul, Cleveland vs Los Angeles, Dec. 26, 1955 (1 interception for touchdown)
49 Dante Magnani, Chicago Bears vs New York Giants, Dec. 15, 1946 (2 interceptions)
45 Leonard Ford, Cleveland vs Detroit, Dec. 26, 1954 (2 interceptions)
41 Garrard Ramsey, Chicago Cardinals vs Philadelphia, Dec. 28, 1947 (1 interception)
39 Sidney Luckman, Chicago Bears vs Washington, Dec. 26, 1943 (2 interceptions)
    Dante Magnani, Chicago Bears vs New York Giants, Dec. 15, 1946 (2 interceptions) (1 TD)
35 Marvin Johnson, Los Angeles vs Cleveland Browns, Dec. 23, 1951 (1 interception)
34 George McAfee, Chicago Bears vs Washington, Dec. 8, 1940 (1 interception) (TD)

Longest Return of Intercepted Pass—Yards

65 Don Paul, Cleveland vs Los Angeles, Dec. 26, 1955
45 Leonard Ford, Cleveland vs Detroit, Dec. 26, 1954
42 John Sample, Baltimore vs New York, Dec. 27, 1959 (TD)
41 Garrard Ramsey, Chicago Cardinals vs Philadelphia, Dec. 28, 1947
39 Dante Magnani, Chicago Bears vs New York Giants, Dec. 15, 1946 (TD)
35 Marvin Johnson, Los Angeles vs Cleveland Browns, Dec. 23, 1951
34 George McAfee, Chicago Bears vs Washington, Dec. 8, 1940 (TD)
33 Kenneth Gorgal, Cleveland Browns vs Los Angeles, Dec. 24, 1950

PUNTING

Most Punts

26 Robert Waterfield, Cleveland and Los Angeles Rams (Played in 4 games)
24 Horace Gillom, Cleveland (Played in 6 games)
19 Joseph Muha, Philadelphia (Played in 3 games)
16 Ray Mallouf, Chicago Cardinals (Played in 2 games)

14 Samuel Baugh, Washington (Played in 5 games)

13 Keith Molesworth, Chicago Bears (Played in 3 games)

Most Punts (one game)

11 Kenneth Strong, New York Giants vs Chicago Bears, Dec. 17, 1933

10 Keith Molesworth, Chicago Bears vs New York Giants, Dec. 17, 1933

Best Punting Average

44.5 Don Chandler, New York Giants (Played in 3 games)

41.0 Robert Waterfield, Cleveland and Los Angeles Rams (Played in 4 games)

Best Punting Average (one game)

50.8 Robert Waterfield, Los Angeles vs Cleveland Browns, Dec. 24, 1950 (4 punts)

50.8 Ray Brown, Baltimore vs New York Giants, Dec. 28, 1958

Longest Punt (Yards)

85 Samuel Baugh, Washington vs Chicago Bears, Dec. 13. 1942

72 Robert Yale Lary, Detroit vs Cleveland, Dec. 27, 1953

69 Joseph Muha, Philadelphia vs Chicago Cardinals, Dec. 28, 1947

68 Horace Gillom, Cleveland Browns vs Los Angeles, Dec. 24, 1950

Shortest Punt (Yards)

4 Joseph Muha, Philadelphia vs Chicago Cardinals, Dec. 28, 1947

PUNT RETURNS

Most Punt Returns

8 Keith Molesworth, Chicago Bears (Played in 3 games)

7 William Reynolds, Cleveland (Played in 3 games)

5 Harry Newman, New York Giants (Played in 3 games)

4 Several

Most Punt Returns (one game)

4 Irving Comp, Green Bay vs New York Giants, Dec. 17, 1944
Steven Bagarus, Washington vs Cleveland Rams, Dec. 16, 1945
Ray Renfro, Cleveland vs Detroit, Dec. 28, 1952
Carl Taseff, Baltimore vs New York Giants, Dec. 28, 1958

3 Several

Most Yards Punts Returned

113 Charles Trippi, Chicago Cardinals (4 returns in 2 games)

97 William Reynolds, Cleveland vs Detroit, Dec. 27, 1953 (7 returns in 3 games)

55 Irving Comp, Green Bay (4 returns in 1 game)

52 Steven Bagarus, Washington (4 returns in 1 game)

42 Sidney Luckman, Chicago Bears (4 returns in 5 games)

38 Alphonse Leemans, New York Giants (2 returns in 3 games)

Most Yards Punts Returned (one game)

102 Charles Trippi, Chicago Cardinals vs Philadelphia, Dec. 28, 1947 (2 returns)

55 Irving Comp, Green Bay vs New York Giants, Dec. 17, 1944 (4 returns)

52 Steven Bagarus, Washington vs Cleveland Rams, Dec. 16, 1944 (4 returns)

Longest Punt Return (Yards)

75 Charles Trippi, Chicago Cardinals vs Philadelphia, Dec. 28, 1947

42 William Reynolds, Cleveland vs Detroit, Dec. 26, 1954

37 John Cochran, Chicago Cardinals vs Philadelphia, Dec. 28, 1947

35 Jerry Williams, Los Angeles vs Cleveland Browns, Dec. 24, 1950

26 Harry Newman, New York Giants vs Chicago Bears, Dec. 17, 1933

SCORING

Most Points Scored

40 Lou Groza, Cleveland (22 extra points, 6 field goals) (Played in 7 games)

36 Kenneth Strong, New York Giants (Played in 5 games) (4 touchdowns; 9 extra points; 1 field goal)

33 Jack Manders, Chicago Bears (Played in 4 games) (2 touchdowns; 6 extra points; 5 field goals)

Most Points Scored (one game)

18 Otto Graham, Cleveland vs Detroit, Dec. 26, 1954

17 Kenneth Strong, New York Giants vs Chicago Bears, Dec. 9, 1934 (2 touchdowns; 2 extra points; 1 field goal)

15 Jack Manders, Chicago Bears vs Washington, Dec. 12, 1937 (2 touchdowns; 3 extra points)

Most Touchdowns

5 Otto Graham, Cleveland (Played in 6 games)

4 Kenneth Strong, New York Giants (Played in 5 games)
Harry Clark, Chicago Bears (Played in 4 games)

3 Kenneth Kavanaugh, Chicago Bears (Played in 3 games)
Andrew Farkas, Washington (Played in 3 games)
Dante Magnani, Chicago Bears

(Played in 2 games)
Richard Hoerner, Los Angeles
(Played in 3 games)
2 Several

Most Touchdowns (one game)

3 Otto Graham, Cleveland vs Detroit, Dec. 26, 1954
2 Several

Most Extra Points

22 Lou Groza, Cleveland (Played in 7 games)
9 Kenneth Strong, New York Giants (Played in 5 games)
8 Robert Waterfield, Cleveland and Los Angeles Rams (Played in 4 games)
Robert Snyder, Chicago Bears (Played in 3 games)
8 James Martin, Detroit (Played in 4 games)
6 Jack Manders, Chicago Bears (Played in 4 games)
John Patton, Philadelphia (Played in 3 games)

Most Extra Points (one game)

8 James Martin, Detroit vs Cleveland, Dec. 29, 1957
8 Lou Groza, Cleveland vs Detroit, Dec. 26, 1954
5 Robert Snyder, Chicago Bears vs Washington, Dec. 26, 1943
Lou Groza, Cleveland vs Los Angeles, Dec. 26, 1955
Ben Agajanian, New York Giants vs Chicago Bears, Dec. 30, 1956
4 Marlin Harder, Chicago Cardinals vs Philadelphia, Dec. 28, 1947
Robert Waterfield, Los Angeles vs Cleveland Browns, Dec. 24, 1950
Riley Smith, Washington vs Chicago Bears, Dec. 12, 1937
3 Several

Most Field Goals

6 Lou Groza, Cleveland (Played in 7 games)
5 Jack Manders, Chicago Bears (Played in 4 games)
3 Robert Snyder, Chicago Bears (Played in 3 games)

Most Field Goals (one game)

3 Jack Manders, Chicago Bears vs New York Giants, Dec. 17, 1933 (16, 40, 18 yards)
Robert Snyder, Chicago Bears vs New York Giants, Dec. 21, 1941 (14, 39, 37 yards)
Lou Groza, Cleveland vs Detroit, Dec. 27, 1953 (13, 15, 43 yards)

George Summerall, New York vs Baltimore, Dec. 27, 1959 (23, 37 and 22 yards)

Most Field Goals Attempted

12 Lou Groza, Cleveland (Played in 7 games
10 Jack Manners, Chicago Bears (Played in 4 games)
5 Ward Cuff, New York Giants (Played in 3 games)

Most Field Goals Attempted (one game)

4 Jack Manders (twice), Chicago Bears vs New York Giants, Dec. 17, 1933 and Dec. 9, 1934
Lou Groza, Cleveland vs Detroit, Dec. 27, 1953
3 Several

Longest Field Goal (Yards)

52 Louis Groza, Cleveland Browns vs Los Angeles, Dec. 23, 1951
43 Lou Groza, Cleveland vs Los Angeles, Dec. 27, 1953
Ben Agajanian, New York Giants vs Chicago Bears, Dec. 30, 1956
42 Ward Cuff, New York Giants vs Green Bay, Dec. 11, 1938
Ernest Smith, Green Bay vs New York Giants, Dec. 10, 1939
40 Jack Manders, Chicago Bears vs New York Giants, Dec. 17, 1933

KICK-OFF RETURNS

Most Kick-off Returns

9 Kenneth Carpenter, Cleveland Browns (Played in 5 games)
7 Donald Bingham, Chicago Bears (Played in 1 game)
6 William Reynolds, Cleveland (Played in 3 games)
5 Verda Smith, Los Angeles (Played in 3 games)
3 Several

Most Kick-off Returns (one game)

7 Don Bingham, Chicago Bears vs New York Giants, Dec. 30, 1956
5 Kenneth Carpenter, Cleveland Browns vs Los Angeles, Dec. 23, 1951

Longest Kick-off Return (Yards)

62 Max Krause, Washington vs Chicago Bears, Dec. 8, 1940
58 Ted Dean, Philadelphia vs Green Bay, Dec. 26, 1960
50 James Brown, Cleveland vs Detroit, Dec. 29, 1957
46 Boris Dimancheff, Chicago Cardinals vs Philadelphia, Dec. 28, 1947

William Reynolds, Cleveland vs Detroit, Dec. 26, 1954

40   Harry Newman, New York Giants vs
Detroit, Dec. 15, 1935

Most Yards Gained Kick-off Returns (Yards)

208   Kenneth Carpenter, Cleveland
(Played in 5 games)

143   William Reynolds, Cleveland (Played
in 3 games)

99   Verda Smith, Los Angeles (Played in
3 games)

90   Boris Dimancheff, Chicago Cardinals
(Played in 2 games)

THE ALL-TIME ROSTER

AAFC—Indicates years played in All America Football Conference

**ABBEY, JOSEPH—End—Texas State
North**
1948–49 Chicago Bears
1949 New York Bulldogs

**ABBOTT, LAFAYETTE—Back—
Syracuse**
1921–29 Dayton Triangles

**ABBRUZZI, LOUIS—Back—Rhode
Island State**
1946 Boston Yanks

ABELL, EARL—Back—Colgate
1926 Milwaukee Badgers

ABERSON, CLIFFORD—Back
1946 Green Bay Packers

ABRAMS, NATHAN—End
1921 Green Bay Packers

**ABRAMSON, GEORGE—Tackle—
Minnesota**
1925 Green Bay Packers

**ABRUZZINO, FRANK—Center—
Colgate**
1931 Brooklyn Dodgers
1933 Cincinnati Reds

ACHUI, WALTER—Back—Dayton
1927–28 Dayton Triangles

**ADAMLE, ANTHONY—Back—Ohio
State**
1947–49 Cleveland Browns (AAFC)
1950–51, 54 Cleveland Browns

ADAMS, CHESTER—Tackle—Ohio
1939–42 Cleveland Rams
1942–43 Green Bay Packers
1946–48 Cleveland Browns (AAFC)
1949 Buffalo Bills (AAFC)
1950 New York Yanks

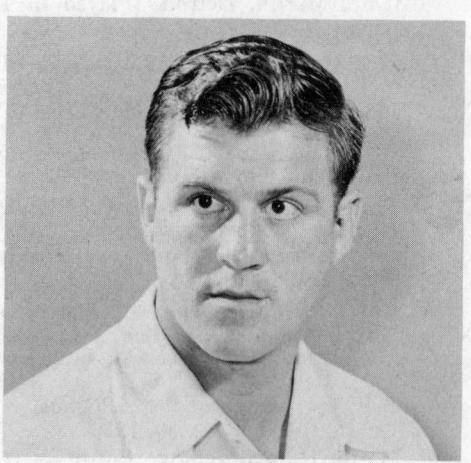

ANTHONY ADAMLE

ADAMS, HENRY—Center—Pittsburgh
1939 Chicago Cardinals

ADAMS, JAMES—Tackle
1924 Rochester Kodaks

ADAMS, JOHN—Tackle—Notre Dame
1945–49 Washington Redskins

**ADAMS, JOHN—Back—Los Angeles
STATE**
1959–60 Chicago Bears

ADAMS, O'NEAL—End—Arkansas
1941–45 New York Giants
1946–47 Brooklyn Dodgers (AAFC)

**ADAMS, VERLIN—Tackle—Morris
Harvey**
1942–45 New York Giants

**ADAMSON, KENNETH—Guard—
Notre Dame**
1960 Denver Broncos (AFL)

ADDAMS, ABRAHAM—End—Indiana
1949 Detroit Lions

**ADDISON, THOMAS—Back—South-
ern California**
1960 Boston Patriots (AFL)

**ADDUCCI, NICHOLAS—Back—
Nebraska**
1954–55 Washington Redskins

ADKINS, ROBERT—End—Marshall
1940–41, 45–46 Green Bay Packers

AFFLIS, RICHARD—Guard—Nevada
1951–54 Green Bay Packers

**AGAJANIAN, BENJAMIN—Kicker—
New Mexico**
1945 Pittsburgh Steelers
1945 Philadelphia Eagles
1947–48 Los Angeles Dons (AAFC)
1949 New York Giants
1953 Los Angeles Rams
1954–57 New York Giants
1960 Los Angeles Chargers (AFL)

**AGASE, ALEXANDER—Guard—
Illinois**
1947 Los Angeles Dons (AAFC)
1947 Chicago Rockets (AAFC)
1948–49 Cleveland Browns (AAFC)
1950–51 Cleveland Browns
1953 Baltimore Colts

AGEE, SAMUEL—Back—Vanderbilt
1938–39 Chicago Cardinals

AGLER, HARRY—End—California
1948 Los Angeles Dons (AAFC)

AGLER, ROBERT—Back—Otterbein
1948–49 Los Angeles Rams

**AGUIRRE, JOSEPH—End—St. Mary's
(Cal.)**
1941–45 Washington Redskins
1946–49 Los Angeles Dons (AAFC)
1945 #1 Field goals

**AIELLO, ANTHONY—Back—
Youngstown**
1944 Detroit Lions
1944 Brooklyn Tigers

**AILINGER, JAMES—Tackle—
Buffalo Univ.**
1924 Buffalo All Americans

AKIN, LEONARD—Guard—Baylor
1942 Chicago Bears

**AKINS, ALBERT—Back—Washington
State**
1946 Cleveland Browns (AAFC)
1947–48 Brooklyn Dodgers (AAFC)
1948 Buffalo Bills (AAFC)

**AKINS, FRANK—Back—Washington
State**
1943–46 Washington Redskins
1947 Baltimore Colts (AAFC)

**ALBAN, RICHARD—Back—
Northwestern**
1952–55 Washington Redskins
1956–59 Pittsburgh Steelers

RICHARD ALBAN

**ALBANESE, DONALD—End—
Tulane**
1925 Columbus Tigers

**ALBANESE, VINCENT—Back—
Syracuse**
1937–38 Brooklyn Dodgers

**ALBERGHINI, THOMAS—Guard—
Holy Cross**
1945 Pittsburgh Steelers

ALBERT, FRANK—Back—Stanford
1946–49 San Francisco 49ers (AAFC)
1950–51 San Francisco 49ers

**ALBRECHT, ARTHUR—Tackle—
Wisconsin**
1941 Green Bay Packers
1942 Pittsburgh Steelers
1943 Chicago Cardinals
1944 Boston Yanks

**ALBRIGHT, WILLIAM—Guard—
Wisconsin**
1951–54 New York Giants

FRANK ALBERT

ALDERMAN, GRADY—Guard— Detroit
1960   Detroit Lions

ALDERTON, JOHN—End—Maryland
1953   Pittsburgh Steelers

ALDRICH, CHARLES—Center—TCU
1939–40   Chicago Cardinals
1940–43, 45–47   Washington Redskins

ALDRIDGE, BENJAMIN—Back— Oklahoma A & M
1950–51   New York Yanks
1952   Dallas Texans
1952–53   San Francisco 49ers
1953   Green Bay Packers

ALEXANDER, JOHN—Tackle— Rutgers
1922   Milwaukee Badgers
1926   New York Giants

ALEXANDER, JOSEPH—Guard— Syracuse
1921–22   Rochester Kodaks
1922   Milwaukee Badgers
1925–27   New York Giants

ALFONSE, JULES—Back—Minnesota
1937–38   Cleveland Rams

ALFORD, EUGENE—Back—Texas Tech.
1931–33   Portsmouth Spartans
1934   Cincinnati Reds
1934   St. Louis Gunners

ALFORD, HERBERT BRUCE— End—TCU
1946–49   New York Yankees (AAFC)
1950–51   New York Yanks

ALFSON, WARREN—Guard— Nebraska
1941   Brooklyn Dodgers

ALLEN, CARL—Back—Oklahoma City Univ.
1948   Brooklyn Dodgers (AAFC)

ALLEN, DALVA—End—Houston
1960   Houston Oilers (AFL)

ALLEN, DONALD—Back—Texas
1960   Denver Broncos (AFL)

ALLEN, EDMUND—End—Colgate
1928   Chicago Cardinals

ALLEN, EDWARD—Back— Pennsylvania
1947   Chicago Bears

ALLEN, ERMAL—Back—Kentucky
1947   Cleveland Browns (AAFC)

ALLEN, JOHN—Center—Purdue
1955–58   Washington Redskins

ALLEN, LOUIS—Tackle—Duke
1950–51   Pittsburgh Steelers

ALLEN, SAMUEL—Tackle
1931   Frankford Yellowjackets

ALLISON, JAMES—End—Texas A & M
1926–27   Buffalo Bisons
1928   New York Giants

ALLISTON, VAUGHAN—Back Mississippi
1960   Denver Broncos (AFL)

ALLMAN, ROBERT —End— Michigan State
1936   Chicago Bears

ALLTON, JOSEPH—Tackle— Oklahoma
1942   Chicago Cardinals

AMBERG, JOHN—Back—Kansas
1951–52   New York Giants

AMBROSE, JOHN—Guard—Catholic Univ.
1932   Brooklyn Dodgers

AMBROSE, WALTER—End—Carroll
1930   Portsmouth Spartans

AMECHE, ALAN—Back—Wisconsin
1955–60   Baltimore Colts
1955   #1 Ball Carrying

AMSTUTZ, JOSEPH—Center— Indiana
1957   Cleveland Browns

ALAN AMECHE

Fran Byrne

HEARTLEY ANDERSON

AMUNDSEN, NORMAN—Guard—Wisconsin
1957 Green Bay Packers

ANANIS, VITO—Back—Boston College
1945 Washington Redskins

ANDABAKER, RUDOLPH—Guard—Pittsburgh
1952, 54 Pittsburgh Steelers

ANDERSEN, STANLEY—End—Stanford
1940–41 Cleveland Rams
1941 Detroit Lions

ANDERSON, CHARLES—End—Louisiana Tech.
1956 Chicago Cardinals

ANDERSON, CLIFTON—End—Indiana
1952–53 Chicago Cardinals
1953 New York Giants

ANDERSON, EDWARD—End—Notre Dame
1922 Rochester Jeffersons
1923 Rock Island Independents
1923 Chicago Bears
1923–25 Chicago Cardinals

ANDERSON, EZZRET—End—Kentucky State
1947 Los Angeles Dons (AAFC)

ANDERSON, HEARTLEY—Guard—Notre Dame
1922–25 Chicago Bears

ANDERSON, HENRY—Guard—Northwestern
1931 Chicago Bears

ANDERSON, OSCAR—Back—Colgate
1921–22 Buffalo All Americans

ANDERSON, RALPH—End—Los Angeles State
1958 Chicago Bears
1960 Los Angeles Chargers (AFL)
Died Nov. 26, 1960, of diabetic attack.

ANDERSON, THOMAS—Back—Haskell
1924 Kansas City Cowboys

ANDERSON, WALTER "BILL"—Back—Tennessee
1958–60 Washington Redskins

ANDERSON, WILLARD—Back—Syracuse
1922, 24 Rochester Jeffersons
1923 Cleveland Indians
1925 Rock Island Independents

ANDERSON, WILLIAM—Back—Tennessee
1958 Washington Redskins

ANDERSON, WILLIAM—Back—Compton Jr.
1953–54 Chicago Bears

ANDERSON, WILLIAM—End—West Virginia
1945 Boston Yanks

ANDERSON, WINSTON—End—Colgate
1936 New York Giants

ANDRAKO, STEPHEN—Center—
Ohio State
1940   Washington Redskins
1941   Cleveland Rams

ANDREWS, LEROY—Back—Kansas
State Teachers
1923   St. Louis Browns
1924–26   Kansas City Cowboys
1927   Cleveland Bulldogs
1934   Philadelphia Eagles

ANDROS, PLATO—Guard—
Oklahoma
1947–50   Chicago Cardinals

ANDRULEWICZ, THEODORE—
Back—Villanova
1930   Newark

ANDRUSKING, SIGMUND—Guard—
Detroit
1937   Brooklyn Dodgers

ANE, CHARLES—Center—
Southern California
1953–59   Detroit Lions

ANGLE, ROBERT—Back—Iowa State
1950   Chicago Cardinals

ELMER ANGSMAN

ANGSMAN, ELMER—Back—Notre
Dame
1946–52   Chicago Cardinals

ANNAN, DUNCAN—Back—Brown
1923–26   Hammond Independents
1925   Akron Steels

APOLSKIS, CHARLES—End—DePaul
1938–39   Chicago Bears

APOLSKIS, RAYMOND—Guard—
Marquette
1941–42, 45–50   Chicago Cardinals

APSIT, MARGER—Back—Southern
California
1931   Frankford Yellowjackets
1931   Brooklyn Dodgers
1932   Green Bay Packers
1933   Boston Redskins

ARCHOSKA, JULIUS—End—Syracuse
1930   Staten Island Stapletons

ARENA, ANTHONY—Center
Michigan State
1942, 46   Detroit Lions

ARENAS, JOSEPH—Back—Omaha
Univ.
1951–57   San Francisco 49ers

ARENZ, ARNOLD—Back—St. Louis
1934   Boston Redskins

ARGUS, ROBERT—Back
1921–25   Rochester Kodaks

ARIAIL, DAVID—End—Alabama
Polytech.
1934   Brooklyn Dodgers
1934   Cincinnati Reds

ARMS, LLOYD—Guard—Oklahoma
A & M
1946–48   Chicago Cardinals

ARMSTRONG, CHARLES—Back—
Mississippi
1946   Brooklyn Dodgers (AAFC)

ARMSTRONG, GRAHAM—Tackle—
John Carroll
1941, 45   Cleveland Rams
1947–48   Buffalo Bills (AAFC)

ARMSTRONG, JOHN—Back—
Columbia
1922   Milwaukee Badgers
1923–25   Rock Island Independents

ARMSTRONG, NEIL—End—
Oklahoma A & M
1947–51   Philadelphia Eagles

ARMSTRONG, RAMON—Guard—
TCU
1960   Oakland Raiders (AFL)

ARMSTRONG, ROBERT—Tackle—
Missouri
1931–32   Portsmouth Spartans

ARNDT, ALFRED—Guard—South
Dakota State
1935   Pittsburgh Pirates
1935   Boston Redskins

ARNETT, JON—Back—Southern
California
1957–60   Los Angeles Rams

NEIL ARMSTRONG

ARNOLD, JAY—Back—Texas
1937–40 Philadelphia Eagles
1941 Pittsburgh Steelers

ARROWHEAD—End
1923 Oorang Indians

JON ARNETT

ARTERBURN, ELMER—Back—Texas Tech.
1954 Chicago Cardinals

ARTMAN, CORWAN—Tackle—Stanford
1931 New York Giants
1932 Boston Braves
1933 Pittsburgh Pirates

ARTOE, LEE—Tackle—California
1940–42, 45 Chicago Bears
1946–47 Los Angeles Dons (AAFC)
1948 Baltimore Colts (AAFC)

ASAD, DOUGLAS—End—Northwstern
1960 Oakland Raiders (AFL)

ASCHBACHER, DARREL—Guard—Oregon
1959 Philadelphia Eagles

ASCHENBRENNER, FRANK—Back—Northwestern
1949 Chicago Hornets (AAFC)

ASH, JULIAN—Guard—Oregon State
1926 Los Angeles

ASHBAUGH, WILLIAM—Back—Pittsburgh
1924 Rock Island Independents

ASHBURNE, CLIFFORD—Guard—Nebraska
1924–25 Kansas City Cowboys
1929 New York Giants
1930 Chicago Bears

ASHCOM, RICHARD—Tackle—Oregon
1943 Detroit Lions

ASHMORE, ROGER—Tackle—Gonzaga
1926 Milwaukee Badgers
1927 Duluth Eskimos
1927 Chicago Bears
1928–29 Green Bay Packers

ASPATORE, EDWARD—Tackle—Marquette
1934 Cincinnati Reds
1934 Chicago Bears

ATCHASON, JACK—End—Illinois Western
1960 Boston Patriots (AFL)
1960 Houston Oilers (AFL)

ATKESON, DALE—Back
1954–56 Washington Redskins

ATKINS, DOUGLAS—End—Tennessee
1953–54 Cleveland Browns
1955–60 Chicago Bears

ATKINS, GEORGE—Guard—Auburn
1955 Detroit Lions

ATKINS, WILLIAM—Back—Auburn
1958 San Francisco 49ers
1960 Buffalo Bills (AFL)

ATTACHE, REGINALD—Back
1922 Oorang Indians

ATTY, ALEXANDER—Guard—West Virginia
1939 Cleveland Rams
1941 Detroit Lions

ATWOOD, JOHN—Back—Wisconsin
1948   New York Giants

AUBNER—End
1921   Columbus Tigers

AUDET, EARL—Tackle—Southern California
1945   Washington Redskins
1946–48   Los Angeles Dons (AAFC)

AUER, HOWARD—Tackle—Michigan
1933   Chicago Cardinals
1933   Philadelphia Eagles

AUGUST, EDWARD—Back—Villanova
1931   Providence Steamrollers

AUGUSTERFER, EUGENE—Guard—Catholic Univ.
1935   Pittsburgh Pirates

AULT, WAYNE—Tackle—Oklahoma A & M
1924–25   Cleveland Indians

AUSTIN, JAMES—End—St. Mary's (Cal.)
1937–38   Brooklyn Dodgers
1939   Detroit Lions

AUSTIN, WILLIAM—Tackle—Oregon State
1949–50, 53–57   New York Giants

AUTREY, WILLIAM—Center—Austin
1953   Chicago Bears

AVEDISIAN, CHARLES—Guard—Providence
1942–44   New York Giants

AVENI, JOHN—End—Indiana
1959–60   Chicago Bears

AVERNO, SISTO—Guard—Muhlenberg
1950   Baltimore Colts
1951   New York Giants
1952   Dallas Texans
1953–54   Baltimore Colts

AVERY, DONALD—Tackle—California
1946–47   Washington Redskins
1948   Los Angeles Dons (AAFC)

AVINGER, CLARENCE—Back—Alabama
1953   New York Giants

BABARTSKY, ALBERT—Tackle—Fordham

1938–42   Chicago Cardinals
1943–45   Chicago Bears

BABB, EUGENE—Back—Austin
1957–58   San Francisco 49ers
1960   Dallas Cowboys

BABCOCK, HARRY—End—Georgia
1953–55   San Francisco 49ers

BABCOCK, SAMUEL—Back—Michigan
1926   Canton Bulldogs

BACCHUS, CARL—End—Missouri
1927   Cleveland Bulldogs
1928   Detroit Wolverines

BACHMAIER, JOSEPH—Guard
1921–24   Rochester Kodaks

BACHOR, LUDWIG—Tackle—Detroit
1928   Detroit Wolverines

BACON, FRANCIS—Back—Wabash
1921–26   Dayton Triangles

BADACZEWSKI, JOHN—Guard—Western Reserve
1946–48   Boston Yanks
1948   Chicago Cardinals
1949–51   Washington Redskins
1953   Chicago Bears

BADGRO, MORRIS—End—Southern California
1927–28   New York Yankees
1929–36   New York Giants
1936   Brooklyn Dodgers

BAGARUS, STEPHEN—Back—Notre Dame
1945–46, 48   Washington Redskins
1947   Los Angeles Rams

BAGBY, HERMAN—Back—Arkansas
1926   Brooklyn Dodgers
1927   Cleveland Bulldogs

BAGDON, EDWARD—Guard—Michigan State
1950–51   Chicago Cardinals
1952   Washington Redskins

BAGGETT, WILLIAM—Back—Louisiana State Univ.
1952   Dallas Texans

BAHAN, LEONARD—Back—Notre Dame
1923   Cleveland Indians

BAHNSEN, KENNETH—Back—Texas State North
1953   San Francisco 49ers

**BAILEY, BYRON—Back—
Washington State**
1952–53   Detroit Lions
1953   Green Bay Packers

BAILEY, EDGAR—End—Duke
1940–41   Brooklyn Dodgers
1946   Boston Yanks

**BAILEY, HOWARD—Tackle—
Tennessee**
1935   Philadelphia Eagles

**BAILEY, JAMES—Guard—West
Virginia State**
1949   Chicago Hornets (AAFC)

**BAILEY, RUSSELL—Center—West
Virginia**
1921   Akron Steels

**BAISI, ALBERT—Guard—West
Virginia**
1940–41, 46   Chicago Bears
1947   Philadelphia Eagles

**BAKER, CONWAY—Tackle—
Centenary**
1936–43, 45   Chicago Cardinals
1944   Card-Pitt

BAKER, DAVID—Back—Oklahoma
1959–60   San Francisco 49ers
1960   #1 Interceptions (tied with G.
Norton)

DAVID BAKER

BAKER, FRANK—End—Northwestern
1931   Green Bay Packers

**BAKER, JOHN—Tackle—
North Carolina College**

1958–60   Los Angeles Rams

JOHN BAKER

BAKER, JON—Guard—California
1949–52   New York Giants

**BAKER, LAWRENCE—Tackle—
Bowling Green**
1960   New York Titans (AFL)

**BAKER, LORIS "SAM"—Back—
Oregon State**
1953, 56–59   Washington Redskins
1957   #1 Scoring (tied with Groza)
1958   #1 Punting
1960   Cleveland Browns

**BAKER, ROY—Back—Southern
California**
1927   New York Yankees
1928–29   Green Bay Packers
1930   Chicago Cardinals
1931   Staten Island Stapletons

BALATTI, EDWARD—Tackle
1946–48   San Francisco 49ers (AAFC)
1948   New York Yankees (AAFC)
1948   Buffalo Bills (AAFC)

BALAZS, FRANK—Back—Iowa
1939–41   Green Bay Packers
1941, 45   Chicago Cardinals

**BALDACCI, LOUIS—Back—Michigan
State**
1956   Pittsburgh Steelers

BALDWIN, ALTON—End—Arkansas
1947–49   Buffalo Bills (AAFC)
1950   Green Bay Packers

BALDWIN, BURR—End—UCLA
1947–49   Los Angeles Dons (AAFC)

BALDWIN, GEORGE—End—Virginia
1925   Cleveland Indians

BALDWIN, JOHN—Center—
Centenary
1946–47   New York Yankees (AAFC)
1947   San Francisco 49ers (AAFC)
1948   Buffalo Bills (AAFC)

BALOG, ROBERT—Center—Denver
1949–50   Pittsburgh Steelers

BALTZELL, VICTOR—Back—
Southwestern
1935   Boston Redskins

BANAS, STEPHEN—Back—Notre
Dame
1935   Detroit Lions
1935   Philadelphia Eagles

BANCROFT, HUGH—End—Alfred
1923   Rochester Kodaks

BANDUCCI, BRUNO—Guard—
Stanford
1944–45   Philadelphia Eagles
1946–49   San Francisco 49ers (AAFC)
1950–54   San Francisco 49ers

BANDURA, JOHN—End—
Southwestern
1943   Brooklyn Dodgers

BANET, HERBERT—Back—
Manchester
1937   Green Bay Packers

BANFIELD, JAMES—Back—
Oklahoma State
1960   Houston Oilers (AFL)

BANJAVIC, EMIL—Back—Arizona
1942   Detroit Lions

BANONIS, VINCENT—Center—
Detroit
1942–43, 46–50   Chicago Cardinals
1951–53   Detroit Lions

BANSAVAGE, ALBERT—Back—
Southern California
1960   Los Angeles Chargers (AFL)

BANTA, HERBERT JACK—Back—
Southern California
1941   Washington Redskins
1941, 44–45   Philadelphia Eagles
1946–48   Los Angeles Rams

BARALTI—Center
1922   Milwaukee Badgers

BARBEE, JOSEPH—Tackle—Kent
State
1960   Oakland Raiders (AFL)

BARBER, BENJAMIN—Tackle—
Virginia Military Inst.
1925   Buffalo Bisons

HERBERT
"JACK" BANTA

BARBER, ERNEST—Center—San
Francisco Univ.
1945   Washington Redskins
1945   New York Giants

BARBER, HENRY—Tackle—
Dartmouth
1932   Boston Braves

BARBER, JAMES—Tackle—San
Francisco Univ.
1935–36   Boston Redskins
1937–41   Washington Redskins

BARBER, MARK—Back—South
Dakota State
1937   Cleveland Rams

BARBOLAK, PETER—Tackle—
Purdue
1949   Pittsburgh Steelers

BARBOUR, WESLEY—Back—
Wake Forest
1945   New York Giants

BARBUTI, RAYMOND—Back—
Syracuse
1930   Staten Island Stapletons

BARCLAY, GEORGE—Guard—North
Carolina
1935   Brooklyn Dodgers

BARFIELD, KENNETH—Guard—
Mississippi
1954   Washington Redskins

BARIL, ADRIAN—Tackle—St.
Thomas
1923–24   Minneapolis Marines
1925   Milwaukee Badgers

BARKER, EDWARD—End—
Washington State
1953 Pittsburgh Steelers
1954 Washington Redskins

BARKER, HUBERT—Back—
Arkansas
1942–45 New York Giants

BARKER, RICHARD—Guard—Iowa
State
1921 Chicago Bears
1921 Rock Island Independents

BARKMAN, RALPH—Back—Albright
1929 Orange
1930 Newark

BARLE, LOUIS—Back—None
1938 Detroit Lions
1939 Cleveland Rams

BARNA, GEORGE—End—Hobart
1929 Frankford Yellowjackets

BARNARD, CHARLES—End—
Oklahoma State
1938 New York Giants

BARNES, EMERY—End—Oregon
1956 Green Bay Packers

BARNES, ERICH—Back—Purdue
1958–60 Chicago Bears

BARNES, ERNEST—Tackle—North
Carolina College
1960 New York Titans (AFL)

WILLIAM BARNES

BARNES, LAWRENCE—Back
Colorado A & M
1957 San Francisco 49ers
1960 Oakland Raiders (AFL)

BARNES, WALTER—Guard—LSU
1948–51 Philadelphia Eagles

BARNES, WILLIAM—Back—
Wake Forest
1957–60 Philadelphia Eagles

BARNETT, SOLON—Tackle—Baylor
1945–46 Green Bay Packers

BARNETT, THOMAS—Back—
Purdue
1959–60 Pittsburgh Steelers

BARNHART —Back—
Centenary
1934 Philadelphia Eagles

BARNI, ROY—Back—San Francisco
1952–53 Chicago Cardinals
1954–55 Philadelphia Eagles
1955–56 Washington Redskins

BARNIKOW, EDWARD—Back
1926 Hartford Blues

BARNUM, LEONARD—Back—West
Virginia Wesleyan
1938–40 New York Giants
1940–42 Philadelphia Eagles

TERRY BARR

BARNUM, ROBERT—Back—West
Virginia
1926 Columbus Tigers

BARR, TERRY—Back—Michigan
1957–60 Detroit Lions

BARR, WALLACE—Back—Wisconsin
1923–24, 26 Racine Legion
1925 Milwaukee Badgers

BARRABEE, ROBERT—End—
New York Univ.
1931 Staten Island Stapletons

**BARRAGER, NATHAN—Center—
Southern California**
1930 Minneapolis Redjackets
1930–31 Frankford Yellowjackets
1931–35 Green Bay Packers

BARREL—Center—Carlisle
1922–23 Oorang Indians

**BARRETT, EMMETT—Center—
Portland**
1942–44 New York Giants

BARRETT, JEFFREY—End—LSU
1936–38 Brooklyn Dodgers

BARRETT, JOHN—Tackle—Detroit
1922–23 Hammond Pros
1924–25 Akron Steels
1926, 28 Detroit Panthers
1927 Pottsville Maroons

**BARRETT, ROBERT—End—
Baldwin-Wallace**
1960 Buffalo Bills (AFL)

**BARRON, JAMES—Tackle—
Georgetown**
1921 Rochester Kodaks

**BARRY, ALBERT—Guard—Southern
California**
1954, 57 Green Bay Packers
1958–59 New York Giants
1960 Los Angeles Chargers (AFL)

BARRY, GEORGE—Guard—Beloit
1922 Racine Legion
1922–24, 26 Hammond Independents
1924–26 Akron Steels

**BARRY, NORMAN—Back—Notre
Dame**
1921 Chicago Cardinals
1921 Green Bay Packers

BARRY, PAUL—Back—Tulsa
1950, 52 Los Angeles Rams
1953 Washington Redskins
1954 Chicago Cardinals

**BARTHOLOMEW, SAMUEL—
Back—Tennessee**
1941 Philadelphia Eagles

BARTON, DONALD—Back—Texas
1953 Green Bay Packers

BARTON, JAMES—Center—Marshall
1960 Dallas Texans (AFL)

**BARTOS, HENRY—Guard—North
Carolina**
1938 Washington Redskins

**BARTOS, JOSEPH—Back—
Annapolis**
1950 Washington Redskins

**BARWEGAN, RICHARD—Guard—
Purdue**
1947 New York Yankees (AAFC)
1948–49 Baltimore Colts (AAFC)
1950, 53–54 Baltimore Colts
1950–52 Chicago Bears

**BARZILAUSKAS, FRANCIS—
Guard—Yale**
1947–48 Boston Yanks
1949 New York Bulldogs
1951 New York Giants

RICHARD BARWEGAN

BASCA, MICHAEL—Back—Villanova
1941 Philadelphia Eagles
       Killed in France on Armistice
       Day, 1944 with Patton's Third
       Army

**BASING, MYRTLE—Back—
Lawrence**
1923–27 Green Bay Packers

**BASRAK, MICHAEL—Center—
Duquesne**
1937–38 Pittsburgh Steelers

**BASS, RICHARD—Back—
College of Pacific**
1960 Los Angeles Rams

BASS, WILLIAM—Back—Nevada
1947 Chicago Rockets (AAFC)

**BASSETT, HENRY—Tackle—
Nebraska**
1924 Kansas City Cowboys

**BASSETT, MAURICE—Back—
Langston**
1954–56 Cleveland Browns

**BASSI, RICHARD—Guard—Santa
Clara**
1938–39 Chicago Bears

1940 Philadelphia Eagles
1941 Pittsburgh Steelers
1946–47 San Francisco 49ers (AAFC)

**BASSMAN, HERMAN—Back—
Ursinus**
1936–37 Philadelphia Eagles

**BASTON, ALBERT—End—
Minnesota**
1922–24 Hammond Pros

**BATCHELLOR, DONALD—Tackle—
Grove City**
1922 Canton Bulldogs
1923 Toledo Maroons

**BATES, THEODORE—Tackle—
Oregon State**
1959 Chicago Cardinals
1960 St. Louis Cardinals

**BATINSKI, STANLEY—Guard—
Temple**
1941–47 Detroit Lions
1948 Boston Yanks
1949 New York Bulldogs
1949 New York Yankees (AAFC)

RICHARD BASS

BATORSKI, JOHN—End—Colgate
1946 Buffalo Bills (AAFC)

**BATTLES, CLIFFORD—Back—West
Virginia Wesleyan**
1932–36 Boston Redskins
1937 Washington Redskins
1933, 37 #1 Ball Carrying

BATTLES, WILLIAM—End—Brown
1939 Chicago Bears

BAUER, JOHN—Guard—Illinois
1954 New York Giants

**BAUER, HERBERT—Tackle—
Baldwin-Wallace**
1923 Racine Legion
1925 Cleveland Indians

BAUGH, SAMUEL—Back—TCU
1937–52 Washington Redskins
1937, 40, 43, 45, 47, 49 #1 Passing
    (tied with Luckman 1945)
1940, 41, 42, 43 #1 Punting
1943 #1 Interceptions

**BAUGHAN, MAX—Center—Georgia
Tech**
1960 Philadelphia Eagles

**BAUJAN, HARRY—End—Notre
Dame**
1921 Cleveland Indians

**BAUMAN, ALFRED—Tackle—
Northwestern**
1947 Chicago Rockets (AAFC)
1947 Philadelphia Eagles
1948–50 Chicago Bears

**BAUMGARDNER, MAX—End—
Texas**
1948 Detroit Lions

**BAUMGARTNER, WILLIAM—
End—Minnesota**
1947 Baltimore Colts (AAFC)

BAUSCH, FRANK—Center—Kansas
1934–36 Boston Redskins
1937–40 Chicago Bears
1940–41 Philadelphia Eagles

BAUSCH, JAMES—Back—Kansas
1933 Cincinnati Reds
1933 Chicago Cardinals

**BAWEL, EDWARD—Back—
Evansville**
1952, 55–56 Philadelphia Eagles

BAXTER, ERNEST—Back—Centre
1923 Racine Legion
1924 Kenosha

BAXTER, LLOYD—Tackle—SMU
1948 Green Bay Packers

BAYLEY, JOHN—Tackle—Syracuse
1927 New York Yankees

BAZE, WINFORD—End—Texas Tech.
1937 Philadelphia Eagles

**BEACH, WALTER—Back—
Michigan Central**
1960 Boston Patriots (AFL)

BEALS, ALYN—End—Santa Clara
1946–49 San Francisco 49ers (AAFC)
1950–51 San Francisco 49ers

**BEAMS, BYRON—Tackle—
Notre Dame**
1959–60   Pittsburgh Steelers

BEASEY, JOHN—Back—South Dakota
1924   Green Bay Packers

BEASLEY, JOHN—Guard—Earlham
1923   Dayton Triangles

**BEATTIE, ROBERT—Tackle—
Princeton**
1927   New York Yankees
1929   Orange
1930   Newark

**BEATTY, EDWARD—Center—
Mississippi**
1955–56   San Francisco 49ers
1957–60   Pittsburgh Steelers

BECHTOL, HUBERT—End—Texas
1947–49   Baltimore Colts (AAFC)

BECK, CARL—Back—West Virginia
1921   Buffalo All Americans
1921, 24   Akron Steels
1925   Pottsville Maroons

**BECK, CLARENCE—Tackle—Penn.
State**
1925–28   Pottsville Maroons

**BECK, KENNETH—Tackle—
Texas A & M**
1959–60   Green Bay Packers

**BECK, RAYMOND—Guard—
Georgia Tech.**
1952, 55–57   New York Giants

BECKER, JOHN—Tackle—Denison
1926–29   Dayton Triangles

**BECKER, WAYLAND—End—
Marquette**
1934   Chicago Bears
1934–35   Brooklyn Dodgers
1936–38   Green Bay Packers
1939   Pittsburgh Steelers

**BECKLEY, ARTHUR—Back—
Michigan State**
1926   Dayton Triangles

**BEDFORD, WILLIAM EUGENE—
End—SMU**
1925   Rochester Jeffersons

**BEDNAR, ALBERT—Guard—
Lafayette**
1924–25   Frankford Yellowjackets
1925–26   New York Giants

**BEDNARIK, CHARLES—Center—
Pennsylvania**

1949–60   Philadelphia Eagles

BEEBE, KEITH—Back—Occidental
1944   New York Giants

**BEEKLEY, EUGENE—Guard—
Miami (Ohio)**
1921   Cincinnati Celts

BEHAN, CHARLES—End—DeKalb
1942   Detroit Lions
        Killed by Japanese gunfire on
        Okinawa, May 18, 1945, Lt. in
        U.S. Army

**BEHMAN, RUSSELL—Tackle—
Dickinson**
1924–31   Frankford Yellowjackets

**BEIL, LAWRENCE—Tackle—
Portland**
1948   New York Giants

**BEINOR, J. EDWARD—Tackle—
Notre Dame**
1940–41   Chicago Cardinals
1941–42   Washington Redskins

**BELANICH, WILLIAM—Tackle
Dayton**
1927–29   Dayton Triangles

BELDEN, CHARLES—Back
1927   Duluth Eskimos
1930–31   Chicago Cardinals

BELDING, LESTER—End—Iowa
1925   Rock Island Independents

**BELICHECK, Stephen—Back—
Western Reserve**
1941   Detroit Lions

BELL, EDWARD—Guard—Indiana
1946   Miami Seahawks (AAFC)
1947–49   Green Bay Packers

**BELL, EDWARD—Back—
Pennsylvania**
1955–58   Philadelphia Eagles
1960   New York Titans (AFL)

BELL, HENRY—Back
1960   Denver Broncos (AFL)

**BELL, KAY—Tackle—Washington
State**
1937   Chicago Bears
1942   New York Giants

**BELLINGER, ROBERT—Tackle—
Gonzaga**
1934–35   New York Giants

**BELOTTI, GEORGE—Center
Southern California**
1960   Houston Oilers (AFL)

EDWARD BELL *(Eagles)*

BENKERT, HENRY—Back—Rutgers
1925   New York Giants
1926   Pottsville Maroons
1929   Orange
1930   Newark

BENNERS, FRED—Back—SMU
1952   New York Giants

**BENNETT, CHARLES—Back—
Indiana**
1930   Portsmouth Spartans

**BENNETT, EARL—Guard—Hardin-
Simmons**
1946   Green Bay Packers

BENNETT, PHILIP—Back—Miami
1960   Boston Patriots (AFL)

BENNETT—Tackle
1922   Milwaukee Badgers

**BENSON, GEORGE—Back—
Northwestern**
1947   Brooklyn Dodgers (AAFC)

**BENSON, HARRY—Guard—Western
Maryland**
1935   Philadelphia Eagles

BENTON, JAMES—End—Arkansas
1938–42   Cleveland Rams
1943   Chicago Bears
1944–45   Cleveland Rams
1946–47   Los Angeles Rams
1946   #1 Pass Receiving

BENTZ, EDWARD—End
1922   Rochester Kodaks

BENTZ, ROMAN—Tackle—Tulane
1946–48   New York Yankees (AAFC)
1948   San Francisco 49ers (AAFC)

**BENTZIEN, ALFRED—Guard—
Marquette**
1924   Racine Legion

**BERCICH, ROBERT—Back—
Michigan State**
1960   Dallas Cowboys

**BEREZNEY, PAUL—Tackle—
Fordham**
1942–44   Green Bay Packers
1946   Miami Seahawks (AAFC)

**BEREZNEY, PETER—Tackle—Notre
Dame**
1947   Los Angeles Dons (AAFC)
1948   Baltimore Colts (AAFC)

BERGER
1924   Milwaukee Badgers

**BERGERSON, GILBERT—Tackle—
Oregon State**
1932–33   Chicago Bears
1933–34   Chicago Cardinals
1935–36   Brooklyn Dodgers

**BERGIN, WILLIAM—Guard—
Marquette**
1922   Toledo Maroons

BERNARD, GEORGE—Guard
1926   Racine Legion

**BERNARD, CHARLES—Center—
Michigan**
1934   Detroit Lions

**BERNARD, DAVID—Back—
Mississippi**
1942   Pittsburgh Steelers
1944–45   Cleveland Rams

**BERNARDI, FRANK—Back—
Colorado**
1955–57   Chicago Cardinals
1960   Denver Broncos (AFL)

BERNET, EDWARD—End—SMU
1955   Pittsburgh Steelers
1960   Dallas Texans (AFL)

**BERNHARDT, GEORGE—Guard—
Illinois**
1946–48   Brooklyn Dodgers (AAFC)
1948   Chicago Rockets (AAFC)

**BERNOSKE, DANIEL—Guard—
Indiana**
1926   Louisville Colonels

BERNS, WILLIAM—Guard—Purdue
1922–23   Dayton Triangles

**BERNSTEIN, JOSEPH—Guard—
Tulsa**

1923–24 Rock Island Independents
1924 Hammond Pros

BERQUIST, JAY—Guard—Nebraska
1924–26 Kansas City Cowboys
1927 Chicago Cardinals

**BERRANG, EDWARD—End—
Villanova**
1949–52 Washington Redskins
1951 Detroit Lions

**BERREHSEN, WILLIAM—Tackle—
Washington & Jefferson**
1926 Columbus Tigers

BERRY, CHARLES—End—Lafayette
1925–26 Pottsville Maroons

**BERRY, CORNELIUS—End—North
Carolina State**
1939 Detroit Lions
1940 Cleveland Rams
1941–46 Chicago Bears
1947 Chicago Rockets (AAFC)

BERRY, GILBERT—Back—Illinois
1935 Chicago Cardinals

**BERRY, HOWARD—Back—
Pennsylvania**
1921 Rochester Kodaks

BERRY, RAYMOND—End—SMU
1955–60 Baltimore Colts
1958–60 #1 Pass Receiving
        (Tie with P. Retzlaff 1958)

BERRY, REX—Back—Brigham Young
1951 San Francisco 49ers

BERRY, WAYNE—Back—Wash. State
1954 New York Giants

**BERRYMAN, ROBERT—Back—
Cornell**
1924 Frankford Yellowjackets

**BERSCHET, MARVIN—Guard—
Illinois**
1954–55 Washington Redskins

**BERTAGNOLLI, LIBERO—Guard—
Washington (St. Louis)**
1942, 45 Chicago Cardinals

**BERTELLI, ANGELO—Back—Notre
Dame**
1946–47 Los Angeles Dons (AAFC)
1947–48 Chicago Rockets (AAFC)

**BERTOGLIO, JAMES—Back—
Creighton**
1926 Columbus Tigers

**BERWICK, EDWARD—Center—
Loyola (Chicago)**
1926 Louisville Colonels

**BERZINSKI, WILLIAM—Back—
Wisconsin State**
1956 Philadelphia Eagles

**BESON, WARREN—Center—
Minnesota**
1949 Baltimore Colts (AAFC)

BESTA—Back
1924 Hammond Pros

**BETTENCOURT, LAWRENCE—
Center—St. Mary's (Cal.)**
1932 Boston Braves
1933 Green Bay Packers

BETTIS, THOMAS—Guard—Purdue
1955–60 Green Bay Packers

THOMAS BETTIS

**BETTRIDGE, JOHN—Back—Ohio
State**
1937 Cleveland Rams
1937 Chicago Bears

BEUTHEL, LLOYD—Guard—Colgate
1927 Buffalo Bisons

**BIANCONE, JOHN—Back—Oregon
State**
1936 Brooklyn Dodgers

**BIEBERSTEIN, ADOLPH—Guard—
Wisconsin**
1926 Racine Legion
1926 Green Bay

**BIELSKI, RICHARD—Back—
Maryland**
1955–59 Philadelphia Eagles
1960 Dallas Cowboys

**BIENEMANN, THOMAS—End—
Drake**
1951–56 Chicago Cardinals

RICHARD BIELSKI

BIERCE, BRUCE—End—Akron Univ.
1921, 25 Akron Steels
1922–24 Cleveland Indians

BIG BEAR—Tackle
1922–23 Oorang Indians

BIG TWIG—Guard
1929 Buffalo Bisons

BIGGS, RILEY—Center—Baylor
1926–27 New York Giants

BIGHEAD, JACK—End—Pepperdine
1954 Baltimore Colts
1955 Los Angeles Rams

BILBO, JONATHAN—Tackle—Mississippi
1938–39 Chicago Cardinals

BILDA, RICHARD—Back—Marquette
1944 Green Bay Packers

BILLMAN, JOHN—Guard—Minnesota
1946 Brooklyn Dodgers (AAFC)
1947 Chicago Rockets (AAFC)

BILLOCK, FRANK—Guard—Wisconsin State
1937 Pittsburgh Pirates

BINGAMAN, LESTER—Guard—Illinois
1948–54 Detroit Lions

BINGHAM, DONALD—Back—Sul Ross State
1956 Chicago Bears

BINOTTO, JOHN—Back—Duquesne
1942 Pittsburgh Steelers
1942 Philadelphia Eagles

BIOLO, JOHN—Guard—Lake Forest
1939 Green Bay Packers

BIRK, FERDINAND—Back—Purdue
1922 Hammond Pros

BIRLEM, KEITH—Back—San Jose State
1939 Chicago Cardinals
1939 Washington Redskins
Killed in England, May 7, 1943, attempting to land crippled B-17 after raid over Europe. Major, U.S.A.F.

BISBEE, BERTIN—End—Minnesota
1922 Milwaukee Badgers

BISCAHA, JOSEPH—End—Richmond
1959 New York Giants
1960 Boston Patriots (AFL)

BISHOP, DONALD—End—Los Angeles College
1958–59 Pittsburgh Steelers
1959 Chicago Bears
1960 Dallas Cowboys

BISHOP, WILLIAM—Tackle—Texas State North
1952–60 Chicago Bears

BISSELL, FREDERICK—End—Fordham
1925–26 Akron Steels

BIVINS, CHARLES—Back—Morris Brown
1960 Chicago Bears

BIZER, HERBERT—Back—Carroll (Wis.)
1929 Buffalo Bisons

BJORK, DELBERT—Tackle—Oregon
1937–38 Chicago Bears

BJORKLUND, ROBERT—Center—Minnesota
1941 Philadelphia Eagles

BLACK, CHARLES—End—Kansas
1925 Duluth Kelleys

BLACK, JOHN—Back—Mississippi State
1946 New York Yankees (AAFC)
1946–47 Buffalo Bills (AAFC)
1947 Baltimore Colts (AAFC)

BLACK BEAR—End
1922–23 Oorang Indians

BLACKBURN, J. A.—Tackle
1923 Chicago Bears

BLACKBURN, WILLIAM—Center—Rice
1946–50 Chicago Cardinals

BLACKLOCK, HUGH—Tackle— Michigan State
1921-25 Chicago Bears
1923 Milwaukee Badgers
1925 Akron Steels
1926 Brooklyn Dodgers

BLACKMAN, E. LENNON—Tackle— Tulsa
1930 Chicago Bears

BLACKWELL, HAROLD—Back— Southern Carolina
1945 Chicago Cardinals

BLAKE, THOMAS—Tackle— Cincinnati
1949 New York Bulldogs

BLANDA, GEORGE —Back— Kentucky
1950 Baltimore Colts
1949-58 Chicago Bears
1960 Houston Oilers (AFL)

BLANDIN, ERNEST—Tackle— Tulane
1946-47 Cleveland Browns (AAFC)
1948-49 Baltimore Colts (AAFC)
1950, 53 Baltimore Colts

BLAZER, PHILIP—Guard— North Carolina
1960 Buffalo Bills (AFL)

BLAZINE, ANTHONY—Tackle— Illinois Wesleyan
1935-40 Chicago Cardinals
1940-41 New York Giants

BLEEKER, MALCOLM—Center— Columbia
1930 Brooklyn Dodgers

BLEEKER, MELVIN—Back—Southern California
1944-46 Philadelphia Eagles
1947 Los Angeles Rams

BLESSING, PAUL—End—Nebraska State Teachers
1944 Detroit Lions

BLISS, GERALD—Back—Ohio State
1921 Columbus Panhandles

BLISS, HOMER—Guard—Washington & Jefferson
1928 Chicago Cardinals

BLONDIN, THOMAS—Guard—West Virginia Wesleyan
1933 Cincinnati Reds

BLOODGOOD, ELBERT—Back— Nebraska
1925-26 Kansas City Cowboys
1927 Cleveland Bulldogs

1928 New York Giants
1930 Green Bay Packers

BLOODWORTH, LOWE—Guard
1923 Louisville Colonels

BLOUNT, LAMAR—End—Mississippi State
1946 Miami Seahawks (AAFC)
1947 Buffalo Bills (AAFC)
1947 Baltimore Colts (AAFC)

BLOZIS, ALBERT—Tackle— Georgetown
1942-44 New York Giants
Killed by German machine-gun fire in Vosges Mountains of France, Jan. 31, 1945. Lt. in U.S. Army.

BLUMENSTOCK, JAMES—Back— Fordham
1947 New York Giants

BLUMENTHAL, MORRIS—Back— Northwestern
1925 Chicago Cardinals

BLUMER, HERBERT—Tackle— Missouri
1925-30, 33 Chicago Cardinals

BOBO, HUBERT—Back—Ohio State
1960 Los Angeles Chargers (AFL)

BOCK, WAYNE—Tackle—Illinois
1957 Chicago Cardinals

BODENGER, MORRIS—Guard— Tulane
1931-33 Portsmouth Spartans
1934 Detroit Lions

BOEDECKER, WILLIAM—Back— DePaul
1946 Chicago Rockets (AAFC)
1947-49 Cleveland Browns (AAFC)
1950 Green Bay Packers
1950 Philadelphia Eagles

BOEKE, JAMES—Tackle— Heidelberg
1960 Los Angeles Rams

BOENSCH, FRED—Guard—Stanford
1947-49 Washington Redskins

BOETTCHER, FRED—Back—Rice
1926 Racine Legion

BOGGAN, REX—Tackle—Mississippi
1955 New York Giants

BOGREN, VINCENT—End— New Mexico
1944 Philadelphia Eagles

BOGUE, GEORGE—Back—Stanford
1930 Chicago Cardinals
1930 Newark

BOHLING, DEWEY—Back—
Hardin-Simmons
1960   New York Titans (AFL)

BOHLMANN, FRANK—Guard—
Centenary
1941   Chicago Cardinals

BOHREN, KARL—Back—Pittsburgh
1927   Buffalo Bills

BOLAN, GEORGE—Back—Purdue
1921–24   Chicago Bears

BOLDEN, LEROY—Back—
Michigan State
1958–59   Cleveland Browns

BOLDT, CHASE—Back
1922–23   Louisville Colonels

BOLKOVAC, NICHOLAS—Tackle—
Pittsburgh
1953–54   Pittsburgh Steelers

BOLL, DONALD—Tackle—Nebraska
1953–59   Washington Redskins
1960   New York Giants

BOLLINGER, EDWARD—Guard—
Bucknell
1930   Frankford Yellowjackets

BOMAR, LYNN—End—Vanderbilt
1925–26   New York Giants

BONADIES, JOHN—Back
1926   Hartford Blues

BOND, CHARLES—Tackle—
Washington
1937–38   Washington Redskins

BOND, JAMES—Guard—Pittsburgh
1926   Brooklyn Dodgers

BOND, RANDALL—Back—
Washington
1938   Washington Redskins
1939–40   Pittsburgh Steelers

BONELLI, ERNEST—Back—
Pittsburgh
1945   Chicago Cardinals
1946   Pittsburgh Steelers

BONDURANT, J. BOURBON—
Guard—DePauw
1921–22   Evansville Crimson Giants
1922   Chicago Bears

BONOWITZ, ELLIOTT—Back—
Wilmington
1923   Columbus Tigers
1924–25   Dayton Triangles

BOOKMAN, JOHN—Back—Miami
1957   New York Giants

1960   Dallas Texans (AFL)

BOOKOUT, WILLIAM—Back—
Austin
1955–56   Green Bay Packers

BOOKS, ROBERT—Back—Dickinson
1926   Frankford Yellowjackets

BOONE, J. R.—Back—Tulsa
1948–51   Chicago Bears
1952   San Francisco 49ers
1953   Green Bay Packers

BOONE, ROBERT—Back—Elon
1942   Cleveland Rams

BOOTH, CLARENCE—Tackle—
SMU
1943   Chicago Cardinals
1944   Card-Pitt

BOOTH, RICHARD—Back—Western
Reserve
1941, 45   Detroit Lions

BORAK, FRITZ—End—Creighton
1938   Green Bay Packers

BORDEN, NATHANIEL—End—
Indiana
1955–59   Green Bay Packers
1960   Dallas Cowboys

DONALD BOLL

BORDEN, LESTER—End—Fordham
1935   New York Giants

BORNTRAEGER, WILLIAM—
Guard
1923   Louisville Colonels

BORRELLI, NICHOLAS—Back—
Muhlenberg
1930   Newark

BORTON, JOHN—Back—Ohio State
1957   Cleveland Browns

NATHAN BORDEN

BOSLEY, BRUCE—Tackle—
West Virginia
1956–60   San Francisco 49ers

BRUCE BOSLEY

BOSSELER, DONALD—Back—Miami
1957–60   Washington Redskins

BOSTICK, LEWIS—Guard—Alabama
1939, 42   Cleveland Rams

BOSWELL, BENJAMIN—Tackle—
TCU
1933   Portsmouth Spartans
1934   Boston Redskins

BOTCHAN, RONALD—Back—
Occidental
1960   Los Angeles Chargers (AFL)

BOULEY, GILBERT—Tackle—
Boston College
1945   Cleveland Rams

1946–50   Los Angeles Rams

BOVA, ANTHONY—End—St. Francis
1942, 45–47   Pittsburgh Steelers
1943   Phil-Pitt
1944   Card-Pitt

DONALD BOSSELER

BOVE, PETER—Guard—Holy Cross
1930   Newark

BOWDOIN, JAMES—Guard—
Alabama
1928–31   Green Bay Packers
1932   New York Giants
1932, 34   Brooklyn Dodgers
1933   Portsmouth Spartans

BOWERS, WILLIAM—Back—
So. California
1954   Los Angeles Rams

GILBERT BOULEY

BOWMAN, WILLIAM—Back—
  William & Mary
1954, 56   Detroit Lions
1957   Pittsburgh Steelers

BOWSER, ARDA—Back—Bucknell
1922   Canton Bulldogs
1923   Cleveland Indians

BOX, CLOYCE—End—West Texas
  State Teachers
1949–50, 52–54   Detroit Lions

BOYD, ROBERT—Back—Oklahoma
1960   Baltimore Colts

BOYD, ROBERT—End—Loyola
1950–51, 53–57   Los Angeles Rams

ROBERT BOYD (RAMS)

BOYD, SAMUEL—End—Baylor
1939–40   Pittsburgh Steelers

BOYD, WALTER—Back—
  Westminister
1930–31   Chicago Cardinals

BOYDA, MICHAEL—Back—
  Washington & Lee
1949   New York Bulldogs
1949   #1 Punting

BOYDSTON, MAX—End—Oklahoma
1955–58   Chicago Cardinals
1960   Dallas Texans (AFL)

BOYER, VERDI—Guard—UCLA
1936   Brooklyn Dodgers

BOYLE, WILLIAM—Tackle—None
1934   New York Giants
1934   Pittsburgh Pirates

BOYNTON, BENJAMIN—Back—
  WILLIAMS
1921–22   Rochester Kodaks
1924   Buffalo Bisons

BRAASE, ORDELL—End—
  South Dakota
1957–60   Baltimore Colts

ORDELL BRAASE

BRAATZ, THOMAS—End—
  Marquette
1957–59   Washington Redskins
1958   Los Angeles Rams
1960   Dallas Cowboys

BRACE, ROBERT—Guard—Brown
1921–22   Buffalo All Americans

BRACKET, MARTIN LUTHER—
  Tackle—Auburn
1956–57   Chicago Bears
1958   New York Giants

BRACKINS, CHARLES—Back—
  Prairie View
1955   Green Bay Packers

BRADEN, DAVID—Guard—
  Marquette
1945   Chicago Cardinals

BRADFUTE, BYRON—Tackle—
  Mississippi Southern
1960   Dallas Cowboys

BRADLEY, EDWARD—End—Wake
  Forest
1950, 52   Chicago Bears

BRADLEY, GERALD—Back—
  Wittenberg
1928   Dayton Triangles

BRADLEY, HAROLD—Guard—Iowa
1954–57   Cleveland Browns
1958   Philadelphia Eagles

BRADLEY, HAROLD—End—Elon
1938–39   Chicago Cardinals
1938–39   Washington Redskins

BRADLEY, ROBERT—Guard—
Ohio State
1928   Chicago Cardinals

BRADSHAW, CHARLES—Tackle—
Baylor
1958–60   Los Angeles Rams

CHARLES BRADSHAW

BRADSHAW, JAMES—Back—Nevada
1924   Kansas City Cowboys

BRADSHAW, WESLEY—Back—
Baylor
1924   Rock Island Independents
1926   Buffalo Bisons

BRADY, PATRICK—Back—Nevada
1952–54   Pittsburgh Steelers
1953, 54   #1 Punting

BRAHM, LAWRENCE—Guard—
Temple
1942   Cleveland Rams
1943   New York Giants

BRAIDWOOD, CHARLES—End—
Chattanooga
1930   Portsmouth Spartans
1931   Cleveland Indians
1932   Chicago Bears
1933   Cincinnati Reds
         Killed in action in South Pacific in winter of 1944–45.
         Member of Red Cross.

BRAMAN, WILLIAM—Tackle—
Colgate
1923   Racine Legion
1925   Cleveland Bulldogs

BRAMHALL, ARTHUR—Back—
De Paul
1931   Chicago Bears

BRANCATO, GEORGE—Back—LSU

1954   Chicago Cardinals

BRANCH, MELVIN—End—LSU
1960   Dallas Texans (AFL)

BRANDAU, ARTHUR—Center—
Tennessee
1945–46   Pittsburgh Steelers

BRANDT, JAMES—Back—St. Thomas
1952–54   Pittsburgh Steelers

BRANEY, JOHN—Guard—Syracuse
1925–26   Providence Steamrollers

BRANNAN—Tackle
1923   Racine Legion
1925   Cleveland Indians

BRATKOWSKI, EDMUND—Back—
Georgia
1954, 57–60   Chicago Bears

BRATT, EDWARD—End—
Wisconsin State
1924   Duluth Kelleys

BRAVO, ALEXANDER—Back—
Cal. Poly.
1957–58   Los Angeles Rams
1960   Oakland Raiders (AFL)

BRAWLEY, EDWARD—Guard—
Holy Cross
1921   Cleveland Indians

BRAY, MAURICE—Tackle—SMU
1935–36   Pittsburgh Pirates

BRAY, RAYMOND—Guard—Western
Michigan
1939–42, 46–51   Chicago Bears
1952   Green Bay Packers

BRAZELL, CARL—Back—Baylor
1938   Cleveland Rams

BRAZINSKY, SAMUEL—Back—
Villanova
1946   Buffalo Bisons (AAFC)

BREDDE, WILLIAM—Back—
Oklahoma A & M
1954   Chicago Cardinals

BREDICE, JOHN—End—
Boston College
1956   Philadelphia Eagles

BREEDLOVE, RODNEY—Guard—
Maryland
1960   Washington Redskins

BREEDON, WILLIAM—Back—
Oklahoma
1937   Pittsburgh Pirates

BRENKERT, WAYNE—Back—
Washington & Lee
1923–24   Akron Steels

**BRENNAN, JOHN—Guard—
Michigan**
1939 Green Bay Packers

**BRENNAN, LEO—Tackle—Holy
Cross**
1942 Philadelphia Eagles

**BRENNAN, MATTHEW—Guard—
Lafayette**
1925 New York Giants
1926 Brooklyn Dodgers

BRENNAN, PAUL—Back—Fordham
1925 Canton Bulldogs

BRENNAN, PHILIP—End—Columbia
1930 Newark

**BRENNAN, ROBERT—End—
Georgetown**
1931 Providence Steamrollers

BRENNAN, WILLIS—Guard
1921–27 Chicago Cardinals

**BRETHAUER, MONTE—End—
Oregon**
1953, 55 Baltimore Colts

**BRETT, EDWIN—End—
Washington State**
1936 Chicago Cardinals
1936–37 Pittsburgh Pirates

**BRETTSCHNEIDER, CARL—Guard
—Iowa State**
1956–58 Chicago Cardinals
1959 Detroit Lions

**BREWER, BROOKE—Back—
Maryland**
1922 Akron Steels

**BREWER, HOMER—Back—
Mississippi**
1960 Washington Redskins

**BREWER, JOHN—Back—Georgia
Tech**
1929 Dayton Triangles

BREWER, JOHN—Back—Louisville
1952–53 Philadelphia Eagles

**BREWSTER, DARRELL—End—
Purdue**
1952–58 Cleveland Browns
1959–60 Pittsburgh Steelers

**BREWSTER, JAMES—End—West
Virginia**
1929 Buffalo Bisons

**BRIAN, HARRY—Back—Grove
City**
1926 Hartford Blues

**BRIAN, WILLIAM—Tackle—
Gonzaga**

DARRELL BREWSTER

1935 Chicago Cardinals
1935–36 Philadelphia Eagles

**BRIANTE, FRANK—Back—New
York Univ.**
1929 Staten Island Stapletons
1930 Newark

BRIDGEFORD, LANE—Back—Knox
1921–22 Rock Island Independents

BRIGGS, PAUL—Tackle—Colorado
1948 Detroit Lions

BRILL, HAROLD—Back—Wichita
1939 Detroit Lions

BRILL, MARTIN—Back—Notre Dame
1931 Staten Island Stapletons

BRINDLEY, WALTER—Back—Drake
1921–22 Rock Island Independents

**BRINK, LAWRENCE—End—
Northern Illinois State**
1948–53 Los Angeles Rams
1954 Chicago Bears

**BRISTOW, GEORGE—Back—
Nebraska**
1925 Providence Steamrollers

**BRISTOW, Gordon—Back—
Oklahoma**
1924–26 Kansas City Cowboys

**BRITO, EUGENE—End—Loyola
(Los Angeles)**
1951–53, 55–58 Washington Redskins
1959–60 Los Angeles Rams

BRITT, CHARLES—Back—Georgia
1960 Los Angeles Rams

**BRITT, EDWARD—Back—Holy
Cross**
1936 Boston Redskins

1937 Washington Redskins
1938 Brooklyn Dodgers

BRITT, MAURICE—End—Arkansas
1941 Detroit Lions

CHARLES BRITT

**BRITT, OSCAR—Guard—
Mississippi**
1946 Washington Redskins

**BRITT, RANKIN—End—Texas
A & M**
1939–40 Philadelphia Eagles
1941 Detroit Lions

BRITTON, EARL—Back—Illinois
1925 Chicago Bears
1926 Brooklyn Dodgers
1927 Frankford Yellowjackets
1927–28 Dayton Triangles
1929 Chicago Cardinals

BROADLEY, KARL—Guard—Bethany
1925 Cleveland Indians

**BROADSTONE, MARION—Tackle—
Nebraska**
1931 New York Giants

**BROCK, CHARLES—Center—
Nebraska**
1939–47 Green Bay Packers

BROCK, J. LOUIS—Back—Purdue
1940–45 Green Bay Packers

**BROCKMAN, EDWARD—Back—
Oklahoma**
1930 Chicago Bears

BRODA, HAROLD—End—Brown
1927 Cleveland Bulldogs

BRODIE, JOHN—Back—Stanford
1957–60 San Francisco 49ers

JOHN BRODIE

**BRODHEAD, ROBERT—Back—
Duke**
1960 Buffalo Bills (AFL)

**BRODNAX, GEORGE—End—
Georgia Tech.**
1949 Detroit Lions

BRODNAX, JOHN—Back—LSU
1960 Denver Broncos (AFL)

**BRODNICKI, CHARLES—Center—
Temple**
1934 Philadelphia Eagles
1934 Brooklyn Dodgers

**BROOKS, WILLIAM—Guard—
Arkansas**
1955 Detroit Lions

THOMAS BROOKSHIER

**BROOKSHIER, THOMAS—Back—
Colorado**
1953, 55–60 Philadelphia Eagles

BROSKY, ALBERT—Back—Illinois
1954 Chicago Cardinals

BROUSSARD, FRED—Center—
Louisiana N.W.
1955 Pittsburgh Steelers
1955 New York Giants
1960 Denver Broncos (AFL)

BROVARNEY, CASIMIR—Tackle—
Detroit
1941 New York Giants

BROVELLI, ANGELO—Back—St.
Mary's (Cal.)
1933-34 Pittsburgh Pirates

BROVELLI, ANGELO—Guard—
Washington State
1960 Los Angeles Rams

BROWN, DONALD—Back—Houston
1960 Houston Oilers (AFL)

BROWN, CHARLES EDWARD
—Back—San Francisco
1954-60 Chicago Bears
1956 #1 Passing

BROWN, DANIEL—End—Villanova
1950 Washington Redskins

BROWN, DAVID—Back—Alabama
1943, 46-47 New York Giants

BROWN, FREDERICK—Back—New
York Univ.
1930 Staten Island Stapletons

BROWN, GEORGE—Guard—TCU
1949 New York Yankees (AAFC)
1950 New York Yanks

BROWN, HARDY—Back—Tulsa
1948 Brooklyn Dodgers (AAFC)
1949 Chicago Rockets (AAFC)
1950 Baltimore Colts
1950 Washington Redskins
1951-55 San Francisco 49ers
1956 Chicago Cardinals
1960 Denver Broncos (AFL)

BROWN, HOWARD—Guard—
Indiana
1948-50 Detroit Lions

BROWN, JACK R.—Center—Dayton
1926-29 Dayton Triangles

BROWN, JAMES—Back—Syracuse
1957-60 Cleveland Browns
1957-60 #1 Ball Carrying
1958 #1 Scoring

BROWN, JESSE—Back—Pittsburgh
1926 Pottsville Maroons

JACK R. BROWN

BROWN, JOHN—Center—North
Carolina College
1947-49 Los Angeles Dons (AAFC)

BROWN, MARVIN—Back—
Texas State East
1957 Detroit Lions

BROWN, PETER—Center—
Georgia Tech.
1953-54 San Francisco 49ers

BROWN, RAYMOND—Back—
Mississippi
1958-60 Baltimore Colts

BROWN, RICHARD—Center—Iowa
1930 Portsmouth Spartans

BROWN, ROGER—Tackle—
Maryland State
1960 Detroit Lions

BROWN, ROOSEVELT—Tackle—
Morgan
1953-60 New York Giants

BROWN, THOMAS—End—William &
Mary
1942 Pittsburgh Steelers

BROWN, THOMAS—Back—
Indiana Teachers
1959 Green Bay Packers
1960 Philadelphia Eagles

BROWN, WILLIAM—Back—Marshall
1943-44 Brooklyn Dodgers

BROWN, WILLIAM—Guard—
Arkansas
1951-52 Washington Redskins
1953-56 Green Bay Packers

BROWN, WILLIAM—Center—
Syracuse

1960   Boston Patriots (AFL)

BROWNING, GREGORY—End—Denver
1947   New York Giants

BROWN—Back
1922   Milwaukee Badgers

BROWNING, R.—Back—Westminster (Mo.)
1925   Kansas City Cowboys

BRUBAKER, RICHARD—End—Ohio State
1955, 57   Chicago Cardinals
1960   Buffalo Bills (AFL)

BRUCE, GAIL—End—Washington
1948–49   San Francisco 49ers (AAFC)
1950–51   San Francisco 49ers

BRUCKNER, LESLIE—Back—Michigan State
1945   Chicago Cardinals

BRUDER, HENRY—Back—Northwestern
1931–39   Green Bay Packers
1940   Pittsburgh Steelers

BRUDER, WOODRUFF—Back—West Virginia
1925   Buffalo Bisons
1925–26   Frankford Yellowjackets

BRUECKMAN, CHARLES—Center—Pittsburgh
1958   San Francisco 49ers
1958   Washington Redskins
1960   Los Angeles Chargers (AFL)

BRUMBAUGH, BOYD—Back—Duquesne
1938–39   Brooklyn Dodgers
1939–41   Pittsburgh Steelers

BRUMBAUGH, CARL—Back—Florida
1930–36, 38   Chicago Bears
1937   Brooklyn Dodgers
1937   Cleveland Rams

BRUMBAUGH, JUSTIN—Back—Bucknell
1931   Frankford Yellowjackets

BRUMFIELD, JACKSON—End—Mississippi Southern
1954   San Francisco 49ers

BRUMLEY, ROBERT—Back—Rice
1945   Detroit Lions

BRUMM, ROMAN—Guard—Wisconsin
1922, 24, 26   Racine Legion
1925   Milwaukee Badgers

BRUNCKLACHER, AUSTIN—Guard
1922–23   Louisville Colonels

BRUNDAGE, DEWEY—End—Brigham Young
1954   Pittsburgh Steelers

BRUNEY, FRED—Back—Ohio State
1953–56   San Francisco 49ers
1956–57   Pittsburgh Steelers
1958   Los Angeles Rams
1960   Boston Patriots (AFL)

BRUNSKI, ANDREW—Center—Temple
1943   Phil-Pitt

BRUTZ, JAMES—Tackle—Notre Dame
1946, 48   Chicago Rockets (AAFC)

BRYANT, JOHN—Back—Chicago
1922   Chicago Cardinals
1923–25, 27   Chicago Bears
1925–26   Milwaukee Badgers

BRYANT, LOWELL—Back—Clemson
1941   Detroit Lions

BRYANT, ROBERT—Tackle—Texas Tech
1946–49   San Francisco 49ers (AAFC)

BRYANT, ROBERT—End—Texas
1960   Dallas Texans (AFL)

BRYANT, WALTER—Back—Texas Tech
1955   Baltimore Colts

BUCCHIANERI, AMADEO—Guard—Indiana
1941, 44–45   Green Bay Packers

BUCEK, FELIX—Guard—Texas A & M
1946   Pittsburgh Steelers

BUCHANAN, STEPHEN—Back—Miami (Ohio)
1929   Dayton Triangles

BUCHER, FRANK—End—Detroit
1925   Detroit Panthers
1925–26   Pottsville Maroons

BUCK, ARTHUR—Back—John Carroll
1941   Chicago Bears

BUCK, HOWARD—Tackle—Wisconsin
1921–25   Green Bay Packers

BUCKEYE, GARLAND—Guard—Wabash
1921–24   Chicago Cardinals

BUCKLER, WILLIAM—Guard—Alabama

1926–28, 31–33   Chicago Bears

BUCKLEW, PHILIP—End—Xavier
1937   Cleveland Rams

**BUCKLEY, EDWARD—Back—
Fordham**
1930   Staten Island Stapletons

BUCKLIN, THOMAS—Back—Idaho
1927   Chicago Cardinals
1931   New York Giants

BUDA, CARL—Guard—Tulsa
1945   Pittsburgh Steelers

BUDD, JOHN—Tackle—Lafayette
1926   Frankford Yellowjackets
1927–28   Pottsville Maroons

BUFFALO—Guard
1922–23   Oorang Indians

**BUFFINGTON, HARRY—Guard—
Oklahoma A & M**
1942   New York Giants
1946–48   Brooklyn Dodgers (AAFC)

**BUHLER, LAWRENCE—Back—
Minnesota**
1939–41   Green Bay Packers

**BUIVID, RAYMOND—Back—
Marquette**
1937–38   Chicago Bears

**BUKANT, JOSEPH—Back—
Washington of Mo.**
1938–40   Philadelphia Eagles
1941–43   Chicago Cardinals

**BUKICH, RUDOLPH—Back—
Southern California**
1953, 56   Los Angeles Rams
1957–58   Washington Redskins
1958–59   Chicago Bears
1960   Pittsburgh Steelers

BUKSAR, GEORGE—Back—Purdue
1949   Chicago Hornets (AAFC)
1950   Baltimore Colts
1951–52   Washington Redskins

BULAND, WALTER—Tackle
1921, 24   Rock Island Independents
1924   Green Bay Packers
1926   Duluth Eskimos

**BULGER, CHESTER—Tackle—
Alabama Polytech.**
1942–43, 45–49   Chicago Cardinals
1944   Card-Pitt
1950   Detroit Lions

**BULLMAN, GALE—End—West
Virginia Wesleyan**
1925   Columbus Tigers

**BULLOUGH, HENRY—Guard—
Michigan State**
1955, 58   Green Bay Packers

**BULTMAN, ARTHUR—Center—
Marquette**
1931   Brooklyn Dodgers
1932–34   Green Bay Packers

**BUMGARDNER, REX—Back—
West Virginia**
1948–49   Buffalo Bills (AAFC)
1950–52   Cleveland Browns

**BUNYAN, JOHN—Guard—New York
Univ.**
1929–30, 32   Staten Island Stapletons
1932   Brooklyn Dodgers

BURDICK, LLOYD—Tackle—Illinois
1931–32   Chicago Bears
1933   Cincinnati Reds

**BURFORD, CHRISTOPHER—End—
Stanford**
1960   Dallas Texans (AFL)

BURGESS, GLEN—Tackle—Tulsa
1945   Chicago Bears

BURGNER, EARL—Back—Wittenberg
1923   Dayton Triangles

BURK, ADRIAN—Back—Baylor
1950   Baltimore Colts
1951–57   Philadelphia Eagles

ADRIAN BURK

**BURKE, CHARLES—Back—
Dartmouth**
1925–26   Providence Steamrollers

**BURKE, DONALD—Back—Southern
California**
1950–54   San Francisco 49ers

BURKE, ROBERT—Tackle—Detroit
1927   Duluth Eskimos

BURKETT, JEFFREY—End—LSU
1947 Chicago Cardinals

**BURKHARDT, ARTHUR—Guard—
Rutgers**
1928 New York Giants

**BURKS, JOSEPH—Center—
Washington State**
1926 Milwaukee Badgers

BURL, ALEX—Back—Colorado A&M
1956 Chicago Cardinals

BURLESON, JOHN—Guard—SMU
1933 Pittsburgh Steelers
1933 Cincinnati Reds
1933 Portsmouth Spartans

**BURMEISTER, FORREST—Back—
Purdue**
1937 Cleveland Rams

BURNELL, MAX—Back—Notre Dame
1944 Chicago Bears

**BURNETT, DALE—Back—Emporia
Teachers**
1931–39 New York Giants

**BURNETTE, THOMAS—Back—
North Carolina**
1938 Pittsburgh Steelers
1939 Philadelphia Eagles

**BURNHAM, STANLEY—Back—
Harvard**
1925 Frankford Yellowjackets

**BURNINE, HAROLD—End—
Missouri**
1956 New York Giants
1956–57 Philadelphia Eagles

BURNSIDE—Back
1926 Racine Legion

BURRIS, PAUL—Guard—Oklahoma
1949–51 Green Bay Packers

**BURROUGHS, DONALD—Back—
Colorado A&M**
1955–59 Los Angeles Rams
1960 Philadelphia Eagles

**BURRUS, HARRY—End—Hardin-
Simmons**
1946–47 New York Yankees (AAFC)
1948 Brooklyn Dodgers (AAFC)
1948 Chicago Rockets (AAFC)

BURT, HAROLD—Guard—Kansas
1925 Cleveland Bulldogs

BURT, RUSSELL—Guard—Canisius
1925 Buffalo Bisons

**BURTON, LEON—Back—Arizona
State**
1960 New York Titans (AFL)

BURTON, LYLE—Guard—DePauw
1924–25 Rock Island Independents

**BURTON, RONALD—Back—
Northwestern**
1960 Boston Patriots (AFL)

**BUSBY, SHERRILL—End—
Alabama State Teachers**
1940 Brooklyn Dodgers

BUSCH, ELMER—Guard—Carlisle
1922–23 Oorang Indians

BUSH, RAYMOND—End—Loyola
1926 Louisville Colonels

**BUSHBY, THOMAS—Back—
Kansas State**
1934 Cincinnati Reds
1935 Philadelphia Eagles

BUSICH, SAMUEL—End—Ohio State
1936 Boston Redskins
1937 Cleveland Rams
1943 Detroit Lions

**BUSLER, RAYMOND—Tackle—
Marquette**
1940–41, 45 Chicago Cardinals

**BUSS, ARTHUR—Tackle—Michigan
State**
1934–35 Chicago Bears
1936–37 Philadelphia Eagles

BUSSE, ELLIS—Back—Chicago
1929 Chicago Cardinals

BUSSEY, YOUNG—Back—LSU
1940–41 Chicago Bears
          Killed leading landing party
          on first day of Lingayen op-
          eration in Philippines. Lt. in
          U.S. Marines

**BUTCHER, WENDELL—Back—
Gustavus-Adolphus**
1938–42 Brooklyn Dodgers

**BUTKUS, CARL—Tackle—George
Washington**
1948 Washington Redskins
1948 New York Yankees (AAFC)
1949 New York Giants

**BUTLER, EDWARD "SOL"—Back—
Loras**
1923 Hammond Pros
1924 Akron Steels

**BUTLER, FRANK—Center—
Michigan State**
1934–36, 38 Green Bay Packers

BUTLER, JOHN—Back—Tennessee
1943 Phil-Pitt
1944 Card-Pitt
1944 Brooklyn Dodgers

1945   Philadelphia Eagles

BUTLER, JOHN—End—St. Bonaventure
1951–59   Pittsburgh Steelers
1957   #1 Interceptions (tied by M. Davis, Christiansen)

BUTLER, WILLIAM—Back— Marquette
1923   Rock Island Independents
1923–24, 26   Hammond Pros
1926   Canton Bulldogs

BUTLER, WILLIAM—Back— Chattanooga
1959   Green Bay Packers
1960   Dallas Cowboys

BUTTS, EDWARD—Back— Chico State
1929   Chicago Cardinals

BUZYNSKI, BERNARD—Guard— Holy Cross
1960   Buffalo Bills (AFL)

BYLER, JOSEPH—Tackle—Nebraska
1946   New York Giants

* * *

CABRELLI, LAWRENCE—End— Colgate
1941–42, 44–47   Philadelphia Eagles
1943   Phil-Pitt

CABHRINA, AUGUST—Back— Dayton
1927   Dayton Triangles

CADDEL, ERNEST—Back—Stanford
1933   Portsmouth Spartans
1934–38   Detroit Lions

CAFEGO, GEORGE—Back— Tennessee
1940–43   Brooklyn Dodgers
1943   Washington Redskins
1944–45   Boston Yanks

CAGLE, CHRISTIAN—Back—West Point
1930–32   New York Giants
1933–34   Brooklyn Dodgers

CAHILL, RONALD—Back—Holy Cross
1943   Chicago Cardinals

CAHOON, IVAN—Tackle—Gonzaga
1926–29   Green Bay Packers

CAIN, JAMES—End—Alabama
1949   Chicago Cardinals
1950, 53–55   Detroit Lions

CALAC, PETER—End—Carlisle
1921   Cleveland Indians

1922   Canton Bulldogs
1922–23   Oorang Indians
1924   Buffalo Bisons
1925–26   Canton Bulldogs

CALCAGNI, RALPH—Tackle— Pennsylvania
1945–46   Boston Yanks
1947–48   Pittsburgh Steelers

CALDWELL, BRUCE—Back—Yale
1928   New York Giants

CALDWELL, CYRIL—Tackle— Baldwin-Wallace
1925–26   Akron Steels

CALEB, JAMIE—Back—Grambling
1960   Cleveland Browns

CALHOUN, ERIC—Tackle—Denison
1926   Dayton Triangles

CALL, JOHN—Back—Colgate
1957–58   Baltimore Colts
1959   Pittsburgh Steelers

CALLAHAN, DANIEL—End—Akron
1960   New York Titans (AFL)

CALLAHAN, JAMES—Back—Texas
1946   Detroit Lions

CALLAHAN, ROBERT—Center— Michigan
1947   Brooklyn Dodgers (AAFC)
1948   Buffalo Bills (AAFC)

CALLEN, FRANK—Guard—St. Mary's (Cal.)
1947   New York Yankees (AAFC)

CALLIGARO, LEONARD—Back— Wisconsin
1944–45   New York Giants

CALLIHAN, WILLIAM—Back— Nebraska
1940–45   Detroit Lions

CALVELLI, ANTHONY—Center— Stanford
1939–40   Detroit Lions
1947   San Francisco 49ers (AAFC)

CALVIN, THOMAS—Back—Alabama
1952–55   Pittsburgh Steelers

CAMERON, EDMUND—Guard— Washington & Lee
1926   Detroit Panthers

CAMERON, PAUL—Back—U.C.L.A.
1954   Pittsburgh Steelers

CAMP, JAMES—Back—North Carolina
1948   Brooklyn Dodgers (AAFC)

CAMPANA, ALBERT—Back— Youngstown

1950–52 Chicago Bears
1953 Chicago Cardinals

CAMPANELLA, JOSEPH—Tackle—Ohio State
1952 Dallas Texans
1953–57 Baltimore Colts

**CAMPBELL, DONALD—Tackle
Carnegie Tech**
1935, 39–40 Pittsburgh Steelers

**CAMPBELL, GLENN—End
Kansas State Teachers**
1929–33 New York Giants
1935 Pittsburgh Pirates
1935 Philadelphia Eagles

**CAMPBELL, KENNETH—End—
West Chester**
1960 New York Titans (AFL)

CAMPBELL, LEON—Back—Arkansas
1950 Baltimore Colts
1952–54 Chicago Bears
1955 Pittsburgh Steelers

**CAMPBELL, MARION—Tackle—
Georgia**
1954–55 San Francisco 49ers
1956–60 Philadelphia Eagles

**CAMPBELL, MILTON—Back—
Indiana**
1957 Cleveland Browns

**CAMPBELL, RAYMOND "DICK"—
—Center—Marquette**
1958–60 Pittsburgh Steelers

**CAMPBELL, STANLEY—Guard—
Iowa State**
1952, 55–58 Detroit Lions
1959–60 Philadelphia Eagles

**CAMPBELL, WILLIAM—Back—
Oklahoma**
1945–49 Chicago Cardinals
1949 New York Bulldogs

**CAMPIGLIO, ROBERT—Back—West
Liberty Teachers**
1932 Staten Island Stapletons
1933 Boston Redskins
1933 Brooklyn Dodgers
1932 #1 Ball Carrying

**CAMPION, THOMAS—Tackle—
Louisiana Southern**
1947 Philadelphia Eagles

**CAMPOFREDA, NICHOLAS—
Center—Western Maryland**
1944 Washington Redskins

**CAMPORA, DONALD—Tackle—
College of the Pacific**

1950, 52 San Francisco 49ers
1953 Washington Redskins

**CANADEO, ANTHONY—Back—
Gonzaga**
1941–44, 46–51 Green Bay Packers

CANADY, JAMES—Back—Texas
1948–49 Chicago Bears
1949 New York Bulldogs

**CANALE, ROCCO—Guard—Boston
College**
1943 Phil-Pitt
1944–45 Philadelphia Eagles
1946–47 Boston Yanks

CANNADY, JOHN—Back—Indiana
1947–54 New York Giants

**CANNAMELA, PATRICK—Guard—
Southern California**
1952 Dallas Texans

**CANNAVA, ANTHONY—Back—
Boston College**
1950 Green Bay Packers

**CANNAVINO, JOSEPH—Back—
Ohio State**
1960 Oakland Raiders (AFL)

**CANNELLA, JOHN—Tackle—
Fordham**
1933–34 New York Giants
1934 Brooklyn Dodgers

CANNON, WILLIAM—Back—LSU
1960 Houston Oilers (AFL)

WILLIAM CANNON

CANTOR, LEO—Back—UCLA
1942 New York Giants
1945 Chicago Cardinals

**CAPPELLETTI, GINO—Back—
Minnesota**

1960 Boston Patriots (AFL)

CAPPS, WILBUR—Tackle
Oklahoma State
1929 New York Giants
1929–30 Frankford Yellowjackets
1930 Minneapolis Redjackets

CAPUZZI, JAMES—Back—Cincinnati
1955–56 Green Bay Packers

CARA, DOMINIC—End—North
Carolina
1937–38 Pittsburgh Pirates

CARANCI, ROLAND—Tackle—
Colorado
1944 New York Giants

CARAPELLA, ALBERT—Tackle—
Miami (Fla.)
1951–55 San Francisco 49ers

CARBERRY, GLENN—End—Notre
Dame
1923–24 Buffalo All Americans
1925 Cleveland Indians

CARD, J. HARPER—Tackle
1922 Louisville Colonels

CARDARELLI, CARL—Center
1924 Akron Steels

CARDINAL, FRED—Back—
Baldwin-Wallace
1947 New York Yankees (AAFC)

CARDWELL, JOHN—Back
1923 St. Louis Browns

CARDWELL, JOSEPH—Tackle—
Duke
1937–38 Pittsburgh Pirates

CARDWELL, LLOYD—Back—
Nebraska
1937–43 Detroit Lions

CAREY, JOSEPH—Guard
1921 Green Bay Packers

CAREY, ROBERT—End—
Michigan State
1952, 54, 56 Los Angeles Rams
1958 Chicago Bears

CARL, HARLAND—Back—Wisconsin
1956 Chicago Bears

CARLSON, IRVIN—Guard—St. Johns
1924 Kenosha
1926 Green Bay Packers

CARLSON, JULES—Guard—Oregon
State
1928–36 Chicago Bears
1937 Chicago Cardinals

CARLSON, OKE EUGENE—Guard—
Iowa State
1924–27 Duluth Eskimos

CARLSON, RAYMOND—Back—
Marquette
1947 Buffalo Bills (AAFC)

CARLSON, ROY—End—Bradley
1929 Dayton Triangles

CARLTON, WRAY—Back—Duke
1960 Buffalo Bills (AFL)

CARMAN, EDMUND—Tackle—
Purdue
1922, 25 Hammond Pros
1925 Buffalo Bisons

CARMICHAEL, ALBERT—Back—
Southern California
1953–58 Green Bay Packers
1960 Denver Broncos (AFL)

CARNELLY, RAYMOND—Back—
Carnegie Tech.
1939 Brooklyn Dodgers

CARNEY, ARTHUR—Guard—
Annapolis
1925–26 New York Giants

CARNEY, HAROLD—End—Albright
1931 Providence Steamrollers

CAROLINE, JAMES C.—Back—
Illinois
1956–60 Chicago Bears

JAMES C. CAROLINE

CAROTHERS, DONALD—End—
Bradley
1960 Denver Broncos (AFL)

CARPE, JOSEPH—Tackle—Millikin
1926–27 Frankford Yellowjackets

1928   Pottsville Maroons
1929   Minneapolis Redjackets
1929   Boston Braves
1933   Philadelphia Eagles

**CARPENTER, JOHN—Tackle—
Missouri, Michigan**
1947–49   Buffalo Bills (AAFC)
1949   San Francisco 49ers (AAFC)

**CARPENTER, KENNETH—Back—
Oregon**
1950–53   Cleveland Browns
1960   Denver Broncos (AFL)

**CARPENTER, LEWIS—Back—
Arkansas**
1953–55   Detroit Lions
1957–58   Cleveland Browns
1959–60   Green Bay Packers

LEWIS CARPENTER

**CARPENTER, PRESTON—Back—
Arkansas**
1956–59   Cleveland Browns
1960   Pittsburgh Steelers

CARR, CHARLES—Back—Syracuse
1926   Akron Steels
1927–28   Pottsville Maroons

CARR, EDWIN—Back
1947–49   San Francisco 49ers (AAFC)
1950   San Francisco 49ers

CARR, HARLAN—Back—Canisius
1927   Buffalo Bisons

CARR, JAMES—Back—Morris Harvey
1955, 57   Chicago Cardinals
1959–60   Philadelphia Eagles

CARR, LUTHER—Back—Washington
1960   Oakland Raiders

CARR, PAUL—Back—Houston
1955–57   San Francisco 49ers

**CARROCCIO, RUSSELL—Guard—
Virginia**
1954–55   New York Giants
1955   Philadelphia Eagles

**CARROLL, EDWARD—End—
Washington & Jefferson**
1921–23, 25   Canton Bulldogs

**CARROLL, VICTOR—Tackle—
Nevada**
1936   Boston Redskins
1937–42   Washington Redskins
1943–47   New York Giants

CARSON, JOHN—End—Georgia
1954–59   Washington Redskins
1960   Houston Oilers (AFL)

CARTER, JOSEPH—End—SMU
1933–40   Philadelphia Eagles
1942   Green Bay Packers
1944   Brooklyn Tigers
1945   Chicago Cardinals
1934   #1 Pass Receiving

CARTER, ROSS—Guard—Oregon
1936–39   Chicago Cardinals

**CARTER, WILLIE—Back—
Tennessee State**
1953   Chicago Cardinals

**CARTIN, CHARLES—Tackle—Holy
Cross**
1925   Frankford Yellowjackets

CARVEL—End
1922   Columbus Tigers

**CASANEGA, KENNETH—Back—
Santa Clara**
1946, 48   San Francisco 49ers (AAFC)

CASARES, RICK—Back—Florida
1955–60   Chicago Bears
1956   #1 Ball Carrying

CASE, ERNEST—Back—UCLA
1947   Baltimore Colts (AAFC)

CASEY, ALBERT—Back—Arkansas
1923   St. Louis Browns

**CASEY, THOMAS—Back—Hampton
Inst.**
1948   New York Yankees (AAFC)

CASEY—Tackle
1926   Akron Steels

**CASNER, KENNETH—Tackle—
Baylor**
1952   Los Angeles Rams

CASON, JAMES—Back—LSU
1948–49 San Francisco 49ers – (AAFC)
1950–52, 54 San Francisco 49ers
1955–56 Los Angeles Rams

CASPER, CHARLES—Back—TCU
1934 St. Louis Gunners
1934 Green Bay Packers
1935 Pittsburgh Pirates

HOWARD "HOPALONG" CASSADY

**CASSADY, HOWARD—Back—
Ohio State**
1956–60 Detroit Lions

**CASSARA, FRANK—Back—
St. Mary's Cal.**
1954 San Francisco 49ers

**CASSIANO, RICHARD—Back—
Pittsburgh**
1940 Brooklyn Dodgers

CASSIDY, WILLIAM—End—Detroit
1924 Kenosha

CASTEEL, MILES—Back—Kalamazoo
1922 Rock Island Independents

**CASTETE, JESSE—Back—
McNeese State**
1956 Chicago Bears
1957 Los Angeles Rams

**CASTIGLIA, JAMES—Back—
Georgetown**
1941, 45–46 Philadelphia Eagles
1947 Baltimore Colts (AAFC)
1947–48 Washington Redskins

**CATHCART, ROYAL—Back—Santa
Barbara**
1950 San Francisco 49ers

**CATHCART, SAMUEL—Back—Santa
Barbara**
1949 San Francisco 49ers (AAFC)
1950, 52 San Francisco 49ers

**CATLIN, THOMAS—Center—
Oklahoma**
1953–54, 57–58 Cleveland Browns
1959 Philadelphia Eagles

CATO, DARYL—Center—Arkansas
1946 Miami Seahawks (AAFC)

**CAVALLI, CARMEN—End—
Richmond**
1960 Oakland Raiders (AFL)

**CAVELLI, ANTHONY—Center—
Stanford**
1939 Detroit Lions
1947 San Francisco 49ers (AAFC)

CAVOSIE, JOHN—Back—Butler
1931–33 Portsmouth Spartans

**CAYWOOD, LESTER—Guard—St.
John's**
1926 Buffalo Bisons
1927 Cleveland Bulldogs
1927 Pottsville Maroons
1928 Detroit Wolverines
1929–32 New York Giants
1932 Brooklyn Dodgers
1933–34 Cincinnati Reds

**CEARING, LLOYD—Back—
Valparaiso**
1922–23 Hammond Pros

CELERI, ROBERT—Back—California
1951 New York Yanks
1952 Dallas Texans

**CEMORE, ANTHONY—Guard—
Creighton**
1941 Philadelphia Eagles

CENCI, JOHN—Center—Pittsburgh
1956 Pittsburgh Steelers

**CHALMERS, GEORGE—Center—
New York Univ.**
1933 Brooklyn Dodgers

**CHAMBERLAIN, DANIEL—End—
Sacramento**
1960 Buffalo Bills (AFL)

**CHAMBERLAIN, GARTH—Guard—
Brigham Young**
1945 Pittsburgh Steelers

**CHAMBERLAIN, GUY—End—
Nebraska**
1921 Chicago Bears (Staleys)

1921–23 Canton Bulldogs
1924 Cleveland Bulldogs
1925–26 Frankford Yellowjackets
1927–28 Chicago Cardinals

**CHAMBERS, WILLIAM—Tackle—
U.C.L.A.**
1948–49 New York Yankees (AAFC)

**CHAMPAGNE, EDWARD—Tackle—
LSU**
1947–50 Los Angeles Rams

**CHAMPION, JAMES—Guard—
Mississippi State**
1950–51 New York Yanks

**CHANDLER, DONALD—Back—
Florida**
1956–60 New York Giants
1957 #1 Punting

**CHANDNOIS, LYNN—Back—
Michigan State**
1950–56 Pittsburgh Steelers

**CHANTILES, THOMAS—Tackle—
Southern California**
1942 Detroit Lions

**CHAPMAN, THOMAS—Tackle—
Mt. St. Mary's**
1925 Pottsville Maroons

CHAPPEL—Guard
1921 Chicago Cardinals

**CHAPPUIS, ROBERT—Back—
Michigan**
1948 Brooklyn Dodgers (AAFC)
1949 Chicago Hornets (AAFC)

**CHARLES, WINSTON—Back—
William & Mary**
1927 Pottsville Maroons
1928 Dayton Triangles

**CHASE, BENJAMIN—Guard—
Annapolis**
1947 Detroit Lions

CHASE, RALPH—Tackle—Pittsburgh
1926 Akron Steels
1926 Hammond Independents

**CHEATHAM, ERNEST—Tackle—
Loyola**
1954 Pittsburgh Steelers
1954 Baltimore Colts

**CHEATHAM, LLOYD—Back—
Alabama Polytech**
1942 Chicago Cardinals
1946–48 New York Yankees (AAFC)

CHELF, DONALD—Guard—Iowa
1960 Buffalo Bills (AFL)

**CHERNE, HAROLD—Tackle—
DePaul**
1933 Boston Redskins

**CHEROKE, GEORGE—Center—Ohio
State**
1946 Cleveland Browns (AAFC)

**CHERRY, EDGAR—Back—
Hardin-Simmons**
1938–39 Chicago Cardinals
1939 Pittsburgh Pirates

**CHERUNDULO, CHARLES—
Center—Penn State**
1937–39 Cleveland Rams
1940 Philadelphia Eagles
1941–42, 45–48 Pittsburgh Steelers

**CHESBRO, MARCEL—Guard—
Colgate**
1938 Cleveland Rams

**CHESNEY, CHESTER—Center—
DePaul**
1939–40 Chicago Bears

**CHEVERKO, GEORGE—Back—
Fordham**
1947–48 New York Giants
1948 Washington Redskins

CHICKEN, FRED—Back
1921 Rock Island Independents
1922–24 Minneapolis Marines

**CHICKERNEO, JOHN—Back—
Pittsburgh**
1942 New York Giants

**CHICKILLO, NICHOLAS—Guard—
Miami**
1953 Chicago Cardinals

CHILDRESS, JOSEPH—Auburn
1956–59 Chicago Cardinals
1960 St. Louis Cardinals

**CHIPLEY, WILLIAM—End—
Washington & Lee**
1947–48 Boston Yanks
1949 New York Bulldogs

**CHISICK, ANDREW—Center—
Villanova**
1940–41 Chicago Cardinals

CHOATE—Guard—Haskell
1924 Kansas City Cowboys

**CHOROVICH, RICHARD—Tackle—
Miami (Ohio)**
1955–56 Baltimore Colts
1960 Los Angeles Chargers (AFL)

CHRISTENSEN, FRANK—Back—Utah
1934–37 Detroit Lions

CHRISTENSEN, GEORGE—Tackle—Oregon
1931–33 Portsmouth Spartans
1934–38 Detroit Lions

CHRISTENSEN, KOESTER—End—Michigan State
1930 Portsmouth Spartans

CHRISTENSEN, MARTIN—Back—Minnesota
1940 Chicago Cardinals

CHRISTIANSEN, JOHN—Back—Colorado A & M
1951–58 Detroit Lions
1957 #1 Interceptions (tied by M. Davis, Butler)

CHRISTIANSON—End
1922–24 Minneapolis Marines

CHRISTMAN, FLOYD—Back—Thiel
1925 Buffalo Bison

PAUL CHRISTMAN

CHRISTMAN, PAUL—Back—Missouri
1945–49 Chicago Cardinals
1950 Green Bay Packers

CHRISTY, RICHARD—Back—North Carolina State
1958 Pittsburgh Steelers
1960 Boston Patriots (AFL)

CHURCHMAN, CHARLES—Back—Virginia
1925 Columbus Tigers

CHURCHWELL, HANSON—Guard—Mississippi

1959 Washington Redskins
1960 Oakland Raiders (AFL)

CIBULAS, JOSEPH—Tackle—Duquesne
1945 Pittsburgh Steelers

CICCONE, BENJAMIN—Center—Duquesne
1934–35 Pittsburgh Pirates

CICCONE, WILLIAM—Guard—West Virginia Wesleyan
1942 Chicago Cardinals

CICHOWSKI, EUGENE—Back—Indiana
1957 Pittsburgh Steelers
1958–59 Washington Redskins

CIFELLI, AUGUST—Tackle—Notre Dame
1950–52 Detroit Lions
1953 Green Bay Packers
1954 Philadelphia Eagles
1954 Pittsburgh Steelers

CIFERS, EDWARD—End—Tennessee
1941–42, 46 Washington Redskins
1947–48 Chicago Bears

CIFERS, ROBERT—Back—Tennessee
1944, 46 Detroit Lions
1947–48 Pittsburgh Steelers
1949 Green Bay Packers

CIVILETTO, FRANK—Back—Springfield
1923 Cleveland Indians

CLAGO, WALTER—End—Detroit
1922 Rock Island Independents

CLAIR, FRANK—End—Ohio State
1941 Washington Redskins

CLANCY, STUART—Back—Holy Cross
1930 Newark
1931–32 Staten Island Stapletons
1933–35 New York Giants

CLARK, ARTHUR—Back—Nevada
1927 Frankford Yellowjackets

CLARK, BERYL—Back—Oklahoma
1940 Chicago Cardinals

CLARK, CHARLES—Guard—Harvard
1924 Chicago Cardinals

CLARK, DONALD—Guard—Southern California
1948–49 San Francisco 49ers (AAFC)

CLARK, EARL—Back—Colorado College

1931–33 Portsmouth Spartans
1934–38 Detroit Lions
1932, 35–36 #1 Scoring
1932 #1 Field Goals
1939–42 Cleveland Rams—Head Coach

**CLARK, GEORGE "POTSY"—Back—
College of Pacific**
1927 Duluth Eskimos

CLARK, HAROLD—End—Fordham
1922–25 Rochester Kodaks

**CLARK, HARRY—Back—West
Virginia**
1940–43 Chicago Bears
1946–47 Los Angeles Dons (AAFC)
1948 Chicago Rockets (AAFC)

**CLARK, HERMAN—Tackle—
Orgeon State**
1952, 54–57 Chicago Bears
1960 Los Angeles Chargers (AFL)

**CLARK, JAMES—Tackle—
Oregon State**
1952–53 Washington Redskins

CLARK, JAMES—Back—Pittsburgh
1933–34 Pittsburgh Pirates

**CLARK, MONTE—Tackle— Southern
California**
1959–60 San Francisco 49ers

CLARK, MYERS—Back—Oregon State
1930 Brooklyn Dodgers
1931 Cleveland Indians
1932 Boston Braves
1933–34 Cincinnati Reds
1934 Philadelphia Eagles

CLARK, WAYNE—End—Utah
1944–45 Detroit Lions

**CLARKE, FRANKLIN—End—
Colorado**
1957–59 Cleveland Browns
1960 Dallas Cowboys

**CLARKE, LEON—End—
Southern California**
1956–59 Los Angeles Rams
1960 Cleveland Browns

**CLARKIN, WILLIAM—Tackle—
St. Benedict**
1929 Orange

**CLARKSON, STUART—Center—
Texas A & M**
1942, 46–51 Chicago Bears

**CLATT, CORWIN—Back—Notre
Dame**
1948–49 Chicago Cardinals

**CLATTERBUCK, ROBERT—Back—
Houston**
1954–57 New York Giants
1960 Los Angeles Chargers (AFL)

CLAY, BOYD—Tackle—Tennessee
1940–42, 44 Cleveland Rams

CLAY, RANDALL—Back—Texas
1950, 53 New York Giants

CLAY, ROY—Back—Colorado State
1944 New York Giants

CLAY, WALTER—Back—Colorado
1946–47 Chicago Rockets (AAFC)
1947–48 Los Angeles Dons (AAFC)

**CLAYPOOL, RALPH—Center—
Purdue**
1925–26, 28 Chicago Cardinals

CLAYTON, DONALD—Tackle
1936 Philadelphia Eagles

**CLEARY, PAUL—End—Southern
California**
1948 New York Yankees (AAFC)
1949 Chicago Hornets (AAFC)

**CLEMENS, CALVIN—Back—Southern
California**
1936 Green Bay Packers

CLEMENS, ROBERT—Back—Georgia
1955 Green Bay Packers

CLEMENT, Alex—Back—Williams
1925 Frankford Yellowjackets

CLEMENT, JOHN—Back—SMU
1941 Chicago Cardinals
1946–48 Pittsburgh Steelers
1949 Chicago Hornets (AAFC)

**CLEMENTS, GEORGE—Tackle—
Washington & Jefferson**
1925 Akron Steels

**CLEMONS, RAYMOND—Guard—
Oklahoma State Central**
1939 Detroit Lions

**CLEMONS, RAYMOND—Guard—St.
Mary's (Cal.)**
1947 Green Bay Packers

CLEVE, EINAR—Back—St. Olaf
1922–24 Minneapolis Marines

CLINE, DOUGLAS—Back—Clemson
1960 Houston Oilers (AFL)

CLINE, OLIVER—Back—Ohio State
1948 Cleveland Browns (AAFC)
1949 Buffalo Bills (AAFC)
1950–51 Detroit Lions

**CLOUD, JOHN—Back—William &
Mary**

1950–51 Green Bay Packers
1952–53 Washington Redskins

**CLOW, HERBERT—Back—
Minnesota**
1924 Duluth Kelleys

**CLOWES, JOHN—Tackle—William &
Mary**
1948 Brooklyn Dodgers (AAFC)
1949 Chicago Hornets (AAFC)
1950–51 New York Yanks
1951 Detroit Lions

COAKER, JOHN—Tackle
1924 Rochester Jeffersons

COATES, RAYMOND—Back—LSU
1948–49 New York Giants

COBB, ALFRED—Guard—Syracuse
1921–22 Akron Steels
1923–25 Cleveland Bulldogs

**COBB, THOMAS—Tackle—
Oklahoma N. E. Teachers**
1926 Kansas City Cowboys
1927 Cleveland Bulldogs
1928 Detroit Panthers
1931 Chicago Cardinals

**COBB, WILLIAM—Tackle—
Kansas State**
1924–26 Duluth Eskimos

**COCHRAN, JOHN—Back—Wake
Forest**
1947–50 Chicago Cardinals

**COCHRAN, THOMAS—Back—
Auburn**
1949 Washington Redskins

**COCKRELL, EUGENE—Tackle—
Hardin-Simmons**
1960 New York Titans (AFL)

CODY, EDWARD—Back—Purdue
1947–48 Green Bay Packers
1949–50 Chicago Bears

COFFEE, JAMES—Back—LSU
1937–38 Chicago Cardinals

**COGDILL, GAIL—End—
Washington State**
1960 Detroit Lions

**COHEN, ABRAHAM—Guard—
Chattanooga**
1960 Boston Patriots (AFL)

**COIA, ANGELO—End—Southern
California**
1960 Chicago Bears

COLAHAN, JOHN—Guard
1928 New York Yankees

EDWARD CODY

**COLCHICO, DANIEL—End—
San Jose State**
1960 San Francisco 49ers

**COLCLOUGH, JAMES—End—
Boston College**
1960 Boston Patriots (AFL)

COLE, EMERSON—Back—Toledo
1950–52 Cleveland Browns
1952 Chicago Bears

**COLE, FREDERICK—Guard—
Maryland**
1960 Los Angels Chargers (AFL)

COLE, JOHN—Back—St. Joseph (Pa.)
1938–40 Philadelphia Eagles

**COLE, PETER—Guard—Trinity
(Texas)**
1934 Cincinnati Reds
1937–40 New York Giants

**COLELLA, THOMAS—Back—
Canisius**
1941–43 Detroit Lions
1944–45 Cleveland Rams
1946–48 Cleveland Browns (AAFC)
1949 Buffalo Bills (AAFC)

**COLEMAN, HERBERT—Center—
Notre Dame**
1946–48 Chicago Rockets (AAFC)
1948 Baltimore Colts (AAFC)

**COLHOUER, JACOB—Guard—
Oklahoma**
1946–48 Chicago Cardinals
1949 New York Giants

**COLLIER, FLOYD—Tackle—San Jose
State**
1948 San Francisco 49ers (AAFC)

COLLIER, ROBERT—Tackle—SMU
1951   Los Angeles Rams

COLLINS, ALBIN—Back—LSU
1949   Chicago Hornets (AAFC)
1950   Baltimore Colts
1951   Green Bay Packers

COLLINS, JOHN—Guard—Canisius
1924   Buffalo Bisons

COLLINS, PAUL—End—Pittsburgh
1932–35   Boston Redskins

COLLINS, PAUL—Back—Missouri
1945   Chicago Cardinals

COLLINS, RAYMOND—Tackle—LSU
1950–52   San Francisco 49ers
1954   New York Giants
1960   Dallas Texans (AFL)

COLLINS, WILLIAM—Guard—Texas
1947   Boston Yanks

COLMER, JOHN—Back—Miramonte Jr. College
1946–48   Brooklyn Dodgers (AAFC)
1949   New York Yankees (AAFC)

COLO, DONALD—Tackle—Brown
1950   Baltimore Colts
1951   New York Yanks
1952   Dallas Texans
1953–58   Cleveland Browns

COLTERYAHN, LLOYD—End—Maryland
1953   Pittsburgh Steelers
1954–56   Baltimore Colts

COLTI—Tackle
1928   Pottsville Maroons

COLVIN, JAMES—Tackle—Houston
1960   Baltimore Colts

COMBS, WILLIAM—End—Purdue
1942   Philadelphia Eagles

COMER—Back
1926   Canton Bulldogs

COMER, MARTIN—End—Tulane
1946–48   Buffalo Bills

COMISKEY, FRANK—End—Ohio State
1937   Brooklyn Dodgers

COMP, H. IRVIN—Back—St. Benedict's (Kan.)
1943–49   Green Bay Packers

COMPAGNO, ANTHONY—Back—St. Mary's (Cal.)
1945–49   Pittsburgh Steelers

COMPTON, OGDEN—Back—Hardin-Simmons

1955   Chicago Cardinals

COMSTOCK, EDWIN—Guard—Washington of Mo.
1929   Buffalo Bisons
1930   Brooklyn Dodgers
1931   Staten Island Stapletons

COMSTOCK, RUDOLPH—Guard—Georgetown
1923, 25   Canton Bulldogs
1924   Cleveland Bulldogs
1926–29   Frankford Yellowjackets
1930   New York Giants
1931–33   Green Bay Packers

CONCANNON, ERNEST—Guard—New York Univ.
1933   Brooklyn Dodgers
1934–36   Boston Redskins

CONDIT, MERLYN—Back—Carnegie Tech.
1940, 46   Pittsburgh Steelers
1941–43   Brooklyn Dodgers
1945   Washington Redskins

CONE, FRED—Back—Clemson
1951–57   Green Bay Packers
1955   #1 Field Goals
1960   Dallas Cowboys

CONERLY, CHARLES—Back—Mississippi
1948–60   New York Giants
1959   #1 Passing

CONGER, MELVIN—End—Georgia
1946–47   New York Yankees (AAFC)
1947   Brooklyn Dodgers (AAFC)

CONKWRIGHT, WILLIAM—Tackle—Oklahoma
1937–38   Chicago Bears
1939–42, 44–45   Cleveland Rams
1943   Washington Redskins
1943   Brooklyn Dodgers

CONLEE, GERALD—Center—St. Mary's (Cal.)
1938   Cleveland Rams
1943   Detroit Lions
1946–47   San Francisco 49ers (AAFC)

CONLEY, JOHN—Tackle—Ohio Northern
1922, 26   Columbus Tigers

CONNAUGHTON, HARRY—Guard—Georgetown
1927   Frankford Yellowjackets

CONNELL, JAMES—Back—Catholic Univ.
1926   Chicago Cardinals

CONNELLY, MICHAEL—Center—Utah State

1960 Dallas Cowboys

CONNER, CLYDE —End—
College of Pacific
1956–60 San Francisco 49ers

CLYDE CONNER

CONNER, EMERSON—Guard—
Texas
1935 Detroit Lions

CONNOLLY, HARRY—Back—Boston
College
1946 Brooklyn Dodgers (AAFC)

CONNOLLY, THEODORE—Guard—
Santa Clara
1954, 56–60 San Francisco 49ers

THEODORE
CONNOLLY

CONNOLLY, WILLIAM—Guard—
Texas
1946 Chicago Cardinals

CONNOR, GEORGE—Tackle—Notre
Dame
1948–55 Chicago Bears

CONNOR, WILLIAM—Tackle—
Catholic Univ.
1929 Boston Braves
1930 Newark

CONNORS, STAFFORD—Back—
New Hampshire
1925 Providence Steamrollers
1926 Brooklyn Dodgers

CONNORS, HAMILTON—End
1925 Rochester Jeffersons

CONOVER, LAWRENCE—Center—
Penn State
1923 Canton Bulldogs
1924–25 Cleveland Bulldogs
1926 Frankford Yellowjackets

CONRAD, MARTIN—Center—
Kalamazoo
1922–23 Toledo Maroons
1924 Kenosha
1925 Akron Steels

CONRAD, ROBERT—Back—
Texas A & M
1958–59 Chicago Cardinals
1960 St. Louis Cardinals

CONSTANTINE, IRVING—Back—
Syracuse
1931 Staten Island Stapletons

CONTI, ENIO—Guard—Bucknell
1941–42, 44–45 Philadelphia Eagles
1943 Phil-Pitt

CONZELMAN, JAMES—Back—
Washington (St. Louis)
1920 Chicago Bears (Staleys)
1921–22 Rock Island Independents
1923–24 Milwaukee Badgers
1925–26 Detroit Panthers
1927–30 Providence Steamrollers

COOK, DAVID—Back—Illinois
1934–36 Chicago Cardinals
1936 Brooklyn Dodgers

COOK, EDWARD—Tackle—
Notre Dame
1958–59 Chicago Cardinals
1960 St. Louis Cardinals

COOK, EUGENE—Back—Michigan
1928 Dayton Triangles

COOK, EUGENE—End—Toledo
1959 Detroit Lions

COOK, JAMES—Guard—Wisconsin
1921 Green Bay Packers

COOK, THEODORE—End—Alabama
1947   Detroit Lions
1948–50   Green Bay Packers

COOKE, EDWARD—End—Maryland
1958   Chicago Bears
1958   Philadelphia Eagles
1959   Baltimore Colts
1960   New York Titans (AFL)

COOKMAN—End
1926   Hartford Blues

COOMER, JOSEPH—Tackle
1941, 45–46   Pittsburgh Steelers
1944   Card-Pitt
1947–49   Chicago Cardinals

COON, EDWARD—Guard—North Carolina State
1940–41   Brooklyn Dodgers

COOPER, HAROLD—Guard—Detroit
1937   Detroit Lions

COOPER, JAMES—Center—North Texas State
1948   Brooklyn Dodgers (AAFC)

COOPER, KENNETH—Guard—Vanderbilt
1949   Baltimore Colts (AAFC)
1950   Baltimore Colts

COOPER, NORMAN—Center—Howard
1937–38   Brooklyn Dodgers

COOPER, SAMUEL—Tackle—Geneva
1933   Pittsburgh Pirates

COOPER, THURLOW—End—Maine
1960   New York Titans (AFL)

COOPER, WILLIAM—Tackle—Oberlin
1937   Cleveland Rams

COPE, FRANK—Tackle—Santa Clara
1938–47   New York Giants

COPLEY, CHARLES—Tackle—Missouri School of Mines
1921   Akron Steels
1922   Milwaukee Badgers

COPPAGE, ALTON—End—Oklahoma
1940–42   Chicago Cardinals
1946   Cleveland Browns (AAFC)
1947   Buffalo Bills (AAFC)

CORBETT, GEORGE—Back—Millikin
1932–38   Chicago Bears

CORBITT, DONALD—Center—Arizona
1948   Washington Redskins

CORBO, THOMAS—Guard—Duquesne
1944   Cleveland Rams

CORCORAN, GERALD—Center—Illinois
1930   Minneapolis Redjackets

CORCORAN, ARTHUR—Back—Georgetown
1921   Cleveland Indians
1922   Akron Steels
1922   Milwaukee Badgers
1923   Buffalo All Americans
1923   Frankford Yellowjackets

CORDILEONE, LOUIS—Guard—Clemson
1960   New York Giants

CORDILL, OLIVER—Back—Rice
1940   Cleveland Rams

CORDOVANO, SAMUEL—Guard—Georgetown
1930   Newark

COREY, WALTER—Back—Miami
1960   Dallas Texans (AFL)

CORGAN, CHARLES—End—Kansas
1924–26   Kansas City Cowboys
1926   Hartford Blues
1927   New York Giants

CORGAN, MICHAEL—Back—Notre Dame
1943   Detroit Lions

CORLEY, ELBERT—Center—Mississippi State
1947   Buffalo Bills (AAFC)
1948   Baltimore Colts (AAFC)

CORN, JOSEPH—Back
1948   Los Angeles Rams

CORNELISON, JERRY—Tackle—SMU
1960   Dallas Texans (AFL)

CORNSWEET, ALBERT—Back—Brown
1931   Cleveland Indians

CORTEMEGLIA, CHRISTOPHER—Back—SMU
1927   Frankford Yellowjackets

CORZINE, LESTER—Back—Davis & Elkins
1933–34   Cincinnati Reds
1934   St. Louis Gunners
1935–37   New York Giants
1938   Chicago Bears

COSNER, DONALD—Tackle—Montana State

1939   Chicago Cardinals

COSTELLO, RORY—Center
1921   Cincinnati Celts

**COSTELLO, VINCENT—Guard—
Ohio**
1957–60   Cleveland Browns

**COSTON, FREDERICK—Center—
Texas A & M**
1939   Philadelphia Eagles

**COTHREN, PAIGE—Back—
Mississippi**
1957–58   Los Angeles Rams
1958   #1 Field Goals (tied by Miner)
1959   Philadelphia Eagles

**COTTON, FORREST—Tackle—
Notre Dame**
1923, 25   Rock Island Independents

**COTTON, RUSSELL—Back—Texas
Mines**
1941   Brooklyn Dodgers
1942   Pittsburgh Steelers

**COUGHLIN, FRANK—Tackle—
Notre Dame**
1921   Detroit Panthers
1921   Green Bay Packers
1921   Rock Island Independents
1923   Minneapolis Marines

**COULTER, DeWITT—Tackle—West
Point**
1946–49, 51–52   New York Giants

**COUMIER, ULYSSES—Back—
Louisiana College**
1929   Buffalo Bisons

COUPPEE, ALBERT—Guard—Iowa
1946   Washington Redskins

**COURTNEY, GERARD—Back—
Syracuse**
1942   Brooklyn Dodgers

**COUTRE, LAWRENCE—Back—
Notre Dame**
1950, 53   Green Bay Packers
1953   Baltimore Colts

COWAN, LESLIE—Tackle—McMurry
1951   Chicago Bears

COWAN, ROBERT—Back—Indiana
1947–48   Cleveland Browns (AAFC)
1949   Baltimore Colts (AAFC)

**COWHIG, GERARD—Back—Notre
Dame**
1947–49   Los Angeles Rams
1950   Chicago Cardinals
1951   Philadelphia Eagles

COX, JAMES—Guard—Stanford
1948   San Francisco 49ers (AAFC)

GERARD COWHIG

COX, JOHN—Guard—Oregon State
1932   Boston Braves

COX, NORMAN—Back—TCU
1946–47   Chicago Rockets (AAFC)

COX, WILLIAM—End—Duke
1951–52, 56   Washington Redskins

COYLE, FRANK—End—Detroit
1924–25   Rock Island Independents

COYNE
1924   Milwaukee Badgers

**CRABTREE, CLEMENT—Tackle—
Wake Forest**
1940–41   Detroit Lions

CRABTREE, CLYDE—Back—Florida
1930   Frankford Yellowjackets
1930   Minneapolis Redjackets

CRAFT, RUSSELL—Back—Alabama
1946–53   Philadelphia Eagles
1954   Pittsburgh Steelers

CRAIG, CLARK—End—Pennsylvania
1925   Frankford Yellowjackets

**CRAIG, LAWRENCE—Back—South
Carolina**
1939–49   Green Bay Packers

CRAIN, MILTON—Back—Baylor
1944   Boston Yanks

**CRAKES, JOSEPH—End—South
Dakota**
1933   Cincinnati Reds

CRAMER, EARL—Back—Hamline
1921–26   Akron Steels

CRANGLE, JOHN—Back—Illinois
1923   Chicago Cardinals

CRASS, WILLIAM—Back—LSU
1937   Chicago Cardinals

RUSSELL CRAFT

CRAWFORD, DENVER—Tackle— Tennessee
1948   New York Yankees (AAFC)

CRAWFORD, EDWARD—Back— Mississippi
1957   New York Giants

CRAWFORD, FREDERICK— Tackle—Duke
1934–35   Chicago Bears

CRAWFORD, JAMES—Back— Wyoming
1960   Boston Patriots (AFL)

CRAWFORD, KENNETH—Back— Miami (Ohio)
1921   Cincinnati Celts
1923   Dayton Triangles
1925   Hammond Pros

CRAWFORD, WALTER—Tackle— Illinois
1925   Chicago Bears

CRAWFORD, WILLIAM—Guard— British Columbia
1960   New York Giants

CRAYNE, RICHARD—Back—Iowa
1936–37   Brooklyn Dodgers

CREEKMUR, LOUIS—Guard— William & Mary
1950–59   Detroit Lions

CREGAR, WILLIAM—Guard—Holy Cross
1947–48   Pittsburgh Steelers

CREIGHTON, MILAN—End— Arkansas
1931–37   Chicago Cardinals

CREMER, THEODORE—End— Auburn

1946–48   Detroit Lions
1948   Green Bay Packers

CRIMMINS, BERNARD—Guard— Notre Dame
1945   Green Bay Packers

CRISLER, HAROLD—End—San Jose State
1946–47   Boston Yanks
1948–49   Washington Redskins
1950   Baltimore Colts

CRITCHFIELD, LAWRENCE— Guard—Grove City
1931   Cleveland Indians
1933   Pittsburgh Pirates

CRITTENDON, JOHN—End— Wayne
1954   Chicago Cardinals

CROCKETT, MONTE—End— Highlands
1960   Buffalo Bills (AFL)

CROFT, JACK—Guard—Utah State
1924   Racine Legion

CROFT, ABRAHAM—End—SMU
1944–45   Chicago Bears

CROFT, MILBURN—Tackle—Ripon
1942–47   Green Bay Packers

CROFT, WINFIELD—Guard—Utah
1935   Brooklyn Dodgers
1936   Pittsburgh Pirates

CRONIN, EUGENE—Guard— College of Pacific
1956–59   Detroit Lions
1960   Dallas Cowboys

CRONIN, FRANCIS—End— St. Mary's (Minn.)
1927   Duluth Eskimos

CRONIN, JOHN—Back—Boston College
1927–30   Providence Steamrollers

CRONIN, THOMAS—Back— Marquette
1922   Green Bay Packers

CRONIN, WILLIAM—Back—Boston College
1927–30   Providence Steamrollers
1932   Brooklyn Dodgers

CRONKHITE, HENRY—End— Kansas State
1934   Brooklyn Dodgers

CROOK, ALBERT—Center— Washington & Jefferson

1925–26 Detroit Panthers
1926 Kansas City Cowboys

CROSS, ROBERT—Tackle—Austin
1952 Chicago Bears
1954–55 Los Angeles Rams
1956–58 San Francisco 49ers
1958–59 Chicago Cardinals
1960 Boston Patriots (AFL)

CROSS, WILLIAM—Back—West Texas State
1951–53 Chicago Cardinals

CROTTY, JAMES—Back—Notre Dame
1960 Washington Redskins

CROUTHAMEL, JOHN JACOB—Back—Dartmouth
1960 Boston Patriots (AFL)

CROW, ALBERT—Tackle—William & Mary
1960 Boston Patriots (AFL)

CROW, JOHN—Back—Texas A & M
1958–59 Chicago Cardinals
1960 St. Louis Cardinals

CROW, LINDON—Back—Southern California
1955–57 Chicago Cardinals
1958–60 New York Giants
1956 #1 Interceptions

LINDON CROW

CROW, ORIEN—Center—Haskell
1933–34 Boston Redskins

CROW, WAYNE—Back—California
1960 Oakland Raiders (AFL)

CROWDER, EARL—Back—Oklahoma
1939 Chicago Cardinals
1940 Cleveland Rams

CROWE, PAUL—Back—St. Mary's (Cal.)
1948–49 Los Angeles Dons (AAFC)
1949 San Francisco 49ers (AAFC)
1951 New York Yanks

CROWELL, ODIS—Tackle—Hardin-Simmons
1947 San Francisco 49ers (AAFC)

CROWL, RICHARD—Center—Rutgers
1930 Brooklyn Dodgers

CROWLEY, JAMES—Back—Notre Dame
1925 Green Bay Packers
1925 Providence Steamrollers

CROWLEY, JOSEPH—End—Dartmouth
1944–45 Boston Yanks

CROWTHERS, RAE—Tackle—Colgate
1925–26 Frankford Yellowjackets

CROWTHERS, SAVILLE—End—Colgate
1925–26 Frankford Yellowjackets

CUBA, PAUL—Tackle—Pittsburgh
1933–35 Philadelphia Eagles

CUDZIK, WALTER—Center—Purdue
1954 Washington Redskins
1960 Boston Patriots (AFL)

CUFF, WARD—Back—Marquette
1937–45 New York Giants
1946 Chicago Cardinals
1947 Green Bay Packers
1938, 39 #1 Field Goals (tie by Kercheval, 1938)

CULLEN, RONALD—Tackle—Oklahoma
1922 Milwaukee Badgers

CULLEN, THOMAS—Guard—Georgetown
1931 Cleveland Indians

CULLOM, JAMES—Guard—California
1951 New York Yanks

CULPEPPER, EDWARD—Guard—Alabama
1958–59 Chicago Cardinals
1960 St. Louis Cardinals

CULVER, ALVIN—Tackle—Notre Dame
1932 Chicago Bears
1932 Green Bay Packers

CULVER, FRANK—Center—Syracuse
1923–24 Buffalo Bisons
1924 Rochester Kodaks
1925 Canton Bulldogs

CULWELL, VAL—Guard—Oregon
1942 New York Giants

CUNEO, EDWARD—Guard— Columbia
1929 Orange
1930 Brooklyn Dodgers

CUNNINGHAM, HAROLD—End— Ohio State
1927 Cleveland Bulldogs
1929 Chicago Bears
1931 Staten Island Stapletons

CUNNINGHAM, LEON—Center— South Carolina
1955 Detroit Lions

CUPPOLETTI, BREE—Guard— Oregon
1934–38 Chicago Cardinals
1939–40 Philadelphia Eagles

CURCILLO, ANTHONY—Guard— Ohio State
1953 Chicago Cardinals

CURE, ARMAND—Back—Rhode Island State
1947 Baltimore Colts (AAFC)

CURRAN, HARRY—Back— Boston College
1921 Chicago Cardinals

CURRIE, DANIEL—Center— Michigan State
1958–60 Green Bay Packers

DANIEL CURRIE

CURRIVAN, DONALD—End—Boston College

1943 Chicago Cardinals
1944 Card-Pitt
1945–48 Boston Yanks
1949 Los Angeles Rams

DONALD CURRIVAN

CURTIN, DONALD—Back— Marquette
1926 Milwaukee Badgers

CURZON, HARRY—End—Michigan
1925 Buffalo Bisons
1925–26 Hammond Pros
1928 Chicago Cardinals

CVERCKO, ANDREW—Guard— Northwestern
1959–60 Green Bay Packers

CYRE, HECTOR—Tackle—Gonzaga
1926, 28 Green Bay Packers
1928 New York Yankees

CZAROBSKI, ZYGMONT—Tackle— Notre Dame
1948–49 Chicago Rockets (AAFC)

* * *

DADDIO, WILLIAM—End— Pittsburgh
1940–42 Chicago Cardinals
1946 Buffalo Bisons (AAFC)
1942 #1 Field Goals

DAFFER, TERRELL—Guard— Tennessee
1954 Chicago Bears

DAGATA, FREDERICK—Back— Providence College
1931 Providence Steamrollers

D'AGOSTINO, FRANK—Guard— Auburn
1956 Philadelphia Eagles
1960 New York Titans (AFL)

**DAHLGREN, GEORGE—Guard—
Beloit**
1924 Kenosha
1925–26 Hammond Pros

**DAHMS, THOMAS—Tackle—San
Diego State**
1951–54 Los Angeles Rams
1955 Green Bay Packers
1956 Chicago Cardinals
1957 San Franciso 49ers

**DAILEY, THEODORE—End—
Pittsburgh**
1933 Pittsburgh Pirates

DALE, CARROLL—End—VPI
1960 Los Angeles Rams

CARROLL DALE

DALE, ROLAND—End—Mississippi
1950 Washington Redskins

**DALEY, WILLIAM—Back—
Minnesota, Michigan**
1946 Miami Seahawks (AAFC)
1946 Brooklyn Dodgers (AAFC)
1947 Chicago Rockets (AAFC)
1948 New York Yankees (AAFC)

DALLY—Guard
1926 Hartford Blues

**D'ALONZO, PETER—Back—
Villanova**
1951–52 Detroit Lions

**DALRYMPLE, ROBERT—Center—
Wabash**
1922 Evansville Crimson Giants

**DALSASSO, CHRISTOPHER—
Tackle—Indiana**
1937 Cleveland Rams

DALTON—Back
1922 Racine

**DAMIANI, FRANCIS—Tackle—
Manhattan**
1944 New York Giants

**DAMORE, JOHN—Guard—
Northwestern**
1957, 59 Chicago Bears

**DANCEWICZ, FRANCIS—Back—
Notre Dame**
1946–48 Boston Yanks

**DANAHE, RICHARD—Tackle—
Southern California**
1947–48 Los Angeles Dons (AAFC)

**DANENHAUER, ELDON—Tackle—
Kansas State Teachers**
1960 Denver Broncos (AFL)

**DANENHAUER, WILLIAM—End—
Kansas State Teachers**
1960 Denver Broncos (AFL)
1960 Boston Patriots (AFL)

**DANIELL, AVERELL—Tackle—
Pittsburgh**
1937 Green Bay Packers
1937–38 Brooklyn Dodgers

**DANIELL, JAMES—Tackle—Ohio
State**
1945 Chicago Bears
1946 Cleveland Browns (AAFC)

**DANIELS, CLEMON—Back—
Prairie View**
1960 Dallas Texans (AFL)

DANJEAN, ERNEST—Back—Auburn
1957 Green Bay Packers

**DANOWSKI, EDWARD—Back—
Fordham**
1934–39, 41 New York Giants
1935, 38 #1 Passing

**DARLING, BERNARD—Center—
Beloit**
1927–31 Green Bay Packers

**DASSTLING, DANE—Tackle—
Marietta**
1921 Cincinnati Celts

**DAUGHERTY, RICHARD—Guard—
Oregon**
1951–53, 56–58 Los Angeles Rams

**DAUGHTERY, RUSSELL—Back—
Illinois**
1927 Frankford Yellowjackets

DAUKAS, LOUIS—Center—Cornell
1947 Brooklyn Dodgers (AAFC)

**DAUKAS, NICHOLAS—Tackle—
Dartmouth**
1946–47 Brooklyn Dodgers (AAFC)

DAUM, CARL—End—Akron Univ.
1922–26 Akron Steels

DAVENPORT, WAYNE—Back—
Hardin-Simmons
1931 Green Bay Packers

DAVID, JAMES—Back—Colorado
A & M
1952–59 Detroit Lions

DAVID, ROBERT—Guard—
Villanova
1947–48 Los Angeles Rams (AAFC)
1948 Chicago Rockets (AAFC)

DAVIDOVITZ, ARTHUR—Tackle—
Lehigh
1930 Frankford Yellowjackets

DAVIDSON, FRANCIS—Back—Baylor
1954, 57 Baltimore Colts
1960 Dallas Texans (AFL)

DAVIDSON, JOSEPH—Guard—
Colgate
1928 Chicago Cardinals
1930 Newark

DAVIDSON, PETER—End—Citadel
1960 Houston Oilers (AFL)

DAVIDSON, WILLIAM—Back—
Temple
1937–39 Pittsburgh Steelers

DAVIS, ANDREW—Back—George
Washington
1952–53 Washington Redskins

DAVIS, ARTHUR—Tackle—Alabama
State
1953–54 Chicago Bears

DAVIS, ARTHUR—Back—Mississippi
State
1956 Pittsburgh Steelers

DAVIS, CARL—Tackle—West
Virginia
1926 Akron Steels
1927 Frankford Yellowjackets

DAVIS, CORBETT—Back—Indiana
1938–42 Cleveland Rams

DAVIS, FREDERICK—Tackle—
Alabama
1941–42, 45 Washington Redskins
1946–51 Chicago Bears

DAVIS, GAINES—Guard—Texas
Teachers
1936 New York Giants

DAVIS, GLENN—Back—West Point
1950–51 Los Angeles Rams

GLENN DAVIS

DAVIS, HARPER—Back—Mississippi
State
1949 Los Angeles Dons (AAFC)
1950 Chicago Bears
1951 Green Bay Packers

DAVIS, HERBERT—Back—Xavier
1925–26 Columbus Tigers

DAVIS, HERMIT—End—
Birmingham-Southern
1935 Brooklyn Dodgers

DAVIS, JACK—Guard—Maryland
1960 Boston Patriots (AFL)

DAVIS, JEROME—Back—
Southeastern Louisiana
1948–51 Chicago Cardinals
1952 Dallas Texans

DAVIS, JOSEPH—End—Southern
California
1943 Brooklyn Dodgers
1946 Brooklyn Dodgers (AAFC)

DAVIS, R. LAMAR—End—Georgia
1946 Miami Seahawks (AAFC)
1947–49 Baltimore Colts (AAFC)

DAVIS, MILTON—Back—U.C.L.A.
1956 Detroit Lions
1957–60 Baltimore Colts
1957 #1 Interceptions (tied by
          Christiansen and Butler)
1959 #1 Interceptions (tied by Derby,
          Shinnick)

DAVIS, PAUL—Guard—Marquette
1921 Dayton Triangles
1922 Green Bay Packers

DAVIS, PAUL—Back—Otterbein
1947–48 Pittsburgh Steelers

DAVIS, RALPH—Guard—Wisconsin

1947–48 Green Bay Packers

DAVIS, RAYMOND—End—Alabama
1935 Chicago Cardinals

MILTON DAVIS

DAVIS, ROBERT—End—Penn State
1946–50 Pittsburgh Steelers

DAVIS, ROBERT—Back—Kentucky
1938 Cleveland Rams
1942 Philadelphia Eagles
1944–47 Boston Yanks

DAVIS, ROBERT—Tackle—Georgia Tech.
1948 Boston Yanks

DAVIS, ROGER—Guard—Syracuse
1960 Chicago Bears

DAVIS, SYLVESTER—Back—Geneva
1932–33 Portsmouth Spartans
1933 Philadelphia Eagles

DAVIS, THOMAS—Kicker—Louisiana State Univ.
1959–60 San Francisco 49ers
1960 #1 Field Goals

DAVIS, VAN—End—Georgia
1947–49 New York Yankees (AAFC)

DAVIS, WILLIAM—Tackle—Texas Tech.
1940–41 Chicago Cardinals
1942 Brooklyn Dodgers
1946 Miami Seahawks (AAFC)

DAVIS, WILLIE—End—Grambling
1956 Detroit Lions
1958–59 Cleveland Browns
1960 Green Bay Packers

DAVLIN, MICHAEL—Tackle—Notre Dame

1955 Washington Redskins

DAWLEY, FREDERICK—Back—Michigan
1944 Detroit Lions

DAWSON, GILBERT—Back—Texas
1953 Green Bay Packers

DAWSON, LEONARD—Back—Purdue
1957–59 Pittsburgh Steelers
1960 Cleveland Browns

DAY, ALBERT—Back—Michigan Eastern
1960 Denver Broncos (AFL)

DAY, HERMAN EAGLE—Back—Mississippi
1959–60 Washington Redskins

DAY, THOMAS—Guard—North Carolina A & T
1960 St. Louis Cardinals

DAYHOFF, HARRY—Back—Bucknell
1924 Frankford Yellowjackets
1925 Pottsville Maroons

DEADEYE—Tackle
1922–23 Oorang Indians

DEAL, RUFUS—Center—Alabama Polytech.
1942 Washington Redskins

DEAN, HAROLD—Guard—Ohio State
1947–49 Los Angeles Rams

DEAN, THEODORE—Back—Wichita
1960 Philadelphia Eagles

DEAN, THOMAS—Tackle—SMU
1946–47 Boston Yanks

DECARBO, NICHOLAS—Guard—Duquesne

THOMAS DAVIS

1933 Pittsburgh Pirates

**DeCARLO, ARTHUR—Back—
Georgia**
1953 Pittsburgh Steelers
1956–57 Washington Redskins
1957–60 Baltimore Colts

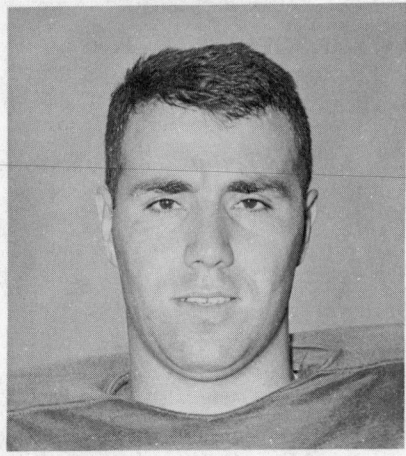

ARTHUR DeCARLO

**DeCLERK, FRANK—Center—
St. Ambrose**
1921–25 Rock Island Independents

**DeCORREVONT, WILLIAM—
Back—Northwestern**
1945 Washington Redskins
1946 Detroit Lions
1947–48 Chicago Cardinals
1948–49 Chicago Bears

DEE, ROBERT—End—Holy Cross
1957–58 Washington Redskins
1960 Boston Patriots (AFL)

**DEEKS, DONALD—Tackle—
Washington**
1945–47 Boston Yanks
1947 Washington Redskins
1948 Green Bay Packers

**DEES, ROBERT—Guard—Missouri
State Southwest**
1952 Green Bay Packers

**DeFILIPPO, DAVID—Guard—
Villanova**
1941 Philadelphia Eagles

**DEFILIPPO, LOUIS—Center—
Fordham**
1941, 45–48 New York Giants

**DeFRUITER, ROBERT—Back—
Nebraska**
1945–47 Washington Redskins
1947 Detroit Lions
1948 Los Angeles Rams

**DeGREE, WALTER—Guard—Notre
Dame**
1921 Detroit Panthers

**DEIBEL, ARTHUR—Tackle—
Lafayette**
1926 Canton Bulldogs

**DEKDEBRUN, ALLEN—Back—
Cornell**
1946 Buffalo Bisons (AAFC)
1947 Chicago Rockets (AAFC)
1948 New York Yankees (AAFC)
1948 Boston Yanks (AAFC)

**DEKKER, PAUL—End—Michigan
State**
1953 Washington Redskins

**DeLAUER, ROBERT—Center—
Southern California**
1945 Cleveland Rams
1946 Los Angeles Rams

DEL BELLO, JOHN—Back—Miami
1953 Baltimore Colts

**DELEVAN, BURTON—Tackle—
College of Pacific**
1955–56 Chicago Cardinals

**DELL ISOLA, JOHN—Center—
Fordham**
1934–40 New York Giants

**DELLERBA, SPIRO—Back—Ohio
State**
1947 Cleveland Browns (AAFC)
1948–49 Baltimore Colts (AAFC)

DELLINGER, LAWRENCE—Guard
1921–23 Dayton Triangles

**DeLUCA, SAMUEL—Tackle—
South Carolina**
1960 Los Angeles Charges (AFL)

**DeLUCCA, GERALD—Tackle—
Tennessee**
1959 Philadelphia Eagles
1960 Boston Patriots (AFL)

**DeMAO, ALBERT—Center—
Duquesne**
1945–53 Washington Redskins

DeMARCO, MARIO—Guard—Miami
1949 Detroit Lions

**DEMAS, GEORGE—Guard—
Washington & Jefferson**
1932 Staten Island Stapletons
1933 Philadelphia Eagles
1934 Brooklyn Dodgers

DeMOE, WILLIAM—End—Beloit
1921 Green Bay Packers

DeMOSS, ROBERT—Back—Purdue
1949   New York Bulldogs

DEMPSEY, FRANK—Tackle—Florida
1950–53   Chicago Bears

DEMPSEY, JOHN—Tackle—Bucknell
1934   Pittsburgh Pirates
1934–37   Philadelphia Eagles

DEMYANOVICH, JOHN—Tackle
1930–32   Staten Island Stapletons

DENFIELD, FREDERICK—Tackle—
   Annapolis
1925   Duluth Kelleys

DENNERLEIN, GERALD—Tackle—
   St. Mary's (Cal.)
1937, 40   New York Giants

DENNERY, VINCENT—End—
   Fordham
1941   New York Giants

DENTON, ROBERT—End—
   College of Pacific
1960   Cleveland Browns

DePAUL, HENRY—Guard—Duquesne
1945   Pittsburgh Steelers

DEPLER, JOHN—Center—Illinois
1929   Orange
1930   Newark

DePRATO, NICHOLAS—Back—
   Michigan State
1921   Detroit Panthers

DERBY, DEAN—Back—Washington
1957–60   Pittsburgh Steelers
1959   #1 Interceptions (tied by M. Davis,
   Shinnick)

DEREMER, ARTHUR—Center—
   Niagara
1942   Brooklyn Dodgers

DeROGATIS, ALBERT—Tackle—
   Duke
1949–52   New York Giants

DeSANTIS, DANIEL—Back—Niagara
1941   Philadelphia Eagles

DESCHAINE, RICHARD—End
1955–57   Green Bay Packers
1958   Cleveland Browns

DeSHANE, CHARLES—Back—
   Alabama
1945–49   Detroit Lions

DesJARDIEN, PAUL—Guard—
   Chicago
1921   Rock Island Independents

DESKIN, VERSIL—End—Drake
1935–39   Chicago Cardinals

DESKINS, DONALD—Guard—
   Michigan
1960   Oakland Raiders (AFL)

DESS, DARRELL—Tackle—North
   Carolina State
1958   Pittsburgh Steelers
1959–60   New York Giants

DeSTEFANO, FREDERICK—Back—
   Northwestern
1924–25   Chicago Cardinals

DETWILER, JOHN—Back—Kansas
1923–24   Hammond Pros

DEWAR, JAMES—Back—Indiana
1947   Cleveland Browns (AAFC)
1948   Brooklyn Dodgers (AAFC)

DeWEESE, BYRNE—Guard—
   Cincinnati
1927–28   Dayton Triangles
1930   Portsmouth Spartans

DEWELL, WILLIAM—End—SMU
1940–41, 45–49   Chicago Cardinals

DEWVEALL, WILLARD—End—SMU
1959–60   Chicago Bears

DeWITZ, HERBERT—Back—
   Nebraska
1924–26   Kansas City Cowboys
1927   Cleveland Indians

DIAL, GILBERT—End—Rice
1959–60   Pittsburgh Steelers

DIAMOND, CHARLES—Tackle—
   Miami
1960   Dallas Texans (AFL)

DIBB, JOHN—Tackle—West Point
1930   Newark

DIBBLE, DORNE—End—Michigan
   State
1951, 53–57   Detroit Lions

DICENZO, ANTHONY—Tackle—
   Michigan State
1960   Boston Patriots (AFL)
1960   Buffalo Bills (AFL)

DICKENS, MARION—Back—Georgia
1932   Boston Braves

DICKEY, LEONARD—Tackle—
   Kilgore Jr. College
1947   New York Yankees (AAFC)

DICKINSON, RICHARD—Back—
   Mississippi Southern
1960   Dallas Texans (AFL)

DICKSON, PAUL—Tackle—Baylor
1959   Los Angeles Rams
1960   Dallas Cowboys

DIEHL, DAVID—End—Michigan State

1939–40, 44–45   Detroit Lions

DIEHL, GORDON—Back—Idaho
1930–31   Chicago Cardinals
1933   Cincinnati Reds
1934   St. Louis Gunners

DIEHL, WALTER—Back—Bucknell
1928–30   Frankford Yellowjackets

**DIETER, HERBERT—Guard—
Pennsylvania**
1922   Buffalo All Americans

**DIGRIS, BERNARD—Tackle—Holy
Cross**
1943   Chicago Bears

DILLON, ROBERT—Back—Texas
1952–59   Green Bay Packers

**DILWEG, LAVERN—End—
Marquette**
1926   Milwaukee Badgers
1927–34   Green Bay Packers

**DIMANCHEFF, BORIS—Back—
Purdue**
1945–46   Boston Yanks
1947–50   Chicago Cardinals
1952   Chicago Bears

**DIMITROFF, THOMAS—Back—
Miami-Ohio**
1960   Boston Patriots (AFL)

**DIMMICK, DONALD—Back—
Bethany**
1926–27   Buffalo Bisons

**DIMMICK, THOMAS—Guard—
Houston**
1956   Philadelphia Eagles

**DiPIERRO, RAYMOND—Guard—
Ohio State**
1950–51   Green Bay Packers

DISEND, LEO—Tackle—Albright
1938–40   Brooklyn Dodgers
1940   Green Bay Packers
1943   Philadelphia Eagles

**DITTRICH, JOHN—Guard—
Wisconsin**
1956   Chicago Cardinals
1959   Green Bay Packers
1960   Oakland Raiders (AFL)

**DIXON, FELIX—Tackle—Boston
Univ.**
1938   Brooklyn Dodgers

DOANE, JOSEPH—Back—Tufts
1922–24   Milwaukee Badgers
1925–26   Detroit Panthers
1927   Pottsville Maroons
1927   Providence Steamrollers

DOBBS, GLENN—Back—Tulsa
1946–47   Brooklyn Dodgers (AAFC)
1948–49   Los Angeles Dons (AAFC)

**DOBELSTEIN, ROBERT—Guard—
Tennessee**
1946–48   New York Giants
1949   Los Angeles Dons (AAFC)

**DOBELEIT, ROBERT—Back—
Ohio State**
1925–26   Dayton Triangles

DOBREY, E. A.—End
1928   Frankford Yellowjackets

**DOBRUS, PETER—Tackle—Carnegie
Tech.**
1941   Brooklyn Dodgers

**DODRILL, DALE—Guard—Colorado
A & M**
1951–59   Pittsburgh Steelers

DODSON, LESLIE—Back—Mississippi
1941   Pittsburgh Steelers

DOEHRING, JOHN—Back
1932–37   Chicago Bears

**DOELLING, FREDERICK—Back—
Pennsylvania**
1960   Dallas Cowboys

**DOGGETT, KEITH—Tackle—
Wichita**
1942   New York Giants

**DOHERTY, GEORGE—Guard—
Louisiana Tech.**
1944   Brooklyn Dodgers
1945   Boston Yanks
1946   New York Yankees (AAFC)
1946–47   Buffalo Bills (AAFC)

**DOHERTY, WILLIAM—Center—
Marietta**
1921   Cincinnati Celts

**DOLL, DONALD—Back—Southern
California**
1949–52   Detroit Lions
1953   Washington Redskins
1954   Los Angeles Rams

**DOLLY, RICHARD—End—
West Virginia**
1941, 45   Pittsburgh Steelers

**DOLOWAY, CLIFFORD—Back—
Carnegie Tech**
1935   Pittsburgh Pirates

**DOMBROWSKI, LEON—Center—
Delaware**
1960   New York Titans (AFL)

DOMNANOVICH, JOSEPH—
Center—Alabama
Alabama
1946–48 Boston Yanks
1949 New York Bulldogs
1950–51 New York Yanks

DONAHUE, JOHN—Tackle—Boston
College
1926 Providence Steamrollers

DONALDSON, EUGENE—Guard—
Kentucky
1953 Cleveland Browns

DONALDSON, JOHN—Back—
Georgia
1949 Chicago Hornets (AAFC)
1949 Los Angeles Dons (AAFC)

DON CARLOS, WILLIAM—Center—
Drake
1931 Green Bay Packers

DONELLI, ALDO—Back—Duquesne
1941–42 Pittsburgh Steelers

DONLAN, JAMES—Guard
1926 Hartford Blues

DONNAHOO, ROGER—Back—
Michigan State
1960 New York Titans (AFL)

DONNELL, BENJAMIN—End—
Vanderbilt
1960 Los Angeles Chargers (AFL)

DONNELL, JOHN—Back—Oregon
1930 Brooklyn Dodgers

DONOHOE, WILLIAM—Back—
Carnegie Tech
1927 Frankford Yellowjackets

DONOVAN, ARTHUR—Tackle—
Boston College
1950, 53–60 Baltimore Colts
1951 New York Yanks
1952 Dallas Texans

DONOVAN, JOHN—Tackle—
Holy Cross
1931 Providence Steamrollers

DOOLAN, GEORGE—Center
1922 Racine Legion

DOOLAN, JOHN—Back—Georgetown
1945 Washington Redskins
1945–46 New York Giants
1947–48 Chicago Cardinals

DOOLEY, JAMES—Back—Miami
1952–54, 56–60 Chicago Bears

DOOLEY, JOHN—Guard—Syracuse
1922–25 Rochester Jeffersons

JAMES DORAN

DORAN, JAMES—End—Iowa State
1951–59 Detroit Lions
1960 Dallas Cowboys

D'ORAZIO, JOSEPH—Tackle—Ithaca
College
1944 Detroit Lions

DORFMAN, ARTHUR—Guard—
Boston Univ.
1929 Buffalo Bisons

DOROW, ALBERT—Back—
Michigan State
1954–56 Washington Redskins
1957 Philadelphia Eagles
1960 New York Titans (AFL)

DOSS, NOBLE—Back—Texas
1947–48 Philadelphia Eagles
1949 New York Yankees (AAFC)

DOTTLEY, JOHN—Back—Mississippi
1951–53 Chicago Bears

DOUDS, FORREST—Tackle—
Washington & Jefferson
1930 Providence Steamrollers
1930–31 Portsmouth Spartans
1932 Chicago Cardinals
1933–35 Pittsburgh Pirates

DOUGHERTY, GEORGE—Back—
Howard
1940 Brooklyn Dodgers

DOUGHERTY, PHILIP—Back—Santa
Clara
1938 Chicago Cardinals

DOUGHERTY, ROBERT—Center—
Kentucky
1957 Los Angeles Rams
1958 Pittsburgh Steelers
1960 Oakland Raiders (AFL)

DOUGLAS, BENJAMIN—Back—Cornell
1933 Brooklyn Dodgers

DOUGLAS, CLARENCE—Back—Kansas
1938 Pittsburgh Steelers

DOUGLAS, EVERETT—Tackle—Florida
1953 New York Giants

DOUGLAS, GEORGE—Center—Marquette
1921 Green Bay Packers
1926 Milwaukee Badgers

DOUGLAS, LEO—Back—Lehigh
1926 Brooklyn Dodgers
1926 Frankford Yellowjackets

DOUGLAS, MERRILL—Back—Utah
1958–60 Chicago Bears

DOUGLAS, OTIS—Tackle—William & Mary
1946–49 Philadelphia Eagles

DOVE, EDWARD—Back—Colorado
1959–60 San Francisco 49ers

EDWARD DOVE

DOVE, ROBERT—End—Notre Dame
1946–47 Chicago Rockets (AAFC)
1948–53 Chicago Cardinals
1953–54 Detroit Lions

DOW, HARLEY—Guard—San Jose State
1950 San Francisco 49ers

DOW, JESS ELWOOD—Back—Texas State West
1938–40 Philadelphia Eagles

DOW, KENNETH—Back—Oregon State
1941 Washington Redskins

DOWD, GERALD—Center—St. Mary's (Cal.)
1939 Cleveland Rams

DOWDA, HARRY—Back—Wake Forest
1949–53 Washington Redskins
1954–55 Philadelphia Eagles

DOWDEN, STEPHAN—Tackle—Baylor
1952 Green Bay Packers

DOWDLE, DON MICHAEL—Back—Texas
1960 Dallas Cowboys

DOWELL, GWYN—Back—Texas Tech.
1935–36 Chicago Cardinals

DOWLER, BOYD—End—Colorado
1959–60 Green Bay Packers

DOWLER, THOMAS—Back—Colgate
1931 Brooklyn Dodgers

DOWLING, PATRICK—End—DePaul
1929 Chicago Cardinals

DOWNS, ROBERT—Guard—Southern California
1951 San Francisco 49ers

DOYLE, EDWARD—End—West Point
1924 Frankford Yellowjackets
1925 Pottsville Maroons
Killed—First officer killed in African invasion, 1943. Captain, U.S. Army.

DOYLE, EDWARD—Guard—Canisius
1927 Buffalo Bisons

DOYLE, RICHARD—Back—Ohio State
1955 Pittsburgh Steelers
1960 Boston Patriots (AFL)
1960 Denver Broncos (AFL)

DOYLE, THEODORE—Tackle—Nebraska
1938–42, 45 Pittsburgh Pirates
1943 Phil-Pitt
1944 Card-Pitt

DRAKE, JOHN—Back—Purdue
1937–41 Cleveland Rams

DRAVELING, LEO—Tackle—Michigan
1933 Cincinnati Reds

DRAYER, CLARENCE—Tackle—Illinois
1925–26 Dayton Triangles

DRAZENOVICH, CHARLES—Back—
Penn State
1950–59 Washington Redskins

DREHER, FERDINAND—End—
Denver
1938 Chicago Bears

DRESSEN, CHARLES—Back
1920 Chicago Bears (Staleys)
1922–23 Racine Legion

DREWS, THEODORE—End—
Princeton
1926 Brooklyn Dodgers
1928 Chicago Bears

DREYER, WALTER—Back—
Wisconsin
1949 Chicago Bears
1950–51 Green Bay Packers

DRISCOLL, JOHN—Back—
Northwestern
1921–25 Chicago Cardinals
1926–29 Chicago Bears

DRISKILL, JOSEPH—Back—
Louisiana State N. E.
1960 St. Louis Cardinals

DRUEHL, WILLIAM—Back—Colby
1929 Boston Braves

DRULIS, ALBERT—Back—Temple
1945–46 Chicago Cardinals
1947 Pittsburgh Steelers
1948 Washington Redskins

DRULIS, CHARLES—Guard—Temple
1942, 45–49 Chicago Bears
1950 Green Bay Packers

DRURY, LYLE—End—St. Louis Univ.
1930–31 Chicago Bears

DRUZE, JOHN—End—Fordham
1938 Brooklyn Dodgers

DRYDEN—Back
1930 Staten Island Stapletons

DRZEWIECKI, RONALD—Back—
Marquette
1955, 57 Chicago Bears

DUBENION, ELBERT—Back—
Bluffton
1960 Buffalo Bills (AFL)

DUBLINSKI, THOMAS—Back—Utah
1952–54 Detroit Lions
1958 New York Giants
1960 Denver Broncos (AFL)

DUBOFSKY, MAURICE—Guard—
Georgetown
1932 New York Giants

DUBZINSKI, WALTER—Guard—
Boston College
1941 Detroit Lions
1943 New York Giants
1944 Boston Yanks

DUCKWORTH, JOSEPH—End—
Colgate
1947 Washington Redskins
1948 Boston Yanks

DUDEN, RICHARD—End—
Annapolis
1949 New York Giants

DUDISH, ANDREW—Center—
Georgia
1946 Buffalo Bisons (AAFC)
1947 Baltimore Colts (AAFC)
1948 Brooklyn Dodgers (AAFC)
1948 Detroit Lions

DUDLEY, WILLIAM—Back—
Virginia
1942, 45–46 Pittsburgh Steelers
1947–49 Detroit Lions
1950–51, 53 Washington Redskins
1942, 46 #1 Ball Carrying
1946 #1 Interceptions

DUFFT, JAMES—Guard—Rutgers
1922 Milwaukee Badgers

DUFFY, PATRICK—Back—Dayton
1929 Dayton Triangles
1929 Providence Steamrollers

DUFORD, WILFRED—Back—
Marquette
1924 Green Bay Packers

DUGAN, FRED—End—Dayton
1958–59 San Francisco 49ers
1960 Dallas Cowboys

DUGAN, LEONARD—Center—
Wichita
1936 New York Giants
1937–39 Chicago Cardinals

DUGGAN, EDWARD—Back—Notre
Dame
1921 Rock Island Independents

DUGGAN, GILFORD—Tackle—
Oklahoma
1940 New York Giants
1941–43, 45 Chicago Cardinals
1944 Card-Pitt
1946 Los Angeles Dons (AAFC)
1947 Buffalo Bisons (AAFC)

DUGGER, JOHN—End—Ohio State
1946 Buffalo Bisons (AAFC)
1947–48 Detroit Lions
1949 Chicago Bears

DUGGINS, GEORGE—End—
Purdue
1933–34 Chicago Cardinals

DUHART, PAUL—Back—Florida
1944 Green Bay Packers
1945 Pittsburgh Steelers
1945 Boston Yanks

DUKE, PAUL—Center—Georgia Tech.
1947 New York Yankees (AAFC)

DUKES, MICHAEL—Back—Clemson
1959 San Francisco 49ers
1960 Houston Oilers (AFL)

DUMOE, JOSEPH—End—Syracuse
1921 Rochester Kodaks

DUNCAN, JAMES—End—Wake
Forest
1950 Detroit Lions
1950–53 New York Giants

DUNCAN, MAURICE—Back—
San Jose State
1954–55 San Francisco 49ers

DUNIGAN, MERTON—Tackle—
Minnesota
1924 Minneapolis Marines
1925–26 Milwaukee Badgers

DUNLAP, ROBERT—Back—
Oklahoma
1935 Chicago Bears
1936 New York Giants

DUNN, COYE—Back—Southern
California
1943 Washington Redskins

DUNN, JOSEPH—Back—Marquette
1924–25 Milwaukee Badgers
1925–26 Chicago Cardinals
1927–31 Green Bay Packers

DUNN, ROBERT—Center—New
York Univ.
1929 Staten Island Stapletons

DUNN, RODERICK, Guard—
Syracuse
1923 Duluth Eskimos

DUNNIGAN, WALTER—End—
Minnesota
1922 Green Bay Packers

DUNSTAN, W. ELWYN—Tackle—
Portland
1938–39 Chicago Cardinals
1939–41 Cleveland Rams

DUPRE, CHARLES—Back—Baylor
1960 New York Titans (AFL)

DUPRE, LOUIS—Back—Baylor
1955–59 Baltimore Colts
1960 Dallas Cowboys

DURDAN, DONALD—Back—Oregon
State
1946–47 San Francisco (AAFC)

DURISHAN, JOHN—Tackle—
Pittsburgh
1947 New York Yankees (AAFC)

DURKO, JOHN—End—Albright
1944 Philadelphia Eagles
1945 Chicago Cardinals

DURKOTA, JEFFREY—Back—Penn
State
1948 Los Angeles Dons (AAFC)

DUTTON, WILLIAM—Back—
Pittsburgh
1946 Pittsburgh Steelers
1947 New York Yankees (AAFC)

DUVALL, EARL—Guard—
Ohio State
1924–26 Columbus Tigers

DVORAK, BENJAMIN—Back—
Minnesota
1922 Minneapolis Marines

DWORSKY, DANIEL—Back—
Michigan
1949 Los Angeles Dons (AAFC)

DWYER, JOHN—Back—Loyola
(Los Angeles)
1951 Washington Redskins
1952–54 Los Angeles Rams

DWYER, ROBERT—Back—
Georgetown
1929 Orange

DYE, LESTER—End—Syracuse
1944–45 Washington Redskins

* * *

EAGLE, ALEXANDER—Tackle—
Oregon
1935 Brooklyn Dodgers

EAGLE FEATHER—Back
1922–23 Oorang Indians

EAKIN, KAY—Back—Arkansas
1940–41 New York Giants
1946 Miami Seahawks (AAFC)

EARHART, RALPH—Back—Texas
Tech.
1948–49 Green Bay Packers

EARON, BLAINE—End—Duke
1952–53 Detroit Lions

EARPE, FRANCIS—Guard—
Monmouth
1921–22 Rock Island Independents
1922–32 Green Bay Packers

1927   New York Giants

EASON, ROGER—Tackle—Oklahoma
1945   Cleveland Rams
1946–48   Los Angeles Rams
1949   Green Bay Packers

**EATON, LOUIS—Tackle—
California**
1945   New York Giants

EATON, VICTOR—Back—Missouri
1955   Pittsburgh Steelers

**EBDING, HARRY—End—St. Mary's
(Cal.)**
1930–33   Portsmouth Spartans
1934–37   Detroit Lions

EBERDT, JESS—Center—Alabama
1932   Brooklyn Dodgers

**EBERSOLE, HAROLD—Guard—
Cornell**
1923   Cleveland Indians

**EBERTS, BERNARD—Guard—
Carleton**
1924   Minneapolis Marines

**EBLI, RAYMOND—End—Notre
Dame**
1942   Chicago Cardinals
1946   Buffalo Bisons (AAFC)
1947   Chicago Rockets (AAFC)

EBY, BYRON—Back—Ohio State
1930   Portsmouth Spartans

**ECKER, ENRIQUE—Tackle—John
Carroll**
1947, 49   Chicago Bears
1948   Chicago Rockets (AAFC)
1950–51   Green Bay Packers
1952   Washington Redskins

ECKHARDT, OSCAR—Back—Texas
1928   New York Giants

ECKL, ROBERT—Tackle—Wisconsin
1945   Chicago Cardinals

**ECKLUND, BRADLEY—Center—
Oregon**
1949   New York Yankees (AAFC)
1950–51   New York Yanks
1952   Dallas Texans
1953   Baltimore Colts

**ECKSTEIN, ALDOPH—Center—
Brown**
1925–26   Providence Steamrollers

**EDGAR, WILLIAM—Back—
Pittsburgh**
1923   Buffalo All Americans
1923   Akron Steels

**EDGINGTON, DANIEL—End—
Florida**
1960   Oakland Raiders (AFL)

**EDLER, ROBERT—Back—Ohio
Wesleyan**
1923   Cleveland Indians

**EDMONDSON, VAN—Center—
Oklahoma**
1926   Buffalo Bisons

**EDWARDS, ALBERT GLEN—
Tackle—Washington State**
1932–36   Boston Redskins
1937–40   Washington Redskins

EDWARDS, CHARLES—Back—Brown
1930–31   Providence Steamrollers

EDWARDS, DANIEL—End—Georgia
1948   Brooklyn Dodgers (AAFC)
1949   Chicago Hornets (AAFC)
1950–51   New York Yanks
1952   Dallas Texans
1953–54, 57   Baltimore Colts

**EDWARDS, EUGENE—Guard—Notre
Dame**
1921   Canton Bulldogs
1922   Toledo Maroons
1923–25   Cleveland Indians

**EDWARDS, LESLIE—Back—
Washington & Jefferson**
1930   Providence

**EDWARDS, MARSHALL—Back—
Wake Forest**
1943   Brooklyn Dodgers

**EDWARDS, THOMAS—Tackle—
Michigan**
1926   Detroit Panthers

EDWARDS, WELDON—Tackle—TCU
1948   Washington Redskins

**EDWARDS, WILLIAM—Back—
Baylor**
1941–42, 46   New York Giants

EDWARDS, WILLIAM—Back
1926   Hartford Blues

EGAN, RICHARD—End—Chicago
1921–23   Chicago Cardinals
1924   Kenosha
1924   Dayton Triangles

**EGGERS, DOUGLAS—Guard—
South Dakota State**
1954–57   Baltimore Colts
1958   Chicago Cardinals

**EHRHARDT, CLYDE—Center—
Georgia**
1946, 48–49   Washington Redskins

EIBNER, JOHN—Tackle—Kentucky
1941–42, 46   Philadelphia Eagles

EICHENLAUB, RAY—Back—Notre Dame
1925 Columbus Tigers
1925 Cleveland Indians

EIDEN, JAMES—Tackle—Knox
1926 Louisville Colonels

EIDEN, EDMUND—Back—Scranton
1944 Philadelphia Eagles
1944 Detroit Lions

EIKENBERG, VIRGIL—Back—Rice
1948 Chicago Cardinals

ELIASON, DONALD—End—Hamline
1942 Brooklyn Dodgers
1946 Boston Yanks

ELKINS, EVERETT—Back—Marshall
1940 Chicago Cardinals

ELKINS, FAIT—Back—Haskell
1929 Frankford Yellowjackets
1929 Chicago Cardinals
1932 Boston Braves
1933 Cincinnati Reds

ELLENA, JACK—Guard—U.C.L.A.
1955–56 Los Angeles Rams

ELLENSON, EUGENE—Tackle—Georgia
1946 Miami Seahawks (AAFC)

ELLERSICK, DONALD—Back—Washington State
1960 Los Angeles Rams

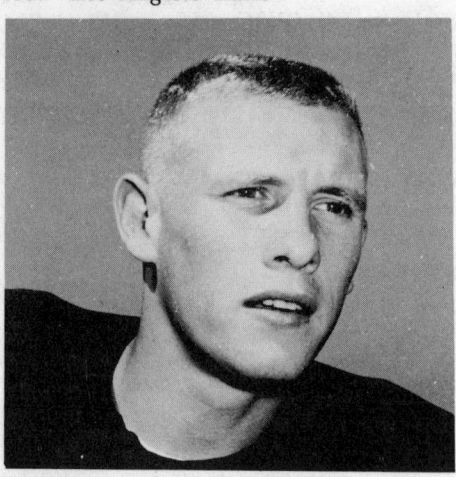

DONALD ELLERSICK

ELLIOTT, ALVAH—Back—Wisconsin
1922–24 Racine Legion
1925 Rock Island Independents

ELLIOTT, BURTON—Back—Marquette
1921 Green Bay Packers

ELLIOTT, CARLTON—End—Virginia
1951–54 Green Bay Packers

ELLIOTT, CHARLES—Tackle—Oregon
1947 New York Yankees (AAFC)
1948 Chicago Rockets (AAFC)
1948 San Francisco 49ers (AAFC)

ELLIOTT, WALLACE—Back—Lafayette
1922–23 Canton Bulldogs
1924–25 Cleveland Indians

ELLIS, DREW—Tackle—TCU
1938–39 Philadelphia Eagles

ELLIS, HERBERT—Center—Texas A & M
1949 New York Bulldogs

ELLIS, JOHN—Guard—Vanderbilt
1944 Brooklyn Dodgers

ELLIS, LAWRENCE—Back—Syracuse
1948 Detroit Lions

ELLIS, ROGER—Center—Maine
1960 New York Titans (AFL)

ELLIS, WALTER—Tackle—Detroit
1924–25 Columbus Tigers
1925 Detroit Panthers
1927 Chicago Cardinals

ELLOR, ALBERT—Guard—Bucknell
1930 Newark

ELLSTROM, MARVIN—Back—Oklahoma
1934 Boston Redskins
1934 Philadelphia Eagles
1935 Pittsburgh Pirates
1936 Chicago Cardinals

ELLZEY, CHARLES—Back—Mississippi Southern
1960 St. Louis Cardinals

ELNESS, LELAND—Back—Bradley
1929 Chicago Bears

ELSER, EARL—Back—Butler
1933 Portsmouth Spartans
1934 Cincinnati Reds
1934 St. Louis Gunners

ELSEY, EARL—Back—Loyola (Los Angeles)
1946 Los Angeles Dons (AAFC)

ELSTON, ARTHUR—Center—Southern California
1942 Cleveland Rams
1946–48 San Francisco 49ers (AAFC)

ELTER, LEO—Back—Villanova
1953–54, 58–59 Pittsburgh Steelers

1955–57 Washington Redskins

ELY, HAROLD—Tackle—Iowa
1932 Chicago Bears
1933–34 Brooklyn Dodgers

EMBREE, MELVIN—End—
 Pepperdine
1953 Baltimore Colts
1954 Chicago Cardinals

EMERICK, ROBERT—Tackle—
 Miami—Ohio
1934 Detroit Lions
1937 Cleveland Rams

EMERSON, GROVER—Guard—Texas
1931–33 Portsmouth Spartans
1934–37 Detroit Lions
1938 Brooklyn Dodgers

EMMONS, FRANKLIN—Back—
 Oregon
1940 Philadelphia Eagles

EMSLIE—Guard
1923 Rochester Kodaks

ENDRISS, ALBERT—End—
 San Francisco State
1952 San Francisco 49ers

ENGEBRETSEN, PAUL—Guard—
 Northwestern
1932 Chicago Bears
1933 Pittsburgh Pirates
1933 Chicago Cardinals
1934 Detroit Lions
1934 Brooklyn Dodgers
1934–41 Green Bay Packers

ENGELMANN, WUERT—Back—
 South Dakota State
1930–33 Green Bay Packers

ENGLUND, HARRY—End
1921–22, 24 Chicago Bears

ENGSTROM, GEORGE—Guard—
 Wisconsin
1924 Duluth Kelleys

ENICH, STEPHEN—Guard—
 Marquette
1945 Chicago Cardinals

ENIS, HUNTER—Back—TCU
1960 Dallas Texans (AFL)

ENKE, FREDERICK—Back—
 Arizona
1948–51 Detroit Lions
1952 Philadelphia Eagles
1953–54 Baltimore Colts

ENRIGHT, REX—Back—Notre Dame
1926–27 Green Bay Packers

EPPERSON, JOHN PATRICK—
 End—Adams State

1960 Denver Broncos (AFL)

EPPS, ROBERT—Back—Pittsburgh
1954–55, 57 New York Giants

ERDLITZ, RICHARD—Back—
 Northwestern
1942, 45 Philadelphia Eagles
1946 Miami Seahawks (AAFC)

ERICKSON, CARLETON—Center—
 Washington
1938–39 Washington Redskins

ERICKSON, HAROLD—Back—
 Washington-Jefferson
1923 Green Bay Packers
1923–24 Milwaukee Badgers
1925 Chicago Bears
1925–28 Chicago Cardinals
1929–30 Minneapolis Marines

ERICKSON, MICHAEL—Center—
 Northwestern
1930–31 Chicago Cardinals
1932 Boston Braves

FREDERICK ENKE

ERICKSON, WALDEN—Tackle—
 Washington
1927 Pottsville Maroons

ERICKSON, WELDON—End—
 South Dakota
1922 Minneapolis Marines

ERICKSON, WILLIAM—Guard—
 Mississippi
1948 New York Giants
1949 New York Yankees (AAFC)

ERNST, JOHN—Back—Lafayette
1925, 30 Frankford Yellowjackets
1925–28 Pottsville Maroons
1928 New York Yankees
1929 Boston Braves

ESCHBACH, HERBERT—Center—
Penn State
1930–31   Providence Steamrollers

ESHMONT, LEONARD—Back—
Fordham
1940–41   New York Giants
1946–49   San Francisco 49ers (AAFC)

ESSER, CLARENCE—End—
Wisconsin
1947   Chicago Cardinals

ETHRIDGE, JOSEPH—Tackle—
SMU
1949   Green Bay Packers

ETTINGER, DONALD—Guard—
Kansas
1948–50   New York Giants

EVANS, EARL—Tackle—Harvard
1925   Chicago Cardinals
1926–29   Chicago Bears

EVANS, FREDERICK—Back—Notre
Dame
1946   Cleveland Browns (AAFC)
1947   Buffalo Bills (AAFC)
1947–48   Chicago Rockets (AAFC)
1948   Chicago Bears

EVANS, JOHN—Back—California
1929   Green Bay Packers

EVANS, JON—End—Oklahoma State
1958   Pittsburgh Steelers

EVANS, LON—Guard—TCU
1933–37   Green Bay Packers

EVANS, MURRAY—Back—Hardin-
Simmons
1942–43   Detroit Lions

EVANS, RAY—Back—Kansas
1948   Pittsburgh Steelers

EVANS, RAYMOND—Tackle—Texas
Mines
1949   San Francisco 49ers (AAFC)
1950   San Francisco 49ers

EVANS. RICHARD—End—Iowa
1940, 43   Green Bay Packers
1941–42   Chicago Cardinals

EVANSEN, PAUL—Guard—Oregon
State
1948   San Francisco 49ers

EWALD, GEORGE—Back—Louisville
1922–23   Louisville Colonels

EWALD, HENRY—Back
1922–23   Louisville Colonels

* * *

FAGIOLI, CARL—Guard—Notre
Dame
1944   Philadelphia Eagles

FAHAY, JOHN—End—Marquette
1926   Racine Legion
1926   Louisville Colonels
1929   Minneapolis Redjackets

FAILING, FRED—Guard—Central
1930   Chicago Cardinals

FAIRCLOTH, ARTHUR—Back—
North Carolina
1947–48   New York Giants

FALASCHI, NELLO—Back—Santa
Clara
1938–41   New York Giants

FALCON, GILBERT—Back—Wabash
1921   Canton Bulldogs
1922–23   Toledo Maroons
1924–25   Hammond Pros
1925   Akron Steels

FALKENSTEIN, ANTHONY—Back—
St. Mary's (Cal.)
1943   Green Bay Packers
1944   Brooklyn Dodgers
1944   Boston Yanks

FALLON, MICHAEL—Guard—
Syracuse
1922   Milwaukee Badgers

FALLS, MICHAEL—Guard—
Minnesota
1960   Dallas Cowboys

FAMIGLIETTI, GARY—Back—
Boston Univ.
1938–45   Chicago Bears
1946   Boston Yanks

FANNING, STANLEY—Tackle—
Idaho
1960   Chicago Bears

FANUCCHI, LEDIO—Tackle—
Fresno State
1954   Chicago Cardinals

FARKAS, ANDREW—Back—Detroit
1938–44   Washington Redskins
1945   Detroit Lions
1939   #1 Scoring

FARMAN, RICHARD—Guard—
Washington State
1939–43   Washington Redskins

FARMER, THOMAS—Back—Iowa
1946   Los Angeles Rams
1947–48   Washington Redskins

RICHARD FARMAN

FARRAGUT, KENNETH—Center—Mississippi
1951–54 Philadelphia Eagles

KENNETH FARRAGUT

FARRAR, VINCENT—Guard—North Carolina State
1938–39 Pittsburgh Steelers
1939 Washington Redskins

FARRELL, EDWARD—Back—Muhlenberg
1938 Pittsburgh Pirates
1938–39 Brooklyn Dodgers

FARRINGTON, JOHN—End—Prairie View
1960 Chicago Bears

FARRIS, THOMAS—Back—Wisconsin
1941, 46–47 Chicago Bears
1948 Chicago Rockets (AAFC)

FARROH, SHIPLEY—Guard—Iowa
1938 Pittsburgh Pirates

FAUNCE, EVERETT—Back—Minnesota
1949 Baltimore Colts (AAFC)

FAUSCH, FRANKLIN—Back—Kalamazoo
1921–22 Evansville Crimson Giants

FAUST, GEORGE—Back—Minnesota
1939 Chicago Cardinals

FAUST, RICHARD—Tackle—Otterbein
1924, 28–29 Dayton Triangles

FAVERTY, HAROLD—Center—Wisconsin
1952 Green Bay Packers

FAWCETT, JACOB—Tackle—SMU
1942, 44 Cleveland Rams
1943 Brooklyn Dodgers
1946 Los Angeles Rams

FAY, JAMES—Back—Canisius
1926 Buffalo Bisons

FAYE, ALLEN—End—Marquette
1922 Green Bay Packers

FEAMSTER, THOMAS—End—Florida State
1956–57 Baltimore Colts

FEARS, THOMAS—End—UCLA
1948–51 Los Angeles Rams
1948, 49, 50 #1 Pass Receiving

FEASTER, WILLIAM—Tackle—Fordham
1929 Orange
1930 Newark

FEATHER, ELVIN—Back—Kansas State Agr.
1927 Cleveland Indians
1928 Detroit Wolverines
1929–30, 32–33 New York Giants
1931 Staten Island Stapletons
1932 Brooklyn Dodgers
1933 Philadelphia Eagles
1934 Cincinnati Reds

FEATHERS, BEATTIE—Back—Tennessee
1934–37 Chicago Bears
1938–39 Brooklyn Dodgers
1940 Green Bay Packers
1934 #1 Ball Carrying

FEBEL, FRED—Guard—Purdue
1935 Chicago Bears

FEDEROVICH, JOHN—Tackle—Davis & Elkins
1941, 46 Chicago Bears

FEDORA, WALTER—Back—George Washington
1942   Brooklyn Dodgers

FEENEY, FRANCIS—Center—Notre Dame
1921   Canton Bulldogs

FEHER, NICHOLAS—Guard—Georgia
1951–54   San Francisco 49ers
1955   Pittsburgh Steelers

FEIST, LOUIS—Tackle—Canisius
1924–26   Buffalo Bisons

FEKETE, EUGENE—Back—Ohio State
1946   Cleveland Browns (AAFC)
1946   Buffalo Bisons (AAFC)

FELBER, FREDERICK—End—North Dakota
1932   Boston Braves
1933   Philadelphia Eagles

FELDHAUS, WILLIAM—Tackle—Cincinnati
1937–40   Detroit Lions

FELKER, ARTHUR—End—Marquette
1951   Green Bay Packers

FELKER, EUGENE—End—Wisconsin
1952   Dallas Texans

FELT, RICHARD—Back—Brigham-Young
1960   New York Titans (AFL)

FELTON, RALPH—Back—Maryland
1954–60   Washington Redskins

FENA, JOSEPH—Guard—Denver
1937   Detroit Lions

FENCL, RICHARD—End—Northwestern
1933   Philadelphia Eagles

FENENBOCK, CHARLES—Back—UCLA
1943–45   Detroit Lions
1946–48   Los Angeles Dons (AAFC)
1948   Chicago Rockets (AAFC)

FENIMORE, ROBERT—Back—Oklahoma A & M
1947   Chicago Bears

FENNEMA, CARL—Center—Washington
1948–49   New York Giants

FENNER, LEE—End—Miami (Ohio)
1923–25   Dayton Triangles

FERGUSON, J. B.—Guard
1932   Chicago Bears
1935   Brooklyn Dodgers

FERGUSON, HOWARD—Back
1953–58   Green Bay Packers
1960   Los Angeles Chargers (AFL)

HOWARD FERGUSON

FERKO, JOHN—Guard—West Chester
1937–38   Philadelphia Eagles

JACK FERRANTE

FERRANTE, JACK—End—None
1941, 1944–50   Philadelphia Eagles

FERRANTI, ORLANDO—Guard—Southern California
1960   Los Angeles Chargers (AFL)

FERRIS, NEIL—Back—Loyola (Los Angeles)
1951–52   Washington Redskins
1952   Philadelphia Eagles

1953   Los Angeles Rams

FERRY, LOUIS—Tackle—Villanova
1949   Green Bay Packers
1951   Chicago Cardinals
1952-55   Pittsburgh Steelers

FETZ, GUSTAVE—Back
1923   Chicago Bears
1923   Canton Bulldogs

FICHMAN, LEON—Tackle—Alabama
1946-47   Detroit Lions

FICHTNER, ROSS—Back—Purdue
1960   Cleveland Browns

**FIEDLER, WILLIAM—Guard—
Pennsylvania**
1938   Philadelphia Eagles

**FIELD, HARRY—Tackle—Oregon
State**
1934-36   Chicago Cardinals

**FIELD, RICHARD—Guard—
Columbia**
1939-40   Philadelphia Eagles

FIELDS, GEORGE—End—Bakersfield
1960   Oakland Raiders (AFL)

FIFE, RALPH—Guard—Pittsburgh
1942, 45   Chicago Cardinals
1946   Pittsburgh Steelers

FIGNER, GEORGE—Back—Colorado
1953   Chicago Bears

FILAK, JOHN—Tackle—Penn State
1926-29   Frankford Yellowjackets

FILCHOCK, FRANK—Back—Indiana
1938   Pittsburgh Pirates
1938-41, 44-55   Washington Redskins
1946   New York Giants
1950   Baltimore Colts
1944   #1 Passing

**FILIPOWICZ, STEPHEN—Back—
Fordham**
1945-46   New York Giants

**FILIPSKI, EUGENE—Back—
Villanova**
1956-57   New York Giants

FINCH, OLIN—Back—Whittier
1926   Los Angeles

FINKS, JAMES—Back—Tulsa
1949-55   Pittsburgh Steelers

FINLAY, JOHN—Guard—UCLA
1947-51   Los Angeles Rams

**FINLEY, JAMES—Guard—Michigan
State**
1942   Green Bay Packers

JOHN FINLAY

FINN, BERNARD—Back—Holy Cross
1930   Newark
1930, 32   Staten Island Stapletons
1933   Chicago Cardinals

FINN, JOHN—Back—Villanova
1924   Frankford Yellowjackets

**FINNERAN, GARRY—Tackle—
Southern California**
1960   Los Angeles Chargers (AFL)

FINNIN, THOMAS—Tackle—Detroit
1953-56   Baltimore Colts
1957   Chicago Cardinals

**FIORENTINO, ALBERT—Guard—
Boston College**
1943-44   Washington Redskins
1945   Boston Yanks

**FIORENTINO, EDWARD—End—
Boston College**
1944, 47   Boston Yanks

FISCHER, CLETUS—Back—Nebraska
1949   New York Giants

**FISCHER, WILLIAM—Tackle—
Notre Dame**
1949-53   Chicago Cardinals

FISHEL, RICHARD—Back—Syracuse
1933-34   Brooklyn Dodgers

**FISHER, CLARK—Back—Catholic
Univ.**
1926   Milwaukee Badgers

FISHER, DARRELL—Back—Iowa
1925   Buffalo Bisons
1925   Canton Bulldogs

**FISHER, EVERETT—Back—Santa
Clara**
1938-39   Chicago Cardinals
1940   Pittsburgh Steelers

FISHER, RAYMOND—Tackle— Illinois State East
1959 Pittsburgh Steelers

FISHER, ROBERT—Tackle— Southern California
1940 Washington Redskins

FISHMAN, ABRAHAM—Guard
1921–22 Evansville Crimson Giants

FISHMAN, ALEXANDER—Tackle
1921–22 Evansville Crimson Giants

FISK, WILLIAM—End—Southern California
1940–43 Detroit Lions
1946–47 San Francisco 49ers (AAFC)
1948 Los Angeles Dons (AAFC)

FISKE, MAX—Back—DePaul
1936–38 Pittsburgh Steelers
1937 Chicago Cardinals

FISS, GALEN—Back—Kansas
1956–60 Cleveland Browns

FITZGERALD, DONALD—Center— Holy Cross
1930 Staten Island Stapletons
1931 Providence Steamrollers

FITZGERALD, FREEMAN—Back— Notre Dame
1921 Rock Island Independents
1923 Toledo Maroons

FITZGIBBONS, PAUL—Back— Creighton
1926 Detroit Panthers
1927 Frankford Yellowjackets
1928 Chicago Cardinals
1930–32 Green Bay Packers

FITZKE, ROBERT—Back—Idaho
1925 Frankford Yellowjackets

FLAGERMAN, JOHN—Center—St. Mary's (Cal.)
1948 Los Angeles Dons (AAFC)

FLAHERTY, PAT—End—Marquette
1923 Chicago Bears

FLAHERTY, RAY—End—Gonzaga
1927–28 New York Yankees
1928–35 New York Giants

FLAHERTY, RICHARD—End— Marquette
1926–27 Green Bay Packers

FLANAGAN, LATHAM—End— Carnegie Tech.
1931 Chicago Bears
1931 Chicago Cardinals

FLANAGAN, RICHARD—Guard— Ohio State

1948–49 Chicago Bears
1950–52 Detroit Lions
1953–56 Pittsburgh Steelers

FLANAGAN, WILLIAM—Back— Pittsburgh
1925–26 Pottsville Maroons

FLATTERY, WILSON—Back— Wooster
1925–26 Canton Bulldogs

FLAVIN, JOHN—Back—Georgetown
1923–24 Buffalo Bisons

FLECKENSTEIN, WILLIAM— Center—Iowa
1925–30 Chicago Bears
1930 Portsmouth Spartans
1931 Frankford Yellowjackets
1931 Brooklyn Dodgers

FLEISCHMAN, GODFREY—Guard— Purdue
1925–26 Detroit Panthers
1927–29 Providence Steamrollers

FLEMING, DONALD—Back— Florida
1960 Cleveland Browns

FLEMING, MALCOLM—Back— Washington & Jefferson
1925 Canton Bulldogs

FLENNIKEN, MAX—Back— Centenary
1930 Chicago Cardinals
1930–31 New York Giants

FLETCHER, OLIVER—Guard— Southern California
1949 Los Angeles Dons (AAFC)
1950 Baltimore Colts

FLOHR, LESTER—Tackle—Bethany
1927 Cleveland Bulldogs

FLORES, THOMAS—Back— College of Pacific
1960 Oakland Raiders (AFL)

FLOWER, JAMES—Tackle—Ohio State
1921–24 Akron Steels

FLOWERS, BERNARD—End— Purdue
1956 Baltimore Colts

FLOWERS, CHARLES—Back— Mississippi
1960 Los Angeles Chargers (AFL)

FLOWERS, KEITH—Center—TCU
1952 Detroit Lions
1952 Dallas Texans
1953 Baltimore Colts

FLOWERS, RICHARD—Back—
Northwestern
1953   Baltimore Colts

FLOWERS, ROBERT—Center—
Texas Tech.
1942–49   Green Bay Packers

FLOYD, BOBBY JACK—Back—TCU
1952   Green Bay Packers
1953   Chicago Bears

FLOYD, DONALD—End—TCU
1960   Houston Oilers (AFL)

FLOYD, JOHN—Tackle—Ouachita
1935   Boston Redskins

FLYNN, DONALD—Back—Houston
1960   Dallas Texans (AFL)

FLYNN, FURLONG—End—Cornell
1926   Hartford Blues

FLYNN, PAUL—Back—Minnesota
1922–23   Minneapolis Marines

FOLDBERG, HENRY—End—West
Point
1948   Brooklyn Dodgers (AAFC)
1949   Chicago Hornets (AAFC)

FOLEY, JAMES—Back—Syracuse
1926   Hartford Blues

FOLK, RICHARD—Guard—Clemson
1939   Brooklyn Dodgers

FOLLET, BERYL—Back—New York
Univ.
1930–31   Staten Island Stapletons

FOLTZ, VERNON—Center—St.
Vincent's
1944   Washington Redskins
1945   Pittsburgh Steelers

FOLZ, ARTHUR—Back—Chicago
1923–25   Chicago Cardinals

FORD, ADRIAN—Back—Lafayette
1927   Pottsville Maroons
1927   Frankford Yellowjackets

FORD, FREDERICK—Back—
California Polytech
1960   Buffalo Bills (AFL)
1960   Los Angeles Chargers (AFL)

FORD, HENRY—Back—Pittsburgh
1956   Pittsburgh Steelers

FORD, LEONARD—End—Michigan
1948–49   Los Angeles Dons (AAFC)
1950–57   Cleveland Browns
1958   Green Bay Packers

FORD, SALEM—Back—Louisville
1922–23   Louisville Colonels

FORDHAM, JAMES—Back—Georgia
1944–45   Chicago Bears

FORESTER, HERSCHEL—Guard—
SMU
1954–57   Cleveland Browns

FORESTER, GEORGE "BILL"—
Guard—SMU
1953–60   Green Bay Packers

FORKOVITCH, NICHOLAS—
Back—William & Mary
1948   Brooklyn Dodgers (AAFC)

FORREST, EDWARD—Center—
Santa Clara
1946–47   San Francisco 49ers (AAFC)

FORTE, ALDO—Guard—Montana
1939–41, 46   Chicago Bears
1946   Detroit Lions
1947   Green Bay Packers

ALDO FORTE

FORTE, ROBERT—Back—Arkansas
1946–50, 52–53   Green Bay Packers

FORTMANN, DANIEL—Guard—
Colgate
1936–46   Chicago Bears

FORTMEYER, ALBEN—Back
1921   Cincinnati Celts

FORTUNATO, JOSEPH—Back—
Mississippi State
1955–60   Chicago Bears

FORTUNE, BURNELL—Guard—
DePaul
1923   Minneapolis Marines
1924   Kenosha
1924–25   Hammond Pros
1926   Louisville Colonels

FOSDICK, ROBERT—Guard—Iowa

1923 Minneapolis Marines

**FOSTER, FREDERICK—Tackle—
Syracuse**
1923 Buffalo Bisons
1923–24 Rochester Jeffersons
1924 Milwaukee Badgers

FOSTER, JAMES—Back—Bucknell
1925 Buffalo Bisons

**FOSTER, RALPH—Tackle—
Oklahoma A & M**
1945–46 Chicago Cardinals

FOSTER, ROBERT—Tackle
1922–23 Racine Legion

FOURNET, SIDNEY—Guard—LSU
1955–56 Los Angeles Rams
1957 Pittsburgh Steeler
1960 Dallas Texans (AFL)

**FOWLER, AUBREY—Back—
Arkansas**
1948 Baltimore Colts (AAFC)

**FOWLER, WILLMER—Back—
Northwestern**
1960 Buffalo Bills (AFL)

FOX, SAMUEL—End—Ohio State
1945–46 New York Giants

FOX, TERRANCE—Back—Miami
1941, 45 Philadelphia Eagles
1946 Miami Seahawks (AAFC)

FRAHM, HERALD—Back—Nebraska
1932 Staten Island Stapletons
1935 Boston Redskins
1935 Philadelphia Eagles

**FRANCESCHI, PETER—Back—San
Francisco**
1946 San Francisco 49ers (AAFC)

FRANCIS, EUGENE—Back—Chicago
1926 Chicago Cardinals

**FRANCIS, JOSEPH—Back—Oregon
State**
1958–59 Green Bay Packers

**FRANCIS, SAMUEL—Back—
Nebraska**
1937–38 Chicago Bears
1939 Pittsburgh Steelers
1939–40 Brooklyn Dodgers

**FRANCK, GEORGE—Back—
Minnesota**
1941, 45–47 New York Giants

**FRANCKHAUSER, THOMAS—
Back—Purdue**
1959 Los Angeles Rams
1960 Dallas Cowboys

**FRANCO, EDWARD—Guard—
Fordham**
1944 Boston Redskins

FRANK, HARRY—Back—Temple
1930 Newark

FRANK, JAMES—Back—Penn. State
1930 Newark

**FRANK, JOSEPH—Tackle—
Georgetown**
1941–42 Philadelphia Eagles
1943 Phil-Pitt

**FRANKIAN, MALCOLM—End—St.
Mary's (Cal.)**
1933 Boston Redskins
1934–35 New York Giants

**FRANKLIN, NORMAN—Back—
Oregon State**
1935–37 Brooklyn Dodgers

**FRANKLIN, PAUL—End—Franklin
College**
1930–33, 35 Chicago Bears

**FRANKLIN, ROBERT—Back—
Mississippi**
1960 Cleveland Browns

**FRANKOWSKI, RAYMOND—
Guard—Washington**
1945 Green Bay Packers
1946–48 Los Angeles Dons (AAFC)

**FRANTA, HERBERT—Tackle—St.
Thomas**
1929–30 Minneapolis Redjackets
1930 Green Bay Packers

**FRASER, GEORGE—Back—
Rutgers**
1927 New York Yankees

FREEMAN, JOHN—Guard—Texas
1946 Brooklyn Dodgers (AAFC)

**FREEMAN, ROBERT—Back—
Auburn**
1957–58 Cleveland Browns
1959 Green Bay Packers
1960 Philadelphia Eagles

FREITAS, JESSE—Back—Santa Clara
1946–47 San Francisco 49ers (AAFC)
1948 Chicago Rockets (AAFC)
1949 Buffalo Bills (AAFC)

FRENCH, BARRY—Guard—Purdue
1947–49 Baltimore Colts (AAFC)
1950 Baltimore Colts
1951 Detroit Lions

**FRENCH, WALTER—Back—West
Point**
1922 Rochester Jeffersons

1925   Pottsville Maroons
FREY, GLENN—Back—Temple
1936–37   Philadelphia Eagles

ROBERT FREEMAN

FREY, RICHARD—End—Texas A&M
1960   Dallas Texans (AFL)

**FRICK, RAYMOND—Center—
Pennsylvania**
1941   Brooklyn Dodgers

**FRIENDLUND, ROBERT—End—
Michigan State**
1946   Philadelphia Eagles

**FRIEDMAN, BENJAMIN—Back—
Michigan**
1927   Cleveland Indians
1928   Detroit Wolverines
1929–31   New York Giants
1932–33   Brooklyn Dodgers

FRIEDMAN, JACOB—End
1926   Hartford Blues

**FRIEDMAN, ROBERT—Guard—
Washington**
1944   Philadelphia Eagles

FRIEND, BENJAMIN—Tackle—LSU
1939   Cleveland Rams

**FRIES, SHERWOOD—Guard—
Colorado State**
1943   Green Bay Packers

FRITSCH
1921   Evansville Crimson Giants

FRITSCH, ERNEST—Center—Detroit
1960   St. Louis Cardinals

**FRITSCH, THEODORE—Back—
Wisconsin State**
1942–50   Green Bay Packers
1946   #1 Scoring
1946   #1 Field Goals

**FRITTS, GEORGE—Tackle—
Clemson**
1945   Philadelphia Eagles

FRITZ, RALPH—Guard—Michigan
1941   Philadelphia Eagles

**FRKETICH, LEONARD—Tackle—
Penn State**
1945   Pittsburgh Steelers

**FROHM, MARTIN—Tackle—
Mississippi State**
1944   Brooklyn Dodgers

**FRONCZEK, ANDREW—Tackle—
Richmond**
1941   Brooklyn Dodgers

**FRUGONNE, JAMES—Back—
Syracuse**
1925   New York Giants

**FRUMP, MILTON—Guard—Ohio
Wesleyan**
1930   Chicago Bears

**FRUTIG, EDWARD—End—
Michigan**
1941, 45   Green Bay Packers
1945–46   Detroit Lions

FRY, ROBERT—Tackle—Kentucky
1953, 56–59   Los Angeles Rams
1960   Dallas Cowboys

FRY, WESLEY—Back—Iowa
1927   New York Yankees
1932   Staten Island Stapletons

**FRYER, KENNETH—Back—West
Virginia**
1944   Brooklyn Dodgers

FUCCI, DOMINIC—Back—Kentucky
1955   Detroit Lions

**FUGLER, RICHARD—Tackle—
Tulane**
1952   Pittsburgh Steelers

**FULCHER, WILLIAM—Tackle—
Georgia Tech.**
1956–58   Washington Redskins

FULLER, FRANK—Tackle—Kentucky
1953, 55, 57–58   Los Angeles Rams
1959   Chicago Cardinals
1960   St. Louis Cardinals

FULLER, LAWRENCE—Back
1944–45   Washington Redskins
1945   Chicago Cardinals

**FULLERTON, EDWARD—Back—
Maryland**
1953   Pittsburgh Steelers

FULTON, THEODORE—Guard—
Oglethorpe
1931–32   Brooklyn Dodgers

FUQUA, RAYMOND—End—SMU
1935–36   Brooklyn Dodgers

FURST, ANTHONY—Tackle—Dayton
1940–41, 45   Detroit Lions

* * *

GAFFNEY, JAMES—Back—
Tennessee
1945–47   Washington Redskins

GAFFORD, ROY—Back—Auburn
1946   Miami Seahawks (AAFC)
1946–48   Brooklyn Dodgers (AAFC)

GAGE, ROBERT—Back—Clemson
1949–50   Pittsburgh Steelers

GAGNON, ROY—Guard—Oregon
1935   Detroit Lions

GAIN, ROBERT—Tackle—Kentucky
1952, 54–60   Cleveland Browns

GAINER, CHARLES—End—North
Dakota
1939   Chicago Cardinals

GAIVER, EINAR—Back—
North Dakota
1922   Hammond Pros
1923   Rock Island
1924   Racine Legion
1925   Hammond Independents
1926   Louisville Colonels

GALAZIN, STANLEY—Center
Villanova
1937–39   New York Giants

GALIFFA, ARNOLD—Back—West
Point
1953   New York Giants
1954   San Francisco 49ers

GALIMORE, WILLIE—Back—
Florida A & M
1957–60   Chicago Bears

GALLAGHER, BERNARD—Guard—
Pennsylvania
1947   Los Angeles Dons (AAFC)

GALLAGHER, EDWARD—Tackle—
Washington & Jefferson
1928   New York Yankees
1928   New York Giants

GALLARNEAU, HUGH—Back—
Stanford
1940–42, 45–47   Chicago Bears

GALLOVICH, ANTHONY—Back—
Wake Forest
1941   Cleveland Rams

GALVIN, JOHN—Back—Purdue
1947   Baltimore Colts (AAFC)

GAMBINO, LUCIEN—Back—
Maryland
1948–49   Baltimore Colts

GAMBOLD, ROBERT—Back—
Washington State
1953   Philadelphia Eagles

GAMERIO—Guard
1930   Newark

GANDEE, SHERWIN—End—Ohio
State
1952   Dallas Texans
1952–56   Detroit Lions

SHERWIN GANDEE

GANSBERG, ALFRED—Tackle—
Miami—Ohio
1926   Louisville Colonels

GANTENBEIN, MILTON—End—
Wisconsin
1931–40   Green Bay Packers
1932   Staten Island Stapletons

GAONA, ROBERT—Tackle—Wake
Forest
1953–56   Pittsburgh Steelers
1957   Philadelphia Eagles

GARDELLA, AUGUSTUS—Back—
Holy Cross
1922   Green Bay Packers

GARDNER, GEORGE—End—Carlisle
1923–24   Cleveland Indians

GARDNER, MILTON—Guard—
Wisconsin
1921   Detroit Panthers
1921   Buffalo All American
1922–26   Green Bay Packers
1924   Kenosha

GARLIN, DONALD—Back—
Southern California
1949 San Francisco 49ers (AAFC)
1950 San Francisco 49ers

GARNAAS, WILFORD—Back—
Minnesota
1946–47 Pittsburgh Steelers

GARNER, ROBERT—Guard
1945 New York Giants

GARNER, ROBERT—Back—
Fresno State
1960 Los Angeles Chargers (AFL)

GARNJOST, DONALD—Guard—
Columbia
1921 Evansville Crimson Giants

GARRETT, ALFRED—End—
Rutgers
1922 Milwaukee Badgers

GARRETT, ROBERT—Back—
Stanford
1954 Green Bay Packers

GARRETT, THURMAN—Center—
Oklahoma A & M
1947–48 Chicago Bears

GARRETT, WILLIAM—Guard—
Mississippi State
1948–49 Baltimore Colts (AAFC)
1950 Chicago Bears

GARRON, LAWRENCE—Back—
Illinois Western
1960 Boston Patriots (AFL)

GARVEY, ARTHUR "HEC"—Tackle
—Notre Dame
1922–25 Chicago Bears
1926 Hartford Blues
1926, 30 Brooklyn Dodgers
1927–28 New York Giants
1929 Providence Steamrollers
1931 Staten Island Stapletons

GARVEY, FRANCIS—Tackle—Holy
Cross
1925–26 Providence Steamrollers

GARZA, DANIEL—End—Oregon
1948 New York Yankees (AAFC)
1951 New York Yanks

GARZONI, MICHAEL—Guard—
Southern California
1947 Washington Redskins
1948 New York Giants
1948 New York Yankees (AAFC)

GASPARELLA, JOSEPH—Back—
Notre Dame
1948, 50–51 Pittsburgh Steelers
1951 Chicago Cardinals

GATEWOOD, LESTER—Center—
Baylor
1946–47 Green Bay Packers

GATSKI, FRANK—Center—Marshall
1946–49 Cleveland Browns (AAFC)
1950–56 Cleveland Browns
1957 Detroit Lions

GAUDIO, ROBERT—Guard—Ohio
State
1947–49 Cleveland Browns (AAFC)
1951 Cleveland Browns

GAUER, CHARLES—Back—
Colgate
1943 Phil-Pitt
1944–45 Philadelphia Eagles

GAUL, FRANK—Tackle—Notre Dame
1949 New York Bulldogs

GAULKE, HAROLD—Back
1921–22 Columbus Tigers

GAUSTAD, ARTHUR—Guard
1922–23 Minneapolis Marines

GAUTT, PRENTICE—Back—
Oklahoma
1960 Cleveland Browns

GAVIER, WILLIAM—Back—
Notre Dame
1924 Racine Legion

GAVIGAN, MICHAEL—Back—
St. Bonaventure
1923 Rochester Kodaks

GAVIN, CHARLES—End—
Tennessee A & I
1960 Denver Broncos (AFL)

GAVIN, FRITZ—End—Marquette
1921, 23 Green Bay Packers

GAVIN, PATRICK "BUCK"—Back
1921 Detroit Panthers
1921–25 Rock Island Independents
1922 Buffalo All Americans
1926 Hammond Pros

GAY, KENNETH—Tackle—Minnesota
1925 Buffalo Bisons
1926 Racine Legion
1926 Milwaukee Badgers

GAY, WILLIAM—Back—Notre Dame
1951–52 Chicago Cardinals

GAYER, WALTER—Tackle—
Creighton
1926 Duluth Eskimos

GAZIANO, FRANK—Guard—Holy
Cross
1944 Boston Yanks

GEDMAN, EUGENE—Back—Indiana
1953, 56–58 Detroit Lions

GEHRKE, BRUCE—End—Columbia
1948   New York Giants

GEHRKE, CLARENCE FRED—
Back—Utah
1940, 45   Cleveland Rams
1946–49   Los Angeles Rams
1950   San Francisco 49ers
1950   Chicago Cardinals

GELATKA, CHARLES—End—
Mississippi State
1937–40   New York Giants

GENTRY, BYRON—Guard—Southern
California
1937–38   Pittsburgh Pirates
1939   Pittsburgh Steelers

GENTRY, CASSIUS—Guard—
Oklahoma
1930–31   Providence Steamrollers

GENTRY, DALE—End—Washington
State
1946–48   Los Angeles Dons (AAFC)

GENTRY, ELMER—Back—Tulsa
1941   Washington Redskins

GEORGE, KARL—Center—Carroll
1922   Racine Legion

GEORGE, RAYMOND—Tackle—
Southern California
1939   Detroit Lions
1940   Philadelphia Eagles

GEORGE, WILLIAM—Guard—Wake
Forest
1952–60   Chicago Bears

GERBER, ELWOOD—Guard—
Alabama
1942   Philadelphia Eagles
1945   Washington Redskins

GEREMSKY, THADDEUS—End—
Pittsburgh
1951   Detroit Lions

GERI, JOSEPH—Back—Georgia
1949–51   Pittsburgh Steelers
1952   Chicago Cardinals

GERMAN, JAMES—Back—Centre
1939   Washington Redskins
1940   Chicago Cardinals

GETCHELL, GORHAM—End—
Temple
1943   Philadelphia Eagles
1947   Baltimore Colts

GETZ, FREDERICK—End—
Chattanooga
1930   Brooklyn Dodgers

GEYER, WILLIAM—Back—Colgate
1941–43, 46   Chicago Bears

GHECAS, LOUIS—Back—Georgetown
1941   Philadelphia Eagles

GHEE, MILTON—Back—Dartmouth
1921–22   Canton Bulldogs
1922–23   Hammond Pros

GHERSANICH, VERNON—Guard—
Alabama Polytech.
1942–43   Chicago Cardinals

GIANCANELLI, HAROLD—Back—
Loyola
1953–56   Philadelphia Eagles

HAROLD GIANCANELLI

GIANNELLI, MARIO—Guard—
Boston College
1948–51   Philadelphia Eagles

GIANNONI, JOHN—End—St. Mary's
(Cal.)
1938   Cleveland Rams

GIBBONS, JAMES—End—Iowa
1958–60   Detroit Lions

GIBRON, ABRAHAM—Guard—
Purdue
1949   Buffalo Bills (AAFC)
1950–56   Cleveland Browns
1956–57   Philadelphia Eagles
1958–59   Chicago Bears

GIBSON, BILLY JOE—Center—Tulsa
1942–44   Cleveland Rams
1943   Washington Redskins
1946–47   Brooklyn Dodgers (AAFC)

GIBSON, DENVER—Guard—Grove
City
1930–34   New York Giants

GIBSON, GEORGE—Guard—
Minnesota
1929   Chicago Cardinals
1930   Frankford Yellowjackets
1930   Minneapolis Marines

**GIBSON, PAUL—End—North
Carolina State**
1947–49   Buffalo Bills (AAFC)

GIBSON, RICHARD—Guard—Centre
1922–23   Louisville Colonels

**GIDDENS, HERSCHEL—Tackle—
Louisiana Tech.**
1938   Philadelphia Eagles
1944   Boston Redskins

**GIFFORD, FRANK—Back—Southern
California**
1952–60   New York Giants

GIFFORD, ROBERT—Back—Denver
1942   Brooklyn Dodgers

GIFT, WAYNE—Back—Purdue
1937   Cleveland Rams

**GILBERT, KLINE—Tackle—
Mississippi**
1953–57   Chicago Bears

**GILBERT, WALTER—Back—
Valparaiso**
1923–26   Duluth Kelleys

**GILCHRIST, GEORGE—Tackle—
Tennessee State**
1953   Chicago Cardinals

**GILDEA, DENNIS—Center—Holy
Cross**
1926   Hartford Blues

**GILDEA, JOHN—Back—St.
Bonaventure**
1935–37   Pittsburgh Pirates
1938   New York Giants

GILL, SLOKO—Guard—Youngstown
1942   Detroit Lions

**GILLETTE, JAMES—Back—
Virginia**
1940, 44–45   Cleveland Rams
1946   Boston Yanks
1947   Washington Redskins
1947   Green Bay Packers
1948   Detroit Lions

**GILLIES, FREDERICK—Tackle—
Cornell**
1921–28   Chicago Cardinals
1923   Toledo Maroons
1923   Canton Bulldogs

GILLIS, DANIEL—Center—Rice
1958–59   Chicago Cardinals
1960   St. Louis Cardinals

GILLO, HENRY—Back—Colgate
1922–24, 26   Racine Legion
1925   Milwaukee Badgers

GILLOM, HORACE—End—Nevada

1947–49   Cleveland Browns (AAFC)
1950–56   Cleveland Browns
1951   #1 Punting

GILLORY, BYRON—Back—Texas
1949   Baltimore Colts (AAFC)

GILMER, HARRY—Back—Alabama
1948–54   Washington Redskins
1955–56   Detroit Lions

GILSON, ROBERT—Guard—Colgate
1930   Minneapolis Redjackets
1930   Frankford Yellowjackets
1931   Brooklyn Dodgers

**GINNEY, JERRY—Guard—Santa
Clara**
1940   Philadelphia Eagles

**GINSBERG, ISRAEL—End—South
Dakota**
1935   Boston Redskins

GIRARD, EARL—Back—Wisconsin
1948–51   Green Bay Packers
1952–56   Detroit Lions
1957   Pittsburgh Steelers

**GLADCHUK, CHESTER—Center—
Boston College**
1940–41, 46–47   New York Giants

CHESTER GLADCHUK

**GLADDEN, JAMES MACK—End—
Missouri**
1934   St. Louis Gunners

GLAMP, JOSEPH—Back—LSU
1947–49   Pittsburgh Steelers

GLASS, WILLIAM—Center—Baylor
1958–60   Detroit Lions

GLASSGOW, WILLIS—Back—Iowa
1930   Portsmouth Spartans
1931   Chicago Cardinals

GLASSMAN, MORRIS—Guard—Wilmington
1921–22   Columbus Tigers
1929   Buffalo Bisons

GLATZ, FRED—End—Pittsburgh
1956   Pittsburgh Steelers

GLENN, HOWARD—Guard—Linfield
1960   New York Titans (AFL)
      Died Oct. 9, 1960, after game against Houston.

GLENN, WILLIAM—Back—Illinois Teachers
1941, 44   Chicago Bears

GLENNIE—End
1926   Racine Legion

GLICK, EDWARD—Back—Marquette
1921–22   Green Bay Packers

GLICK, FRED—Back—Colorado A&M
1959   Chicago Cardinals
1960   St. Louis Cardinals

GLICK, GARY—Back—Colorado A & M
1956–59   Pittsburgh Steelers
1959–60   Washington Redskins

GARY GLICK

GLODEN, FREDERICK—Back—Tulane
1941   Philadelphia Eagles
1946   Miami Seahawks (AAFC)

GOAD, PAUL—Back—Abilene Christian
1956   San Francisco 49ers

GOB, ARTHUR—End—Pittsburgh
1959   Washington Redskins
1960   Los Angeles Chargers (AFL)

GOBLE, LESTER—Back—Temple
1954–55   Chicago Cardinals

GODDARD, EDWARD—Back—Washington State
1936–37   Brooklyn Dodgers
1937–38   Cleveland Rams

GODFREY, HERBERT—End—Washington State
1942   Cleveland Rams

GODWIN, WALTER—Guard—Georgia Tech.
1929   Staten Island Stapletons

GODWIN, WILLIAM—Center—Georgia
1947–48   Boston Yanks

GOEBEL, PAUL—End—Michigan
1923–25   Columbus Tigers
1925   Chicago Bears

GOETZ, ANGUS—Tackle—Michigan
1922   Buffalo All Americans
1923   Columbus Tigers

GOFF, CLARK—Tackle—Florida
1940   Pittsburgh Steelers

GOLDBERG, MARSHALL—Back—Pittsburgh
1939–43, 46–48   Chicago Cardinals

GOLDENBERG, CHARLES—Guard—Wisconsin
1933–45   Green Bay Packers

GOLDFEIN, JERSEY—Back—Wisconsin State
1927   Duluth Eskimos

GOLDING, JOSEPH—Back—Oklahoma
1947–48   Boston Yanks
1949   New York Bulldogs
1950–51   New York Yanks

GOLDMAN, SAMUEL—End—Howard
1944–47   Boston Yanks
1948   Chicago Cardinals
1949   Detroit Lions

GOLDSBERRY, JOHN—Tackle—Indiana
1949–50   Chicago Cardinals

GOLDSMITH, EARL—End
1921–22   Evansville Crimson Giants

GOLDSTEIN, ALAN—End—North Carolina
1960   Oakland Raiders (AFL)

GOLDSTON, RALPH—Back—Youngstown
1952, 54–55   Philadelphia Eagles

RALPH GOLDSTON

GOLEMBESKI, ANTHONY—End—
Holy Cross
1925–26, 29 Providence Steamrollers

GOLEMGESKE, GORN—Tackle—
Wisconsin
1937–40 Brooklyn Dodgers

GOLLOMB, RUDOLPH—Guard—
Wisconsin
1936 Philadelphia Eagles

GOLSEN, EUGENE—Back—
Georgetown
1926 Louisville Colonels

GOLSEN, THOMAS—Back—
Georgetown
1926 Louisville Colonels

GOMPERS, WILLIAM—Back—Notre
Dame
1948 Buffalo Bills (AAFC)

GONDA, GEORGE—Back—Duquesne
1942, 45–46 Pittsburgh Steelers

GONSOULIN, AUSTIN—Back—
Baylor
1960 Denver Broncos (AFL)

GONYA, ROBERT—Tackle—
Northwestern
1933–34 Philadelphia Eagles

GONZAGA, JOHN—Tackle—
Northwestern
1956–59 San Francisco 49ers
1960 Dallas Cowboys

GOODBREAD, ROYCE—Back—
Florida
1930 Frankford Yellowjackets
1930 Minneapolis Redjackets
1931 Providence Steamrollers

GOODE, ROBERT—Back—Texas
A & M
1949–51, 54–55 Washington Redskins
1955 Philadelphia Eagles

GOODMAN, AUBREY—Tackle—
Chicago
1927 Chicago Cardinals

GOODMAN, HENRY—Tackle—West
Virginia
1942 Detroit Lions

GOODNIGHT, CLYDE—End—Tulsa
1945–48 Green Bay Packers
1949–50 Washington Redskins

GOODNIGHT, OWEN—Back—
Hardin-Simmons
1941 Cleveland Rams
1946 Chicago Bears

GOODWIN, EARL—Tackle—
Bucknell
1928 Pottsville Maroons

GOODWIN, MYRL—Back—Bucknell
1928 Pottsville Maroons

GOODWIN, TOD—End—West
Virginia
1935–36 New York Giants
1935 #1 Pass Receiving

GOODYEAR, JOHN—Back—
Marquette
1942 Washington Redskins

GOOLSBY, JAMES—End—
Mississippi State
1940 Cleveland Rams

GORDON, LOUIS—Tackle—Illinois
1930–35 Chicago Cardinals
1931 Brooklyn Dodgers
1936–37 Green Bay Packers
1938 Chicago Bears

GORDON, ROBERT—Back—
Tennessee
1958 Chicago Cardinals
1960 Houston Oilers (AFL)

GORDY, JOHN—Tackle—Tennessee
1957, 59–60 Detroit Lions

GORE, GORDON—Back—Oklahoma
Southwest Teachers
1938–39 Detroit Lions

GORGAL, ALEX—Back
1923 Rock Island Independents

GORGAL, KENNETH—Back—Purdue
1950, 53–54 Cleveland Browns
1955 Chicago Bears
1956 Green Bay Packers

KENNETH GORGAL

GORGONE, PETER—Back—
Muhlenberg
1946 New York Giants

GORINSKI, WALTER—Back—LSU
1946 Pittsburgh Steelers

GORMAN, EARL—Guard
1921 Evansville Crimson Giants
1922–23 Racine Legion
1924 Kenosha

GORRILL, CHARLES—End—Ohio
State
1926 Columbus Tigers

GOSS, DONALD—Tackle—SMU
1956 Cleveland Browns

GOSS, NORMAN—Tackle—Case
1923 Toledo Maroons

GOSSAGE, EUGENE—Tackle—
Northwestern
1960 Philadelphia Eagles

GOVERNALI, PAUL—Back—
Columbia
1946–47 Boston Yanks
1948–49 New York Giants

GRABFELDER, EARL—Back—
Kentucky
1926 Louisville Colonels

GRABINSKI, THADDEUS—Center
1939–40 Pittsburgh Steelers

GRACE, LESLIE—End—Temple
1930 Newark

GRAHAM, ALFRED—Guard—Ohio
1925–29 Dayton Triangles
1930–31 Providence Steamrollers
1932–33 Chicago Cardinals

GRAHAM, CLARENCE—Back
1928 Dayton Triangles

GRAHAM, FRED—End—West
Virginia
1926 Frankford Yellowjackets

GRAHAM, LESTER—Guard—Tulsa
1938 Detroit Lions

GRAHAM, LYLE—Center—Richmond
1941 Philadelphia Eagles

GRAHAM, MICHAEL—Back—
Cincinnati
1948 Los Angeles Dons (AAFC)

GRAHAM, OTTO—Back—
Northwestern
1947–49 Cleveland Browns (AAFC)
1950–55 Cleveland Browns
1953, 55 #1 Passing

GRAHAM, THOMAS—Guard—
Temple
1935 Philadelphia Eagles

GRAIN, EDWIN—Guard—
Pennsylvania
1947 New York Yankees (AAFC)
1947–48 Baltimore Colts (AAFC)

GRANATO, SAMUEL—Tackle
1943 Brooklyn Dodgers

GRANDELIUS, EVERETT—Back—
Michigan State
1953 New York Giants

GRANDERSON, RUFUS—Tackle—
Prairie View
1960 Dallas Texans (AFL)

GRANDINETTE, GEORGE—
Guard—Fordham
1943 Brooklyn Dodgers

GRANGE, GARLAND—End—Illinois
1929–31 Chicago Bears

GRANGE, HAROLD—Back—Illinois
1925, 28–34 Chicago Bears
1927 New York Yankees

GRANT, AARON—Center—
Chattanooga
1930 Portsmouth Spartans

GRANT, HARRY—End—Minnesota
1951–52 Philadelphia Eagles

GRANT, HUGH—Back—St. Mary's
(Cal.)
1928 Chicago Cardinals

GRANT, LEONARD—Tackle—New
York Univ.
1930–37 New York Giants

GRANT, ROSS—Guard—New York
Univ.

1932 Staten Island Stapletons
1933–34 Cincinnati Reds

GRANTHAM, LAWRENCE—Guard
—Mississippi
1960 New York Titans (AFL)

GRAU, ARTHUR—Guard
1923 St. Louis
1924 Kenosha

GRATE, CARL—Center—Georgia
1945 New York Giants

GRAVES, RAYMOND—Center—
Tennessee
1942, 46 Philadelphia Eagles
1943 Phil-Pitt

GRAY, KENNETH—Back—
Howard-Payne
1958–59 Chicago Cardinals
1960 St. Louis Cardinals

GRAY, SAMUEL—End—Tulsa
1946–47 Pittsburgh Steélers

GRAY, WILLIAM—Guard—Oregon
State
1947–48 Washington Redskins

GRAY HORSE—Back
1922 Oorang Indians

GREAVES, GARY—Guard—Miami
(Fla.)
1960 Houston Oilers (AFL)

GREEN, FRANK—Back—Tulsa
1934 Chicago Cardinals

GREEN, J. B.—Tackle
1926 Louisville Colonels
1926–27 Chicago Cardinals

GREEN, JEROME—End—Georgia
Tech
1960 Boston Patriots (AFL)

GREEN, JOHN—End—Tulsa
1947–51 Philadelphia Eagles

GREEN, JOHN—Back—Chattanooga
1960 Buffalo Bills (AFL)

GREEN, NELSON—Tackle—Tulsa
1948 New York Yankees (AAFC)

GREEN, ROBERT—Back—Florida
1960 Pittsburgh Steelers

GREENBERG, BENJAMIN—Back—
Rutgers
1930 Brooklyn Dodgers

GREENE, JOHN—End—Michigan
1944–51 Detroit Lions

GREENE, THEODORE—Center—
Tampa
1960 Dallas Texans (AFL)

JOHN GREEN

GREENE, THOMAS—Back—
Holy Cross
1960 Boston Patriots (AFL)

GREENEY, NORMAN—Guard—
Notre Dame
1933 Green Bay Packers
1934 Pittsburgh Pirates

GREENFIELD, THOMAS—Center—
Arizona
1939–41 Green Bay Packers

GREENHALGH, ROBERT—Back—
San Francisco
1949 New York Giants

GREENSHIELDS, DONN—Tackle—
Penn. State
1932–33 Brooklyn Dodgers

GREENWOOD, DONALD—Back—
Missouri & Illinois
1945 Cleveland Rams
1946–47 Cleveland Browns (AAFC)

GREENWOOD, GLENN—Back—
Iowa
1924 Chicago Bears
1926 Louisville Colonels

GREER, JAMES—End—North
Carolina Teachers
1960 Denver Broncos (AFL)

GREFE, THEODORE—End—
Northwestern
1945 Detroit Lions

GREGG, EDWARD—End—Kentucky
1922 Louisville Colonels

GREGG, FORREST—Tackle—SMU
1956–60 Green Bay Backers

GREGORY, BRUCE—Back—
Michigan

1926 Detroit Panthers

GREGORY, FRANK—Back—Williams
1924 Buffalo Bisons

**GREGORY, GARLAND—Guard—
Louisiana Tech.**
1946–47 San Francisco 49ers (AAFC)

**GREGORY, JOHN—Guard—
Chattanooga**
1941–42 Cleveland Rams

**GREGORY, MICHAEL—Guard—
Denison**
1931 Cleveland Indians

**GREMMINGER, HENRY—Back—
Baylor**
1956–60 Green Bay Packers

HENRY GREMMINGER

**GRGICH, VISCO—Guard—Santa
Clara**
1946–49 San Francisco 49ers (AAFC)
1950–52 San Francisco 49ers

**GRIER, ROOSEVELT—Tackle—
Penn State**
1955–56, 58–60 New York Giants

GRIFFEN, HAROLD—Center—Iowa
1928 Green Bay Packers
1930–32 Portsmouth Spartans

GRIFFIN, DONALD—Back—Illinois
1946 Chicago Rockets (AAFC)

GRIFFIN, ROBERT—Back—Baylor
1951 New York Yanks

**GRIFFIN, ROBERT—Guard—
Arkansas**
1953–57 Los Angeles Rams
1958 Detroit Lions

**GRIFFITH, FORREST—Back—
Kansas**
1950–51 New York Giants

**GRIFFITHS, HOMER—Back—Santa
Clara**
1934 Chicago Cardinals

**GRIFFITHS, PAUL—Guard—Penn
State**
1921 Canton Bulldogs

GRIGAS, JOHN—Back—Holy Cross
1943 Chicago Cardinals
1944 Card-Pitt
1945–47 Boston Yanks

GRIGG, CECIL—Back—Austin
1921–23 Canton Bulldogs
1925 Rochester Kodaks
1926 Akron Steels
1926 New York Giants
1927 Frankford Yellowjackets

GRIGG, FORREST—Tackle—Tulsa
1946–47 Buffalo Bills (AAFC)
1947 Chicago Rockets (AAFC)
1948–49 Cleveland Browns (AAFC)
1950–51 Cleveland Browns
1952 Dallas Texans

**GRIGONAS, FRANK—Back—
Chattanooga**
1942 Detroit Lions

GRIMES, GEORGE—Back—Virginia
1948 Detroit Lions

**GRIMES, WILLIAM—Back—
Oklahoma A & M**
1949 Los Angeles Dons
1950–52 Green Bay Packers

**GROMAN, WILLIAM—Back—
Heidelberg**
1960 Houston Oilers (AFL)

**GROOME, JEROME—Center—Notre
Dame**
1951–55 Chicago Cardinals

**GROOMES, MELVIN—Back—
Indiana**
1948–49 Detroit Lions

**GROSSCUP, CLYDE LEE—Back—
Utah**
1960 New York Giants

GROSSMAN, JOHN—Back—Rutgers
1932–36 Brooklyn Dodgers

GROSSMAN, REX—Back—Indiana
1948–49 Baltimore Colts (AAFC)
1950 Baltimore Colts
1950 Detroit Lions

**GROSVENOR, GEORGE—Back—
Colorado**
1935–36 Chicago Bears
1936–37 Chicago Cardinals

GROTTKAU, ROBERT—Guard—Oregon
1959–60 Detroit Lions

GROVE, ROGER—Back—Michigan State
1931–35 Green Bay Packers
1937 Brooklyn Dodgers

GROVES, GEORGE—Guard—Marquette
1946 Cleveland Browns (AAFC)
1947 Buffalo Bills (AAFC)
1948 Baltimore Colts (AAFC)

GROZA, LOUIS—Tackle—Ohio State
1946–49 Cleveland Browns (AAFC)
1950–59 Cleveland Browns
1950, 52, 53, 54, 57 #1 Field Goals
1957 #1 Scoring

GRUBE, CHARLES—End—Michigan
1926 Detroit Panthers

GRUBE, FRANK—End—Lafayette
1922–23 Louisville Colonels

GRUBER, HERBERT—End
1920–23 Louisville Colonels

GRYCO, ALBERT—Back—South Carolina
1944–45 Chicago Bears

GUARNERI, ALBERT—End—Canisius
1924 Buffalo Bisons

GUDAUSKAS, PETER—Guard—Murray State
1940 Cleveland Rams
1942, 45 Green Bay Packers
1943–44 Chicago Bears
1948 Chicago Rockets (AAFC)

GUDD, LEONARD—End—Temple
1934 Philadelphia Eagles

GUDE, HENRY—Guard—Vanderbilt
1946 Philadelphia Eagles

GUDMUNDSON, SCOTT—Back—George Washington
1944–45 Boston Yanks

GUESMAN, RICHARD—Tackle—West Virginia
1960 New York Titans (AFL)

GUFFEY, ROY—End—Oklahoma
1926 Buffalo Bisons

GUGLIELMI, RALPH—Back—Notre Dame
1955, 58–60 Washington Redskins

GUIGLIANO, PASQUALE—Back

1923 Louisville Colonels

GULIAN, MICHAEL—Tackle—Brown
1923 Buffalo All Americans
1924 Frankford Yellowjackets
1925–27 Providence Steamrollers

RALPH GUGLIELMI

GULYANICS, GEORGE—Back
1947–52 Chicago Bears

GUMP—Guard
1922 Columbus Tigers

GUNDERMAN, ROBERT—Back—Virginia
1957 Pittsburgh Steelers

GUNDERSON, BORGE—Guard—Wisconsin
1921 Rock Island Independents

GUNDERSON, HARRY—Center
1922–23 Minneapolis Marines

GUNDLACH, HERMAN—Guard—Harvard
1935 Boston Redskins

GUNNELS, JOHN—Tackle—Georgia
1960 Philadelphia Eagles

GUSSIE, MICHAEL—Guard—West Virginia
1940 Brooklyn Dodgers

GUSTAFSON, EDSEL—Center—George Washington
1947–48 Brooklyn Dodgers (AAFC)

GUTKNECHT, ALBERT—Guard—Niagara
1943 Brooklyn Dodgers
1944 Cleveland Rams

GUTOWSKY, LEROY—Back—Oklahoma City Univ.

1931   New York Giants
1932–33   Portsmouth Spartans
1934–38   Detroit Lions
1939   Brooklyn Dodgers

LEROY "ACE"
GUTOWSKY

JOHN GUZIK

GUTTORMSEN, GEORGE—Back
   Washington
1926   Los Angeles

GUY, CHARLES—Center—
   Washington & Jefferson
1921   Detroit Panthers
1921–22   Buffalo All Americans
1923   Cleveland Indians
1925   Dayton Triangles
1925   Columbus Tigers

GUY, MELWOOD—Tackle—Duke
1958–59   New York Giants
1960   Dallas Cowboys

GUYON, JOSEPH—Back—Carlisle
1921   Cleveland Indians
1922   Oorang Indians
1924   Rock Island Independents
1924–25   Kansas City Cowboys
1927   New York Giants

GUZIK, JOHN—Tackle—Pittsburgh
1959–60   Los Angeles Rams

GWOSDEN, MILO—End—Pittsburgh
1925   Buffalo Bisons

* * *

HAAK, ROBERT—Tackle—Indiana
1937   Brooklyn Dodgers

HAAS—Back
1921   Cleveland Indians

HAAS, ROBERT—Back—Purdue
1929   Dayton Triangles

HACHTEN, WILLIAM—Guard—
   Stanford
1947   New York Giants

HACKBART, DALE—Back—
   Wisconsin
1960   Green Bay Packers

HACKENBRUCK, JOHN—Tackle—
   Oregon State
1940   Detroit Lions

HACKNEY, ELMER—Back—Kansas
   State
1940–41   Philadelphia Eagles
1941   Pittsburgh Steelers
1942–46   Detroit Lions

HADDON, ALDOUS—Back—
   Washington & Jefferson
1925–26   Detroit Panthers
1927–28   Providence Steamrollers
1928   Chicago Bears
1929–30   Providence Steamrollers

HADEN, JOHN—Tackle—Arkansas
1936–38   New York Giants

HAFEN, BARNARD—End—Utah
1949–50   Detroit Lions

HAGBERG, RUDOLPH—Center—
   West Virginia
1929   Buffalo Bisons
1930   Brooklyn Dodgers

HAGENBUCKLE, VERNON—End—
   Dartmouth
1926   Providence Steamrollers

HAGERTY, LORIS—Back—Iowa
1930   Brooklyn Dodgers

HAGERTY, JOHN—Back—
   Georgetown
1926–30, 32   New York Giants

HAHN, RAY—End—Bethany (Kansas)
1926   Hammond Pros

HAINES, BYRON—Back—Washington
1937   Pittsburgh Pirates

HAINES, HARRY—Tackle—Colgate
1930–31   Brooklyn Dodgers

HAINES, HENRY—Back—Penn State
1925–29   New York Giants
1930–31   Staten Island Stapletons

HAJEK, CHARLES—Center—
   Northwestern
1934   Philadelphia Eagles

HALAS, GEORGE—End—Illinois
1921–30   Chicago Bears

HALEY, ARTHUR—Back—Akron
1923   Akron Steels

HALEY, GEORGE RICHARD—
   Back—Pittsburgh
1959–60   Washington Redskins

HALICKI, EDWARD—Back—
   Bucknell
1929–30   Frankford Yellowjackets

HALL, FORREST—Back—Duquesne,
   Southern California
1948   San Francisco 49ers (AAFC)

HALL, HAROLD—Center
1942   New York Giants

HALL, IRVING—Back—Brown
1942   Philadelphia Eagles

HALL, JOHN—End—Iowa
1955   New York Giants

HALL, JOHN—Back—TCU
1940   Chicago Cardinals
1942   Detroit Lions

HALL, KENNETH—Back—Texas
   A & M
1958   Baltimore Colts
1959   Chicago Cardinals
1960   Houston Oilers (AFL)

HALL, PARKER—Back—Mississippi
1939–42   Cleveland Rams
1946   San Francisco 49ers (AAFC)
1939   #1 Passing

HALL, RAYMOND—Tackle—Illinois
1927   New York Yankees

HALL, RONALD—Back—
   Missouri Valley
1959   Pittsburgh Steelers

HALLADAY, RICHARD—End—
   Chicago
1922–24   Racine Legion

HALLECK—Back
1924   Columbus Tigers

HALLECK, PAUL—Back—Ohio
1937   Cleveland Rams

HALLIDAY, JOHN—Tackle—SMU
1951   Los Angeles Rams

HALLORAN, J.—Back
1926   Hartford Blues

HALPERN, ROBERT—Guard—
   CCNY
1930   Staten Island Stapletons
1932   Brooklyn Dodgers

HALUSKA, JAMES—Back—Wisconsin
1956   Chicago Bears

HALVERSON, WILLIAM—Tackle—
   Oregon State
1942   Philadelphia Eagles

HAMAN, JOHN—Center—
   Northwestern
1940–41   Cleveland Rams

HAMAS, STEVEN—Back—
   Pennsylvania State
1929   Orange

HAMBACKER, ERNEST—Back—
   Bucknell
1929   Orange

HAMER, ERNEST—Back—Penn-
   sylvania
1924–27   Frankford Yellowjackets

HAMILTON, RAYMOND—End—
   Arkansas
1938, 44–45   Cleveland Rams
1939   Detroit Lions
1946–47   Los Angeles Rams

RICHARD HALEY

HAMITY, LEWIS—Back—Chicago
1941   Chicago Bears

**HAMMACK, MALCOLM—Back—
Florida**
1955, 57–59   Chicago Cardinals
1960   St. Louis Cardinals

**HAMMER, KENNETH—Center—
Oregon State**
1932   Boston Braves

**HAMMOND, HENRY—End—
Southwestern**
1937   Chicago Bears

HANDLER, PHILIP—Guard—TCU
1930–36   Chicago Cardinals

**HANDLEY, RICHARD—Center—
Fresno State**
1947   San Francisco 49ers (AAFC)
1947   Baltimore Colts (AAFC)

HANKE, CARL—End—Minnesota
1923   Hammond Pros
1924–25   Chicago Cardinals

HANKE, J.—Guard
1922   Chicago Bears

**HANKEN, RAYMOND—End—George
Washington**
1937–38   New York Giants

**HANLEY, RICHARD—Back—
Washington State**
1924   Racine Legion

HANLON, ROBERT—Back—Loras
1948   Chicago Cardinals
1949–50   Pittsburgh Steelers

**HANNA, ELZAPHAN—Guard—
Southern Carolina**
1945   Washington Redskins

**HANNAH, HERBERT—Tackle—
Alabama**
1951   New York Giants

**HANNEMAN, CHARLES—End—
Michigan State Normal**
1937–41   Detroit Lions

**HANNER, JOEL "DAVE"—Tackle—
Arkansas**
1952–60   Green Bay Packers

HANNIGAN, WILLIAM—Tackle
1926   Louisville Colonels

HANNY, FRANK—Tackle—Indiana
1923–27   Chicago Bears
1928–29   Providence Steamrollers
1930   Portsmouth Spartans
1930   Green Bay Packers

HANRICUS, RALPH—Back
1922   Rochester Kodaks

HANSEN, CLIFFORD—Back—Luther
1933   Chicago Bears

**HANSEN, DALE—Tackle—Michigan
State**
1944, 48–49   Detroit Lions

**HANSEN, RONALD—Guard—
Minnesota**
1954   Washington Redskins

**HANSEN, ROSCOE—Tackle—North
Carolina**
1951   Philadelphia Eagles

**HANSEN, WAYNE—Guard—Texas
Western**
1950–58   Chicago Bears
1960   Dallas Cowboys

**HANSON, HAROLD—Guard—
Minnesota**
1928–30   Frankford Yellowjackets
1930   Minneapolis Marines

**HANSON, HOMER—Back—Kansas
State**
1934   Cincinnati Reds
1935–36   Chicago Cardinals

HANSON, JOHN—Back—Temple
1937   Brooklyn Dodgers
1938   Pittsburgh Steelers

HANSON, ROY—Back—Marquette
1921   Rock Island Independents
1923   Columbus Tigers
1923   Minneapolis Marines
1923   Green Bay Packers

HANSON, STEVEN—End
1925   Kansas City Cowboys
1926   Louisville Colonels

HANSON, THOMAS—Back—Temple
1931   Brooklyn Dodgers
1932   Staten Island Stapletons
1933–37   Philadelphia Eagles
1934   Cincinnati Reds
1938   Pittsburgh Pirates

HANTLA, ROBERT—Guard—Kansas
1954–55   San Francisco 49ers

**HANULAK, CHESTER—Back—
Maryland**
1954, 57   Cleveland Browns

HAPES, MERLE—Back—Mississippi
1942, 46   New York Giants

**HARDER, MARLIN—Back—
Wisconsin**
1946–50   Chicago Cardinals

1951–53 Detroit Lions
1947 #1 Field Goals
1947, 48, 49 #1 Scoring (1947 - tied by
Roberts)

**HARDING, ROGER—Center—
California**
1945 Cleveland Rams
1946 Los Angeles Rams
1947 Philadelphia Eagles
1948 Detroit Lions
1949 Green Bay Packers
1949 New York Bulldogs

HARDY, CARROLL—Back—Colorado
1955 San Francisco 49ers

**HARDY, CHARLES—End—San Jose
State**
1960 Oakland Raiders (AFL)

**HARDY, ISHAM—Guard—William &
Mary**
1923 Akron Steels
1926 Racine Legion

**HARDY, JAMES—Back—Southern
California**
1946–48 Los Angeles Rams
1949–51 Chicago Cardinals
1952 Detroit Lions

JAMES HARDY

HARE, CECIL—Back—Gonzaga
1941–42, 45 Washington Redskins
1946 New York Giants

HARE, RAYMOND—Back—Gonzaga
1940–43 Washington Redskins
1944 Brooklyn Tigers
1946 New York Yankees

**HARKEY, LEMUEL—Back—Kansas
State Teacher**
1955 Pittsburgh Steelers
1955 San Francisco 49ers

**HARLAN, JULIAN—Back—
Georgia Tech**
1922 Hammond Pros

**HARLEY, CHARLES—Back—Ohio
State**
1921 Chicago Bears

**HARMON, HAMILTON—Center—
Tulsa**
1937 Chicago Cardinals

**HARMON, THOMAS—Back—
Michigan**
1946–47 Los Angeles Rams

THOMAS HARMON

**HARMS, ARTHUR—Tackle—
Vermont**
1925–27 Frankford Yellowjackets
1926–27 New York Giants

**HARNESS, JAMES—Back—Mississippi
State**
1956 Baltimore Colts

**HARPER, DARRELL—Back—
Michigan**
1960 Buffalo Bills (AFL)

HARPER, MAURICE—Center—None
1937–40 Philadelphia Eagles
1941 Pittsburgh Steelers

**HARRINGTON, JOHN—End—
Marquette**
1946 Cleveland Browns (AAFC)
1947 Chicago Rockets (AAFC)

**HARRIS, AMOS—Guard—Mississippi
State**
1947–48 Brooklyn Dodgers (AAFC)

HARRIS, BRYAN—Back—Grove City
1926 Hartford Blues

HARRIS, ELMORE—Back—Morgan

1947 Brooklyn Dodgers (AAFC)

HARRIS, HENRY—Guard—Texas
1947–48 Washington Redskins

HARRIS, JAMES—Back—Oklahoma
1957 Philadelphia Eagles
1958 Los Angeles Rams
1960 Dallas Texans (AFL)

HARRIS, JOHN—Back—Wisconsin
1925–26 Green Bay Packers
1926 Hartford Blues

HARRIS, JOHN—Back—Santa Monica
1960 Oakland Raiders (AFL)

HARRIS, KENNETH—Back—Syracuse
1923–24 Duluth Eskimos

HARRIS, OLIVER—End—Geneva
1926 New York Giants

HARRIS, RICHARD—Back—Louisiana State (McNeese)
1960 Los Angeles Chargers (AFL)

HARRIS, THOMAS—Tackle—Ohio State
1930 Portsmouth Spartans
1930 Brooklyn Dodgers

HARRIS, WILLIAM—End—Hardin-Simmons
1937 Pittsburgh Pirates

HARRISON, EDWARD—End—Boston College
1927 Brooklyn Dodgers
1928 New York Giants

HARRISON, GRANVILLE—End—Mississippi State
1940 New York Giants
1941 Philadelphia Eagles
1942 Detroit Lions

HARRISON, JOSEPH—Tackle—Kansas State
1937 Brooklyn Dodgers

HARRISON, MAXWELL—End—Auburn
1940 New York Giants

HARRISON, RICHARD—End—Boston College
1944 Boston Redskins

HARRISON, ROBERT—Back—Oklahoma
1959–60 San Francisco 49ers

HART, DEE "PETE"—Back—Hardin-Simmons
1960 New York Titans (AFL)

HART, LEON—End—Notre Dame
1950–57 Detroit Lions

HART, LESLIE—Back—Colgate
1931 Staten Island Stapletons

HARTLEY, HOWARD—Back—Duke
1948 Washington Redskins
1949–52 Pittsburgh Steelers

HARTMAN, FREDERICK—Tackle—Rice
1947 Chicago Bears
1948 Philadelphia Eagles

HARTMAN, JAMES—End—Colorado State
1936 Brooklyn Dodgers

HARTMAN, WILLIAM—Back—Georgia
1938 Washington Redskins

HARTONG, GEORGE—Guard—Chicago
1923 Racine Legion
1924 Chicago Cardinals

HARTSHORN, LAWRENCE—Guard—Kansas State
1955 Chicago Cardinals

HARTZOG, HOWARD—Tackle—Baylor
1928 New York Giants

HARVEY, NORMAN—Tackle—Detroit
1925, 27 Buffalo Bisons
1926 Detroit Panthers
1927 New York Yankees
1928–29 Providence Steamrollers

HASBROUCK, JOHN—Back—Rutgers
1921 Rock Island Independents
1921 Rochester Kodaks

HASTINGS, GEORGE—Tackle—Ohio
1931 Portsmouth Spartans

HATHAWAY, RUSSELL—Tackle—Indiana
1921–25 Dayton Triangles
1926–27 Pottsville Maroons
1927 Buffalo Bisons

HATLEY, JOHN—Tackle—Sul Ross State
1953 Chicago Bears
1954–55 Chicago Cardinals
1960 Denver Broncos (AFL)

HAUSER, ARTHUR—Guard—Xavier
1954–57 Los Angeles Rams
1959 Chicago Cardinals
1959 New York Giants
1960 Boston Patriots (AFL)

HAUSER, EARL—End—Miami (Ohio)
1921 Cincinnati Celts

HAUSER, HAROLD—Back—Kansas
1927 Buffalo Bisons
1930 Newark

HAVEN, JOHN—End—Hamline
1923 Duluth Kelleys

HAVENS, CHARLES—Center—Western Maryland
1930 Frankford Yellowjackets

HAWKINS, ALEX—Back—South Carolina
1959-60 Baltimore Colts

ALEX HAWKINS

HAWKINS, JOHN—Tackle—Southern California
1926 Los Angeles

HAWKINS, WAYNE—Guard—College of Pacific
1960 Oakland Raiders (AFL)

HAWS, HARVEY—Back—Dartmouth
1924-25 Frankford Yellowjackets

HAYCRAFT, KENNETH—End—Minnesota
1929-30 Minneapolis Redjackets
1930 Green Bay Packers

HAYDEN, JOHN—Tackle—Arkansas
1936-38 New York Giants

HAYDEN, KENNETH—Center—Arkansas
1942 Philadelphia Eagles
1943 Washington Redskins

HAYDUK, HENRY—Guard—Washington State
1935 Pittsburgh Pirates
1935 Brooklyn Dodgers

HAYES, GERALD—End—Notre Dame

1921 Rock Island Independents

HAYES, NORBERT—End—Marquette
1922 Racine Legion
1923 Green Bay Packers

HAYES, RICHARD—Back—Clemson
1959-60 Pittsburgh Steelers

HAYNES, ABNER—Back—North Texas
1960 Dallas Texans (AFL)

HAYNES, HALL—Back—Santa Clara
1950, 53 Washington Redskins
1954-55 Los Angeles Rams

HAYNES, JOSEPH—Guard—Tulsa
1947 Buffalo Bills

HAYS, DAVID—End—Notre Dame
1921-22 Green Bay Packers

HAYS, GEORGE—End—St. Bonaventure
1950-52 Pittsburgh Steelers
1953 Green Bay Packers

HAZBURG—Tackle
1930 Brooklyn Dodgers

HAZELHURST, ROBERT—Back—Denver
1948 Boston Yanks
1949 New York Bulldogs

HAZELTINE, MATTHEW—Center—California
1955-60 San Francisco 49ers

MATTHEW HAZELTINE

HAZELWOOD, THEODORE—Tackle—North Carolina
1949 Chicago Hornets (AAFC)
1953 Washington Redskins

HEADRICK, SHERRILL—Back—TCU
1960 Dallas Texans (AFL)

HEALY, MICHAEL DONALD—
Tackle—Maryland
1958–59   Chicago Bears
1960   Dallas Cowboys

HEALY, EDWARD—Tackle—
Dartmouth
1921–22   Rock Island Independents
1922–27   Chicago Bears

HEAP, JOSEPH—Back—Notre Dame
1955   New York Giants

HEAP, WALTER—Back—Texas
1947–48   Los Angeles Dons (AAFC)

HEARDEN, LEONARD—End—Ripon
1924   Green Bay Packers

HEARDEN, THOMAS—Back—
Notre Dame
1927–28   Green Bay Packers
1929   Chicago Bears

HEATER, WILLIAM—Tackle—
Syracuse
1940   Brooklyn Dodgers

HEATH, LEON—Back—Oklahoma
1951–53   Washington Redskins

HEATH, STANLEY—Back—Nevada
1949   Green Bay Packers

HECHT, ALFRED—Guard—
Alabama
1947   Chicago Rockets (AAFC)

HECK, ROBERT—End—Purdue
1949   Chicago Hornets (AAFC)

HECKER, NORBERT—End—
Baldwin-Wallace
1951–53   Los Angeles Rams
1955–57   Washington Redskins

HECKER, ROBERT—Back—
Baldwin-Wallace
1952   Los Angeles Rams
1952   Chicago Cardinals

HEENAN, PATRICK—End—
Notre Dame
1960   Washington Redskins

HEFTI, JAMES—Back—St. Lawrence
1947   Washington Redskins

HEGARTY, WILLIAM—Tackle—
Villanova
1953   Pittsburgh Steelers
1953   Washington Redskins

HEIKKENEN, RALPH—Guard—
Michigan
1939   Brooklyn Dodgers

HEILEMAN, CHARLES—End—Iowa
State
1939   Chicago Bears

HEIMSCH, JOHN—Back—Marquette
1926   Milwaukee Badgers

HEIN, HERBERT—End—Minnesota
1947   Brooklyn Dodgers (AAFC)

HEIN, MELVIN—Center—Washington
State
1931–45   New York Giants

HEIN, ROBERT—End—Kent
1947   Brooklyn Dodgers

HEINEMAN, KENNETH—Back—
Texas Mines
1940–41   Cleveland Rams
1943   Brooklyn Dodgers

HEINISCH, FRED—Tackle
1923, 26   Racine Legion
1924   Kenosha
1926   Duluth Eskimos
1926   Milwaukee Badgers

HEINRICH, DONALD—Back—
Washington
1954–59   New York Giants
1960   Dallas Cowboys

DONALD HEINRICH

HEKKERS, GEORGE—Tackle—
Wisconsin
1946   Miami Seahawks (AAFC)
1947   Baltimore Colts (AAFC)
1947–49   Detroit Lions

HELD, PAUL—Back—San Jose State
1954   Pittsburgh Steelers
1955   Green Bay Packers
1955   Detroit Lions

HELDT, CARL—Tackle—Purdue
1935–36   Brooklyn Dodgers

HELDT, JOHN—Center—Iowa State
1923, 26   Columbus Tigers

HELLER, WARREN—Back—
Pittsburgh
1934–36   Pittsburgh Pirates

HELLSTROM, NORTON—Back—
Illinois
1921   Chicago Cardinals

HELLUIN, FRANCIS—Tackle—
Tulane
1952–53   Cleveland Browns
1954–57   Green Bay Packers
1960   Houston Oilers (AFL)

HELMS, JOHN—End—Georgia Tech.
1946   Detroit Lions

HELWIG, JOHN—Back—Notre Dame
1953–56   Chicago Bears

HEMPEL, WILLIAM—Tackle—John
Carroll
1941–42   Chicago Bears

HENDERSON, HERBERT—Back—
Ohio State
1921–22   Evansville Crimson Giants

HENDLEY, RICHARD—Back—
Clemson
1951   Pittsburgh Steelers

HENDREN, JOHN—Back—Bucknell
1921   Cleveland Indians

HENDREN, ROBERT—Tackle—
Southern California
1949–51   Washington Redskins

HENDRIAN, WARREN—Back—
Pittsburgh
1921   Cleveland Indians
1922–23   Canton Bulldogs
1923   Akron Steels
1924   Green Bay Packers
1925   Rock Island Independents
1925   New York Giants

HENKE, EDGAR—Guard—Southern
California
1949   Los Angeles Dons (AAFC)
1951–52, 56–60   San Francisco 49ers

HENNESSEY, JEROME—End—Santa
Clara
1950–51   Chicago Cardinals
1952–53   Washington Redskins

HENNIGAN, CHARLES—Back—
Louisiana N.W.
1960   Houston Oilers (AFL)

HENRY, MICHAEL—Back—
Southern California
1959–60   Pittsburgh Steelers

HENRY, WILBUR—Tackle—
Washington & Jefferson

1921–23, 25–26   Canton Bulldogs
1925   Akron Steels
1926   New York Giants
1927–28   Pottsville Maroons
1930   Staten Island Stapletons

EDGAR HENKE

HENSLEY, RICHARD—End—
Kentucky
1949   New York Giants
1952   Pittsburgh Steelers
1953   Chicago Bears

HERBER, ARNOLD—Back—Regis
1930–41   Green Bay Packers
1944–45   New York Giants
1932, 34, 36   #1 Passing

HERCHMAN, WILLIAM—Tackle—
Texas Tech.
1956–59   San Francisco 49ers
1960   Dallas Cowboys

HERGERT, JOSEPH—Back—Florida
1960   Buffalo Bills (AFL)

HERMAN, EDWARD—End—
Northwestern
1925   Rock Island Independents

HERMANN, JOHN—Back—U.C.L.A.
1956   New York Giants
1956   Baltimore Colts

HERNDON, DONALD—Back—Tulsa
1960   New York Titans (AFL)

HERRIN, HOUSTON—Guard—
St. Mary's Cal.
1931   Cleveland Indians

HERRING, GEORGE—Back—
Mississippi Southern
1960   Denver Broncos

HERRING, HAROLD—Center—
Alabama Polytech.
1949   Buffalo Bills (AAFC)
1950–51   Cleveland Browns

HERSHEY, KIRK—End—Cornell
1941 Philadelphia Eagles
1941 Cleveland Rams

HERTZ, FRANK—End—Carroll (Wis.)
1926 Milwaukee Badgers

HESS, ARTHUR—Back—Indiana
1922–25 Hammond Pros
1924 Kenosha

HEWITT, WILLIAM—End—Michigan
1932–36 Chicago Bears
1936–39 Philadelphia Eagles
1943 Phil-Pitt

HEYWOOD, RALPH—End—Southern Californa
1946 Chicago Rockets (AAFC)
1947 Detroit Lions
1948 Boston Yanks
1949 New York Bulldogs

HIBBS, JESSE—Tackle—Southern California
1931 Chicago Bears

HICKERSON, EDWARD—Guard—Alabama
1941 Washington Redskins

HICKERSON, EUGENE—Tackle—Mississippi
1958–60 Cleveland Browns

HICKEY, HOWARD—End—Arkansas
1941, 45 Cleveland Rams
1946–48 Los Angeles Rams

HICKMAN, HERMAN—Guard—Tennessee
1932–34 Brooklyn Dodgers

HICKMAN, LAWRENCE—Back—Baylor
1959 Chicago Cardinals
1960 Green Bay Packers

HIEMSTRA, EDWARD—Guard—Sterling
1942 New York Giants

HIGGINS, AUSTIN—Center
1922–23 Louisville Colonels

HIGGINS, JOHN—Guard—Trinity
1941 Chicago Cardinals

HIGGINS, LUKE—Guard—Notre Dame
1947 Baltimore Colts (AAFC)

HIGGINS, ROBERT—Back—Penn State
1921 Canton Bulldogs

1925 Providence Steamrollers
1925 Columbus Tigers

HIGGINS, THOMAS—Tackle—North Carolina
1953 Chicago Cardinals
1954–55 Philadelphia Eagles

HIGHTOWER, JOHN—End—Sam Houston
1942 Cleveland Rams
1943 Detroit Lions

HILL, CHARLES—Back—Baker
1924–26 Kansas City Cowboys
1926 New York Giants

HILL, DONALD—Back—Stanford
1929 Green Bay Packers
1929–30 Chicago Cardinals

HILL, HARLON—End—Alabama State Teachers
1954–60 Chicago Bears

HILL, HAROLD—End—Howard
1938–40 Brooklyn Dodgers

HILL, HARRY—Back—Oklahoma
1923 Toledo Maroons
1924–26 Kansas City Cowboys

HILL, IRVING—Back—Trinity
1931–32 Chicago Cardinals

HILL, JAMES—Back—Sam Houston
1955–59 Chicago Cardinals
1960 St. Louis Cardinals

HILL, JAMES—Back—Tennessee
1951–52 Detroit Lions
1955 Detroit Lions

HILL, KING—Back—Rice
1958–59 Chicago Cardinals
1960 St. Louis Cardinals

HILL, ROBERT—Guard—Haskell
1922 Oorang Indians

HILLENBRAND, WILLIAM—Back—Indiana
1946 Chicago Rockets (AAFC)
1947–48 Baltimore Colts (AAFC)

HILLHOUSE, ANDREW—Back—Brown
1921 Buffalo All Americans

HILLMAN, WILLIAM—Back—Tennessee
1947 Detroit Lions

HILPERT, HAROLD—Back—Oklahoma City Univ.
1930 New York Giants
1931 Chicago Cardinals
1933 Cincinnati Reds

HINCHMAN, HUBERT—Back—Butler
1933-34 Chicago Cardinals
1934 Detroit Lions

HINKLE, CLARKE—Back—Bucknell
1932-41 Green Bay Packers
1938 #1 Scoring
1940, 41 #1 Field Goals

HINKLE, JOHN—Back—Syracuse
1940 New York Giants
1941-42, 44-47 Philadelphia Eagles
1943 Phil-Pitt

HINTE, HAROLD—End—Pittsburgh
1942 Green Bay Packers
1942 Pittsburgh Steelers

HINTON, J. W.—Back—TCU
1932 Staten Island Stapletons
Killed in East Indies on flight mission, Dec. 10, 1944. Lt. Col., U.S. Air Force.

HIPPA, SAMUEL—End—Dayton
1927-28 Dayton Triangles

HIRSCH, EDWARD—Back—Northwestern
1947-49 Buffalo Bills (AAFC)

HIRSCH, ELROY—End—Wisconsin
1946-48 Chicago Rockets (AAFC)
1949-57 Los Angeles Rams
1951 #1 Pass Receiving

HITT, JOEL—End—Mississippi College
1939 Cleveland Rams

HIX, WILLIAM—End—Arkansas
1950 Philadelphia Eagles

HOAGUE, JOSEPH—Back—Colgate
1941-42 Pittsburgh Steelers
1943 Phil-Pitt
1944 Card-Pitt
1946 Boston Yanks

HOBBS, HOMER—Guard—Georgia
1949 San Francisco 49ers (AAFC)
1950 San Francisco 49ers

HOBSCHEID, FRANK—Guard—Chicago
1926 Racine Legion
1927 Chicago Bears

HOBSON, BENJAMIN—Back—Wabash
1926-27 Buffalo Bisons

HOCK, JOHN—Tackle—Santa Clara
1950 Chicago Cardinals
1953, 55-56 Los Angeles Rams

HODEL, MERWIN—Back—Colorado
1953 New York Giants

HODGES, HERMAN—End—Howard
1939-42 Brooklyn Dodgers

HOEL, ROBERT—Guard—Pittsburgh
1935 Pittsburgh Pirates
1937-38 Chicago Cardinals

HOERNER, RICHARD—Back—Iowa
1947-51 Los Angeles Rams
1952 Dallas Texans

RICHARD HOERNER

HOERNSCHEMEYER, ROBERT—Back—Indiana
1946-47, 49 Chicago Rockets
1947-48 Brooklyn Dodgers
1950-55 Detroit Lions

HOFFMAN, ARNOLD—Tackle—Syracuse
1925 Rochester Jeffersons

HOFFMAN, JACK—End—Xavier
1952, 55-58 Chicago Bears

HOFFMAN, JOHN—Back—Arkansas
1949-56 Chicago Bears

HOFFMAN, ROBERT—Back—Southern California
1940-41 Washington Redskins
1946-49 Los Angeles Rams

HOFFMAN, WILLIAM—Guard—Lehigh
1924-26 Frankford Yellowjackets
1927 Pottsville Maroons

HOGAN, DARRELL—Guard—Trinity
1949-53 Pittsburgh Steelers

HOGAN, PAUL—Back—Detroit
1924 Akron Steels
1925-26, 28 Detroit Panthers
1925 Canton Bulldogs
1926 Frankford Yellowjackets

1926 New York Giants

HOGLAND, DOUGLAS—Guard—Oregon State
1953–55 San Francisco 49ers
1956–58 Chicago Cardinals
1958 Detroit Lions

HOGUE, MURRELL—Back—Centenary
1928 New York Yankees
1929–30 Chicago Cardinals
1930 Minneapolis Redjackets

HOISINGTON, ALLAN—End—Pasadena
1960 Oakland Raiders (AFL)
1960 Buffalo Bills (AFL)

HOKUF, STEPHEN—End—Nebraska
1933–35 Boston Redskins

HOLCOMB, WILLIAM—Tackle—Texas Tech.
1937 Pittsburgh Pirates
1937 Philadelphia Eagles

HOLDER, LEWIS—End—Texas
1949 Los Angeles Dons (AAFC)

HOLLADAY, ROBERT—Back—Tulsa
1956–57 San Francisco 49ers

HOLLAR, JOHN—Back—Appalachian State
1948–49 Washington Redskins
1949 Detroit Lions

HOLLERAN, THOMAS—Back—Pittsburgh
1923 Buffalo All Americans

HOLLEY, KENNETH—Back—Holy Cross
1946 Miami Seahawks (AAFC)

HOLLINGSWORTH, JOSEPH—Back—East Kentucky State
1949–51 Pittsburgh Steelers

HOLLQUIST—Back
1926 Milwaukee Badgers

HOLM, BERNARD—Back—Alabama
1930 Providence Steamrollers
1931 Portsmouth Spartans
1932 Chicago Cardinals
1933 Pittsburgh Pirates

HOLMER, WALTER—Back—Northwestern
1929–30 Chicago Bears
1931–32 Chicago Cardinals
1933 Boston Redskins
1933 Pittsburgh Pirates

HOLOVAK, MICHAEL—Back—Boston College
1946 Los Angeles Rams

1947–48 Chicago Bears

HOLTZMAN, GLEN—Tackle—Texas State North
1955–58 Los Angeles Rams
1960 Los Angeles Chargers (AFL)
1960 Oakland Raiders (AFL)

HOLZ, GORDON—Tackle—Minnesota
1960 Denver Broncos (AFL)

HOMAN, HENRY—Back—Lebanon Valley
1925–30 Frankford Yellowjackets

HONAKER, CHARLES—End—Ohio State
1924 Cleveland Bulldogs

HOOD, FRANKLIN—Back—Pittsburgh
1933 Pittsburgh Pirates

HOOLEY, ROBERT—Guard—Detroit
1924 Minneapolis Marines

HOPKINS, THEODORE—End—Pennsylvania
1922 Columbus Tigers

HOPP, HARRY—Back—Nebraska
1940–43 Detroit Lions
1946 Miami Seahawks (AAFC)
1946 Buffalo Bisons (AAFC)
1947 Los Angeles Dons (AAFC)

HOPTOWIT, ALBERT—Tackle—Washington State
1941–45 Chicago Bears

HORNBEAK, JAY—Back—Washington
1935 Brooklyn Dodgers

HORD, AMBROSE ROY—Guard—Duke
1960 Los Angeles Rams

HORN, RICHARD—Back—Stanford
1958 Baltimore Colts

HORNE, RICHARD—End—Oregon
1941 New York Giants
1946 Miami Seahawks (AAFC)
1946 Buffalo Bisons (AAFC)
1947 San Francisco 49ers (AAFC)

HORNER, SAMUEL—Back—VMI
1960 Washington Redskins

HORNICK, WILLIAM—Tackle—Tulane
1947 Pittsburgh Steelers

HORNING, CLARENCE—Tackle—Colgate
1921 Detroit Panthers

1921   Buffalo All Americans
1922–23   Toledo Maroons

SAMUEL HORNER

HORNUNG, PAUL—Back—Notre Dame
1957–60   Green Bay Packers
1959–60   #1 Scoring

HORRELL, WILLIAM—Guard—Michigan State
1952, 55   Philadelphia Eagles

HORSTMANN, ROY—Back—Purdue
1933   Boston Redskins
1934   Chicago Cardinals

HORTON, LESTER—Back—Rutgers
1930   Newark

HORVATH, LESLIE—Back—Ohio State
1947–48   Los Angeles Rams (AAFC)
1949   Cleveland Browns (AAFC)

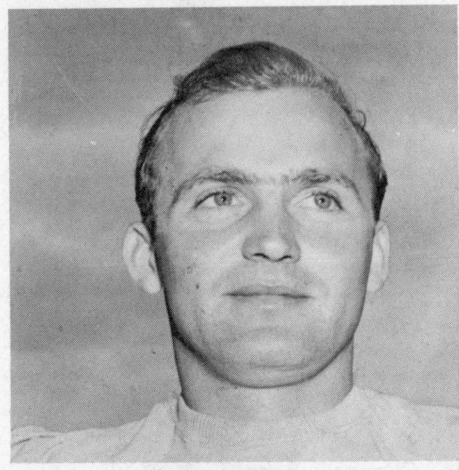

LESLIE HORVATH

HORWEEN, ARNOLD—Back—Harvard
1921–24   Chicago Cardinals

HORWEEN, RALPH—Back—Harvard
1921–23   Chicago Cardinals

HOUCK, JOSEPH—Guard
1921   Columbus Tigers

HOUGHTON, JERRY—Tackle—Washington State
1950   Washington Redskins
1951   Chicago Cardinals

HOULE, WILFRED—Back—St. Thomas (Minn.)
1924   Minneapolis Marines

HOUSER, JOHN—Guard—Redlands
1957–59   Los Angeles Rams
1960   Dallas Cowboys

HOUSTON, JAMES—End—Ohio State
1960   Cleveland Browns

HOUSTON, LINDELL—Guard—Ohio State
1946–49   Cleveland Browns (AAFC)
1950–53   Cleveland Browns

LINDELL HOUSTON

HOUSTON, WALTER—Guard—Purdue
1955   Washington Redskins

HOVIOUS, JOHN—Back—Mississippi
1945   New York Giants

HOWARD, ALBERT—Guard—Princeton
1926   Brooklyn Dodgers
1927   New York Giants

HOWARD, LYNN—Back—Indiana
1921–22   Green Bay Packers

HOWARD, ROBERT—Guard—
Marietta
1924–26 Kansas City Cowboys
1927 Cleveland Bulldogs
1928 Detroit Wolverines
1929–30 New York Giants

HOWARD, SHERMAN—Back—
Nevada
1949 New York Yankees (AAFC)
1950–51 New York Yanks
1952–53 Cleveland Browns

HOWARD, WILLIAM—Back—
Southern California
1939 Detroit Lions

HOWELL, CLARENCE—End—
Texas A & M
1948 San Francisco 49ers

HOWELL, EARL—Back—
Mississippi
1949 Los Angeles Dons

HOWELL, FOSTER—Tackle—
Texas Christian
1934 Cincinnati Reds

HOWELL, JAMES LEE—End—
Arkansas
1937–42, 46–48 New York Giants

HOWELL, JOHN—Back—Nebraska
1938 Green Bay Packers

HOWELL, MILLARD—Back—
Alabama
1937 Washington Redskins

HOWELL, WILFRED—End—
Catholic Univ.
1929 Boston Braves

HOWLEY, CHARLES—Center—West
Virginia
1958–59 Chicago Bears

HOWTON, WILLIAM—End—Rice
1952–58 Green Bay Packers
1959 Cleveland Browns
1960 Dallas Cowboys

HRABETIN, FRANK—Tackle—
Loyola (Los Angeles)
1942 Philadelphia Eagles
1946 Miami Seahawks (AAFC)
1946 Brooklyn Dodgers (AAFC)

HUBBARD, ROBERT—Tackle—
Geneva
1927–28, 36 New York Giants
1929–35 Green Bay Packers
1936 Pittsburgh Pirates

HUBBARD, WESLEY—End—
San Jose State

1935 Brooklyn Dodgers

HUBBELL, FRANKLIN—End—
Tennessee
1947–49 Los Angeles Rams

HUBKA, EUGENE—Back—Temple
1947 Pittsburgh Steelers

HUDOCK, MICHAEL—Center—
Miami
1960 New York Titans (AFL)

HUDSON, RICHARD—Back
1923 Minneapolis Marines
1925–26 Hammond Pros

HUDSON, MARTIN—Guard—
Michigan
1931 Cleveland Indians

HUDSON, ROBERT—End—Clemson
1951–52 New York Giants
1953–55, 57–58 Philadelphia Eagles
1959 Washington Redskins
1960 Dallas Texans (AFL)
1960 Denver Broncos (AFL)

HUFF, ROBERT LEE "SAM"—
Guard—West Virginia
1956–60 New York Giants

HUFFINE, KENNETH—Back—
Purdue
1921 Chicago Bears
1921–26 Dayton Triangles

HUFFMAN, FRANK—Guard—
Marshall
1939–41 Chicago Cardinals

HUFFMAN, IOLAS—Tackle—Ohio
State
1923 Cleveland Indians
1924 Buffalo Bisons

HUFFMAN, RICHARD—Tackle—
Tennessee
1947–50 Los Angeles Rams

HUFFMAN, VERNON—Back—
Indiana
1937–38 Detroit Lions

HUFFORD, DARRELL—End—
California
1926 Los Angeles

HUGASIAN, HARRY—Back—
Stanford
1955 Chicago Bears
1955 Baltimore Colts

HUGGINS, ROY—Back—
Vanderbilt
1944 Cleveland Rams

HUGHES, BERNARD—Center—
Oregon

1934–36 Chicago Cardinals
1941 Chicago Bears

1925–26 Providence Steamrollers
1926 Kansas City Cowboys

RICHARD HUFFMAN

RICHARD HUMBERT

**HUGHES, DENNIS—Center—
Georgetown**
1925 Pottsville Maroon

HUGHES, EDWARD—Back—Tulsa
1954–55 Los Angeles Rams
1956–58 New York Giants

**HUGHES, GEORGE—Guard—
William & Mary**
1950–54 Pittsburgh Steelers

**HUGHES, HENRY—Back—Oregon
State**
1932 Boston Braves

HUGHES, WILLIAM—Center—Texas
1937–40 Philadelphia Eagles
1940–41 Chicago Bears

**HUGHITT, ERNEST—Back—
Michigan**
1921–24 Buffalo All Americans

**HUGRET, JOSEPH—End—New York
Univ.**
1933–34 Brooklyn Dodgers

**HULTMAN, VIVIAN—End—
Michigan State**
1925–26 Detroit Panthers
1927 Pottsville Maroons

**HUMBERT, RICHARD—End—
Richmond**
1941, 45–49 Philadelphia Eagles

HUMBLE, WELDON—Guard—Rice
1947–49 Cleveland Browns (AAFC)
1950 Cleveland Browns
1952 Dallas Texans

**HUMMELL, CHARLES—Back—
Lafayette**

HUMMON, JOHN—End—Wittenberg
1926–28 Dayton Triangles

HUMPHREY, LOYIE—Back—Baylor
1959–60 Los Angeles Rams

HUMPHREY, PAUL—Center—Purdue
1939 Brooklyn Dodgers

**HUNEKE, CHARLES—Tackle—St.
Benedict's**
1946–47 Chicago Rockets (AAFC)
1947–48 Brooklyn Dodgers (AAFC)

**HUNSINGER, CHARLES—Back—
Florida**
1950–51 Chicago Bears

HUNT, BEN—Tackle—Alabama
1923 Toledo Maroons

**HUNT, EDWARD—Back—
Georgetown**
1926 Hartford Blues

HUNT, JAMES—End—Prairie View
1960 Boston Patriots (AFL)

HUNT, JOHN—Back—Marshall
1945 Chicago Bears

**HUNTER, ARTHUR—Center—Notre
Dame**
1954 Green Bay Packers
1956–59 Cleveland Browns
1960 Los Angeles Rams

**HUNTER, ROMNEY—Back—
Marshall**
1933 Portsmouth Spartans

HUNTER—Guard
1925–26 Hammond Pros

**HUPKE, THOMAS—Guard—
Alabama**

1934–37 Detroit Lions
1938–39 Cleveland Rams

ARTHUR HUNTER

HURLBURT, JOHN—Back—Chicago
1924–25 Chicago Cardinals

HURLEY, GEORGE—Guard—
Washington State
1932–33 Boston Redskins

HURLEY, JOHN—End—
Washington State
1931 Cleveland Indians

HURST, WILLIAM—Guard—
Oregon Univ.
1924 Chicago Bears
1924 Kenosha

HURTJUN—Back
1923 Rochester Kodaks

HUSMANN, EDWARD—Guard—
Nebraska
1953, 56–59 Chicago Cardinals
1960 Dallas Cowboys

HUST, ALBERT—End—Tennessee
1946 Chicago Cardinals

HUTCHINSON, ELVIN—Back—
Whittier
1939 Detroit Lions

HUTCHINSON, RALPH—Tackle—
Chattanooga
1949 New York Giants

HUTCHINSON, WILLIAM—Back—
Dartmouth
1942 New York Giants

HUTH, GERALD—Guard—Wake
Forest
1956 New York Giants

1959–60 Philadelphia Eagles

HUTSON, DONALD—End—Alabama
1935–45 Green Bay Packers
1940, 41, 42, 43, 44 #1 Scoring
1936, 37, 39, 41, 42, 43, 44, 45 #1 Pass
    Receiving
1943 #1 Field Goals

HUTSON, MERLE—Guard—
Heidelberg
1931 Cleveland Indians

HUTTON, LEON—Back—Purdue
1930 Frankford Yellowjackets

HUXHOLD, KENNETH—Guard—
Wisconsin
1954–58 Philadelphia Eagles

HUZVAR, JOHN—Back—North
Carolina
1952 Philadelphia Eagles
1953–54 Baltimore Colts

• • •

ILLMAN, EDWARD—Back—
Montana State
1928 Chicago Cardinals
1933 Philadelphia Eagles

ILLOWIT, ROY—Tackle—CCNY
1937 Brooklyn Dodgers

IMAN, KENNETH—Center—
Southwestern
1960 Green Bay Packers

IMLAY, TALMA—Back—California
1926 Los Angeles
1927 New York Giants

INGALLS, ROBERT, Center—
Michigan
1942 Green Bay Packers

INGLE—Back
1921 Evansville Crimson Giants

INGLEHART, FLOYD—Back—Wiley
(Tex.)
1958 Los Angeles Rams

INGWERSON, BERT—Tackle—
Illinois
1921 Chicago Bears (Staleys)

INTRIERI, MARNE—Guard—
Loyola (Md.)
1932 Staten Island Stapletons
1933–34 Boston Redskins

IPPOLITO, ANTHONY—Guard—
Purdue
1943 Chicago Bears

IRGENS, EINAR—Back
1922–24 Minneapolis Marines

IRGENS, NEWMAN—Back
1922 Minneapolis Marines

**IRVIN, BARLOW—Guard—Texas
A & M**
1926–27 Buffalo Bisons

**IRVIN, CECIL—Tackle—Davis &
Elkins**
1931 Providence Steamrollers
1932–35 New York Giants

**IRVIN, WILLIAM—End—Florida
A & M**
1953 Philadelphia Eagles

IRWIN, DONALD—Back—Colgate
1936 Boston Redskins
1937–40 Washington Redskins

IRWIN, JAMES—Back
1922–23 Louisville Colonels

**ISAACSON, THEODORE—Tackle—
Washington**
1934–35 Chicago Cardinals

ISABEL, WILMER—Back—Ohio State
1923–24 Columbus Tigers

ISBELL, CECIL—Back—Purdue
1938–42 Green Bay Packers
1941, 42 #1 Passing

CECIL ISBELL

**ISSELHARDT, RALPH—Guard—
Franklin**
1937 Detroit Lions
1937 Cleveland Rams

ITZEL, JOHN—Back—Pittsburgh
1945 Pittsburgh Steelers

**IVERSON, CHRISTOPHER—Back—
Oregon**
1947 New York Giants
1948–49 New York Yankees (AAFC)

1950–51 New York Yanks

IVY, FRANK—End—Oklahoma
1940 Pittsburgh Steelers
1940–42, 45–47 Chicago Cardinals

IZO, GEORGE—Back—Notre Dame
1960 St. Louis Cardinals

* * *

JACKSON, CHARLES—Back—SMU
1958 Chicago Cardinals
1960 Dallas Texans (AFL)

**JACKSON, COLVILLE—End—
Chicago**
1922 Hammond Pros

**JACKSON, DONALD—Back—North
Carolina**
1936 Philadelphia Eagles

**JACKSON, GRADY—Tackle—
Oklahoma State Southwest**
1928–30 Providence Steamrollers

JACKSON, HENRY—Back—Missouri
1928 Detroit Panthers

**JACKSON, KENNETH—Tackle—
Texas**
1952 Dallas Texans
1953–57 Baltimore Colts

**JACKSON, LAWRENCE—Back—
Loyola**
1926 Louisville Colonels

**JACKSON, ROBERT—Back—North
Carolina**
1950–51 New York Giants

**JACKSON, ROBERT—Back—
Alabama**
1960 Philadelphia Eagles

JACOBS, HARRY—End—Bradley
1960 Boston Patriots (AFL)

JACOBS, JACK—Back—Oklahoma
1942, 45 Cleveland Rams
1946 Washington Redskins
1947–49 Green Bay Packers
1947 #1 Punting (tied by Reagen)

JACOBS, MARVIN—Tackle
1948 Chicago Cardinals

**JACOBS, PROVERB—Tackle—
California**
1958 Philadelphia Eagles
1960 New York Giants

JACUNSKI, HARRY—End—Fordham
1939–44 Green Bay Packers

JAFFUR, JOHN—Guard—Penn State
1946 Washington Redskins

PROVERB JACOBS

JAGADE, HARRY—Back—Indiana
1949   Baltimore Colts (AAFC)
1951–53   Cleveland Browns
1954–55   Chicago Bears

**JAGIELSKI, HARRY—Guard—
Indiana**
1956   Chicago Cardinals
1956   Washington Redskins
1960   Boston Patriots (AFL)

**JAMERSON, CHARLES—End—
Arkansas**
1926   Hartford Blues

JAMES, DANIEL—Center—Ohio State
1960   Pittsburgh Steelers

JAMES, GEORGE—Guard—Nebraska
1929   Frankford Yellowjackets

JAMES, RICHARD—Back—Oregon
1956–60   Washington Redskins

RICHARD JAMES

JAMES, THOMAS—Back—Ohio State
1948–51   Cleveland Browns

**JAMIESON, RICHARD—Back—
Bradley**
1960   New York Titans (AFL)

**JAMISON, ALFRED—Tackle—
Colgate**
1960   Houston Oilers (AFL)

**JAMISON, LEON—End—Tennessee
A & I**
1958   Pittsburgh Steelers

**JANECEK, CLARENCE—Guard—
Purdue**
1933   Pittsburgh Pirates

**JANERETTE, CHARLES—Guard—
Penn State**
1960   Los Angeles Rams

JANIAK, LEONARD—Back—Ohio
1939   Brooklyn Dodgers
1940–42   Cleveland Rams

**JANKOVICH, KEEVER—Center—
College of Pacific**
1952   Dallas Texans
1953   Chicago Cardinals

**JANKOWSKI, EDWARD—Back—
Wisconsin**
1936–41   Green Bay Packers

**JANNISEN, RAYMOND—Tackle—
South Dakota**
1931   Green Bay Packers

**JANOWICZ, VICTOR—Back—Ohio
State**
1954–55   Washington Redskins

**JANSANTE, VALERIO—End—
Duquesne**
1946–51   Pittsburgh Steelers
1951   Green Bay Packers

JANSING, L.—End
1922   Louisville Colonels

JAPPE, PAUL—Guard—Syracuse
1925, 27–28   New York Giants
1926   Brooklyn Dodgers

JAQUITH—Back
1926   Kansas City Cowboys

**JARMOLUK, MICHAEL—Tackle—
Temple**
1946–47   Chicago Bears
1948   Boston Yanks
1949   New York Bulldogs
1950–55   Philadelphia Eagles

**JARVI, TOIMI—Back—North
Illinois State**

1944   Philadelphia Eagles
1945   Pittsburgh Steelers

**JASZEWSKI, FLOYD—Tackle—
Minnesota**
1950–51   Detroit Lions

**JAWISH, HENRY—Guard—
Georgetown**
1926   Pottsville Maroons

JEAN, WALTER—Guard—Bethany
1922–23   Akron Steels
1924   Milwaukee Badgers
1925–26   Green Bay Packers
1927   Pottsville Maroons

**JECHA, RALPH—Guard—
Northwestern**
1955   Chicago Bears
1956   Pittsburgh Steelers

**JEFFERS, EDWARD—Guard—
Oklahoma A & M**
1947   Brooklyn Dodgers (AAFC)

**JEFFERSON, WILLIAM—Back—
Mississippi State**
1941   Detroit Lions
1942   Brooklyn Dodgers
1942   Philadelphia Eagles

**JEFFRIES, ROBERT—Guard—
Howard**
1942   Brooklyn Dodgers

JELACIC, JON—End—Minnesota
1958   New York Giants

**JELLEY, THOMAS—End—Miami
(Fla.)**
1951   Pittsburgh Steelers

**JENISON, RAYMOND—Tackle—
South Dakota**
1931   Green Bay Packers

**JENKINS, JACQUE—Back—
Vanderbilt**
1943, 46–47   Washington Redskins

**JENKINS, JONATHAN—Tackle—
Tackle—Dartmouth**
1949   Baltimore Colts (AAFC)
1950   Baltimore Colts
1950   New York Yanks

JENKINS, WALTER—End—Tackle
1955   Detroit Lions

JENNINGS, JAMES—End—Missouri
1955   Green Bay Packers

**JENNINGS, JOHN—Tackle—Ohio
State**
1950–57   Chicago Cardinals

**JENNINGS, WILLIAM—Center—
Haskell**

1929   Providence Steamrollers
1930   Portsmouth Spartans

JENSEN, ROBERT—End—Iowa State
1948–49   Chicago Rockets (AAFC)
1950   Baltimore Colts

JENSVOLD, LEO—Back—Iowa
1931   Chicago Bears
1931   Cleveland Indians

JESSEN, ERNEST—Tackle—Iowa
1931   Cleveland Indians

**JESSUP, WILLIAM—End—
Southern California**
1951–52, 54–58   San Francisco 49ers
1960   Denver Broncos (AFL)

**JETER, PERRY—Back—California
Polytech.**
1956–57   Chicago Bears

JETT, JOHN—End—Wake Forest
1941   Detroit Lions

**JEWETT, ROBERT—End—Michigan
State**
1958   Chicago Bears

JOBKO, WILLIAM—Guard—Ohio
1958–60   Los Angeles Rams

WILLIAM JOBKO

**JOCHER, ARTHUR—Guard—
Manhattan**
1940–42   Brooklyn Dodgers

JOE, LAWRENCE—Back—Penn State
1949   Buffalo Bills (AAFC)

**JOESTING, HERBERT—Back—
Minnesota**
1929–30   Minneapolis Redjackets
1930–31   Frankford Yellowjackets
1931–32   Chicago Bears

JOHNS, JAMES—Guard—Michigan

1923–24   Cleveland Bulldogs
1924   Minneapolis Marines

**JOHNSON, ALBERT—Back—
Kentucky**
1937   Brooklyn Dodgers
1938   Chicago Bears
1939–41   Chicago Cardinals
1942   Philadelphia Eagles

**JOHNSON, ALVIN—Back—Hardin-
Simmons**
1948   Philadelphia Eagles

**JOHNSON, ARTHUR—Tackle—
Fordham**
1923–27   Duluth Kelleys

**JOHNSON, CECIL—Back—East
Texas**
1942   Philadelphia Eagles
1943–44   Brooklyn Dodgers

**JOHNSON, CLYDE—Tackle—
Kentucky**
1946–47   Los Angeles Rams
1948   Los Angeles Dons (AAFC)

**JOHNSON, DONALD—Back—
California**
1953–55   Philadelphia Eagles

**JOHNSON, DONALD—Center—
Northwestern**
1942   Cleveland Rams

**JOHNSON, EUGENE—Back—
Cincinnati**
1959–60   Philadelphia Eagles

**JOHNSON, FARNHAM—End—
Wisconsin & Michigan**
1948   Chicago Rockets (AAFC)

**JOHNSON, FREDERIC—Back—
Notre Dame**
1922   Rock Island Independents
1922–24   Racine Legions
1924   Chicago Bears

JOHNSON, GILBERT—Back—SMU
1949   New York Yankees (AAFC)

**JOHNSON, GLENN—Tackle—
Arizona State**
1948   New York Yankees (AAFC)
1949   Green Bay Packers

**JOHNSON, HARVEY—Back—
William & Mary**
1946–49   New York Yankees (AAFC)
1951   New York Yanks

**JOHNSON, HERBERT—Back—West
Point**
1954   New York Giants

**JOHNSON, HOWARD—Guard—
Georgia**

1940–41   Green Bay Packers
    Killed ninth day of Iwo Jima
    invasion. Capt., U.S. Marines.

JOHNSON, JACK—Back—Miami
1957–59   Chicago Bears
1960   Buffalo Bills (AFL)

JOHNSON, JOHN—Tackle—Utah
1934–40   Detroit Lions

**JOHNSON, JOHN CURLEY—Back—
Houston**
1960   Dallas Texans (AFL)

JOHN HENRY JOHNSON

**JOHNSON, JOHN HENRY—
St. Mary's Cal.**
1954–56   San Francisco 49ers
1957–59   Detroit Lions
1960   Pittsburgh Steelers

**JOHNSON, JOSEPH—Back—
Mississippi**
1948   New York Giants

**JOHNSON, KOSSE "JOE"—Back—
Boston College**
1954–58   Green Bay Packers
1960   Boston Patriots (AFL)

**JOHNSON, LAWRENCE—Center—
Haskell**
1933–35   Boston Redskins
1936–39   New York Giants
1944   Washington Redskins

JOHNSON, LEON—End—Columbia
1929   Orange

**JOHNSON, MARVIN—Back—San
Jose State**
1951–52   Los Angeles Rams
1952–53   Green Bay Packers

**JOHNSON, NATHAN—Tackle—
Illinois**
1946–47   New York Yankees (AAFC)
1948–49   Chicago Rockets

1950 New York Yanks

JOHNSON, OSCAR—Back—Vermont
1929 Boston Braves

**JOHNSON, PETER—Back—
Virginia Military Inst.**
1959 Chicago Bears

**JOHNSON, RAYMOND—Back—
Denver**
1940 Chicago Cardinals

**JOHNSON, ROBERT—Tackle—
Chattanooga**
1930 Portsmouth Spartans

**JOHNSON, THEODORE—Tackle—
South Dakota**
1921 Akron Steels

**JOHNSON, THOMAS—Tackle—
Michigan**
1952 Green Bay Packers

**JOHNSON, WILLIAM—Guard—
SMU**
1947 Chicago Bears

**JOHNSON, WILLIAM—End—
Minnesota**
1940 Green Bay Packers

**JOHNSON, WILLIAM—Center—
Tyler, Tex. JC**
1948–56 San Francisco 49ers

**JOHNSOS, LUKE—End—
Northwestern**
1929–36, 38 Chicago Bears

**JOHNSTONE, CHESTER—Back—
Elmhurst**
1931, 34–38 Green Bay Packers
1934 St. Louis Gunners
1939–40 Pittsburgh Pirates

**JOHNSTON, JAMES—Back—
Washington**
1939–40 Washington Redskins
1946 Chicago Cardinals

**JOHNSTON, MARK—Back—
Northwestern**
1960 Houston Oilers (AFL)

**JOHNSTON, PRESTON—Back—
SMU**
1946 Miami Seahawks (AAFC)
1946 Buffalo Bisons (AAFC)

**JOHNSTON, REX—Back—
Southern California**
1960 Pittsburgh Steelers

JOLLEY, ALFRED—Tackle—Marietta
1922, 26 Akron Steels
1923 Dayton Triangles
1929 Buffalo Bisons

1930 Brooklyn Dodgers
1931 Cleveland Indians

JONAS—MARVIN—Center—Utah
1931 Brooklyn Dodgers

JONASEN, CHARLES—Back
1923 Minneapolis Marines

JONES, ARTHUR—Back—Richmond
1941, 45–46 Pittsburgh Steelers

JONES, BEN—Back—Grove City
1921 Akron Steels
1923, 25 Canton Bulldogs
1924 Dayton Triangles
1924–25 Cleveland Indians
1925–26 Frankford Yellowjackets
1927–28 Chicago Cardinals

JONES, BRUCE—Guard—Alabama
1927–28 Green Bay Packers
1930 Newark
1931–34 Brooklyn Dodgers

**JONES, CHARLES—End—
George Washington**
1955 Washington Redskins

**JONES, DONALD—Back—
Washington**
1940 Philadelphia Eagles

JONES, EDGAR—Back—Pittsburgh
1945 Chicago Bears
1946–49 Cleveland Browns (AAFC)

JONES, ELLIS—Guard—Tulsa
1945 Boston Yanks

**JONES, ELMER—Guard—Wake
Forest**
1946 Buffalo Bisons (AAFC)
1947–48 Detroit Lions

JONES, HARVEY—Back—Baylor
1944–45 Cleveland Rams
1947 Washington Redskins

**JONES, JAMES "CASEY"—Back—
Union Tenn.**
1946 Detroit Lions

JONES, JAMES—Back—Washington
1958 Los Angeles Rams

**JONES, JERRY—Tackle—Notre
Dame**
1921 Chicago Bears (Staleys)
1922 Rock Island Independents
1923 Toledo Maroons
1924 Cleveland Indians

**JONES, KENNETH—Back—
Franklin-Marshall**
1924 Buffalo Bisons

**JONES, LEWIS—Guard—
Weatherford**
1943 Brooklyn Dodgers

JONES, RALPH—End—Alabama
1946 Detroit Lions
1947 Baltimore Colts (AAFC)

JONES, ROBERT—Guard—Indiana
1934 Green Bay Packers

**JONES, STANLEY—Tackle—
Maryland**
1954–60 Chicago Bears

**JONES, THOMAS—Guard—
Bucknell**
1930 Minneapolis Marines
1929–31 Frankford Yellowjackets
1932–36 New York Giants
1938 Green Bay Packers

**JONES, THOMAS—Tackle—
Miami (Ohio)**
1955 Cleveland Browns

**JONES, THURMAN—Back—
Abilene Christian**
1941–43 Brooklyn Dodgers

**JONES, WILLIAM—Back—Tulane &
LSU**
1946 Miami Seahawks (AAFC)
1946–47 Brooklyn Dodgers (AAFC)
1948–49 Cleveland Browns (AAFC)
1950–55 Cleveland Browns

**JONES, WILLIAM—Guard—West
Virginia Wesleyan**
1937 Brooklyn Dodgers

JORDAN, HENRY—Tackle—Virginia
1957–58 Cleveland Browns
1959–60 Green Bay Packers

**JORGENSEN, CARL—Tackle—St.
Mary's (Cal.)**
1934 Green Bay Packers
1935 Philadelphia Eagles

**JORGENSEN, WAGNER—Center—St.
Mary's (Cal.)**
1936–37 Brooklyn Dodgers

JOSEPH, R.—End
1927 Dayton Triangles

**JOSEPH, ZERN—Center—Miami
(Ohio)**
1925, 27 Dayton Triangles
1930 Portsmouth Spartans
1931 Cleveland Indians

JOYCE, DONALD—Tackle—Tulane
1951–53 Chicago Cardinals
1954–60 Baltimore Colts

JOYNER, L. C.—Back—Diablo Valley
1960 Oakland Raiders (AFL)

JUDD, SAXON—End—Tulsa
1946–48 Brooklyn Dodgers (AAFC)

DONALD JOYCE

**JULIAN, FREDERICK—Back—
Michigan**
1960 New York Titans (AFL)

**JUNGMICHEL, HAROLD—Guard—
Texas**
1946 Miami Seahawks (AAFC)

JUNKER, STEPHAN—End—Xavier
1957, 59–60 Detroit Lions

**JURGENSEN, CHRISTIAN—Back—
Duke**
1957–60 Philadelphia Eagles

**JURICH, MICHAEL—Tackle—
Denver**
1941–42 Brooklyn Dodgers

**JURKIEWICZ, WALTER—Center—
Indiana**
1946 Detroit Lions

**JUSTER, RUBIN—Tackle—
Minnesota**
1946 Boston Yanks

**JUSTICE, CHARLES—Back—North
Carolina**
1950, 52–54 Washington Redskins

JUSTICE, EDWARD—Back—Gonzaga
1936 Boston Redskins
1937–42 Washington Redskins

**JUZWIK, STEPHEN—Back—Notre
Dame**
1942 Washington Redskins
1946–47 Buffalo Bills (AAFC)
1948 Chicago Rockets (AAFC)

* * *

**KABEALO, MICHAEL—Back—Ohio
State**
1944 Cleveland Rams

KADESKY, MAX—End—Iowa
1923   Rock Island Independents

KAER, MORTON—Back—Southern
   California
1931   Frankford Yellowjackets
1931   Brooklyn Dodgers

KAHL, CYRUS—Back—North Dakota
1930–31   Portsmouth Spartans

KAHLER, ROBERT—Back—
   Nebraska
1940–44   Green Bay Packers

KAHLER, ROYAL—Tackle—
   Nebraska
1941   Pittsburgh Steelers
1942   Green Bay Packers

KAHN, EDWARD—Guard—North
   Carolina
1935–36   Boston Redskins
1937   Washington Redskins
   Died of wounds in Leyte invasion, Feb. 17, 1945. Lt., U.S.
   Marines.

KAKASIC, GEORGE—Guard—
   Duquesne
1936–39   Pittsburgh Steelers

KAKELA, WAYNE—Center—
   Minnesota
1930   Minneapolis Redjackets

KALLINO, EDWARD—Tackle—
   Illinois
1928   Chicago Bears

KALMANIR, THOMAS—Back—
   Nevada
1949–51   Los Angeles Rams
1952   Dallas Texans
1953   Baltimore Colts

KAMP, JAMES—Tackle—Oklahoma
   City Univ.
1932   Staten Island Stapletons
1933   Boston Redskins

KANE, CARL—Back—St. Louis Univ.
1936   Philadelphia Eagles

KANE, HERBERT—Tackle—
   Oklahoma Teachers
1944–45   New York Giants

KANYA, ROBERT—Tackle—New
   York Univ.
1931–32   Staten Island Stapletons

KAPELE, JOHN—Tackle—
   Brigham Young
1960   Pittsburgh Steelers

KAPITANSKY, BERNARD—Guard—
   Long Island Univ.
1942   Brooklyn Dodgers

KAPLAN, BERNARD—Guard—
   Western Maryland
1935–36   New York Giants
1942   Philadelphia Eagles

KAPLAN, SIDNEY—Back—Hamline
1923   Minneapolis Marines

KAPLANOFF, CARL—Tackle—Ohio
   State
1939   Brooklyn Dodgers

KAPORCH, ALBERT—Tackle—St.
   Bonaventure
1943–45   Detroit Lions

KAPTER, ALEXANDER—Guard—
   Northwestern
1946   Cleveland Browns (AAFC)

KARAMATIC, GEORGE—Back—
   Gonzaga
1938   Washington Redskins

KARAS, EMIL—Guard—Dayton
1959   Washington Redskins
1960   Los Angeles Chargers (AFL)

KARCH, ROBERT—Tackle—Ohio
   State
1921–22   Columbus Tigers
1923   Louisville Colonels

KARCHER, JAMES—Guard—Ohio
   State
1936   Boston Redskins
1937–39   Washington Redskins

KARCIS, JOHN—Back—Carnegie
   Tech.
1932–35   Brooklyn Dodgers
1936–38   Pittsburgh Pirates
1938–39   New York Giants

KARILIVACZ, CARL—Back—
   Syracuse
1953–58   Detroit Lions
1958   New York Giants
1959–60   Los Angeles Rams

KARMAZIN, MICHAEL—Guard—
   Duke
1946–47   New York Yankees (AAFC)

KARNOFSKY, ABRAHAM—Back—
   Arizona
1945   Philadelphia Eagles
1946   Boston Yanks

KARPOWICH, EDWARD—Tackle—
   Catholic Univ.
1936–39   Pittsburgh Pirates

CARL KARILIVACZ

KARR, WILLIAM—End—West Virginia
1933-38   Chicago Bears

KARRAS, ALEXANDER—Tackle—Iowa
1958-60   Detroit Lions

KARRAS, JOHN—Back—Illinois
1952   Chicago Cardinals

KARRAS, LOUIS—Tackle—Purdue
1950-52   Washington Redskins

KARRAS, THEODORE—Tackle—Indiana
1958-59   Pittsburgh Steelers
1960   Chicago Bears

KARRS, JOHN—Back—Duquesne
1944   Cleveland Rams

KARSTENS, GEORGE—Center—Indiana
1949   Detroit Lions

KARWALES, JOHN—End—Michigan
1945, 47   Chicago Bears
1947   Chicago Cardinals

KASAP, MICHAEL—Tackle—Illinois & Purdue
1947   Buffalo Colts (AAFC)
1947   Buffalo Bills (AAFC)

KASKA, ANTHONY—Back—Illinois Wesleyan
1935   Detroit Lions
1936-38   Brooklyn Dodgers

KASKY, EDWARD—Tackle—Villanova
1942   Philadelphia Eagles

KASPER, THOMAS—Back—Notre Dame

1923   Rochester Jeffersons

KASSEL, CHARLES—End—Illinois
1927   Chicago Bears
1927-28   Frankford Yellowjackets
1929-33   Chicago Cardinals

KATALINES, LEO—Tackle—Catholic Univ.
1937   Green Bay Packers

KATCAVAGE, JAMES—End—Dayton
1956-60   New York Giants

KATCIK, JOSEPH—Tackle—Notre Dame
1960   New York Titans (AFL)

KATRISHEN, MICHAEL—Tackle—George Washington
1947-49   Washington Redskins

KAUFMAN, JOHN—Tackle—Pennsylvania
1929   Dayton Triangles

KAVANAUGH, KENNETH—End—LSU
1940, 41, 45-50   Chicago Bears

KAVEL, GEORGE—Back—Carnegie Tech.
1934   Philadelphia Eagles
1934   Pittsburgh Steelers

KAW, EDWARD—Back—Cornell
1924   Buffalo Bisons

KAWAL, EDWARD—Center—Illinois
1931-36   Chicago Bears
1937   Washington Redskins

KEAHEY, EULIS—Tackle—George Washington
1942   New York Giants
1942   Brooklyn Dodgers

KEANE, JAMES—End—Iowa
1946-51   Chicago Bears
1952   Green Bay Packers
1947   #1 Pass Receiving

KEANE, THOMAS—Back—West Virginia
1948-51   Los Angeles Rams
1952   Dallas Texans
1953-54   Baltimore Colts
1955   Chicago Cards

KEARNS, THOMAS—Tackle—Miami (Fla.)
1945   New York Giants
1946   Chicago Cardinals

KECK, STANLEY—Guard—Princeton
1923   Cleveland Indians

KEEBLE, JOSEPH—Back—UCLA
1937   Cleveland Rams

KEEFE, EMMETT—Guard—Notre Dame
1921   Green Bay Packers
1921–22   Rock Island Independents
1922   Milwaukee Badgers

KEEFER, JACKSON—Back—Brown
1926   Providence Steamrollers
1928   Dayton Triangles

KEELING, RAYMOND—Tackle—Texas
1938–39   Philadelphia Eagles

KEEN, ALLEN—Back—Arkansas
1937–38   Philadelphia Eagles

KEENAN, EDWARD—Guard—Washington
1926   Hartford Blues

KEENAN, JOHN—Guard—Southern Carolina
1944–45, 51   Washington Redskins

KEENE, ROBERT—Back—Detroit
1943–45   Detroit Lions

KEKERIS, JAMES—Tackle—Missouri
1947   Philadelphia Eagles
1948   Green Bay Packers

KELCH—End
1930   Brooklyn Dodgers

KELL, PAUL—Tackle—Notre Dame
1939–40   Green Bay Packers

KELLAGHER, WILLIAM—Back—Fordham
1946–48   Chicago Rockets (AAFC)

KELLER, KENNETH—Back—North Carolina
1956–57   Philadelphia Eagles

KELLEY, EDWARD—Tackle—Texas
1949   Los Angeles Dons (AAFC)

KELLEY, GORDON—Back—Georgia
1960   San Francisco 49ers

KELLEY, ROBERT—Center—Texas State West
1955–56   Philadelphia Eagles

KELLEY, WILLIAM—End—Texas Tech.
1949   Green Bay Packers

KELLISON, JOHN—Tackle—West Virginia Wesleyan
1921   Canton Bulldogs

KELLOGG, CLARENCE—Back—St. Mary's (Cal.)
1936   Chicago Cardinals

KELLOGG, ROBERT—Back—Tulane
1940   Chicago Cardinals

KELLOGG, WILLIAM—Back—Syracuse
1924   Frankford Yellowjackets
1925   Rochester Jeffersons
1926   Chicago Cardinals

KELLY, CHARLES—Back—Northwestern
1922   Toledo Maroons
1923–26   Duluth Kelleys
1925   Rochester Kodaks

KELLY, ELLISON—Guard—Michigan State
1959   New York Giants

KELLY, ELMER—End—Wichita
1944   Chicago Bears

KELLY, JOHN SIMMS—Back—Kentucky
1932   New York Giants
1933–34, 37   Brooklyn Dodgers

KELLY, ROBERT—Back—Notre Dame
1947–48   Los Angeles Dons (AAFC)
1949   Baltimore Colts (AAFC)

KELLY, WILLIAM—Back—Montana
1927   Cleveland Indians
1927–28   New York Yankees
1929   Orange
1929   Frankford Yellowjackets
1929–30   Brooklyn Dodgers

KELSCH, CHRISTIAN—Back—None
1933–34   Pittsburgh Pirates

KELSH, MATTHEW—End—Iowa
1930   Brooklyn Dodgers

KEMP, JOHN—Back—Occidental
1957–58   Pittsburgh Steelers
1958   New York Giants
1959   San Francisco 49ers
1960   Los Angeles Chargers (AFL)

KEMP, RAYMOND—Tackle—Duquesne
1933   Pittsburgh Pirates

KEMPINSKA, CHARLES—Guard—Mississippi
1960   Los Angeles Chargers (AFL)

KEMPTON, HERBERT—Back—Yale
1921   Canton Bulldogs

KENDALL, CHARLES—Back—UCLA
1960   Houston Oilers (AFL)

KENDRICKS, JAMES—Tackle—Texas A & M
1922   Toledo Maroons

1922   Canton Bulldogs
1923   Louisville Colonels
1924   Chicago Bears
1925   Hammond Pros
1925–26   Buffalo Bisons
1927   New York Giants

JOHN KEMP

KENERSON, JOHN—Guard—Kentucky State
1960   Los Angeles Rams

KENNARD, GEORGE—Guard—Kansas
1952–55   New York Giants

KENNEALLY, GEORGE—End—St. Bonaventure
1926–28   Pottsville Maroons
1929, 32   Boston Braves
1930   Chicago Cardinals
1933–35   Philadelphia Eagles

KENNEDY, JOSEPH—Back—Columbia
1925   Buffalo Bisons

KENNEDY, ROBERT—Back—Washington State
1946–49   New York Yankees (AAFC)
1950   New York Yanks

KENNEDY, ROBERT—Back—North Carolina
1949   Los Angeles Dons (AAFC)

KENNEDY, WILLIAM—End—Michigan State
1942, 44   Detroit Lions
1947   Boston Yanks

KENNY, CHARLES—Guard—San Francisco
1947   San Francisco 49ers (AAFC)

KENYON, CROWELL—Guard—Ripon
1923   Green Bay Packers

KENYON, WILLIAM—Back—Georgetown
1925   New York Giants

KERCHER, RICHARD—Back—Tulsa
1954   Detroit Lions

KERCHER, ROBERT—End—Georgetown
1944   Green Bay Packers

KERCHEVAL, RALPH—Back—Kentucky
1934–40   Brooklyn Dodgers
1938   #1 Field Goals (tied by Cuff)

KERIASOTIS, NICHOLAS—Guard—St. Ambrose
1941–42, 45   Chicago Bears

KERKORIAN, GARY—Back—Stanford
1952   Pittsburgh Steelers
1954–55, 58   Baltimore Colts

KERN, WILLIAM—Tackle—Pittsburgh
1929–30   Green Bay Packers

KERNS, JOHN—Tackle—Ohio
1947–49   Buffalo Bills (AAFC)

KERNWEIN, GRAHAM—Back—Chicago
1926   Racine Legion
1927   Chicago Bears

KERR, WILLIAM—End—Notre Dame
1946   Los Angeles Dons (AAFC)

KERRIGAN, THOMAS—Guard—Columbia
1930   New York Giants
1930   Newark

KERSHAW, GEORGE—End—Colgate
1949   New York Giants

KETZKO, ALEXANDER—Tackle—Michigan State
1942   New York Giants
1943   Detroit Lions
          Killed in France with Patch's
          7th Army, Dec. 23, 1944. Sergeant, U.S. Army.

KEUPER, KENNETH—Back—Georgia
1945–47   Green Bay Packers
1948   New York Giants

KEYES, ROBERT—Back—San Diego
1960   Oakland Raiders (AFL)

**KEYS, HOWARD—Tackle—
    Oklahoma State**
1960 Philadelphia Eagles

**KHAYAT, EDWARD—Tackle—
    Tulane**
1957 Washington Redskins
1958–60 Philadelphia Eagles

**KHAYAT, ROBERT—Guard—
    Mississippi**
1960 Washington Redskins

KIBLER, WILLIAM—Back
1922 Buffalo Bisons

**KICHEFSKI, WALTER—End—
    Miami (Fla.)**
1940–42 Pittsburgh Steelers
1944 Card-Pitt

KIEJEL—End
1934 Chicago Cardinals

KIELBASA, MAX—Back—Duquesne
1946 Pittsburgh Steelers

KIELEY, HOWARD—Tackle—
1923–25 Duluth Kelleys
1926 Chicago Cardinals

**KIESLING, WALTER—Guard—St.
    Thomas**
1926–27 Duluth Eskimos
1928 Pottsville Maroons
1929 Boston Braves
1929–33 Chicago Cardinals
1934 Chicago Bears
1935–36 Green Bay Packers
1937–38 Pittsburgh

KIICK, GEORGE—Back—Bucknell
1940, 45 Pittsburgh Steelers

**KILBOURNE, WARREN—Tackle—
    Michigan**
1939 Green Bay Packers

**KILCULLEN, ROBERT—Tackle—
    Texas Tech.**
1957–60 Chicago Bears

KILEY, ROGER—End—Notre Dame
1923 Chicago Cardinals

**KILLINGER, GLENN—Back—
    Penn. State**
1926 New York Giants

KILROY, FRANK—Tackle—Temple
1943 Phil-Pitt
1944–56 Philadelphia Eagles

**KIMBER, WILLIAM—End—
    Florida State**
1959–60 New York Giants

**KIMBLE, FRANK—End—West
    Virginia**
1945 Pittsburgh Steelers

**KIMBROUGH, JOHN—Back—Texas
    A & M**
1946–48 Los Angeles Dons (AAFC)

KIMMEL, J. D.—Tackle—Houston
1955–57 Washington Redskins
1958 Green Bay Packers

**KINARD, FRANK—Tackle—
    Mississippi**
1938–44 Brooklyn Dodgers
1946–47 New York Yankees (AAFC)

**KINARD, GEORGE—Guard—
    Mississippi**
1941–42 Brooklyn Dodgers
1946 New York Yankees (AAFC)

**KINARD, WILLIAM—Back—
    Mississippi**
1956 Cleveland Browns
1957–58 Green Bay Packers
1960 Buffalo Bills (AFL)

**KINCAID, JAMES—Back—
    South Carolina**
1954 Washington Redskins

KINDERDINE, GEORGE—Center—
1921–29 Dayton Triangles

KINDT, DONALD—Back—Wisconsin
1947–55 Chicago Bears

KINEK, GEORGE—Back—Tulane
1954 Chicago Cardinals

**KINEK, MICHAEL—End—Michigan
    State**
1940 Cleveland Rams

KING, ANDREW—Back—West Virginia
1921 Akron Steels
1922 Toledo Maroons
1922 Milwaukee Badgers
1925 Hammond Pros

KING, DONALD—Tackle—Kentucky
1954 Cleveland Browns
1956 Philadelphia Eagles
1956 Green Bay Packers
1960 Denver Broncos (AFL)

**KING, EDWARD—End—Boston
    College**
1948–49 Buffalo Bills (AAFC)
1950 Baltimore Colts

KING, EMMETT—Back
1954 Chicago Cardinals

KING, HENRY—End—Georgia
1946–47 Buffalo Bills (AAFC)
1948–49 Chicago Rockets (AAFC)

KING, PHILIP—Back—Vanderbilt
1958–60 New York Giants

KING, RALPH—Tackle—Chicago

1924   Racine Legions
1925   Chicago Bears

PHILIP KING

KING, RICHARD—Back—Harvard
1921   Rochester Jeffersons
1923   St. Louis Browns
1923–24   Chicago Cardinals

KINGERY, ELLSWORTH—Back—Tulane
1954   Chicago Cardinals

KINGERY, WAYNE—Back—LSU
1949   Baltimore Colts (AAFC)

KINSCHERF, CARL—Back—Colgate
1943–44   New York Giants

KIPP, JAMES—Tackle—Montana State
1942   Detroit Lions

KIRBY, JOHN—Back—Southern California
1949   Green Bay Packers

KIRCHNER, ADOLPH—Tackle
1926   Louisville Colonels

KIRK, BERNARD—Center—Michigan
1926   Buffalo Bisons

KIRK, KENNETH—Center—Mississippi
1960   Chicago Bears

KIRKGARD—Back
1923   Toledo Maroons

KIRKLAND, B'HO—Guard—Alabama
1935–36   Brooklyn Dodgers

KIRKLESKI, FRANK—Back—Lafayette
1927–28   Pottsville Maroons
1929   Orange
1930   Newark
1931   Brooklyn Dodgers

KIRKMAN, ROGER—Back—Washington & Jefferson
1933–35   Philadelphia Eagles

KISH, BENJAMIN—Back—Pittsburgh
1940–41   Brooklyn Dodgers
1942   44–49   Philadelphia Eagles
1943   Phil-Pitt

KISIDAY, GEORGE—End—Duquesne
1948   Buffalo Bills (AAFC)

KISSELL, ADOLPH—Back—Boston College
1942   Chicago Bears

KISSELL, EDWARD—Back—Wake Forest
1952, 54   Pittsburgh Steelers

KISSELL, JOHN—Tackle—Boston College
1948–49   Buffalo Bills (AAFC)
1950–52, 54–56   Cleveland Browns

KISSELL, VITO—Back—Holy Cross
1949   Buffalo Bills (AAFC)
1950   Baltimore Colts
1951   New York Yanks

KITTREDGE, PAUL—Back—Holy Cross
1929   Boston Braves

KITZMILLER, JOHN—Back—Oregon
1931   New York Giants

KIZZIRE, LEE—Back—Wyoming
1937   Detroit Lions
       Killed when shot down over
       New Guinea, Dec. 5, 1943.
       Captain, U.S. Air Force.

KLAPSTEIN, EARL—Tackle—College of Pacific
1946   Pittsburgh Steelers

KLASNIC, JOHN—Back—None
1948   Brooklyn Dodgers

KLASOSKUS, ALBIN—Tackle—Holy Cross
1941–42   New York Giants

KLAUS, FEE—Center—None
1921   Green Bay Packers

KLAWITTER, RICHARD—Center—South Dakota State
1956   Chicago Bears

KLEIN, RICHARD—Tackle—Iowa
1958–59   Chicago Bears
1960   Dallas Cowboys

KLENK, QUENTIN—End—Southern California

1946   Buffalo Bisons (AAFC)
1946   Chicago Rockets (AAFC)

KLEWICKI, EDWARD—End—
   Michigan State
1935–38   Detroit Lions

KLIEBHAN, ROGER—Back—
   Milwaukee Teachers
1921   Green Bay Packers

KLIMEK, ANTHONY—End—Illinois
1951–52   Chicago Cardinals

KLINE, GEORGE—Back
1937   Brooklyn Dodgers

KLINE, HARRY—End—Emporia
   Teachers
1939–40, 42   New York Giants

KLING—Back
1937   Brooklyn Dodgers

KLOPPENBERG, HARRY—End—
   Fordham
1930   Staten Island Stapletons
1931, 33–34   Brooklyn Dodgers
1936   Philadelphia Eagles

KLOSTERMAN, DONALD—Back—
   Loyola
1952   Los Angeles Rams

KLOTOVICH, MICHAEL—Back—
   St. Mary's (Cal.)
1941   Chicago Cardinals
1945   New York Giants

KLOTZ, JOHN—Tackle—
   Penn Military
1960   New York Titans (AFL)

KLUG, ALFRED—Tackle—Marquette
1946   Buffalo Bisons (AAFC)
1947–48   Baltimore Colts (AAFC)

KLUMB, JOHN—End—Washington
   State
1939   Chicago Cardinals
1940   Detroit Lions
1940   Pittsburgh Steelers

KLUTKA, NICHOLAS—End—
   Florida
1946   Buffalo Bisons (AAFC)

KMETOVIC, PETER—Back—
   Stanford
1946   Philadelphia Eagles
1947   Detroit Lions

KNABB, CHESTER—Back
1921   Cincinnati Celts

KNAFELC, GARY—End—Colorado
1954   Chicago Cardinals
1954–60   Green Bay Packers

GARY KNAFELC

KNAPPER, JOSEPH—Back—
   Ottawa-Kan.
1934   Philadelphia Eagles

KNECHT, WILLIAM—Tackle—
   Xavier (Cincinnati)
1925–26   Dayton Triangles

KNIGHT, PATRICK—Back—SMU
1952, 54–55   New York Giants

KNOLLA, JOHN—Back—Creighton
1942, 45   Chicago Cardinals

KNOP, OSCAR—Back—Illinois
1922–23   Hammond Pros
1923–27   Chicago Bears

KNORR, LAWRENCE—End—Dayton
1942, 45   Detroit Lions

KNOX, CHARLES—Tackle—St.
   Edmonds
1937   Philadelphia Eagles

KNOX, FRANK SAMUEL—Guard—
   New Hampshire
1934–36   Detroit Lions

KNOX, RONALD—Back—U.C.L.A.
1957   Chicago Bears

KNUTSON, EUGENE—End—
   Michigan
1954, 56   Green Bay Packers

KOBOLINSKI, STANLEY—Center—
   Boston College
1926   Brooklyn Dodgers

KOBROSKI, MILTON—Back—
   Trinity
1937   New York Giants

KOCH, GEORGE—Back—Baylor
1945   Cleveland Rams

1947   Buffalo Bills (AAFC)

**KOCHEL, MICHAEL—Guard—
Fordham**
1939   Chicago Cardinals

**KOCOUREK, DAVID—End—
Wisconsin**
1960   Los Angeles Chargers (AFL)

KODBA, JOSEPH—Center—Purdue
1947   Baltimore Colts (AAFC)
1947   Buffalo Bills (AAFC)

**KOEHLER, ROBERT—Back—
Northwestern**
1921   Chicago Bears (Staleys)
1921–26   Chicago Cardinals

**KOENINGER, ARTHUR—Center—
Chattanooga**
1932   Staten Island Stapletons
1933   Philadelphia Eagles

**KOEPFER, KARL—Guard—
Bowling Green**
1958   Detroit Lions

**KOKEN, MICHAEL—Back—Notre
Dame**
1933   Chicago Cardinals

**KOLBERG, ELMER—Back—Oregon
State**
1939–40   Philadelphia Eagles
1941   Pittsburgh Steelers

**KOLESAR, ROBERT—Guard—
Michigan**
1946   Cleveland Browns (AAFC)

**KOLLS, LOUIS—Center—St.
Ambrose**
1921–25   Rock Island Independents
1927   New York Yankees

**KOLMAN, EDWARD—Tackle—
Temple**
1940–42, 46–47   Chicago Bears
1949   New York Giants

**KOMAN, WILLIAM—Guard—
North Carolina**
1956   Baltimore Colts
1957–58   Philadelphia Eagles
1959   Chicago Cardinals
1960   St. Louis Cardinals

**KOMPARA, JOHN—Tackle—
South Carolina**
1960   Los Angeles Chargers (AFL)

**KONDRIA, JOHN—Tackle—St.
Vincent's**
1945   Pittsburgh Steelers

KONETSKY, FLOYD—End—Florida
1944–45   Cleveland Rams

1946   Pittsburgh Steelers
1947   Baltimore Colts (AAFC)
1947   Buffalo Bills (AAFC)

**KONISZEWSKI, JOHN—Tackle—
George Washington**
1945–46, 48   Washington Redskins

KONOPKA, JOHN—Back—Temple
1936   Philadelphia Eagles

**KONOVSKY, ROBERT—Guard—
Wisconsin**
1956–58   Chicago Cardinals
1960   Chicago Bears

KOONS, JOSEPH—Center—Scranton
1941   Brooklyn Dodgers

KONZ, KENNETH—Back—L.S.U.
1953–59   Cleveland Browns

**KOPCHA, JOSEPH—Guard—
Chattanooga**
1929, 32–35   Chicago Bears
1936   Detroit Lions

**KOPLAW, JOSEPH—Tackle—Boston
College**
1926   Providence Steamrollers

**KOPPISCH, WALTER—Back—
Columbia**
1925   Buffalo Bisons
1925–26   New York Giants

**KORISKY, EDWARD—Center—
Villanova**
1944   Boston Yanks

KOSEL, STANLEY—Back—Albright
1938–39   Brooklyn Dodgers

**KOSHLAP, JULES—Back—
Georgetown**
1940   Brooklyn Dodgers

**KOSIKOWSKI, FRANK—End—
Marquette, Notre Dame**
1948   Cleveland Browns (AAFC)
1948   Buffalo Bills (AAFC)

**KOSLOWSKI, JOSEPH—Tackle—
Boston College**
1925–27, 30   Providence Steamrollers
1929   Boston Braves

**KOSLOWSKI, STANLEY—Back—
Holy Cross**
1946   Miami Seahawks (AAFC)

**KOSTIUK, MICHAEL—Tackle—
Detroit**
1945   Detroit Lions
1946   Buffalo Bills (AAFC)

**KOSTKA, STANLEY—Back—
Minnesota**

1935 Brooklyn Dodgers

KOSTOS, ANTHONY—End—Bucknell
1927–31 Frankford Yellowjackets
1930 Minneapolis Redjackets
1933 Philadelphia Eagles

KOSTOS, MARTIN—End—Albright
1929–30 Frankford Yellowjackets

KOTAL, EDWARD—Back—Lawrence
1925–29 Green Bay Packers

KOTTLER, MARTIN—Back—Centre
1933 Pittsburgh Pirates

KOVAC, Edward—Back—Cincinnati
1960 Baltimore Colts

KOVASCY, WILLIAM—Tackle—Illinois
1923 Hammond Pros

KOVATCH, JOHN—End—Notre Dame
1941–42, 46 Washington Redskins
1947 Green Bay Packers

KOVATCH, JOHN—End—Northwestern
1938 Cleveland Rams

KOWALCZYK, WALTER—Back—Michigan State
1958–59 Philadelphia Eagles
1960 Dallas Cowboys

WALTER KOWALCZYK

KOWALSKI, ADOLPH—Back—Tulsa
1947 Brooklyn Dodgers (AAFC)

KOWALSKI, ANDREW—End—Mississippi State
1943–44 Brooklyn Dodgers
1945 Boston Yanks

KOZEL, CHESTER—Tackle—Mississippi
1947–48 Buffalo Bills (AAFC)
1948 Chicago Rockets (AAFC)

KOZIAK, MICHAEL—Guard—Notre Dame
1924–25 Duluth Kelleys

KRACUM, GEORGE—Back—Pittsburgh
1941 Brooklyn Dodgers

KRAEHE, OLIVER—Guard—Washington of Mo.
1922 Rock Island Independents
1923 St. Louis Browns

KRAEMER, ELDRED—Guard—Pittsburgh
1955 San Francisco 49ers

KRAFT, REYNOLD—End—Illinois
1922 Minneapolis Marines

KRALL, GERARD—Back—Ohio State
1950 Detroit Lions

KRAMER, FREDERICK—Guard—Washington State
1927–28 New York Yankees

KRAMER, GEORGE—Guard
1921 Akron Steels
1922–24 Minneapolis Marines
1924 Rock Island Independents

KRAMER, GERALD—Guard—Idaho
1958–60 Green Bay Packers

KRAMER, JOHN—Tackle—Marquette
1946 Buffalo Bisons (AAFC)

KRAMER, RONALD—End—Michigan
1957, 59–60 Green Bay Packers

KRANZ, KENNETH—Back—Milwaukee State
1949 Green Bay Packers

KRAUS, FRANCIS—Tackle—Hobart
1924 Buffalo Bisons

KRAUSE, HENRY—Center—St. Louis Univ.
1936 Brooklyn Dodgers
1937–38 Washington Redskins

KRAUSE, MAX—Back—Gonzaga
1933–36 New York Giants
1937–40 Washington Redskins

KRAUSE, PAUL—Guard—De Paul
1938 Cleveland Rams

KREAMCHECK, JOHN—Guard—William & Mary

1953–55   Chicago Bears

RONALD KRAMER

KREINHEDER, WALTER—Guard—Michigan
1922   Akron Steels
1923   St. Louis Browns
1925   Cleveland Indians

KREITLING, RICHARD—End—Illinois
1959–60   Cleveland Browns

KRESKY, JOSEPH—Guard—Wisconsin
1930   Green Bay Packers
1932   Boston Braves
1933–35   Philadelphia Eagles
1935   Pittsburgh Pirates

KRIEGER, EARL—Back—Ohio
1922   Columbus Tigers

KRIEGER, ROBERT—End—Dartmouth
1940–41, 46   Philadelphia Eagles

KRIEL, EMMETT—Guard—Baylor
1939   Philadelphia Eagles

KRING, FRANK—Back—TCU
1945   Detroit Lions

KRISHER, WILLIAM—Guard—Oklahoma
1958   Pittsburgh Steelers
1960   Dallas Texans (AFL)

KRISS, HOWARD—Back—Ohio State
1931   Cleveland Indians

KRISTUFEK, FRANK—Tackle—Pittsburgh
1940–41   Brooklyn Dodgers

KRIVONAK, JOSEPH—Guard—Southern Carolina

1946   Miami Seahawks (AAFC)

KROL, JOSEPH—Back—West Ontario
1945   Detroit Lions

KROUSE, RAYMOND—Tackle—Maryland
1951–55   New York Giants
1956–57   Detroit Lions
1958–59   Baltimore Colts
1960   Washington Redskins

KREUCK, EDWARD—End
1921   Cincinnati Celts

KRUEGER, ALBERT—Tackle—Drake
1924   Kansas City Cowboys

KRUEGER, ALVIN—End—Southern California
1940–42   Washington Redskins
1946   Los Angeles Dons (AAFC)

KREUGER, CHARLES—End—Texas A&M
1959–60   San Francisco 49ers

KRUEZ, ALBERT—Back—Pennsylvania
1931   Frankford Yellowjackets

KRUPA, JOSEPH—Guard—Purdue
1956–60   Pittsburgh Steelers

KRUTKO, LAWRENCE—Back—West Virginia
1958–60   Pittsburgh Steelers

KRYSL, JERRY—Tackle—Kansas State
1927   Cleveland Indians

KSIONZYK, JOHN—Back—St. Bonaventure
1947   Los Angeles Rams

KUCHARSKI, THEODORE—End—Holy Cross
1930   Providence Steamrollers

KUCHTA, FRANK—Center—Notre Dame
1958   Washington Redskins
1960   Denver Broncos (AFL)

KUCZINSKI, BERNARD—End—Pennsylvania
1943   Detroit Lions
1946   Philadelphia Eagles

KUEHL, RAYMOND—Back—Dubuque
1921   Detroit Panthers
1921–22   Buffalo All Americans
1922   Hammond Pros
1923   Rock Island Independents

1924   Dayton Triangles

CHARLES KRUEGER

KUEHNER, OSCAR—Guard
1921   Columbus Panhandles

**KUFFEL, RAYMOND—End—
Marquette**
1947   Buffalo Bills (AAFC)
1948–49   Chicago Hornets (AAFC)

**KUHARICH, JOSEPH—Guard—
Notre Dame**
1940-41, 45   Chicago Cardinals

KUICK, STANLEY—Guard—Beloit
1926   Green Bay Packers
1926   Milwaukee Badgers

KULBACKI, JOSEPH—Back—Purdue
1960   Buffalo Bills (AFL)

**KULBITSKI, VICTOR—Back—
Minnesota, Notre Dame**
1946–48   Buffalo Bills

**KUPCINET, IRVING—Back—North
Dakota**
1935   Philadelphia Eagles

KURRASCH, ROY—End—UCLA
1947   New York Yankees (AAFC)
1948   Pittsburgh Steelers

**KURTH, JOSEPH—Tackle—Notre
Dame**
1933–34   Green Bay Packers

KUSKO, JOHN—Back—Temple
1936–38   Philadelphia Eagles

**KUSSEROW, LOUIS—Back—
Columbia**
1949   New York Yankees (AAFC)
1950   New York Yanks

KUTNER, MALCOLM—End—Texas
1946–50   Chicago Cardinals

**KUUSISTO, WILLIAM—Guard—
Minnesota**
1941–46   Green Bay Packers

KUZCO, PAUL—Back—Villanova
1929   Staten Island Stapletons

KUZMAN, JOHN—Tackle—Fordham
1941   Chicago Cardinals
1946   San Francisco 49ers (AAFC)
1947   Chicago Rockets (AAFC)

**KVATERNICK, ZVONIMIR—
Guard—Kansas**
1934   Pittsburgh Pirates

KYLE, JAMES—Center—Gettysburg
1925–26   Canton Bulldogs

KYLE, JOHN—Back—Indiana
1923   Cleveland Indians

* * *

**LAACK, GALEN—Guard—College of
Pacific**
1958   Philadelphia Eagles

**LABENGOOD, HOWARD—Back—
Villanova**
1925   Pottsville Maroons

**LA BISSONIERE, JOSEPH—Center—
St. Thomas**
1922   Hammond Pros

LACH, STEPHEN—Back—Duke
1942   Chicago Cardinals
1946–47   Pittsburgh Steelers

LACKMAN, RICHARD—Back
1933–35   Philadelphia Eagles

LADD, JAMES—End—Bowling Green
1954   Chicago Cardinals

LADROW, WALTER—Guard
1921   Green Bay Packers

LADYGO, PETER—Guard—Maryland
1952–54   Pittsburgh Steelers

**LaFITTE, WILLIAM—End—
Ouchita**
1944   Brooklyn Tigers

**LaFLEUR, JOSEPH—Back—
Marquette**
1922–24   Chicago Bears

**LAGOD, CHESTER—Guard—
Chattanooga**
1953   New York Giants

**LAHAR, HAROLD—Guard—
Oklahoma**
1940–41   Chicago Bears
1946–48   Buffalo Bills (AAFC)

LAHEY, THOMAS—End—John Carroll
1946–47   Chicago Rockets (AAFC)

LAHR, WARREN—Back—Western Reserve
1948–49   Cleveland Browns (AAFC)
1950–59   Cleveland Browns

LAINHART, PORTER—Back—Oregon
1933   Chicago Cardinals
1933   Philadelphia Eagles

LAIRD, JAMES—Back—Colgate
1921   Rochester Kodaks
1921–22   Buffalo All Americans
1925–28   Providence Steamrollers
1931   Staten Island Stapletons

LAJOVSKY, WILLIAM—Guard—Catholic Univ.
1936   Pittsburgh Pirates

LAMANA, PETER—Center—Boston Univ.
1947–48   Chicago Rockets (AAFC)

LAMAS, JOSEPH—Guard—Mt. St. Mary's
1942   Pittsburgh Steelers

LAMB, ROY—Back—Lombard
1925   Rock Island Independents
1926–27, 33   Chicago Cardinals

LAMB, WALTER—End—Oklahoma
1946   Chicago Bears

LAMBEAU, EARL—Back—Notre Dame
1921–30   Green Bay Packers

LAMME, EMERALD—End—Ohio Wesleyan
1931   Cleveland Indians

LAND, FREDERICK—Tackle—LSU
1948   San Francisco 49ers (AAFC)

LANDE, CLIFFORD—End—John Carroll
1921   Green Bay Packers

LANDRIGAN, JAMES—Tackle—Holy Cross
1947   Baltimore Colts (AAFC)

LANDRUM, JAMES—Guard
1922–23   Louisville Colonels

LANDRY, THOMAS—Back—Texas
1949   New York Yankees (AAFC)
1950–55   New York Giants

LANDSBERG, MORTIMER—Back—Cornell
1941   Philadelphia Eagles
1947   Los Angeles Dons (AAFC)

LANE, CLAYTON—Tackle—New Hampshire
1948   New York Yankees (AAFC)

LANE, FRANK—Guard
1921   Cincinnati Celts

LANE, LEWIS—Back—St. Mary's—Kansas
1924   Kansas City Cowboys

LANE, OSCAR—Tackle—Marquette
1926   Milwaukee Badgers

LANE, RICHARD—Back—Scottsbluff
1952–53   Los Angeles Rams
1954–59   Chicago Cardinals
1952, 54   #1 Interceptions
1960   Detroit Lions

LANGAS, ROBERT—End—Wayne
1954   Baltimore Colts

LANGE, CLIFFORD—End—Montana
1927   Duluth Eskimos
1929   Chicago Cardinals

LANGE, WILLIAM—Guard—Dayton
1951–52   Los Angeles Rams
1953   Baltimore Colts
1954–55   Chicago Cardinals

LANGHOFF, IRVING—Back—Marquette
1922–23   Racine Legion

LANKAS, JAMES—Back—St. Mary's (Texas)
1942   Brooklyn Dodgers
1942   Philadelphia Eagles
1943   Green Bay Packers

LANPHEAR, DANIEL—End—Wisconsin
1960   Houston Oilers (AFL)

LANSDELL, GRANVILLE—Back—Southern California
1940   New York Giants

LANSFORD, ALEX—Tackle—Texas
1952   Dallas Texans
1955–58   Philadelphia Eagles
1958–60   Los Angeles Rams

LANTZ, MONTGOMERY—Center—Grove City
1933   Pittsburgh Pirates

LANUM, RALPH,—Back—Illinois
1921–24   Chicago Bears

LAPHAM, WILLIAM—Center—Iowa
1960   Philadelphia Eagles

LAPKA, THEODORE—End—St. Ambrose
1943–44, 46   Washington Redskins

ALEX LANSFORD

LAPORT, JOHN—Guard
1924   Columbus Tigers
1925–26   Dayton Triangles

**LaPRESTA, BENJAMIN—Back—
St. Louis Univ.**
1933   Boston Redskins
1934   St. Louis Gunners

**LARABA, ROBERT—Back—
Texas Western**
1960   Los Angeles Chargers (AFL)

LARAWAY, JACK—Back—Purdue
1960   Buffalo Bills (AFL)

LA ROSA, PAUL—End
1921   Chicago Cardinals

LARPENTER, CARL—Tackle—Texas
1960   Denver Broncos (AFL)

**LARSCHEID, JACK—Back—
College of Pacific**
1960   Oakland Raiders (AFL)

**LARSON, FREDERICK—Center—
Notre Dame**
1922   Chicago Bears
1923–24   Milwaukee Badgers
1925   Green Bay Packers
1929   Chicago Cardinals

LARSON, LLOYD—Back—Wisconsin
1926   Duluth Eskimos
1929   Chicago Cardinals

LARSON, PAUL—Back—California
1957   Chicago Cardinals
1960   Oakland Raiders (AFL)

**LARSON, WILLIAM—Back—
Illinois Western**
1960   Boston Patriots (AFL)

**LARY, ROBERT YALE—Back—
Texas A & M**

1952–53, 56–60   Detroit Lions
1959   #1 Punting

LASCARI, JOHN—End—Georgetown
1942   New York Giants

**LASSA, NICHOLAS—Center—Carlisle
(Long Time Sleep)**
1922–23   Oorang Indians

PAUL LARSON

**LASSAHN, LOUIS—End—
Western Maryland**
1938   Pittsburgh Pirates

LASSE, RICHARD—End—Syracuse
1958–59   Pittsburgh Steelers
1960   Washington Redskins

LATONE, ANTHONY—Back
1925–28   Pottsville Maroons
1929   Boston Braves
1930–31   Providence Steamrollers

**LATTNER, JOHN—Back—
Notre Dame**
1954   Pittsburgh Steelers

LAUER, HAROLD—Back—Detroit
1922   Rock Island Independents
1922   Green Bay Packers
1923   Toledo Maroons
1925–26   Detroit Panthers

**LAUER, LAWRENCE—Center—
Alabama**
1955   Chicago Bears
1956   Green Bay Packers

LAUER, PETER—Back—Iowa
1921–22 Evansville Crimson Giants

LAUGHING GAS—Back
1922   Oorang Indians

**LAUGHLIN, HENRY—Back—
Kansas**
1955   San Francisco 49ers

LAURICELLA, HENRY—Back—
Tennessee
1952   Dallas Texans

LAURINAITIS, FRED—Center—
Richmond
1947   Brooklyn Dodgers (AAFC)

LAURO, LINDELL—Back—
Pittsburgh
1951   Chicago Cardinals

LAUX, THEODORE—Back—St.
Joseph (Pa.)
1942, 44   Philadelphia Eagles
1943   Phil-Pitt

LAVELLI, DANTE—End—Ohio State
1946–49   Cleveland Browns (AAFC)
1950–56   Cleveland Browns

DONALD LAWRENCE

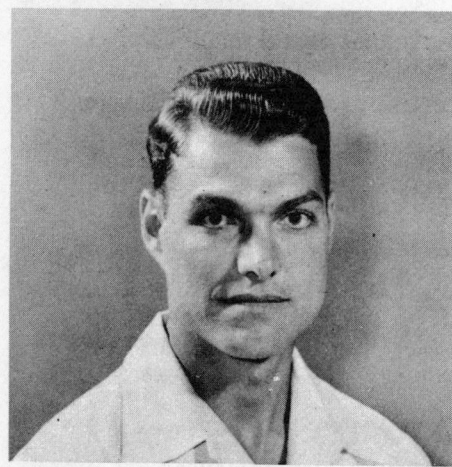

DANTE LAVELLI

LAW, HUBBARD—Guard—Sam
Houston
1942, 45   Pittsburgh Steelers

LAW, JOHN—Tackle—Notre Dame
1929   Orange
1930   Newark

LAWLER, ALLEN—Back—Texas
1948   Chicago Bears

LAWRENCE, DONALD—Tackle—
Notre Dame
1959–60   Washington Redskins

LAWRENCE, EDWARD—Back—
Brown
1929   Boston Braves
1930   Staten Island Stapletons

LAWRENCE, JAMES—Back—TCU
1936–38   Chicago Cardinals
1939   Green Bay Packers

LAWS, JOSEPH—Back—Iowa
1934–45   Green Bay Packers

LAWSON, JAMES—End—Stanford
1927   New York Yankees

LAY, RUSSELL—Guard—Michigan
State
1934   Detroit Lions
1934   Cincinnati Reds
1934   St. Louis Gunners

LAYDEN, PETER—Back—Texas
1948–49   New York Yankees (AAFC)
1950   New York Yanks

LAYDEN, ROBERT—End—
Kansas State Teachers
1943   Detroit Lions

LAYNE, ROBERT—Back—Texas
1948   Chicago Bears
1949   New York Bulldogs
1950–58   Detroit Lions
1958–60   Pittsburgh Steelers
1956   #1 Scoring

LAYPORT, JOHN—Back—Wooster
1924   Columbus Tigers
1925   Dayton Triangles

LAZETICH, MILAN—Guard—
Michigan
1945   Cleveland Rams
1946–50   Los Angeles Rams

LAZETICH, WILLIAM—Back—
Montana
1939, 41–42   Cleveland Rams

LEA, PAUL—Tackle—Tulane
1951   Pittsburgh Steelers

LEAD, GARFIELD—Tackle—Syracuse
1926   Louisville Colonels

LEAHY, BERNARD—Back—
Notre Dame
1932   Chicago Bears

LEAHY, GERALD—Tackle—
Colorado
1957   Pittsburgh Steelers

LEAPER, WESLEY—End—
Wisconsin
1921, 23   Green Bay Packers

LEAR, LESLIE—Guard—Manitoba
Univ.
1944–45   Cleveland Rams
1946   Los Angeles Rams
1947   Detroit Lions

LEARY, THOMAS—End—Fordham
1927–29, 31   Frankford Yellowjackets
1929   Staten Island Stapletons
1930   Newark

LEATHERMAN, PAUL—End—
Chicago
1922   Hammond Pros

LEATHERS, MILTON—Guard—
Georgia
1933   Philadelphia Eagles

LeBARON, EDWARD—Back—
College of Pacific
1952–53, 55–59   Washington Redskins
1960   Dallas Cowboys
1958   #1 Passing

LeBEAU, RICHARD—Back—
Ohio State
1959–60   Detroit Lions

LEBERMAN, ROBERT—Back—
Syracuse
1954   Baltimore Colts

LECHNER, EDGAR—Tackle—
Minnesota
1942   New York Giants

LECHTHALER, ROY—Guard—
Lebanon Valley
1933   Philadelphia Eagles

LECKONBY, WILLIAM—Back—St.
Lawrence
1939–41   Brooklyn Dodgers

LeCLERC, ROGER—Guard—
Trinity (Conn.)
1960   Chicago Bears

LECTURE, JAMES—Guard—
Northwestern
1946   Buffalo Bisons (AAFC)

LEDBETTER, HOMER—Back—
Arkansas
1932   Staten Island Stapletons
1932–33   Chicago Cardinals

LEDBETTER, TOY—Back—
Oklahoma A & M

1950, 53–55   Philadelphia Eagles

TOY LEDBETTER

LEDYARD, HAROLD—Back—
Chattanooga
1953   San Francisco 49ers

LEE, BERNARD—Back—Villanova
1938   Philadelphia Eagles
1938   Pittsburgh Pirates

LEE, EUGENE—Center—Florida
1946   Boston Yanks

LEE, HERMAN WILLIE—Tackle—
Florida A & M
1957   Pittsburgh Steelers
1958–60   Chicago Bears

LEE, HILARY—Guard—Oklahoma
1931   Cleveland Indians
1931   Portsmouth Spartans
1933–34   Cincinnati Reds

LEE, JACK—Back—Cincinnati
1960   Houston Oilers (AFL)

LEE, JOHN—Back—Carnegie Tech.
1939   Pittsburgh Steelers

LEE, ROBERT—Tackle—Missouri
1960   Boston Patriots (AFL)

LEE, WILLIAM—Tackle—Alabama
1935–37   Brooklyn Dodgers
1937–42, 46   Green Bay Packers

LEEMANS, ALPHONSE—Back—
George Washington
1936–43   New York Giants
1936   #1 Ball Carrying

LeFEBRE, GILBERT—Back
1933–34   Cincinnati Reds
1935   Detroit Lions

LeFORCE, CLYDE—Back—Tulsa
1947–49   Detroit Lions

LEGGETT, DAVID—Back—
Ohio State

1955   Chicago Cardinals

LEGGETT, EARL—Tackle—LSU
1957–60   Chicago Bears

**LEHECKA, JOSEPH—Back—
Lafayette**
1933   Frankford Yellowjackets

LEHRER, CHRISTOPHER—Back
1922   Rochester Kodaks

LEICHT, JACOB—Back—Oregon
1948–49   Baltimore Colts (AAFC)

LEISK, WARDELL—Guard—LSU
1937   Brooklyn Dodgers

**LEITH, ALBERT—Back—
Pennsylvania**
1926   Brooklyn Dodgers

**LEMEK, RAYMOND—Tackle—
Notre Dame**
1957–60   Washington Redskins

LEMON, CLIFFORD—End—Centre
1926   Chicago Bears

LENC, GEORGE—End—Augustana
1939   Brooklyn Dodgers

GEORGE LENC

LENNAN, BURGESS REID—Guard
1945   Washington Redskins
1947   Los Angeles Dons (AAFC)

**LENSING, VINCENT—Guard—
Notre Dame**
1921   Evansville Crimson Giants

LEO, CHARLES—Guard—Indiana
1960   Boston Patriots (AFL)

LEO, JAMES—Back—Cincinnati
1960   New York Giants

LEON, ANTHONY—Guard—Alabama
1943   Washington Redskins

1944   Brooklyn Tigers
1945–46   Boston Yanks

LEONARD, JAMES—Guard—Colgate
1924   Chicago Bears

**LEONARD, JAMES—Back—Notre
Dame**
1934–37   Philadelphia Eagles

LEONARD, JOHN—Guard—Indiana
1922–23   Chicago Cardinals

**LEONARD, WILLIAM—End—Notre
Dame**
1949   Baltimore Colts (AAFC)

**LEONETTI, ROBERT—Guard—
Wake Forest**
1948   Buffalo Bills
1948   Brooklyn Dodgers

LESANE, JAMES—Back—Virginia
1952, 54   Chicago Bears
1954   Baltimore Colts

LESTER, DARRELL—Center—TCU
1937–38   Green Bay Packers

**LESTER, HAROLD—End—
Providence**
1926   Providence Steamrollers

**LETLOW, RUSSELL—Guard—San
Francisco**
1936–42, 46   Green Bay Packers

**LETSINGER, HOWARD—Guard—
Purdue**
1933   Pittsburgh Pirates

**LEVANITIS, STEPHEN—Tackle—
Boston College**
1942   Philadelphia Eagles

LEVANTI, LOUIS—Guard—Illinois
1951–52   Pittsburgh Steelers

LEVEY, JAMES—Back—None
1935–36   Pittsburgh Pirates

LEVY, HARVEY—Guard—Syracuse
1928   New York Giants
1928   New York Yankees

**LEVY, LEONARD—Guard—
Minnesota**
1945   Cleveland Rams
1946   Los Angeles Rams
1947–48   Los Angeles Dons (AAFC)

**LEWELLEN, VERNE—Back—
Nebraska**
1924–32   Green Bay Packers
1927   New York Yankees

LEWIS, ARTHUR—Tackle—Ohio
1936   New York Giants
1938–39   Cleveland Rams

LEWIS, ARTHUR—Tackle—
West Virginia
1921   Cincinnati Celts

LEWIS, CHARLES "MAC"—Tackle—
Iowa
1959   Chicago Cardinals

LEWIS, CLIFFORD—Back—Duke
1946–49   Cleveland Browns (AAFC)
1950–51   Cleveland Browns

LEWIS, DANIEL—Back—Wisconsin
1958–60   Detroit Lions

LEWIS, ERNEST—Back—Colorado
1947–49   Chicago Rockets

LEWIS, HAROLD—Back—Houston
1959   Baltimore Colts
1960   Buffalo Bills (AFL)

LEWIS, JOSEPH—Tackle—
Compton Jr.
1958–60   Pittsburgh Steelers

LEWIS, LOREN—Back—
Northwestern
1930   Portsmouth Spartans
1931   Cleveland Indians
1934   Cincinnati Reds

LEWIS, WOODLEY—Back—
Oregon
1950–55   Los Angeles Rams
1956–59   Chicago Cardinals
1960   Dallas Cowboys

LEYENDECKER, CHARLES—
Tackle—Vanderbilt
1933   Philadelphia Eagles

LEYSENAAR, HARRY—Back—
Marquette
1941   Chicago Cardinals

LIDBERG, CARL—Back—Minnesota
1926–30   Green Bay Packers

LIDDICK, DAVID—Tackle—George
Washington
1957   Pittsburgh Steelers
1960   Denver Broncos (AFL)

LIEBEL, FRANK—End—Norwich
1942–47   New York Giants
1948   Chicago Cardinals

LIEBERUM, DONALD—Back—
Manchester (Ind.)
1942   New York Giants

LIGHTNER, JOSEPH—Back—Penn
State
1933   Frankford Yellowjackets

LILES, ELVIN—Guard—Oklahoma
A & M

1943–45   Detroit Lions
1945   Cleveland Rams

LILLARD, JOSEPH—Back—Oregon
1932–33   Chicago Cardinals

LILLYWHITE, VERL—Back—
Southern California
1948–49   San Francisco 49ers (AAFC)
1950–51   San Francisco 49ers

LIND, ALBERT—Center—
Northwestern
1936   Chicago Cardinals

LINDAHL, VIRGIL—Guard—
Kentucky
1945   New York Giants

LINDON, LUTHER—Tackle—
Kentucky
1944–45   Detroit Lions
1945   Chicago Cardinals

LINDSEY, MENZIES—Back—Wabash
1921–22   Evansville Crimson Giants

LINDSKOG, VICTOR—Center—
Stanford
1944–51   Philadelphia Eagles

LINDSTROM
1922   Racine Legion

LININGER, RAYMOND—Center—
Ohio State
1950–51   Detroit Lions

LINNAN, FRANCIS—Tackle—
Marquette
1922, 26   Racine Legion

LINTZENICH, JOSEPH—Tackle— St.
Louis Univ.
1930–31   Chicago Bears

LIO, AUGUSTINO—Guard—
Georgetown
1940–43   Detroit Lions
1944–45   Boston Yanks
1946   Philadelphia Eagles
1947   Baltimore Colts (AAFC)

LIPOSTAD, EDWARD—Guard—
Wake Forest
1952   Chicago Cardinals

LIPSCOMB, EUGENE—Tackle
1953–55   Los Angeles Rams
1956–60   Baltimore Colts

LIPSCOMB, PAUL—Tackle—
Tennessee
1945–49   Green Bay Packers
1950–54   Washington Redskins
1954   Chicago Bears

LIPSKI, JOHN—Center—Temple

1933–34 Philadelphia Eagles

LISTON, PAUL—Tackle—Georgetown
1930 Newark

PAUL LIPSCOMB

**LITTLE, JACK—Tackle—
Texas A & M**
1953–54 Baltimore Colts

LITTLE, JAMES—Tackle—Kentucky
1945 New York Giants

**LITTLE, LOUIS—Tackle—
Pennsylvania**
1921 Buffalo All Americans

LITTLE TWIG—Tackle—Carlisle
1922–23 Oorang Indians
1924–25 Rock Island Independents
1926 Akron Legions
1926 Canton Bulldogs

**LITTLEFIELD, CARL—Back—
Washington State**
1938 Cleveland Rams
1939 Pittsburgh Steelers

**LIVINGSTON, CLIFFORD—End—
U.C.L.A.**
1954–60 New York Giants

**LIVINGSTON, HOWARD—Back—
None**
1944–47 New York Giants
1948–50 Washington Redskins
1950 San Francisco 49ers

**LIVINGSTON, ROBERT—Back—
Notre Dame**
1948–49 Chicago Hornets (AAFC)
1949 Buffalo Bills (AAFC)
1950 Baltimore Colts

**LIVINGSTON, THEODORE—
Tackle—Indiana**
1937–40 Cleveland Rams

CLIFFORD LIVINGSTON

**LIVINSTON, WALTER—Back—
Heidelberg**
1960 Boston Patriots (AFL)

LLOYD, DAVID—Center—Georgia
1959–60 Cleveland Browns

LO BOUTWELL—Back—Carlisle
1922 Oorang Indians

**LOCKLIN, WILLIAM—Back—
New Mexico State**
1960 Oakland Raiders (AFL)

**LOEPFE, RICHARD—Tackle—
Wisconsin**
1948–49 Chicago Cardinals

**LOFTON, OSCAR—End—
Southeastern (La.)**
1960 Boston Patriots (AFL)

**LOGAN, ANDREW—Tackle—
Western Reserve**
1941 Detroit Lions

LOGAN, JAMES—Guard—Indiana
1942–43 Chicago Bears

**LOGAN, RICHARD—Guard—
Ohio State**
1952–53 Green Bay Packers

LOGEL, ROBERT—End
1949 Buffalo Bills

LOGUS—Center
1934 Cincinnati Reds

**LOKANC, JOSEPH—Guard—
Northwestern**
1941 Chicago Cardinals

LOLLAR, GEORGE—Back—Howard
1928 Green Bay Packers

LOLOTAI, ALBERT—Guard— Weber
1945 Washington Redskins

1946–49 Los Angeles Dons (AAFC)

LOMASNEY, THOMAS—End—
Villanova
1929 Staten Island Stapletons

LONE WOLF—Guard—Carlisle
1922–23 Oorang Indians

LONG, BUFORD—Back—Florida
1953–55 New York Giants

LONG, HARVEY—Tackle—Detroit
1929 Chicago Bears
1930 Frankford Yellowjackets

LONG, JOHN—Back—Colgate
1944–45 Chicago Bears

LONG, LOUIS—Tackle—SMU
1931 Portsmouth Spartans

LONG, MICHAEL—End—Brandeis
1960 Boston Patriots (AFL)

LONG, ROBERT—Back—Tennessee
1947 Boston Yanks

LONG, ROBERT—Back—U.C.L.A.
1955–59 Detroit Lions
1955, 60 Los Angeles Rams

ROBERT LONG

LONG, THOMAS—Guard—Ohio State
1923 Racine Legion
1925 Columbus Tigers

LONG, WILLIAM—End—Oklahoma
A & M
1949–50 Pittsburgh Steelers

LONG TIME SLEEP (NICHOLAS
LASSA)—Center—Carlisle
1922 Oorang Indians

LONGENECKER, KENNETH—
Tackle—Lebanon Valley
1960 Pittsburgh Steelers

LONGO, ANTONIO—Guard—
Connecticut State

1928 Providence Steamrollers

LONGO, CHARLES—Back—
San Jose State
1960 Los Angeles Rams
1960 Oakland Raiders (AFL)

LONGSTREET, ROY—Center—Iowa
State
1926 Racine Legion

LONGUA, PAUL—End—Villanova
1929 Orange
1930 Newark

LOOKABAUGH, JOHN—End—
Maryland
1946–47 Washington Redskins

LOOMIS, ACE—Back—Wisconsin
State
1951–53 Green Bay Packers

LOONEY, DONALD—Back—TCU
1940 Philadelphia Eagles
1941–42 Pittsburgh Steelers
1940 #1 Pass Receiving

LORD, JACK—Guard—Rutgers
1929 Staten Island Stapletons

LOSCH, JOHN—Back—Miami
1956 Green Bay Packers

LOTT, JOHN—Tackle—
Bucknell
1929 Orange
1930 Brooklyn Dodgers

LOTT, WILLIAM—Back—Mississippi
1958 New York Giants
1960 Oakland Raiders (AFL)

LOUDD, ROMMIE—Back—UCLA
1960 Los Angeles Chargers (AFL)

LOUDERBACK, THOMAS—Guard—
San Jose State
1958–59 Philadelphia Eagles
1960 Oakland Raiders (AFL)

LOVE, JOHN—Tackle—Pittsburgh
1934 Pittsburgh Steelers

LOVETERE, JOHN—Tackle—
Compton
1959–60 Los Angeles Rams

LOVIN—Guard
1929 Minneapolis Redjackets

LOVUOLO, EDMOND—Tackle—
1947 Brooklyn Dodgers (AAFC)

LOVUOLO, FRANK—End—St.
Bonaventure
1949 New York Giants

LOWE, GEORGE—End—Fordham
1921 Cleveland Indians
1922 Buffalo All Americans

1923   Rock Island Independents
1924–26   Frankford Yellowjackets
1925, 27   Providence Steamrollers

JOHN LOVETERE

LOWE, GARY—Back—Michigan State
1956–57   Washington Redskins
1957–60   Detroit Lions

LOWE, LLOYD—Back—Texas State North
1953–54   Chicago Bears

LOWE, PAUL—Back—Oregon State
1960   Los Angeles Chargers (AFL)

PAUL LOWE

LOWE, WILLIAM—Back—Tennessee
1925–26   Frankford Yellowjackets

LOWERY, DARBY—Tackle—Ursinus
1921–25   Rochester Jefferson

LOWTHER, RUSSELL—Back—Detroit
1944   Detroit Lions
1945   Pittsburgh Steelers

LOYD, ALEXANDER—End—Oklahoma A & M
1950   San Francisco 49ers

LUBRATOVICH, MILO—Tackle—Wisconsin
1931–35   Brooklyn Dodgers

LUCAS, RICHARD—End—Boston College
1958   Pittsburgh Steelers
1960   Philadelphia Eagles

LUCAS, RICHARD—Back—Penn State
1960   Buffalo Bills (AFL)

LUCENTE, JOHN—Back—West Virginia
1945   Pittsburgh Steelers

LUCKMAN, SIDNEY—Back—Columbia
1939–50   Chicago Bears
1945   #1 Passing (Tied by Baugh)

LUCKY, WILLIAM—Tackle—Baylor
1955   Green Bay Packers

LUDTKE, NORMAN—Guard—John Carroll
1924   Green Bay Packers

LUFT, DONALD—End—Indiana
1954   Philadelphia Eagles

LUHN, NOLAN—End—Tulsa
1945–49   Green Bay Packers

LUJACK, JOHN—Back—Notre Dame
1948–51   Chicago Bears

JOHN LUJACK

LUKENS, JAMES—End—Washington & Lee
1949   Buffalo Bisons   (AAFC)

LUMMUS, JOHN—End—Baylor
1940–41   New York Giants
Killed by land mine while leading infantry-tank attack against last Japanese stronghold on Iwo Jima. Lt., U.S. Army

LUMPKIN, ROY—Back—Georgia Tech.
1930–33   Portsmouth Spartans
1934   Detroit Lions
1935–37   Brooklyn Dodgers

LUNA, ROBERT—Back—Alabama
1955   San Francisco 49ers
1959   Pittsburgh Steelers

LUNCEFORD, DAVID—Tackle—Baylor
1957   Chicago Cardinals

LUND, WILLIAM—Back—Case
1946–47   Cleveland Browns (AAFC)

LUNDAY, KENNETH—Center—Arkansas
1937–41, 46–47   New York Giants

LUNDE, LESTER—Guard—Ripon
1922–24   Racine Legions

LUNDELL, ROBERT—End—Gustavus-Adolphus
1929–30   Minneapolis Redjackets
1930   Staten Island Stapletons

LUNGREN, CHARLES—Back—Swarthmore
1923   Rock Island Independents

LUNDY, LAMAR—End—Purdue
1957–60   Los Angeles Rams

LAMAR LUNDY

LUNZ, GERALD—Guard—Marquette
1925–26   Chicago Cardinals
1930   Frankford Yellowjackets

LUSK, ROBERT—Center—William & Mary
1956   Detroit Lions

LYLE, DEWEY—Guard—Minnesota
1921–22   Rock Island Independents
1922–23   Green Bay Packers

LYLES, LEONARD—Back—Louisville
1958   Baltimore Colts
1959–60   San Francisco 49ers

LYMAN, DELBERT—Tackle—UCLA
1941   Green Bay Packers
1941, 44   Cleveland Rams

LYMAN, ROY—Tackle—Nebraska
1922–23, 25   Canton Bulldogs
1923–24   Cleveland Indians
1925–34   Chicago Bears

LYNCH, EDWARD—End—Catholic Univ.
1925   Rochester Jeffersons
1926   Detroit Panthers
1926   Hartford Blues
1927   Providence Steamrollers
1929   Orange

LYNCH, LYNN—Guard—Illinois
1951   Chicago Cardinals

LYNCH, PAUL—Back—Ohio Northern
1925   Columbus Tigers

LYNCH, RICHARD—Back—Notre Dame
1958   Washington Redskins
1959–60   New York Giants

RICHARD LYNCH

LYONS, GEORGE—Tackle—Tulsa
1929   Chicago Bears
1929   New York Giants
1930   Portsmouth Spartans
1931   Cleveland Indians
1932–33   Brooklyn Dodgers

1934 St. Louis Gunners

* * *

**MacAFEE, KENNETH—End—
Alabama**
1954–58 New York Giants
1959 Philadelphia Eagles
1959 Washington Redskins

MacAULIFFE, JOHN—Back—Beloit
1926 Green Bay Packers

**MacCOLLUM, MAXWELL—End—
Centre**
1922 Louisville Colonels

**MacPHEE, WALTER—Back—
Princeton**
1925–26 Providence Steamrollers

**McADAMS, DEAN—Back—
Washington**
1940–43 Brooklyn Dodgers

McAFEE, GEORGE—Back—Duke
1940–41, 45–50 Chicago Bears

McAFEE, WESLEY—Back—Duke
1941 Philadelphia Eagles

**McARTHUR, JOHN—Center—
Santa Clara**
1926 Los Angeles
1927 Buffalo Bisons
1927–28 New York Yankees
1929 Orange
1930 Newark
1930, 33 Brooklyn Dodgers
1930 Frankford Yellowjackets
1930–31 Providence Steamrollers

McBRIDE, JOHN—Back—Syracuse
1925–28, 32–34 New York Giants
1929 Providence Steamrollers
1930–32 Brooklyn Dodgers
1935 Chicago Cardinals

**McCABE, RICHARD—Back—
Pittsburgh**
1955, 57–58 Pittsburgh Steelers
1959 Washington Redskins
1960 Buffalo Bills (AFL)

**McCAIN, ROBERT—End—
Mississippi**
1946 Brooklyn Dodgers

**McCAFFERTY, DONALD—End—
Ohio State**
1946 New York Giants

**McCAFFRAY, ARTHUR—Tackle—
College of Pacific**
1946 Pittsburgh Steelers

McCAIN, ROBERT—End—Mississippi
1946 Brooklyn Dodgers

**McCANN, ERNEST—Tackle—Penn
State**
1926 Hartford Blues

**McCARTHY, HOWARD—Back—
Notre Dame**
1924–25 Rock Island Independents

**McCARTHY, JAMES—Tackle—
California**
1927 Duluth Eskimos

McCARTHY, JAMES—End—Illinois
1946–47 Brooklyn Dodgers (AAFC)
1948–49 Chicago Rockets (AAFC)

**McCARTHY, THOMAS—Back—
St. Francis**
1944 Card-Pitt

McCAUSLAND, LEO—End—Detroit
1922 Akron Steels

McCAW, WILLIAM—End—Indiana
1923 Racine Legion
1926 Louisville Colonels
        Died in Service. Capt. of Infantry
        assigned to ROTC at Indiana

**McCHESNEY, ROBERT—End—
Hardin-Simmons**
1950 Philadelphia Eagles
1950–51 New York Giants

**McCHESNEY, ROBERT—End—
UCLA**
1936 Boston Redskins
1937–43 Washington Redskins

McCLAIN, CLINTON—Back—SMU
1940–41 New York Giants

McCLAIN, MAYES—Guard—Iowa
1930–31 Portsmouth Spartans

**McCLAIREN, JACK—Back—
Bethune-Cookman**
1955–60 Pittsburgh Steelers

**McCLUNG, WILLIE—Tackle—
Florida A & M**
1955–57 Pittsburgh Steelers
1958–59 Cleveland Browns
1960 Detroit Lions

**McCLURE, ROBERT—Guard—
Nevada**
1947–48 Boston Yanks

McCOLL, WILLIAM—End—Stanford
1954–59 Chicago Bears

**McCOLLUM, HARLEY—Tackle—
Tulane**
1946 New York Yankees (AAFC)
1947 Chicago Rockets (AAFC)

**McCOMBS, DONALD—End—
Villanova**

1960   Boston Patriots (AFL)

McCOMBS—Tackle
1929   Buffalo Bisons

McCONNELL, DEWEY—End— Wyoming
1954   Pittsburgh Steelers

McCONNELL, FELTON—Guard— Georgia Tech.
1927   Buffalo Bisons

DARRIS McCORD

McCORD, DARRIS—Tackle— Tennessee
1955–60   Detroit Lions

McCORMACK, MICHAEL—Tackle— Kansas
1951   New York Yanks
1954–60   Cleveland Browns

McCORMICK, ELMER—Guard— Detroit
1923–25   Buffalo Bisons
1925   Frankford Yellowjackets
1926   Hartford Blues

McCORMICK, FELIX—Back— Bucknell
1929   Orange
1930   Newark

McCORMICK, LEONARD—Center— Baylor
1948   Baltimore Colts (AAFC)

McCORMICK, THOMAS—Back— College of Pacific
1953–55   Los Angeles Rams
1956   San Francisco 49ers

McCORMICK, WALTER—Center— Southern California
1948   San Francisco 49ers (AAFC)

McCOY, JOEL—Back—Alabama

1946   Detroit Lions

McCRARY, HURDIS—Back—Georgia
1929–33   Green Bay Packers

McCRILLIS, EDWARD—Guard— Brown
1929   Boston Braves

McCULLOCH, JAMES—Guard— Holy Cross
1926   Brooklyn Dodgers

McCULLOUGH, HAROLD—Back— Cornell
1942   Brooklyn Dodgers

McCULLOUGH, HUGH—Back— Oklahoma
1939   Pittsburgh Steelers
1940–41   Chicago Cardinals
1943   Phil-Pitt
1945   Boston Yanks

McCUSKER, JAMES—Tackle— Pittsburgh
1958   Chicago Cardinals
1959–60   Philadelphia Eagles

McDANIEL, WAHOO—Guard— Oklahoma
1960   Houston Oilers (AFL)

McDADE, WILLIAM—Center— Portland
1938   Pittsburgh Pirates

McDERMOTT, LLOYD—Tackle— Kentucky
1950   Detroit Lions
1950–51   Chicago Cardinals

McDONALD, DONALD—End— Oklahoma
1944–46   Philadelphia Eagles
1948   New York Yankees

McDONALD, EDWARD—Back— Duquesne
1936   Pittsburgh Pirates

McDONALD, JAMES—Back—Ohio State
1938–40   Detroit Lions

McDONALD, JOHN—Tackle
1926   Louisville Colonels

McDONALD, LESTER—End— Nebraska
1937–39   Chicago Bears
1940   Philadelphia Eagles

McDONALD, THOMAS—Back— Oklahoma
1957–60   Philadelphia Eagles

McDONALD, WALTER—Center— Utah

1935   Brooklyn Dodgers

**McDONALD, WALTER—Back—
Tulane**
1946   Miami Seahawks (AAFC)
1946–48   Brooklyn Dodgers (AAFC)
1949   Chicago Hornets (AAFC)

THOMAS McDONALD

**McDONNELL, JOHN—Back—
Creighton**
1924–25   Duluth Kelleys
1925   Hammond Pros
1926   Detroit Panthers
1926–30   Chicago Cardinals
1931   Frankford Yellowjackets

**McDONOUGH, COLEY—Back—
Dayton**
1939   Chicago Cardinals
1939–41   Pittsburgh Steelers
1944   Card-Pitt

McDONOUGH, PAUL—End—Utah
1938   Pittsburgh Pirates
1939–41   Cleveland Rams

**McDONOUGH, ROBERT—Guard—
Duke**
1942, 46   Philadelphia Eagles

**McDOUGAL, ROBERT—Back—
Miami (Fla.)**
1947   Green Bay Packers

**McDOWELL, JAY—End—
Washington**
1946–51   Philadelphia Eagles

**McELHENNY, HUGH—Back—
Washington**
1952–60   San Francisco 49ers

**McELVOY, EDWARD—Back—
Spring Hill**
1926   Hartford Blues

**McELWAIN, WILLIAM—Back—
Northwestern**
1924, 26   Chicago Cardinals
1925   Chicago Bears
1926   Racine Legion

**McENULTY, DOUGLAS—Back—
Wichita**
1942–44   Chicago Bears

**McFADDEN, BANKS—Back—
Clemson**
1940   Brooklyn Dodgers

**McFADDEN, MARVIN—Guard—
Michigan State**
1953, 56   Pittsburgh Steelers

McFADIN, LOUIS—Guard—Texas
1952–56   Los Angeles Rams
1960   Denver Broncos (AFL)

**McFARLANE, NYLE—Back—
Brigham Young**
1960   Oakland Raiders (AFL)

**McGARRY, BERNARD—Guard—
Utah**
1939–42   Cleveland Rams

McGAW, WALTER—Guard—Beloit
1926   Green Bay Packers

McGEHEAN, ROBERT—Back
1923   Louisville Colonels

**McGEARY, CLARENCE—Tackle—
North Dakota**
1950   Green Bay Packers

McGEE, EDWARD—Tackle—Temple
1940   New York Giants
1945–46   Boston Yanks

McGEE, GEORGE—Tackle—Southern
1960   Boston Patriots (AFL)

**McGEE, HOWARD—Guard—Kansas
State**
1927   Cleveland Indians
1929, 32   Staten Island Stapletons
1930   Newark

McGEE, MICHAEL—Guard—Duke
1960   St. Louis Cardinals

**McGEE, WILLIAM MAX—End—
Tulane**
1954, 57–60   Green Bay Packers

**McGIBBONY, CHARLES—Back—
Arkansas State**
1944   Brooklyn Tigers

**McGILBRA, SANFORD—Tackle—
Redlands**
1926   Buffalo Bisons

McGILL—Center
1922   Racine Legion

WILLIAM MAX McGEE

McGINLEY, EDWARD—Tackle—Pennsylvania
1925 New York Giants

McGINNIS, LAWRENCE—End—Marquette
1923–24 Milwaukee Badgers

McGIRL, LEONARD—Guard—Missouri
1931–32 Frankford Yellowjackets
1933 Chicago Cardinals
1934 St. Louis Gunners

McGLONE, JOSEPH—Back—Harvard
1926 Providence Steamrollers

McGOLDRICK, HUGH—Tackle—Lehigh
1925 Providence Steamrollers

McGRATH, BRYAN—Guard—New York University
1922 Louisville Colonels

McGRATH, FRANK—End—Georgetown
1927 Frankford Yellowjackets
1928 New York Yankees

McGRATH, RICHARD—End—Holy Cross
1926 Brooklyn Dodgers

McGRAW, THURMAN—Tackle—Colorado A & M
1950–54 Detroit Lions

McGREGORY—Back
1923 Buffalo All Americans

McGREW, DANIEL—Center—Purdue
1960 Buffalo Bills (AFL)

McGUIRK, WARREN—Tackle—Boston College

1929–30 Providence Steamrollers

McHAN, LAMAR—Back—Arkansas
1954–58 Chicago Cardinals
1959–60 Green Bay Packers

THURMAN McGRAW

McHUGH, PAT—Back—Georgia Tech.
1947–51 Philadelphia Eagles

PAT McHUGH

McILHENNY, DONALD—Back—SMU
1956 Detroit Lions
1957–59 Green Bay Packers
1960 Dallas Cowboys

McINERNEY, ARNOLD—Center—Notre Dame
1921–27 Chicago Cardinals

McINNIS, HUGH—End—Mississippi Southern
1960 St. Louis Cardinals

McINTOSH, DANIEL—Back—Rhode Island State
1925–26 Providence Steamrollers

**McKALIP, WILLIAM—End—
Oregon State**
1931–32 Portsmouth Spartans
1934, 36 Detroit Lions

McKAY, ROY—Back—Texas
1944–47 Green Bay Packers
1945, 46 #1 Punting

McKEE, PAUL—End—Syracuse
1947–48 Washington Redskins

McKETES—Back
1926 Hammond Pros

**McKISSACK, RICHARD—Back—
SMU**
1952 Dallas Texans

**McLAIN, JOSEPH—Guard—
St. John's**
1928 New York Yankees

**McLAUGHLIN, JAMES—Back—
Villanova**
1934 St. Louis Gunners

**McLAUGHLIN, LEE—Guard—
Virginia**
1941 Green Bay Packers

**McLAUGHLIN, LEON—Center—
UCLA**
1951 Los Angeles Rams

McLAUGHRY, JOHN—Back—Brown
1940 New York Giants

McLEAN, RAYMOND—Back
1921 Green Bay Packers

**McLEAN, RAYMOND—Back—St.
Anselm's**
1940–47 Chicago Bears

**McLEAN, STUART—Tackle—
Indiana**
1922–23 Louisville Colonels

**McLEMORE, EMMETT—Back—
Haskell**
1922 Oorang Indians
1924 Kansas City Cowboys

**McLEOD, ARTHUR—Center—St.
Louis Univ.**
1934 St. Louis Gunners

**McLEOD, ROBERT—Back—
Dartmouth**
1939–40 Chicago Bears

McMAHAN—Back—Heidelberg
1921 Cincinnati Celts

**McMICHAELS, JOHN—Back—
Birmingham Southern**
1944 Brooklyn Tigers

**McMILLAN, CHARLES—Back—
John Carroll**
1954 Baltimore Colts

**McMILLAN, STEWART—Center—
North Dakota**
1931 Cleveland Indians

**McMILLEN, JAMES—Guard—
Illinois**
1924–31, 35 Chicago Bears

McMILLIN, ALVIN—Back—Centre
1922–23 Milwaukee Badgers
1923 Cleveland Indians

**McMULLAN, JOHN—Guard—
Notre Dame**
1960 New York Titans (AFL)

**McMULLEN, DANIEL—Guard—
Nebraska**
1929 New York Giants
1930–31 Chicago Bears
1932 Portsmouth Spartans

**McMURDO, JAMES—Tackle—
Pittsburgh**
1932–33 Boston Redskins
1934–37 Philadelphia Eagles

**McMURTRY, CHARLES—Tackle—
Whittier**
1960 Buffalo Bills (AFL)

**McNALLY, FRANK—Center—St.
Mary's**
1931–34 Chicago Cardinals

**McNALLY, JOHN "BLOOD"—
Back—St. John (Minn.)**
1925–27 Milwaukee Badgers
1926–27 Duluth Eskimos
1928 Pottsville Maroons
1928–36 Green Bay Packers
1937–39 Pittsburgh Steelers

**McNAMARA, EDMUND—Tackle—
Holy Cross**
1945 Pittsburgh Steelers

**McNAMARA, ROBERT—Back—
Minnesota**
1960 Denver Broncos (AFL)

**McNAMARA, THOMAS—Guard—
Detroit**
1923 Toledo Maroons
1925–26 Detroit Panthers

**McNEIL, CHARLES—Back—
Compton Jr.**
1960 Los Angeles Chargers (AFL)

**McNEIL, FRANCIS—End—
Washington & Jefferson**
1932 Brooklyn Dodgers

McNELLIS, WILLIAM—Back—St. Thomas
1927 Duluth Eskimos

McNULTY, PAUL—Back—Notre Dame
1924-25 Chicago Cardinals

McPEAK, WILLIAM—End— Pittsburgh
1949-58 Pittsburgh Steelers

WILLIAM McPEAK

McPHAIL, HAROLD—Back—Xavier
1934-35 Boston Redskins

McPHAIL, HOWARD—Back— Oklahoma
1953, 56 Baltimore Colts

McPHEE, FRANK—End—Princeton
1955 Chicago Cardinals

McPHERSON, FORREST—Tackle— Nebraska
1935 Chicago Bears
1935-37 Philadelphia Eagles
1943-45 Green Bay Packers

McQUADE, JOHN—Back— Georgetown
1922 Canton Bulldogs

McQUARY, JOHN—Back— California
1946 Los Angeles Dons (AAFC)

McRAE, STANLEY—Back— Michigan State
1946 Washington Redskins

McRAVEN, WILLIAM—Back— Murray State Teachers
1939 Cleveland Rams

McSHEA, JOSEPH—Guard— Rochester
1923 Rochester Kodaks

McTIGUE—Back
1926 Hartford Blues

McWILLIAMS, THOMAS—Back— Mississippi State
1949 Los Angeles Rams
1950 Pittsburgh Steelers

McWILLIAMS, WILLIAM—Back— Jordan College
1934 Detroit Lions

MAACK, HERBERT—Tackle— Columbia
1946 Brooklyn Dodgers (AAFC)

MACEAU, MELVIN—Guard— Marquette
1946-48 Cleveland Browns (AAFC)

MACERELLI, JOHN—Guard— St. Vincent's
1956 _ Cleveland Browns

MACIOSZCZYK, ARTHUR—Back— Western Michigan
1944, 47 Philadelphia Eagles
1948 Washington Redskins

MACKENROTH, JOHN—Center— North Dakota
1938 Detroit Lions

MACKERT, ROBERT—Tackle— West Virginia
1925 Rochester Jeffersons

MACKEY, DEE—End—Texas Etate East
1960 San Francisco 49ers

MACKORELL, JOHN—Back— Davidson
1935 New York Giants

MACKRIDES, WILLIAM—Back— Nevada
1947-51 Philadelphia Eagles
1953 Pittsburgh Steelers
1953 New York Giants

MACON, EDWARD—Back— College of Pacific
1952-53 Chicago Bears
1960 Oakland Raiders (AFL)

MADAR, ELMER—End—Michigan
1947 Baltimore Colts (AAFC)

MADARIK, ELMER—Back—Detroit
1945-47 Detroit Lions
1948 Washington Redskins

MADDEN, LLOYD—Back—Colorado Mines
1940 Chicago Cardinals

MADDOCK, ROBERT—Guard— Notre Dame

1942, 46   Chicago Cardinals

**MADDOX, GEORGE—Tackle—
Kansas State**
1935   Green Bay Packers

**MADEROS, GEORGE—Back—
Chico State**
1955–56   San Francisco 49ers

**MADIGAN, FRANK—Center—St.
Mary's (Minn.)**
1922, 24   Minneapolis Marines
1923   Duluth Kelleys

**MAEDA, CHESTER—Back—Colorado
State**
1945   Chicago Cardinals

**MAEDER, ALBERT—Tackle—
Minnesota**
1929   Minneapolis Redjackets

**MAGAG, MICHAEL—Guard—
Missouri**
1960   San Francisco 49ers

**MAGEE, JAMES—Center—
Villanova**
1945–46   Boston Yanks

MAGEE, JOHN—Guard—Rice
1948–51   Philadelphia Eagles

**MAGGIOLO, ACHILLE—Back—
Illinois**
1948   Buffalo Bills (AAFC)
1949   Detroit Lions
1950   Baltimore Colts

MAGLIOLO, JOSEPH—Back—Texas
1948   New York Yankees (AAFC)

**MAGLISCEAU, ALBERT—Tackle—
Geneva**
1929   Frankford Yellowjackets

**MAGNANI, DANTE—Back—St.
Mary's (Cal.)**
1940–42   Cleveland Rams
1942–43, 46, 49   Chicago Bears
1947–48   Los Angeles Rams
1950   Detroit Lions

**MAGNER, JAMES—Back—North
Carolina**
1931   Frankford Yellowjackets

**MAGNUSSON, GLEN—Center—
Northwestern**
1925   Hammond Pros

MAGUIRE, PAUL—Back—Citadel
1960   Los Angeles Chargers (AFL)

**MAGULICK, GEORGE—Back—St.
Francis**
1944   Card-Pitt

MAHAN, R.—Back

1929   Buffalo Bisons
1930   Brooklyn Dodgers

**MAHAN, WALTER—Guard—West
Virginia**
1926   Frankford Yellowjackets

MAHER, BRUCE—Back—Detroit
1960   Detroit Lions

MAHER, FRANCIS—Back—Toledo
1940–41   Pittsburgh Steelers
1941   Cleveland Rams

**MAHONEY, FRANK "IKE"—Back—
Creighton**
1925–28, 31   Chicago Cardinals

MAHONEY, JOHN—Back—Detroit
1923   Buffalo Bisons

**MAHONEY, ROGER—Center—
Penn State**
1928–30   Frankford Yellowjackets
1930   Minneapolis Marines

**MAHRT, ALPHONSE—Back—
Dayton**
1922–23   Dayton Triangles

MAHRT, JOHN—End—Dayton
1925   Dayton Triangles
1925   Pottsville Maroons

MAHRT, LOUIS—Back—Dayton
1926–27   Dayton Triangles

**MAIKKULA, KENNETH—End—
Connecticut**
1942   New York Giants

**MAILLARD, RALPH—Tackle—
Creighton**
1929   Chicago Bears

MAINES, THOMAS—Back—Syracuse
1946   Brooklyn Dodgers

**MAINS, GILBERT—Tackle—
Murray State**
1953–60   Detroit Lions

**MALCOLM, CARVEL—Tackle—
Franklin Marshall**
1926   Frankford Yellowjackets

**MALCOLM, HARRY—Tackle—
Washington & Jefferson**
1929   Frankford Yellowjackets

MALEY, HOWARD—Back—SMU
1946–47   Boston Yanks

**MALINOWSKI, EUGENE—Back—
Detroit**
1948   Boston Yanks
1949   Detroit Lions

MALKOVICH, JOSEPH—Center—Duquesne
1935 Pittsburgh Pirates

MALLOUF, RAYMOND—Back—SMU
1941, 46–48 Chicago Cardinals
1949 New York Giants

MALLOY, LESTER—Back—Loyola
1931–33 Chicago Cardinals

MALONE, CHARLES—End—Texas A & M
1933 Chicago Bears
1934–36 Boston Redskins
1937–40, 42 Washington Redskins

MALONE, GROVER—Back—Notre Dame
1921 Green Bay Packers
1921 Rock Island Independents
1923 Akron Steels

MALONEY, GERALD—End—Dartmouth
1925 Providence Steamrollers
1927 New York Yankees
1929 Boston Braves

MALONEY, NORMAN—End—Purdue
1948–49 San Francisco 49ers (AAFC)

MANCHA, VAUGHN—Center—Alabama
1948 Boston Yanks

MANDARINO, MICHAEL—Center—LaSalle
1944–45 Philadelphia Eagles

MANDERS, CLARENCE—Back—Drake
1939–44 Brooklyn Dodgers
1945 Boston Yanks
1946 New York Yankees (AAFC)
1947 Buffalo Bills (AAFC)
1941 #1 Ball Carrying

MANDERS, JOHN—Back—Minnesota
1933–40 Chicago Bears
1934, 37 #1 Scoring
1933, 34, 36, 37 #1 Field Goals
(1933 tied by Presnell, 1936 tied by Niccolai)

MANELLA—Guard
1928 New York Yankees

MANFREDA, ANTHONY—Back—Holy Cross
1930 Newark

MANGUM, PETER—Back—Mississippi
1954 New York Giants
1960 Denver Broncos (AFL)

MANIACI, JOSEPH—Back—Fordham
1936–38 Brooklyn Dodgers
1939–41 Chicago Bears

MANION, JAMES—Guard—St. Thomas (Minn.)
1926–27 Duluth Eskimos

MANKAT, CARL—Guard—Colgate
1928–29 Dayton Triangles

MANLEY, JOSEPH—Center—Mississippi State
1953 San Francisco 49ers

MANLEY, LEON—Guard—Oklahoma
1950–51 Green Bay Packers

MANN, DAVID—Back—Oregon State
1955–57 Chicago Cardinals

MANN, ROBERT—End—Michigan
1948–49 Detroit Lions
1950–54 Green Bay Packers

ROBERT MANN

MANNING, JOSEPH—Back—Fordham
1926 Hartford Blues
1926 Providence Steamrollers

MANNING, PETER—Back—Wake Forest
1960 Chicago Bears

MANOURIAN, DONALD—Guard—Stanford
1960 Oakland Raiders (AFL)

MANSFIELD, JERRY—Back
1921 Rock Island Independents

MANSKE, EDGAR—End—Northwestern
1935, 37, 39–40 Chicago Bears
1935–36 Philadelphia Eagles

**MANTELL, JOSEPH—Guard—
Canisius**
1924   Columbus Tigers

MANTON, TALDON—Back—TCU
1936–38   New York Giants
1938   Washington Redskins
1940   Philadelphia Eagles
1943   Brooklyn Dodgers

**MANZINI, BAPTISTE—Center—St.
Vincent's**
1944–45, 49   Philadelphia Eagles

**MANZO, JOSEPH—Tackle—Boston
College**
1945   Detroit Lions

**MAPLE, HOWARD—Back—Oregon
State**
1930   Chicago Cardinals
1934   Cincinnati Reds

MARAS, JOSEPH—Center—Duquesne
1938–40   Pittsburgh Steelers

**MARCHETTI, GINO—End—San
Francisco**
1952   Dallas Texans
1953–60   Baltimore Colts

**MARCHI, BASILIO—Center—New
York Univ.**
1934   Pittsburgh Pirates
1941–42   Philadelphia Eagles

**MARCHIBRODA, THEODORE—
Back—St. Bonaventure**
1953, 55–56   Pittsburgh Steelers
1957   Chicago Cardinals

**MARCINIAK, RONALD—Guard—
Kansas State**
1955   Washington Redskins

**MARCOLINI, HUGO—Back—St.
Bonaventure**
1948   Brooklyn Dodgers (AAFC)

**MARCONI, JOSEPH—Back—West
Virginia**
1956–60   Los Angeles Rams

**MARCUS, ALEXANDER—End—
Temple**
1933   Philadelphia Eagles

MARCUS, PETER—End—Kentucky
1944   Washington Redskins

**MAREFOS, ANDREW—Back—St.
Mary's (Cal.)**
1940–41   New York Giants
1946   Los Angeles Dons (AAFC)

**MAREK, JOSEPH—Back—Texas
Tech.**

1943   Brooklyn Dodgers

**MARELLI, RAY—Guard—Notre
Dame**
1928   Chicago Cardinals

JOSEPH MARCONI

**MARGARITA, HENRY—Back—
Brown**
1944–46   Chicago Bears

**MARGUCCI, JOSEPH—Back—
Southern California**
1947–48   Detroit Lions

**MARINO, VICTOR—Guard—Ohio
State**
1947   Baltimore Colts (AAFC)

MARINO—Back
1928   Pottsville Maroons

MARION, PHILIP—Back—Michigan
1925–26   Detroit Panthers

**MARK, LOUIS—End—
North Carolina State**
1938–40   Brooklyn Dodgers
1945   Boston Yanks

**MARKER, CLIFFORD—Back—
Washington State**
1926   Canton Bulldogs
1927   Frankford Yellowjackets
1927   New York Giants

**MARKER, HENRY—Back—
West Virginia**
1934   Brooklyn Dodgers
1934   Pittsburgh Pirates

MARKO—Back
1944   Brooklyn Dodgers

**MARKOV, VICTOR—Tackle—
Washington**
1938   Cleveland Rams

**MARKS, LAWRENCE—Back—
Indiana**

1926   Akron Steels
1927   New York Yankees
1928   Green Bay Packers
1931   Portsmouth Spartans

**MARONE, JOHN—Guard—
Manhattan**
1943   New York Giants

DUSAN MARONIC

MARONIC, DUSAN—Guard
1944–50   Philadelphia Eagles
1951   New York Giants

**MARONIC, STEPHEN—Tackle—
North Carolina**
1939–40   Detroit Lions

MAROTTI, LOUIS—Guard—Toledo
1943, 45   Chicago Cardinals
1944   Card-Pitt

MARQUARDT, JOHN—End—Illinois
1921   Chicago Cardinals

**MARQUES, ROBERT—Center—
Boston Univ.**
1960   New York Titans (AFL)

**MARSH, HOWARD—Back—
Oklahoma**
1921   Canton Bulldogs

**MARSH, RICHARD—Guard—
Oklahoma**
1933   New York Giants

**MARSHALL, CLOYD—End—New
York Univ.**
1931–32   Staten Island Stapletons

**MARSHALL, JAMES—Tackle—
Ohio State**
1960   Cleveland Browns

**MARSHALL, ROBERT—End—
Minnesota**
1921   Rock Island Independents
1922–24   Minneapolis Marines

1923–27   Duluth Eskimos

**MARSTON, RALPH—Back—Boston
Univ.**
1929   Boston Braves

MARTELL, HERMAN—End
1921   Green Bay Packers

**MARTIN, BLANCHE—Back—
Michigan State**
1960   New York Titans (AFL)
1960   Los Angeles Chargers (AFL)

**MARTIN, CALEB—Tackle—
Louisiana Tech.**
1947   Chicago Cardinals

**MARTIN, FRANK—Back—
Alabama**
1943–44   Brooklyn Dodgers
1945   New York Giants
1945   Boston Yanks

**MARTIN, HERSCHEL—Back—
Missouri**
1929   Staten Island Stapletons
1930   Newark
1932   Chicago Cardinals

**MARTIN, JAMES—Guard—
Notre Dame**
1950   Cleveland Browns
1951–60   Detroit Lions

**MARTIN, JOHN (PEPPER)—
Kicker—None**
1948   Brooklyn Dodgers

MARTIN, JOHN—Back—Oklahoma
1941–43   Chicago Cardinals
1944   Card-Pitt
1944–45   Boston Yanks

MARTIN, JOHN—Center—Annapolis
1947–49   Los Angeles Rams

MARTIN, VERNON—Back—Texas
1942   Pittsburgh Steelers

**MARTINEAU, ROY—Back—
Syracuse**
1923   Buffalo All Americans
1924–25   Rochester Jeffersons

**MARTINELLI, JAMES—Center—
Scranton**
1946   Buffalo Bisons (AAFC)

**MARTINKOVIC, JOHN—End—
Xavier**
1951–56   Green Bay Packers
1957   New York Giants

**MARTINOVICH, PHILIP—Guard—
College of Pacific**
1939   Detroit Lions

1940 Chicago Bears
1946–47 Brooklyn Dodgers (AAFC)

MASINI, LEONARD—Back—Fresno State
1947–48 San Francisco 49ers (AAFC)
1948 Los Angeles Dons (AAFC)

MASKAS, JOHN—Guard—Virginia Polytech
1947, 49 Buffalo Bills (AAFC)

MASON, JOEL—End—Western Michigan
1939 Chicago Cardinals
1941–45 Green Bay Packers

MASON, SAMUEL—Back— Virginia Military Inst.
1922 Minneapolis Marines
1925 Milwaukee Badgers

MASON, WALTER—End—Colgate
1928 Chicago Cardinals

MASSEY, CARLETON—End—Texas
1954–56 Cleveland Browns
1957–58 Green Bay Packers

MASTERS, NORMAN—Tackle— Michigan State
1957–60 Green Bay Packers

NORMAN MASTERS

MASTERS, ROBERT—Back—Baylor
1935–38, 41–42 Philadelphia Eagles
1939 Pittsburgh Steelers
1942 Washington Redskins
1943 Phil-Pitt
1943–44 Chicago Bears

MASTERS, WALTER—Back— Pennsylvania
1942–43 Chicago Cardinals
1944 Card-Pitt

MASTERSON, BERNARD—Back— Nebraska

1934–40 Chicago Bears

MASTERSON, FOREST—Center— Iowa
1945 Chicago Bears

MASTERSON, ROBERT—End— Miami
1938–43 Washington Redskins
1944–45 Boston Yanks
1946 New York Yankees (AAFC)

MASTRANGELO, JOHN—Guard— Notre Dame
1947–48 Pittsburgh Steelers
1949 New York Yankees (AAFC)
1950 New York Giants

MASTROGANY, AUGUST—End— Iowa
1931 Chicago Bears
1931 Brooklyn Dodgers

MATESIC, EDWARD—Back— Pittsburgh
1934–35 Philadelphia Eagles
1936 Pittsburgh Pirates

MATESIC, JOSEPH—Tackle—End— Arizona State
1954 Pittsburgh Steelers

MATHESON, JOHN—End—Western Michigan
1943–46 Detroit Lions
1947 Chicago Bears

MATHESON, RILEY—Guard—Texas Mines
1939–42, 44–45 Cleveland Rams
1943 Detroit Lions
1946–47 Los Angeles Rams
1948 San Francisco 49ers (AAFC)

MATHEWS, BOB ORR—End— Annapolis
1926 Racine Legion

MATHEWS, EDWARD—Back— UCLA
1940–43 Detroit Lions
1945 Boston Yanks
1946 Chicago Rockets (AAFC)
1946–47 San Francisco 49ers (AAFC)

MATHEWS, NEIL—Tackle— Pennsylvania
1921–22 Canton Bulldogs

MATHEWS, RAYMOND—Back— Clemson
1951–59 Pittsburgh Steelers
1960 Dallas Cowboys

MATHEWSON, MORLEY—End— California
1941 Detroit Lions

MATHIS, WILLIAM—Back—
   Clemson
1960 New York Titans (AFL)

MATHYS, CHARLES—Back—Indiana
1922–26 Green Bay Packers

MATISI, ANTHONY—Tackle—
   Pittsburgh
1938 Detroit Lions

MATISI, JOHN—Tackle—Duquesne
1943 Brooklyn Dodgers
1946 Buffalo Bisons (AAFC)

MATSOS, ARCHIBALD—Center—
   Michigan State
1960 Buffalo Bills (AFL)

MATSON, OLIVER—Back—San
   Francisco
1952, 54–58 Chicago Cardinals
1959–60 Los Angeles Rams

MATSU, ARTHUR—Back—William
   & Mary
1928 Dayton Triangles

MATTEO, FRANCIS—Tackle—
   Syracuse
1922–25 Rochester Jeffersons

MATTHEWS, CLAY—Tackle—
   Georgia Tech.
1950, 53–55 San Francisco 49ers

MATTIFORD, JOHN—Guard—
   Marshall
1941 Detroit Lions

MATTINGLY, FRANCIS—Guard—
   Texas A & I
1947 Chicago Rockets (AAFC)

MATTIOLI, FRANCIS—Guard—
   Pittsburgh
1946 Pittsburgh Steelers

MATTISON, RALPH—Guard—
   Davis-Elkins
1930 Brooklyn Dodgers

MATTOS, HARRY—Back—St. Mary's
   (Cal.)
1936 Green Bay Packers
1937 Cleveland Rams

MATTOX, MARVIN—Back—
   Washington & Lee
1923 Milwaukee Badgers

MATUZA, ALBERT—Center—
   Georgetown
1941–43, 46 Chicago Bears

MATUSZAK, MARVIN—Center—
   Tulsa
1953, 55–56 Pittsburgh Steelers

1957–58 San Francisco 49ers
1958 Green Bay Packers
1959–60 Baltimore Colts

MAUL, C. NEWELL—Back—
   California
1926 Los Angeles

MAULDIN, STANLEY—Tackle—
   Texas
1946–48 Chicago Cardinals
Died Sept. 1948 after game against
Philadelphia.

MAVES, EARL—Back—Wisconsin
1948 Detroit Lions
1948 Baltimore Colts (AAFC)

MAVRAIDES, MENIL—Guard—
   Notre Dame
1954–57 Philadelphia Eagles

MAXWELL, JOSEPH—End—Notre
   Dame
1927–29 Frankford Yellowjackets

MAY, FRANCIS—Center—Centenary
1933 Cleveland Rams

MAY, WILLIAM—Back—LSU
1937–38 Chicago Cardinals

MAYER, ERNEST—Tackle—Catholic
1926 Duluth Eskimos
1927 Pottsville Maroons

MAYER, FRANK—Guard—Notre
   Dame
1927 Green Bay Packers

MAYES, CARL—Back—Texas
1952 Los Angeles Rams

MAYHEW, HAYDEN—Guard—Texas
   Mines
1936–38 Pittsburgh Steelers

MAYL, EUGENE—End—Notre Dame
1925–26 Dayton Triangles

MAYNARD, DONALD—Back—Texas
   Western
1958 New York Giants
1960 New York Titans (AFL)

MAYNARD, LESTER—Back—Rider
1932 Staten Island Stapletons
1933 Philadelphia Eagles

MAYNAUGH, ROLAND—Guard—St.
   Thomas
1924 Minneapolis Marines

MAYNE, LEWIS—Back—Texas
1946 Brooklyn Dodgers (AAFC)
1947 Cleveland Browns (AAFC)
1948 Baltimore Colts (AAFC)

MAZNICKI, FRANK—Back—Boston
   College

1941–42, 46 Chicago Bears
1947 Boston Yanks

MAZUREK, EDWARD—Tackle—Xavier (O.)
1960 New York Giants

MAZZA, VINCENT—End—Trott Vocational
1945–46 Detroit Lions
1947–49 Buffalo Bills (AAFC)

MAZZANTI, GINO—Back—Arkansas
1950 Baltimore Colts

MEAD, JOHN—End—Wisconsin
1946–47 New York Giants

MEADE, JAMES—Back—Maryland
1939–40 Washington Redskins

MEADOR, EDWARD—Back—Arkansas Tech
1959–60 Los Angeles Rams

EDWARD MEADOR

MEADOWS, EDWARD—End—Duke
1954, 56–57 Chicago Bears
1955 Pittsburgh Steelers
1958 Philadelphia Eagles
1959 Washington Redskins

MEADOWS, ERIC—Back—Pittsburgh
1923 Milwaukee Badgers

MECHAM, CURTIS—Back—Oregon
1942 Brooklyn Dodgers

MEEKER, HERBERT—Back—Washington State
1930–31 Providence Steamrollers

MEEKS, BRYANT—Center—South Carolina
1947–48 Pittsburgh Steelers

MEEKS, EDWARD—Back—Louisville
1922 Louisville Colonels

MEESE, WARD—End—Wabash
1922 Milwaukee Badgers
1923 St. Louis Browns
1924 Kenosha
1925 Hammond Pros

MEHELICH, CHARLES—End—Duquesne
1946–51 Pittsburgh Steelers

MEHELICH, THOMAS—Guard—St. Mary's
1929 Minneapolis Redjackets

MEHRE, HENRY—Center—Notre Dame
1923–24 Minneapolis Marines

MEHRINGER, PETER—Tackle—Kansas
1934–36 Chicago Cardinals

MEILINGER, STEVEN—End—Kentucky
1956–57 Washington Redskins
1958, 60 Green Bay Packers

MEINERT, DALE—Guard—Oklahoma State
1958–59 Chicago Cardinals
1960 St. Louis Cardinals

MEINHARDT, GEORGE—Guard—St. Louis Univ.
1923 St. Louis Browns

MEISENHEIMER, DARRELL—Back—Oklahoma A & M
1951 New York Yanks

MELLEKAS, JOHN—Tackle—Arizona
1956, 58–60 Chicago Bears

MELLO, JAMES—Back—Notre Dame
1947 Boston Yanks
1948 Chicago Rockets (AAFC)
1948–49 Los Angeles Rams
1949 Detroit Lions

MELLUS, JOHN—Tackle—Villanova
1938–41 New York Giants
1946 San Francisco 49ers (AAFC)
1947–49 Baltimore Colts (AAFC)

MELVIN—End—Marietta
1921 Cincinnati Celts

MEMMELAAR, DALE—Guard—Wyoming
1959 Chicago Cardinals
1960 St. Louis Cardinals

MENASCO, DONALD—Back—Texas
1952–53 New York Giants
1954 Washington Redskins

MENEFEE, VICTOR—End
1921 Rock Island Independents

MERCER, JAMES—Back—Oregon State
1942–43   New York Giants

MERCER, KENNETH—Back—Simpson
1927–29   Frankford Yellowjackets

MEREDITH, DONALD—Back—SMU
1960   Dallas Cowboys

MEREDITH, RUSSELL—Guard—West Virginia
1923   Louisville Colonels
1925   Cleveland Indians

MERGEN, MICHAEL—Tackle—San Francisco
1952   Chicago Cardinals

MERGENTHAL, ARTHUR—Guard—Notre Dame
1945   Cleveland Rams
1946   Los Angeles Rams

MERILLAT, LOUIS—End—Annapolis
1925   Canton Bulldogs

MERKEL, MONTE—Guard—Kansas
1942–43   Chicago Bears

MERKLE, EDWARD—Guard—Oklahoma A & M
1943   Chicago Bears
1944   Washington Redskins

MERKOVSKY, ALBERT—Tackle—Pittsburgh
1944   Card-Pitt
1945–46   Pittsburgh Steelers

MERLIN, EDWARD—Guard—Vanderbilt
1938–39   Brooklyn Dodgers

MERLONI, PETER—End—Arkansas
1929   Boston Braves

MERRILL, WALTER—Tackle—Alabama
1940–42   Brooklyn Dodgers

MERTENS, GERALD—End—Drake
1958–60   San Francisco 49ers

MERTES, BERNARD—Back—Iowa
1945   Chicago Cardinals
1946   Los Angeles Dons (AAFC)
1947–49   Baltimore Colts
1949   New York Giants

MESAK, RICHARD—Tackle—St. Mary's (Cal.)
1945   Detroit Lions

MESSNER, MAX—Back—Cincinnati
1960   Detroit Lions

GERALD MERTENS

MESTNIK, FRANK—Back—Marquette
1960   St. Louis Cardinals

METHOD, RUSSELL—Back—North Dakota
1923–27   Duluth Eskimos
1928   Chicago Cardinals

METRICK—Back
1935   Brooklyn Dodgers

METZGER, LOUIS—Back—Georgetown
1926   Louisville Colonels

MEYER, EDWARD—Tackle—West Texas State
1960   Buffalo Bills (AFL)

MEYER, ERNEST—Guard—Geneva
1930   Portsmouth Spartans

MEYER, FREDERICK—End—Stanford
1942, 45   Philadelphia Eagles

MEYERS, GILBERT—End—Wake Forest
1947   Baltimore Colts (AAFC)

MEYERS, PAUL—End—Wisconsin
1923   Racine Legion

MEYERS, ROBERT—Back—Stanford
1952–53   San Francisco 49ers

MICHAEL, RICHARD—Tackle—Ohio State
1960   Houston Oilers (AFL)

MICHAEL, WILLIAM—Guard—Ohio State
1957   Pittsburgh Steelers

MICHAELS, ALTON—Back—Heidelberg

1923–24 Akron Steels
1925 Cleveland Indians

MICHAELS, EDWARD—Guard—Villanova
1936 Chicago Bears
1937 Washington Redskins
1943 Phil-Pitt
1944–46 Philadelphia Eagles

MICHAELS, JOHN—Guard—Tennessee
1953 Philadelphia Eagles

MICHAELS, LOUIS—Tackle—Kentucky
1958–60 Los Angeles Rams

LOUIS MICHAELS

MICHAELS, WALTER—Guard—Washington & Lee
1951 Green Bay Packers
1952–60 Cleveland Browns

MICHALIK, ARTHUR—Guard—St. Ambrose
1953–54 San Francisco 49ers
1955–56 Pittsburgh Steelers

MICHALSKE, AUGUST—Guard—Penn State
1927–28 New York Yankees
1929–35, 37 Green Bay Packers

MICKA, MICHAEL—Back—Colgate
1944–45 Washington Redskins
1945–48 Boston Yanks

MIDDLETON, DAVID—End—Auburn
1955–60 Detroit Lions

MIDLER, LOUIS—Guard—Minnesota
1939 Pittsburgh Steelers
1940 Green Bay Packers

MIELZINER, SAUL—Center—Carnegie Tech.
1929–30 New York Giants
1931–34 Brooklyn Dodgers

MIESZKOWSKI, EDWARD—Tackle—Notre Dame
1946–47 Brooklyn Dodgers (AAFC)

MIHAJLOVICH, LOUIS—End—Minnesota
1948 Los Angeles Dons (AAFC)

MIHAL, JOSEPH—Tackle—Purdue
1940–41 Chicago Bears
1946 Los Angeles Dons (AAFC)
1947 Chicago Rockets (AAFC)

MIKE, ROBERT—Tackle—UCLA
1948–49 San Francisco 49ers (AAFC)

MIKETA, ANDREW—Center—North Carolina
1954–55 Detroit Lions

MIKLICH, WILLIAM—Back—Idaho
1947–48 New York Giants
1948 Detroit Lions

MIKULA, THOMAS—Back—William & Mary
1948 Brooklyn Dodgers (AAFC)

MIKULAK, MICHAEL—Back—Oregon
1934–36 Chicago Cardinals

MILAM, BARNES—Guard—Austin
1934 Philadelphia Eagles

MILAN, JOSEPH—Back—Phillips
1925 Kansas City Cowboys

MILANO, ARCH—End—St. Francis
1945 Detroit Lions

MILES, LEO—Back—Virginia State
1953 New York Giants

MILLER, ALFRED—Back—Harvard
1929 Boston Braves
1930 Minneapolis Redjackets

MILLER, ALAN—Back—Boston College
1960 Boston Patriots (AFL)

MILLER, BEN—Center—Tennessee
1946 Chicago Rockets (AAFC)

MILLER, BLAKE—End—Michigan State
1921 Detroit Lions

MILLER, CHARLES—Center–Purdue
1932–37 Chicago Bears
1937 Cleveland Rams
1938 Green Bay Packers

MILLER, DONALD—Back—Notre Dame
1925 Providence Steamrollers

MILLER, DONALD—Back—Wisconsin
1941–42 Green Bay Packers

MILLER, DONALD—Back—SMU
1954 Green Bay Packers
1954 Philadelphia Eagles

MILLER, EDWARD—Back—New Mexico State
1939–40 New York Giants

MILLER, FREDERICK—Tackle—College of Pacific
1945 Washington Redskins

MILLER, HAROLD—Tackle—Georgia Tech.
1953 San Francisco 49ers

MILLER, HENRY—End—Penn State
1921 Buffalo All Americans
1922–23 Racine Legion
1923–24 Frankford Yellowjackets
1925 Milwaukee Badgers

MILLER, JAMES—Tackle—New York Univ.
1929, 31 Staten Island Stapletons
1930 Brooklyn Dodgers

MILLER, JOHN—Tackle—Boston College
1956–59 Washington Redskins
1960 Green Bay Packers

MILLER, LLOYD—Back
1922–23 Louisville Colonels

MILLER, MILFORD—Guard—Nebraska State
1935 Chicago Bears
1936–37 Chicago Cardinals

MILLER, PAUL—Back—South Dakota
1936–38 Green Bay Packers

MILLER, PAUL—End—LSU
1954–57 Los Angeles Rams
1960 Dallas Texans (AFL)

MILLER, RALPH—Tackle—Rice
1937–38 Cleveland Rams

MILLER, J. ROBERT—Center—Wittenberg
1931 Portsmouth Spartans

MILLER, ROBERT—Tackle—Virginia
1952–58 Detroit Lions

MILLER, RONALD—End—Southern California
1956 Los Angeles Rams

ROBERT MILLER

MILLER, THOMAS—End—Hampton-Sydney
1942, 44 Philadelphia Eagles
1943 Phil-Pitt
1945 Washington Redskins
1946 Green Bay Packers

MILLMAN, ROBERT—Back—Lafayette
1926–27 Pottsville Maroons

MILLNER, WAYNE—End—Notre Dame
1936 Boston Redskins
1937–41, 45 Washington Redskins

MILLS, DENVER—End—William & Mary
1952 Chicago Cardinals

MILLS, JOSEPH—Center—Carnegie Tech
1922–25 Akron Steels

MILLS, THOMAS—Back—Penn State
1922–23 Green Bay Packers

MILNER, WILLIAM—Guard—Duke
1947–49 Chicago Bears
1950 New York Giants

MILSTEAD, CENTURY—Tackle—Yale
1925, 27–28 New York Giants

MILSTEAD, CHARLES—Back—Texas A. & M.
1960 Houston Oilers (AFL)

MILTON, JOHN—End—Southern California
1923 Milwaukee Badgers
1923 St. Louis Browns
1924 Kansas City Cowboys

MILTON, THOMAS—End—Lake Forrest

1923 St. Louis Browns
1924 Kansas City Cowboys
1924 Green Bay Packers

**MINARIK, HENRY—End—Michigan
State**
1951 Pittsburgh Steelers

MINER, THOMAS—End—Tulsa
1958 Pittsburgh Steelers
1958 #1 Field Goals
        (tied by P. Cothren)

MINGO, EUGENE—Back
1960 Denver Broncos (AFL)

MINICK, PAUL—Guard—Iowa
1927 Buffalo Bisons
1928–29 Green Bay Packers

**MININI, FRANK—Back—San Jose
State**
1947–49 Chicago Bears
1949 Pittsburgh Steelers

**MINISI, ANTHONY—Back—
Pennsylvania**
1948 New York Giants

MINTUN, JOHN—Center
1923–24, 26 Racine Legion
1925 Kansas City Cowboys

**MIODUSZEWSKI, EDWARD—Back—
William & Mary**
1953 Baltimore Colts

**MISCHAK, ROBERT—Guard—West
Point**
1958 New York Giants
1960 New York Titans (AFL)

MISHEL, DAVID—Back—Brown
1927 Providence Steamrollers
1931 Cleveland Indians

**MITCHAM, EUGENE—End—Arizona
State**
1958 Philadelphia Eagles

**MITCHELL, ALBERT—Tackle—
Thiel**
1924 Buffalo Bisons

**MITCHELL, CHARLES—Back—
Tulsa**
1945 Chicago Bears
1946 Green Bay Packers

**MITCHELL, FONDREN—Back—
Florida**
1946 Miami Seahawks (AAFC)

**MITCHELL, FREDERICK—Center—
Bucknell**
1929 Orange
1930 Newark

**MITCHELL, GRANVILLE—End—
David & Elkins**
1931–33 Portsmouth Spartans
1934–35 Detroit Lions
1935–36 New York Giants
1937 Brooklyn Dodgers

**MITCHELL, HAROLD—Tackle—
U.C.L.A.**
1952 New York Giants

**MITCHELL, PAUL—Tackle—
Minnesota**
1946–48 Los Angeles Dons (AAFC)
1948–49 New York Yankees (AAFC)
1950–51 New York Yanks

ROBERT MITCHELL *(Browns)*

**MITCHELL, ROBERT—Back—
Illinois**
1958–60 Cleveland Browns

**MITCHELL, ROBERT—Back—
Stanford**
1946–48 Los Angeles Dons

**MITRICK, FRANK—Tackle—
Oglethorpe**
1945 Detroit Lions

**MIX, RONALD—Tackle—
Southern California**
1960 Los Angeles Chargers (AFL)

MIXON, WILLIAM—Back—Georgia
1953–54 San Francisco 49ers

**MIZELL, WARNER—Back—Georgia
Tech.**
1931 Brooklyn Dodgers
1931 Frankford Yellowjackets

**MOAN, EMMETT—Back—West
Virginia**
1939 Cleveland Rams

**MOBLEY, RUDOLPH—Back—
Hardin-Simmons**
1947 Baltimore Colts (AAFC)

RONALD MIX

MODZELEWSKI, EDWARD—Back—Maryland
1952 Pittsburgh Steelers
1955–59 Cleveland Browns

MODZELEWSKI, RICHARD—Tackle—Maryland
1953–54 Washington Redskins
1955 Pittsburgh Steelers
1956–60 New York Giants

MOE, HAROLD—Back—Oregon State
1933 Chicago Cardinals

MOEGLE, RICHARD—Back—Rice
1955–59 San Francisco 49ers
1960 Pittsburgh Steelers

MOHARDT, JOHN—Back—Notre Dame
1922–23 Chicago Cardinals
1924 Racine Legion
1925–26 Chicago Bears

MOHS, LOUIS—End—St. Thomas
1923–24 Minneapolis Marines

MOLENDA, JOHN—Back—Michigan
1927–28 New York Yankees
1929–32 Green Bay Packers
1932–35 New York Giants

MOLESWORTH, KEITH—Back—Monmouth
1930 Portsmouth Spartans
1931–37 Chicago Bears

MOLINET, LOUIS—Back—Cornell
1927 Frankford Yellowjackets

MOMSEN, ANTHONY—Center—Michigan
1951 Pittsburgh Steelers
1952 Washington Redskins

MOMSEN, ROBERT—Guard—Ohio State
1951 Detroit Lions
1952 San Francisco 49ers

MONACHINO, JAMES—Back—California
1951, 53 San Francisco 49ers
1954 New York Giants
1955 Washington Redskins

MONACO, RAYMOND—Guard—Holy Cross
1944 Washington Redskins
1945 Cleveland Rams

MONAHAN, REGIS—Guard—Ohio State
1935–38 Detroit Lions
1939 Chicago Cardinals

MONELIE, WILLIAM—Back—St. Mary's—Minn.
1927 Duluth Eskimos

MONFORT, AVERY—Back—New Mexico
1941 Chicago Cardinals

MONNETT, ROBERT—Back—Michigan State
1933–38 Green Bay Packers

MONT, THOMAS—Back—Maryland
1947–49 Washington Redskins

MONTGOMERY, WILLIAM—Back—LSU
1946 Chicago Cardinals

MONTGOMERY, CLIFFORD—Back—Columbia
1934 Brooklyn Dodgers

MONTGOMERY, JAMES—Tackle—Texas A & M
1946 Detroit Lions

MONTGOMERY, RALPH—Tackle—Centre College
1923 Chicago Cardinals
1927 Frankford Yellowjackets

MONTGOMERY, WILLIAM—Tackle—St. Louis Univ.
1934 St. Louis Gunners

MOODY, WILKIE—Back—Denison
1924–25 Columbus Tigers

MOONEY, BOW TIPP—Back—Abline Christian
1944–46 Chicago Bears

MOONEY, GEORGE—Back—Georgetown
1922–24 Milwaukee Badgers

MOONEY, JAMES—End—Georgia
1930   Newark
1930–31   Brooklyn Dodgers
1933–34   Cincinnati Reds
1935   Chicago Cardinals
1935   Chicago Bears
       Killed by sniper's bullet in France,
       Aug. 12, 1944. Private, U.S. Army.

MOONEY, TEX—Southern California
  (O. T. SCHUPBACH)
1943   Brooklyn Dodgers

MOORE, ALLEN—Back—Loyola
  (of N. O.)
1932   Chicago Cardinals
1933   Pittsburgh Pirates
1934   Cincinnati Reds

MOORE, ALLEN—Back—
  Northwestern
1932   Chicago Bears

MOORE, ALLEN—End—Texas
  A & M
1939   Green Bay Packers

MOORE, EUGENE—Center—
  Colorado
1938   Brooklyn Dodgers

MOORE, HENRY—Back—Arkansas
1956   New York Giants
1957   Baltimore Colts

MOORE, KENNETH—Center—West
  Virginia Wesleyan
1940   New York Giants

MOORE, LEONARD—Back—Penn.
  State
1956–60   Baltimore Colts

MOORE, LEROY—End—
  Ft. Valley State
1960   Buffalo Bills (AFL)

MOORE, McNEIL—Back—Sam
  Houston
1954, 56–57   Chicago Bears

MOORE, PAUL—Back—
  Presbyterian
1940–41   Detroit Lions

MOORE, THOMAS—Back—
  Vanderbilt
1960   Green Bay Packers

MOORE, WALTER—Back—Lafayette
1927   Pottsville Maroons

MOORE, WILBUR—Back—
  Minnesota
1939–47   Washington Redskins

MOORE, WILLIAM—Back—Loyola
  (New Orleans)

1939–41   Detroit Lions

MOORE, WILLIAM—Guard—Penn
  State
1947–49   Pittsburgh Steelers

MOOTY, JAMES—Back—Arizona
1960   Dallas Cowboys

MORALES, GONZALES—Back—St.
  Mary's (Cal.)
1947–48   Pittsburgh Steelers

MORAN, DALE—Back—Carnegie
  Tech.
1925–27   Frankford Yellowjackets
1928–34   New York Giants

MORAN, FRANCIS—Back—Grinnell
1927   Chicago Cardinals
1928   Pottsville Maroons

MORAN, JAMES—Guard—Holy Cross
1935–36   Boston Redskins

MORAN, THOMAS—Back—Center
1925   New York Giants

MORELLI, JOHN—Guard—
  Georgetown
1944–45   Boston Yanks

MORGAN, BOYD—Back—Southern
  California
1939–40   Washington Redskins

MORGAN, JOSEPH—Tackle—
  Mississippi Southern
1949   San Francisco 49ers (AAFC)

MORGAN, ROBERT—Tackle—
  Maryland
1954   Chicago Cardinals
1954   Washington Redskins

MORGAN, WILLIAM—Tackle—
  Oregon
1933–36   New York Giants

MORLEY, SAMUEL—End—Stanford
1954   Washington Redskins

MORLOCK, JOHN—Back—
  Marshall
1940   Detroit Lions

MORRALL, EARL—Back—Michigan
  State
1956   San Francisco 49ers
1957–58   Pittsburgh Steelers
1958–60   Detroit Lions

MORRIS, DENNIT—Guard—
  Oklahoma
1958   San Francisco 49ers
1960   Houston Oilers (AFL)

MORRIS, FRANCIS—Back—Boston
  Univ.
1942   Chicago Bears

**MORRIS, GEORGE—Center—
GeorgiaTech**
1956 San Francisco 49ers

**MORRIS, GEORGE—Back—Baldwin-
Wallace**
1941–42 Cleveland Rams

**MORRIS, GLEN—End—Colorado
State**
1940 Detroit Lions

MORRIS, JOHN—Back—Oregon State
1958–60 Los Angeles Rams
1960 Pittsburgh Steelers

**MORRIS, JOHN—Back—Santa
Barbara**
1958–60 Chicago Bears

**MORRIS, LAWRENCE—Center—
Georgia Tech**
1955–57 Los Angeles Rams
1959–60 Chicago Bears

MORRIS, MAX—End—Northwestern
1946–47 Chicago Rockets (AAFC)
1948 Brooklyn Dodgers (AAFC)

**MORRIS, RILEY—Back—
Florida A&M**
1960 Oakland Raiders (AFL)

MORRIS, ROBERT—Guard—Cornell
1926 Brooklyn Dodgers

**MORRISEY, FRANK—Tackle—
Boston College**
1921 Rochester Kodaks
1922–24 Buffalo Bisons
1924 Milwaukee Badgers

**MORRISON, FRED—Back—Ohio
State**
1950–53 Chicago Bears
1954–56 Cleveland Browns

**MORRISON, JOSEPH—Back—
Cincinnati**
1959–60 New York Giants

**MORRISON, MAYNARD—Center—
Michigan**
1933–34 Brooklyn Dodgers

**MORRISON, RONALD—Tackle—
New Mexico**
1960 Houston Oilers (AFL)
1960 Boston Patriots (AFL)

**MORROW, JAMES—Back—
Pittsburgh**
1921 Canton Bulldogs
1922 Buffalo All Americans

**MORROW, JOHN—Guard—
Michigan**
1956, 58–59 Los Angeles Rams
1960 Cleveland Browns

MORROW, JOHN—Back—Alabama
1937–38 Chicago Cardinals

**MORROW, ROBERT—Back—
Illinois Wesleyan**
1940–43 Chicago Cardinals
1945 New York Giants
1946 New York Yankees (AAFC)

**MORROW, RUSSELL,—Center—
Tennessee**
1946–47 Brooklyn Dodgers (AAFC)

MORSE, RAYMOND—End—Oregon
1935–38, 40 Detroit Lions

MORSE, ROBERT—Guard—Carlton
1923 Duluth Kelleys

**MORTELL, EMMETT—Back—
Wisconsin**
1937–39 Philadelphia Eagles

MORTON, JOHN—Back—TCU
1953 San Francisco 49ers

**MORTON, JOHN—End—Missouri,
Purdue**
1945 Chicago Bears
1946 Los Angeles Dons (AAFC)
1947 Buffalo Bills (AAFC)

MORTON, LOCK—Back—Arkansas
1930 Newark

**MORZE, FRANK—Center—Boston
College**
1957–60 San Francisco 49ers

FRANK MORZE

MOSCRIP, JAMES—End—Stanford
1938–39 Detroit Lions

**MOSELLE, DONALD—Back—
Wisconsin State Teachers**
1950 Cleveland Browns
1951 Green Bay Packers

MOSER, ROBERT—Center—College of Pacific
1951–53 Chicago Bears

MOSER, THEODORE—Guard
1926 Louisville Colonels

MOSES, HOWARD—End—Washington State
1933 Cincinnati Reds

MOSHER, CLURE—Center—Louisville
1942 Pittsburgh Steelers

MOSLEY, HENRY—Back—Morris-Brown
1955 Chicago Bears

MOSLEY, NORMAN—Back—Alabama
1948 Pittsburgh Steelers

MOSLEY, RUSSELL—Back—Alabama
1945–46 Green Bay Packers

MOSS, PAUL—End—Purdue
1933 Pittsburgh Pirates
1934 St. Louis Gunners

MOSS, PERRY—Back—Illinois
1948 Green Bay Packers

MOSTARDO, RICHARD—Back—Kent State
1960 Cleveland Browns

MOTE, KELLY—End—Duke
1947–49 Detroit Lions
1950–52 New York Giants

MOTL, ROBERT—End—Northwestern
1946 Chicago Rockets (AAFC)

MOTLEY, MARION—Back—Nevada
1946–49 Cleveland Browns (AAFC)
1950–53 Cleveland Browns
1955 Pittsburgh Steelers
1950 #1 Ball Carrying

MOTT, NORMAN—Back—Georgia
1933 Green Bay Packers
1934 Cincinnati Reds
1934 Pittsburgh Pirates

MOYNIHAN, RICHARD—Back—Villanova
1927 Frankford Yellowjackets

MOYNIHAN, TIMOTHY—Center—Notre Dame
1932–33 Chicago Cardinals

MRKONIC, GEORGE—Guard—Kansas
1953 Philadelphia Eagles

MUCHA, CHARLES—Guard—Washington
1935 Chicago Bears

MUCHA, RUDOLPH—Back—Washington
1941, 45 Cleveland Rams
1945–46 Chicago Bears

MUELHAUPT, EDWARD—Guard—Iowa State
1960 Buffalo Bills (AFL)

MUEHLHEUSER, FRANK—Back—Colgate
1948 Boston Yanks
1949 New York Bulldogs

MUELLER, EWALD—Guard—Northwestern
1922–24 Racine Legion

MUELLNER, WILLIAM—End—De Paul
1937 Chicago Cardinals

MUGG, GARVIN—Tackle—North Texas State
1945 Detroit Lions

MUHA, JOSEPH—Back—Virginia Military Inst.
1946–50 Philadelphia Eagles
1948 #1 Punting

MUIRHEAD, STANLEY—Guard—Michigan
1924 Dayton Triangles
1924 Cleveland Bulldogs

MULBARGER, JOSEPH—Tackle—Broaddus
1922–26 Columbus Tigers

MULDOON, MATTHEW—Tackle—St. Mary's (Cal.)
1922 Rochester Kodaks

MULLEN, THOMAS—End—Chicago
1927–28 Pottsville Maroons

MULLEN, VERNE—Back—Nebraska
1921 Evansville Crimson Giants
1923 Canton Bulldogs
1924–27 Chicago Bears
1927 Chicago Cardinals

MULLENEAUX, CARL—End—Utah State
1938–41, 45–46 Green Bay Packers

MULLENEAUX, LEE—Back—Arizona
1932 New York Giants
1933–34 Cincinnati Reds
1934 St. Louis Gunners
1935–37 Pittsburgh Pirates
1938 Green Bay Packers
1938 Chicago Cardinals

MULLER, HAROLD—End—
California
1926   Los Angeles

MULLIGAN, GEORGE—Back—
Catholic Univ.
1936   Philadelphia Eagles

MULLINS, NOAH—Back—Kentucky
1946–49   Chicago Bears
1949   New York Giants

MULREADY, GERALD—End—North
Dakota State
1947   Chicago Rockets

MULVEY, VINCENT—Back—
Syracuse
1923   Buffalo All Americans

MUMLEY, NICHOLAS—End—Purdue
1960   New York Titans (AFL)

MUNDAY, GEORGE—Tackle—
Emporia Teachers
1931–32   New York Giants
1933–34   Cincinnati Reds
1934   St. Louis Gunners

MUNDEE, FREDERICK—Tackle—
Notre Dame
1942–45   Chicago Bears

MUNGER—Tackle
1924   Chicago Cardinals

MUNN, LYLE—End—Kansas State
1925–26   Kansas City Cowboys
1927   Cleveland Bulldogs
1928   Detroit Wolverines
1929   New York Giants

MUNN, MONTE—End—Nebraska
1925   Kansas City Cowboys

MUNN, WAYNE—Tackle—Nebraska
1925   Kansas City Cowboys

MUNNS, GEORGE—Back—
Miami (Ohio)
1921   Cincinnati Celts

MURAKOWSKI, ARTHUR—Back—
Northwestern
1951   Detroit Lions

MURLEY, RICHARD—Guard—
Purdue
1956   Pittsburgh Steelers
1956   Philadelphia Eagles

MURPHY, FREDERICK—End—
Georgia Tech
1960   Cleveland Browns

MURPHY, GEORGE—Back—Southern
California
1949   Los Angeles Dons (AAFC)

MURPHY, GEORGE—Back—
Dartmouth

1926   Milwaukee Badgers
1928   Chicago Cardinals

MURPHY, HARVEY—End—
Mississippi
1940   Cleveland Rams

MURPHY, JAMES—Back—St. Thomas
1926   Racine Legion
1926   Columbus Tigers

MURPHY, JOSEPH—Guard—
Dartmouth
1921   Cleveland Indians

MURPHY, PHILIP—Center—
Marquette
1926   Duluth Eskimos

MURPHY, THOMAS—Back—
St. Mary's (Kan.)
1926   Kansas City Cowboys

MURPHY, THOMAS—Back—
Arkansas
1934   Chicago Cardinals

MURPHY, WILLIAM—Guard—
Washington of Mo.
1940–41   Chicago Cardinals

MURRAH, W. E.—Tackle—Texas
A & M
1922   Canton Bulldogs
1922–24   Racine Legion
1923   St. Louis Browns

MURRAY, EARL—Guard—Purdue
1950   Baltimore Colts
1951   New York Giants
1952   Pittsburgh Steelers

MURRAY, FRANCIS—Back—
Pennsylvania
1939–40   Philadelphia Eagles

MURRAY, JOHN—End—St. Thomas
1924   Duluth Kelleys

MURRAY, RICHARD—Tackle—
Marquette
1921–24   Green Bay Packers
1925   Chicago Bears

MURRY, DONALD—Tackle—
Wisconsin
1924–32   Chicago Bears

MURTAGH, GEORGE—Center—
Georgetown
1926   Providence Steamrollers
1926–32   New York Giants

MUSICK, JAMES—Back—Southern
California
1932–36   Boston Redskins

MUSSO, GEORGE—Guard—Millikin
1933–44   Chicago Bears

MUTRYN, CHESTER—Back—Xavier
1946–49 Buffalo Bisons (AAFC)
1950 Baltimore Colts

MUTSCHELLER, JAMES—End—Notre Dame
1954–60 Baltimore Colts

MYER, DENNIS—Guard—Iowa
1930–31 Brooklyn Dodgers
1931 Chicago Bears

MYERS, BRADFORD—Back—Bucknell
1953, 56 Los Angeles Rams
1958 Philadelphia Eagles

MYERS, CYRIL—End—Ohio State
1922 Toledo Maroons
1923 Racine Legion
1923, 25 Cleveland Indians

MYERS, DAVID—Guard—New York Univ.
1930 Staten Island Stapletons

MYERS, JOHN—Back—UCLA
1948–50 Philadelphia Eagles
1952 Los Angeles Rams

JOHN MYERS

MYERS, ROBERT—Tackle—Ohio State
1955–56 Baltimore Colts

MYERS, THOMAS—Back—Fordham
1925 New York Giants
1926 Brooklyn Dodgers

MYHRA, STEVEN—Guard—North Dakota
1957–60 Baltimore Colts

MYLES—End
1929 Buffalo Bisons
1930 Newark

* * *

STEVEN MYHRA

NABORS, ROLAND—Center—Texas Tech.
1948 New York Yankees (AAFC)

NACRELLI, ANDREW—End—Fordham
1958 Philadelphia Eagles

NADOLNEY, ROMANUS—Guard—Notre Dame
1922 Green Bay Packers
1923–25 Milwaukee Badgers

NAGEL, RAYMOND—Back—U.C.L.A.
1950–51 New York Yanks
1953 Chicago Cardinals

NAGEL, ROSS—Tackle—St. Louis Univ.
1942 Chicago Cardinals

NAGIDA—Back
1926 Hammond Independents

NAGLER, GERN—End—Santa Clara
1953–58 Chicago Cardinals
1959 Pittsburgh Steelers
1960 Cleveland Browns

NAGURSKI, BRONKO—Back—Minnesota
1930–37, 43 Chicago Bears

NAIOTI, JOHN—Back—St. Francis
1942, 45 Pittsburgh Steelers
1944 Card-Pitt

NAPIER, WALTER—Tackle—Paul Quinn
1960 Dallas Texans (AFL)

NARDACCI, NICHOLAS—Back—West Virginia
1925 Cleveland Indians

NARDI, RICHARD—Back—Ohio State
1938   Detroit Lions
1939   Brooklyn Dodgers
1939   Pittsburgh Steelers

NARRAN, ROGER—End
1926   Buffalo Bisons

NASH, ROBERT—Tackle—Rutgers
1921–23   Buffalo All Americans
1925   New York Giants

NASH, THOMAS—End—Georgia
1928–32   Green Bay Packers
1933–34   Brooklyn Dodgers

NATOWICH, ANDREW—Back—Holy Cross
1944   Washington Redskins

NAUMETZ, FREDERICK—Center—Boston College
1946–50   Los Angeles Rams

FREDERICK NAUMETZ

NAUMU, JOHN—Back—Southern California
1948   Los Angeles Dons (AAFC)

NEACY, CLEMENT—End—Colgate
1924–26   Milwaukee Badgers
1927   Duluth Eskimos
1927   Chicago Bears
1928   Chicago Cardinals

NEAL, THOMAS—Guard—Duke
1924–26   Hammond Pros

NEAL, WILLIAM "ED"—Tackle—Tulane, LSU
1945–51   Green Bay Packers
1951   Chicago Bears

NEELY, JESS—Tackle—Vanderbilt
1926   Hartford Blues

NEGUS, FREDERICK—Center—Wisconsin
1947–49   Chicago Rockets (AAFC)
1950   Chicago Bears

NEIHAUS, FRANCIS—Back—Washington & Jefferson
1925   Akron Steels
1926   Pottsville Maroons

NEIHAUS, RALPH—Tackle—Dayton
1939   Cleveland Rams

NEILL, JAMES—Back—Texas Tech.
1937   New York Giants

NELSON, ANDREW—Back—Memphis State
1957–60   Baltimore Colts

ANDREW NELSON

NELSON, DONALD—Center—Ohio Wesleyan
1926   Hammond Pros
1926   Canton Bulldogs

NELSON, DONALD—Guard—Iowa
1937   Brooklyn Dodgers

NELSON, EVERETT—Tackle—Illinois
1929   Chicago Bears

NELSON, FRANK—Back—Utah
1948   Boston Yanks
1949   New York Bulldogs

NELSON, HERBERT—End—Pennsylvania
1946   Buffalo Bisons (AAFC)
1947–48   Brooklyn Dodgers (AAFC)

NELSON, JAMES—Back—Alabama
1946   Miami Seahawks (AAFC)

NELSON, REED—Center—Brigham Young

1947   Detroit Lions

NELSON, ROBERT—Center—Baylor
1941–45   Detroit Lions
1946–49   Los Angeles Dons (AAFC)
1950   Baltimore Colts

NEMECEK, ANDREW—Guard—Ohio State
1923–25   Columbus Tigers

NEMECEK, GERALD—End—New York Univ.
1931   Brooklyn Dodgers

NEMETH, STEPHEN—Back—Notre Dame
1945   Cleveland Rams
1946   Chicago Rockets (AAFC)
1947   Baltimore Colts (AAFC)

NEMZEK, ALBERT—Guard—North Dakota State
1930   Minneapolis Marines

NERY, CARL—Guard—Duquesne
1940–41   Pittsburgh Steelers

NERY, RONALD—End—Kansas State
1960   Los Angeles Chargers (AFL)

NESBITT, RICHARD—Back—Drake
1930–33   Chicago Bears
1933   Chicago Cardinals
1934–35   Brooklyn Dodgers

NESS, VAL—Guard
1922   Minneapolis Marines

NESSER, AL—End
1921–25   Akron Steels
1925–26   Columbus Tigers
1926   Akron Steels
1927–28   New York Giants
1931   Cleveland Indians

NESSER, FRANK—Back
1921, 26   Columbus Tigers

NESSER, FRED—Guard
1921–22   Columbus Tigers

NESSER, JOHN—Back
1921   Columbus Tigers

NESSER, PHILIP—Back
1921   Columbus Tigers

NESSER, THEODORE—Center
1921   Columbus Tigers

NETHERTON, WILLIAM—End—Kentucky
1922   Louisville Colonels

NEVERS, ERNEST—Back—Stanford
1926–27   Duluth Eskimos
1929–31   Chicago Cardinals

NEWASHE—Tackle—Carlisle
1922   Oorang Indians

NEWMAN, HARRY—Back—Michigan
1933–35   New York Giants
1933   #1 Passing

NEWMAN, OLIN—Tackle—Carnegie Tech.
1924–25   Akron Steels
1926   Hammond Pros

NEWMAN, ROBERT—End—Wesleyan
1934–36   Chicago Cardinals

NEWMEYER, DONALD—Tackle—California
1926   Los Angeles

NEWTON, CHARLES—Tackle—Washington
1939–40   Philadelphia Eagles

NICCOLAI, ARMAND—Tackle—Duquesne
1934–42   Pittsburgh Pirates
1935, 36   #1 Field Goals (1935 tied by Smith, W; 1936 tied by Manders)

NICELY, JOHN—Tackle—Gettysburg
1930   Staten Island Stapletons

NICHELINI, ALBERT—Back—St. Mary's
1935–36   Chicago Cardinals

NICHOLS, ALLEN—Back—Temple
1945   Pittsburgh Steelers

NICHOLS, HAMILTON—Guard—Rice
1947–49   Chicago Cardinals
1951   Green Bay Packers

NICHOLS, JOHN—Guard—Ohio State
1926   Canton Bulldogs

NICHOLS, MICHAEL—Center—Arkansas A & M
1960   Denver Broncos (AFL)

NICHOLS, RALPH—Tackle—Kansas State
1926   Hartford Blues

NICHOLS, SIDNEY—Guard—Illinois
1921   Rock Island Independents

NICKEL, ELBERT—End—Cincinnati
1947–57   Pittsburgh Steelers

NICKLA, EDWARD—Tackle—Maryland
1959   Chicago Bears

NICKSICH, GEORGE—Guard—St. Bonaventure
1950–51   Pittsburgh Steelers

**NICKSICH, MICHAEL—Back—
Pittsburgh**
1935 Pittsburgh Steelers
1942 Brooklyn Dodgers

NIEDZIELA, BRUNO—Tackle—Iowa
1947 Chicago Rockets (AAFC)

**NIELSEN, WALTER—Back—
Arizona**
1940 New York Giants

**NIEMANN, WALTER—Center—
Michigan**
1922–24 Green Bay Packers

**NIEMI, LAURIE—Tackle—
Washington State**
1949–53 Washington Redskins

NILES, JERRY—Back—Iowa
1946–47 New York Giants

**NINOWSKI, JAMES—Back—
Michigan State**
1958–59 Cleveland Browns
1960 Detroit Lions

JAMES NINOWSKI

NIPP, MAURICE—Guard—Loyola
1952–53, 56 Philadelphia Eagles

NISBET, DAVID—End—Washington
1933 Chicago Cardinals

**NISBY, JOHN—Tackle—College of
Pacific**
1957–60 Pittsburgh Steelers

**NITSCHKE, RAYMOND—Back—
Illinois**
1958–60 Green Bay Packers

NIX, DOYLE—Back—SMU
1955 Green Bay Packers
1958–59 Washington Redskins

1960 Los Angeles Chargers (AFL)

RAYMOND NITSCHKE

NIX, EMERY—Back—TCU
1943, 46 New York Giants

NIX, EMORY—Tackle—Haskell
1926 Buffalo Bisons
1926 Akron Steels

NIX, JOHN—Back—Mississippi State
1940 Cleveland Rams

**NIX, JOHN—End—Southern
California**
1950 San Francisco 49ers

NIXON, GEORGE—Back—Idaho
1942 Brooklyn Dodgers

**NIXON, MICHAEL—Back—
Pittsburgh**
1941–42 Brooklyn Dodgers

NOBILE, LEO—Guard—Penn State
1947 Washington Redskins
1948–49 Pittsburgh Steelers

NOBLE, DAVID—Back—Nebraska
1924–25 Cleveland Indians

NOBLE, JAMES—Back—Syracuse
1925 Buffalo Bisons

**NOBLE, RICHARD—Guard—
Trinity—Conn.**
1926 Hartford Blues

NOCERA, JOHN—Center—Iowa
1959–60 Philadelphia Eagles

NOLAN, EARL—Tackle—Arizona
1937–38 Chicago Cardinals

NOLAN, JOHN—Guard—Santa Clara
1926 Los Angeles

NOLAN, JOHN—Tackle—Penn State
1948 Boston Yanks
1949 New York Bulldogs
1950 New York Yanks

**NOLAN, RICHARD—Back—
Maryland**
1954–57, 59–60   New York Giants
1958   Chicago Cardinals

**NOLANDER, DONALD—Center—
Minnesota**
1946   Los Angeles Dons (AAFC)
1947   Baltimore Colts (AAFC)

NOLL, CHARLES—Guard—Dayton
1953–59   Cleveland Browns

NOLTING, RAY—Back—Cincinnati
1936–44   Chicago Bears

**NOMELLINI, LEO—Tackle—
Minnesota**
1950–60   San Francisco 49ers

**NONNEMAKER, GUSTAVUS—End—
Wittenberg**
1926   Columbus Tigers

**NOONAN, GERALD—Back—
Fordham**
1921–24   Rochester Kodaks

**NOPPENBERG, JOHN—Back—
Miami (Fla.)**
1940–41   Pittsburgh Steelers
1941   Detroit Lions

NORBERG, HENRY—End—Stanford
1946–47   San Francisco 49ers (AAFC)
1948   Chicago Bears

NORBY, JOHN—Back—Idaho
1934   St. Louis Gunners
1934   Philadelphia Eagles
1934   New York Giants
1935   Brooklyn Dodgers

**NORDSTROM, HARRY—Guard—
Trinity (Conn.)**
1925   New York Giants
1926   Brooklyn Dodgers

NOREENE, OLAF—Back—Minnesota
1921   Evansville Crimson Giants

NORGARD, ALVAR—End—Stanford
1934   Green Bay Packers

NORI, REINO—Back—DeKalb
1937   Detroit Lions
1937   Brooklyn Dodgers
1938   Chicago Bears

**NORMAN, HALDO—End—
Gustavus-Adolphus**
1952   San Francisco 49ers

NORMAN, JAMES—Guard
1955   Washington Redskins

NORMAN, ROBERT—Center—None
1945   Chicago Cardinals

**NORMAN, WILLARD—Back—
Washington & Jefferson**
1928   Pottsville Maroons

**NORRIS, HAROLD—Back—
California**
1955–56   Washington Redskins

NORRIS, JOHN—End—Maryland
1932   Staten Island Stapletons

**NORTH, JAMES—Tackle—Central
Washington**
1944   Washington Redskins

NORTH, JOHN—End—Vanderbilt
1948–49   Baltimore Colts (AAFC)
1950   Baltimore Colts

NORTON, DONALD—End—Iowa
1960   Los Angeles Chargers (AFL)

NORTON, GERALD—Back—SMU
1954–58   Philadelphia Eagles
1959   Chicago Cardinals
1960   St. Louis Cardinals
1960   #1 Interceptions (Tie with
          D. Baker)
1960   #1 Punting

NORTON, JAMES—Back—Idaho
1960   Houston Oilers (AFL)

**NORTON, MARTIN—Back—
Carleton**
1922, 24   Minneapolis Marines
1925   Green Bay Packers

**NORTON, RAY—Back—San Jose
State**
1960   San Francisco 49ers

NOSICH, JOHN—Tackle
1938   Pittsburgh Pirates

NOTT, DOUGLAS—Back—Detroit
1935   Detroit Lions
1935–36   Boston Redskins

NOVACK, EDWARD—Back
1921–22, 25   Rock Island Independents
1924   Minneapolis Marines

**NOVOTNY, RAYMOND—Back—
Ashland**
1930   Portsmouth Spartans
1931   Cleveland Indians
1932   Brooklyn Dodgers

NOWAK, WALTER—End—Villanova
1944   Philadelphia Eagles

**NOWASKEY, ROBERT—End—
George Washington**
1940–42   Chicago Bears
1946–47   Los Angeles Dons (AAFC)
1948–49   Baltimore Colts (AAFC)
1950   Baltimore Colts

**NOYES, LEONARD—Tackle—
Montana**

1938 Brooklyn Dodgers

NUGENT—Back
1924 Cleveland Bulldogs

NUNNERY, ROBERT—Tackle—LSU
1960 Dallas Texans (AFL)

**NUSSBAUMER, ROBERT—Back—
Michigan**
1946 Green Bay Packers
1947–48 Washington Redskins
1949–50 Chicago Cardinals
1951 Green Bay Packers
1949 #1 Interceptions

**NUTT, RICHARD—Back—Texas
State North**
1949 New York Giants

**NUTTER, MADISON—Center—
Virginia Polytech.**
1954–60 Baltimore Colts

MADISON NUTTER

**NUZUM, GERALD—Back—New
Mexico A & M**
1948–51 Pittsburgh Steelers

**NYDALL, MALCOLM—Back—
Minnesota**
1929–30 Minneapolis Redjackets
1930–31 Frankford Yellowjackets

**NYERS, RICHARD—Back—
Indiana Central**
1956–57 Baltimore Colts

**NYGREN, BERNARD—Back—San
Jose State**
1946 Los Angeles Dons (AAFC)
1947 Brooklyn Dodgers (AAFC)

* * *

OAKES, WILLIAM—Tackle—Haskell
1921 Green Bay Packers

OAKLEY, CHARLES—Back—LSU
1954 Chicago Cardinals

**OAS, ARNOLD—Center—St. Mary's—
Minn.**
1929 Minneapolis Marines

**OBECK, VICTOR—Guard—
Springfield**
1945 Chicago Cardinals
1946 Brooklyn Dodgers

OBEE, DUNCAN—Center—Dayton
1941 Detroit Lions

OBERBRUCKINGER—Tackle
1924 Kenosha

**O'BOYLE, HARRY—Back—Notre
Dame**
1928–29, 32 Green Bay Packers
1933 Philadelphia Eagles

**O'BRIEN, FRANCIS—Tackle—
Michigan State**
1959 Cleveland Browns
1960 Washington Redskins

O'BRIEN, GAIL—Tackle—Nebraska
1935–36 Boston Redskins

O'BRIEN, JOHN—End—Florida
1954–56 Pittsburgh Steelers

**O'BRIEN, ROBERT DAVID—Back—
TCU**
1939–40 Philadelphia Eagles

O'BRIEN, WILLIAM—Back
1947 Detroit Lions

OBST, HENRY—End—Syracuse
1931 Staten Island Stapletons
1933 Philadelphia Eagles

**O'CONNELL, GRATTAN—Guard—
Boston College**
1926 Hartford Blues
1927 Providence Steamrollers

**O'CONNELL, J. F.—Center—Penn
State**
1924 Chicago Bears

**O'CONNELL, MILTON—End—
Penn State**
1924–25 Frankford Yellowjackets

**O'CONNELL, THOMAS—Back—
Illinois**
1953 Chicago Bears
1956–57 Cleveland Browns
1957 #1 Passing
1960 Buffalo Bills (AFL)

**O'CONNOR, DANIEL—Guard—
Georgetown**
1921 Cleveland Indians
1921–24 Chicago Cardinals

**O'CONNOR, FRANCIS—Tackle—
Holy Cross**

1926   Hartford Blues

**O'CONNOR, ROBERT—Guard—
Stanford**
1935   Green Bay Packers

**O'CONNOR, WILLIAM—End—Notre
Dame**
1948   Buffalo Bills (AAFC)
1949   Cleveland Browns (AAFC)
1951   New York Yanks

O'DELLI, MELVIN—Back—Duquesne
1944   Card-Pitt
1945   Pittsburgh Steelers

ODEN, OLAF—Back—Brown
1925–31   Providence Steamrollers
1932   Boston Braves

**O'DONAHUE, PATRICK—End—
Wisconsin**
1952   San Francisco 49ers
1955   Green Bay Packers

**O'DONNELL, RICHARD—End—
Minnesota**
1923   Duluth Kelleys
1924–30   Green Bay Packers
1931   Brooklyn Dodgers

**ODSON, URBAN—Tackle—
Minnesota**
1946–49   Green Bay Packers

OECH, VERNE—Tackle—Minnesota
1936   Chicago Bears

OEHLER, JOHN—Center—Purdue
1933–34   Pittsburgh Pirates
1935–36   Brooklyn Dodgers

**OEHLRICH, ARNOLD—Back—
Nebraska**
1928–29   Frankford Yellowjackets

**OELERICH, JOHN—Back—
St. Ambrose**
1938   Pittsburgh Steelers
1938   Chicago Bears

OGLESBY, PAUL—Tackle—UCLA
1960   Oakland Raiders (AFL)

**O'HANLEY, ROSS—Back—
Boston College**
1960   Boston Patriots (AFL)

O'HEARN, JOHN—Back—Cornell
1921   Buffalo All Americans

**OHLGREN, EARL—End—Texas
A & M**
1942   Green Bay Packers

**OLDERSHAW, DOUGLAS—Guard—
Santa Barbara**
1939–41   New York Giants

OLDHAM—End
1926   Racine Legion

**OLEJNICZAK, STANLEY—Tackle—
Pittsburgh**
1935   Pittsburgh Pirates

**OLENSKI, MITCHELL—Tackle—
Alabama**
1946   Miami Seahawks (AAFC)
1947   Detroit Lions
1948   Pittsburgh Steelers

**OLIKER, AARON—End—West
Virginia**
1926   Pottsville Maroons

**OLIPHANT, ELMER—Back—West
Point**
1921   Buffalo All Americans

OLIVER, VINCENT—Back—Indiana
1945   Chicago Cardinals

**OLIVER, WILLIAM—Guard—
Alabama**
1926   Pottsville Maroons
1927   New York Yankees

OLMSTEAD, LAWRENCE—Guard
1922–23   Louisville Colonels

OLSEN, RALPH—End—Utah
1949   Green Bay Packers

OLSEN,   —Tackle
1944– Cleveland Rams

OLSON, CARL—Tackle—UCLA
1942   Chicago Cardinals

OLSON, FORREST—Guard—Iowa
1927   New York Yankees

OLSON, HAROLD—Tackle—Clemson
1960   Buffalo Bills (AFL)

**OLSON, RAYMOND—Tackle—
Tulane**
1944   Cleveland Rams

**OLSONOSKI, LAWRENCE—Guard—
Minnesota**
1948–49   Green Bay Packers
1949   New York Bulldogs

OLSSON, LESTER—Guard—Mercer
1934–36   Boston Redskins
1937–38   Washington Redskins

**OLSZEWSKI, ALBERT—End—Penn
State & Pittsburgh**
1945   Pittsburgh Steelers

**OLSZEWSKI, JOHN—Back—
California**
1953–57   Chicago Cardinals
1958–60   Washington Redskins

**OLTZ, RUSSELL—Center—
Washington & Jefferson**

1922–25 Hammond Pros
1924 Kenosha

JOHN OLSZEWSKI

O'MALLEY, JOSEPH—End—Georgia
1955–56 Pittsburgh Steelers

**O'MALLEY, ROBERT—Back—
Cincinnati**
1950 Green Bay Packers

O'NEAL, JAMES—Guard—TCU
1946–47 Chicago Rockets (AAFC)

**O'NEIL, CHARLES—Center—
Connecticut State**
1926 Hartford Blues

**O'NEIL, ROBERT—Guard—Notre
Dame**
1956–57 Pittsburgh Steelers

**O'NEILL, THOMAS—End—St. Mary's
(Minn.)**
1923 Toledo Maroons
1925 Duluth Kelleys

**O'NEIL, WILLIAM—End—
Marquette**
1921 Evansville Crimson Giants

**O'NEILL, WILLIAM—Back—George
Washington**
1937 Cleveland Rams

**OPALEWSKI, EDWARD—Tackle—
Michigan Normal**
1943–44 Detroit Lions

O'QUINN, JOHN—End—Wake Forest
1950–51 Chicago Bears
1951 Philadelphia Eagles

**ORDWAY, WILLIAM—Back—
N. Dakota**
1939 Philadelphia Eagles

O'REILLY—Guard
1924 Racine Legion

ORF, ROLAND—End—Missouri
1941 Chicago Cardinals

**ORISTAGLIO, ROBERT—End—
Pennsylvania**
1949 Buffalo Bills (AAFC)
1950 Baltimore Colts
1951 Cleveland Browns
1952 Philadelphia Eagles

ORLICH, DANIEL—End—Nevada
1949–51 Green Bay Packers

**ORMSBEE, ELLIOTT—Back—
Bradley Tech.**
1946 Philadelphia Eagles

**O'ROURKE, CHARLES—Back—
Boston College**
1942 Chicago Bears
1946–47 Los Angeles Dons (AAFC)
1948–49 Baltimore Colts (AAFC)

ORR, JAMES—End—Georgia
1958–60 Pittsburgh Steelers

**ORTH, HENRY—Guard—
Miami (Ohio)**
1921 Cincinnati Celts

**ORTMAN, CHARLES—Back—
Michigan**
1951 Pittsburgh Steelers
1952 Dallas Texans

ORWELL—Back
1926 Milwaukee Badgers

**OSBORN, ROBERT—Guard—
Penn State**
1921–23 Canton Bulldogs
1924 Cleveland Bulldogs
1925–28 Pottsville Maroons

**OSBORNE, CLARENCE—Back—
Arizona State**
1959–60 San Francisco 49ers

**OSBORNE, THOMAS—Back—
Hastings**
1960 Washington Redskins
1960 San Francisco 49ers

**OSMANSKI, JOSEPH—Back—Holy
Cross**
1946–49 Chicago Bears
1949 New York Bulldogs

**OSMANSKI, WILLIAM—Back—Holy
Cross**
1939–43, 46–47 Chicago Bears
1939 #1 Ball Carrying

**OSSOWSKI, THEODORE—Tackle—
Oregon State**
1947 New York Yankees (AAFC)

**OSTENDARP, JAMES—Back—
Bucknell**

1950–51 New York Giants

**OSTROWSKI, CHESTER—End—
Notre Dame**
1954–59 Washington Redskins

**O'TOOLE, WILLIAM—Guard—St.
Mary's (Minn.)**
1924 Duluth Kelleys

OTTE, F. LOWELL—End—Iowa
1927 Buffalo Bisons

**OTTELE, RICHARD—Back—
Washington**
1948 Los Angeles Dons (AAFC)

OTTO, A.—Center
1922–23 Louisville Colonels

OTTO, JAMES—Center—Miami
1960 Oakland Raiders (AFL)

OWEN, ALTON—Back—Mercer
1939–40, 42 New York Giants

OWEN, STEPHEN—Tackle—Phillips
1924–26 Kansas City Cowboys
1926–36 New York Giants

**OWEN, VILAS—Back—Wisconsin
State Teachers**
1942 New York Giants

**OWEN, WILLIAM—Tackle—
Oklahoma A & M**
1925–26 Kansas City Cowboys
1927 Cleveland Bulldogs
1928 Detroit Lions
1929–36 New York Giants

**OWENS, DELMER—Back—North
Idaho**
1947 New York Yankees (AAFC)

**OWENS, DONALD—Tackle—
Mississippi Southern**
1957 Washington Redskins
1958–60 Philadelphia Eagles
1960 St. Louis Cardinals

**OWENS, HARRY—Guard—Lake
Forest**
1922 Green Bay Packers

OWENS, ISAIAH—End—Illinois
1948 Chicago Rockets (AAFC)

OWENS, JAMES—End—Oklahoma
1950 Baltimore Colts

OWENS, LUKE—Tackle—Kent State
1957 Baltimore Colts
1958–59 Chicago Cardinals
1960 St. Louis Cardinals

**OWENS, RALEIGH—End—Idaho
College**
1957–60 San Francisco 49ers

RALEIGH OWENS

**OWENS, TRUET—Guard—Texas
Tech.**
1943 Brooklyn Dodgers

* * *

PACE, JAMES—Back—Michigan
1958–59 San Francisco 49ers

**PACEWIC, VINCENT—Back—San
Francisco**
1947 Washington Redskins

PADAN, ROBERT—Back—Ohio State
1922 Louisville Colonels

**PADGEN, NICHOLAS—Center—
Creighton**
1940 Chicago Cardinals

PADLOW, MAX—End—Ohio State
1935 Philadelphia Eagles
1936 Cleveland Rams

**PAFFRATH, ROBERT—Back—
Minnesota**
1946 Miami Seahawks (AAFC)
1946 Brooklyn Dodgers (AAFC)

PAGE, PAUL—Back—SMU
1949 Baltimore Colts (AAFC)

PAGLIEI, JOSEPH—Back—Clemson
1959 Philadelphia Eagles
1960 New York Titans (AFL)

PAHL, LOUIS—Back—St. Thomas
1923–24 Minneapolis Marines

PAINE, HOMER—Tackle—Oklahoma
1949 Chicago Hornets (AAFC)

**PALATELLA, LOUIS—Guard—
Pittsburgh**
1955–58 San Francisco 49ers

**PALAZZI, LOUIS—Center—Penn
State**

1946–47   New York Giants

PALM, MICHAEL—Back—Penn State
1925   New York Giants
1933   Cincinnati Reds

**PALMER, CHARLES—Back—
Northwestern**
1924   Racine Legions
1926   Louisville Colonels

PALMER, DARRELL—Tackle—TCU
1946–48   New York Yankees (AAFC)
1949   Cleveland Browns (AAFC)
1950–53   Cleveland Browns

**PALMER, LESLIE—Back—North
Carolina State**
1948   Philadelphia Eagles

**PALMER, THOMAS—Tackle—Wake
Forest**
1953–54   Pittsburgh Steelers

PALUCK, JOHN—Tackle—Pittsburgh
1956, 59–60   Washington Redskins

**PALUMBO, SAMUEL—Center—Notre
Dame**
1955–56   Cleveland Browns
1957   Green Bay Packers
1960   Buffalo Bills (AFL)

**PANACCION, VICTOR—Tackle—
Penn. State**
1930   Frankford Yellowjackets

**PANCIERA, DONALD—Back—San
Francisco**
1949   New York Yankees (AAFC)
1950   Detroit Lions
1952   Chicago Cardinals

**PANELLI, JOHN—Back—Notre
Dame**
1949–50   Detroit Lions
1951–53   Chicago Cardinals

**PANFIL, KENNETH—Tackle—
Purdue**
1956–58   Los Angeles Rams
1959   Chicago Cardinals
1960   St. Louis Cardinals

**PANGLE, HAROLD—Back—Oregon
State**
1935–38   Chicago Cardinals

**PANNELL, ERNEST—Tackle—
Texas A & M**
1941–42, 45   Green Bay Packers

PAOLUCCI, BEN—Tackle—Wayne
1959   Detroit Lions

PAPACH, GEORGE—Back—Purdue
1948–49   Pittsburgh Steelers

PAPE, ORRIN—Back—Iowa
1930   Green Bay Packers
1930   Minneapolis Redjackets
1931   Providence Steamrollers
1932   Boston Braves
1932   Staten Island Stapletons
1933   Philadelphia Eagles

PAPIT, JOHN—Back—Virginia
1951–53   Washington Redskins
1953   Green Bay Packers

PAPPIO, JOSEPH—Back—Haskell
1930   Chicago Cardinaals

**PARDEE, JOHN—Center—
Texas A & M**
1957–60   Los Angeles Rams

JOHN PARDEE

PARDONEER, PAUL—Back—Purdue
1934–35   Chicago Cardinals

PARILLI, VITO—Back—Kentucky
1952–53, 57–58   Green Bay Packers
1956   Cleveland Browns
1960   Oakland Raiders (AFL)

PARKER, CLARENCE—Back—Duke
1937–41   Brooklyn Dodgers
1945   Boston Redskins
1946   New York Yankees (AAFC)

**PARKER, DAVID—End—Hardin-
Simmons**
1941   Brooklyn Dodgers

PARKER, HOWARD—Back—SMU
1948   New York Yankees (AAFC)

**PARKER, JAMES—Tackle—Ohio
State**
1957–60   Baltimore Colts

PARKER, JOSEPH—End—Texas
1946–47   Chicago Cardinals

JAMES PARKER

PARKER, RAYMOND—Back—
Centenary
1935–36 Detroit Lions
1937–43 Chicago Cardinals

PARKINSON, THOMAS—Back—
Pittsburgh
1931 Staten Island Stapletons

PARKS—Tackle—Washington & Lee
1926 Frankford Yellowjackets

PARKS, EDWARD—Center—
Oklahoma
1938–40 Washington Redskins
1946 Chicago Rockets (AAFC)

PARMER, JAMES—Back—Oklahoma
A & M
1948–56 Philadelphia Eagles

JAMES PARMER

PARNELL, FREDERICK—Tackle—
Colgate
1925–27 New York Giants

PARRIOTT, WILLIAM—End—
West Virginia
1934 Cincinnati Reds

PARRISH, BERNARD—Back—
Florida
1959–60 Cleveland Browns

PARRY, OWEN—Tackle—Baylor
1937–39 New York Giants

PARSEGHIAN, ARA—Back—Miami
(Ohio)
1948–49 Cleveland Browns (AAFC)

PARSONS, EARLE—Back—Southern
California
1946–47 San Francisco 49ers (AAFC)

PARSONS, LLOYD—Back—Gustavus-
Adolphus
1941 Detroit Lions

PARTLOW, LOUIS—Back—
Dayton
1921–29 Dayton Triangles
1923–24 Cleveland Indians

PASCHAL, WILLIAM—Back—
Georgia Tech.
1943–47 New York Giants
1947–48 Boston Yanks
1943, 44 #1 Ball Carrying

PASCHKA, GORDON—Guard—
Minnesota
1943 Phil-Pitt
1947 New York Giants

PASKVAN, GEORGE—Back—
Wisconsin
1941 Green Bay Packers

PASQUA, BERNARD—Tackle—
Southern Methodist
1941–42 Cleveland Rams
1942–43 Washington Redskins
1946 Los Angeles Rams

PASQUARIELLO, RALPH—Back—
Villanova
1950 Los Angeles Rams
1951–52 Chicago Cardinals

PASQUESI, ANTHONY—Tackle—
Notre Dame
1955–57 Chicago Cardinals

PASSUELO, WILLIAM—Guard
1923 Columbus Tigers

PASTIN, FRANK—Guard—Waynes-
burg
1942 Pittsburgh Steelers

PATANELLI, MICHAEL—End—
Ball State Teachers (Ind.)
1947 Brooklyn Dodgers (AAFC)

PATE, RUPERT—Guard—Wake Forest
1940 Chicago Cardinals
1942 Philadelphia Eagles

PATERA, JOHN—Guard—Oregon
1955–57 Baltimore Colts
1958–59 Chicago Cardinals
1960 Dallas Cowboys

PATERNOSTER, ANGELO—Guard —Georgia
1943 Washington Redskins

PATRICK, FRANK—Back—Pittsburgh
1938–39 Chicago Cardinals
1940 Pittsburgh Steelers

PATRICK, JOHN—Back—Penn State
1941, 45–46 Pittsburgh Steelers

PATT, MAURICE—End—Carnegie Tech.
1938 Detroit Lions
1939–42 Cleveland Rams

JOHN "CLIFF" PATTON

PATTERSON, PAUL—Back—Illinois
1949 Chicago Hornets (AAFC)

PATTERSON, WILLIAM—Back—Baylor
1939 Chicago Bears
1940 Pittsburgh Steelers

PATTISON—Guard—Michigan
1924 Kenosha

PATTON, JAMES—Back—Mississippi
1955–60 New York Giants
1958 #1 Interceptions

PATTON, JOHN—Guard—TCU
1946–50 Philadelphia Eagles

1951 Chicago Cardinals
1948, 49 #1 Field Goals
(1949 tied by Waterfield)

PATTON, ROBERT—Tackle—Clemson
1952 New York Giants

PAUL, DON—Center—UCLA
1948–54 Los Angeles Rams

PAUL, DON—Back—Washington State
1950–53 Chicago Cardinals
1954–58 Cleveland Browns

PAULEKAS, ANTHONY—Center—Washington & Jefferson
1936 Green Bay Packers

PAULEY, FRANK—Tackle—Washington & Jefferson
1930 Chicago Bears

PAVELEC, THEODORE—Guard—Detroit
1940–43 Detroit Lions

PAVKOV, STONKO—Guard—Idaho
1939–40 Pittsburgh Steelers

PAVLICH, CHARLES—Guard
1946 San Francisco 49ers (AAFC)

PAYNE, OTTO—Back—Texas A & M
1937 Detroit Lions

PEACE, LAWRENCE—Back—Pittsburgh
1941 Brooklyn Dodgers

PEACOCK, MERRILL—End—San Francisco
1952 Chicago Cardinals

PEAKS, CLARENCE—Back—Michigan State
1957–60 Philadelphia Eagles

CLARENCE PEAKS

PEARCE, HARLEY—End—
Ohio Wesleyan
1926 Columbus Tigers

PEARCE, WALTER—Back—Illinois
1921–22 Chicago Bears
1924 Kenosha
1925 Providence Steamrollers

PEARCY, JAMES—Guard—Marshall
1946–49 Chicago Rockets (AAFC)

PEARLMAN, I. R.—Guard—
Pittsburgh
1921 Cleveland Indians
1924 Rochester Kodaks

PEARSON, DUDLEY—Back—
Notre Dame
1922 Racine Legion

PEARSON, LINDELL—Back—
Oklahoma
1950–52 Detroit Lions
1952 Green Bay Packers

PEARSON, MADISON "BERT"—
Center—Kansas State
1929–34 Chicago Bears
1935–36 Chicago Cardinals

PEASE, GEORGE—Back—Columbia
1929 Orange

PEDERSON, JAMES—End—Augsburg
1930 Minneapolis Marines
1930–31 Frankford Yellowjackets
1932 Chicago Bears

PEDERSON, WINFIELD—Tackle—
Minnesota
1941, 45 New York Giants
1946 Boston Yanks

PEEBLES, JAMES—End—Vanderbilt
1946–51 Washington Redskins

PEERY, GORDON—Back—Oklahoma
1927 Cleveland Bulldogs

PEGG, HAROLD—Center—Bucknell
1940 Philadelphia Eagles

PELFREY, RAYMOND—Back—East
Kentucky State
1951–52 Green Bay Packers
1952 Dallas Texans
1952 Chicago Cardinals
1953 New York Giants

PELLEGRINI, ROBERT—Center—
Maryland
1956, 58–60 Philadelphia Eagles

PELLINGTON, WILLIAM—Guard—
Rutgers
1953–56, 58–60 Baltimore Colts

PENSE, LEON—Center—Arkansas

1945 Pittsburgh Steelers

PEPPER, EUGENE—Guard—Missouri
1950–53 Washington Redskins
1954 Baltimore Colts

PERANTONI, FRANCIS—Center—
Princeton
1948–49 New York Yankees (AAFC)

PERDUE, WILLARD—End—Duke
1940 Washington Redskins
1940 New York Giants
1946 Miami Seahawks (AAFC)
1946 Brooklyn Dodgers (AAFC)

PEREZ, PETER—Guard—Illinois
1945 Chicago Bears

PERINA, ROBERT—Back—Princeton
1946 New York Yankees (AAFC)
1947 Brooklyn Dodgers (AAFC)
1948 Chicago Rockets (AAFC)
1949–50 Chicago Bears
1950 Baltimore Colts

PERINI, EVO—Back—Ohio State
1954 Baltimore Colts
1954–55 Chicago Bears
1955 Cleveland Browns

PERKINS, DONALD—Back—
Plattsville Teachers
1943–45 Green Bay Packers
1945–46 Chicago Bears

PERKO, JOHN—Guard—Duquesne
1937–40, 45–47 Pittsburgh Steelers
1944 Card-Pitt

PERKO, JOHN—Guard—Minnesota
1946 Buffalo Bisons (AAFC)

PERLMAN, IRWIN—Guard—Pitts-
burgh
1921 Cleveland Indians
1924 Rochester Kodaks

PERLO, PHILIP—Back—Maryland
1960 Houston Oilers (AFL)

PERPICH, GEORGE—Tackle—
Georgetown
1946 Brooklyn Dodgers (AAFC)
1947 Baltimore Colts (AAFC)

PERRIN, JOHN—Back—Chicago
1926 Hartford Blues

PERROTTI, MICHAEL—Tackle—
Cincinnati
1948–49 Los Angeles Dons (AAFC)

PERRY, CLAUDE—Tackle—Alabama
1927–35 Green Bay Packers
1931 Brooklyn Dodgers

PERRY, FLETCHER—Back—
Compton, Jr.
1948–49 San Francisco 49ers (AAFC)

1950–60   San Francisco 49ers
1953, 54   #1 Ball Carrying

**PERRY, GERARD—Tackle—
California**
1954, 56–59   Detroit Lions
1960   St. Louis Cardinals

PERRY, LOWELL—Back—Michigan
1956   Pittsburgh Steelers

**PESHMALYAN, BARUYR—End—
West Point, Yale**
1922   Hammond Professionals
1924   Chicago Bears

**PESONEN, RICHARD—Back—
Minnesota**
1960   Green Bay Packers

**PESSALANO, LOUIS—Tackle—
Villanova**
1929   Staten Island Stapletons

PETCHEL, JOHN—Back—Duquesne
1941, 44   Cleveland Rams
1944   Card-Pitt
1945   Pittsburgh Steelers

**PETCOFF, BONI—Tackle—Ohio
State**
1924–26   Columbus Tigers

**PETERS, FLOYD—End—
San Francisco**
1959–60   Cleveland Browns

PETERS, FOREST—Back—Illinois
1930   Providence Steamrollers
1930–31   Brooklyn Dodgers
1932   Chicago Cardinals

**PETERS, VOLNEY—Tackle—
Southern California**
1952–53   Chicago Cardinals
1954–57   Washington Redskins
1958   Philadelphia Eagles
1960   Los Angeles Chargers (AFL)

**PETERSON, GERALD—Tackle—
Texas**
1956   Baltimore Colts

**PETERSON, KENNETH—Back—
Gonzaga**
1935   Chicago Cardinals
1936   Detroit Panthers

**PETERSON, LEONARD—End—
Nebraska State Teachers**
1924   Kansas City Cowboys

PETERSON, LESTER—End—Texas
1931   Portsmouth Spartans
1932   Staten Island Stapletons
1932, 34–35   Green Bay Packers
1933-34   Brooklyn Dodgers

**PETERSON, NELSON—Back—West
Virginia Wesleyan**
1937   Washington Redskins
1938   Cleveland Rams

**PETERSON, PHILIP—Back—
Wisconsin**
1932   Green Bay Packers

**PETERSON, RAYMOND—Back—
San Francisco**
1937   Green Bay Packers

**PETERSON, RUSSELL—Tackle—
Montana**
1932   Boston Redskins

**PETITBON, JOHN—Back—
Notre Dame**
1952   Dallas Texans
1955–56   Cleveland Browns
1957   Green Bay Packers

**PETITBON, RICHARD—Back—
Tulane**
1959–60   Chicago Bears

**PETRELLA, JOHN—Back—Penn
State**
1945   Pittsburgh Steelers

PETRILAS, WILLIAM—End—None
1944–45   New York Giants

**PETRO, STEPHEN—Guard—Pitts-
burgh**
1940–41   Brooklyn Dodgers

**PETROVICH, GEORGE—Tackle—
Texas**
1949–50   Chicago Cardinals

PETTY, JOHN—Back—Purdue
1942   Chicago Bears

**PEVIANI, ROBERT—Guard—
Southern California**
1953   New York Giants

PEYTON, LEO—Back
1923–24   Rochester Jeffersons
1926   Buffalo Bisons

PFOHL, ROBERT—Back—Purdue
1948–49   Baltimore Colts (AAFC)

**PFUHL, RICHARD—Back—St. Louis
Univ.**
1947   Buffalo Bills (AAFC)

**PHARMER, ARTHUR—Back—
Minnesota**
1930   Minneapolis Redjackets
1930–31   Frankford Yellowjackets

**PHELAN, ROBERT—Back—Notre
Dame**

1922   Toledo Maroons
1923-24   Rock Island Independents

PHELPS, DONALD—Back—Kentucky
1950-52   Cleveland Browns

**PHILLIPS, EWELL—Guard—
Oklahoma Baptist**
1936-37   New York Giants

PHILLIPS, GEORGE—Back—UCLA
1945   Cleveland Rams

PHILLIPS, JAMES—End—Auburn
1958-60   Los Angeles Rams

JAMES PHILLIPS

**PHILLIPS, MICHAEL—Center—
Western Maryland**
1947   Baltimore Colts (AAFC)

**PHILPOTT, DEAN—Back—
Fresno State**
1958   Chicago Cardinals

PIASECKY, ALBERT—End—Duke
1942   Philadelphia Eagles
1943-45   Washington Redskins

**PICCOLO, WILLIAM—Center—
Canisius**
1943-45   New York Giants

**PIEPUL, MILTON—Back—Notre
Dame**
1941   Detroit Lions

PIERCE, BEMUS—Back—Carlisle
1922   Oorang Indians
1926   Columbus Tigers

PIERCE, DONALD—Center—Kansas
1941   Brooklyn Dodgers
1942-43   Chicago Cardinals

**PIEROTTI, ALBERT—Center—
Washington & Lee**
1922-24   Milwaukee Badgers

1927-28   Providence Steamrollers
1929, 32   Boston Braves

PIERRE, JOHN—End—Pittsburgh
1945   Pittsburgh Steelers

**PIETROSANTE, NICHOLAS—
Back—Notre Dame**
1959-60   Detroit Lions

**PIFFERINI, ROBERT—Center—San
Jose State**
1949   Detroit Lions

PIGGOTT, BERT—Back—Illinois
1947   Los Angeles Dons (AAFC)

PIGNATELLI, CARL—Back—Iowa
1931   Cleveland Indians

PIHOS, PETER—End—Indiana
1947-55   Philadelphia Eagles
1953, 54, 55   #1 Pass Receiving
1955   (Tied by Wilson, W.)

PILCONIS, JOSEPH—End—Temple
1934, 36-37   Philadelphia Eagles

**PINCKERT, ERNEST—Back—
Southern California**
1932-36   Boston Redskins
1937-40   Washington Redskins

**PINCURA, STANLEY—Back—Ohio
State**
1937-38   Cleveland Rams

**PINGEL, JOHN—Back—Michigan
State**
1939   Detroit Lions

PIPKIN, JOYCE—End—Arkansas
1948   New York Giants
1949   Los Angeles Dons (AAFC)

PIRO, HENRY—End—Syracuse
1941   Philadelphia Eagles

**PIRRO, ROCCO—Guard—Catholic
Univ.**
1940-41, 45   Pittsburgh Steelers
1946   Buffalo Bisons (AAFC)
1947-49   Buffalo Bills (AAFC)

PISKOR, ROMAN—Tackle—Niagara
1946   New York Yankees (AAFC)
1947   Cleveland Browns (AAFC)
1948   Chicago Rockets (AAFC)

**PITTMAN, MELVIN—Center—
Hardin-Simmons**
1935   Pittsburgh Pirates

PITTS, EDWIN "ALABAMA"—Back
1935   Philadelphia Eagles

PITTS, HUGH—Center—TCU
1956   Los Angeles Rams
1960   Houston Oilers (AFL)

PIVARNICK, JOSEPH—Guard—
Notre Dame
1936 Philadelphia Eagles
1942 Brooklyn Dodgers

PLANK, EARL—End
1926 Columbus Tigers
1929 Buffalo Bisons
1930 Brooklyn Dodgers

PLANSKY, ANTHONY—Back—
Georgetown
1928–29 New York Giants
1932 Boston Braves

PLANUTIS, GERALD—Back—
Michigan State
1956 Washington Redskins

PLASMAN, RICHARD—End—
Vanderbilt
1937–41, 44 Chicago Bears
1946–47 Chicago Cardinals

PLATUKIS, GEORGE—End—
Duquesne
1938–41 Pittsburgh Steelers
1941–42 Cleveland Rams

PLUM, MILTON—Back—Penn. State
1957–60 Cleveland Browns
1960 #1 Passing

PLUMRIDGE, THEODORE—
Center—St. John's
1926 Brooklyn Dodgers

PLUNKETT, SHERMAN—Tackle—
Maryland State
1958–60 Baltimore Colts

SHERMAN PLUNKETT

PLUNKETT, WARREN—Back—
Minnesota
1941 Cleveland Rams

PODMAJERSKI, PAUL—Guard—
Illinois
1944 Chicago Bears

PODOLEY, JAMES—Back—Michigan
Central
1957–60 Washington Redskins

JAMES PODOLEY

POHLMAN, JOHN—Back—Brown
1925 Providence Steamrollers

POILLON, RICHARD—Back—
Canisius
1942, 46–49 Washington Redskins

POLANSKI, JOHN—Back—Wake
Forest
1942 Detroit Lions
1946 Los Angeles Dons (AAFC)
1947 Brooklyn Dodgers (AAFC)

POLISKI, JOHN—Tackle—Notre
Dame
1929 Chicago Bears

POLLARD, ALBERT—Back—
West Point
1951 New York Yanks
1951–53 Philadelphia Eagles

POLLARD, FRITZ—Back—Brown
1921 Akron Steels
1922 Milwaukee Badgers
1923–25 Hammond Pros
1925–26 Akron Steels
1925 Providence Steamrollers

POLLOCK, WILLIAM—Back—Penn.
Military Academy
1935–36 Chicago Bears
1937, 42–43 Philadelphia Eagles

POLOFSKY, GORDON—Guard—
Tennessee
1952–54 Chicago Cardinals

POLSFOOT, FRANCIS—End—
Washington State
1950–52   Chicago Cardinals
1953   Washington Redskins

POOL, HAMPTON—End—Stanford
1940–43   Chicago Bears
1946   Miami Seahawks (AAFC)

POOLE, G. BARNEY—End—West
Point & Mississippi
1949   New York Yankees (AAFC)
1950–51   New York Yanks
1952   Dallas Texans
1953   Baltimore Colts
1954   New York Giants

POOLE, JAMES—End—Mississippi
1937–41, 46   New York Giants
1945   Chicago Cardinals

POOLE, OLIVER—End—Mississippi
1947   New York Yankees (AAFC)
1948   Baltimore Colts (AAFC)
1949   Detroit Lions

POOLE, RAY—End—Mississippi
1947–52   New York Giants

POPA, ELI—Back—Illinois
1952   Chicago Cardinals

POPE, LESTER—Back—Connecticut
1931   Providence Steamrollers

POPE, LEWIS—Back—Purdue
1933–34   Cincinnati Reds

POPOVICH, JOHN—Back—St.
Vincent's
1944   Card-Pitt
1945   Pittsburgh Steelers

POPOVICH, MILTON—Back—
Montana
1938–42   Chicago Cardinals

POSTEL—End
1925   Chicago Cardinals

POSTUS, ALBERT—Back—Villanova
1945   Pittsburgh Steelers

POTH, PHILIP—Guard—Gonzaga
1934   Philadelphia Eagles

POTO, JOHN—Back
1947–48   Boston Yanks

POTTEIGER, EARL—Back—Ursinus
1921   Chicago Cardinals
1922   Milwaukee Badgers
1924   Kenosha
1925–28   New York Giants

POTTS, ROBERT—Tackle—Clemson
1926   Frankford Yellowjackets

POTTS, WILLIAM—Back—Villanova
1934   Pittsburgh Pirates

POWELL, ARTHUR—Back—
San Jose State
1959   Philadelphia Eagles
1960   New York Titans (AFL)

POWELL, CHARLES—End
1952–53, 55–57   San Francisco 49ers
1960   Oakland Raiders

POWELL, RICHARD—End—
Davis-Elkins
1931   New York Giants
1933–34   Cincinnati Reds

POWELL, STANCIL—Guard—
Carlisle
1922   Oorang Indians
1926   Buffalo Bisons

POWERS, JAMES—Back—Southern
California
1950–53   San Francisco 49ers

POWERS, SAMUEL—Guard—
Northern Michigan
1921   Green Bay Packers

PRATHER, DALE—End—George
Washington
1937–38   Cleveland Rams

PRCHLIK, JOHN—Tackle—Yale
1949–53   Detroit Lions

JOHN PRCHLIK

PREAS, GEORGE—Guard—
Virginia Polytech.
1955–60   Baltimore Colts

PREBOLA, EUGENE—End—
Boston Univ.
1960   Oakland Raiders (AFL)

PREGULMAN, MERVIN—Guard—
Michigan
1946   Green Bay Packers
1947–48   Detroit Lions
1949   New York Bulldogs

PRESCOTT, HAROLD—End—
Hardin-Simmons
1946 Green Bay Packers
1947–49 Philadelphia Eagles
1949 New York Bulldogs
1949 Detroit Lions

GEORGE PREAS

PRESNELL, GLENN—Back—
Nebraska
1931–33 Portsmouth Spartans
1934–36 Detroit Lions
1933 # 1 Field Goals
(Tied by Manders)

PRESSLEY, LEE—Center—Oklahoma
1945 Washington Redskins

PRESTEL, JAMES—Tackle—Idaho
1960 Cleveland Browns

PRESTON, PATTISON—Guard—
Wake Forest
1946–49 Chicago Bears

PREWITT, FELTON—Center—
Tulsa
1946–48 Buffalo Bills (AAFC)
1949 Baltimore Colts (AAFC)

PRIATKO, WILLIAM—Guard—
Pittsburgh
1957 Pittsburgh Steelers
1957 Green Bay Packers

PRICE, CHARLES—Back—Texas
A & M
1940–41, 45 Detroit Lions
1946 Miami Seahawks (AAFC)

PRICE, EDWARD—Back—Tulane
1950–55 New York Giants
1951 # 1 Ball Carrying

PRICER, WILLIAM—Back—
Oklahoma
1957–60 Baltimore Colts

WILLIAM PRICER

PRIEST, JAMES—Back—Centre
1923 Louisville Colonels

PRIESTLEY, ROBERT—End—Brown
1941–42 Philadelphia Eagles

PRINCIPE, DOMINIC—Back—
Fordham
1940–41 New York Giants
1946 Brooklyn Dodgers

PRISCO, NICHOLAS—Back—Rutgers
1933 Philadelphia Eagles

PRITCHARD, ABISHA—Back—
Virginia Military Inst.
1942 Cleveland Rams
1946–51 Philadelphia Eagles
1951 New York Giants

ABISHA PRITCHARD

PRITCHARD, WILLIAM—Back—
Pennsylvania
1927–28 Providence Streamrollers
1928 New York Yankees

PRITKO, STEPHEN—End—Villanova
1943   New York Giants
1944-45   Cleveland Rams
1946-47   Los Angeles Rams
1948   Boston Yanks
1949   New York Bulldogs
1949-50   Green Bay Packers

**PROCHASKA, RAYMOND—End—
Nebraska**
1941   Cleveland Rams

PROCTOR, DEWEY—Back—Furman
1946-47, 49   New York Yankees (AAFC)
1948   Chicago Rockets (AAFC)

PROCTOR, REX—Back—Rice
1953   Chicago Bears

**PROKOP, EDWARD—Back—
Georgia Tech.**
1946-47, 49   New York Yankees (AAFC)
1948   Chicago Rockets (AAFC)

PROKOP, JOSEPH—Back—Bradley
1948   Chicago Rockets (AAFC)

**PROMUTO, VINCENT—Guard—
Holy Cross**
1960   Washington Redskins

VINCENT PROMUTO

**PROVENCIAL, KENNETH—Back—
Georgetown**
1930   Frankford Yellowjackets

**PROVO, FREDERICK—Back—
Washington**
1948   Green Bay Packers

**PSALTIS, JAMES—Back—Southern
California**
1953, 55   Chicago Cardinals
1954   Green Bay Packers

**PTACEK, Robert—Back—
Michigan State**

1959   Cleveland Browns

PUCCI, BENITO—Tackle
1946-47   Buffalo Bills (AAFC)
1947   Chicago Rockets (AAFC)
1948   Cleveland Browns (AAFC)

**PUDDY, HAROLD—Tackle—Oregon
State**
1948   San Francisco 49ers (AAFC)

**PUDLOSKI, CHESTER—Tackle—
Villanova**
1944   Cleveland Rams

PUGH—Tackle
1922   Milwaukee Badgers

**PUGH, MARION—Back—Texas
A & M**
1940-41, 45   New York Giants
1946   Miami Seahawks (AAFC)

**PUPLIS, ANDREW—Back—Notre
Dame**
1943   Chicago Cardinals

PURDIN, CALVIN—Back—Tulsa
1943   Chicago Cardinals
1946   Miami Seahawks (AAFC)
1946   Brooklyn Dodgers (AAFC)

PURDY, CLAIR—Q—Brown
1922   Milwaukee Badgers

PURDY, EVERETT—Back—Beloit
1922   Milwaukee Badgers
1926-27   Green Bay Packers

**PURNELL, FRANK—Back—Alcorn
A & M**
1957   Green Bay Packers

**PUTMAN, EARL—Center—Arizona
State**
1957   Chicago Cardinals

**PUTNAM, DUANE—Guard—College
of Pacific**
1952-59   Los Angeles Rams
1960   Dallas Cowboys

**PUTZIER, FREDERICK—Back—
St. Olaf**
1924   Minneapolis Marines

PYEATT, JOHN—Back
1960   Denver Broncos (AFL)

**PYLE, PALMER—Tackle—
Michigan State**
1960   Baltimore Colts

**PYLMAN, ROBERT—Tackle—
South Dakota State**
1938-39   Philadelphia Eagles

**PYNE, JOHN—Tackle—Boston
College**

1931   Providence Steamrollers
* * *

DUANE PUTNAM

VOLNEY QUINLAN

QUAM, CHARLES—Back
1926   Duluth Eskimos

QUAST, JOHN HENRY—End—
Purdue
1923   Louisville Colonels

QUATSE, JESS—Tackle—Pittsburgh
1933   Green Bay Packers
1933–34   Pittsburgh Pirates
1935   New York Giants

QUILLEN, FRANK—End—
Pennsylvania
1946–47   Chicago Rockets (AAFC)

QUILTER, CHARLES—Tackle
1949   San Francisco 49ers (AAFC)
1950   San Francisco 49ers

QUINLAN, VOLNEY—Back—
San Diego
1952–56   Los Angeles Rams
1956   Cleveland Browns

QUINLAN, WILLIAM—End—
Michigan
1957–58   Cleveland Browns
1959–60   Green Bay Packers

QUINN, GEORGE—Back
1921   Rock Island Independents

QUINN, IVAN—Guard—Carroll
1924   Kansas City Cowboys

QUIRK, EDWARD—Back—Missouri
1948–51   Washington Redskins

* * *

RABB, WARREN—Back—LSU
1960   Detroit Lions

RABOLD, MICHAEL—Guard—
Indiana
1959   Detroit Lions
1960   St. Louis Cardinals

RABORN, CARROLL—Center—SMU
1936–37   Pittsburgh Pirates

RACIS, FRANK—Guard
1925–28   Pottsville Maroons
1928   New York Yankees
1929   Boston Braves
1930   Providence Steamrollers
1931   Frankford Yellowjackets

RADICK, KENNETH—End—
Marquette
1930–31   Green Bay Packers
1931   Brooklyn Dodgers

RADO, ALEX—Back—
West Virginia Tech
1934   Pittsburgh Pirates

RADO, GEORGE—Guard—Duquesne
1935–37   Pittsburgh Pirates

RADOSEVICH, GEORGE—Center—
Pittsburgh
1954–56   Baltimore Colts

RADOVICH, WILLIAM—Guard—
Southern California
1938–41, 45   Detroit Lions
1946–47   Los Angeles Dons (AAFC)

RADZIEVITCH, VICTOR—Back—
Connecticut
1926   Hartford Blues

RAEMER, NORBERT—Guard—
Kansas State
1941   Brooklyn Dodgers

RAFFEL, WILLIAM—End—
Pennsylvania
1932 Brooklyn Dodgers

RAGAZZO, PHILIP—Tackle—
Western Reserve
1938–39 Cleveland Rams
1940–41 Philadelphia Eagles
1945–47 New York Giants

RAGUNAS, VINCENT—Back—
Virginia Military Inst.
1949 Pittsburgh Steelers

RAIMONDI, BENJAMIN—Back—
Indiana
1947 New York Yankees (AAFC)

RAJKOVICH, PETER—Back—
Detroit
1934 Pittsburgh Pirates

RAMONA, JOSEPH—Guard—Santa
Clara
1953 New York Giants

RAMSEY, FRANK—Tackle—Oregon
State
1945 Chicago Bears

RAMSEY, GARRARD—Guard—
William & Mary
1946–51 Chicago Cardinals

RAMSEY, HERSCHEL—End—Texas
Tech.
1938–40, 45 Philadelphia Eagles

RAMSEY, KNOX—Guard— William &
Mary
1948–49 Los Angeles Dons (AAFC)
1950–51 Chicago Cardinals
1952 Philadelphia Eagles
1952–53 Washington Redskins

RAMSEY, RAY—Back—Bradley
1948–49 Chicago Rockets (AAFC)
1948 Brooklyn Dodgers (AAFC)
1950–51 Chicago Cardinals

RANDALL, PROCTOR—End—
Kansas State
1925 Kansas City Cowboys

RANDELS, HORACE—End—Kansas
State
1926 Kansas City Cowboys
1927 Cleveland Bulldogs
1928 Detroit Lions

RANDLE, ULMO—End—Virginia
1959 Chicago Cardinals
1960 St. Louis Cardinals

RANDOLPH, CLARE—Center—
Indiana
1930 Chicago Cardinals
1931–33 Portsmouth Spartans
1934–36 Detroit Lions

RANDOLPH—Back
1923 Columbus Tigers

RANKIN, WALTER—Back—Texas
Tech.
1941–43, 45–47 Chicago Cardinals
1944 Card-Pitt

RANSPOT, KEITH—End—SMU
1940 Chicago Cardinals
1941 Detroit Lions
1942 Green Bay Packers
1942–43 Brooklyn Dodgers
1944–45 Boston Yanks

RAPACZ, JOHN—Center—Oklahoma
1948–49 Chicago Hornets (AAFC)
1950–54 New York Giants

RAPP, HERBERT—Center—Xavier
1929 Buffalo Bisons
1930–31 Staten Island Stapletons

RAPP, MANUEL—Back—St. Louis
Univ.
1934 St. Louis Gunners
1941–42 Cleveland Rams

RAPP, ROBERT—Back
1922–26 Columbus Tigers

RASCHER, AMBROSE—Back—
Indiana
1932 Portsmouth Spartans

RASKOWSKI, LEO—Tackle—Ohio
State
1932 Staten Island Stapletons
1933 Brooklyn Dodgers
1933 Pittsburgh Pirates
1935 Philadelphia Eagles

RATE, EDWIN—Back—Purdue
1923 Milwaukee Badgers

RATICA, JOSEPH—Center—St.
Vincent's
1939 Brooklyn Dodgers

RATTERMAN, GEORGE—Back—
Notre Dame
1947–49 Buffalo Bills (AAFC)
1950–51 New York Yanks
1952–56 Cleveland Browns

RAUCH—Guard
1921 Columbus Tigers

RAUSCH, JOHN—Back—Georgia
1949 New York Bulldogs
1950–51 New York Yanks
1951 Philadelphia Eagles

RAUSCH, RICHARD—Guard—
Penn State

1925 Pottsville Maroons
1928 New York Yankees
1929 Boston Braves

1960 Pittsburgh Steelers

GEORGE RATTERMAN

FRANK REAGAN

**RAVENSBURG, ROBERT—End—
  Indiana**
1948–49 Chicago Cardinals

**RAWLINGS, ROBERT—Back—
  Georgetown**
1922 Buffalo All Americans

RAY, BUFORD—Tackle—Vanderbilt
1938–48 Green Bay Packers

RAYBURN, VAN—End—Tennessee
1933 Brooklyn Dodgers

**READER, RUSSELL—Back—
  Michigan State**
1947 Chicago Bears

**REAGAN, FRANK—Back—
  Pennsylvania**
1941, 46–48 New York Giants
1949–51 Philadelphia Eagles
1947 #1 Interceptions
      (Tied by Seno)
1947 #1 Punting

REAGEN—Tackle
1926 Brooklyn Dodgers

**REAM, CHARLES—Tackle—Ohio
  State**
1938 Cleveland Rams

**REBSEAMAN, PAUL—Center—
  Centenary**
1927 Pottsville Maroons

**RECHICHAR, ALBERT—Back—
  Tennessee**
1952 Cleveland Browns
1953–59 Baltimore Colts

**RECKMARCK, RAYMOND—Back—
  Syracuse**
1937 Detroit Lions
1937 Brooklyn Dodgers

ALBERT RECHICHAR

RED FANG—Tackle
1922–23 Oorang Indians

RED FOOT—End
1923 Oorang Indians

RED FOX—Back
1922–23 Oorang Indians

REDINGER, OTIS—Back—Colgate
1925 Canton Bulldogs

REDMOND, GUS—Guard
1921, 24 Dayton Triangles

**REDMOND, THOMAS—End—
  Vanderbilt**

1960   St. Louis Cardinals

REECE, DONALD—Tackle—Missouri
1946   Miami Seahawks (AAFC)

REED, JOSEPH—Back—LSU
1937–39   Chicago Cardinals

REED, LEROY—End—Mississippi
1958   Pittsburgh Steelers

REED, MAX—Center—Bucknell
1925   Buffalo Bisons
1926–27   Frankford Yellowjackets
1928   New York Giants

REEDINGER, OTIS—Back—Penn. State
1925   Canton Bulldogs

REESE, DAVID—End—Denison
1921–23   Dayton Triangles

REESE, HENRY—Center—Temple
1933–34   New York Giants
1935–39   Philadelphia Eagles

REESE, KENNETH—Back—Alabama
1947   Detroit Lions

REESE, LLOYD—Back—Tennessee
1946   Chicago Bears

REGAN, JAMES—Back—Still
1925   Columbus Tigers

REGER, JOHN—Back—Pittsburgh
1955–60   Pittsburgh Steelers

REGNIER, PETER—Back—Minnesota
1922   Green Bay Packers
1922   Minneapolis Marines

REICHARDT, WILLIAM—Back—Iowa
1952   Green Bay Packers

REICHLE, LOUIS—End—Butler
1926   Columbus Tigers

REICHLE, RICHARD—End—Illinois
1923   Milwaukee Badgers

REICHOW, GERALD—End—Iowa
1956–59   Detroit Lions
1960   Philadelphia Eagles

REICHOW, CHARLES—Back—St. Thomas
1926   Racine Legion

REID, FLOYD—Back—Georgia
1950–56   Green Bay Packers

REID, Joseph—Center—LSU
1951   Los Angeles Rams
1952   Dallas Texans

REIFSNYDER, ROBERT—End—Annapolis
1960   New York Titans (AFL)

REINHARD, ROBERT—Tackle—California
1946–49   Los Angeles Dons (AAFC)
1950   Los Angeles Rams

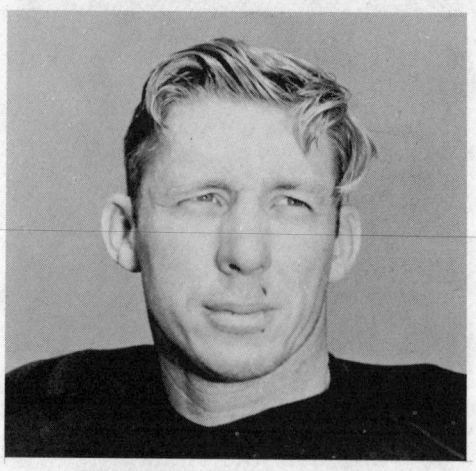

ROBERT REINHARD

REINHARD, WILLIAM—Back—California
1947–48   Los Angeles Dons (AAFC)

REISER, EARL—End
1923   Louisville Colonels

REISSIG, WILLIAM—Back
1938–39   Brooklyn Dodgers

REISZ, ALBERT—Back—Southeastern Louisiana
1944–45   Cleveland Rams
1946   Los Angeles Rams
1947   Buffalo Bills (AAFC)

REITER, WILBUR—Guard—West Virginia Wesleyan
1926–27   Dayton Triangles

REMINGTON, WILLIAM—Center—Washington State
1946   San Francisco 49ers

REMMERT, DENNIS—Tackle—Iowa State
1960   Buffalo Bills (AFL)

RENFRO, DEAN—Back—Texas State North
1955   Baltimore Colts
1960   Dallas Texans (AFL)

RENFRO, RAYMOND—Back—Texas State North
1952–60   Cleveland Browns

RENFRO, RICHARD—Back—Washington State
1946   San Francisco 49ers (AAFC)

RAYMOND RENFRO

**RENFRO, WILLIAM—Guard—
Memphis State**
1957–59 Washington Redskins
1960 Pittsburgh Steelers

**RENGEL, NEIL—Back—Davis &
Elkins**
1930 Frankford Yellowjackets

**RENTNER, ERNEST—Back—
Northwestern**
1934–36 Boston Redskins
1936–37 Chicago Bears

**REPKO, JOSEPH—Tackle—Boston
College**
1946–47 Pittsburgh Steelers
1948–49 Los Angeles Rams

RESTIC, JOSEPH—End—Villanova
1952 Philadelphia Eagles

**RETZLAFF, PALMER—End—South
Dakota State**
1956–60 Philadelphia Eagles
1956–58 Philadelphia Eagles
1958 #1 Pass Receiving
      (Tied by Berry, R.)

**REUTER, VICTOR—Center—
Lafayette**
1932 Staten Island Stapletons

**REUTT, RAYMOND—End—Virginia
Military Inst.**
1943 Philadelphia Eagles

**REX, RAYMOND—Back—North
Carolina State**
1935 Boston Redskins

REXER, FREEMAN—End—Tulane
1943, 45 Chicago Cardinals
1944 Detroit Lions

REYNOLDS, ALLAN—Guard—Tarkio
1960 Dallas Texans (AFL)

**REYNOLDS, HOMER—Guard—
Tulsa**
1934 St. Louis Gunners

**REYNOLDS, JAMES—Back—
Oklahoma A & M**
1946 Pittsburgh Steelers

**REYNOLDS, JAMES—Back—
Alabama Polytech.**
1946 Miami Seahawks (AAFC)

REYNOLDS, JOHN—Center—Baylor
1937 Chicago Cardinals

**REYNOLDS, MACK CHARLES—
Back—SMU**
1958–59 Chicago Cardinals
1960 Washington Redskins

REYNOLDS, OWEN—End—Georgia
1925 New York Giants
1926 Brooklyn Dodgers

**REYNOLDS, QUENTIN—Tackle—
Brown**
1926 Brooklyn Dodgers

**REYNOLDS, ROBERT—Center—
Stanford**
1937–38 Detroit Lions

**REYNOLDS, ROBERT—Back—
Mississippi**
1944 Brooklyn Dodgers
1945 Chicago Cardinals

**REYNOLDS, WILLIAM—Back—
Pittsburgh**
1953–54, 56–57 Cleveland Browns
1958 Pittsburgh Steelers
1960 Oakland Raiders (AFL)

RHEA, FLOYD—Guard—Oregon
1943 Chicago Cardinals
1944 Brooklyn Dodgers
1945 Boston Yanks
1947 Detroit Lions

RHEA, HUGH—Guard—Nebraska
1932 Boston Redskins
1933 Brooklyn Dodgers

**RHENQUIST, MILTON—Center—
Bethany**
1924–26 Kansas City Cowboys
1927 Cleveland Indians
1928–31 Providence Steamrollers
1931 New York Giants
1932 Boston Braves

RHENSTROM—End
1922 Racine Legion

RHOADS, DONALD—Tackle—
Washington & Jefferson
1933 Pittsburgh Pirates
1937 Cleveland Rams

RHODEMYRE, JAY—Center—
Kentucky
1948–49, 51–52 Green Bay Packers

RIBAR, FRANK—Guard—Duke
1943 Washington Redskins

RIBBLE, LORAN—Guard—
Hardin-Simmons
1932 Portsmouth Spartans
1933 Chicago Cardinals
1934–35 Pittsburgh Pirates

RIBLETT, PAUL—End—
Pennsylvania
1932–36 Brooklyn Dodgers

RICCA, JAMES—Tackle—Georgetown
1951–54 Washington Redskins
1955 Detroit Lions
1955–56 Philadelphia Eagles

RICE, WILLIAM—Back—Norwich
1929 New York Giants

RICH, HERBERT—Back—Vanderbilt
1950 Baltimore Colts
1951–53 Los Angeles Rams
1954–56 New York Giants

RICHARDS, ELVIN—Back—Simpson
1933–39 New York Giants

RICHARDS, PERRY—End—Detroit
1957 Pittsburgh Steelers
1958 Detroit Lions
1959 Chicago Cardinals
1960 St. Louis Cardinals

RICHARDS, PETER—Center—
Swarthmore
1927 Frankford Yellowjackets

RICHARDS, RAY—Guard—Nebraska
1930 Frankford Yellowjackets
1932–33, 35–36 Chicago Bears
1934 Detroit Lions

RICHARDS, RICHARD—Back—
Kentucky
1933 Brooklyn Dodgers

RICHARDSON, ALVIN—End—
Grambling
1960 Boston Patriots (AFL)

RICHARDSON, GERALD—End—
Wofford
1959–60 Baltimore Colts

RICHARDSON, JESS—Tackle—
Alabama
1953–60 Philadelphia Eagles

JESS RICHARDSON

RICHESON, RAYMOND—Guard—
Alabama
1949 Chicago Hornets (AAFC)
1950 Pittsburgh Steelers

RICHINS, ALDO—Back—Utah
1935 Detroit Lions

RICHMAN, HARRY—Guard—Illinois
1929 Chicago Bears

LESTER RICHTER

RICHTER, LESTER—Guard—
California
1954–60 Los Angeles Rams

RICKARD, PAUL—Back—
Pittsburgh
1948 Los Angeles Rams

RIDDICK, RAYMOND—End—
Fordham
1940–42, 46 Green Bay Packers

**RIDLER, DONALD—Tackle—
Michigan State**
1931   Cleveland Indians

RIDLON, JAMES—Back—Syracuse
1957–60   San Francisco 49ers

**RIETH, WILLIAM—Center—
Carnegie Tech.**
1941–42, 44–45   Cleveland Rams

**RIFENBURG, RICHARD—End—
Michigan**
1950   Detroit Lions

**RIFFLE, CHARLES—Guard—Notre
Dame**
1944   Cleveland Rams
1946–48   New York Yankees (AAFL)

**RIFFLE, RICHARD—Back—
Albright**
1938–40   Philadelphia Eagles
1941–42   Pittsburgh Steelers

**RIGGS, THRON—Tackle—
Washington Univ.**
1944   Boston Yanks

**RILEY, JOHN—Tackle—
Northwestern**
1933   Boston Redskins

RILEY, LEON—Back—Detroit
1955   Detroit Lions
1956–59   Philadelphia Eagles
1960   New York Giants

RINGO, JAMES—Center—Syracuse
1953–60   Green Bay Packers

JAMES RINGO

**RINGWALT, CARROLL—Center—
Indiana**
1930   Portsmouth Spartans
1931   Frankford Yellowjackets

**RIOPEL, ALBERT—Back—Holy
Cross**
1925   Providence Steamrollers

**RIORDAN, CHARLES—Back—New
York Univ.**
1929   Staten Island Stapletons

RISK, EDWARD—Back—Purdue
1932   Chicago Cardinals

RISLEY, ELLIOTT—Tackle—Indiana
1922–23   Hammond Pros

RISVOLD—Back
1927–28   Chicago Cardinals

**RITCHHART, DELBERT—Center—
Colorado**
1936–37   Detroit Lions

ROACH, JOHN—Back—Notre Dame
1927   Chicago Cardinals

ROACH, JOHN—Back—SMU
1956, 59   Chicago Cardinals
1960   St. Louis Cardinals

ROBB, HARRY—Back—Penn State
1921–23, 25–26   Canton Bulldogs

ROBB, JOSEPH—End—TCU
1959–60   Philadelphia Eagles

ROBB, STANLEY—End—Center
1925–26   Canton Bulldogs

ROBBINS, JOHN—Back—Arkansas
1938–39   Chicago Cardinals

**ROBERTS, CHARLES—Back—Iowa
State**
1927   Pottsville Maroons

**ROBERTS, CORNELIUS—Back—
Southern California**
1959–60   San Francisco 49ers

**ROBERTS, EUGENE—Back—
Chattanooga**
1947–50   New York Giants
1949   #1 Scoring
       (Tied by Harder)

ROBERTS, FRED—Tackle—Iowa
1930–32   Portsmouth Spartans

ROBERTS, JAMES—End—Centre
1922   Toledo Maroons
1923   Akron Steels
1925–26   Canton Bulldogs

ROBERTS, JOHN—Back—Georgia
1932   Boston Braves
1932   Staten Island Stapletons
1933–34   Philadelphia Eagles
1934   Pittsburgh Pirates

**ROBERTS, THOMAS—Tackle—
DePaul**

1943 New York Giants
1944–45 Chicago Bears

ROBERTS, WALCOTT—Back—Annapolis
1922–23 Canton Bulldogs
1922–24 Hammond Pros
1924–25 Cleveland Bulldogs
1924 Rock Island Independents
1926 Frankford Yellowjackets

ROBERTS, WILLIAM—Back—Dartmouth
1956 Green Bay Packers
1956 Los Angeles Rams

ROBERTSON, HARRY—Tackle—Syracuse
1922 Rochester Kodaks

ROBERTSON, JAMES—Back—Carnegie Tech.
1924–25 Akron Steels

ROBERTSON, LAKE—End—Mississippi
1945 Detroit Lions

ROBERTSON, ROBERT—Back—Southern California
1942 Brooklyn Dodgers

ROBERTSON, THOMAS—Center—Tulsa
1940–42 Brooklyn Dodgers
1946 New York Yankees (AAFC)

ROBESON, PAUL—End—Rutgers
1921 Akron Steels
1922 Milwaukee Badgers

ROBINSON, EDWARD—Back—North Carolina
1923–25 Hammond Pros
1926 Louisville Colonels

ROBINSON, FREDERICK—Guard—Washington
1957 Cleveland Browns

ROBINSON, GILBERT—End—Catawba
1933 Pittsburgh Pirates

ROBINSON, JOHN—Tackle—Missouri State Northeast
1935–36 Brooklyn Dodgers
1936–38 Chicago Cardinals
1938 Cleveland Rams
1938 Pittsburgh Pirates

ROBINSON, JOHN—Back—LSU
1960 Dallas Texans (AFL)

ROBINSON, WAYNE—Center—Minnesota
1952–56 Philadelphia Eagles

ROBINSON, WILLIAM—Back—Lincoln

1952 Green Bay Packers
1960 New York Titans (AFL)

JOHN ROBINSON

ROBISON, BURLE—End—Brigham Young
1935 Philadelphia Eagles

WAYNE ROBINSON

ROBISON, GEORGE—Guard—Virginia Military Inst.
1952 Dallas Texans

ROBL, HAROLD—Back—Wisconsin State Teachers
1945 Chicago Cardinals

ROBNETT, EDWARD—Back—Texas Tech.
1947 San Francisco 49ers (AAFC)

ROBNETT, MARSHALL—Center—Texas A & M
1943, 45 Chicago Cardinals
1944 Card-Pitt

**ROBUSTELLI, ANDREW—End—
Arnold**
1951–55   Los Angeles Rams
1956–60   New York Giants

ROBY, DOUGLAS—Back—Michigan
1923   Cleveland Indians

**ROCHESTER, PAUL—End—
Michigan State**
1960   Dallas Texans (AFL)

**ROCKONBACH, LYLE—Guard—
Michigan State**
1943   Detroit Lions

**ROCKWELL, HENRY—Center—
Arizona State**
1940–42   Cleveland Rams
1946–48   Los Angeles Dons (AAFC)

**RODAK, MICHAEL—Guard—
Western Reserve**
1939–40   Cleveland Rams
1942   Pittsburgh Steelers

**RODERICK, BENJAMIN—Back—
Columbia**
1923   Buffalo All Americans
1923, 25–26   Canton Bulldogs
1927   Buffalo Bisons

**RODGERS, HOSEA—Back—North
Carolina**
1949   Los Angeles Dons (AAFC)

**RODGERS, THOMAS—Tackle—
Bucknell**
1947   Boston Yanks

**RODGERS, WALTER—Back—
Washington of Mo.**
1922   Columbus Tigers

RODRIGUEZ, JESS—Back—Salem
1929   Buffalo Bisons
1930   Frankford Yellowjackets
1930   Minneapolis Redjackets

**RODRIGUEZ, KELLY—Back—West
Virginia Wesleyan**
1935   Boston Redskins

**ROEHNELT, WILLIAM—Guard—
Bradley**
1958–59   Chicago Bears
1960   Washington Redskins

ROEPKE, JOHN—Back—Penn State
1928   Frankford Yellowjackets

ROESSLER, FRITZ—End—Marquette
1922–24   Racine Legion
1923   Toledo Maroons
1925   Milwaukee Badgers

**ROFFLER, WILLIAM—Back—
Washington State**
1954   Philadelphia Eagles

ROGALLA, JOHN—Back—Scranton
1945   Philadelphia Eagles

ROGAS, DANIEL—Guard—Tulane
1951   Detroit Lions
1952   Philadelphia Eagles

ROGEL, FRANK—Back—Penn State
1950–57   Pittsburgh Steelers

**ROGERS, CHARLES—Back—
Pennsylvania**
1927–29   Frankford Yellowjackets

**ROGERS, CULLEN—Back—Texas
A & M**
1946   Pittsburgh Steelers

**ROGERS, DONALD—Center—
Southern California**
1960   Los Angeles Chargers (AFL)

**ROGERS, GLYNN—Guard—
Texas Christian Univ.**
1938–39   Chicago Cardinals

**ROGERS, JOHN—Center—Notre
Dame**
1933–34   Cincinnati Reds

**ROGERS, WILLIAM—Tackle—
Villanova**
1938   Chicago Cardinals
1938–40, 44   Detroit Lions

ROGGE, GEORGE—End—Iowa
1931–33   Chicago Cardinals
1934   St. Louis Gunners

**ROGGEMAN, THOMAS—Tackle—
Purdue**
1956   Chicago Bears

**RHODE, LEONARD—End—
Utah State**
1960   San Francisco 49ers

**ROHLEDER, GEORGE—End—
Wittenberg**
1925   Columbus Tigers
1926   Akron Steels

**ROHRIG, HERMAN—Back—
Nebraska**
1941, 46–47   Green Bay Packers

ROKISKY, JOHN—End—Duquesne
1946   Cleveland Browns (AAFC)
1947   Chicago Rockets (AAFC)
1948   New York Yankees (AAFC)

ROLLE, DAVID—Back—Oklahoma
1960   Denver Broncos (AFL)

ROMAN, GEORGE—Tackle—Western Reserve
1948   Boston Yanks
1949   New York Bulldogs
1950   New York Giants

ROMANIK, STEPHEN—Back—Villanova
1950–53   Chicago Bears
1953–54   Chicago Cardinals

ROMBOLI, RUDOLPH—Back
1946–48   Boston Yanks

ROMERO, RAYMOND—Guard—Kansas
1951   Philadelphia Eagles

ROMINE, ALTON—End—Alabama State Teachers
1955, 58   Green Bay Packers
1960   Denver Broncos (AFL)

ROMNEY, MILTON—Back—Chicago
1923–24   Racine Legion
1925–28   Chicago Bears

RONZANI, GENE—Back—Marquette
1933–38, 44–45   Chicago Bears

ROONEY, COBB—Back—Colorado Mines
1923–27   Duluth Kelleys
1925   New York Giants
1928   New York Yankees
1929–30   Chicago Cardinals

ROONEY, JOSEPH—End
1924–25   Rock Island Independents
1923–24, 26–27   Duluth Eskimos
1928   Pottsville Maroons

ROONEY, WILLIAM—Back
1923–27   Duluth Eskimos
1929   Chicago Cardinals

ROOT, JAMES—Back—Miami (Ohio)
1953, 56   Chicago Cardinals

RORISON, JAMES—Tackle—Southern California
1938   Pittsburgh Steelers

ROSATO, SALVATORE—Back—Villanova
1945–47   Washington Redskins

ROSATTI, ROMAN—Tackle—Michigan
1923   Cleveland Indians
1924, 26–27   Green Bay Packers
1928   New York Giants

ROSE, ALFRED—End—Texas
1930–31   Providence Steamrollers
1930   Staten Island Stapletons
1932–36   Green Bay Packers

ROSE, EUGENE—Back—Wisconsin
1929–31   Chicago Cardinals

ROSE, ROY—End—Tennessee
1936   New York Giants

ROSEN, STANLEY—Back—Rutgers
1929   Buffalo Bisons

ROSENBERGER—Tackle
1921   Evansville Crimson Giants

ROSENOW, AUGUST—Back—Ripon
1921   Green Bay Packers

ROSEQUIST, THEODORE—Tackle—Ohio State
1934–36   Chicago Bears
1937   Cleveland Rams

ROSKIE, KENNETH—Back—South Carolina
1946   San Francisco 49ers (AAFC)
1948   Detroit Lions
1948   Green Bay Packers

ROSS, DAVID—End—Los Angeles State
1960   New York Titans (AFL)

ROSSO, GEORGE—Back—Ohio State
1954   Washington Redskins

ROSTECK, ERNEST—Center
1944   Detroit Lions

ROTE, KYLE—Back—SMU
1951–60   New York Giants

ROTE, TOBIN—Back—Rice
1950–56   Green Bay Packers
1957–59   Detroit Lions

TOBIN ROTE

ROTHROCK, CLIFFORD—Center—North Dakota State
1947   Chicago Rockets (AAFC)

ROTON, HERBERT—End—Auburn
1937   Philadelphia Eagles

**ROUDEBUSH, GEORGE—Back—
Denison**
1921   Dayton Triangles

ROUSE, STILLMAN—End—Missouri
1940   Detroit Lions

**ROUSSOS, MICHAEL—Tackle—
Pittsburgh**
1948–49   Washington Redskins
1949   Detroit Lions

**ROVINSKI, ANTHONY—Back—Holy
Cross**
1933   New York Giants
1934   Brooklyn Dodgers

ROWAN, JAMES—Back—Tennessee
1923   Louisville Colonels

**ROWAN, EVERETT—End—Ohio
State**
1930, 32–33   Brooklyn Dodgers
1933   Philadelphia Eagles

**ROWE, HARMON—Back—San
Francisco**
1947–49   New York Yankees (AAFC)
1950–52   New York Giants

ROWE, ROBERT—Back—Colgate
1934   Detroit Lions
1935   Philadelphia Eagles

**ROWLAND, BRADLEY—Back—
McMurry**
1951   Chicago Bears

ROWLAND, JUSTIN—End—TCU
1960   Chicago Bears

ROY, ELMER—End
1921–25   Rochester Jeffersons
1927   Buffalo Bisons

**ROYSTON, EDWARD—Guard—
Wake Forest**
1948–49   New York Giants

**ROZELLE, AUBREY—Guard—
Delta State**
1957   Pittsburgh Steelers

**RUBINO, ANTHONY—Guard—
Wake Forest**
1943–46   Detroit Lions

**RUBKE, CARL—Center—
Southern California**
1957–60   San Francisco 49ers

**RUBY, MARTIN—Tackle—Texas
A & M**
1946–48   Brooklyn Dodgers (AAFC)
1949   New York Yankees (AAFC)
1950   New York Yanks

RUCINSKI, EDWARD—End—Indiana
1940–41   Brooklyn Dodgers

1943, 45–46   Chicago Cardinals
1944   Card-Pitt

RUCKA, LEO—Center—Rice
1956   San Francisco 49ers

**RUDOLPH, JOHN—Back—
Georgia Tech**
1960   Boston Patriots (AFL)

RUETZ, HOWARD—Tackle—Loras
1951–53   Green Bay Packers

**RUETZ, JOSEPH—Guard—Notre
Dame**
1946, 48   Chicago Rockets (AAFC)

**RUH, EMMETT—Back—
Davis-Elkins**
1921–25   Columbus Tigers

RUH, HOMER—End
1921–26   Columbus Tigers

RUKAS, JUSTIN—Guard—LSU
1936   Brooklyn Dodgers

**RUNDQUIST, ELMER—Tackle—
Illinois**
1922   Chicago Cardinals
1923–26   Duluth Eskimos

**RUNNELS, THOMAS—Back—Texas
State North**
1956–57   Washington Redskins

RUNNING DEER—End
1922   Oorang Indians

RUNSEY, ROY—Tackle
1921   Evansville Crimson Giants

RUPP, NELSON—Back—Denison
1921   Chicago Bears

RUSH, ARDEN—End—Ohio
1922–24   Columbus Tigers

RUSH, CLIVE—Back—Miami (Ohio)
1953   Green Bay Packers

RUSH, JAMES—Back—Minnesota
1922   Minneapolis Marines

**RUSHING, MARION—Guard—
Southern Illinois**
1959   Chicago Cardinals

**RUSKUSKY, RAYMOND—End—St.
Mary's (Cal.)**
1947   New York Yankees (AAFC)

**RUSSAS, ALBERT—Tackle—
Tennessee**
1949   Detroit Lions

RUSSELL. DOUGAL—Back—Kansas
1934–38   Chicago Cardinals
1935   #1 Ball Carrying

ALBERT RUSSAS

**RUSSELL, EDWARD—Guard—
Pennsylvania**
1921–22   Canton Bulldogs

RUSSELL, JAMES—Tackle—Temple
1936–37   Philadelphia Eagles

RUSSELL, JOHN—End—Baylor
1946–49   New York Yankees (AAFC)
1950   New York Yanks

**RUSSELL, KENNETH—Tackle—
Bowling Green**
1957–59   Detroit Lions

**RUSSELL, LAFAYETTE—Back—
Northwestern**
1933   New York Giants
1933   Philadelphia Eagles

RUSSELL, LLOYD—Back—Baylor
1939   Cleveland Rams

**RUSSELL, REGINALD—End—
Northwestern**
1928   Chicago Bears

**RUSSELL, TORRANCE—Tackle—
Auburn**
1939–40   Washington Redskins

**RUST, REGINALD—Back—Oregon
State**
1932   Boston Braves

RUTHSTROM, RALPH—Back—SMU
1945   Cleveland Rams
1946   Los Angeles Rams
1947–48   Washington Redskins
1949   Baltimore Colts (AAFC)

**RUTKOWSKI, CHARLES—End—
Ripon**
1960   Buffalo Bills (AFL)

**RUZICH, STEVEN—Guard—Ohio
State**
1952–54   Green Bay Packers

**RYAN, CLARENCE—Back—
West Virginia**
1929   Buffalo Bisons

**RYAN, DAVID—Back—Hardin-
Simmons**
1945–46   Detroit Lions
1948   Boston Yanks

**RYAN, EDWARD—End—St. Mary's
(Cal.)**
1948   Pittsburgh Steelers

RYAN, FRANK—Back—Rice
1958–60   Los Angeles Rams

FRANK RYAN

RYAN, JAMES—Back—Notre Dame
1924   Rock Island Independents
1924   Chicago Cardinals

RYAN, JOHN—Back—Illinois
1956–58   Philadelphia Eagles
1958   Chicago Bears

RYAN, JOHN—Tackle—Detroit
1929   Chicago Bears
1930   Portsmouth Spartans

RYAN, JOSEPH—End—Villanova
1960   New York Titans (AFL)

RYAN, KENT—Back—Utah State
1938–40   Detroit Lions

**RYCHLEC, THOMAS—End—
American International**
1958   Detroit Lions
1960   Buffalo Bills (AFL)

**RYDZEWSKI, FRANK—Tackle—
Notre Dame**
1921   Chicago Cardinals

1922–26 Hammond Pros
1923 Chicago Bears
1925 Milwaukee Badgers

RYKOVICH, JULIUS—Back—Illinois
1947–48 Buffalo Bills (AAFC)
1948 Chicago Rockets (AAFC)
1949–51 Chicago Bears

RYKOWSKI, FRANK—Guard—Purdue
1940 Pittsburgh Steelers

RYMKUS, LOUIS—Tackle—Notre Dame
1943 Washington Redskins
1946–49 Cleveland Browns (AAFC)
1950–51 Cleveland Browns

* * *

SABADOS, ANDREW—Guard—Citadel
1939–41 Chicago Cardinals

SABAL, RONALD—Tackle—Purdue
1960 Oakland Raiders (AFL)

SABAN, LOUIS—Back—Indiana
1946–49 Cleveland Browns (AAFC)

LOUIS SABAN

SABASTEANKSI, JOSEPH—Center—Fordham
1946–48 Boston Yanks
1949 New York Bulldogs

SABUCO, TINO—Center—San Francisco
1949 San Francisco 49ers (AAFC)

SACHS, LEONARD—End—Loyola
1921–23, 25 Chicago Cardinals
1923 Columbus Tigers
1923–24 Milwaukee Badgers
1924–25 Hammond Pros
1926 Louisville Colonels

SACHSE, FRANCIS—Back—Texas Tech.
1942 Chicago Cardinals
1943–44 Brooklyn Dodgers
1945 Boston Yanks

SACHSE, JOHN—Center—Texas
1945 Boston Yanks

SACK, JOHN—Guard—Pittsburgh
1923, 25 Columbus Tigers
1926 Canton Bulldogs

SACKSTEDER, NORBERT—Back—Dayton
1921 Detroit Panthers
1922–24 Canton Bulldogs
1925 Dayton Triangles

SACRINTY, NICHOLAS—Back—Wake Forest
1947 Chicago Bears

SADER, STEVEN—Back
1943 Philadelphia Eagles

SADOWSKY, LEONARD—Back—Ohio
1936 Cleveland Rams

SAENZ, EDWARD—Back—Southern California
1946–51 Washington Redskins

SAGELY, FLOYD—End—Arkansas
1954, 56 San Francisco 49ers
1957 Chicago Cardinals

SAIDOCK, THOMAS—Tackle—Michigan State
1957 Philadelphia Eagles
1960 New York Titans (AFL)

ST. CLAIR, ROBERT—Tackle—San Francisco
1953–60 San Francisco 49ers

ROBERT ST. CLAIR

ST. GERMAINE, THEODORE—
Guard—Carlisle
1922   Oorang Indians

ST. JOHN, HERBERT—Guard—
Georgia
1948   Brooklyn Dodgers (AAFC)
1949   Chicago Hornets (AAFC)

SALATA, ANDREW—Guard—
Pittsburgh
1929   Orange
1930   Newark

SALATA, PAUL—End—Southern
California
1949   San Francisco 49ers (AAFC)
1950   San Francisco 49ers
1950   Baltimore Colts

SALEM, EDWARD—Back—Alabama
1951   Washington Redskins

SALEMI, SAMUEL—Back—St.
Johns (N. Y.)
1928   New York Yankees

SALSBURY, JAMES—Guard—
U.C.L.A.
1955–56   Detroit Lions
1957–58   Green Bay Packers

SALSCHNEIDER, JOHN—Back—St.
Thomas
1949   New York Giants

SAMPLE, CHARLES—Back—Toledo
1942, 45   Green Bay Packers

SAMPLE, JOHN—Back—Maryland
State
1958–60   Baltimore Colts

JOHN SAMPLE

SAMPSON, ARTHUR—Back
1921   Dayton Triangles

SAMPSON, SENECA—Back—Brown
1926   Providence Steamrollers

SAMUELS, DONALD—Back—Oregon
State
1949–50   Pittsburgh Steelers

SAMUELSON, CARL—Tackle—
Nebraska
1948–51   Pittsburgh Steelers

SANCHEZ, JOHN—Tackle—San
Francisco
1947   Chicago Rockets (AAFC)
1947   New York Yankees (AAFC)
1947   Detroit Lions
1947–49   Washington Redskins
1949–50   New York Giants

SANDBERG, ROY—Back—
Washington State
1926   Los Angeles

SANDBERG, SIGMUND—Tackle—
Iowa Wesleyan
1933   Chicago Cardinals
1934   St. Louis Gunners
1935–37   Pittsburgh Pirates
1937   Brooklyn Dodgers

SANDEFUR, MAYNE—Back—
Purdue
1936–37   Pittsburgh Steelers

SANDERS, JOHN—Back—SMU
1940–41   Pittsburgh Steelers
1943   Phil-Pitt
1945   Philadelphia Eagles

SANDERS, ORBAN—Back—Texas
1946–48   New York Yankees (AAFC)
1950   New York Yankees

SANDERS, PAUL—Back—Utah State
1944   Boston Yanks

SANDIFER, DANIEL—Back—
Louisana State
1948–49   Washington Redskins
1950   Detroit Lions
1950   San Francisco 49ers
1950–51   Philadelphia Eagles
1952–53   Green Bay Packers
1953   Chicago Cardinals
1948   # 1 Interceptions

SANDIG, CURTIS—Back—St. Mary's
(Tex.)
1942   Pittsburgh Steelers
1946   Buffalo Bisons (AAFC)

SANDUSKY, ALEX—End—Penn. State
1954–60   Baltimore Colts

SANDUSKY, JOHN—Tackle—
Villanova
1950–55   Cleveland Browns
1956   Green Bay Packers

ALEX SANDUSKY

SANDUSKY, MICHAEL—Tackle—Maryland
1957–60 Pittsburgh Steelers

SANFORD, HAYWARD—End—Alabama
1940 Washington Redskins

SANFORD, JAMES—Tackle—Lehigh Lehigh
1924 Duluth Kelleys

SANFORD, LEO OTIS—Guard—LSU
1951–57 Chicago Cardinals
1958 Baltimore Colts

SANSEN, OLIVER—Back—Iowa
1932–35 Brooklyn Dodgers

SANTONE—Guard
1926 Hartford Blues

SANZOTTA, DOMINIC—Back—Western Reserve
1942, 46 Detroit Lions

SAPIENZA, RICHARD—Back—Villanova
1960 New York Titans (AFL)

SAPP, THERON—Back—Georgia
1959–60 Philadelphia Eagles

SARAFINY, ALBERT—Center—St. Edwards
1933 Green Bay Packers

SARAUSKY, ANTHONY—Back—Fordham
1935–37 New York Giants
1938 Brooklyn Dodgers

SARBOE, PHILIP—Back—Washington State
1934 Boston Redskins
1934–36 Chicago Cardinals
1936 Brooklyn Dodgers

SARDISCO, ANTHONY—Guard—Tulane
1956 Washington Redskins
1956 San Francisco 49ers
1960 Boston Patriots (AFL)

SARK, HARVEY—Guard
1931 New York Giants
1934 Cincinnati Reds

SARRATT, CHARLES—Back—Oklahoma
1948 Detroit Lions

SARRINGHAUS, PAUL—Back—Ohio State
1946 Chicago Cardinals
1948 Detroit Lions

SARTORI, LAWRENCE—Guard—Fordham
1942, 45 Detroit Lions
1944 Boston Yanks

SATENSTEIN, BERNARD—Guard—New York Univ.
1929–32 Staten Island Stapletons
1933 New York Giants

SATTERFIELD, ALFRED—Tackle—Vanderbilt
1947 San Francisco 49ers (AAFC)

SAUER, EDWARD—Tackle—Miami (Ohio)
1921–26 Dayton Triangles

SAUER, GEORGE—Back—Nebraska
1935–37 Green Bay Packers

SAULIS, SAMUEL—Guard
1938 Pittsburgh Pirates

SAUMER, SYLVESTER—Back—St. Olaf
1934 Cincinnati Reds
1934 Pittsburgh Pirates
1934 Boston Redskins

SAUNDERS, RUSSELL—Back—Southern California
1931 Green Bay Packers

SAUNOOK—End—Carlisle
1922 Oorang Indians

SAVATSKY, OLIVER—End—Miami (Ohio)
1937 Cleveland Rams

SAVITSKY, GEORGE—Tackle—Pennsylvania
1948–49 Philadelphia Eagles

SAVOLDI, JOSEPH—Back—Notre Dame
1930 Chicago Bears

SAWYER, HERMAN—Tackle—Syracuse

1922   Rochester Kodaks

SAZIO, RALPH—Tackle—William & Mary
1948   Brooklyn Dodgers (AAFC)

SCAFIDE, JOHN—Tackle—Tulane
1933   Boston Redskins

SCALES, CHARLES—Back—Indiana
1960   Pittsburgh Steelers

SCALISSI, THEODORE—Back— Ripon
1947   Chicago Rockets (AAFC)

SCALZI, JOHN—Back—Georgetown
1931   Brooklyn Dodgers

SCANLON, DEWEY—Back— Valparaiso
1926   Duluth Eskimos

SCANLON, JOHN—Back—De Paul
1921   Chicago Cardinals
1926   Louisville Colonels

SCARBATH, JOHN—Back— Maryland
1953–54   Washington Redskins
1956   Pittsburgh Steelers

SCARDINE, CARMEN—Back
1932   Chicago Cardinals

SCARRY, MICHAEL—Center— Waynesburg
1944–45   Cleveland Rams
1946–47   Cleveland Browns (AAFC)

SCHAAKE, ELMER—Back—Kansas
1933   Portsmouth Spartans

SCHABARUM, PETER—Back— California
1951, 53–54   San Francisco 49ers

SCHAEFER, DONALD—Back— Notre Dame
1956   Philadelphia Eagles

SCHAFFER, JOSEPH—Back— Tennessee
1960   Buffalo Bills (AFL)

SCHAFFNIT, PETER—End— California
1926   Los Angeles

SCHAFRATH, RICHARD—End— Ohio State
1959–60   Cleveland Browns

SCHAMMELL, FRANCIS—Guard— Iowa
1937   Green Bay Packers

SCHARER, EDWARD—Back—Notre Dame

1926–28   Detroit Panthers
1927   Pottsville Maroons
1930   Portsmouth Spartans

SCHEIN, JOSEPH—Tackle—Brown
1931   Providence Steamrollers

SCHELL, HERBERT—Back— Ohio State
1924   Columbus Tigers

SCHENKER, NATHAN—Tackle— Howard
1939   Cleveland Rams

SCHERER, BERNARD—End— Nebraska
1936–38   Green Bay Packers
1939   Pittsburgh Steelers

SCHEVER, ABRAHAM—End
1934   Brooklyn Dodgers

SCHIBANOFF, ALEXANDER— Tackle—Franklin-Marshall
1942   Detroit Lions

SCHIEB, LEE—Center— West Virginia Wesleyan
1930   Brooklyn Dodgers

SCHIEBEL, ARTHUR—Back— Colgate
1932   Staten Island Stapletons

SCHIECHL, JOHN—Center—Santa Clara
1941–42   Pittsburgh Steelers
1942   Detroit Lions
1945–46   Chicago Bears
1947   San Francisco 49ers (AAFC)

SCHILLING, RALPH—End— Oklahoma City Univ.
1946   Washington Redskins
1946   Buffalo Bisons (AAFC)

SCHIMMEL—Back
1925   Rock Island Independents

SCHLEICH, VICTOR—Tackle— Nebraska
1947   New York Yankees (AAFC)

SCHLEICHER, MAURICE—End— Penn State
1959   Chicago Cardinals
1960   Los Angeles Chargers (AFL)

SCHLINKMAN, WALTER—Back— Texas Tech.
1946–50   Green Bay Packers
1951   Chicago Cardinals

SCHLUESNER, VINCENT—Tackle— Iowa
1930–31   Portsmouth Spartans

SCHMAEHL, ARTHUR—Back

1921   Green Bay Packers

SCHMAAR, HERMAN—End—
Catholic
1943   Brooklyn Dodgers

SCHMEELK, GARRY—Tackle—
Manhattan
1942   New York Giants

SCHMIDT, GEORGE—Center—Lewis
1952   Green Bay Packers
1953   Chicago Cardinals

SCHMIDT, HENRY—Tackle—
Southern California
1959–60   San Francisco 49ers

SCHMIDT, JOHN—Center—Carnegie
Tech
1940   Pittsburgh Steelers

SCHMIDT, JOSEPH—Guard—
Pittsburgh
1953–60   Detroit Lions

SCHMIDT, KERMIT—End—
California Polytech.
1932   Boston Braves
1933   Cincinnati Reds

SCHMIDT, ROBERT—Tackle—
Minnesota
1959–60   New York Giants

SCHMIDT, THEODORE—Center—
Pittsburgh
1938–40   Philadelphia Eagles

SCHNEIDER, DONALD—Back—
Pennsylvania
1948   Buffalo Bills (AAFC)

SCHNEIDER, LEROY—Tackle—
Tulane
1947   Brooklyn Dodgers (AAFC)

SCHNEIDMAN, HERMAN—Back—
Iowa
1935–39   Green Bay Packers
1940   Chicago Cardinals

SCHNELKER, ROBERT—End—
Bowling Green
1953   Philadelphia Eagles
1954–60   New York Giants

SCHNELLBACHER, OTTO—Back—
Kansas
1948–49   New York Yankees (AAFC)
1950–51   New York Giants
1951   #1 Interceptions

SCHNELLER, JOHN—Back—
Wisconsin
1933   Portsmouth Spartans
1934–36   Detroit Lions

SCHOEMANN, ROY—Center—
Marquette
1938   Green Bay Packers

SCHOLL, ROY—Guard—Lehigh
1929   Boston Braves

SCHOLTZ, ROBERT—Center—
Notre Dame
1960   Detroit Lions

SCHOTTEL, IVAN—Back—
Missouri State Teachers
1946, 48   Detroit Lions

SCHRADER, JAMES—Center—Notre
Dame
1954, 57–60   Washington Redskins

SCHROEDER, EUGENE—End—
Virginia
1951–52, 54–57   Chicago Bears

SCHROEDER, WILLIAM—Back—
Wisconsin
1946–47   Chicago Rockets (AAFC)

SCHROLL, CHARLES—Back—LSU
1949   Buffalo Bills (AAFC)
1950   Detroit Lions
1951   Green Bay Packers

SCHUBER, JAMES—Back—Navy
1930   Brooklyn Dodgers

SCHUELKE, KARL "JAKE"—Back—
Rice
1939   Philadelphia Eagles

SCHUELKE, WARREN—Back—
Wisconsin
1939   Pittsburgh Steelers

SCHUESSLER, ERWIN—Tackle
1921   Cincinnati Celts

SCHUETTE, CARL—Back
Marquette
1948–49   Buffalo Bills (AAFC)
1950–51   Green Bay Packers

SCHUETTE, PAUL—Guard—
Wisconsin
1928   New York Giants
1930–32   Chicago Bears
1932   Boston Braves

SCHULER, WILLIAM—Tackle—
Yale
1947–48   New York Giants

SCHULTZ, CHARLES—Tackle—
Minnesota
1939–41   Green Bay Packers

SCHULTZ, EBERLE—Guard—Oregon
State
1940, 42   Philadelphia Eagles
1941   Pittsburgh Steelers

1943   Phil-Pitt
1944   Card-Pitt
1945   Cleveland Rams
1946–47   Los Angeles Rams

SCHUPBACH, O. T.—Tackle—West Texas State
(Tex Mooney)
1941–42   Cleveland Rams
1943   Brooklyn Dodgers

SCHUPE, WALTER—Tackle—Miami, Ohio
1921   Cincinnati Celts

SCHUSTER, RICHARD—End—Penn State
1925   Canton Bulldogs

SCHWAB, RAYMOND—Back—Oklahoma City Univ.
1931   New York Giants
1932   Staten Island Stapletons

SCHWALL, VICTOR—Back—Northwestern
1947–50   Chicago Cardinals

SCHWAMMEL, ADOLPH—Tackle—Oregon State
1934–36, 43–44   Green Bay Packers

SCHWARTZ, ELMER—Back—Washington State
1931   Portsmouth Spartans
1932   Chicago Cardinals
1933   Pittsburgh Pirates

SCHWARTZ, PERRY—End—California
1938–42   Brooklyn Dodgers
1946   New York Yankees (AAFC)

SCHWARZER, THEODORE—Guard—Centenary
1926   Buffalo Bisons

SCHWEDER, JOHN—Guard—Pennsylvania
1950   Baltimore Colts
1951   Pittsburgh Steelers

SCHWEDES, GERHARD—Back—Syracuse
1960   New York Titans (AFL)
1960   Boston Patriots (AFL)

SCHWEIDLER, RICHARD—Back—St. Louis Univ.
1938–39, 46   Chicago Bears

SCHWENK, WILSON—Back—Washington (St. Louis)
1942   Chicago Cardinals
1946   Cleveland Browns (AAFC)
1947   Baltimore Colts (AAFC)
1947   Buffalo Bills (AAFC)
1948   New York Yankees (AAFC)

SCOLLARD, NICHOLAS—End—St. Josephs
1946–48   Boston Yanks
1949   New York Bulldogs

CLYDE SCOTT

SCOTT, CLYDE—Back—Arkansas
1949–52   Philadelphia Eagles
1952   Detroit Lions

SCOTT, EDWARD—Guard—Monmouth
1924   Rock Island Independents

SCOTT, EUGENE—Guard—Hamline
1923   Akron Steels
1924   Minneapolis Marines

SCOTT, GEORGE—Back—Miami, Ohio
1959   New York Giants

SCOTT, JOHN—Back—Lafayette
1921–23   Buffalo All Americans
1924   Frankford Yellowjackets

SCOTT, JOHN—Tackle—Ohio State
1960   Buffalo Bills (AFL)

SCOTT, JOSEPH—Back—San Francisco
1948–53   New York Giants

SCOTT, PERRY—End—Muhlenberg
1942   Detroit Lions

SCOTT, PRINCE—End—Texas Tech.
1946   Miami Seahawks (AAFC)

SCOTT, RALPH—Tackle—Wisconsin
1921–25   Chicago Bears
1926   Providence Steamrollers
1927   New York Yankees
1929   Orange

SCOTT, THOMAS—End—Virginia
1953–58   Philadelphia Eagles

1959–60 New York Giants

SCOTT, VINCENT—Guard—Notre Dame
1947–48 Buffalo Bills (AAFC)

SCOTTI, BENJAMIN—Back—Maryland
1959–60 Washington Redskins

SCRABIS, ROBERT—Back—Penn State
1960 New York Titans (AFL)

SCRUGGS, EDWIN—End—Rice
1947–48 Brooklyn Dodgers (AAFC)

SCUDERO, JAMES—Back—San Francisco
1954–58 Washington Redskins
1960 Pittsburgh

SEABRIGHT, CHARLES—Back—West Virginia
1941 Cleveland Rams
1946–50 Pittsburgh Steelers

SEARS, JAMES—Back—Southern California
1954, 57–58 Chicago Cardinals
1960 Los Angeles Chargers (AFL)

JAMES SEARS

SEARS, RICHARD—Back—Kansas State
1924 Kansas City Cowboys

SEARS, VICTOR—Tackle—Oregon State
1941–42, 44–51 Philadelphia Eagles
1943 Phil-Pitt

SEASHOLTZ, GEORGE—Back—Lafayette
1922 Milwaukee Badgers
1924 Kenosha

SEBASTIAN, MICHAEL—Back—Pittsburgh

1934 Cincinnati Reds
1935 Philadelphia Eagles
1935 Pittsburgh Pirates
1935 Boston Redskins
1937 Cleveland Indians

SEBEK, NICHOLAS—Back—Indiana
1951 Washington Redskins

SEBO, SAM—Back—Syracuse
1930 Newark

SEBORG, HENRY—Back—Kalamazoo
1929–30 Minneapolis Redjackets
1930 Minneapolis Redjackets
1930–31 Frankford Yellowjackets

SECHRIST, WALTER—Guard—West Virginia
1924 Akron Steels
1925 Frankford Yellowjackets
1926 Hammond Pros
1926 Louisville Colonels

SECORD, JOSEPH—Center
1922 Green Bay Packers

SEDBROOK, LEONARD—Back—Oklahoma City Univ.
1928 Detroit Wolverines
1929–31 New York Giants

SEDLOCK, ROBERT—Tackle—Georgia
1960 Buffalo Bills (AFL)

SEEDS—Back
1926 Canton Bulldogs

SEEMAN, GEORGE—End—Nebraska
1940 Green Bay Packers

SEFTON, FREDERICK—End—Colgate
1921–22 Canton Bulldogs

SEGRETTA, ROCCO—End
1926 Hartford Blues

SEIBERLING, GERALD—Back—Drake
1932 Chicago Bears

SEIBERT, EDWARD—Guard—Otterbein
1923 Hammond Pros
1927–28 Dayton Triangles

SEIBOLD, CHAMP—Tackle—Wisconsin
1934–38, 40–41 Green Bay Packers
1942 Chicago Cardinals

SEICK, EARL—Guard—Manhattan
1942–43 New York Giants

SEIDELSON, HARRY—Guard—Pittsburgh
1925 Frankford Yellowjackets

1926   Akron Steels

SEIFERLING, JOHN—Back—Fresno State
1947   Chicago Bears

SEIGEL—End
1925   Cleveland Indians

SELAWSKI, EUGENE—Tackle—Purdue
1959   Los Angeles Rams
1960   Cleveland Browns

SELF, CLARENCE—Back—Wisconsin
1949   Chicago Cardinals
1950–52   Detroit Lions
1952, 54–55   Green Bay Packers

SELTZER, HARRY—Back—Morris-Harvey
1942   Detroit Lions

SEMES, BERNARD—Back—Duquesne
1944   Card-Pitt

SENN, WILLIAM—Back—Knox
1926–31   Chicago Bears
1931   Brooklyn Dodgers
1934   St. Louis Gunners

SENO, FRANK—Back—George Washington
1943–44, 49   Washington Redskins
1945–46   Chicago Cardinals
1947–48   Boston Yanks
1947   #1 Interceptions
          (Tied by Reagen)

SENSENBAUGHER, DEAN—Back—Ohio State
1948   Cleveland Browns (AAFC)
1949   New York Bulldogs

SERGIENKO, GEORGE—Tackle—American International
1943–44   Brooklyn Dodgers
1945   Boston Yanks
1946   Brooklyn Dodgers (AAFC)

SERINI, WASHINGTON—Guard—Kentucky
1948–51   Chicago Bears
1952   Green Bay Packers

SERMON, RAY—Back—Warrensburg
1925   Kansas City Cowboys

SETCAVAGE, JOSEPH—Back—Duquesne
1942–43   Brooklyn Dodgers

SETRON, JOSEPH—Guard—West Virginia
1923   Cleveland Indians

HARLEY SEWELL

SEWELL, HARLEY—Guard—Texas
1953–60   Detroit Lions

SEXTON, LINWOOD—Back—Wichita
1948   Los Angeles Dons (AAFC)

SEYFRIT, MICHAEL—End—Notre Dame
1923   Toledo Maroons
1924   Hammond Pros

SEYMOUR, ROBERT—Back—Oklahoma
1940–45   Washington Redskins
1946   Los Angeles Dons (AAFC)

SHAFFER, GEORGE—Back—Washington & Jefferson
1933   Pittsburgh Pirates

SHAFFER, LELAND—Back—Kansas State
1935–45   New York Giants

SHANLEY, JAMES—Back—Oregon
1958   Green Bay Packers

SHAPIRO, JOHN—Back—New York Univ.
1929   Staten Island Stapletons

SHARE, NATHAN—Guard—Tufts
1925   Providence Steamrollers

SHARKEY, EDWARD—Guard—Nevada, Duke
1947–49   New York Yankees (AAFC)
1950   New York Yanks
1952   Cleveland Browns
1953   Baltimore Colts
1954–55   Philadelphia Eagles
1955–56   San Francisco 49ers

SHARP, EVERETT—Tackle—
California Polytech.
1944–45 Washington Redskins

SHAUB, HARRY—Guard—Cornell
1935 Philadelphia Eagles

SHAW, CHARLES—Guard—
Oklahoma A & M
1950 San Francisco 49ers

SHAW, EDWARD—Back—Nebraska
1922 Canton Bulldogs
1923 Akron Steels

SHAW, GEORGE—Back—Oregon
1955–58 Baltimore Colts
1959–60 New York Giants

SHAW, GLEN—Back—Kentucky
1960 Chicago Bears

SHAW, JESSE—Guard—Southern
California
1931 Chicago Cardinals

SHAW, ROBERT—End—Ohio State
1945 Cleveland Rams
1946, 49 Los Angeles Rams
1950 Chicago Cardinals

SHEARD, ALFRED—Back—St.
Lawrence
1923–25 Rochester Jeffersons

SHEDLOSKY, EDMOND—Back—
Tulsa & Fordham
1945 New York Giants

SHEEKS, PAUL—Back—South Dakota
1921–22 Akron Steels

SHEHAN, JOHN—Guard—Boston
College
1925 Providence Steamrollers

SHELBURNE, JOHN—Back—
Dartmouth
1922 Hammond Pros

SHELDON, JAMES—End—Brown
1926 Brooklyn Dodgers

SHELETON, VINCENT—Guard—
Marquette
1922 Racine Legions

SHELLOGG, ALEXANDER—
Tackle—Notre Dame
1939 Brooklyn Dodgers

SHELLY, DEXTER—Back—Texas
1931 Providence Steamrollers
1931 Portsmouth Spartans
1932 Chicago Cardinals
1932–33 Green Bay Packers

SHELTON, MURRAY—End—
Cornell

1921–22 Buffalo Bisons

SHENEFELT, PAUL—Tackle—
Manchester
1934–35 Chicago Cardinals

SHEPARD, CHARLES—Back—Texas
State North
1956 Pittsburgh Steelers

SHEPARD, WILLIAM—Back—
Western Maryland
1935 Boston Redskins
1935–40 Detroit Lions

SHERER, DAVID—End—SMU
1959 Baltimore Colts
1960 Dallas Cowboys

SHERIFF, STANLEY—Guard—
California Polytech
1954 Pittsburgh Steelers
1956–57 San Francisco 49ers
1957 Cleveland Browns

SHERMAN, ALEX—Back—Brooklyn
College
1943 Phil-Pitt
1944–47 Philadelphia Eagles

SHERMAN, SAUL—Back—Chicago
1939–40 Chicago Bears

SHERMAN, WILLARD—Back—
St. Mary's Cal.
1952 Dallas Texans
1954–60 Los Angeles Rams
1955 #1 Interceptions

WILLARD SHERMAN

SHERROD, HORACE—End—
Tennessee
1952 New York Giants

SHERRY, GERALD—Back—Loyola
1926 Louisville Colonels

SHETLEY, RHOTEN—Back—
Furman
1940–42, 46 Brooklyn Dodgers

SHIELDS, LEBRON—Tackle—
Tennessee
1960 Baltimore Colts

SHINNICK, DONALD—Back—
U.C.L.A.
1957–60 Baltimore Colts
1959 #1 Interceptions
(Tied by M. Davis, Derby)

DONALD SHINNICK

SHIPKEY, JERRY—Back—UCLA
1948–52 Pittsburgh Steelers
1953 Chicago Bears

SHIPP, WILLIAM—Tackle—Alabama
1954 New York Giants

SHIRES, MARSHALL—Back—
Tennessee
1945 Philadelphia Eagles

SHIREY, FREDERICK—Tackle—
Nebraska
1940–41 Cleveland Rams

SHIRK, JOHN—End—Oklahoma
1940 Chicago Cardinals

SHIRKEY, GEORGE—Tackle—Austin
1960 Houston Oilers (AFL)

SHIRLEY, MARION—Tackle—
Oklahoma City Univ.
1948–49 New York Yankees (AAFC)

SHIVER, RAYMOND—Back—Miami
1956 Los Angeles Rams

SHOCKLEY, ARNOLD—Guard—
Southwestern State
1928–29 Providence Steamrollers
1929 Boston Braves

SHOCKLEY, WILLIAM—Back—
West Chester
1960 New York Titans (AFL)

SHOEMAKER, HUBBARD—Guard—
Illinois
1921 Chicago Bears (Staleys)

SHOENER, HAROLD—End—Iowa
1948–49 San Francisco 49ers (AAFC)
1950 San Francisco 49ers

SHOENER, HERBERT—End—Iowa
1948–49 Washington Redskins

SHOFNER, DELBERT—Back—Baylor
1957–60 Los Angeles Rams

DELBERT SHOFNER

SHOFNER, JAMES—Back—TCU
1958–60 Cleveland Browns

SHONK, JOHN—End—West Virginia
1941 Philadelphia Eagles

SHONTA, CHARLES—Back—
Michigan Eastern
1960 Boston Patriots (AFL)

SHOOK, FREDERICK—Center—TCU
1940–41 Chicago Cardinals

SHOULTS, PAUL—Back—Miami
(Ohio)
1949 New York Bulldogs

SHUGART, CLYDE—Guard—Iowa
State
1939–44 Washington Redskins

SHULA, DONALD—John Carroll
1951–52 Cleveland Browns
1953–56 Baltimore Colts
1957 Washington Redskins

SHULTZ, JOHN—Back—Temple
1930 Frankford Yellowjackets

SHURNAS, MARSHALL—End—
Missouri
1947 Cleveland Browns (AAFC)

SHURTLEFF, BERTRAND—Back—
Brown
1925–26 Providence Steamrollers
1929 Boston Braves
1929 Buffalo Bisons

SHURTZ, HUBERT—Tackle—LSU
1948 Pittsburgh Steelers

SIANO, ANTHONY—Center—
Fordham
1932 Boston Braves
1934 Brooklyn Dodgers

SIDORIK, ALEXANDER—Tackle—
Mississippi State
1947 Boston Yanks
1948–49 Baltimore Colts (AAFC)

SIEGAL, JOHN—End—Columbia
1939–43 Chicago Bears

SIEGERT, HERBERT—Guard—
Illinois
1949–51 Washington Redskins
1951 Detroit Lions
1951 New York Yanks

SIEGFRIED, ORVILLE—Back—
Washington & Jefferson
1923 St. Louis Browns

SIEGLE, JULES—Back—Northwestern
1948 New York Giants

SIEMERING, LAWRENCE—Center—
San Francisco
1935–36 Boston Redskins

SIERADZKI, STEPHEN—Back—
Michigan State
1948 New York Yankees (AAFC)
1948 Brooklyn Dodgers (AAFC)

SIEROCINSKI, STEPHEN—Tackle
1946 Boston Yanks

SIES, DALE—Guard—Pittsburgh
1921–22, 24 Dayton Triangles
1923 Rock Island Independents
1924 Kenosha

SIGILLO, DOMINIC—Tackle—
Xavier (Cincinnati)
1943–44 Chicago Bears
1945 Detroit Lions

SIGNAIGO, JOSEPH—Guard—Notre
Dame
1948–49 New York Yankees (AAFC)
1950 New York Yanks

SIGURDSON, SIGURD—End—
Pacific Lutheran

1947 Baltimore Colts (AAFC)

SIKICH, RUDOLPH—Tackle—
Minnesota
1945 Cleveland Rams

SIKORA, MICHAEL—Guard—Oregon
1952 Chicago Cardinals

SILLIN, FRANK—Back—Western
Maryland
1927–29 Dayton Triangles

SILVERMAN—Tackle
1929 Boston Braves

SIMAS, WILLIAM—Back—St. Mary's
(Cal.)
1932–33 Chicago Cardinals

SIMENDINGER, KENNETH—Back
—Holy Cross
1926 Hartford Blues

SIMENSON, DONALD—Tackle—St.
Thomas
1951–52 Los Angeles Rams

SIMERSON, JOHN—Tackle—Purdue
1957–58 Philadelphia Eagles
1958 Pittsburgh Steelers
1960 Houston Oilers (AFL)

SIMINGTON, MILTON—Guard—
Arkansas
1941 Cleveland Rams
1942 Pittsburgh Steelers

SIMMONS, FLOYD—Back—Notre
Dame
1948 Chicago Rockets (AAFC)

SIMMONS, JAMES—Back—Oklahoma
State Southwest
1928 Providence Steamrollers

SIMMONS, JOHN—Guard—Detroit
1948 Baltimore Colts (AAFC)
1949–50 Detroit Lions
1950–56 Chicago Cardinals

SIMMONS, ROY—Back—Syracuse
1927 Cleveland Indians

SIMMS, ROBERT—End—Rutgers
1960 New York Giants

SIMON—End—Hamline
1924 Minneapolis Marines

SIMONETTI, LEONARD—Tackle—
Tennessee
1946–48 Cleveland Browns (AAFC)

SIMPSON, EBER—Back—Wisconsin
1922 Toledo Maroons
1923 St. Louis Browns
1923–24 Minneapolis Marines

SIMPSON, J. FELIX—Back—
Detroit Univ.
1924   Kenosha

SIMPSON, JACKIE—Back—Florida
1958–60   Baltimore Colts

SIMS, GEORGE—Back—Baylor
1949–50   Los Angeles Rams

SINGER, MILTON—Center—
Syracuse
1935   New York Giants

SINGER, WALTER—End—Syracuse
1935–37   New York Giants

SINGLETON, JOHN—Back—Wabash
1929   Dayton Triangles

SINKO, STEPHEN—Tackle—
Duquesne
1934–36   Boston Redskins

SINKOVITZ, FRANK—Center—
Duke
1947–51   Pittsburgh Steelers
1952   Dallas Texans

SINKWICH, FRANK—Back—Georgia
1943–44   Detroit Lions
1946–47   New York Yankees (AAFC)
1947   Baltimore Colts (AAFC)
1944   #1 Punting

SIROCHMAN, GEORGE—Guard—
Duquesne
1942   Pittsburgh Steelers
1944   Detroit Lions

SISK, JOHN—Back—Marquette
1932–36   Chicago Bears

SITES, VINCENT—End—Pittsburgh
1936–37   Pittsburgh Pirates

SITKO, EMIL—Back—Notre Dame
1950   San Francisco 49ers
1951–52   Chicago Cardinals

SIVELL, RALPH—Guard—Auburn
1938–42   Brooklyn Dodgers
1944–45   New York Giants
1946   Miami Seahawks (AAFC)

SKEATE, GILBERT—Back—Gonzaga
1927   Green Bay Packers

SKIBINSKI, JOSEPH—Guard—
Purdue
1952   Cleveland Browns
1955–56   Green Bay Packers

SKLADANY, JOSEPH—End—
Pittsburgh
1934   Pittsburgh Steelers

SKLADANY, LEO—End—Pittsburgh
1949   Philadelphia Eagles

1950   New York Giants

SKOCZEN, STANLEY—Back—
Western Reserve
1944   Cleveland Rams

SKOGLUND, ROBERT—End—
Notre Dame
1947   Green Bay Packers

SKORICH, NICHOLAS—Guard—
Cincinnati
1946–48   Pittsburgh Steelers

SKORONSKI, EDWARD—Center—
Purdue
1935–36   Pittsburgh Pirates
1937   Brooklyn Dodgers
1937   Cleveland Rams

SKORONSKI, ROBERT—Tackle—
Indiana
1956, 59–60   Green Bay Packers

ROBERT SKORONSKI

SKUDIN, DAVID—Guard—New York
Univ.
1929   Staten Island Stapletons

SLACKFORD, DAVID—Back—Notre
Dame
1921   Canton Bulldogs

SLAGLE, GEORGE—Tackle
1926   Louisville Colonels

SLATER, FRED—Tackle—Iowa
1922–25   Rock Island Independents
1922, 26   Milwaukee Badgers
1927–31   Chicago Cardinals

SLATER, WALTER—Back—
Tennessee
1947   Pittsburgh Steelers

SLEIGHT, ELMER—Tackle—Purdue
1930–31   Green Bay Packers

SLIVINSKI, STEPHEN—Guard—
Washington
1939–43 Washington Redskins

SLOAN, DWIGHT—Back—Arkansas
1938 Chicago Cardinals
1939–40 Detroit Lions

SLOSBURG, PHILIP—Back—
Temple
1948 Boston Yanks
1949 New York Bulldogs

SLOUGH, ELMER—Back—Oklahoma
1926 Buffalo Bisons

SLOVAK, MARTIN—Back—Toledo
1939–41 Cleveland Rams

SMEJA, RUDOLPH—End—Michigan
1944–45 Chicago Bears
1946 Philadelphia Eagles

SMITH, BEN—End—Alabama
1933 Green Bay Packers
1934–35 Pittsburgh Pirates
1937 Washington Redskins

SMITH, BILLY RAY—Guard—
Arkansas
1957 Los Angeles Rams
1958–60 Pittsburgh Steelers

SMITH, BRUCE—Back—Minnesota
1945–48 Green Bay Packers
1949 Los Angeles Rams

SMITH, CARL—Back—Tennessee
1960 Buffalo Bills (AFL)

SMITH, CEDRIC "PAT"—Back—
Michigan
1921–23 Buffalo Bisons
1923–24 Frankford Yellowjackets

SMITH, CHARLES—End—Abilene
Christian
1956 San Francisco 49ers

SMITH, CHARLES—Back—Georgia
1947 Chicago Cardinals

SMITH, CLYDE—Back—Missouri
1926 Kansas City Cowboys
1926–27 Cleveland Bulldogs
1927–30 Providence Steamrollers
1930–31 Portsmouth Spartans

SMITH, DAVID—Back—Ripon
1960 Houston Oilers (AFL)

SMITH, DEWEY—Guard
1930 Newark

SMITH, EARL—Tackle—Ripon
1922 Green Bay Packers
1923 Rock Island Independents
1923–24 Milwaukee Badgers
1923, 26 Hammond Pros
1923–24 Racine Legion

1925 Detroit Panthers

SMITH, EDWARD—Back—
New York Univ.
1936 Boston Redskins
1937 Green Bay Packers

SMITH, ERNEST—Back—
Compton Jr.
1955–56 San Francisco 49ers

SMITH, ERNEST—Tackle—
Southern California
1935–39 Green Bay Packers

SMITH, EUGENE—Guard—Georgia
Tech.
1930 Chicago Bears

SMITH, GAYLON—Back—
Southwestern Univ.
1939–42 Cleveland Rams
1946 Cleveland Browns (AAFC)

SMITH, GEORGE—Guard—Georgia
1930 Frankford Yellowjackets

SMITH, GEORGE—Center—
California
1937, 40–43 Washington Redskins
1944 Brooklyn Tigers
1945 Boston Yanks
1947 San Francisco 49ers (AAFC)

SMITH, HAROLD—Tackle—UCLA
1960 Boston Patriots (AFL)

SMITH, HARRY—Tackle—Southern
California
1940 Detroit Lions

SMITH, HENRY—Center—Lancaster
1921–25 Rochester Jeffersons

SMITH, HOUSTON ALLEN—End—
Mississippi
1947–48 Chicago Bears

SMITH, J. D.—Back—North Carolina
A & T
1956 Chicago Bears
1956–60 San Francisco 49ers

SMITH, JAMES—Tackle—Colorado
1945 Philadelphia Eagles
1947 Los Angeles Dons (AAFC)

SMITH, JAMES—Back—Iowa
1948 Brooklyn Dodgers (AAFC)
1948 Buffalo Bills (AAFC)
1949 Chicago Hornets (AAFC)
1949–54 Detroit Lions

SMITH, JAMES "JETSTREAM"—
Back—Compton Jr.
1960 Oakland Raiders (AFL)

SMITH, JAMES RAY—Guard—Baylor
1956–60 Cleveland Browns

J. D. SMITH

SMITH, JERALD—Guard—Wisconsin
1952–53, 56 San Francisco 49ers
1956 Green Bay Packers

JAMES RAY SMITH

SMITH, JESS D.—Tackle—Rice
1959–60 Philadelphia Eagles

SMITH, JOHN—End—Stanford
1942 Philadelphia Eagles
1943 Washington Redskins

SMITH, JOSEPH—End—Texas Tech.
1948 Baltimore Colts (AAFC)

SMITH, LEO—End—Providence
1928 Providence Steamrollers

SMITH, MILTON—End—UCLA
1945 Philadelphia Eagles

**SMITH, OLIN—Tackle—Ohio
    Wesleyan**
1924 Cleveland Bulldogs

SMITH, ORLAND—Tackle—Brown
1927–29 Providence Steamrollers

SMITH, OSCAR—Back—Texas Mines
1948 Green Bay Packers
1949 New York Bulldogs

SMITH, RAY—Center—Missouri
1931 Providence Steamrollers
1933 Philadelphia Eagles
1933 Boston Redskins

SMITH, RAY—Back—Midwestern
1954–57 Chicago Bears

**SMITH, REX—End—LaCrosse
    Teachers**
1922 Green Bay Packers

**SMITH, RICHARD—Guard—Notre
    Dame**
1927, 29 Green Bay Packers
1928 New York Yankees
1930 Newark
1930–31 New York Giants

SMITH, RILEY—Back—Alabama
1936 Boston Redskins
1937–38 Washington Redskins

**SMITH, ROBERT—Back—Texas
    A & M**
1953–54 Detroit Lions

ROBERT SMITH

SMITH, ROBERT—Back—Nebraska
1955–56 Cleveland Browns
1956 Philadelphia Eagles

SMITH, ROBERT—Tackle—Southern
1948 Brooklyn Dodgers (AAFC)

**SMITH, ROGER "ZEKE"—Guard—
    Auburn**
1960 Baltimore Colts

SMITH, RUSSELL—Guard—Illinois

1921–22   Chicago Bears
1921–22, 25   Chicago Cardinals
1924   Cleveland

SMITH, STUART—Back—Bucknell
1937–38   Pittsburgh Pirates

SMITH, TRUETT—Back—Wyoming, Mississippi State
1950–51   Pittsburgh Steelers

VERDA SMITH

SMITH, VERDA—Back—Abilene Christian
1949–51   Los Angeles Rams

SMITH, WARREN—Center—Carlton
1921   Green Bay Packers

SMITH, WILFRED—End—DePauw
1922   Hammond Pros
1923–25   Chicago Cardinals

SMITH, WILLIAM—End—Washington
1934–39   Chicago Cardinals
1935   #1 Field Goals (tied by Niccolai)

SMITH, WILLIAM—Tackle—North Carolina
1948   Chicago Rockets (AAFC)
1948   Los Angeles Dons (AAFC)

SMITH, WILLIE—Tackle—Michigan
1960   Denver Broncos (AFL)

SMITH, WILLIS—Back—Idaho
1934–35   New York Giants

SMUKLER, DAVID—Back—Temple
1936–39   Philadelphia Eagles
1940   Detroit Lions
1944   Boston Yanks

SMYTH, JAMES—Back—Centre
1922–23   Canton Bulldogs
1925–26   Providence Steamrollers

1926   Frankford Yellowjackets

SMYTH, WILLIAM—Tackle—Cincinnati
1947–50   Los Angeles Rams

SMYTHE, LOUIS—Back—Texas
1924–25   Rochester Jeffersons
1926   Hartford Blues
1926   Providence Steamrollers

SNEDDON, ROBERT—Back—St. Mary's
1944   Washington Redskins
1945   Detroit Lions
1946   Los Angeles Dons (AAFC)

SNELL, GEORGE—Back—Penn State
1926   Brooklyn Dodgers
1927   Buffalo Bisons

SNELLING, KENNETH—Back—UCLA
1945   Green Bay Packers

SNOOTS, J. LEE—Back
1921–25   Columbus Tigers

SNYDER, GERALD—Back—Maryland
1929   New York Giants
1930   Staten Island Stapletons

SNYDER, KENNETH—Tackle—Georgia Tech.
1952–55, 58   Philadelphia Eagles

SNYDER, ROBERT—Back—Ohio
1937–38   Cleveland Rams
1939–43   Chicago Bears

SOAR, HENRY—Back—Providence
1937–44, 46   New York Giants

SOBOLESKI, JOSEPH—Tackle—Michigan
1949   Chicago Hornets (AAFC)
1949   Washington Redskins
1950   Detroit Lions
1951   New York Yanks
1952   Dallas Texans

SOFISH, ALEXANDER—Guard—Grove City
1931   Providence Steamrollers

SOHN, BENJAMIN—Guard—Southern California
1941   New York Giants

SOKOLIS, STANLEY—Tackle—Pennsylvania
1933   Philadelphia Eagles

SOLTAU, GORDON—End—Minnesota
1950–58   San Francisco 49ers
1952, 53   #1 Scoring

SOLTIS, ROBERT—Back—Minnesota
1960   Boston Patriots (AFL)

**SOMERS, GEORGE—Tackle—
    LaSalle (Pa.)**
1939–40   Philadelphia Eagles
1941–42   Pittsburgh Steelers

**SOMMER, MICHAEL—Back—George
    Washington**
1958–59   Washington Redskins
1959–60   Baltimore Colts
1960   Dallas Cowboys

SOMMERS, JOHN—Center—UCLA
1947   Washington Redskins

**SONGIN, EDWARD—Back—
    Boston College**
1960   Boston Patriots (AFL)

**SONNENBERG, GUSTAVE—Guard—
    Dartmouth**
1923   Columbus Tigers
1924   Pottsville Maroons
1925–26   Detroit Panthers
1927–28,30   Providence Steamrollers
        Died at Great Lakes Training Sta-
        tion, Sept. 13, 1944. Chief Specialist,
        U.S. Navy.

SORCE, ROSS—Tackle—Georgetown
1945   Pittsburgh Steelers

SORENSON, GLEN—Guard—Utah
1943–45   Green Bay Packers

**SOREY, JAMES—Guard—
    Texas Southern**
1960   Buffalo Bills (AFL)

**SORTET, WILBUR—End—West
    Virginia**
1933–40   Pittsburgh Steelers

**SOSSAMON, LOUIS—Center—
    South Carolina**
1946–49   New York Yankees (AAFC)

**SOUCHAK, FRANK—End—
    Pittsburgh**
1939   Pittsburgh Steelers

SOUDERS, CECIL—End—Ohio State
1947–49   Detroit Lions

**SPADACCINI, VICTOR—Back—
    Minnesota**
1938–40   Cleveland Rams

SPAGNA, JOSEPH—Center—Lehigh
1921   Buffalo All Americans
1924–25   Frankford Yellowjackets

SPAIN, RICHARD—Guard
1921   Evansville Crimson Giants

**SPANGLER, EUGENE—Back—
    Tulsa**
1946   Detroit Lions

**SPANIEL, FRANK—Back—Notre
    Dame**
1950   Baltimore Colts
1950   Washington Redskins

**SPARKMAN, ALAN—Tackle—Texas
    A & M**
1948–49   Los Angeles Rams

**SPARKS, DAVID—Guard—South
    Carolina**
1951   San Francisco 49ers
1954   Washington Redskins
Died Dec. 5, 1954, after game against
Cleveland.

SPARLIS, ALBERT—Guard—UCLA
1946   Green Bay Packers

SPARR, EDWIN—Tackle—Carroll
1926   Racine Legion

**SPAVITAL, JAMES—Back—
    Oklahoma A & M**
1949   Los Angeles Dons (AAFC)
1950   Baltimore Colts

SPEAR, GLEN—Back—Drake
1926   Kansas City Cowboys

**SPEARS, CLARENCE—Tackle—
    Dartmouth**
1921–22   Canton Bulldogs

**SPECHT, NORMAN "DUTCH"—
    Guard**
1921   Evansville Crimson Giants
1921–23, 25–26   Canton Bulldogs
1924   Akron Steels

SPEEDIE, MAC—End—Utah
1946–49   Cleveland Browns (AAFC)
1950–51   Cleveland Browns

**SPEEGLE, CLIFTON—Center—
    Oklahoma**
1945   Chicago Cardinals

**SPEELMAN, HARRY—Guard—
    Michigan State**
1940   Detroit Lions

SPELLACY—End
1922   Buffalo All Americans

SPELLMAN, JOHN—End—Brown
1925–31   Providence Steamrollers
1929, 32   Boston Braves

**SPENCE, JULIAN—Back—Sam
    Houston**
1956   Chicago Cardinals
1957   San Francisco 49ers
1960   Houston Oilers (AFL)

SPENCER, JAMES—Guard—Dayton
1928–29   Dayton Triangles

**SPENCER, JOSEPH—Tackle—
Oklahoma A & M**
1948   Brooklyn Dodgers (AAFC)
1949   Cleveland Browns (AAFC)
1950–51   Green Bay Packers

SPENCER, OLIVER—Tackle—Kansas
1953, 56, 59–60   Detroit Lions
1957–58   Green Bay Packers

**SPETH, GEORGE—Tackle—Murray
State Teachers**
1942   Detroit Lions

**SPIEGEL, CLARENCE—Tackle—
Notre Dame**
1921–22   Evansville Crimson Giants

**SPIERS, ROBERT—Tackle—Ohio
State**
1922   Akron Steels
1925   Cleveland Indians

SPIKES, JACK—Back—TCU
1960   Dallas Texans (AFL)

ARTHUR SPINNEY

**SPRINGER, HAROLD—End—
Oklahoma Teachers**
1945   New York Giants

**SPRINGSTEEN, WILLIAM—Center—
Lehigh**
1925–26   Frankford Yellowjackets
1927–28   Chicago Cardinals

**SPRINKLE, EDWARD—End—
Hardin-Simmons**
1944–55   Chicago Bears

**SPRINKLE, HUBERT—Tackle—
Carnegie Tech.**
1923–24   Akron Steels
1925   Cleveland Indians

SPRUILL, JAMES—Tackle—Rice
1948–49   Baltimore Colts (AAFC)

SQUYRES, SEAMAN—Back—Rice
1933   Cincinnati Reds

STACCO, EDWARD—Tackle—Colgate
1947   Detroit Lions
1947–48   Washington Redskins

**STACKPOOL, JOHN—Back—
Washington**
1942   Philadelphia Eagles

STACY, JAMES—Tackle—Oklahoma
1935–37   Detroit Lions

**STACY, WILLIAM—Back—
Mississippi State**
1959   Chicago Cardinals
1960   St. Louis Cardinals

**STAFFORD, HARRISON—Back—
Texas**
1934   New York Giants

**STAHLMAN, RICHARD—End—
DePaul**
1924   Hammond Pros

JACK SPIKES

**SPILLERS, RAYMOND—Tackle—
Arkansas**
1937   Philadelphia Eagles

**SPINKS, JACK—Guard—Alcorn
A & M**
1952–53   Pittsburgh Steelers
1953   Chicago Cardinals
1955–56   Green Bay Packers
1956–57   New York Giants

**SPINNEY, ARTHUR—End—Boston
College**
1950, 53–60   Baltimore Colts

SPIRIDA, JOHN—End—St. Anselm's
1939–40   Washington Redskins

**SPONAUGLE, ROBERT—End—
Pennsylvania**
1949   New York Bulldogs

1924   Kenosha
1924–25   Akron Steels
1927, 30   New York Giants
1931–32   Green Bay Packers
1933   Chicago Bears

STALCUP, JERRY—Guard—Wisconsin
1960   Los Angeles Rams

STALLINGS, ALVA DONALD—Tackle—North Carolina
1960   Washington Redskins

STANDLEE, NORMAN—Back—Stanford
1941   Chicago Bears
1946–49   San Francisco 49ers (AAFC)
1950–52   San Francisco 49ers

NORMAN STANDLEE

STANFEL, RICHARD—Guard—San Francisco
1952–55   Detroit Lions
1956–58   Washington Redskins

STANLEY, C. E.—Tackle—Tulsa
1946   Buffalo Bills (AAFC)

STANSAUK, DONALD—Tackle—Denver
1950–51   Green Bay Packers

STANTON, HENRY—End—Arizona
1946–47   New York Yankees (AAFC)

STANTON, WILLIAM—End—North Carolina State
1949   Buffalo Bills (AAFC)

STARK, HARRY—Back—Syracuse
1935   Boston Redskins

STARK, HOWARD—Tackle—Wisconsin
1923   Racine Legion

RICHARD STANFEL

STARR, BRYAN—Back—Alabama
1956–60   Green Bay Packers

BRYAN STARR

STARR, WALLACE—Back—Wisconsin
1926   Racine Legion

STARRET, BENJAMIN—Back—St. Mary's (Cal.)
1941   Pittsburgh Steelers
1941–45   Green Bay Packers

STASICA, LEO—Back—Colorado
1941   Brooklyn Dodgers
1941   Philadelphia Eagles
1943   Washington Redskins
1944   Boston Yanks

STASICA, STANLEY—Back—South Carolina

1946 Miami Seahawks (AAFC)

STATON, JAMES—Tackle—Wake Forest
1951 Washington Redskins

STATUTO, ARTHUR—Center— Notre Dame
1948–49 Buffalo Bills (AAFC)
1950 Los Angeles Rams

STAUTBERG, GERALD—Guard— Cincinnati
1951 Chicago Bears

STAUTNER, ERNEST—Tackle— Boston College
1950–60 Pittsburgh Steelers

STAUTZENBERGER, ODELL— Guard—Texas A & M
1949 Buffalo Bills (AAFC)

STEBER, JOHN—Guard—Georgia Tech.
1946–50 Washington Redskins

STEELE, CLIFFORD—Back— Syracuse
1921–22 Rochester Kodaks
1922 Akron Steels

STEELE, ERNEST—Back— Washington
1942, 44–48 Philadelphia Eagles
1943 Phil-Pitt

STEEN, FRANK—End—Rice
1939 Green Bay Packers

STEEN, JAMES—Tackle—Syracuse
1935–36 Detroit Lions

STEERE, RICHARD—Tackle—Drake
1951 Philadelphia Eagles

STEFFEN, JAMES—Back—UCLA
1959–60 Detroit Lions

STEFIK, ROBERT—End—Niagara
1948 Buffalo Bills (AAFC)

STEGER, PETER—Back
1921 Chicago Cardinals

STEHOWER, RONALD—Tackle— Colorado State
1960 Pittsburgh Steelers

STEIN, HERBERT—Tackle— Washington & Jefferson
1921 Buffalo All Americans
1922 Toledo Maroons
1924 Frankford Yellowjackets
1925–26, 28 Pottsville Maroons
1928–29 Chicago Cardinals

STEIN, RUSSELL—Tackle— Pittsburgh
1922 Toledo Maroons
1924 Frankford Yellowjackets
1925 Pottsville Maroons
1926 Canton Bulldogs

STEIN, SAMUEL—End
1929–30 Staten Island Stapletons
1931 New York Giants
1932 Brooklyn Dodgers

STEIN, WILLIAM—Guard—Fordham
1923–27 Duluth Eskimos

STEINBACH, LAURENCE—Tackle— St. Thomas
1930–31 Chicago Bears
1932 Chicago Cardinals
1933 Philadelphia Eagles

STEINBRUNNER, DONALD—End— Washington State
1953 Cleveland Browns

STEINER, ROY—End—Alabama
1950–51 Green Bay Packers

STEINKE, GILBERT—Back—Texas A & M
1945–48 Philadelphia Eagles

STEINKEMPER, WILLIAM— Tackle—Notre Dame
1942–43 Chicago Bears

STEINMETZ, KENNETH—Back
1944–45 Boston Yanks

STENN, PAUL—Tackle—Villanova
1942 New York Giants
1946 Washington Redskins
1947 Pittsburgh Steelers
1948–51 Chicago Bears

STENNET, FRED—Back—St. Mary's (Cal.)
1931 Portsmouth Spartans
1932 Chicago Cardinals

STEPANOVICH, ANTHONY— Guard—Southern California
1930 Minneapolis Redjackets
1930 Frankford Yellowjackets

STEPANOVICH, MICHAEL—Guard —St. Mary's Cal
1933 Boston Redskins

STEPHEN, THOMAS—Back— Syracuse
1960 Boston Patriots (AFL)

STEPHENS, JOHN—End—Marshall
1938 Cleveland Rams

STEPHENS, LAWRENCE—End— Texas
1960 Cleveland Browns

STEPHENS, LESLIE—Center—Idaho
1927–28   New York Yankees

STEPHENS, LOUIS—Guard—San Francisco
1955–60   Washington Redskins

LOUIS STEPHENS

STEPHENS, WILLIAM—Center—Brown
1926   Brooklyn Dodgers
1926   New York Giants

STEPHENSON, DAVID—Guard—West Virginia
1950   Los Angeles Rams
1951–56   Green Bay Packers

STERNAMAN, EDWARD—Back—Illinois
1921–30   Chicago Bears

STERNAMAN, JOSEPH—Back—Illinois
1922–30   Chicago Bears
1923   Duluth Kellys

STEUBER, ROBERT—Back—Missouri
1942–43   Chicago Bears
1946   Cleveland Browns (AAFC)
1947   Los Angeles Dons (AAFC)
1948   Buffalo Bills (AAFC)

STEVENS, DONALD—Back—Illinois
1952, 54   Philadelphia Eagles

STEVENS, PETER—Center—Temple
1936   Philadelphia Eagles

STEVENS, THEODORE—Center—Brown
1926   Brooklyn Dodgers

STEVENSON, ARTHUR—Guard—Fordham
1928   New York Yankees

STEVENSON, MARTIN—Guard—Notre Dame
1922   Columbus Panhandles

STEVENSON, RALPH—Guard—Oklahoma
1940   Cleveland Rams

STEVERSON, NORRIS—Tackle—Arizona State
1934   Cincinnati Reds

STEWARD, DEAN—Back—Ursinus
1943   Phil-Pitt

STEWART, CHARLES—Tackle—Carnegie Tech.
1943   Phil-Pitt

STEWART, CHARLES—Guard—Colgate
1921–22   Canton Bulldogs
1923   Akron Steels

STEWART, RALPH—Center—Missouri, Notre Dame
1947–48   New York Yankees (AAFC)
1948   Baltimore Colts (AAFC)

STEWART, VAUGHN—Center—Alabama
1942, 44   Brooklyn Dodgers
1943   Chicago Cardinals
1944   Boston Redskins

STICKEL, WALTER—Tackle—Pennsylvania
1946–49   Chicago Bears
1950–51   Philadelphia Eagles

STICKLES, MONTFORD—End—Notre Dame
1960   San Francisco 49ers

STIFLER, JAMES—End—Brown
1926–27   Providence Steamrollers

STILL, JAMES—Back—Georgia Tech.
1948–49   Buffalo Bills (AAFC)

STINCHCOMB, GAYLORD—Back—Ohio State
1921–22   Chicago Bears
1923   Columbus Tigers
1926   Louisville Colonels

STITS, WILLIAM—Back—U.C.L.A.
1954–56   Detroit Lions
1957–58   San Francisco 49ers
1959   Washington Redskins
1959–60   New York Giants

STOBBS, WILLIAM—Back—Washington & Jefferson
1921   Detroit Panthers

STOCK, HERBERT—Back—Kenyon

1924–25 Columbus Tigers

WILLIAM STITS

STOCK, JOHN—End—Pittsburgh
1956 Pittsburgh Steelers

**STOCKTON, HERSCHEL—Guard—
Gonzaga**
1937–38 Philadelphia Eagles

**STOCKTON, HOUSTON—Back—
Gonzaga**
1925–26 Frankford Yellowjackets
1929 Providence Steamrollers
1929 Boston Braves

**STOFER, KENNETH—Back—
Cornell**
1946 Buffalo Bisons (AAFC)

**STOFKO, EDWARD—Back—Wake
Forest**
1945 Pittsburgh Steelers

**STOJACK, FRANK—Guard—
Washington State**
1935–36 Brooklyn Dodgers

STOKES, LEE—Center—Centenary
1937–39 Detroit Lions
1943 Chicago Cardinals

STOLFA, ALTON—Back—Luther
1939 Chicago Bears

**STOLHANDSKE, THOMAS—End—
Texas**
1955 San Francisco 49ers

STONE, AVATUS—Back—Syracuse
1958 Baltimore Colts

STONE, JACK—Tackle—Oregon
1960 Dallas Texans (AFL)

STONE, WILLIAM—Back—Bradley
1949 Baltimore Colts (AAFC)
1950 Baltimore Colts
1951–54 Chicago Bears

**STONEBRAKER, JOHN—End—
Southern California**
1942 Green Bay Packers

**STONESIFER, DONALD—End—
Northwestern**
1951–56 Chicago Cardinals

STORER, JOHN—Back—Lehigh
1924 Frankford Yellowjackets

**STORM, EDWARD—Back—Santa
Clara**
1934–35 Philadelphia Eagles

**STOTSBERG, HAROLD—Tackle—
Xavier**
1930 Brooklyn Dodgers

STOUGH, GLEN—Tackle—Duke
1945 Pittsburgh Steelers

STOUT, PETER—Back—TCU
1949–50 Washington Redskins

**STOVALL, RICHARD—Center—
Abilene Christian**
1947–48 Detroit Lions
1949 Washington Redskins

**STOVER, STEWART—Back—
Louisiana State N.E.**
1960 Dallas Texans

**STRACK, CHARLES—Guard—
Colgate**
1928 Chicago Cardinals

**STRADER, NORMAN—Back—St.
Mary's (Cal.)**
1927 Chicago Cardinals

**STRALKA, CLEMENT—Guard—
Georgetown**
1938–42, 45–46 Washington Redskins

STRAND, LIEF—Center—Fordham
1923–27 Duluth Kelleys

**STRANSKY, ROBERT—Back—
Colorado**
1960 Denver Broncos (AFL)

STRASSER—End
1925 Canton Bulldogs

**STRAUSBAUGH, JAMES—Back—
Ohio State**
1946 Chicago Cardinals

**STRAUSS, ARTHUR—Back—
Phillips**
1923 Toledo Maroons
1924 Kansas City Cowboys

**STRIBLING, MAJURE—End—
Mississippi**
1951–53 New York Giants

1955–57 Philadelphia Eagles

STRICKLAND, BISHOP—Back—South Carolina
1951 San Francisco 49ers

STRICKLAND, DAVIS—Back—Memphis State
1960 Denver Broncos (AFL)

STRICKLAND, LAWRENCE—Center—Texas State North
1954–59 Chicago Bears

STRICKLAND, WILLIAM—Guard—Lombard
1923 Milwaukee Badgers
1923 Racine Legion

STRIEGEL, WILLIAM—Guard—College of Pacific
1959 Philadelphia Eagles
1960 Boston Patriots (AFL)

STRINGER, EUGENE—Back—John Carroll
1925 Cleveland Indians

STRINGER, ROBERT—Back—Tulsa
1952–53 Philadelphia Eagles

STRINGFELLOW, JOSEPH—End—Mississippi Southern
1942 Detroit Lions

STRODE, WOODROW—End—UCLA
1946 Los Angeles Rams

STROHMEYER, GEORGE—Center—Notre Dame
1948 Brooklyn Dodgers (AAFC)
1949 Chicago Hornets (AAFC)

STROM, FRANK—Tackle—Oklahoma Military Academy
1944 Brooklyn Dodgers

STROMIELLO, MICHAEL—End—Colgate
1930–34 Brooklyn Dodgers

STRONG, KENNETH—Back—New York Univ.
1929–32 Staten Island Stapletons
1933–35, 39, 43–47 New York Giants
1933 #1 Scoring (tied by Presnell)
1944 #1 Field Goals

STROSCHEIN, BROCK—End—UCLA
1951 New York Yanks

STROSNIDER, AUBREY—Guard—Dayton
1928 Dayton Triangles

STROSSER, WALTER—Back—St. Vincent
1940 Brooklyn Dodgers

STROUD, JACK—Guard—Tennessee
1953–60 New York Giants

STRUESSI—Tackle
1926 Chicago Cardinals

STRUGAR, GEORGE—Back—Washington
1957–60 Los Angeles Rams

GEORGE STRUGAR

STRUTT, ARTHUR—Back—Duquesne
1935–36 Pittsburgh Pirates

STRZYKALSKI, JOHN—Back—Marquette
1946–49 San Francisco 49ers (AAFC)
1950–52 San Francisco 49ers

STUART, JAMES—Tackle—Oregon
1938, 41–42 Washington Redskins

STUART, ROY—Back—Tulsa
1942 Cleveland Rams
1943 Phil-Pitt
1943 Detroit Lions
1946 Buffalo Bisons (AAFC)

STUCKEY, WILLIAM—Back—Loyola
1926 Louisville Colonels

STUHLDREHER, HARRY—Back—Notre Dame
1926 Brooklyn Dodgers

STURGEON, CECIL—Tackle—North Dakota State
1941 Philadelphia Eagles

STURGEON, LYLE—Tackle—North Dakota State
1937 Green Bay Packers

STURTRIDGE, DONALD—Back—DePaul
1928–29 Chicago Bears

**STYDAHAR, JOSEPH—Tackle—
West Virginia**
1936–42, 45–46   Chicago Bears

**STYNCHULA, ANDREW—Tackle—
Penn State**
1960   Washington Redskins

ANDREW STYNCHULA

SUCHY, PAUL—End
1925   Cleveland Indians

SUCIC, STEPHEN—Back—Illinois
1946   Los Angeles Rams
1947   Boston Yanks
1947–48   Detroit Lions

**SUESS, RAYMOND—Tackle—
Villanova**
1923–27   Duluth Eskimos

**SUFFRIDGE, ROBERT—Guard—
Tennessee**
1941, 45   Philadelphia Eagles

SUGAR, LEO—End—Purdue
1954–59   Chicago Cardinals
1960   St. Louis Cardinals

**SUHEY, STEPHEN—Guard—Penn
State**
1948–49   Pittsburgh Steelers

SULAITIS, JOSEPH—Back
1943–45, 47–51   New York Giants
1946   Boston Yanks

**SULIMA, GEORGE—End—Boston
Univ.**
1952–54   Pittsburgh Steelers

SULLIVAN—Back
1922   Evansville Crimson Giants

**SULLIVAN, FRANK—Center—
Loyola (New Orleans)**
1935–39   Chicago Bears

1940   Pittsburgh Steelers

**SULLIVAN, GEORGE—Back—
Pennsylvania**
1924–25   Frankford Yellowjackets

**SULLIVAN, GEORGE—End—Notre
Dame**
1949   New York Bulldogs

SULLIVAN, JOHN—Back—Rochester
1921   Buffalo Bisons

**SULLIVAN, ROBERT—Back—Holy
Cross, Iowa**
1947   Pittsburgh Steelers
1948   San Francisco 49ers (AAFC)
1948   Brooklyn Dodgers (AAFC)
1948   Chicago Rockets (AAFC)

**SULLIVAN, WALTER—Guard—
Beloit**
1921   Green Bay Packers
1922   Milwaukee Badgers
1923–24   Hammond Pros

**SUMINSKI, DAVID—Tackle—
Wisconsin**
1953   Washington Redskins
1953   Chicago Cardinals

**SUMMERALL, GEORGE—End—
Arkansas**
1952   Detroit Lions
1953–57   Chicago Cardinals
1958–60   New York Giants
1959   #1 Field Goals

**SUMMERHAYS, ROBERT—Back—
Utah**
1949–51   Green Bay Packers

**SUMNER, CHARLES—Back—William
& Mary**
1955, 57–60   Chicago Bears

SUMPTER, ANTHONY—Guard—
1946–48   Chicago Rockets (AAFC)

**SUPULSKI, LEONARD—End—
Dickinson**
1942   Philadelphia Eagles
Killed in plane crash in Nebraska. Lt.,
U.S. Air Force.

**SURABIAN, ZAREH—Tackle—
Williams**
1927   Providence Steamrollers
1929   Boston Braves

**SUSEOFF, NICHOLAS—End—
Washington State**
1946–49   San Francisco 49ers (AAFC)

**SUSTERIC, EDWARD—Back—
Findlay**
1949   Cleveland Browns (AAFC)

SUTCH, GEORGE—Back—Temple
1946   Chicago Cardinals

SUTHERIN, DONALD—Back—Ohio State
1959   New York Giants
1959–60   Pittsburgh Steelers

SUTTON, EDWARD—Back—North Carolina
1957–59   Washington Redskins
1960   New York Giants

EDWARD SUTTON

SUTTON, JOSEPH—Back—Temple
1949   Buffalo Bills (AAFC)
1950–51   Philadelphia Eagles

SVARE, HARLAND—Guard—Washington State
1953–54   Los Angeles Rams
1955–60   New York Giants

SVENDSEN, EARL—Guard—Minnesota
1937–40   Green Bay Packers
1940–43   Brooklyn Dodgers

SVENDSEN, GEORGE—Center—Minnesota
1935–37, 39–41   Green Bay Packers

SVOBODA, WILLIAM—Back—Tulane
1950–53   Chicago Cardinals
1954–58   New York Giants

SWAIN, GLADSTONE—End—Trinity (Tex.)
1926   Buffalo Bisons

SWANSON, EYAR—End—Lombard
1924   Milwaukee Badgers
1925   Rock Island Independents
1925–27   Chicago Cardinals

SWEENEY, JAMES—Tackle—Cincinnati
1944   Chicago Bears

SWEET, FREDERICK—Back—Brown
1925–26   Providence Steamrollers

SWEIGER, ROBERT—Back—Minnesota
1946–48   New York Yankees (AAFC)
1949   Chicago Hornets (AAFC)

SWIACKI, WILLIAM—End—Columbia
1948–50   New York Giants
1951–52   Detroit Lions

SWIADON, PHILIP—Guard—New York Univ.
1943   Brooklyn Dodgers

SWINK, JAMES—Back—TCU
1960   Dallas Texans (AFL)

JAMES SWINK

SWISHER, ROBERT—Back—Northwestern
1938–41, 45   Chicago Bears

SWISTOWICZ, MICHAEL—Back—Notre Dame
1950   New York Yanks
1950   Chicago Cardinals

SWITZER, VERYL—Back—Kansas State
1954–55   Green Bay Packers

SYKES, ROBERT—Back—San Jose State
1952   Washington Redskins

SYLVESTER, JOHN—Back—Temple
1947   New York Yankees (AAFC)
1948   Baltimore Colts (AAFC)

SYMANK, JOHN—Back—Florida
1957–60   Green Bay Packers

JOHN SYMANK

SZAFARYN, LEONARD—Tackle—North Carolina
1949 Washington Redskins
1950, 53–56 Green Bay Packers
1957–58 Philadelphia Eagles

SZAKASH, PAUL—Back—Montana
1938–42 Detroit Lions

SZOT, WALTER—Tackle—Bucknell
1946–48 Chicago Cardinals
1949–50 Pittsburgh Steelers

SZYMANSKI, FRANK—Center—Notre Dame
1945–47 Detroit Lions
1948 Philadelphia Eagles
1949 Chicago Bears

SZYMANSKI, RICHARD—Center—Notre Dame
1955, 57–60 Baltimore Colts

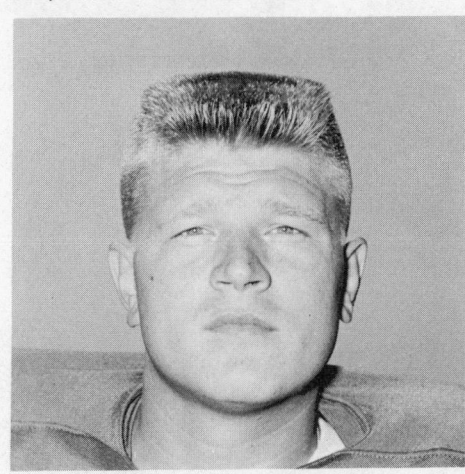

RICHARD SZYMANSKI

* * *

TACKETT, DOYLE—Back
1946–48 Brooklyn Dodgers (AAFC)

TACKWELL, CHARLES—End—Kansas State
1930–31 Frankford Yellowjackets
1931–33 Chicago Bears
1933–34 Cincinnati Reds

TAFT, MERRILL—Back—Wisconsin
1924 Chicago Bears

TAIT, ARTHUR—End—Mississippi State
1951 New York Yanks
1952 Dallas Texans

TALAMINI, ROBERT—Guard—Kentucky
1960 Houston Oilers (AFL)

TALBOT, JOHN—End—Brown
1926 Providence Steamrollers

TALCOTT, DONALD—Tackle—Nevada
1947 Philadelphia Eagles

TALIAFERRO, GEORGE—Back—Indiana
1949 Los Angeles Dons (AAFC)
1950–51 New York Yanks
1952 Dallas Texans
1953–54 Baltimore Colts
1955 Philadelphia Eagles

TALLANT, DAVID—Tackle—Grove City
1922–25 Hammond Pros

TALLY
1921 Evansville Crimson Giants

TAMBURO, SAMUEL—End—Penn State
1949 New York Bulldogs

TANDY, GEORGE—Center—North Carolina
1921 Cleveland Indians

TANGUAY, JAMES—Back—New York Univ.
1933 Pittsburgh Pirates

TANNER, HAMPTON—Tackle—Georgia
1951 San Francisco 49ers
1952 Dallas Texans

TANNER, JOHN—End—Centre
1922 Toledo Maroons
1923–24 Cleveland Indians

TANNER, ROBERT—End—Minnesota
1930 Frankford Yellowjackets
1930 Minneapolis Marines

TARASOVIC, GEORGE—End—LSU
1952–53, 56–60 Pittsburgh Steelers

TARR, JAMES—End—Missouri
1931 Cleveland Indians

TARRANT, JAMES—Back—Howard, Tennessee
1946 Miami Seahawks (AAFC)

TARRANT, ROBERT—End—Kansas State Teachers
1936 New York Giants

TASEFF, CARL—Back—John Carroll
1951 Cleveland Browns
1953–60 Baltimore Colts

CARL TASEFF

TASSOS, DAMON—Guard—Texas A & M
1945–46 Detroit Lions
1947–49 Green Bay Packers

TATUM, JESS—End—North Carolina State
1938 Pittsburgh Pirates

TAUGHER, CLAUDE—Back—Marquette
1922 Green Bay Packers
1924 Milwaukee Badgers

TAVENOR, JOHN—Center—Indiana
1946 Miami Seahawks (AAFC)
1946 Brooklyn Dodgers (AAFC)

TAYLOR, CECIL—Back—Kansas State
1955, 57 Los Angeles Rams

TAYLOR, CHARLES—Guard—Stanford
1946 Miami Seahawks (AAFC)

TAYLOR, CHARLES—Back—Auburn
1944 Brooklyn Dodgers

TAYLOR, ERQUIET—Guard—Auburn
1931 Staten Island Stapletons

TAYLOR, HUGH—End—Oklahoma City Univ.
1947–54 Washington Redskins

TAYLOR, JAMES—Center—Baylor
1956 Pittsburgh Steelers
1957–58 Chicago Cardinals

TAYLOR, JAMES—Back—LSU
1958–60 Green Bay Packers

TAYLOR, JOHN—Tackle—Ohio State
1921 Chicago Bears
1922–23 Canton Bulldogs
1926 Brooklyn Dodgers

TAYLOR, LIONEL—End—Highlands
1959 Chicago Bears
1960 Denver Broncos (AFL)

TAYS, JAMES—Back
1925 Chicago Cardinals
1927 Dayton Triangles
1930 Newark
1930 Staten Island Stapletons

TEBELL, GUSTAVUS—End—Wisconsin
1923–24 Columbus Tigers

TEETER, ALAN—End—Minnesota
1932 Staten Island Stapletons

TEEUWS, LEONARD—Tackle—Tulane
1952–56 Los Angeles
1957 Chicago Cardinals

TEMP, JAMES—End—Wisconsin
1957–60 Green Bay Packers

JAMES TEMP

TEMPLE, MARK—Back—Oregon State

1936 Brooklyn Dodgers
1936 Boston Redskins

TENNANT, JOHN—Back—Wisconsin
1941 Pittsburgh Steelers

**TENNER, ROBERT—End—
Minnesota**
1935 Green Bay Packers

TEPE, LOUIS—Center—Duke
1953–55 Pittsburgh Steelers

TEPO, GEORGE—End—Fordham
1942 New York Giants
1946 Boston Yanks

**TERESA, ANTHONY—Back—San
Jose State**
1958 San Francisco 49ers
1960 Oakland Raiders (AFL)

**TERESHINSKI, JOSEPH—End—
Georgia**
1947–54 Washington Redskins

**TERLEP, GEORGE—Back—Notre
Dame**
1946–48 Buffalo Bills (AAFC)
1948 Cleveland Browns (AAFC)

**TERRELL, MARVIN—Guard—
Mississippi**
1960 Dallas Texans (AFL)

**TERRELL, RAYMOND—Back—
Mississippi**
1946–47 Cleveland Browns (AAFC)
1947 Baltimore Colts (AAFC)

TERSCH, RUDOLPH—Tackle
1922–23 Minneapolis Marines

**TESSER, RAYMOND—End—
Carnegie Tech.**
1933–34 Pittsburgh Pirates

**TETEAK, DARREL—Guard—
Wisconsin**
1952–56 Green Bay Packers

**TEVIS, LEEK—Back—Washington &
Miami**
1947–48 Brooklyn Dodgers (AAFC)

TEW, LOWELL—Back—Alabama
1948–49 New York Yankees (AAFC)

**THACKER, ALVIN—Back—Morris-
Harvey**
1941 Philadelphia Eagles

THARP, THOMAS—Back—Alabama
1960 New York Titans (AFL)

**THAYER, HARRY—Tackle—
Tennessee**
1933 Portsmouth Spartans

THIBAUT, JAMES—Back—Tulane
1946 Buffalo Bisons (AAFC)

THIELE, CARL—End—Denison
1921–23 Dayton Triangles

**THOMAS, ALFRED—Back—
Pennsylvania**
1926 Hartford Blues

THOMAS, CALVIN—Guard—Tulsa
1939–40 Detroit Lions

**THOMAS, CARL—Guard—
Pennsylvania**
1921, 24 Rochester Kodaks
1922 Milwaukee Badgers
1922–23 Buffalo Bisons

**THOMAS, CLENDON—Back—
Oklahoma**
1958–60 Los Angeles Rams

CLENDON THOMAS

**THOMAS, GEORGE—Back—
Oklahoma**
1950–51 Washington Redskins
1952 New York Giants

**THOMAS, JAMES—Guard—
Oklahoma**
1938–39 Chicago Cardinals

**THOMAS, JESSE—Back—Michigan
State**
1955–57 Baltimore Colts
1960 Los Angeles Chargers (AFL)

**THOMAS, JOHN—Back—College of
Pacific**
1958–60 San Francisco 49ers

**THOMAS, RALPH—End—San
Francisco**
1952 Chicago Cardinals
1955 Washington Redskins

THOMAS, REX—Back—St. John's

1926, 30–31 Brooklyn Dodgers
1927 Cleveland Indians
1928 Detroit Wolverines

**THOMAS, RUSSELL—TACKLE—
Ohio State**
1946–49 Detroit Lions

**THOMAS, WILLIAM—Back—Penn
State**
1924 Frankford Yellowjackets
1925–26 Providence Steamrollers

**THOMASON, JAMES—Back—Texas
A & M**
1945 Detroit Lions

**THOMASON, JOHN—Back—Georgia
Tech.**
1930–34 Brooklyn Dodgers
1935–36 Philadelphia Eagles

**THOMASON, ROBERT—Back—
Virginia Military Inst.**
1949 Los Angeles Rams
1951 Green Bay Packers
1952–57 Philadelphia Eagles

ROBERT THOMASON

**THOMPSON, ALVIN—Tackle—
Nebraska**
1925 Kansas City Cowboys

**THOMPSON, CLARENCE—Back—
Minnesota**
1937–38 Pittsburgh Pirates
1939 Green Bay Packers

**THOMPSON, DONALD—Guard—
Redlands**
1926 Los Angeles

THOMPSON, GEORGE—End
1923–25 Rock Island Independents

**THOMPSON, GEORGE—Guard—
Syracuse**

1922 Rochester Kodaks

**THOMPSON, HAROLD—End—
Delaware**
1947–48 Brooklyn Dodgers (AAFC)

**THOMPSON, HARRY—Guard—
UCLA**
1950–54 Los Angeles Rams
1955 Chicago Cardinals

**THOMPSON, JOHN—Tackle—
Lafayette**
1929 Frankford Yellowjackets

**THOMPSON, RUSSELL—Tackle—
Nebraska**
1936–39 Chicago Bears
1940 Philadelphia Eagles

**THOMPSON, THOMAS—Back—
Tulsa**
1940 Pittsburgh Steelers
1940–42, 45–50 Philadelphia Eagles
1948 #1 Passing

**THOMPSON, THOMAS—Center—
William & Mary**
1949 Cleveland Browns (AAFC)
1950–53 Cleveland Browns

**THOMPSON, WILLIAM—Guard—
Washburn**
1924–25 Kansas City Cowboys

**THORNTON, RICHARD—Back—
Missouri Mines**
1933 Philadelphia Eagles

**THORNTON, ROBERT—Guard—
Santa Clara**
1946–47 San Francisco 49ers (AAFC)

THORPE, JACK—Guard
1922–23 Oorang Indians

THORPE, JAMES—Back—Carlisle
1921 Cleveland Indians
1922, 26 Canton Bulldogs
1922–23 Oorang Indians
1923 Toledo Maroons
1924–25 Rock Island Independents
1925 New York Giants

**THORPE, WILFRED—End—
Arkansas**
1940–42 Cleveland Rams

**THROWER, WILLIE—Back—
Michigan State**
1953 Chicago Bears

**THUERK, OWEN—End—St. Joseph
(Ind.)**
1940 Detroit Lions

THURBON, ROBERT—Back—Pittsburgh
1943   Phil-Pitt
1944   Card-Pitt
1946   Buffalo Bisons (AAFC)

THURMAN, JOHN—Tackle—Pennsylvania
1926   Los Angeles

THURSTON, FRED—Guard—Valparaiso
1958   Baltimore Colts
1959–60   Green Bay Packers

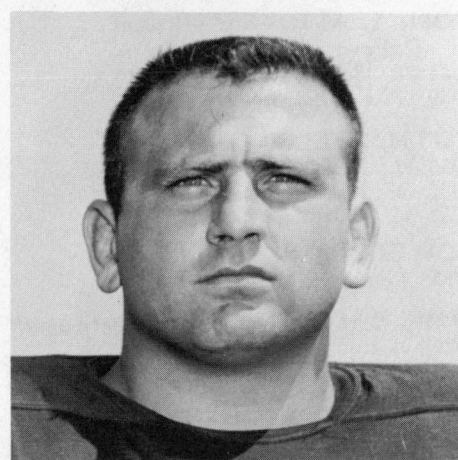

FREDERICK
THURSTON

TIDD, GLENN—Tackle
1921–24   Dayton Triangles

TIDWELL, TRAVIS—Back—Auburn
1950–51   New York Giants

TIDWELL, WILLIAM—Back—Texas A & M
1954   San Francisco 49ers

TIERNEY, FREDERICK—Guard—Minnesota
1922   Hammond Pros
1923–24   Minneapolis Marines
1925   Milwaukee Badgers

TILLER, MORGAN—End—Denver
1941, 45   Pittsburgh Steelers
1944   Boston Yanks

TILLMAN, ALONZO—Center—Oklahoma
1949   Baltimore Colts (AAFC)

TIMBERLAKE, GEORGE—Guard—Southern California
1955   Green Bay Packers

TIMMONS, CHARLES—Back—Clemson
1946   Brooklyn Dodgers (AAFC)

TINSLEY, GAYNELL—End—LSU
1937–38, 40   Chicago Cardinals
1938   #1 Pass Receiving

TINSLEY, JESS—Tackle—LSU
1929–33   Chicago Cardinals

TINSLEY, PETER—Guard—Georgia
1938–45   Green Bay Packers

TINSLEY, ROBERT—Tackle—Baylor
1949   Los Angeles Dons (AAFC)

TINSLEY, SIDNEY—Back—Clemson
1945   Pittsburgh Steelers

TIPTON, HOWARD—Back—Southern California
1933–37   Chicago Cardinals

TITCHENAL, ROBERT—Center—San Jose State
1940–42   Washington Redskins
1946   San Francisco 49ers (AAFC)
1947   Los Angeles Dons (AAFC)

TITMAS, HERBERT—Back—Syracuse
1931   Providence Steamrollers

TITTLE, YELVERTON—Back—LSU
1948–49   Baltimore Colts (AAFC)
1950   Baltimore Colts
1951–60   San Francisco 49ers

TITUS, GEORGE—Center—Holy Cross
1945–46   Pittsburgh Steelers

TITUS, SILAS—End—Holy Cross
1940–42   Brooklyn Dodgers

TOBIN, ELGIE—End—Penn State
1920–21   Akron Steels

TOBIN, GEORGE—Guard—Notre Dame
1947   New York Giants

TOBIN, REX—End—Minnesota
1925   Duluth Eskimos

TODD, RICHARD—Back—Texas A & M
1939–42, 45–48   Washington Redskins

TOFIL, JOSEPH—End—Indiana
1942   Brooklyn Dodgers

TOLAR, CHARLES—Back—Louisiana N.W.
1960   Houston Oilers (AFL)

TOLLEFSON, CHARLES—Guard—Iowa
1944–46   Green Bay Packers

TOLLEY, EDWARD—Guard
1929   Dayton Triangles

TOMAHAWK—Back—Carlisle
1922–23 Oorang Indians

TOMAINI, ARMY—Tackle—Catawba
1945 New York Giants

TOMAINI, JOHN—End—Georgetown
1929 Orange
1930 Newark
1930–32 Brooklyn Dodgers

TOMASETTI, LOUIS—Back—Bucknell
1939–40 Pittsburgh Steelers
1940–42 Philadelphia Eagles
1941 Detroit Lions
1946–49 Buffalo Bills (AAFC)

TOMASIC, ANDREW—Back—Temple
1942, 46 Pittsburgh Steelers

TOMLIN, THOMAS—Guard—Syracuse
1921 Akron Steels
1922 Milwaukee Badgers
1925–26 New York Giants

TOMLINSON, RICHARD—Guard—Kansas
1950–51 Pittsburgh Steelers

TOMMERSON, CLARENCE—Back—Wisconsin
1938 Pittsburgh Pirates

TONEFF, ROBERT—Tackle—Notre Dame
1952, 54–58 San Francisco 49ers
1959–60 Washington Redskins

TONELLI, AMERIGO—Center—Southern California
1939 Detroit Lions

TONELLI, MARIO—Back—Notre Dame
1939 Detroit Lions

TONNEMAKER, CLAYTON—Center—Minnesota
1950, 53–54 Green Bay Packers

TOOGOOD, CHARLES—Tackle—Nebraska
1951–56 Los Angeles Rams
1957 Chicago Cardinals

TOPER, THEODORE—Back—Michigan
1955 Detroit Lions

TOPP, ROBERT—End—Michigan
1954, 56 New York Giants

TORCZON, LAVERNE—End—Nebraska
1960 Buffalo Bills (AFL)

TORGESON, LAVERN—Center—Washington State
1951–54 Detroit Lions
1955–57 Washington Redskins

TORRANCE, JOHN—Tackle—LSU
1939–40 Chicago Bears

TOSCANI, FRANCIS—Back—St. Mary's (Cal.)
1932 Brooklyn Dodgers
1932 Chicago Cardinals

TOSI, FLAVIO—End—Boston College
1934–36 Boston Redskins
1939 Pittsburgh Steelers

TOTH, ZOLLIE—Back—LSU
1950–51 New York Yanks
1952 Dallas Texans
1953–54 Baltimore Colts

TOWELL—Back—Carlisle
1922 Oorang Indians

TOWLE, THURSTON—End—Brown
1929 Boston Braves

TOWLER, DANIEL—Back—Washington & Jefferson
1950–55 Los Angeles Rams
1952 #1 Ball Carrying

TOWNS, ROBERT—Back—Georgia
1960 St. Louis Cardinals

TOWNSEND, OTTO—Guard
1922 Minneapolis Marines

TRACEY, JOHN—End—Texas A&M
1959 Chicago Cardinals
1960 St. Louis Cardinals

TRACY, JOHN THOMAS—Back—Tennessee
1956–57 Detroit Lions
1958–60 Pittsburgh Steelers

TRAFTON, GEORGE—Center—Notre Dame
1921–32 Chicago Bears

TRASK, ORVILLE—Tackle—Rice
1960 Houston Oilers (AFL)

TRAVIS, J. EDWARD—Tackle—Missouri
1921 Rock Island Independents
1923 St. Louis Browns

TRAYNOR, BERNARD—Center—Colgate
1925 Milwaukee Badgers

TRAYNOR, MICHAEL—Back—Canisius

1923–24   Buffalo Bisons

**TREADAWAY, JOHN—Tackle—
Hardin-Simmons**
1947–48   New York Giants
1949   Detroit Lions

**TREBOTICH, IVAN—Back—St.
Mary's (Cal.)**
1944–45   Detroit Lions
1947   Baltimore Colts (AAFC)

**TRESSA, THOMAS—Guard—
Davis-Elkins**
1942   Detroit Lions

TRIGGS, JOHN—Back—Providence
1926   Providence Steamrollers

**TRIGILIO, FRANK—Back—
Alfred & Vermont**
1946   Miami Seahawks (AAFC)
1946   Los Angeles Dons (AAFC)

TRIPLETT, MELVIN—Back—Toledo
1955–60   New York Giants

**TRIPLETT, WALLACE—Back—
Penn State**
1949–50   Detroit Lions
1952–53   Chicago Cardinals

TRIPPI, CHARLES—Back—Georgia
1947–55   Chicago Cardinals

**TRIPSON, JOHN—Tackle—
Mississippi State**
1941   Detroit Lions

**TRIPUCKA, FRANK—Back—Notre
Dame**
1949   Philadelphia Eagles
1949   Detroit Lions
1950–52   Chicago Cardinals
1952   Dallas Texans
1960   Denver Broncos (AFL)

**TROCOLOR, ROBERT—Back—
Alabama**
1942–44   New York Giants
1944   Brooklyn Dodgers

**TROST, MILTON—Tackle—
Marquette**
1935–39   Chicago Bears
1940   Philadelphia Eagles

TRUAX, DALTON—Tackle—Tulane
1960   Oakland Raiders (AFL)

TRYON, EDWARD—Back—Colgate
1927   New York Yankees

**TSOUTSOUVAS, JOHN—Center—
Oregon State**
1940   Detroit Lions

**TSOUTSOUVAS, LOUIS—Center—
Stanford**

1938   Pittsburgh Pirates

**TUBBS, GERALD—Center—
Oklahoma**
1957–58   Chicago Cardinals
1958–59   San Francisco 49ers
1960   Dallas Cowboys

**TUCKEY, RICHARD—Back—
Manhattan**
1938   Washington Redskins
1938   Cleveland Rams

**TULIS, ROBERT—Guard—Texas
A & M**
1948   Detroit Lions

**TULLY, DARRELL—Back—Texas
State Teachers**
1939   Detroit Lions

TULLY, GEORGE—End—Dartmouth
1927   Frankford Yellowjackets

TUNNELL, EMLEN—Back—Iowa
1948–58   New York Giants
1959–60   Green Bay Packers

**TURBERT, FRANCIS—Back—
Morris-Harvey**
1943   New York Giants
1944   Boston Redskins

TURLEY, DOUGLAS—End—Scranton
1944–48   Washington Redskins

**TURLEY, JOHN—Back—Ohio
Wesleyan**
1935–36   Pittsburgh Pirates

**TURNBOW, GUY—Tackle—
Mississippi**
1933–34   Philadelphia Eagles

**TURNER, CLYDE—Center—Hardin-
Simmons**
1940–52   Chicago Bears
1942   #1 Interceptions

**TURNER, HAROLD—End—
Tennessee State**
1954   Detroit Lions

**TURNER, JAMES—Back—North-
western**
1923   Milwaukee Badgers

**TURNER, JAMES—Center—
Oklahoma A & M**
1937   Cleveland Rams

**TURNER, JAY LEWIS—Back—
George Washington**
1938–39   Washington Redskins

**TUTTLE, ORVILLE—Guard—
Oklahoma City Univ.**
1937–41, 46   New York Giants

TUTTLE, RICHARD—End—
Minnesota
1927   Green Bay Packers

TWEDELL, FRANCIS—Guard—
Minnesota
1939   Green Bay Packers

TYLER—End
1926   Chicago Bears

TYLER, PETER—Back—Hardin-
Simmons
1937–38   Chicago Cardinals
1938   New York Giants

TYNES, DAVID—Back—Texas
1924–25   Columbus Tigers

TYREE, JAMES—End—Oklahoma
1948   Boston Yanks
1949   New York Bulldogs

TYRRELL, JOSEPH—Guard—
Temple
1952   Philadelphia Eagles

* * *

UCOVICH, MITCHELL—Tackle—
San Jose State
1944   Washington Redskins
1945   Chicago Cardinals

UGOCCIONI, ENRICO—End—
Kentucky
1944   Brooklyn Dodgers

ULINSKI, EDWARD—Guard—
Marshall
1946–49   Cleveland Browns

ULINSKI, HARRY—Center—
Kentucky
1950–51, 53–56   Washington Redskins

ULLERY, WILLIAM—Back—Penn
State
1922   Dayton Triangles

ULRICH, CHARLES—Tackle—
Illinois
1954–58   Chicago Cardinals

ULRICH, HUBERT—End—Kansas
1946   Miami Seahawks (AAFC)

UMONT, FRANK—Tackle
1943–45   New York Giants

UNDERWOOD, FORREST—Tackle—
Davis & Elkins
1937   Cleveland Rams

UNDERWOOD, JOHN—Guard—
1923   Milwaukee Badgers
1924–27   Duluth Eskimos

UNDERWOOD, RONALD—Back—
Arkansas
1957   Chicago Bears

UNGERER, JOSEPH—Tackle—
Fordham
1944–45   Washington Redskins

UNITAS, JOHN—Back—Louisville
1956–60   Baltimore Colts

JOHN UNITAS

URAM, ANDREW—Back—
Minnesota
1938–43   Green Bay Packers

URBAN, ALEXANDER—End—
Southern Carolina
1941, 44–45   Green Bay Packers

URBAN, GASPER—Guard—Notre
Dame
1948   Chicago Rockets (AAFC)

URBAN, LUKE—End—Boston
College
1921–24   Buffalo Bisons

UREMOVICH, EMIL—Tackle—
Indiana
1940–42, 45–46   Detroit Lions
1948   Chicago Rockets (AAFC)

UREVIG, CLAUDE—Back—North
Dakota
1934–35   Philadelphia Eagles

URSELLA, REUBEN—Back—
Minnesota
1921, 24–25   Rock Island Independents
1926   Akron Steels
1926   Hammond Pros
1929   Minneapolis Redjackets

USHER, EDWARD—Back—
Michigan
1921   Buffalo All Americans

1922 Rock Island Independents
1922, 24 Green Bay Packers
1924–25 Kansas City Cowboys

USHER, LOUIS—Tackle—Syracuse
1921, 23 Chicago Bears
1921 Rochester Kodaks
1923–24 Milwaukee Badgers
1923–24, 26 Hammond Pros
1924 Kenosha

UZDAVINIS, WALTER—End—Fordham
1937 Cleveland Rams

* * *

VACANTI, SAMUEL—Back—Nebraska
1947–48 Chicago Rockets (AAFC)
1948–49 Baltimore Colts (AAFC)

VAINOWSKI, PETER—Guard
1926 Louisville Colonels

VAIRO, DOMINIC—End—Notre Dame
1935 Green Bay Packers

VALDEZ, VERNON—Back
1960 Los Angeles Rams

VERNON VALDEZ

VAN BROCKLIN, NORMAN—Back—Oregon
1949–57 Los Angeles Rams
1958–60 Philadelphia Eagles
1950, 52, 54 #1 Passing
1955, 56 #1 Punting

VAN BUREN, EBERT—Back—LSU
1951–53 Philadelphia Eagles

VAN BUREN, STEPHEN—Back—LSU
1944–52 Philadelphia Eagles
1945, 47, 48, 49 #1 Ball Carrying
1945 #1 Scoring

VANCE, JOSEPH—Back—Southwestern
1931 Brooklyn Dodgers

VANDELLO—Center
1921 Rock Island Independents

VANDEWEGHE, ALFRED—End—William & Mary
1946 Buffalo Bisons (AAFC)

VAN DOREN, ROBERT—End—Southern California
1953 San Francisco 49ers

VAN DYKE, JAMES—Back
1922–23 Louisville Colonels

VAN DYNE, CHARLES—Tackle—Missouri
1925 Buffalo Bisons

VAN EVERY, HAROLD—Back—Minnesota
1940–41 Green Bay Packers

VAN HORNE, CHARLES—Back—Washington & Lee
1927 Buffalo Bisons
1929 Orange

VAN SICKLE, CLYDE—Center—Arkansas
1930 Frankford Yellowjackets
1932–33 Green Bay Packers

VAN TONE, ARTHUR—Back—Mississippi
1943–45 Detroit Lions
1946 Brooklyn Dodgers (AAFC)

VANT, HULL, FREDERICK—Guard—Minnesota
1942 Green Bay Packers
1946 Los Angeles Dons (AAFC)

VANZO, FREDERICK—Back—Northwestern
1938–41 Detroit Lions
1941 Chicago Cardinals

VARDIAN, JOHN—Back
1946 Miami Seahawks (AAFC)
1947–48 Baltimore Colts (AAFC)

VARRICHIONE, FRANK—Tackle—Notre Dame
1955–60 Pittsburgh Steelers

VASICEK, VICTOR—Guard—Texas
1949 Buffalo Bills (AAFC)
1950 Los Angeles Rams

VASSAU, ROY—Tackle—St. Thomas
1923 Milwaukee Badgers

VAUGHN, CHARLES—Back—Tennessee

1935–36   Detroit Lions

VAUGHN, John—Back—Bellfont
1933–35   Pittsburgh Pirates
1936   Chicago Cardinals

VAUGHN, WILLIAM—Back—SMU
1926   Buffalo Bisons

VAUGHT, THOMAS—End—TCU
1955   San Francisco 49ers

VEDDER, NORTON—Back
1927   Buffalo Bisons

VENUTO, SAMUEL—Back—Guilford
1952   Washington Redskins

VENTURELLI, FRED—Tackle
1948   Chicago Bears

VEREB, EDWARD—Back—Maryland
1960   Washington Redskins

VEREEN, CARL—Tackle—Georgia Tech
1957   Green Bay Packers

VERGARA, GEORGE—End—Notre Dame
1925   Green Bay Packers

VERRY, NORMAN—Tackle—Southern California
1946–47   Chicago Rockets (AAFC)

VESSELS, WILLIAM—Back—Oklahoma
1956   Baltimore Colts

VESSER, JOHN—End—Idaho
1927, 30–31   Chicago Cardinals

VETRANO, JOSEPH—Back—Mississippi Southern
1946–49   San Francisco 49ers (AAFC)

VETTER, JOHN—Back—McPherson
1942   Brooklyn Dodgers

VEXALL, ROY—Back
1923–25   Duluth Kelleys

VEZMAR, WALTER—Guard—Michigan State
1946–47   Detroit Lions

VICK, HENRY "ERNIE"—Back—Michigan
1924   Kenosha
1925, 28   Detroit Panthers
1925, 27–28   Chicago Bears

VICK, RICHARD—Back—Washington & Jefferson
1925–26   Detroit Panthers
1926   Canton Bulldogs

VIDONI, VICTOR—End—Duquesne
1935–36   Pittsburgh Pirates

VILLANUEVA, DANIEL—Kicker—New Mexico State
1960   Los Angeles Rams

DANIEL VILLANEUVA

VINCE, RALPH—Guard—Washington & Jefferson
1923–25   Cleveland Indians

VINNOLA, PAUL—Back—Santa Clara
1946   Los Angeles Dons (AAFC)

VISNIC, LAWRENCE—Guard—St. Benedict's (Kansas)
1943–45   New York Giants

VODICKA, JOSEPH—Back
1943–45   Chicago Bears
1945   Chicago Cardinals

VOGDS, EVAN—Guard—Wisconsin
1946–47   Chicago Rockets (AAFC)
1948–49   Green Bay Packers

VOGELAAR, CARROLL—Tackle—San Francisco
1947–48   Boston Yanks
1949   New York Bulldogs
1950   New York Yanks

VOGT, ALOIS—Back—Marquette
1946   Buffalo Bisons (AAFC)

VOIGHT—Guard
1921   Chicago Cardinals

VOKATY, OTTO—Back—Heidelberg
1931   Cleveland Indians
1932   New York Giants
1933   Chicago Cardinals
1934   Cincinnati Reds

VOLOK, WILLIAM—Guard—Tulsa
1934–39   Chicago Cardinals

VOLZ, PETER—End
1921   Cincinnati Celts

VOLZ, WILBUR—Back—Missouri

1949 Buffalo Bills (AAFC)

**VOSBERG, DONALD—End—
Marquette**
1940–41 New York Giants

VOSS, WALTER—End—Detroit
1921, 25 Detroit Panthers
1921, 29 Buffalo All Americans
1922 Rock Island Independents
1922–24 Dayton Triangles
1923 Toledo Maroons
1924 Green Bay Packers
1926 New York Giants
1927–28 Chicago Bears

VOYTEK, EDWARD—Guard—Purdue
1957–58 Washington Redskins

**VUCINICH, MILTON—Center—
Stanford**
1945 Chicago Bears

* * *

**WADE, JAMES—Back—Oklahoma
City Univ.**
1949 New York Bulldogs

WADE, WILLIAM—Back—Vanderbilt
1954–60 Los Angeles Rams

WILLIAM WADE

**WAGER, CLINTON—End—St.
Mary's (Minn.)**
1941–42 Chicago Bears
1943, 45 Chicago Cardinals
1944 Card-Pitt

WAGER, JOHN—Center—Carthage
1930 Newark
1931–33 Portsmouth Spartans

**WAGNER, BUFFTON—Back—
Northern Michigan**
1921 Green Bay Packers

**WAGNER, LOWELL—Back—
Southern California**

1946–48 New York Yankees (AAFC)
1949–51 San Francisco 49ers

**WAGNER, RAYMOND—End—
Columbia**
1931 Brooklyn Dodgers

**WAGNER, SIDNEY—Guard—
Michigan State**
1936–38 Detroit Lions

**WAGSTAFF, JAMES—Back—
Idaho State**
1959 Chicago Cardinals
1960 Buffalo Bills (AFL)

WAITE, CARL—End—Georgetown
1928 Frankford Yellowjackets
1929 Orange
1930 Newark

WAITE, WILLARD—Guard
1921 Columbus Panhandles

**WALBRIDGE, LYMAN—Center—
Fordham**
1925 New York Giants

**WALDRON, AUSTIN—Guard—
Gonzaga**
1927 Chicago Cardinals

**WALDSMITH, RALPH—Guard—
Akron**
1921 Cleveland Indians
1922 Canton Bulldogs

**WALKER, EWELL DOAK—Back—
SMU**
1950–55 Detroit Lions
1950, 55 #1 Scoring

WALKER, PAUL—End—Yale
1948 New York Giants

WALKER, VAL JOE—Back—SMU
1953–56 Green Bay Packers
1957 San Francisco 49ers

WALKER, WAYNE—Center—Idaho
1958–60 Detroit Lions

**WALKER, WILLIAM—Guard—
Virginia Military Inst.**
1945 Boston Yanks

**WALL, EDWARD—Back—Grove
City**
1930 Frankford Yellowjackets

**WALLACE, BEVERLY—Back
Compton Jr.**
1947–49 San Francisco 49ers (AAFC)
1951 New York Yanks

WALLACE, FRED—Guard—Akron
1923–24, 26 Akron Steels
1925 Cleveland Indians
1926 Canton Bulldogs

WALLACE, HENRY—Back—
College of Pacific
1960 Los Angeles Chargers (AFL)

WALLACE, JOSEPH—End—Notre
Dame
1928 Chicago Bears
1929 Dayton Triangles

WALLACE, STANLEY—Back—Illinois
1954, 56–58 Chicago Bears

WALLER, RONALD—Back—
Maryland
1955–58 Los Angeles Rams
1960 Los Angeles Chargers (AFL)

WALLER, WILLIAM—End—
Illinois
1938 Brooklyn Dodgers

WALLNER, FREDERICK—Guard—
Notre Dame
1951–52, 54–55 Chicago Cardinals
1960 Houston Oilers (AFL)

WALLS, WILLIAM—End—TCU
1938–43 New York Giants

WALQUIST, LAURIE—Back—
Illinois
1922–31 Chicago Bears

WALSH, WILLIAM—Center—
Notre Dame
1949–54 Pittsburgh Steelers

WALSTON, ROBERT—End—
Georgia
1951–60 Philadelphia Eagles
1954 #1 Scoring

WALTERS, LESTER—End—Penn.
State
1958 Washington Redskins

WALTERS—Back
1924 Kenosha

WALTON, FRANK—Guard—
Pittsburgh
1934 Boston Redskins
1944–45 Washington Redskins

WALTON, JOSEPH—End—Pittsburgh
1957–60 Washington Redskins

WANDLESS, GEORGE—Back
1922 Louisville Colonels

WARD, DAVID—Tackle—
New Mexico
1933 Boston Redskins

WARD, ELMER—Center—Utah
1935–36 Detroit Lions

JOSEPH WALTON

WARD, GILBERT—Tackle—Notre
Dame
1921 Buffalo All Americans
1923 Dayton Triangles

WARD, JOHN—Tackle—Southern
California
1930 Frankford Yellowjackets
1930 Minneapolis Redjackets

WARD, WILLIAM—Guard—
Washington State
1946–47 Washington Redskins
1947–49 Detroit Lions

WARDLOW, DUANE—End—
Washington
1954–56 Los Angeles Rams

WARNER, ROBERT—Back—
Wisconsin
1927 Duluth Eskimos

WARREN, BUSIT—Back—Tennessee
1945 Philadelphia Eagles
1945 Pittsburgh Steelers

WARREN, MORRISON—Back—
Arizona State
1948 Brooklyn Dodgers (AAFC)

WARRINGTON, CALEB—Center—
William & Mary, Ala. Polytech.
1946–48 Brooklyn Dodgers (AAFC)

WARWEG
1921 Evansville Crimson Giants

WARZEKA, RONALD—Tackle—
Montana State
1960 Oakland Raiders (AFL)

WASHINGTON, CLYDE—Back—
Purdue
1960 Boston Patriots (AFL)

**WASHINGTON, KENNETH—Back—
UCLA**
1946–48 Los Angeles Rams

KENNETH
WASHINGTON

**WASSERBACH, LLOYD—Tackle—
Wisconsin**
1946–47 Chicago Rockets (AAFC)

**WATERFIELD, ROBERT—Back—
UCLA**
1945 Cleveland Rams
1946–52 Los Angeles Rams
1946, 51 #1 Passing
1949 #1 Field Goals (tied by Patton)

WATERS, DALE—End—Florida
1931 Cleveland Indians
1932–33 Boston Redskins

**WATERS, ROBERT—Back—
Presbyterian**
1960 San Francisco 49ers

**WATFORD, GERALD—End—
Alabama**
1953–54 Chicago Cardinals

**WATKINS, FORREST—Back—West
Texas State**
1940–41 Philadelphia Eagles

**WATKINS, GORDON—Tackle—
Georgia Tech.**
1930 Minneapolis Marines
1930 Frankford Yellowjackets
1931 Brooklyn Dodgers

**WATKINS, ROBERT—Back—
Ohio State**
1955–57 Chicago Bears
1958 Chicago Cardinals

WATSON, GRADY—Back—Texas
1922–23 Toledo Maroons

1924 Kenosha
1924–25 Hammond Pros
1927 Buffalo Bisons

**WATSON, JAMES—Center—College
of Pacific**
1945 Washington Redskins

WATSON, JOSEPH—Center—Rice
1950 Detroit Lions

**WATSON, SIDNEY—Back—
Northeastern**
1955–57 Pittsburgh Steelers
1958 Washington Redskins

WATT, JOSEPH—Back—Syracuse
1947 Boston Yanks
1947–48 Detroit Lions
1949 New York Bulldogs

**WATT, WALTER—Back—Miami
(Fla.)**
1945 Chicago Cardinals

**WATTERS, LEONARD—End—
Springfield**
1924 Buffalo Bisons

**WATTS, GEORGE—Tackle—
Appalachian State**
1942 Washington Redskins

WAY, CHARLES—Back—Penn State
1921 Canton Bulldogs
1924 Frankford Yellowjackets

**WEAR, ROBERT—Center—Penn
State**
1942 Philadelphia Eagles
1944 Brooklyn Dodgers

**WEATHERALL, JAMES—Tackle—
Oklahoma**
1955–57 Philadelphia Eagles
1958 Washington Redskins
1959–60 Detroit Lions

**WEATHERLEY, GERALD—Center—
Rice**
1950, 52–54 Chicago Bears

WEATHERS, GUY—Guard—Baylor
1926 Buffalo Bisons

**WEAVER, CHARLES—Guard—
Chicago**
1930 Chicago Cardinals
1930 Portsmouth Spartans

WEAVER, JAMES—Center—Centre
1923 Columbus Tigers

**WEAVER, JOHN—Guard—Miami
(Ohio)**
1949 New York Bulldogs

**WEAVER, LARRYE—Back—
Fullerton Jr.**

1955 New York Giants

WEBB, GEORGE—End—Texas Tech.
1943 Brooklyn Dodgers

WEBB, KENNETH—Back—
Presbyterian
1958–60 Detroit Lions

WEBB—Tackle
1922 Milwaukee Badgers

WEBER, CHARLES—Guard—
Westchester
1955–56 Cleveland Browns
1956–58 Chicago Cardinals
1959–60 Philadelphia Eagles

WEBER, ELMER—Back—Nebraska
1927 Cleveland Bulldogs

WEBBER, CHARLES—Guard—
Colgate
1926 Brooklyn Dodgers

WEBBER, HARRY—End—Nebraska
1923 Rock Island Independents

WEBBER, HOWARD—End—Kansas
State
1924–25 Kansas City Cowboys
1926 Hartford Blues
1926 New York Giants
1927 Cleveland Indians
1928 Green Bay Packers
1930 Providence Steamrollers
1930 Newark

WEBBER, RICHARD—Back—St.
Louis Univ.
1945 Detroit Lions

WEBSTER, ALEX—Back—North
Carolina
1955–60 New York Giants

ALEX WEBSTER

WEBSTER, DAVID—Back—
Prairie View
1960 Dallas Texans (AFL)

WEBSTER, FREDERICK—Back—
Colgate
1924 Racine Legion

WEDEL, RICHARD—Guard—Wake
Forest
1948 Chicago Cardinals

WEDEMEYER, HERMAN—Back—St.
Mary's (Cal.)
1948 Los Angeles Dons (AAFC)
1949 Baltimore Colts (AAFC)

WEED, THURLOW—Back—Ohio
State
1955 Pittsburgh Steelers

WEEDON, DONALD—Guard—Texas
1947 Philadelphia Eagles

WEEKS, GEORGE—End—Alabama
1944 Brooklyn Dodgers

WEGERT, THEODORE—Back
1955–56 Philadelphia Eagles
1960 New York Titans (AFL)
1960 Denver Broncos (AFL)

WEHBA, RAYMOND—End—
Southern California
1943 Brooklyn Dodgers
1944 Green Bay Packers

WEIMER, CHARLES—Back—
Wilmington
1929 Buffalo Bisons
1930 Brooklyn Dodgers
1931 Cleveland Indians

WEINBERG, HENRY—Guard—
Duquesne
1934 Pittsburgh Pirates

WEINBERG, SAUL—Tackle
1923 Cleveland Indians

WEINER, ALBERT—Back—
Muhlenberg
1934 Philadelphia Eagles

WEINER, ARTHUR—End—North
Carolina
1950 New York Yanks

WEINER, BERNARD—Tackle—
Kansas State
1942 Brooklyn Dodgers

WEINMEISTER, ARNOLD—
Tackle—Washington
1948–49 New York Yankees (AAFC)
1950–53 New York Giants

WEINSTOCK, ISADORE—Back—
Pittsburgh

1935 Philadelphia Eagles
1937–38 Pittsburgh Pirates

WEIR, EDWARD—Tackle—Nebraska
1926–28 Frankford Yellowjackets

WEIR, JOSEPH—Guard—Nebraska
1927 Frankford Yellowjackets

WEISENBAUGH, HENRY—Back—Pittsburgh
1935 Pittsburgh Steelers
1935–36 Boston Redskins

WEISGERBER, RICHARD—Back—Willamette
1938 Cleveland Rams
1938–40, 42 Green Bay Packers

WEISS, HOWARD—Back—Wisconsin
1939–40 Detroit Lions

WEISS, JOHN—End
1944–47 New York Giants

WELCH, GILBERT—Back—Pittsburgh
1928 New York Yankees
1929 Providence Steamrollers

WELCH, JAMES—Back—SMU
1960 Baltimore Colts

WELDIN, HAROLD—Center—Northwestern
1934 St. Louis Gunners

WELDON, JOHN—Back—Lafayette
1921–22 Buffalo Bisons

WELDON, LAWRENCE—Back—Presbyterian
1944–45 Washington Redskins

WELLER, LOUIS—Back—Haskell
1933 Boston Redskins

WELLER, RAYMOND—Tackle—Nebraska
1923 St. Louis Browns
1924 Milwaukee Badgers
1926–27 Chicago Cardinals
1928 Frankford Yellowjackets

WELLS, DONALD—End—Georgia
1946–49 Green Bay Packers

WELLS, WILLIAM—Back—Michigan State
1954, 56–57 Washington Redskins
1957 Pittsburgh Steelers
1958 Philadelphia Eagles
1960 Boston Patriots (AFL)

WELMUS, WOODCHUCK—End—Carlisle
1922–23 Oorang Indians

WELSH, JAMES—Guard—Colgate

1924–25 Frankford Yellowjackets
1925–27 Pottsville Maroons

WELTMAN, LAWRENCE—Back—Syracuse
1922 Rochester Jeffersons

WEMPLE, DONALD—End—Colgate
1941 Brooklyn Dodgers
Killed piloting Army transport in India.
Lt., U.S. Air Force.

WENDELL, MARTIN—Guard—Notre Dame
1949 Chicago Hornets (AAFC)

WENDLER, HAROLD—Back—Ohio State
1926 Akron Steels
1926 Hammond Pros

WENDLICK, JOSEPH—End—Oregon State
1940 Philadelphia Eagles
1941 Pittsburgh Steelers

WENIG, OBE—End—Morningside
1921–22 Rock Island Independents

WENKE, ADOLPH—Tackle—Nebraska
1923 Milwaukee Badgers

WENTWORTH, SHIRLEY—Back—New Hampshire
1925–26 Providence Steamrollers
1929 Boston Braves

WENTZ, BYRON—Back—Penn State
1925–28 Pottsville Maroons
1929 Boston Braves
1930–31 Providence Steamrollers

WENZEL, RALPH—End—Tulane
1941 Pittsburgh Steelers

WERDER, RICHARD—Guard—Georgetown
1948 New York Yankees (AAFC)

WERNER, SOX—Back—Missouri State
1923 St. Louis Brown

WERWAISS, ELBERT—Tackle—Dean Jr.
1926 Hartford Blues

WESLEY, LECIL—Center—Alabama
1926–27 Providence Steamrollers
1928 New York Giants
1930 Portsmouth Spartans

WEST, DAVID—Tackle—Colgate
1921 Canton Bulldogs

WEST, HODGES—Tackle—Tennessee
1941 Philadelphia Eagles

WEST, PAT—Back—Southern California
1944–45   Cleveland Rams
1946–48   Los Angeles Rams
1948   Green Bay Packers

WEST, STANLEY—Guard—Oklahoma
1950–54   Los Angeles Rams
1955   New York Giants
1956   Chicago Cardinals

WEST, WILLIE—Back—Oregon
1960   St. Louis Cardinals

WESTFALL, EDGAR—Back—Ohio Wesleyan
1932–33   Pittsburgh Pirates
1933   Boston Redskins

WESTFALL, ROBERT—Back—Michigan
1944–47   Detroit Lions

WESTOPHAL, JOSEPH—Center—Nebraska
1926   Kansas City Cowboys
1928   Detroit Wolverines
1929–30   New York Giants

WETOSKA, ROBERT—Tackle—Notre Dame
1960   Chicago Bears

WETTERLUND, CHESTER—Back—Illinois Wesleyan
1942   Chicago Cardinals
Killed flying Navy Hellcat on night patrol off New Jersey coast, Sept. 5, 1944. Lt., U.S. Navy.

WETZ, HARLAN—Tackle—Texas
1947   Brooklyn Dodgers (AAFC)

WETZEL, DAMON—Back—Ohio State
1935   Chicago Bears
1935   Pittsburgh Pirates

WHALEN, GERALD—Center—Canisius
1948   Buffalo Bills (AAFC)

WHALEN, THOMAS—Back—Catholic Univ.
1933   Pittsburgh Pirates

WHALEN, WILLIAM—Guard
1921–24   Chicago Cardinals

WHALEY, BENJAMIN—Guard—Virginia State
1949   Los Angeles Dons (AAFC)

WHAM, THOMAS—End—Furman
1949–51   Chicago Cardinals

WHARTON, HOGAN—Guard—Houston
1960   Houston Oilers (AFL)

WHATELY, JAMES—End—Alabama
1936–38   Brooklyn Dodgers

WHEELER, ERNEST—Back—North Dakota State
1939   Pittsburgh Steelers
1939, 42   Chicago Cardinals

WHEELER, LYLE—End—Ripon
1921–23   Green Bay Packers

WHELAN, THOMAS—Center—Georgetown
1921   Cleveland Indians

WHIRE, JOHN—Back—Alabama
1933   Philadelphia Eagles

WHITE, ARTHUR—Guard—Alabama
1937–39, 45   New York Giants
1940–41   Chicago Cardinals

WHITE, BYRON—Back—Minnesota
1926   Los Angeles

WHITE, BYRON—Back—Colorado
1938   Pittsburgh Pirates
1940–41   Detroit Lions
1938, 40   #1 Ball Carrying

WHITE, EUGENE—Guard—Indiana
1946   Buffalo Bisons (AAFC)

WHITE, EUGENE—Back—Georgia
1954   Green Bay Packers

WHITE, HARVEY—Back—Clemson
1960   Boston Patriots (AFL)

WHITE, JAMES—Tackle—Notre Dame
1945–50   New York Giants

WHITE, JOHN—End—Texas Southern
1960   Houston Oilers (AFL)

WHITE, PAUL—Back—Michigan
1947   Pittsburgh Steelers

WHITE, PHILIP—End—Oklahoma
1924–25   Kansas City Cowboys
1925–27   New York Giants
1928   New York Yankees

WHITE, ROBERT—End
1923   Louisville Colonels

WHITE, ROBERT—Back—Stanford
1951–52   San Francisco 49ers
1955   Cleveland Browns
1955   Baltimore Colts

WHITE, ROBERT—Back—Ohio State
1960   Houston Oilers (AFL)

WHITE, ROY—Back—Northwestern
1924–25, 27–29   Chicago Bears

WHITE, THOMAS "ALLIE"—
Tackle—TCU
1939　Philadelphia Eagles

WHITE, WILBUR—Back—Colorado
State
1935　Brooklyn Dodgers
1936　Detroit Lions

WHITE, WILBUR—End—Marietta
1922-23　Toledo Maroons

WHITE, WILFORD—Back—
Arizona State
1951-52　Chicago Bears

WHITED, MARVIN—Back—
Oklahoma
1942, 45　Washington Redskins

WHITEHEAD
1921　Evansville Crimson Giants

WHITLEY, HALL—Back—Texas A&I
1960　New York Titans (AFL)

WHITLOW, KENNETH—Center—
Rice
1946　Miami Seahawks (AAFC)

WHITLOW, ROBERT—Center—
Arizona
1960　Washington Redskins

WHITMAN, S. J. LAVERNE—Back—
Tulsa
1951　Chicago Cardinals

WHITSELL, DAVID—Back—Indiana
1958-60　Detroit Lions

WHITTENTON, JESSE—Back—
Texas Western
1956-57　Los Angeles
1958　Chicago Bears
1958-60　Green Bay Packers

WIATRAK, JOHN—Center—
Washington
1939　Philadelphia Eagles
1939　Detroit Lions

WIBERG, OSCAR—Back—Nebraska
Wesleyan
1927　Cleveland Indians
1928　Detroit Panthers
1930　New York Giants
1932　Brooklyn Dodgers
1933　Cincinnati Reds

WICKETT, LLOYD—Tackle—Oregon
State
1943, 46　Detroit Lions

WIDSETH, EDWIN—Tackle—
Minnesota
1937-40　New York Giants

WIEDERQUIST, CHESTER—
Tackle—Washington & Jefferson
1923-24　Milwaukee Badgers
1925　Rock Island Independents
1928　Chicago Cardinals
1928　Detroit Lions
1929　Minneapolis Redjackets

WIEDICH, RALPH—Tackle—
Kansas State Teachers
1924　Kansas City Cowboys
1926　Rock Island Independents

WIEHL, JOSEPH—Tackle—
Duquesne
1935　Pittsburgh Pirates

WIESE, ROBERT—Back—Michigan
1947-48　Detroit Lions

WIETECHA, RAYMOND—Center—
Northwestern
1953-60　New York Giants

WIETHE, JOHN—Guard—Xavier
(Cincinnati)
1939-42　Detroit Lions

WIGGIN, PAUL—End—Stanford
1957-60　Cleveland Browns

WIGGS, HUBERT—Back—
Vanderbilt
1922-23　Louisville Colonels

WIGHTKIN, WILLIAM—End—
Notre Dame
1950-57　Chicago Bears

WILCOX, EDWARD—Back—Swarth-
more
1926-27　Frankford Yellowjackets
1930　Staten Island Stapletons

WILCOX, JOHN—Tackle—Oklahoma
1926　Buffalo Bisons

WILCOX, JOHN—Tackle—Oregon
1960　Philadelphia Eagles

WILDE, GEORGE—Back—
Texas A & M
1947　Washington Redskins

WILDER, HAROLD—Guard—
Nebraska
1923　St. Louis Browns

WILDUNG, RICHARD—Guard—
Minnesota
1946-51, 53　Green Bay Packers

WILEY, JOHN—Tackle—Waynesburg
1946-50　Pittsburgh Steelers

WILGING, COLEMAN—Tackle—
Xavier
1934　Cincinnati Reds

WILKERSON, BASIL—End—
Oklahoma City Univ.
1932　Staten Island Stapletons
1932　Boston Braves

1934 Cincinnati Reds

RICHARD WILDUNG

A. W. WILLIAMS

**WILKIN, WILBUR—Tackle—
St. Mary's (Cal.)**
1938–43 Washington Redskins
1946 Chicago Rockets (AAFC)

WILKINS, RICHARD—End—Oregon
1949 Los Angeles Dons (AAFC)
1952 Dallas Texans
1954 New York Giants

WILKINS, ROY—End—Georgia
1958–59 Los Angeles Rams
1960 Washington Redskins

**WILKINS, THEODORE—End—
Indiana**
1925 Green Bay Packers

**WILKINSON, ROBERT—End—
UCLA**
1951–52 New York Giants

**WILKINSON, WILLIAM—End—
Bucknell**
1936 Boston Redskins

**WILLEGALLE, HENRY—Back—
Carleton**
1929 Minneapolis Redjackets

WILLERT—Guard
1922 Hammond Pros

WILLEY, NORMAN—End—Marshall
1950–57 Philadelphia Eagles

**WILLIAMS, A. W.—Back—
College of Pacific**
1959 Green Bay Packers
1960 Cleveland Browns

**WILLIAMS, ARTHUR—Back—
Connecticut State**
1928–31 Providence Steamrollers

WILLIAMS, BOYD—Center—Syracuse
1947 Philadelphia Eagles

**WILLIAMS, BROUGHTON—End—
Florida**
1947 Chicago Bears

**WILLIAMS, BURTON "CY"—
Guard—Florida**
1929–30 Staten Island Stapletons
1931 Brooklyn Dodgers

**WILLIAMS, DANIEL—Guard—
Minnesota State Teachers**
1923–27 Duluth Eskimos

**WILLIAMS, DONALD—Guard—
Texas**
1941 Pittsburgh Steelers

**WILLIAMS, ELLERY—End—Santa
Clara**
1950 New York Giants

**WILLIAMS, FRANK—Back—Utah
State**
1948 New York Giants

**WILLIAMS, FRED—Tackle—
Arkansas**
1952–60 Chicago Bears

**WILLIAMS, GARLAND—Tackle—
Georgia**
1947–48 Brooklyn Dodgers (AAFC)
1949 Chicago Rockets (AAFC)

**WILLIAMS, IVAN—Back—
Georgia Tech**
1929 Staten Island Stapletons

WILLIAMS, JACOB—Tackle—TCU
1929–33 Chicago Cardinals

**WILLIAMS, JAY "INKY"—End—
Brown**

1921–26 Hammond Pros
1924 Kenosha
1925 Cleveland Indians

**WILLIAMS, JEROME—Back—
Washington State**
1949–52 Los Angeles Rams
1953–54 Philadelphia Eagles

JEROME WILLIAMS

WILLIAMS, JOEL—Center—Texas
1948 San Francisco 49ers (AAFC)
1950 Baltimore Colts

**WILLIAMS, JOHN—Center—
Auburn**
1942 Philadelphia Eagles
1946 Miami Seahawks (AAFC)

**WILLIAMS, JOHN—Back—Southern
California**
1952–53 Washington Redskins
1954 San Francisco 49ers

**WILLIAMS, JOSEPH—Guard—
Lafayette**
1923 Canton Bulldogs
1925–26 New York Giants

**WILLIAMS, JOSEPH—Back—
Ohio State**
1939 Pittsburgh Steelers

**WILLIAMS, REX—Center—Texas
Tech.**
1945 Detroit Lions

**WILLIAMS, ROBERT—Back—Notre
Dame**
1951–52, 55 Chicago Bears

**WILLIAMS, ROLLAND—Back—
Wisconsin**
1921 Green Bay
1923 Minneapolis Marines
1923 Racine Legion

**WILLIAMS, SAMUEL—End—
Michigan State**
1959 Los Angeles Rams
1960 Detroit Lions

WILLIAMS, STANLEY—End—Baylor
1952 Dallas Texans

**WILLIAMS, THEODORE—Back—
Boston College**
1942 Philadelphia Eagles
1942 Washington Redskins
1944 Boston Yanks

WILLIAMS, TRAVIS—Back
1921 Evansville Crimson Giants

**WILLIAMS, WALTER—Back—
Boston Univ.**
1946 Chicago Rockets (AAFC)
1947 Boston Yanks

WILLIAMS, WINDELL—End—Rice
1948–49 Baltimore Colts (AAFC)

**WILLIAMSON, ERNEST—Tackle—
North Carolina**
1947 Washington Redskins
1948 New York Giants
1949 Los Angeles Dons (AAFC)

**WILLIAMSON, FREDERICK—
End—Northwestern**
1960 Pittsburgh Steelers

**WILLIAMSON, IVAN—Tackle—
Michigan**
1932 Chicago Cardinals

**WILLIS, WILLIAM—Guard—Ohio
State**
1946–49 Cleveland Browns (AAFC)
1950–53 Cleveland Browns

**WILLSON, JOSEPH—Guard—
Pennsylvania**
1926–27 Buffalo Bisons

**WILLSON, OSBORNE—Guard—
Pennsylvania**
1933–35 Philadelphia Eagles

**WILSBACH, FRANK—Guard—
Bucknell**
1925 Frankford Yellowjackets

**WILSON, ABRAHAM—Guard—
George Washington**
1927–29 Providence Steamrollers

WILSON, CAMP—Back—Tulsa
1946–49 Detroit Lions

WILSON, ENID—Back—Penn State
1926 Hartford Blues

WILSON, EUGENE—End—SMU

1947–48   Green Bay Packers

WILSON, FAYE—Back—Texas A & M
1926   Buffalo Bisons
1927–32   New York Giants
1931   Green Bay Packers
1932–33   Portsmouth Spartans
1934   Brooklyn Dodgers

**WILSON, GEORGE—Back—
Washington**
1927–29   Providence Steamrollers

WILSON, GERALD—End—Auburn
1959–60   Philadelphia Eagles
1960   San Francisco 49ers

**WILSON, GEORGE—End—North-
western**
1937–47   Chicago Bears

WILSON, GEORGE—Back—Lafayette
1929–30   Frankford Yellowjackets

**WILSON, GORDON—Tackle—Texas
Mines**
1941   Cleveland Rams
1942–43, 45   Chicago Cardinals
1944   Brooklyn Dodgers

WILSON, JAMES—End—Cornell
1922   Rochester Kodaks
1922   Buffalo All Americans

**WILSON, JOHN—End—Western
Reserve**
1938   Pittsburgh Pirates
1939–42   Cleveland Rams

WILSON, JOHN—Back—Baylor
1946–47   Los Angeles Rams

WILSON, LAWRENCE—Back—Utah
1960   St. Louis Cardinals

WILSON, LELAND—Back—Cornell
1929–30   Minneapolis Marines
1930–31   Frankford Yellowjackets

**WILSON, MILTON—Tackle—
Wisconsin State Teachers**
1921   Green Bay Packers
1923–24   Akron Steels

WILSON, OLIVER—End—SMU
1947–48   Green Bay Packers

WILSON, ROBERT—Back—SMU
1936   Brooklyn Dodgers

**WILSON, SAMUEL "MIKE"—End—
Lehigh**
1923–24, 26   Rock Island Independents

**WILSON, STUART—End—
Washington & Jefferson**
1932   Staten Island Stapletons

WILSON, THOMAS—Back

1956–60   Los Angeles Rams

THOMAS WILSON

WILSON, WILLIAM—End—Gonzaga
1935–37   Chicago Cardinals
1938   Pittsburgh Pirates
1938   Philadelphia Eagles

**WILSON, WILLIAM—End—San Jose
State**
1951–58   San Francisco 49ers
1954, 56, 60   #1 Pass Receiving
(1954 Tied by Pihos)

WIMBERLY, ABNER—End—LSU
1949   Los Angeles Dons (AAFC)
1950–52   Green Bay Packers

**WIMBERLY, BYRON—Guard—
Washington & Jefferson**
1925   Detroit Panthers

WINDBIELE, JOSEPH—Center
1921–22   Evansville Crimson Giants

**WINDBURN, ERNEST—End—
Missouri State**
1923   St. Louis Browns

WINGATE, ELMER—End—Maryland
1953   Baltimore Colts

**WINKELMAN, BENJAMIN—End—
Arkansas**
1922–24   Milwaukee Badgers

**WINKLER, BERNARD—Tackle—
Texas Tech.**
1948   Los Angeles Dons (AAFC)

**WINKLER, JAMES—Tackle—
Texas A & M**
1951–52   Los Angeles Rams
1953   Baltimore Colts

**WINKLER, JOSEPH—Center—
Purdue**
1945   Cleveland Rams

WINNESCHICK—Center—Carlisle
1922 Oorang Indians

WINSLOW, PAUL—Back—
North Carolina College
1960 Green Bay Packers

WINSLOW, ROBERT—End—
Southern California
1940 Brooklyn Dodgers
1940 Detroit Lions

WINTERS, ARNOLD—Tackle
1941 Green Bay Packers

WINTERS, LINDELL—Back—Ohio
Wesleyan
1923–24 Columbus Tigers

WIPER, DONALD—Back—Ohio State
1922 Columbus Tigers

WISENER, GARY—End—Baylor
1960 Dallas Cowboys

WISINGER, ZONAR—Guard—
Pittsburgh
1926 Pottsville Maroons

WISMANN, PETER—Center—
St. Louis Univ.
1949 San Francisco 49ers (AAFC)
1950–52 San Francisco 49ers

WISTERT, ALBERT—Tackle—
Michigan
1943 Phil-Pitt
1944–51 Philadelphia Eagles

WITCHER, THOMAS "AL"—Back—
Baylor
1960 Houston Oilers (AFL)

WITTE, EARL—Back—Gustavus-
Adolphus
1934 Green Bay Packers

WITTENBORN, JOHN—Guard—
Missouri Southeast
1958–60 San Francisco 49ers
1960 Philadelphia Eagles

WITTER, RAYMOND—Center—
Syracuse
1921, 23 Rochester Kodaks

WITUCKI, CASIMIR—Guard—
Indiana
1950–51, 53–56 Washington Redskins

WIZBICKI, ALEXANDER—Back—
Holy Cross
1947–49 Buffalo Bills (AAFC)
1950 Green Bay Packers

WOERNER, ERWIN—Tackle—
Bucknell
1930 Newark

WOIT, RICHARD—Back—Arkansas
State
1955 Detroit Lions

WOJCIECHOWICZ, ALEXANDER—
Center—Fordham
1938–46 Detroit Lions
1946–50 Philadelphia Eagles

WOLF, RICHARD—Back—Miami
(Ohio)
1923–25, 27 Cleveland Indians

WOLFE, HUGH—Back—Texas
1938 New York Giants

WOLTMAN, CLEMENT—Tackle—
Purdue
1938–40 Philadelphia Eagles

WOMACK, BRUCE—Guard—Texas
State West
1951 Detroit Lions

WOMBLE, ROYCE—Back—Texas
State North
1954 Baltimore Colts
1960 Los Angeles Chargers (AFL)

ROYCE WOMBLE

WOOD, DUANE—Back—Oklahoma
State
1960 Dallas Texans (AFL)

WOOD, JAMES—Guard
1921–24 Rochester Kodaks
1924 Kenosha

WOOD, ROBERT—Tackle—Alabama
1940 Chicago Cardinals

WOOD, WILLIE—Back—USC
1960 Green Bay Packers

WOODIN, HOWARD—Guard—
Marquette
1922–31 Green Bay Packers
1922 Racine Legion

WOODRUFF—End
1926 Chicago Cardinals
1929 Buffalo Bisons

**WOODRUFF, LEE—Back—
Mississippi**
1931 Providence Steamrollers
1932 Boston Braves
1933 Philadelphia Eagles

WOODS, GERALD—Back—Butler
1926 Columbus Tigers

WOODSON, ABE—Back—Illinois
1958–60 San Francisco 49ers

ABE WOODSON

**WOODWARD, RICHARD—Center—
Iowa**
1949 Los Angeles Dons (AAFC)
1950–51 New York Giants

WOOLFORD, BARD—Tackle
1922–24 Columbus Tigers

WOOTEN, JOHN—Tackle—Colorado
1959–60 Cleveland Browns

**WORDEN, JAMES—Back—Waynes-
burgh**
1945 Cleveland Rams

WORDEN, NEIL—Back—Notre Dame
1954, 57 Philadelphia Eagles

**WORDEN, STUART—Guard—
Hampden-Sidney**
1930, 32–34 Brooklyn Dodgers

WORK, JACK—Back—Denver
1960 Denver Broncos (AFL)

**WORK, JOSEPH—Back—Miami
(Ohio)**
1923–25 Cleveland Indians

WORKMAN, BLAKE—Back—Tulsa

1932 New York Giants
1933 Cincinnati Reds
1934 St. Louis Gunners

**WORKMAN, HARRY—Back—Ohio
State**
1924 Cleveland Bulldogs

**WORKMAN, HOGE—Back—
Ohio State**
1931 Cleveland Indians

**WOUDENBERG, JOHN—Tackle—
Denver**
1940–42 Pittsburgh Steelers
1946–49 San Francisco 49ers (AAFC)

WOZNIAK, JOHN—Guard—Alabama
1948 Brooklyn Dodgers (AAFC)
1949 New York Yankees (AAFC)
1950–51 New York Yanks
1952 Dallas Texans

**WRAY, LUDLOW—Center—
Pennsylvania**
1921 Buffalo All Americans
1922 Rochester Kodaks

WREN, LOWE—Back—Missouri
1956–59 Cleveland Browns
1960 Pittsburgh Steelers

**WRIGHT, ALBERT—Back—
Oklahoma A & M**
1930 Frankford Yellowjackets

**WRIGHT, ERNEST—Tackle—
Ohio State**
1960 Los Angeles Chargers (AFL)

**WRIGHT, FRANK—Tackle—
Kentucky**
1933 Brooklyn Dodgers

WRIGHT, JAMES—Guard—SMU
1947 Boston Yanks

WRIGHT, JOHN—Back—Maryland
1947 Baltimore Colts (AAFC)

**WRIGHT, THEODORE—Back—
Texas Tech.**
1934–35 Boston Redskins
1935 Brooklyn Dodgers

WRINKLE MEAT—Guard
1922 Oorang Indians

**WUKITS, ALBERT—Center—
Duquesne**
1943 Phil-Pitt
1944 Card-Pitt
1945 Pittsburgh Steelers
1946 Miami Seahawks (AAFC)
1946 Buffalo Bisons (AAFC)

**WULFF, JAMES—Back—Michigan
State**
1960 Washington Redskins

WUNSCH, HARRY—Guard—Notre Dame
1934   Green Bay Packers

WYANT, FRED—Back—West Virginia
1956   Washington Redskins

WYCOFF, DOUGLAS—Back—Georgia Tech.
1927, 31   New York Giants
1929–30, 32   Staten Island Stapletons
1933   Brooklyn Dodgers
1934   Boston Redskins

WYCOFF, LEE—Tackle—Washburn
1923   St. Louis Browns

WYDO, Frank—Tackle—Cornell
1947–51   Pittsburgh Steelers
1951–57   Philadelphia Eagles

WYHONIC, JOHN—Guard—Alabama
1946–47   Philadelphia Eagles
1948–49   Buffalo Bills (AAFC)

WYMAN, ARNOLD—Back—Minnesota
1921   Rock Island Independents

WYNNE, CHESTER—Back—Notre Dame
1922   Rochester Kodaks
1928   Chicago Bears
1929   Dayton Triangles
1929   Providence Steamrollers

WYNNE, HARRY—End—Arkansas
1944   Boston Yanks
1945   New York Giants

* * *

YABLOK, JULIUS—Back—Colgate
1930–31   Brooklyn Dodgers
1931   Staten Island Stapletons

YABLONSKI, VENTAN—Back—Columbia
1948–51   Chicago Cardinals

YACHANICH, Joseph—Guard—Fordham
1946–48   New York Yankees

YAGIELLO, RAYMOND—Guard—Catawba
1948–49   Los Angeles Rams

YARR, THOMAS—Center—Notre Dame
1933   Chicago Cardinals

YEAGER, HOWARD—Back—Santa Barbara State
1940–41   New York Giants

YEAGER, JAMES—Tackle—Lehigh

1926   Brooklyn Dodgers

YEISLEY—End
1928   Chicago Cardinals

YELVERTON, WILLIAM—End—Mississippi
1960   Denver Broncos (AFL)

YELVINGTON, RICHARD—Tackle—Georgia
1952–57   New York Giants

YEZERSKI, JOHN—Tackle—St. Mary's
1936   Brooklyn Dodgers

YOHO, MACK—End—Miami (Ohio)
1960   Buffalo Bills (AFL)

YOKAS, FRANK—Guard
1946   Los Angeles Dons (AAFC)
1947   Baltimore Colts (AAFC)

YONAKER, JOHN—End—Notre Dame
1946–49   Cleveland Browns (AAFC)
1950   New York Yanks
1952   Washington Redskins

YONAMINE, WALLACE—Back—
1947   San Francisco 49ers (AAFC)

YOUEL, JAMES—Back—Iowa
1946–48   Washington Redskins
1948   Los Angeles Rams
1948   Boston Yanks

YOUMANS, MAURICE—End—Syracuse
1960   Chicago Bears

YOUNCE, LEONARD—Guard—Oregon State
1941–44, 46–48   New York Giants

YOUNG, CLAUDE—Back—Illinois
1947–49   New York Yankees (AAFC)
1950–51   New York Yanks
1952   Dallas Texans
1953–56   Baltimore Colts

YOUNG, GEORGE—End—Georgia
1946–49   Cleveland Browns (AAFC)
1950–53   Cleveland Browns

YOUNG, GLEN—Back—Purdue
1956–57   Green Bay Packers

YOUNG, HERMAN—End—Detroit
1930   Providence Steamrollers

YOUNG, JOHN—Back—California
1926   Los Angeles

YOUNG, JOSEPH—End—Arizona
1960   Denver Broncos (AFL)

YOUNG, LESLIE—Back—North Dakota

1925–26   Dayton Triangles
1925–27   Providence Steamrollers

YOUNG, PAUL—Center—Oklahoma
1933   Green Bay Packers

**YOUNG, RICHARD—Back—
Chattanooga**
1955–56   Baltimore Colts
1957   Pittsburgh Steelers

YOUNG, ROY—Tackle—Texas A & M
1938   Washington Redskins

**YOUNG, SAMUEL—Tackle—North
Dakota**
1925–27   Providence Steamrollers
1929–30   Minneapolis Marines

YOUNG, WALTER—End—Oklahoma
1939–40   Brooklyn Dodgers
Killed returning from first B-29 raid
over Tokyo when he dropped out of
formation to cover a crippled col-
league, on Jan. 9, 1945. Captain,
U.S. Air Force.

**YOUNG, WILLIAM—Tackle—
Alabama**
1937–42, 46   Washington Redskins

**YOUNG, WILLIAM—Guard—Ohio
State**
1929   Green Bay Packers

**YOUNGELMAN, SIDNEY—Guard—
Alabama**
1955   San Francisco 49ers
1956–58   Philadelphia Eagles
1959   Cleveland Browns
1960   New York Titans (AFL)

YOUNGER, PAUL—Back—Grambling
1949–57   Los Angeles Rams
1958   Pittsburgh Steelers

PAUL YOUNGER

**YOUNGFLEISCH, FRANCIS—
Center—Villanova**
1926–27   Pottsville Maroons

**YOUNGSTROM, ADOLPH—Guard—
Dartmouth**
1921–25   Buffalo Bisons
1926–27   Frankford Yellowjackets

YOURIST, ABE—End
1923   Chicago Bears

YOUSO, FRANK—Tackle—Minnesota
1958–60   New York Giants

YOVISIN, JOHN—End—Gettysburg
1944   Philadelphia Eagles

**YOWARSKY, WALTER—End—
Kentucky**
1951, 54   Washington Redskins
1955   Detroit Lions
1955–57   New York Giants
1958   San Francisco 49ers

YURCHEY, JOHN—Back—Duquesne
1940   Pittsburgh Steelers

* * *

**ZADWORNEY, FRANK—Back—
Ohio State**
1940   Brooklyn Dodgers

**ZAGERS, ALBERT—Back—
Michigan State**
1955, 57–58   Washington Redskins

ALBERT ZAGERS

**ZALEJSKI, ERNEST—Back—Notre
Dame**
1950   Baltimore Colts

**ZAMLYNSKI, ZIGMOND—Back—
Villanova**
1946   San Francisco 49ers (AAFC)

**ZANINELLI, SILVIO—Back—
Duquesne**

1934–37   Pittsburgh Pirates

ZAPUSTAS, JOSEPH—End—Fordham
1933   New York Giants

ZARNAS, AUGUSTUS—Guard—Ohio State
1938   Chicago Bears
1939   Brooklyn Dodgers
1939–40   Green Bay Packers

ZARUBA, CARROLL—Back—Nebraska
1960   Dallas Texans (AFL)

ROGER ZATKOFF

ZATKOFF, ROGER—Tackle—Michigan
1953–56   Green Bay Packers
1957–58   Detroit Lions

ZEHRER, HENRY—Back
1926   Hartford Blues

ZELENCIK, FRANK—Tackle—Oglethorpe
1939   Chicago Cardinals

ZELLER, JEROME—Back
1921–22   Evansville Crimson Giants

ZELLER, JOSEPH—Guard—Indiana
1932   Green Bay Packers
1933–38   Chicago Bears

ZEMAN, ROBERT—Back—Wisconsin
1960   Los Angeles Chargers (AFL)

ZENO, JOSEPH—Guard—Holy Cross
1942–44   Washington Redskins
1946–47   Boston Yanks

ZERBE—End
1926   Canton Bulldogs

ZIEGLER, FRANCIS—Back—Clemson
1922   Columbus Tigers

ZIEGLER, FRANK—Back—Georgia Tech
1949–51   Philadelphia Eagles

ZIFF, DAVID—End—Syracuse
1925   Rochester
1926   Brooklyn Dodgers

ZILLY, JOHN—End—Notre Dame
1947–51   Los Angeles Rams
1952   Philadelphia Eagles

JOHN ZILLY

ZIMMERMAN, GUY—Back—Akron
1924   Akron Steels
1925   Canton Bulldogs

ZIMMERMAN, LEROY—Back—San Jose State
1940–42   Washington Redskins
1942, 44–46   Philadelphia Eagles
1943   Phil-Pitt
1947   Detroit Lions
1948   Boston Yanks
1945   #1 Interceptions

ZIMMERMAN, PLEASANT—Guard—Purdue
1927–29   Dayton Triangles

ZIMNY, ROBERT—Tackle—Indiana
1945–49   Chicago Cardinals

ZIRINSKY, WALTER—Back—Lafayette
1945   Cleveland Rams

ZIZAK, VINCENT—Tackle—Villanova
1934–37   Philadelphia Eagles

ZOIA, CLYDE—Guard—Notre Dame
1921–23   Chicago Cardinals

ZOLL, CARL—Guard
1921–22   Green Bay Packers

ZOLL, MARTIN—Guard
1921   Green Bay Packers

ZOLL, RICHARD—Guard—Indiana
1937–38   Cleveland Rams
1939   Green Bay Packers

ZUCCO VICTOR—Back—Michigan State
1957–60   Chicago Bears

ZUIDMULDER, DAVID—Back— St. Ambrose
1929–31   Green Bay Packers

ZUNKER, CHARLES—Tackle— Texas State Southwest
1934   Cincinnati Reds

ZUPEK, ALBERT—Back—Lawrence
1946   Green Bay Packers

ZUVER, MERLE—Center—Nebraska
1930   Green Bay Packers

ZUZZIO, ANTHONY—Guard— Muhlenberg
1942   Detroit Lions

ZOMBEK, JOSEPH—End—Pittsburgh
1954–55   Pittsburgh Steelers

ZONTINI, LOUIS—Back—Notre Dame
1940–41   Chicago Cardinals
1944   Cleveland Rams
1946   Buffalo Bisons (AAFC)

ZOPETTI, FRANK—Back—Duquesne
1941   Pittsburgh Steelers

ZORICH, GEORGE—Guard—Northwestern
1944–46   Chicago Bears
1946   Miami Seahawks (AAFC)
1947   Baltimore Colts (AAFC)

ZYNTELL, JAMES—Guard—Holy Cross
1933   New York Giants
1933–35   Philadelphia Eagles

THE ALL-TIME ROSTER
BY TEAMS

AKRON STEELS (1921–1926)
(Also played as Indians and Pros)

Annan, Duncan (Brown) –B–1925–26
Bailey, Russell (West Virginia) –C–1921
Barrett, John (Detroit) –G–1924–25
Barry, George (Beloit) –G–1925–26
Beck, Carl (West Virginia) –B–1921, 24, 26
Bierce, Bruce (Akron) –E–1921–25
Bissell, Frederick (Fordham) –E–1925–26
Blacklock,Hugh (Michigan State) –T –1925
Brenkert, Wayne (Washington & Lee) –B –1923–24
Brewer, Brooke (Maryland) –B–1922
Butler, Edward "Sol" (Loras) –B–1924
Caldwell, Cyril (Baldwin Wallace) –T –1925–26
Cardarelli, Carl–C–1924
Carr, Charles (Syracuse) –B–1926
Casey, H. (Baldwin Wallace) –T–1926
Chase, Ralph (Pittsburgh) –T–1926
Clements, George (Washington & Jefferson) –T–1925
Cobb, Alfred (Syracuse) –G–1921–22
Conrad, Martin (Kalamazoo) –C–1925
Copley, Charles (Missouri) –T–1921
Corcoran, Arthur (Georgetown) –E–1922
Cramer, Earl (Hamline) –B–1921–26
Daum, Carl (Akron) –E–1922–26
Davis, Carl (West Virginia) –T–1926
Edgar, William (Pittsburgh) –B–1923
Falcon, Gilbert (Wabash) –B–1925
Flower, James (Ohio State) –T–1921–24
Grigg, Cecil (Austin) –B–1926
Haley, Arthur (Akron) –B–1923
Hendrian, Warren (Pittsburgh) –B–1923
Hardy, Isham (William & Mary) –G–1923
Henry, Wilbur (Washington & Jefferson) –T–1925
Hogan, Paul (Detroit) –B–1924
Jean, Walter (Bethany) –G–1922–23
Johnson, Theodore (South Dakota) –T –1921
Jolley, Alfred (Marietta) –T–1922, 26
Jones, Ben (Grove City) –B–1921
King, Andrew (West Virginia) –B–1921
Kramer, George (West Virginia) –B–1921
Kreinheder, Walter (Michigan) –G–1922
Little Twig (Carlisle) –T–1926
McCausland, Leo (Detroit) –E–1922
Malone, Grover (Notre Dame) –B–1923
Marks, Lawrence (Indiana) –Q–1926

Michaels, Alton (Heidelberg) –B–1923–24
Mills, Joseph (Carnegie Tech) –E– 1923–26
Neihaus, Francis (Washington & Jefferson) –B–1925
Nesser, Alfred–E–1921–26
Newman, Olin (Carnegie Tech) –T –1924–26
Nix (Haskell) –T–1926
Pollard, Fritz (Brown) –B–1921, 25–26
Roberts, James (Centre) –B–1923
Robertson, James (Carnegie Tech) –B –1924–25
Robeson, Paul (Rutgers) –E–1921
Rohleder, George (Wittenberg) –E–1926
Scott, Eugene (Monmouth) –G–1923
Sechrist, Walter (West Virginia) –G–1924
Seidelson, Harry (Pittsburgh) –G–1926
Shaw, Edward (Nebraska) –B–1923
Sheeks, Paul (South Dakota) –B–1921–22
Speck, Norman "Dutch"–G–1924
Spiers, Robert (Ohio State) –T–1922
Sprinkle, Hubert (Carnegie Tech) –T –1923–24
Stahlman, Richard (De Paul) –E–1924–25
Steele, Harold (Syracuse) –B–1922
Stewart, Charles (Colgate) –G–1923
Tobin, Elgie (Penn. State) –E–1921
Tomlin, Thomas (Syracuse) –G–1921
Ursella, Rueben–B–1926
Wallace, Fred (Bethany) –G–1923–24, 26
Wendler, Harold (Ohio State) –B–1926
Wilson, Milton (Wisconsin Teachers) –T –1923–24
Zimmerman, Guy (Akron) –B–1924

BALTIMORE COLTS (1950–60)

Agase, Alex (Illinois) –G–1953
Ameche, Alan (Wisconsin) –B–1955–60
Averno, Sisto (Muhlenberg) –G –1950, 53–54
Barwegan, Richard (Purdue) –G –1950, 53–54
Berry, Raymond (Southern Methodist Univ.) –E–1955–60
Bighead, Jack (Pepperdine) –E–1954
Blanda, George (Kentucky) –Q–1950
Blandin, Ernest (Tulane) –T–1950, 53
Boyd, Robert (Oklahoma) –B–1960
Braase, Ordell (South Dakota)–E–1957–60
Brethauer, Monte (Oregon) –E–1953, 55
Brown, Hardy (Tulsa) –C–1950

Brown, Raymond (Mississippi) —B—
1958–60
Bryan, Walter (Texas Tech.) —B—1955
Buskar, George (Purdue) —B—1950
Burk, Adrian (Baylor) —Q—1950
Call, John (Colgate) —1957–58
Campanella, Joseph (Ohio State) —T
—1953–57
Campbell, Leon (Arkansas) —B—1950
Cheatham, Ernest (Loyola, L.A.) —E—1954
Chorovich, Richard (Miami, Ohio) —T
—1955–56
Collins, Albin (Louisiana State Univ.) —B
—1950
Colo, Donald (Brown) —T—1950
Colteryahn, Lloyd (Maryland) —E—1954–56
Colvin, James (Houston) —T—1960
Cooke, Edward (Maryland) —E—1959
Cooper, Kenneth (Vanderbilt) —G—1950
Coutre, Lawrence (Notre Dame) —B—1953
Crisler, Harold (San Jose State) —E—1950
Davidson, Francis (Baylor) —Q—1954, 57
Davis, Milton (U.C.L.A.) —B—1957–60
DeCarlo, Arthur (Georgia) —B—1957–60
DelBello, John (Miami) —B—1953
Donovan, Arthur (Boston College) —T
—1950, 53–60
Dupre, Louis (Baylor) —B—1955–59
Ecklund, Bradley (Oregon) —C—1953
Edwards, Daniel (Georgia) —E—1953–54,
57
Eggers, Douglas (South Dakota State) —G
—1954–57
Embree, Melvin (Pepperdine) —E—1953
Enke, Frederick (Arizona) —Q—1953–54
Feamster, Thomas (Florida State) —E—
1956–57
Filchock, Frank (Purdue) —Q—1950
Finnin, Thomas (Detroit) —T—1953–56
Fletcher, Oliver (Southern California) —G
—1950
Flowers, Bernard (Purdue) —E—1956
Flowers, Keith (Texas Christian Univ.) —G
—1953
Flowers, Richard (Northwestern) —B—1953
French, Barry (Purdue) —G—1950
Grossman, Rex (Indiana) —B—1950
Hall, Kenneth (Texas A & M) —B—1958
Harness, James (Mississippi State) —B
—1956
Hawkins, Alex (South Carolina) —B—
1959–60
Hermann, John (U.C.L.A.) —B—1956
Horn, Richard (Stanford) —B—1958
Hugasian, Harry (Stanford) —B—1955
Huzvar, John (Pittsburgh) —B—1953–54
Jackson, Kenneth (Texas) —T—1952–57
James, Thomas (Ohio State) —B—1956
Jenkins, Jonathan (Dartmouth) —T—1950
Jensen,Robert (Iowa State) —E—1950
Joyce, Donald (Tulane) —T—1954–60
Kalmanir, Thomas (Nevada) —B—1953
Keane, Thomas (West Virginia) —B—
—1953–54

Kerkorian, Gary (Stanford) —Q
—1954–55, 58
King, Edward (Boston College) —E—1950
Kissell, Vito (Holy Cross) —B—1950
Koman, William (North Carolina) —G
—1956
Kovac, Edward (Cincinnati) —B—1960
Krouse, Raymond (Maryland) —T—1958–59
Langas, Robert (Wayne) —E—1954
Lange, William (Dayton) —G—1953
Leberman, Robert (Syracuse) —B—1954
Lesane, James (Virginia) —B—1954
Lewis, Harold (Houston) —B—1959
Lipscomb, Eugene—T—1956–60
Little, John (Texas A & M) —T—1953–54
Livingston, Robert (Notre Dame) —B—1950
Lyles, Leonard (Louisville) —B—1958
McMillan, Charles (John Carroll) —B—1954
McPhail, Howard (Oklahoma) —B—1953, 56
Maggioli, Achille (Illinois) —B—1950
Marchetti, Gino (San Francisco) —E
—1953–60
Matuszak, Marvin (Tulsa) —C—1959–60
Mazzanti, Gino (Arkansas) —B—1950
Mioduszewski, Edward (William & Mary)
—B—1953
Moore, Henry (Arkansas) —B—1957
Moore, Leonard (Penn. State)—B—1956–60
Murray, Earl (Purdue) —G—1950
Mutryn, Chester (Xavier) —B—1950
Mutscheller, James (Notre Dame) —E
—1954–60
Myers, Robert (Ohio State) —T—1955–56
Myhra, Steven (North Dakota) —G
—1957–60
Nelson, Andrew (Memphis State) —B
—1957–60
North, John (Vanderbilt) —E—1950
Nowaskey, Robert (George Washington)
—E—1950
Nutter, Madison (Virginia Polytech.) —C
—1954–60
Nyers, Richard (Indiana Central) —B
—1956–57
Oristaglio, Robert (Pennsylvania) —E—1950
Owens, James (Oklahoma) —E—1950
Owens, Luke (Kent State) —T—1957
Parker, James (Ohio State) —T—1957–60
Patera, John (Oregon) —G—1955–57
Pellington, William (Rutgers) —G—1953–60
—1960
Pepper, Eugene (Missouri) —G—1954
Perina, Robert (Princeton) —G—1950
Perini, Evo (Ohio State) —B—1954
Peterson, Gerald (Texas) —T—1956
Plunkett, Sherman (Maryland State) —T
—1958–60
Poole, G. Barney (Mississippi) —E—1953
Preas, George (Virginia Polytech.) —G
—1955–60
Pricer, William (Oklahoma) —B—1957–60
Pyle, Palmer (Michigan State) —T—1960
Radosevich, George (Pittsburgh) —G
—1954–56

Rechichar, Albert (Tennessee) —B—1953–59

Renfro, Dean (Texas State North) —B —1955

Rich, Herbert (Vanderbilt) —B—1950

Richardson, Gerard (Wofford) —E—1959–60

Salata, Paul (Southern California) —E—1950

Sample, John (Maryland State) —B— 1958–60

Sandusky, Alexander (Penn. State Teachers) —E—1954–60

Sanford, Leo (Louisiana Polytech.) —G —1958

Schweder, John (Pennsylvania) —G—1950

Sharkey, Edward (Nevada & Duke) —G —1953

Shaw, George (Oregon) —Q—1955–58

Sherer, David (Southern Methodist Univ.) —E—1959

Shieds, Lebron (Tennessee) —T—1960

Shields, Burrel (John Carroll) —B—1955

Shinnick, Donald (U.C.L.A.) —G—1957–60

Shula, Donald (John Carroll) —B—1953–56

Simpson, Jackie (Florida) —B—1958

Smith, Roger "Zeke" (Auburn) —G—1960

Sommer, Michael (George Washington) —B—1959–60

Spaniel, Frank (Notre Dame) —B—1950

Spavital, James (Oklahoma A & M) —B —1950

Spinney, Arthur (Boston College) —E —1950, 53–60

Stone, Avatus (Syracuse) —B—1958

Stone, William (Bradley) —B—1950

Szymanski, Richard (Notre Dame) —C —1955, 57–60

Taliaferro, George (Indiana) —B—1953–54

Taseff, Carl (John Carroll) —B—1953–60

Thomas, Jesse (Michigan State) —B —1955–57

Thurston, Fred (Valparaiso) —G—1958

Tittle, Yelverton A. (Louisiana State Univ.) —Q—1950

Toth, Zollie (Louisiana State Univ.) —B —1953–54

Unitas, John (Louisville) —Q—1956–60

Vessels, William (Oklahoma) —B—1956

Welch, James (Southern Methodist Univ.) —B—1960

White, Robert (Stanford) —B—1955

Williams, Joel (Texas) —C—1950

Wingate, Elmer (Maryland) —E—1953

Winkler, James (Texas A&M) —T—1953

Womble, Royce (Texas State North) —B —1954–57

Young, Claude (Illinois) —B—1953–56

Young, Richard (Chattanooga) —B —1955–56

Zalejski, Ernest (Notre Dame) —B—1950

BOSTON REDSKINS
(Also played as Braves)
(1929, 1932—1936)

Apsit, Marger (Southern California) —B —1933

Arenz, Arnold (St. Louis) —B—1934

Arndt, Alfred (South Dakota State) —G —1935

Artman, Corwan (Stanford) —T—1932

Baltzell, Victor (Southwestern) —B—1935

Barber, Henry (Dartmouth) —T—1932

Barber, James (San Francisco) —T—1935–36

Battles, Clifford (West Virginia Wesleyan) —B—1932–36

Bausch, Frank (Kansas) —C—1934–36

Bettencourt, Lawrence (St. Mary's Cal.) —C —1932

Boswell, Benjamin (Texas Christian Univ.) —T—1934

Britt, Eddie (Holy Cross) —B—1936

Busich, Samuel (Ohio State) —E—1936

Campiglio, Robert (West Virginia Teachers) —B—1933

Carp, Joseph (Millikin) —T—1929

Carroll, Victor (Nevada) —T—1936

Cherne, Harold (DePaul) —T—1933

Clark, Myers (Ohio State) —B—1932

Collins, Paul (Pittsburgh) —E—1932–35

Concannon, Ernest (New York Univ.) —G —1934–36

Connor, William (Catholic Univ.) —T —1929

Cox, John (Oregon State) —G—1932

Crow, Orien (Haskell) —C—1933–34

Dickens, Marion (Georgia) —B—1932

Druehl, William (Colby) —B—1929

Edwards, Albert (Washington State) —T —1932–36

Elkins, Fait (Haskell) —B—1932

Ellstrom, Marvin (Waynesburg) —B—1934

Erickson, Michael (Northwestern) —C—1932

Ernst, John (Lafayette) —B—1929

Felber, Fred (North Dakota) —E—1932

Floyd, John (Ouachita) —T—1935

Frahm, Herald (Nebraska) —B—1935

Frankian, Malcolm (St. Mary's Cal.) —E —1933

Ginsberg, Israel (South Dakota State) —E —1935

Gundlach, Herman (Harvard) —G—1935

Hammer, Kenneth (Oregon State) —C —1932

Hokuf, Steven (Nebraska) —E—1933–35

Holmer, Walter (Northwestern) —B—1933

Horstman, Roy (Purdue) —B—1933

Howell, Wilfred (Catholic Univ.) —E—1929

Hughes, Henry (Oregon State) —B—1932

Hurley, George (Washington State) —G —1932–33

Intrieri, Marne (Loyola Md.) —G—1933–34

Irwin, Donald (Colgate) —B—1936

Johnson, Lawrence (Haskell) —C—1933–35

Johnson, Oscar (Vermont) —B—1929

Justice, Edward (Gonzaga) —B—1936

Kahn, Edward (North Carolina) —G —1935–36

Kamp, James (Oklahoma City Univ.) —T —1933

Karcher, James (Ohio State) —G—1936

Kenneally, George (St. Bonaventure) —B —1929, 32
Kittredge, Paul (Holy Cross) —B—1929
Koplaw, Joseph (Boston Univ.) —T—1929
Koslowski, Joseph (Boston College) —T —1929
Kresky, Joseph (Wisconsin) —G—1932
LaPresta, Benjamin (St. Louis) —B—1933
Latone, Anthony—B—1929
Lawrence, Edward (Brown) —B—1929
McChesney, Robert (U.C.L.A.) —E—1936
McCrillis, Edward (Brown) —G—1929
McMurdo, James (Pittsburgh) —T—1932–33
McPhail, Harold (Xavier) —B—1934–35
Malone, Charles (Texas A & M) —E —1934–36
Maloney, Gerald (Dartmouth) —E—1929
Marston, Ralph (Boston Univ.) —B—1929
Merloni, Peter (Arkansas) —E—1929
Miller, Alfred (Harvard) —B—1929
Millner, Wayne (Notre Dame) —E—1936
Moran, James (Holy Cross) —G—1935–36
Musick, James (Southern California) —B —1932–36
Nott, Douglas (Detroit) —B—1935
O'Brien, Gail (Nebraska) —T—1934–36
Oden, Olaf (Brown) —B—1932
Olsson, Lester (Mercer) —G—1934–36
Pape, Orrin (Iowa) —B—1932
Peterson, Russell (Montana) —T—1932
Pierotti, Albert (Washington & Lee) —C —1929, 32
Pinckert, Ernest (Southern California) — B—1932–36
Plansky, Anthony (Georgetown) —B—1932
Racis, Frank—G—1929
Rauch, Richard (Penn. State) —G—1929
Rentner, Ernest (Northwestern) —B —1934–36
Rex, Raymond (North Carolina State) — B—1935
Rhenquist, Milton (Bethany) —C—1932
Riley, John (Northwestern) —T—1933
Roberts, John (Georgia) —B—1932
Rust, Reginald (Oregon State) —B—1932
Sarboe, Philip (Washington State) —B —1934
Saumer, Sylvester (St. Olaf) —B—1934
Scafide, John (Tulane) —T—1933
Scholl, Roy (Lehigh) —G—1929
Schmidt, Kermit (California Poly Tech.) — E—1932
Schuette, Paul (Wisconsin) —G—1932
Sebastian, Michael (Pittsburgh) —B—1935
Shepard, William (Western Maryland) —B —1935
Shockley, Arnold (Southwestern) —G—1929
Shurtleff, Bertrand (Brown) —T—1929
Siano, Anthony (Fordham) —C—1932
Siemering, Lawrence (San Francisco) —C 1935–36
Silverman—T—1929
Sinko, Steven (Duquesne) —T—1934–36
Smith, Edward (New York Univ.) —B—1936

Smith, Raymond (Missouri) —C—1933
Smith, Riley (Alabama) —B—1936
Stark, Harry (Syracuse) —B—1935
Spellman, John (Brown) —E—1932
Stepanovich, Michael (St. Mary's, Cal.) — G—1933
Stockton, Houston (Gonzaga) —B—1929
Surabian, Zareh (Williams) —T—1929
Temple, Mark (Oregon State) —B—1936
Tosi, Flavio (Boston College) —E—1934–36
Towles, Thurston (Brown) —E—1929
Walton, Frank (Pittsburgh) —G—1934–35
Ward, David (New Mexico) —G—1933
Waters, Dale (Florida) —E—1932–33
Weisenbaugh, Henry (Pittsburgh) —B —1935–36
Weller, Louis (Haskell) —B—1933
Wentworth, Shirley (New Hampshire) —B —1929
Wentz, Byron (Penn. State) —B—1929
Westfall, Edgar (Ohio Wesleyan) —B —1932–33
Wilkerson, Basil (Oklahoma City Univ.) —E—1932
Wilkinson, William (Bucknell) —E—1936
Woodruff, Lee (Mississippi) —B—1932
Wright, Theodore (Texas State Teachers) —B—1934–35
Wycoff, Douglas (Georgia Tech.) —B—1934

BOSTON YANKS (1944–1948)

Abbruzzi, Louis (Rhode Island State) —B —1946
Albrecht, Arthur (Wisconsin) —T—1944
Anderson, William (West Virginia) —E —1945
Bailey, Edgar (Duke) —E—1946
Badaczewski, John (Western Reserve) —G —1946–48
Barzilauskas, Francis (Yale) —G—1947–48
Batinski, Stanley (Temple) —G—1948
Cafego, George (Tennessee) —B—1944–45
Calcagni, Ralph (Pennsylvania) —T —1945–46
Canale, Rocco (Boston College) —G 1946–47
Chipley, William (Washington & Lee) —E —1947–48
Collins, William (Texas) —G—1947
Crain, Milton (Baylor) —B—1944
Crisler, Harold (San Jose State) —E —1946–47
Crowley, Joseph (Dartmouth) —E—1944–45
Currivan, Donald (Boston College) —E 1945–48
Dancewicz, Frank (Notre Dame) —Q —1946–48
Davis, Robert (Kentucky) —B—1944–47
Davis, Robert (Georgia Tech.) —T—1948
Dean, Thomas (Southern Methodist Univ.) —T—1946–47
Deeks, Donald (Washington) —T—1945–47
Dekdebrun, Allen (Cornell) —Q—1948
Dimancheff, Boris (Purdue) —B—1945–46

Doherty, George (Louisiana Tech.) —G —1945

Domnanovich, Joseph (Alabama) —C —1946–48

Dubzinski, Walter (Boston College) —G —1944

Duckworth, Joseph (Colgate) —E—1948

Duhart, Paul (Florida) —B—1945

Eliason, Donald (Hamline) —E—1946

Falkenstein, Anthony (St. Mary's —California) —B—1944

Famiglietti, Gary (Boston) —B—1946

Fiorentino, Albert (Boston College) —G —1945

Fiorentino, Edward (Boston College) —E —1944, 47

Franco, Edward (Fordham) —G—1944

Gaziano, Frank (Holy Cross) —G—1944

Giddens, Herschel (Louisiana Tech.) —T —1944

Gillette, James (Virginia) —B—1946

Goodwin, William (Georgia) —C—1947–48

Golding, Joseph (Oklahoma) —B—1947–48

Goldman, Samuel (Howard College) —E —1944–47

Governali, Paul (Columbia) —Q—1946–47

Grigas, John (Holy Cross) —B—1945–47

Gudmunson, Scott (George Washington) —B—1944–45

Hazelhurst, Robert (Denver) —G—1948

Hoague, Joseph (Colgate) —B—1946

Jarmoluk, Michael (Temple) —T—1948

Jones, Ellis (Tulsa) —G—1945

Juster, Rubin (Minnesota) —T—1946

Karnofsky, Abraham (Arizona) —B—1946

Kennedy, William (Michigan State) —E —1947

Korisky, Edward (Villanova) —C—1944

Lee, Eugene (Florida) —C—1946

Leon, Anthony (Alabama) —G—1945–46

Lio, Agostino (Georgetown) —T—1944–45

Long, Robert (Tennessee) —B—1947

Magee, James (Villanova) —C—1944–46

Maley, Howard (Southern Methodist Univ.) —B—1946–47

Malinowski, Eugene (Detroit) —B—1948

Mancha, Vaughn (Alabama) —C—1948

Manders, Clarence (Drake) —B—1945

Mark, Louis (North Carolina) —E—1945

Martin, Frank (Alabama) —B—1945

Martin, John (Oklahoma) —B—1944–45

Masterson, Robert (Miami) —E—1945

Mathews, Edward (U.C.L.A.) —B—1945

Maznicki, Frank (Boston College) —B—1947

McClure, Robert (Nevada) —G—1947–48

McCullough, Hugh (Oklahoma) —B—1945

McGee, Edward (Temple) —T—1944–46

Micka, Michael (Colgate) —B—1945–48

Morelli, John (Georgetown) —G—1944–45

Muehlheuser, Frank (Colgate) —B—1948

Nelson, D. Frank (Utah) —B—1948

Nolan, John (Penn. State) —T—1948

Parker, Clarence (Duke) —B—1945

Paschal, William (Georgia Tech.) —B —1947–48

Pederson, Winfield (Minneapolis) —T —1946

Poto, John—B—1947–48

Pritko, Steven (Villanova) —E—1948

Ransport, Keith (Southern Methodist Univ.) —E—1944–45

Rhea, Floyd (Oregon) —G—1945

Riggs, Thron (Washington Univ.) —T— 1944

Rodgers, Thomas (Bucknell) —T—1947

Roman, George (Western Reserve) —T —1948

Romboli, Rudolph—B—1946–48

Ryan, David (Hardin-Simmons) —B—1948

Sabasteanski, Joseph (Fordham) —C —1946–48

Sachse, Francis (Texas Tech.) —B—1945

Sachse, John (Texas) —C—1945

Sanders, Paul (Utah State) —B—1944

Sartori, Lawrence (Fordham) —G—1944

Scollard, Nicholas (St. Joseph's) —E —1946–48

Seno, Frank (George Washington) —B —1947–48

Sergienko, George (American International) —T—1945

Sierocinski, Stephen—T—1946

Slosburg, Phillip (Temple) —B—1948

Smith, George (California) —C—1945

Smukler, David (Temple) —B—1944

Stasica, Leo (Colorado) —B—1944

Steinmetz, Kenneth—B—1944–45

Stewart, Vaughn (Alabama) —C—1944

Sucic, Steven (Illinois) —B—1947

Sulatis, Joseph—B—1946

Tepo, George (Fordham) —E—1946

Tiller, Morgan (Denver) —E—1944

Turbert, Francis (Morris Harvey) —B—1944

Tyree, James (Oklahoma) —E—1948

Walker, William (Virginia Military Inst.) —B—1944–45

Watt, Joseph (Syracuse) —B—1947

Williams, Theodore (Boston College) —B —1944

Wright, James (Southern Methodist Univ.) —B—1947

Wynne, Harry (Arkansas) —E—1944

Vogelaar, Carroll (San Francisco) —T —1947–48

Youel, James (Iowa) —B—1948

Zeno, Joseph (Holy Cross) —G—1946–47

BROOKLYN DODGERS)
(Also played as Tigers)
(1926, 1930—1944)

Abruzzino, Frank (Colgate) —C—1931

Aiello, Anthony (Youngstown) —B—1944

Albanese, Vincent (Syracuse) —B—1937–38

Alfson, Warren (Nebraska) —G—1941

Ambrose, John (Catholic Univ.) —G—1932

Andrusking, Sigmund (Detroit) —G—1937

Apsit, Marger (Southern California) —B —1931

Arial, David (Auburn) —E—1934

Austin, James (St. Mary's Cal.) —E
  —1937–38
Badgro, Morris (Southern California) —E
  —1936
Bagby, Herman (Arkansas) —B—1926
Bailey, Edgar (Duke) —E—1940–41
Bandura, John (Southwestern) —E—1943
Barrett, Jeffrey (Louisiana State Univ.) —E
  —1936–38
Barclay, George (North Carolina) —G—1935
Becker, Wayland (Marquette) —E—1934–35
Bergerson, Gilbert (Oregon State) —T
  —1935–36
Biancone, John (Oregon State) —B—1936
Blacklock, Hugh (Michigan State) —T
  —1926
Bleeker, Malcolm (Columbia) —C—1930
Bond, James (Pittsburgh) —G—1926
Bowdoin, James (Alabama) —G—1932, 34
Boyer, Verdi (U.C.L.A.) —G—1936
Brennan, Matthew (Lafayette) —B—1926
Britt, Edward (Holy Cross) —B—1936–38
Britton, Earl (Illinois) —B—1926
Brodnicki, Charles (Temple) —G—1934
Brown, William (Marshall) —B—1943–44
Brumbaugh, Boyd (Duquesne) —B
  —1938–39
Brumbaugh, Carl (Florida) —B—1937
Bultman, Arthur (Marquette) —C—1931
Bunyan, John (New York Univ.) —G—1932
Busby, Sherrill (Alabama State Teachers)
  —E—1940
Butcher, Wendell (Gustavus-Adolphus) —B
  —1938–42
Cafego, George (Tennessee) —Q
  —1940–41, 43
Cagle, Christian (West Point) —B—1933–34
Cannela, John (Fordham) —T—1934
Carnelly, Raymond (Carnegie Tech.) —B
  —1939
Carter, Joseph (Southern Methodist Univ.)
  —E—1944
Cassiano, Richard (Pitsburgh) —B—1940
Caywood, Lester (St. John's) —G—1932
Chalmers, George (New York Univ.) —C
  —1933
Clark, Myers (Oregon State) —B—1930
Comiskey, Franky (Ohio State) —E—1937
Comstock, Edwin (Washington of Mo.) —G
  —1930
Condit, Merlyn (Carnegie Tech.) —B
  —1941–43
Conkright, William (Oklahoma) —C—1943
Connors, Stafford (New Hampshire) —B
  —1926
Cook, David (Illinois) —B—1936
Coon, Edward (North Carolina State) —G
  —1940–41
Cooper, Norman (Howard) —C—1937–38
Cotton, Russell (Texas Mines) —Q—1941
Courtney, Gerard (Syracuse) —B—1942
Crayne, Richard (Iowa) —B—1936–37
Croft, Winston (Utah) —G—1935

Cronin, William (Boston College) —B
  —1931
Cronkhite, Henry (Kansas State) —E—1934
Crowl, Richard (Rutgers) —C—1930
Cumisky, Frank (Ohio State) —E—1937–38
Cuneo, Edward (Columbia) —G—1930
Daniell, Averell (Pittsburgh) —T—1937–38
Davis, Hermit (Birmingham Southern) —
  E—1935
Davis, Joseph (Southern California) —E
  —1943
Davis, William (Texas Tech.) —T—1942–43
Demas, George (Washington & Jefferson)
  —G—1934
Deremer, Arthur (Niagara) —C—1942
Disend, Leo (Albright) —T—1938–40
Dixon, Felix (Boston Univ.) —T—1938
Dobrus, Peter (Carnegie Tech.) —T—1941
Doherty, George (Louisiana Tech.) —G
  —1944
Donnell, John (Oregon) —B—1930
Dougherty, George (Howard) —B—1940
Douglas, Benjamin (Cornell) —B—1933
Douglas, Leo (Lehigh) —B—1926
Dowler, Thomas (Colgate) —B—1931
Drews, Theodore (Princeton) —E—1926
Druze, John (Fordham) —E—1938
Eagle, Alexander (Oregon) —T—1935
Eberdt, Jess (Alabama) —C—1932
Edwards, Marshall (Wake Forest) —B—1943
Eliason, Donald (Hamline) —E—1942
Ellis, John (Vanderbilt) —G—1944
Ely, Harold (Iowa) —T—1932–34
Engebretsen, Paul (Northwestern) —G
  —1934
Falkenstein, Anthony (St. Mary's Cal.) —B
  —1944
Farrell, Edward (Muhlenberg) —B—1938–39
Fawcett, Jacob (Southern Methodist Univ.)
  —T—1943
Feathers, Beattie (Tennessee) —B—1938–39
Fedora, Walter (George Washington) —B
  —1942
Ferguson, J. B.—G—1935
Fishel, Richard (Syracuse) —B—1933–34
Fleckenstein, William (Iowa) —G—1931
Folk, Richard (Clemson) —G—1939
Francis, Samuel (Nebraska) —B—1939–40
Franklin, Norman (Oregon State) —B
  —1935–37
Frick, Raymond (Pennsylvania) —C—1941
Friedman, Benjamin (Michigan) —Q
  —1932–33
Frohm, Martin (Mississippi State)—T—1944
Fronczek, Andrew (Richmond) —T—1941
Fryer, Kenneth (West Virginia) —B—1944
Fulton, Theodore (Oglethorpe) —G
  —1931–32
Fuqua, Raymond (Southern Methodist
  Univ.) —E—1935–36
Garvey, Arthur (Notre Dame) —T
  —1926, 30
Getz, Frederick (Chattanooga) —E—1930
Gifford, Robert (Denver) —B—1941

Gillson, Robert (Colgate) —G—1930–31
Goddard, Edward (Washington State) —B —1937
Golemgeske, Gorn (Wisconsin) —T —1937–40
Gordon, Louis (Illinois) —T—1931
Granato, Samuel—T—1943
Grandinette, George (Fordham) —G—1943
Greenberg, Benjamin (Rutgers) —B—1930
Greenshields, Donn (Penn. State) —T —1932–33
Grossman, John (Rutgers) —B—1932–36
Grove, Roger (Michigan State) —B—1937
Gussie, Michael (West Virginia) —G—1940
Gutknecht, Albert (Niagara) —G—1943
Gutowsky, Leroy· (Oklahoma City Univ.) —B—1939
Haak, Robert (Indiana) —T—1939
Hagberg, Rudolph (West Virginia) —C —1930
Hagerty, Loris (Iowa State) —B—1930
Haines, Harry (Colgate) —T—1930–31
Halpren, Roy (City College N.Y.) —G —1932
Hanson, Thomas (Temple) —B—1931, 37
Hare, Raymond (Gonzaga) —B—1944
Harris, Thomas (Ohio State) —T—1930
Harrison, Edward (Boston College) —E —1926
Harrison, John (Kansas State) —T—1937
Hartman, James (Colorado State) —E—1936
Hayduk, Henry (Washington State) —G —1935
Heater, William (Syracuse) —T—1940
Heikkinen, Ralph (Michigan) —G—1939
Hein, Herbert (Minnesota) —E—1947
Heineman, Kenneth (Texas Mines) —B —1943
Heldt, Carl (Purdue) —T—1935–36
Hickmann, Herman (Tennessee) —G —1932–34
Hill, Harold (Howard) —E—1938–40
Hodges, Herman (Howard) —E—1939–42
Hornbeak, Jay (Washington) —B—1935
Howard, Albert (Princeton) —G—1926
Hubbard, Wesley (San Jose State) —E— 1935
Hugret, Joseph (New York Univ.) —E —1933–34
Humphrey, Paul (Purdue) —C—1939
Ilowit, Roy (City College N.Y.) —T—1937
Janiak, Leonard (Ohio) —B—1939
Jappe, Paul (Syracuse) —E—1926
Jefferson, William (Mississippi State) —C —1942
Jeffries, Robert (Missouri) —G—1941
Jocher, Arthur (Manhattan) —G—1940–42
Johnson, Albert (Kentucky) —B—1937
Johnson, Cecil, (Texas State East) —B —1943–44
Jolley, Alfred (Marietta) —T—1930
Jonas, Marvin (Utah) —C—1931
Jones, Bruce (Alabama) —G—1931–34
Jones, Thurman (Abilene Christian) —B —1941–43

Jones, William (West Virginia Wesleyan) —G—1937
Jorgenson, Wagner (St. Mary's Cal.) —C —1936–37
Jurich, Michael (Denver) —T—1941–42
Kapitansky, Bernard (Long Island Univ.) —G—1942
Kaplanoff, Carl (Ohio State) —T—1939
Karcis, John (Carnegie Tech.) —B—1932–35
Kaska, Anthony (Illinois Wesleyan) —B —1936–38
Keahey, Eulis (George Washington) —G —1942
Kelsh, Matthew (Iowa) —E—1930
Kelly, John Simms (Kentucky) —B —1933–34, 37
Kelly, William (Montana) —B—1929–30
Kercheval, Ralph (Kentucky) —B—1934–40
Kinard, Frank (Mississippi) —T—1938–44
Kinard, George (Mississippi) —G—1941–42
Kirkland, B'ho (Alabama) —G—1935–36
Kirkleski, Frank (Lafayette) —B—1931
Kish, Benjamin (Pittsburgh) —Q—1940–41
Kline, George—B—1937
Kloppenberg, Harry (Fordham) —E —1931, 33–34
Kobolinski, Stanley (Boston College) —C —1926
Koons, Joseph (Scranton) —C—1941
Kosel, Stanley (Albright) —B—1938–39
Koshlap, Jules (Georgetown) —B—1941
Kostka, Stanley (Minnesota) —B—1935
Kowalski, Andrew (Mississippi State) —E 1943–44
Kracum, George (Pittsburgh) —B—1941
Krause, Henry (St. Louis) —C—1936–37
Kristufek, Frank (Pittsburgh) —T—1940–41
LaFitte, William (Ouachita) —E—1944
Lankas, James (St. Mary's Tex.) —B—1942
Leckonby, William (St. Lawrence) —B —1939–41
Lee, William (Alabama) —T—1935–37
Leisk, Wardell (Louisiana State Univ.) —G —1937
Leith, Albert (Pennsylvania) —B—1926
Lenc, George (Augustana) —E—1939
Leon, Anthony (Alabama) —G—1944
Lott, John (Bucknell) —T—1930
Lubratovich, Milo (Wisconsin) —T —1931–35
Lumpkin, Roy (Georgia Tech.) —B —1936–37
Lyons, George (Kansas State) —T—1932–33
McAdams, Dean (Washington) —B —1941–43
McArthur, John (Santa Clara) —C—1930, 33
McBride, John (Syracuse) —B—1930–32
McCullough, James (Holy Cross) —G—1926
McCullough, Harold (Cornell) —B—1942
McDonald, Walter (Utah) —C—1935
McFaden, Banks (Clemson) —B—1940
McGibbony, Charles (Arkansas State) —B —1944
McGrath, Richard (Holy Cross) —T—1926

McMichaels, John (Birmingham) —B—1944
McNeil, Francis (Washington & Jefferson)
—E—1932
Mahan, R. (Washington of Mo.) —B—1930
Manders, Clarence (Drake) —B—1939–43
Maniaci, Joseph (Fordham) —B—1936–38
Manton, Taldon (Texas Christian Univ.)
—Q—1943
Marek, Joseph (Texas Tech.) —Q—1943
Mark, Louis (North Carolina State) —E—
1938–40, 44
Marker, Henry (West Virginia) —B—1934
Martin, Frank (Alabama) —B—1943–44
Masterson, Robert (Miami) —E—1944
Mastrogany, August (Iowa) —E—1931
Matisi, John (Duquesne) —T—1943
Mattison, Ralph (Davis-Elkins) —G—1930
Mecham, Curtis (Oregon) —B—1942
Merlin, Edward (Vanderbilt) —G—1938–39
Merrill, Walter (Alabama) —T—1940–42
Mielziner, Saul (Carnegie Tech.) —C
—1931–34
Miller, James (New York Univ.) —T—1930
Mitchell, Granville (Davis-Elkins) —E—1937
Mizell, Warner (Georgia Tech.) —B—1931
Montgomery, Clifford (Columbia) —B
—1934
Mooney, James (Georgetown) —E—1930–31
Moore, Vernon (Oregon) —C—1938
Morris, Robert (Cornell) —G—1926
Morrison, Maynard (Michigan) —C
—1933–34
Myers, Dennis (Iowa) —G—1930–31
Myers, Thomas (Fordham) —B—1926
Nardi, Richard (Ohio State) —B—1939
Nash, Thomas (Georgia) —E—1933–34
Nelson, Donald (Iowa) —G—1937
Nemeck, Gerald (New York Univ.) —E
—1931
Nesbitt, Richard (Drake) —B—1934–35
Nicksick, Michael (Pittsburgh) —B—1942
Nixon, George (Idaho) —B—1942
Norby, John (Idaho) —B—1935
Nordstrom, Harry (Trinity, Conn.) —G
—1926
Nori, Reino (DeKalb) —B—1937–38
Novotny, Raymond (Ashland) —B—1932
Noyes, Leonard (Montana) —T—1938
O'Donnell, Richard (Minnesota) —E—1931
Oehler, John (Purdue) —C—1935–36
Owens, Truett (Texas Tech.) —G—1943
Parker, Clarence (Duke) —B—1937–41
Parker, David (Hardin- Simmons) —E—1941
Peace, Lawrence (Pittsburgh) —B—1941
Perry, Claude (Alabama) —T—1931
Peters, Forest (Illinois) —B—1930–31
Peterson, Lester (Texas) —E—1933–34
Petro, Steven (Pittsburgh) —G—1940–41
Pierce, Donald (Kansas) —C—1942
Pivarnik, Joseph (Notre Dame) —G—1942
Plank, Anthony (Georgetown) —B—1930
Plank, Earl—E—1930
Plumridge, Theodore (St. John's) —C—1926
Radick, Kenneth (Marquette) —E—1931

Raemer, Norbert (Kansas State) —G—1942
Raffel, William (Pennsylvania) —E—1932
Ranspot, Keith (Southern Methodist
Univ.) —E—1942–43
Raskowski, Leo (Ohio State) —T—1933
Ratica, Joseph (St. Vincent's) —C—1939
Rayburn, Van (Tennessee) —E—1933
Reagen—T—1926
Rechmarck, Raymond (Syracuse) —B—1937
Reissig, William (Kansas State Teachers)
—B—1938–39
Reynolds, Owen (Georgia) —E—1926
Reynolds, Quentin (Brown) —T—1926
Reynolds, Robert (Mississippi) —B—1944
Rhea, Floyd (Oregon) —G—1944
Rhea, Hugh (Nebraska) —G—1933
Riblett, Paul (Pennsylvania) —E—1932–36
Richards, Richard (Kentucky) —B—1933
Robertson, Robert (Southern California)
—B—1942
Robertson, Thomas (Tulsa) —C—1940–42
Robinson, John (Missouri State Northeast)
—T—1935–36
Rooney, Cobb (Colorado) —B—1926
Rovinski, Anthony (Holy Cross) —B—1934
Rowan, Everett (Ohio State) —E
—1930, 32–33
Rucinski, Edward (Indiana) —E—1941–42
Rukas, Justin (Louisiana State Univ.) —G
—1936
Sachse, Francis (Texas Tech.) —B—1943–44
Sandberg, Sigmund (Iowa Wesleyan) —T
—1937
Sansen, Oliver (Iowa) —B—1932–35
Sarausky, Anthony (Fordham) —B—1938
Sarboe, Philip (Washington State) —B
—1936
Scalzi, John (Georgetown) —B—1931
Scheuer, Abraham—E—1934
Schieb, Lee (W. Virginia Wesleyan) —C—
1930
Schmarr, Herman (Catholic Univ.) —E
—1943
Schuber, James (Annapolis) —B—1930
Schupbach, O. T. Jr. alias "Tex Mooney"
(Texas State West) —T—1943
Schwartz, Perry (California) —E—1940–42
Senn, William (Knox) —B—1931
Sergienko, George (American International)
—T—1943–44
Setcavage, Joseph (Duquesne) —Q—1942–43
Sheldon, James (Brown) —E—1926
Shellogg, Alexander (Notre Dame) —T
—1939
Shetley, Rhoten (Furman) —B—1940–42
Siano, Anthony (Fordham) —C—1934
Sivell, Ralph (Auburn) —G—1938–42
Skoronski, Edward (Purdue) —C—1937
Smith, George (California) —C—1944
Snell, George (Penn. State) —B—1926
Stasica, Leo (Colorado) —B—1941
Stein, Samuel—E—1932
Stephen, William (Brown) —C—1926
Stevens, Theodore (Brown) —C—1926

Stevenson, Arthur (Fordham) —G—1926
Stewart, Ralph (Missouri) —C—1944
Stewart, Vaughn (Alabama) —C—1942, 44
Stojack, Frank (Washington State) —G
—1935–36
Stotsberg, Harold (Xavier) —T—1930
Strom, Frank (Oklahoma Military Acad.) —
T—1944
Stromiello, Michael (Colgate) —E—1930–34
Strosser, Walter (St. Vincent) —B—1940
Stuhldreher, Harry (Notre Dame) —Q
—1926
Svendsen, Earl (Minnesota) —G—1939–41
Swiadon, Philip (New York Univ.) —G
—1943
Taylor—B—1944
Taylor, John (Ohio State) —T—1926
Temple, Mark (Oregon State) —B—1936
Thomas, Rex (St. John's) —B—1926, 30–31
Thomason, John (Georgia Tech.) —B
—1930–34
Titus, Silas (Holy Cross) —E—1940–42
Tofil, Joseph (Indiana) —E—1942
Tomaini, John (Georgetown) —E—1930–32
Toscani, Francis (St. Mary's Cal.) —B—1932
Ugoccioni, Enrico (Murray State) —E—1944
Vance, Joseph (Texas State Southwest) —B
—1931
Vetter, John (McPherson) —B—1942
Wagner, Raymond (Columbia) —E—1931
Waller, William (Illinois) —E—1938
Watkins, Gordon (Georgia Tech.) —T
—1931
Wear, Robert (Penn. State) —C—1944
Webb, George (Texas Tech.) —E—1943
Webber, Charles (Colgate) —G—1926
Weeks, George (Alabama) —E—1944
Wehba, Raymond (Southern California)
—E—1943
Weimer, Charles (Wilmington) —B—1930
Weiner, Bernard (Kansas State) —G—1942
Wemple, Donald (Colgate) —E—1941
Whately, James (Alabama) —T—1936–38
White, Wilbur (Colorado State) —B—1935
Wiberg, Oscar (Nebraska Wesleyan) —B
—1932
Williams, Burton "Cy" (Florida) —G—1931
Wilson, Fay (Texas A & M) —B—1934
Wilson, Robert (Southern Methodist
Univ.) —B—1936
Winslow, Robert (Southern California) —E
—E—1940
Worden, Stuart (Hampden-Sydney) —G
—1930, 32–34
Wright, Frank (Kentucky) —T—1933
Wright, Theodore (Texas State Teachers)
—B—1935
Wycoff, Douglas (Georgia Tech.) —B—1933
Yablok, Julius (Colgate) —B—1930–31
Yeager, James (Lehigh) —T—1926
Yezerski, John (St. Mary's Cal.) —T—1936
Young, Walter (Oklahoma) —E—1939–40
Zadworney, Frank (Ohio State) —B—1940
Zarnas, Augustus (Ohio State) —G—1939
Ziff, David (Syracuse) —E—1926

BUFFALO BISONS
(Also Played as
All Americans, Bulldogs)
(1921–1927, 1929)

Ailinger, James (Buffalo) —T—1924
Allison, James (Texas A & M) —E—1926–27
Anderson, Oscar (Colgate) —B—1921–22
Barber, Benjamin (Virginia Military Inst.)
—T—1925
Beck, Carl (West Virginia) —B—1921
Beuthel, Lloyd (Colgate) —G—1927
Bierce, Bruce (Akron) —E—1923
Big Twig—G—1929
Bizer, Herbert (Carroll) —B—1929
Bohren, Karl (Pittsburgh) —B—1927
Boynton, Ben (Williams) —B—1924
Brace, William (Brown) —G—1921–22
Bradshaw, Wesley (Baylor) —B—1926
Brewster, James (West Virginia) —E—1929
Bruder, Woodie (West Virginia) —B—1925
Burt, Russell (Canisius) —G—1925
Calac, Peter (Carlisle) —B—1924

PETER CALAC

Carberry, Glenn (Notre Dame) —E
—1923–24
Carman, Edmund (Purdue) —T—1925
Carr, Harlan (Syracuse) —B—1927
Christman, Floyd (Thiel) —B—1925
Collins, John (Canisius) —G—1924
Comstock, Edwin (Washington of Mo.) —G
—1929
Connors, Stafford (New Hampshire) —B—
1923–24
Corcoran, Arthur (Georgetown) —E—1923
Coumier, Ulysses (Louisiana College) —B
—1929
Culver, Frank (Syracuse) —C—1923–24
Curzon, Harry (Illinois) —E—1925
Dieter, Herbert (Pennsylvania) —G—1922
Dimmick, Donald (Bethany) —1926–27
Dorfman, Arthur (Boston Univ.) —G—1929
Doyle, Edward (Canisius) —G—1927
Edgar, William (Pittsburgh) —B—1923

Edmonson, Van (Oklahoma) —C—1926
Fay, James (Canisius) —B—1926
Feist, Louis (Canisius) —T—1924–26
Fisher, Darrell (Iowa) —G—1925
Flavin, John (Georgetown) —B—1923–24
Foster, Fred (Syracuse) —B—1923
Foster, James (Bucknell) —B—1925
Gardner, Milton (Wisconsin) —G—1921
Gavin, Patrick "Buck"—B—1922
Gay, Kenneth (Minnesota) —T—1925
Glassman, Morris (Wilmington College) —G—1929
Goetz, Angus (Michigan) —T—1922
Grace—G—1921
Gregory, Frank (Williams) —B—1924
Guarneri, Albert (Canisius) —E—1924
Guffey, Roy (Oklahoma) —E—1926
Gulian, Michael (Brown) —T—1923
Guy, Charles (Washington & Jefferson) —C —1921–22
Gwosden, Milo (Pittsburgh) —E—1925
Hagberg, Rudolph (West Virginia) —C —1929
Harvey, Norman (Detroit) —T—1925, 27
Hauser, Kenneth (Washington & Jefferson) —B—1927
Hillhouse, Andrew (Brown) —B—1921
Hobson, Benjamin (Wabash) —B—1926–27
Holleran, Thomas (Pittsburgh) —B—1923
Horning, Clarence (Colgate) —T—1921
Huffman, Iolas (Ohio State) —T—1924
Hughitt, Ernest (Michigan) —B—1921–24
Irvin, Barlow (Texas A & M) —G—1926–27
Jolley, Alfred (Marietta) —T—1929
Jones, Kenneth (Franklin & Marshall) —B —1924
Kaw, Edward (Cornell) —B—1924
Kelly, Clancy (Olympia) —G—1923
Kendricks, James (Texas A & M) —T —1925–26
Kennedy, Joseph (Columbia) —B—1925
Kibler, William—B—1922
Kirk, Bernard (Baylor) —C—1926
Koppisch, Walter (Columbia) —B—1925
Krause, Francis (Hobart) —T—1924
Kuehl, Raymond (Dubuque) —B—1921–22
Laird, James (Colgate) —B—1921–22
Little, Louis (Pennsylvania) —T—1921
Lowe, George (Fordham) —E—1922
McArthur, John (Santa Clara) —C—1927
McCombs—T—1929
McConnell, Felton (Georgia Tech.) —G —1927
McCormick, Elmer (Detroit) —G—1923–25
McGilbra, Sanford (Redlands) —T—1926
McGregory—B—1923
Mahan, Edward (Washington of Mo.) —B —1929
Mahoney, John (Detroit) —B—1923
Martineau, Roy (Syracuse) —B—1923
Miller, Henry (Penn. State) —E—1921
Minick, Paul (Iowa) —G—1927
Mitchell, Albert (Thiel) —T—1924
Morrisey, Frank (Boston College) —T —1922–24

Morrow, James (Pittsburgh) —B—1922
Mulvey, Vincent (Syracuse) —B—1923
Myles—E—1929
Narran, Roger—E—1926
Nash, Robert (Rutgers) —T—1921–23
Nix, Emory (Haskell) —T—1926
Noble, James (Syracuse) —B—1925
O'Hearn, John (Cornell) —B—1921
Oliphant, Elmer (West Point) —B—1921
Otte, Lowell (Iowa) —E—1927
Plank, Earl—E—1929
Powell, Stancil (Carlisle) —G—1926

STANCIL POWELL

Rawlings, Robert (Georgetown) —B—1922
Reed, Max (Bucknell) —C—1925
Roderick, Benjamin (Columbia) —B—1923
Rodriguez, Jess (Salem) —B—1929
Rosen, Stanley (Rutgers) —B—1929
Roy, Elmer—E—1927
Ryan, Clarence (West Virginia) —B—1929
Schwarzer, Theodore (Centenary)—G—1926
Scott, John (Lafayette) —B—1921–23
Shelton, Murray (Cornell) —E—1921–22
Shurtleff, Bertrand (Brown) —B—1929
Slough, Elmer (Oklahoma) —B—1926
Smith, Cedric (Michigan) —B—1921, 23
Spagna, Joseph (Lehigh) —C—1921
Spellacy—E—1922
Stein, Herbert (Washington & Jefferson) —T—1921
Sullivan, John (Rochester) —B—1921
Swain, Gladstone (Trinity, Tex.) —E—1926
Thomas, Carl (Pennsylvania) —G—1922–23
Traynor, Michael (Canisius) —B—1923–24
Urban, Luke (Boston College) —E—1921–24
Usher, Edward (Michigan) —B—1921
VanDyne, Charles (Missouri) —T—1925
VanHorn, Charles (Washington & Lee) —B —1927
Vaughn, William (Southern Methodist Univ.) —B—1926
Vedder, Norton—B—1927
Voss, Walter (Detroit) —E—1921, 29
Ward, Gilbert (Notre Dame) —T—1921
Watson, Grady (Texas) —B—1927
Watters, Leonard (Springfield) —E—1924
Weathers, Guy (Baylor) —G—1926
Weldon, John (Lafayette) —B—1921–22
Wilcox, John (Oklahoma) —T—1926

Willson, Joseph (Pennsylvania) —G—
  1926–27
Wilson, Lafayette (Texas A & M) —B—1926
Wilson, James (Cornell) —E—1922
Woodruff—E—1929
Wray, Ludlow (Pennsylvania) —C—1921
Youngstrom, Adolph (Dartmouth) —G
  —1921–25

CANTON BULLDOGS
(1921–1923, 1925–1926)

Babcock, Samuel (Michigan) —B—1926
Batchelor, Donald (Grove City) —T—1922
Bowser, Arda (Bucknell) —B—1922
Brennan, Paul (Fordham) —B—1925
Butler, William (Marquette) —B—1926
Calac, Peter, (Carlisle) —B—1922, 25–26
Carroll, Edward (Washington & Jefferson)
  —E—1921–23, 25
Chamberlain, Guy (Nebraska) —E—1921–23
Comer—B—1926
Comstock, Ralph (Georgetown) —G
  —1923, 25
Conover, Lawrence (Penn. State) —C—1923
Culver, Frank (Syracuse) —C—1923, 25
Deibel, Arthur (Lafayette) —T—1926
Edwards, Eugene (Notre Dame) —G—1921
Elliott, Wallace (Lafayette) —B—1922–23
Falcon, Gilbert (Wabash) —B—1921
Feeney, Francis (Notre Dame) —C—1921
Fetz, Gustave—B—1923
Fisher, Darrell (Iowa) —B—1925
Flattery, Wilson (Wooster) —B—1925–26
Fleming, Malcolm (Washington &
  Jefferson) —B—1925
Ghee, Milton (Dartmouth) —B—1921–22
Gillies, Frederick (Cornell) —T—1923
Griffiths, Paul (Penn. State) —G—1921
Griggs, Cecil (Austin) —B—1921–23
Hendrian, Warren (Pittsburgh) —B—1923
Henry, Wilbur (Washington & Jefferson)
  —T—1921–23
Higgins, Robert (Penn. State) —B—1921
Hogan, Paul (Detroit) —B—1925
Jones, Benjamin (Grove City) —B—1923, 25
Kellison, John (West Virginia Wesleyan)
  —T—1921
Kempton, Herbert (Yale) —Q—1921
Kendricks, James (Texas A & M) —B—1922
Kyle, James (Gettysburg) —C—1925–26
Little Twig (Carlisle) —T—1926
Lyman, Roy (Nebraska) —T—1922–23, 25
McQuade, John (Georgetown) —B—1922
Marker, Clifford (Washington State) —B
  —1926
Marsh, Howard (Oklahoma) —B—1921
Matthews, Neil (Pennsylvania) —T—
  1921–22
Merillat, Louis (Annapolis) —E—1925
Morrow, James (Pittsburgh) —B—1921
Mullen, Vern (Nebraska) —E—1923
Murrah, William (Texas A & M) —T—1922
Nelson, Donald (Ohio Wesleyan) —C—1926

Nichols, John (Ohio State) —G—1926
Osborn, Robert (Penn. State) —G—1921–23
Reed, Max (Bucknell) —C—1925
Reedinger, Otis (Penn. State) —B—1925
Robb, Harry (Penn. State) —B
  —1921–22, 25–26
Robb, Stanley (Centre) —E—1926
Roberts, James (Centre) —C—1925–26
Roberts, Walcott (Annapolis) —B—1922–23
Roderick, Benjamin (Columbia) —B
  —1923, 25–26
Russell, Edward (Pennsylvania) —G—
  1921–22
Sacksteder, Norbert (Dayton) —1922–24
Schuster, Richard (Penn. State) —E—1925
Shaw, Edward (Nebraska) —B—1922–23
Seeds—B—1926
Sefton, Frederick (Colgate) —E—1921–22
Slackford, Frederick (Notre Dame) —B
  —1921
Smythe, James (Centre) —B—1922–23
Spears, Clarence (Dartmouth) —T—1921–22
Speck, Norman "Dutch"—G—1921–23,
  25–26
Stewart, Charles (Colgate) —T—1921–22
Strasser—E—1925
Stein, Russell (Pittsburgh) —T—1926
Taylor, John (Ohio State) —T—1922–23
Thorpe, James (Carlisle) —B—1926
Vick, Richard (Washington & Jefferson)
  —B—1926
Waldsmith, Ralph (Akron) —G—1922
Wallace, Frederick (Bethany) —G—1926
Way, Charles (Penn. State) —B—1921
West, David (Colgate) —T—1921
Williams, Joseph (Lafayette) —G—1923
Zerbe—E—1926
Zimmerman, Guy (Akron) —B—1925

CHICAGO BEARS
(Also played as Staley Bears)
(1921—1960)

Abbey, Joseph (North Texas State) —E
  —1948–49
Adams, John (Los Angeles State) —B—
  1959–60
Akin, Leonard (Baylor) —G—1942
Allen, Edward (Penn. U.) —B—1947
Allman, Robert (Mich. State) —E—1936
Anderson, Edward (Notre Dame) —E—1923
Anderson, Heartley (Notre Dame) —G
  —1922–25
Anderson, Henry (Northwestern) —G—1931
Anderson, Ralph (Los Angeles State) —E
  —1958
Anderson, William (Compton Jr.) —B
  —1953–54
Apolskis, Charles (DePaul) —E—1938–39
Artoe, Lee (California) —T—1940–42, 45
Ashburn, Clifford (Nebraska) —G—1930
Ashmore, Roger (Gonzaga) —T—1927
Aspatore, Edward (Marquette) —T—1934
Atkins, Douglas (Tennessee) —E—1955–60

Autrey, William (Texas Tech.) —C—1953
Aveni, John (Indiana) —E—1959–60
Babartsky, Albert (Fordham) —T—1943–45
Badaczewski, John (Western Reserve) —G
    —1953
Baisi, Albert (West Virginia) —G—
    —1940–41, 46
Barker, Richard (Iowa State) —G—1921
Barnes, Erich (Purdue) —B—1958–60
Barwegan, Richard (Purdue) —G—1950–52
Bassi, Richard (Santa Clara) —G—1938–39
Battles, William (Brown) —E—1939
Bauman, Alfred (Northwestern) —T—
    —1949–50
Bausch, Frank (Kansas) —C—1937–40
Becker, Wayland (Marquette) —E—1934
Bell, Kay (Washington State) —T—1937
Benton, James (Arkansas) —E—1943
Bergerson, Gilbert (Oregon State) —T
    —1932
Berry, Cornelius (North Carolina State) —B
    —1942–46
Bettridge, John (Ohio State) —B—1937
Bingham, Donald (Sul Ross Teachers) —E
    —1956
Bishop, Donald (Los Angeles C. C.) —E—
    1959
Bishop, William (North Texas State) —T
    —1952–60
Bivins, Charles (Morris Brown) —B—1960
Bjork, Delbert (Oregon Univ.) —T
    —1937–38
Blackburn, J.—T—1923
Blacklock, Hugh (Michigan State) —T
    —1921–25
Blackman, E. Lennon (Tulsa) —T—1930
Blanda, George (Kentucky) —Q—1949–58
Bolan, George (Purdue) —B—1921–24
Bondurant, J. Bourbon (DePauw) —G—
    1922
Boone, J. R. (Tulsa) —B—1948–51
Brackett, Martin (Auburn) —G—1956–57
Bradley, Edward (Wake Forest) —E
    —1950, 52
Braidwood, Charles (Chattanooga) —E
    —1932
Bramhall, Arthur (DePaul) —B—1931
Bratkowski, Edmund (Georgia) —Q
    —1954, 1957–60
Bray, Raymond (Western Michigan) —B
    —1939–42, 1946–51
Brink, Lawrence (North Illinois State) —E
    —1954
Britton, Earl (Illinois) —B—1925
Brown, Charles Edward (San Fran. Univ.)
    —Q—1954–60
Brumbaugh, Carl (Florida) —Q—1930–38
Bryan, John (Chicago) —B—1922–25, 27
Buck, Arthur (Carroll) —B—1941
Buckler, William (Alabama) —G
    —1926–28, 31–33
Buivid, Raymond (Marquette) —B
    —1937–38
Bukich, Rudolph (So. Cal.) —Q—1958–59
Burdick, Lloyd (Illinois) —T—1931

Burgeis, Glen (Tulsa) —T—1945
Burnell, Max (Notre Dame) —B—1944
Buss, Arthur (Michigan State) —T—1934–35
Bussey, Young (Louisiana State Univ.) —B
    —1940–41
Campana, Albert (Youngstown) —B
    —1950–52
Campbell, Leon (Arkansas) —B—1952–54
Canaday, James (Texas) —B—1948–49
Carey, Robert (Michigan State) —E—1958
Carl, Harland (Wisconsin) —B—1956
Carlson, Jules (Oregon State) —G—1928–36
Caroline, James C. (Illinois) —B—1956–60
Casares, Richard (Florida) —B—1955–60
Casteete, Jesse (McNeese State) —B—1956
Chamberlain, Guy (Nebraska) —E—1921
Chesney, Chester (DePaul) —C—1939–40
Cifers, Edward (Tennessee) —E—1947–48
Clark, Harry (West Virginia) —B—1940–43
Clark, Herman (Oregon State) —T
    —1952, 54–57
Clarkson, Stuart (Texas A & M) —C
    —1942, 46–51
Cody, Edward (Purdue) —B—1949–50
Coia, Angelo (Southern California) —E—
    1960
Cole, Emerson (Toledo) —B—1952
Conkright, William (Oklahoma) —C—1938
Connor, George (Notre Dame) —T
    —1948–55
Cooke, Edward (Maryland) —E—1958
Corbett, George (Millikin) —B—1932–38
Corzine, Lester (Davis-Elkins) —B—1938
Cowan, Leslie (McMurry) —T—1951
Crawford, Fred (Duke) —T—1934–35
Crawford, Walter (Illinois) —T—1925
Croft, Abe (Southern Methodist U.) —E
    —1944–45
Cross, Robert (Austin) —T—1952
Culver, Alvin (Notre Dame) —T—1932
Cunningham, Harold (Ohio State) —E
    —1929
Daffer, Terrell (Tennessee) —E—1954
Damore, John (Northwestern) —G—1957,
    59
Daniell, James (Ohio State) —T—1945
Davis, Arthur (Alabama State) —T
    —1953–54
Davis, Fred (Alabama Univ.) —T—1947–51
Davis, Harper (Mississippi State) —B—1950
Davis, Roger (Syracuse) —G—1960
DeCorrevant, William (Northwestern) —B
    —1948–49
Dempsey, Frank (Florida) —T—1950–53
Dewveall, Willard (Southern Methodist
    Univ.) —E—1959–60
Digris, Bernard (Holy Cross) —T—1943
Dimanscheff, Boris (Purdue) —B—1952
Doehring, John—B—1932–37
Dooley, James (Miami) —B—1952–54,
    56–57, 59–60
Dottley, John (Mississippi) —B—1951–53
Douglas, Merrill (Utah) —B—1958–60
Dreher, Ferdinand (Denver Univ.) —E
    —1938

Dreyer, Walter (Wisconsin) —B—1949

Drews, Theodore (Princeton) —E—1928

Driscoll, John (Northwestern) —B—1926–29

Drulis, Charles (Temple) —G —1942, 1945–49

Drury, Lyle (St. Louis Univ.) —E—1930–31

Drzewiecki, Ronald (Marquette) —B —1955, 57

Dugger, John (Ohio State) —E—1949

Dunlap, Robert (Oklahoma) —B—1935

Ecker, Enrique (John Carroll)—T—1947, 49

Elness, Leland (Bradley) —B—1929

Ely, Harold (Iowa) —T—1932

Engebretsen, Paul (Northwestern) —G —1932

Englund, Harry—E—1921–22, 24

Erickson, Harold (Washington & Jefferson) —B—1925

Evans, Earl (Harvard) —T—1926–29

Evans, Frederick (Notre Dame) —B—1948

Famiglietti, Gary (Boston Univ.) —B —1938–45

Fanning, Stanley (Idaho) —T—1960

Farrington, John (Prairie View) —E—1960

Farris, Thomas (Wisconsin) —Q—1946–47

Feathers, Beattie (Tennessee) —B—1934–37

Febel, Fred (Purdue) —G—1935

Federovich, John (Davis-Elkins) —T —1941, 46

Fenimore, Robert (Oklahoma A & M) —B —1947

Ferguson, J. B.—G—1932

Fetz, Gustave—B—1923

Figner, George (Colorado) —B—1953

Flaherty, Pat (Marquette) —E—1923

Flanagan, Latham (Carnegie Tech.) —E —1931

Flanagan, Richard (Ohio State) —G —1948–49

Fleckenstein, William (Iowa) —G—1925–30

Floyd, Robert Jack (Texas Christian U.) —B—1953

Fordham, James (Georgia) —B—1944–45

Forte, Aldo (Montana) —G—1939–41, 46

Fortmann, Daniel (Colgate) —G—1936–46

Fortunato, Joseph (Mississippi State) —B —1955–60

Francis, Samuel (Nebraska) —B—1937–38

Franklin, Paul (Franklin Coll.) —E —1930–33, 35

Frump, Milton (Ohio Wesleyan) —G—1930

Galimore, Willie (Florida A & M) —B —1957–60

Gallarneau, Hugh (Stanford) —B —1941–42, 45–47

Garrett, Thurman (Oklahoma A & M) —C —1947–48

PETE RETZLAFF OF THE PHILADELPHIA EAGLES GOES CLOUD-BUSTING TO TAKE A PASS AGAINST THE CHICAGO BEARS IN A PRE-SEASON GAME IN THE EARLY FALL OF 1958. BEAR JOE FORTUNATO (31) IS ABOUT TO TACKLE RETZLAFF AND VIC ZUCCO (48) IS MOVING IN.

Garrett, William (Mississippi State) —G
—1950
Garvey, Arthur "Hec" (Notre Dame) —
E—1922–25
George, William (Wake Forest) —G
—1952–60
Geyer, William (Colgate) —B—1942–43, 46
Gibron, Abraham (Purdue) —G—1958–59
Gilbert, Kline (Mississippi) —T—1953–57
Glenn, William (East Illinois Teachers) —B
—1941, 44
Goebel, Paul (Michigan) —E—1925
Goodnight, Owen (Hardin-Simmons) —B
—1941, 46
Gordon, Louis (Illinois) —T—1938
Gorgal, Kenneth (Purdue) —B—1955–56
Grange, Garland (Illinois) —E—1929–31
Grange, Harold (Illinois) —B—1925, 28–34
Greenwood, Glen (Iowa) —B—1924
Grosvenor, George (Colorado) —B—1935–36
Grygo, Albert (South Carolina) —B
—1944–45
Gudauskas, Peter (Murray State) —G
—1943–45
Gulyanics, George—B—1947–52
Haddon, Aldous (Washington & Jefferson)
—B—1928
Halas, George (Illinois) —E—1921–30
Haluska, James (Wisconsin) —B—1956
Hamity, Lewis (Chicago) —B—1941
Hammond, Henry (Southwestern) —E
—1937
Hanke, J.—G—1922
Hanny, Frank (Indiana) —T—1923–27
Hansen, Clifford (Luther) —B—1933
Hansen, Wayne (Texas Western) —G
—1950–58
Harley, Charles (Ohio State) —B—1921
Hartman, Fred (Rice) —T—1947
Hatley, John (Baylor) —G—1953
Healy, Michael Donald (Maryland) —T—
1958–59
Healy, Edward (Dartmouth) —T—1922–27
Hearnden, Thomas (Notre Dame) —B
—1929
Heileman, Charles (Iowa State) —E—1939
Helwig, John (Notre Dame) —B—1953–56
Hempel, William (Carroll) —T—1941–42
Hensley, Richard (Kentucky) —E—1953
Hewitt, William (Michigan) —E—1932–36
Hibbs, Jesse (Southern California) —T
—1931
Hill, Harlon (Alabama Teachers) —E
—1954–60
Hobscheid, Frank (Chicago) —G—1927
Hoffman, Jack (Xavier) —E—1952, 55–58
Hoffman, John (Arkansas) —E—1949–56
Holmer, Walter (Northwestern) —B
—1929–30
Holovak, Michael (Boston College) —B
—1947–48
Hoptowit, Albert (Washington State) —T
—1941–45
Howley, Charles (West Virginia) —C—
1958–59

Huffine, Kenneth (Purdue) —B—1921
Hugasian, Harry (Stanford) —B—1955
Hughes, William (Texas) —C—1940–41
Hunsinger, Charles (Florida) —B—1950–52
Hunt, John (Marshall) —B—1945
Hurst, William—G—1924
Ingwersen, Bert (Illinois) —T—1921
Ippolito, Anthony (Purdue) —G—1943
Jagade, Harry (Indiana) —B—1954–55
Jarmoluk, Michael (Temple) —T—1946–47
Jecha, Ray (Northwestern) —G—1955
Jensvold, Leo (Iowa) —B—1931
Jeter, Perry (California Polytech) —B
—1956–57
Jewett, Robert (Michigan State) —E—1958
Joesting, Herbert (Minnesota) —B—1931–32
Johnson, Albert (Kentucky) —B—1938
Johnson, Jack (Miami) —E—1957–59
Johnson, Fred (Notre Dame) —B—1924
Johnson, Peter (Virginia Military Inst.) —
B—1959
Johnson, William (Southern Methodist
Univ.) —G—1946–47
Johnsos, Luke (Northwestern) —E—1929–38
Jones, Edgar (Pittsburgh) —B—1945
Jones, Jerry (Notre Dame) —T—1921
Jones, Stanley (Maryland) —T—1954–60
Kallino, Edward (Illinois) —T—1928
Karr, William (West Virginia) —E—1933–38
Karras, Ted (Indiana) —T—1960
Karwales, John (Michigan) —E—1945, 47
Kassel, Charles (Illinois) —E—1927
Kavanaugh, Kenneth (Louisiana State
Univ.) —E—1940–41, 45–50
Kawal, Edward (Illinois) —C—1931–36
Keane, James (Iowa) —E—1946–51
Kelly, Elmer (Wichita) —E—1944
Kendricks, James (Texas A & M) —B—1924
Keriasotis, Nicholas (St. Ambrose) —G
—1941–42, 45
Kernwein, Graham (Chicago) —B—1927
Kiesling, Walter (St. Thomas) —G—1934
Kilcullen, Robert (Texas Tech.) —T
—1957–58, 60
Kindt, Donald (Wisconsin) —B—1947–55
King, Ralph (Chicago) —T—1925
Kirk, Kenneth (Mississippi) —C—1960
Kissell, Adolph (Boston College) —B—1942
Klawitter, Dominic (South Dakota State)
—C—1956
Klein, Richard (Iowa) —T—1958–59
Knop, Oscar (Illinois) —B—1923–27
Knox, Ronald (U.C.L.A.) —B—1957
Koehler, Robert (Northwestern) —B—1921
Kolman, Edward (Temple) —T
—1940–42, 46–47
Konovsky, Robert (Wisconsin)
Kopcha, Joseph (Chattanooga) —G
—1929, 32–35
Kreamcheck, John (William & Mary) —G
—1953–55
LaFleur, Joseph (Marquette) —B—1922–24
Lahar, Harold (Oklahoma) —G—1941
Lamb, Walter (Oklahoma) —E—1946

Lanum, Ralph (Illinois) —B—1921–24
Larson, Frederic (Notre Dame) —C—1922
Lawler, Allen (Texas) —B—1948
Layne, Robert (Texas) —Q—1948
Leahy, Bernard (Notre Dame) —B—1932
LeClerc, Roger (Trinity, Conn.) —G—1960
Lee, Herman Willie (Florida A & M) —T —1958–60
Leggett, Earl (Louisiana State Univ.) —T —1957–60
Lemon, Clifford (Centre) —E—1926
Leonard, James (Colgate) —T—1924
Lesane, James (Virginia) —B—1952, 54
Lintzenich, Joseph (St. Louis) —B—1930–31
Lipscomb, Paul (Tennessee) —T—1954
Livingston, Howard—B—1953
Logan, James (Indiana) —G—1942–43
Long, Harvey (Detroit) —T—1929
Long, John (Colgate) —B—1944–45
Lowe, Loyd (Texas State North) —B —1953–54
Luckman, Sidney (Columbia) —Q—1939–50
Lujack John (Notre Dame) —Q—1948–51
Lyman, Roy (Nebraska) —T—1926–34
Lyon, George (Kansas State) —T—1929
McAfee, George (Duke) —B —1940–41, 45–50
McColl, William (Stanford) —E—1952–59
McDonald, Lester (Nebraska) —E—1937–39
McEnulty, Douglas (Wichita) —B—1943–44
McIlwain, Roy (Illinois) —B—1925
McLean, Raymond (St. Anselm's) —B —1940–47
McLeod, Robert (Dartmouth) —B—1939–40
McMillen, James (Illinois) —B—1924–28
McMullen, Daniel (Nebraska) —G—1930–31
McPherson, Forrest (Nebraska) —T—1935
Macon, Edward (College of Pacific) —B —1952–53
Magnani, Dante (St. Mary's Cal.) —B —1942–43, 46, 49
Maillard, Ralph (Creighton) —T—1929
Manders, John (Minnesota) —B—1933–41
Maniaci, Joseph (Fordham) —B—1938–41
Manning, Peter (Wake Forest) —B—1960
Manske, Edgar (Northwestern) —E —1935, 37–40
Margarita, Henry (Brown) —B—1944–46
Martinovich, Philip (College of Pacific) —G —1940
Masters, Robert (Baylor) —B—1943–44
Masterson, Bernard (Nebraska) —B —1934–40
Masterson, Forest (Iowa) —C—1945
Mastrogany, August (Iowa) —E—1931
Matheson, John (Western Michigan) —E —1947
Matuza, Albert (Georgetown) —C —1941–43, 46
Maznicki, Frank (Boston College) —B —1942, 46
Meadows, Edward (Duke) —E—1954, 56–57
Mellekas, John (Arizona) —T—1956, 58–60
Merkel, Monte (Kansas) —G—1942–43
Michaels, Edward (Villanova) —G—1936

Mihal, Joseph (Purdue) —T—1940–41
Miller, Charles (Purdue) —C—1932–36
Miller, Milford (Nebraska State) —G—1935
Milner, William (Duke) —G—1947–49
Minini, Frank (San Jose) —B—1947–49
Mintun, John—C—1921
Mitchell, Charles (Tulsa) —B—1945
Mohardt, John (Notre Dame) —B—1925–26
Molesworth, Keith (Monmouth) —Q —1931–37
Mooney, Bow Tipp (Abilene Christian) —B —1944–46
Mooney, James (Georgetown) —E—1935
Moore, Allen (Northwestern) —B—1932
Moore, McNeil (Sam Houston) —B —1954, 56–57
Morris, Francis (Boston Univ.) —B—1942
Morris, John (Santa Barbara) —B—1958–60
Morris, Lawrence (Georgia Tech.) —G— 1959–60
Morrison, Fred (Ohio State) —B—1950–53
Morton, John (Missouri) —E—1945
Moser, Robert (College of Pacific) —C 1951–53
Mosley, Henry (Morris Brown) —B—1955
Mucha, Charles (Washington) —G—1935
Mucha, Rudolph (Washington) —G —1945–46
Mullen, Vern (Nebraska) —E—1924–27
Mullins, Noah (Kentucky) —B—1946–49
Mundee, Fred (Notre Dame) —T—1943–45
Murray, Richard (Marquette) —T—1925
Murry, Donald (Wisconsin) —T—1924–32
Musso, George (Millikin) —G—1933–44
Myers, Dennis (Iowa) —G—1931
Nagurski, Bronko (Minnesota) —B —1930–37, 43
Neacy, Clement (Colgate) —E—1927
Neal, William Edward (Louisiana State Univ.) —T—1951
Negus, Frederick (Wisconsin) —C—1950
Nelson, Everett (Illinois) —T—1929
Nesbitt, Richard (Drake) —B—1930–33
Nickla, Edward (Maryland) —T—1959
Nolting, Ray (Cincinnati) —B—1936–44
Norberg, Henry (Stanford) —E—1948
Nori, Reino (DeKalb) —B—1938
Nowaskey, Robert (Geo. Washington) —E —1940–42
O'Connell, J. F. (Penn. State) —C—1924
O'Connell, Thomas (Illinois) —Q—1953
Oelerich, John (St. Ambrose) —B—1938
Oech, Vern (Minnesota) —T—1936
O'Quinn, John (Wake Forest) —E—1950–51
O'Rourke, Charles (Boston Coll.) —Q—1942
Osmanski, Joseph (Holy Cross) —B —1946–49
Osmanski, William (Holy Cross) —B —1939–43, 46–47
Patterson, William (Baylor) —B—1939
Pauley, Frank (Washington & Jefferson) —T—1930
Pearce, Walter (Illinois) —B—1921–22
Pearson, Madison "Bert" (Kansas State) — C—1929–36
Pederson, James (Augsburg) —E—1932

Perez, Peter (Illinois) —G—1945
Perina, Robert (Princeton) —B—1949–50
Perini, Evo (Ohio State) —B—1954–55
Perkins, Donald (Plattesville) —B—1945–46
Petitbon, Richard (Tulane) —B—1959–60
Peshmalyan, Baruyr (West Point) —E—1924
Petty, John (Purdue) —B—1942
Plasman, Richard (Vanderbilt) —E
—1937–41, 44
Podmajersky, Paul (Illinois) —G—1944
Poliski, John (Notre Dame) —T—1929
Pollock, William (Penn. Military) —B
—1935–36
Pool, J. Hampton (Stanford) —E—1940–43
Preston, Pattison (Wake Forest) —G
—1946–49
Proctor, Rex (Rice) —B—1953
Ramsey, Frank (Oregon State) —T—1945
Reader, Russell (Michigan State) —B—1947
Reese, Lloyd (Tennessee) —B—1946
Rentner, Ernest (Northwestern) —B–1936–37
Richard, Raymond (Nebraska) —G
—1932–33, 35–36
Richman, Harry (Illinois) —G—1929
Roberts, Thomas (DePaul) —T—1944
Roehnelt, William (Bradley) —G—1958–59
Roggeman, Thomas (Purdue) —G—1956–57
Romanik, Steven (Villanova) —Q—1950–53
Romney, Milton (Chicago) —B—1924–28
Ronzani, Gene (Marquette) —Q
—1933–38, 44–45
Rosequist, Theodore (Ohio State) —T
—1934–36
Rowland, Bradley (McMurry) —B—1951
Rowland, Justin (Texas Christian Univ.)
—E—1960
Rupp, Nelson (Denison) —B—1921
Ryan, John (Detroit) —B—1929
Ryan, John (Illinois) —B—1958

Rydzewski, Frank (Notre Dame) —T—1923
Rykovich, Julius (Illinois) —B—1949–51
Sacrinty, Nicholas (Wake Forest) —Q—1947
Savoldi, Joseph (Notre Dame) —B—1930
Schiechl, John (Santa Clara) —C—1945–46
Schroeder, Eugene (Virginia) —E
—1951–52, 54–57
Schuette, Paul (Wisconsin) —G—1930–32
Schweidler, Richard (St. Louis) —B
—1938–39, 46
Scott, Ralph (Wisconsin) —E—1921–25
Seiberling, Gerald (Drake) —B—1932
Seiferling, John (Fresno State) —Q—1947
Senn, William (Knox) —B—1926–31
Serini, Washington (Kentucky) —G
—1948–51
Shaw, Glen (Kentucky) —B—1960
Sherman, Saul (Chicago) —Q—1939–40
Shipkey, Gerald (U.C.L.A.) —B—1953
Shoemaker, Hubbard (Illinois) —G—1921
Siegel, John (Columbia) —E—1939–43
Sigillo, Dominic (Xavier) —T—1943–44
Sisk, John (Marquette) —B—1932–36
Smeja, Rudolph (Michigan) —E—1944–45
Smith, Eugene (Georgia Tech.) —G—1930
Smith, Houston Allen (Mississippi) —E
—1947–48
Smith, J. (North Carolina A & T) —B—1956
Smith, Raymond (Midwestern) —B
—1954–57
Smith, Russell (Illinois) —G—1921–22
Snyder, Robert (Ohio Univ.) —Q—1939–43
Sprinkle, Edward (Hardin-Simmons) —E
—1944–55
Stahlman, Richard (DePaul) —E—1933
Standlee, Norman (Stanford) —B—1941
Stautberg, Gerald (Cincinnati) —G—1951
Steinbach, Laurence (St. Thomas) —T
—1930–31

Nate Fine Photo

REDSKIN WILBUR MOORE, WHO MADE A HABIT OF SLAUGHTERING BEARS, ROLLS OUT
FROM A REVERSE DURING GAME IN 1943. SOLID BLOCKING FORMS OUT IN FRONT.

Steinkemper, William (Notre Dame) —T
—1942–43

Stenn, Paul (Villanova) —T—1948–51

Sternaman, Edward (Illinois) —B—1921–30

Sternaman, Joseph (Illinois) —B—1922–30

Steuber, Robert (Missouri) —B—1943

Stickel, Walter (Penn. Univ.) —T—1946–49

Stinchcomb, Gaylord (Illinois) —B—1921–22

Stolfa, Alton (Luther) —B—1939

Stone, William (Bradley) —B—1951–54

Strickland, Lawrence (Texas State North)
—G—1954–59

Sturtridge, Donald (DePauw) —B—1928–29

Stydahar, Joseph (West Virginia) —T
—1936–42, 45–46

Sullivan, Frank (Loyola) —C—1935–39

Sumner, Charles (William & Mary) —B
—1955, 57–60

Sweeney, James (Cincinnati) —T—1944

Swisher, Robert (Northwestern) —B
—1938–41, 45

Szymanski, Frank (Notre Dame) —C—1949

Tackwell, Charles (Kansas State) —E
—1931–33

Taft, Merrill (Wisconsin) —B—1924

Taylor, John (Ohio State) —T—1921

Taylor, Lionel (Highlands) —E—1959

Thompson, Russell (Nebraska) —T
—1936–39

Thrower, Willie (Michigan State)—Q—1953

Torrance, John (Louisiana State Univ.) —T
—1939–40

Trafton, George (Notre Dame) —C
—1921–32

Trost, Milton (Marquette) —T—1935–39

Turner, Clyde (Hardin-Simmons) —C
—1940–52

Tyler—E—1926

Underwood, Ronald (Arkansas) —B—1957

Usher, Louis (Syracuse) —T—1921, 23

Venturelli, Fred—T—1948

Vick, Henry "Ernie" (Michigan) —C—
1925, 27–28

Vick, Richard (Washington & Jefferson) —B
—1925

Vodicka, Joseph (Lewis) —B—1943–45

Voss, Walter (Detroit) —E—1927–28

Vucinich, Milton (Stanford) —C—1945

Wager, Clinton (St. Mary's Minn.) —E
—1941–42

Wallace, Joseph (Notre Dame) —E—1928

Wallace, Stanley (Illinois) —B—1954, 56–58

Walquist, Laurie (Illinois) —B—1922–31

Watkins, Robert (Ohio State) —B—1955–58

Weatherly, Gerald (Rice) —C—1950–54

Wetoska, Robert (Notre Dame) —T—1960

Wetzel, Damon (Ohio State) —B—1935

White, Roy (Valparaiso) —B—1924–29

White, Wilford (Arizona State) —B
—1951–52

Whitman, S. J. Laverne (Tulsa) —B
—1953–54

Whittenton, Jesse (Texas Western) —B
—1958

Wightkin, William (Notre Dame) —E
—1950–57

Williams, Broughton (Florida) —E—1947

Williams, Fred (Arkansas) —T—1952–60

Williams, Robert (Notre Dame) —Q
—1951–52, 55

Wilson, George (Northwestern) —E
—1937–47

Wynne, Chester (Notre Dame) —B—1928

Youmans, Maurice (Syracuse) —E—1960

Yourist, Abe—E—1923

Zarnas, Augustus (Ohio State) —G—1938

Zeller, Joseph (Indiana) —G—1933–38

Zizak, Vincent (Villanova) —T—1934

Zorich, George (Northwestern) —G
—1944–46

Zucco, Victor (Wayne) —B—1957–60

CHICAGO CARDINALS (1921–59)

Adams, Henry (Pittsburgh) —C—1939

Agee, Samuel (Vanderbilt) —B—1938–39

Albrecht, Arthur (Wisconsin) —T—1943

Aldrich, Charles "Ki" (Texas Christian
Univ.) —C—1939–40

Allen, Edmund (Creighton) —E—1928

Allston, Joseph (Oklahoma) —T—1942

Anderson, Charles (Louisiana Polytech) —E
—1956

Anderson, Clifton (Indiana) —E—1952–53

Anderson, Edward (Notre Dame) —E
—1922–25

Andros, Plato (Oklahoma) —G—1947–50

Angle, Robert (Iowa State) —T—1950

Angsman, Elmer (Notre Dame) —B
—1946–52

Apolskis, Raymond (Marquette) —G
—1941–42, 45–50

Arms, Lloyd (Oklahoma A & M) —G
—1946–48

Arterburn, Elmer (Texas Tech.) —B—1954

Auer, Howard (Michigan) —T—1933

Babartsky, Albert (Fordham) —T—1938–42

Badaczewski, John (Western Reserve) —G
—1948

Bagdon, Edward (Michigan State) —G
—1950–51

Baker, Conway (Centenary) —T
—1936–43, 45

Baker, Roy (Southern California) —B
—1929–30

Balaz, Frank (Iowa) —B—1941, 45

Banonis, Vincent (Detroit) —C
—1942–43, 46–50

Barni, Roy (San Francisco) —B—1952

Barry, Norman (Notre Dame) —Q—1921

Barry, Paul (Tulsa) —B—1954

Bates, Theodore (Oregon State) —T—1959

Bausch, James (Kansas Univ.) —B—1933

Beinor, Edward (Notre Dame) —T
—1940–41

Belden, Charles—B—1930–31

Bergerson, Gilbert (Oregon State) —T
—1933–34

Bernardi, Frank (Colorado) —B—1955–57
Berquist, Jay (Nebraska) —G—1927
Berry, Gilbert (Illinois) —B—1935
Bertagnolli, Libero (Washington of Mo.) —G—1942, 45
Bienemann, Thomas (Drake) —E—1951–56
Bilbo, Jonathan (Mississippi) —T—1938–39
Birlem, Keith (San Jose State) —B—1939
Blackburn, William (Rice) —C—1946–50
Blackwell, Harold (South Carolina) —B —1945
Blazine, Anthony (Illinois Wesleyan) —T —1935–40
Bliss, Homer (Washington & Jefferson) —G —1928
Blumenthal, Morris (Northewestern) —B —1925
Blumer, Herbert (Missouri) —E —1925–30, 33
Bock, Wayne (Illinois) —T—1957
Bogue, George (Stanford) —B—1930
Bohlman, Frank (Centenary) —G—1942
Bonelli, Ernest (Pittsburgh) —B—1945
Booth, Clarence (Southern Methodist Univ.) —T—1943
Boyd, Walter (Westminster) —B—1930–31
Boydston, Max (Oklahoma) —E—1955–58
Braden, David (Marquette) —G—1945
Bradley, Harold (Elon) —E—1938–39
Bradley, R. (Ohio State) —G—1928
Brancato, George (Louisiana State Univ.) —B—1954
Bredde, William (Oklahoma A & M) —B —1954
Brennan, Willis—G—1921–27
Brett, Edwin (Washington State) —E—1936
Brettschneider, Carl (Iowa State) —B —1956–59
Brian, William (Gonzaga) —T—1935
Britton, Earl (Illinois) —B—1929
Brosky, Albert (Illinois) —B—1954
Brown, Hardy (Tulsa) —B—1956
Brubaker, Richard (Ohio State) —E —1955, 57
Bruckner, Leslie (Michigan State) —B—1945
Bryan, John (Chicago) —B—1922
Buckeye, Garland (Wabash) —G—1921–24
Bucklin, Thomas (Idaho) —B—1927
Bukant, Joseph (Washington of Mo.) —B —1941–43
Bulger, Chester (Auburn) —T —1942–43, 45–49
Burkett, Jeffrey (Louisiana State Univ.) —E —1947
Burnett, Dale (Kansas Teachers) —B—1938
Burl, Alexander (Colorado A & M) —B —1956
Busler, Raymond (Marquette) —T —1940–41, 45
Busse, Ellis (Chicago) —B—1929
Butts, Edward (Chico State) —B—1929
Cahill, Ronald (Holy Cross) —B—1943
Cain, James (Alabama) —E—1949
Campana, Albert (Youngstown) —B—1953
Campbell, William (Oklahoma) —B —1945–49

Cantor, Leo (U.C.L.A.) —B—1945
Carlson, Jules (Oregon State) —G—1937
Carr, James (Morris Harvey) —B—1955, 57
Carter, Ross (Oregon) —G—1936–39
Carter, Willie (Tennessee State) —B—1953
Chamberlain, Guy (Nebraska) —E—1927–28
Chappel—G—1921
Cheatham, Lloyd (Auburn) —B—1942
Cherry, Edgar (Hardin-Simmons) —B —1938–39
Chickillo, Nicholas (Miami) —G—1953
Childress, Joseph (Auburn) —B—1956–59
Chisick, Andrew (Villanova) —C—1940–41
Christenson, Martin (Minnesota) —B—1940
Christman, Paul (Missouri) —Q—1945–49
Ciccone, William (W. Virginia Wesleyan) —G—1942
Clark, Beryl (Oklahoma) —B—1940
Clark, Charles (Harvard) —G—1924
Clatt, Corwin (Notre Dame) —B—1948–49
Claypool, Ralph (Purdue) —C—1925–26, 28
Clement, John (Southern Methodist Univ.) —B—1941
Cobb, Thomas (Okla. N.E. Teachers) — T—1931
Cochran, John (Wake Forest) —B—1947–50
Coffee, James (Louisiana State Univ.) —B —1937–38
Colhouer, Jacob (Oklahoma) —G—1946–48
Collins, Paul (Missouri) —B—1945
Compton, Ogden (Hardin-Simmons) —B —1955
Connell, James (Catholic Univ.) —B—1926
Connolly, William (Texas) —G—1946
Conrad, Robert (Texas A&M) —B—1958–59
Cook, David (Illinois) —B—1934–36
Cook, Edward (Notre Dame) —T—1958–59
Coomer, Joseph—T—1947–49
Coppage, Alton (Oklahoma) —E—1940–42
Cosner, Donald (Montana State) —T—1939
Cowhig, Gerald (Notre Dame) —B—1950
Crangle, John (Illinois) —B—1923
Crass, William (Louisiana State Univ.) —B —1937
Creighton, Milan (Arkansas) —E—1931–37
Crittendon, John (Wayne) —E—1954
Cross, Robert (Austin) —T—1958–59
Cross, William (Texas State West) —B —1951–53
Crow, John (Texas A & M) —B—1959–59
Crow, Lindon (Southern California) —B —1955–57
Crowder, Earl (Oklahoma) —B—1939
Cuff, Ward (Marquette) —B—1946
Culpepper, Edward (Alabama)—G—1958–59
Cuppoletti, Bree (Oregon) —G—1934–38
Curcillo, Anthony (Ohio State) —G—1953
Curran, Harry (Boston College) —B—1921
Currivan, Donald (Boston College) —E —1943
Curzon, Harry—B—1928
Daddio, William (Pittsburgh) —E—1940–42
Dahms, Thomas (San Diego State) —T —1956
Davidson, Joseph (Colgate) —G—1928

Davis, Jerome (Louisiana Southeastern) —B
—1948–51
Davis, Raymond (Alabama) —E—1935
Davis, William (Texas Tech.) —T—1940–41
DeCorrevont, William (Northwestern) —B
—1947–48
Delevan, Burton (College of Pacific) —T
1955–56
Deskin, Versil (Drake) —E—1935–39
DeStefano, Frederick (Northwestern) —B
—1924–25
Dewell, William (Southern Methodist
Univ.) —E—1940–41, 45–49
Diehl, Gordon (Idaho) —G—1930–31
Dimancheff, Boris (Purdue) —B—1947–50
Dittrich, John (Wisconsin) —G—1956
Doolan, John (Georgetown) —B—1947–48
Douds, Forrest (Washington & Jefferson)
—T—1932
Dougherty, Philip (Santa Clara) —B—1938
Dove, Robert (Notre Dame) —E—1948–53
Dowell, Gwyn (Texas Tech.) —B—1935–36
Dowling, Patrick (DePaul) —E—1929
Driscoll, John (Northwestern) —B—1921–25
Drulis, Albert (Temple) —B—1945–46
Dugan, Leonard (Wichita) —C—1937–39
Duggan, Gilford (Oklahoma) —T
—1941–43, 45
Duggins, George (Purdue) —E—1933–34
Dunn, Joseph (Marquette) —B—1925–26
Dunstan, Elwyn (Portland) —T—1938–39
Durko, John (Albright) —E—1945
Ebli, Raymond (Notre Dame) —E—1942
Eckl, Robert (Wisconsin) —T—1945
Egan, Richard (Chicago) —E—1921–23
Eggers, Douglas (South Dakota State) —G
—1958
Eikenberg, Charles (Rice) —Q—1948
Elkins, Everett (Marshall) —B—1940
Elkins, Fait (Haskell) —B—1929
Ellis, Walter (Detroit) —T—1926–27
Embree, Melvin (Pepperdine) —E—1954
Engebretsen, Paul (Northwestern) —G
—1933
Enich, Steven (Marquette) —G—1945
Erickson, Harold (Washington & Jefferson)
—B—1925–28
Erickson, Michael (Northwestern) —C
—1930–31
Esser, Clarence (Wisconsin) —E—1947
Evans, Earl (Harvard) —T—1925
Evans, Richard (Iowa) —E—1941–42
Failing, Fred (Central College) —G—1930
Fanucchi, Ledio (Fresno State) —T—1954
Faust, George (Minnesota) —B—1939
Ferry, Louis (Villanova) —T—1951
Field, Harry (Oregon State) —T—1934–36
Fife, Ralph (Pittsburgh) —G—1942, 45
Finn, Bernard (Holy Cross) —B—1933
Finnin, Thomas (Detroit) —T—1957
Fischer, William (Notre Dame) —T
—1949–53
Fisher, Everett (Santa Clara) —B—1938–39
Fiske, Max (DePaul) —B—1937
Fitzgibbons, Paul (Creighton) —B—1928
Flanagan, Latham (Carnegie Tech.) —E

—1931
Flenniken, Max (Geneva) —B—1930
Folz, Arthur (Chicago) —B—1923–25
Foster, Ralph (Oklahoma A & M) —T
1945–46
Francis, Eugene (Chicago) —B—1926
Fugler, Richard (Tulane) —T—1954
Fuller, Frank (Kentucky) —T—1959
Fuller, Lawrence—B—1945
Gainer, Charles (North Dakota) —E—1939
Gasperella, Joseph (Notre Dame) —B—1951
Gay, William (Notre Dame) —B—1951
Gehrke, C. Fred (Los Angeles) —B—1950
Geri, Joseph (Georgia) —B—1952
German, James (Centre) —B—1940
Ghersanich, Vernon (Auburn) —G—1942–43
Gibbons, James (DePaul) —C—1929
Gibson, George (Minnesota) —G—1929
Gilchrist, George (Tennessee State) —T
—1953
Gillies, Fred (Cornell) —T—1921–28
Gillis, Daniel (Rice) —C—1958–59
Glassgow, Willis (Iowa) —B—1931
Glick, Fred (Colorado A & M) —B—1959
Goble, Lester (Alfred) —B—1954–55
Goldberg, Marshall (Pittsburgh) —B
—1939–43, 46–48
Goldman, Samuel (Howard) —E—1948
Goldsberry, John (Indiana) —T—1949–50
Goodman, Aubrey (Chicago) —T—1927
Gordon, Louis (Illinois) —T—1930–35
Gordon, Robert (Tennessee) —B—1958
Graham, Alfred (Dayton) —G—1932–33
Grant, Hugh (St. Mary's Cal.) —B—1928
Gray, Kenneth (Howard Payne) —B—
1958–59
Green, Frank (Tulsa) —B—1934
Greene—T—1921
Green—T—1926–27
Griffiths, Homer (Southern California) —B
—1934
Grigas, John (Holy Cross) —B—1942–43
Groom, Jerome (Notre Dame)—T—1951–55
Grosvenor, George (Colorado) —B—1936–37
Hall, John (Texas Christian Univ.) —B
—1940–43
Hall, Kenneth (Texas A & M) —B—1959
—1955, 57–59
Hammack, Malcolm (Florida) —B
1955, 57–59
Handler, Philip (Texas Christian Univ.)
—G—1930–36
Hanke, Carl (Minnesota) —E—1924–25
Hanlon, Robert (Notre Dame) —B—1948
Hanson, Homer (Kansas State) —B—
1935–36
Harder, Marlin (Wisconsin) —B—1946–50
Hardy, James (Southern California) —Q
—1949–51
Harmon, Hamilton (Tulsa) —C—1937
Hartong, George (Chicago) —G—1924
Hartshorn, Lawrence (Kansas State) —G
—1955
Hatley, John (Baylor) —G—1954–55
Hauser, Arthur (Xavier) —T—1959
Hecker, Norbert (Baldwin-Wallace) —E

—1952

Hellstrom, Norton (Illinois) —B—1921
Hennessey, Jerome (Santa Clara) —E—1950—51
Hickman, Lawrence (Baylor) —B—1959
Higgins, John (Trinity) —G—1941
Higgins, Thomas (North Carolina) —T—1953
Hill, Donald (Stanford) —B—1929—30
Hill, Irving (Trinity) —B—1931—32
Hill, James (Sam Houston) —B—1955—59
Hill, King (Rice) —Q—1958—59
Hilpert, Harold (Oklahoma City) —E—1931
Hinchman, Hubert (Butler) —B—1933—34
Hock, John (Santa Clara) —T—1950
Hoel, Robert (Pittsburgh) —G—1937—38
Hogue, Murrell (Centenary) —T—1929—30
Holm, Bernard (Alabama) —B—1932
Horstman, Roy (Purdue) —B—1934
Horween, Arnold (Harvard) —B—1921—24
Horween, Ralph (Harvard) —B—1921—23
Houghton, Gerald (Washington State) —T—1951
Huffman, Frank (Marshall) —G—1939—41
Hughes, Bernard (Oregon) —C—1934—36
Hummell, Charles (Lafayette) —G—1927
Hurlburt, John (Chicago) —B—1924—25
Husmann, Edward (Nebraska) —T—1953, 56—59
Hust, Albert (Tennessee) —E—1946
Illman, Edward (Montana State) —B—1928
Isaacson, Theodore (Washington) —T—1934—35
Ivy, Frank (Oklahoma) —E—1940—41, 45—57
Jackson, Charles (Southern Methodist Univ.) —B—1958
Jacobs, Marvin—T—1948
Jagielski, Harry (Indiana) —T—1956
Jankovich, Keever (College of Pacific) —E—1953
Jennings, John (Ohio State) —T—1950—57
Jones, Ben (Grove City) —B—1927—28
Johnson, Albert (Kentucky) —B—1939—41
Johnson, Raymond (Denver) —B—1940
Johnston, James (Washington) —B—1946
Joyce, Donald (Tulane) —T—1951—53
Karras, John (Illinois) —B—1952
Karwales, John (Michigan) —E—1947
Kassel, Charles (Illinois) —E—1929—33
Keane, Thomas (West Virginia) —B—1955
Kearns, Thomas (Miami) —T—1946
Kellogg, Clarence (St. Mary's Cal.) —B—1936
Kellogg, Robert (Tulane) —B—1940
Kellogg, William (Syracuse) —B—1926
Kenneally, George (St. Bonaventure) —B—1930
Kieley, Howard—T—1926
Kiesling, Walter (St. Thomas) —T—1929—33
Kiley, Roger (Notre Dame) —E—1923
Kinek, George (Tulane) —B—1954
King, Emmett—B—1954
King, Richard (Harvard) —B—1923—24
Kingery, Ellsworth (Tulane) —B—1954
Klimek, Anthony (Illinois) —E—1951—52

Klotovich, Michael (St. Mary's Cal.) —B—1941
Klumb, John (Washington State) —E—1939
Knafelc, Gary (Colorado) —E—1954
Knight, Charles—C—1921
Knolla, John (Creighton) —B—1942, 45
Kochel, Michael (Fordham) —G—1939
Koehler, Robert (Northwestern) —B—1921—26
Koken, Michael (Notre Dame) —B—1933
Koman, William (North Carolina) —G—1959
Konovsky, Robert (Wisconsin) —T—1956—58
Kuharich, Joseph (Notre Dame) —G—1940—41, 45
Kutner, Malcom (Texas) —E—1946—50

DOUBLE TROUBLE—MAL KUTNER, (*left*) AND
BILL DEWELL, OFFENSIVE ENDS FOR THE
CHICAGO CARDINALS IN THE GLORY YEARS OF
1947 AND 1948, WORKED ALONG WITH THE
FAMOUS "DREAM BACKFIELD" OF CHRISTMAN,
HARDER, TRIPPI, AND ANGSMAN TO BRING
TERROR TO THE DEFENSIVE TEAMS OF THEIR
OPPONENTS IN THE NATIONAL FOOTBALL
LEAGUE.

Kuzman, John (Fordham) —T—1941
Lach, Steven (Duke) —B—1942
Ladd, James (Bowling Green) —E—1954
Lainhart, Porter (Oregon) —B—1933
Lamb, Roy (Lombard) —B—1926—27, 33
Lane, Richard—B—1954—59
Lange, Clifford (Montana) —E—1929
Lange, William (Dayton) —G—1954—55
LaRosa, Paul—E—1921
Larson, Frederic (Notre Dame) —C—1929
Larson, Lloyd (Wisconsin) —B—1929
Larson, Paul (California) —B—1957
Lauro, Lindell (Pittsburgh) —B—1951
Lawrence, James (Texas Christian Univ.) —B—1936—37
Ledbetter, Homer (Arkansas) —B—1932—33
Leggett, David (Ohio State) —B—1955

Leonard, John (Indiana) —G—1922–23
Lewis, Charles Mac (Iowa) —T—1959
Lewis, Woodley (Oregon) —B—1956–59
Leysenaar, Harry (Marquette) —B—1942
Liebel, Frank (Norwich) —E—1948
Lillard, Joseph (Oregon) —B—1932–33
Lind, Albert (Northwestern) —C—1936
Lindon, Luther (Kentucky) —T—1945
Lipinski, James (Fairmont State) —T—1950
Lipostad, Edward (Wake Forest) —T—1952
Loepfe, Richard (Wisconsin) —T—1948–49
Lokanc, Joseph (Northwestern) —G—1941
Lunceford, David (Baylor) —T—1957
Lunz, Gerald (Marquette) —G—1925–26
Lynch, Lynn (Illinois) —G—1951
McBride, John (Syracuse) —B—1935
McCullough, Hugh (Oklahoma) —B
  —1940–41
McCusker, James (Pittsburgh) —T—1958
McDermott, Lloyd (Kentucky) —T
  —1950–51
McDonnell, John (Creighton) —B—1926–30
McDonough, Coley (Dayton) —B—1939
McElwain, William (Northwestern) —B
  —1924, 26
McGirl, Leonard (Missouri) —G—1933
McHan, Lamar (Arkansas) —Q—1954–58
McInerney, Arnold (Notre Dame) —E
  —1921–27
McNally, Frank (St. Mary's Cal.) —C
  —1931–34
McNulty, Paul (Notre Dame) —B—1924–25
McPhee, Frank (Princeton) —E—1955
Madden, Lloyd (Colorado Mines) —B—1940
Maddock, Robert (Notre Dame) G—
  —1942, 46
Maeda, Chester (Colorado State) —B—1945
Mahoney, Frank "Ike" (Creighton) —B
  —1925–28, 31
Mallouf, Ray (Southern Methodist Univ.)
  —Q—1941, 46–48
Malloy, Lester (Loyola) —B—1931–33
Mann, David (Oregon State) —B—1955–57
Maple, Howard (Oregon State) —B—1930
Marchibroda, Theodore (Detroit) —Q—1957
Marelli, Ray (Notre Dame) —G—1928
Marotti, Louis (Toledo) —G—1943, 45
Marquardt, John (Illinois) —E—1921
Martin, Caleb (Louisiana Tech.) —T—1947
Martin, Herschel (New York Univ.) —B
  —1932
Martin, John (Oklahoma) —B—1941–43
Mason, Joel (Western Michigan) —E—1939
Mason, Walter (Colgate) --E—1928
Masters, Walter (Pennsylvania) —Q
  —1942–43
Matson, Oliver (San Francisco) —B
  —1952–58
Mauldin, Stanley (Texas) —T—1946–48
May, William (Louisiana State Univ.) —B
  —1937–38
Mehringer, Peter (Kansas) —T—1934–36
Meinert, Dale (Oklahoma State) —G—
  1958–59
Memmelaar, Dale (Wyoming) —G—1959

Mergen, Michael (San Francisco) —T—1952
Mertes, Bernard (Iowa) —B—1945
Method, Russell (North Dakota) —B—1929
Mikulak, Michael (Oregon) —B—1934–36
Miller, Milford (Nebraska State) —G
  —1936–37
Mills, Denver (William & Mary) —E—1952
Moe, Harold (Oregon State) —B—1933
Mohardt, John (Notre Dame) —B—1922–23
Monahan, Regis (Ohio State) —G—1939
Montfort, Avery (New Mexico) —B—1941
Montgomery, William (Louisiana State
  Univ.) —B—1946
Montgomery, Ralph (Centre) —T—1923
Mooney, James (Georgetown) —E—1935
Moore, Allen (Loyola of N. O.) —B—1932
Moran, Francis (Grinnell) —B—1927
Morrow, John (Alabama) —B—1937–38
Morrow, Robert (Illinois Wesleyan) —B
  1941–43
Moynihan, Timothy (Notre Dame) —C
  1932–33
Muellner, William (DePaul) —E—1937
Mullen, Vern (Nebraska) —E—1927
Mulleneaux, Lee (Arizona) —B—1938
Munger—T—1924
Murphy, George (Dartmouth) —B—1928
Murphy, Thomas (Arkansas) —B—1934
Murphy, William (Washington of Mo.) —
  G—1940–41
Nagel, Ray (U.C.L.A.) —B—1953
Nagel, Ross (St. Louis) —T—1942
Nagler, Gern (Santa Clara) —B—1953–58
Neacy, Clement (Colgate) —E—1928
Nesbitt, Richard (Drake) —B—1933
Nevers, Ernest (Stanford) —B—1929–31
Newman, Robert (Illinois Wesleyan) —E
  —1934–36
Nichelini, Allen (St. Mary's Cal.) —B
  —1935–36
Nichols, Hamilton (Rice) —G—1947–49
Nisbet, David (Washington) —E—1933
Nolan, Earl (Arizona) —T—1937–38
Norman, Robert—C—1945
Norton, Jerry (Southern Methodist Univ.)
  —B—1959
Nussbaumer, Robert (Michigan) —B
  —1949–50
Oakley, Charles (Louisiana State Univ.)
  —B—1954
Obeck, Victor (Springfield) —G—1945
O'Connor, Daniel (Georgetown) —G
  —1921–22, 24
Oliver, Vincent (Indiana) —B—1945
Olson, Carl (U.C.L.A.) —T—1942
Olszewski, John (California) —B—1953–57
Orf, Roland (Missouri) —E—1941
Owens, Luke (Kent State) —T—1958–59
Padgen, Nicholas (Creighton) —C—1940
Panciera, Donald (San Francisco) —B—1952
Panelli, John (Notre Dame) —B—1951–53
Panfil, Kenneth (Purdue) —T—1959
Pangle, Harold (Oregon State)—B—1935–38
Pappio, Joseph (Haskell) —B—1930
Pardoneer, Paul (Purdue) —B—1934–35

Parker, Joseph (Texas) —E—1946–47
Parker, Raymond (Centenary) —B—1937–42
Pasquariello, Ralph (Villanova) —B —1951–52
Pasquesi, Anthony (Notre Dame) —T —1955–57
Pate, Rupert (Wake Forest) —G—1940
Patera, John (Oregon) —G—1958–59
Patrick, Frank (Pittsburgh) —B—1938–39
Patton, John (Texas Christian Univ.) —G —1951
Paul, Donald (Washington State) —B —1950–53
Peacock, Merrill (San Francisco) —E—1952
Pearson, Madison "Bert" (Kansas State) — C—1935–36
Peters, Forest (Illinois) —B—1932
Peters, Volney (Southern California) —T —1952–53
Peterson, Kenneth (Gonzaga) —B—1935
Petrovich, George (Texas) —T—1949–50
Philpott, Dean (Fresno State) —B—1958
Pierce, Donald (Kansas) —C—1942–43
Plasman, Richard (Vanderbilt) —E 1946–47
Polofsky, Gordon (Tennessee) —B—1952–54
Polsfoot, Francis (Washington State) —E 1950–52
Poole, James (Mississippi) —E—1945
Popa, Eli (Illinois) —B—1952
Popovich, Milton (Montana) —B—1938–42
Psaltis, James (Southern California) —B —1953–55
Puplis, Andrew (Notre Dame) —Q—1943
Purdin, Calvin (Tulsa) —B—1943
Ramsey, Garrard (William & Mary) —G —1946–50
Ramsey, Knox (William & Mary) —G —1950–51
Ramsey, Ray (Bradley) —B—1950–53
Randle, Ulmo (Virginia) —E—1959
Randolph, Clare (Indiana) —C—1930
Rankin, Walter (Texas Tech.) —B —1942–43, 45–47
Ranspot, Keith (Southern Methodist Univ.) —E—1940
Ravensburg, Robert (Indiana) —E—1948–49
Reed, Joseph (Louisiana State Univ.) —B 1937–39
Rexer, Freeman (Tulane) —E—1943, 45
Reynolds, John (Baylor) —C—1937
Reynolds, Mack Charles (Louisiana State Univ.) —Q—1958–59
Reynolds, Robert (Mississippi) —B—1945
Rhea, Floyd (Oregon) —G—1943
Ribble, Loran (Hardin-Simmons) —G— 1933
Richards, Perry (Detroit) —E—1959
Risk, Edward (Purdue) —B—1932
Risvold—B—1927–28
Roach, John (Notre Dame) —B—1927
Roach, John (Southern Methodist Univ.) —B—1956, 1959
Robbins, John (Arkansas) —B—1938–39
Robinson, John (Missouri State Northeast)

—T—1936–38
Robl, Harold (Wisconsin Teachers) —B —1945
Robnett, Marshall (Texas A & M) —C —1943, 45
Rogers, Glynn (Texas Christian Univ.) — G—1938–39
Rogge, George (Iowa) —E—1931–33
Romanik, Steven (Villanova) —Q—1953–54
Rooney, Cobb (Colorado) —B—1929–30
Rooney, William—B—1929
Root, James (Miami) —B—1953, 56
Rose, Eugene (Wisconsin) —B—1929–32
Rucinski, Edward (Indiana) —E—1943, 45–46
Rundquist, Elmer (Illinois) —T—1922
Rushing, Marion (Southern Illinois) —G —1959
Russell, Dougal (Kansas) —B—1934–37
Ryan—B—1924
Ryszewski, Frank (Notre Dame) —T—1921
Sabados, Andrew (Citadel) —G—1939–41
Sachs, Leonard (Loyola) —E—1921–23, 25
Sachse, Francis (Texas Tech.) —B—1942
Sandberg, Sigmund (Iowa Wesleyan) —T —1933
Sandifer, Daniel (Louisiana State Univ.) —B—1953
Sanford, Leo (Louisiana Tech.) —G —1951–57
Sarbo, Philip (Washington State) —B 1934–36
Sarringhaus, Paul (Ohio State) —B—1946
Scanlon, John (DePaul) —B—1921
Scardine, Carmen—B—1932
Schleicher, Maurice (Penn State) —E—1959
Schlinkman, Walter (Texas Tech.) —B —1951
Schmidt, George (Lewis College) —C—1953
Schneidman, Herman (Iowa) —B—1940
Schwall, Victor (Northwestern) —B —1947–50
Schwartz, Elmer (Washington State) —B —1932
Schwenk, Wilson (Washington of Mo.) —B —1942
Sears, James (Southern California) —B —1954, 57–58
Self, Clarence (Wisconsin) —B—1949
Seno, Frank (George Washington) —B —1945–46
Shaw, Jesse (Southern California) —G—1931
Shaw, Robert (Ohio State) —E—1950
Shelly, Dexter (Texas) —B—1932
Shenefelt, Paul—T—1934–35
Shirk, John (Oklahoma) —E—1940
Shook, Fred (Texas Christian Univ.) —C —1940–41
Sikora, Michael (Oregon) —G—1952
Simas, William (St. Mary's Cal.) —B— 1932–33
Simmons, John (Detroit) —G—1950–56
Sitko, Emil (Notre Dame) —B—1951–52
Slater, Fred (Iowa) —T—1926–31
Sloan, Dwight (Arkansas) —B—1938
Smith, Charles (Georgia) —B—1947
Smith, George (Villanova) —B—1943

Smith, Russell (Illinois) —G—1922, 25
Smith, Wilfred (DePauw) —G—1923–25
Smith, William (Washington) —E—1934–39
Speegle, Clifton (Oklahoma) —C—1945
Spence, Julian (Sam Houston) —B—1956
Spinks, Jack (Alcorn A & M) —G—1953
Springsteen, William (Lehigh) —E—1927–28
Stacy, William (Mississippi State) —B—1959
Steger, Peter—B—1921
Stein, Herbert (Washington & Jefferson) —G—1928–29
Stennet, Fred (St. Mary's Cal.) —B—1932
Stewart, Vaughn (Alabama) —C—1943
Stokes, Lee (Centenary) —C—1943
Stonesifer, Donald (Northwestern) —E —1951–56
Strack, Charles (Colgate) —G—1928
Strader, Norman (St. Mary's Cal.) —B—1927
Strausbaugh, James (Ohio State) —B—1946
Sugar, Leo (Purdue) —E—1954–59
Suminski, David (Wisconsin) —G—1953
Summerall, George (Arkansas) —E—1953–57
Sutch, George (Temple) —B—1946
Svoboda, William (Tulane) —B—1950–53
Swanson, Eyar (Lombard) —E—1925–27
Swistowicz, Michael (Notre Dame) B—1950
Szot, Walter (Bucknell) —T—1946–48
Taylor, James (Baylor) —C—1957–58
Tays, James—B—1925
Teeuws, Leonard (Tulane) —T—1954–57
Thomas, Ralph (San Francisco) —E—1952
Thompson, Harry (U.C.L.A.) —G—1955
Tinsley, Gaynell (Louisiana State Univ.) —E—1937–38, 40
Tinsley, Jess (Louisiana State Univ.) —T —1929–33
Tipton, Howard (Southern California) —B —1933–37
Tonelli, Mario (Notre Dame) —B—1940–45
Toogood, Charles (Nebraska) —T—1957
Toscani, Francis (St. Mary's Cal.) —B—1932
Tracey, John (Texas A & M) —E—1959
Triplett, Wallace (Penn. State) —B —1952–53
Trippi, Charles (Georgia) —B—1947–55
Tripucka, Frank (Notre Dame) —Q —1950–52
Tubbs, Gerald (Oklahoma) —B—1957–58
Tyler, Peter (Hardin-Simmons) —B —1937–38
Ucovich, Mitchell (San Jose State) —T —1945
Ulrich, Charles (Illinois) —T—1954–58
Underwood, John (Iowa State) —G—1929
Vanzo, Fred (Northwestern) —Q—1941
Vaughn, Charles (Tennessee) —B—1936
Vesser, John (Idaho) —E—1927, 30–31
Vodicka, Joseph (Lewis) —B—1945
Voight—G—1921
Vokaty, Otto (Heidelberg) —B—1933
Volok, William (Tulsa) —G—1934–39
Wager, Clinton (St. Mary's Minn.) —E —1943, 45
Wagstaff, James (Idaho State) —B—1959
Waldron, Austin (Gonzaga) —G—1927

Wallner, Fred (Notre Dame) —G —1951–52, 54–55
Watford, Gerald (Alabama) —E—1953–54
Watkins, Robert (Ohio State) —B—1958
Watt, Walter (Miami) —B—1945
Weaver, Charles (Chicago) —C—1930
Weber, Charles (Westchester) —E—1956–58
Wedel, Richard (Wake Forest) —G—1948
Weller, Truman (Nebraska) —T—1926–27
West, Stanley (Oklahoma) —G—1956–57
Wetterlund, Chester (Illinois Wesleyan) —B—1942
Whalen, William—G—1921–24
Wham, Thomas (Furman) —E—1949–51
Wheeler, Ernest (North Dakota State) —B —1939, 42
White, Arthur (Alabama) —G—1940–41 —G—1940–41
Whitman, S. J. Laverne (Tulsa) —B —1951–53
Wiederquist, Chester (Washington & Jefferson) —T—1928
Williams, Jacob (Texas Christian Univ.) —T—1929–33
Williamson, Ivan (Michigan) —T—1932
Wilson, Gordon (Texas Mines) —G 1942–43, 45
Wilson, William (Gonzaga) —E—1935–37
Wood, Robert (Alabama) —T—1940
Woodruff—E—1926
Yablonski, Ventan (Columbia)—B—1948–51
Yarr, Thomas (Notre Dame) —C—1933
Yeisley—E—1928
Zelencik, Frank (Oglethorpe) —T—1939
Zimny, Robert (Indiana) —T—1945–49
Zoia, Clyde (Notre Dame) —G—1921–23
Zontini, Louis (Notre Dame) —B—1940–41

CARD PITT (Merger) (1944)

Baker, Conway (Centenary) —T—1944
Booth, Clarence (Southern Methodist Univ.) —T—1944
Bove, Anthony (St. Francis) —E—1944
Bulger, Chester (Auburn) —T—1944
Butler, John (Tennessee) —B—1944
Coomer, Joseph—T—1944
Currivan, Donald (Boston College) —E —1944
Doyle, Theodore (Nebraska) —T—1944
Duggan, Cilford (Oklahoma) —T—1944
Grigas, John (Holy Cross) —B—1944
Hoague, Joseph (Colgate) —B—1944
Kichefski, Walter (Miami) —E—1944
McCarthy, James (Illinois) —E—1944
McCarthy, Thomas (St. Francis) —B—1944
McDonough, Coley (Dayton) —B—1944
Magulick, George (St. Francis) —B—1944
Marotti, Louis (Toledo) —G—1944
Martin, John (Oklahoma) —B—1944
Masters, Walter (Pennsylvania) —Q—1944
Merkovsky, Elmer (Pittsburgh) —T—1944
Naioti, John (St. Francis) —B—1944
O'Dell, Melvin (Duquesne) —B—1944
Perko, John (Duquesne) —G—1944

DREAM COMES TRUE—CHARLES TRIPPI (*left*) SIGNS HIS FIRST CONTRACT WITH THE CHICAGO
CARDINALS EARLY IN 1947 TO COMPLETE THE "DREAM BACKFIELD" THAT THE LATE
CHARLES BIDWELL (*right*), THEN OWNER OF THE CARDINALS, HAD WANTED. JIM
CONZELMAN, HEAD COACH OF THE TEAM, LOOKS ON. BIDWELL'S DREAM WAS (*bottom
picture, left to right*): PAUL CHRISTMAN, QB; PAT HARDER, FB; MARSHALL GOLDBERG
AND TRIPPI, HBS. WHEN THE TEAM WON ITS FIRST CHAMPIONSHIP THAT FALL, BIDWELL
WAS DEAD. ELMER ANGSMAN WAS ONE OF THE HALFBACKS, AND GOLDBERG HAD BECOME
ONE OF THE FINEST DEFENSIVE SAFETYMEN IN LEAGUE HISTORY.

Petchell, John (Duquesne)—B—1944
Popovich, John (St. Vincent's)—B—1944
Rankin, Walter (Texas Tech.)—B—1944
Robnett, Marshall (Texas A & M)—C—1944
Rucinski, Edward (Indiana)—E—1944
Schultz, Eberle (Oregon State)—G—1944
Semes, Bernard (Duquesne)—B—1944
Thurbon, Robert (Pittsburgh)—B—1944
Wager, Clinton (St. Mary's Minn.)—E—1944
Wukits, Albert (Duquesne)—C—1944

CINCINNATI CELTS (1921)

Beekley, Eugene (Miami, Ohoi)—G—1921
Costello, Rory—C—1921
Crawford, Kenneth (Miami, Ohio)—B—1921
Dasstling, Dane (Marietta)—T—1921
Doherty, William (Marietta)—C—1921
Fortmeyer, Alben—B—1921
Green
Hauser, Earl (Miami, Ohio) E—1921
Knabb, Chester—B—1921
Krueck, Edward—E—1921
Lane, Frank—G—1921
Lewis, Arthur (West Virginia)—T—1921
McMahan (Heidelberg)
Melvin (Marietta)
Munns, George (Miami, Ohio)—B—1921
Orth, Henry (Miami, Ohio)—G—1921
Schuessler, Erwin—T—1921
Schupe, Walter (Miami, Ohio)—T—1921
Thompson
Volz, Peter—E—1921

CINCINNATI REDS (1933—34)

Abruzzino, Frank (Colgate)—C—1933
Alford, Eugene (Texas Tech.)—B—1934
Ariail, David (Auburn)—E—1934
Aspatore, Edward (Marquette)—T—1934
Bausch, James (Kansas)—B—1933
Blondin, Thomas (West Virginia Wesleyan)—G—1933
Braidwood, Charles (Chattanooga)—E—1933
Burdick, Lloyd (Illinois)—T—1933
Burleson, John (Southern Methodist Univ.)—G—1933
Bushby, Thomas (Kansas State)—T—1934
Caywood, Lester (St. John's)—G—1933—34
Clark, Myers (Oregon State)—B—1933—34
Cole, Peter (Trinity-Tex.)—G—1934
Corzine, Lester (Davis & Elkins)—B—1933—34
Crakes, Joseph (South Dakota)—E—1933
Diehl, Gordon (Idaho)—T—1933
Draveling, Leo (Michigan)—T—1933
Elkins, Fait (Haskell)—B—1933
Elser, Earl (Butler)—B—1934
Feather, Elwin (Kansas State)—B—1934
Grant, Ross (New York Univ.)—G—1933—34

Hanson, Homer (Kansas State)—B—1934
Hilpert, Harold (Oklahoma City Univ.)—B—1933
Howell, Foster (Texas Christian Univ.)—T—1934
Lee, Hilary (Oklahoma)—G—1933—34
LeFebre, Gilbert—B—1933—34
Lewis, Loren (Northwestern)—B—1934
Logus—C—1934
Maples, Talmadge (Tennessee)—B—1934
Mooney, James (Georgetown)—E—1933—34
Moore, Allen (Loyola-N. O.)—B—1934
Moses, Howard (Washington State)—E—1933
Mott, Norman (Georgia)—B—1934
Mulleneaux, Lee (Arizona)—B—1933—34—1933—34
Munday, George (Emporia Teachers)—T—1933—34
Palm, Michael (Penn. State)—B—1933
Parriott, William (West Virginia)—E—1934
Pope, Lewis (Purdue)—B—1933—34
Powell, Richard (Davis-Elkins)—E—1933—34
Rogers, John (Notre Dame)—C—1933—34
Sark, Harvey (Phillips)—G—1934
Saumer, Sylvester (St. Olaf)—B—1934
Schmidt, Kermit (California Polytech)—E—1933
Sebastian, Michael (Pittsburgh)—B—1934
Squyres, Seaman, (Rice)—B—1933
Steverson, Norris (Arizona State)—T—1934
Tackwell, Charles (Kansas State)—E—1933—34
Vokaty, Otto (Heidelberg)—B—1934
Wiberg, Oscar (Nebraska Wesleyan)—B—1933
Wilging, Coleman (Xavier)—T—1934
Wilkerson, Basil (Oklahoma City Univ.)—E—1934
Workman, Blake (Tulsa)—B—1933
Zunker, Charles (Texas State Southwest)—T—1934

CLEVELAND RAMS (1921, 1923—25, 1927, 1931, 1937—42, 1944—45) (Also played as Indians, Bulldogs,then transferred to Los Angeles as the Rams)

Adams, Chester (Ohio)—T—1939—42
Alfonse, Jules (Minnesota)—B—1937—38
Anderson, Stanley (Stanford)—E—1940—41
Anderson, Willard (Syracuse)—B—1923
Andrako, Stephen (Ohio State)—C—1941
Andrews, Leroy (Kansas State Teachers)—G—1927
Armstrong, Graham (John Carroll)—T—1941, 45
Atty, Alexander (West Virginia)—G—1939
Ault, Wayne (Oklahoma A & M)—T—1924—25
Bacchus, Carl (Missouri)—E—1927
Bagby, Herman (Arkansas)—B—1927
Bahan, Leonard (Notre Dame)—B—1923
Baldwin, George (Virginia)—E—1925

Barber, Mark (South Dakota State) —B —1937
Barle, Louis—T—1939
Bauer, Herbert (Baldwin-Wallace) —T —1925
Baujan, Harry (Notre Dame) —E—1921
Benton, James (Arkansas) —E —1938–42, 44–45
Bernard, David (Mississippi) —B—1944–45
Berry, Cornelius (North Carolina State) —E —1940
Bettridge, John (Ohio State) —B—1937
Bierce, Bruce (Akron) —E—1922–24
Bloodgood, Elbert (Nebraska) —B—1927
Bostick, Lewis (Alabama) —G—1939–42
Boone, Robert (Elon) —B—1942
Bouley, Gilbert (Boston College) —T—1945
Bowser, Arda (Bucknell) —B—1923
Brahm, Lawrence (Temple) —G—1942
Braidwood, Charles (Chattanooga) —E —1931
Braman, William (Colgate) —T—1925
Brawley, Edward (Holy Cross) —G—1921
Brazell, Carl (Baylor) —B—1938
Broadley, Karl (Bethany) —G—1925
Broda, Harold (Brown) —E—1927
Brumbaugh, Carl (Florida) —B—1937
Bucklew, Philip (Xavier) —E—1937
Burmeister, Forrest (Purdue) —B—1937
Burt, Harold (Kansas) —G—1925
Busich, Samuel (Ohio State) —E—1937
Calac, Peter (Carlisle) —B—1921
Carberry, Glenn (Notre Dame) —E—1925
Chamberlain, Guy (Nebraska) —B—1924
Cherundolo, Charles (Penn. State) —C —1937–39
Chesbro, Marcel (Colgate) —G—1938
Civiletto, Frank (Springfield) —B—1923
Clark, Myers (Oregon State) —B—1931
Clay, Boyd (Tennessee) —T—1940–42, 44
Cobb, Alfred (Syracuse) —G—1923–25
Cobb, Thomas (Okla. N.E. Teachers) — T—1927
Colella, Thomas (Canisius) —B—1944–45
Comstock, Rudolph (Georgetown) —G —1924
Conkright, William (Oklahoma) —C —1939–45
Conlee, Gerald (St. Mary's Cal.) —C—1938
Conover, Lawrence (Penn. State) —C —1924–25
Cooper, William (Oberlin) —T—1937
Corbo, Thomas (Duquesne) —G—1944
Corcoran, Arthur (Georgetown) —E—1921
Cordill, Oliver (Rice) —B—1940
Cornsweet, Albert (Brown) —B—1931
Crowder, Earl (Oklahoma) —B—1940
Critchfield, Lawrence (Grove City) —G —1931
Cullen, Thomas (Georgetown) —G—1931
Cunningham, Harold (Ohio State) —E —1927
Dalsasso, Christopher (Indiana) —T—1937
Davis, Corbett (Indiana) —Q—1938–42
DeLauer, Robert (Southern California) —C

—1945
DeWitz, Herbert (Nebraska) —B—1927
Dowd, Gerald (St. Mary's Cal.) —C—1939
Drake, John (Purdue) —B—1937–41
Dunstan, Elwyn (Portland) —T—1939–41
Eason, Roger (Oklahoma) —T—1945
Ebersole, Harold (Cornell) —G—1923
Edler, Robert (Ohio Wesleyan) —B—1923
Edwards, Eugene (Notre Dame) —G —1923–25
Eichenlaub, Raymond (Notre Dame) —B —1925
Elston, Arthur (Southern California) —C —1942
Elliott, Wallace (Lafayette) —B—1924–25
Emerick, Robert (Miami—Ohio) —T—1937
Fawcett, Jacob (Southern Methodist Univ.) —T—1942, 44
Feather, Elwin (Kansas State) —B—1927
Flohr, Lester (Bethany) —T—1927
Friedman, Benjamin (Michigan) —B—1927
Friend, Benjamin (Louisiana State Univ.) —T—1939
Gardner, George (Carlisle) —E—1923–24
Gallovich, Anthony (Wake Forest) —B —1941
Gehrke, Clarence Fred (Utah) —B—1940, 45
Ghee, Milton (Dartmouth) —B—1921
Giannoni, John (St. Mary's Cal.) —E—1938
Gibson, Billy Joe (Tulsa) —C—1942, 44
Gift, Wayne (Purdue) —B—1937
Goddard, Edward (Washington State) —B —1937–38
Godfrey, Herbert (Washington State) —E —1942
Goodnight, Owen (Hardin-Simmons) —B —1941
Greenwood, Donald (Missouri) —B—1945
Gregory, John (Chattanooga) —G—1941–42
Gregory, Michael (Denison) —G—1931
Goolsby, James (Mississippi State) —C —1940
Gudauskas, Peter (Murray State) —G—1940
Gutknecht, Albert (Niagara) —G—1944
Guy, Charles (Washington & Jefferson) —C —1923
Guyon, Joseph (Carlisle) —B—1921
Haas—B—1921
Hall, Parker (Mississippi) —Q—1939–42
Halleck, Paul (Ohio) —B—1937
Haman, John (Northwestern) —C—1940–41
Hamilton, Raymond (Arkansas) —E —1938, 44–45
Heineman, Kenneth (Texas Mines) —B —1940–41
Hendren, John (Bucknell) —B—1921
Hendrian, Warren (Pittsburgh) —B—1921
Herrin, Houston (St. Mary's) —G—1931
Hershey, Kirk (Cornell) —E—1941
Hickey, Howard (Arkansas) —E—1941, 45
Hightower, John (Sam Houston) —E—1942
Hitt, Joel (Mississippi College) —E—1939
Honaker, Charles (Ohio State) —E—1924
Howard, Robert (Marietta) —G—1927
Huffman, Iolas (Ohio State) —T—1923

Wide World Photo

GEORGE "PAT" SUMMERALL OF THE NEW YORK GIANTS BOOTS A FIELD GOAL IN FINAL
TWO MINUTES OF PLAY AGAINST CLEVELAND BROWNS AT YANKEE STADIUM, DECEMBER
14, 1958, TO GIVE THE GIANTS THE MARGIN OF VICTORY, 13–10. QUARTERBACK CHARLES
CONERLY HOLDS THE BALL. THE BOOT, FROM THE 49-YARD LINE, SET UP THE PLAYOFF
GAME ON DECEMBER 21 BETWEEN THE GIANTS AND THE BROWNS TO DECIDE THE WINNER
OF THE EASTERN DIVISION TITLE. THE GIANTS WON THAT GAME, THEN LOST TO THE
BALTIMORE COLTS IN THE CHAMPIONSHIP GAME THE FOLLOWING WEEK.

Huggins, Roy (Vanderbilt) —B—1944
Hupke, Thomas (Alabama) —G—1938–39
Hurley, John (Washington State) —E—1931
Hutson, Merle (Heidelberg) —G—1931
Isselhardt, Ralph (Franklin) —G—1937
Jacobs, Jack (Oklahoma) —Q—1942, 45
Janiak, Leonard (Ohio) —B—1940–42
Jensvold, Leo (Iowa) —B—1931
Jessen, Ernest (Iowa State) —T—1931
Johns, James (Michigan) —G—1923–24
Johnson, Donald (Northwestern) —C—1942
Jolley, Alfred (Marietta) —T—1931
Jones, Benjamin (Grove City) —B—1924–25
Jones, Jerry (Notre Dame) —T—1924
Jones, Harvey (Baylor) —B—1944–45
Joseph, Zern (Miami—Ohio) —C—1931
Kabealo, Michael (Ohio State) —B—1944
Karrs, John (Duquesne) —B—1944
Keck, Stanley (Princeton) —T—1923
Keeble, Joseph (U.C.L.A.) —B—1937
Kelly, William (Montana) —B—1927
Kinek, Michael (Michigan State) —E—1940
Koch, George (Baylor) —B—1945
Konetsky, Floyd (Florida) —E—1944–45
Kovatch, John (Northwestern) —E—1938
Kreinheder, Walter (Michigan) —G—1925
Kriss, Howard (Ohio State).—B—1931
Krause, Paul (DePaul) —G—1938
Krysol, Gerald (Kansas State) —T—1927
Kyle, John (Indiana) —B—1923
Lamme, Emerald (Ohio Wesleyan) —E
  —1931
Lazetich, Milan (Michigan) —G—1945
Lazetich, William (Montana) —B
  —1939, 41–42
Lear, Leslie (Manitoba) —G—1944–45
Lee, Hilary (Oklahoma) —G—1931
Levy, Leonard (Minnesota) —G—1945
Lewis, Arthur (Ohio) —T—1938–39
Lewis, Loren (Northwestern) —B—1931
Liles, Elvin (Oklahoma A & M) —G—1945
Littlefield, Carl (Washington State) —B
  —1938
Livingston, Theodore (Indiana) —T
  —1937–40
Lowe, George (Fordham) —B—1921
Lyman, Delbert (U.C.L.A.) —T—1941, 44
Lyman, Roy (Nebraska) —T—1923–24
Lyon, George (Kansas State) —T—1931
McDonough, Paul (Utah) —E—1939–41
McGarry, Bernard (Utah) —G—1939–42
McGee, Howard (Kansas State) —G—1927
McMillan, S. (North Dakota) —C—1931
McMillen, James (Illinois) —G—1923
McMillin, Alvin (Centre) —B—1923
McRaven, William (Murray State) —B
  —1939
Magnani, Dante (St. Mary's Cal.) —B
  —1940–42
Maher, Francis (Toledo) —B—1941
Markov, Victor (Washington) —T—1938
Matheson, Riley (Texas Mines) —G
  —1939–42, 44–45
Mattos, Harry (St. Mary's Cal.) —B—1937
May, Francis (Centenary) —C—1933

Meredith, Russell (West Virginia) —G—1925
Mergenthal, Arthur (Notre Dame) —G
  —1945
Michaels, Alton (Heidelberg) —B—1925
Miller, Charles (Purdue) —C—1937
Miller, Ralph (Rice) —T—1937–38
Mishel, David (Brown) —B—1931
Moan, Emmett (West Virginia) —B—1939
Monaco, Raymond (Holy Cross) —G—1945
Morris, George (Baldwin-Wallace) —B
  —1941–42
Mucha, Rudolph (Washington) —Q
  —1941, 45
Muirhead, Stanley (Michigan) —G—1924
Munn, Lyle (Kansas State) —E—1927
Murphy, Harvey (Mississippi) —E—1940
Murphy, Joseph (Dartmouth) —G—1921
Myers, Cyril (Ohio State) —E—1923, 25
Nardacci, Nicholas (West Virginia) —B
  —1925
Neihaus, Ralph (Dayton) —T—1939
Nemeth, Steven (Notre Dame) —B—1945
Nesser, Al—T—1925, 31
Nix, John (Mississippi State) —B—1940
Noble, David (Nebraska) —B—1924–25
Novotny, Raymond (Ashland) —B—1931
Nugent—B—1924
O'Connor, Daniel (Georgetown) —G—1921
Olson, Raymond (Tulane) —T—1944
O'Neill, William (George Washington) —B
  —1937
Osborn, Robert (Penn. State) —G—1924
Owen, William (Oklahoma A & M) —T
  —1927
Partlow, Eugene (Dayton) —B—1923–24
Pasqua, Joseph (Southern Methodist
  Univ.) —T—1942
Patt, Maurice (Carnegie Tech.) —E
  —1939–42
Pearlman, Lester (Pittsburgh) —G—1921
Peery, Gordon (Oklahoma) —B—1927
Petchell, John (Duquesne) —B—1942, 44
Peterson, Nelson (West Virginia Wesleyan)
  —B—1938
Phillips, George (U.C.L.A.) —B—1945
Pincura, Stanley (Ohio State) —B—1937–38
Pignatelli, Carl (Iowa) —B—1931
Platukas, George (Duquesne) —E—1941–42
Plunkett, Warren (Minnesota) —B—1942
Prather, Dale (George Washington) —E
  —1938–39
Pritchard, Abisha (Virginia Military Inst.)
  —B—1942
Prochaska, Raymond (Nebraska) —E—1941
Pudloski, Chester (Villanova) —T—1944
Ragazzo, Philip (Western Reserve) —T
  —1938–39
Randels, Horace (Kansas State) —E—1927
Rapp, Manuel (St. Louis) —B—1941–42
Ream, Charles (Ohio State) —T—1938
Reisz, Albert (Louisiana Southeast) —B
  —1944–45
Rhenquist, Milton (Bethany) —C—1927
Rhoads, Donald (Washington & Jefferson)
  —T—1936

Ridler, Donald (Michigan State) —T—1931
Rieth, William (Carnegie Tech.) —C —1941–42, 44–45
Riffle, Charles (Notre Dame) —G—1944
Roberts, Walcott (Annapolis) —B—1924–25
Robinson, John (Missouri State Northeast) —T—1938
Roby, Douglas (Michigan) —B—1923
Rockwell, Henry (Arizona State) —C —1940–42
Rodak, Michael (Western Reserve) —G —1939–40
Rosatti, Roman (Michigan) —T—1923
Rosequist, Theodore (Ohio State) —T —1937
Russell, Douglas (Kansas) —B—1939
Russell, Lloyd (Baylor) —B—1939
Ruthstrom, Ralph (Southern Methodist Univ.) —B—1945
Savatsky, Oliver (Miami—Ohio) —E—1937
Scarry, Michael (Waynesburg) —C—1944–45
Schenken, Nathan (Howard) —T—1939
Schupbach, O. T. (Also known as Tex Mooney) (Texas State West) —T —1941–42
Seabright, Charles (West Virginia) —Q —1941
Sebastian, Michael (Pittsburgh) —B—1937
Seigel—E—1925
Setron, Joseph (West Virginia) —G—1923
Shaw, Robert (Ohio State) —E—1945
Shirey, Fred (Nebraska) —T—1940–41
Sikich, Rudolph (Minnesota) —T—1945
Simington, Milton (Arkansas) —G—1941
Simmons, Roy (Syracuse) —B—1927
Skooczen, Stanley (Western Reserve) —B —1944
Skoronski, Edward (Purdue) —C—1937
Slovak, Martin (Toledo) —B—1939–41
Smith, Clyde (Missouri) —B—1927
Smith, Gaylon (Southwestern) —B—1939–42
Smith, Olin (Ohio Wesleyan) —T—1924
Smith, Russell (Illinois) —G—1924
Snyder, Robert (Ohio) —B—1937–38
Spadaccini, Victor (Minnesota) —B —1938–40
Spiers, Robert (Ohio State) —T—1925
Sprinkle, Hubert (Carnegie Tech.) —T —1925
Stephens, John (Marshall) —E—1938
Stevenson, Ralph (Oklahoma) —G—1940
Stringer, Eugene (John Carroll) —B—1925
Stuart, Roy (Tulsa) —B—1942
Suchy, Paul—E—1925
Tandy, George (North Carolina) —C—1921
Tanner, John (Centre) —E—1923–24
Tarr, James (Missouri) —E—1931
Thomas, Rex (St. John's) —B—1927
Thorp, Wilfred (Arkansas) —C—1940–42
Thorpe, James (Carlisle) —B—1921
Tuckey, Richard (Manhattan) —B—1938
Turner, James (Oklahoma A & M) —C —1937
Underwood, Forrest (Davis-Elkins) —T —1937

Uzdavinis, Walter (Fordham) —E—1937
Vince, Ralph (Washington & Jefferson) —G —1923–25
Vokaty, Otto (Heidelberg) —B—1931
Waldsmith, Ralph (Akron) —G—1921
Wallace, Fred (Bethany) —G—1925
Waterfield, Robert (U.C.L.A.) —Q—1945
Waters, Dale (Florida) —E—1931
Webber, Howard (Kansas State) —E—1927
Weber, Elmer (Nebraska) —B—1927
Weimer, Howard (Wilmington) —B—1931
Weinberg, Saul—T—1923
Weisgerber, Richard (Willamette) —B —1938
West, Patrick (Southern California) —B —1944–45
Whelan, Thomas (Georgetown) —C—1921
Wiberg, Oscar (Nebraska Wesleyan) —B —1927
Williams, Jay (Brown—E—1925
Wilson, Gordon (Texas Mines) —T—1941
Wilson, John (Western Reserve) —E —1939–42
Winkler, Joseph (Purdue) —C—1945
Wolf, Richard (Miami—Ohio) —B —1923–25, 27
Worden, James (Waynesburg) —B—1945
Work, Joseph (Miami—Ohio) —B—1923–25
Workman, Harry (Ohio State) —B—1924
Workman, Hoge (Ohio State) —B—1931
Zirinsky, Walter (Lafayette) —B—1945
Zoll, Richard (Indiana) —G—1937–38

CLEVELAND BROWNS (1950—60)

Adamle, Anthony (Ohio State) —B —1950–51, 54
Agase, Alexander (Illinois) —G—1950–51
Amstutz, Joseph (Indiana) —C—1957
Atkins, Douglas (Tennessee) —E—1953–54
Baker, Loris "Sam" (Oregon State) —B— 1960
Bassett, Maurice (Langston) —B—1954–56
Bolden, Leroy (Michigan State) —B— 1958–59
Borton, John (Ohio State) —B—1957
Bradley, Harold (Iowa State) —G—1954–57
Brewster, Darrell (Purdue) —E—1952–58
Brown, James (Syracuse) —B—1957–60
Bumgardner, Rex (West Virginia) —B —1950–52
Caleb, James (Grambling) —B—1960
Campbell, Milton (Indiana) —B—1957
Carpenter, Kenneth (Oregon State) —B —1950–53
Carpenter, Lewis (Arkansas) —B—1957–58
Carpenter, Preston (Arkansas) —B—1956–59
Catlin, Thomas (Oklahoma) —G —1953–54, 57–58
Clarke, Frank (Colorado) —E—1957–59
Clarke, Leon (Southern California) —E— 1960
Cole, Emerson (Toledo) —B—1950–52
Colo, Donald (Brown) —T—1953–58
Costello, Vincent (Ohio) —G—1957–60

Davis, Willie (Grambling) —B—1958–59
Dawson, Leonard (Purdue) —Q—1960
Denton, Robert (College of Pacific) —E— 1960
Deschaine, Richard—E—1958
Donaldson, Eugene (Kentucky) —G—1953
Fichtner, Ross (Purdue) —B—1960
Fiss, Galen (Kansas) —B—1956–60
Fleming, Donald (Florida) —B—1960
Ford, Leonard (Michigan) —E—1950–57
Forester, Herschel (Southern Methodist Univ.) —G—1954–57
Franklin, Robert (Mississippi) —B—1960
Freeman, Robert (Auburn) —B—1957–58
Gain, Robert (Kentucky) —T—1952, 54–60
Gatski, Frank (Marshall) —C—1950–56
Gaudio, Robert (Ohio State) —G—1951
Gautt, Prentice (Oklahoma) —B—1960
Gibron, Abraham (Purdue) —G—1950–56
Gillom, Horace (Nevada) —E—1950–56
Gorgal, Kenneth (Purdue) —B—1950, 53–54
Goss, Donald (Southern Methodist Univ.) —T—1956
Graham, Otto (Northwestern) —Q—1950–55
Grigg, Forrest (Tulsa) —T—1950–51
Groza, Louis (Ohio State) —T—1950–59
Hanulak, Chester (Maryland) —B—1954, 57
Helluin, Frances (Tulane) —T—1952–53
Herring, Harold (Auburn) —C—1950–52
Hickerson, Eugene (Mississippi) —T— 1958–60
Houston, James (Ohio State) —E—1960
Houston, Lindell (Ohio State)—G—1950–53
Howard, Sherman (Nevada) —B—1952–53
Howton, William (Rice) —E—1959
Humble, Weldon (Rice) —G—1950
Hunter, Arthur (Notre Dame)—T—1956–59
Jagade, Harry (Indiana) —B—1951–53
James, Thomas (Ohio State) —B—1950–55
Jones, Thomas (Miami, Ohio) —T—1955
Jones, William (Tulane) —B—1950–55
Jordan, Henry (Virginia) —T—1957–58
Kinard, William (Mississippi) —B—1956
King, Donald (Kentucky) —T—1954
Kissell, John (Boston College) —T —1950–52, 54–56
Konz, Kenneth (Louisiana State Univ.) —B —1953–59
Kreitling, Richard (Illinois) —E—1959–60
Lahr, Warren (Western Reserve) —B —1950–59
Lavelli, Dante (Ohio State) —E—1950–56
Lewis, Clifford (Duke) —B—1950–51
Lloyd, David (Georgia) —C—1959–60
McClung, William (Florida A & M) —T— 1958–60
McCormack, Michael (Kansas) —G —1954–60
Macerelli, John (St. Vincent) —T—1956
Marshall, James (Ohio State) —T—1960
Martin, James (Notre Dame) —G—1950
Massey, Carlton (Texas) —E—1954–56
Michaels, Walter (Washington Lee) —G —1952–60
Mitchell, Robert (Illinois) —B—1958–60
Modzelewski, Edward (Maryland) —B

—1955–59
Morrison, Fred (Ohio State) —B—1954–56
Morrow, John (Michigan) —T—1960
Moselle, Donald (Wisconsin State) —B —1950
Mostardo, Richard (Kent State) —Q—1960
Motley, Marion (Nevada) —B—1950–53
Murphy, Frederick (Georgia Tech) —E— 1960
Nagler, Gern (Santa Clara) —E—1960
Ninowski, James (Michigan State) —Q —1958–60
Noll, Charles (Dayton) —G—1953–59
O'Brien, Francis (Michigan State) —T— 1959
O'Connell, Thomas (Illinois) —Q—1956–57
Oristaglio, Robert (Pennsylvania) —E—1951
Palmer, Darrell (Texas Christian Univ.) —T—1950–53
Palumbo, Samuel (Notre Dame) —C —1955–56
Parilli, Vito (Kentucky) —Q—1956
Parrish, Bernard (Florida) —B—1959–60
Paul, Donald (Washington State) —B —1954–58
Perini, Evo (Ohio State) —B—1955
Peters, Floyd (San Francisco State) —E— 1959–60
Petitbon, John (Notre Dame) —B—1955–56
Phelps, Donald (Kentucky) —B—1950–52
Plum, Milton (Penn. State) —Q—1957–60
Prestel, James (Idaho) —T—1960
Ptacek, Robert (Michigan) —B—1959
Quinlan, Volney (San Diego State) —B —1956
Quinlan, William (Michigan State) —E —1957–58
Ratterman, George (Notre Dame) —Q —1952–56
Rechichar, Albert (Tennessee) —B—1952
Renfro, Ray (Texas State North) —B —1952–60
Reynolds, William (Pittsburgh) —B —1953–54, 57
Robinson, Fred (Washington) —G—1957
Rymkus, Louis (Notre Dame) —T —1950–51
Sandusky, John (Villanova) —T—1950–55
Schafrath, Richard (Ohio State) —E— 1859–60
Selawski, Eugene (Purdue) —T—1960
Sharkey, Edward (Nevada & Duke) —G —1952
Sheriff, Stanley (California Polytech.) — G—1957
Shofner, James (Texas Christian Univ.) —B —1958–60
Shula, Donald (John Carroll) —B—1951–52
Skibinski, Joseph (Purdue) —G—1952
Smith, James Ray (Baylor) —G—1956–60
Smith, Robert (Nebraska) —B—1955–56
Speedie, Mac (Utah) —E—1950–52
Steinbrunner, Donald (Washington State) —T—1953
Stephens, Lawrence (Texas) —E—1960

Taseff, Carl (John Carroll) —B—1951

Thompson, Thomas (William & Mary) —C —1950-53

Weber, Charles (Westchester State) —E —1955-56

White, Robert (Stanford) —B—1955

Wiggin, Paul (Stanford) —T—1957-60

Williams, A. D. (College of Pacific—B— 1960

Willis, William (Ohio State) —G—1950-53

Wooten, John (Colorado) —G—1959-60

Wren, Lowe (Missouri) —B—1956-59

Young, George (Georgia) —E—1950-53

Youngelman, Sidney (Alabama) —G—1959

COLUMBUS TIGERS (1921—26)

Albanese, Donald (Tulane) —E—1925

Aubner—E—1921

Barnum, Robert (West Virginia) —B—1926

Berrehsen, William (Washington & Jefferson) —T—1926

Bertoglio, James (Creighton) —B—1926

Bliss, Gerald (Ohio State) —Q—1921

Bonowitz, Elliott (Wilmington College) —B—1923

Bullman, Gale (West Virginia Western)—E —1925

Carvel—E—1922

Churchman, Charles (Virginia) —B—1925

Conley, John (Ohio Northern) —T —1922, 26

Davis, Herbert (Xavier) —B—1925-26

Duvall, Earl (Ohio State) —G—1924-26

Eichenlaub, Roy (Notre Dame) —B—1925

Ellis, Walter (Detroit) —T—1924-25

Gaulke, Harold—B—1922

Glassman, Morris—E—1921-22

Goebel, Paul (Michigan) —E—1923-25

Goetz, Angus (Michigan) —T—1923

Gorrill, Charles (Ohio State) —E—1926

Gump—G—1922

Guy, Charles (Washington & Jefferson) —C—1925

Halleck—B—1924

Heldt, John (Iowa) —C—1923, 26

Higgins, Robert (Penn. State) —B—1925

Hopkins, Theodore (Pennsylvania) —E —1922

Houck, Joseph—G—1921

Isabel, Wilmer (Ohio State) —B—1923-24

Karch, Robert (Ohio State) —T—1921-22

Krieger, Earl (Ohio State) —B—1922

Kuehner, Oscar—G—1921

Laprot, John—G—1924

Long, Thomas (Ohio State) —G—1925

Lynch, Paul (Ohio Northern) —B—1925

Mantell, Joseph (Canisius) —G—1924

Moody, Wilkie (Denison) —B—1924-25

Mulbarger, Joseph (Broaddus)—T—1921-26

Murphy, James (St. Thomas) —B—1926

Nemecek, Andrew (Ohio State) —G —1923-25

Nesser, Al—E—1925-26

Nesser, Frank—B—1921, 26

Nesser, Fred—G—1921-22

Nesser, John—B—1921

Nesser, Philip—C—1921

Nesser, Theodore—C—1924

Nonnemaker, Gustavus (Wittenberg) —E —1926

Passuelo, William—G—1923

Pearce, Harley (Ohio Wesleyan) —E—1926

Petcoff, Boni (Ohio State) —T—1924-26

Pierce, Bemus (Carlisle) —B—1926

Plank, Earl—E—1926

Randolph—B—1923

Rapp, Robert—B—1922-26

Rauck—G—1921

Regan, James—Q

Reichle, Louis (Butler) —C—1926

Rodgers, Walter (Washington of Mo.) —B —1922

Rohleder, George (Wittenberg) —E—1925

Ruh, Emmett (Davis-Elkins) —B—1921-25

Ruh, Homer—E—1921-26

Rush, Arden (Ohio) —E—1922-24

Sack, John (Pittsburgh) —G—1923, 25

Schell, Herbert—B—1924

Snoots, J. Lee—B—1922-25

Sonnenberg, Gustavus (Dartmouth) —G— 1923

Stevenson, Mark (Notre Dame) —G—1922

Stinchomb, Gaylord (Ohio State) —B— 1923

Stock, Herbert (Kenyon) —B—1924-25

Tebell, Gustavus (Wisconsin) —E—1923-24

Tynes, David (Texas) —B—1924-25

Waite, Willard—G—1921

Weaver, James (Centre) —C—1923

Wiper, Donald (Ohio State) —B—1922

Winters, Lindel (Ohio Wesleyan) —B —1923-24

Woods, Gerald (Butler) —B—1926

Wolford, Bard—T—1922, 24

Ziegler, Francis (Clemson) —B—1922

DALLAS COWBOYS (1960)

Babb, Eugene (Austin) —B—1960

Bercich, Robert (Michigan State) —B—1960

Bielski, Richard (Maryland) —B—1960

Bishop, Donald (Los Angeles C. C.) —E— 1960

Borden, Nathaniel (Indiana) —E—1960

Braatz, Thomas (Marquette) —E—1960

Bradfute, Byron (Mississippi Southern) — T—1960

Butler, William (Chattanooga) —B—1960

Clarke, Franklin (Colorado) —E—1960

Cone, Frederick (Clemson) —B—1960

Connelly, Michael (Utah State) —C—1960

Cronin, Eugene (College of Pacific) —E— 1960

Dickson, Paul (Baylor) —T—1960

Doelling, Frederick (Pennsylvania) —B— 1960

Doran, James (Iowa State) —E—1960

Dowd, Don Michael (Texas) —B—1960

- NESSER BROTHERS -

TED IS THE FATHER OF FRED. ONE BROTHER WHO PLAYED WITH THEM IS
MISSING FROM THE PICTURE.

Dugan, Frederick (Dayton) —B—1960
Dupre, Louis (Baylor) —B—1960
Falls, Michael (Minnesota) —G—1960
Franckhauser, Thomas (Purdue) —B—1960
Fry, Robert (Kentucky) —T—1960
Gonzaga, John—C—1960
Guy, Melwood (Duke) —T—1960
Hansen, Wayne (Texas Western) —G—1960
Healy, Michael Donald (Maryland) —T—1960
Heinrich, Donald (Washington) —Q—1960
Herchman, William (Texas Tech) —T—1960
Houser, John (Redlands) —C—1960
Howton, William (Rice) —E—1960
Husmann, Edward (Nebraska) —T—1960
Klein, Richard (Iowa) —T—1960
Kowalczyk, Walter (Michigan State) —B—1960
LeBaron, Edward (College of Pacific) —Q—1960
Lewis, Woodley (Oregon) —B—1960
McIlhenny, Donald (Southern Methodist Univ.) —B—1960
Mathews, Raymond (Clemson) —B—1960
Meredith, Donald (Southern Methodist Univ.) —Q—1960
Mooty, James (Arkansas) —B—1960
Patera, John (Oregon) —G—1960
Putnam, Duane (College of Pacific) —G—1960
Sherer, David (Southern Methodist Univ.) —E—1960
Sommer, Michael (George Washington) —B—1960
Tubbs, Jerry (Oklahoma) —B—1960
Wisener, Gary (Baylor) —E—1960

DALLAS TEXANS (1952)

Aldridge, Bennie (Oklahoma A & M) —B—1952
Averno, Sisto (Muhlenberg) —G—1952
Baggett, William (Louisiana State Univ.) —B—1952
Campanella, Joseph (Ohio State) —T—1952
Cannamella, Patrick (Southern California) —G—1952
Celeri, Robert (California) —Q—1952
Colo, Donald (Brown) —T—1952
Davis, Jerome (Louisiana State Southeast) —B—1952
Donovan, Arthur (Boston College) —T—1952
Ecklund, Bradley (Oregon) —C—1952
Edwards, Daniel (Georgia) —E—1952
Felker, Eugene (Wisconsin) —E—1952
Flowers, Keith (Texas Christian Univ.) —G—1952
Gandee, Sherwin (Ohio State) —E—1952
Grigg, Forrest (Tulsa) —T—1952
Hoerner, Richard (Iowa) —B—1952
Humble, Weldon (Rice) —G—1952
Jackson, Kenneth (Texas) —T—1952
Jankovich, Keever (College of Pacific) —E—1952
Kalmanir, Thomas (Nevada) —B—1952
Keane, Thomas (West Virginia) —B—1952
Lansford, James (Texas) —T—1952
Lauricella, Henry (Tennessee) —B—1952
McKissack, Richard (Southern Methodist Univ.) —B—1952
Marchetti, Gino (San Francisco) —E—1952
Ortman, Charles (Michigan) —B—1952
Pelfrey, Raymond (Kentucky State East) —B—1952
Petitbon, John (Notre Dame) —B—1952

Poole, Barney (Mississippi) —E—1952
Reid, Joseph (Louisiana State Univ.) —C —1952
Robison, George (Virginia Military Inst.) —G—1952
Sherman, Willard (St. Mary's, Cal.) —E —1952
Sinkovitz, Frank (Duke) —C—1952
Soboleski, Joseph (Michigan) —T—1952
Tait, Arthur (Mississippi State) —E—1952
Taliaferro, George (Indiana) —B—1952
Tanner, Hampton (Georgia) —T—1952
Toth, Zollie (Louisiana) —B—1952
Tripucka, Frank (Notre Dame) —Q—1952
Wilkins, Richard (Oregon) —E—1952
Williams, Stanley (Baylor) —E—1952
Wozniak, John (Alabama) —G—1952

DAYTON TRIANGLES (1921—29)

Abbott, Lafayette (Syracuse) —B—1921—29
Achui, Walter (Dayton) —B—1927—28
Bacon, Francis (Wabash) —B—1921—26
Beasley, John (Earlham) —G—1923
Becker, John (Denison) —T—1926—29
Beckley, Arthur (Michigan) —B—1926
Belanich, William (Dayton) —T—1927—29
Berns, William (Purdue) —G—1922—23
Bonowitz, Elliott (Wilmington) —G —1923—25
Bradley, Gerald (Wittenberg) —B—1928
Brewer, John (Georgia Tech) —B—1929
Britton, Earl (Illinois) —B—1927—28
Brown, Jack R. (Dayton) —C—1927—29
Buchanan, Stephen (Miami, Ohio) —B —1929
Burgner, Earl (Wittenberg) —B—1923
Cabhrina, August (Dayton) —B—1927
Calhoun, Eric (Denison) —T—1926
Carlson, Roy (Bradley) —E—1929
Charles, Winston (William and Mary) —B—1928
Cook, Eugene (Michigan) —B—1928
Crawford, Kenneth (Miami, Ohio) —G —1923
Davis, Paul (Marquette) —G—1921
Dellinger, Lawrence—G—1921—23
DeWeese, Byrne (Cincinnati) —G—1927—28
Dobeleit, Richard (Ohio State) —B— 1925—26
Drayer, Clarence (Illinois) —T—1925—26
Duffy, Patrick (Dayton) —B—1929
Egan, Richard (Chicago) —E—1924
Faust, Richard (Otterbein) —T —1924, 28—29
Fenner, Lee (Miami, Ohio) —E—1923—25
Gabler, John (West Virginia Wesleyan) —C—1926
Graham, Alfred—G—1925—29
Graham, Clarence—B—1928
Guy, Charles (Washington & Jefferson) —C—1925
Haas, Robert (Purdue) —B—1929
Hathaway, Russell (Indiana) —T—1921—24
Hippa, Samuel (Dayton) —E—1927—28

Huffine, Kenneth (Purdue) —B—1921—25
Hummons, John (Wittenberg) —E —1926—28
Jolley, Alfred (Marietta) —T—1923
Jones, Benjamin (Grove City) —B—1924
Joseph, A.—E—1927
Joseph, Zern (Miami, Ohio) —E—1925, 27
Kaufman, John (Pennsylvania) —T—1929
Keefer, Jackson (Brown) —B—1928
Kinderdine, George—C—1921—29
Knecht, William (Xavier) —T—1925—26
Kuehl, Raymond (Dubuque) —B—1924
Lauer, Harold (Detroit) —B—1923
Layport, John (Wooster) —G—1925—26
Mahrt, Alphonse (Dayton) —B—1922—23
Mahrt, John (Dayton) —E—1925
Mahrt, Louis (Dayton) —Q—1926—27
Mankat, Carl (Colgate) —G—1928—29
Matsu, Arthur (William and Mary) —B —1928
Mayl, Eugene (Notre Dame) —E—1925—26
Muirhead, Stanley (Michigan) —G—1924
Partlow, Louis—B—1921—27, 29
Redmond—G—1921, 24
Reese, David (Denison) —E—1921—23
Reiter, Wilbur (West Virginia Wesleyan) —G—1926—27
Roudebush, George (Denison) —B—1921
Sacksteder, Norbert (Dayton) —B—1925
Sampson, Arthur—G—1921
Sauer, Edward (Miami, Ohio) —T—1921—26
Seibert, Edward (Otterbein) —C—1927—28
Sies, Dale (Pittsburgh) —G—1921—22, 24
Sillin, Frank (West Maryland) —B —1927—29
Singleton, John (Wabash) —B—1929
Spencer, James (Dayton) —G—1928—29
Strosnider, Aubrey (Dayton) —G—1928
Tays, James—B—1927
Thiele, Carl (Denison) —E—1921—23
Tidd, Glenn—T—1921—24
Tolley, Edward—G—1929
Ullery, William (Pennsylvania State) —B—1922
Voss, Walter (Detroit) —E—1922—24
Wallace, Joseph (Notre Dame) —E—1929
Ward, Gilbert (Notre Dame) —T—1923
Wynne, Chester (Notre Dame) —B—1929
Young, Leslie (North Dakota) —B—1925
Zimmerman, Pleasant (Purdue) —G —1927—29

DETROIT LIONS
(1921, 1925—26, 1928, 1934—60)
(Also played as Panthers, Wolverines)

Addams, Abraham (Indiana) —E—1949
Aiello, Anthony (Youngstown) —B—1944
Alderman, Grady (Detroit) —G—1960
Anderson, Stanley (Stanford) —E—1941
Ane, Charles (Southern California) —T —1953—59
Ashcom, Richard (Oregon) —T—1943
Atkins, George (Auburn) —G—1955

Atty, Alexander (West Virginia) —G—1941
Austin, James (St. Mary's, Cal.) —E—1939
Bacchus, Carl (Missouri) —E—1928
Bachor, Ludwig (Detroit) —T—1928
Bailey, Byron (Washington State) —B —1952–53
Banas, Steven (Notre Dame) —B—1935
Banjavic, Emil (Arizona) —B—1942
Banonis, Vincent (Detroit) —C—1951–53
Barle, Louis (Duluth) —G—1938
Barr, Terry (Michigan) —B—1957–60
Barrett, John (Detroit) —T—1926, 28
Batinski, Stanley (Temple) —G—1941–47
Baumgardner, Max (Texas) —E—1948
Behan, Charles (DeKalb) —E—1942
Belichick, Stephen (Western Reserve) B—1941
Bernard, Charles (Michigan) —C—1934
Berrang, Edward (Villanova) —E—1951
Berry, Cornelius (North Carolina State) —E—1939
Bingaman, Lester (Illinois) —G—1948–54
Blessing, Paul (Nebraska State Teachers) —E—1944
Bodenger, Morris (Tulane) —G—1934
Booth, Richard (Western Reserve) —B —1941, 45
Bowman, William (William & Mary) —B —1954, 56
Box, Cloyce (Texas State Teachers) —E —1949–50, 52–54
Brettschneider, Carl (Iowa State) —B—1960
Briggs, Paul (Colorado) —T—1948
Brill, Harold (Wichita) —B—1939
Britt, Maurice (Arkansas) —E—1941
Britt, Rankin (Texas A & M) —E—1941
Brodnax, George (Georgia Tech.) —E —1949
Brooks, William (Arkansas) —G—1955
Brown, Howard (Indiana) —G—1948–50
Brown, Marvin (Texas State East) —B —1957
Brown, Roger (Maryland State) —T—1960
Brumley, Robert (Rice) —B—1945
Bryant, Lowell (Clemson) —B—1941
Bucher, Frank (Detroit) —E—1925
Bulger, Chester (Auburn) —T—1950
Busich, Samuel (Ohio State) —E—1943
Caddel, Ernest (Stanford) —B—1934–38
Cain, James (Alabama) —E—1950, 53–55
Callahan, James (Texas) —B—1946
Callihan, William (Nebraska) —Q—1940–45
Calvelli, Anthony (Stanford) —C—1939–40
Campbell, Stanley (Iowa State) —G— 1952–55–58
Cameron, Edmund (Washington & Lee) —G—1926
Cardwell, Lloyd (Nebraska) —B—1937–43
Carpenter, Lewis (Arkansas) —B—1953–55
Cassady, Howard (Ohio State) —B—1956–60
Caywood, Lester (St. Johns) —G—1928
Chantiles, Thomas (Southern California) —T—1942
Chase, Benjamin (Annapolis) —G—1947
Christensen, Frank (Utah) —B—1934–37

Christensen, George (Oregon) —T —1934–38
Christiansen, John (Colorado A & M) —B —1951–58
Cifelli, August (Notre Dame) —T—1950–52
Cifers, Robert (Tennessee) —Q—1944, 46
Clark, Earl (Colorado College) —Q— 1934–38
Clark, Wayne (Utah) —E—1944–45
Clemons, Raymond (St. Mary's) —G—1939
Cline, Oliver (Ohio State) —B—1950–53
Cloves, John (William & Mary) —T—1951
Cobb, Thomas (Okla. N.E. Teachers) —T —1928
Cogdill, Gail (Washington State) —E—1960
Colella, Thomas (Canisius) —B—1942–43
Conlee, Gerald (St. Mary's, Cal.) —C—1943
Conner, Emerson (Texas) —G—1935
Conzelman, James (Washington of Mo.) —B—1925–26
Cook, Albert (Washington & Jefferson) —C —1925–26
Cook, Eugene (Toledo) —E—1959
Cook, Theodore (Alabama) —E—1947
Cooper, Harold (Detroit) —G—1937
Corgan, Michael (Notre Dame) —B—1943
Coughlin, Frank (Notre Dame) —T—1921
Crabtree, Clem (Wake Forest) —T —1940–41
Creekmur, Louis (William & Mary) —G —1950–59
Cremer, Theodore (Auburn) —E—1946–48
Cronin, Eugene (College of Pacific) —E —1956–59
Crook, Albert (Washington & Jefferson) — —1925–26
Cunningham, Leon (South Carolina) —C —1955
D'Alonzo, Peter (Villanova) —B—1951–52
David, James (Colorado A & M) —B —1952–59
Davis, Glenn (Ohio State) —E—1960
Davis, Willie (Grambling) —B—1956
Dawley, Fred (Michigan) —B—1944
DeCorrevont, William (Northwestern) —B —1946
DeFruiter, Robert (Nebraska) —B—1947
DeGree, Walter (Notre Dame) —G—1921
DeMarco, Mario (Miami) —G—1949
DePrato, Nicholas (Michigan State) —B —1921
DeShane, Charles (Alabama) —B—1945–49
Dibble, Dorne (Michigan State) —E —1951–57
Diehl, David (Michigan State) —E —1939–40, 44–45
Doane, Joseph (Tufts) —B—1925–26
Doll, Donald (Southern California) —B —1949–52
Doran, James (Iowa State) —E—1951–59
D'Orazio, Joseph (Ithaca) —G—1944
Dove, Robert (Notre Dame) —E—1953–54
Dublinksi, Thomas (Utah) —Q—1952–54
Dubzinski, Walter (Boston College) —G— 1941

Dudish, Andrew (Georgia) —B—1948
Dudley, William (Virginia) —B—1947–49
Dugger, John (Ohio State) —E—1946–48
Duncan, James (Wake Forest) —E—1950
Earon, Blaine (Duke) —E—1952–53
Ebding, Harry (St. Mary's, Cal.) —E —1934–37
Edwards, Thomas (Michigan) —G—1926
Eiden, Edmund (Scranton) —B—1944
Ellis, Lawrence (Syracuse) —G—1948
Ellis, Walter (Detroit) —T—1925
Emerick, Robert (Miami, Ohio) —T—1934
Emerson, Grover (Texas) —G—1934–37
Engebretson, Paul (Northwestern) —G— 1934
Enke, Fred (Arizona) —Q—1948–51
Evans, Murray (Hardin-Simmons) —B —1942–43
Farkas, Andrew (Detroit) —B—1945
Feather, Elwin (Kansas State) —B—1928
Feldhaus, William (Cincinnati) —T —1937–40
Fena, Joseph (Denver) —G—1936–37
Fenenbock, Charles (U.C.L.A.) —B —1943, 45
Fichman, Leon (Alabama) —T—1946–47
Fisk, William (Southern California) —E —1940–43
Flanagan, Richard (Ohio State) —G —1950–52

Fleischman, Godfrey (Purdue) —G —1925–26
Flowers, Keith (Texas Christian Univ.) —G—1950
Forte, Aldo (Montana State) —G—1946
French, Barry (Purdue) —G—1951
Friedman, Benjamin (Michigan) —B—1928
Frutig, Edward (Michigan) —E—1945–46
Fucci, Dominic (Kentucky) —B—1955
Furst, Anthony (Dayton) —T—1940–41, 44
Gagnon, Roy (Oregon) —G—1935
Gandee, Sherwin (Ohio State) —E —1952–56
Gardner, Milton (Wisconsin) —G—1921
Gatski, Frank (Marshall) —G—1957
Gavin, Patrick "Buck"—B—1921
Gedman, Eugene (Indiana) —B —1953, 56–58
George, Raymond (Southern California) —T—1939
Geremsky, Thaddeus (Pittsburgh) —E —1951
Gibbons, James (Iowa) —E—1958–60
Gill, Sloko (Youngstown) —G—1942
Gillette, James (Virginia) —B—1948
Gilmer, Harry (Alabama) —Q—1955–56
Girard, Earl (Wisconsin) —B—1952–56
Glass, William (Baylor) —C—1958–60
Goldman, Samuel (Howard) —E—1949

Nate Fine Photo

REDSKIN ANDY FARKAS INTERCEPTS A PASS AGAINST DETROIT IN 1943. TWO YEARS LATER ANDY WAS PLAYING FOR THE LIONS.

Goodman, Henry (West Virginia) —T
 —1942
Gordy, John (Tennessee) —T—1957, 59–60
Gore, Gordon (Oklahoma Teachers) —B
 —1938–39
Graham, Lester (Tulsa) —G—1938
Greene, John (Michigan) —E—1944–50
Grefe, Theodore (Northwestern) —E—1945
Gregory, Bruce (Michigan) —B—1926
Griffin, Robert (Arkansas) —C—1958
Grigonis, Frank (Chattanooga) —B—1942
Grimes, George (Virginia) —B—1948
Groomes, Melvin (Indiana) —B—1948–49
Grossman, Rex (Indiana) —B—1950
Grottkau, Robert (Oregon) —G—1959–60
Grube, Charles (Michigan) —E—1926
Gutowsky, Leroy (Oklahoma City Univ.)
 —B—1934–38
Guy, Charles (Washington & Jefferson)
 —C—1921
Hackenbrush, John (Oregon State) —T
 —1940
Hackney, Elmer (Kansas State) —B
 —1942–46
Haddon, Aldous (Washington & Jefferson)
 —B—1925–26
Hafen, Bernard (Utah) —E—1949–50
Hall, John (Texas Christian Univ.) —B
 —1942
Hamilton, Raymond (Arkansas) —E—1939
Hanneman, Charles (Michigan State
 Normal) —E—1937–41
Hansen, Dale (Michigan State) —T
 —1944, 48–49
Harder, Marlin (Wisconsin) —B—1951–53
Harding, Roger (California) —C—1948
Hardy, James (Southern California) —B
 —1952
Harrison, Granville (Mississippi State) —E
 —1942
Hart, Leon (Notre Dame) —E—1950–57
Harvey, Norman (Detroit) —T—1926
Hekkers, George (Wisconsin) —T—1947–49
Held, Paul (San Diego State) —Q—1955
Helms, John (Georgia Tech.) —E—1946
Heywood, Ralph (Southern California)
 —E—1947
Hightower, John (Sam Houston) —E—1943
Hill, James (Tennessee) —B—1951–52
Hillman, William (Tennessee) —B—1947
Hinchman, Hubert (Butler) —B—1934
Hoernschemeyer, Robert (Indiana) —B
 —1950–55
Hogan, Paul (Detroit) —T—1925–26, 28
Hogland, Douglas (Oregon State) —T
 —1958
Hollar, John (Appalachian State) —B—1949
Hopp, Harry (Nebraska) —Q—1941–43
Horning, Clarence (Colgate) —T—1921
Howard, Robert (Marietta) —G—1928
Howard, William (Southern California)
 —B—1939
Huffman, Vernon (Indiana) —B—1937–38
Hultman, Vivian (Michigan State) —E
 —1925–26
Hupke, Thomas (Alabama) —G—1934–37

Hutchinson, Elvin (Whittier) —B—1939
Isselhardt, Ralph (Franklin) —G—1937
Jackson, Henry (Missouri) —B—1928
James, Thomas (Ohio State) —B—1947
Jaszewski, Floyd (Minnesota) —T—1950–51
Jefferson, William (Mississippi State) —B
 —1941
Jenkins, Walter (Wayne) —E—1955
Jett, John (Wake Forest) —E—1941
Johnson, John (Utah) —T—1934–40
Johnson, John Henry (Arizona State)
 —B—1957–59
Jones, C. (Union) —B—1946
Jones, Elmer (Wake Forest) —G—1948
Jones, Ralph (Alabama) —E—1946
Junker, Steven (Xavier) —E—1957, 59–60
Jurkiewicz, Walter (Indiana) —C—1946
Kaporch, Albert (St. Bonaventure) —T
 —1944–45
Karilivacz, Carl (Syracuse) —B—1953–57
Karras, Alexander (Iowa) —T—1958–60
Karstens, George (Indiana) —C—1949
Kaska, Anthony (Illinois Wesleyan) —B
 —1935
Keene, Robert (Detroit) —B—1943–45
Kennedy, William (Michigan State) —E
 —1942, 44
Kercher, Richard (Tulsa) —B—1954
Ketzko, Alexander (Michigan State) —T
 —1943
Kipp, James (Montana State) —T—1942
Kizzier, Lee (Wyoming) —B—1937
Klewicki, Edward (Michigan State) —E
 —1935–38
Klumb, John (Washington State) —E—1940
Kmetovic, Peter (Stanford) —B—1947
Knorr, Lawrence (Dayton) —E—1942, 45
Knox, Samuel (New Hampshire) —G—
 1934–36
Koepfer, Karl (Bowling Green) —G—1958
Kopcha, Joseph (Chattanooga) —G—1936
Kostiuk, Michael (Detroit) —T—1945
Krall, Gerard (Ohio State) —B—1950
Kring, Frank (Texas Christian Univ.) —B
 —1945
Krol, Joseph (West Ontario) —B—1945
Krouse, Raymond (Maryland) —T
 —1956–57
Kuczinski, Albert (Pennsylvania) —E—1943
Kuehl, Raymond (Dubuque) —B—1921
Lane, Richard—B—1960
Lary, Robert Yale (Texas A & M) —B
 —1952–53, 56–60
Lauer, Harold (Detroit) —B—1925–26
Lay, Russell (Michigan State) —G—1934
Layden, Robert (Kansas Southwestern) —E
 —1943
Layne, Robert (Texas) —Q—1950–58
Lear, Leslie (Manitoba) —G—1947
LeBeau, Richard (Ohio State) —B—1959–60
Lewis, Daniel (Wisconsin) —B—1958–60
LeFebre, Gilbert—B—1935
LeForce, Clyde (Tulsa) —Q—1947–48
Lewis, Daniel (Wisconsin) —B—1958
Liles, Elvin (Oklahoma A & M) —G

—1943–45

Lindon, Luther (Kentucky) —T—1944–45

Lininger, Raymond (Ohio State) —C —1950–51

Lio, Augustino (Georgetown) —T—1941–43

Logan, Andrew (Western Reserve) —T —1941

Long, Robert (U.C.L.A.) —E—1955–60

Lowe, Gary (Michigan State) —B—1957–60

Lowther, Russell (Detroit) —B—1944

Lumpkin, Roy (Georgia Tech.) —B—1934

Lusk, Robert (William & Mary) —C—1956

Lynch, Edward (Holy Cross) —E—1926

McClung, William (Florida A & M) —T— 1960

McCord, Darris (Tennessee) —T—1955–60

McCoy, Joel (Alabama) —B—1946

McDermott, Lloyd (Kentucky) —T—1950

McDonald, James (Ohio State) —B —1938–40

McDonnell, John (Creighton) —B—1926

McGraw, Thurman (Colorado A & M) —T —1950–54

McIlhenny, Donald (Southern Methodist Univ.) —B—1956

McKalip, William (Oregon State) —E —1934, 36

McNamara, Thomas (Detroit) —G —1925–26

McWilliams, William (Jordan) —B—1934

Mackenroth, John (North Dakota) —C —1938

Madarik, Elmer (Detroit) —B—1945–47

Maggioli, Achille (Illinois) —B—1949

Magnani, Dante (St. Mary's, Cal.) —B —1950

Maher, Bruce (Detroit) —B—1960

Mains, Gilbert (Murray State, Ky.) —E —1953–60

Malinowski, Eugene (Detroit) —B—1949

Mann, Robert (Michigan) —E—1948–49

Manzo, Joseph (Boston College) —T—1945

Margucci, Joseph (Southern California) —Q—1947–48

Marion, Philip (Michigan) —B—1925–26

Maronic, Steven (North Carolina) —T —1939–40

Martin, James (Notre Dame) —G—1951–60

Martinovich, Philip (College of Pacific) —G—1939

Matheson, John (Western Reserve) —E —1943–46

Matheson, Riley (Texas Mines) —G—1943

Mathews, Edward (U.C.L.A.) —B—1941–43

Mathewson, M. (California) —E—1941

Matisi, Anthony (Pittsburgh) —T—1938

Mattiford, John (Marshall) —G—1941

Maves, Earl (Wisconsin) —B—1948

Mazza, Vincent—E—1945–46

Mello, James (Notre Dame) —B—1949

Mesak, Richard (St. Mary's, Cal.) —T—1945

Messner, Max (Cincinnati) —B—1960

Middleton, David (Auburn) —B—1955–60

Miketa, Andrew (North Carolina) —C —1954–55

Miklich, William (Idaho) —B—1948

Milano, Arch (St. Francis) —E—1945

Miller, Blake (Michigan State) —E—1921

Miller, Robert (Virginia) —T—1952–58

Mitchell, Granville (Davis-Elkins) —E —1934–35

Mitrick, Frank (Oglethorpe) —T—1945

Momsen, Robert (Ohio State) —G—1951

Monahan, Regis (Ohio State) —G—1935–38

Montgomery, James (Texas A & M) —T —1946

Moore, Paul (Presbyterian) —Q—1940–41

Moore, William (Loyola) —B—1939

Morlock, John (Marshall) —B—1940

Morrall, Earl (Michigan State) —Q— 1958–60

Morris, Glen (Colorado State) —E—1940

Morse, Raymond (Oregon) —E —1935–38, 40

Moscrip, James (Stanford) —E—1938–39

Mote, Kelly (Duke) —E—1947–49

Mugg, Garvin (Texas State North) —T —1945

Munn, Lyle (Kansas State) —E—1928

Murakowski, Arthur (Northwestern) —B —1951

Nardi, Richard (Ohio State) —B—1938

Nelson, Reed (Brigham Young) —C—1947

Nelson, Robert (Baylor) —C—1941, 45

Ninowski, James (Michigan State) —Q— 1960

Noppenberg, John (Miami) —B—1941

Nori, Reino (DeKalb) —B—1937

Nott, Douglas (Detroit) —B—1935

Obee, Duncan (Dayton) —T—1941

O'Brien, William—B—1947

Olenski, Mitchell (Alabama) —T—1947

Opalewski, Edward (Michigan State Normal—T—1943–44

Owen, William (Oklahoma A & M) —T —1928

Panciera, Donald (San Francisco) —B—1950

Panelli, John (Notre Dame) —B—1949–50

Paolucci, Benjamin (Wayne) —T—1959

Parker, Raymond (Centenary) —B —1935–36

Parsons, Lloyd (Gustavus Adolphus) —B —1941

Patt, Maurice (Carnegie Tech.) —E—1938

Pavelec, Theodore (Detroit) —G—1941–43

Payne, Otto (Texas A & M) —B—1937

Pearson, Lindell (Oklahoma) —B—1950–52

Perry, Gerald (California) —T—1954–59

Peterson, Kenneth (Gonzaga) —B—1936

Piepul, Milton (Notre Dame) —B—1941

Pietrosante, Nicholas (Notre Dame) —B— 1959–60

Pifferini, Robert (San Jose State) —C—1949

Pingel, John (Michigan State) —B—1939

Polanski, John (Wake Forest) —B—1942

Poole, Oliver (Mississippi) —E—1949

Prchlik, John (Yale) —T—1949–53

Pregulman, Mervin (Michigan) —G —1947–48

Prescott, Harold (Hardin-Simmons) —E

—1949
Presnell, Glenn (Nebraska) —B—1934–36
Price, Charles (Texas A & M) —Q
—1940–41, 45
Rabb, Warren (Louisiana State Univ.) —
Q—1960
Rabold, Michael (Indiana) —G—1959
Radovich, William (Southern California)
—G—1938–41, 45
Randels, Horace (Kansas State) —E—1928
Randolph, Clare (Indiana) —C—1934–36
Ranspot, Keith (Southern Methodist
Univ.) —E—1941
Rechmarck, Raymond (Syracuse) —B—1937
Reese, Kenneth (Alabama) —B—1947
Reichow, Garet (Iowa) —B—1956–57, 59–60
Rexer, Freeman (Tulane) —E—1944
Reynolds, Robert (Stanford) —C—1937–38
Rhea, Floyd (Oregon) —G—1947
Ricca, James (Georgetown) —T—1955
Richards, Perry (Detroit) —E—1958
Richards, Ray (Nebraska) —G—1934
Richins, Aldo (Utah) —B—1935
Rifenburg, Richard (Michigan) —E—1950
Riley, Leon (Detroit) —B—1955
Ritchhart, Delbert (Colorado) —C—1936–37
Roberson, Lake (Mississippi) —E—1945
Rockenback, Lyle (Michigan State) —G
—1943
Rogas, Daniel (Tulane) —G—1951
Rogers, William (Villanova) —T
—1938–40, 44
Roskie, Kenneth (South Carolina) —B
—1948
Rosteck, Ernest—C—1944
Rote, Tobin (Rice) —Q—1957–59
Rouse, Stillman (Missouri) —E—1940
Roussos, Michael (Pittsburgh) —T—1949
Rowe, Robert (Colgate) —B—1934
Rubino, Anthony (Wake Forest) —G
—1943, 46
Russas. Albert (Tennessee) —T—1949
Russell, Kenneth (Bowling Green) —T
—1957–59
Ryan, David (Hardin-Simmons) —B
—1945–46
Ryan, Kent (Utah State) —B—1938–40
Rychlec, Thomas (American International)
—E—1958
Sacksteder, Norbert (Dayton) —B—1921
Salsbury, James (U.C.L.A.) —G—1955–56
Sanchez, John (San Francisco) —T—1947
Sandifer, Daniel (Louisiana State Univ.)
—1950
Sanzotta, Dominic (Western Reserve) —B
—1942–46
Sarratt, Charles (Oklahoma) —Q—1948
Sarringhaus, Paul (Ohio State) —B—1946
Sartori, Lawrence (Fordham) —G—1942, 45
Scharer, Edward (Notre Dame) —B
—1926, 28
Schibanoff, Alexander (Franklin-Marshall)
—T—1942
Schiechl, John (Santa Clara) —C—1942
Schmidt, Joseph (Pittsburgh) —G—1953–60

Schneller, John (Wisconsin) —B—1934–36
Scholtz, Robert (Notre Dame) —C—1960
Schottel, Ivan (Missouri State Teachers)
—Q—1946–48
Schroll, Charles (Louisiana State Univ.)
—B—1950–51
Scott, Clyde (Arkansas) —B—1952
Scott, Perry (Muhlenberg) —E—1942
Sedbrook, Leonard (Oklahoma City Univ.)
—B—1928
Self, Clarence (Wisconsin) —B—1950–51
Seltzer, Harry (Morris Harvey) —B—1942
Sewell, Harley (Texas) —G—1953–60
Shepard, William (Western Maryland) —B
—1935–40
Siegert, Herbert (Illinois) —G—1951
Sigillo, Dominic (Xavier) —T—1945
Simmons, John (Detroit) —G—1949–50
Sinkwich, Frank (Georgia) —B—1943–44
Sirochman, George (Duquesne) —G—1944
Sloan, Dwight (Arkansas) —B—1939–40
Smith, Earl (Ripon) —T—1925
Smith, Harry (Southern California) —T
—1940
Smith, James (Iowa) —B—1949–54
Smith, Robert (Texas A & M) —B—1953–54
Smukler, David (Temple) —B—1940
Sneddon, Robert (St. Mary's, Cal.) —B
—1945
Soboleski, Joseph (Michigan) —T—1950
Sonnenberg, Gustave (Dartmouth) —T
—1925–26
Souders, Cecil (Ohio State) —E—1947–49
Spangler, Eugene (Tulsa) —B—1946
Speelman, Harry (Michigan State) —G
—1940
Spencer, Oliver (Kansas) —G—1953, 56,
59–60
Speth, George (Murray State, Ky.) —T
—1942
Stacco, Edward (Colgate) —T—1947
Stacey, James (Oklahoma) —T—1935–37
Stanfel, Richard (San Francisco) —G
—1952–55
Steen, James (Syracuse) —T—1935–36
Steffen, James (UCLA) —B—1959–60
Stits, William (U.C.L.A.) —B—1954–56
Stobbs, William (Washington & Jefferson)
—B—1921
Stokes, Lee (Centenary) —C—1937–39
Stovall, Richard (Abilene Christian) —C
—1947–48
Stringfellow, Joseph (Mississippi Southern)
—E—1942
Stuart, Roy (Tulsa) —B—1943
Sucic, Steven (Illinois) —B—1947–48
Summerall, George (Arkansas) —E—1952
Swiacki, William (Columbia) —E—1951–52
Szakash, Paul (Montana) —B—1938–42
Szymanski, Frank (Notre Dame) —C
—1945–47
Tassos, Damon (Texas A & M) —G
—1945–46
Thomas, Calvin (Tulsa) —G—1939–40
Thomas, James (Oklahoma) —G—1939

Thomas, Rex (St. Johns) —B—1928
Thomas, Russell (Ohio State) —T—1946–49
Thomason, James (Texas A & M) —B—1945
Thuerk, Owen (St. Joseph) —E—1940
Tomasetti, Louis (Bucknell) —B—1941
Tonelli, Amerigo (Southern California) —C—1939
Topor, Theodore (Michigan State) —T —1955
Torgeson, Lavern (Washington State) —C —1951–54
Tracy, Thomas (Tennessee) —B—1956–57
Treadaway, John (Hardin-Simmons) —T —1949
Trebotich, Ivan (St. Mary's, Cal.) —B —1944–45
Tressa, Thomas (Davis-Elkins) —G—1942
Triplett, Wallace (Penn. State) —B 1949–50, 52
Tripson, John (Mississippi State) —T—1941
Tripucka, Frank (Notre Dame) —Q—1949
Tsoutsouvas, John (Oregon State) —C— 1940
Tulis, Robert (Texas A & M) —G—1948
Tully, Darrell (Texas Teachers East) —B —1939
Turner, Harold (Tennessee) —E—1954
Uremovich, Emil (Indiana) —T —1941–42, 45–46
VanTone, Arthur (Mississippi) —B —1943–45
Vanzo, Frederick (Northwestern) —B —1938–41
Vaughan, Charles (Tennessee) —B —1935–36
Vezmar, Walter (Michigan State) —G —1946–47
Vick, Henry "Ernie" (Michigan) —B— 1925, 28
Vick, Richard (Washington & Jefferson) —B—1925–26
Voss, Walter (Detroit) —E—1921, 25
Wagner, Sidney (Michigan State) —G —1936–38
Walker, Ewell Doak (Southern Methodist Univ.) —B—1950–55
Walker, Wayne (Idaho) —C—1958–60
Ward, Elmer (Utah State) —C—1935–36
Ward, William (Washington State) —G —1947–49
Watson, Joseph (Rice) —C—1950
Watt, Joseph (Syracuse) —B—1947–48
Weatherall, James (Oklahoma) —T— 1959–60
Webb, Kenneth (Presbyterian) —B— 1958–60
Weber, Richard (St. Louis Univ.) —B—1945
Weiss, Howard (Wisconsin) —B—1939–40
Westfall, Robert (Michigan) —B—1944–47
Westoupal, Joseph (Nebraska) —C—1928
White, Byron (Colorado) —B—1940–41
White, Wilbur (Colorado State) —B—1936
Whitsell, David (Indiana) —B—1958–60
Wiatrak, John (Washington) —C—1939
Wiberg, Oscar (Nebraska Wesleyan) —B

—1928
Wickett, Lloyd (Oregon State) —T —1943, 46
Wiederquist, Chester (Washington & Jefferson) —T—1928
Wiese, Robert (Michigan) —B—1947–48
Wiethe, John (Xavier) —G—1939–42
Williams, Rex (Texas Tech.) —C—1945
Williams, Samuels (Michigan State) —E— 1960
Wilson, Camp (Tulsa) —B—1946–49
Wimberly, Bryon (Washington & Jefferson) —G—1925
Winslow, Robert (Southern California) —E —1940
Woit, Richard (Arkansas State) —B—1955
Wojciechowicz, Alexander (Fordham) —C —1938–46
Womack, Bruce (Texas State West) —G —1951
Wyhonic, John (Alabama) —G—1941
Yowarsky, Walter (Kentucky) —C—1955
Zatkoff, Roger (Michigan) —G—1957–58
Zimmerman, Leroy (San Jose State) —Q —1947
Zuzzio, Anthony (Muhlenberg) —G—1942

DULUTH ESKIMOS
(1923—27)
(Also played as Kellys)

Ashmore, Roger (Gonzaga) —T—1927
Belden, Charles—B—1927
Black, Charles (Kansas) —E—1925
Bratt, Edward (Wisconsin State) —E—1924
Buland, Walter—T—1926
Burke, Robert (Detroit) —T—1927
Carlson, Eugene (Iowa State) —G—1924–27
Clark, Arthur (Nevada) —B—1927
Clow, Herbert (Minnesota) —B—1924
Cobb, William (Kansas State) —T—1924–26
Cronin, Francis (St. Mary's, Minn.) —E —1927
Denfield, Frederick (Annapolis) —T—1925
Dunn, Roderick (Syracuse) —G—1923
Engstrom, George (Superior State) —G— 1924
Fitzgibbons, Paul (Creighton) —B—1926
Gayer, Walter (Creighton) —T—1926
Gilbert, Walter (Valparaiso) —B—1923–26
Goldfein, Jersey (Superior State) —B—1927
Harris, Kenneth (Syracuse) —B—1923–24
Haven, John (Hamline) —E—1923
Heinisch, Fred—B—1926
Johnson, Arthur (Fordham) —T—1923–27
Kelly, Charles (Northwestern) —B—1923–26
Kieley, Howard—E—1923–25
Kiesling, Walter (St. Thomas) —G —1926–27
Koziak, Michael (Notre Dame) —G —1924–25
Lange, Clifford (Montana) —T—1927
Larson, Lloyd (Wisconsin) —B—1926
McCarthy, James (California) —T—1927
McDonnell, John (Creighton) —B—1924–25

McNally, John (St. John's, Minn.) —B
—1926–27
McNellis, William (St. Thomas) —B—1927
Madigan, Frank (St. Mary's, Minn.) —C
—1923
Manion, James (St. Thomas, Minn.) —G
—1926–27
Marshall, Robert (Minnesota) —E—1923–27
Mayer, Frank (Notre Dame) —G—1926
Method, Russell (North Dakota) —B
—1923–27
Monelie, William (St. Mary's, Minn.) —B
—1927
Morse, Robert (Carlton) —G—1923
Murray, John (St. Thomas) —E—1926
Murphy, Philip (Marquette) —C—1926
Neacy, Clement (Colgate) —E—1927
Nevers, Ernest (Stanford) —B—1926–27
O'Donnell, Richard (Minnesota) —E—1923
O'Neill, Thomas (St. Mary's, Minn.) —E
—1925
O'Toole, William (St. Mary's, Minn.) —G
—1924
Quam, Charles—B—1926
Rooney, Cobb (Colorado) —B—1923–27
Rooney, Joseph—E—1923–24, 26–27
Rooney, William—B—1923–27
Rundquist, Elmer (Illinois) —T—1923–26
Sanford, James (Lehigh) —T—1924
Scanlon, Dewey (Valparaiso) —B—1926
Stein, William (Fordham) —E—1923–27
Sternaman, Joseph (Illinois) —B—1923
Strand, Lief (Fordham) —C—1924
Suess, Raymond (Villanova) —T—1926–27
Tobin, Elgie (Pennsylvania State) —E
—1925
Tobin, Rex (Minnesota) —E—1925
Underwood, John (Iowa State) —E
—1924–26
Vexall, Roy—B—1923–25
Warner, Robert (Wisconsin) —B—1927
Williams, Daniel (Minnesota) —G—1923–27

EVANSVILLE (IND.) CRIMSON GIANTS (1921—22)

Bondurant, J. Bourbon (DePauw) —G—
1921–22
Dalrymple, Robert (Wabash) —C—1922
Fausch, Franklin (Kalamazoo) —B—1921–22
Fishman, Abraham—G—1921–22
Fishman, Alexander—T—1921–22
Fritsch
Garnjost, Donald (Columbia) —G—1921
Goldsmith, Earl—E—1921–22
Gorman, Earl—G—1921
Henderson, Herbert (Ohio State) —B—
1921–22
Ingle—B—1921
Lauer, Peter (Iowa) B—1921–22
Lensing, Vincent (Notre Dame) —G—1921
Lindsey, Menzies (Wabash) —Q—1921–22
Mullen, Vern (Nebraska) —E—1921
Noreene, Olaf (Minnesota) —B—1921
O'Neill, William (Marquette) —E—1921

Rosenberger—T—1921
Runsey, Roy—T—1921
Spain, Richard—G—1921
Specht, Norman "Dutch"—G—1921
Spiegel, Clarence (Notre Dame) —T—
1921–22
Sullivan, Steven (Montana) —Q—1922
Tally
Warweg
Whitehead
Williams, Travis—B—1921
Windbiele, Joseph—C—1921–22
Zeller, Jerry—B—1921–22

FRANKFORD YELLOWJACKETS (1924—31)

Allen, Samuel (Pennsylvania Military)
—T—1931
Apsit, Marger (Southern California) —B
—1931
Barna, George (Hobart) —E—1929
Barrager, Nathan (Southern California)
—C—1930–31
Bednar, Albert (Lafayette) —G—1924–25
Behman, Russell (Dickinson) —T—1924–31
Berryman, Robert (Cornell) —B—1924
Bollinger, Edward (Bucknell) —G—1930
Books, Robert (Dickinson) —B—1926
Britton, Earl (Illinois) —B—1927
Bruder, Woodie (West Virginia) —B
—1925–26
Brumbaugh, Justin (Bucknell) —B—1931
Budd, John (Lafayette) —T—1926
Burnham, Stanley (Harvard) —B—1925
Capps, Wilbur (Oklahoma State East) —T
—1929–30
Carpe, Joseph (Millikin) —T—1926–27
Cartin, Charles (Holy Cross) —T—1925
Chamberlain, Guy (Nebraska) —E—1925–26
Clark, Arthur (Nevada) —B—1927
Clement, Alexander (Williams) —B—1925
Comstock, Rudolph (Georgetown) —G
—1926–29
Connaughton, Harry (Georgetown) —G
—1927
Conover, Lawrence (Penn. State) —C—1926
Corcoran, Arthur (Georgetown) —E—1923
Cortemeglia, Christopher (Southern
Methodist Univ.) —B—1927
Crabtree, Clyde (Florida) —B—1930
Craig, Clark (Pennsylvania) —E—1925
Crowthers, Rae (Colgate) —E—1925–26
Crowthers, Saville (Colgate) —G—1925
Daugherty, Russell (Illinois) —T—1927
Davidovitz, Arthur (Lehigh) —T—1930
Davis, Carl (West Virginia) —T—1927
Dayhoff, Harry (Bucknell) —B—1924
Diehl, Walter (Bucknell) —B—1928–30
Dobrey, E.—E—1928
Donohoe, William (Carnegie Tech.) —B
—1927
Douglas, Leo (Lehigh) —B—1926
Doyle, Edward (West Point) —E—1924
Elkins, Fait (Haskell) —B—1928–29

Ernst, John (Lafayette) —B—1925, 30
Filak, John (Penn. State) —T—1927–29
Finn, John (Villanova) —B—1924
Fitzgibbons, Paul (Creighton) —B—1927
Fitzke, Robert (Idaho) —B—1925
Fleckenstein, William (Iowa) —G—1931
Ford, Adrian (Lafayette) —B—1927
Graham, Frederick (West Virginia) —E
  —1926
Gibson, George (Minnesota) —G—1930
Gillson, Robert (Colgate) —G—1930
Goodbread, Royce (Florida) —B—1930
Grigg, Cecil (Austin) —B—1927
Gulian, Michael (Brown) —T—1924
Halicki, Edward (Bucknell) —B—1929–30
Hamer, Ernest (Pennsylvania) —B
  —1924–28
Hanson, Harold (Minnesota) —G—1928–30
Harms, Arthur (Vermont) —T—1925–26
Havens, Charles (Western Maryland) —C
  —1930
Haws, Harvey (Dartmouth) —B—1924–25
Hoffman, William (Lehigh) —G—1924–26
Hogan, Paul (Detroit) —B—1926
Homan, Henry (Lebanon Valley) —B
  —1925–30
Hutton, Leon (Purdue) —B—1930
James, George (Nebraska) —G—1929
Joesting, Herbert (Minnesota) —B
  —1930–31
Jones, Benjamin (Grove City) —B—1925–26
Jones, Thomas (Bucknell) —G—1930–31
Kaer, Morton (Southern California) —B
  —1931
Kassel, Charles (Illinois) —E—1927–28
Kellogg, William (Syracuse) —B—1924
Kelly, William (Montana) —B—1929
Kostos, Anthony (Bucknell) —E—1927–31
Kostos, Martin (Albright) —E—1929–30
Kruez, Albert (Pennsylvania) —B—1931
Leary, Thomas (Fordham) —E—1927–29, 31
Long, Harvey (Detroit) —T—1924
Lowe, George (Fordham) —E—1924–26
Lunz, Gerald (Marquette) —G—1930
McArthur, John (Santa Clara) —C—1930
McCormick, Edward (Detroit) —G—1925
McDonnell, John (Creighton) —B—1931
McGirl, Leonard (Missouri) —G—1931
McGrath, Frank (Georgetown) —E—1927
Maglisceau, Albert (Geneva) —T—1929
Magner, James (North Carolina) —B—1931
Mahan, Walter (West Virginia) —G—1926
Mahoney, Roger (Penn. State) —C
  —1928–30
Malcolm, Carvel (Franklin Marshall) —G—
  1926
Malcolm, Harry (Washington & Jefferson)
  —T—1929
Maxwell, Joseph (Notre Dame) —E
  —1927–29
Mercer, Kenneth (Simpson) —B—1927–29
Mizell, Warner (Georgia Tech) —B—1931
Molinet, Louis (Cornell) —B—1927
Montgomery, Ralph "Sully" (Centre) —T
  —1927

Moran, Dale (Carnegie Tech.) —B
  —1925–27
Moynahan, Richard (Villanova) —B—1927
Nydall, Malcolm (Minnesota) —B—1930–31
O'Connell, Milton (Lafayette) —E
  —1924–25
Oehlrich, Arnold (Nebraska) —B—1928–29
Panaccion, Victor (Penn. State) —T—1930
Parks (Washington & Lee) —T—1926
Pederson, James (Augsberg) —E—1930–31
Pharmer, Arthur (Minnesota) —B—1930–31
Potts, Robert (Washington & Lee) —T
  —1926
Provencial, Kenneth (Georgetown) —B
  —1930
Racis, Frank—G—1931
Reed, Max (Bucknell) —C—1926–27
Rengel, Neil (Davis-Elkins) —B—1930
Richards, Peter (Swarthmore) —C—1927
Richards, Raymond (Nebraska) —G—1930
Ringwalt, Carroll (Indiana) —C—1931
Roberts, Walcott (Annapolis) —B—1926
Rodriguez, Jess (Salem) —B—1930
Roepke, John (Penn. State) —B—1928
Rogers, Charles (Pennsylvania) —B
  —1927–29
Scott, John (Lafayette) —B—1924
Seborg, Henry (Kalamazoo) —B—1930–31
Sechrist, Walter (West Virginia) —G—1925
Seidelson, Harry (Pittsburgh) —G—1925
Schultz, John (Temple) —B—1930
Smith, George (Georgia) —G—1930
Smythe, James (Centre) —B—1926
Spagna, Joseph (Lehigh) —C—1924–25
Springsteen, William (Lehigh) —C
  —1925–26
Stein, Russell (Pittsburgh) —T—1924
Stepanovich, Anthony (Southern
  California) —G—1930
Stockton, Houston (Gonzaga) —B
  1925–26, 28–29
Storer, John (Lehigh) —B—1924
Sullivan, George (Pennsylvania) —B
  —1924–25
Tackwell, Charles (Kansas State) —E
  —1930–31
Tanner, Robert (Minnesota) —E—1930
Thomas, William (Penn. State) —B—1924
Thompson, John (Lafayette) —T—1929
Tully, George (Dartmouth) —E—1927
VanSickle, Clyde (Arkansas) —C—1930
Waite, Carl (Georgetown) —E—1928
Wall, Edward (Grove City) —B—1930
Ward, John (Southern California) —T
  —1930
Watkins, Gordon (Georgia Tech.) —T
  —1930
Way, Charles (Penn. State) —B—1924
Weir, Edward (Nebraska) —T—1926–28
Weir, Joseph (Nebraska) —E—1927
Weller, Truman (Nebraska) —T—1928
Welsh, James (Colgate) —G—1924–25
Wilcox, Edward (Swarthmore) —B—1926–27
Wilsbach, Frank (Bucknell) —G—1925
Wilson, George (Lafayette) —B—1929–30

Wilson, Leland (Cornell) —B—1930–31
Wright, Albert (Oklahoma A & M) —B
—1930
Youngstrom, Adolph (Dartmouth) —G
1926–27

GREEN BAY PACKERS (1921—60)

Aberson, Clifford—B—1946
Abrams, Nathan—E—1921
Abramson, George (Virginia) —T—1925
Adams, Chester (Ohio) —T—1942–43
Adkins, Robert (Marshall) —B
—1940–41, 45–46
Afflis, Richard (Nevada) —G—1951–54
Albrecht, Arthur (Wisconsin) —T—1941
Aldridge, Benjamin (Oklahoma A & M) —B
—1953
Amundsen, Norman (Wisconsin) —C—1957
Apsit, Marger (Southern California) —B
—1932
Ashmore, Roger (Gonzaga) —T—1928–29
Bailey, Byron (Washington State) —B—1953
Baker, Frank (Northwestern) —E—1931
Baker, Roy (Southern California) —B
—1928–29
Balaz, Frank (Iowa) —B—1939–41
Baldwin, Alton (Arkansas) —E—1950
Banet, Herbert (Manchester) —B—1937
Barnes, Emery (Oregon) —E—1956
Barnett, Solon (Baylor) —T—1945–46
Barrager, Nathan (Southern California) —C
—1931–35
Barry, Albert (Southern California) —G
—1954, 57
Barry, Norman (Notre Dame) —B—1921
Barton, Donald (Texas) —B—1953
Basing, Myrtle (Lawrence) —B—1923–27
Baxter, Lloyd (Southern Methodist Univ.)
—T—1948
Beasley, John (South Dakota) —B—1924
Beck, Kenneth (Texas A & M) —1959–60
Becker, Wayland (Marquette) —E—1936–38
Bell, Edward (Indiana) —G—1947–49
Bennett, Earl (Hardin-Simmons) —G—1946
Berezney, Paul (Fordham) —T—1942–44
Berrang, Edward (Villanova) —E—1952
Berry, Cornelius (North Carolina State) —E
—1940
Bettencourt, Lawrence (St. Mary's Cal.) —C
—1933
Bettis, Thomas (Purdue) —G—1955–60
Bieberstein, Adolph (Wisconsin) —G—1926
Bilda, Richard (Marquette) —B—1944
Biolo, John (Lake Forest) —G—1939
Bloodgood, Elbert (Nebraska) —B—1930
Boedeker, William (Kalamazoo) —B—1950
Bookout, William (Austin) —B—1955–56
Boone, J. R. (Tulsa) —B—1953
Borak, Fritz (Creighton) —E—1938
Borden, Nathan (Indiana) —E—1955–59
Bowdoin, James (Alabama) —G—1928–32
Brackins, Charles (Prairie View A & M) —B
—1955
Bray, Ray (Western Michigan) —G—1952
Brennan, John (Michigan) —G—1939

Brock, Charles (Nebraska) —C—1939–47
Brock, Louis (Purdue) —B—1940–45
Brown, Thomas (Ball State) —B—1959
Brown, William (Arkansas) —G—1953–56
Bruder, Henry (Northwestern) —B
—1931–39
Bucchianeri, Amadeo (Indiana) —G
—1941, 44–45
Buck, Howard (Wisconsin) —T—1921–25
Buhler, Lawrence (Minnesota)—Q—1939–41
Buland, Walter—T—1924
Bullough, Harry (Michigan State) —G
—1955, 58
Bultman, Arthur (Marquette) —C—1932–34
Burris, Paul (Oklahoma) —G—1949–51
Butler, Frank (Michigan State) —C
—1934–36, 38
Butler, William (Chattanooga) —B—1959
Cahoon, Ivan (Gonzaga) —T—1926–29
Canadeo, Anthony (Gonzaga) —B—1941–52
Cannava, Anthony (Boston College) —B
—1950
Capuzzi, James (Cincinnati) —B—1955–56
Carey, Joseph—G—1921
Carlson, Irvin (St. John's) —G—1926
Carmichael, Albert (Southern California)
—B—1953–58
Carpenter, Lewis (Arkansas) —B—1959–60
Casper, Charles (Texas Christian Univ.)
—B—1934
Christman, Paul (Missouri) —Q—1950
Cifelli, August (Notre Dame) —T—1953
Clemens, Calvin (Southern California) —B
—1936
Clemens, Robert (Georgia) —B—1955
Clemons, Ray (St. Mary's Cal.) —G—1947
Cloud, John (William & Mary) —B
—1950–51
Cody, Edward (Purdue) —B—1947–48
Collins, Albin (Louisiana State Univ.) —B
—1951
Comp, Irvin (St. Benedict's) —Q—1943–49
Comstock, Rudolph (Georgetown) —G
—1931–33
Cook, James (Wisconsin) —G—1921
Cone, Fred (Clemson) —B—1951–57
Cook, Theodore (Alabama) —E—1948–50
Coughlin, Frank (Notre Dame) —B—1921
Coutre, Lawrence (Notre Dame) —B
—1950, 53
Craig, Lawrence (South Carolina) —Q
—1939–49
Cremer, Theodore (Auburn) —E—1948
Crimmins, Bernard (Notre Dame)—G—1945
Croft, Milburn (Ripon) —T—1942–47
Cronin, Thomas (Marquette) —B—1922
Crowley, James (Notre Dame) —B—1925
Cuff, Ward (Marquette) —B—1947
Culver, Alvin (Notre Dame) —T—1932
Currie, Daniel (Michigan State) —C—
1958–60
Cvercko, Andrew (Northwestern) —G—
1959–60
Cyre, Hector (Gonzaga) —T—1926–28
Dahms, Thomas (San Diego State) —T
—1955

Daniell, Averell (Pittsburgh) —T—1937
Danjean, Ernest (Auburn) —G—1957
Darling, Bernard (Beloit) —C—1927–31
Davenport, Wayne (Hardin-Simmons) —B —1931
Davis, Harper (Mississippi State) —B—1951
Davis, Paul (Marquette) —G—1922
Davis, Ralph (Wisconsin) —G—1947–48
Davis, William (Grambling) —B—1960
Dawson, Gilbert (Texas) —B—1953
Deeks, Donald (Washington) —T—1948
Dees, Robert (Missouri State Southwest) —T—1952
DeMoe, William (Beloit) —E—1921
Deschaine, Richard—E—1955–57
Dillon, Robert Dan (Texas) —B—1952–59
Dilweg, Lavern (Marquette) —E—1927–34
DiPierro, Raymond (Ohio State) —T —1950–51
Disend, Leo (Albright) —T—1940
Dittrich, John (Wisconsin) —G—1959
Doncarlos, William (Drake) —C—1931
Douglas, George (Marquette) —C—1921
Dowden, Steven (Baylor) —T—1952
Dowler, Boyd (Colorado) —E—1959–60
Dreyer, Walter (Wisconsin) —B—1950–51
Drulis, Charles (Temple) —G—1950
Duford, Wilfred (Marquette) —B—1924
Duhart, Paul (Florida) —B—1944
Dunn, Joseph (Marquette) —B—1927–31
Dunnigan, Walter (Minnesota) —E—1922
Earhart, Ralph (Texas Tech.) —B—1948–49
Earpe, Francis (Monmouth) —T—1922–32
Eason, Roger (Oklahoma) —T—1949
Ecker, Enrique (John Carroll)—T—1950–51
Elliott, Burton (Marquette) —B—1921
Elliot, Carleton (Virginia) —E—1951–54
Engebretsen, Paul (Northwestern) —G 1934–41
Engelmann, Wuert (South Dakota State) —B—1930–33
Enright, Rex (Notre Dame) —B—1926–27
Ethridge, Joseph (Southern Methodist Univ.) —T—1949
Evans, John (California) —B—1929
Evans, Lon (Texas Christian Univ.) —G —1933–37
Evans, Richard (Iowa) —E—1940, 43
Falkenstein, Anthony (St. Mary's—Cal.) —B —1943
Faverty, Harold (Wisconsin) —C—1952
Faye, Allen (Marquette) —E—1922
Feathers, Beattie (Tennessee) —B—1940
Felker, Arthur (Marquette) —E—1951
Ferguson, Howard—B—1953–58
Ferry, Louis (Villanova) —T—1949
Finley, James (Michigan State) —G—1942
Finnin, Thomas (Detroit) —T—1957
Fitzgibbons, Paul (Creighton) —B—1930–32
Flaherty, Richard (Marquette) —E—1926–27
Flowers, Robert (Texas Tech.) —C —1942–49
Floyd, Robert Jack (Texas Christian Univ.) —B—1952, 54
Ford, Leonard (Michigan) —E—1958

Forester, George "Bill" (Southern Methodist Univ.) —T—1953–60
Forte, Robert (Arkansas) —B—1946–53
Francis, Joseph (Oregon State) —B—1958
Frankowski, Raymond (Washington) —G —1945
Francis, Joseph (Oregon State)—B—1958–59
Franta, Herbert (St. Thomas) —T—1930
Freeman, Robert (Auburn) —B—1959
Fries, Sherwood (Colorado State) —G—1943
Fritsch, Theodore (Wisconsin State) —B —1942–50
Frutig, Edward (Michigan) —E—1941, 45
Gantenbein, Milton (Wisconsin) —E —1931–40
Gardella, Augustus (Holy Cross) —B—1922
Gardner, Milton (Wisconsin) —G—1922–26
Garrett, Robert (Stanford) —B—1954
Gatewood, Lester (Baylor) —B—1946–47
Gavin, Fritz (Marquette) —E—1921, 23
Gillette, James (Virginia) —B—1947
Glick, Edward (Marquette) —B—1921–22
Goldenberg, Charles (Wisconsin) —G —1933–45
Goodnight, Clyde (Tulsa) —E—1945–49
Gordon, Louis (Illinois) —T—1936–37
Greeney, Norman (Notre Dame) —G—1933
Greenfield, Thomas (Arizona) —C—1939–41
Gregg, Forest (Southern Methodist Univ.) —T—1956, 58–60
Gremminger, Henry (Baylor) —B—1956–60
Griffen, Harold (Iowa) —C—1928
Grimes, William (Oklahoma A & M) —B —1950–52
Grove, Roger (Michigan State)—B—1931–35
Gudauskas, Peter (Murray State) —G —1942, 45
Hackbart, Dale (Wisconsin) —B—1960
Hanner, Joel "Dave" (Arkansas) —T— 1952–60
Hanny, Frank (Indiana) —T—1930
Hanson, Roy (Marquette) —B—1923
Harding, Roger (California) —C—1949
Harris, John (Wisconsin) —B—1925–26
Haycraft, Kenneth (Minnesota) —E—1930
Hayes, Norbert (Marquette) —E—1923
Hays, David (Notre Dame) —E—1921–22
Hays, George (St. Bonaventure) —E—1953
Hearden, Leonard (Ripon) —B—1924
Hearden, Thomas (Notre Dame) —B —1927–28
Heath, Stanley (Nevada) —Q—1949
Held, Paul (San Diego State) —B—1955
Helluin, Francis (Tulane) —T—1955–57
Hendrian, Warren (Pittsburgh) —B—1924
Herber, Arnold (Regis) —Q—1931–41
Hickman, Lawrence (Baylor) —B—1960
Hill, Donald (Stanford) —B—1929
Hinkle, Clarke (Bucknell) —B—1932–41
Hinte, Harold (Pittsburgh) —E—1941
Hornung, Paul (Notre Dame) —B—1957–60
Howard, Lynn (Indiana) —B—1921–22
Howell, John (Nebraska) —B—1938
Howton, William (Rice) —E—1952–58
Hubbard, Robert "Cal" (Geneva) —T

DON HUTSON COULD RUN, TOO. HERE HE GOES FOR A TOUCHDOWN AGAINST THE CHICAGO CARDINALS IN 1941. GEORGE SVENDSEN (66) IS COMING ALONG TO BLOCK IF NEEDED. GREEN BAY WON 17–9.

—1929–35

Hunter, Arthur (Notre Dame) —T—1954
Hutson, Donald (Alabama) —E—1935–45
Iman, Kenneth (Southeastern) —C—1960
Ingalls, Robert (Michigan) —C—1942
Isbell, Cecil (Purdue) —Q—1938–42
Jacobs, Jack (Oklahoma) —Q—1947–49
Jacunski, Harry (Fordham) —E—1939–44
Jankowski, Edward (Wisconsin) —B —1937–41
Jansante, Valerio (Duquesne) —E—1951
Jean, Walter (Bethany) —G—1925–26
Jenison, Ray (South Dakota) —T—1931
Jennings, James (Missouri) —E—1955
Johnson, Glenn (Arizona State) —T—1949
Johnson, Howard (Georgia) —G—1940–41
Johnson, Kosse "Joe" (Rice) —B—1954–58
Johnson, Marvin (San Jose State) —B —1952–53
Johnson, Thomas (Michigan) —T—1952
Johnson, William (Minnesota) —E—1941
Johnstone, Chester (Elmhurst) —B —1931, 34–38
Jones, Bruce (Alabama) —G—1927–28
Jones, Robert (Indiana) —G—1934
Jones, Thomas (Bucknell) —G—1938
Jordan, Henry (Virginia) —T—1959–60
Jorgenson, Carl (St. Mary's–Cal.—T—1934
Kahler, Robert (Nebraska) —B—1941–44
Kahler, Royal (Nebraska) —T—1942
Katalinas, Leo (Catholic Univ.) —T—1938
Keane, James (Iowa) —E—1952
Keefe, Emmett (Notre Dame) —G—1921
Kell, Paul (Notre Dame) —T—1939–40
Kelley, William (Texas Tech.) —E—1949
Kenyon, Crowell (Ripon) —G—1923
Kercher, Robert (Georgetown) —E—1944
Kern, William (Pittsburgh) —T—1929–30
Keuper, Kenneth (Georgia) —B—1945–47
Kiesling, Walter (St. Thomas) —T—1935–36

Kilbourne, Warren (Michigan) —T—1939
Kimmel, J. D. (Houston) —T—1958
Kinnard, William (Mississippi) —B —1957–58
King, Donald (Kentucky) —T—1956
Kirby, John (Southern California) —B —1949
Klaus, Fee—C—1921
Kliebhan, Roger (Milwaukee Teachers) —B —1921
Knafelc, Gary (Colorado) —E—1954–60
Knutson, Eugene (Michigan) —E—1954, 56
Kotal, Edward (Lawrence) —B—1925–29
Kovatch, John (Notre Dame) —E—1947
Kramer, Gerald (Idaho) —G—1959–60
Kramer, Ronald (Michigan) —E—1957, 59–60
Kranz, Kenneth (Milwaukee Teachers) —B —1949
Kresky, Joseph (Wisconsin) —G—1930
Kuick, Stanley (Beloit) —G—1926
Kurth, Joseph (Notre Dame) —T—1933–34
Kuusisto, William (Minnesota) —G —1941–46
Ladrow, Walter—B—1921
Lambeau, Earl (Notre Dame) —B—1921–30
Lande, Clifford (Carroll) —E—1921
Lankas, James (St. Mary's–Tex.) —B—1943
Larson, Frederic (Notre Dame) —C—1925
Lauer, Harold (Detroit) —B—1922
Lauer, Lawrence (Alabama) —C—1956–57
Lawrence, James (Texas Christian Univ.) —B—1939
Laws, Joseph (Iowa) —B—1934–45
Leaper, Wesley (Wisconsin) —E—1921, 23
Lee, William (Alabama) —T—1937–42, 46
Lester, Darrell (Texas Christian Univ.) —C —1937–38
Letlow, Russell (San Francisco) —G —1936–42, 46
Lewellen, Verne (Nebraska) —B—1924–32

Lidberg, Carl (Minnesota) —B—1926–30
Lipscomb, Paul (Tennessee) —T—1945–49
Logan, Richard (Ohio State) —T—1952–53
Lollar, George (Howard) —B—1928
Loomis, Ace (Wisconsin State) —B—1951–53
Losch, John (Miami) —B—1956
Lucky, William (Baylor) —T—1955
Ludtke, Norman (Carroll) —G—1924
Luhn, Nolan (Tulsa) —E—1945–49
Lyle, Dewey (Minnesota) —E—1922–23
Lyman, Delbert (U.C.L.A.) —T—1941
MacAuliffe, John (Beloit) —B—1926
McCrary, Hurdis (Georgia) —B—1929–33
McDougal, Robert (Miami) —B—1947
McGaw, Walter (Beloit) —G—1926
McGeary, Clarence (North Dakota State) —T—1950
McGee, William Max (Tulane) —E— 1954, 57–60
McHan, Lamar (Arkansas) —Q—1959–60
McIlhenny, Donald (Southern Methodist Univ.) —B—1957–59
McKay, Roy (Texas) —B—1945–47
McLaughlin, Lee (Virginia) —G—1941
McLean, Ray—B—1921
McNally, John "Blood" (St. John) —B —1928–36
McPherson, Forrest (Nebraska) —T —1943–45

Maddox, George (Kansas State) —T—1935
Malone, Grover (Notre Dame) —B—1921
Manley, Leon (Oklahoma) —G—1950–51
Mann, Robert (Michigan) —E—1950–54
Marks, Lawrence (Indiana) —B—1928
Martell, Herman—E—1921
Martinkovich, John (Xavier) —E—1951–56
Mason, Joel (Western Michigan) —E —1941–45
Massey, Carleton (Texas) —E—1957–58
Masters, Norman (Michigan State) —T —1957–60
Mathys, Charles (Indiana) —B—1922–26
Mattos, Harry (St. Mary's—Cal.) —B—1936
Matuszak, Marvin (Tulsa) —C—1958
Mayer, Frank (Notre Dame) —G—1927
Meilinger, Stephan (Kentucky) —E— 1958, 60
Michaels, Walter (Washington & Lee) —G —1951
Michalske, August (Penn. State) —G —1929–37
Midler, Louis (Northwestern) —G—1941
Miller, Charles (Purdue) —C—1938
Miller, Donald (Southern Methodist Univ.) —B—1954
Miller, Donald (Wisconsin) —B—1941–42
Miller, John (Boston College) —T—1960
Miller, Paul (South Dakota) —B—1936–38

Nate Fine Photo

REDSKIN SAM BAUGH INTERCEPTS A PASS THROWN TO GREEN BAY END NOLAN LUHN IN
1943. EARLY IN HIS CAREER BAUGH WAS A TOP DEFENSIVE BACK, LEADING THE LEAGUE
IN INTERCEPTIONS IN 1943.

Mills, Thomas (Penn. State) —B—1922–23
Milton, Thomas (Lake Forest) —E—1924
Minick, Paul (Iowa) —G—1928–29
Mitchell, Charles (Tulsa) —B—1946
Molenda, John (Michigan) —B—1929–32
Monnett, Robert (Michigan State) —B
—1933–38
Moore, Allen (Texas A & M) —E—1939
Moore, Thomas (Vanderbilt) —B—1960
Moselle, Don (Wisconsin State) —B
—1951–52
Mosley, Russell (Alabama) —B—1945–46
Moss, Perry (Illinois) —B—1948
Mott, Norman (Georgia) —B—1933
Mulleneaux, Carl (Utah State) —E
—1938–41, 45–46
Mulleneaux, Lee (Arizona State) —T—1938
Murray, Richard (Marquette) —T—1921–24
Nadolney, Romanus (Notre Dame) —G
—1922
Nash, Thomas (George Washington) —E
—1928–32
Neal, William "Ed" (Tulane) —T—1945–51
Nichols, Hamilton (Rice) —G—1951
Niemann, Walter (Michigan) —C—1922–24
Nitschke, Raymond (Illinois) —B—1958–60
Nix, Doyle (Southern Methodist Univ.) —B
—1955
Norgard, Albert (Stanford) —E—1934
Norton, Martin (Carleton) —B—1925–28
Nussbaumer, Robert (Michigan) —B
—1946, 51
Oakes, William (Haskell) —T—1921
O'Boyle, Harry (Notre Dame) —B
1928–29, 32
O'Connor, Robert (Stanford) —T—1935
O'Donahue, Patrick (Wisconsin) —E—1955
O'Donnell, Richard (Minnesota) —E
—1924–30
Odson, Urban (Minnesota) —T—1946–49
Ohlgren, Earl (Minnesota) —E—1942
Olsen, Ralph (Utah) —E—1949
Olsonoski, Lawrence (Minnesota) —G
—1948–49
O'Malley, Robert (Cincinnati) —B—1950
Orlich, Daniel (Nevada) —E—1949–51
Owens, Henry (Lake Forest) —G—1922
Pannell, Ernest (Texas A & M) —T
—1941–42, 45
Parilli, Vito (Kentucky)—Q—1952–53, 56–58
Pape, Orrin (Iowa) —B—1930
Paskvan, George (Wisconsin) —B—1941
Paulekas, Anthony (Washington &
Jefferson) —C—1936
Pearson, Lindell (Oklahoma) —B—1952
Pelfrey, Raymond (Kentucky State East)
—B—1951–52
Perkins, Donald (Plattsville Teachers) —B
—1943–45
Perry, Claude (Alabama) —T—1927–35
Pesonen, Richard (Minnesota) —B—1960
Peterson, Lester (Texas) —E—1932–35
Peterson, Philip (Wisconsin) —B—1932
Peterson, Raymond (San Francisco) —B
—1937
Petitbon, John (Notre Dame) —B—1957

Powers, Samuel (Michigan North) —G
—1921
Pregulman, Mervin (Michigan) —G—1946
Prescott, Harold (Hardin-Simmons) —E
—1946
Priatko, William (Pittsburgh) —G—1957
Pritko, Steven (Villanova) —E—1949–50
Provo, Frederick (Washington) —B—1948
Psaltis, James (Southern California) —B
—1954
Purdy, Everett (Beloit) —B—1926–27
Purnell, Frank (Alcorn A & M) —B—1957
Putman, Earl (Arizona State) —C—1957
Quatse, Jess (Pittsburgh) —T—1933
Quinlan, William (Michigan State) —E
—1959–60
Radick, Kenneth (Marquette) —E—1930–31
Ranspot, Keith (Southern Methodist
Univ.) —E—1942
Ray, Buford (Vanderbilt) —T—1938–48
Regnier, Peter (Minnesota) —B—1922
Reichardt, William (Iowa) —B—1952
Reid, Floyd (Georgia) —B—1950–56
Rhodemyre, Jay (Kentucky) —C—1948–52
Riddick, Raymond (Fordham) —E
—1940–42, 46
Ringo, James (Syracuse) —C—1953–60
Roberts, William (Dartmouth) —B—1956
Robinson, William (Lincoln) —B—1952
Rohrig, Herman (Nebraska) —B
—1941, 46–47
Romine, Alton (Alabama) —E—1955, 58
Rosatti, Roman (Michigan) —T
—1924, 26–27
Rose, Alfred (Texas) —E—1932–36
Rosenow, August (Ripon) —B—1921
Roskie, Kenneth (South Carolina) —B
—1948
Rote, Tobin (Rice) —Q—1950–56
Ruetz, Howard (Loras) —T—1951–53
Rush, Clive (Miami) —E—1953
Ruzich, Stephan (Ohio State) —G—1952–54
Salsbury, James (U.C.L.A.) —G—1957–58
Sample, Charles (Toledo) —B—1942, 45
Sandifer, Daniel (Louisiana State Univ.)
—B—1952–53
Sarafiny, Albert (St. Edwards) —C—1933
Sauer, George (Nebraska) —B—1935–37
Saunders, Russell (Southern California) —B
—1931
Schammel, Francis (Iowa) —G—1937
Scherer, Bernard (Nebraska) —E—1936–38
Schlinkman, Walter (Texas Tech.) —B
—1946–50
Schmaehl, Arthur—B—1921
Schmidt, George (Lewis) —C—1952–53
Schneidman, Herman (Iowa) —B—1935–39
Schoemann, Roy (Marquette) —C—1938
Schroll, Charles (Louisiana State Univ.) —B
—1951
Schuette, Carl (Marquette) —B—1950–51
Schultz, Charles (Minnesota) —T—1939–41
Schwammel, Adolph (Oregon State) —T
—1934–37, 43–44
Secord, Joseph—C—1922
Seeman, George (Nebraska) —E—1940

Seibold, Champ (Wisconsin) —T—1934–41
Self, Clarence (Wisconsin) —B—1952, 54–55
Serini, Washington (Kentucky) —G—1952
Shanley, James (Oregon) —B—1958
Shelly, Dexter (Texas) —B—1932–33
Skeate, Gilbert (Gonzaga) —B—1927
Skibinski, Joseph (Purdue) —G—1955–56
Skoglund, Robert (Notre Dame) —E—1947
Skoronski, Robert (Indiana) —T—1956, 59–60
Sleight, Elmer (Purdue) —T—1930–31
Smith, Ben (Alabama) —E—1933
Smith, Bruce (Minnesota) —B—1945–48
Smith, Earl (Ripon) —T—1922
Smith, Edward (New York Univ.) —B—1937
Smith, Ernest (Southern California) —T —1935–37, 39
Smith, Gerald (Wisconsin) —G—1956
Smith, Oscar (Texas Mines) —B—1948
Smith, Rex (Wisconsin Teachers) —E—1922
Smith, Richard (Notre Dame) —G—1927–29
Smith, Warren (Carlton) —C—1921
Snelling, Kenneth (U.C.L.A.) —B—1945
Sorenson, Glen (Utah State) —G—1943–45
Sparlis, Albert (U.C.L.A.) —G—1946
Spencer, Joseph (Oklahoma A & M) —T —1950–51
Spencer, Oliver (Texas) —G—1957–58
Spinks, Jack (Alcorn A & M) —G—1955–56
Stahlman, Richard (DePaul) —E—1931–32
Stansauk, Donald (Denver) —T—1950–51
Starr, Bryan (Alabama) —B—1956–60
Starret, Benjamin (St. Mary's-Cal.) —B —1941–45
Steen, Frank (Rice) —E—1939
Steiner, Roy (Alabama) —E—1950–51
Stephenson, David (West Virginia) —G —1951–54
Stonebraker, John (Southern California) —E—1942
Sturgeon, Lyle (North Dakota State) —T —1937
Sullivan, Walter (Beloit) —G—1921
Summerhays, Robert (Utah) —B—1949–51
Svendsen, Earl (Minnesota) —C—1937–40
Svendsen, George (Minnesota) —C —1935–41
Switzer, Veryl (Kansas State) —B—1954–55
Symank, John (Florida) —B—1957–60
Szafaryn, Leonard (North Carolina) —T —1950, 53–56
Tassos, Damon (Texas A & M) —G —1947–49
Taugher, Claude (Marquette) —B—1922
Taylor, James (Louisiana State Univ.) —B —1958–60
Temp, James (Wisconsin) —E—1957–60
Tenner, Robert (Minnesota) —E—1935
Teteak, Deral (Wisconsin) —G—1952–56
Thomason, Robert (Virginia Military Inst.) —B—1951
Thompson, Clarence (Minnesota) —B—1939
Thurston, Frederick (Valparaiso) —G— 1959–60
Timberlake, George (Southern California)

—C—1955
Tinsley, Peter (Georgia) —G—1938–45
Tollefson, Charles (Iowa) —G—1944–46
Tonnemaker, Clayton (Minnesota) —C —1950, 53–54
Tunnell, Emlen (Iowa) —B—1959–60
Tuttle, Richard (Minnesota) —E—1927
Twedell, Francis (Minnesota) —G—1939
Uram, Andrew (Minnesota) —B—1938–43
Urban, Alex (South Carolina) —E —1941, 44–45
Usher, Edward (Michigan) —B—1922, 24
Vairo, Dominic (Notre Dame) —E—1935
VanEvery, Harold (Minnesota) —B —1940–41
VanSickle, Clyde (Arkansas) —C—1932–33
Vant Hull, Fred (Minnesota) —G—1942
Vereen, Carl (Georgia Tech.) —T—1957
Vegara, George (Notre Dame) —E—1925
Vogds, Evan (Wisconsin) —G—1948–49
Voss, Walter (Detroit) —E—1924
Wagner, Buffton (Michigan North) —B —1921
Walker, Val Joe (Southern Methodist Univ.) —B—1953–56
Webber, Howard (Kansas State) —E—1928
Wehba, Raymond (Southern California) —E—1944
Weisgerber, Richard (Willamette) —B —1938–40, 42
Wells, Donald (Georgia) —E—1946–49
West, Pat (Southern California) —B—1948
Wheeler, Lyle (Ripon) —E—1921–23
White, Eugene (Georgia) —B—1954
Whittenton, Jesse (Texas Western) —B —1958–60
Wildung, Richard (Minnesota) —G —1946–53
Wilkins, Theodore (Indiana) —E—1925
Williams, A. D. (College of Pacific) —B —1959
Williams, Richard (Wisconsin) —B—1921
Wilson, Eugene (Southern Methodist Univ.) —E—1947–48
Wilson, Milton (Wisconsin State Teachers) —T—1921
Wimberly, Abner (Louisiana State Univ.) —E—1950–52
Winslow, Paul (North Carolina Coll.) —B—1960
Winters, Arnold—T—1941
Witte, Earl (Gustavus-Adolphus) —B—1934
Wizbicki, Alexander (Holy Cross) —B—1950
Wood, William (Southern California) —B—1960
Woodin, Howard (Marquette) —G —1922–30
Wunsch, Harry (Notre Dame) —G—1934
Young, Glenn (Purdue) —B—1956–57
Young, Paul (Oklahoma) —C—1933
Young, William (Ohio State) —G—1929
Zarnas, Augustus (Ohio State) —G—1939–40
Zatkoff, Roger (Michigan) —G—1953–56
Zeller, Joseph (Indiana) —G—1932
Zoll, Carl—G—1921–22
Zoll, Martin—G—1921

Zoll, Richard (Indiana) —G—1939
Zuidmulder, David (St. Ambrose) —B
—1929—31
Zupek, Albert (Lawrence) —E—1946
Zuver, Merle (Nebraska) —C—1930

HAMMOND PROS (1922—26)

Annan, Duncan (Brown) —B—1923—26
Barrett, John (Washington & Lee) —B—
1922—23
Barry, George (Beloit) —G—1922—24
Baston, Albert (Minnesota) —E—1922—24
Bernstein, Joseph (Tulsa) —G—1925
Besta—B—1924
Birk, Ferdinand (Purdue) —B—1922
Butler, Edward "Sol" (Loras) —B—1923
Butler, William (Marquette) —B
—1923—24, 26
Carman, Edmund (Purdue) —T—1922, 25
Cearing, Lloyd (Valparaiso) —B—1922—23
Chase, Ralph (Pittsburgh) —T—1926
Crawford, Kenneth (Miami—Ohio) —B
—1925
Curzon, Harry—B—1925—26
Dahlgren, George (Beloit) —G—1925—26
Detwiler, John (Kansas) —B—1923—24
Falcon, Gilbert (Wabash) —B—1924—25
Fortune, Burnell (DePauw) —G—1924—25
Gaiver, Einar (North Dakota) —E—1922,
1925
Gavin, Patrick "Buck"—B—1926
Ghee, Milton (Dartmouth) —B—1922—23
Hahn, Ray (Bethany) —E—1926
Hanke, Carl (Minnesota) —E—1923
Harlon, Julian (Georgia Tech) —B—1922
Hess, Arthur (Indiana) —B—1922—25
Hudson, Richard—B—1925—26
Hunter—G—1925
Jackson, Colville (Chicago) —E—1922
Kendricks, James (Texas A & M) —B—1925
King, Andrew (West Virginia) —B—1925
Knop, Oscar (Illinois) —B—1922—23
Kovascy, William (Illinois) —T—1923
Kuehl, Walter (Dubuque) —B—1922
Labissoniere, Joseph (St. Thomas, Minn.)
—C—1922
Leatherman, Paul (Chicago) —E—1922
Magnusson, Glenn (Northwestern) —C
—1925
McDonnell, John (Creighton) —B—1925
McKetes—B—1926
Meese, Ward (Wabash) —E—1925
Nagida—B—1926
Neal, Thomas (Duke) —G—1924—26
Nelson, Donald (Ohio Wesleyan) —C—1926
Newman, Olin (Carnegie Tech.) —T—1926
Oltz, Russell (Washington & Jefferson) —C
—1922—25
Peshmalyan, Baruyr (Yale) —E—1922
Pollard, Fritz (Brown) —B—1923—25
Risley, Elliott (Indiana) —T—1922—23
Roberts, Walcott (Annapolis) —E—1922,
1924
Robinson, Edward (North Carolina) —B—
1923—25

Rydzewski, Frank (Notre Dame) —T
—1922—26
Sachs, Leonard (Loyola Chicago) —E
—1924—25
Sechrist, Walter (West Virginia) —G—1926
Seibert, Edward (Otterbein) —G—1923
Seyfrit, Michael (Notre Dame) —E—1924
Shelburne, John (Dartmouth) —B—1922
Siefers—E—1924
Smith, Earl (Ripon) —E—1923, 26
Smith, Wilfred (DePaul) —E—1922
Stahlman, Richard (DePaul) —E—1924
Sullivan, Walter (Beloit) —G—1923—24
Tallant, David (Grove City) —T—1922—25
Tierney, Frederick (Minnesota) —G—1922
Ursella, Rueben—B—1926
Usher, Louis (Syracuse) —T—1923—24, 26
Watson, Grady (Texas) —B—1924—25
Wendler, H. (Ohio State) —B—1926
Willert—G—1922
Williams, Jay Mayo (Brown) —E—1922—26

HARTFORD BLUES (1926)

Barnikow, Edward—B—1926
Bonadies, John—B—1926
Brian, Harry (Grove City) —B—1926
Cookman—E—1926
Corgan, Charles (Kansas) —E—1926
Dally—G—1926
Donlan, James—G—1926
Edwards, William—B—1926
Flynn, Furlonge (Cornell) —E—1926
Foley, James (Syracuse) —B—1926
Friedman, Jacob—E—1926
Garvey, Arthur "Hec" (Notre Dame) —
C—1926
Gildea, Dennis (Holy Cross) —C—1926
Halloran, James—B—1926
Harris, John—B—1926
Hunt, Edward (Georgetown) —B—1926
Jamerson, Charles (Arkansas) —E—1926
Keenan, Edward (Washington State) —G
—1926
Lynch, Edward (Catholic Univ.) —E—1926
McCann, Ernest (Penn. State) —T—1926
McCormick, Elmer (Detroit) —G—1926
McEvoy, Edward (Spring Hill) —B—1926
McMahon, Harry (Holy Cross) —B—1926
McTigue, Robert (Georgia) —B—1926
Manning, Joseph (Fordham) —B—1926
Neely, Jess (Vanderbilt) —T—1926
Nichols, Ralph (Kansas State) —T—1926
Noble, Richard (Trinity-Conn.) —G—1926
O'Connell, Grattan (Boston College) —E
—1926
O'Connor, Francis (Holy Cross) —T—1926
O'Neil, Charles (Connecticut) —C—1926
Perrin, John (Chicago) —B—1926
Radzievitch, Victor (Connecticut) —B—1926
Santone, Al—G—1926
Segretta, Rocco—E—1926
Simendinger, Kenneth (Holy Cross) —B
—1926
Smythe, Louis (Texas) —B—1926

Thomas, Alfred (Pennsylvania) —B—1926
Thomas, Enid (Pennsylvania) —B—1926
Webber, Howard (Kansas State) —E—1926
Werwaiss, Elbert (Dean) —T—1926
Wilson, Enid (Penn. State) —B—1926
Zehrer, Henry—B—1926

KANSAS CITY COWBOYS (1924—26)

Anderson, Thomas (Haskell) —B—1924
Andrews, Leroy (Kansas State Teachers) —B—1924—26
Ashburn, Clifford (Nebraska) —G—1924—25
Bassett, Henry (Nebraska) —T—1924
Berquist, Jay (Nebraska) —G—1924—26
Bloodgood, Elbert (Nebraska) —B—1925—26
Bradshaw, James (Nevada) —B—1924
Bristow, Gordon (Oklahoma) —B—1924—26
Browning, R. (Westminster—Mo.) —Q —1925
Choate (Haskell) —G—1924
Cobb, Thomas (Okla. N. E. Teachers) —T —1926
Corgan, Charles (Arkansas) —E—1924—26
Crook, Albert (Washington & Jefferson) —C—1926
DeWitz, Herbert (Nebraska) —B—1924—26
Guyon, Joseph (Carlisle) —B—1924—25
Hanson, Steven—B—1925
Hill, Charles (Baker) —B—1924—26
Hill, Harry (Oklahoma) —B—1924—26
Howard, Albert (Princeton) —G—1924—25
Howard, Robert (Marietta) —G—1924—26
Hummell, Charles (Lafayette) —B—1926
Jaquith—B—1926
Krueger, Albert (Drake) —T—1924
Lane, Lewis (St. Mary's—Kan.) —Q—1924
McLemore, Emmett (Haskell) —B—1924
Milan, Joseph (Phillips) —B—1924—25
Milton, John (So. California) —E—1924
Milton, Thomas (Lake Forest) —E—1924
Mintun, John—C—1924—25
Munn, Lyle (Kansas State) —E—1925—26
Munn, Monte (Nebraska) —E—1924
Munn, Wayne (Nebraska) —T—1924
Murphy, Thomas (St. Mary's, Kan.) —B— 1926
Owen, Stephen (Phillips) —T—1924—26
Owen, William (Oklahoma A & M) —T —1925—26
Peterson, Leonard (Nebraska State Teachers) —E—1924
Quinn, Ivan (Carroll) —G—1924
Randall, Proctor (Kansas State) —E—1925
Randels, Horace (Kansas State) —E—1926
Rhenquist, Milton (Bethany) —C—1924—26
Sears, Richard (Kansas State) —B—1924
Sermon, Ray (Missouri State) —Q—1925
Smith, Clyde (Missouri) —C—1926
Spear, Glen (Drake) —B—1926
Strauss, Arthur (Phillips) —B—1924
Thompson, Alvin (Iowa) —T—1925
Thompson, William (Washburn) —G —1924—25
Usher, Edward (Michigan) —E—1924
Webber, Howard (Kansas State) —E —1924—25

Westophal, Joseph (Nebraska) —C—1926
White, Philip (Oklahoma) —E—1924—25
Wiedich, Ralph (Kansas State Teachers) —T—1924

KENOSHA (1924)

Baxter, Ernest (Centre) —B—1924
Carlson, Irvin (St. John's) —G—1924
Cassidy, William (Detroit) —E—1924
Conrad, Marty (Kalamazoo) —C—1924
Dahlgren, George (Beloit) —G—1924
Egan, Richard (Chicago) —E—1924
Fortune, Burnell (DePaul) —G—1924
Gardner, Milton (Wisconsin) —G—1924
Gorman, Earl—G—1924
Grau, Arthur—G—1924
Heinisch, Fred—B—1924
Hess, Arthur (Indiana) —B—1924
Hurst, William (Oregon Univ.) —G—1924
Meese, Ward (Wabash) —E—1924
Oberbruckinger—T—1924
Oltz, Russell (Washington & Jefferson) — C—1924
Pattison (Michigan) —G—1924
Pearce, Walter (Illinois) —B—1924
Potteiger, Earl (Ursinus) —Q—1924
Seasholtz, George (Lafayette) —B—1924
Sies, Dale (Pittsburgh) —G—1924
Simpson, J. Felix (Detroit) —B—1924
Stahlman, Richard (DePaul) —E—1924
Usher, Louis (Syracuse) —T—1924
Vick, Henry "Ernie" (Michigan) —B—1924
Walters—B—1924
Watson, Grady (Texas) —B—1924
Williams, Jay (Brown) —E—1924
Wood (Lafayette) —G—1924

LOS ANGELES (1926)

Ash, Julian (Oregon State) —G—1926
Finch, Olin (Whittier) —B—1926
Guttormsen, George (Washington) —B —1926
Hawkins, John (Southern California) —T —1926
Hufford, Darrell (California) —E—1926
Imlay, Talma (California) —Q—1926
McArthur, John (Santa Clara) —C —1926
Maul, C. Newell (California) —B—1926
Muller, Harold (California) —E—1926
Newmeyer, Donald (California) —T—1926
Nolan, John (Santa Clara) —G—1926
Sandberg, Roy (Washington State) —B —1926
Schaffnit, Peter (California) —E—1926
Thompson, Donald (Redlands) —G—1926
Thurman, John (Pennsylvania) —T—1926
White, Byron (Minnesota) —B—1926
Young, John "Al" (California) —B—1926

LOS ANGELES RAMS (1946—60)
(Formerly Cleveland Rams)

Agajanian, Benjamin (New Mexico) —B —1953

Agler, Robert (Otterbein) —H—1948–49

Arnett, Jon (Southern California) —B —1957–60

Bagarus, Steven (Notre Dame) —B—1947

Baker, Jon (North Carolina State) —T— 1958–60

Banta, Herbert (Southern California) —B —1946–48

Barry, Paul (Tulsa) —B—1950, 52

Bass, Richard (College of Pacific) —B—1960

Benton, James (Arkansas) —E—1946–47

Bighead, Jack (Pepperdine) —E—1955

Bleeker, Melvin (Southern California) —B —1947

Boeke, James (Heidelberg) —T—1960

Bouley, Gilbert (Boston College) —T —1946–50

Bowers, William (Southern California) —B —1954

Boyd, Robert (Loyola, L.A.) —E —1950–51, 53–57

Braatz, Thomas (Marquette) —E—1958

Bradshaw, Charles (Baylor) —T—1958–60

Bravo, Alex (California Polytech.) —B —1957–58

Brink, Lawrence (Illinois State Northern) —E—1948–53

Brito, Eugene (Loyola, La.) —E—1959–60

Britt, Charles (Georgia) —B—1960

Brovelli, Angelo (Washington State) —G— 1960

Bruney, Fred (Ohio State) —B—1958

Bukich, Rudolph (Southern California) —Q—1953–56

Burroughs, Donald (Colorado A & M) —B —1955–60

Carey, Robert (Michigan State) —E —1952, 54, 56

Casner, Kenneth (Baylor) —T—1952

Cason, James (Louisiana State) —B —1955–56

Castete, Jesse (McNeese State) —B —1956–57

Champagne, Edward (Louisiana State) —T —1947–50

Clarke, Leon (Southern California) —E —1956–59

Collier, Robert (Southern Methodist Univ.) —T—1951

Corn, Joseph—B—1948

Cothren, Paige (Mississippi) —B—1957–58

Cowhig, Gerard (Notre Dame) —B —1947–49

Cross, Robert (Austin) —T—1954–55

Currivan, Donald (Boston College) —E —1948–49

Dahms, Thomas (San Diego State) —T —1951–54

Dale, Carroll (V.P.I.) —E—1960

David, Robert (Villanova) —B—1947–48

Davis, Glenn (West Point) —B—1950–51

Daugherty, Richard (Oregon) —G —1951–53, 56–58

Dean, Harold (Ohio State) —G—1947–49

DeFruiter, Robert (Nebraska) —B—1948

DeLauer, Robert (Southern California) —C—1946

Dickson, Paul (Baylor) —T—1959

Doll, Donald (Southern California) —B —1954

Dougherty, Robert (Kentucky) —E—1957

Dwyer, John (Loyola, L.A.) —B—1952–55

Eason, Roger (Oklahoma) —T—1946–48

Ellena, Jack (U.C.L.A.) —G—1955–56

Ellersick, Donald (Washington State) —B —1960

Farmer, Thomas (Iowa) —B—1946

Fawcett, Jacob (Southern Methodist Univ.) —T—1946

Fears, Thomas (U.C.L.A.) —E—1948–56

Ferris, Neil (Loyola, L.A.) —B—1953

Finlay, John (U.C.L.A.) —G—1947–51

Fournet, Sidney (Louisiana State Univ.) —G—1955–56

Franckhauser, Thomas (Purdue) —B—1959

Fry, Robert (Kentucky) —T—1953, 56–59

Fuller, Frank (Kentucky) —T —1953, 55, 57–58

Gehrke, Fred (Utah) —B—1946–49

Griffin, Robert (Arkansas) —C—1953–57

Guzik, John (Pittsburgh) —T—1959–60

Halliday, John (Southern Methodist Univ.) —T—1951

Hamilton, Ray (Arkansas) —E—1946–47

Harding, Roger (California) —C—1946

Hardy, James (Southern California) —B —1946–48

Harmon, Thomas (Michigan) —B—1946–47

Harris, James (Oklahoma) —B—1958

Hauser, Arthur (Xavier, Ohio) —T —1954–57

Haynes, Hall (Santa Clara) —B—1954–55

Hecker, Norbert (Baldwin-Wallace) —E —1951–53

Hecker, Robert (Baldwin-Wallace) —B —1952–53

Hickey, Howard (Arkansas) —E—1946–48

Hirsch, Elroy (Wisconsin) —B—1949–57

Hock, John (Santa Clara) —T—1953, 55–57

Hoerner, Richard (Iowa) —B—1947–51

Hoffman, Robert (Southern California) —B —1946–49

Holovak, Michael (Boston College) —B —1946

Holtzman, Glen (Texas State Northern) —T—1955–58

Hord, Ambrose Roy (Duke) —G—1960

Horvath, Leslie (Ohio State) —B—1947–48

Houser, John (Redlands) —C—1957–59

Hubbell, Frank (Tennessee) —E—1947–49

Huffman, Richard (Tennessee) —T —1947–50

Hughes, Edward (Tulsa) —B—1954–56

Humphrey, Loyie (Baylor) —Q—1959–60

Hunter, Arthur (Notre Dame) —T—1960

Inglehart, Floyd (Wiley College, Texas) —B—1958

Janerette, Charles (Penn State) —G—1960

Jobko, William (Ohio State) —G—1958–60

Johnson, Clyde (Kentucky) —T—1946–47

Johnson, Marvin (San Jose State) —B
—1951–52

Jones, James (Washington) —B—1958

Kalmanir, Thomas (Nevada) —B—1949–51

Karilivacz, Carl (Syracuse) —B—1959–60

Keane, Thomas (West Virginia) —B
—1948–51

Kenerson, John (Kentucky State) —G—1960

Klosterman, Don (Loyola, L. A.) —B—1952

Ksionzyk, John (St. Bonaventure) —Q
—1947

Lane, Richard—E—1952–53

Lange, William (Dayton) —G—1951–52

Lansford, Alex (Texas) —T—1958–60

Lazetich, Milan (Michigan) —G—1946–50

Lear, Leslie (Manitoba University) —G
—1946

Levy, Leonard (Minnesota) —G—1946

Lewis, Woodley (Oregon) —B—1950–55

Lipscomb, Eugene—E—1953–55

Long, Robert (U.C.L.A.) —B—1960

Longo, Charles (San Jose State) —B—1960

Lovetere, John (Compton) —T—1959–60

Lundy, Lamar (Purdue) —E—1957–60

McCormick, Thomas (College of Pacific)
—B—1953–55

McFadin, Lewis (Texas) —G—1952–56

McLaughlin, Leon (U.C.L.A.) —C—1951–55

Magnani, Dante (St. Mary's) —B—1947–48

Marconi, Joseph (West Virginia) —B
—1956–60

Martin, John (Annapolis) —C—1947–49

Matheson, Riley (Texas Mines) —G
—1946–47

Matson, Oliver (San Francisco) —B
—1959–60

Mayes, Carl (Texas) —B—1952

Meador, Edward (Arkansas Tech) —B—
1959–60

Mello, James (Notre Dame) —B—1948

Mergenthal, Arthur (Notre Dame) —G
—1946

Michaels, Louis (Kentucky) —T—1958–60

Miller, Paul (Louisiana State) —E—1954–57

Miller, Ronald (Southern California) —E
—1956

Morris, John (Oregon) —B—1958–60

Morris, Lawrence (Georgia Tech.) —G
—1955–57

Morrow, John (Michigan) —T—1956, 58–59

Myers, Bradford (Bucknell) —B—1953, 56

Myers, John (U.C.L.A.) —B—1952

Naumetz, Fred (Boston College) —C
—1946–50

Panfil, Kenneth (Purdue) —T—1956–58

Pardee, John (Texas A & M) —C—1957–60

Pasqua, Joseph (Southern Methodist Univ.)
—T—1946

Pasquariello, Ralph (Villanova) —B—1950

Paul, Donald (U.C.L.A.) —C—1948–55

Phillips, James (Auburn) —E—1958–60

Pitts, Hugh (Texas Christian Univ.) —C
—1956

Pritko, Steven (Villanova) —E—1946–47

Putnam, Duane (College of Pacific) —G

—1952–59

Quinlan, Volney (San Diego State) —B
—1952–56

Reid, Joseph (Louisiana State Univ.) —C
—1951

Reinhard, Robert (California) —T—1950

Reiz, Albert (Louisiana Southeastern) —Q
—1946

Repko, Joseph (Boston College) —T
—1948–49

Rich, Herbert (Vanderbilt) —B—1951–53

Richter, Lester (California) —G—1954–60

Rickards, Paul (Pittsburgh) —B—1948

Roberts, William (Dartmouth) —B—1956

Robustelli, Andrew (Arnold) —E—1951–55

Ruthstrom, Ralph (Southern Methodist
Univ.) —B—1946

Ryan, Frank (Rice) —B—1958–60

Schultz, Eberle (Oregon State) —G
—1946–47

Selawski, Eugene (Purdue) —T—1959

Shaw, Robert (Ohio State) —E—1946, 49

Sherman, Willard (St. Mary's, Cal.) —E
—1954–60

Shiver, Raymond (Miami) —B—1956

Shofner, Delbert (Baylor) —B—1957–60

Simensen, Donald (St. Thomas) —T
—1951–52

Sims, George (Baylor) —B—1949–50

Smith, Billy Ray (Arkansas) —G—1957

Smith, Bruce (Minnesota) —B—1949

Smith, James (Colorado) —T—1947

Smith, Verda (Abilene Christian) —B
—1949–53

Smyth, William (Cincinnati) —T—1947–50

Sparkman, Allen (Texas A & M) —T
—1948–49

Stalcup, Jerry (Wisconsin) —G—1960

Statuto, Arthur (Notre Dame) —C—1950

Stephenson, David (West Virginia) —G
—1950

Strode, Woodrow (U.C.L.A.) —E—1946

Strugar, George (Washington) —T
—1957–60

Sucic, Steven (Illinois) —B—1946

Svare, Harland (Washington State) —E
—1953–54

Taylor, Cecil (Kansas State) —B—1955, 57

Teeuws, Leonard (Tulane) —T—1952–57

Thomas, Clendon (Oklahoma) —B—
1958–60

Thomason, Robert (Virginia Military Inst.)
—B—1949

Thompson, Harry (U.C.L.A.) —G—1950–54

Toogood, Charles (Nebraska) —T—1951–56

Towler, Daniel (Washington & Jefferson)
—B—1950–55

Valdez, Vernon—B—1960

Van Brocklin, Norman (Oregon) —Q
—1949–57

Vasicek, Victor (Texas) —G—1950

Villanueva, Daniel (New Mexico State)
—K—1960

Wade, William (Vanderbilt) —Q—1954–60

Waller, Ronald (Maryland) —B—1955–58

Wardlow, Duane (Washington)—E
—1954, 56
Washington, Kenneth (U.C.L.A.)—B
—1946-48
Waterfield, Robert (U.C.L.A.)—Q
—1946-52
West, Patrick (Southern California)—B
—1946-48
West, Stanley (Oklahoma)—G—1950-54
Whittenton, Jesse (Texas Western)—B
—1956-57
Wilkins, Roy (Georgia)—E—1958-59
Williams, Jerome (Washington State)—B
—1949-52
Williams, Samuel (Michigan State)—E—
1959
Wilson, John (Baylor)—B—1946-47
Wilson, Thomas—B—1956-60
Winkler, James (Texas A & M)—T
—1951-52
Yagiello, Ray (Catawba)—G—1948-49
Younger, Paul (Grambling)—B—1949-57
Zilly, John (Notre Dame)—E—1947-51

LOUISVILLE COLONELS
(1922—23, 1926)

Bernoske, Daniel (Indiana)—G—1926
Berwick, Edward (Loyola, Chi.)—C—1926
Bloodworth, Lowe—G—1923
Boldt, S. Chase—B—1922-23
Borntraeger, William —G—1923
Brunchlacher, Austin—G—1922-23
Bush, Raymond (Loyola, Chi.)—E—1926
Card, J. Harper—T—1922
Curzon, Harry (Michigan)—E—1926
Eiden, James (Knox)—T—1926
Ewald, George (Louisville)—B—1922-23
Ewald, Henry—B—1922-23
Fahay, John (Marquette)—E—1926
Ford, Salem (Louisville)—B—1922-23
Fortune, Burnell (DePauw)—G—1926
Gaiver, Einar (North Dakota)—E—1926
Gansberg, Alfred (Miami, Ohio)—T—1926
Gibson, Richard (Centre)—G—1922
Golsen, Eugene (Georgetown)—B—1926
Golsen, Thomas (Georgetown)—B—1926
Grabfelder, Earl (Kentucky)—B—1923
Green, J. B. H.—T—1926
Greenwood, Glenn (Iowa)—B—1926
Gregg, Edward (Kentucky)—E—1922
Grubert, Herbert—E—1922-23
Guigliano, Pasquale—B—1923
Hannigan, William—T—1926
Hanson, Steven—E—1926
Higgins, Austin—C—1922-23
Irwin, James—B—1922-23
Jackson, Lawrence (Loyola)—B—1926
Jansing, L.—E—1922
Karch, Robert (Ohio State)—T—1923
Kendricks, James (Texas A & M)—T—1923
Kirchner, Adolph—T—1926
Landrum, James—1922-23
Lead, Garfield (Syracuse)—T—1926

MacCollum (Centre)—E—1922
McCaw, William (Indiana)—E—1926
McDonald, John—T—1926
McGehean, Robert—B—1923
McGrath, Bryan (N. Y. U.)—G—1922
McLean, Stuart (Indiana)—T—1922-23
Meeks, Edward (Louisville)—B—1922
Meredith, Russell (West Virginia)—G
—1923
Metzger, Louis (Georgetown)—B—1926
Miller, Lloyd—B—1922-23
Moser, Theodore—G—1922-23
Netherton, William (Kentucky)—E—1922
Olmstead, Lawrence—G—1922-23
Otto, A.—C—1922-23
Padan, Robert (Ohio State)—B—1922
Palmer, Charles (Northwestern)—B—1926
Priest, James (Centre)—B—1923
Quast, John (Purdue)—E—1923
Reiser, Earl—E—1923
Robinson, Edward (North Carolina)—B
—1926
Rowan, James (Tennessee)—B—1923
Sachs, Leonard (Loyola, Chi.)—E—1926
Scanlon, John (DePaul)—B—1926
Sechrist, Walter (West Virginia)—G
—1926
Sherry, Gerald (Loyola)—B—1926
Slagle, George—T—1926
Stinchcomb, Gaylord (Illinois)—B—1926
Stuckey, William (Loyola)—B—1926
Vainowski, Peter—G—1926
Van Dyke, James—B—1922-23
Wandless, George B—1922-23
White, Robert—E—1923
Wiggs, Hubert (Vanderbilt)—B—1922-23

MARION (OHIO) (1922)
See Oorang Indians

MILWAUKEE BADGERS (1922—26)
Abell—B—1926
Alexander, John (Rutgers)—T—1922
Armstrong, John (Columbia)—B—1922
Ashmore, Roger (Gonzaga)—T—1926
Baralti—C—1922
Baril, Adrian (St. Thomas)—T—1925
Barr, Wallace (Wisconsin)—B—1925
Bennett—T—1922
Berger—1924
Bisbee, Bertin (Minnesota)—E—1922
Blacklock, Hugh (Michigan State)—T
—1923
Brown—B—1922
Brumm, Roman (Wisconsin)—G—1925
Bryant, John (Chicago)—B—1925-26
Burks, Joseph (Washington State)—C
—1926
Conzelman, James (Washington of Mo.)
—B—1922-24
Copley, Charles (Mo. Sch. Mines)—T—1922
Corcoran, Arthur (Georgetown)—E—1922
Coyne—1924
Cullen, Ronald (Oklahoma)—T—1922

Curtin, Donald (Marquette) —B—1926
Dilweg, Lavern (Marquette) —E—1926
Doane, Joseph (Tufts) —B—1922–24
Dooley, John (Syracuse) —G—1923
Douglas, George (Marquette) —T—1926
Dufft, James (Rutgers) —G—1922
Dunigan, Merton (Minnesota) —T
—1925–26
Dunn, Joseph (Marquette) —B—1924–25
Erickson, Harold (Washington & Jefferson)
—B—1923–24
Fallon, Michael (Syracuse) —G—1922
Fisher, Clark (Catholic Univ.) —B—1926
Foster, Frederick (Syracuse) —T—1924
Garrett, Alfred (Rutgers) —E—1922
Gay, Kenneth (Minnesota) —T—1926
Gillo, Henry (Colgate) —B—1925
Green (Holy Cross) —B—1922
Heimsch, John (Marquette) —B—1926
Hertz, Frank (Carroll) —E—1926
Hollquist—B—1926
Jean, Walter (Bethany) —G—1924
Keefe, Emmett (Notre Dame) —G—1922
King, Andrew (West Virginia) —B—1922
Kuick, Stanley (Beloit) —G—1926
Lane, Oscar (Marquette) —T—1926
Larson, Frederic (Notre Dame) —C
—1923–24
McGinnis, Lawrence (Marquette) —E
—1923–24
McMillen, James (Illinois) —B—1923
McMillin, Alvin "Bo" (Centre) —Q—
1922–23
McNally, John "Blood" (St. John) —B
1925–26
Mason, Samuel (Virginia Military Inst.)
—B—1925
Mattox, Marvin (Washington & Lee) —B
—1923
Meadows, Eric (Pittsburgh) —B—1923
Meese, Ward (Wabash) —E—1922
Miller, Henry (Penn. State) —E—1925
Milton, John (Southern California)
—E—1923
Mooney, George (Georgetown)—B—1922–24
Morrisey, Frank (Boston College) —T
—1924
Murphy, George (Dartmouth) —B—1926
Nadolney, Romanus (Notre Dame) —G
—1923–25
Neacy, Clement (Colgate) —E—1924–26
Orwell—B—1926
Pierotti, Albert (Washington & Lee) —C
—1922–24
Pollard, Fritz (Brown) —B—1922
Potteiger, Earl (Ursinus) —B—1922
Pugh—T—1922
Purdy, Clair (Brown) —B—1922
Rate, Edwin (Purdue) —B—1923
Reichle, Richard (Illinois) —E—1923
Robeson, Paul (Rutgers) —E—1922
Roessler, Fritz (Marquette) —E—1925
Rydzewski, Frank (Notre Dame) —T—1925
Sachs, Leonard (Loyola) —E—1923–24
Seasholtz, George (Lafayette) —B—1922

Slater, Fred (Iowa) —T—1922, 26
Smith, Earl (Ripon) —T—1923–24
Strickland, William (Lombard) —G—1923
Sullivan, Walter (Beloit) —B—1922
Swanson, Eyar (Lombard) —E—1924
Taugher, Claude (Marquette) —B—1924
Thomas, Carl (Pennsylvania) —T—1922
Tierney, Frederick (Minnesota) —G—1925
Tomlin, Thomas (Syracuse) —G—1922
Traynor, Bernard (Colgate) —C—1925
Traynor, Michael (Canisius) —B—1925
Turner, James (Northwestern) —B—1923
Underwood, John (Iowa State) —G—1923
Usher, Louis (Syracuse) —T—1923–24
Vassau, Roy (St. Thomas) —T—1923
Webb—T—1922
Weller, Truman (Nebraska) —T—1924
Wenke, Adolph (Nebraska) —T—1923
Wiederquist, Chester (Washington &
Jefferson) —T—1923–24
Winkleman, Benjamin (Arkansas) —E
—1922–24

MINNEAPOLIS MARINES
(1922–24, 1929–30)

Baril, Adrian (St. Thomas) —T—1923–24
Barragar, Nathan (Southern California)
—C—1930
Capps, Wilbur (Oklahoma State East) —T
—1930
Chicken, Frederick—B—1922–24
Christenson—E—1922–24
Cleve, Einar (St. Olaf) —B—1922–24
Corcoran, Gerald (Illinois) —C—1930
Coughlin, Frank (Notre Dame) —B—1923
Crabtree, Clyde (Florida) —B—1930
Dunigan, Merton (Minnesota) —T—1924
Dvorak, Benjamin (Minnesota) —B—1922
Eberts, Bernard (Carleton) —B—1924
Erickson, Harold (Washington & Jefferson)
—B—1929–30
Erickson, Weldon (South Dakota) —E
—1922
Fahay, John (Marquette) —E—1929
Flynn, Paul (Minnesota) —T—1922–23
Fosdick, Robert (Iowa) —G—1923
Franta, Herbert (St. Thomas) —T—1929–30
Gaustad, Arthur—G—1922–23
Gibson, George (Minnesota) —G—1930
Gillson, Robert (Colgate) —G—1930
Goodbread, Royce (Florida) —B—1930
Gunderson, Harry—C—1922–23
Hanson, Harold (Minnesota) —G—1930
Hanson, Roy (Marquette) —B—1923
Haycraft, Kenneth (Minnesota) —E
—1929–30
Hogue, Murrel (Centenary) —B—1930
Hooley, Robert (Detroit) —G—1924
Houle, Wilfred (St. Thomas) —B—1924
Hudson, Richard—B—1923
Irgens, Einar—B—1922–24
Irgens, Newman—B—1922
Joesting, Herbert ,(Minnesota) —B
—1929–30

Johns, James (Michigan) —G—1924
Jonasen, Charles—B—1923
Jones, Thomas (Bucknell) —G—1930
Kakela, Wayne (Minnesota) —C—1930
Kaplan, Sidney (Hamline) —B—1923
Kostos, Anthony (Bucknell) —E—1930
Kraft, Reynolds (Illinois) —E—1922
Kramer, George—G—1922–24
Lovin—G—1929
Lundell, Robert (Gustavus Adolphus) —E
  —1929–30
Madigan, Frank (St. Mary's, Minn.) —C
  —1922, 24
Maeder, Albert (Minnesota) —T—1929
Mahoney, Roger (Penn. State) —C—1930
Marshall, Robert (Minnesota) —E—1922–23
Mason, Samuel (Virginia Military Inst.) —
  B—1922
Maynaugh, Roland (St. Thomas) —G—1924
Mehelich, Thomas (St. Mary's, Minn.) —G
  —1929
Mehre, Henry (Notre Dame) —C—1923–24
Miller, Alfred (Harvard) —B—1930
Mohs, Louis (St. Thomas) —E—1923–24
Nemzek, Albert (North Dakota State) —G
  —1930
Ness, Val—G—1922
Norton, Martin (Carleton) —B—1922–24
Novack, Edward—B—1924
Nydall, Malcoln (Minnesota) —B—1929–30
Oas, Arnold (St. Mary's, Minn.) —C—1929
Pahl, Louis (St. Thomas) —B—1923–24
Pape, Orrin (Iowa) —B—1930
Pederson, James (Augsberg) —E—1930
Pharmer, Arthur (Minnesota) —B—1930
Putzier, Frederick (St. Olaf) —B—1924
Regnier, Peter (Minneapolis) —B—1922
Rodriguez, Jess (Salem) —B—1930
  —B—1930
Rush, James (Minnesota) —B—1922
Scott, Eugene (Hamline) —G—1924
Seborg, Henry (Kalamazoo) —B—1929–30
Simon (Hamline) —E—1924
Simpson, Eber (Wisconsin) —B—1923–24
Stepanovich, Anthony (Southern
  California) —G—1930
Tanner, Robert (Minnesota) —E—1930
Tersch, Rudolph—T—1922–24
Tierney, Fred (Minnesota) —G—1923–24
Townsend, Otto—G—1922
Ursella, Reuben (Minnesota) —B—1929
Ward, John (Southern California) —T
  —1930
Watkins, Gordon (Georgia Tech.) —T
  —1930
Weiderquist, Chester (Washington-
  Jefferson) —T—1929
Willegalle, Henry (Carleton) —B—1929
Williams, Richard (Wisconsin) —B—1923
Wilson, Leland (Cornell) —B—1929–30
Young, Samuel (Detroit) —E—1929–30

MINNESOTA VIKINGS
(Three players contributed by twelve

teams, all except Dallas, and trades from
other teams to create basic Viking squad
before 1961 season.)

Alderman, Grady (Detroit) —G
Barnett, Thomas (Purdue) —B
Beams, Byron (Notre Dame) —T
Beck, Kenneth (Texas A & M) —T
Bishop, William (North Texas State) —T
Bell, Donald (Nebraska) —T
Culpepper, Edward (Alabama) —G
Ellersick, Donald (Washington State) —B
Haley, George Richard (Pittsburgh) —B
Huth, Gerald (Wake Forest) —G
Johnson, Eugene (Cincinnati) —B
Joyce, Donald (Tulane) —E
Kimber, William (Florida State) —E
Lapham, William (Iowa) —C
McElhenny, Hugh (Washington) —B
Middleton, David (Auburn) —E
Morris, John (Oregon) —B
Mostardo, Richard (Kent State) —B
Murphy, Frederick (Georgia Tech.) —E
Osborne, Clarence (Arizona State) —B
Pesonen, Richard (Minnesota) —B
Rabold, Michael (Indiana) —G
Richards, Perry (Detroit) —E
Roehnelt, William (Bradley) —G
Rubke, Karl (Southern California) —C
Selawski, Eugene (Purdue) —T
*Shaw, George (Oregon) —Q
Shaw, Glenn (Kentucky) —B
Shields, LeBron (Tennessee) —T
Smith, Roger "Zeke" (Auburn) —G
Stalcup, Jerry (Wisconsin) —G
Stephens, Louis (San Francisco) —G
Sumner, Charles (William & Mary) —B
Whitsell, David (Indiana) —B
Winslow, Paul (North Carolina Coll.) —B
Youso, Frank (Minnesota) —T

*By trade

NEW YORK BULLDOGS (1949)
Abbey, Joseph (Texas State North) —E
  —1949
Barzilauskas, Francis (Yale) —G—1949
Batinski, Stanley (Temple) —G—1949
Blake, Thomas (Cincinnati) —T—1949
Boyda, Michael (Washington & Lee) —B
  —1949
Campbell, William (Oklahoma) —B—1949
Canady, James (Texas) —B—1949
Chipley, William (Washington & Lee) —E
  —1949
DeMoss, Robert (Purdue) —Q—1949
Ellis, Herbert (Texas A & M) —C—1949
Domnanovich, Joseph (Alabama) —C—1949
Gaul, Frank (Notre Dame) —T—1949
Golding, Joseph (Oklahoma) —B—1949
Harding, Roger (California) —C—1949
Hazelhurst, Robert (Denver) —G—1949
Heywood, Ralph (Southern California) —E
  —1949
Jarmoluk, Michael (Temple) —T—1949

SAM BAUGH TRADES A RIPPED JERSEY FOR SOME YARDAGE AGAINST THE NEW YORK GIANTS
IN 1945.

Layne, Robert (Texas) —Q—1949
Muehlheuser, Frank (Colgate) —B—1949
Nelson, Frank (Utah) —B—1949
Nolan, John (Penn. State) —T—1949
Olsonoski, Lawrence (Minnesota) —G
  —1949
Osmanski, Joseph (Holy Cross) —B—1949
Pregulman, Mervin (Michigan) —G—1949
Prescott, Harold (Hardin-Simmons) —E
  —1949
Pritko, Steven (Villanova) —E—1949
Rauch, John (Georgia) —Q—1949
Roman, George (Western Reserve) —T
  —1949
Sabasteanski, Joseph (Fordham) —C—1949
Scollard, Nicholas (St. Joseph's) —E—1949
Sensenbaugher, Dean (Ohio State) —B
  —1949
Shoults, Paul (Miami, Ohio) —B—1949
Slosburg, Philip (Temple) —B—1949
Smith, Oscar (Texas Mines) —B—1949
Sponaugle, Robert (Pennsylvania) —E
  —1949
Sullivan, George (Notre Dame) —E—1949
Tamburo, Samuel (Penn. State) —E—1949
Tyree, James (Oklahoma) —E—1949
Vogelaar, Carroll (San Francisco) —T—1949
Wade, James (Oklahoma City Univ.) —B
  —1949
Watt, Joseph (Syracuse) —B—1949
Weaver, John (Miami, Ohio) —G—1949

NEW YORK GIANTS (1925—60)

Adams, O'Neal (Arkansas) —E—1941–45
Adams, Verlin (Morris-Harvey) —T
  —1942–45
Agajanian, Ben (New Mexico) —K
  —1949, 54–57

Albright, William (Wisconsin) —G
  —1951–54
Alexander, John (Rutgers) —T—1926
Alexander, Joseph (Syracuse) —G—1925–27
Allison, James (Texas A & M) —E—1928
Amberg, John (Kansas) —B—1951–52
Anderson, Clifton (Indiana) —E—1953
Anderson, Winston (Colgate) —E—1936
Artman, Corwan (Stanford) —T—1931
Ashburn, Clifford (Nebraska) —G—1929
Atwood, John (Wisconsin) —B—1948
Austin, William (Oregon State) —T
  —1949–50, 53–57
Avedisian, Charles (Providence) —G
  —1942–44
Averno, Sisto (Muhlenberg) —G—1951
Avinger, Clarence (Alabama) —B—1953
Badgro, Morris (Southern California) —E
  —1927–35
Baker, Jon (California) —G—1949–52
Barber, Ernest (San Francisco) —C—1945
Barbour, Wesley (Wake Forest) —Q—1945
Barker, Hubert (Arkansas) —B—1942–45
Barnard, Charles (Oklahoma State,
  Edmond) —E—1938
Barnum, Leonard (West Virginia
  Wesleyan) —Q—1938–40
Barrett, Emmett (Portland) —C—1942–44
Barry, Albert (Southern California) —G
  —1958–59
Barzilauskas, Fritz (Yale) —G—1951
Bauer, John (Illinois) —G—1954
Beck, Ray (Georgia Tech) —G—1952, 55–57
Bednar, Albert (Lafayette) —G—1925–26
Beebe, Keith (Occidental) —B—1944
Beil, Lawrence (Portland) —T—1948
Bell, Kay (Washington State) —T—1942
Bellinger, Robert (Gonzaga) —T—1934–35
Benkert, Henry (Rutgers) —B—1925

Benners, Frederick (Southern Methodist Univ.) —Q—1952

Berry, Wayne (Washington State) —B —1954

Biggs, Riley (Baylor) —C—1926–27

Biscaha, Joseph (Richmond) —E—1959

Blazine, Anthony (Illinois Wesleyan) —T —1940–41

Bloodgood, Elbert (Nebraska) —B—1928

Blozis, Albert (Georgetown) —T—1942–44

Blumenstock, James (Fordham) —B—1947

Boggan, Rex (Mississippi) —T—1955

Boll, Donald (Nebraska) —T—1960

Bookman, John (Miami) —B—1957

Bomar, Lynn (Vanderbilt) —E—1925–26

Borden, Lester (Fordham) —E—1935

Bowdoin, James (Alabama) —G—1932

Boyle, William—T—1934

Brackett, Martin (Auburn) —G—1958

Brahm, Lawrence (Temple) —G—1943

Brennan, Matthew (Lafayette) —B—1925

Broadstone, Marion (Nebraska) —T—1931

Broussard, Fred (Louisiana Northwest) —C —1955

Brovarney, Casimir (Detroit) —T—1941

Brown, David (Alabama) —B—1943, 46–47

Brown, Roosevelt (Morgan State) —T —1953–60

Browning, Gregory (Denver) —E—1947

Bucklin, Thomas (Idaho) —B—1931

Buffington, Harry (Oklahoma A & M) —G —1942

Burkhardt, Arthur (Rutgers) —G—1928

Burnett, Dale (Kansas Teachers) —B —1930–39

Burnine, Harold (Missouri) —E—1956

Butkus, Carl (George Washington) —T —1949

Byler, Joseph (Nebraska) —T—1946

Cagle, Christian (West Point) —B—1930–32

Caldwell, Bruce (Yale) —B—1928

Calligaro, Leonard (Wisconsin) —B —1944–45

Campbell, Glenn (Kansas Teachers) —E —1929–33

Cannady, John (Indiana) —B—1947–54

Cannela, John (Fordham) —T—1933–34

Cantor, Leo (U.C.L.A.) —B—1942

Capps, Wilbur (Oklahoma State Central) —1929

Caranci, Roland (Colorado) —T—1944

Carney, Arthur (Annapolis) —G—1925–26

Carroccio, Russell (Virginia) —G—1954–55

Carroll, Victor (Nevada) —T—1943–47

Caywood, Lester (St. John's) —G—1929–32

Chandler, Donald (Florida) —B—1956–60

Cheverko, George (Fordham) —B—1947–48

Chickerneo, John (Pittsburgh) —B—1942

Clancy, Stuart (Holy Cross) —B—1933–35

Clatterbuck, Robert (Houston) —Q

Wide World Photo

NEW YORK GIANTS PULL A DOUBLE HANDOFF AND LATERAL AGAINST CLEVELAND BROWNS FOR ONLY TOUCHDOWN OF THE EASTERN DIVISION PLAYOFF GAME AT THE YANKEE STADIUM ON DECEMBER 21, 1958. AS PLAY STARTS ON BROWNS 19-YARD LINE, QUARTER-BACK CHARLES CONERLY (42) HANDS OFF BALL TO ALEX WEBSTER (29), WHO HANDS OFF BALL TO FRANK GIFFORD (16). WITH BLOCK BY AL BARRY (68), GIFFORD BREAKS AWAY TO THE 12-YARD LINE WHERE HE LATERALS BALL TO CONERLY. CONERLY IS CHASED BY BROWNS' BOB GAIN (79), HIT BY BROWNS' JUNIOR WREN (42), BUT FALLS ACROSS THE GOAL LINE. GIANTS WON 10–0.

—1954–57

Clay, Randall (Texas) —B—1950, 53
Clay, Roy (Colorado) —B—1944
Coates, Ray (Louisiana State Univ.) —B 1948–49
Cole, Peter (Trinity, Tex.) —G—1937–40
Colhouer, Jacob (Oklahoma) —G—1949
Collins, Ray (Louisiana State Univ.) —T —1954
Comstock, Rudolph (Georgetown) —G —1930
Conerly, Charles (Mississippi)—Q—1948–60
Cope, Frank (Santa Clara) —T—1938–47
Cordileone, Louis (Clemson) —G—1960
Corgan, Charles (Arkansas) —E—1927
Corzine, Lester (Davis-Elkins) —B—1934–37
Coulter, DeWitt (West Point) —T —1946–52
Crawford, Edward (Mississippi) —B—1957
Crawford, William (British Columbia) —G —1960
Crow, Lindon (Southern California) —B —1958–60
Cuff, Ward (Marquette) —B—1937–45
Culwell, Val (Oregon) —G—1942
Damiani, Francis (Manhattan) —T—1944
Danowski, Edward (Fordham) —Q —1934–41
Davis, Gaines (Texas Tech) —G—1936
DeFilippo, Louis (Fordham) —C —1941, 45–48
Dell Isola, John (Fordham) —C—1934–40
Dennerlien, Gerald (St. Mary's, Cal.) —T 1937–40
Dennery, Vincent (Fordham) —E—1941
Derogatis, Albert (Duke) —T—1949–52
Dess, Darrell (North Carolina State) —G— 1959–60
Dobelstein, Robert (Tennessee) —G —1946–48
Doggett, Keith (Wichita) —T—1942
Doolan, John (Georgetown) —B—1945–46
Douglas, Everett (Florida) —T—1953
Dublinski, Thomas (Utah) —Q—1958
Dubofsky, Maurice (Georgetown) —G —1932
Dubzinski, Walter (Boston College) —G —1943
Duden, Richard (Annapolis) —E—1949
Dugan, Leonard (Wichita) —C—1936
Duggan, Gilford (Oklahoma) —T—1940
Duncan, James (Wake Forest) —E— —1950–53
Dunlap, Robert (Oklahoma) —B—1936
Eakin, Kay (Arkansas) —B—1940–41
Eaton, Louis (California) —T—1945
Eckhardt, Oscar (Texas) —B—1928
Edwards, William (Baylor) —G —1941–42, 46
Epps, Robert (Pittsburgh) —B—1954–55, 57
Erickson, William (Mississippi) —G—1948
Eshmont, Leonard (Fordham) —B—1940–41
Ettinger, Donald (Kansas) —G—1948–50
Faircloth, Arthur (North Carolina) —B —1947–48
Falaschi, Nello (Santa Clara) —B—1938–41

Feather, Elwin (Kansas State) —B —1929–30, 32–33
Fennema, Carl (Washington) —C—1948–49
Filchock, Frank (Indiana) —Q—1946
Filipowicz, Steven (Fordham) —B—1945–46
Filipski, Eugene (Villanova) —B—1956–57
Fischer, Cletus (Nebraska) —B—1949
Flaherty, Ray (Gonzaga) —E—1928–35
Flenniken, Max (Geneva) —B—1930–31
Fox, Samuel (Ohio State) —E—1945–46
Franck, George (Minnesota) —B —1941, 45–48
Frankian, Malcolm (St. Mary's, Cal.) —E 1934–35
Friedman, Benjamin (Michigan) —Q —1929–31
Frugonne, James (Syracuse) —B—1925
Galazin, Stanley (Villanova) —C—1937–39
Galiffa, Arnold (West Point) —Q—1953
Gallagher, Edward (Washington & Jefferson) —T—1928
Garner, Robert—G—1945
Garvey, Arthur "Hec" (Notre Dame) —G —1927–28
Garzoni, Michael (Southern California) —G—1948
Gehrke, Bruce (Columbia) —E—1948
Gelatka, Charles (Mississippi State) —E —1937–40
Gibson, Denver (Grove City) —G—1930–34
Gifford, Francis (Southern California) —B —1952–60
Gildea, John (St. Bonaventure) —B—1938
Gladchuk, Chester (Boston College) —C —1941, 46–47
Goodwin, Tod (West Virginia) —E —1935–36
Gorgone, Peter (Muhlenberg) —B—1946
Governali, Paul (Columbia) —Q—1947–48
Grandelius, Everett (Michigan State) —B —1953
Grant, Leonard (New York Univ.) —T —1930–37
Grate, Carl (Georgia) —C—1945
Greenhalgh, Robert (San Francisco) —B —1949
Grier, Roosevelt (Penn. State) —T —1955–56, 58–60
Griffith, Forrest (Kansas) —B—1950–51
Grigg, Cecil (Austin) —B—1926
Grosscup, Clyde Lee (Utah) —Q—1960
Gutowsky, Leroy (Oklahoma City Univ.) —B—1931
Guy, Melwood (Duke) —T—1958–59
Guyon, Joseph (Carlisle) —B—1927
Hachten, William (Stanford) —G—1947
Haden, John (Arkansas) —T—1936–38
Hagerty, John (Georgetown) —B—1926–30
Haines, Henry (Penn State) —B—1925–29
Hall, Harold—C—1942
Hall, John (Iowa) —E—1955
Hanken, Raymond (George Washington) —E—1937–38
Hannah, Herbert (Alabama) —T—1951
Hapes, Merle (Mississippi) —B—1942, 46

Hare, Cecil (Gonzaga) —B—1946
Harms, Arthur (Vermont) —T—1926-27
Harris, Oliver (Geneva) —E—1926
Harrison, Edward (Boston College) —E
    —1928
Harrison, Granville (Mississippi State) —E
    —1941
Harrison, Maxwell (Auburn) —E—1940
Hartzog, Howard (Baylor) —T—1928
Hauser, Arthur (Xavier, Ohio) —T—1959
Heap, Joseph (Notre Dame) —B—1955
Hein, Melvin (Washington State) —C
    —1931-45
Heinrich, Donald (Washington) —Q
    —1954-59
Hendrian, Warren (Pittsburgh) —B—1925
Henry, Wilbur (Washington & Jefferson)
    —T—1927
Hensley, Richard (Kentucky) —E—1949
Herber, Arnold (Regis) —Q—1944-45
Hermann, John (U.C.L.A.) —B—1956
Hiemstra, Edward (Sterling) —C—1942
Hill, Charles (Baker) —B—1926
Hilpert, Harold (Oklahoma City Univ.)
    —B—1930
Hodel, Merwin (Colorado) —B—1953
Hogan, Paul (Detroit) —B—1926
Horne, Richard (Oregon) —G—1941
Hovious, John (Mississippi) —B—1945
Howard, Albert (Princeton) —G—1927
Howard, Robert (Marietta) —G—1929-30
Howell, James Lee (Arkansas) —E
    —1937-42, 46-48
Hubbard, Robert "Cal" (Geneva) —T
    —1927-29, 36
Hudson, Robert (Clemson) —E—1951-52
Huff, Robert Lee (West Virginia) —G
    —1956-60
Hughes, Edward (Tulsa) —B—1956-58
Hutchinson, Ralph (Chattanooga) —T
    —1949
Hutchinson, William (Dartmouth) —B
    —1942
Huth, Gerald (Wake Forest) —G—1956
Imlay, Talma (California) —B—1927
Irvin, Cecil (Davis-Elkins) —T—1932-35
Iverson, Christopher (Oregon) —B—1947
Jackson, Robert (North Carolina A & T)
    —B—1950-51
Jacobs, Proverb (California) —T—1960
Jappe, Paul (Syracuse) —E—1925, 27-28
Jelacic, Jon (Minnesota) —E—1958
Johnson, Herbert—B—1954
Johnson, Joseph (Mississippi) —B—1948
Johnson, Lawrence (Haskell) —C—1936-39
Jones, Thomas (Bucknell) —G—1932-36
Kaplan, Bernard (Western Maryland) —G
    —1935-36
Kane, Herbert (Oklahoma Teachers) —T
    —1944-45
Karcis, John (Carnegie Tech) —B
    —1938-39, 43
Karilivacz, Carl (Syracuse) —B—1958
Katcavage, James (Dayton) —E—1956-60
Keahey, Eulis (George Washington) —G
    —1942

Kearns, Thomas (Miami) —T—1945
Kelly, Ellison (Michigan State) —G—1959
Kelly, John Simms (Kentucky) —B—1932
Kemp, John (Occidental) —B—1958
Kendricks, James (Texas A & M) —T—1927
Kennard, George (Kansas) —G—1952-55
Kenyon, William (Georgetown) —B—1925
Kerrigan, Thomas (Columbia) —G—1930
Kershaw, George (Colgate) —E—1949
Ketzko, Alex (Michigan State) —T—1942
Keuper, Kenneth (Georgia) —B—1948
Killinger, Glenn (Penn. State) —B—1926
Kimber, William (Florida State) —E—
    1959-60
King, Philip (Vanderbilt) —B—1958-60
Kinscherf, Carl (Colgate) —B—1943-44
Kitzmiller, John (Oregon) —B—1931
Klasoskus, Albin (Holy Cross) —T
    —1941-42
Kline, Harry (Kansas Teachers) —E
    1939-41
Klotovich, Michael (St. Mary's, Cal.) —B
    —1945
Knight, Patrick (Southern Methodist
    Univ.) —B—1952, 54-55
Kobrosky, Milton (Trinity, Conn.) —B
    —1937
Kolman, Edward (Temple) —T—1949
Koppisch, Walter (Columbia) —B—1925-26
Krause, Max (Gonzaga) —B—1933-36
Krouse, Raymond (Maryland) —T
    —1951-55
Lagod, Chester (Chattanooga) —G—1953
Landrey, Thomas (Texas) —B—1950-55
Lansdell, Granville (Southern California)
    —B—1940
Lascari, John (Georgetown) —E—1942
Lechner, Edgar (Minnesota) —T—1942
Leemans, Alphonse (George Washington)
    —B—1936-43
Leo, James (Cincinnati) —B—1960
Levy, Harvey (Syracuse) —G—1928
Lewis, Arthur (Ohio) —T—1936
Liebel, Frank (Norwich) —E—1942-47
Lieberum, Donald (Manchester) —B—1942
Lindahl, Virgil (Nebraska State) —G—1945
Little, James (Kentucky) —T—1945
Livingston, Clifford (U.C.L.A.) —B
    —1954-60
Livingston, Howard—B—1944-47
Long, Buford (Florida) —B—1953-55
Lott, William (Mississippi) —B—1958
Lovuolo, Frank (St. Bonaventure) —E
    —1949
Lummus, John (Baylor) —E—1941
Lunday, Kenneth (Arkansas) —C
    —1937-41, 46-47
Lynch, Richard (Notre Dame)—B—1959-60
Lyons, George (Kansas State) —T—1929
MacAfee, Kenneth (Alabama) —E—1954-58
McBride, John (Syracuse) —B
    —1925-28, 32-34
McCafferty, Donald (Ohio State) —E—1946
McChesney, Robert (Hardin-Simmons) —E
    —1950-52
McClain, Clinton (Southern Methodist

Univ.) —B—1941

McGee, Edward (Temple) —T—1940

McGinley, Edward (Pennsylvania) —T
—1925

McLaughry, John (Brown) —B—1940

McMullen, Daniel (Nebraska) —G—1929

Mackorell, John (Davidson) —B—1935

Mackrides, William (Nevada) —Q—1953

Maikkula, Kenneth (Connecticut) —E
—1942

Mallouf, Raymond (Southern Methodist
Univ.) —Q—1949

Mangum, Peter (Mississippi) —B—1954

Manton, Taldon (Texas Christian Univ.)
—B—1936–38

Marefos, Andrew (St. Mary's, Cal.) —B
—1941–42

Marker, Clifford (Washington State) —B
1927

Marone, John (Manhattan) —G—1943

Maronic, Dusan—G—1951

Marsh, Richard (Oklahoma) —G—1933

Martin, Frank (Alabama) —B—1945

Martinkovich, John (Xavier) —E—1957

Mastrangelo, John (Notre Dame) —G—1950

Maynard, Donald (Texas Western) —B
—1958

Mazurek, Edward (Xavier, O.) —T—1960

Mead, John (Wisconsin) —E—1946–47

Mellus, John (Villanova) —T—1938–41

Menasco, Donald (Texas) —B—1952–53

Mercer, James (Oregon State) —Q—1942–43

Mertes, Bernard (Iowa) —B—1949

Mielziner, Saul (Carnegie Tech) —C
—1929–30

Miklich, William (Idaho) —B—1947–48

Miles, Leo (Virginia State) —B—1953

Miller, Edward (New Mexico State) —B
—1939–40

Milner, William (Duke) —G—1950

Milstead, Century (Yale) —T—1925, 27–28

Minisi, Anthony (Pennsylvania) —B—1948

Mischak, Robert (West Point) —G—1958

Mitchell, Granville (Davis-Elkins) —E—1935

Mitchell, Harold (U.C.L.A.) —T—1952

Modzelewski, Richard (Maryland) —T
—1956–60

Molenda, John (Michigan) —B—1932–35

Moore, Henry (Arkansas) —B—1956

Moore, Kenneth (West Virginia Wesleyan)
—C—1940

Moran, Dale (Carnegie Tech) —B—1928–34

Moran, Thomas (Centre) —B—1925

Morgan, William (Oregon) —T—1933–36

Morrison, Joseph (Cincinnati)—B—1959–60

Morrow, Robert (Illinois Wesleyan) —B
—1945

Mote, Kelly (Duke) —E—1950–52

Mulleneaux, Lee (Arizona) —B—1932

Mullins, Noah (Kentucky) —B—1949

Munday, George (Kansas Teachers) —T
—1931–32

Munn, Lyle (Kansas State) —E—1929

Murray, Earl (Purdue) —G—1951

Murtagh, George (Georgetown) —C
—1926–32

Myers, Thomas (Fordham) —B—1925–26

Nash, Robert (Rutgers) —T—1925

Neill, James (Texas Tech) —B—1937

Nesser, Albert—E—1926–28

Newman, Harry (Michigan) —Q—1933–35

Nielsen, Walter (Arizona) —B—1940

Niles, Gerald (Iowa) —B—1946–47

Nix, Emery (Texas Christian Univ.) —Q
—1943, 46

Nolan, Richard (Maryland) —B—
1954–57, 59–60

Norby, John (Idaho) —B—1934

Nordstrom, Harry (Trinity, Conn.) —G
—1925

Nutt, Richard (Texas State North) —B
—1949

Oldershaw, Douglas (Santa Barbara) —G
—1939–41

Ostendarp, James (Bucknell) —B—1950–51

Owen, Alton (Mercer) —B—1939–41

Owen, Steven (Phillips) —T—1926–36

Owen, Vilas (Wisconsin Teachers) —Q
—1942

Owen, William (Oklahoma A & M) —T
—1929–37

Palazzi, Louis (Penn. State) —C—1946–47

Palm, Michael (Penn. State) —B—1925–26

Parnell, Fred (Colgate) —T—1925–27

Parry, Owen (Baylor) —T—1937–39

Paschal, William (Georgia Tech) —B
—1943–47

Paschka, Gordon (Minnesota) —G—1947

Patton, James (Mississippi) —B—1955–60

Patton, Robert (Clemson) —T—1952

Pederson, Winfield (Minnesota) —T
1941, 45

Pelfrey, Ray (Kentucky State East) —B
—1953

Perdue, Willard (Duke) —E—1940

Petrilas, William—E—1944–45

Peviani, Robert (Southern California) —G
—1953

Phillips, Ewell (Oklahoma Baptist) —G
—1936–37

Piccolo, William (Canisius) —C—1943–45

Pipkin, Joyce (Arkansas) —E—1948

Plansky, Anthony (Georgetown) —B
1928–29

Poole, G. Barney (Mississippi) —E—1954–55

Poole, James (Mississippi) —E—1937–41, 46

Poole, Ray (Mississippi) —E—1947–52

Potteiger, Earl (Ursinus) —B—1925–28

Powell, Richard (Davis-Elkins) —E—1931

Price, Edward (Tulane) —B—1950–55

Principe, Dominic (Fordham) —B—1940–42

Pritchard, Abisha (Virginia Military Inst.)
—B—1951

Pritko, Steven (Villanova) —E—1943

Pugh, Marion (Texas A & M) —Q—1941, 45

Quatse, Jess (Pittsburgh) —T—1935

Ragazzo, Philip (Western Reserve) —T
—1945–47

Ramona, Joseph (Santa Clara) —G—1953

Rapacz, John (Oklahoma) —C—1950–54

Reagan, Frank (Pennsylvania) —B
1941, 46–48

Reed, Max (Bucknell) —C—1928

Reese, Henry (Temple) —C—1933–34

Reynolds, Owen (Georgia) —E—1925
Rhenquist, Milton (Bethany) —C—1931
Rice, William (Norwich) —B—1929
Rich, Herbert (Vanderbilt) —B—1954–56
Richards, Elvin (Simpson) —B—1933–39
Riley, Leon (Detroit) —B—1960
Roberts, Eugene (Chattanooga) —B —1947–50
Roberts, Thomas (DePaul) —T—1943
Robustelli, Andrew (Arnold) —E—1956–60
Roman, George (Western Reserve) —T —1950
Rooney, Cobb (Colorado) —B—1925
Rosatti, Roman (Michigan) —T—1928
Rose, Roy Eugene (Tennessee) —E—1936
Rote, Kyle (Southern Methodist Univ.) —E —1951–60
Rovinski, Anthony (Holy Cross) —B—1933
Rowe, Harmon (San Francisco) —B —1950–52
Royston, Edward (Wake Forest) —G —1948–49
Russell, Lafayette (Northwestern)—B—1933
Salscheider, John (St. Thomas) —B—1949
Sanchez, John (San Francisco) —T—1949–50
Sarausky, Anthony (Fordham) —B—1935–37
Sark, Harvey (Phillips) —G—1931
Satenstein, Bernard (New York Univ.) —G —1933
Schmeelk, Gary (Manhattan) —T—1942
Schmidt, Robert (Minnesota) —T—1959–60
Schnelker, Robert (Bowling Green) —E —1954–60
Schnellbacher, Otto (Kansas) —B—1950–51
Schuette, Paul (Wisconsin) —G—1928
Schuler, William (Yale) —T—1947–48
Schwab, Raymond (Oklahoma City Univ.) —B—1931
Scott, George (Miami, Ohio) —B—1959
Scott, Joseph (San Francisco) —B—1948–53
Scott, Thomas (Virginia) —E—1959–60
Sedbrook, Leonard (Oklahoma City Univ.) —B—1929–31
Seick, Earl (Manhattan) —G—1942–43
Shaffer, Leland (Kansas State) —Q —1935–43, 45
Shaw, George (Oregon) —Q—1959–60
Shedlosky, Edmond (Tulsa) —B—1945
Sherrod, Horace (Tennessee) —E—1952
Shipp, William (Alabama) —T—1954
Siegle, Jules (Northwestern) —B—1948
Simms, Robert (Rutgers) —E—1960
Singer, Milton (Syracuse) —C—1935
Singer, Walter (Syracuse) —E—1935–37
Sivell, Ralph (Auburn) —G—1944–45
Skladany, Leo (Pittsburgh) —E—1950
Smith, Richard (Notre Dame) —G—1930–31
Smith, Willis (Idaho) —B—1934–35
Snyder, Gerald (Maryland) —B—1929
Soar, Henry (Providence) —B—1937–44, 46
Sohn, Ben (Southern California) —G—1941
Spinks, Jack (Alcorn A & M) —G—1956–57
Springer, Harold (Oklahoma State Central) —E—1945
Stafford, Harrison (Texas) —B—1934

Stahlman, Richard (DePaul) —E—1927, 30
Stein, Samuel—E—1931
Stenn, Paul (Villanova) —T—1942
Stevens, Theodore (Brown) —C—1926
Stits, William (UCLA) —B—1959–60
Stribling, Majure (Mississippi) —E—1951–53
Strong, Kenneth (New York Univ.) —B —1933-35, 43–47
Stroud, Jack (Tennessee) —G—1953–60
Sulaitis, Joseph—B—1943–53
Summerall, George (Arkansas) —E— 1958–60
Sutherin, Donald (Ohio State) —B—1959
Sutton, Edward (North Carolina) —B—1960
Svare, Harland (Washington State) —B 1955–60
Svoboda, William (Tulane) —B—1954–58
Swiacki, William (Columbia) —E—1948–50
Tarrant, Robert (Kansas State Teachers) —E—1936
Thomas, George (Oklahoma) —B—1952
Thorpe, James (Carlisle) —B—1925
Tidwell, Travis (Auburn) —Q—1950–51
Tobin, George (Notre Dame) —G—1947
Tomaini, Army (Catawba) —T—1945
Tomlin, Thomas (Syracuse) —G—1925–26
Topp, Robert (Michigan) —E—1954, 56
Treadaway, John (Hardin-Simmons) —T —1947–48
Triplett, Melvin (Toledo) —B—1955–60
Trocolor, Robert (Alabama) —B—1942–44
Tunnell, Emlen (Iowa) —B—1948–58
Turbert, Francis (Morris Harvey) —B—1943
Tuttle, Orville (Oklahoma City Univ.) —G —1937–41, 46
Tyler, Peter (Hardin-Simmons) —B—1938
Umont, Frank—T—1943–45
Visnic, Lawrence (St. Benedict, Kan.) —G —1943–45
Vokaty, Otto (Heidelberg) —B—1932
Vosberg, Donald (Marquette) —E—1941
Voss, Walter (Detroit) —E—1926
Walbridge, Lyman (Fordham) —G—1925
Walker, Paul (Yale) —E—1948
Walls, William (Texas Christian Univ.) —E —1937–43
Weaver, Larrye (Fullerton) —B—1955
Webber, Howard (Kansas State) —E—1926
Webster, Alex (North Carolina State) —B —1955–60
Weinmeister, Arnold (Washington) —T —1950–53
Weiss, John—E—1944–47
Wesley, Lecil (Alabama) —C—1928
West, Stanley (Oklahoma) —G—1955
Westoupal, Joseph (Nebraska)—C—1929–30
White, Arthur (Alabama) —G—1937–39, 45
White, James (Notre Dame) —T—1945–50
White, Philip (Oklahoma) —B—1925–27
White, Philip (Oklahoma) —E—1925–27
Wiberg, Oscar (Nebraska Wesleyan) —B —1930
Widseth, Edward (Minnesota) —T—1937–40
Wietecha, Ray (Northwestern)—C—1953–60
Wilkins, Richard (Oregon) —E—1954

EMLEN TUNNELL, THE NEW YORK GIANTS' GREAT SAFETY MAN FOR MANY YEARS, LEAVES
THREE PITTSBURGH STEELERS BEHIND IN A 1956 GAME. FRED GLATZ HAS JUST MISSED
HIM WHILE MC FADDEN (61) AND MATUSZAK (64) WONDER HOW HE GOT AWAY.

Wilkinson, Robert (U.C.L.A.) —E—1951–52
Williams, Ellery (Santa Clara) —E—1950
Williams, Frank (Utah State) —B—1948
Williams, Joseph (Lafayette) —G—1925–26
Williamson, Ernest (North Carolina) —T
  —1948
Wilson, Fay (Texas A & M) —B—1927–32
Wolfe, Hugh (Texas) —B—1938
Woodward, Richard (Iowa) —C
  —1950–51, 53
Workman, Blake (Tulsa) —B—1932
Wycoff, Douglas (Georgia Tech) —B
  —1927, 31
Wynne, Harry (Arkansas) —E—1945
Yeager, Howard (Santa Barbara) —B
  —1940–41
Yelvington, Richard (Georgia) —T
  —1952–57
Younce, Leonard (Oregon State) —G
  —1941–48
Youso, Frank (Minnesota) —T—1958–60
Yowarsky, Walter (Kentucky) —E—1955–57
Zapustas, Joseph (Fordham) —E—1933
Zyntell, James (Holy Cross) —G—1933

NEW YORK YANKEES (1927–28)

Badgro, Morris (Southern California) —E
  —1927–28
Baker, Roy (Southern California) —B—1927
Bayley, John (Syracuse) —T—1927
Beattie, Robert (Princeton) —T—1927
Crawford, Walter (Illinois) —T—1927
Colahan, John—G—1928
Cyre, Hector (Gonzaga) —T—1928
Earpe, Francis (Monmouth) —G—1927
Flaherty, Ray (Gonzaga) —E—1927–28

Fraser, George (Rutgers) —B—1927
Fry, Wesley (Iowa) —B—1927
Gallagher, Edward (Washington &
  Jefferson) —T—1928
Grange, Harold (Illinois) —B—1927
Grube, Frank (Lafayette) —E—1928
Hall, Raymond (Illinois) —T—1927
Harvey, Norman (Detroit) T—1927
Hogue, Murrel (Centenary) —B—1928
Kelly, William (Montana) —B—1927–28
Kramer, Fred (Washington State) —G
  —1927–28
Kolls, Louis (St. Ambrose) —C—1927
Lawson, James (Stanford) —E—1927
Levy, Harvey (Syracuse) —G—1928
Lewellen, Vern (Nebraska) —B—1927
McArthur, John (Santa Clara) —C
  —1927–28
McGrath, Frank (Georgetown) —E—1928
McLain, Joseph (St. John's) —G—1928
Maloney, Gerald (Dartmouth) —E—1927
Manella—G—1928
Marker, Clifford (Washington State) —B
  —1927
Marks, Lawrence (Indiana) —Q—1927
Michalske, August (Penn. State) —G
  —1927–28
Molenda, John (Michigan) —B—1927–28
Oliver, William (Alabama) —G—1927
Olson, Forrest (Iowa) —G—1927
Pritchard, William (Penn. State) —B—1928
Racis, Frank—G—1928
Rauch, Richard (Penn. State) —G—1928
Rooney, Cobb (Colorado) —B—1928
Salemi, Samuel (St. John's—N.Y.) —B—1928
Scott, Ralph (Wisconsin) —T—1927
Smith, Richard (Notre Dame) —B—1928

Stephens, Leslie (Idaho) —C—1927–28
Stevenson, Arthur (Fordham) —G—1928
Tryon, Edward (Colgate) —B—1927
Welch, Gilbert (Pittsburgh) —B—1928
White, Philip (Oklahoma) —E—1928

NEW YORK YANKS (1950–51)

Adams, Chester (Ohio) —T—1950
Aldridge, Benjamin (Oklahoma A & M) —B
—1950–51
Alford, Herbert (Texas Christian Univ.)
—E—1950–51
Brown, George (Texas Christian Univ.) —G
—1950
Celeri, Robert (California) —Q—1951
Champion, James (Mississippi State) —G
—1950–51
Clowes, John (William & Mary) —T
—1950–51
Colo, Donald (Brown) —E—1951
Crowe, Paul (St. Mary's—Cal.) —B—1951
Cullom, James (California) —G—1951
Donovan, Arthur (Boston College) —T
—1951
Ecklund, Bradley (Oregon) —C—1950–51
Edwards, Daniel (Georgia) —E—1950–51
Garza, Daniel (Oregon) —E—1951
Griffin, Robert (Baylor) —B—1951
Howard, Sherman (Nevada) —B—1950–51
Iverson, Christopher (Oregon) —B—1950–51
Jenkins, Jonathan (Dartmouth) —T—1950
Johnson, Harvey (William & Mary) —B
—1951
Johnson, Nathan (Illinois) —E—1950
Kennedy, Robert (Washington State) —B
—1950
Kusserow, Louis (Columbia) —B—1950
Layden, Peter (Texas) —B—1950
Meisenheimer, Darrell (Oklahoma A & M)
—B—1951
Mitchell, Paul (Minnesota) —T—1950–51
Nagel, Ross (St. Louis) —T—1951
O'Connor, William (Notre Dame)—E—1951
Poole, Barney (Mississippi) —E—1950–51
Ratterman, George (Notre Dame) —Q
—1950–51
Ruby, Martin (Texas A & M) —T—1950
Russell, John (Baylor) —E—1950
Sanders, Orban (Texas) —B—1950
Sharkey, Edward (Nevada) —G—1950
Signaigo, Joseph (Notre Dame) —C—1950
Soboleski, Joseph (Michigan) —T—1950–51
Stroschein, Brock (U.C.L.A.) —E—1951
Swistowicz, Michael (Notre Dame) —B
—1950
Tait, Arthur (Mississippi State) —E—1951
Taliaferro, George (Indiana) —B—1950–51
Toth, Zollie (Louisiana) —B—1950–51
Weiner, Arthur (North Carolina) —E—1950
Wozniak, John (Alabama) —G—1950–51
Yonaker, John (Notre Dame) —E—1950

NEWARK 1930

Andrulewicz, Theodore (Villanova) —B
—1930

Barkman, Ralph (Albright) —B—1930
Beattie, Robert (Princeton) —T—1930
Benkert, Henry (Rutgers) —B—1930
Bogue, George (Stanford) —B—1930
Borrelli, Nicholas (Muhlenberg) —B—1930
Bove, Peter (Holy Cross) —G—1930
Brennan, Philip (Columbia) —E—1930
Briante, Frank (New York Univ.)—Q—1930
Clancy, Stuart (Holy Cross) —B—1930
Connor, William (Catholic Univ.) —G
—1930
Cordavano, Samuel (Georgetown)—G—1930
Davidson, Joseph (Colgate) —G—1930
Depler, John (Illinois) —C—1930
Dibbs, John (West Point) —T—1930
Ellor, Albert (Bucknell) —G—1930
Feaster, William (Fordham) —T—1930
Finn, Bernard (Holy Cross) —B—1930
Franks, James (Penn. State) —B—1930
Gamerio (Ohio State) —E—1930
Grace, Leslie (Temple) —E—1930
Hauser, Kenneth (Washington & Jefferson)
—B—1930
Horton, Lester (Rutgers) —B—1930
Jones, Bruce (Alabama) —G—1930
Kerrigan, Thomas (Columbia) —G—1930
Kirkleski, Frank (Lafayette) —Q—1930
Leary, Thomas (Fordham) —E—1930
Liston, Paul (Georgetown) —T—1930
Longua, Paul (Villanova) —E—1930
McCormick, Felix (Bucknell) —B—1930
McGee, Howard (Kansas State) —G—1930
Manfreda, Anthony (Holy Cross) —B—1930
Martin, Herschel (Missouri) —B—1930
Mitchell, Frederick (Bucknell) —C—1930
Mooney, James (Georgetown) —E—1930
Morton, Lock (Arkansas) —B—1930
Myles—E—1930
Salata, Andrew (Pittsburgh) —G—1930
Sebo, Samuel (Syracuse) —B—1930
Smith, Dewey—G—1930
Smith, Richard (Notre Dame) —G—1930
Tays, James—B—1930
Tomaini, John (Georgetown) —E—1930
Wager, John (Carthage) —C—1930
Wagner, Raymond (Columbia) —E—1930
Waite, Carl (Georgetown) —E—1930
Webber, Howard (Kansas State) —E—1930
Woerner, Erwin (Bucknell) —T—1930

OORANG INDIANS (1922–23)
(Represented Marion, Ohio)

Arrowhead—E—1922
Attache, Reginald—B—1922
Barrel (Carlisle) —C—1922
Big Bear—T—1922–23
Black Bear—E—1922–23
Buffalo—G—1922–23
Busch, Elmer (Carlisle) —G—1922
Calac, Peter (Carlisle) —B—1922–23
Deadeye—T—1922
Eagle Feather—B—1922–23
Gray Horse—B—1922
Guyon, Joseph (Carlisle) —B—1922

ELMER BUSCH   BEMUS PIERCE   "WOODCHUCK" WELMUS

Hill, Robert (Haskell) —G—1922
Lassa, Nicholas "Long Time Sleep" (Carlisle) —C—1922–23
Laughing Gas—B—1922
Lo Boutwell—Q—1922
Little Twig (Carlisle) —E—1922–23
Lone Wolf (Carlisle) —G—1922–23
Newashe (Carlisle) —T—1922
Pierce, Bemus (Carlisle) —B—1922
Powell, Stancil (Carlisle) —G—1922
Red Fang—T—1922–23
Red Foot—E—1923
Red Fox—B—1922–23
Running Deer—E—1922
St. Germaine, Theodore (Carlisle)—G—1922
Saunook (Carlisle) —E—1922
Thorpe, Jack—G—1922–23
Thorpe, James (Carlisle) —1922–23
Tomahawk—B—1922–23
Towell (Carlisle) —B—1922
Welmus, Woodchuck (Carlisle) —E—1922–23
Winneschick (Carlisle) —C—1922
Wrinkle Meat—G—1922

ORANGE (1929)

Barkman, Ralph (Albright) —B—1929
Beattie, Robert (Princeton) —T—1929
Benkert, Henry (Rutgers) —B—1929
Clarkin, William (St. Benedict) —T—1929
Cunec, Edward (Columbia) —G—1929
Depler, John (Illinois) —C—1929
Dwyer, Robert (Georgetown) —B—1929
Feaster, William (Fordham) —T—1929
Hamas, Steven (Penn. State) —B—1929
Hambacker, Ernest (Bucknell) —B—1929
Johnson, Leon (Columbia) —E—1929
Kelly—T—1929
Kirkleski, Frank (Lafayette) —Q—1929
Law, John (Notre Dame) —T—1929
Longua, Paul (Villanova) —E—1929
Lott, John (Bucknell) —T—1929
Lynch, Edward (Holy Cross) —E—1929
McArthur, John (Santa Clara) —C—1929
McCormick, Felix (Bucknell) —B—1929
Mitchell, Frederick (Bucknell) —C—1929
Pease, George (Columbia) —Q—1929
Salata, Andrew (Pittsburgh) —G—1929
Scott, P.—G—1929

Tomaini, John (Georgetown) —E—1929
Van Horn, Charles (Washington Lee) —B—1929
Waite, Carl (Georgetown) —E—1929

PHILADELPHIA EAGLES
(1933—60)

Agajanian, Benjamin (New Mexico) —B—1945
Andrews, Leroy (Kansas State Teachers) —G—1934
Armstrong, Neil (Oklahoma A & M) —E—1947–51
Arnold, Jay (Texas) —B—1937–40
Aschbacher, Darrel (Oregon) —G—1959
Auer, Howard (Michigan) —T—1933
Bailey, Howard (Tennessee) —T—1935
Baisi, Albert (West Virginia) —G—1947
Banas, Steven (Notre Dame) —B—1935
Banducci, Bruno (Stanford) —G—1944–45
Banta, Herbert Jack (Southern California) —B—1941, 44–45
Barnes, Walter (Louisiana) —G—1948–51
Barnes, William (Wake Forest) —B—1957–60
Barnhart, Daniel (Centenary) —B—1934
Barni, Roy (San Francisco) —B—1954–55
Barnum, Leonard (West Virginia Wesleyan) —Q—1940–42
Bartholomew, Samuel (Tennessee) —B—1941
Basca, Michael (Villanova) —B—1941
Bassi, Richard (Santa Clara) —G—1940
Bassman, Herman (Ursinus) —B—1936–37
Baughan, Max (Georgia Tech.) —C—1960
Bauman, Alfred (Northwestern) —T—1947
Bausch, Frank (Kansas) —C—1940–41
Bawel, Edward (Evansville) —E—1952, 54–56
Baze, Winford (Texas Tech) —B—1937
Bednarik, Charles (Pennsylvania) —C—1949–60
Bell, Edward (Pennsylvania) —E—1955–58
Benson, Harry (Western Maryland) —G—1935
Berzinski, William (Wisconsin State) —B—1956
Bielski, Richard (Maryland) —B—1955–59
Binotto, John (Duquesne) —B—1942
Bjorklund, Robert (Minnesota) —C—1941

Bleeker, Melvin (Southern California) —B —1944–47

Boedecker, William (Kalamazoo) —B—1950

Bogren, Vincent (New Mexico) —E—1944

Bradley, Harold (Iowa State) —G—1958

Bredice, John (Boston Univ.) —E—1956

Brennan, Leo (Holy Cross) —T—1942

Brewer, John (Louisville) —B—1952–53

Brian, William (Gonzaga) —T—1935–36

Britt, Rankin (Texas A & M) —E—1939–40

Brodnicki, Charles (Temple) —C—1934

Brookshier, Thomas (Colorado) —E —1953, 55–60

Brown, Thomas (Ball State) —B—1960

Bukant, Joseph (Washington of Mo.) —B —1938–40

Burk, Adrian (Baylor) —Q—1951–57

Burnette, Thomas (North Carolina) —B —1938

Burnine, Harold (Missouri) —E—1956–57

Burrough, Donald (Colorado A & M) —B —1960

Bushby, Thomas (Kansas State) —B—1935

Buss, Athur (Michigan State) —T—1936–37

Butler, John (Tennessee) —B—1943–45

Cabrelli, Lawrence (Colgate) —E —1941–42, 44–47

Campbell, Glenn (Kansas State Teachers) —E—1935

Campbell, Marion (Georgia) —T—1956–60

Campbell, Stanley (Iowa State) —G— 1959–60

Campion, Thomas (Louisiana Southeast) —T—1947

Canale, Rocco (Boston College) —G —1943–45

Carpe, Joseph (Millikin) —T—1933

Carr, James (Morris Harvey) —B—1959–60

Carroccio, Russell (Virginia) —G—1955

Carter, Joseph (Southern Methodist Univ.) —E—1933–40

Castiglia, James (Georgetown) —B —1941, 45–46

Catlin, Thomas (Oklahoma) —G—1959

Cemore, Anthony (Creighton) —G—1941

Cherundulo, Charles (Penn. State) —C —1940

Cifelli, August (Notre Dame) —T—1954

Clark, Myers (Oregon State) —B—1934

Clayton, Donald—T—1936

Cole, John (St. Joseph) —B—1938–40

Combs, William (Purdue) —E—1942

Conti, Enio (Bucknell) —G—1941–43, 44–45

Cooke, Edward (Maryland) —E—1958

Coston, Fred (Texas A & M) —C—1939

Cothren, Paige (Mississippi) —B—1959

Cowhig, Gerald (Notre Dame) —B—1951

Craft, Russell (Alabama) —B—1946–54

Cuba, Paul (Pittsburgh) —T—1933–35, 38

Cuppoletti, Bree (Oregon) —G—1939–40

D'Agostino, Frank (Auburn) —G—1956

Davis, Robert (Kentucky) —B—1942

Davis, Sylvester (Geneva) —B—1933

Dean, Theodore (Wichita) —B—1960

DeFilippo, David (Villanova) —G—1941

DeLuca, Gerald (Tennessee) —T—1959

Demas, George (Washington & Jefferson) —G—1933

Dempsey, John (Bucknell) —T—1934, 37

DeSantis, Daniel (Niagara) —B—1941

Dimmick, Thomas (Houston) —G—1956

Disend, Leo (Albright) —T—1943

Dorow, Albert (Michigan State) —Q—1957

Doss, Noble (Texas) —B—1947–48

Douglas, Otis (William & Mary) —T —1946–49

Dow, Elwood (Texas State West) —B —1938–40

Dowda, Harry (Wake Forest) —B—1954–55

Durko, John (Albright) —E—1944

Eibner, John (Kentucky) —T—1941–42, 46

Eiden, Edmund (Scranton) —B—1944

Ellis, Drew (Texas Christian Univ.) —T —1938–40

Ellstrom, Marvin (Oklahoma) —B—1934

Emmons, Franklin (Oregon) —B—1940

Enke, Fred (Arizona) —Q—1952

Erdlitz, Richard (Northwestern) —B —1942, 45

Fagioli, Carl (Notre Dame) —G—1944

Farragut, Kenneth (Mississippi) —C —1951–54

Feather, Elwin (Kansas State) —B—1933

Felber, Fred (North Dakota) —E—1933

Fencl, Richard (Northwestern) —E—1933

Ferko, John (Westchester) —T—1937–38

Ferrante, Jack—E—1938, 41, 44–50

Ferris, Neil (Loyola L.A.) —B—1953

Fiedler, William (Pennsylvania) —G—1938

Field, Richard (Columbia) —G—1939–40

Fox, Terence (Miami) —B—1941–45

Frahm, Herald (Nebraska) —B—1935

Frank, Joseph (Georgetown) —T—1941–42

Freeman, Robert (Auburn) —B—1960

Frey, Glenn (Temple) —B—1936–37

Friedlund, Robert (Michigan State) —E —1946

Friedman, Robert (Washington) —G—1944

Fritts, George (Clemson) —T—1945

Fritz, Ralph (Michigan) —G—1941

Gambold, Robert (Washington State) —B —1953

Gaona, Robert (Wake Forest) —T—1957

Gauer, Charles (Colgate) —B—1944–45

George, Ray (Southern California) —T —1940

Gerber, Elwood (Alabama) —G—1941–42

Getchell, Gorham (Temple) —E—1943

Ghecas, Louis (Georgetown) —B—1941

Giancanelli, Harold (Loyola Cal.) —B —1953–56

Gianelli, Mario (Boston College) —G —1948–51

Gibron, Abraham (Purdue) —G—1957

Giddens, Herschel (Louisiana Teachers) —T—1928–39

Ginney, Jerry (Santa Clara) —G—1940

Gloden, Fred (Tulane) —B—1941

Goldston, Ralph (Youngstown) —B —1952, 54–55

"BOSH" PRITCHARD (30) OF THE PHILADELPHIA EAGLES TAKES OFF AGAINST THE LOS ANGELES RAMS DURING A GAME AT PHILADELPHIA IN 1948. RUSSELL CRAFT (33) AND AL WISTERT (70) MOVE INTO THE BLOCKING PATTERN.

Gollomb, Ralph (Wisconsin) —G—1936
Gonya, Robert (Northwestern) —T —1933–34
Goode, Robert (Texas A & M) —B—1955
Gossage, Eugene (Northwestern) —T—1960
Graham, Lyle (Richmond) —C—1940
Graham, Thomas (Temple) —G—1935
Grant, Harry (Minnesota) —E—1951–52
Graves, Ray (Tennessee) —C—1942, 46
Green, John (Tulsa) —E—1945, 47, 49–51
Gudd, Leonard (Temple) —E—1934
Gude, Henry (Vanderbilt) —G—1946
Gunnels, John (Georgia) —T—1960
Hackney, Elmer (Kansas State) —B —1940–41
Hajek, Charles (Northwestern) —C—1934
Hall, Irving (Brown) —B—1942
Halverson, William (Oregon State) —T —1942
Hansen, Roscoe (North Carolina)—T—1951
Hanson, Thomas (Temple) —B—1933–37
Harding, Roger (California) —C—1947
Harper, Maurice (Austin) —C—1937–41
Harris, James (Oklahoma) —B—1957
Harrison, Granville (Mississippi State) —E —1941
Hartman, Fred (Rice) —T—1948
Hayden, Kenneth (Arkansas) —C—1942
Hershey, Kirk (Cornell) —E—1941
Hewitt, William (Michigan) —E—1937–39
Higgins, Thomas (North Carolina) —T —1954–55
Hinkle, John (Syracuse) —1941–42, 44–47
Hix, William (Arkansas) —E—1950
Holcomb, William (Texas Tech.)—T—1937
Horrell, William (Michigan State) —G —1952, 55
Hrabetin, Frank (Loyola) —T—1942
Hudson, Robert (Clemson) —E—1953–58
Hughes, William (Texas) —C—1937–40

Humbert, Richard (Richmond) —E —1941, 45–49
Huth, Gerald (Wake Forest) —G—1959–60
Huxhold, Kenneth (Wisconsin) —G —1954–58
Huzvar, John (Pittsburgh) —B—1952
Ignatius, James (Holy Cross) —G—1935
Illman, Edward (Montana State) —B—1933
Irvin, William (Florida A & M) —E—1953
Jackson, Donald (North Carolina) —B —1936
Jackson, Robert (Alabama) —B—1960
Jacobs, Proverb (California) —G—1958
Jarmoluk, Michael (Temple) —T—1949–55
Jarvi, Toimi (Illinois State North) —B —1944
Jefferson, William (Mississippi State) —B —1942
Johnson, Albert (Kentucky) —B—1942
Johnson, Alvin (Hardin-Simmons) —Q —1948
Johnson, Cecil (Texas State East) —B—1942
Johnson, Donald (California) —B—1953–55
Johnson, Eugene (Cincinnati) —B—1959–60
Jones, Donald (Washington) —B—1940
Jorgenson, Carl (St. Mary's Cal.) —T—1935
Jurgensen, Christian (Duke) —Q—1957–60
Kane, Carl (St. Louis) —B—1936
Kaplan, Bernard (Western Maryland) —G —1942
Karnofsky, Abraham (Arizona) —B—1945
Kasky, Edward (Villanova) —T—1942
Kavel, George (Carnegie Tech) —B—1934
Keeling, Raymond (Texas) —T—1938–39
Keen, Delbert (Arkansas) —B—1937–38
Kekeris, James (Missouri) —T—1947
Keller, Kenneth (North Carolina) —B —1956–57
Kelley, Robert (Western Maryland) —C —1955–56
Kenneally, George (St. Bonaventure) —E

—1933–35

Keys, Howard (Oklahoma State) —T—1960

Khayat, Edward (Tulane) —T—1958–60

Kilroy, Frank (Temple) —T—1944–56

King, Donald (Kentucky) —T—1956

Kirkman, Roger (Washington & Jefferson) —B—1933–35

Kish, Benjamin (Pittsburgh) —Q —1942, 1944–49

Kloppenberg, Harry (Fordham) —T—1936

Kmetovic, Peter (Stanford) —B—1946

Knapper, Joseph—B—1934

Knox, Charles (St. Edmonds) —T—1937

Koeninger, Arthur (Chattanooga) —C—1933

Kolberg, Elmer (Oregon State) —Q —1939–41

Koman, William (North Carolina) —G —1957–58

Konopka, John (Temple) —B—1936

Kostos, Anthony (Bucknell) —E—1933

Kowalczyk, Walter (Michigan State) —B —1958–59

Kresky, Joseph (Wisconsin) —G—1933–35

Krieger, Robert (Dartmouth) —E—1940– 41, 46

Kriel, Emmett (Baylor) —G—1939

Kuczinski, Albert (Pennsylvania) —E—1946

Kupcinet, Irving (North Dakota) —Q—1935

Kusko, John (Temple) —B—1936–38

Laack, Galen (College of Pacific) —G—1958

Lackman, Richard—B—1933–35

Lainhart, Porter (Oregon) —B—1933

Landsberg, Mortimer (Cornell) —B—1941

Lankas, James (St. Mary's—Tex.) —B—1942

Lansford, Alexander (Texas) —T—1955–57

Lapham, William (Iowa) —C—1960

Laux, Theodore (St. Joseph) —Q—1942–44

Leathers, Milton (Georgia) —G—1933

Lechthaler, Roy (Lebanon Valley) —G —1933

Ledbetter, Toy (Oklahoma A & M) —B —1950, 53–55

Lee, Bernard (Villanova) —B—1938

Leonard, James (Notre Dame) —B—1934–37

Levanitis, Stephen (Boston College) —T —1942

Leyendecker, Charles (Vanderbilt) —T —1933

Lindskog, Victor (Stanford) —C—1944–51

Lio, Augustino (Georgetown) —G—1946

Lipski, John (Temple) —C—1933–34

Looney, Donald (Texas Christian Univ.) —B—1940

Louderback, Thomas (San Jose State) —G —1958–59

Lucas, Richard (Boston College) —E—1960

Luft, Donald (Indiana) —E—1954

MacAfee, Kenneth (Alabama) —E—1959

McAfee, Wesley (Duke) —B—1941

McChesney, Robert (Hardin-Simmons) —E —1950

McCusker, James (Pittsburgh)—T—1959–60

McDonald, Donald (Oklahoma) —E —1944–45

McDonald, Lester (Nebraska) —E—1940

McDonald, Thomas (Oklahoma) —B —1957–60

McDonough, Robert (Duke) —G—1942, 46

McDowell, Jay (Washington) —E—1946–51

McHugh, Patrick (Georgia Tech) —B —1947–51

McMurdo, James (Pittsburgh) —T—1934–37

McPherson, Forrest (Nebraska) —C —1935–37

Macioszczyk, Arthur (Western Michigan) —B—1944, 47

Mackrides, William (Nevada) —Q—1947–51

Magee, John (Rice) —G—1948–55

Mandarino, Michael (LaSalle) —C—1944–45

Manske, Edward (Northwestern) —E —1935–36

Manton, Taldon (Texas Christian Univ.) —B—1940

Manzini, Baptiste (St. Vincent) —C —1944–45, 48

Marchi, Basilio (New York Univ.) —C —1941–42

Marcus, Alexander (Temple) —E—1933

Maronic, Dusan—G—1944–50

Masters, Robert (Baylor) —B—1937, 41–42

Masters, Walter (Pennsylvania) —Q—1936

Matesic, Edward (Pittsburgh) —B—1934–35

Mavraides, Menil (Notre Dame) —G —1954, 57

Maynard, Lester (Rider) —B—1933

Meadows, Edward (Duke) —E—1958

Meyer, Fred (Stanford) —E—1942, 45

Michaels, Edward (Villanova) —G—1944–46

Michaels, John (Tennessee) —G—1953

Milam, Barnes (Austin) —G—1934

Miller, Donald (Southern Methodist Univ.) —B—1954

Miller, Thomas (Hampton-Sidney) —E —1942, 44

Mitcham, Eugene (Arizona State) —E—1958

Mortell, Emmett (Wisconsin) —B—1937–39

Moselle, Donald (Wisconsin State) —B —1954

Mrkonic, George (Kansas) —T—1953

Muha, Joseph (Virginia Military Inst.) —B —1946–50

Mulligan, George (Catholic Univ.) —B —1936

Murley, Richard (Purdue) —T—1956

Murray, Francis (Pennsylvania) —B —1939–40

Myers, Bradford (Bucknell) —B—1958

Myers, John (U.C.L.A.) —B—1948–50

Nacrelli, Andrew (Fordham) —E—1958

Newton, Charles (Washington) —T —1939–40

Nipp, Maurice (Loyola, La.) —G— —1952–53, 56

Nocera, John (Iowa) —G—1959–60

Norby, John (Idaho) —B—1934

Norton, Gerald (Southern Methodist Univ.) —B—1954–58

Nowak, Walter (Villanova) —E—1944

O'Boyle, Harry (Notre Dame) —B—1933

O'Brien, Robert David (Texas Christian

Univ.) —Q—1939–40

Obst, Henry (Syracuse) —G—1933

O'Quinn, John (Wake Forest) —E—1951

Ordway, William (North Dakota) —B—1939

Oristaglio, Robert (Pennsylvania) —E—1952

Ormsbee, Elliott (Bradley) —B—1946

Owens, Donald (Mississippi Southern) —T —1958–60

Padlow, Max (Oregon State) —E—1935

Pagliei, Joseph (Clemson) —B—1959

Palmer, Leslie (North Carolina State) —B —1948

Pape, Orrin (Iowa) —B—1933

Parmer, James (Oklahoma A & M) —B —1948–56

Pate, Rupert (Wake Forest) —G—1942

Patton, John (Texas Christian Univ.) —G —1946–50

Peaks, Clarence (Michigan State) —B —1957–60

Pegg, Harold (Bucknell) —C—1940

Pellegrini, Robert (Maryland) —C—1956–60

Peters, Volney (Southern California) —T —1958

Piasecky, Alexander (Duke) —E—1942

Pihos, Peter (Indiana) —E—1947–55

Pilconis, Joseph (Temple) —E—1934, 36–37

Piro, Henry (Syracuse) —E—1941

Pitts, Edwin (Alabama) —B—1935

Pivarnik, Joseph (Notre Dame) —G—1936

Pollard, Alfred (West Point) —B—1951–53

Pollock, William—B—1937, 42–43

Poth, Philip (Gonzaga) —G—1934

Powell, Arthur (San Jose State) —B—1959

Prescott, Harold (Hardin-Simmons) —E —1947–49

Priestly, Robert (Brown) —E—1942

Prisco, Nicholas (Rutgers) —B—1933

Pritchard, Abisha (Virginia Military Inst.) —B—1942, 46–51

Pylman, Robert (South Dakota State) —T —1938–39

Rado, George (Duquesne) —G—1938

Ragazzo, Philip (Western Reserve) —T —1940–41

Ramsay, Herschel (Texas Tech) —E —1938–40, 45

Ramsey, Knox (William & Mary) —G—1952

Raskowski, Leo (Ohio State) —T—1935

Rauch, John (Georgia) —Q—1951

Reagan, Frank (Pennsylvania) —B—1949–51

Reese, Henry (Temple) —C—1935–39

Reichow, Garet (Iowa) —Q—1960

Restic, Joseph (Villanova) —E—1952

Retzlaff, Palmer (South Dakota State) —E —1956–60

Reutt, Raymond (Virginia Military Inst.) —E—1943

Ricca, James (Georgetown) —T—1955–6

Richardson, Jess (Alabama) —T—1953–60

Riffle, Richard (Albright) —B—1938–40

Riley, Leon (Detroit) —B—1956, 58–59

Robb, Joseph (Texas Christian Univ.) —E —1959–60

Roberts, John (Georgia) —B—1933–34

Robinson, Wayne (Minnesota) —C —1952–56

Robison, Burle (Brigham Young) —E —1935

Roffler, William (Washington State) —B —1954

Rogalla, John (Scranton) —B—1945

Rogas, Daniel (Tulane) —G—1952

Romero, Raymond (Kansas State) —G —1951

Roton, Herbert (Auburn) —E—1937

Rowan, Everett (Ohio State) —E—1933

Rowe, Robert (Colgate) —B—1935

Russell, Lafayette (Northwestern) —B— 1933

Russell, James (Temple) —T—1936–37

Ryan, John (Illinois) —B—1956–58

Saidock, Thomas (Michigan State) —T —1957

Sanders, John (Southern Methodist Univ.) —G—1945

Sandifer, Daniel (Louisiana State Univ.) —B—1950–51

Sapp, Theron (Georgia) —B—1959

Savitsky, George (Pennsylvania) —T —1948–49

Schaefer, Donald (Notre Dame) —B—1956

Schmidt, Theodore (Pittsburgh) —C —1938–40

Schnelker, Robert (Bowling Green) —E —1953

Schuelke, Karl "Jake" (Rice) —B—1939

Schultz, Eberle (Oregon State) —G—1940

Scott, Clyde (Arkansas) —B—1949–52

Scott, Thomas (Virginia) —E—1953–58

Sears, Victor (Oregon State) —T —1941–42, 44–53

Sebastian, Michael (Pittsburgh) —B—1935

Sharkey, Edward (Nevada) —G—1954–55

Shaub, Harry (Cornell) —G—1935

Sherman, Alex (Brooklyn) —Q—1944–47

Shires, Marshall (Tennessee) —Q—1945

Shonk, John (W. Virginia) —E—1941

Simerson, John (Purdue) —C—1957–58

Skladany, Leo (Pittsburgh) —E—1949

Smeja, Rudolph (Michigan) —E—1946

Smith, James (Colorado) —T—1945

Smith, Jess D. (Rice) —T—1959–60

Smith, John (Stanford) —E—1942

Smith, Milton (U.C.L.A.) —E—1945

Smith, Ray (Missouri) —C—1933

Smith, Robert (Nebraska) —B—1956

Smukler, David (Temple) —B—1936–39

Snyder, Kenneth (Georgia Tech) —T —1952–55, 58

Sokolis, Stanley (Pennsylvania) —T—1933

Sommers, George (LaSalle) —T—1939–40

Spillers, Ray (Arkansas) —T—1937

Stackpool, John (Washington) —B—1942

Stasica, Leo (Colorado) —B—1941

Steele, Ernest (Washington) —B—1944–48

Steere, Richard (Drake) —T—1951

Steinbach, Laurence (St. Thomas) —T —1933

Steinke, Gilbert (Texas A & I) —B—1945–48

PHILADELPHIA EAGLES FOOTBALL TEAM 1958

Front Row: (Left to right) Gene Mitcham, e; Jerry Norton, b; Tommy McDonald,
b; Sonny Jurgensen, b; Billy Barnes, b; Tom Brookshier, b; Lee Riley, b;
Brad Myers, b; Billy Wells, b; Bobby Walston, e; Galen Laack, g.
Second Row: Fred Schubach, equipment manager; Frank O'Neill, trainer; Jerry
Williams, assistant coach; Bruno Banducci, assistant coach; Harold Bradley, g;
Bob Hudson, lb; Pete Retzlaff, b; Ken Huxhold, g; Tom Louderback, lb;
Marion Campbell, t; Norman Van Brocklin, b; Ed Meadows, e; Bob Pellegrini,
lb; Walt Kowalczyk, b; Buck Shaw, head coach.
Back Row: Clarence Peaks, b; Don Owens, t; Proverb Jacobs, t; Dick Bielski, e;
Sid Youngelman, t; Tom Scott, e; Jess Richardson, t; Eddie Bell, b; Len Szafaryn,
t; Volney Peters, t; Lum Snyder, t; Chuck Bednarik, c; Bill Koman, lb.

Stevens, Donald (Illinois) —B—1952, 54
Stevens, Peter (Temple) —C—1936
Stickel, Walter (Pennsylvania)—T—1950-51
Stockton, H. Vard (California) —G
—1937-38
Storm, Edward (Santa Clara) —B—1934-35
Stribling, Majure (Mississippi) —E—1955-57
Striegel, William (College of Pacific) —G—
1959
Stringer, Robert (Tulsa) —B—1952-53
Sturgeon, Cecil (North Dakota State) —T
—1941
Suffridge, Robert (Tennessee) —G—1941, 45
Supulski, Leonard (Dickinson) —E—1942
Sutton, Joseph (Temple) —B—1950-52
Szafaryn, Leonard (North Carolina) —T
—1957-58
Szymanski, Frank (Notre Dame) —C—1948
Talcott, Donald (Nevada) —T—1947
Taliaferro, George (Indiana) —B—1955
Thacker, Alvin (Morris-Harvey) —B—1941
Thomason, John (Georgia Tech) —B
—1935-36
Thomason, Robert (Virginia Military
Inst.) —Q—1953-57
Thompson, Russell (Nebraska) —T—1940
Thompson, Thomas (Tulsa) —Q
—1940-42, 45-50
Thornton, Richard (Missouri Mines) —B
—1933
Tomasetti, Louis (Bucknell) —B—1940-42
Tripucka, Frank (Notre Dame) —Q—1949
Trost, Milton (Marquette) —T—1940
Turnbow, Guy (Mississippi) —T—1933-34
Tyrrell, Joseph (Temple) —G—1952
Urevig, Claude (North Dakota) —B—1934-
35

Van Brocklin, Norman (Oregon) —Q—
1958-60
VanBuren, Ebert (Louisiana State Univ.)
—B—1950-51, 53
VanBuren, Steven (Louisiana State Univ.)
—B—1944-51
Walston, Robert (Georgia) —E—1951-60
Warren, Busit (Tennessee) —B—1945
Watkins, Forrest (Texas State West) —Q
—1940-41
Wear, Robert (Penn. State) —C—1942
Weatherall, James (Oklahoma) —T
—1955-57
Weber, Charles (Westchester State) —E—
1959-60
Weedon, Donald (Texas) —G—1947
Wegert, Theodore—B—1955-56
Weiner, Albert (Muhlenberg) —B—1934
Weinstock, Isadore (Pittsburgh) —B—1935
Wells, William (Michigan State) —B—1958
Wendlick, Joseph (Oregon State) —E—1940
West, Hodges (Tennessee) —T—1941
Whire, John (Georgia) —B—1933
White, Thomas (Texas Christian Univ.)
—G—1939
Wiatrak, John (Washington) —C—1939
Wilcox, John (Oregon) —T—1960
Willey, Norman (Marshall) —E—1950-57
Williams, Boyd (Syracuse) —C—1947
Williams, Jerome (Washington State) —B
—1953-54
Williams, John (Auburn) —G—1942
Williams, Theodore (Boston College) —B
—1942
Willson, Osborne (Pennsylvania) —G
—1933-35

Wilson, Gerald (Auburn) —E—1959–60
Wilson, William (Gonzaga) —E—1938
Wistert, Albert (Michigan) —T—1944–51
Wittenborn, John (Missouri Southeast) —
G—1960
Wojciechowicz, Alexander (Fordham) —C
—1946–50
Woltman, Clement (Purdue) —T—1938–40
Woodruff, Lee (Mississippi) —B—1933
Worden, Neil (Notre Dame) —B—1954, 57
Wydo, Frank (Cornell) —T—1951–57
Wyhonic, John (Alabama) —G—1946–47
Youngelman, Sidney (Alabama) —G
1956–57
Yovisin, John (Gettysburg) —E—1944
Ziegler, Frank (Georgia Tech) —B—1949–53
Zilly, John (Notre Dame) —E—1952
Zimmerman, Leroy (San Jose State) —Q
—1942, 44–46
Zizak, Vincent (Villanova) —T—1934–37
Zyntell, James (Holy Cross) —G—1933–35

PHIL-PITT (Merger) (1943)

Bova, Anthony (St. Francis) —E—1943
Brunksi, Andrew (Temple) —C—1943
Butler, John (Tennessee) —B—1943
Cabrelli, Lawrence (Colgate) —E—1943
Conti, Enio (Bucknell) —G—1943
Doyle, Theodore (Nebraska) —T—1943

Frank, Joseph (Georgetown) —T—1943
Gauer, Charles (Colgate) —B—1943
Graves, Raymond (Tennessee) —C—1943
Hewitt, William (Michigan) —E—1943
Hinkle, John (Syracuse) —B—1943
Hoague, Joseph (Colgate) —B—1943
Kilroy, Frank (Temple) —G—1943
Kish, Ben (Pittsburgh) —Q—1943
Laux, Theodore (St. Joseph's) —Q—1943
McCullough, Hugh (Oklahoma) —B—1943
Masters, Robert (Baylor) —B—1943
Michaels, Edward (Villanova) —G—1943
Miller, Thomas (Hampton-Sidney) —E
—1943
Paschka, Gordon (Minnesota) —G—1943
Sader, Steven—B—1943
Sanders, John (Southern Methodist Univ.)
—G—1943
Schultz, Eberle (Oregon State) —G—1943
Sears, Victor (Oregon State) —T—1943
Sherman, Alex (Brooklyn) —Q—1943
Steele, Ernest (Washington) —B—1943
Steward, Dean (Ursinus) —B—1943
Stewart, Charles (Carnegie Tech) —T—1943
Stuart, Raymond (Tulsa) —B—1943
Thurbon, Robert (Pittsburgh) —B—1943
Wistert, Albert (Michigan) —T—1943
Wukits, Albert (Duquesne) —C—1943
Zimmerman, Leroy (San Jose State) —Q
—1943

Nate Fine Photo

WILBUR MOORE OF WASHINGTON ABOUT TO CATCH ONE OF SAM BAUGH'S PASSES AND
GO FOR A TOUCHDOWN AGAINST THE PHILADELPHIA EAGLES DURING A 1943 GAME.
THE EAGLE TRYING TO BREAK IT UP (7) IS LEROY ZIMMERMAN, FORMER REDSKIN
QUARTERBACK.

PITTSBURGH STEELERS
(1933—60)
(Formerly played as Pirates)

Agajanian, Ben (New Mexico)—B—1945
Alban, Richard (Northwestern)—B 1956—59
Alberghini, Thomas (Holy Cross)—G—1945
Alderton, John (Maryland)—E—1953
Allen, Louis (Duke)—T—1950–51
Andabaker, Rudolph (Pittsburgh)—G —1952–54
Arndt, Alfred (South Dakota State)—G —1935
Arnold, Jay (Texas)—B—1941
Artman, Corwan (Stanford)—T—1933
Augusterfer, Eugene (Catholic Univ.)—G —1935
Baldacci, Louis (Michigan)—B—1956
Balog, Robert (Denver)—C—1949–50
Barbolak, Peter (Purdue)—T—1949
Barker, Edward (Washington State)—E —1953
Barnett, Thomas (Purdue)—B—1959–60
Basrak, Michael (Duquesne)—C—1937–38
Bassi, Richard (Santa Clara)—G—1941
Beams, Byron (Notre Dame)—T—1959–60
Beatty, Edward (Mississippi)—C—1957–60
Bernard, David (Mississippi)—B—1942
Bernet, Edward (Southern Methodist Univ.)—E—1955
Billock, Frank (LaCrosse)—G—1937
Binotto, John (Duquesne)—B—1942
Bishop, Donald (Los Angeles City College) —E—1958–59
Bolkovak, Nicholas (Pittsburgh)—T —1953–54
Bond, Randall (Washington)—B—1939–40
Bonelli, Ernest (Pittsburgh)—B—1946
Bova, Anthony (St. Francis)—E —1942, 45–47
Bowman, William (William & Mary)—B —1957
Boyd, Samuel (Baylor)—T—1939–40
Boyle, William—T—1934
Brady, Patrick (Nevada)—B—1952–54
Brandau, Arthur (Tennessee)—C—1945–46
Brandt, James (St. Thomas)—B—1952–54
Bray, Maurice (Southern Methodist Univ.) —T—1935–36
Breedon, William (Oklahoma)—B—1937
Brett, Edward (Washington State)—E —1936–37
Brewster, Darrel (Purdue)—E—1959–60
Broussard, Fred (Louisiana Northwest) —C—1955
Brovelli, Angelo (St. Mary's, Cal.)—B —1933–34
Brown, Thomas (William & Mary)—E —1942
Bruder, Henry (Northwestern)—B—1940
Brumbaugh, Boyd (Duquesne)—B —1939–41
Brundage, Dewey (Brigham Young)—E —1954
Bruney, Fred (Ohio State)—B—1956–57

Bucek, Felix (Texas A & M)—G—1946
Buda, Carl (Tulsa)—G—1945
Bukich, Rudolph (Southern California)— Q—1960
Burleson, John (Southern Methodist Univ.)—G—1933
Burnette, Thomas (North Carolina)—B —1938
Butler, John (St. Bonaventure)—E —1951–59
Calcagni, Ralph (Pennsylvania)—T —1947–48
Call, John (Colgate)—B—1959
Calvin, Thomas (Alabama)—B—1952–55
Cameron, Paul (U.C.L.A.)—B—1954
Campbell, Donald (Carnegie Tech)—T —1939–40
Campbell, Glenn (Kansas State Teachers) —E—1935
Campbell, Leon (Arkansas)—B—1955
Campbell, Raymond "Dick" (Marquette) —C—1958–60
Cara, Dominic (North Carolina State)—E —1937–38
Cardwell, Joseph (Duke)—T—1937–38
Carpenter, Preston (Arkansas)—B—1960
Casper, Charles (Texas Christian Univ.) —B—1935
Cenci, John (Pittsburgh)—C—1956
Chamberlain, Garth (Brigham Young)—G —1945
Chandnois, Lynn (Michigan State)—B —1950–56
Cheatham, Ernest (Loyola, L. A.)—E—1954
Cherry, Edgar (Hardin-Simmons)—B— 1939
Cherundolo, Charles (Penn. State)—C —1941–42, 45–48
Christy, Richard (North Carolina State) —B—1958
Cibulas, Joseph (Duquesne)—T—1945
Cichowski, Eugene (Indiana)—B—1957
Ciccone, Benjamin (Duquesne)—C —1934–35
Cifelli, August (Notre Dame)—T—1954
Cifers, Robert (Tennessee)—Q—1947–48
Clark, James (Pittsburgh)—B—1933–34
Clement, John (Southern Methodist Univ.) —Q—1946–48
Compagno, Anthony (St. Mary's, Cal.)—B —1945–49
Condit, Merlyn (Carnegie Tech)—B —1940, 46
Coomer, Joseph—T—1941, 45–46
Cooper, Samuel (Geneva)—T—1933
Cotton, Russell (Texas Mines)—Q—1942
Craft, Russell (Alabama)—B—1954
Cregar, William (Holy Cross)—G—1947–48
Critchfield, Lawrence (Grove City)—G —1933
Croft, Winfield (Utah)—G—1936
Dailey, Theodore (Pittsburgh)—E—1933
Davidson, William (Temple)—B—1937–39
Davis, Arthur (Mississippi State)—B—1956
Davis, Paul (Otterbein)—B—1947–48

Davis, Robert (Penn. State) —E—1946–50
Dawson, Leonard (Purdue) —B—1957–59
DeCarbo, Nicholas (Duquesne) —G—1933
DeCarlo, Arthur (Georgia) —B—1953–54
Dempsey, John (Bucknell) —T—1934
DePaul, Henry (Duquesne) —G—1945
Derby, Dean (Washington) —B—1957–60
Dess, Darrell (North Carolina State) —T —1958
Dial, Gilbert (Rice) —E—1959–60
Dodrill, Dale (Colorado A & M) —G —1951–59
Dodson, Leslie (Mississippi) —B—1941
Doehring, John—B—1935
Doloway, Clifford (Carnegie Tech) —B —1935
Dolly, Richard (West Virginia) —E —1941, 45
Donelli, Aldo (Duquesne) —B—1941–42
Douds, Forrest (Washington & Jefferson) —T—1933–34
Dougherty, Robert (Kentucky) —E—1958
Douglas, Clarence (Kansas) —B—1938
Doyle, Richard (Ohio State) —B—1955
Doyle, Theodore (Nebraska) —T —1938–42, 45
Drulis, Albert (Temple) —B—1947
Dudley, William (Virginia) —B —1942, 45–46

Duhart, Paul (Florida) —B—1945
Dutton, William (Pittsburgh) —B—1946
Eaton, Victor (Missouri) —B—1955
Elter, Leo (Duquesne) —1953–54, 58–59
Engebretsen, Paul (Northwestern) —G —1933
Evans, Jon (Oklahoma State) —E—1958
Evans, Raymond (Kansas) —B—1948
Farrar, Vincent (North Carolina State) —B—1938–39
Farrell, Edward (Muhlenberg) —B—1938
Farroh, Shipley (Iowa) —G—1938
Feher, Nicholas (Georgia) —G—1955
Ferry, Louis (Villanova) —T—1952–55
Fife, Ralph (Pittsburgh) —G—1946
Filchock, Frank (Indiana) —B—1938
Finks, James (Tulsa) —B—1949–55
Fisher, Everett (Santa Clara) —B—1940
Fisher, Raymond (Illinois State East) —T —1959
Fiske, Max (DePaul) —B—1936–38
Flanagan, Richard (Ohio State) —G —1953–55
Foltz, Vernon (St. Vincent's) —C—1945
Ford, Henry (Pittsburgh) —B—1956
Fournet, Sidney (Louisiana State Univ.) —G—1957
Francis, Samuel (Nebraska) —B—1939
Frketich, Leonard (Penn. State) —T—1945

A PITTSBURGH SPREAD PATTERN TAKES THE GREEN BAY DEFENSE APART AND JOE GERI (35) WHIPS A PASS TO END HANK MINARIK (82) DURING 1951 GAME. MINARIK WAS CAUGHT FROM BEHIND BY ACE LOOMIS (7).

Fugler, Richard (Tulane) —T—1952
Fullerton, Edward (Maryland) —B—1953
Gage, Robert (Clemson) —B—1949–50
Gaona, Robert (Wake Forest) —T—1953–57
Garnaas, Wilford (Minnesota) —B
—1946–47
Gasparella, Joseph (Notre Damé) —B
—1948, 50–51
Gentry, Byron (Southern California) —G
—1937–40
Geri, Joseph (Georgia) —B—1949–51
Gildea, John (St. Bonaventure) —B
—1935–37
Girard, Earl (Wisconsin) —B—1957
Glamp, Joseph (Louisiana State Univ.)
—B—1947–49
Glatz, Fred (Pittsburgh) —E—1956
Glick, Gary (Colorado) —B—1956–59
Goff, Clark (Florida) —T—1940
Gonda, George (Duquesne) —B
—1942, 45–46
Gorinski, Walter (Louisiana State Univ.)
—B—1946
Grabinski, Thaddeus (Duquesne) —C
—1939–40
Gray, Samuel (Tulsa) —E—1946–47
Green, Robert (Florida) —1960
Greeney, Norman (Notre Dame) —G
—1934–35
Gunderman, Robert (Virginia) —B—1957
Hackney, Elmer (Kansas State) —B—1941
Haines, Byron (Washington) —B—1937
Hall, Ronald (Missouri Valley) —B—1959
Hanlon, Robert (Notre Dame) —B
—1949–50
Hanson, Thomas (Temple) —B—1938
Harkey, Lemuel (Kansas State Teachers)
—B—1955
Harper, Maurice (Austin) —C—1941
Harris, William (Hardin-Simmons) —E—
1937
Hartley, Howard (Duke) —B—1949–52
Hayduk, Henry (Washington State) —G
—1935
Hayes, Richard (Clemson) —B—1959—60
Hays, George (St. Bonaventure) —E
1950–52
Hegarty, William (Villanova) —T—1953
Held, Paul (San Diego State) —B—1954
Heller, Warren (Pittsburgh) —B—1934–36
Hendley, Richard (Clemson) —B—1951
Henry, Michael (Southern California) —
B—1959–60
Hensley, Richard (Kentucky) —E—1952
Hill, James (Tennessee) —B—1955
Hinte, Harold (Pittsburgh) —E—1942
Hipps, Claude (Georgia) —B—1952–53
Hoague, Joseph (Colgate) —B—1941–42
Hoel, Robert (Pittsburgh) —G—1935
Hogan, Darrell (Trinity, Tex.) —G
—1949–53
Holcomb, William (Texas Tech) —T—1937
Hollingsworth, Joseph (Kentucky State
East) —B—1949–51

Holm, Bernard (Alabama) —B—1933
Holmer, Walter (Northwestern) —B—1933

Hood, Franklin (Pittsburgh) —B—1933
Hornick, William (Tulane) —T—1947
Hubbard, Robert "Cal" (Geneva) —T
—1936
Hubka, Eugene (Bucknell) —B—1947
Hughes, George (William & Mary) —G
—1950–54
Hughes, Richard (Tulsa) —B—1957
Itzel, John (Georgetown) —B—1945
Ivy, Frank (Oklahoma) —E—1940
James, Daniel (Ohio State) —C—1960
Jamison, Leon (Tennessee A & I) —E—1958
Janecek, Clarence (Purdue) —G—1933
Jansante, Valerio (Duquesne) —E—1946–51
Jarvi, Toimi (Illinois State North) —B
—1945
Jecha, Raymond (Northwestern) —G—1956
Jelley, Thomas (Miami) —E—1951
Johnson, John Henry (Arizona State) —B
—1960
Johnston, Chester (Elmhurst) —B—1939–40
Johnston, Rex (Southern California) —B
—1960
Jones, Arthur (Richmond) —B—1941, 45–46
Kahler, Royal (Nebraska) —T—1941
Kakasic, George (Duquesne) —G—1936–39
Kapele, John (Brigham Young) —T—1960
Kapriva, Frank (Wake Forest) —G—1946
Karcis, John (Carnegie Tech) —B—1936–38
Karpowich, Edward (Catholic Univ.) —T
—1936–39
Karras, Theodore (Indiana) —T—1958–59
Kavel, George (Carnegie Tech) —B—1934
Kelsch, Christian—B—1933–34
Kemp, John (Occidental) —Q—1957–58
Kemp, Raymond (Duquesne) —T—1933
Kerkorian, Gary (Stanford) —Q—1952
Kichefski, Walter (Miami) —E—1940–42
Kielbasa, Max (Duquesne) —B—1946
Kiesling, Walter (St. Thomas) —G
—1937–38
Kiick, George (Bucknell) —B—1940–45
Kimble, Frank (West Virginia) —E—1945
Kissell, Edward (Wake Forest) —B
—1952, 54
Klapstein, Earl (College of Pacific) —T
—1946
Klumb, John (Washington State) —E—1940
Kolberg, Elmer (Oregon State) —Q—1941
Kondria, John (St. Vincent) —T—1945
Kottler, Martin (Centre) —B—1933
Kresky, Joseph (Wisconsin) —G—1935
Krisher, William (Oklahoma) —G—1958
Krupa, Joseph (Purdue) —G—1956–60
Krutko, Lawrence (West Virginia) —B
—1958–60
Kurrasch, Roy (U.C.L.A.) —E—1948
Kvaternik, Zvonimir (Kansas) —G—1934
Lach, Steven (Duke) —B—1946–47
Ladygo, Peter (Maryland) —T—1952–54
Lajovsky, William (Catholic Univ.) —G
—1936
Lamas, Joseph (Mt. St. Mary's) —G—1942
Lantz, Montgomery (Grove City) —C—1933
Lassahn, Louis (Western Maryland) —E
—1938

Lasse, Richard (Syracuse) —E—1958–59
Lattner, John (Notre Dame) —B—1954
Law, Hubbard (Sam Houston) —G —1952, 45
Layne, Robert (Texas) —Q—1958–60
Lea. Paul (Tulane) —T—1951
Leahy, Gerald (Colorado) —T—1957
Lee, Bernard (Villanova) —B—1938
Lee, John (Carnegie Tech) —B—1939
Lee, Willie (Florida A & M) —T—1957
Letsinger, Howard (Purdue) —G—1933
Levanti, Louis (Illinois) —C—1951–52
Levey, James—B—1934–36
Lewis, Joseph (Compton) —T—1958–60
Liddick, David (George Washington) —T —1957
Littlefield, Carl (Washington State) —B —1939
Long, William (Oklahoma A & M) —E —1949–50
Longenecker, Kenneth (Lebanon Valley) — T—1960
Looney, Donald (Texas Christian Univ.) —B—1941–42
Love, John (Pittsburgh) —T—1934
Lowther, Russell (Detroit) —B—1945
Lucas, Richard (Boston College) —E—1958
Lucente, John (West Virginia) —B—1945
Luna, Robert (Alabama) —B—1959
McCabe, Richard (Pittsburgh) —B —1955, 57–58
McCafferty, Arthur (Santa Clara) —T—1946
McClairan, Jack (Bethune-Cookman) —E —1955–60
McClung, William (Florida A & M) —T —1955–57
McConnell, Dewey (Wyoming) —E—1954
McCullough, Hugh (Oklahoma) —B—1939
McDade, William (Portland) —C—1938
McDonald, Edward (Duquesne) —B—1936
McDonough, Coley (Dayton) —B—1939–41
McDonough, Paul (Utah) —E—1938
McFadden, Marvin (Michigan State) —T —1953, 56
McNally, John "Blood" (St. John) —B —1934, 37–39
McPeak, William (Pittsburgh) —E—1949–58
McWilliams, Thomas (Mississippi State) —B—1950
Mackrides, William (Nevada) —Q—1953
Maher, Francis (Toledo) —B—1940–41
Malkovich, Joseph (Duquesne) —C—1935
Manske, Edward (Northwestern) —E—1938
Maras, Joseph (Duquesne) —C—1938–40
Marchi, Basilio (New York Univ.) —C —1934
Marchibroda, Theodore (Detroit) —Q —1953, 55–56
Marker, Henry (West Virginia) —B—1934
Martin, Vernon (Texas) —B—1942
Masters, Robert (Baylor) —B—1939
Mastrangelo, John (Notre Dame) —G —1947–48
Matesic, Edward (Pittsburgh) —B—1936
Matesic, Joseph (Arizona State) —T—1954
Mathews, Raymond (Clemson) —B

—1951–59
Mattioli, Francis (Pittsburgh) —G—1946
Matuszak, Martin (Tulsa) —C—1953, 55–56
Mayhew, Hayden (Texas Mines) —G —1936–38
Meadows, Edward (Duke) —E—1955
Meeks, Bryant (South Carolina) —C —1947–48
Mehelich, Charles (Duquesne) —E —1946–51
Merkovsky, Elmer (Pittsburgh) —T —1945–46
Michael, William (Ohio State) —G—1957
Michalik, Arthur (St. Ambrose) —G —1955–56
Midler, Louis (Northwestern) —G—1940
Minarik, Henry (Michigan State) —E—1951
Miner, Thomas (Tulsa) —E—1958
Minini, Frank (San Jose State) —B—1949
Modzelewski, Edward (Maryland) —B —1952
Modzelewski, Richard (Maryland) —T —1955
Moegle, Richard (Rice) —B—1960
Momsen, Anthony (Michigan) —C—1951
Moore, Allen (Loyola, N.O.) —B—1933
Moore, William (Penn. State) —G—1947–49
Morales, Gonzales (St. Mary's, Cal.) —B —1947–48
Morrall, Earl (Michigan State) —Q —1957–58
Morris, John (Oregon) —B—1960
Mosher, Clure (Louisville) —C—1942
Mosley, Norman (Alabama) —B—1948
Moss, Paul (Purdue) —E—1933
Motley, Marion (Nevada) —B—1955
Mott, Norman (Georgia) —B—1934
Mulleneaux, Lee (Arizona) —B—1935–37
Murley, Richard (Purdue) —G—1956
Murray, Earl (Purdue) —G—1952
Nagler, Gern (Santa Clara) —E—1959
Naioti, John (St. Francis) —B—1942, 45
Nardi, Richard (Ohio State) —B—1939
Nery, Carl (Duquesne) —G—1940–41
Niccolai, Armand (Duquesne) —T —1934–42
Nichols, Allen (Temple) —B—1945
Nickel, Elbie (Cincinnati) —E—1947–57
Nicksick, George (St. Bonaventure) —G —1950–51
Nicksick, Michael (Pittsburgh) —B—1935
Nisby, John (College of Pacific) —E —1957–60
Nobile, Leo (Penn. State) —G—1948–49
Noppenberg, John (Miami) —B—1940–41
Nosich, John—T—1938
Nuzum, Gerald (New Mexico A & M) —B —1948–51
O'Brien, John (Florida) —E—1954–56
O'Delli, Melvin (Duquesne) —B—1945
Oehler, John (Purdue) —C—1933–34
Oelerich, John (St. Ambrose) —B—1938
Olejniczak, Stanley (Pittsburgh) —T—1935
Olenski, Mitchell (Alabama) —T—1948
Olszewski, Albert (Pittsburgh) —E—1945

O'Malley, Joseph (Georgia) —E—1955–56
O'Neil, Robert (Notre Dame) —E—1956–57
Orr, James (Georgia) —E—1958–60
Ortman, Charles (Michigan) —Q—1951
Palmer, Thomas (Wake Forest) —T
—1953–54
Papach, George (Purdue) —B—1948–49
Pastin, Frank (Waynesburg) —G—1942
Patrick, Frank (Pittsburgh) —B—1940
Patrick, John (Penn. State) —Q
—1941, 45–46
Patterson, William (Baylor) —B—1940
Pavko, Stonko (Idaho) —G—1939–40
Pense, Leon (Arkansas) —B—1945
Perko, John (Duquesne) —G
—1937–40, 45–47
Perry, Lowell (Michigan) —E—1956
Petchel, John (Duquesne) —B—1945
Petrella, John (Penn. State) —B—1945
Pierre, John (Pittsburgh) —E—1945
Pirro, Rocco (Catholic Univ.) —G
—1940–41, 45
Pittman, Melvin (Hardin-Simmons) —C
—1935
Platukas, George (Duquesne) —E—1938–41
Popovich, John (St. Vincent's) —B—1945
Postus, Albert (Villanova) —B—1945
Potts, William (Villanova) —B—1934
Priatko, William (Pittsburgh) —G—1957
Quatse, Jess (Pittsburgh) —T—1933–34
Raborn, Carroll (Southern Methodist
Univ.) —C—1936–37
Rado, Alex (West Virginia Tech.) —B—
1934
Rado, George (Duquesne) —G—1935–37
Ragunis, Vincent (Virginia Military Inst.)
—B—1949
Rajkovich, Peter (Detroit) —B—1934
Raskowski, Leo (Ohio State) —T—1933
Rechichar, Albert (Tennessee) —B—1960
Reed, Leroy (Mississippi) —E—1958
Reger, John (Pittsburgh) —C—1955–60
Renfro, William (Memphis State) —T—
1960
Repko, Joseph (Boston College) —T
—1946–47
Reynolds, James (Oklahoma A & M) —B
—1946
Reynolds, William (Pittsburgh) —B—1958
Rhoads, Donald (Washington & Jefferson)
—T—1933
Ribble, Loran (Hardin-Simmons) —G
—1934–35
Richards, Perry (Detroit) —E—1957
Richeson, Raymond (Alabama) —G—1950
Riffle, Richard (Albright) —B—1941–42
Roberts, John (Georgia) —B—1934
Robinson, Gilbert (Catawba) —E—1933
Robinson, John (Missouri State Northeast)
—T—1938
Rodack, Michael (Western Reserve) —G
—1942
Rogel, Frank (Penn. State) —B—1950–57
Rogers, Cullen (Texas A & M) —B—1946
Rorison, James (Southern California) —T
—1938

Rozelle, Aubrey (Delta State) —E—1957
Ryan, Edward (St. Mary's, Cal.) —E—1948
Rykowski, Frank (Purdue) —G—1940
Samuel, Donald (Oregon State) —B
—1949–50
Samuelson, Carl (Nebraska) —T—1948–51
Sandberg, Sigmund (Iowa Wesleyan) —T
—1935–37
Sandefur, Wayne (Purdue) —B—1936
Sanders, John (Southern Methodist Univ.)
—1940–42
Sandig, Curtis (St. Mary's, Tex.) —B—1942
Sandusky, Michael (Maryland) —G
—1957–60
Saulis, Samuel—G—1938
Saumer, Sylvester (St. Olaf) —B—1934
Scales, Charles (Indiana) —B—1960
Scarbath, Jack (Maryland) —Q—1956
Scherer, Bernard (Nebraska) —E—1939
Schiechl, John (Santa Clara) —C—1941–42
Schmidt, John (Carnegie Tech) —C—1940
Schuecke, Warren (Wisconsin) —B—1939
Schultz, Eberle (Oregon State) —G
—1941–42
Schwartz, Elmer (Washington State) —B
—1933
Schweder, John (Pennsylvania) —G
—1951–55
Scudero, Joseph (San Francisco) —B—1960
Seabright, Charles (West Virginia) —Q
—1946–50
Sebastian, Michael (Pittsburgh) —B—1935
Shaffer, George (Washington & Jefferson)
—Q—1933
Shepard, Charles (Texas State North) —B
—1956
Sheriff, Stanley (California Polytech.) —G
—1954
Shields, Burrel (John Carroll) —B—1954
Shipkey, Gerald (U.C.L.A.) —B—1948–52
Shurtz, Hubert (Louisiana State Univ.)
—T—1948
Simerson, John (Purdue) —C—1958
Simington, Milton (Arkansas) —G—1942
Sinkovitz, Frank (Duke) —C—1947–52
Sirochman, George (Duquesne) —G—1942
Sites, Vincent (Pittsburgh) —E—1936–37
Skladany, Joseph (Pittsburgh) —E—1934
Skorich, Nicholas (Cincinnati) —G
—1946–48
Skoronski, Edward (Purdue) —C—1935–36
Slater, Walter (Tennessee) —B—1947
Smith, Benjamin (Alabama) —E—1934–35
Smith, Billy Ray (Arkansas) —G—1958–60
Smith, Stuart (Bucknell) —B—1937–38
Smith, Truett (Mississippi State) —B
—1950–51
Snyder, William (Ohio) —G—1934–35
Sommers, George (LaSalle) —T—1941–42
Sorce, Ross (Georgetown) —T—1945
Sortet, William (West Virginia) —E
—1933–40
Souchak, Frank (Pittsburgh) —E—1939
Spinks, Jack (Alcorn A & M) —B—1952–53
Starret, Benjamin (St. Mary's—Cal.) —B
—1941

Stautner, Ernest (Boston College) —T
—1950–60
Stehower, Ronald (Colorado State) —T—
1960
Stenn, Paul (Villanova) —T—1947
Stock, John (Pittsburgh) —E—1956
Stofko, Edward (Wake Forest) —B—1945
Stough, Glen (Duke) —T—1945
Strutt, Arthur (Duquesne) —B—1935–36
Suhey, Steven (Penn. State) —G—1948–49
Sulima, George (Boston Univ.) —E
—1952–54
Sullivan, Frank (Loyola, La.) —C—1940
Sullivan, Robert (Holy Cross) —B—1947
Sutherin, Donald (Ohio State) —B—1959–60
Szot, Walter (Bucknell) —T—1949–50
Tanguay, James (New York Univ.) —B
—1933
Tarasovic, George (Louisiana State Univ.)
—C—1952–60
Tatum, James (North Carolina State) —E
—1938
Taylor, Jess (Baylor) —C—1956
Tennant, John (Wisconsin) —B—1941
Tepe, Louis (Duke) —C—1953–55
Tesser, Raymond (Carnegie Tech) —E
—1933–34
Thompson, Thomas (Tulsa) —B
—1937–38, 40
Tiller, Morgan (Denver) —E—1941, 45
Tinsley, Sidney (Clemson) —B—1945
Titus, George (Holy Cross) —C—1945–46
Tomasetti, Louis (Bucknell) —B—1939–40
Tomasio, Andrew (Temple) —B—1942, 46
Tomlinson, Richard (Kansas) —G—1950–51
Tommerson, Clarence (Wisconsin) —B
—1938
Tosi, Flavio (Boston College) —E—1939
Tracy, John Thomas (Tennessee) —B—
1958–60
Tsoutsouvas, Louis (Stanford) —C—1938
Turley, John (Ohio Wesleyan) —B
—1935–36
Varrichione, Frank (Notre Dame) —T
—1955–60
Vaughn, John (Bellfont) —B—1933–35
Vidoni, Victor (Duquesne) —E—1935–36
Walsh, William (Notre Dame) —C—1949–54
Warren, Busit (Tennessee) —B—1945
Watson, Sidney (Northeastern) —B
—1955–57
Weed, Thurlow (Ohio State) —B—1955
Weinberg, Henry (Duquesne) —G—1934
Weinstock, Isadore (Pittsburgh) —B
—1937–38
Weisenbaugh, Henry (Pittsburgh) —B
—1935
Wells, William (Michigan State) —B—1957
Wendlick, Joseph (Oregon State) —E—1941
Wenzel, Ralph (Tulane) —E—1941
Westfall, Edgar (Ohio Wesleyan) —B—1933
Wetzel, Damon (Ohio State) —B—1935
Whalen, Thomas (Catholic Univ.) —B
—1933
Wheeler, Ernest (North Dakota State) —B
—1939

White, Byron (Colorado) —B—1938
White, Paul (Michigan) —B—1947
Wiehl, Joseph (Duquesne) —T—1935
Wiley, John (Waynesburg) —T—1946–50
Williams, Donald (Texas) —G—1941
Williams, Joseph (Ohio State) —B—1939
Williamson, Frederick (Northwestern)
—B—1960
Wilson, John (Western Reserve) —E—1938
Wilson, William (Gonzaga) —E—1938
Woudenberg, John (Denver) —T—1940–42
Wren, Lowe (Missouri) —B—1960
Wukits, Albert (Duquesne) —C—1945
Wydo, Frank (Cornell) —T—1947–57
Young, Richard (Chattanooga) —B—1957
Younger, Paul (Grambling) —B—1958
Yurchey, John (Duquesne) —B—1940
Zaninello, Silvio (Duquesne) —Q—1934–37
Zombek, Joseph (Pittsburgh) —E—1954–55
Zopetti, Frank (Duquesne) —B—1941

PORTSMOUTH SPARTANS
(1930–33)

Alford, Eugene (Texas Tech) —B—1931–33
Ambrose, Walter (Carroll) —T—1930
Armstrong, Robert (Missouri) —T—1931–32
Bennett, Charles (Indiana) —B—1930
Bodenger, Morris (Tulane) —G—1931–33
Boswell, Benjamin (Texas Christian Univ.)
—T—1933
Bowdoin, James (Alabama) —G—1933
Braidwood, Charles (Chattanooga) —E
—1930
Brown, Richard (Iowa State) —C—1930
Burleson, John (Southern Methodist
Univ.) —G—1923
Caddell, Ernest (Stanford) —B—1933
Cavosie, John (Butler) —B—1931–33
Christensen, George (Oregon)—T—1931–33
Christenson, Koester (Michigan State) —E
—1930
Clark, Earl (Colorado College)—Q—1931–33
Davis, Sylvester (Geneva) —B—1932–33
DeWeese, Byrne (Cincinnati) —G—1930
Douds, Forrest (Washington & Jefferson)
—T—1930–31
Edbing, Harry (St. Mary's—Cal.) —E
—1930–33
Eby, Byron (Ohio State) —B—1930
Elser, Earl (Butler) —B—1933
Emerson, Grover (Texas) —G—1931–33
Fleckenstein, William (Iowa) —C—1930
Glassgow, Willis (Iowa) —B—1930
Grant, Aaron (Chattanooga) —C—1930
Griffen, Harold (Iowa) —C—1930–32
Gutowsky, Leroy (Oklahoma City Univ.)
—B—1932–33
Hanny, Frank (Indiana) —T—1930
Harris, Thomas (Ohio State) —T—1930
Hastings, George (Ohio) —T—1931
Holm, Bernard (Alabama) —B—1931
Hunter, Romey (Marshall) —B—1933
Jennings, William (Haskell) —E—1930
Johnson, Robert (Chattanooga) —T—1930
Joseph, Zern (Miami—Ohio) —E—1930

Kahl, Cyrus (North Dakota) —B—1930–31
Lee, Hilary (Oklahoma) —G—1931
Lewis, Loren (Northwestern) —B—1930
Long, Louis (Southern Methodist Univ.)
—T—1931
Lumpkin, Roy (Georgia Tech) —B
—1930–33
Lyon, George (Kansas State) —T—1930
McClain, Mayes (Iowa) —B—1930–31
McKalip, William (Oregon State) —E
—1931–32
McMullen, Daniel (Nebraska) —G—1933
Marks, Lawrence (Indiana) —B—1931
Meyer, Ernest (Geneva) —G—1930
Miller, J. Robert (Wittenberg) —C—1931
Mitchell, Granville (Davis-Elkins) —E
—1931–33
Molesworth, Keith (Monmouth) —Q—1930
Novotny, Raymond (Ashland) —B—1930
Peterson, Lester (Texas) —E—1930–31
Presnell, Glenn (Nebraska) —Q—1931–33
Randolph, Clare (Indiana) —C—1931–33
Rascher, Ambrose (Indiana) —G—1932
Ringwalt, Carroll (Indiana) —C—1930
Robert, Frederick (Iowa) —T—1930–32
Ryan, John (Detroit) —T—1930
Schaake, Elmer (Kansas) —B—1933
Scharer, Edward (Notre Dame) —B—1930
Schluesner, Vincent (Iowa) —T—1930–31
Schneller, John (Wisconsin) —B—1933
Schwartz, Elmer (Washington State) —B
—1931
Shelly, Dexter (Texas) —B—1931
Smith, Clyde (Missouri) —B—1930–31
Stennett, Frederick (St. Mary's Cal.) —B
—1931
Thayer, Harry (Tennessee) —T—1933
Wager, John (Carthage) —C—1931–33
Waters, Dale (Florida) —E—1931
Weaver, Charles (Chicago) —C—1930
Wesley, Lecil (Alabama) —C—1930

POTTSVILLE MAROONS (1925–28)
Barrett, John (Detroit) —C—1927
Beck, Clarence (Penn. State) —T—1925–28
Benkert, Henry (Rutgers) —B—1926
Berry, Charles (Lafayette) —E—1925–26
Brown, Jesse (Pittsburgh) —B—1926
Bucher, Frank (Detroit) —E—1925–26
Budd, John (Lafayette) —T—1927–28
Carpe, Joseph (Millikin) —T—1928
Carr, Charles (Syracuse) —B—1927–28
Caywood, Lester (St. John's) —G—1927
Chapman, Thomas (Mt. St. Mary's) —T
—1925
Charles, Winston (William & Mary) —B
—1927
Colt—T—1928
Dayhoff, Harry (Bucknell) —B—1925
Doane, Joseph (Tufts) —B—1927
Doyle, Edward (West Point) —E—1925
Erickson, Walden (Washington) —T—1927
Ernst, John (Lafayette) —B—1925–28
Flanagan, William (Pittsburgh) —B
—1925–26

Ford, Adrian (Lafayette) —B—1927
French, Walter (West Point) —B—1925

International News Photo

CHARLES BERRY *(left)*, CAPTAIN OF THE POTTS-
VILLE MAROONS, GREETS GEORGE TRAFTON,
HEAD MAN OF THE CHICAGO BEARS, BEFORE
A GAME IN 1925. BERRY LATER BECAME A
TOP UMPIRE IN MAJOR LEAGUE BASEBALL
AND AN OFFICIAL IN THE NATIONAL FOOT-
BALL LEAGUE

Goodwin, Earl (Bucknell) —E—1928
Goodwin, Myrl (Bucknell) —B—1928
Hathaway, Russell (Indiana) —T—1925–26
Henry, Wilbur (Washington & Jefferson)
—T—1927–28
Hoffman, William (Lehigh) —G—1927
Hughes, Dennis (Georgetown) —C—1925
Hultman, Vivian (Michigan State) —E
—1927
Jawish, Henry (Georgetown) —G—1926
Jean, Walter (Bethany) —G—1927
Kenneally, George (St. Bonaventure) —B
—1926–28
Kiesling, Walter (St. Thomas) —G—1928
Kirkleski, Frank (Lafayette) —B—1927–28
Labengood, Howard (Villanova) —B—1925
Latone, Anthony—B—1925–28
McNally, John (St. John—Minnesota) —B
—1928
Mahrt, Armin (West Virginia) —B—1925
Marino—B—1928
Maver, Ernest (Catholic Univ.) —E—1927
Millman, Robert (Lafayette) —B—1926–27
Moore, Walter (Lafayette) —B—1927
Moran, Francis (Grinnell) —B—1928
Mullen, Thomas (Chicago) —E—1927–28
Neihaus, Francis (Washington & Jefferson)
—B—1926
Norman, Willard (Washington & Jefferson)

—B—1928
Oliker, Aaron (West Virginia) —E—1926
Osborn, Robert (Penn. State) —G—1925—28
Racis, Frank—G—1925—28
Rauch, Richard (Penn. State) —G—1925
Rebseaman, Paul (Centenary) —C—1927
Roberts, Charles (Iowa State) —B—1927
Rooney, Joseph—E—1928
Scharer Edward (Notre Dame) —B—1927
Sonnenberg, Gustave (Dartmouth) —T —1925
Stein, Herbert (Washington & Jefferson) —C—1925—26, 28
Stein, Russell (Pittsburgh) —T—1925
Underwood, John (Iowa State) —G—1927
Wedge, Utley (Pennsylvania) —T—1927
Welsh, James (Colgate) —G—1926—27
Wentz, Byron (Penn State) —B—1925—28
Wissinger, Zonar (Pittsburgh) —G—1926
Youngfleish, Francis (Villanova) —C—1927

PROVIDENCE STEAMROLLERS
(1925—31)

August, Edward (Villanova) —B—1931
Braney, John (Syracuse) —G—1925—26
Brennan, Robert (Georgetown) —E—1931
Bristow, George (Nebraska) —B—1925
Burke, Charles (Dartmouth) —B—1925—26
Carney, Harold (Albright) —E—1931
Connors, Stafford (New Hampshire) —B —1925
Conzelman, James (Washington of Mo.) —B—1927—30
Cronin, John (Boston College) —B
Cronin, William (Boston College) —B —1927—31
Crowley, James (Notre Dame) —B—1925
Dacata, Frederick (Providence College) —B —1931
Doane, Joseph (Tufts) —B—1927
Donahue, John (Boston College) —T—1926
Donovan, John (Holy Cross) —T—1931
Douds, Forrest (Washington & Jefferson) —T—1930
Duffy, Patrick (Dayton) —B—1929 —1927—30
Eckstein, Adolph (Brown) —C—1925—26
Edwards, Charles (Brown) —B—1930—31
Edward, Leslie (Washington & Jefferson) —B—1930
Eschbach, Herbert (Penn. State) —C —1930—31
Fitzgerald, Donald (Holy Cross) —C—1931
Fleischman, Godfrey (Purdue) —G —1927—29
Garvey, Arthur "Hec" (Notre Dame) —C— 1929
Garvey, Francis (Holy Cross) —T—1925—26
Gentry, Cassius (Oklahoma) —G—1930—31
Golembeski, Anthony (Holy Cross) —E —1925—26, 29
Goodbread, Royce (Florida) —B—1931
Graham, Alfred (Dayton) —G—1930—31
Griggs, Cecil (Austin) —B—1926
Gulian, Michael (Brown) —T—1925—27

Haddon, Aldous (Washington & Jefferson) —B—1927—30
Hagenbuckle, Vernon (Dartmouth) —E —1926
Hanny, Frank (Indiana) —T—1928—30
Harvey, Norman (Detroit) —E—1928—29
Higgins, Robert (Penn. State) —B—1925
Holm, Anthony (Alabama) —B—1930
Hummell, Charles (Lafayette) —B—1925—26
Irvin, Cecil (Davis-Elkins) —T—1931
Jackson, Grady (Southwestern) —T —1928—30
Jennings, William (Haskell) —E—1929
Keefer, Jackson (Brown) —B—1926
Koplaw, Joseph (Boston College) —T—1926
Koslowski, Joseph (Boston College) —T —1925—27, 30
Kucharski, Theodore (Holy Cross) —E —1930—31
Laird, James (Colgate) —B—1925—28
Latone, Anthony—B—1930—31
Lester, Harold (Providence College) —E —1926
Longo, Anthony (Conn. State) —G—1928
Lowe, George (Lafayette) —E—1925, 27
Lynch, Edward (Holy Cross) —E—1927
McArthur, John (Santa Clara) —C —1930—31
McBride, John (Syracuse) —B—1929
McCrillis, Edward (Brown) —G—1926
McGlone, Joseph (Harvard) —B—1926
McGoldrick, Hugh (Lehigh) —B—1925
McGuirk, Warren (Boston College) —T —1929—30
McIntosh, Daniel (Rhode Island State) —B —1925—26
MacPhee, Walter (Princeton) —B—1925—26
Maloney, Gerald (Dartmouth) —E—1925
Manning, Joseph (Fordham) —B—1926
Meeker, Herbert (Washington State) —B —1930—31
Miller, Don (Notre Dame) —B—1925
Mishel, David (Brown) —B—1927
Murtagh, George (Georgetown) —E—1926
O'Connell, Grattman (Boston College) —E —1927
Oden, Olaf (Brown) —B—1925—31
Pape, Orrin (Iowa) —B—1931
Pearce, Walter (Illinois) —B—1925
Peters, Forest (Illinois) —1930
Pierotti, Albert (Washington Lee) —C —1927—28
Pohlman, John (Brown) —B—1928
Pollard, Fritz (Brown) —B—1925
Pope, Lester (Connecticut) —B—1931
Pritchard, William (Penn. State) —B —1927—28
Pyne, John (Boston College) —T—1931
Racis, Frank—G—1930
Rhenquist, Milton (Bethany) —C—1928—31
Riopel, Albert (Holy Cross) —B—1925
Rose, Alfred (Texas) —E—1930—31
Sampson, Seneca (Brown) —B—1926
Schein, Joseph (Brown) —T—1931
Scott, Ralph (Wisconsin) —T—1926
Share, Nathan (Tufts) —G—1925—26

Sheehan, John (Boston College) —B—1925
Shelly, Dexter (Texas) —B—1931
Shockley, Arnold (Southwestern State
  College) —G—1928—29

Shurtleff, Bertrand (Brown) —T—1925
Simmons, James (Oklahoma Southwest)
  —B—1928
Smith, Clyde (Missouri) —C—1928—30
Smith, Leo (Providence) —E—1928
Smith, Orland (Brown) —T—1927—29
Smith, Ray (Missouri) —C—1931
Smythe, James (Centre) —B—1926
Sofish, Alexander (Grove City) —G—1931
Sonnenberg, Gustave (Dartmouth) —T
  —1927—28, 30
Spellman, John (Brown) —E—1925—31
Stifler, James (Brown) —E—1926—27
Surabian, Zareh (Williams) —T—1927
Sweet, Frederick (Brown) —B—1925—27
Talbot, John (Brown) —E—1926
Thomas, William (Penn. State) —B
  —1925—26
Titmas, Herbert (Syracuse) —B—1931
Triggs, John (Providence College) —B
  —1926
Webber, Howard (Kansas State) —E—1930
Welch, Gilbert (Pittsburgh) —B—1929
Wentworth, Shirley (New Hampshire) —B
  —1925—26
Wentz, Byron (Penn. State) —B—1930—31
Wesley, Lecil (Alabama) —C—1926—27
Williams, Arthur (Connecticut State) —B
  —1928—30
Wilson, Abraham (Washington) —G
  —1927—29
Wilson, George (Washington) —B—1927—29
Woodruff, Lee (Mississippi) —B—1931
Wynne, Chester (Notre Dame) —B—1929
Young, Herman (Detroit) —E—1930
Young, Leslie (North Dakota) —B—1925—27
Young, Sam (Detroit) —E—1930

RACINE LEGION (1922—24, 1926)

Barr, Wallace (Wisconsin) —B—1923—24, 26
Barry, George (Beloit) —T—1922
Bauer, Herbert (Baldwin-Wallace) —T
  —1923
Baxter, Ernest (Centre) —B—1923
Bernard, George—G—1926
Bentzien, Alfred (Marquette) —G—1924
Bieberstein, Adolph (Wisconsin) —G—1926
Boettcher, Fred (Rice) —B—1926
Braman, William (Colgate) —T—1923
Brumm, Roman (Wisconsin) —G
  —1922, 24, 26
Burnside—B—1926
Croft, Jack (Utah State) —G—1924
Dalton (Beloit) —B—1922
Doolan, George—C—1922
Dressen, Charles—Q—1922—23
Elliott, Alvah (Wisconsin) —B—1922—24
Fahay, John (Marquette) —B—1926
Foster, Robert—T—1922—23
Gaiver, Einar (North Dakota) —E—1924

Gavier, William (Notre Dame) —B—1924
Gay, Kenneth (Minnesota) —T—1926
George, Karl (Carroll) —G—1922
Gillo, Henry (Colgate) —B—1922—24, 26
Glennie—E—1926
Gorman, Earl—G—1922—23
Halladay, Richard (Chicago) —E—1922—24
Hanley, Richard (Washington State) —B
  —1924
Hardy, Isham (William & Mary) —G—1926
Hartong, George (Chicago) —G—1922—24
Hayes, Norbert (Marquette) —E—1922
Heinisch, Fred—B—1923—26
Hobscheid, Frank (Chicago) —G—1926
Johnson, Frederick (Notre Dame) —B
  —1922—24
Kernwein, Graham (Chicago) —B—1926
King, Ralph (Chicago) —T—1924
Langhoff, Irving (Marquette) —B—1922—23
Lindstrom—1922
Linnan, Francis (Marquette) —T—1922, 26
Long, Thomas (Ohio State) —G—1923
Longstreet, Roy (Iowa State) —C—1926
Lunde, Lester (Ripon) —G—1922—24
McCaw, William (Indiana) —E—1923
McElwain, William (Northwestern) —B
  —1926
McGill—C—1922
Mathews, Bob Orr (Annapolis) —E—1926
Meyers, Paul (Wisconsin) —E—1923
Miller, Henry (Pennsylvania State) —E
  —1922—23
Mintun, John—C—1923—24, 26
Mohardt, John (Notre Dame) —B—1924
Mueller, Ewald (Northwestern) —G
  1922—24
Murphy, James (St. Thomas) —B—1926
Murrah, W. E. (Texas A & M)—T—1922—24
Myers, Cyril (Ohio State) —E—1923
Oldham—E—1926
O'Reilly—G—1924
Palmer, Charles (Northwestern) —B—1924
Pearson, Dudley (Notre Dame) —B—1922
Reichow, Charles (St. Thomas,Minn.) —
  B—1926
Rhenstrom—E—1922
Roessler, Fritz (Marquette) —E—1922—24
Romney, Milton (Chicago) —B—1923—24
Shekleton, Vincent (Marquette) —G—1922
Smith, Earl (Ripon) —E—1923—24
Strickland, William (Lombard) —G—1923
Starr, Wallace (Wisconsin) —B—1926
Stark, Howard (Wisconsin) —T—1923
Sparr, Edwin (Carroll) —T—1926
Webster, Fred (Colgate) —B—1924
Williams, Rolland (Wisconsin) —B—1923
Woodin, Howard (Marquette) —G—1922

ROCHESTER KODAKS (1921—25)

(Also played as Jeffersons)

Adams, Joseph—T—1924
Alexander, Joseph (Syracuse) —G—1921—22
Anderson, Edward (Notre Dame) —E—1922
Anderson, Willard (Syracuse) —B—1922, 24
Argus, Robert—B—1921—25

Bachmaier, Joseph—G—1921–24
Bancroft, Hugh (Alfred)—E—1923
Barron, James (Georgetown)—T—1921
Bedford, William Eugene (Southern Methodist Univ.)—E—1925
Bentz, Edward—E—1922
Berry, Howard (Pennsylvania)—B—1921
Boynton, Benjamin (Williams)—Q—1922
Clark, Harold "Butch" (Fordham)—E—1922–25
Coaker, John—T—1924
Connors, Hamilton—E—1925
Culver, Frank (Syracuse)—C—1924
Dooley, John (Syracuse)—G—1922, 24–25
Dumoe, Joseph (Syracuse)—E—1921
Emslie—G—1923
Foster, Fred (Syracuse)—B—1923–24
French, Walter (West Point)—B—1922
Gavigan, Michael (St. Bonaventure)—B—1923
Grigg, Cecil (Austin)—Q—1925
Hanricus, Ralph—B—1922
Hasbrouck, John (Rutgers)—B—1921
Hoffman, Arnold (Syracuse)—T—1925
Hurtjun—B—1923
Kasper, Thomas (Notre Dame)—B—1923
Kellogg, William (Syracuse)—B—1925
Kelly, Charles (Northwestern)—C—1925
King, Richard (Harvard)—B—1922
Laird, James (Colgate)—B—1921
Lehrer, Christopher—B—1922
Lowery, Darby (Ursinus)—T—1921–25
Lynch, Edward (Catholic Univ.)—E—1925
McShea, Joseph (Rochester)—G—1923
Mackert, Robert (West Virginia)—T—1925
Martineau, Roy (Syracuse)—B—1924–25
Matteo, Francis (Syracuse)—T—1922–25
Morrisey, Frank (Boston College)—T—1921
Muldoon, Matthew (St. Mary's Cal.)—T—1922
Mulvey, Vincent (Syracuse)—B—1923
Noonan, Gerald (Fordham)—B—1921–24
Peyton, Leo—B—1923–24
Pearlman, Lester (Pittsburgh)—G—1924
Robertson, Harry (Syracuse)—T—1922
Roy, Elmer—E—1921–22, 25
Sawyers, Herman (Syracuse)—T—1922
Sheard, Alfred (St. Lawrence)—B—1923–25
Smith, Henry (Lancaster)—C—1921–25
Smythe, Louis (Texas)—B—1924–25
Steele, Clifford (Syracuse)—B—1921–22
Thomas, Carl (Pennsylvania)—G—1921
Thompson, George (Syracuse)—G—1922
Weltman, Lawrence (Syracuse)—B—1922
Witter, Raymond (Syracuse)—C—1921–23
Wood, James—G—1921–25
Wray, Ludlow (Pennsylvania)—C—1922
Wynne, Chester (Notre Dame)—B—1922
Usher, Louis (Syracuse)—T—1921
Ziff, David (Syracuse)—E—1925

ROCK ISLAND (1921—25)

Anderson, Edward (Notre Dame)—E—1923
Anderson, Willard (Syracuse)—B—1925
Anderson, Oscar (Colgate)—B—1925

Armstrong, John (Columbia)—B—1923–25
Ashbaugh, William (Pittsburgh)—B—1924
Barker, Richard (Iowa State)—G—1921
Belding, Lester (Iowa)—E—1925
Bernstein, Joseph (Tulsa)—G—1923–25
Bradshaw, Wesley (Baylor)—B—1924
Bridgeford, Lane (Knox College)—B—1921–22
Brindley, Walter (Drake)—B—1921–22
Buland, Walter—T—1921, 24
Burton, Lyle (DePauw)—G—1924–25
Butler, William (Marquette)—B—1923
Casteel, Miles (Kalamazoo)—B—1922
Chicken, Fred—B—1921
Clago, Walter (Detroit)—E—1922
Conzelman, James (Washington of Mo.)—B—1921–22
Cotton, Forrest (Notre Dame)—T—1923, 25
Coughlin, Frank (Notre Dame)—B—1921
Coyle, Frank (Detroit)—E—1924–25
DeClerk, Frank (St. Ambrose)—C—1921–25
DesJardiens, Paul (Chicago)—G—1921
Duggan, Edward (Notre Dame)—B—1921
Earpe, Francis (Monmoth)—G—1921, 22
Elliott, Alvah (Wisconsin)—B—1925
Fitzgerald, Freeman (Notre Dame)—B—1921
Gaiver, Einar (Georgia Tech.)—B—1923
Gavin, Patrick "Buck"—B—1921–25—1922–25
Gorgal, Alexander—B—1923
Gunderson, Borge (Wisconsin)—G—1921
Guyon, Joseph (Carlisle)—B—1924
Hasbrouck, John (Rutgers)—B—1921
Hayes, Gerald (Notre Dame)—E—1921
Healy, Edward (Dartmouth)—T—1921, 22
Hendrian, Warren (Pittsburgh)—B—1925
Herman, Edward (Northwestern)—E—1925
Johnson, Frederick (Notre Dame)—B—1922
Jones, Jerry (Notre Dame)—T—1922
Kadesky, Max (Iowa)—E—1923
Keefe, Emmett (Notre Dame)—G—1921–22
Kolls, Louis (St. Ambrose)—C—1921–25
Kraehe, Oliver (Washington of Mo.)—G—1922
Kramer—G—1924
Kuehl, Walter (Dubuque)—B—1923
Lamb, Roy (Lombard)—B—1925
Lauer, Harold (Detroit)—B—1922
Little Twig (Carlisle)—T—1924–25
Lowe, George (Fordham)—B—1923
Lungren, Charles (Swarthmore)—B—1923
Lyle, Dewey (Minnesota)—E—1921–22
Malone, Grover (Notre Dame)—B—1921
Mansfield, Jerry—B—1921
Marshall, Robert (Minnesota)—E—1921
McCarthy, Howard (Notre Dame)—B—1924–25
Menepee, Victor—E—1921
Nichols, Sidney (Illinois)—T—1921
Novack, Edward—B—1921-22, 25
Phelan, Robert (Notre Dame)—B—1923–24
Quinn, George—B—1921
Roberts, Walcott (Annapolis)—E—1924
Rooney, Joseph—E—1924–25

photo by Eckman

ROCK ISLAND FOOTBALL TEAM—1923

Bottom row (*left to right*): Walter Kuehl, b; Robert Phelan, b; John Armstrong, b;
William Gavier, b.
Middle row: Samuel "Mike" Wilson, e; Fred Slater, t; Dale Sies, g; Louis Kolls, c;
Earl Smith, e; Joseph Bernstein, g; Max Kadesky, e.
Top row: Thompson, president; Alexander Gorgal, b; George Lowe, b; Pha,
trainer; Charles Lungren, b; Frank DeClerk, c; Rimmerman, manager.

Ryan, James (Notre Dame) —B—1924
Scott, Edward (Monmouth) —G—1924
Schimmel—B—1925
Sies, Dale (Pittsburgh) —G—1923
Slater, Fred (Iowa) —T—1922-25
Smith, Earl (Ripon) —E—1923
Swanson, Eyar (Lombard) —E—1925
Thompson, George —E —1923-25
Thorpe, James (Carlisle) —B—1924, 25
Travis, J. Edward (Missouri) —T—1921
Ursella, Rueben—B—1921, 24-25
Usher, Edward (Michigan) —E—1922
Vandello—C—1921
Voss, Walter (Detroit) —E—1922
Webber, Harry (Nebraska) —E—1923
Wenig, Obe (Morningside) —E—1921-22
Wiederquist, Chester (Washington &
Jefferson) —T—1925
Wiedich, Ralph (Kansas State Teachers)
—T—1926
Wilson, Samuel (Lehigh) —E—1923-24
Wyman, Arnold (Minnesota) —B—1921

. ST. LOUIS BROWNS (1923)

Andrews, Leroy (Kansas State Teachers)
—B—1923
Cardwell, John—B—1923
Casey, Albert (Arkansas) —B—1923
Grau, Arthur—E—1923
King, Richard (Harvard) —B—1923
Kraehe, Oliver (Washington of Mo.) —G
—1923
Kreinheder, Walter (Michigan) —C—1923
Meinhardt, George (St. Louis) —G—1923
Meese, Ward (Wabash) —E—1923
Milton, John (Southern California) —E—
1923
Murrah, W. E. (Texas A & M) —T—1923
Siegfreid, Orville (Washington & Jefferson)
—B—1923
Simpson, Eber (Wisconsin) —Q—1923
Travis, J. Edward (Missouri) —T—1923
Weller, Raymond (Nebraska) —T—1923
Werner, Sox (Missouri State) —B—1923
Wilder, Harold (Nebraska) —G—1923

Windburn, Ernest (Missouri State) —E —1923

Wycoff, Lee (Washburn) —T—1923

ST. LOUIS CARDINALS
(Formerly Chicago Cardinals)

Bates, Theodore (Oregon State) —T—1960
Childress, Joseph (Auburn) —B—1960
Conrad, Robert (Texas A & M) —B—1960
Cook, Edward (Notre Dame) —T—1960
Crow, John (Texas A & M) —B—1960
Culpepper, Edward (Alabama) —G—1960
Day, Thomas (North Carolina A & T) —G —1960
Driskill, Joseph (Louisiana State N.E.) — B—1960
Ellzey, Charles (Mississippi Southern) — B—1960
Fritsch, Ernest (Detroit) —C—1960
Fuller, Frank (Kentucky) —T—1960
Gillis, Daniel (Rice) —C—1960
Glick, Frederick (Colorado A & M) —B— 1960
Gray, Kenneth (Howard Payne) —B—1960
Hammack, Malcolm (Florida) —B—1960
Hill, James (Sam Houston) —B—1960
Hill, King (Rice) —Q—1960
Izo, George (Notre Dame) —Q—1960
Koman, William (North Carolina) —G— 1960
McGee, Michael (Duke) —G—1960
McInnis, Hugh (Mississippi Southern) — E—1960
Meinert, Dale (Oklahoma State) —G—1960
Memmelaar, Dale (Wyoming) —G—1960
Mestnik, Frank (Marquette) —B—1960
Norton, Jerry (Southern Methodist Univ.) —B—1960
Owens, Donald (Mississippi Southern) —T—1960
Owens, Luke (Kent State) —T—1960
Panfil, Kenneth (Purdue) —T—1960
Perry, Gerald (California) —T—1960
Rabold, Michael (Indiana) —G—1960
Randle, Ulmo (Virginia) —E—1960
Redmond, Thomas (Vanderbilt) —E—1960
Richards, Perry (Detroit) —E—1960
Roach, John (Southern Methodist Univ.) —Q—1960
Stacy, William (Mississippi State) —B—1960
Sugar, Leo (Purdue) —E—1960
Towns, Robert (Georgia) B—1960
Tracey, John (Texas A & M) —E—1960
West, William (Oregon) —B—1960
Wilson, Lawrence (Utah) —B—1960

ST. LOUIS GUNNERS (1934)

Alford, Eugene (Texas Tech.) —B—1934
Casper, Charles (Texas Christian Univ.) —B—1934
Corzine, Lester (Davis-Elkins) —B—1934
Diehl, Gordon (Idaho) —G—1934
Elser, Earl (Butler) —B—1934
Gladden, James Mack (Missouri) —E—1934

Herber—G—1934
Johnstone, Chester (Elmhurst) —B—1936
LaPresta, Ben (St. Louis) —B—1934
Lay, Russell (Michigan State) —G—1934
Lyon, George (Kansas State) —T—1934
McGirl, Leonard (Missouri) —G—1934
McLaughlin, James (Villanova) —B—1934
McLeod, Arthur (St. Louis) —C—1934
Montgomery, William (St. Louis) —T—1934
Moss, Paul (Purdue) —E—1934
Mulleneaux, Lee (Arizona) —B—1934
Munday, George (Kansas State Teachers) —T—1934
Norby, John (Idaho) —B—1934
Rapp, Manuel (St. Louis) —B—1934
Reynolds, Homer (Tulsa) —G—1934
Rogge, George (Iowa) —E—1934
Sandberg, Sigmund (Iowa Western) —T —1934
Senn, William (Knox) —B—1934
Weldin, Harold (Northwestern) —C—1934
Workman, Blake (Tulsa) —B—1934

SAN FRANCISCO 49ers (1950—60)

Albert, Frank (Stanford) —Q—1950—52
Aldridge, Benjamin (Oklahoma A & M) —B—1952
Arenas, Joseph (Omaha) —B—1951—57
Atkins, William (Auburn) —B—1958—59
Babb, Eugene (Austin) —B—1957—58
Babcock, Harry (Georgia) —E—1953—55
Bahnsen, Kenneth (Texas State Northern) —B—1953
Baker, David (Oklahoma) —B—1959—60
Banducci, Bruno (Stanford) —G—1950—54
Barnes, Lawrence (Colorado A & M) —B —1957
Beals, Alyn (Santa Clara) —E—1950—51
Beatty, Edward (Mississippi) —C—1955—56
Berry, Rex (Brigham Young) —B—1951—56
Boone, J. R. (Tulsa) —B—1952
Bosley, Bruce (West Virginia) —T—1956—60
Brodie, John (Stanford) —Q—1957—60
Brown, Hardy (Tulsa) —B—1952—56
Brown, Peter (Georgia Tech) —C—1953—54
Bruce, Gail (Washington) —E—1950—51
Brueckman, Charles (Pittsburgh) —C—1958
Brumfield, Jackson (Mississippi Southern) —E—1954
Bruney, Fred (Ohio State) —B—1953, 56
Burke, Donald (Southern California) —B —1950—54
Campbell, Marion (Georgia) —T—1954—55
Campora, Donald (College of Pacific) —T —1950, 52
Carapella, Albert (Miami) —T—1951—55
Carr, Edwin—B—1950
Carr, Paul (Houston) —B—1955—57
Cason, James (Louisiana State Univ.) —B —1950—52, 54
Cassara, Frank (St. Mary's—Cal.) —B—1954
Cathcart, Royal (Santa Barbara) —B—1950
Cathcart, Samuel (Santa Barbara) —B —1950, 52
Clark, Monte (Southern California) —T—

1959–60

Colchico, Daniel (San Jose State) –E–1960

Collins, Raymond (Louisiana State Univ.) –T–1950–52

Conner, Clyde (College of Pacific) –E –1956–60

Connolly, Theodore (Santa Clara) –G –1954, 56–60

Cross, Robert (Austin) –T–1956–57

Dahms, Thomas (San Diego) –T–1957

Davis, Thomas (Louisiana State Univ.) – K–1959–60

Dove, Edward (Colorado) –B–1959–60

Dow, Harley (San Jose State) –G–1950

Downs, Robert (Southern California) –G –1951

Dugan, Fred (Dayton) –E–1958–59

Dukes, Michael (Clemson) –B–1959

Duncan, Maurice (San Francisco State) –B –1954–55

Endress, Albert (San Francisco State) –E –1952

Evans, Raymond (Texas Mines) –T–1950

Feher, Nicholas (Georgia) –G–1951–54

Galiffa, Arnold (West Point) –B–1954

Garlin, Donald (Southern California) –B –1950

Gehrke, Clarence (Utah) –B–1950

Goad, Paul (Abilene Christian) –B–1956

Gonzaga, John–C–1956–59

Grgich, Visco (Santa Clara) –G–1950–52

Hantla, Robert (Kansas) –G–1954–55

Hardy, Carroll (Colorado) –B–1955

Harrison, Robert (Oklahoma) –B– 1959–60

Harkey, Lemuel (Kansas State Teachers) –B–1955

Hazeltine, Matthew (California) –C –1955–60

Henke, Edgar (Southern California) –E –1951–52, 56–60

Herchman, William (Texas Tech) –T –1956–59

Hobbs, Homer (Georgia) –G–1950

Hogland, Douglas (Oregon State) –T –1953–55

Holladay, Robert (Tulsa) –B–1956–57

Jessup, William (Southern California) –E –1951–52, 54, 56–58

Johnson, John (Arizona State) –B–1954–56

Johnson, William (Tyler, Tex. J. C.) –C –1951–56

Kelley, Gordon (Georgia) –B–1960

Kemp, John (Occidental) –Q–1959

Kraemer, Eldred (Pittsburgh) –G–1955

Krueger, Charles (Texas A & M) –E– 1959–60

Laughlin, Henry (Kansas) –B–1955

Ledyard, Harold (Chattanooga) –B–1953

Lillywhite, Verl (Southern California) –B –1950–51

Livingston, Howard–B–1950

Loyd, Alex (Oklahoma A & M) –E–1950

Luna, Robert (Alabama) –B–1955

Lyles, Leonard (Louisville) –B–1959–60

McCormick, Thomas (College of Pacific) –B–1956

McElhenny, Hugh (Washington) –B –1952–60

Mackey, Dee (Texas State East) –E–1960

Maderos, George (Chico State) –B –1955–56

Magac, Michael (Missouri) –G–1960

Manley, Joseph (Mississippi) –C–1953

Matthews, William (Georgia Tech) –T –1950, 53–55

Matuszak, Marvin (Tulsa) –C–1957–58

Mertens, Gerald (Drake) –E–1958–60

Meyers, Robert (Stanford) –B–1952

Michalik, Arthur (St. Ambrose) –G –1953–54

Miller, Harlon (Georgia Tech) –T–1953

Mixon, William (Georgia) –B–1953–54

Moegle, Richard (Rice) –B–1955–59

Momsen, Robert (Ohio State) –G–1952

Monachino, James (California) –B –1951, 53

Morrall, Earl (Michigan State) –Q–1956

Morris, Dennit (Oklahoma) –G–1958

Morris, George (Georgia Tech) –C–1956

Morton, John (Texas Christian Univ.) –B –1953

Morze, Frank (Boston College) –C –1957–60

Nix, John (Southern California) –E–1950

Nomellini, Leo (Minnesota) –T–1950–60

Norman, Haldo (Gustavus Adolphus) –E –1952

Norton, Jerry (Southern Methodist Univ.) –B–1960

O'Donahue, Patrick (Wisconsin) –E–1952

Osborne, Clarence (Arizona State) –B– 1959–60

Osborne, Thomas (Hastings) –E–1960

Owens, Raleigh (College of Idaho) –B –1957–60

Pace, James (Michigan) –B–1958–59

Palatella, Louis (Pittsburgh) –G–1955–58

Perry, Fletcher (Compton) –B–1950–60

Powell, Charles–E–1952–53, 55–57

Powers, James (Southern California) –B –1950–53

Quilter, Charles–T–1950

Rhode, Leonard (Utah State) –E–1960

Ridlon, James (Syracuse) –B–1957–60

Roberts, Cornelius (Southern California) –B–1959–60

Rubke, Karl (Southern California) –C –1957–60

Rucka, Leo (Rice) –C–1956

St. Clair, Robert (San Francisco) –T –1953–60

Sagely, Floyd (Arkansas) –E–1954

Salata, Paul (Southern California) –E –1950

Sandifer, Daniel (Louisiana State) –B –1950

Sardisco, Anthony (Tulane) –G–1956

Schabarum, Peter (California) –B –1951, 53–54

SAN FRANCISCO 49ers FOOTBALL TEAM 1951

First Row: *(Left to right)* Bill Johnson, Bruno Banducci, Frank Albert, Captain Norm Standlee, Visco Grgich, Al Beals, John Strzykalski.

Second Row: Jim Cason, Verl Lillywhite, Pete Wismann, Jim Lawson, Buck Shaw, Phil Bengston, Lowell Wagner, Joe Perry.

Third Row: Pete Schabarum, Ray Collins, Billy Wilson, Gordy Soltau, Leo Nomellini, Nick Feher, Al Carapella.

Fourth Row: Y. A. Tittle, Bishop Strickland, Don Burke, Joe Arenas, Jim Powers, Bill Jessup, Dave Sparks, Rex Berry.

Fifth Row: Frank Clark, Hamp Tanner, Bobby White. Jim Monachino, Hardy Brown, Ed Henke, Bob Kleckner.

Schmidt, Henry (Southern California) T—1959–60

Sharkey, Edward (Nevada and Duke) —G —1955–56

Shaw, Charles (Oklahoma A & M)—G—1950

Sherriff, Stanley (California Polytech.) —G —1956–57

Shoener, Harold (Iowa) —E—1950

Sitko, Emil (Notre Dame) —B—1950

Smith, Charles (Abilene Christian) —E —1956 ·

Smith, Ernest (Compton) —B—1955–56

Smith, J. D. (North Carolina A & T) —B —1956–60

Smith, Jerry (Wisconsin) —G—1952–56

Soltau, Gordon (Minnesota) —E—1950–58

Sparks, David (South Carolina) —G—1951

Spence, Julian (Sam Houston) —B—1957

Standlee, Norman (Stanford) —B—1950–52

Stickles, Montford (Notre Dame) —E—1960

Stits, William (U.C.L.A.) —B—1957–58

Stolhandske, Thomas (Texas) —E—1955

Strickland, Bishop (South Carolina) —B —1951

Strzykalski, John (Marquette) —B—1950–52

Tanner, Hampton (Georgia) —T—1951

Teresa, Anthony (San Jose State) —B—1958

Thomas, John (College of Pacific) — B—1958–60

Tidwell, William (Texas A & M) —B—1954

Tittle, Yelverton (Louisiana State) —Q —1951–60

Toneff, Robert (Notre Dame) —T —1952, 54–58

Tubbs, Jerry (Oklahoma) —B—1958–59

Van Doren, Robert (Southern California) —E—1953

Vaught, Theodore (Texas Christian Univ.) —E—1955

Wagner, Lowell (Southern California) —B —1950–53, 55

Walker, Val Joe (Southern Methodist Univ.) —B—1957

Waters, Robert (Presbyterian) —Q—1960

White, Robert (Stanford) —B—1951–52

Williams, John (Southern California) —B —1954

Wilson, Gerald (Auburn) —E—1960

Wilson, William (San Jose State) —E —1951–60

Wissmann, Peter (St. Louis) —C —1950–52, 54

Wittenborn, John (Missouri Southeastern) —G—1958–60

Woodson, Abe (Illinois) —B—1958–60

Youngelman, Sidney (Alabama) —G—1955

Yowarsky, Walter (Kentucky) —E—1958

STATEN ISLAND STAPLETONS
(1929—32)

Archoska, Julius (Syracuse) —E—1930
Baker, Roy (Southern California) —B—1931
Barabee, Robert (New York Univ.) —E —1931
Barbuti, Raymond (Syracuse) —B—1930
Brill, Martin (Notre Dame) —B—1931
Briante, Frank (New York Univ.) —B—1929
Brown, Frederick (New York Univ.) —B —1930
Buckley, Edward (Fordham) —B—1930
Bunyan, John (New York Univ.) —G —1929—30, 32
Campiglio, Robert (West Virginia Teachers) —B—1932
Clancy, Stuart (Holy Cross) —B—1931—32
Comstock, Edwin (Washington of Mo.) —G —1931
Constantine, Irving (Syracuse) —B—1931
Cunningham, Harold (Ohio State) —E —1931
Demas, George (Washington & Jefferson) —G—1932
Demyanovich, John—T—1930—32
Dryden —B—1930
Dunn, Robert (New York Univ.) —C—1929
Feather, Elwin (Kansas State) —B—1931
Finn, Bernard (Holy Cross) —B—1930, 32
Fitzgerald, Donald (Holy Cross) —C —1930—31
Follet, Beryl (New York Univ.) —B —1930—31
Frahm, Herald (Nebraska) —B—1932
Fry, Wesley (Iowa) —B—1932
Gantenbein, Milton (La Crosse) —E—1932
Garvey, Arthur "Hec" (Notre Dame) — —C—1931
Godwin, Walter (Georgia Tech) —G—1929
Grant, Ross (New York Univ.) —G—1932
Haines, Henry (Penn. State) —B—1930—31
Halpern, Robert (City College N.Y.) —G —1930
Hanson, Thomas (Temple) —B—1932
Hart, J. Leslie (Colgate) —B—1931
Henry, Wilbur (Washington & Jefferson) —T—1930
Hinton, J. W. "Grassy"' (Texas Christian Univ.) —B—1932
Intrieri, Marne (Loyola—Md.) —G—1932
Kamp, James (Oklahoma City Univ.) —T —1932
Kanya, Albert (Syracuse) —T—1931—32
Kloppenberg, Harry (Fordham) —E—1930
Koeninger, Arthur (Chattanooga) —C—1932
Kuzco, Paul (Villanova) —B—1929
Laird, James (Colgate) —G—1931
Lawrence, Edward (Brown) —B—1930
Leary, Thomas (Fordham) —E—1929
Ledbetter, Chester (Arkansas) —B—1932
Lomasney, Thomas (Villanova) —E—1929
Lord, John (Rutgers) —G—1929
Lundell, Robert (Gustavus-Adolphus) — E—1930

McClain, Mayes (Iowa) —B—1931
McGee, Howard (Kansas State) —G —1929, 32
Marshall, Cloyd (New York Univ.) —E —1931—32
Martin, Herschel (Missouri) —B—1929
Maynard, Lester (Rider) —B—1932
Miller, James (New York Univ.) —T —1929—31
Myers, David (New York Univ.) —G—1930
Nicely, John (Gettysburg) —T—1930
Norris, John (Maryland) —E—1932
Obst, Henry (Syracuse) —G—1931
Pape, Orrin (Iowa) —B—1932
Parkinson, Thomas (Pittsburgh) —B—1931
Pessalano, Louis (Villanova) —T—1929
Peterson, Lester (Texas) —E—1932
Rapp, Herbert (Xavier) —C—1930—31
Raskowski, Leo (Ohio State) —T—1932
Reuter, Victor (Lafayette) —C—1932
Riordan, Charles (New York Univ.) —B —1929
Roberts, John (Georgia) —B—1932
Rose, Alfred (Texas) —E—1930
Satenstein, Bernard (New York Univ.) —G —1929—32
Schiebel, Arthur (Colgate) —B—1932
Schwab, Raymond (Oklahoma City Univ.) —B—1932
Shapiro, John (New York Univ.) —B—1929
Skudin, David (New York Univ.) —G—1929
Snyder, Gerald (Maryland) —B—1930
Stein, Samuel (Pennsylvania) —E—1929—30
Stromiello, Michael (Colgate) —E—1932
Strong, Kenneth (New York Univ.) —B —1929—32
Taylor, Erquiet (Auburn) —G—1931
Tays, James—B—1930
Teeter, Alan (Minnesota) —E—1932
Wilcox, Edward (Swarthmore) —B—1930
Williams, Burton "Cy" (Florida) —G —1929—30
Williams, Ivan (Georgia Tech.) —B—1929
Wilson. Faye (Texas A & M) —B—1930
Wilson, Stuart (Washington & Jefferson) — E—1932
Wycoff, Douglas (Georgia Tech) —Q —1929—30, 32
Yablok, Julius (Colgate) —B—1931

TOLEDO MAROONS (1922—23)

Batchelor, Donald (Grove City) —T—1923
Bergin, William (Marquette) —G—1922
Conrad, Martin (Kalamazoo) —C—1922—23
Edwards, Eugene (Notre Dame) —G—1922
Falcon, Gilbert (Wabash) —B—1922—23
Fitzgerald, Freeman (Notre Dame) —B —1923
Gillies, Fred (Cornell) —T—1923
Hill, Harry (Oklahoma) —B—1923
Horning, Clarence (Colgate) —T—1922—23
Hunt, Benjamin (Alabama) —T—1923
Jones, Jerry (Notre Dame) —T—1923
Kelly, Charles (Northwestern) —T—1922

Kendricks, James (Texas A & M) —B—1922
King, Andrew (West Virginia) —E—1922
Kirkgard—B—1923
Lauer, Harold (Detroit) —B—1923
McNamara, Thomas (Detroit) —G—1923
Myers, Cyril (Ohio State) —E—1922
O'Neill, Thomas (St. Mary's Minn.) —E
—1923
Phelan, Robert (Notre Dame) —B—1922
Roberts, James (Centre) —B—1922
Roessler, Fritz (Marquette) —B—1923
Seyfrit, Michael (Notre Dame) —E—1923
Simpson, Eber (Wisconsin) —B—1922
Stein, Herbert (Washington & Jefferson)
—C—1922
Stein, Russell (Pittsburgh) —T—1922
Strauss, Arthur (Phillips) —B—1923
Tanner, John (Centre) —E—1922–23
Thorpe, James (Carlisle) —B—1923
Voss, Walter (Detroit) —E—1923
Watson, Grady (Texas) —B—1922–23
White, Wilbur (Marietta) —E—1922–23

WASHINGTON REDSKINS
(1937—60)

Adams, John (Notre Dame) —T—1945–49
Adducci, Nicholas (Nebraska) —B—1954–55
Aguirre, Joseph (St. Mary's Cal.) —E
—1941–45
Akins, Frank (Washington State) —B
—1943–46
Alban, Richard (Northwestern Univ.) —B
—1952–55
Aldrich, Charles (Texas Christian Univ.)
—C—1940–43, 45–47
Allen, John (Purdue) —G—1955–58
Ananis, Vito (Boston College) —B—1945
Anderson, Walter "Bill" (Tennessee)
—B—1958–60
Andrako, Stephen (Ohio State) —C—1940
Atkeson, Dale—B—1954–56
Audet, Earl (Southern California) —T
—1945
Avery, Donald (California) —T—1946–47
Badazewski, John (Western Reserve) —G
—1949–51
Bagarus, Steven (Notre Dame)—B—1945–46
Bagdon, Edward (Michigan State)—G—1952
Baker, Loris "Sam" (Oregon State) —B
—1953, 56–59
Banta, Herbert (Southern California) —B
—1941
Barber, Ernest (San Francisco) —C—1945
Barber, James (San Francisco) —T—1937–41
Barfield, Kenneth (Mississippi) —G—1954
Barker, Edward (Washington State) —E
—1954
Barni, Roy (San Francisco) —B—1955–56
Barry, Paul (Tulsa) —B—1953
Bartos, Henry (North Carolina) —G—1938
Bartos, Joseph (Annapolis) —B—1950
Battles, Clifford (West Virginia Wesleyan)
—B—1937
Baugh, Samuel (Texas Christian Univ.)
—Q—1937–52

Beinor, J. Edward (Notre Dame) —T
—1941–42
Berrang, Edward (Villanova) —E—1949–52
Berschet, Marvin (Illinois) —G—1954–55
Birlem, Keith (San Jose State) —B—1939
Boensch, Fred (Stanford) —G—1947–49
Boll, Donald (Nebraska) —T—1953–59
Bond, Charles (Washington) —T—1937–38
Bond, Randal (Washington) —B—1938
Bosseler, Donald (Miami University) —B
—1957–60
Braatz, Thomas (Marquette) —E—1957–59
Bradley, Harold (Elon College) —E
—1938–39
Breedlove, Rodney (Maryland) —G—1960
Brewer, Homer (Mississippi) —B—1960
Brito, Eugene (Loyola—L.A.) —E
—1951–53, 55–58
Britt, Edward (Holy Cross) —B—1937
Britt, Oscar (Mississippi) —G—1946
Brown, Daniel (Villanova) —E—1950
Brown, Hardy (Tulsa) —B—1950
Brown, William (Arkansas) —G—1951–52
Brueckman, Charles (Pittsburgh) —C—1958
Bukich, Rudolph (Southern California)
—Q—1957–58
Buksar, George (Purdue) —B—1951–52
Butkas, Carl (George Washington) —T
—1948
Cafego, George (Tennessee) —B—1943
Campofreda, Nicholas (Western Maryland)
—C—1944
Campora, Donald (College of Pacific) —T
—1953
Carroll, Victor (Nevada) —T—1937–41
Carson, John (Georgia) —E—1954–59
Castiglia, James (Georgetown) —B—1947–48
Cheverko, George (Fordham) —B—1948
Churchwell, Hanson (Mississippi) —G—
1959
Cichowski, Eugene (Indiana) —B—1958–59
Cifers, Edward (Tennessee) —E
—1941–42, 46
Clair, Frank (Ohio State) —E—1941
Clark, James (Oregon State) —G—1952–53
Cochran, Thomas (Auburn) —B—1949
Condit, Merlyn (Carnegie Tech) —B—1945
Conkright, William (Oklahoma) —C—1943
Corbitt, Donald (Arizona) —C—1948
Couppee, Albert (Iowa) —G—1946
Cox, William (Duke) —E—1951–52, 55
Crisler, Harold (San Jose State) —E
—1948–49
Crotty, James (Notre Dame) —B—1960
Cudzik, Walter (Purdue) —C—1954
Dale, Roland (Mississippi) —E—1950
Davis, Andrew (George Washington) —B
—1952–53
Davis, Fred (Alabama) —T—1941–42, 45
Davlin, Michael (Notre Dame) —T—1955
Day, Herman "Eagle" (Mississippi) —B—
1959–60
Deal, Rufus (Auburn) —C—1942
DeCarlo, Arthur (Georgia) —B—1956–57
DeCorrevont, William (Northwestern) —B

Wide World Photo

ROY BARNI (21), WASHINGTON DEFENSIVE BACK, BREAKS UP A TOUCHDOWN PASS THAT
WAS HEADING FOR THE ARMS OF NEW YORK GIANT HALFBACK GENE FILIPSKI IN A
1956 GAME.

—1945
Dee, Robert (Holy Cross) —E—1957–58
Deeks, Donald (Washington) —T—1947
DeFruiter, Robert (Nebraska) —B—1945–47
Dekker, Paul (Michigan State) —E—1953
DeMao, Albert (Duquesne) —C—1945–53
Doll, Donald (Southern California) —B
    —1953
Doolan, John (Georgetown) —B—1945
Dorow, Albert (Michigan State) —Q
    —1954–56
Dow, Kenneth (Oregon State) —B—1941
Dowda, Harry (Wake Forest) —B—1949–53
Drazenovich, Charles (Penn. State) —B
    —1950–59
Drulis, Albert (Temple) —B—1947
Duckworth, Joseph (Colgate) —E—1947
Dudley, William (Virginia)—B—1950–51, 53
Dunn, Coye (Southern California)—B—1943
Dwyer, John (Loyola—L.A.) —B—1951
Dye, Lester (Syracuse) —E—1944–45
Ecker, Enrique (John Carroll) —T—1952
Edwards, Albert (Washington State) —T
    —1937–40
Edwards, Weldon (Texas Christian Univ.)
    —T—1948
Ehrhardt, Clyde (Georgia) —C—1946–48, 49
Elter, Leo (Duquesne) —B—1955–57
Erikson, Carleton (Washington) —C
    —1938–39
Farkas, Andrew (Detroit) —B—1938–44
Farman, Richard (Washington State) —G
    —1939–43
Farmer, Thomas (Iowa) —B—1947–48

Farrar, Vincent (North Carolina State) —B
    —1939
Felton, Ralph (Maryland) —B—1954–60
Ferris, Neil (Loyola—L.A.) —B—1951–52
Filchock, Frank (Indiana) —Q
    —1938–40, 44–45
Fiorentino, Albert (Boston College) —G
    —1943–44
Fisher, Robert (Southern California) —T
    —1940
Foltz, Vernon (St. Vincent's) —C—1944
Fulcher, William (Georgia Tech) —G
    1956–58
Fuller, Lawrence—B—1944–45
Gaffney, James (Tennessee) —B—1945–47
Garzoni, Michael (Southern California) —G
    —1947
Gentry, Elmer (Tulsa) —B—1941
Gerber, Elwood (Alabama) —G—1945
German, James (Centre) —B—1939
Gibson, Billy Joe (Tulsa) —C—1943
Gillette, James (Virginia) —B—1947
Gilmer, Harry (Alabama) —Q—1948–54
Glick, Gary (Colorado A & M)—B—1959–60
Gob, Arthur (Pittsburgh) —G—1959
Goode, Robert (Texas A & M) —B
    —1949–51, 54–55
Goodnight, Clyde (Tulsa) —E—1949–50
Goodyear, John (Marquette) —B—1942
Gray, William (Oregon State) —G—1947–48
Guglielmi, Ralph (Notre Dame) —Q
    —1955, 58–60
Haley, George Richard (Pittsburgh) —B
    —1959–60

Morgan, Boyd (Southern California) —B
    —1939–40
Morgan, Robert (Maryland) —T—1954
Morley, Samuel (Stanford) —T—1954
Moss, Joseph (Maryland) —T—1952
Natowich, Andrew (Holy Cross) —B—1944
Niemi, Laurie (Washington State) —T
    —1949–53
Nix, Doyle (Southern Methodist Univ.)
    —1958–59
Nobile, Leo (Penn. State) —G—1947
Norman, James—G—1955
Norris, Harold (California) —B—1955
North, James (Washington State Central)
    —T—1944
Nussbaumer, Robert (Michigan) —B
    —1947–48
O'Brien, Francis (Michigan State) —T—
    1960
Olsson, Lester (Mercer) —G—1937–38
Olszewski, John (California) —B—1958–60
Osborne, Thomas (Hastings) —B—1960
Ostroski, Chester (Notre Dame) —E
    —1954–59
Owens, Donald (Mississippi Southern) —T
    —1957
Pacewic, Vincent (San Francisco) —B—1947
Paluck, John (Pittsburgh) —E—1956, 59–60
Papit, John (Virginia) —B—1951–53
Parks, Edward (Oklahoma) —C—1938–40
Pasqua, Joseph (Southern Methodist
    Univ.) —T—1942–43
Paternoster, Angelo (Georgetown) —G
    —1943
Peebles, James (Vanderbilt) —E—1946–51
Pepper, Eugene (Missouri) —G—1950–53
Perdue, Willard (Duke) —E—1940
Peters, Volney (Southern California) —T
    —1954–57
Peterson, Nelson (West Virginia Wesleyan)
    —B—1937
Piasecky, Alex (Duke) —E—1943–45
Planutis, Gerald (Michigan State) —B
    —1956
Podoley, James (Michigan Central) —B
    —1957–60
Poillon, Richard (Canisius) —B
    —1942, 46–49
Polsfoot, Francis (Washington State) —E
    —1953
Pressley, Lee (Oklahoma) —C—1945
Promuto, Vincent (Holy Cross) —G—1960
Quirk, Edward (Missouri) —B—1948–51
Ramsey, Knox (William & Mary) —G
    —1952–53
Renfro, William (Memphis State) —T
    —1957–59
Reynolds, Mack Charles (Louisiana State
    Univ.) —Q—1960
Ribar, Frank (Duke) —G—1943
Ricca, James (Georgetown) —T—1951–55
Roehnelt, William (Bradley) —G—1960
Rosato, Salvatore (Villanova) —B—1945–47
Rosso, George (Ohio State) —B—1954
Roussos, Michael (Pittsburgh) —T

    —1948–49
Runnels, Thomas (Texas State North) —B
    —1956–57
Russell, Torrance (Auburn) —T—1939–40
Ruthstrom, Ralph (Southern Methodist
    Univ.) —B—1947–48
Rykovich, Julius (Illinois) —B—1952–53
Rymkus, Louis (Notre Dame) —T—1943
Saenz, Edward (Southern California) —B
    —1946–51
Salem, Edward (Alabama) —B—1951
Sanchez, John (San Francisco) —T—
    —1948–49
Sandifer, Daniel (Louisiana State Univ.)
    —B—1948–49
Sanford, Hayward (Alabama) —E—1940
Sardisco, Anthony (Tulane) —G—1956
Scarbath, Jack (Maryland) —Q—1953–54
Schilling, Ralph (Oklahoma) —E—1946
Schrader, James (Notre Dame) —C
    —1954–60
Scotti, Benjamin (Maryland) —B—1959–60
Scudero, Joseph (San Francisco) —B
    —1954–58
Sebek, Nicholas (Indiana) —B—1950
Seno, Frank (George Washington) —B
    —1943–44, 49
Seymour, Robert (Oklahoma) —B—1940–45
Sharp, Everett (California Polytech.) —T
    —1944–45
Shoener, Herbert (Iowa) —E—1948–49
Shugart, Clyde (Iowa State) —G—1939–44
Shula, Donald (John Carroll) —B—1957
Siegert, Herbert (Illinois) —G—1949–51
Slivinski, Steven (Washington) —G
    —1939–43
Smith, Benjamin (Alabama) —E—1937
Smith, George (California) —C
    —1937, 40–43
Smith, John (Stanford) —E—1943
Smith, Riley (Alabama) —Q—1937–38
Sneddon, Robert (St. Mary's, Cal.) —B
    —1944
Soboleski, Joseph (Michigan) —T—1949
Sommer, Michael (George Washington)
    —B—1958
Sommers, John (U.C.L.A.) —C—1947
Spaniel, Frank (Notre Dame) —B—1950
Sparks, David (South Carolina) —G—1951
Spirida, John (St. Anselm's) —E—1939–40
Stacco, Edward (Colgate) —T—1947–48
Stallings, Alva Donald (North Carolina)
    —T—1960
Stanfel, Richard (San Francisco) —G
    —1956–58
Stasica, Leo (Colorado) —B—1943
Staton, James (Wake Forest) —T—1951
Steber, John (Georgia Tech) —T—1946–50
Stenn, Paul (Villanova) —T—1946
Stephens, Louis (San Francisco) —G
    —1955–60
Stout, Peter (Texas Christian Univ.) —B
    —1949–50
Stovall, Richard (Abilene Christian) —C
    —1949

Stralka, Clem (Georgetown) —G
—1938–42, 45–46
Stuart, James (Oregon) —T—1938, 41–42
Stynchula, Andrew (Penn State) —T—1960
Suminski, David (Wisconsin) —G—1953
Sutton, Edward (North Carolina) —B
—1957–59
Sykes, Robert (San Jose State) —B—1952
Szafaryn, Leonard (North Carolina) —T
—1949
Taylor, Hugh (Oklahoma City Univ.) —E
—1947–54
Tereshinski, Joseph (Georgia) —E
—1947–54
Thomas, George (Oklahoma) —B—1950–51
Thomas, Ralph (San Francisco) —E—1952
Titchenal, Robert (San Jose State) —E
—1941–42
Todd, Richard (Texas A & M) —B
—1939–42, 45–48
Toneff, Robert (Notre Dame)—T—1959–60
Torgeson, Lavern (Washington State) —C
—1955–57
Tuckey, Richard (Manhattan) —B—1938
Turley, Douglas (Scranton) —E—1944–48
Turner, Jay Lewis (George Washington)
—B—1938–39
Ucovich, Mitchell (San Jose State) —T
—1944
Ulinski, Harry (Kentucky) —C—1950–56
Ungerer, Joseph (Fordham) —T—1944–45
Venuto, Samuel (Guilford) —B—1952
Vereb, Edward (Maryland) —B—1960
Voytek, Edward (Purdue) —G—1957–58
Walters, Lester (Penn. State) —E—1958
Walton, Frank (Pittsburgh) —G—1944–45
Walton, Joseph (Pittsburgh) —E—1957–60
Ward, William (Washington State) —G
—1946–47

Watson, James (College of Pacific) —C
—1945
Watson, Sidney (Northeastern) —B—1958
Watts, George (Appalachian State) —T
—1942
Weatherall, James (Oklahoma) —T—1958
Weldon, Lawrence (Presbyterian) —Q
—1944–45
Wells, William (Michigan State) —B
—1954, 56–57
Whited, Marvin (Oklahoma) —B—1942, 45
Whitlow, Robert (Arizona) —C—1960
Wilde, George (Texas A & M) —B—1947
Wilkin, Wilbur (St. Mary's, Cal.) —T
—1938–43
Wilkins, Roy (Georgia) —E—1960
Williams, Garland (Georgia) —T—1947
Williams, John (Southern California) —B
—1952–53
Williams, Theodore (Boston College) —B
—1942
Williamson, Ernest (North Carolina) —T
—1947
Witucki, Casimir (Indiana) —G
—1950–51, 53–54
Woodward, Richard (Iowa) —C—1952
Wulff, James (Michigan State) —B—1960
Wyant, Frederick (West Virginia) —Q
—1956
Yonaker, John (Notre Dame) —E—1952
Youel, James (Iowa) —Q—1946–48
Young, Roy (Texas A & M) —T—1938
Young, William (Alabama) —T
—1937–42, 46
Yowarsky, Walter (Kentucky) —E—1951, 54
Zagers, Albert (Michigan State) —B
—1955, 57–58
Zeno, Joseph (Holy Cross) —G—1942–44
Zimmerman, Leroy (San Jose State) —Q
—1940–42

THE AMERICAN FOOTBALL LEAGUE

BOSTON PATRIOTS (1960)

Addison, Thomas (Southern California)
—B—1960
Beach, Walter (Michigan Central) —B—
1960
Bennett, Philip (Miami) —B—1960
Biscaha, Joseph (Richmond) —E—1960
Brown, William (Syracuse) —C—1960
Bruney, Frederick (Ohio State) —B—1960
Burton, Ronald (Northwestern) —B—1960
Cappelletti, Gino (Minnesota) —B—1960
Christy, Richard (North Carolina State) —
B—1960
Cohen, Abraham (Chattanooga) —G—1960
Colclough, James (Boston College) —E—
1960
Crawford, James (Wyoming) —B—1960
Cross, Robert (Austin) —T—1960

Crouthamel, John Jacob (Dartmouth) —
B—1960
Crow, Albert (William & Mary) —T—1960
Cudzik, Walter (Purdue) —C—1960
Danenhauer, William (Kansas State
Teachers) —E—1960
Davis, Jack (Maryland) —G—1960
Dee, Robert (Holy Cross) —E—1960
DeLucca, Gerald (Tennessee) —T—1960
Dicenzo, Anthony (Michigan State) —T
—1960
Dimitroff, Thomas (Miami-Ohio)—Q—1960
Garron, Lawrence (Illinois Western) —B
—1960
Green, Jerome (Georgia Tech) —E—1960
Greene, Thomas (Holy Cross) —Q—1960
Hauser, Arthur (Xavier) —T—1960
Hunt, James (Prairie View) —E—1960
Jacobs, Harry (Bradley) —E—1960

Jagielski, Harry (Indiana) —T—1960
Johnson, Kosse "Joe" (Boston College) —B—1960
Larson, William (Illinois Western) —B—1960
Lee, Robert (Missouri) —T—1960
Leo, Charles (Indiana) —G—1960
Livingston, Walter (Heidelberg) —B—1960
Lofton, Oscar (Louisiana Southeastern) —E—1960
Long, Michael (Brandeis) —E—1960
McCombs, Donald (Villanova) —E—1960
McGee, George (Southern) —T—1960
Miller, Alan (Boston College) —B—1960
Morrison, Ronald (New Mexico) —T—1960
O'Hanley, Ross (Boston College) —B—1960
Richardson, Alvin (Grambling) —E—1960
Rudolph, John (Georgia Tech) —B—1960
Sardisco, Anthony (Tulane) —G—1960
Schwedes, Gerhard (Syracuse) —B—1960
Shonta, Charles (Michigan Eastern) —B—1960
Smith, Harold (U.C.L.A.) —T—1960
Soltis, Robert (Minnesota) —B—1960
Songin, Edward (Boston College) —Q—1960
Stephen, Thomas (Syracuse) —B—1960 —1960
Striegel, William (College of Pacific) —G
Washington, Clyde (Purdue) —B—1960
Wells, William (Michigan State) —B—1960
White, Harvey (Clemson) —Q—1960

BUFFALO BILLS (1960)

Barrett, Robert (Baldwin-Wallace) —E—1960
Blazer, Philip (North Carolina) —G—1960
Brodhead, Robert (Duke) —Q—1960
Brudbaker, Richard (Ohio State) —E—1960
Buzynski, Bernard (Holy Cross) —G—1960
Carlson, Wray (Duke) —B—1960
Chamberlain, Daniel (Sacramento) —E—1960
Chelf, Donald (Iowa) —G—1960
Crockett, Monte (Highlands) —E—1960
Dicenzo, Anthony (Michigan State) —T —1960
Dubenion, Elbert (Bluffton) —B—1960
Ford, Frederick (California Poly Tech.) —B—1960
Fowler, Willmer (Northwestern) —B—1960
Green, John (Chattanooga) —Q—1960
Harper, Darrell (Michigan) —B—1960
Hoisington, Allan (Pasadena) —E—1960
Hergert, Joseph (Florida) —B—1960
Johnson, Jack (Miami) —B—1960
Kinard, William (Mississippi) —B—1960
Kulbacki, Joseph (Purdue) —B—1960
Laraway, Jack (Purdue) —B—1960
Lewis, Harold (Houston) —B—1960
Lucas, Richard (Penn State) —B—1960
McCabe, Richard (Pittsburgh) —B—1960
McGrew, Daniel (Purdue) —C—1960
McMurtry, Charles (Whittier) —T—1960
Matsos, Archibald (Michigan State) —C—1960

Meyer, Edward (West Texas State) —T—1960
Moore, Leroy (Ft. Valley State) —E—1960
Muelhaupt, Edward (Iowa State) —G—1960
O'Connell, Thomas (Illinois) —Q—1960
Olson, Harold (Clemson) —T—1960
Palumbo, Samuel (Notre Dame) —C—1960
Remmert, Dennis (Iowa State) —T—1960
Rutkowski, Charles (Ripon) —E—1960
Rychlec, Thomas (American International) —E—1960
Schaffer, Joseph (Tennessee) —B—1960
Scott, John (Ohio State) —T—1960
Sedlock, Robert (Georgia) —T—1960
Smith, Carl (Tennessee) —B—1960
Sorey, James (Texas Southern) —G—1960
Torczon, Laverne (Nebraska) —E—1960
Wagstaff, James (Idaho State) —B—1960
Yoho, Mack (Miami, Ohio) —E—1960

DALLAS TEXANS (1960)

Barton, James (Marshall) —C—1960
Bernet, Edward (Southern Methodist Univ.) —E—1960
Bookman, John (Miami) —B—1960
Boydston, Max (Oklahoma) —E—1960
Branch, Melvin (Louisiana State Univ.) —E—1960
Bryant, Robert (Texas) —E—1960
Burford, Christopher (Stanford) —E—1960
Collins, Raymond (Louisiana State Univ.) —T—1960
Corey, Walter (Miami) —B—1960
Cornelison, Jerry (Southern Methodist Univ.) —T—1960
Daniels, Clemon (Prairie View) —B—1960
Davidson, Francis (Baylor) —Q—1960
Diamond, Charles (Miami) —T—1960
Dickinson, Richard (Mississippi Southern) —B—1960
Dimmick, Thomas (Houston) —G—1960
Enis, Hunter (Texas Christian Univ.) —Q—1960
Flynn, Donald (Houston) —B—1960
Fournet, Sidney (Louisiana State Univ.) —G—1960
Frey, Richard (Texas A & M) —E—1960
Granderson, Rufus (Prairie View) —T—1960
Greene, Theodore (Tampa) —C—1960
Harris, James (Oklahoma) —B—1960
Haynes, Abner (North Texas) —B—1960
Headrick, Sherrill (Texas Christian Univ.) —B—1960
Hudson, Robert (Clemson) —B—1960
Jackson, Charles (Southern Methodist Univ.) —B—1960
Johnson, John Curley (Houston) —B —1960
Krisher, William (Oklahoma) —G—1960
Miller, Paul (Louisiana State Univ.) —E—1960
Napier, Walter (Paul Quinn) —T—1960
Nunnery, Robert (Louisiana State Univ.) —T—1960

Renfro, Dean (North Texas State) —B—1960
Reynolds, Allan (Tarkio) —G—1960
Robinson, John (Louisiana State Univ.) —B—1960
Rochester, Paul (Michigan State) —E—1960
Spikes, Jack (Texan Christian Univ.) — B—1960
Stone, Jack (Oregon) —T—1960
Stover, Stewart (Louisiana State Northeast) —B—1960
Swink, James (Texas Christian Univ.) —B —1960
Terrell, Marvin (Mississippi) —G—1960
Webster, David (Prairie View) —B—1960
Wood, Duane (Oklahoma State) —B—1960
Zaruba, Carroll (Nebraska) —B—1960

DENVER BRONCOS (1960)

Adamson, Kenneth (Notre Dame) —G—1960
Allen, Donald (Texas) —B—1960
Alliston, Vaughan (Mississippi) —B—1960
Bell, Henry—B—1960
Bernardi, Frank (Colorado) —B—1960
Brodnax, John (Louisiana State Univ.) — B—1960
Broussard, Frederick (Louisiana Northwest) —C—1960
Brown, Hardy (Tulsa) —B—1960
Carmichael, Albert (Southern California) —B—1960
Carothers, Donald (Bradley) —E—1960
Carpenter, Kenneth (Oregon State) —B—1960
Danenhauer, Eldon (Kansas State Teachers) —T—1960
Danenhauer, William (Kansas State Teachers) —E—1960
Day, Albert (Michigan) —B—1960
Doyle, Richard (Ohio State) —B—1960
Dublinski, Thomas (Utah) —Q—1960
Epperson, John Patrick (Adams State) —E—1960
Gavin, Charles (Tennessee A & I)—E—1960
Gonsoulin, Austin (Baylor) —B—1960
Greer, James (North Carolina Teachers) —E—1960
Hatley, John (Baylor) —G—1960
Herring, George (Mississippi Southern) —Q—1960
Holz, Gordon (Minnesota) —T—1960
Hudson, Robert (Clemson) —G—1960
Jessup, William (Southern California) —E—1960
King, Donald (Kentucky) —O—T—1960
Kuchta, Frank (Notre Dame) —C—1960
Larpenter, Carl (Texas) —T—1960
Liddick, David (George Washington) —T —1960
McFadin, Lewis (Texas) —G—1960
McNamara, Robert (Minnesota) —B—1960
Mangum, Peter (Mississippi) —B—1960
Mingo, Eugene—B—1960
Nichols, Michael (Arkansas A & M) —C—1960

Pyeatt, John—B—1960
Rolle, David (Oklahoma) —B—1960
Romine, Alton (Alabama Teachers) — —E—1960
Smith, William (Michigan) —T—1960
Stransky, Robert (Colorado) —B—1960
Strickland, Davis (Memphis State) —B—1960
Taylor, Lionel (Highlands) —E—1960
Tripucka, Frank (Notre Dame) —Q—1960
Wegert, Theodore—B—1960
Work, Jack (Denver) —B—1960
Yelverton, William (Mississippi) —E—1960
Young, Joseph (Arizona) —E—1960

HOUSTON OILERS (1960)

Allen, Dalva (Houston) —E—1960
Atchason, Jack (Illinois Western) —E—1960
Banfield, James "Tony" (Oklahoma State) —B—1960
Belotti, George (Southern California) — C—1960
Blanda, George (Kentucky) —Q—1960
Brown, Donald (Houston) —B—1960
Cannon, William (Louisiana State Univ.)— B—1960
Carson, John (Georgia) —E—1960
Cline, Douglas (Clemson) —B—1960
Davidson, Peter (Citadel) —E—1960
Dukes, Michael (Clemson) —B—1960
Floyd, Donald (Texas Christian Univ.) — E—1960
Gordon, Robert (Tennessee) —B—1960
Greaves, Gary (Miami, Fla.) —G—1960
Groman, William (Heidelberg) —B—1960
Hall, Kenneth (Texas A & M) —B—1960
Helluin, Frances "Jerry" (Tulane) —T—1960
Hennigan, Charles (Louisiana Northwest) —B—1960
Jamison, Alfred (Colgate) —T—1960
Johnson, Mark (Northwestern) —B—1960
Kendall, Charles (U.C.L.A.) —1960
Lanphear, Daniel (Wisconsin) —E—1960
Lee, Jack (Cincinnati) —Q—1960
McDaniels, Wahoo (Oklahoma) —G—1960
Michael, Richard (Ohio State) —T—1960
Milstead, Charles (Texas A & M) —Q—1960
Morris, Dennit (Oklahoma) —G—1960
Norton, James (Idaho) —B—1960
Perlo, Philip (Maryland) —B—1960
Pitts, Hugh (Texas Christian Univ.) — —C—1960
Shirkey, George (Austin) —T—1960
Simerson, John (Purdue) —C—1960
Smith, David (Ripon) —B—1960
Spence, Julian (Sam Houston) —B—1960
Talamini, Robert (Kentucky) —G—1960
Tolar, Charles (Louisiana Northwest) — B—1960
Trask, Orville (Rice) —T—1960
Wallner, Frederick (Notre Dame) —G—1960
Wharton, Hogan (Houston) —G—1960
White, John (Texas Southern) —E—1960

White, Robert (Ohio State) —B—1960
Witcher, Thomas "Al" (Baylor) —B—1960

LOS ANGELES CHARGERS (1960)

Agajanian, Benjamin (New Mexico) —K—1960
Anderson, Ralph (Los Angeles State) —E—1960
Bansavage, Albert (Southern California) —B—1960
Barry, Albert (California) —G—1960
Bobo, Hubert (Ohio State) —B—1960
Botchan, Ronald (Occidental) —B—1960
Brueckman, Charles (Pittsburgh) —C—1960
Chorovich, Richard (Miami, Ohio) —T—1960
Clark, Howard (Chattanooga) —E—1960
Clatterbuck, Robert (Houston) —Q—1960
Cole, Frederick (Maryland) —G—1960
DeLuca, Samuel (South Carolina)—T—1960
Donnell, Benjamin (Vanderbilt) —E—1960
Ferguson, Howard—B—1960
Ferranti, Orlando (Southern California) —G—1960
Finneran, Gary (Southern California) —T—1960
Flowers, Charles (Mississippi) —B—1960
Ford, Frederick (Cal. Poly.) —B—1960
Garner, Robert (Fresno State) —B—1960
Gob, Arthur (Pittsburgh) —E—1960
Harris, Robert (McNeese State) —B—1960
Karas, Emil (Dayton) —G—1960
Kemp, John (Occidental) —Q—1960
Kempinska, Charles (Mississippi) —G—1960
Kocourek, David (Wisconsin) —E—1960
Kompara, John (South Carolina) —T—1960
Laraba, Robert (Texas Western) —Q—1960

Loudd, Rommie Lee (U.C.L.A.) —B—1960
Lowe, Paul (Oregon State) —B—1960
McNeil, Charles (Compton Jr.) —B—1960
Maguire, Paul (Citadel) —B—1960
Martin, Blanche (Michigan State)—B—1960
Mix, Ronald (Southern California) —T—1960
Nery, Ronald (Kansas State) —E—1960
Nix, Doyle (Southern Methodist Univ.) —B—1960
Norris, Donald (Iowa) —E—1960
Peters, Volney (Southern California) —T—1960
Rogers, Donald (South Carolina) —C—1960
Schleicher, Maurice (Penn State) —E—1960
Sears, James (Southern California) —B—1960
Thomas, Jesse (Michigan State) —B—1960
Wallace, Henry (College of Pacific) —B—1960
Waller, Ronald (Maryland) —B—1960
Womble, Royce (North Texas State) —B—1960
Wright, Ernest (Ohio State) —T—1960
Zeman, Robert (Wisconsin) —B—1960

NEW YORK TITANS (1960)

Baker, Lawrence (Bowling Green) —T—1960
Barnes, Ernest (North Carolina Coll.) —T—1960
Bell, Edward (Pennsylvania) —G—1960
Bohling, Dewey (Hardin-Simmons) —B—1960
Burton, Leon (Arizona State) —B—1960
Callahan, Daniel (Akron) —G—1960
Campbell, Kenneth (West Chester) —E—1960
Cockrell, Eugene (Hardin-Simmons) —T—1960
Cooke, Edward (Maryland) —E—1960
Cooper, Thurlow (Maine) —E—1960
D'Agostino, Frank (Auburn) —G—1960
Dombrowski, Leon (Delaware) —C—1960
Donnahoo, Roger (Michigan State) —B—1960
Dorow, Albert (Michigan State) —Q—1960
Dupre, Charles (Baylor) —Q—1960
Ellis, Roger (Maine) —C—1960
Felt, Richard (Brigham Young) —B—1960
Glenn, Howard (Linfield) —G—1960
Grantham, Lawrence (Mississippi) —G—1960
Guesman, Richard (West Virginia) —T—1960
Hart, Dee "Pete" (Hardin-Simmons) —B—1960
Herndon, Donald (Tampa) —B—1960
Hudock, Michael (Miami) —C—1960
Jamieson, Richard (Bradley) —Q—1960
Julian, Frederick (Michigan) —B—1960
Katcik, Joseph (Notre Dame) —T—1960
Klotz, John (Penn Military Coll.)—T—1960
McMullan, John (Notre Dame) —G—1960
Marques, Robert (Boston Univ.) —C—1960
Martin, Blanche (Michigan State) —B—1960
Mathis, William (Clemson) —B—1960
Maynard, Donald (Texas Western) —E—1960
Mischak, Robert (West Point) —G—1960
Mumley, Nicholas (Purdue) —E—1960
Pagliei, Joseph (Clemson) —B—1960
Powell, Arthur (San Jose State) —E—1960
Reifsnyder, Robert (Annapolis) —E—1960
Robinson, William (Lincoln) —B—1960
Ross, David (Los Angeles State) —E—1960
Ryan, Joseph (Villanova) —E—1960
Saidock, Thomas (Michigan State) —T—1960
Sapienza, Richard (Villanova) —B—1960
Schwedes, Gerhard (Syracuse) —B—1960
Scrabis, Robert (Penn State) —Q—1960
Shockley, William (West Chester)—B—1960
Tharp, Thomas (Alabama) —Q—1960
Wegert, Theodore—B—1960
Whitley, Hall (Texas A & I) —B—1960
Youngelman, Sidney (Alabama) —G—1960

OAKLAND RAIDERS (1960)

Armstrong, Ramon (Texas Christian Univ.) —G—1960
Asad, Douglas (Northwestern) —E—1960
Barbee, Joseph (Kent State) —T—1960
Barnes, Lawrence (Colorado A & M) —B—1960
Bravo, Alexander (California Polytech) —B—1960
Cannavino, Joseph (Ohio State) —B—1960
Carr, Luther (Washington) —B—1960
Cavalli, Carmen (Richmond) —E—1960
Churchwell, Hanson (Mississippi)—G—1960
Crow, Wayne (California) —B—1960
Deskins, Donald (Michigan) —G—1960
Dittrich, John (Wisconsin) —G—1960
Dougherty, Robert (Kentucky) —E—1960
Edgington, Daniel (Florida) —E—1960
Fields, George (Bakersfield) —E—1960
Flores, Thomas (College of Pacific) —Q—1960
Goldstein, Alan (North Carolina) —E—1960
Hardy, Charles (San Jose State) —E—1960
Harris, John (Santa Monica) —B—1960
Hawkins, Wayne (College of Pacific) —G—1960
Hoisington, Allan (Pasadena) —E—1960
Holtzman, Glen (North Texas State) —T—1960

Joyner, L. C. (Diablo Valley) —B—1960
Keyes, Robert (San Diego) —B—1960
Larscheid, Jack (College of Pacific) —B—1960
Larson, Paul (California) —Q—1960
Locklin, William (New Mexico State) —1960
Lott, William (Mississippi) —B—1960
Louderback, Thomas (San Jose State) —G—1960
McFarlane, Nyle (Brigham Young) —B—1960
Macon, Edward (College of Pacific) —B—1960
Manoukian, Donald (Stanford) —G—1960
Morris, Riley (Florida A & M) —B—1960
Oglesby, Paul (U.C.L.A.) —T—1960
Otto, James (Miami) —C—1960
Parilli, Vito (Kentucky) —Q—1960
Powell, Charles—E—1960
Prebola, Eugene (Boston Univ.) —E—1960
Reynolds, William (Pittsburgh) —B—1960
Sabal, Ronald (Purdue) —T—1960
Smith, James (Compton Jr.) —B—1960
Teresa, Anthony (San Jose State) —B—1960
Truax, Dalton (Tulane) —T—1960
Warzeka, Ronald (Montana State) —T—1960

THE ALL AMERICA FOOTBALL CONFERENCE
1946—49

BALTIMORE COLTS (1947—49 only)

Akins, Frank (Washington State) —B—1947
Artoe, Lee (California) —T—1948
Barwegan, Richard (Purdue) —G—1948–49
Baumgartner, William (Minnesota) —E—1947
Bechtol, Hubert (Texas) —E—1947–49
Berezney, Peter (Notre Dame) —T—1948
Beson, Warren (Minnesota) —C—1949
Black, John (Mississippi State) —B—1947
Blandin, Ernest (Tulane) —T—1948–49
Blount, Lamar (Mississippi State) —E—1947
Case, Ernest (U.C.L.A.) —B—1947
Castiglia, James (Georgetown) —B—1947
Cleman, Herbert (Notre Dame) —C—1948
Cooper, Kenneth (Vanderbilt) —G—1949
Corley, Elbert (Mississippi State) —C—1948
Cowan, Robert (Indiana) —B—1949
Cure, Armand (Rhode Island) —B—1947
Davis, R. Lamar (Georgia) —E—1947–49
Dellerba, Spiro (Ohio State) —B—1948–49
Dudish, Andrew (Georgia) —B—1947
Faunce, Everett (Minnesota) —B—1949
Fowler, Aubrey (Arkansas) —B—1948
French, Barry (Purdue) —G—1947–49
Galvin, John (Purdue) —B—1947
Gambino, Lucien (Maryland) —B—1948–49
Garrett, William (Mississippi State) —G—1948–48
Getchell, Gorham (Temple) —E—1947
Gillory, Byron (Texas) —B—1949

Grain, Edwin (Pennsylvania) —G—1947–48
Grossman, Rex (Indiana) —B—1948–49
Groves, George (Marquette) —G—1948
Handley, Richard (Fresno State) —C—1947
Hekkers, George (Wisconsin) —T—1947
Higgins, Luke (Notre Dame) —G—1947
Hillenbrand, William (Indiana) —B—1947–48
Jagade, Harry (Indiana) —B—1949
Jenkins, Jonathan (Dartmouth) —T—1949
Jones, Ralph (Alabama) —E—1947
Kasap, Michael (Purdue) —T—1947
Kelly, Robert (Notre Dame) —B—1949
Kingery, Wayne (Louisiana State Univ.) —B—1949
Klug, Alfred (Marquette) —T—1947–48
Kobda, Joseph (Purdue) —C—1947
Konetsky, Floyd (Florida) —E—1947
Landrigan, James (Holy Cross) —T—1947
Leicht, Jacob (Oregon) —B—1948–49
Leonard, William (Notre Dame) —E—1949
Lio, Augustine (Georgetown) —G—1947
McCormick, Leonard (Baylor) —C—1948
Madar, Elmer (Michigan) —E—1947
Marino, Victor (Ohio State) —G—1947
Maves, Earl (Wisconsin) —B—1948
Mayne, Louis (Texas) —B—1948
Mellus, John (Villanova) —T—1947–49
Mertes, Bernard (Iowa) —B—1947–49
Meyers, Gilbert (Wake Forest) —E—1947
Mobley, Rudolph (Hardin-Simmons) —B—

1947

Nemeth, Steven (Notre Dame) —B—1947
Nolander, Donald (Minnesota) —C—1947
North, John (Vanderbilt) —E—1948–49
Nowaskey, Robert (George Washington) —E—1948–49
O'Rourke, Charles (Boston College) — Q—1948–49
Page, Paul (Southern Methodist Univ.) — B—1949
Perpich, George (Georgetown) —T—1947
Pfohl, Robert (Purdue) —B—1948–49
Phillips, Michael (Western Maryland) —C—1947
Poole, Oliver (Mississippi) —E—1948
Prewitt, Felton (Tulsa) —C—1949
Ruthstrom, Ralph (Southern Methodist Univ.) —B—1949
Schwenk, Wilson (Washington, Mo.) — B—1947
Sidorik, Alexander (Mississippi State) —T— 1948–49
Sigurdson, Sigurd (Pacific Lutheran) —E—1947
Simmons, John (Detroit) —G—1948
Sinkwich, Frank (Georgia) —B—1947
Smith, Joseph (Texas Tech) —E—1948
Spruill, James (Rice) —E—1948–49
Stewart, Ralph (Notre Dame) —C—1948
Stone, William (Bradley) —B—1949
Sylvester, John (Temple) —B—1948
Terrell, Raymond (Mississippi) —B—1947
Tillman, Alonzo (Oklahoma) —C—1949
Tittle, Yelverton A. (Louisiana State Univ.) —Q—1948–49
Trebotich, Ivan (St. Mary's, Cal.) —B—1947
Vacanti, Samuel (Nebraska) —Q—1948–49
Vardian, John—B—1947–48
Wedemeyer, Herman (St. Mary's, Cal.) — B—1949
Williams, Wendell (Rice) —E—1948–49
Wright, John (Maryland) —B—1947
Yokas, Frank—G—1947
Zorich, George (Northwestern) —G—1947

BROOKLYN DODGERS

Akins, Albert (Washington State) —B— 1947–48
Allen, Carl (Oklahoma City Univ.) — B—1948
Armstrong, Charles (Mississippi) —B—1946
Benson, George (Northwestern) —B—1947
Bernhardt, George (Illinois) —G—1946–48
Billman, John (Minnesota) —G—1946
Brown, Hardy (Tulsa) —B—1948
Buffington, Harry (Oklahoma A & M) — G—1946–48
Burrus, Harry (Hardin-Simmons) —E—1948
Callahan, Robert (Michigan) —C—1947
Camp, James (North Carolina) —B—1948
Chappuis, Robert (Michigan) —B—1948
Clowes, John (William & Mary) —T—1948
Colmer, John—B—1946–48
Conger, Melvin (Georgia) —E—1947
Connolly, Harry (Boston College)—B—1946

Cooper, James (North Texas State) —C— 1948
Daley, William (Minnesota) —B—1946
Daukas, Louis (Cornell) —C—1947
Daukas, Nicholas (Dartmouth) —T— 1946–47
Davis, Joseph (Southern California) —E— 1946
Dewar, James (Indiana) —B—1948
Dobbs, Glenn (Tulsa) —B—1946–47
Edwards, Daniel (Georgia) —E—1948
Foldberg, Henry (West Point) —Q—1948
Forkovitch, Nicholas (William & Mary) — B—1948
Freeman, John (Texas) —G—1946
Gafford, Roy (Auburn) —B—1946–48
Gibson, Billy Joe (Tulsa) —C—1946–47
Gustafson, Edsel (George Washington) — C—1947–48
Harris, Amos (Mississippi State) —G— 1947–48
Harris, Elmore (Morgan State) —B—1947
Hein, Herbert (Minnesota) —E—1947
Hoernschemeyer, Robert (Indiana) —B— 1947
Hrabetin, Frank (Loyola, Cal.) —T—1946
Huneke, Charles (St. Benedict's) —T— 1947–48
Jeffers, Edward (Oklahoma A & M) —G— 1947
Jones, Lewis (Weatherford) —G—1948
Jones, William "Dub" (Tulane & Louisiana State Univ.) —B—1946–47
Judd, Saxon (Tulsa) —T—1946–48
Klasnic, John —B—1948
Kowalski, Adolph (Tulsa) —B—1947
Lauriaitis, Fred (Richmond) —C—1947
Leonetti, Robert (Wake Forest) —G—1948
Lovuolo, Edmund—T—1947
McCain, Robert (Mississippi) —E—1946
McCarthy, James (Illinois) —E—1946–47
McDonald, Walter (Tulane) —Q—1946–48
Maack, Herbert (Columbia) —T—1946
Maines, Thomas (Syracuse) —B—1946
Marcolini, Hugo (St. Bonaventure) —B— 1948
Martin, Jon—K—1948
Martinovich, Philip (College of Pacific) — G—1946–47
Mayne, Louis (Texas) —B—1946 1946–47
Mieszkowski, Edward (Notre Dame) —T— 1946–47
Mikula, Thomas (Williama & Mary) — B—1948
Morris, Max (Northwestern) —E—1948
Morrow, Russell (Tennessee) —C—1946–47
Nelson, Herbert (Pennsylvania) —E— 1947–48
Nygre, Bernard (San Jose State) —B—1947
Obeck, Victor (Springfield) —G—1946
Paffrath, Robert (Minnesota) —B—1946
Patanelli, Michael (Ball State Teachers) — E—1947
Perdue, Willard (Duke) —E—1946
Perina, Robert (Princeton) —B—1947

Perpich, George (Georgetown) —T—1946
Polanski, John (Wake Forest) —B—1947
Principe, Dominic (Fordham) —B—1946
Purdin, Calvin (Tulsa) —B—1946
Ramsey, Raymond (Bradley) —B—1948
Ruby, Martin (Texas A & M) —T—1946–48
Schneider, Leroy (Tulane) —T—1947
Scruggs, Edwin (Rice) —E—1947–48
Sergienko, George (American International) —T—1946
Shetley, Rhoten (Furman) —B—1946
Spencer, Joseph (Oklahoma A & M) —T—1948
St. John, Herbert (Georgia) —G—1948
Strohmeyer, George (Notre Dame) —C—1948
Sullivan, Robert (Holy Cross) —B—1948
Tackett, Doyle—B—1946–48
Tavenor, John (Indiana) —C—1946
Tevis, Leek (Washington, Mo.) —B—1947–48
Thompson, Harold (Delaware) —E—1947–48
Timmons, Charles (Clemson) —B—1946
Van Tone, Arthur (Mississippi Southern) —B—1946
Warren, Morrison (Arizona State)—B—1948
Warrington, Caleb (William & Mary) —C—1946–48
Wetz, Harlan (Texas) —T—1947
Williams, Garland (Georgia) —T—1947–48
Wozniak, John (Alabama) —G—1948

BUFFALO BILLS
(also played as BISONS)

Akins, Albert (Washington State) —B—1948
Armstrong, Graham (John Carroll) —T—1947–48
Balatti, Edward—E—1948
Baldwin, Alton (Arkansas) —E—1947–49
Baldwin, John (Centenary) —C—1948
Batorski, John (Colgate) —E—1946
Black, John (Mississippi State) —B—1946–47
Blount, Lamar (Mississippi State) —E—1947
Brazinsky, Samuel (Villanova) —C—1946
Bumgardner, Rex (West Virginia) —B—1948–49
Callahan, Robert (Michigan) —C—1948
Carlson, Raymond (Marquette) —B—1947
Carpenter, John (Michigan) —T—1947–49
Cline, Oliver (Ohio State) —B—1949
Colella, Thomas (Canisius) —B—1949
Comer, Martin (Tulane) —E—1946–48
Coppage, Alton (Oklahoma) —E—1947
Corley, Elbert (Mississippi State) —C—1947
Daddio, William (Pittsburgh) —E—1946
Dekdebrun, Allen (Cornell) —Q—1946
Doherty, George (Louisiana Tech.) —G—1946–47
Dudish, Andrew (Georgia) —B—1946
Duggan, Gilford (Oklahoma) —T—1947
Dugger, John (Ohio State) —E—1946
Ebli, Raymond (Notre Dame) —E—1946
Evans, Frederick (Notre Dame) —B—1947

Fekete, Eugene (Ohio State) —B—1946
Freitas, Jesse (Santa Clara) —Q—1949
Gibson, Paul (North Carolina State) —E—1947–49
Gompers, William (Notre Dame) —B—1948
Grigg, Forrest (Tulsa) —T—1946–47
Grover, George (Marquette) —G—1947
Haynes, Joseph (Tulsa) —C—1947
Herring, Harold (Auburn) —C—1949
Hirsch, Edward (Northwestern) —B—1947–49
Hopp, Harry (Nebraska) —Q—1946
Horne, Richard (Oregon) —G—1946
Joe, Lawrence (Penn State) —B—1949
Johnston, Preston (Southern Methodist Univ.) —B—1946
Jones, Elmer (Wake Forest) —G—1946
Juzwik, Steven (Notre Dame) —B—1946–47
Kasap, Michael (Purdue) —T—1947
Kerns, John (Ohio) —T—1947–49
King, Edward (Boston College) —E—1948–49
King, Henry (Georgia) —E—1946–47
Kisiday, George (Duquesne) —E—1948
Kissell, John (Boston College) —T—1948–49
Kissell, Veto (Holy Cross) —B—1949
Klenk, Quentin (Southern California) —E—1946
Klug, Alfred (Marquette) —T—1946
Klutka, Nicholas (Florida) —E—1946
Koch, George (Baylor) —B—1947
Kodba, Joseph (Purdue) —C—1947
Konetsky, Floyd (Florida) —E—1947
Kosikowski, Frank (Marquette) —E—1948
Kozel, Chester (Mississippi) —T—1947–48
Kramer, John (Marquette) —T—1946
Kuffel, Raymond (Marquette) —E—1947
Kulbitski, Victor (Minnesota) —B—1946–48
Lahar, Harold (Oklahoma) —G—1946–48
Lecture, James (Northwestern) —G—1946
Leonetti, Robert (Wake Forest) —G—1948
Livingstone, Robert (Notre Dame) —B—1949
Logel, Robert—E—1949
Lukens, James (Washington & Lee) —E—1949
Maggiole, Achille (Illinois) —B—1948
Manders, Clarence (Drake) —B—1947
Martinelli, James (Scranton) —C—1946
Maskas, John (Virginia Polytech) —G—1947, 49
Matsis, John (Duquesne) —T—1946
Mazza, Vincent—E—1947–49
Morton, John (Missouri) —E—1947
Mutryn, Chester (Xavier) —B—1946–49
Nelson, Herbert (Pennsylvania) —E—1946
O'Connor, William (Notre Dame) —E—1948
Oristaglio, Robert (Pennsylvania) —E—1949
Perko, John (Minnesota) —G—1946
Pfuhl, Richard (St. Louis) —B—1947
Pirro, Rocco (Catholic Univ.) —G—1946–49
Prewitt, Felton (Tulsa) —C—1946–48
Pucci, Benito—T—1946–47
Ratterman, George (Notre Dame) —Q—

1947–49

Reisz, Albert (Southeastern Louisiana) — **B–1947**

Rykovich, Julius (Illinois) —B–1947–48

Sandig, Curtis (St. Mary's—Tex.) —B–1946

Schilling, Ralph (Oklahoma City Univ.) —E–1946

Schneider, Donald (Pennsylvania) —B–1948

Schroll, Charles (Louisiana State Univ.) — —1949

Schuette, Carl (Marquette) —B–1948–49

Schwenck, Wilson (Washington, Mo.) — B–1947

Scott, Vincent (Notre Dame) —G–1947–48

Smith, James (Iowa) —B–1948

Stanley C. (Tulsa) —T–1946

Stanton, William (North Carolina State) — E–1949

Statuto, Arthur (Notre Dame) —C– 1948–49

Stautzenberger, Odell (Texas A & M) —G –1949

Stefik, Robert (Niagara) —E–1948

Steuber, Robert (Missouri) —B–1948

Still, James (Georgia Tech.) —B–1948–49

Stofer, Kenneth (Cornell) —B–1946

Stuart, Raymond (Tulsa) —B–1946

Sutton, Joseph (Temple) —B–1949

Terlep, George (Notre Dame)—Q–1946–48

Thibaut, James (Tulane) —B–1946

Thurbon, Robert (Pittsburgh) —B–1946

Thomasetti, Louis (Bucknell) —B–1946–49

Vandeweghe, Alfred (William & Mary) — B–1946

Vasicek, Victor (Texas) —G–1949

Vogt, Alois (Marquette) —Q–1946

Volz, Wilbur (Missouri) —B–1949

Whalen, Gerald (Canisius) —C–1948

White, Eugene (Indiana) —G–1946

Wizbicki, Alexander (Holy Cross) —B– 1947–49

Wukits, Albert (Duquesne) —C–1946

Wyhonic, John (Alabama) —G–1948–49

Zontini, Louis (Notre Dame) —B–1946

CHICAGO ROCKETS
(also played as HORNETS)

Agase, Alexander (Illinois) —G–1947

Aschenbrenner, Frank (Northwestern) — B–1949

Bailey, James (West Virginia State) —G– 1949

Bass, William (Nevada) —B–1947

Bauman, Alfred (Northwestern) —T–1947

Bernhardt, George (Illinois) —G–1948

Berry, Cornelius (North Carolina State) — E–1947

Bertelli, Angelo (Notre Dame) —Q– 1947–48

Billman, John (Minnesota) —G–1947

Boedecker, William (Kalamazoo) —B–1946

Brown, Hardy (Tulsa) —B–1949

Brutz, James (Notre Dame) —T–1946, 48

Buksar, George (Purdue) —B–1949

Burrus, Harry (Hardin-Simmons) —E–1948

Chappuis, Robert (Michigan) —B–1949

Clark, Harry, (West Virginia) —B–1948

Clay, Walter (Colorado) —B–1946–47

Cleary, Paul (Santa Ana & So. Cal.) —E –1949

Clement, John (Southern Methodist Univ.) —Q–1949

Clowes, John (William & Mary) —T–1949

Coleman, Herbert (Notre Dame) —C– 1946–48

Coolins, Albin (Louisiana State Univ.) — B–1949

Cox, Norman (Texas Christian Univ.) —B–1946–47

Czarobski, Zygmont (Notre Dame) —T– 1948–49

Daley, William (Minnesota) —B–1947

David, Robert (Villanova) —B–1948

Dekdebrun, Allen (Cornell) —Q–1947

Donaldson, John (Georgia) —B–1949

Dove, Robert (Notre Dame) —E–1946–47

Ebli, Raymond (Notre Dame) —E–1947

Ecker, Enrique (John Carroll) —T–1948

Edwards, Daniel (Georgia) —E–1949

Elliott, Charles (Oregon) —T–1948

Evans, Frederick (Notre Dame) —B– 1947–48

Farris, Thomas (Wisconsin) —Q–1948

Fenenbock, Charles (U.C.L.A.) —B–1948

Foldberg, Henry (West Point) —E–1949

Freitas, Jesse (Santa Clara) —Q–1948

Griffin, Donald (Illinois) —B–1946

Grigg, Forrest (Tulsa) —T–1947

Gudauskas, Peter (Murray State) —G–1948

Harrington, John (Marquette) —E–1947

Hazelwood, Theodore (North Carolina) — T–1949

Hecht, Alfred (Alabama) —**G–1947**

Heck Robert (Purdue) —E–1949

Heywood, Ralph (Southern California) — E–1946

Hillenbrand, William (Indiana) —B–1946

Hirsch, Elroy (Wisconsin) —B–1946–48

Hoernschemeyer, Robert (Indiana) —B– 1946–47, 49

Huneke, Charles (St. Benedict's) —T– 1946–47

Jensen, Robert (Iowa State) —E–1948–49

Johnson, Farnham (Wisconsin) —E–1948

Johnson, Nathan (Illinois) —T–1948–49

Juzwik, Steven (Notre Dame) —B–1948

Kellagher, William (Fordham) —B– 1946–48

King, Henry (Georgia) —E–1948–49

Klenk, Quentin (Southern California) — T–1946

Kozel, Chester (Mississippi) —T–1948

Kuffel, Raymond (Marquette) —E–1948–49

Kuzman, John (Fordham) —T–1947

Lahey, Thomas (John Carroll) —E– 1946–47

Lamana, Peter (Boston Univ.) —C–1946–48

Lewis, Ernest (Colorado) —B–1946–49

Livingstone, Robert (Notre Dame) —B– 1948–49

McCarthy, James (Illinois) —E—1948–49
McCollum, Harley (Tulane) —T—1947
McDonald, Walter (Tulane) —Q—1949
Maddock, George (Northwestern) —T—1949
Mathews, Edward (U.C.L.A.) —B—1946
Mattingly, Francis (Texas A & I) —B—1947
Mello, James (Notre Dame) —B—1948–49
Mihal, Joseph (Purdue) —T—1947
Miller Benjamin (Tennessee) —C—1946
Morris, Max (Northwestern) —E—1946–47
Motl, Robert (Northwestern) —E—1946
Mulready, Gerald (North Dakota State) —E—1947
Negus, Frederick (Wisconsin) —C—1947–49
Nemeth, Steven (Notre Dame) —B—1946
Niedziela, Bruno (Iowa) —T—1947
O'Neal, James (Texas Christian Univ.) —G—1946–47
Owens, Isaiah (Illinois) —E—1948
Paine, Homer (Oklahoma) —T—1949
Parks Edward (Oklahoma) —C—1946
Patterson, Paul (Illinois) —B—1949
Pearcy, James (Marshall) —G—1946–49
Perina, Robert (Princeton) —B—1948
Piskor, Roman (Niagara) —T—1948
Proctor, Dewey (Furman) —B—1948
Prokop, Edward (Georgia Tech.) —B—1948
Prokop, Joseph (Bradley) —B—1948
Pucci, Benito—T—1947
Quillen, Frank (Pennsylvania) —E—1946–47
Ramsey, Raymond (Bradley) —B—1947–49
Rapacz, John (Oklahoma) —C—1948–49
Richeson, Raymond (Alabama) —G—1949
Rokisky, John (Duquesne) —E—1947
Rothrock, Clifford (North Dakota State) —C—1947
Ruetz, Joseph (Notre Dame) —G—1946, 48
Rykovich, Julius (Illinois) —B—1948–49
St. John, Herbert (Georgia) —G—1949
Sanchez, John (San Francisco) —T—1947
Scalissi, Theodore (Ripon) —G—1947
Schroeder, William (Wisconsin) —B—1946–47
Simmons, Floyd (Notre Dame) —B—1948
Simmons, John (Detroit) —G—1948
Smith, James (Iowa) —B—1949
Smith, William (North Carolina) —T—1948
Soboleski, Joseph (Michigan) —T—1949
Strohmeyer, George (Notre Dame) —C—1949
Sullivan, Robert (Holy Cross) —B—1948
Sumpter, Anthony (Cameron Jr.) —G—1946–48
Sweiger, Robert (Minnesota) —B—1949
Urban, Gasper (Notre Dame) —G—1948
Uremovich, Emil (Indiana) —T—1948
Vacanti, Samuel (Nebraska) —Q—1947–48
Verry, Norman (Southern California) —T—1946–47
Vogds, Evan (Wisconsin) —G—1946–47
Wasserbach, Lloyd (Wisconsin) —T—1946–47
Wendell, Martin (Notre Dame) —G—1949
Wilkin, Wilbur (St. Mary's, Cal.) —T—1946
Williams, Walter (Boston Univ.) —B—1946

CLEVELAND BROWNS

Adamle, Anthony (Ohio State) —B—1947–49
Adams, Chester (Ohio Univ.) —T—1946–49
Agase, Alexander (Illinois) —G—1948–49
Akins, Albert (Washington State) —G—1946
Allen, Ermal (Kentucky) —B—1947
Blandin, Ernest (Tulane) —T—1946–47
Boedeker, William (Kalamazoo) —B—1947–49
Cheroke, George (Ohio State) —G—1946
Cline, Oliver (Ohio State) —B—1948
Colella, Thomas (Canisius) —B—1946–48
Coppage, Alton (Oklahoma) —E—1946
Cowan, Robert (Indiana) —B—1947–48
Daniell, James (Ohio State) —T—1946
Dellerba, Spiro (Ohio State) —B—1947
Dewar, James (Indiana) —B—1947
Evans, Frederick (Notre Dame) —B—1946
Fekete, Eugene (Ohio State) —B—1946
Gatski, Frank (Marshall) —C—1946–49
Gaudio, Robert (Ohio State) —G—1947–49
Gillom, Horace (Nevada) —E—1947–49
Graham, Otto (Northwestern) —Q—1946–49
Greenwood, Donald (Missouri) —B—1946–47
Grigg, Forrest (Tulsa) —T—1948–49
Groves, George (Marquette) —G—1946
Groza, Louis (Ohio State) —T—1946–49
Harrington, John (Marquette) —E—1946
Houston, Lindell (Ohio State) —G—1946–49
Humble, Weldon (Rice) —G—1947–49
James, Thomas (Ohio State) —B—1948–49
Jones, Edgar (Pittsburgh) —B—1946–49
Jones, William "Dub" (Tulane) —B—1948–49
Kolesar, Robert (Michigan) —G—1946
Kosilkowski, Frank (Marquette) —E—1948
Lahr, Warren (Western Reserve) —B—1948–49
Lavelli, Dante (Ohio State) —E—1946–49
Lewis, Clifford (Duke) —B—1946–49
Lund, William (Case) —B—1946–47
Maceau, Melvin (Marquette) —G—1946–48
Mayne, Louis (Texas) —E—1947
Motley, Marion (Nevada) —B—1946–49
O'Connor, William (Notre Dame) —E—1949
Palmer, Darrell (Texas Christian Univ.) —T—1949
Parseghian, Ara (Miami, Ohio) —B—1948–49
Piskor, Roman (Niagara) —T—1947
Pucci, Benito—T—1948
Rokisky, John (Duquesne) —E—1946
Rymkus, Louis (Notre Dame) —T—1946–49
Saban, Louis (Indiana) —G—1946–49
Scarry, Michael (Waynesburg) —C—1946–47

Schwenk, Wilson (Washington, Mo.) —B —1946

Sensenbaugher, Dean (Ohio State) —B— 1948

Shirnas, Marshall (Missouri) —E—1947

Simonetti, Leonard (Tennessee) —T— 1946-48

Smith, Gaylon (Southwestern) —B—1946

Speedie, Mac (Utah) —E—1946-49

Spencer, Joseph (Oklahoma A & M) —T— 1949

Susteric, Edward (Findlay) —B—1949

Terlep, George (Notre Dame) —Q—1948 1946-47

Terrell, Raymond (Mississippi) —B—

Thompson, Thomas (William & Mary) — C—1949

Ulinski, Edward (Marshall) —G—1946-49

Willis, William (Ohio State) —G—1946-49

Yonaker, John (Notre Dame) —E—1946-49

Young, George (Georgia) —E—1946-49

LOS ANGELES DONS

Agajanian, Benjamin (New Mexico) —K— 1947-48

Agase, Alexander (Illinois) —G—1947

Agler, Harry (California) —E—1948

Agler, Robert (Otterbein) —B—1948-49

Aguire, Joseph (St. Mary's, Cal.) —E— 1946-49

Anderson, Ezzret (Kentucky State) —E —1947

Artoe, Lee (California) —T—1946-47

Audet, Earl (Southern California) —T —1946-48

Avery, Donald (California) —T—1948

Baldwin, Burr (U.C.L.A.) —E—1947-49

Berezney, Peter (Notre Dame) —T—1947

Bertelli, Angelo (Notre Dame) —Q— 1946-47

Brown, John (North Carolina Coll.) —C —1947-49

Clark, Harry (West Virginia) —B—1946-48

Clay, Walter (Colorado) —B—1947-49

Crowe, Paul (St. Mary's, Cal.) —B—1948-49

Danehe, Richard (Southern California) — T—1947-48

Davis, Harper (Mississippi State) —B—1949

Dobbs, Glenn (Tulsa) —B—1947-49

Dobelstein, Robert (Tennessee) —G—1949

Donaldson, John (Georgia) —B—1949

Duggan, Gilford (Oklahoma) —T—1946

Durkota, Jeffrey (Penn State) —B—1948

Dworsky, Daniel (Michigan) —B—1949

Elsey, Earl (Loyola, La.) —B—1946

Fenenbock, Charles (U.C.L.A.) —B— 1946-48

Fisk, William (Southern California) —E —1948

Flagerman, John (St, Mary's, Cal.) —C— 1948

Fletcher, Oliver (Southern California) —G—1949

Ford, Leonard (Michigan) —E—1948-49

Frankowski, Raymond (Washington) — G—1946-48

Gallagher, Bernard (Pennsylvania) —G— 1947

Gentry, Dale (Washington State) —E— 1946-48

Graham, Michael (Cincinnati) —B—1948

Grimes, William (Oklahoma A & M) — B—1949

Heap, Walter (Texas) —B—1947-48

Hoffman, Robert (Southern California) — B—1949

Holder, Lewis (Texas) —E—1949

Hopp, Harry (Nebraska) —Q—1947

Howell, Earl (Mississippi) —B—1949

Johnson, Clyde (Kentucky) —T—1946-48

Kelley, Edward (Texas) —T—1949

Kelly, Robert (Notre Dame) —B—1947-48

Kennedy, Robert (North Carolina) —B— 1949

Kerr, William (Notre Dame) —E—1946

Kimbrough, John (Texas A & M) —B— 1946-48

Kreuger, Alvin (Southern California) — E—1946

Landsburg, Mortimer (Cornell) —B—1947

Lennan, Burgess—G—1947

Levy, Leonard (Minnesota) —G—1947-48

Lolotai, Albert (Weber) —G—1946-48

McQuarry, John (California) —B—1946-47

McWilliams, Thomas (Mississippi State) — B—1949

Marefos, Andrew (St. Mary's, Cal.) —B— 1946

Masini, Leonard (Fresno State) —B—1948

Mertes, Bernard (Iowa) —B—1946

Mihajlovich, Louis (Indiana) —E—1948

Mihal, Joseph (Purdue) —T—1946

Mitchell, Paul (Minnesota) —T—1946-48

Mitchell, Robert (Stanford) —B—1946-48

Morton, John (Missouri) —E—1946

Murphy, George (Southern California) — B—1949

Naumu, John (Southern California) —B— 1948

Nelson, Robert (Baylor) —C—1946-49

Nolander, Donald (Minnesota) —C—1946

Nowaskey, Robert (George Washington) —E—1946-48

Nygrem, Bernard (San Jose State) —B— 1946

O'Rourke, Charles (Boston College) — Q—1946-47

Ottele, Richard (Washington) —B—1948

Perrotti, Michael (Cincinnati)—T—1948-49

Piggott, Albert (Illinois) —B—1947

Pipkin, Joyce (Arkansas) —E—1949

Polanski, John (Wake Forest) —B—1946

Radovich, William (Southern California) —G—1946-47

Ramsey, Knox (William & Mary) —G— 1948-49

Reinhard, Robert (California) —T— 1946-48

Reinhard, William (California) —B— 1947-48

Rockwell, Henry (Arizona State) —C— 1946–48
Rodgers, Hosea (North Carolina) —B—1949
Sexton, Linwood (Wichita) —B—1948
Seymour, Robert (Oklahoma) —B—1946
Smith, William (North Carolina) —T—1948
Sneddon, Robert (St. Mary's, Cal.) —B— 1946
Spavital, James (Oklahoma A & M) —B— 1949
Steuber, Robert (Missouri) —B—1947
Taliaferro, George (Indiana) —B—1949
Tinsley, Robert (Baylor) —T—1949
Titchenal, Robert (San Jose State) —E— 1947
Trigilio, Frank (Alfred) —B—1946
Vant Hull, Frederick (Minnesota) —G— 1946
Vinnola, Paul (Santa Clara) —B—1946
Wedemeyer, Herman (St. Mary's, Cal.) — B—1948
Whaley, Benjamin (Virginia) —G—1949
Wilkins, Richard (Oregon) —E—1949
Williamson, Ernest (North Carolina) — T—1949
Wimberly, Abner (Louisiana State Univ.) —E—1949
Winkler, Bernard (Texas Tech) —T—1948
Woodward, Richard (Iowa) —C—1949
Yokas, Frank—G—1946

MIAMI SEAHAWKS (1946 only)

Bell, Edward (Indiana) —G
Berezney, Paul (Fordham) —T
Blount, Lamar (Mississippi State) —E
Cato, Daryl (Arkansas) —C
Daley, William (Minnesota) —B
Davis, Lamar (Georgia) —E
Davis, William (Texas Tech) —T
Eakin, Kay (Arkansas) —B
Ellenson, Eugene (Georgia) —T
Erdlitz, Richard (Northwestern) —B
Fox, Terrence (Miami) —B
Gafford, Roy (Auburn) —B
Gloden, Frederick (Tulane) —B
Hekkers, George (Wisconsin) —T
Holley, Kenneth (Holy Cross) —Q
Hopp, Harry (Nebraska) —Q
Horne, Richard (Oregon) —G
Hrabetin, Frank (Loyola, Cal.) —T
Johnston, Preston (Southern Methodist Univ.) —B
Jungmichel, Harold (Texas) —G
Koslowski, Stanley (Holy Cross) —B
Krivonak, Joseph (South Carolina) —G
McDonald, Walter (Tulane) —Q
Mitchell, Fondren (Florida) —B
Nelson, James (Alabama) —B
Olenski, Mitchell (Alabama) —T
Paffrath, Robert (Minnesota) —B
Perdue, Willard (Duke) —E
Price, Charles (Texas A & M) —Q
Pugh, Marion (Texas A & M) —Q
Purdin, Calvin (Tulsa) —B
Reece, Donald (Missouri) —T

Reynolds, James (Auburn) —B
Scott, Prince (Texas Tech) —E
Sivell, Ralph (Auburn) —G
Stasica, Stanley (South Carolina) —B
Tarrant, James (Howard) —Q
Tavenor, John (Indiana) —C
Taylor, Charles (Stanford) —G
Trigilio, Frank (Alfred) —B
Ulrich, Hubert (Kansas) —E
Vardian, John—B
Whitlow, Kenneth (Rice) —C
Williams, John (Auburn) —C
Wukits, Albert (Duquesne) —C
Zorich, George (Northwestern) —G

NEW YORK YANKEES

Alford, Herbert Bruce (Texas Christian Univ.) —E—1946–49
Balatti, Edward—E—1948
Baldwin, John (Centenary) —C—1946–47
Barwegan, Richard (Purdue) —G—1947
Batinski, Stanley (Temple) —G—1949
Bentz, Roman (Tulane) —T—1946–48
Black, John (Mississippi State) —B—1946
Brown, George (Texas Christian Univ.) —G—1949
Burrus, Harry (Hardin-Simmons) —E— 1946–47
Butkus, Carl (George Washington) — T—1948
Callen, Frank (St. Mary's, Cal.) —G—1947
Cardinal, Fred (Baldwin Wallace) —B— 1947
Casey, Thomas (Hampton) —B—1948
Chambers, William (Alabama) —T— 1948–49
Cheatham, Lloyd (Auburn) —B—1946–48
Cleary, Paul (Santa Ana) —E—1948
Colmer, John—B—1949
Conger, Melvin (Georgia) —E—1946–47
Crawford, Denver (Tennessee) —T—1948
Daley, William (Minnesota) —B—1948
Davis, Van (Georgia) —E—1947–49
Dekdebrun, Allen (Cornell) —Q—1948
Dickey, Leonard—T—1947
Doherty, George (Louisiana Tech) —G— 1946
Doss, Noble (Texas) —B—1949
Durishan, John (Pittsburgh) —T—1947
Dutton, William (Pittsburgh) —B—1946
Elliott, Charles (Oregon) —T—1947
Erickson, William (Mississippi) —G—1949
Garzoni, Michael (Southern California) — G—1948
Grain, Edwin (Pennsylvania) —G—1947
Green, Nelson (Tulsa) —T—1948
Hare, Ray (Gonzaga) —B—1946
Howard, Sherman (Nevada) —B—1949
Iverson, Christopher (Oregon) —B—1948
Johnson, Gilbert (Southern Methodist Univ.) —B—1949
Johnson, Glenn (Arizona State) —T—1948
Johnson, Hargey (William & Mary) —B— 1946–49
Johnson, Nathan (Illinois) —T—1946–47

Kennedy, Robert (Washington State) —
  B—1946–49
Kinard, Frank (Mississippi) —T—1946–47
Kinard, George (Mississippi) —G—1946
Kurrasch, Roy (U.C.L.A.) —E—1947
Kusserow, Louis (Columbia) —B—1949
Landry, Thomas (Texas) —B—1949
Lane, Clayton (New Hampshire) —T—1948
Layden, Peter (Texas) —B—1948–49
McCollum, Harley, (Tulane) —T—1946
McDonald, Donald (Oklahoma) —E—1948
Magliolo, Joseph (Texas) —B—1948
Manders, Clarence (Drake) —B—1946
Masterson, Robert (Miami) —E—1946
Mastrangelo, John (Notre Dame) —G—1949
Mitchell, Paul (Minnesota) —T—1948–49
Nabors, Roland (Texas Tech) —C—1948
Ossowski, Theodore (Oregon State) —
  T—1947
Owens, Delmer (North Idaho) —B—1947
Palmer, Darrell (Texas Christian Univ.) —
  T—1946–48
Panciera, Donald (San Francisco) —B—1949
Parker, Clarence (Duke) —B—1946
Parker, Howard (Southern Methodist
  Univ.) —B—1948
Perina, Robert (Princeton) —B—1946
Piskor, Roman (Niagara) —T—1946
Poole, G. Barney (Mississippi) —E—1949
Poole, Oliver (Mississippi) —E—1947
Proctor, Dewey (Furman) —B—1946–47, 49
Prokop, Edward (Georgia Tech) —B—
  1946–47, 49
Raimondi, Benjamin (Indiana) —B—1947
Riffle, Charles (Notre Dame) —G—1946–47
Robertson, Thomas (Tulsa) —C—1946
Rokisky, John (Duquesne) —E—1948
Rowe, Harmon (San Francisco) —B—
  1947–49
Ruby, Martin (Texas A & M) —T—1949
Ruskusky, Raymond (St. Mary's, Cal.) —
  E—1947
Russell, John (Baylor) —E—1946–49
Sanchez, John (San Francisco) —T—1947
Sanders, Orban (Texas) —B—1946–48
Schleich, Victor (Nebraska) —T—1947
Schnellbacher, Otto (Kansas) —E—1948–49
Schwartz, Perry (California) —E—1946
Schwenk, Wilson (Washington, Mo.)
  —B—1948
Sharkey, Edward (Nevada) —G—1947–49
Shirley, Marion (Oklahoma City Univ.) —
  T—1948–49
Sieradski, Stephen (Michigan State) —B—
  1948
Signaigo, Joseph (Notre Dame) —G—
  1948–49
Sinkwich, Frank (Georgia) —B—1946–47
Sossamon, Louis (South Carolina) —C—
  1946–49
Stanton, Henry (Arizona) —E—1946–47
Stewart, Ralph (Missouri) —C—1947–48
Sweiger, Robert (Minnesota) —B—1946–48
Sylvester, John (Temple) —B—1947
Tew, Lowell (Alabama) —B—1948–49
Wagner, Lowell (Southern California) —

B—1946–48
Weinmeister, Arnold (Washington) —T—
  1948–49
Werder, Richard (Georgetown) —G—1948
Wozniak, John (Alabama) —G—1949
Yachanich, Joseph (Fordham) —G—1946–48
Young, Claude "Buddy" (Illinois) —B—
  1947–49

SAN FRANCISCO 49ers

Albert, Frank (Stanford) —Q—1946–49
Baldwin, John (Centenary) —C—1947
Balatti, Edward—T—1946–48
Banducci, Bruno (Stanford) —G—1946–49
Bassi, Richard (Santa Clara) —G—1946–47
Beals, Alyn (Santa Clara) —E—1946–49
Bentz, Roman (Tulane) —T—1948
Bryant, Robert (Texas Tech) —T—1946–49
Calvelli, Anthony (Stanford) —C—1947
Carpenter, John (Michigan) —T—1949
Carr, Edwin—B—1947–49
Casenega, Kenneth (Santa Clara) —B—
  1946–48
Cason, James (Louisiana State Univ.) —
  B—1948–49
Cathcart, Samuel (Santa Barbara) —B—1949
Clark, Donald (Southern California) —
  G—1948–49
Collier, Floyd (San Jose State) —T—1948
Conlee, Gerald (St. Mary's, Cal.) —C—
  1946–47
Cox, James (Stanford) —G—1948
Crowe, Paul (St. Mary's, Cal.) —B—1948
Crowell, Odis (Hardin-Simmons) —T—
  1947
Durdan, Donald (Oregon State) —B—
  1946–47
Elliott, Charles (Oregon) —T—1948
Elston, Arthur (Southern California) —
  C—1946–48
Eshmont, Leonard (Fordham) —B—1946–49
Evans, Raymond (Texas Mines) —T—1949
Evansen, Paul (Oregon State) —G—1948
Fisk, William (Southern California) —E
  —1946–47
Forrest, Edward (Santa Clara) —C—1946–47
Franschi, Peter (San Francisco) —B—1946
Freitas, Jesse (Santa Clara) —Q—1946–47
Garlin, Donald (Southern California) —B
  —1949
Gregory, Garland (Louisiana Tech) —G—
  1946–47
Grgich, Visco (Santa Clara) —G—1946–49
Hall, Forrest (Duquesne) —B—1948
Hall, Parker (Mississippi) —Q—1946
Handley, Richard (Fresno State) —C—1947
Hobbs, Homer (Georgia) —G—1949
Horne, Richard (Oregon) —E—1947
Howell, Clarence (Texas A & M) —E—1948
Johnson, William (Tyler Jr.) —C—1948–49
Kenny, Charles (San Francisco) —G—1947
Kuzman, John (Fordham) —T—1946
Land, Frederick (Louisiana State Univ.) —
  G—1948
Lillywhite, Verl (Southern California) —

B—1948–49

McCormick, Walter (Southern California) —C—1948

Maloney, Norman (Purdue) —E—1948–49

Masini, Leonard (Fresno State) —B— 1947–48

Matheson, Riley (Texas Mines) —G—1948

Mathews, Edward (U.C.L.A.) —B—1946–47

Mellus, John (Villanova) —T—1946

Mike, Robert (U.C.L.A.) —T—1948–49

Morgan, Joseph (Mississippi Southern) — T—1949

Norberg, Henry (Stanford) —E—1946–47

Parsons, Earle (Southern California) —B —1946–47

Pavlich, Charles—G—1946

Puddy, Harold (Oregon State) —T—1948

Quilter, Charles—T—1949

Remington, Joseph (Washington State) — C—1946

Renfro, Richard (Washington State) —B 1946

Robnett, Edward (Texas Tech) —B—1947

Roskie, Kenneth (South Carolina) —B— 1946

Sabuco, Tino (San Francisco) —C—1949

Salata, Paul (Southern California) —E—1949

Satterfield, Alfred (Vanderbilt) —T—1947

Schiechl, John (Santa Clara) —C—1947

Shoener, Harold (Iowa) —E—1948–49

Smith, George (California) —C—1947

Standlee, Norman (Stanford) —B—1946–49

Strzykalski, John (Marquette) —B—1946–49

Sullivan, Robert (Holy Cross) —B—1948

Susoeff, Nicholas (Washington State) —E —1946–49

Thornton, Robert (Santa Clara) —G— 1946–47

Titchenal, Robert (San Jose State) —E— 1946

Vetrano, Joseph (Mississippi Southern) — B—1946–49

Wagner, Lowell (Southern California) —B —1949

Wallace, Beverly (Compton Jr.) —B— 1947–49

Williams, Joel (Texas) —C—1948

Wissman, Peter (St. Louis) —C—1949

Woudenberg, John (Denver) —T—1946–49

Yonamine, Wallace—B—1947

Zamlynski, Zigmond (Villanova) —B—1946

THE ALL-TIME ROSTER BY COLLEGES

The following pages list all major league football players (since 1921) under the names of the colleges which produced them. Here also are players who attended no college, or whose background is obscured. It must be admitted too that a few mastodons of the early days sometimes coyly added the name of a prominent university to their own without going through the formality of becoming a student thereof, thereby clouding the scene from the standpoint of research in later years. This will explain why some last names have universities attached but lack first names, for all colleges were queried about the identity of these athletes.

These same players are listed under the Player Roster, and the Team Rosters along with their playing records and any departmental championships they earned.

ABILENE CHRISTIAN
Goad, Paul
Jones, Thurman
Mooney, Bow Tipp
Smith, Charles
Smith, Verda
Stovall, Richard

ADAMS STATE, COLO.
Epperson, John
Epperson, Pat

AKRON UNIVERSITY
Bierce, Bruce
Callahan, Daniel
Daum, Carl
Haley, Arthur
Waldsmith, Ralph
Wallace, Fred
Zimmerman, Guy

ALABAMA STATE
Davis, Arthur

ALABAMA STATE TEACHERS

Busby, Sherrill
Hill, Harlon
Romine, Alton

ALABAMA UNIVERSITY
Avinger, Clarence
Bostick, Lewis
Bowdoin, James
Brown, David
Buckler, William
Cain, James
Calvin, Thomas
Chambers, William
Cook, Theodore
Craft, Russell
Culpepper, Edward
Davis, Frederick
Davis, Raymond
DeShane, Charles
Domnanovich, Joseph
Eberdt, Jess
Fichman, Leon
Gerber, Elwood
Gilmer, Harry
Hannah, Herbert

Hecht, Alfred
Hickerson, Edward
Holm, Bernard
Howell, Millard
Hunt, Ben
Hupke, Thomas
Hutson, Donald
Jackson, Robert
Jones, Bruce
Jones, Ralph
Kirkland, B'ho
Lauer, Lawrence
Lee, William
Leon, Anthony
MacAfee, Kenneth
McCoy, Joel
Mancha, Vaughn
Martin, Frank
Merrill, Walter
Morrow, John
Mosley, Norman
Mosley, Russell
Nelson, James
Olenski, Mitchell

Oliver, William
Perry, Claude
Reese, Kenneth
Richardson, Ray
Richeson, Ray
Salem, Edward
Sanford, Hayward
Shipp, William
Smith, Ben
Smith, Riley
Starr, Bryan
Steiner, Roy
Stewart, Vaughn
Tew, Lowell
Tharp, Thomas
Trocolor, Robert
Watford, Gerald
Weeks, George
Wesley, Lecil
Whatley, James
Whire, John
White, Arthur
Wood, Robert
Wozniak, John
Wyhonic, John
Young, William
Youngelman, Sidney

ALBRIGHT
Barkman, Ralph
Carney, Harold
Disend, Leo
Durko, John
Kosel, Stanley
Kostos, Martin
Riffle, Richard
Taylor, George

ALCORN A & M
Purnell, Frank
Spinks, Jack

ALFRED
Bancroft, Hugh
Goble, Lester
Trigilio, Frank

AMERICAN
Rychlec, Thomas
Sergienko, George

ANNAPOLIS
Bartos, Joseph
Carney, Arthur
Chase, Ben
Denfield, Frank
Duden, Richard
Martin, John
Mathews, Bob Orr
Merillat, Louis
Reifsnyder, Robert
Roberts, Walcott
Schuber, James

APPALACHIAN STATE
Hollar, John
Watts, George

ARIZONA STATE
Burton, Leon
Johnson, Glenn
Johnson, John Henry
McGibbony, Charles
Matesic, Joseph
Mitcham, Eugene
Osborne, Clarence
Putman, Earl
Rockwell, Henry
Warren, Morrison
White, Wilford

ARIZONA UNIVERSITY
Banjavic, Emil
Corbitt, John
Enke, Fred
Greenfield, Thomas
Karnofsky, Abraham
Mellekas, John
Mulleneaux, Lee
Nielsen, Walter
Nolan, Earl
Stanton, Henry
Whitlow, Robert
Young, Joseph

ARKANSAS A & M
Nichols, Michael

ARKANSAS POLYTECH
Meador, Edward
Taylor, Charles

ARKANSAS STATE
Woit, Richard

ARKANSAS UNIVERSITY
Adams, O'Neal
Bagby, Herman
Baldwin, Alton
Barker, Hubert
Benton, James
Britt, Maurice
Brooks, William
Brown, William
Campbell, Leon
Carpenter, Lewis
Carpenter, Preston
Casey, Albert
Cato, Daryl
Creighton, Milan
Eakin, Kay
Forte, Robert
Fowler, Aubrey
Griffin, Robert
Hamilton, Ray
Hanner, Joel
Hayden, John
Hayden, Kenneth
Hickey, Howard
Hix, William
Hoffman, John
Howell, James Lee
Jamerson, Charles
Keen, Delbert
Ledbetter, Homer
Lunday, Kenneth
McHan, Lamar
Mazzanti, Gino
Merloni, Peter
Moore, Henry
Mooty, James
Morton, Lock
Murphy, Thomas
Pense, Leon
Pipkin, Joyce
Robbins, John
Sagely, Floyd
Scott, Clyde
Simington, Milton
Sloan, Dwight
Smith, Billy Ray
Spillers, Ray
Summerall, George
Thorpe, Wilfred
Underwood, Ronald
Van Sickle, Clyde
Williams, Fred
Winkelman, Ben
Wynne, Harry

ARNOLD
Robustelli, Andrew

ASHLAND
Novotny, Raymond

AUBURN (Ala. Polytech)
Ariail, David
Atkins, George
Atkins, William
Brackett, M. L.
Bulger, Chester
Cheatham, Lloyd
Childress, Joseph
Cochran, Thomas
Cremer, Theodore
D'Agostino, Frank
Danjean, Ernest
Deal, Rufus
Freeman, Robert
Gafford, Roy
Ghersanich, Vernon
Harper, Maurice
Harrison, Maxwell
Herring, Harold
Middleton, David
Phillips, James
Reynolds, James
Roton, Herbert

Russell, Torrance
Sivell, J. Ralph
Smith, Roger
Taylor, Erquiet
Tidwell, Travis
Warrington, Caleb
Williams, John
Wilson, Gerald

AUGSBURG
Pederson, James

AUGUSTANA
Leng, George

AUSTIN
Babb, Eugene
Bookout, William
Cross, Robert
Grigg, Cecil
Milam, Barnes
Shirkey, George

BAKER UNIVERSITY
Hill, Charles

BAKERSFIELD
Fields, George

BALDWIN-WALLACE
Barrett, Robert
Bauer, Herbert
Caldwell, Cyril
Cardinal, Frank
Hecker, Norbert
Hecker, Robert
Morris, George

BALL STATE TEACHERS
Patanelli, Michael

BAYLOR
Akin, Leonard
Barnett, Solon
Biggs, Riley
Boyd, Samuel
Bradshaw, Charles
Bradshaw, Wesley
Brazell, Carl
Burk, Adrian
Casner, Kenneth
Crain, Milton
Davidson, Frances
Dickson, Paul
Dowden, Steven
Dupre, Charles
Dupre, Louis
Edwards, William
Gatewood, Lester
Glass, William
Gonsoulin, Austin
Gremminger, Henry
Griffin, Robert
Hartzog, Howard
Hatley, John
Hickman, Lawrence
Humphrey, Loyie
Jones, Harvey
Kirk, Bernard
Koch, George
Kriel, Emmett
Lucky, William
Lummus, John
Lunceford, David
McCormick, Leonard
Masters, Robert
Nelson, Robert
Parry, Owen
Patterson, William
Paxton,
Reynolds, John
Russell, John
Russell, Lloyd
Shofner, Del
Sims, George
Smith, James Ray
Taylor, James
Tinsley, Robert
Weathers, Guy
Williams, Stanley
Wilson, John
Wisener, Gary
Witcher, Thomas, "Al"

BELOIT

Barry, George
Dahlgren, George
Dalton
Darling, Bernard
DeMoe, William
Kuick, Stanley
MacAuliffe, John
McGaw, Walter
Purdy, Everett
Sullivan, Walter

BETHANY, MO.
Broadlet, Karl
Dimmick, Donald
Flohr, Lester
Hahn, Ray
Jean, Walter
Rhenquist, Milton

BIRMINGHAM, SOUTHERN
Davis, Hermit
McMichaels, John

BETHUNE-COOKMAN
McClairan, Jack

BLUFFTON
Dubenion, Elbert

BOSTON COLLEGE
Ananis, Vito
Bouley, Gilbert
Canale, Rocco
Cannava, Anthony
Colclough, James
Connolly, Harry
Cronin, John
Cronin, William
Curran, Harry
Currivan, Donald
Donahue, John
Donovan, Arthur
Dubinski, Walter
Fiorentino, Albert
Giannelli, Mario
Gladchuk, Chester
Harrison, Edward
Holovak, Michael
Johnson, Kosse
Kaplan, Joseph
King, Edward
Kissell, Adolph
Kissell, John
Kobolinski, Stanley
Koslowski, Joseph
Levanitis, Stephen
Lucas, Richard
McGurik, Warren
Manzo, Frank
Marston, Ralph
Maznicki, Frank
Miller, Alan
Miller, John
Morrisey, Frank
Morze, Frank
Naumetz, Fred
O'Connell, Grattan
O'Hanley, Ross
O'Rourke, Charles
Repko, Joseph
Sheehan, John
Songin, Edward
Spinney, Arthur
Stautner, Ernest
Tosi, Flavio
Urban, Luke
Williams, Theodore

BOSTON UNIVERSITY
Bredice, John
Dixon, Felix
Dorfman, Arthur
Famiglietti, Gary
Lamana, Peter
Marques, Robert
Morris, Francis
Prebola, Eugene
Sulima, George
Williams, Walter

BOWLING GREEN
Baker, Lawrence
Koepfer, Karl

Ladd, James
Russell, Kenneth
Schnelker, Robert

BRADLEY
Carlson, Roy
Carothers, Donald
Elness, Leland
Jacobs, Harry
Jamieson, Richard
Ormsbee, Elliott
Prokop, Joseph
Ramsey, Ray
Roehnelt, William
Stone, William

BRANDEIS
Long, Michael

BRIGHAM YOUNG
Berry, Rex
Brundage, Dewey
Chamberlain, Garth
Felt, Richard
Kapele, John
McFarlane, Nyle
Nelson, Reed
Robison, Burle

BRITISH COLUMBIA
Crawford, William

BROADDUS
Mulbarger, Joseph

BROOKLYN COLLEGE
Sherman, Alex

BROWN
Annan, Duncan
Battles, William
Brace, Robert
Broda, Harold
Colo, Don
Cornsweet, Albert
Eckstein, Adolph
Edwards, Charles
Gulian, Michael
Hall, Irving
Hillhouse, Andrew
Keefer, Jackson
Lawrence, Edward
McCrillis, Edward
McLaughry, John
Margarita, Henry
Mishel, David
Oden, Olaf
Pohlman, John
Pollard, Fritz
Priestley, Robert
Purdy, Clair
Reynolds, Quentin
Sampson, Seneca
Schein, Joseph
Sheldon, James
Shurtleff, Bertrand
Smith, Orland
Stephan, W. A.
Stevens, Theodore
Spellman, John
Stifler, James
Sweet, Frederick
Talbot, John
Williams, Jay "Inky"

BUCKNELL
Bollinger, Edward
Bowser, Arda
Brumbaugh, Justin
Conti, Enio
Dayhoff, Harry
Dempsey, John
Diehl, Walter
Ellor, Albert
Foster, James
Goodwin, Myrl
Halicki, Edward
Hambacker, Ernest
Hendren, John
Hubka, Eugene
Jones, Thomas
Kiick, George
Kostos, Anthony
Lott, John

McCormick, Felix
Mitchell, Frederick
Myers, Bradford
Ostendarp, James
Pegg, Harold
Reed, Max
Rodgers, Thomas
Smith, Stuart
Szot, Walter
Tomasetti, Louis
Wilkinson, William
Wilsbach, Frank
Woerner, Erwin

BUFFALO
Ailinger, James

BUTLER
Cavosie, John
Elser, Earl
Hinchman, Hubert
Reichle, Louis
Woods, Gerald

CALIFORNIA STATE POLY
Bravo, Alex
Ford, Frederick
Jeter, Perry
Schmidt, Kermit
Sharp, Everett
Sheriff, Stanley

CALIFORNIA (SOUTHERN)
Addison, Thomas
Ane, Charles
Apsit, Marger
Arnett, Jon
Audet, Earl
Badgro, Morris
Baker, Roy
Bansavage, Albert
Banta, Herbert
Barrager, Nathan
Barry, Albert
Belotti, George
Bleeker, Melvin
Bowers, William
Bukich, Rudolph
Burke, Donald
Cannamela, Pat
Carmichael, Albert
Chantiles, Thomas
Clark, Donald
Clark, Monte
Clarke, Leon
Cleary, Paul
Clemens, Calvin
Coia, Angelo
Crow, Lindon
Danehe, Richard
Davis, Joseph
DeLauer, Robert
Doll, Donald
Downs, Robert
Dunn, Coye
Elston, Arthur
Ferranti, Orlando
Finneran, Garry
Fisher, Robert
Fisk, William
Fletcher, Oliver
Garlin, Donald
Garzoni, Michael
Gentry, Michael
George, Raymond
Gifford, Francis
Griffiths, Homer
Hardy, James
Hendren, Robert
Hawkins, John
Henke, Edgar
Henry, Michael
Heywood, Ralph
Hibbs, Jesse
Hoffman, Robert
Hoffman, Wayne
Howard, William
Jessup, William
Johnston, Rex
Kaer, Morton
Kirby, John
Klenk, Quentin
Krueger, Alvin

Lansdell, Granville
Lillywhite, Verl
McCormick, Walter
Margucci, Joseph
Miller, Ronald
Milton, John
Mix, Ronald
Mooney, "Tex"
  (O. P. Schupbach)
Morgan, Boyd
Murphy, George
Musick, James
Naumi, John
Nix, John
Parsons, Earle
Peters, Volney
Peviani, Robert
Pinckert, Ernest
Powers, James
Psaltis, James
Radovich, William
Roberts, Cornelius
Robertson, Robert
Rorison, James
Rubke, Karl
Saenz, Edward
Salata, Paul
Saunders, Russell
Schmidt, Henry
Sears, James
Shaw, Jesse
Smith, Ernest
Smith, Harry
Sohn, Benjamin
Steponovich, Anthony
Stonebraker, John
Timberlake, George
Tipton, Howard
Tonelli, Amerigo
VanDoren, Robert
Verry, Norman
Ward, John
Wehba, Raymond
West, Pat
Williams, John
Winslow, Robert
Wood, William

CALIFORNIA U.
Agler, Harry
Artoe, Lee
Avery, Donald
Baker, Jon
Celeri, Robert
Crow, Wayne
Cullom, James
Eaton, Louis
Evans, John
Harding, Roger
Hazeltine, Matthew
Hufford, Darrell
Imlay, Talma
Jacobs, Proverb
Johnson, Donald
Larson, Paul
McCarthy, James
McQuary, John
Mathewson, M.
Maul, C. Newell
Monachino, James
Muller, Harold
Newmeyer, Donald
Norris, Harold
Olszewski, John
Perry, Gerald
Reinhard, Robert
Reinhard, William
Richter, Lester
Schabarum, Peter
Schaffnit, Peter
Schwartz, Perry
Smith, George
Wagner, Lowell
Young, John

CALIFORNIA UNIVERSITY
(at Los Angeles, UCLA)
Baldwin, Burr
Boyer, Verdi
Cameron, Paul
Cantor, Leo
Case, Ernest
Davis, Milton
Ellena, Jack
Fears, Thomas
Fenenbock, Charles

Finlay, John
Hermann, John
Keeble, Joseph
Kendall, Charles
Knox, Ronald
Kurrasch, Roy
Livingston, Clifford
Long, Robert
Loudd, Rommie Lee
Lyman, Delbert
McChesney, Robert
McLaughlin, Leon
Mathews, Ned
Mike, Robert
Mitchell, Harold
Myers, John
Nagel, Ray
Oglesby, Paul
Olson, Carl
Paul, Don
Phillips, George
Salsbury, James
Shinnick, Donald
Shipkey, Gerald
Smith, Harold
Smith, Milton
Snelling, Kenneth
Sommers, John
Sparlis, Albert
Steffen, James
Stits, William
Strode, Woodrow
Stroschein, Brock
Thompson, Harry
Washington, Kenneth
Waterfield, Robert
Wilkinson, Robert

CAMERON JR.
Sumpter, Anthony

CANISIUS
Burt, Russell
Carr, Harlan
Colella, Thomas
Collins, John
Doyle, Edward
Fay, James
Feist, Louis
Guarneri, Albert
Mantell, Joseph
Piccolo, William
Poillon, Richard
Trayner, Michael
Whalen, Gerald

CARLETON
Eberts, Bernard
Morse, Robert
Norton, Martin
Smith, Warren
Willegalle, Henry

CARLISLE
Barrel
Busch, Elmer
Calac, Peter
Gardner, George
Guyon, Joseph
Little Twig
Lone Wolf
Long Time Sleep
  (Nikolas Lassa)
Newashe
Pierce, Bemus
Powell, Stancil
Saunook
St. Germaine, Theodore
Thorpe, Jack
Thorpe, James
Tomahawk
Towell
Welmus, Woodchuck
Winneschick

CARNEGIE TECH
Campbell, Donald
Carnelly, Ray
Condit, Merlyn
Dobrus, Peter
Dolaway, Clifford
Donohoe, William
Flanagan, Latham
Karcis, John
Kavel, George

Lee, John
Mielziner, Saul
Mills, Joseph
Moran, Dale
Newman, Olin
Patt, Maurice
Rieth, William
Robertson, James
Schmidt, John
Spisak, Charles
Sprinkle, Hubert
Stewart, Charles
Tesser, Ray

CARROLL COLLEGE
Ambrose, Walter
Bizer, Herbert
Buck, Arthur
George, Karl
Hempel, William
Hertz, Frank
Lande, Clifford
Ludtke, Norman
Quinn, Ivan
Sparr, Edwin

CARTHAGE
Wager, John

CASE
Goss, Norman
Lund, William

CATAWBA
Robinson, Gilbert
Tomaini, Army
Yagiello, Ray

CATHOLIC
UNIVERSITY
Ambrose, John
Augusterfer, Eugene
Connell, James
Connor, William
Fisher, Clark
Howell, Wilfred
Karpowich, Edward
Katalinas, Leo
Lajovsky, William
Lynch, Edward
Mayer, Ernest
Mulligan, George
Pirro, Rocco
Schmarr, Herman
Whalen, Thomas

CENTENARY
Baker, Conway
Baldwin, Jack
Barnhart, Daniel
Bohlmann, Frank
Hogue, Murrel
May, Francis
Parker, Raymond
Rebseaman, Paul
Schwarzer, Theodore
Stoker, Lee

CENTRAL COLLEGE
Failing, Frederick

CENTRE COLLEGE
Baxter, Ernest
German, James
Gibson, Richard
Kottler, Martin
Lemon, Clifford
MacCollum, Maxwell
McMillin, Alvin
Montgomery, Ralph
Moran, Thomas
Priest, James
Robb, Stanley
Roberts, James
Smythe, James
Tanner, John
Weaver, James

CHATTANOOGA
Braidwood, Charles
Butler, William
Clark, Howard
Cohen, Abraham
Getz, Fred
Grant, Aaron

Green, John
Gregory, Jack
Grigonis, Frank
Hutchinson, Ralph
Johnson, Robert
Lagod, Chester
Ledyard, Harold
Koeninger, Arthur
Kopcha, Joseph
Roberts, Eugene
Young, Richard

CHICAGO UNIV.
Bryant, John
Busse, Ellis
DesJardins, Paul
Egan, Richard
Folz, Arthur
Francis, Eugene
Goodman, Aubrey
Halladay, Richard
Hamity, Lewis
Hartong, George
Hobscheid, Frank
Hurlburt, John
Jackson, Colville
Kernwein, Graham
King, Ralph
Leatherman, Paul
Mullen, Thomas
Perrin, John
Romney, Milton
Sherman, Saul
Weaver, Charles

CHICO STATE
Butts, Edward
Maderos, George

CINCINNATI
Blake, Thomas
Capuzzi, James
DeWeese, Byrne
Feldhaus, William
Graham, Michael
Johnson, Eugene
Kovac, Edward
Lee, Jack
Lee, James
Messner, Max
Morrison, Joseph
Nickel, Elbie
Nolting, Ray
O'Malley, Robert
Perrotti, Michael
Skorich, Nicholas
Smyth, William
Stautberg, Gerald
Sweeney, Jake

CITADEL
Davidson, Peter
Maguire, Paul
Sabados, Andrew

CLEMSON
Bryant, Lowell
Cline, Douglas
Cone, Fred
Cordileone, Louis
Dukes, Michael
Folk, Richard
Fritts, George
Gage, Robert
Hayes, Richard
Hendley, Richard
Hudson, Robert
McFadden, Banks
Mathews, Ray
Mathis, William
Olson, Harold
Pagliei, Joseph
Patton, Robert
Timmons, Charles
Tinsley, Sidney
White, Harvey
Ziegler, Francis

COLBY COLLEGE
Druehl, William

COLGATE
Abruzzino, Frank
Anderson, Oscar

Anderson, Winston
Batorski, John
Beuthel, Lloyd
Cabrelli, Lawrence
Call, John
Chesbro, Marcel
Crowthers, Rae
Crowthers, Saville
Davidson, Joseph
Dowler, Thomas
Duckworth, Joseph
Fortmann, Daniel
Gauer, Charles
Geyer, William
Gillo, Henry
Gilson, Robert
Haines, Harry
Hart, J. Leslie
Hoague, Joseph
Horning, Clarence
Irwin, Donald
Jamison, Alfred
Kershaw, George
Kinscherf, Carl
Laird, James
Leonard, James
Long, John
Mankat, Carl
Mason, Walter
Micka, Michael
Muehlheuser, Frank
Neacy, Clement
Parnell, Fred
Rowe, Robert
Schiebel, Arthur
Sefton, Frederick
Stacco, Edward
Stewart, Charles
Strack, Charles
Stromiello, Michael
Traynor, B. P.
Tryon, Edward
Webber, Charles
Webster, Fred
Welsh, James
Wemple, Donald
West, David
Yablok, Julius

COLORADO A. & M.
Barnes, Lawrence
Burl, Alex
Burroughs, Donald
Christiansen, John
Clay, Roy
David, James
Dodrill, Dale
Fries, Sherwood
Glick, Fred
Glick, Gary
Hartman, James
McGraw, Thurman
Maeda, Chester
Morris, Glen
Stehower, Ronald
White, Wilbur

COLORADO MINES
Madden, Lloyd
Rooney, Cobb

COLORADO UNIV.
Bernardi, Frank
Briggs, Paul
Brookshier, Thomas
Caranci, Roland
Clark, Earl
Clarke, Frank
Clay, Walter
Dove, Edward
Dowler, Boyd
Figner, George
Grosvernor, George
Hardy, Carroll
Hodel, Merwin
Knafelc, Gary
Leahy, Gerald
Lewis, Ernest
Moore, Eugene
Ritchart, Delbert
Smith, James
Stransky, Robert
Stasica, Leo
White, Byron
Wooten, John

COLUMBIA
Armstrong, John
Bleeker, Malcolm
Brennan, Philip
Cuneo, Edward
Field, Richard
Garnjost, Donald
Gehrke, Bruce
Governali, Paul
Johnson, Leon
Kennedy, Joseph
Kerrigan, Thomas
Kisiday, George
Koppisch, Walter
Kusserow, Lou
Luckman, Sidney
Maack, Herbert
Montgomery, Clifford
Pease, George
Roderick, Benjamin
Siegal, John
Swiacki, William
Wagner, Raymond
Yablonski, Ventan

COMPTON JR.
Anderson, William
Lewis, Joseph
LoVetere, John
MtNeil, Charles
Perry, Fletcher
Smith, Ernest
Smith, James
Wallace, Beverly

CONNECTICUT STATE
Longo, Anthony
Maikkula, Kenneth
O'Neil, Charles
Radzievitch, Victor
Williams, Arthur

CORNELL
Berryman, Robert
Daukas, Louis
Dekdebrun, Allen
Douglas, Benjamin
Ebersole, Harold
Flynn, Frank
Gillies, Fred
Hershey, Kirk
Kaw, Edward
Landsburg, Mortimer
McCullough, Harold
Molinet, Louis
Morris, Robert
O'Hearn, John
Shaub, Harry
Shelton, Murray
Stofer, Kenneth
Wilson, James
Wydo, Frank

CREIGHTON
Allen, Edmund
Bertoglio, James
Borak, Anthony
Cemore, Anthony
Fitzgibbons, Paul
Gayer, Walter
Knolla, John
McDonnell, John
Mahoney, Frank
Maillard, Ralph
Padgen, Nicholas

DARTMOUTH
Barber, Henry
Burke, Charles
Crouthamel, John
Crowley, Joseph
Daukas, Nicholas
Ghee, Milton
Hagenbuckle, Vernon
Haws, Harvey
Healy, Edward
Hutchinson, William
Jenkins, Jonathan
Krieger, Robert
McLeod, Robert
Maloney, Gerald
Murphy, Joseph
Roberts, William
Shelburne, John
Sonnenberg, Gustave
Spears, Clarence

Thielscher, Karl
Tully, George
Youngstrom, Adolph

DAVIDSON
Mackorell, John

DAVIS & ELKINS
Corzine, Lester
Federovich, John
Irvin, Cecil
Mattison, Ralph
Mitchell, Granville
Powell, Richard
Rengel, Neil
Ruh, Emmett
Tressa, Thomas
Underwood, Forrest

DAYTON UNIVERSITY
Achui, Walter
Belanich, William
Brown, Jack R.
Cabhrina, August
Duffy, Patrick
Dugan, Fred
Furst, Anthony
Graham, Alfred
Hippa, Samuel
Karas, Emil
Katcavage, James
Knorr, Lawrence
Lange, William
McDonough, Coley
Mahrt, Al
Mahrt, Armin
Mahrt, John
Neihaus, Ralph
Noll, Charles
Obee, Duncan
Spencer, James
Strosnider, Aubrey

DEKALB
Behan, Charles
Brink, Lawrence
Jarvi, Toimi
Nori, Reino

DELAWARE
Dombroski, Leon
Thompson, Harold

DENISON
Becker, John
Calhoun, Eric
Gregory, Michael
Moody, Wilkie
Reese, David
Roudebush, George
Rupp, Nelson
Thiele, Carl

DENVER UNIVERSITY
Balog, Robert
Browning, Gregory
Dreher, Ferdinand
Fena, Joseph
Gifford, Robert
Hazelhurst, Robert
Johnson, Raymond
Jurich, Michael
Stansauk, Donald
Tiller, Morgan
Work, Jack
Woudenberg, John

DE PAUL
Apolskis, Charles
Bramhall, Arthur
Cherne, Harold
Dowling, Patrick
Fiske, Max
Gibbons, James
Krause, Paul
Muellner, William
Roberts, Thomas
Scanlon, John
Stahlman, Richard

DE PAUW
Bondurant
Burton, Lyle
Fortune, Burnell
Smith, Wilfred
Sturtridge, Donald

DETROIT UNIVERSITY
Alderman, Grady
Andrusking, Sigmund
Bachor, Ludwig
Banonis, Vincent
Barrett, John
Brovarney, Casimer
Bucher, Frank
Burke, Robert
Cassidy, William
Clago, Walter
Cooper, Harold
Coyle, Frank
Ellis, Walter
Farkas, Andrew
Finnin, Thomas
Fritsch, Ernest
Harvey, Norman
Hogan, Paul
Hooley, Robert
Keene, Robert
Kostiuk, Michael
Lauer, Harold
Long, Harvey
Lowther, Russell
McCausland, Leo
McCormick, Elmer
McNamara, Thomas
Madarik, Elmer
Maher, Bruce
Mahoney, John
Malinowski, Eugene
Marchibroda, Theodore
Nott, Douglas
Pavelec, Theodore
Raskovich, Peter
Richards, Perry
Riley, Leon
Ryan, John
Simmons, John
Simpson, J. Felix
Voss, Walter
Young, Herman

DIABLO VALLEY
Joyner, L. C.

DICKINSON
Behman, Russell
Books, Robert
Supulski, Leonard

DRAKE
Bienemann, Thomas
Brindley, Walter
Deskin, Versil
Don Carlos, William
Krueger, Albert
Manders, Clarence
Mertens, Jerry
Nesbitt, Richard
Seiberling, Gerald
Spear, Glen
Steere, Richard

DUKE
Allen, Louis
Bailey, Edgar
Brodhead, Robert
Cardwell, Joseph
Carleton, Wray
Cox, William
Crawford, Frederick
DeRogatis, Albert
Earon, Blaine
Guy, Melwood
Hartley, Howard
Hord, Ambrose Roy
Jurgensen, Christian
Karmazin, Michael
Lach, Steven
Lewis, Clifford
McAfee, George
McAfee, Wesley
McDonough, Robert
Meadows, Edward
Milner, William
Mote, Kelly
Neal, Thomas
Parker, Clarence
Perdue, Willard
Piasecky, Alexander
Ribar, Frank
Sharkey, Edward
Sinkovitz, Frank
Stough, Glen
Tepe, Louis

DUQUESNE
Basrak, Michael
Bonotto, John
Brumbaugh, Boyd
Cibulas, Joseph
Ciccone, Benjamin
Corbo, Thomas
DeCarbo, Nicholas
DeMao, Albert
DePaul, Henry
Elter, Leo
Gonda, George
Grabinski, Thaddeus
Hall, Forrest
Jansante, Valerio
Kakasic, George
Karrs, George
Kemp, Ray
Kielbasa, Max
McDonald, Edward
Malkovich, Joseph
Maras, Joseph
Matisis, John
Mehelich, Charles
Nery, Carl
Niccolai, Armand
O'Dell, Melvin
Perko, John
Petchell, John
Platukas, George
Rado, George
Rokisky, John
Semes, Bernard
Setcavage, Joseph
Sinko, Steven
Sirochman, George
Strutt, Arthur
Vidoni, Victor
Weinberg, Henry
Wiehl, Joseph
Wukits, Albert
Yurchey, John
Zaninello, Silvio
Zoppetti, Frank

EARLHAM
Beasley, John

ELLISVILLE JR.
Gulyanics, George

ELMHURST
Johnston, Chester

ELON
Boone, Robert
Bradley, Harold

EMPORIA TEACHERS
Burnett, Dale
Campbell, Glenn
Harkey, Lemuel
Kline, Harry
Munday, George

EVANSVILLE
Bawel, Edward

FINDLAY
Susteric, Edward

FLORIDA A & M
Galimore, Willie
Lee, Willie
McClung, William
Morris, Riley

FLORIDA STATE COLLEGE
Feamster, Thomas
Kimber, William

FLORIDA UNIVERSITY
Brumbaugh, Carl
Casares, Richard
Chandler, Donald
Crabtree, Clyde
Dempsey, Frank
Douglas, Everett
Duhart, Paul
Edgington, Daniel
Fleming, Donald
Goff, Clark
Goodbread, Royce
Green, Robert
Hammack, Malcolm
Herbert, Joseph
Hunsinger, Charles

Klutka, Nicholas
Konetsky, Floyd
Lee, Eugene
Long, Buford
Mitchell, Fondren
O'Brien, John
Parrish, Bernard
Simpson, Jackie
Symank, John
Waters, Dale
Williams, Broughton
Williams, Burton

FORDHAM
Barbartsky, Albert
Berezney, Paul
Bissell, Frederick
Blumenstock, James
Borden, Lester
Brennan, Paul
Buckley, Edward
Cannela, John
Cheverko, George
Clark, Frank
Danowski, Edward
DeFillipo, Louis
Dell Isola, John
Dennery, Vincent
Druze, John
Eshmont, Leonard
Feaster, William
Filipowicz, Steven
Franco, Edward
Grandinette, George
Jacunski, Harry
Johnson, Arthur
Kellagher, William
Kloppenberg, Harry
Kochel, Michael
Kuzman, John
Leary, Thomas
Lowe, George
Maniaci, Joseph
Manning, Joseph
Myers, Thomas
Nacrelli, Andrew
Noonan, Gerald
Principe, Dominic
Riddick, Raymond
Sabasteanski, Joseph
Sarausky, Anthony
Sartori, Lawrence
Siano, Anthony
Stein, William
Stevenson, Arthur
Strand, Lief
Tepo, George
Ungerer, Joseph
Uzdavinis, Walter
Walbridge, Lyman
Wojciechowicz, Alex
Yackanich, Joseph
Zapustas, Joseph

FT. HAYS, TEACHERS
Reissig, William

FT. VALLEY STATE
Moore, Leroy

FRANKLIN
Franklin, Paul
Isselhardt, Ralph

FRANKLIN MARSHALL
Jones, Kenneth
Malcolm, Carvel
Schibanoff, Alex

FRESNO STATE
Fanucchi, Ledio
Garner, Robert
Handley, Richard
Masini, Leonard
Philpott, Dean
Seiferling, John

FULLERTON JR.
Livingston, Howard
Weaver, Larrye

FURMAN
Proctor, Dewey
Shetley, Rhoten
Wham, Thomas

GENESEE WESLEYAN
Webb,

GENEVA
Cooper, Samuel
Davis, Sylvester
Flenniken, Max
Harris, Oliver
Hubbard, Robert
Magisceau, Albert
Meyer, Ernest

GEORGE WASHINGTON
Butkus, Carl
Davis, Andrew
Fedora, Walter
Gudmundson, Scott
Gustafson, Edsel
Hanken, Ray
Jones, Charles
Katrishen, Michael
Keahey, Eulis
Koniszewski, John
Leemans, Alphonse
Nash, Thomas
Nowaskey, Robert
O'Neill, William
Prather, Dale
Seno, Frank
Sommer, Michael
Turner, Jay Turner
Wilson, Abraham

GEORGETOWN
Barron, James
Blozis, Al
Brennan, Ralph
Castiglia, James
Comstock, Rudolph
Connaughton, Harry
Corcoran, Arthur
Cordavano, Samuel
Cullen, Thomas
Doolan, John
Dubofsky, Maurice
Dwyer, Robert
Flavin, John
Frank, Joseph
Ghecas, Louis
Golsen, Eugene
Golsen, Thomas
Hagerty, John
Hughes, Dennis
Hunt, Edward
Itzel, John
Jawish, Henry
Kenyon, William
Kercher, Robert
Koshlap, Jules
Lascari, John
Lio, Augustino
Liston, Paul
McGrath, Frank
McQuade, John
Matuza, Albert
Metzger, Louis
Mooney, George
Morelli, John
Murtagh, George
O'Connor, Daniel
Paternoster, Angelo
Perpich, George
Plansky, Anthony
Provencial, Kenneth
Rawlings, Robert
Ricca, James
Scalzi, John
Sorce, Ross
Stralka, Clement
Tomaini, John
Waite, Carl
Werder, Richard
Whelan, Thomas

GEORGIA TECH
Baughan, Max
Beck, Ray
Brewer, John
Brodnax, George
Brown, Peter
Davis, Robert
Duke, Paul
Fulcher, William
Godwin, Walter
Green, Jerome
Harlan, Julian
Helms, John
Lumpkin, Roy
McConnell, Felton
McHugh, Pat
Matthews, Clay

Miller, Harold
Mizell, Warner
Morris, George
Morris, Lawrence
Murphy, Frederick
Murphy, Robert
Paschal, William
Prokop, Edward
Rudolph, John
Snyder, Kenneth
Steber, John
Still, James
Thomason, John
Vereen, Carl
Watkins, Gordon
Williams, Ivan
Wycoff, Douglas
Ziegler, Frank

GEORGIA UNIVERSITY
Babcock, Harry
Bratkowski, Edmund
Britt, Charles
Campbell, Marion
Carson, John
Clement, Robert
Conger, Melvin
Davis, R. Lamar
Davis, Van
DeCarlo, Arthur
Dickens, Marion
Donaldson, John
Dudish, Andrew
Edwards, Daniel
Ehrhardt, Clyde
Ellenson, Eugene
Feher, Nicholas
Fordham, James
Geri, Joseph
Godwin, William
Grate, Carl
Gunnels, John
Hartman, William
Hobbs, Homer
Johnson, Howard
Kelley, Gordon
Keuper, Kenneth
King, Henry
Leathers, Milron
Lloyd, David
Metigue, Robert
McCrary,
Mooney,
Mott,
Paternoster,
Rausch, John
Reid, Floyd
Reynolds, Owen
Roberts, John
St. John, Herbert
Sapp, Theron
Sedlock, Robert
Sinkwich, Frank
Smith, Charles
Smith, George
Tanner, Hampton
Tereshinski, Joseph
Tinsley, Peter
Trippi, Charles
Walston, Robert
Wells, Donald
Whire, John
White, Eugene
Wilkins, Roy
Williams, Garland
Yelvington, Richard
Young, George

GETTYSBURG
Kyle, James
Nicely, John
Yovisin, John

GONZAGA
Ashmore, Roger
Bellinger, Robert
Brian, William
Cahoon, Ivan
Canadeo, Anthony
Cyre, Hector
Flaherty, Ray
Hare, Cecil
Hare, Ray
Justice, Edward
Karamatic, George
Krause, Max
Peterson, Kenneth
Poth, Philip

Skeate, Gilbert
Stockton, Herschel
Stockton, Houston
Waldron, Austin
Wilson, William

GRAMBLING
Caleb, James
Davis, Willie
Richardson, Alvin
Younger, Paul

GRINNELL
Moran, Francis

GROVE CITY
Batchelor, Donald
Brian, Harry
Critchfield, Lawrence
Gibson, Denver
Jones, Ben
Lantz, Montgomery
Sofish, Alexander
Tallant, David
Wall, Edward

GUSTAVUS ADOLPHUS
Butcher, Wendell
Lundell, Robert
Norman, Haldo
Parsons, Lloyd
Witte, Earl

GUILFORD
Venuto, Sam

HAMLINE
Cramer, Earl
Eliason, Donald
Haven, John
Kaplan, Sidney
Scott, Eugene

HAMPTON INSTITUTE
Casey, Thomas

HAMPDEN-SYDNEY
Miller, Thomas
Worden, Stuart

HARDIN-SIMMONS
Bennett, Earl
Bohling, Dewey
Burrus, Harry
Cherry, Edgar
Cockrell, Eugene
Compton, Ogden
Crowell, Odis
Davenport, Wayne
Evans, Murray
Goodnight, Owen
Harris, William
Hart, Dee
Johnson, Alvin
McChesney, Robert
Mobley, Rudolph
Parker, David
Pittman, Melvin
Prescott, Harold
Ribble, Loran
Ryan, David
Sprinkle, Edward
Treadaway, John
Turner, Clyde
Tyler, Peter

HARVARD
Burnham, Stanley
Casey, Edward
Clark, Charles
Dadman, Harrie
Doane, Joseph
Evans, Earl
Gundlach, Herman
Horween, Arnold *
Horween, Ralph *
King, Richard
McGlone, Joseph
Miller, Alfred
*Played as "McMahon"

HASKELL
Anderson, Thomas
Choate
Crow, Orien
Elkins, Fait
Hill, Robert

Jennings,
Johnson, Lawrence
McLemore, Emmett
Nix, Emory
Oakes, William
Pappio, Joseph
Weller, Louis

HASTINGS
Osborne, Thomas

HEIDELBERG
Boehe, James
Hutson, Merle
Groman, William
Livingston, Walter
Michaels, Alton
Vokaty, Otto

HIGHLANDS
Crockett, Monte
Taylor, Lionel

HOBART
Barna, George
Kraus, Francis

HOLY CROSS
Alberghini, Thomas
Bove, Peter
Brawley, Edward
Brennan, Leo
Britt, Edward
Buzynski, Bernard
Cahill, Ronald
Cartin, Charles
Clancy, Stuart
Cregar, William
Dee, Robert
Digris, Bernard
Donovan, John
Finn, Bernard
Fitzgerald, Donald
Gardella, Augustus
Garvey, Francis
Gaziano, Frank
Gildea, Dennis
Golembeske, Anthony
Greene, Thomas
Grigas, John
Holley, Kenneth
Ignatius, James
Kissel, Veto
Kittredge, Paul
Klasoskus, Albin
Koslowski, Stanley
Kucharski, Theodore
Landrigan, James
McCulloch, James
McGrath, Richard
McMahon, Harry
McNamara, Edmund
Manfreda, Anthony
Monaco, Raymond
Moran, James
Natowich, Andrew
O'Connor, Francis
Osmanski, Joseph
Osmanski, William
Promuto, Vincent
Pyne, George
Riopel, Albert
Rovinski, Anthony
Simendinger, Kenneth
Strotny, Theodore
Sullivan, Robert
Titus, George
Titus, Silas
Wizbicki, Alexander
Zeno, Joseph
Zyntell, James

HOUSTON
Allen, Dalva
Brown, Donald
Carr, Paul
Clatterbuck, Robert
Colvin, James
Dimmick, Thomas
Flynn, Donald
Johnson, John
Kimmel, J.
Lewis, Harold
Wharton, Hogan

HOWARD
Cooper, Norman
Daugherty, George

Goldman, Samuel
Gray, Kenneth
Hill, Harold
Hodges, Herman
Lollar, George
Schenker, Nathan
Tarrant, James

IDAHO
Bucklin, Thomas
Diehl, Gordon
Fanning, Stanley
Fitzke, Robert
Miklich, William
Nixon, George
Norby, John
Norton, James
Owens, Delmer
Pavkov. Stonko
Prestel, James
Smith, Willis
Stephens, Leslie
Vesser, John
Walker, Wayne

IDAHO, COLLEGE OF
Owens, Raleigh

IDAHO STATE
Wagstaff, James

ILLINOIS EASTERN
Fisher, Raymond

ILLINOIS SOUTHERN
Rushing, Marion

ILLINOIS TEACHERS
Glenn, William

ILLINOIS UNIVERSITY
Agase, Alexander
Bauer, John
Bernhardt, George
Berschet, Marvin
Berry, Gilbert
Bingaman, Lester
Bock, Wayne
Boerio, Charles
Britton, Earl
Brosky, Albert
Burdick, Lloyd
Caroline, James
Cook, David
Corcoran, Gerald
Crangle, John
Crawford, Walter
Daugherty, Russell
Depler, John
Drayer, Clarence
Gordon, Louis
Grange, Garland
Grange, Harold
Griffin, Donald
Halas, George
Hall, Raymond
Hellstrom, Norton
Ingwersen, Bert
Johnson, Nathan
Kallino, Edward
Karras, John
Kasap, Michael
Kassel, Charles
Kawal, Edward
Klimek, Anthony
Knop, Oscar
Kovacsy, William
Kraft, Reynold
Kreitling, Richard
Lanum, Ralph
Lynch, Lynn
McCarthy, James
McMillen, James
Maggioli, Achille
Marquardt, John
Mitchell, Robert
Morris, G. Max
Moss, Perry
Nelson, Everett
Nichols, Sidney
Nitschke, Ray
O'Connell, Thomas
Owens, Isaiah
Patterson, Paul
Pearce, Walter
Perez. Peter
Peters, Forest
Petty, Ross
Piggott, Bert

Podmajersky, Paul
Popa, Eli
Reichle, Richard
Richman, Harry
Rundquist, Elmer
Ryan, John
Rykovich, Julius
Shoemaker, Hubbard
Siegert, Herbert
Smith, Russell
Sternaman, Edward
Sternaman, Joseph
Stevens, Donald
Stichcomb, Gaylord
Sucic, Steven
Ulrich, Charles
Walquist, Laurie
Wallace, Stanley
Waller, William
Woodson, Abe
Young, Claude

ILLINOIS WESLEYAN
Atcheson
Blazine, Anthony
Kaska, Anthony
Morrow, Robert
Newman, Robert
Wetterlund, Chester

ILLINOIS WESTERN
Atchason, Jack
Garron, Lawrence
Larson, William

INDIANA CENTRAL
Nyers, Richard

INDIANA UNIVERSITY
Addams, Abraham
Amstutz, Joseph
Anderson, Clifton
Aveni, John
Bell, Edward
Bennett, Charles
Bernoske, Daniel
Borden, Nathan
Brown, Howard
Bucchianeri, Amadeo
Campbell, Milton
Cannady, John
Cichowski, Eugene
Cowan, Robert
Dalsasso, Christopher
Davis, Corbett
Dewar, James
Filchock, Frank
Gedman, Eugene
Goldsberry, John
Groomes, Melvin
Grossman, Rex
Haak, Robert
Hanny, Frank
Hathaway, Russell
Hess, Arthur
Hillenbrand, William
Hoernschmeyer, Robert
Howard, Lynn
Huffman, Vernon
Jagade, Harry
Jagielski, Harry
Jones, Robert
Jurkewicz, Walter
Karras, Theodore
Karstens, George
Kyle, John
Leo, Charles
Leonard, John
Livingston, Theodore
Logan, James
Luft, Donald
McCaw, William
McLean, Stuart
Marks, Lawrence
Mathys, Charles
Oliver, Vincent
Pihos, Peter
Rabold, Michael
Randolph, Clare
Raimondi, Benjamin
Randolph, Clare
Rascher, Ambrose
Ravensburg, Robert
Ringwalt, Carroll
Risley, Elliott
Rucinski, Edward
Saban, Louis
Scales, Charles

Sebek, Nicholas
Skoronski, Robert
Taliaferro, George
Tavenor, John
Tofil, Joseph
Uremovich, Emil
White, Eugene
Whitsell, David
Wilkins, Theodore
Witucki, Casimir
Zeller, Joseph
Zimny, Robert
Zoll, Richard

IOWA STATE
Angle, Robert
Barker, Richard
Bradley, Harold
Brettschneider, Carl
Brown, Richard
Campbell, Stanley
Carlson, Oke
Doran, James
Hagerty, Loris
Heileman, Charles
Jensen, Robert
Jessen, Ernest
Longstreet, Roy
Muelhaupt, Edward
Remmert, Dennis
Roberts, Charles
Shugart, Clyde

IOWA UNIVERSITY
Balazs, Frank
Belding, Lester
Chelf, Donald
Couppee, Albert
Crayne, Richard
Ely, Harold
Evans, Richard
Farmer, Thomas
Farroh, Shipley
Fisher, Darrell
Fleckenstein, William
Fosdick, Robert
Fry, Wesley
Gibbons, James
Glasgow, Willis
Greenwood, Glenn
Griffin, Harold
Hall, John
Herdt, John
Hoerner, Richard
Jensvold, Leo
Kadesky, Max
Karras, Alex
Keane, James
Kelsh, Matthew
Klein, Richard
Lapham, William
Lauer, Peter
Laws, Joseph
Lewis, Charles
McClain, Mayes
Masterson, Forest
Mastrogony, August
Mertes, Bernard
Minick, Paul
Myers, Dennis
Nelson, Donald
Niedziela, Bruno
Niles, Jerry
Nocera, John
Norton, Donald
Olson, Forrest
Otte, F. Lowell
Pape, Orrin
Pignatelli, Carl
Reichardt, William
Reichow, Garet
Roberts, Fred
Rogge, George
Sansen, Oliver
Schammel, Francis
Schluesner, Vincent
Schneidman, Herman
Shoener, Harold
Shoener, Herbert
Slater, Fred
Smith, James
Smith, Robert
Thompson, George
Tollefson, Charles
Tunnell, Emlen
Woodward, Richard
Youel, James

IOWA WESLEYAN
Sandberg, Sigmund

ITHACA COLLEGE
D'Orazio, Joseph

JOHN CARROLL
Armstrong, Graham
Ecker, Enrique
Lahey, Thomas
McMillan, Charles
Shields, Burrel
Shula, Donald
Stringer, Eugene
Taseff, Carl

JORDAN
McWilliams, William

KALAMAZOO
Boedecker, William
Casteel, Miles
Conrad, Martin
Fausch, Franklin
Seborg, Henry

KANSAS SOUTHWESTERN
Hammond, Henry
Layden, Robert
Shockley, Arnold
Smith, Gaylon

KANSAS STATE
Bushby, Thomas
Cobb, William
Cronkhite, Henry
Feather, Elwin
Hackney, Elmer
Hanson, Homer
Harrison, John
Hartshorn, Lawrence
Krysl, Gerald
Lyon, George
McGee, Howard
Maddox, George
Marciniak, Ronald
Munn, Lyle
Nery, Ronald
Nichols, Ralph
Pearson, Madison
Raemer, Norbert
Randall, Proctor
Randels, Horace
Romero, Ray
Sears, Richard
Shaffer, Leland
Switzer, Veryl
Tackwell, Charles
Taylor, Cecil
Webber, Howard
Weiner, Bernard

KANSAS STATE TEACHERS
Andrews, Leroy
Danenhauer, Eldon
Danenhauer, William
Tarrant, Robert
Wiedich, Ralph

KANSAS UNIVERSITY
Amberg, John
Bausch, Frank
Bausch, James
Black, Charles
Burt, Harold
Bushby, Thomas
Corgan, Charles
Detweiler, John
Douglass, Clarence
Ettinger, Donald
Evans, Ray
Fiss, Galen
Griffith, Forrest
Hantla, Robert
Kvaternick, Zvonimir
Laughlin, Henry
McCormack, Michael
Mehringer, Peter
Merkel, Monte
Makonic, George
Pierce, Donald
Russell, Dougal
Schaake, Elmer
Schnellbacher, Otto
Spencer, Oliver
Tomlinson, Richard
Ulrich, Hubert

KENT STATE
Barbee, Joseph
Owens, Luke

KENTUCKY STATE
Anderson, Ezzret
Mostardo, Richard

KENTUCKY STATE EAST
Hollingsworth, Joseph
Kenerson, John
Pelfrey, Ray

KENTUCKY UNIVERSITY
Allen, Ermal
Blanda, George
Davis, Robert
Donaldson, Eugene
Daugherty, Robert
Eibner, John
Fry, Robert
Fucci, Dominic
Fuller, Frank
Gain, Robert
Grabfelder, Earl
Gregg, Edward
Hensley, Richard
Johnson, Albert
Johnson, Clyde
Kelly, John Simms
Kercheval, Ralph
King, Donald
Lindahl, Virgil
Lindon, Luther
Little, James
McDermott, Lloyd
Marcus, Peter
Meilinger, Stephan
Michaels, Louis
Mullins, Noah
Netherton, William
Parilli, Vito
Phelps, Donald
Rhodemyre, Jay
Richards, Richard
Serini, Washington
Shaw, Glenn
Talamini, Robert
Ulinski, Harry
Wright, Frank
Yowarsky, Walter

KENYON
Stock, Herbert

KIRKSVILLE, KAN.
Baltzell, Victor

KNOX
Bridgeford, Lane
Eiden, James
Senn, William
Thompson

LAFAYETTE
Bednar, Albert
Berry, Charles
Brennan, Matthew
Budd, John
Deibel, Arthur
Elliott, Wallace
Ernst, John
Ford, Adrian
Grube, Frank
Hummell, Charles
Kirkleski, Frank
Lehecka, Joseph
Millman, Robert
Moore, Walter
O'Connell, Milton
Reuter, Victor
Scott, John
Seasholtz, George
Thompson, John
Weldon, John
Williams, Joseph
Wilson, George
Wood
Zirinsky, Walter

LAKE FOREST
Biolo, John
Milton, Thomas
Owens, Henry

LANCASTER
Smith, Henry

LANGSTON UNIVERSITY
Bassett, Maurice

LA SALLE
Mandarino, Michael
Sommers, George

LAWRENCE
Basing, Myrtle
Johnstone, Arthur
Kotal, Edward
Zupek, Albert

LEBANON VALLEY
Homan, Henry
Irwin, Walter
Lechthaler, Roy
Longenecker, Kenneth

LEHIGH
Davidovitz, Arthur
Douglas, Leo
Hoffman, William
McGoldrick, Hugh
Sanford, James
Scholl, Roy
Spagna, Joseph
Springsteen, William
Storer, John
Wilson, Samuel
Yeager, James

LEWIS COLLEGE
Schmidt, George
Vodicka, Joseph

LINCOLN UNIVERSITY
Robinson, William

LINFIELD
Glenn, Howard

LOMBARD
Lamb, Roy
Strickland, William
Swanson, Eyar
Thompson, C.

LONG ISLAND UNIVERSITY
Kapitansky, Bernard

LORAS COLLEGE (DUBUQUE)
Butler, Edward
Kuehl, Ray
Ruetz, Howard

LOS ANGELES CITY COLLEGE
Bishop, Donald

LOS ANGELES STATE COLLEGE
Adams, John
Anderson, Ralph
Ross, David

LOUISIANA NORTHEASTERN
Stover, Stewart

LOUISIANA NORTHWESTERN
Broussard, Fred
Hennigan, Charles
Tolar, Charles

LOUISIANA POLY-TECH
Anderson, Charles
Doherty, George
Giddens, Herschel
Gregory, Garland
Martin, Caleb
Sanford, Leo

LOUISIANA SOUTHEASTERN
Bandura, John
Campion, Thomas
Davis, Jerome
Lofton, Oscar
Reisz, Albert

LOUISIANA STATE UNIVERSITY
Baggett, William
Barnes, Walter
Barrett, Jeffrey
Brancato, George
Branch, Melvin
Brodnax, John
Burkett, Jeffrey
Bussey, Young
Cannon, William
Cason, James
Champagne, Edward
Coates, Ray
Coffee, James
Collins, Albin
Collins, Ray

Crass, William
Davis, Thomas
Fournet, Sidney
Friend, Benjamin
Glamp, Joseph
Gorinski, Walter
Jones, William
Kavanaugh, Kenneth
Kingery, Wayne
Konz, Kenneth
Land, Fred
Leggett, Earl
Leisk, Wardell
May, William
Miller, Paul
Montgomery, William
Neal, William
Nunnery, Robert
Oakley, Charles
Rabb, Warren
Reed, Joseph
Reid, Joseph
Reynolds, Mack Charles
Robinson, John
Rukas, Justin
Sandifer, Daniel
Sanford, Otis
Schroll, Charles
Shurtz, Hubert
Tarasovic, George
Taylor, James
Tinsley, Jess
Tittle, Yelverton
Torrance, John
Toth, Zollie
Van Buren, Ebert
Van Buren, Steven
Wimberly, Abner

LOUISVILLE
Brewer, John
Ewald, George
Ford, Salem
Lyles, Leonard
Meeks, Edward
Mosher, Clure
Unitas, John

LOYOLA (CHICAGO)
Berwick, Edward
Bush, Raymond
Jackson, Lawrence
Malloy, Lester
Moore, Allen
Sachs, Leonard
Sherry, Gerald

LOYOLA (MARYLAND)
Intrieri, Marne

LOYOLA (LOS ANGELES)
Boyd, Robert
Brito, Eugene
Cheatham, Ernest
Dwyer, John
Elsey, Earl
Ferris, Neil
Giancanelli, Harold
Hrabetin, Frank
Klosterman, Donald
Moore, William

LOYOLA (NEW ORLEANS)
Moore, William
Nipp, Maurice
Sullivan, Frank

LUTHER
Hansen, Clifford
Stolfa, Alton

MAINE
Cooper, Thurlow
Ellis, Roger

MANCHESTER, MT. MORRIS
Banet, Herbert
Lieberum, Donald
Shenefelt, Paul

MANHATTAN
Damiani, Francis
Jocher, Arthur
Marone, John
Schmeelk, Garry
Seick, Earl
Tuckey, Richard

MANITOBA

Lear, Leslie

MARIETTA COLLEGE
Dasstling, Dane
Howard, Robert
Jolley, Alfred
White, Wilbur

MARQUETTE
Apoiskis, Raymond
Aspatore, Edward
Becker, Wayland
Bentzien, Alfred
Bergin, William
Bilda, Richard
Braatz, Thomas
Braden, David
Buivid, Raymond
Bultman, Arthur
Busler, Raymond
Butler, William
Campbell, Raymond
Carlson, Ray
Cronin, Thomas
Cuff, Ward
Curtin, Donald
Davis, Paul
Dilweg, Lavern
Douglas, George
Drzewjecki, Ronald
Duford, Wilfred
Dunn, Joseph
Elliott, Burton
Enich, Steven
Fahay, John
Faye, Allen
Felker, Arthur
Flaherty, Pat
Flaherty, Richard
Gavin, Fritz
Glick, Edward
Goodyear, John
Groves, George
Hanson, Ray
Harrington, John
Hayes, Norbert
Heimsch, John
Johnstone, Chester
Klug, Alfred
Kosikowski, Frank
Kramer, John
Kuffel, Raymond
LaFleur, Joseph
Lane, Oscar
Langhoff, Irving
Leysenaar, Harry
Linnan, Francis
Lunz, Gerald
McGinnis, Lawrence
Maceau, Melvin
Murphy, Philip
Murray, Richard
O'Neill, William
Radick, Kenneth
Roessler, Fritz
Ronzani, Gene
Schoemann, Roy
Schuette, Carl
Shekleton, Vincent
Sisk, John
Strzykalski, John
Taugher, Claude
Trost, Milton
Vogt, Alois
Vosberg, Donald
Woodin, Howard

MARSHALL
Adkins, Robert
Barton, James
Brown, William
Elkins, Everett
Gatski, Frank
Huffman, Frank
Hunt, John
Mattiford, John
Morlock, John
Pearcy, James
Stephens, John
Ulinski, Edward
Willey, Norman

MARYLAND STATE
Brown, Roger
Fletcher, Andrew
Plunkett, Sherman
Sample, John

MARYLAND UNIVERSITY
Alderton, John
Bielski, Richard
Breedlove, Rodney
Brewer, Brooke
Cole, Frederick
Colteryahn, Lloyd
Cooke, Edward
Davis, Jack
Felton, Ralph
Fullerton, Edward
Gambino, Lucien
Hanulak, Chester
Healy, Donald
Jones, Stanley
Krouse, Ray
Ladygo, Peter
Lookabaugh, John
Meade, James
Modzelewski, Edward
Modzelewski, Richard
Mont, Thomas
Morgan, Robert
Moss, Joseph
Nickla, Edward
Nolan, Richard
Norris, John
Pellegrini, Robert
Perlo, Philip
Sandusky, Michael
Scarbath, Jack
Scotti, Ben
Snyder, Gerald
Vereb, Edward
Waller, Ronald
Wingate, Elmer
Wright, John

MARYLAND WESTERN
Benson, Harry
Campofreda, Nicholas
Havens, Charles
Kaplan, Bernard
Lassahn, Louis
Phillips, Michael
Shepherd, William
Sillin, Frank

McMURRY
Cowan, Leslie
Rowland, Bradley

McNEESE STATE
Castete, Jesse
Harris, Richard

McPHERSON
Vetter, John

MEMPHIS STATE COLLEGE
Nelson, Andrew
Renfro, William
Strickland, Davis

MERCER
Olsson, Lester
Owen, Alton

MIAMI UNIV. of FLORIDA
Bennett, Philip
Bookman, John
Bosseler, Donald
Carapella, Albert
Chickillo, Nicholas
DelBello, John
DeMarco, Mario
Diamond, Charles
Dooley, James
Fox, Terrance
Greaves, Gary
Hudock, Michael
Jelley, Thomas
Johnson, Jack
Kearns, Thomas
Kichefski, Walter
Losch, John
McDougal, Robert
Masterson, Robert
Otto, James
Noppenberg, John
Shiver, Raymond
Tevis, Leek
Watt, Walter

MIAMI UNIV. of OHIO
Buchanan, Stephen
Chorovich, Richard

Corey, Walter
Crawford, Kenneth
Fenner, Lee
Gansberg, Alfred
Hauser, Earl
Jones, Thomas
Joseph, Zern
Parseghian, Ara
Root, James
Rush, Clive
Sauer, Edward
Savatsky, Oliver
Schupe, Walter
Scott, George
Shoults, Paul
Weaver, John
Wolf, Richard
Work, Joseph
Yoho, Mack

MICHIGAN CENTRAL
Beach, Walter
Podoley, James

MICHIGAN EASTERN
Day, Albert
Shonta, Charles

MICHIGAN STATE
Allman, Robert
Bagdon, Edward
Beckley, Arthur
Bercich, Robert
Blacklock, Hugh
Bolden, Leroy
Bruckner, Leslie
Bullough, Harry
Buss, Arthur
Butler, Frank
Carey, Robert
Chandnois, Lynn
Christenson, Koester
Currie, Daniel
Dekker, Paul
DePrato, Nicholas
Dibble, Dorne
Diehl, David
Dienzo, Anthony
Donnahoo, Roger
Finley, James
Friedlund, Robert
Grandelius, Everett
Grove, Roger
Hansen, Dale
Horrell, William
Hultman, Vivian
Jewett, Robert
Kelly, Ellison
Johnson, Farnham
Kennedy, William
Ketzko, Alexander
Kinek, Michael
Klewicki, Edward
Kowalczyk, Walter
Lay, Russell
Lowe, Gary
McFadden, Marvin
McRae, Stanley
Martin, Blanche
Masters, Norman
Matsos, Archibald
Minarik, Henry
Monnett, Robert
Morrall, Earl
Ninowski, James
O'Brien, Francis
Peaks, Clarence
Pingel, John
Planutis, Gerald
Ptacek, Robert
Pyle, Palmer
Quinlan, William
Reader, Russell
Ridler, Donald
Rochenbach, Lyle
Rochester, Paul
Saidock, Thomas
Sieradzki, Stephen
Speelman, Harry
Thomas, Jesse
Thrower, Willie
Topor, Theodore
Vezmar, Walter
Wagner, Sidney
Wells, William
Williams, Samuel
Wulff, James

Zagers, Albert

MICHIGAN STATE NORMAL
Hanneman, Charles
Opalewski, Edward

MICHIGAN STATE NORTH
Powers, Samuel
Wagner, Buffton

MICHIGAN UNIVERSITY
Auer, Howard
Babcock, Samuel
Baldacci, Louis
Barr, Terry
Bernard, Charles
Brennan, John
Callahan, Robert
Carpenter, John
Chappuis, Robert
Cook, Eugene
Curzon, Harry
Daley, William
Dawley, Fred
Deskins, Donald
Draveling, Leo
Dworsky, Daniel
Edwards, Thomas
Ford, Leonard
Friedman, Benjamin
Fritz, Ralph
Frutig, Edward
Goebel, Paul
Goetz, Angus
Greene, John
Gregory, Bruce
Grube, Charles
Harmon, Thomas
Harper, Darrell
Heikkinen, Ralph
Hewitt, William
Hirsch, Elroy
Hudson, Martin
Hughitt, Ernest
Ingalls, Robert
Johns, James
Johnson, Thomas
Julian, Frederick
Karwales, John
Kilbourne, Warren
Knutson, Eugene
Kolesar, Robert
Kramer, Ronald
Kreinheder, Walter
Lazetich, Milan
Madar, Elmer
Mann, Robert
Marion, Philip
Molenda, John
Morrison, Maynard
Morrow, John
Monsen, Anthony
Muirhead, Stanley
Newman, Harry
Nieman, Walter
Nussbaumer, Robert
Ortman, Charles
Pace, James
Perry, Lowell
Pregulman, Mervin
Rifenburg, Richard
Roby, Douglas
Rosatti, Roman
Smeja, Rudolph
Smith, Cedric "Pat"
Smith, William
Soboleski, Joseph
Topp, Robert
Vick, Henry "Ernie"
Westfall, Robert
White, Paul
Wiese, Robert
Williamson, Ivan
Wistert, Albert
Usher, Edward
Zatkoff, Roger

MICHIGAN WESTERN
Bray, Raymond
Macioszczyk, Arthur
Mason, Joel
Matheson, John

MIDWESTERN
Smith, Ray

MILLIKIN
Carpe, Joseph

Corbett, George

MILWAUKEE TEACHERS
Kliebhan, Roger
Kranz, Kenneth

MINNESOTA STATE
Williams, Daniel

MINNESOTA
Abramson, George
Alfonse, Jules
Baston, Albert
Baumgartner, William
Beson, Warren
Billman, John
Bisbee, Bertin
Bjorklund, Robert
Buhler, Lawrence
Cappalletti, Gino
Christenson, Martin
Clow, Herbert
Daley, William
Dunigan, Merton
Dunnigan, Walter
Dvorak, Benjamin
Falls, Michael
Faunce, Everett
Faust, George
Franck, George
Garnaas, Wilford
Gay, Kenneth
Gibson, George
Grant, Harry
Hanke, Carl
Hansen, Ronald
Hanson, Harold
Haycraft, Kenneth
Hein, Robert
Holz, Gordon
Jaszewski, Floyd
Jelacic, Jon
Joesting, Herbert
Johnson, William
Juster, Rubin
Kakela, Wayne
Kostka, Stanley
Kulbitski, Victor
Kuusisto, William
Lechner, Edgar
Levy, Leonard
Lidberg, Carl
Lyle, Dewey
McNamara, Robert
Maeder, Albert
Manders, John
Marshall, Robert
Mihajlovich, Louis
Mitchell, Paul
Moore, Wilbur
Nagurski, Bronko
Nolander, Donald
Nomellini, Leo
Noreene, Olaf
Nydall, Malcolm
O'Donnell, Richard
Odson, Urban
Oech, Vern
Ohlgren, Earl
Olsonoski, Lawrence
Oss, Arnold
Paffrath, Robert
Paschka, Gordon
Pederson, Winfield
Perko, John
Pesonen, Richard
Pharmer, Arthur
Plunkett, Warren
Regnier, Peter
Robinson, Wayne
Rush, James
Schmidt, Robert
Schultz, Charles
Sikich, Rudolph
Smith, Bruce
Soltau, Gordon
Soltis, Robert
Spadaccini, Victor
Svendsen, Earl
Svendsen, George
Sweiger, Robert
Tanner, Robert
Tenner, Robert
Teeter, Alan
Thompson, Clarence
Thompson, Franklin
Tierney, Frederick

Tobin, Rex
Tonnemaker, Clayton
Tuttle, Richard
Twedell, Francis
Uram, Andrew
Ursella, Reuben
Van Every, Harold
Van Hull, Frederick
Widseth, Edwin
Wildung, Richard
Wyman, Arnold
Youso, Frank

MISSISSIPPI COLLEGE
Hitt, Joel

MISSISSIPPI SOUTHERN
Bradfute, Byron
Brumfield, Jackson
Dickinson, Richard
Herring, George
Morgan, Joseph
Owens, Donald
Stringfellow, Joseph
Van Tone, Arthur
Vetrano, Joseph

MISSISSIPPI STATE
Armstrong, Charles
Black, John
Blount, Lamar
Champion, James
Corley, Elbert
Davis, Arthur
Davis, Harper
Fortunato, Joseph
Frohm, Martin
Garrett, William
Gelatka, Charles
Goolsby, James
Harness, James
Harris, Amos
Harrison, Granville
Jefferson, William
Kowalski, Andrew
McWilliams, Thomas
Nix, John
Sermon, Raymond
Sidorik, Alexander
Smith, Truett
Stacy, William
Tait, Arthur
Tripson, John

MISSISSIPPI UNIVERSITY
Alliston, Vaughn
Barfield, Kenneth
Beatty, Edward
Bernard, David
Bilbo, Jonathan
Boggan, Rex
Brewer, Homer
Britt, Oscar
Brown, Raymond
Churchwell, Hanson
Conerly, Charles
Cothren, Paige
Crawford, Edward
Dale, Roland
Day, Herman "Eagle"
Dodson, Leslie
Dottley, John
Erickson, William
Farragut, Kenneth
Flowers, Charles
Franklin, Robert
Gilbert, Kline
Grantham, Lawrence
Hall, L. Parker
Hapes, Merle
Hickerson, Eugene
Hovious, John
Howell, Earl
Johnson, Joseph
Kempinski, Charles
Khayat, Robert
Kinard, Frank
Kinard, George
Kinard, William
Kirk, Kenneth
Kozel, Chester
Lee, Robert
Lott, William
McCain, Robert
Magnum, Peter
Manley, Joseph
Murphy, Harvey

Patton, James
Poole, G. Barney
Poole, James
Poole, Oliver
Poole, Ray
Reed, Leroy
Reynolds, Robert
Reynolds, William
Roberson, Lake
Smith, Houston Allen
Stribling, Majure
Terrell, Marvin
Terrell, Raymond
Turnbow, Guy
Woodruff, Lee
Yelverton, William

MISSOURI MINES
Thornton, Richard

MISSOURI STATE CENTRAL
Werner, Sox
Windburn, Ernest

MISSOURI STATE NORTHEAST
Robinson, John

MISSOURI STATE NORTHWEST
Schottel, Ivan

MISSOURI STATE SOUTHEAST
Wittenborn, John

MISSOURI STATE SOUTHWEST
Dees, Robert

MISSOURI UNIVERSITY
Armstrong, Robert
Bacchus, Carl
Blumer, Herbert
Burnine, Harold
Christman, Paul
Collins, Paul
Copley, Charles
Eaton, Victor
Gladden, James Mack
Greenwood, Donald
Jackson, Henry
Jean, Walter
Jeffries, Robert
Kekeris, James
McGirl, Leonard
Magac, Michael
Martin, Herchel
Morton, John
Pepper, Eugene
Quirk, Edward
Reece, Donald
Rouse, Stillman
Shurnas, Marshall
Smith, Clyde
Smith, Ray
Steuber, Robert
Stewart, Ralph
Tarr, James
Travis, J. Edward
Van Dyne, Charles
Volz, Wilbur
Wren, Lowe

MISSOURI VALLEY
Hall, Ronald

MONMOUTH
Earp, Francis
Molesworth, Keith
Scott, Eugene

MONTANA STATE
Cosner, Donald
Forte, Aldo
Illman, Edward
Kelly, William
Kipp, James
Lange, Clifford
Lazetich, William
Peterson, Russell
Popovich, Milton
Szakash, Paul
Warzeka, Ronald

MONTANA UNIVERSITY
Noyes, Leonard
Sullivan, Steven

MORGAN STATE
Brown, Roosevelt
Harris, Elmore

MORNINGSIDE

Wenig, Obe

MORRIS BROWN
Bivins, Charles
Mosley, Henry

MORRIS HARVEY
Adams, Verlin
Carr, James
Seltzer, Harry
Thacker, Alvin
Turbert, Francis

MT. ST. MARY'S
Chapman, Thomas
Lamas, Joseph

MUHLENBERG
Averno, Sisto
Borrelli, Nicholas
Farrell, Edward
Gorgone, Peter
Scott, L. Perry
Weiner, Albert
Zuzzio, Anthony

MURRAY STATE TEACHERS
Mains, Gilbert
Gudauskas, Peter
McRaven, William
Speth, George

NEBRASKA STATE TEACHERS
Blessing, Paul
Lindahl, Virgil
Miller, Milford
Peterson, Cordie

NEBRASKA UNIVERSITY
Adducci, Nicholas
Alfson, Warren
Ashburne, Clifford
Bassett, Herbert
Berquist, Jay
Boll, Donald
Bristow, George
Broadstone, Marion
Brock, Charles
Byler, Joseph
Callahan, William
Cardwell, Lloyd
Chamberlain, Guy
DeFruiter, Robert
DeWitz, Herbert
Doyle, Theodore
Fischer, Cletus
Frahm, Herald
Francis, Samuel
Hokuf, Steven
Hopp, Harry
Howell, John
Husmann, Edward
James, George
Kahler, Robert
Kahler, Royal
Lewellen, Verne
Lyman, Roy
McDonald, Lester
McMullen, Daniel
McPherson, Forrest
Masterson, Bernard
Mullen, Vern
Munn, Monte
Munn, Wayne
Noble, David
O'Brien, Gail
Oehlrich, Arnold
Presnell, Glenn
Prochaska, Ray
Rhea, Hugh
Richards, Harry
Richards, Raymond
Rohrig, Herman
Samuelson, Carl
Sauer, George
Scherer, Bernard
Schleich, Victor
Seeman, George
Shaw, Edward
Shirey, Frederick
Smith, Robert
Thompson, Alvin
Thompson, Russell
Toogood, Charles
Torczon, Laverne
Vacanti, Samuel
Webber, Harry
Weber, Elmer

Weir, Edward
Weir, Joseph
Weller, Raymond
Wenke, Adolph
Westophal, Joseph
Wilder, Harold Wiedich.
Zaruba, Carroll
Zuver, Merle

NEBRASKA WESLEYAN
Wiberg, Oscar

NEVADA
Afflis, Richard
Bass, William
Bradshaw, James
Carroll, Victor
Clark, Arthur
Gillom, Horace
Heath, Stanley
Howard, Sherman
Kalmanir, Thomas
Lane, Clayton
McClure, Robert
Mackrides, William
Motley, Marion
Orlich, Daniel
Talcott, Donald
Wentworth, Shirley

NEW HAMPSHIRE
Connors, Stafford
Knox, Samuel

NEW MEXICO
Agajanian, Benjamin
Bogren, Vincent
Locklin, William
Miller, Edward
Montfort, Avery
Morrison, Ronald
Ward, David

NEW MEXICO A & M
Nuzum, Jerry
Villanueva, Daniel

NEW YORK CITY COLLEGE
Halpern, Robert
Illowit, Roy

NEW YORK UNIVERSITY
Barabee, Robert
Briante, Frank
Brown, Frederick
Bunyan, John
Chalmers, George
Concannon, Ernest
Dunn, Robert
Follet, Beryl
Grant, Leonard
Grant, Ross
Hugret, Joseph
McGrath, Bryan
Marchi, Basilio
Marshall, Cloyd
Miller, James
Myers, David
Nemeck, Jerald
Riordan, Charles
Satenstein, Bernard
Shapiro, Jack
Skudkin, David
Smith, Edward
Strong, Kenneth
Swiadon, Philip
Tanguay, James

NIAGARA
Deremer, Arthur
DeSantis, Daniel
Gutknecht, Albert
Piskor, Roman
Stefik, Robert

N. CAROLINA A & I
Jackson, Robert
Smith, J

N. CAROLINA STATE
Baker, John
Barnes, Ernest
Berry, Cornelius
Brown, John
Christy, Richard
Coon, Edward
Dees, Darrell
Farrar, Vincent
Gibson, Paul

Greer, James
Mark, Louis
Palmer, Leslie
Rex, Raymond
Stanton, William
Tatum, Jess
Webster, Alex
Winslow, Paul

N. CAROLINA UNIVERSITY
Barclay, George
Bartos, Henry
Blazer, Philip
Burnette, Thomas
Camp, James
Cara, Dominic
Faircloth, Arthur
Goldstein, Alan
Hansen, Roscoe
Hazelwood, Theodore
Higgins, Thomas
Jackson, Donald
Justice, Charles
Kahn, Edward
Keller, Kenneth
Kennedy, Robert
Koman, William
Magner, James
Maronic, Steven
Miketa, Andrew
Robinson, Edward
Rodgers, Hosea
Smith, William
Stallings, Alva Donald
Sutton, Edward
Szafaryn, Leonard
Tandy, George
Weiner, Arthur
Williamson, Ernest

NORTH DAKOTA STATE
Nemzek, Albert

N. DAKOTA
Felber, Frederick
Gainer, Charles
Gaiver, Einar
Kahl, Cyrus
Kupcinet, Irving
McGeary, Clarence
McMillan, Stewart
Mackenroth, John
Mulready, Gerald
Myhra, Steven
Ordway, William
Rothrock, Clifford
Sturgeon, Cecil
Sturgeon, Lyle
Urevig, Claude
Wheeler, Ernest
Young, Leslie

NORTHEASTERN
Watson, Sidney

NORTHWESTERN
Alban, Richard
Anderson, Henry
Asad, Douglas
Aschenbrenner, Frank
Baker, Frank
Bauman, Alfred
Benson, George
Blumenthal, Morris
Bruder, Henry
Burton, Ronald
Cvercko, Andrew
Damore, John
DeCorrevont, William
DeStefano, Frederick
Driscoll, John
Engebretsen, Paul
Erdlitz, Richard
Erickson, Michael
Fencl, Richard
Flowers, Richard
Fowler, Willmer
Gonya, Robert
Gossage, Eugene
Graham, Otto
Grefe, Theodore
Hajek, Charles
Haman, John
Herman, Edward
Hirsch, Edward
Holmer, Walter

Jecha, Ray
Johnson, Donald
Johnsos, Luke
Johnston, Mark
Kapter, Alexander
Kelly, Charles
Koehler, Robert
Kovatch, John
Lecture, James
Lewis, Loren
Lind, Albert
Lokanc, Joseph
McElwain, William
Maddock, George
Magnusson, Glenn
Manske, Edward
Midler, Louis
Motl, Robert
Mueller, Ewald
Murakowski, Arthur
Palmer, Charles
Rentner, Charles
Riley, John
Russell, Lafayette
Russell, Reginald
Schwall, Victor
Siegle, Jules
Stonesifer, Donald
Swisher, Robert
Tuner, James
Vanzo, Frederick
Weldin, Harold
Wietecha, Ray
Williamson, Frederick
Wilson, George
Zorich, George

NORWICH
Liebel, Frank
Rice, William

NOTRE DAME
Adams, John
Adamson, Kenneth
Anderson, Edward
Anderson, Heartley
Angsman, Elmer
Bagarus, Steven
Bahan, Leonard
Banas, Steven
Barry, Norman
Baujan, Harry
Beams, Byron
Beinor, J. Edward
Berezney, Peter
Bertelli, Angelo
Brill, Martin
Brutz, James
Burnell, Max
Carberry, Glenn
Cifelli, August
Clatt, Corwin
Coleman, Herbert
Connor, George
Cook, Edward
Corgan, Michael
Cotton, Forrest
Coughlin, Frank
Coutre, Lawrence
Cowhig, Gerard
Crimmins, Bernard
Crotty, James
Crowley, James
Culver, Alvin
Czarobski, Zygmont
Dancewicz, Frank
Davlin, Michael
Degree, Walter
Dove, Robert
Duggan, Edward
Ebli, Raymond
Edwards, Eugene
Eichenlaub, Raymond
Enright, Rex
Evans, Frederick
Fagioli, Carl
Feeney, Francis
Fischer, William
Fitzgerald, Freeman
Garvey, Arthur
Gasparella, Joseph
Gaul, Frank
Gavier, William
Gay, William
Gompers, William
Greenev, Norman
Groom, Jerome

Guglielmi, Ralph
Hanlon, Robert
Hart, Leon
Hayes, David
Hayes, Gerald
Heap, Joseph
Hearden, Thomas
Heenan, Patrick
Helwig, John
Higgins, Luke
Hornung, Paul
Hunter, Arthur
Jones, Jerry
Juzwik, Steven
Kasper, Thomas
Katcik, Joseph
Keefe, Emmett
Kell, Paul
Kelly, Robert
Kerr, William
Kiley, Roger
Koken, Michael
Kovatch, John
Koziak, Michael
Kuchta, Frank
Kuharich, Joseph
Kurth, Joseph
Lambeau, Earl
Lattner, John
Larson, Fred
Law, John
Lawrence, Donald
Leahy, Bernard
Lemek, Ray
Lensing, Vincent
Leonard, James
Leonard, William
Livingstone, Robert
Lujack, John
Lynch, Richard
McCarthy, Howard
McInerney, Arnold
McMullan, John
McNulty, Paul
Maddock, Robert
Malone, Grover
Marelli, Raymond
Martin, James
Mastrangelo, John
Mavraides, Menil
Mayer, Frank
Mayl, Eugene
Maxwell, Joseph
Mehre, Henry
Mello, James
Merganthal, Arthur
Mieskowski, Edward
Miller, Donald
Millner, Wayne
Mohardt, John
Moynihan, Timothy
Mundee, Frederick
Mutschelier, James
Nadolney, Roman
Nemeth, Steven
O'Boyle, Harry
O'Connor, William
Ostroski, Chester
Palumbo, Sam
Panelli, John
Pasquesi, Anthony
Pearson, Dudley
Pietrosante, Nicholas
Petitbon, John
Phelan, Robert
Piepul, Milton
Pivarnik, Joseph
Polisky, John
Puplis, Andrew
Ratterman, George
Riffle, Charles
Roach, John
Rogers, John
Ruetz, Joseph
Ryan, James
Rydzewski, Frank
Rymkus, Louis
Savoldi, Joseph
Schaeffer, Donald
Scholtz, Robert
Schrader, James
Scharer, Edward
Scott, Vincent
Seyfrit, Michael
Shellogg, Alec
Signaigo, Joseph
Simmons, Floyd
Sitko, Emil

Skoglund, Robert
Slackford, Fred
Smith, Edward
Smith, Richard
Spaniel, Frank
Spiegel, Clarence
Statuto, Arthur
Steinkemper, William
Stevenson, Mark
Stickles, Montford
Strohmeyer, George
Stuhldreyer, Harry
Sullivan, George
Swistowicz, Michael
Szymanski, Frank
Syzmanski, Richard
Terlep, George
Tobin, George
Toneff, Robert
Tonelli, Mario
Trafton, George
Tripucka, Frank
Urban, Gasper
Vairo, Dominic
Varrichione, Frank
Vegara, George
Wallace, Joseph
Wallner, Frederick
Walsh, William
Ward, Gilbert
Wendell, Martin
Wetoska, Robert
White, James
Wightkin, William
Williams, Robert
Worden, Neil
Wunsch, Harry
Wynne, Chester
Yarr, Thomas
Yonaker, John
Yonakor, John
Zalejski, Ernest
Zilly, John
Zontini, Louis
Zoia, Clyde

OBERLIN
Cooper, William

OCCIDENTAL
Beebe, Keith
Botchan, Ronald

OGLETHORPE
Fulton, Theodore
Mitrick, Frank
Zelencik, Frank

OHIO NORTHERN
Conley, John
Lynch, Paul

OHIO STATE
Adamle, Anthony
Andrako, Stephen
Ash, Julian
Bettridge, John
Bobo, Hubert
Borton, John
Bradley, Robert
Brubaker, Richard
Bruney, Fred
Busich, Samuel
Campanella, Joseph
Cannavino, Joseph
Cassady, Howard
Cheroke, George
Clair, Frank
Cline, Oliver
Comiskey, Frank
Cunningham, Harold
Curcillo, Anthony
Daniell, James
Davis, Glenn
Dean, Harold
Dellerba, Spiro
DiPierro, Raymond
Dow, Elwood
Doyle, Richard
Dugger, John
Duvall, Earl
Eby, Byron
Fekete, Eugene
Flanagan, Richard
Flowers, James
Fox, Samuel
Gandee, Sherwin
Gaudio, Robert
Gorrill, Charles

Groza, Louis
Harley, Charles
Harris, Thomas
Henderson, Herbert
Houston, James
Honaker, Charles
Horvath, Leslie
Houston, Lindell
Huffman, Iolas
Isabel, Wilmer
James, Daniel
James, Thomas
Janowicz, Victor
Jennings, John
Jobko, William
Kabealo, Michael
Kaplanoff, Carl
Karch, Robert
Karcher, James
Krall, Gerard
Kriss, Howard
Lavelli, Dante
LeBeau, Richard
Leggett, David
Lininger, Raymond
Logan, Richard
Long, Thomas
McCafferty, Donald
McDonald, James
Marino, Victor
Marshall, James
Michael, Richard
Michaels, Alton
Michaels, William
Momsen, Robert
Monaha, Regis
Morrison, Frederick
Myers, Cyril
Myers, Robert
Nardi, Richard
Nemecek, Andrew
Nichols, John
Padan, Robert
Padlow, Max
Parker, James
Perini, Evo
Petcoff, Boni
Pincura, Stanley
Raskowski, Leo
Ream, Charles
Rosequist, Theodore
Rosso, George
Rowan, Everett
Ruzich, Stephen
Sarringhaus, Paul
Schafrath, Richard
Schell, Herbert
Scott, John
Sensenbaugher, Dean
Shaw, Robert
Souders, Cecil
Spiers, Robert
Stinchcomb, Gaylord
Strausbaugh, James
Sutherin, Donald
Taylor, John
Thomas, Russell
Waite, Willard
Watkins, Robert
Weed, Thurlow
Wendler, Harold
Wetzel, Damon
White, Robert
Williams, Joseph
Willis, William
Wiper, Donald
Workman, Harry
Workman, Hoge
Wright, Ernest
Young, William
Zadworney, Frank
Zarnas, Augustus

OHIO UNIVERSITY
Adams, Chester
Costello, Vincent
Graham, Alfred
Halleck, Paul
Hastings, George
Janiak, Leonard
Kerns, John
Krieger, Earl
Lewis, Arthur
Rush, Arden
Sadowsky, Leonard
Snyder, Robert
Snyder, William

OHIO WESLEYAN
Edler, Robert
Frump, Milton
Lamme, Emerald
Nelson, Donald
Pearce, Harley
Smith, Olin
Turley, John
Westfall, Edgar
Winters, Lindel

OKLAHOMA A. & M.
Aldridge, Benjamin
Arms, Lloyd
Armstrong, Neil
Ault, Wayne
Bredde, William
Buffington, Harry
Fenimore, Robert
Foster, Ralph
Garrett, Thurman
Grimes, William
Jeffers, Edward
Ledbetter, Toy
Liles, Elvin
Long, William
Loyd, Alexander
Meisenheimer, Darrell
Merkle, Edward
Owen, William
Parmer, James
Reynolds, James
Shaw, Charles
Spavital, James
Spencer, Joseph
Turner, James
Wright, Albert

OKLAHOMA BAPTIST
Phillips, Ewell

OKLAHOMA CITY
UNIVERSITY
Allen, Carl
Gutowsky, Leroy
Hilpert, Harold
Kamp, James
Schilling, Ralph
Schwab, Raymond
Sedbrook, Leonard
Shirley, Marion
Taylor, Hugh
Tuttle, Orville
Wade, James
Wilkerson, Basil

OKLAHOMA MILITARY
ACADEMY
Strom, Frank

OKLAHOMA N. E.
TEACHERS
Cobb, Thomas

OKLAHOMA STATE
CENTRAL
Capps, Walter

OKLAHOMA S. W.
TEACHERS
Gore, Gordon
Jackson, Grady
Kane, Herbert
Simmons, James
Springer, Harold

OKLAHOMA STATE
Banfield, James
Barnard, Charles
Evans, Jon
Keys, Howard
Meinert, Dale
Wood, Duane

OKLAHOMA
UNIVERSITY
Allton, Joseph
Andros, Plato
Baker, David
Boyd, Robert
Boydston, Max
Breedon, William
Bristow, Gordon
Brockman, Edward
Burris, Paul
Campbell, William
Catlin, Thomas
Clark, Beryl

Colhouer, Jacob
Conkright, William
Coppage, Alton
Cox, Robert
Crowder, Earl
Cullen, Ronald
Duggan, Gilford
Dunlap, Robert
Eason, Roger
Edmundson, Van
Gautt, Prentice
Gentry, Cassius
Golding, Joseph
Guffey, Roy
Harris, James
Harrison, Robert
Heath, Leon
Hill, Harry
Ivy, Frank
Jacobs, Jack
Krisher, William
Lahar, Harold
Lamb, Walter
Lee, Hilary
McCullough, Hugh
McDaniel, Wahoo
McDonald, Donald
McDonald, Thomas
McPhail, Howard
Manley, Leon
Marsh, Howard
Marsh, Richard
Martin, John
Morris, Dennit
Owens, James
Paine, Homer
Parks, Edward
Pearson, Lindell
Peery, Gordon
Pressley, Lee
Pricer, William
Rapacz, John
Rolle, David
Sarratt, Charles
Seymour, Robert
Shirk, John
Slough, Elmer
Speegle, Clifton
Staey, James
Stevenson, Ralph
Thomas, Clendon
Thomas, George
Thomas, James
Tillman, Alonzo
Tubbs, Gerald
Tyree, James
Vessels, William
Weatherall, James
West, Stanley
White, Philip
Whited, Marvin
Wilcox, John
Young, Paul
Young, Walter

OMAHA UNIVERSITY
Arenas, Joseph

OREGON STATE
Austin, William
Baker, Loris
Bates, Theodore
Bergerson, Gilbert
Biancone, John
Carlson, Jules
Clark, James
Clark, Myers
Cox, John
Dow, Kenneth
Durdan, Donald
Evansen, Paul
Field, Harry
Francis, Joseph
Franklin, Norman
Gray, William
Hackenbrush, John
Halverson, William
Hogland, Douglas
Hughes, Henry
Kolberg, Elmer
Lowe, Paul
McKalip, William
Mann, David
Maple, Howard
Mercer, James
More, Harold
Ossowski, Theodore
Pangle, Harold

Puddy, Harold
Ramsey, Frank
Rust, Reginald
Samuel, Donald
Schultz, Eberle
Schwammel, Adolph
Shanley, James
Sears, Victor
Temple, Mark
Tsoutsouvas John
Wendlick, Joseph
Wickett, Lloyd
Younce, Leonard

OREGON UNIVERSITY
Aschbacher, Darrel
Ashcom, Richard
Barnes, Emery
Bjork, Delbert
Brethauer, Monte
Carter, Ross
Christensen, George
Culwell, Val
Cuppoletti, Bree
Daugherty, Richard
Donnell, John
Eagle, Alexander
Ecklund, Bradley
Elliott, Charles
Emmons, Franklin
Gagnon, Roy
Garza, Daniel
Grottkau, Robert
Horne, Richard
Hughes, Bernard
Hurst, William
Iverson, Christopher
James, Richard
Kitzmiller, John
Lainhart, Porter
Leicht, Jacob
Lewis, Woodley
Lillard, Joseph
Mecham, Curtis
Mikulak, Michael
Morgan, William
Morris, John
Morse, Raymond
Patera, John
Rhea, Floyd
Shanley, James
Shaw, George
Sikora, Michael
Stone, Jack
Stuart, James
Van Brocklin, Norman
West, Willie
Wilcox, John
Wilkins, Richard

OTTAWA, KAN.
Knapper, Joseph

OTTERBEIN
Agler, Robert
Davis, Paul
Faust, Richard
Seibert, Edward

OUCHITA
Floyd, John
LaFitte, William

PACIFIC, COLLEGE of
Bass, Richard
Campora, Donald
Clark, George
Conner, Clyde
Cronin, Eugene
Delavan, Burton
Denton, Robert
Flores, Thomas
Hawkins, Wayne
Jankovich, Keever
Klapstein, Earl
McCaffray, Arthur
McCormick, Thomas
Macon, Edward
Martinovich, Philip
Miller, Fred
Moser, Robert
Laack, Galen
Larscheid, Jack
LeBaron, Edward
Nisby, John
Putnam, Duane
Striegel, William

Thomas, John
Wallace, Henry
Watson, James
Williams, A. D.

PACIFIC LUTHERAN
Sigurdson, Sigurd

PASADENA
Hoisington, Allan

PAUL QUINN COLLEGE
Napier, Walter

PENN MILITARY
Allen, Samuel
Klotz, John

PENN STATE
Beck, Clarence
Cherundulo, Charles
Conover, Lawrence
Davis, Robert
Drazenovich, Charles
Durkota, Jeffrey
Eschbach, Herbert
Filak, John
Frank, James
Frketich, Leonard
Greenshields, Donn
Grier, Roosevelt
Griffiths, Paul
Haines, Henry
Hamas, Steven
Higgins, Robert
Jaffur, John
Janerette, Charles
Joe, Lawrence
Killinger, Glenn
Lightner, Joseph
Lucas, Richard
McCann, Ernest
Mahoney, Roger
Michalske, August
Miller, Henry
Miller, Joseph
Mills, Thomas
Moore, Leonard
Moore, William
Nobile, Leo
Nolan, John
O'Connell, J.
Olszewski, Albert
Osborn, Robert
Palazzi, Louis
Palm, Michael
Patrick, John
Panaccion, Victor
Petrella, John
Plum, Milton
Pritchard, William
Rauch, Richard
Reedinger, Otis
Robb, Harry
Roepke, John
Rogel, Frank
Schleicher, Maurice
Schuster, Richard
Scrabis, Robert
Snell, George
Stynchula, Andrew
Suhey, Steven
Tamburo, Samuel
Thomas, William
Tobin, Elgie
Triplett, Wallace
Ullery, William
Walters, Lester
Way, Charles
Wear, Robert
Wentz, Byron
Werder, Enid
Wilson, E.

PENN STATE TEACHERS
Sandusky, Alex

PENN UNIVERSITY
Allen, Edward
Bednarik, Charles
Bell, Edward
Berray, Howard
Calcagni, Ralph
Craig, Clark
Dieter, Herbert
Doelling, Frederick
Fiedler, William
Frick, Ray
Gallagher, Bernard

Grain, Edwin
Hamer, Ernest
Hopkins, Theodore
Kaufman, John
Kuczinski, Bernard
Leith, Oliver
Little, Louis
McGinley, Edward
Masters, Walter
Matthews, Neil
Milan, Joseph
Minisi, Anthony
Murray, Francis
Nelson, Herbert
Oristaglio, Robert
Quillen, Frank
Raffel, William
Reagan, Frank
Riblett, Paul
Rogers, Charles
Russell, Edward
Savitsky, George
Schneider, Donald
Schweder, John
Sokolis, Stanley
Sponaugle, Robert
Stein, Samuel
Stickel, Walter
Sullivan, George
Sweeney, William
Thomas, Alfred
Thurman, John
Willson, Osborne
Wray, Ludlow

PEPPERDINE
Bighead, Jack
Embree, Melvin

PHILLIPS UNIVERSITY
Owen, Stephen
Sark, Harvey
Strauss, Arthur

PITTSBURGH
Adams, Henry
Andabaker, Rudolph
Ashbaugh, William
Bohren, Karl
Bolkovac, Nicholas
Bonelli, Ernest
Brown, Jesse
Brueckman, Charles
Butler, Jack
Cassiano, Richard
Cenci, John
Chase, Ralph
Chickerneo, John
Clark, James
Collins, Paul
Cosgrove, Raymond
Cuba, Paul
Daddio, Louis
Dailey, Theodore
Daniell, Averell
Durishan, John
Dutton, William
Edgar, William
Epps, Robert
Fife, Ralph
Flanagan, William
Ford, Henry
Geremsky, Thaddeus
Glatz, Fred
Gob, Arthur
Goldberg, Marshall
Guzik, John
Gwosden, Milo
Haley, Richard
Heller, Warren
Hendrian, Warren
Hinte, Harold
Hoel, Robert
Holleran, Thomas
Hood, Franklin
Huzvar, John
Jones, Edgar
Kern, William
Kish, Benjamin
Kracum, George
Kraemer, Eldred
Kristufek, Frank
Lauro, Lindell
Love, John
McCabe, Richard
McCusker, James
McMurdo, James

McPeak, William
Matesic, Edward
Matisi, Anthony
Mattioli, Francis
Meadows, Eric
Merkovsky, Elmer
Morrow, James
Nicksick, Michael
Olezniczak, Stanley
Palatella, Louis
Paluck, John
Parkinson, Thomas
Patrick, Frank
Peace, Lawrence
Pealman, Lester
Petro, Steven
Pierre, John
Priatko, William
Quatse, Jess
Radosevich, George
Reger, John
Reynolds, William
Rickards, Paul
Roussos, Michael
Sack, John
Salata, Andrew
Schmidt, Joseph
Schmitt, Theodore
Sebastian, Michael
Siedelson, Harry
Sies, Dale
Sites, Vincent
Skladany, Joseph
Skladany, Leo
Souchak, Frank
Stein, Russell
Stock, John
Thornhill, Claude
Thurbon, Robert
Walton, Frank
Walton, Joseph
Weinstock, Isadore
Welch, Gilbert
Wiesenbaugh, Henry
Wissinger, Zonar
Zombek, Joseph

PORTLAND
Barrett, Emmett
Beil, Lawrence
Dunstan, Elwyn
McDade, William

PRAIRIE VIEW A & M
Brackins, Charles
Daniels, Clemon
Farrington, John
Granderson, Rufus
Hunt, James
Webster, David

PRESBYTERIAN
Moore, Paul
Waters, Robert
Webb, Kenneth
Weldon, Lawrence

PRINCETON
Beattie, Robert
Drews, Theodore
Howard, Albert
Keck, Stanley
MacPhee, Walter
Perantoni, J. Francis
Perina, Robert
Poole, George

PROVIDENCE
Avedisian, Charles
Dagata, Frederick
Lester, Harold
Smith, Leo
Soar, Henry
Triggs, John

PURDUE
Allen, John
Barbolak, Peter
Barnes, Erich
Barnett, Thomas
Barwegan, Richard
Berne, William
Bettis, Thomas
Birk, Ferdinand
Boland, George
Brewster, Darrell
Brock, J. Louis
Buksar, George

Burmeister, Forrest
Carman, Edmund
Claypool, Ralph
Cody, Edward
Combs, William
Dawson, Leonard
DeMoss, Robert
Dimancheff, Boris
Drake, John
Duggins, George Herbert
Febel, Fred
Fichtner, Ross
Fleischman, Godfrey
Flowers, Bernard
Franckhauser, Thomas
French, Barry
Galvin, John
Gibron, Abraham
Gift, Wayne
Gorgal, Kenneth
Haas, Robert
Heck, Robert
Heldt, Carl
Horstmann, Roy
Houston, Walter
Huffine, Kenneth
Humphrey, Paul
Hutton, Leon
Ippolito, Anthony
Isbell, Cecil
Janecek, Clarence
Karras, Louis
Kodba, Joseph
Krupa, Joseph
Kulbacki, Joseph
Laraway, Jack
Letsinger, James
Lundy, Lamar
McGrew, Daniel
Maloney, Norman
Mihal, Joseph
Miller, Charles
Moss, Paul
Mumley, Nicholas
Murley, Richard
Murray, Earl
Oehler, John
Panfil, Kenneth
Papach, George
Pardonner, Paul
Petty, John
Pfohl, Robert
Pope, Lewis
Quast, John
Rate, Edwin
Risk, Edward
Roggeman, Thomas
Rykowski, Frank
Sabal, Ronald
Sandefur, Wayne
Selawski, Eugene
Simerson, John
Skibinski, Joseph
Skoronski, Edward
Sleight, Elmer
Sugar, Leo
Voytek, Edward
Washington, Clyde
Wellman, Ferdinand
Winkler, Joseph
Woltman, Clement
Young, Glenn
Zimmerman, Gifford

REDLANDS
Housman, John
McGilbra, Sanford
Thompson, Donald

REGIS
Herber, Arnold

RHODE ISLAND STATE
Abbruzzi, Louis
Cure, Armand
McIntosh, Daniel

RICE INSTITUTE
Blackburn, William
Boettcher, Frederick
Brick, Shirley
Brumley, Robert
Cordill, Oliver
Dial, Gilbert
Eikenberg, Charles
Gillis, Daniel
Hartman, Frederick

Hill, King
Howton, William
Humble, Weldon
Magee, John
Miller, Ralph
Moegle, Richard
Nichols, Hamilton
Proctor, Rex
Rote, Tobin
Rucka, Leo
Schuelke, Karl
Scruggs, Edwin
Smith, Jess D.
Spruill, James
Squyres, Seaman
Steen, Frank
Trask, Orville
Watson, Joseph
Weatherly, Gerald
Whitlow, Kenneth
Williams, Wendell

RICHMOND
Biscaha, Joseph
Cavalli, Carmen
Fronczek, Andrew
Graham, S. Lyle
Humbert, Richard
Jones, Arthur
Lauriatis, Fred

RIDER
Maynard, Lester

RIPON
Croft, Milburn
Hearden, Leonard
Kenyon, Crowell
Lunde, Lester
Rosenow, August
Rotkowski, Charles
Scalissi, Theodore
Smith, David
Smith, Earl
Wheeler, Lyle

ROCHESTER
Sullivan, John

RUTGERS
Alexander, John
Benkert, Henry
Burkhardt, Arthur
Crowl, Richard
Duffit, James
Fraser, George
Garrett, Alfred
Greenberg, Benjamin
Grossman, John
Hasbrouck, John
Horton, Lester
Lord, John
Nash, Robert
Pellington, William
Prisco, Nicholas
Rendall, Kenneth
Robeson, Paul
Rosen, Stanley
Simms, Robert

SACRAMENTO
Chamberlain, Daniel

ST. AMBROSE
DeClerk, Frank
Hansen,
Lapka, Theodore
Michalik, Arthur
Keriasotis, Nicholas
Kolls, Louis
Oelerich, John
Zuidmulder, David

ST. ANSELM'S
McLean, Raymond
Spirida, John

ST. BENEDICT'S
Clarkin, William
Comp, Irvin
Hunehe, Charles
Visnic, Lawrence

ST. BONAVENTURE
Butler, John
Gavigan, Michael

Gildae, John
Hays, George
Kaporch, Anbert
Kenneally, George
Ksionzyk, John
Lovuolo, Frank
Marcolini, Hugo
Nicksich, George

ST. EDMONDS
Knox, Charles

ST. EDWARDS
Sarafiny, Albert

ST. FRANCIS
Bova, Anthony
McCarthy, Thomas
Magulick, George
Milano, Arch
Naioti, John

ST. JOHNS (MINN.)
Carlson, Irvin
Caywood, Lester
McNally, John "Blood"

ST. JOHNS (NEW YORK)
McLain, Joseph
Salemi, Samuel

ST. JOSEPH'S (IND.)
Scollard, Nicholas
Thuerk, Owen

ST. JOSEPH'S (PA.)
Cole, John
Laux, Theodore

ST. LAWRENCE
Hefti, James
Leckonby, William
Sheard, Alfred

ST. LOUIS
Arenz, Arnold
Drury, Lyle
Kane, Carl
Krause, Henry
LaPresta, Benjamin
Lintzenich, Joseph
McLeod, Arthur
Meinhardt, George
Montgomery, William
Nagel, Ross
Pfuhl, Richard
Rapp, Manuel
Schweidler, Richard
Weber, Richard
Wissmann, Peter

ST. MARY'S (CAL.)
Aguirre, Joseph
Austin, James
Brovelli Angelo
Callen, Frank
Cassara, Frank
Clemons, Raymond
Compagno, Anthony
Conlee, Gerald
Crowe, Paul
Dennerlien, Gerald
Dowd, Jerry
Ebding, Harry
Falkenstein, Anthony
Flagerman, John
Frankian, Malcolm
Giannoni, John
Grant, Hugh
Herrin, Houston
Jorgenson, Carl
Jorgenson, Wagner
Kellogg, Clarence
Klotovich, Michael
McNally, Frank
Magnani, Dante
Marefos, Andrew
Mattos, Harry
Mesak, Richard
Morales, Gonzales
Muldoon, Matthew
Nichelini, Allen
Ruskusky, Raymond
Ryan, Edward
Sherman, Willard
Simas, William
Starrett, Benjamin
Stennet, Frederick

Stepanovich, Michael
Strader, Norman
Toscani, Francis
Trebotich, Ivan
Wedemeyer, Herman
Wilkin, Wilbur
Yezerski, John

ST MARY'S (KAN.)
Lane, Lewis
Murphy, Thomas

ST. MARY'S (MINN.)
Cronin,
Madigan, Frank
Mehelich,
Monelie, William
Oas, Arnold
O'Neill, Thomas
O'Toole, William
Wager, Clinton

ST. MARY'S (TEXAS)
Bettencourt, Lawrence
Billock, Frank
Lankas, James
Sandig, Curtis

ST. OLAF
Cleve, Einar
Putlier, Fred
Saumer, Sylvester

ST. THOMAS
Baril, Adrian
Brandt, James
Franta, Herbert
Houle, Wilfred
Kiesling, Walter
LaBissoniere, Joseph
McNellis, William
Manion, James
Maynaugh, Roland
Mohs, Louis
Murphy, James
Murray, John
Pahl, Louis
Reichow, Charles
Salscheider, John
Simensen, Donald
Steinbach, Laurence
Vassau, Roy

ST. VINCENT'S
Foltz, Vernon
Kondria, John
Macerelli, John
Manzini, Baptiste
Popovich, John
Ratica, Joseph
Strosser, Walter

SALEM
Rodriguez, Jess

SAM HOUSTON
Hightower, John
Hill, James
Law, Hubbard
Moore, McNeil
Spence, Julian

SAN DIEGO STATE
Dahms, Thomas
Held, Paul
Keyes, Robert
Quinlan, Volney

SAN FRANCISCO
Barber, Ernest
Barber, James
Barni, Roy
Brown, Charles Edward
Duncan, Maurice
Endress, Albert
Franceschi, Peter
Greenhalgh, Robert
Kenny, Charles
Marchetti, Gino
Matson, Oliver
Mergen, Michael
Pacewic, Vincent
Panciera, Donal
Peacock, Merrill
Peters, Floyd
Peterson, Raymond
Letlow, Russell
Rowe, Harmon

Sabuco, Tino
St. Clair, Robert
Sanchez, John
Scott, Joseph
Scudero, Joseph
Siemering, Lawrence
Stanfel, Richard
Stephens, Louis
Vogelaar, Carroll

SAN JOSE STATE
Birlem, Keith
Colchico, Daniel
Collier, Floyd
Crisler, Harold
Dow, Harley
Hardy, Charles
Hubbard, Wesley
Johnson, Marvin
Longo, Charles
Louderback, Thomas
Minini, Frank
Nygren, Bernard
Pifferini, Robert
Powell, Arthur
Sykes, Robert
Teresa, Anthony
Titchenal, Robert
Ucovich, Mitchell
Wilson, William
Zimmerman, Leroy

SANTA BARBARA
Cathcart, Royal
Cathcart, Samuel
Morris, John
Oldershaw, Douglas
Yeager, Howard

SANTA CLARA
Bassi, Richard
Beals, Alyn
Casanega, Kenneth
Connolly, Theodore
Cope, Frank
Dougherty, Philip
Falaschi, Nello
Fisher, Everett
Forrest, Edward
Freitas, Jesse
Ginney, Jerry
Grgich, Visco
Haynes, Hall
Hennessey, Jerome
Hock, John
McArthur, John
McCafferty, Arthur
Nagler, Gern
Nolan, John
Ramona, Joseph
Schiechl, John
Storm, Edward
Thornton, Robert
Vinnola, Paul
Williams, Ellery

SANTA MONICA
Harris, John

SCRANTON
Eiden, Edmund
Koons, Joseph
Martinelli, James
Rogalla, John
Turley, Douglas

SIMPSON
Mercer, Kenneth
Richards, Elvin

S. CAROLINA
Blackwell, Harold
Craig, Lawrence
Cunningham, Leon
Deluca, Sam
Grygo, Albert
Hanna, Elzaphan
Hawkins, Alex
Keenan, John
Kincaid, James
Kompara, John
Krivonak, Joseph
Meeks, Bryant
Rogers, Donald
Roskie, Kenneth
Sparks, David
Sossamon, Louis

Stasica, Stanley
Strickland, Bishop
Urban, Alexander

S. DAKOTA STATE
Arndt, Alfred
Barber, Mark
Beasy, John
Crakes, Joseph
Eggers, Douglas
Engelmann, Wuert
Erickson, Weldon
Ginsberg, Israel
Klawitter, Dominic
Jenison, Raymond
McCormick, Frank
Miller, Paul
Pylman, Robert
Retzlaff, Palmer
Sheeks, Paul

S. DAKOTA UNIVERSITY
Braase, Ordell
Johnson, Theodore

SOUTHERN
McGee, George

SOUTHERN METHODIST UNIVERSITY
Baxter, Lloyd
Bedford, William
Benners, Frederick
Bernet, Edward
Berry, Raymond
Booth, Clarence
Bray, Maurice
Carter, Joseph
Clement, John
Collier, Robert
Cornelison, Jerry
Cortemeglia, Christopher
Croft, Abe
Dean, Thomas
Dewell, William
Dewveall, Willard
Ethridge, Joseph
Fawcett, Jacob
Forester, George
Fuqua, Raymond
Goss, Donald
Gregg, Forest
Halliday, John
Jackson, Charles
Johnson, Gilbert
Johnson, William
Johnston, L. Preston
Knight, Patrick
Long, Louis
McClain, Clinton
McIlhenny, Donald
McKissick, Richard
Maley, Howard
Mallouf, Raymond
Meredith, Donald
Miller, Donald
Nix, Doyle
Norton, Gerald
Page, Paul
Parker, Howard
Pasqua, Joseph
Raborn, Carroll
Ranspot, Keith
Roach, John
Rote, Kyle
Ruthstrom, Ralph
Sanders, John
Sherer, David
Vaughn, W.
Walker, Ewell Doak
Walker, Val Joe
Welch, James
Wilson, Eugene
Wilson, Robert
Wright, James

SOUTHWESTERN, MO.
Baltzell, Victor
Iman, Kenneth

SPRING HILL COLLEGE
McEvoy, Edward

SPRINGFIELD
Civiletto, Frank
Obeck, Victor
Watters, Leonard

STANFORD
Albert, Frank
Anderson, Stanley
Artman, Corwan
Banducci, Bruno
Boensch, Frederick
Bogue, George
Brodie, John
Burford, Christopher
Caddel, Ernest
Calvelli, Anthony
Cavelli, Anthony
Cox, James
Gallarneau, Hugh
Garrett, Robert
Hachten, William
Hill, Donald
Hugasian, Harry
Kerkorian, Gary
Kmetovic, Peter
Lawson, James
Lindskog, Victor
McColl, William
Manoukian, Donald
Meyer, Frederick
Meyers, Robert
Mitchell, Robert
Morley, Samuel
Moscrip, James
Nevers, Ernest
Norberg, Henry
Norgard, Alvar
O'Connor, Robert
Pool, J. Hampton
Reynolds, Robert
Smith, John
Standlee, Norman
Taylor, Charles
Tsoutsouvas, Louis
Vucinich, Milton
White, Robert
Wiggin, Paul

STERLING
Hiemstra, Edward

STILL
Regan, James

SUL ROSS TEACHERS
Bingham, Donald

SWARTHMORE
Clime, Benjamin
Lungren, Charles
Richards, Peter
Wilcox, Edward

SYRACUSE
Abbott, Lafayette
Albanese, Vincent
Alexander, Joseph
Anderson, Willard
Archoski, Julius
Barbuti, Raymond
Bayley, John
Braney, John
Brown, James
Brown, William
Carr, Charles
Cobb, Alfred
Constantine, Irving
Courtney, Gerard
Culver, Frank
Davis, Roger
Dooley, John
Dumoe, Joseph
Dunn, Roderick
Dye, Lester
Ellis, Lawrence
Fallon, Michael
Fishel, Richard
Foley, James
Forsyth, Charles
Foster, Frederick
Frugonne, James
Harris, Kenneth
Herter, William
Hinkle, Jack
Hoffman, Arnold
Jappe, Paul
Kanya, Albert
Karilivacz, Carl
Kellogg, William
Lasse, Richard
Lead, Garfield
Leberman, Robert
Levy, Harvey

McBride, John
McKee, Paul
Maines, Thomas
Martineau, Roy
Matteo, Francis
Mulvey, Vincent
Noble, James
Obst, Henry
Piro, Henry
Reckmarck, Raymond
Ridlon, James
Ringo, James
Robertson, Harry
Sawyer, Herman
Schwedes, Gerhard
Sebo, Samuel
Simmons, Roy
Singer
Singer, Walter
Stark, Harry
Steele, Clifford
Steen, James
Stephen, Thomas
Stone, Avatus
Thompson, George
Titmas, Herbert
Tomlin, Thomas
Usher, Louis
Watt, Joseph
Williams, Boyd
Witter, Ray
Youmans, Maurice
Ziff, David

TAMPA
Greene, Theodore
Herndon, Donald

TARKIO, MO.
Sacksteder, Norman
Reynolds, Allan

TEMPLE
Batinski, Stanley
Brahm, Lawrence
Brodnicki, Charles
Brunski, Andrew
Davidson, William
Drulis, Charles
Frey, Glenn
Getchell, C. Gorham
Grace, Leslie
Graham, Thomas
Gudd, Leonard
Hanson, John
Hanson, Thomas
Jarmoluk, Michael
Kilroy, Frank
Kolman, Edward
Konopka, John
Kusko, John
Lipski, John
McGee, Edward
Marcus, Alexander
Nichols, Allen
Pilconis, Joseph
Reese, Henry
Russell, James
Shults, John
Slosburg, Philip
Smukler, David
Stevens, Peter
Sutch, George
Sutton, Joseph
Sylvester, John
Tomasic, Andrew
Tyrrell, Joseph

TENNESSEE A & I
Gavin, Charles
Jamison, Leon

TENNESSEE STATE
Carter, Willie
Gilchrist, George

TENNESSEE TECH
Smith, Flavious

TENNESSEE UNIVERSITY
Anderson, William
Atkins, Douglas
Bailey, Howard
Bartholomew, Samuel
Brandau, Arthur
Butler, John
Cafego, George
Cifers, Edward
Cifers, Robert

Clay, Boyd
Crawford, Denver
Daffer, Terrell
DeLucca, Gerald
Dobelstein, Robert
Feathers, Beattie
Gaffney, James
Gordon, Robert
Gordy, John
Graves, Raymond
Hickman, Herman
Hill, James
Hillman, William
Hubbell, Franklin
Huffman, Richard
Hust, Albert
Lauricella, Henry
Lipscomb, Paul
Long, Robert
Lowe, William
McCord, Darris
Maples, Talmadge
Michaels, John
Miller, Benjamin
Morrow, Russell
Polofsky, Gordon
Rayburn, Van
Rechichar, Albert
Reese, Lloyd
Rose, Roy Eugene
Rowan, James
Russas, Albert
Schaffer, Joseph
Sherrod, Horace
Shields, Lebron
Shires, Marshall
Simonetti, Leonard
Slater, Walter
Smith, Carl
Stroud, Jack
Suffridge, Robert
Tarrant, James
Thayer, Harry
Tracy, Thomas
Turner, Harold
Vaghan, Charles
Warren, Busit
West, Hodges

TEXAS A. & I.
Mattingly, Francis
Steinke, Gilbert
Whitley, Hall

TEXAS A. & M.
Allison, James
Beck, Kenneth
Britt, Rankin
Bucek, Felix
Clarkson, Stuart
Conrad, Robert
Coston, Frederick
Crow, John
Ellis, Herbert
Frey, Richard
Goode, Robert
Hall, Kenneth
Howell, Clarence
Irvin, Barlow
Kendricks, James
Kimbrough, John
Kreuger, Charles
Lary, Robert Yale
Little, Jack
Malone, Charles
Marek, Joseph
Milstead, Charles
Montgomery, James
Moore, Allen
Murrah, W. E.
Pannell, Ernest
Pardee, John
Payne, Otto
Price, Charles
Pugh, Marion
Robnett, Marshall
Rogers, Cullen
Ruby, Martin
Smith, Robert
Sparkman, Alan
Stautzenberger, Odell
Tassos, Damon
Thomason, James
Tidwell, William
Todd, Richard
Tracey, John
Tulis, Robert
Wilde, George

Wilson, Fay
Winkler, James
Young, Roy

TEXAS CHRISTIAN UNIV.
Aldrich, Charles
Alford, Herbert
Armstrong, Ramon
Baugh, Samuel
Boswell, Benjamin
Brown, George
Casper, Charles
Cox, Norman
Douglass, Astynax
Edwards, Weldon
Ellis, Drew
Ennis, Hunter
Evans. Lon
Floyd, Donald
Hall, John
Handler, Philip
Headrick, Sherrill
Hinton, J. W.
Howell, Foster
Kring, Frank
Lawrence, James
Lester, Darrell
Looney, Donald
Manton, Taldon
Morton, John
Nix, Emery
O'Brien, Robert David
O'Neal, James
Palmer, Darrell
Patton, John
Pitts, Hugh
Robb, Joseph
Rogers, Glynn
Rowland, Justin
Shofner, James
Shook, Frederick
Spikes, Jack
Stout, Peter
Swink, James
Vaught, Theodore
Walls, William
White, Thomas
Williams, Jacob

TEXAS MINES
Cotton, Russell
Evans, Raymond
Heineman, Kenneth
Matheson, Riley
Mayhew, Hayden
Smith, Oscar
Wilson, Gordon

TEXAS SOUTHERN
Sorey, James
White, John

TEXAS STATE EAST
Brown, Marvin
Mackey, Dee

TEXAS STATE NORTH
Abbey, Joseph
Bishop, William
Cooper, James
Haynes, Abner
Holtzman, Glen
Lowe, Lloyd
Mugg, Garvin
Nutt, Richard
Renfro, Ray
Renfro, Dean
Runnels, Thomas
Shepard, Charles
Womble, Royce

TEXAS STATE SOUTHWEST
Vance, Joseph
Zunker, Charles

TEXAS STATE WEST
Box, Cloyce
Cross, William
Dow, Elwood
Hansen. Wayne
Kelley, Robert
Laraba, Robert
Maynard, Donald
Meyer, Edward
Shupbach, O. T.
Watkins, Forrest
Whittenton, Jesse
Womack, Bruce

TEXAS TEACHERS
Davis, Gaines
Johnson, Cecil
Tully, Darrell
Wright, Theodore

TEXAS TECH
Alford, Eugene
Arterburn, Elmer
Autry, William
Baze, Winford
Bryan, Walter
bry. ni Robert
Davis, William
Dowell, Gwyn
Earhart, Ralph
Flowers, Robert
Herchman, William
Holcomb, William
Kelley, William
Kilcullen, Robert
Nabors, Ronald
Neill, James
Owens, Truet
Ramsay, Herschel
Rankin, Walter
Robnett, Edward
Sachse, Francis
Schlinkman, Walter
Scott, Prince
Smith, Joseph
Webb, George
Williams, Rex
Winkler, Bernard

TEXAS UNIVERSITY
Allen, Donald
Arnold, Jay
Barton, Donald
Baumgardner, Max
Bechtol, Hubert
Bryant, Robert
Callahan, James
Canady, James
Clay, Randall
Collins, William
Conner, Emerson
Connolly, William
Dawson, Gilbert
Dillon, Robert
Doss, Noble
Dowdle, Don Michael
Eckhardt, Oscar
Emerson, Grover
Freeman, John
Gillory, Byron
Harris, Henry
Heap, Walter
Holder, Lewis
Hughes, William
Jackson, Kenneth
Jungmichel, Harold
Keeling, Raymond
Kelley, Edward
Kutner, Malcolm
Landry, Thomas
Lansford, Alex
Lansford, James
Larpenter, Carl
Lawler, Allen
Layden, Peter
Layne, Robert
McFadin, Lewis
McKay, Roy
Magliolo, Joseph
Martin, Vernon
Massey, Carleton
Mauldin, Stanley
Mayes, Carlton
Mayne, Louis
Menasco, Donald
Parker, Joseph
Peterson, Gerald
Peterson, Lester
Petrovich, George
Rose, Alfred
Sanders, Orban
Sewell, Harley
Shelley, Dexter
Smyth, Louis
Stafford, Harrison
Stephens, Lawrence
Stolhandske, Thomas
Tynes, David
Vasicek, Victor
Watson, Grady
Weedon, Donald
Wetz, Harlan

Williams, Donald
Williams, Joel
Wolfe, Hugh

THIEL
Christman, Floyd
Mitchell, Albert

TOLEDO
Cole, Emerson
Cook, Eugene
Maher, Francis
Marotti, Louis
Sample, Charles
Slovak, Martin
Triplett, Melvin

TRINITY (CONN.)
Kobrosky, Milton
LeClerc, Roger
Nordstrom, Harry

TRINITY (TEX.)
Cole, Peter
Higgins, John
Hill, Irving
Hogan, Darrell
Noble, Richard
Swain, Gladstone

TROTT VOCATIONAL
Mazza, Vincent

TUFTS
Share, Nathan

TULANE
Albanese, Donald
Bentz, Roman
Bladin, Ernest
Bodenger, Morris
Comer, Martin
Fugler, Richard
Gloden, Frederick
Helluin, Frances
Hornick, William
Joyce, Donald
Kellogg, Robert
Khayat, Edward
Kinek, George
Kingery, Ellsworth
Lea, Paul
McCollum, Harley
McDonald, Walter
McGee, William Max
Olson, Raymond
Petitbon, Richard
Price, Edward
Rexer, Freeman
Sardisco, Anthony
Scafide, John
Schneider, Leroy
Svoboda, William
Teeuws, Leonard
Thibaut, James
Truax, Dalton
Wenzel, Ralph

TULSA UNIVERSITY
Barry, Paul
Bernstein, Joseph
Blackman, E. Lennon
Boone, J. R.
Brown, Hardy
Buda, Carl
Burgeis, Glenn
Dobbs, Glenn
Finks, James
Gentry, Elmer
Gibson, Billy Joe
Goodnight, Clyde
Gray, Samuel
Green, John
Green, Nelson
Greene, Frank
Grigg, Forrest
Harmon, Hamilton
Haynes, Joseph
Holladay, Robert
Hughes, Edward
Hughes, Richard
Jones, Ellis
Judd, Saxon
Kercher, Richard
Kowalski, Adolphe
LeForce, Clyde
Luhn, Nolan
Matuszak, Marvin

Miner, Thomas
Mitchell, Charles
Prewitt, Felton
Purdin, Calvin
Reynolds, Homer
Robertson, Thomas
Rogas, Daniel
Scafide, Albert
Shedlosky, Edmond
Spangler, Eugene
Stanley, G. B.
Stringer, Robert
Stuart, Roy
Thomas, Calvin
Thompson, Thomas
Volok, William
Whitman, S. J. Laverne
Wilson, Camp
Workman, Blake

TYLER (TEXAS) JC
Johnson, William

UNION OF TENNESSEE
Jones, James "Casey"

URSINUS
Bassman, Herman
Lowery, Darby
Potteiger, Earl
Mulleneaux, Carl
Steward, Dean

UTAH STATE
Croft, Jack
Connelly, Michael
Rohde, Leonard
Ryan, Kent
Sanders, Paul
Sorenson, Glen
Ward, Elmer
Williams, Frank

UTAH UNIVERSITY
Christensen, Frank
Clark, Wayne
Croft, Winfield
Douglas, Merrill
Dublinski, Thomas
Gehrke, Clarence
Grosscup, Clyde Lee
Hafen, Banard
Johnson, John
Jonas, Marvin
McDonald, Walter
McDonough, Paul
McGarry, Bernard
Nelson, D. Frank
Olsen, Ralph
Richins, Aldo
Speedie, Mac
Summerhays, Robert

VALPARAISO
Cearing, Lloyd
Gilbert, Walter
Scanlon, Dewey
Thurston, Fred
White, Roy

VANDERBILT
Agee, Samuel
Bomar, Lynn
Cooper, Kenneth
Donnell, Benjamin
Ellis, John
Gude, Henry
Huggins, Roy
Jenkins, Jacque
King, Philip
Leyendecker, Charles
Merlin, Edward
Moore, Thomas
Neely, Jess
North, John
Peebles, James
Plasman, Richard
Ray, Bufford
Rich, Herbert
Satterfield, Alfren
Wade, William
Wiggs, Hubert

VERMONT
Harms, Arthur
Johnson, Oscar

Trigilio, Frank

VILLANOVA
Andrulewicz, Theodore
August, Edward
Basca, Michael
Berrang, Edward
Brazinsky, Samuel
Brown, Daniel
Chisick, Andrew
D'Alonzo, Peter
David, Robert
DeFilippo, David
Ferry, Louis
Filipski, Eugene
Finn, John
Galazin, Stanley
Hegarty, William
Kasky, Edward
Korisky, Edward
Kuzco, Paul
Labengood, Howard
Lee, Bernard
Lomasney, Thomas
Longua, Paul
McCombs, Donald
McLaughlin,
Magee, James
Mellus, John
Michaels, Edward
Moynihan, Richard
Nowak, Walter
Pasquariello, Ralph
Pessalano, Louis
Postus, Albert
Potts, William
Pritko, Steven
Pudloski, Chester
Restic, Joseph
Rogers, William
Romanik, Steven
Rosato, Salvatore
Ryan, Joseph
Sandusky, John
Sapienza, Richard
Smith, George
Stenn, Paul
Suess, Raymond
Youngfleisch, Francis
Zamlynski, Zygmond
Zizak, Vincent

VIRGINIA MILITARY INST.
Barber, Benjamin
Horner, Samuel
Johnson, Peter
Mason, Samuel
Muha, Joseph
Pritchard, Abisha
Ragunis, Vincent
Reutt, Raymond
Robison, George
Thomason, Robert
Walker, William

VIRGINIA POLYTECH INST.
Dale, Carroll
Maskas, John
Nutter, Madison
Preas, George

VIRGINIA UNIVERSITY
Baldwin, George
Carroccio, Russell
Churchman, Charles
Dudley, William
Elliott, Carlton
Gillette, James
Grimes, George
Gunderman, Robert
Jordan, Henry
Lesane, James
McLaughlin, Lee
Miller, Robert
Papit, John
Randle, Ulmo
Schroeder, Eugene
Scott, Thomas
Whaley, Benjamin

VIRGINIA STATE
Miles, Leo

WABASH
Bacon, Francis
Buckeye, Garland

Dalrymple, Robert
Falcon, Gilbert
Griggs, Harold
Hobson, Benjamin
Lindsey, Menzies
Meere, Ward
Robinson, Maurice
Singleton, John

WAKE FOREST
Barbour, Wesley
Barnes, William
Bradley, Edward
Cochran, John
Crabtree, Clement
Dowda, Harry
Duncan, James
Edwards, Marshall
Gallovich, Anthony
Gaona, Robert
George, William
Huth, Gerald
Jett, John
Jones, Elmer
Kapriva, Frank
Kissell, Edward
Leonetti, Robert
Lipgstad, Edward
Manning, Peter
Meyers, Gilbert
O'Quinn, John
Palmer, Thomas
Pate, Rupert
Polanski, John
Preston, Pattison
Royston, Edward
Rubino, Anthony
Sacrinty, Nicholas
Staton, James
Stofko, Edward
Wedel, Richard

WASHBURN
Thompson, William
Wycoff, Lee

WASHINGTON (ST. LOUIS)
Bertagnolli, Libero
Bukant, Joseph
Comstock, Edwin
Conzelman, James
Kraehe, Oliver
Mahan, R.
Murphy, William
Rodgers, Walter
Schwenk, Wilson

WASHINGTON STATE
Akins, Albert
Akins, Frank
Bailey, Byron
Barker, Edward
Bell, Kay
Berry, Wayne
Brett, Edwin
Brovelli, Angelo
Burks, Joseph
Cogdill, Gail
Edwards, Albert Glen
Ellersick, Donald
Farman, Richard
Gambold, Robert
Gentry, Dale
Goddard, Edward
Godfrey, Herbert
Hanley, Richard
Hayduk, Henry
Hein, Melvin
Hoptowit, Al
Houghton, Gerald
Hurley, George
Hurley, John
Keenan, Edward
Kennedy, Robert
Klumb, John
Kramer, Frederick
Littlefield, Carl
Marker, Clifford
Meeker, Herbert
Moses, Howard
Niemi, Laurie
Paul, Donald
Polsfoot, Francis
Remington, Joseph
Renfro, Richard

Roffler, William
Sandberg, Roy
Sarboe, Philip
Schwartz, Elmer
Steinbrunner, Donald
Stojack, Frank
Suseoff, Nicholas
Svare, Harland
Torgeson, Lavern
Ward, William
Williams, Jerome

WASHINGTON CENTRAL
North, James

WASHINGTON UNIVERSITY
Bond, Charles
Bond, Randal
Bruce, Gail
Carr, Luther
Deeks, Donald
Derby, Dean
Erickson, Carleton
Erickson, Walden
Fennema, Carl
Frankowski, Raymond
Friedman, Robert
Guttormsen, George
Haines, Byron
Heinrich, Donald
Hornbeak, Jay
Isaacson, Theodore
Johnston, James
Jones, Donald
Jones, James
McAdams, Dean
McDowell, Jay
McElhenny, Hugh
Markov, Victor
Mucha, Charles
Mucha, Rudolph
Newton, Charles
Nisbet, David
Ottele, Richard
Provo, Frederick
Riggs, Thron
Robinson, Fred
Slivinski, Steven
Smith, William
Stackpool, John
Steele, Ernest
Strugar, George
Tevis, Leek
Wardlow, Duane
Weinmeister, Arnold
Wiatrak, John
Wilson, George

WASHINGTON & JEFFERSON
Berrehsen, William
Bliss, Homer
Carroll, Edward
Clements, George
Crook, Albert
Demas, George
Douds, Forrest
Edwards, Leslie
Erickson, Harold
Erickson, Harry
Fleming, Malcolm
Guy, Charles
Gallagher, Edward
Haddon, Aldous
Hauser, Kenneth
Henry, Wilbur
Kirkman, Roger
McNeil, Francis
Malcolm, Harry
Neihaus, Francis
Norman, Willard
Oltz, Russell
Paulekas, Anthony
Pauley, Frank
Rhoads, Donald
Shaffer, George
Siegfried, Orville
Stein, Herbert
Stobbs, William
Towler, Daniel
Vick, Richard
Vince, Ralph
Wiederquist, Chester
Wimberly, Byron

WASHINGTON & LEE
Boyda, Michael

Brennert, Wayne
Cameron, Edmund
Chipley, William
Lukens, James
Mattox, Marvin
Michaels, Walter
Pierotti, Albert
Potts, Robert
Sweetland, Frederick
Van Horne, Charles

WAYNE UNIVERSITY
Crittenden, John
Jenkins, Walter
Langas, Robert
Paolucci, Ben.
Zucco, Victor

WAYNESBURG
Ellstrom, Marvin
Pastin, Frank
Scarry, Michael
Wiley, John
Worden, James

WEATHERFORD JR. (TEX.)
Jones, Lewis

WEBER JR. (UTAH)
Lolatai, Albert

WEST POINT
Cagle, Christian
Coulter, DeWitt
Davis, Glen
Dibbs, John
Doyle, Edward
Foldberg, Henry
French, Walter
Galiffa, Arnold
Mischak, Robert
Oliphant, Elmer
Peshmalyan, Baruyr
Pollard, Al

WEST VIRGINIA TEACHERS
Campiglio, Robert

WEST VIRGINIA
Anderson, William
Atty, Alexander
Bailey, James
Bailey, Russell
Baisi, Albert
Barnum, Robert
Beck, Carl
Bosley, Bruce
Brewster, James
Bruder, Woodie
Bumgardner, Rex
Clark, Harry
Davis, Carl
Dolly, John
Fryer, Kenneth
Goodman, Harry
Goodwin, Tod
Graham, Fred
Guesman, Richard
Gussie, Michael
Hagburg, Rudolph
Howley, Charles
Huff, Robert
Karr, William
Keane, Thomas
Kimble, Frank
King, Andrew
Krutko, Lawrence
Lewis, Arthur
Lucente, John
Mackert, Robert
Mahan, Walter
Mahrt, Armin
Marconi, Joseph
Marker, Henry
Meredith, Russell
Moan, Emmett
Nardacci, Nicholas
Parriott, William
Ryan, Clarence
Seabright, Charles
Sechrist, Walter
Setron, Joseph
Shonk, John
Sortet, Wilbur
Stephenson, David
Stydahar, Joseph

Wyant, Fred

WEST VIRGINIA TECH.
Rado, Alex

WEST VIRGINIA WESLEYAN
Barnum, Leonard
Battles, Clifford
Blondin, Thomas
Bullman, Gail
Ciccone, William
Gabler, John
Jones, William
Kellison, John
Moore, Kenneth
Peterson, Nelson
Reiter, Wilbur
Rodriguez, Kelly
Schieb, Lee

WESTCHESTER (Ohio)
Campbell, Kenneth
Ferko, John
Shockley, William
Weber, Charles

WESTMINSTER
Boyd, Walter
Browning, R.

WESTERN ONTARIO
Krol, Joseph

WESTERN RESERVE
Badaczewski, John
Belicheck, Stephen
Booth, Richard
Lahr, Warren
Logan, Andrew
Ragazzo, Philip
Rodak, Michael
Roman, George
Sanzotta, Dominic
Skoczen, Stanley
Wilson, John

WHITTIER
Finch, Olin
Hutchinson, Elvin
McMurtry, Charles

WICHITA
Brill, Harold
Dean, Theodore
Doggett, Keith
Dugan, Leonard
Kelly, Elmer
McEnulty, Douglas
Sexton, Linwood

WILEY COLLEGE (Tex.)
Inglehart, Floyd

WILLAMETTE
Weisgerber, Richard

WILLIAM & MARY
Bowman, William
Brown, Thomas
Charles, Winston
Cloud, John
Clowes, John
Creekmur, Louis
Crow, Albert
Douglas, Otis
Forkovitch, Nicholas
Hardy, Isham
Hughes, George
Johnson, Harvey
Kreamcheck, John
Lusk, Robert
Matsu, Arthur
Mikula, Thomas
Mills, Denver
Mioduszewski, Edward
Ramsey, Knox
Sazio, Ralph
Sumner, Charles
Thompson, Thomas
Vandeweghe, Alfred

WILLIAMS
Boynton, Benjamin
Clement, Alexander
Gregory, Frank
Surabian, Zareh

WILMINGTON

Bonowitz, Elliott
Glassman, Morris
Weimer, Charles

WISCONSIN STATE
Berzinski, William
Billock, Frank
Bratt, Edward
Engstrom, George
Fritsch, Theodore
Goldfein, Jersey
Loomis, Ace
Moselle, Donald
Owens, Rex
Perkins, Donald
Robl, Harold
Smith, Rex
Wilson, Milton

WISCONSIN
UNIVERSITY
Albrecht, Arthur
Albright, William
Ameche, Alan
Amundsen, Norman
Atwood, John
Barr, Wallace
Bieberstein, Adolph
Brumm, Roman
Buck, Howard
Calligaro, Leonard
Carl, Harland
Cook, James
Davis, Ralph
Dittrich, John
Dreyer, Walter
Eckle, Robert
Elliott, Alvah
Esser, Clarence
Farris, Thomas
Faverty, Harold
Felker, Eugene
Gantenbein, Milton
Gardner, Milton
Girard, Earl
Goldenburg, Charles
Golemgeske, Gorn
Gollomb, Rudolph
Gunderson, Borge
Hackbart, Dale
Haluska, James
Harder, Marlin
Harris, John
Hekkers, George
Hirsch, Elroy
Huxhold, Kenneth
Kankowski, Edward
Kindt, Donald
Kocourek, David
Konovsky, Robert
Kresky, Joseph
Lanphear, Daniel
Larson, Lloyd
Leaper, Wesley
Lewis, Daniel
Loepfe, Richard
Lubratovich, Milo
Maves, Earl
Mead, John
Meyers, Paul
Miller, Donald
Mortell, Emmett
Murry, Donald
Negus, Frederick
O'Donahue, Patrick
Paskvan, George
Peterson, Philip
Rose, Eugene
Schneller, John
Schroeder, William
Scuelke, Warren
Schuele, Karl
Schuette, Paul
Scott, Ralph
Seibold, Champ
Self, Clarence
Simpson, Eber
Smith, Gerald
Stalcup, Terry
Stark, Howard
Starr, Wallace
Suminski, David
Taft, Merrill
Tebell, Gustavus
Temp, James

Tennant, John
Teteak, Derall
Tommerson, Clarence
Vogds, Evan
Warner, Robert
Wasserbach, Lloyd
Weiss, Howard
Williams, Rolland
Zeman, Robert

WITTENBERG
Bradley, O.
Burgner, Earl
Hummons, John
Miller, J. Robert
Nonnemaker, Gustavus
Rohleder, George

WOFFORD
Richardson, Gerald

WOOSTER
Flattery, Wilson

Laport, John

WYOMING UNIVERSITY
Crawford, James
Kizzier, Lee
McConnell, Dewey
Memmelaar, Dale

XAVIER
Bucklew, Philip
Davis, Herbert
Hauser, Arthur
Hoffman, Jack
Knecht, William
Junker, Steven
McPhail, Harold
Martinovic, John
Mazurek, Edward
Mutryn, Chester
Rapp, Herbert
Sigillo, Dominic
Stotsberg, Harold

Wiethe, John
Wilging, Coleman

YALE
Barzilauskas, Francis
Caldwell, Bruce
Kempton, Herbert
Milstead, Century
Peshmalyan, Baruyr
Prchlik, John
Schuler, William
Walker, Paul

YOUNGSTOWN
Aiello, Anthony
Campana, Al
Gill, Sloko
Goldston, Ralph

CHAPTER 5
THE TEAMS

In modern major league football, thirty-three rather than eleven men make up the team. Limitless combinations of eleven can be made from thirty-three. There is the kick-off team; the kick-off receiving team; the team for the plunge through the middle; the team for skirting the end; the team for forward-passing in endless patterns of deception; the teams for defense against all these and more expected thrusts by the enemy; the team to kick field goals and extra points; the team to defend against them; the punting team; the punt-receiving team. Within these named there are countless combinations of men who do each factor best, so that in a league game, which averages eighty offensive and eighty defensive plays, more than a hundred different line-ups could be found on the field.

The team is the final end product of all the players and coaches listed in previous pages. The headline names, the All-Time All-Stars, are forgotten for the moment. The muscular device made up of twenty-two legs, twenty-two arms and twenty-two eyes must start and accelerate and move as one gigantic creature.

The records of those who did this best will be found at, or near, the top of the ensuing categories and break-downs.

WORLD CHAMPIONSHIP PLAY-OFFS, 1933-60

Year		Winner		Loser	
1933	(Dec. 17 at Chicago)	Chicago Bears	23	New York Giants	21
1934	(Dec. 9 at New York)	New York Giants	30	Chicago Bears	13
1935	(Dec. 15 at Detroit)	Detroit Lions	26	New York Giants	7
1936	(Dec. 13 at New York)	Green Bay Packers	21	Boston Redskins	6
1937	(Dec. 12 at Chicago)	Washington Redskins	28	Chicago Bears	21
1938	(Dec. 11 at New York)	New York Giants	23	Green Bay Packers	17
1939	(Dec. 10 at Milwaukee)	Green Bay Packers	27	New York Giants	0
1940	(Dec. 8 at Washington)	Chicago Bears	73	Washington Redskins	0
1941	(Dec. 21 at Chicago)	Chicago Bears	37	New York Giants	9
1942	(Dec. 13 at Washington)	Washington Redskins	14	Chicago Bears	6
1943	(Dec. 26 at Chicago)	Chicago Bears	41	Washington Redskins	21
1944	(Dec. 17 at New York)	Green Bay Packers	14	New York Giants	7
1945	(Dec. 16 at Cleveland)	Cleveland Rams	15	Washington Redskins	14
1946	(Dec. 15 at New York)	Chicago Bears	24	New York Giants	14
1947	(Dec. 28 at Chicago)	Chicago Cardinals	28	Philadelphia Eagles	21
1948	(Dec. 19 at Philadelphia)	Philadelphia Eagles	7	Chicago Cardinals	0
1949	(Dec. 18 at Los Angeles)	Philadelphia Eagles	14	Los Angeles Rams	0
1950	(Dec. 24 at Cleveland)	Cleveland Browns	30	Los Angeles Rams	28
1951	(Dec. 23 at Los Angeles)	Los Angeles Rams	24	Cleveland Browns	17
1952	(Dec. 28 at Cleveland)	Detroit Lions	17	Cleveland Browns	7
1953	(Dec. 27 at Detroit)	Detroit Lions	17	Cleveland Browns	16
1954	(Dec. 26 at Cleveland)	Cleveland Browns	56	Detroit Lions	10
1955	(Dec. 26 at Los Angeles)	Cleveland Browns	38	Los Angeles Rams	14
1956	(Dec. 30 at New York)	New York Giants	47	Chicago Bears	7
1957	(Dec. 29 at Detroit)	Detroit Lions	59	Cleveland Browns	14
1958	(Dec. 28 at New York)	Baltimore Colts	23	New York Giants	17
		(First period of overtime after tie game.)			
1959	(Dec. 27 at Baltimore)	Baltimore Colts	31	New York Giants	16
1960	(Dec. 26 at Philadelphia)	Philadelphia Eagles	17	Green Bay Packers	13

BERT BELL BENEFIT BOWL

1961—Detroit, 17; Cleveland, 16

PRO BOWL RESULTS

New York
1936—New York, 12; All-Stars, 2
1937—New York, 14; All-Stars, 7
1938—New York, 6; All-Stars, 0
1939—New York, 10; All-Stars, 0
1940—All Stars, 16; New York, 7
1941—New York, 23; All-Stars, 3
1942—Army, 16; New York, 0
1947—New York, 21; All-Stars, 0
1949—All-Stars, 28; New York, 13

Pro-Bowl
*1938—N. Y. Giants, 13; All-Stars, 10
*1939—Green Bay, 16; All-Stars, 7
*1940—Bears, 28; All-Stars, 14
†1941—Bears, 35; All-Stars, 24
‡1942—All-Stars, 17; Washington, 14
*1951—Am. Conf., 28; Nat. Conf., 27
*1952—Nat. Conf., 30; Am. Conf., 13
*1953—Nat Conf., 27; Am. Conf., 7
*1954—East. Conf., 20; West. Conf., 9
*1955—West. Conf., 26; East. Conf., 19
*1956—East. Conf., 31; West. Conf., 30
*1957—West. Conf., 19; East. Conf., 10
*1958—West. Conf., 26; East. Conf., 7
*1959—East. Conf., 28; West. Conf., 21
*1960—West. Conf., 38; East Conf., 21
*1961—West Conf., 34; East Conf., 31

*—Played in Los Angeles.   †—Played in New York.   ‡—Played in Philadelphia.

CITIES WHICH WERE AFFILIATED WITH THE NFL
AND THE YEARS OF THEIR ACTION AS OF 1959

Akron, Ohio (7)   1920, 21, 22, 23, 24, 25, 26.

Baltimore, Md. (7)   1950 and 1953–61

Boston, Mass. (11)   1929, 32, 33, 34, 35, 36, and 1944 to 1948 inclusive.

Brooklyn, N.Y. (16)   1926 only, and 1930 thru 1944 inclusive.

Buffalo, N.Y. (8)   1921, 22, 23, 24, 25, 26, 27, 29.

Canton, Ohio (6)   1920, 21, 22, 23, 25, 26.

Chicago Bears (37)   1920 to present time.

Chicago Cards (38)   1920 to present time. (Longest period for team.)

Cincinnati, Ohio (3) 1921, 1933 and 34.

Cleveland, Ohio (18)   1920, 21, 23, 24, 25, 27, 31, 37, 38, 39, 40, 41, 42, 44, 45, and 1950–61.

Columbus, Ohio (6)   1921, 22, 23, 24, 25, 26.

Dallas, Texas (2)   1952, 1960–61

Dayton, Ohio (10)   1920 to 1929 inclusive.

Detroit, Mich. (23)   1921, 25, 26, 28, 1934 to present time.

Duluth, Minn. (5)   1923 to 1927 inclusive.

Evansville, Ind. (1)   1921 and 22

Frankford, Pa. (8)   1924 to 1931 inclusive.

Green Bay, Wis. (32)   1921 to present time.

Hammond, Ind. (6)   1920, 22, 23, 24, 25, 26.

Hartford, Conn. (1)   1926

Kansas City, Mo. (3)   1924 to 1926 inclusive.

Kenosha, Wis. (1)   1924

Los Angeles, Cal. (8)   1926 only, and also 1946 to present time.

Louisville, Ky. (3)   1922, 23, 26.

Marion, Ohio (2)   1922–23

Milwaukee, Wis. (5)   1922 to 1926 inclusive.

Minneapolis, Minn. (5)   1922, 23, 24, 29, 30 and 1961

Muncie, Ind.   1921

Newark, N.J. (1)   1930

N.Y. Bulldogs (1)   1949

N.Y. Giants (28)   1925 to present time.

N.Y. Yanks (4)   1927, 28, and 1950, 51.

Orange, N.J. (1)   1929

Philadelphia, Pa. (20)   1933 to present time.

Pittsburgh, Pa. (20)   1933 to present time.

Portsmouth, Ohio (4)   1930 to 1933 inclusive.

Pottsville, Pa. (4)   1925 to 1928 inclusive.

Providence, R.I. (7)   1925 to 1931 inclusive.

Racine, Wis. (4)   1922, 23, 24, 26.

Rochester, N.Y. (6)   1921 to 1925 inclusive.

Rock Island, Ill. (6)   1920 to 1925 inclusive.

San Francisco, Cal. (3)   1950 to present time.

Stapleton, N.Y. (4) 1929 to 1932 inclusive.

St. Louis, Mo. (2) 1923 only, and also 1934 and 1960–61.

Toledo, Ohio (2) 1922, 23.

Washington, D.C. (16) 1937 to present time.

SEVENTEEN STATES, PLUS DISTRICT OF COLUMBIA, REPRESENTED IN THE NFL

California (2): Los Angeles and San Francisco

Connecticut (1): Hartford

Illinois (3): Chicago, Decatur, Rock Island

Indiana (3): Evansville, Hammond, Muncie

Kentucky (1): Louisville

Maryland (1): Baltimore

Massachusetts (1): Boston

Michigan (1): Detroit

Minnesota (2): Duluth, Minneapolis

Missouri (2): Kansas City, St. Louis

New Jersey (2): Newark, Orange

New York (5): Brooklyn, Buffalo, New York City, Rochester, Stapleton

Ohio (10): Akron, Canton, Cincinnati, Cleveland, Columbus, Dayton, Marion, Massillon, Portsmouth, Toledo

Pennsylvania (4): Frankford, Philadelphia, Pittsburgh, Pottsville

Rhode Island (1): Providence

Texas (1): Dallas

Wisconsin (4): Green Bay, Kenosha, Milwaukee, Racine

District of Columbia (1): Washington

WORLD CHAMPIONSHIP GAMES, 1933-60

1933 WORLD CHAMPIONSHIP PROFESSIONAL FOOTBALL GAME

(Wrigley Field, Chicago, Ill., Dec. 17)
Attendance 26,000

Chicago Bears (23)	New York Giants (21)
Hewitt—L.E.	Badgro—L.E.
Lyman—L.T.	Grant—L.T.
Carlson—L.G.	Gibson—L.G.
Miller—C.	Hein—C.
Kopcha—R.G.	Jones—R.G.
Musso—R.T.	Owen—R.T.
Karr—R.E.	Flaherty—R.E.
Brumbaugh—Q.B.	Newman—Q.B.
Molesworth—L.H.	Strong—L.H.
Ronzani—R.H.	Burnett—R.H.
Nagurski—F.B.	Molenda—F.B.

Chicago Bears	3	3	10	7—23
New York Giants	0	7	7	7—21

Touchdowns—Karr 2, Badgro, Krause, Strong.

Points after touchdown—Strong 3, Manders 3.

Field goals—Manders 2.

Coaches—George Halas (Chicago), Stephen Owen (New York).

SUBSTITUTIONS

Chicago Bears—Manders, Grange, Richards, Sisk, Corbett.

New York Giants—Richards, Irwin, Clancy, Campbell, Krause, Canella.

Officials: Referee—Thomas Hughitt. Umpire—Robert Cohn. Head Linesman—Robert Karch. Field Judge—Dan Tehan.

THE GAME

Jack Manders opened the scoring for the Bears with a 16-yard field goal in the first quarter to touch off sixty minutes of fireworks that kept the fans standing on their chairs through most of the game.

Manders pumped another one over from 40 yards in the second period before the Giants' Harry Newman whipped a pass to Red Badgro in the end zone for the Giants' first touchdown. Strong converted and the Giants led, 7–6, at the half.

The reliable Manders banged over another field goal from 28 yards away in the third period but Newman engineered a drive for New York that ended when Max Krause plowed over from the Chicago one and Strong again converted to make it 14–9. The Bears came right back to score again on a pass from Bronko Nagurski to Bill Karr and Manders' extra point put them ahead, 16–14, as the third quarter ended.

In the last period the Giants invented a play to score again. Strong, starting from

Wide World Photo

THIS CHICAGO BEARS TEAM, FEATURING THE SMASHING YOUNG FULLBACK, BRONKO NAGURSKI, RULED THE WEST IN 1933 AND 1934. THEY PLAYED THE NEW YORK GIANTS FOR THE CHAMPIONSHIP IN BOTH YEARS, WINNING THE FIRST TIME, LOSING THE SECOND. THE LINE *(left to right):* BILL KARR, GEORGE MUSSO, JOE KOPCHA, CHARLES "OOKIE" MILLER, WALTER KIESLING, ROY LYMAN, AND BILL HEWITT. THE BACKFIELD *(left to right):* GENE RONZANI, THE BRONK, BEATTIE FEATHERS, AND CARL BRUMBAUGH.

the Bears' 8-yard line, was trapped for a loss. In desperation, he lateraled to Newman, who recovered from his surprise in time to flee to the opposite side of the field. When he too was trapped he threw the ball in the general direction of the goal line—and there was Strong to catch it for a touchdown. Strong's conversion put the Giants in the lead again, 21–16. But the Bears came roaring back to the Giants' 36. Nagurski lobbed a pass over the line to Bill Hewitt, who lateraled to Bill Karr, who went the distance, thanks to an earth-shaking block which Gene Ronzani put on Strong to clear the way. Manders' conversion made it 23–21 for the Bears' victory.

1934 WORLD CHAMPIONSHIP PROFESSIONAL FOOTBALL GAME

(Polo Grounds, New York, N.Y., Dec. 9)
Attendance 35,059

New York Giants (30)	Chicago Bears (13)
Frankian—L.E.	Hewitt—L.E.
Morgan—L.T.	Lyman—L.T.
Gibson—L.G.	Pearson—L.G.
Hein—C.	Kawal—C.
Jones—R.G.	Carlson—R.G.
Irwin—R.T.	Musso—R.T.
Flaherty—R.E.	Karr—R.E.
Danowski—Q.B.	Brumbaugh—Q.B.
Burnett—L.H.	Molesworth—L.H.
Strong—R.H.	Ronzani—R.H.
Molenda—F.B.	Nagurski—F.B.

New York Giants	3	0	0	27—30
Chicago Bears	0	10	3	0—13

Touchdowns—Nagurski, Frankian, Strong 2, Danowski.
Points after touchdown—Manders, Strong 3.
Field goals—Manders 2, Strong.
Coaches—Stephen Owen (New York), George Halas (Chicago).

SUBSTITUTIONS

New York Giants—McBride, Richards, Owen, Grant.
Chicago Bears—Manders, Johnsos, Buss, Sisk, Zeller, Rosequist, Masterson.
Officials: Referee—Robert Cahn. Umpire—G. H. Lowe. Head Linesman—George Vergara. Field Judge—O. Meyer.

THE GAME

With the temperature at nine degrees and the Polo Grounds covered with sheet ice, this contest became known as the "Sneaker" game when Steve Owen, New York coach, provided his squad with basketball shoes to open the second half and thus brought about four touchdowns and the rout of the Bears who had beaten the

Giants twice during the regular season.

When the game began, the Bears were carrying a thirteen-consecutive-game winning streak and they had completed thirty-three games in a row without defeat. But Beattie Feathers, the sensational halfback, and Joe Kopcha, their brilliant lineman, were injured too severely to play (as was Harry Newman, Giant quarterback). Still the Bears were heavily favored to win.

Ken Strong got the Giants off on top in the first quarter with a 38-yard field goal which was the only score in that period.

The Bears smashed back for their first touchdown on a one-yard plunge by Nagurski. Manders' extra point and a field goal by Manders gave the Bears a 10–3 lead as the half ended.

Manders booted another from the 24-yard line in the third quarter and then the roof fell in for the Bears.

As the last period began, the New York team was getting used to their new footwear. Ed Danowski started the rout with a 28-yard pass to Ike Frankian. Moments later, Ken Strong galloped 42 yards for another score. Then, so rapidly that the Bears were completely lost, Danowski and Strong ran for touchdowns to turn the game into a track meet. Strong cashed three of four conversion attempts and the score ended at 30–13.

1935 WORLD CHAMPIONSHIP PROFESSIONAL FOOTBALL GAME

(Detroit University Stadium, Detroit, Mich., Dec. 15) Attendance 15,000

Detroit Lions (26)	New York Giants (7)
Klewicki—L.E.	
Johnson—L.T.	Frankian—L.E.
Monahan—L.G.	Morgan—L.T.
Randolph—C.	Jones—L.G.
Emerson—R.G.	Hein—C.
Christensen, G.—R.T.	Owen—R.G.
	Grant—R.T.
Schneller—R.E.	Goodwin—R.E.
Presnell—Q.B.	Danowski—Q.B.
Christensen, F.—L.H.	Strong—L.H.
Caddel—R.H.	Richards—R.H.
Gutowski—F.B.	Corzine—F.B.

Detroit Lions	13	0	0	13—26
New York Giants	0	7	0	0— 7

Touchdowns—Strong, Gutowsky, Clark, Caddel, Parker.

Points after touchdown—Strong, Presnell, Clark.

Coaches—George Clark (Detroit), Stephen Owen (New York).

SUBSTITUTIONS

New York Giants—Ends: Singer, Mitchell; tackle: Irwin; guards: Bellinger, Dell Isola; backs: Newman, Shaffer, Krause.

Detroit Lions—Ends: Morse, Ebding; tackles: Steen, Stacy; guards: Knox, Hopke; center: Ward; backs: Clark, Shepherd, Parker, Vaughn, Kaska.

Officials: Referee—Thomas Hughitt. Umpire—Robert Cahn. Head Linesman—M. J. Meyer. Field Judge—Harry Robb.

THE GAME

The lethal power of the Detroit backfield was evident from the first kick-off which the Lions took right back to a touchdown with Leroy "Ace" Gutowsky plowing over from the 2-yard line. Glenn Presnell kicked the extra point.

The Giants were unable to move successfully and Detroit scored again when Earl "Dutch" Clark broke loose for a 40-yard touchdown romp. Clark tried the conversion and missed.

In the second quarter, which was scoreless, the Giants smashed as far as the Detroit 4-yard line but were unable to go any further. The Lions led, 13–0, at the end of the half.

The Giants racked up their only score in the third quarter when Ed Danowski passed from the Detroit 42. Strong caught the ball in full stride on the 30 and went all the way, kicking the conversion to make it 13–7. But that was the end of the Giants.

In the fourth quarter, the Lions took full charge of the game, capitalizing on New York tactics of desperation passes. George Christensen blocked a punt by Danowski and recovered the ball on the New York 26. The Lions drove to the 4 where Ernie Caddel took the ball over on his favorite reverse play. The extra point was missed. Later in the period, Raymond "Buddy" Parker intercepted Danowski's pass attempt on the Giant 32 and fled to the 9. Buddy then smashed the rest of the way for the final score and Clark picked up the extra point to make it 26–7.

1936 WORLD CHAMPIONSHIP PROFESSIONAL FOOTBALL GAME

(Polo Grounds, New York, N.Y., Dec. 13)
Attendance 29,545

Green Bay Packers (21)	Boston Redskins (6)
Gantenbein—L.E.	Millner—L.E.
Smith, Ernest—L.T.	Edwards—L.T.
Engebretsen—L.G.	Olson—L.G.
Svendsen—C.	Bausch—C.
Evans—R.G.	Karcher—R.G.
Gordon—R.T.	Barber—R.T.
Hutson—R.E.	Malone—R.E.
Bruder—Q.B.	Smith, Riley—Q.B.
Sauer—L.H.	Justice—L.H.
Herber—R.H.	Battles—R.H.
Hinkle—F.B.	Irwin—F.B.

Green Bay Packers	7	0	7	7—21
Boston Redskins	0	6	0	0— 6

Touchdowns—Hutson, Rentner, Gantenbein, Monnett.

Points after touchdown—Ernest Smith 2, Engebretsen.

Coaches—Earl Lambeau (Green Bay), Ray Flaherty (Boston).

SUBSTITUTIONS

Green Bay—Ends: Scherer, Schneidmann; tackles: Schwammel, Seibold; guards: Kiesling, Goldenberg, Paulekas; center: Butler; backs: Miller, Monnett, Laws, Clemens, Johnston, Blood (McNally).

Boston—Ends: Busich, Tosi, McChesney; tackles: O'Brien, Carroll, Sinko; center: Siemering; backs: Pinckert, Britt, Rentner, Temple, Edward Smith.

Officials: Referee—W. G. Crowell. Umpire—Robert Cahn. Head Linesman—M. J. Meyer. Field Judge—William Holleran.

THE GAME

This was the only championship game ever played on a neutral field, a situation resulting from the refusal of Boston fans to support their championship contender. Perfect weather and field conditions were in force at the Polo Grounds and the devastating Packer attack was running at full throttle.

Wide World Photo

PREVIEW OF TITLE GAME—GREEN BAY CAME TO THE POLO GROUNDS IN NOVEMBER OF 1936 TO BEAT THE NEW YORK GIANTS 26–14. THAT'S HERMAN SCHNEIDMAN OF GREEN BAY INTERCEPTING A PASS AND ABOUT TO RUN FOR A TOUCHDOWN. BEHIND SCHNEIDMAN IS DON HUTSON. A MONTH LATER THE PACKERS RETURNED TO NEW YORK AND AGAIN BEAT THE GIANTS, 21–6, FOR THE CHAMPIONSHIP.

Immediately after the kick-off, Lou Gordon recovered Riley Smith's fumble at midfield. Arnold Herber struck through the air at once, heaving a 43-yard touchdown to Don Hutson. Ernie Smith converted to give the Packers a 7-point lead before the game was three minutes old. Right after the next kick-off, the Redskins lost their great halfback, Cliff Battles, who was injured so badly he played no more that day.

The 'Skins got back in the game on the first play of the second period when "Pug" Rentner crashed over from the one-yard line to make it 7–6. Riley Smith missed the conversion.

Herber fired another long one, 52 yards to Johnny "Blood" McNally, to move the Packers to the Boston 8-yard line, and then pitched to Milt Gantenbein in the end zone in the third quarter. Smith converted. The Redskins got a setback in this period when Frank Bausch, their dynamic center, was tossed out of the game for fighting with Frank Butler.

The Packers scored once more in the last period when Monnett went over from the 2 after a Boston punt was blocked. Engebretsen converted to make it 21–6, the final score.

The gross receipts were $33,471, of which each Packer received $250, each Redskin $180.

1937 WORLD CHAMPIONSHIP PROFESSIONAL FOOTBALL GAME

**(Wrigley Field, Chicago, Ill., Dec. 12)
Attendance 15,870**

Washington Redskins (28)	Chicago Bears (21)
Millner—L.E.	Manske—L.E.
Edwards—L.T.	Stydahar—L.T.
Olson—L.G.	Fortmann—L.G.
Kawal—C.	Bausch—C.
Karcher—R.G.	Musso—R.G.
Barber—R.T.	Bjork—R.T.
Malone—R.E.	Wilson—R.E.
Smith, R.—Q.B.	Masterson—Q.B.
Baugh—L.H.	Nolting—L.H.
Pinckert—R.H.	Manders—R.H.
Battles—F.B.	Nagurski—F.B.

Washington Redskins	7	0	7	14—28
Chicago Bears	7	7	7	0—21

Touchdowns—Battles, Millner 2, Justice, Manders 2, Manske.
Points after touchdown—Manders 3, Riley Smith 4.
Coaches—Ray Flaherty (Washington), George Halas (Chicago).

Wide World Photo

REDSKINS WHIP BEARS—WITH SO MANY PASSES WHIZZING PAST THEIR EARS FROM THE HAND OF SAM BAUGH, THE CHICAGO BEARS WERE UNPREPARED FOR A GROUND ATTACK BY THE TEXAS STAR. THIS PHOTOGRAPH SHOWS BAUGH BEING BROUGHT DOWN AFTER A 30-YARD GAIN THROUGH THE CHICAGO LINE AT WRIGLEY FIELD, DECEMBER 12, 1937. THE REDSKINS WON THE CHAMPIONSHIP 28–21.

NEW YORK GIANTS FOOTBALL TEAM—CHAMPIONS 1938

Front Row: (*left to right*) Ward Cuff, Owen Parry, Leonard Barnum, Henry Soar, John Gildea, John Karcis, Arthur White, Orville Tuttle.

Second Row: Lawrence Johnson, Charles Gelatka, Hugh Wolfe, John Haden, Nello Falaschi, Peter Cole, Leland Shaffer, Jim Lee Howell.

Third Row: Raymond Hanken, Alphonse "Tuffy" Leemans, Elvin Richards, Kay Lunday, Will Wells, James Poole, Dale Burnett, Wellington Mara, Steve Owen (coach).

Top Row: John "Bo" Molenda (asst. coach), Edward Widseth, Stanley Galazin, Edward Danowski, Melvin Hein, John dell Isola, Frank Cope, John Mellus.

SUBSTITUTIONS

Washington Redskins—Michaels, Justice, Carroll, Bond, Irwin, Young, Krause, Kahn, G. Smith.

Chicago Bears—Buivid, Plasman, Ronzani, McDonald, Thompson, Rentner, Francis, Molesworth, Conkwright, Feathers, Karr, Zeller, Sullivan, Trost.

Officials: Referee—W. T. Halloran. Umpire—A. W. Cochrane. Field Judge—E. F. Hughitt. Head Linesman—Bobie Cahn.

THE GAME

The Bears bumped into a young rookie by the name of Sam Baugh on this ice-covered field. He immediately began to give them nightmares, and continued to do so for the rest of his career.

Cliff Battles racked up the first Redskin touchdown in the first period, scoring on a 10-yard romp through tackle. Riley Smith's conversion made it 7–0. Jack Manders pounded over for the Bears from 10 yards out and converted to tie the score.

In the second quarter, Bernie Masterson passed 20 yards to Manders for another six-pointer and Manders again converted

to give the Bears a 14–7 lead at the rest period.

Baugh went through the air to Wayne Millner for 55 yards and a touchdown early in the third quarter and Smith kicked the extra point. Masterson passed 3 yards to Manske and Manders converted to put the Bears back in the lead.

The fourth quarter was all Baugh. He passed for a seventy-eight yarder to Wayne Millner for one touchdown and then to Ed Justice for 35 yards on another. Smith kicked both extra points for a final score of 28–21 to take the title to Washington.

1938 WORLD CHAMPIONSHIP PROFESSIONAL FOOTBALL GAME

(Polo Grounds, New York, N.Y., Dec. 11)
Attendance 48,120

New York Giants   Green Bay Packers
(23)   (17)

Poole—L.E.
Widseth—L.T.
Dell Isola—L.G.
Hein—C.
Tuttle—R.G.
Parry—R.T.
Howell—R.E.
Danowski—Q.B.
Soar—L.H.
Cuff—R.H.
Shaffer—F.B.

Becker—L.E.
Seibold—L.T.
Letlow—L.G.
Mulleneaux, L.—C.
Goldenburg—R.G.
Lee—R.T.
Gantenbein—R.E.
Schneidman—Q.B.
Isbell—L.H.
Laws—R.H.
Hinkle—F.B.

New York Giants	9	7	7	0—23
Green Bay Packers	0	14	3	0—17

Touchdowns—Leemans, Barnard, Soar, C. Mulleneaux, Hinkle.

Points after touchdown—Cuff 2, Engebretsen 2.

Field Goals: Engebretsen, Cuff.

Coaches—Stephen Owen (New York), Earl Lambeau (Green Bay).

SUBSTITUTIONS

New York Giants—Ends: Barnard, Gelatka; tackles: Mellus, Cope; guards: Lunday, Cole, White; centers: Galazin, Johnson; backs: Leemans, Barnum, Karcis, Richards, Gildea, Burnett, Falaschi.

Green Bay Packers—Ends: Hutson, C. Mulleneaux, Scherer; tackles: Butler, Ray; guards: Johnson, Engebretsen, Tinsley; centers: Svendsen, O. Miller; backs: P. Miller, Bruder, Jankowski, Uram, Herber, Monett.

Officials: Referee—R. Cahn. Umpire—T. Thorp. Head Linesman—L. Conover. Field Judge—J. L. Meyer.

THE GAME

A real slam-bang, bruising thriller was staged for the largest crowd to turn out for a professional championship game up to that time. The entire league had played to a new high in attendance records, the average being up more than 15 percent above previous marks. The victorious Giants became the first team since 1933 (when the league was split into two divisions) to win the championship twice.

The Giants were off on top when two Green Bay punts were blocked early in the game. Ward Cuff cashed one of these for a 13-yard field goal. Tuffy Leemans smashed over from the 6 for a touchdown on the other. Gildea missed the conversion and the Giants led, 9—0, at the end of the period.

Arnie Herber launched a 50-yard pass to Carl Mulleneaux for a TD early in the second quarter and Engebretsen kicked the conversion. The Giants made it 16—7 when E. Danowski passed 20 yards to Hap Barnard in the end zone and Ward Cuff obliged with the extra point. Clark Hinkle smashed over from the 6 to lead to another conversion by Engebretsen and the Giants led, 16—14, at the half.

The Packers took the second half kickoff back to the Giant 15, where Engebretsen hoisted a field goal. The Giants stormed back to the Packer 23 from where Danowski passed to Hank Soar on the 2 and Soar plowed over for the TD. Cuff added the extra and the score was 23—17. There was no further scoring in this period nor in the next.

1939 WORLD CHAMPIONSHIP PROFESSIONAL FOOTBALL GAME

(State Fair Grounds, Milwaukee, Wis., Dec. 10)
Attendance 32,279

Green Bay Packers (27)	New York Giants (0)
Hutson—L.E.	Poole—L.E.
Ray—L.T.	Cope—L.T.
Letlow—L.G.	Dell Isola—L.G.
Svendsen—C.	Hein—C.
Goldenberg—R.G.	Tuttle—R.G.
Lee—R.T.	Mellus—R.T.
Gantenbein—R.E.	Howell—R.E.
Craig—Q.B.	Danowski—Q.B.
Isbell—L.H.	Richards—L.H.
Laws—R.H.	Cuff—R.H.
Hinkle—F.B.	Falaschi—F.B.

Green Bay Packers	7	0	10	10—27
New York Giants	0	0	0	0— 0

Touchdowns—Gantenbein, Laws, Jankowski.

Points after touchdown—Engebretsen 2, Smith.

Field goals—Engebretsen, Smith.

Coaches—Earl Lambeau (Green Bay), Stephen Owen (New York).

SUBSTITUTIONS

Green Bay Packers—Bruder, Jankowski, Tinsley, Brock, Engebretsen, Herber, Uram, Smith, Jacunski, Schultz, Balacz, Lawrence, Zarnas, Weisgerber, Moore, Greenfield.

New York Giants—Leemans, Lunday, Barnum, Burnett, Shaffer, Walls, Kline, Oldershaw, Parry, Widseth, Cole, Owen, Soar, Miller, Gelatka.

Officials: Referee—W. Halloran. Umpire—E. Cochrane. Head Linesman—T. Thorp. Field Judge—Dan Tehan.

THE GAME

This grudge game, played on dry ground but with a chill 35-mph wind making aerial sorties a bit dubious, brought sweet revenge to Green Bay, who had lost the title to the same Giants the previous year.

Arnie Herber tossed a 7-yard pass to Milt Gantenbein in the end zone and Engebretsen cashed the conversion in the first period. There was no further scoring and the Packers led, 7–0, at the half.

Engebretsen continued his scoring with a 29-yard field goal in the third period. Joe Laws then caught Cecil Isbell's 20-yard pass on the Giant 7 and scooted across. Engebretsen again converted to make it 17–0

Late in the fourth quarter, Ernie Smith kicked a 42-yard field goal. A few plays later an interception led the Packers to the Giant 12. From there, on a double reverse,

Jacunski carried to the one and, on the next play, Jankowski took it over. Smith converted and it was 27–0, the final score.

1940 WORLD CHAMPIONSHIP PROFESSIONAL FOOTBALL GAME

(Griffith Stadium, Washington, D.C., Dec. 8)
Attendance 36,034

Chicago Bears (73)	Washington Redskins (0)
Nowaskey—L.E.	Masterson—L.E.
Stydahar—L.T.	Wilkin—L.T.
Fortmann—L.G.	Farman—L.G.
Turner—C.	Titchenal—C.
Musso—R.G.	Slivinski—R.G.
Artoe—R.T.	Barber—R.T.
Wilson—R.E.	Malone—R.E.
Luckman—Q.B.	Krause—Q.B.
Nolting—L.H.	Baugh—L.H.
McAfee—R.H.	Justice—R.H.
Osmanski, W.—F.B.	Johnston—F.B.

Chicago Bears	21	7	26	19—73
Washington Redskins	0	0	0	0— 0

Touchdowns—Osmanski, Luckman, Maniaci, Kavanaugh, Turner, Pool, Nolting, McAfee, Clark 2, Famiglietti.

Press-Gazette Photo

GREEN BAY PACKERS FOOTBALL TEAM—CHAMPIONS 1939

Front Row: *(left to right)* Earl "Curly" Lambeau (coach), Milton Gantenbein, Andrew Uram, Donald Hutson, Cecil Isbell, Charles Goldenberg, Joseph Laws, Charles Brock, Paul Engebretsen, Henry Bruder, James Lawrence, Edward Jankowski.

Middle Row: Lawrence Craig, Arnold Herber, Clarke Hinkle, Richard Weisgerber, Peter Tinsley, Lawrence Buhler, Thomas Greenfield, Russell Letlow, Lee Mulleneaux, William Lee, Augustus Zarnas, Richard "Red" Smith (asst. coach).

Back Row: David Woodward (trainer), Earl Svendsen, Paul Kell, Charles Schultz, Carl Mulleneaux, Buford Ray, Allen Moore, Harry Jacunski, Ernest Smith, Frank Balasz, Bud Jorgenson (asst. trainer).

Nate Fine Photo

DICK TODD OF THE WASHINGTON REDSKINS SCAMPERS AWAY FROM HAMPTON POOL OF THE CHICAGO BEARS IN THIS 1940 GAME WHICH WASHINGTON WON, 7-3. THREE WEEKS LATER THE SAME TEAMS MET FOR CHAMPIONSHIP AND THE SAME FIGURES APPEARED IN THE FINAL SCORE. BUT IT WAS BEARS 73, WASHINGTON 0.

Points after touchdown—Manders, Snyder 2, Martinovich, Plasman, Stydahar, Maniaci.

Coaches—George Halas (Chicago), Ray Flaherty (Washington).

SUBSTITUTIONS

Chicago Bears—Ends: Plasman, Kavanaugh, Manders, Siegal, Martinovich, Pool, Manske; tackles: Kolman, Mihal; guards: Baisi, Forte, Torrance; center: Bausch; backs: Masterson, Sherman, Clark, Swisher, McLean, Famiglietti, Snyder, Maniaci, Manders.

Washington Redskins—Ends: Millner, McChesney, Sanford; tackles: Russell, Fisher, Parks; guards: Shugart, Stralka; centers: Andrako, Carroll; backs: Pinckert, Hoffman, Morgan, Filchock, Zimmerman, Moore, Seymour, Meade, Todd, Farkas, Hare.

Officials: Referee—William Friesell. Umpire —Harry Robb. Head Linesman—Irving Kupcinet. Field Judge—Fred Young.

THE GAME

The most fantastic exhibition of sheer football power and genius, combined with perfect timing and good luck, fashioned this championship game into one that will be mentioned with awe as long as football is played. Washington was far from an outclassed team. In fact their seasonal record was better (9 wins, 2 losses) than the Bears' (8 wins, 3 losses). They were expected to triumph. Baugh had been having his best year to date—the team was ready.

The Bears received and, on the second play, Bill Osmanski sped around his left end for 68 yards and a touchdown. Jack Manders converted. Sid Luckman scored the next with a one-yard plunge after driving the team 80 yards. Bob Snyder kicked the extra point. Joe Maniaci followed Osmanski's trail around left end

CHICAGO BEARS FOOTBALL TEAM CHAMPIONS—1940
Front Row: (*left to right*) Saul Sherman, Robert Snyder, Robert Nowaskey, Daniel Fortmann, Harry Clarke, George Wilson, Edgar Manske, George McAfee, John Manders, Sidney Luckman, Raymond McLean, Robert Swisher, Albert Baisi, Edward Kolman.
Middle Row: Dr. Davis, Carl Brumbaugh (coach), Andrew Lotshaw (trainer), John Torrance, Aldo Forte, George Musso, John Siegel, Philip Martinovich, Clyde Turner, Raymond Nolting, Robert Masterson, William Osmanski, Heartley Anderson (coach), George Halas (head coach).
Back Row: Frank Bausch, Hampton Poole, Joseph Stydahr, Kenneth Kavanaugh, Joseph Mihal, Lee Artoe, Richard Plasman, Chester Chesney, Gary Famiglietti, Joseph Maniaci, Raymond Bray, Herman Cole (asst. trainer).

for 42 yards and a TD, and Phil Martinovich cashed the conversion to make it 21–0 at the end of the quarter.

The second period was fairly quiet; the only scoring was Luckman's 30-yard pass to Ken Kavanaugh in the end zone and Snyder's second conversion.

Hampton Pool intercepted a Baugh pass to open the second half and ran 19 yards for a touchdown with Dick Plasman converting. Ray Nolting blasted for 23 yards and another score and this time Plasman missed the conversion. George McAfee then intercepted Roy Zimmerman's pass and returned 34 yards for a TD and Joe Stydahar kicked the extra point. Clyde Turner got into the act by intercepting another Zimmerman throw and rumbling 21 yards over the goal. The Redskins blocked Maniaci's conversion attempt. This made it 54–0 as the third quarter ended.

Harry Clark went around his right end for 44 yards and a TD and Gary Famiglietti missed the conversion. A few minutes later, Famiglietti atoned by smashing over from the 2 after Bulldog Turner had re-

covered Frank Filchock's fumble. This time, Sollie Sherman passed to Maniaci for the extra point. Clark scored the final TD from the one-yard line but the Sherman-Maniaci pass-for-conversion attempt went wild.

Ten different Bears had scored eleven touchdowns; six different players had scored seven conversions.

The gross receipts were $112,508.00, a new record at the time. Each Bear received $873.99, each Redskin $606.25. This left a pool of $4,546.45 for the members of the sectional second place clubs (Brooklyn and Green Bay).

1941 WORLD CHAMPIONSHIP PROFESSIONAL FOOTBALL GAME

(Wrigley Field, Chicago, Ill., Dec. 21)
Attendance 13,341

Chicago Bears (37)	New York Giants (9)
Plasman—L.E.	Poole—L.E.
Kolman—L.T.	Mellus—L.T.

Fortmann—L.G.
Turner—C.
Bray—R.G.
Artoe—R.T.
Siegal—R.E.
Luckman—Q.B.
Nolting—L.H.
Gallarneau—R.H.
Standlee—F.B.

Lunday—L.G.
Hein—C.
Younce—R.G.
Edwards—R.T.
Howell—R.E.
Falaschi—Q.B.
Franck—L.H.
Cuff—R.H.
Leemans—F.B.

Chicago Bears	3	6	14	14—37
New York Giants	6	0	3	0— 9

Touchdowns—Franck, Standlee, McAfee, Kavanaugh.
Points after touchdown—Snyder, Maniaci, Artoe, McLean.
Field Goals—Cuff, Snyder 3.
Coaches—George Halas (Chicago), Stephen Owen (New York).

SUBSTITUTIONS

Chicago Bears—Ends: Kavanaugh, Nowaskey, Wilson, Poole; tackles: Stydahar, Mihal, Fedorovitch; guards: Lahar, Baisi, Forte, Musso; center: Matuza; backs: Snyder, Bussey, Swisher, Clark, McLean, McAfee, Famiglietti, Maniaci, W. Osmanski.

New York Giants—Ends: Horne, Walls, Lummis; tackles: Cope, Blazine; guards: Tuttle, Sohn, Oldershaw, Edwards; centers: Gladchuk, Lunday; backs: Principe, Shaffer, Eshmont, Eakin, Yeager, McLain, Marefos, Soar.

Officials: Referee—Emil Heintz. Umpire—John Schommer. Head Linesman—Charles Berry. Field Judge—Chuck Sweeney.

THE GAME

The Giants had won eight, lost three in the East. The Bears had won ten, lost one to tie with the Green Bay Packers in the West. In the play-off game the Bears walloped the Packers 33–14. Pearl Harbor Day was only two weeks past when they met for the championship, a factor which kept the attendance down to ridiculous figures as this great Bear team prepared to break up for the duration. Young Bussey, Bear quarterback, would be killed in action before the war was over. And Jack Lummis, New York, would die on Iwo Jima.

Bob Snyder put the Bears in front with a 14-yard field goal in the first quarter, but the Giants led after the whistle ended the period, because Tuffy Leemans had sent a 4-yard pass to George Franck, who galloped 27 more yards for the touchdown. Johnny Siegal blocked Ward Cuff's conversion attempt.

Snyder continued the long-range bombardment in the second quarter, booting a field goal from the 39 and another from the 37. There was no other scoring and the Bears led 9–6 at the half.

Ward Cuff kicked a three-pointer from the 17 to tie the score early in the third period but that was the end of the Giants. Norm Standlee smashed through right tackle for 2 yards and a TD, Snyder kicking the extra, then Standlee hit for another from 7 yards out and Joe Maniaci converted. This made it 23–9 as the fourth period opened. George McAfee then hit the line for 5 yards and another marker with Lee Artoe kicking the conversion successfully. Ken Kavanaugh added the final TD by scooping up a fumbled lateral pass from Hank Soar that was intended for Andy Marefos and racing 42 yards for the touchdown. This time Ray McLean dropkicked the conversion and it was 37–9.

The gross receipts (including radio) were $46,184.05, each Bear receiving $430.94, each Giant $288.70. This left a pool of $1,564.06 for the members of the sectional second-place clubs (Green Bay Packers and Brooklyn).

1942 WORLD CHAMPIONSHIP PROFESSIONAL FOOTBALL GAME
(Griffith Stadium, Washington, D.C., Dec. 13)
Attendance 36,006

Washington Redskins (14)	Chicago Bears (6)
Masterson—L.E.	Kolman—L.E.
Wilkin—L.T.	Nowaskey—L.T.
Farman—L.G.	Fortmann—L.G.
Aldrich—C.	Turner—C.
Slivinski—R.G.	Bray—R.G.
Young—R.T.	Artoe—R.T.
Cifers—R.E.	Wilson—R.E.
Hare, R.—Q.B.	Luckman—Q.B.
Baugh—L.H.	Nolting—L.H.
Justice—R.H.	Gallarneau—R.H.
Farkas—F.B.	Famiglietti—F.B.

Washington Redskins	0	7	7	0—14
Chicago Bears	0	6	0	0— 6

Touchdowns—Artoe, Moore, Farkas.
Points after touchdown—Masterson 2.
Coaches—Ray Flaherty (Washington),
Coaches—Heartley Anderson, Luke Johnsos (Chicago).

ANDY FARKAS WAS THE BIG MAN OF THE WASHINGTON REDSKINS TEAM IN THEIR
CHAMPIONSHIP VICTORY OVER THE CHICAGO BEARS IN 1942. IN THE THIRD PERIOD OF
THE TIGHT GAME, FARKAS CARRIED THE BALL ON TEN OF TWELVE CONSECUTIVE PLAYS,
COVERED 80 YARDS AND SCORED THE DECISIVE TOUCHDOWN. WHEN HE WAS NOT MOVING
THE BALL HE WAS BUSY TACKLING BEARS, LIKE RAY NOLTING IN THE BOTTOM PICTURE.

SUBSTITUTIONS

Washington Redskins—Tackles: Beinor, F. Davis; guards: Stralka, Shugart; backs: C. Hare, Moore, Todd, Seymour.

Chicago Bears—Ends: Siegal, Pool; tackles: Stydahar, Hoptowit; guards: Drulis, Akin, Musso; backs: O'Rourke, Clark, Maznicki, McLean, Petty, W. Osmanski.

Officials: Referee—Ronald Gibbs. Umpire—Carl Brubaker. Head Linesman—Charles Berry. Field Judge—Chuck Sweeney.

THE GAME

The two top passers of the era were at each other's throats in this championship match, for Sam Baugh and Sid Luckman had led their respective teams through their best seasonal records of history. The Bears had won all eleven of their league contests; the Redskins had won ten and lost but one, an early season defeat by the New York Giants, whom they whipped later on. Baugh at this time was still playing halfback in a single-wing formation although the Bears had been shooting the T for three seasons.

The first period was scoreless. In the second, Lee Artoe snatched up a fumbled pass from center and scampered 50 yards for a touchdown but missed the conversion. Baugh sent a 25-yard touchdown toss to Wilbur Moore which led to Bob Masterson's successful conversion for a 7–6 lead, and a half-time score of 7–6, Redskins.

In the third period, Andy Farkas, carrying the ball on ten out of twelve plays, drove for 80 yards and a touchdown, the scoring smash starting from the Bears' one-yard line. Masterson again converted to make it 14–6; the final period was scoreless.

The gross receipts (including radio) were $113,260.40, each Redskin receiving $965.89, each Bear $637.56. This left a pool of $3,241.90 for members of the sectional second-place clubs (Green Bay Packers and Pittsburgh Steelers).

1943 WORLD CHAMPIONSHIP PROFESSIONAL FOOTBALL GAME

(Wrigley Field, Chicago, Ill., Dec. 26)
Attendance 34,320

Chicago Bears (41) Washington Redskins (21)

Benton—L.E.	Masterson—L.E.
Sigillo—L.T.	Rymkus—L.T.
Fortmann—L.G.	Shugart—L.G.
Turner—C.	Smith, G.–C.
Musso—R.G.	Slivinski—R.G.
Hoptowit—R.T.	Pasqua—R.T.
Wilson—R.E.	Aguirre—R.E.
Snyder—Q.B.	Hare—Q.B.
Clark—L.H.	Seno—L.H.
Magnani—R.H.	Cafego—R.H.
Masters—F.B.	Farkas—F.B.

Chicago Bears	0	14	13	14—41
Washington Redskins	0	7	7	7—21

Touchdowns—Clark 2, Magnani 2, Nagurski, Benton, Farkas 2, Aguirre.

Points after touchdown—Snyder 5, Masterson 2, Aguirre.

Coaches—Heartley Anderson, Luke Johnsos (Chicago), Arthur Bergman (Washington).

SUBSTITUTIONS

Chicago Bears—Ends: Pool, Berry; tackles: Steinkemper, Babartsky, Mundee; guards: Ippolito, Logan; center: Matuza; backs: McLean, Luckman, Famiglietti, Nagurski, McEnulty, Nolting, Vodicka.

Washington Redskins—Ends: Piasecky, Lapka; tackle: Wilkin; guards: Zeno, Fiorentino, Leon; center: Hayden; backs: Baugh, Seymour, Moore, Gibson, F. Akins, Stasica.

Officials: Referee—Ronald Gibbs. Umpire—John Kelly. Head Linesman—Charles Berry. Field Judge—Edward Tryon.

THE GAME

Although all the teams in the league had been depleted of most of their star players by World War II, Sid Luckman of the Bears and Sam Baugh of the Redskins had kept the fans' interest high with their spectacular passing. Against the Giants, Luckman had fashioned the unbelievable record of throwing for seven touchdowns in one game and Baugh had led the Washington team to a divisional tie with the New York Giants and then to a 28–0 victory in the play-off game.

The Bears, supposedly creaking with age, beaten previously by the Redskins during a season game, had lured the aged Bronko Nagurski out of retirement to add his thundering power to the attack, but it was Luckman's splendid passing that saved the title for the Bears. Baugh received a concussion late·in the game which put the Redskins out of contention.

There was no scoring in the first period.

The Redskins clicked first when Andy Farkas plowed one yard to start the second quarter and Bob Masterson converted for 7–0. Luckman fired 31 yards to Harry Clark on a screen-pass for a touchdown and Bob Snyder's extra point tied the game. The Bears led, 14–7, at the half following a 3-yard plunge for a touchdown by Nagurski and Snyder's conversion.

Luckman opened the third period with two touchdown passes, the first traveling 36 yards to Dante Magnani, the second again to Magnani for a 66-yard romp from the flat. Snyder kicked the first conversion, missed the second. The Redskins made it 27–14 at the end of the third quarter after Baugh passed 8 yards to Andy Farkas who ran 9 more for the counter. Masterson converted.

Luckman had two more TD's in his guns for the last period. He threw the first 29 yards to Jim Benton in the end zone, the second 16 yards to Harry Clark, who took it on the goal line. Bob Snyder kicked both conversions. Sam Baugh, just before he was injured, passed 26 yards to Joe Aguirre in the end zone, Aguirre kicked the point and the game ended, 41–21.

The gross receipts (including radio) were $120,500.05, of which each Bear received $1,146.87, each Redskin $765.78. This left a pool of $3,470.57 for members of the sectional second-place clubs (Green Bay Packers and New York Giants).

1944 WORLD CHAMPIONSHIP PROFESSIONAL FOOTBALL GAME

(Polo Grounds, New York, N.Y., Dec. 17)
Attendance 46,016

Green Bay Packers (14)	New York Giants (7)
Hutson—L.E.	Adams, O.—L.E.
Ray—L.T.	Cope—L.T.
Kuusisto—L.G.	Younce—L.G.
Brock, C.—C.	Hein—C.
Goldenberg—R.G.	Sivell—R.G.
Berezney—R.T.	Carroll—R.T.
Jacunski—R.E.	Liebel—R.E.
Craig—Q.B.	Calligaro—Q.B.
Comp—L.H.	Herber—L.H.
Laws—R.H.	Cuff—R.H.
Fritsch—F.B.	Livingston—F.B.

Green Bay Packers	0	14	0	0—14
New York Giants	0	0	0	7— 7

Touchdowns—Fritsch 2, Cuff.
Points after touchdown—Hutson 2, Strong.
Coaches: E. Lambeau (Green Bay), Stephen Owen (New York).

SUBSTITUTIONS

Green Bay Packers—End: Webha; tackle: Croft; guards: Tinsley, Sorenson; backs: L. Brock, Perkins, Duhart.
New York Giants—Ends: Weiss, V. Adams; tackle: Blozis; guard: Avedisian; backs: Petrilas, Paschal, Kinscherf, Sulaitis, Barker, Strong.
Officials: Referee—Ronald Gibbs. Umpire—C. H. Brubaker. Head Linesman—Charles Berry. Field Judge—Eugene Miller. Timer: W. Friesell.

THE GAME

After a scoreless first period, Ted Fritsch put the Packers ahead with a 2-yard touchdown plunge and Don Hutson converted to make it 7–0. Later in the period, Irv Comp passed to Ted Fritsch for 26 yards and another TD with Hutson's conversion giving the Green Bay team a 14–0 lead at half-time.

The third period was scoreless, but, at its end, the Giants were on the Packer one-yard line and Ward Cuff plunged across on the first play of the last quarter. Ken Strong kicked the conversion to make it 14–7 and there was no further scoring.

The gross receipts (including radio) were $146,204.15, of which each Packer received $1,449.71, each Giant $814.36. This left a pool of $8,143.84 for members of the sectional second-place teams (Philadelphia Eagles and both the Chicago Bears and Detroit Lions who tied for second in the West).

1945 WORLD CHAMPIONSHIP PROFESSIONAL FOOTBALL GAME

(Municipal Stadium, Cleveland, Ohio, Dec. 16)
Attendance 32,178

Cleveland Rams (15)	Washington Redskins (14)
Konetsky—L.E.	Millner—L.E.

CLEVELAND RAMS FOOTBALL TEAM—WORLD CHAMPIONS 1945

Front row: (*left to right*) Donald Greenwood, Albie Reisz, Steven Nemeth, Frederick Gehrke, Elvin Liles, Assistant Trainer Bud Leininger.

Second Row: Howard Hickey, Eberle Schultz, Steven Pritko, James Benton, Riley Matheson, Head Coach Adam Walsh, Jim Gillette, David Bernard, Harvey Jones, Raymond Hamilton.

Third row: Line Coach George Trafton, Michael Scarry, Robert DeLauer, Roger Harding, Ralph Ruthstrom, Gilbert Bouley, Robert Shaw, Robert Waterfield, Floyd Konetsky, Milan Lazetich, General Manager Charles Walsh.

Fourth row: Backfield Coach Robert Snyder, Thomas Colella, George Koch, Rudolph Sikich, Leonard Levy, Arthur Mergenthal, Joseph Winkler, Leslie Lear, Walter Zirinsky, Pat West, Trainer Tiny Dippery (Jack Jacobs not present).

Schultz—L.T.	Audet—L.T.
Matheson, R.—L.G.	Adams, J.—L.G.
Scarry—C.	Aldrich—C.
Lazetich—R.G.	Whited—R.G.
Bouley—R.T.	Ungerer—R.T.
Pritko—R.E.	Turley—R.E.
Reisz—Q.B.	Hare, C.—Q.B.
Nemeth—L.H.	Seymour—L.H.
Gillette—R.H.	Condit—R.H.
West—F.B.	Akins, F.—F.B.

Cleveland Rams	2	7	6	0—15
Washington Redskins	0	7	7	0—14

Touchdowns—Benton, Gillette, Bagarus, Seymour.

Points after touchdown—Aguirre 2, Waterfield.

Safety—Automatic.

Coaches: Adam Walsh (Cleveland), Dudley DeGroot (Washington).

SUBSTITUTIONS

Cleveland Rams—Ends: Hamilton, Hickey, Benton; tackles: Lear, Sikich, Eason; guards: Levy, Mergenthal; center: deLauer, Harding; backs: Waterfield, Koch, Greenwood, Gehrke.

Washington Redskins—Ends: Piasecky, Aguirre, Dye; tackles: Davis, Koniszewski; guards: Sharp, Lolotai, Hanna, Stralka; center: DeMao; backs: Bagarus, Baugh, deCorrevont, Filchock, Rosato, Todd, deFruiter.

Officials: Referee—Ronald Gibbs. Umpire—Harry Robb. Head Linesman—Charles Berry. Field Judge—William Downes.

THE GAME

It was so cold in Cleveland on the day of the game that the musical instruments froze, putting the great Redskin band out of action even before the game started. The field had been covered with mountains of straw but was slippery underfoot. The wind was strong and erratic. It was a perfect day for staying home by the fireside but no less than 32,178 eager fans appeared.

Sam Baugh attempted a pass from his end zone in the first quarter. The wind veered the ball into the goal post for an automatic safety to give the Rams a 2-point lead.

In the second period, Frank Filchock passed 26 yards to Steve Bagarus who ran 12 more for the first touchdown. Joe Aguirre converted to put the Redskins ahead 7-2. Waterfield then passed 25 yards

CHICAGO BEARS FOOTBALL TEAM—CHAMPIONS 1946

Front row: (*left to right*) Cole (asst. trainer), Walter Lamb, Richard Schweidler, Thomas Farris, Noah Mullins, Raymond McLean, George McAfee, Robert Margarita, Goldie (equipment).

Second row: Frank Halas, Hugh Gallarneau, William Osmanski, Dante Magnani, George Wilson, Edward Sprinkle, Sidney Luckman, Pattison Preston, Raymond Bray, Fred Davis, Ralph Brizzolara.

Third row: George Halas, Lloyd Reese, Kenneth Kavanaugh, Rudolph Mucha, Clyde Turner, Walter Stickel, Edward Kolman, Aldo Forte, Joseph Osmanski, Heartley Anderson, Luke Johnsos.

Top row: John "Paddy" Driscall, Donald Perkins, Albert Baisi, Cornelius Berry, Stuart Clarkson, Joseph Stydahar, Michael Jarmoluk, James Keane, John Schiechl, Andrew Lotshaw (trainer).

to Jim Benton who added 12 more for a TD and Waterfield's conversion made it 9–7 at the end of the half.

In the third, Waterfield threw 39 yards to Jim Gillette, who then scored from the 14. Waterfield's conversion missed to keep it 15–7.

Filchock passed the 'Skins to within 2 points of the Rams, with an 8-yard pitch to Bob Seymour in the end zone. Aguirre again converted.

The fourth period was scoreless and the game ended 15–14.

The gross receipts (including radio and motion picture rights) were $164,-542.40, of which each Ram received $1,469.74, each Redskin $902.47. This left a pool of $4,763.05 for members of the sectional second-place clubs (Philadelphia Eagles and Detroit Lions).

1946 WORLD CHAMPIONSHIP PROFESSIONAL FOOTBALL GAME

(Polo Grounds, New York, N.Y., Dec. 15)

Attendance 58,346

Chicago Bears (24)	New York Giants (14)
Kavanaugh—L.E.	Poole—L.E.
Davis, F.—L.T.	Coulter—L.T.
Mucha—L.G.	Dobelstein—L.G.
Turner—C.	Gladchuk—C.
Bray—R.G.	Young—R.G.
Jarmoluk—R.T.	White—R.T.
Wilson—R.E.	Howell—R.E.
Osmanski, J.—Q.B.	Filipowicz—Q.B.
Magnani—L.H.	Brown—L.H.
Gallarneau—R.H.	Livingston—R.H.
Osmanski, W.—F.B.	Strong—F.B.

Chicago Bears	14 0 0 10—24
New York Giants	7 0 7 0—14

Touchdowns—Kavanaugh, Magnani, Luckman, Liebel, Filipowicz.

Points after touchdown—Maznicki 3, Strong 2.

Coaches: George Halas (Chicago), Stephen Owen (New York).

SUBSTITUTIONS

Chicago Bears—Ends: Lamb, Keane, Sprinkle; tackles: Stickel, Kolman; guards: Forte, Preston, Drulis; centers: Clarkson, Schiechl; backs: Maznicki, McAfee, Perkins, Margarita, Luckman, Farris, Schweidler, McLean.

New York Giants—Ends: Mead, McCafferty, Liebel; tackles: Cope, Ragazzo, Carroll; guard: Edwards; center: De-Filippo; backs: Soar, Gorgone, Franck, Filchock, Reagan, Doolan.

Officials: Referee—Ronald Gibbs. Umpire—Carl Brubaker. Head Linesman—Charles Berry. Field Judge—William Grimberg.

THE GAME

The Bears had won the Western division championship easily with 8 wins, 2 losses and a tie. The Giants dominated the Eastern with 7 wins, 3 losses and a tie. There was considerable excitement a few days before the game when it was revealed that two New York players had been approached by Broadway characters who wanted them to control the score.

The deadly Sid Luckman-to-Ken Kavanaugh pass combination opened the scoring for the Bears in the first period with a 21-yard toss over the goal and Frank Maznicki's conversion made it 7–0. The Bears increased their lead to 14–0 when Dante Magnani intercepted Filchock's pass and raced 19 yards for the TD, then kicked the extra point. The Giants got their first touchdown in the same period when Frank Filchock passed 38 yards to Frank Liebel. Ken Strong converted.

There was no scoring in the second period.

In the third, the Giants pulled even at 14–14 when Filchock passed 5 yards for a TD to Steve Filipowicz and Strong converted.

Sid Luckman fooled the Giants completely with a "keep-it" play in the fourth quarter, running 19 yards for a touchdown and Maznicki converted again. Later in the quarter, Maznicki booted a field goal from the 26 to make the final score 24–14.

The gross receipts (including radio and motion picture rights) were $282,955.25, a new record at the time. Each Bear received $1,975.82, each Giant $1,295.57. This left a pool of $14,395.33 for members of the sectional second-place clubs (Philadelphia Eagles and Los Angeles Rams).

1947 WORLD CHAMPIONSHIP PROFESSIONAL FOOTBALL GAME

(Comiskey Park, Chicago, Ill., Dec. 28)
Attendance 30,759

Chicago Cardinals (28)	Philadelphia Eagles (21)
Blackburn—L.E.	Ferrante—L.E.
Plasman—L.T.	Sears—L.T.
Arms—L.G.	Patton—L.G.
Banonis—C.	Wojciechowicz—C.
Nichols—R.G.	Kilroy—R.G.
Mauldin—R.T.	Wistert—R.T.
Doolan—R.E.	Pihos—R.E.

ELMER ANGSMAN, CHICAGO CARDINAL HALFBACK, IN ONE OF HIS TWO 70-YARD TOUCHDOWN SCAMPERS AGAINST THE PHILADELPHIA EAGLES IN THE CHAMPIONSHIP GAME OF 1947. TWO MORE LONG TOUCHDOWN DASHES BY CHARLES TRIPPI GAVE THE CARDINALS THE TITLE, 28–21. THE EAGLE PLAYER TRYING FUTILELY FOR A TACKLE IS UNIDENTIFIED.

Campbell—Q.B. McHugh—Q.B.
Cochran—L.H. Van Buren—L.H.
Goldberg—R.H. Pritchard—R.H.
Rankin—F.B. Muha—F.B.

Chicago Cardinals	7	7	7	7—28
Philadelphia Eagles	0	7	7	7—21

Touchdowns—Trippi 2, Angsman 2, Mc-Hugh, Van Buren, Craft.
Points after touchdown—Harder 4, Patton 3.
Coaches: James Conzelman (Chicago), Earle Neale (Philadelphia).

SUBSTITUTIONS

Chicago Cardinals—Ends: Parker, Kutner, Dewell; tackles: Coomer, Bulger; guards: Andros, Ramsey, Apolskis; backs: Mallouf, Dimancheff, DeCorrevont, Angsman, Harder, Christman, Trippi.
Philadelphia Eagles—Ends: Armstrong, Green, Cabrelli, Prescott; tackles: Kekeris, Douglas, McDowell, Harding; guard: Wyhonic; center: Lindskog; backs: Steele, Craft, Kish, Sherman, Thompson.
Officials: Referee—William Downs. Umpire—Harry Robb. Head Linesman—Dan Tehan. Field Judge—Harry Haines. Back Judge—Carl Rebele.

THE GAME

Philadelphia finished the season tied with the Pittsburgh Steelers, each having an 8–4 record, then won the divisional title by beating the Pittsburgh team 21–0 in the play-off. The Cardinals had won 9, lost 3. The field was fast and frozen, the weather frigid when they clashed for the championship. The new eight-man-line defense developed by coach Earle "Greasy" Neale, although highly effective all season, backfired in this game.

In the first period, Charlie Trippi squirted through tackle on a quick-opener and went 44 yards for a touchdown. Harder kicked the conversion.

In the second period, Elmer Angsman, on the same play, went 70 yards for the Cardinals' second score and Harder converted. The Eagles came back to make it 14–7 at the half after Tommy Thompson passed 53 yards to Pat McHugh, who ran 17 more to score, with Cliff Patton converting.

Charlie Trippi ran a punt back for 75 yards and a TD in the third period and Harder again converted to make it 21–7, but the Eagles countered with a 73-yard

drive, Steve Van Buren scoring from the one-yard line and Patton again converting to make it 21–14.

Again on the quick-opener Elmer Angsman burst loose for his second 70-yard touchdown run in the fourth quarter and Harder converted. And again the Eagles smashed through on the ground with Russ Craft crashing from the one and Patton once more converting to end the scoring at 28–21.

The gross receipts (including radio and motion picture rights) were $159,498, of which each Cardinal received $1,132, each Eagle $754. This left a pool of $8,388 for members of the sectional second-place clubs (Chicago Bears and Pittsburgh Steelers).

1948 WORLD CHAMPIONSHIP PROFESSIONAL FOOTBALL GAME

(Shibe Park, Philadelphia, Pa., Dec. 19)
Attendance 36,309

Philadelphia Eagles (7)	Chicago Cardinals (0)
Green—L.E.	Cochran—L.E.
MacDowell—L.T.	Zimny—L.T.
Maronic—L.G.	Ramsey—L.G.
Lindskog—C.	Banonis—C.
Kilroy—R.G.	Andros—R.G.
Wistert—R.T.	Bulger—R.T.
Armstrong—R.E.	Clatt—R.E.
Thompson—Q.B.	Davis—Q.B.
Steele—L.H.	Trippi—L.H.
Craft—R.H.	Angsman—R.H.
Muha—F.B.	Harder—F.B.

Philadelphia Eagles	0	0	0	7—7
Chicago Cardinals	0	0	0	0—0

Touchdown—Van Buren.
Point after touchdown—Patton.
Coaches—Earle Neale (Philadelphia), James Conzelman (Chicago).

SUBSTITUTIONS

Eagles—Ends: Ferrante, Humbert, Pihos; tackles: Sears, Douglas, Savitsky; guards: Patton, Gianelli; center: Wojciechowicz; backs: Van Buren, Pritchard, Myers, McHugh.
Cardinals—Ends: Kutner, Ravensberg, Dewell, Goldman; tackles: Coomer, Szot, Loepfe; guards: Colhouer, Nichols, Apolskis; center: Blackburn; backs: Mallouf,

THE CHAMPIONSHIP GAME OF 1948 WAS PLAYED UNDER THE MOST ATROCIOUS CONDITIONS IMAGINABLE. A SWIRLING BLIZZARD BLEW SNOW THROUGHOUT THE GAME, BLANKETING SHIBE PARK, WIPING OUT LINE MARKERS AND EVERYTHING ELSE. THIS IS STEVE VAN BUREN OF THE EAGLES SCORING THE ONLY TOUCHDOWN WHICH GAVE PHILADELPHIA THE TITLE, 7–0.

Dimancheff, Schwall, Goldberg, Yablonski.

Officials: Referee—Ronald Gibbs. Umpire—Sam Wilson. Head Linesman—Charles Berry. Field Judge—William F. McHugh. Back Judge—Robert C. Austin.

THE GAME

This championship has been described as having taken place in "Blizzard Bowl," the "Arctic Bowl" and otherwise in the worst conditions ever provided by nature for a football game. The field was covered with snow, the line markers were invisible, and one of the worst storms in Philadelphia history raged through the game. Referee Ronald Gibbs and his crew did a remarkable job of officiating under almost impossible conditions.

The 36,309 true fanatics who sat through the game saw the two teams struggle back and forth through the arctic conditions until Frank Kilroy recovered quarterback Ray Mallouf's fumble on the Cardinal 17-yard line in the fourth period after three scoreless sessions. It was now or never for the Eagles and they powered across for the touchdown, Steve Van Buren smashing 5 yards to score. Cliff Patton kicked the extra point to end the scoring.

The gross receipts (including radio, television and motion picture rights) were $223,622.25, of which each Eagle received $1,540.84, each Cardinals $874.39. This left a pool of $10,985.62 for members of the sectional second-place clubs (Washington Redskins and Chicago Bears).

1949 WORLD CHAMPIONSHIP PROFESSIONAL FOOTBALL GAME

(Los Angeles Memorial Coliseum, Los Angeles, Cal., Dec. 18) Attendance 27,980

Philadelphia Eagles (14)	Los Angeles Rams (0)
Ferrante—L.E.	Fears—L.E.
Sears—L.T.	Huffman—L.T.
Patton—L.G.	Dean—L.G.
Lindskog—C.	Martin—C.
Kilroy—R.G.	Yagiello—R.G.
Wistert—R.T.	Bouley—R.T.
Pihos—R.E.	Smyth—R.E.
Thompson—Q.B.	Waterfield—Q.B.
Van Buren—L.H.	Kalmanir—L.H.
Scott—R.H.	Smith, V. T.—R.H.
Myers—F.B.	Hoerner—F.B.

Philadelphia Eagles	0	7	7	0–14
Los Angeles Rams	0	0	0	0– 0

Touchdowns—Pihos, Skladany.
Points after touchdown—Patton 2.
Coaches—Earle Neal (Philadelphia),
   Clark Shaughnessy (Los Angeles).

SUBSTITUTIONS

Philadelphia Eagles—Ends: Armstrong,
   Skladany; tackles: Savitsky, McDowell,
   Jarmoluk; guards: Gianelli, Magee,
   Barnes, Maronic; centers: Wojciechowicz,
   Bednarik; backs: Reagen, Ziegler, Craft,
   Pritchard, Parmer, McHugh, Muha,
   Kish.
Los Angeles Rams—Ends: Fears, Hubbell,
   Currivan, Zilly, Shaw, Keane: tackles:
   Sparkman, Champagne; guards: Finlay,
   Lazetich; centers: Naumetz, Paul; backs:
   Van Brocklin, Gehrke, Hirsch, Younger,
   Williams, Sims, Cowhig.
Officials: Referee—Ronald Gibbs. Umpire—
   Joseph Crowley. Head Linesman—Charles
   Berry. Field Judge—William F. McHugh.
   Back Judge—Robert C. Austin.

WHILE CIVIC LEADERS BLUSHED OVER THE
DRENCHING RAINSTORM AT LOS ANGELES COL-
ISEUM, THE PHILADELPHIA EAGLES WON THEIR
SECOND STRAIGHT CHAMPIONSHIP BY BEATING
THE RAMS 14–0 FOR THE 1949 TITLE. THIS
IS STEVE VAN BUREN OF THE EAGLES CHUG-
GING THROUGH THE MUD FOR ONE OF HIS
CUSTOMARY GAINS.

THE GAME

Drenching rain on this first time the
Rams had played a home game under any
but the best weather conditions held the
crowd down though the Philadelphia Eagles
invaded the West Coast strutting a record
of eleven victories, marred by only one loss
to the Chicago Bears. The Rams had won
eight, lost two and tied two. It was not a
day for passing, a fact which hampered Bob
Waterfield, throwing ace of the Rams, and
added potency to the ground power of the
Eagles, spearheaded by Steve Van Buren.

The game was scoreless until midway
in the second quarter when Tommy
Thompson, Eagle quarterback, threw one
of his few passes and connected with end
Pete Pihos for 31 yards and a touchdown.
Cliff Patton converted and the defending
champions led 7–0.

Late in the third period, Waterfield,
attempting a punt from his own five,
slipped, and the kick was blocked by Ed
Skladany, who grabbed the loose ball for
a touchdown. Patton again converted and
this ended the scoring.

The gross receipts (including radio)
were $149,344.80, of which each Eagle re-
ceived $1094.68, each Ram $739.66. This
left a pool of $7,754.12 for members of the
sectional second-place clubs (Chicago Bears
and Pittsburgh).

1950 WORLD CHAMPIONSHIP PROFESSIONAL FOOTBALL GAME

**(Cleveland Municipal Stadium,
Cleveland, Ohio, Dec. 24)
Attendance 29,751**

Cleveland Browns (30)	Los Angeles Rams (28)
Speedie—L.E.	Fears—L.E.
Groza—L.T.	Huffman—L.T.
Humble—L.G.	Finlay—L.G.
Gatski—C.	Naumetz—C.
Houston—R.G.	Thompson—R.G.
Rymkus—R.T.	Reinhard—R.T.
Lavelli—R.E.	Zilly—R.E.
Graham—Q.B.	Waterfield—Q.B.
Bumgardner—L.H.	Davis, G.—L.H.
Jones, W.—R.H.	Smith, V. T.—R.H.
Motley—F.B.	Hoerner—F.B.

Cleveland Browns	7	6	7	10—30
Los Angeles Rams	14	0	14	0—28

Touchdowns—Jones, Lavelli 2, Bumgard-
   ner, Davis, Hoerner 2, Brink.
Field Goal—Groza.
Points after touchdown—Groza 3, Water-
   field 4.
Coaches—Paul Brown (Cleveland), Joe
   Stydahar (Los Angeles).

SUBSTITUTIONS

Browns—Ends: Young, Martin, Gillom,
   Ford; tackles: Palmer, Grigg, Kissell,

Sandusky; guards: Willis, Gibron, Agase; centers: Herring, Thompson; backs: Gorgal, Carpenter, Cole, Adamle, Lahr, James, Lewis, Moselle, Phelps.

Rams—Ends: Boyd, Brink, Smyth, Hirsch; tackles: Champagne, Bouley, guards: Stephenson, West, Vasicek, Lazetich; centers: Paul, Statuto; backs: Lewis, Towler, Williams, Barry, Keane, Kalmanir, Pasquariello, Van Brocklin, Younger.

Officials: Referee—Ronald Gibbs. Umpire—Samuel Wilson. Head Linesman—Charles Berry. Field Judge—Lloyd Brazil. Back Judge—Norman Duncan.

THE GAME

Treacherous, icy footing could not slow the action of this sixty minutes of mayhem at Cleveland Municipal Stadium. Both teams had won their divisional tie play-offs the week before, the Browns beating the Giants 8–3 after losing to them twice during the season; the Rams knocking out the Bears 24–14 after losing two to the Chicago club.

With efficient lines, evenly matched, this shaped up as a passing duel pitting Otto Graham, quarterback of the Browns, against Bob Waterfield and Norman Van Brocklin, throwing for the Rams; and as a goal kicking duel between Lou Groza of the Browns and the versatile Waterfield.

Only 27 seconds after the kick-off, Waterfield threw to Glenn Davis for 82 yards and a touchdown and converted for 7–0. Graham came right back with a completion to William "Dub" Jones and Groza converted to tie, 7–7. The Rams went ahead again, 14–7, when Hoerner plunged 3 yards to score and Waterfield converted.

In the second quarter, Graham threw another TD to Dante Lavelli, but the attempt at conversion failed when the pass from center was juggled and the Rams still led, 14–13.

Early in the second half, Graham again passed to Lavelli for a score and Groza's conversion made it 20–14. Dick Hoerner's one-yard plunge and Waterfield's conversion put the Rams ahead 21–20, and, seconds later, Larry Brink picked up Motley's fumble on the Brown 6 to score again. Waterfield converted and it was 28–20.

Graham put the Browns back in the game in the last quarter with a TD pitch to

LOU GROZA, TOP PLACE KICKER OF ALL TIME, SCORED A FIELD GOAL WITH TWENTY-EIGHT SECONDS TO GO TO WIN THE 1950 CHAMPIONSHIP TITLE FOR CLEVELAND.

Rex Bumgardner and Groza converted for 28–27. An interception gave the Browns the ball in the closing minutes and, from the 16-yard line, with twenty-eight seconds remaining, Lou Groza booted a 3-pointer to win the game for the Browns 30–28.

The gross receipts (including radio) were $157,078.00, of which each Brown received $1,113.16, each Ram $686.44. This left a pool of $7,627.21 for members of the sectional second-place clubs (Chicago Bears and New York Giants).

1951 WORLD CHAMPIONSHIP PROFESSIONAL FOOTBALL GAME

(Los Angeles Coliseum, Los Angeles, Cal., Dec. 23)
Attendance 59,475

Los Angeles Rams (24)	Cleveland Browns (17)
Fears—L.E.	Speedie—L.E.
Simensen—L.T.	Groza—L.T.
Daugherty—L.G.	Gibron—L.G.
McLaughlin—C.	Gatski—C.
Lange—R.G.	Gaudio—R.G.
Dahms—R.T.	Rymkus—R.T.
Hirsch—R.E.	Lavelli—R.E.

VERDA SMITH, THE RAM WITH THE BALL, THINKS EVERYONE FROM THE CITY OF CLEVE-
LAND IS OUT THERE IN FRONT OF HIM AS THE CLEVELAND BROWNS DEFENSE CLOSES
IN. THE RAMS WON THE CHAMPIONSHIP IN THIS CONTEST OF 1951 BY A 24–17 SCORE.

Waterfield—Q.B.   Graham—Q.B.
Towler—L.H.   Carpenter—L.H.
Younger—R.H.   Jones, W.—R.H.
Hoerner—F.B.   Motley—F.B.

Los Angeles Rams   0   7   7 10—24
Cleveland Browns   0 10   0   7—17

Touchdowns—Hoerner, Towler, Fears,
Jones, Carpenter.
Field Goals—Waterfield, Groza.
Points after touchdown—Waterfield 3,
Groza 2.
Coaches: Paul Brown (Cleveland), Joseph
Stydahar (Los Angeles).

SUBSTITUTIONS

Los Angeles—Ends: Brink, Hecker, Keane,
Robustelli, Boyd; tackles: Winkler, Too-
good, Halliday; guards: West, Finlay,
Thompson, Collier; center: Paul, Reid;
backs: Van Brocklin, G. Davis, Williams,
Johnson, V. Smith, Kalmanir, Lewis,
Rich.
Cleveland—Ends: Young, Gillom, Ford,
Oristaglio; tackles: Kissell, Palmer, San-
dusky, Grigg; guards: Thompson, Agase,
Willis, Houston; center: Herring; backs:
Lewis, Shula, Lahr, Bumgardner, James,
Taseff, Adamle, Cole, Jagade.
Officials: Referee—Ronald Gibbs. Umpire—
Carl Brubaker. Head Linesman—Dan
Tehan. Field Judge—William McHugh.
Back Judge—Robert Austin.

THE GAME

The largest crowd in professional football history (59,475) watched in ideal
weather conditions as the Los Angeles
Rams, after losing the last two championship play-offs, finally beat the Browns for
the first time to win the title. It was the
first time the defending champions had
ever lost a championship after four victorious years in the All America Football Conference and one in the NFL.

After a scoreless first period, Waterfield drove the Rams to the Cleveland one-
yard line, completing two passes on the
way, then gave the ball to Dick Hoerner
who plowed over. Waterfield converted.

Cleveland got its first three points from
a towering 52-yard field goal by Lou Groza,
the longest in championship history but
4 yards short of the all-time big one of 56
yards kicked by Albert Rechichar. The
Browns scored again in the second quarter
on a 17-yard pass from Graham to William
"Dub" Jones and Groza converted to make
the score 10–7 at the half.

The Rams went ahead, 14–10 in the
third period after Larry Brink's crashing
tackle of Graham produced a fumble. The
ball was picked up and hurried to the

Brown one-yard line by Andy Robustelli. Dan Towler banged over for the touchdown and Waterfield converted.

The Browns pulled even early in the fourth period after Waterfield's 17-yard field goal had put the Rams ahead 17–10. They traveled 70 yards with the last one-yard plunge by Ken Carpenter bagging the vital points. Groza again scored the extra point.

Norman Van Brocklin, quarterbacking the Rams through most of the second half, then fired a long pass to Tom Fears behind the Brown defense for a 73-yard touchdown play which proved to be the winner. Waterfield booted his third extra point and the Rams held solidly against the Brown's frantic efforts to get the game even once more.

The gross receipts (including radio and television) were $325,970, of which each Ram received $2,108.44, each Brown $1,483.12. This left a pool of $15,655.14 for members of the sectional second-place clubs (Detroit Lions and New York Giants). All these financial scores were new records.

1952 WORLD CHAMPIONSHIP PROFESSIONAL FOOTBALL GAME

(Played at Cleveland Stadium, Cleveland, Dec. 28)
Attendance 50,934

Detroit Lions (17)	Cleveland Browns (7)
Box—L.E.	Brewster—L.E.
Miller—L.T.	Groza—L.T.
Creekmur—L.G.	Gibron—L.G.
Banonis—C.	Gatski—C
Martin—R.G.	Skibinski—R.G.
Cifelli—R.T.	Sandusky—R.T.
Hart—R.E.	Lavelli—R.E.
Layne—Q.B.	Graham—Q.B.
Walker—L.H.	Carpenter—L.H.
Hoernschemeyer—R.H.	Bumgardner—R.H.
Harder—F.B.	Jagade—F.B.

Detroit Lions	0	7	7	3—17
Cleveland Browns	0	0	7	0— 7

Touchdowns—Layne, Walker (Detroit), Jagade (Cleveland).

Field Goal—Harder (Detroit).

Extra Points—Harder 2 (Detroit); Groza 1 (Cleveland).

Coaches: Raymond Parker (Detroit); Paul Brown (Cleveland).

SUBSTITUTIONS

Detroit—Ends: Doran, Earon, Swiacki; tackles: McGraw, Prchlik; guards: Campbell, Flanagan, Bingaman; center: Torgeson; backs: Lary, Christiansen, Bailey, Cline, Hill, Dublinski, David, Doll, Smith.

Cleveland—Ends: Young, Ford, Gillom; tackles: Helluin, Palmer, Gain; guards: Houston, Willis, Sharkey; centers: Thompson, Herring; backs: Rechichar, Lahr, Renfro, Michaels, Motley, James, Shula.

Officials—Referee, Thomas Timlin; Umpire, Samuel Wilson; Head Linesman, Charles Berry; Field Judge, Lloyd Brazil; Back Judge, John Hamer; alternates, Carl Rebele, John Glascott.

THE GAME

After a scoreless first period, Layne drove the Lions from midfield early in the second and scored the touchdown himself from the 2-yard line. Harder converted. Groza tried and missed field goals from the 44 and 47 and there was no other scoring in the first half.

Doak Walker broke loose for a 67 yard romp and a touchdown in the third period and Harder's second conversion put Detroit ahead 14–0. Cleveland sent Jagade over on a 7-yard smash and Groza converted to go into the fourth period 14–7. The Browns had been as close as Detroit's 5-yard line but were stopped by a solid defense.

Martin recovered a Cleveland fumble in the fourth and Harder booted a 36 yard field goal for the final score. The Detroit defense again halted the Browns inside the 10 to end the game 17–7.

The gross receipts (including radio and TV) were $314,318, of which each Lion received $2,274.77, each Brown $1,712.49. This left a pool of $17,404.51 for members of the sectional second place clubs (Los Angeles, Philadelphia, New York).

1953 WORLD CHAMPIONSHIP PROFESSIONAL FOOTBALL GAME

(Played at Briggs Stadium, Detroit, Dec. 27)
Attendance 54,577

Detroit Lions (17)	Cleveland Browns (16)
Dibble—L.E.	Brewster—L.E.
Creekmur—L.T.	Groza—L.T.

PAT HARDER, WITH BOBBY LAYNE HOLDING, BOOTS A 36-YARD FIELD GOAL IN THE FOURTH PERIOD OF THE 1952 CHAMPIONSHIP GAME TO PUT DETROIT OUT IN FRONT OF CLEVELAND, 17–7. PART OF THE HOLDING OPERATION WAS AN INTERCEPTION OF AN OTTO GRAHAM PASS BY JIM DAVID IN THE PICTURE BELOW.

Wide World Photo

JIM DORAN OF THE DETROIT LIONS GETS HIS HANDS ON A PASS, GOOD FOR 25 YARDS, IN THE FIRST PERIOD OF THE 1953 CHAMPIONSHIP GAME. HE ALSO GETS THE HAND OF KEN GORGAL (15), OF THE CLEVELAND BROWNS, IN HIS FACE. AT LEFT IS WARREN LAHR OF THE BROWNS. THE LIONS WON 17–16.

Sewell—L.G.	Gibron—L.G.
Banonis—C.	Gatski—C.
Stanfel—R.G.	Noll—R.G.
Spencer—R.T.	Sandusky—R.T.
Hart—R.E.	Lavelli—R.E.
Layne—Q.B.	Graham—Q.B.
Walker—L.H.	Carpenter—L.H.
Gedman—R.H.	Reynolds—R.H.
Hoernschemeyer—F.B.	Jagade—F.B.

Detroit Lions	7	3	0	7–17
Cleveland Browns	0	3	7	6–16

Touchdowns—Walker, Doran (Detroit), Jagade (Cleveland).
Conversions—Walker 2 (Detroit), Groza (Cleveland).
Field Goals—Walker (Detroit), Groza 3 (Cleveland).

SUBSTITUTIONS

Detroit—Ends: Doran, Gandee, Cain; tackles: McGraw, Miller, Prchlik; guards: Bingaman, Martin, Schmidt; centers: Ane, Torgeson; backs: Christiansen, Carpenter, Cline, David, Karilivacz, Girard, Lary, J. R. Smith.

Cleveland—Ends: Ford, Young, Atkins, Gillom; tackles: Colo, Palmer, Steinbrunner, Helluin; guards: Houston, Donaldson, Willis; center: Catlin; backs: Gorgal, Ratterman, Konz, Lahr, Renfro, Howard, Michaels, Motley, James.

Officials—Referee, Ronald Gibbs; Umpire, Samuel Wilson; Back Judge, James Hamer; Head Linesman, Dan Tehan; Field Judge, Carl Rebele.

THE GAME

LaVern Torgeson of Detroit knocked the ball out of the hands of Otto Graham early in the first period. Bingaman recovered for Detroit on the Cleveland 13 and Doak Walker soon scored from the one. Walker added the extra point. In the second period Groza kicked a 13-yard field goal for Cleveland and Walker booted one for Detroit from the 23. The Lions led, 10–3 at the half.

Harry Jagade scored Cleveland's only touchdown from nine yards out in the third period and Groza added the extra point to tie the game. Groza kicked two more field goals in the fourth period, from the 15 and 43 yard lines and Cleveland was winning, 16–10, with 2½ minutes to play. Layne then hit four of six passes, the last a 33-yarder to Jim Doran for the touchdown. Walker's conversion put the Lions ahead, 17–16. Karilivacz intercepted Graham's first pass after the kickoff and the Lions ran out the clock for the victory.

The gross receipts (including radio and TV) were $358,693.00 of which each Lion received $2,424.10, each Brown $1,-654.26. This left a pool of $18,840.25 for members of the sectional second place clubs (Philadelphia and San Francisco).

1954 WORLD CHAMPIONSHIP PROFESSIONAL FOOTBALL GAME

(Played in Cleveland Stadium, Cleveland, Dec. 26, 1954)
Attendance 43,827

Cleveland Browns (56)	Detroit Lions (10)
Brewster—L.E.	Dibble—L.E.
Groza—L.T.	Creekmur—L.T.
Gibron—L.G.	Sewell—L.G.
Gatski—C.	Miketa—C.
Noll—R.G.	Martin—R.G.
Sandusky—R.T.	Ane—R.T.
Lavelli—R.E.	Girard—R.E.
Graham—Q.B.	Layne—Q.B.
Renfro—L.H.	Walker—L.H.
Reynolds—R.H.	Carpenter—R.H.
Bassett—F.B.	Bowman—F.B.

Cleveland Browns	14	21	14	7—56
Detroit Lions	3	7	0	0—10

Touchdowns—Renfro 2, Brewster, Graham 3, Morrison, Hanulak (Cleveland), Bowman (Detroit).
Conversions—Groza 8 (Cleveland), Walker (Detroit).
Field Goal—Walker (Detroit).

SUBSTITUTIONS

Cleveland—Ends: Massey, Ford, Atkins, Gillom; tackles: Kissell, Gain, Colo; guards: McCormack, Forester, Bradley; center: Catlin; backs: Konz, Hanulak, Lahr, Paul, James, Jones, Morrison, Michaels.
Detroit—Ends: Dove, Gandee, Doran, Cain,

END OF A BRILLIANT CAREER—OTTO GRAHAM (14), FINE QUARTERBACK OF THE CLEVELAND BROWNS FOR MANY YEARS, CARRIES AGAINST THE LOS ANGELES RAMS IN THE CHAMPIONSHIP GAME OF 1955. RAM (65) IS ART HAUSER. GRAHAM TOSSED TOUCHDOWN PASSES TO RAY RENFRO AND DANTE LAVELLI, AND SCORED TWO MORE HIMSELF TO LEAD THE BROWNS TO THE TITLE, 38-14. IT WAS GRAHAM'S LAST GAME IN THE NATIONAL FOOTBALL LEAGUE.

Hart, Turner, Box; tackles: Mains, Mc-Graw, Miller, Perry; guards: Stanfel, Torgeson, Bingaman; center: Schmidt; backs: Dublinski, Christiansen, David, Stits, Hoernschemeyer, Smith, Karilivacz. Officials—Referee, Thomas Timlin; Umpire, Samuel Wilson; Head Linesman, Dan Tehan; Back Judge, James Hamer; Field Judge, William McHugh.

THE GAME

Doak Walker kicked a 36-yard field goal to open the scoring. Graham tossed touchdown passes to Renfro and Brewster in the same period and Groza's conversion made it 14–3. Graham scored two more in the second himself and passed to Brewster for another. Groza collected all the extra points. Bowman scored one for Detroit and Walker converted for the Lion's last score. It was 35–10 at the half.

Graham crashed over for another as the third half opened and Morrison plowed 13 yards for the Brown's seventh TD in the third period. In the final period Hanulak scored the final and Groza completed eight conversions.

The gross receipts (including radio and TV) were $289,126.43 of which each Brown got $2,478.57, each Lion, $1,585.63. This left a pool of $18,452.42 for members of the sectional second place clubs (Philadelphia and Chicago Bears).

1955 WORLD CHAMPIONSHIP PROFESSIONAL FOOTBALL GAME

(Played in Los Angeles Coliseum, Los Angeles, Dec. 26)
Attendance 85,693

Cleveland Browns (38)	Los Angeles Rams (14)
Brewster—L.E.	Fears—L.E.
Groza—L.T.	Cross—L.T.
Gibron—L.G.	Putnam—L.G.
Gatski—C.	McLaughlin—C.
Bradley—R.G.	Hock—R.G.
McCormack—R.T.	Toogood—R.T.
Lavelli—R.E.	Hirsch—R.E.
Graham—Q.B.	Van Brocklin—Q.B.
Renfro—L.H.	Waller—L.H.
Morrison—R.H.	Quinlan—R.H.
Modzelewski—F.B.	Towler—F.B.

Cleveland Browns	3	14	14	7—38
Los Angeles	0	7	0	7—14

Touchdowns—Graham 2, Renfro, Paul, La-velli (Cleveland), Quinlan, Waller (Los Angeles).
Conversions—Groza 5 (Cleveland), Richter 2 (Los Angeles).
Field Goal—Groza (Cleveland).

SUBSTITUTIONS

Cleveland—Ends: Massey, Weber, Ford, Gillom; tackles: Colo, Sandusky; guards: Gain, Forester; centers: Noll, Palumbo; backs: Ratterman, Lahr, Konz, Smith, Paul, James, Petitbon, Jones, Michaels, Bassett, Perini.

Los Angeles—Ends: Boyd, Miller, Robustelli, Fuller, Lewis; tackles: McFadin, Lipscomb, Holtzman, Hauser; guards: Ellena, Paul, Fournet, Richter; centers: Griffin, Morris; backs: Wade, McCormick, Hughes, Sherman, Burroughs, Cason.

Officials—Referee, Ronald Gibbs; Umpire, Samuel Wilson; Head Linesman, Dan Tehan; Field Judge, William McHugh; Back Judge, Tay Brown.

THE GAME

Groza's 26-yard field goal was the only scoring in the first quarter. Early in the second, Paul intercepted Van Brocklin's pass and ran 65 yards for a touchdown and Groza made it 10–0. On Los Angeles' second play after the kickoff, Van Brocklin threw a 67-yard touchdown to Quinlan and Richter made it 10–7. Late in the half Graham tossed a 50-yard score to Lavelli and Groza converted.

Graham himself scored two touchdowns for Cleveland in the third period and threw another to Renfro in the fourth. Waller scored Los Angeles final TD on a 4-yard run and Richter made it 38–14, the final score. Cleveland had intercepted six of Van Brocklin's passes.

The gross receipts (including radio and TV) were $504,257.00 of which each Brown got $3,508.21 and each Ram received $2,316.26. This left a pool of $27,-666.46 for members of the sectional second place clubs (Washington and Chicago Bears).

1956 WORLD CHAMPIONSHIP PROFESSIONAL FOOTBALL GAME

(Played in Yankee Stadium, New York City, Dec. 30)

New York Giants (47)	Chicago Bears (7)
Rote—L.E.	Jack Hoffman—L.E.

MEL TRIPLETT, NEW YORK GIANT FULLBACK, KNOCKED OVER EVERYTHING EXCEPT YANKEE STADIUM SCORING THIS FIRST TOUCHDOWN AGAINST THE CHICAGO BEARS IN THE 1956 TITLE GAME. THE OFFICIAL HERE IS ABOUT TO BITE THE DUST (WHICH WAS FROZEN SOLID) AS TRIPLETT SMASHES FOR 17 YARDS AND A TOUCHDOWN. THE FUTILE BEARS ARE RAY SMITH (20), J. C. CAROLINE (25), AND MC NEIL MOORE (29). ALEX WEBSTER, GIANT HALFBACK (29) IN WHITE, GOES ALONG FOR MORAL SUPPORT.

Brown—L.T.	Williams—L.T.
Austin—L.G.	George—L.G.
Wietecha—C.	Hansen—C.
Stroud—R.G.	Fortunato—R.G.
Yelvington—R.T.	Bishop—R.T.
MacAfee—R.E.	Meadows—R.E.
Heinrich—Q.B.	Blanda—Q.B.
Gifford—L.H.	Caroline—L.H.
Webster—R.H.	Moore—R.H.
Triplett—F.B.	Wallace—F.B.

New York Giants	13	21	6	7–47
Chicago Bears	0	7	0	0– 7

Touchdowns—Webster 2, Triplett, Rote, H. Moore, Gifford (New York), Casares (Chicago).

Conversions—Agajanian 5 (New York), Blanda (Chicago).

Field Goals—Agajanian 2 (New York).

SUBSTITUTIONS

New York—Ends: Schnelker, Yowarsky, Robustelli, Katcavage; tackles: Modzelewski, Grier; guards: Beck, Huth, Huff; center: Livingston; backs: Tunnell, Hughes, Filipski, Nolan, Patton, Moore, Svoboda, Svare, Chandler.

Chicago Bears—Ends: Atkins, Hill, Dooley, Helwig, McColl, Schroeder; tackles: Mellekas, Wrightkin, Brackett, Gilbert; guards: Clark, Jones, Roggeman; centers: Strickland, Klawitter; backs: Brown, Watkins, Smith, John Hoffman, Bingham, Moore.

Officials—Referee, William Downes; Umpire, Samuel Wilson; Head Linesman, Cleo Diehl; Back Judge, Don Looney; Field Judge, George Rennix.

THE GAME

Triplett smashed 17 yards over the icy ground for the first New York touchdown and Agajanian scored the first of five conversions. The Giants recovered Casares' fumble on the Bear's 15 and Agajanian kicked the first of two field goals from the 17. He kicked the other still in the first period after Patton intercepted Brown's pass. This one was from the 43 yard line.

In the second period Webster crashed over from the 3 and the Bears got their only touchdown when Casares scored from 9 yards out. Webster racked up another on a one-yard plunge. The Giants made it 34–7 at the half when Moore recovered Brown's punt in the end zone after it was blocked by Beck.

Conerly passed to Rote for a 9-yard

touchdowner in the third period and tossed one 14 yards to Gifford in the final period to complete the scoring, at 47–7.

The gross receipts (including radio and TV) were $517,385.00 of which each Giant got $3,779.19 and each Bear $2,485.16. This left a pool of $28,483.81 for members of the sectional second place teams (Detroit and Chicago Cardinals).

1957 WORLD CHAMPIONSHIP PROFESSIONAL FOOTBALL GAME

(Played in Briggs Stadium, Detroit, Dec. 29)
Attendance 55,263

Detroit Lions (59)	Cleveland Browns (14)
Doran—L.E.	Brewster—L.E.
Creekmur—L.T.	Groza—L.T.
Sewell—L.G.	Forester—L.G.
Gatski—C.	Hunter—C.
Campbell—R.G.	Robinson—R.G.
Russell—R.T.	McCormack—R.T.
Junker—R.E.	P. Carpenter—R.E.
Rote—Q.B.	O'Connell—Q.B.
Gedman—L.H.	Renfro—L.H.
Cassady—R.H.	L. Carpenter—R.H.
Johnson—F.B.	Brown—F.B.

Detroit Lions	17	14	14	14–59
Cleveland Browns	0	7	7	0–14

Touchdowns—Rote, Gedman, Junker 2, Barr, Doran, Middleton, Cassady (Detroit), Brown, L. Carpenter, (Cleveland). Conversions—Martin 8 (Detroit), Groza 2 (Cleveland). Field Goal—Martin, 31 yards (Detroit).

SUBSTITUTIONS
Detroit—Ends: Dibble, Middleton, Long, McCord; tackles: Perry, Miller, Krouse, Mains, Ane; guards: Gordy, Cronin, Schmidt, Martin; center: Zatkoff; backs: Reichow, Karilivacz, Christiansen, David, Lary, Barr, Lowe, Tracy, Hart.
Cleveland—Ends: Ford, Clarke, Quinlan, Wiggin; tackles: Jordan, Colo; guards: Gain, Smith; centers: Catlin, Costello; backs: Plum, Campbell, Reynolds, Hanulak, Wren, Lahr, Konz, Paul, Freeman, Michaels, Modzelewski, Fiss.
Officials—Referee, Ronald Gibbs; Umpire, Joseph Connell; Head Linesman, Dan Tehan; Field Judge, Don Looney; Back Judge, Cleo Diehl.

THE GAME
Detroit, playing without quarterback Bobby Layne, whose leg had been broken in a recent game, dominated this contest from start to finish. Martin scored first with a 31-yard field goal. Rote smashed through center for 1-yard and the first touchdown and Gedman got another in the first period on a one-yard thrust.

Brown raced 17 yards around end early in the second period for the first Cleveland score and Groza converted. However, Detroit came back with two more, the first a 26-yard pass from Rote to Junker on a fake field goal play, the second when Barr intercepted a Plum pass on Cleveland's 19 and raced over. It was 31–7 at the half.

Lew Carpenter got Cleveland's other touchdown in the third quarter and Groza made the extra point. Detroit came back with two more in this period. Rote passed from his own 22 to Doran who went all the way for 78 yards, second longest pass touchdown in championship history. Rote threw a 23-yarder for the next.

Rote opened the fourth quarter with a touchdown strike to Middleton over the goal from Cleveland's 23. Later, Reichow, quarterbacking for the Lions, tossed 16 yards to Cassady for Detroit's eighth touchdown. Martin completed all the conversion attempts and the final score was 59–14.

The gross receipts (including radio and TV) were $593,967.50 of which each Lion got $4,295.41 and each Brown $2,750.30. This left a pool of $33,570.78 for members of the sectional second place teams (San Francisco and New York).

1958 WORLD CHAMPIONSHIP PROFESSIONAL FOOTBALL GAME

(Played in Yankee Stadium, New York, Dec. 28)
Attendance 64,185

Baltimore Colts (23)	New York Giants (17)
Berry—L.E.	Rote—L.E.
Parker—L.T.	Brown—L.T.
Spinney—L.G.	Barry—L.G.
Nutter—C.	Wietecha—C.
Sandusky—R.G.	Mischak—R.G.
Preas—R.T.	Youso—R.T.
Mutscheller—R.E.	Schnelker—R.E.
Unitas—Q.B.	Heinrich—Q.B.
Dupre—L.H.	Gifford—L.H.
Moore—R.H.	Webster—R.H.
Ameche—F.B.	Triplett—F.B.

Baltimore Colts	0	14	0	3	6–23
New York Giants	3	0	7	7	0–17

World Wide Photo

HAPPY DAYS FOR THE NEW YORK GIANTS CAME THROUGH 1956 AND 1958 AND 1959. AND THESE THREE WERE THE BACKS TO CARRY THE TEAM INTO THREE CHAMPIONSHIP GAMES. ALEX WEBSTER, LEFT, CHARLES CONERLY, CENTER, AND FRANK GIFFORD BECAME NATION-WIDE HEROES, WELL KNOWN TO EVERY FOOTBALL FAN. IN 1960, INJURIES TOOK THEM ALL OUT OF THE LINE-UP FOR LONG PERIODS AND THE GIANTS DROPPED OUT OF FIRST PLACE.

Touchdowns—Ameche 2, Berry, (Baltimore), Triplett, Gifford, (New York).

Conversions—Myhra 2, (Baltimore), Summerall 2, (New York).

Field Goals—Myhra (20 yards), (Baltimore), Summerall (36 yards), (New York).

SUBSTITUTIONS

Baltimore—Ends: Marchetti, Braase, Joyce; tackles: Donovan, Lipscomb, Krouse; guards: Thurston, Spinney, Plunkett; centers: Shinnick, Sanford; quarterbacks: Shaw, Brown, Rechichar; halfbacks: Taseff, Simpson, Nelson, Sample, Davis, Call, DeCarlo, Lyles; fullbacks: Pellington, Pricer.

New York—Ends: Livingston, Katcavage, Summerall, Robustelli, MacAfee, Svare; tackles: Modzelewski, Grier, Stroud; guards: Brackett, Guy; center: Huff; quarterbacks: Conerly, Tunnell; halfbacks: Crow, Hughes, Maynard, Crow, Lott, King, Patton, Karilivacz; fullbacks: Svoboda, Chandler.

Officials—Referee: Ron Gibbs (St. Thomas). Umpire: Lou Palazzi (Penn State). Head Linesman: Charlie Berry (Lafayette). Field Judge: Charlie Sweeney (Notre Dame). Back Judge: Cleo Diehl (Northwestern).

THE GAME

Half of the opening quarter elapsed before Baltimore registered the game's initial first down, via a 60-yard Unitas to Moore pass play to New York's 25. Myhra's fourth-down field goal attempt from the 27 was blocked by Huff.

Gifford's sweep of 38 yards around left end helped move the Giants from their 27 to the Colt's 29. Summerall's fourth-down field goal from the 36 at 12:58 of the first period made it: New York 3, Baltimore 0.

Krouse recovered Gifford's fumble on the New York 20 on the first play of the second quarter. Five consecutive running

Wide World Photo

THIS SEQUENCE TELLS THE STORY OF THE KEY SITUATION DURING THE OVERTIME PERIOD
IN THE BALTIMORE COLTS-NEW YORK GIANTS PRO CHAMPIONSHIP GAME AT YANKEE
STADIUM IN 1958. TOP: QUARTERBACK JOHN UNITAS OF COLTS HAS BALL IN THIRD-DOWN
PLAY STARTING FROM THE COLTS' 36-YARD LINE, 15 YARDS TO GO. UNITAS IS WAVING
HIS LEFT ARM, MOTIONING END RAY BERRY TO MOVE FARTHER DOWNFIELD. CENTER:
UNITAS, STILL TAKING HIS TIME, WAVES AGAIN TO BERRY, TELLING HIM TO KEEP MOVING.
THEN HE THREW THE PASS. BOTTOM: BERRY CATCHES THE BALL IN FRONT OF THE GIANTS'
BENCH, ON NEW YORK'S 43-YARD LINE, FOR A 21-YARD GAIN AND A CRITICAL FIRST DOWN.
SIX PLAYS LATER BALTIMORE SCORED TO WIN.

ALAN AMECHE (35) OF THE COLTS PLUNGES OVER THE GIANTS' LINE FOR THE WINNING
TOUCHDOWN IN THE 1958 CHAMPIONSHIP GAME. THE FINAL SCORE WAS 23-17.

plays produced a Baltimore touchdown, with Ameche plunging two yards for the score at 2:26. Myhra converted. Baltimore 7, New York 3.

Following Guy's recovery of Simpson's fumble on the Colt's 10, Joyce regained the ball for Baltimore on its 14 by pouncing on Gifford's bobble. Hard running by Moore and Ameche and three Unitas passes for 28 yards advanced the Colts to the Giants' 15, from which point Unitas pegged to Berry in the end zone at 13:40. Myhra converted. Baltimore 14, New York 3.

A Baltimore drive of 58 yards in the third quarter was stalled on the Giants' one, New York taking over on its five, where Ameche was stopped by Livingston on fourth down. Three plays later Conerly floated a pass to Rote, who fumbled upon being hit by Nelson on the Colts' 25—Webster scooped up the loose ball and dashed to the one. Triplett banged across for the score on second down at 11:14. Summerall added the extra point. The long gain aerial, Conerly to Rote to Webster,

covered 86 yards and set up the tally. Baltimore 14, New York 10.

New York launched a TD drive the next time it took possession of the ball on its 19. Conerly threw to Schnelker for gains of 17 and 46 yards to Baltimore's 15, then fired to Gifford for the touchdown at 0:53 of the fourth quarter. Summerall kicked the extra point, New York 17, Baltimore 14.

With less than two minutes remaining Taseff made a fair catch of Chandler's punt on Baltimore's 14. Unitas completed four of seven consecutive passes, the last three to Berry for gains of 25, 15 and 22 yards to the Giants' 13. Myhra booted a field goal from the 20 at 14:53. New York 17, Baltimore 17.

New York won the toss to start the National Football League's first sudden-death playoff and elected to receive. After three plays netted nine yards to the New York 29, Chandler punted to Taseff, who returned the ball one yard to Baltimore's 20-yard line. Unitas connected on four of five passes, two to Berry for 33 yards, as

Colts surged to Giants' one in 12 plays. Ameche shot through a gaping hole in the right side of his line to score the winning touchdown on the 13th play. No conversion was attempted and the game ended after 8:15 of the sudden-death period. Final score: Baltimore 28, New York 17.

The gross receipts (including radio and TV) were $698,646 of which each Colt got $4,718.77 and each Giant $3,111.33. This left a pool of $37,231.06 for the sectional second place teams (Cleveland and Los Angeles, Chicago Bears, the latter two tied in Western Conference).

1959 WORLD CHAMPIONSHIP PROFESSIONAL FOOTBALL GAME

(Played in Municipal Stadium, Baltimore, Md., Dec. 27) Attendance 57,545

Baltimore Colts (31)	New York Giants (16)
Berry—L.E.	Rote—L.E.
Parker—L.T.	Brown—L.T.
Spinney—L.G.	Dess—L.G.
Nutter—C.	Wietecha—C.
Sandusky—R.G.	Stroud—R.G.
Preas—R.T.	Youso—R.T.
Mutscheller—R.E.	Schnelker—R.E.
Unitas—Q.B.	Conerly—Q.B.
Sommer—L.H.	Gifford—L.H.
Moore—R.H.	Webster—R.H.
Ameche—F.B.	Triplett—F.B.

Baltimore Colts	7	0	0	24—31
New York Giants	3	3	3	7—16

Touchdowns—Moore, Unitas, Richardson, Sample (Baltimore), Schnelker (New York).
Conversions—Myhra 4 (Baltimore); Summerall (New York).
Field Goals—Myhra (25 yards) (Baltimore); Summerall 3, (23) (37) (22), (New York).

SUBSTITUTIONS

Baltimore—Ends: Marchetti, Richardson, Braase; tackles: Donovan, Plunkett, Lipscomb, Krouse; guards: Pellington, Myhra, Shinnick, Matuszak; centers: Szymanski; quarterbacks: Brown, Nelson; halfbacks: Taseff, Hawkins, Sample, M. Davis, Lewis, Simpson; fullbacks: Pricer.

New York—Ends: Katcavage, Biscaha, Robustelli, T. Scott, Summerall; tackles: Modzelewski, Guy, Hauser, Grier; guards: Barry, Livingston, Svare, Kelly; centers: Huff, Schmidt; quarterbacks: Heinrich, Shaw, Patton; halfbacks: Crow, Chand-

ler, Stits, Lynch, Morrison, Nolan; fullback: King.

Officials—Referee: Ronald Gibbs (St. Thomas); Umpire—Louis Palazzi (Penn State); Lineman, Charles Berry (Lafayette); Back Judge, Cleo Diehl (Northwestern); Field Judge, Charles Sweeney (Notre Dame).

THE GAME

Baltimore scored from 80 yards out the first time it had the ball, with a 59-yard Unitas to Moore pass ending the drive. Myhra converted to make it 7–0. New York came back in the first period from its own 40 to the Baltimore 23 and Summerail kicked a field goal. It was 7–3 at the end of the first period.

New York moved the score to 7–6 in the second period, during which Summerall's second field goal was the only scoring. It was a 37-yard shot. Myhra of Baltimore missed from the 42.

In the third period New York went ahead 9–7 on Summerall's third field goal, this one from 22 yards out. The New York defense was still making a magnificent stand against the relentless attack of John Unitas and his offensive unit.

Shortly after the fourth quarter started, Unitas put Baltimore ahead with a five-yard touchdown run on a roll-out option play. Myhra's conversion made it Baltimore 14, New York 9. Andrew Nelson intercepted a Conerly pass to set up Baltimore's next score from the New York 14. Unitas passed to Richardson for the touchdown and Myhra again converted to push the lead to 21–9.

With time running out and 12 points needed, Conerly was forced to pass desperately. One of them was picked off by John Sample, defensive back of Baltimore, and run back 42 yards for a touchdown. Myhra's kick made it 28–9.

Sample's second interception of a Conerly pass gave Baltimore the ball on New York's 18 and Myhra booted a field goal from the 25 to make the final score, 31–9.

The gross receipts (including radio and television) were $666,281.00, of which each Colt got $4,674.44 and each Giant $3,083.27. This left a pool of $38,902.02 for the sectional second place teams (Chicago in the Western Conference, and Cleveland and Philadelphia, the latter two tied in the Eastern Conference).

1960 WORLD CHAMPIONSHIP PROFESSIONAL FOOTBALL GAME

(Played at Franklin Field, Philadelphia, Pa., Dec. 26)
Attendance 67,325

Philadelphia Eagles (17)	Green Bay Packers (13)
Retzlaff—L.E.	McGee—L.E.
McCusker—L.T.	Skoronski—L.T.
Huth—L.G.	Thurston—L.G.
Bednarik—C.	Ringo—C.
S. Campbell—R.G.	J. Kramer—R.G.
J. D. Smith—R.T.	Gregg—R.T.
Walston—R.E.	Knafelc—R.E.
Van Brocklin—Q.B.	Starr—Q.B.
Barnes—L.H.	Hornung—L.H.
McDonald—R.H.	Dowler—R.H.
Dean—F.B.	Taylor—F.B.

Philadelphia Eagles	0	10	0	7—17
Green Bay Packers	3	3	0	7—13

Touchdowns: McDonald, Dean (Philadelphia); McGee (Green Bay).

Conversions: Walston 2 (Philadelphia); Hornung (Green Bay).

Field Goals: Hornung 2 (Green Bay); Walston (Philadelphia).

SUBSTITUTIONS

Philadelphia—Ends: Robb, M. Campbell, Reichow, Lucas, Gossage; tackles: Khayat, Richardson, Wilcox, Gunnels, Keys; guards: Wittenborn, Lapham, Weber, Baughan, Nocera; backs: Jurgensen, Peaks, Carr, Brown, Johnson, Jackson, Sapp, Brookshier, Freeman, Burroughs.

Green Bay—Ends: Davis, Quinlan, Beck; tackles: Masters, Hanner, Jordan, Miller; guards: Cvercko, Currie, Forester, Nitschke, Bettis, Iman; backs: McHan, Moore, Carpenter, Winslow, Hickman, Gremminger, Whittenton, Tunnell, Symank, Hackbart, Pesonen, Wood.

Officials—Referee: Ronald Gibbs (St. Thomas); Umpire: Joseph Connell (Pittsburgh); Linesman: John Highberger (Carnegie Tech); Back Judge: Sam Giangreco (Manhattan); Field Judge: Herman Rohrig (Nebraska).

THE GAME

Philadelphia received the kickoff and lost the ball on the first play when Van Brocklin's pass to Barnes in the flat was intercepted by Quinlan on the Eagle 14-yard line. The Packers moved to the six and lost the ball on downs. On the Eagles' third play Dean fumbled and the ball was recovered by Green Bay's Bill Forester on the 22. Philadelphia held on the 13 after six plays and Hornung kicked a field goal from the 20 to put Green Bay ahead 3–0.

Early in the second period Hornung kicked another 3-pointer from the 23 and the Packers led 6–0. Later in the period Philadelphia started from their own 43 following a punt. Van Brocklin passed 22 yards to McDonald and then 35 yards to the same receiver for a touchdown. Walston converted and the Eagles led 7–6. Later in the second period Walston kicked a 15-yard field goal to increase the lead to 10–6. As the half ended Hornung missed a kick from the Eagle 13.

There was no scoring in the third period, but the Packers had a long drive going as the last chapter opened. McGee finally took Starr's seven-yard pass for a touchdown, and Hornung's conversion put Green Bay ahead, 13–10.

This lead lasted only for one series of downs by the Eagles. Ted Dean, rookie fullback, took Hornung's kickoff on the three and flew to Green Bay's 39 before he was smashed out of bounds. Dean and Barnes pounded to the Green Bay five-yard line and then Van Brocklin sent Dean around left end for the touchdown. Walston's conversion produced the final score 17–13. As the game ended Starr was passing desperately against the clock and Taylor was stopped on the Philadelphia 10 by Bednarik.

The gross receipts (including radio and television) were $747,876, a new record. Each Eagle got $5,116.55 and each Packer $3,105.14. This left a pool of $41,-401.85 for the sectional second place teams (Cleveland and Detroit and San Francisco, the latter two tied in the Western Conference).

CHAMPIONSHIP GAME RECORDS

Most Championship Wins

7   Chicago Bears (1921, 1932, 1933, 1940, 1941, 1943, 1946)
6   Green Bay (1929, 1930, 1931, 1936, 1939, 1944)

Most Play-offs Participated In

11   New York Giants (1933, 1934, 1935, 1938, 1939, 1941, 1944, 1946, 1956, 1958, 1959)
9   Chicago Bears (1933, 1934, 1937, 1940, 1941, 1942, 1943, 1946, 1956

GROUND GAINING

Most Yards Gained

2,831   Chicago Bears (9 play-offs)
2,675   New York Giants (11 play-offs)
2,348   Cleveland Browns (7 play-offs)

Most Yards Gained (one game)

501   Chicago Bears vs Washington, Dec. 8. 1940
460   Baltimore vs New York, Dec. 28, 1958
445   Chicago Bears vs Washington, Dec. 26, 1943

Fewest Yards Gained (one game)

116   Boston Redskins vs Green Bay, Dec. 13, 1936
119   Los Angeles vs Philadelphia, Dec. 18, 1949

Most Yards Gained Rushing

1,358   Chicago Bears (9 play-offs)
1,144   Cleveland Browns (7 play-offs)

Most Yards Gained Rushing (one game)

382   Chicago Bears vs Washington, Dec. 8, 1940
274   Philadelphia vs Los Angeles, Dec. 18, 1949

Fewest Yards Gained Rushing (one game)

21   Los Angeles vs Philadelphia, Dec. 18, 1949
22   Washington vs Chicago Bears, Dec. 8, 1940

Most Yards Gained Passing

1,506   New York Giants (102 completions in 11 play-offs)
1,473   Chicago Bears (84 completions in 9 play-offs)
1,238   Cleveland Browns (96 completions in 7 play-offs)

1,037   Washington (67 completions in 5 play-offs)

Most Yards Gained Passing (one game)

371   Washington vs Chicago Bears, Dec. 12, 1937 (22 completions)
349   Baltimore vs New York Giants, Dec. 28, 1958 (26 completions)
312   Los Angeles vs Cleveland Browns, Dec. 24, 1950 (18 completions)

Fewest Yards Gained Passing (one game)

7   Philadelphia vs Chicago Cardinals, Dec. 19, 1948 (2 completions)
9   Cleveland Browns vs Detroit, Dec. 27, 1953 (3 completions)
35   Chicago Cardinals vs Philadelphia, Dec. 19, 1948 (3 completions) .

FIRST DOWNS

Most First Downs

132   New York Giants (11 play-offs)
124   Chicago Bears (9 play-offs)
122   Cleveland Browns (7 play-offs)

Most First Downs (one game)

27   Baltimore vs New York Giants, Dec. 28, 1958

Most First Downs Rushing

74   Chicago Bears (9 play-offs)
65   New York Giants (11 play-offs)
64   Cleveland Browns (7 play-offs)

Most First Downs Rushing (one game)

16   Philadelphia vs Chicago Cardinals, Dec. 19, 1948
15   Cleveland Browns vs Detroit, Dec. 28, 1952
14   Chicago Bears vs New York Giants, Dec. 21, 1941
14   Green Bay vs Philadelphia, Dec. 26, 1960

Most First Downs Passing

57   Cleveland Browns (7 play-offs)
49   New York Giants (11 play-offs)
44   Chicago Bears (9 play-offs)
32   Washington (5 play-offs)

Most First Downs Passing (one game)

17   Baltimore vs New York Giants, Dec. 28, 1958
16   Cleveland Browns vs Los Angeles, Dec. 23, 1951
13   Cleveland Browns vs Los Angeles, Dec. 24, 1950

12   Los Angeles vs Cleveland Browns,
     Dec. 24, 1950

Most First Downs by Penalty

14   New York Giants (11 play-offs)
7   **Washington (5 play-offs)**

FORWARD PASSING

Most Passes Completed

102 New York Giants (226 attempts,
     11 play-offs)
96   Cleveland Browns (185 attempts in
     7 play-offs)
93   Chicago Bears (218 attempts in 9
     play-offs)
67   **Washington (148 attempts in 5
     play-offs)**

Most Passes Completed (one game)

27   Philadelphia vs Chicago Cardinals,
     Dec. 28, 1947 (44 attempts)
26   Baltimore vs New York Giants, Dec.
     28, 1958
22   Washington vs Chicago Bears, Dec.
     12, 1937 (40 attempts)
     Cleveland Browns vs Los Angeles,
     Dec. 24, 1950 (33 attempts)

Fewest Passes Completed (one game)

2   Detroit vs New York Giants, Dec. 15,
     1935 (5 attempts)
     Philadelphia vs Chicago Cardinals,
     Dec. 19, 1948 (12 attempts)

Most Passes Attempted

226 New York Giants (102 completions
     in 11 play-offs)
218 Chicago Bears (93 completions in 9
     play-offs)
184 Cleveland Browns (96 completions
     in 7 play-offs)
148 Washington (67 completions in 5
     play-offs)

Most Passes Attempted (one game)

51   Washington vs Chicago Bears, Dec.
     8, 1940 (20 completions)
47   Chicago Bears vs New York, Dec. 30,
     1956 (20 completions)
44   Philadelphia vs Chicago Cardinals,
     Dec. 28, 1947 (27 completions)

Fewest Passes Attempted (one game)

5   Detroit vs New York Giants, Dec. 15,
     1935 (2 completions)
9   Philadelphia vs Los Angeles, Dec.
     18, 1949 (5 completions)

INTERCEPTIONS

Most Passes Had Intercepted

28   New York Giants (226 attempts in
     11 play-offs)

19   Washington (148 attempts in 5
     play-offs)

Most Passes Had Intercepted (one game)

8   Washington vs Chicago Bears, Dec.
     8, 1940 (51 attempts)
7   Los Angeles vs Cleveland, Dec. 26,
     1955 (28 attempts)
6   New York Giants vs Green Bay,
     Dec. 10, 1939 (26 attempts)
     New York Giants vs Chicago Bears,
     Dec. 15, 1946 (26 attempts)

Most Passes Intercepted By

29   Chicago Bears (8 play-offs)
22   Cleveland (7 play-offs)

Most Passes Intercepted By (one game)

8   Chicago Bears vs Washington, Dec.
     8, 1940
7   Cleveland vs Los Angeles, Dec. 26,
     1955
6   Green Bay vs New York Giants, Dec.
     10, 1939
     Chicago Bears vs New York Giants,
     Dec. 15, 1946
     Cleveland vs Detroit, Dec. 26, 1954

Most Yards Interceptions Returned

355 Chicago Bears (29 interceptions in
     9 play-offs)
288 Cleveland (22 interceptions in 7
     play-offs)
137 Green Bay (8 interceptions in 3
     play-offs)

Most Yards Interceptions Returned (one game)

123 Green Bay vs New York Giants,
     Dec. 10, 1939 (6 interceptions)
122 Cleveland vs Detroit, Dec. 26, 1954
     (6 interceptions)
117 Chicago Bears vs Washington, Dec.
     8, 1940 (8 interceptions)

PUNTS

Most Punts

78   New York Giants (11 play-offs)
55   Chicago Bears (9 play-offs)

Most Punts (one game)

13   New York Giants vs Chicago Bears,
     Dec. 17, 1933
10   New York Giants vs Chicago Bears,
     Dec. 19, 1934

Fewest Punts (one game)

2   Chicago Bears (twice) vs Washing-
     ton, Dec. 8, 1940, and vs New York
     Giants, Dec. 21, 1941
3   Washington vs Chicago Bears, Dec.
     8, 1940

Best Punting Average

43.1 yards Detroit (16 punts in 5 play-offs)

40.7 yards Chicago Bears (47 punts in 8 play-offs)

40.7 yards Cleveland Browns (21 punts, 5 play-offs)

Best Punting Average (one game)

53.5 yards Chicago Bears vs New York Giants, Dec. 21, 1941 (2 punts)

52.5 yards Washington vs Chicago Bears, Dec. 13, 1942 (6 punts)

PUNT RETURNS

Most Punt Returns

31 New York (74 punts in 11 play-offs)

25 Cleveland (33 punts in 7 play-offs)

20 Chicago Bears (57 punts in 9 play-offs)

19 Chicago Bears (54 punts in 8 play-offs)

17 Washington (27 punts in 5 play-offs)

Most Punt Returns (one game)

8 Green Bay vs New York Giants, Dec. 17, 1944

6 Washington vs Chicago Bears, Dec. 13, 1942

Cleveland vs Detroit, Dec. 28, 1952

New York vs Baltimore, Dec. 27, 1959

Most Yards Punts Returned

247 New York Giants (31 returns in 11 play-offs)

193 Chicago Bears (20 returns in 9 play-offs)

169 New York Giants (16 returns in 8 play-offs)

Most Yards Punts Returned (one game)

150 Chicago Cardinals vs Philadelphia, Dec. 28, 1947 (4 returns)

90 Detroit vs New York Giants, Dec. 15, 1935 (4 returns)

KICK-OFF RETURNS

Most Kick-offs Returned

32 New York Giants (11 play-offs)

32 Chicago Bears (9 play-offs)

Cleveland (7 play-offs)

Most Kick-offs Returned (one game)

9 Chicago Bears vs New York, Dec. 30, 1956

8 Washington vs Chicago Bears, Dec. 8, 1940

Cleveland vs Detroit, Dec. 29, 1957

7 Los Angeles vs Cleveland, Dec. 26, 1955

6 New York Giants vs Chicago Bears, Dec. 17, 1933

Washington vs Chicago Bears, Dec. 26, 1943

Most Yards Kick-offs Returned

782 New York Giants (37 returns in 11 play-offs)

632 Cleveland (29 returns in 7 play-offs)

595 New York (29 returns in 9 play-offs)

432 Washington (21 returns in 5 play-offs)

Most Yards Kick-offs Returned (one game)

225 Washington vs Chicago Bears, Dec. 8, 1940 (8 returns)

215 Los Angeles vs Cleveland, Dec. 26, 1955 (7 returns)

149 Washington vs Chicago Bears, Dec. 26, 1943 (6 returns)

PENALTIES

Most Penalties

55 Chicago Bears (470 yards in 9 play-offs)

40 New York Giants (346 yards in 11 play-offs)

Most Penalties (one game)

19 Chicago Bears vs New York Giants, Dec. 21, 1941 (80 yards)

Chicago Cardinals vs Philadelphia, Dec. 28, 1947 (98 yards)

11 New York Giants vs Green Bay, Dec. 17, 1944 (90 yards)

Fewest Penalties (one game)

1 Washington vs Chicago Bears, Dec. 12, 1937 (5 yards)

Chicago Bears vs Washington, Dec. 12, 1937 (15 yards)

Most Yards Penalized

470 Chicago Bears (55 penalties in 9 play-offs)

346 New York Giants (40 penalties in 11 play-offs)

Most Yards Penalized (one game)

102 Chicago Bears vs New York Giants, Dec. 15, 1946 (9 penalties)

98 Chicago Cardinals vs Philadelphia, Dec. 28, 1947 (10 penalties)

Fewest Yards Penalized (one game)

5 Washington vs Chicago Bears, Dec. 12, 1937 (1 penalty)

10 New York Giants vs Green Bay, Dec. 11, 1938 (2 penalties)

Los Angeles vs Cleveland, Dec. 26, 1955

FUMBLES

Most Fumbles

26   New York Giants (11 play-offs)
20   Chicago Bears (9 play-offs)

Most Fumbles (one game, one team)

6   New York vs Baltimore, Dec. 28, 1958
5   Boston Redskins vs Green Bay, Dec. 13, 1936

Most Fumbles Recovered

25   Chicago Bears (14 own; 11 opponents; 38 opportunities in 9 play-offs)

Most Fumbles Recovered (one game)

7   Chicago Bears vs New York Giants (4 own; 3 opponents; 8 opportunities), Dec. 9, 1934
6   Chicago Bears vs Washington (4 own; 2 opponents; 7 opportunities), Dec. 12, 1937

SCORING

Most Points Scored

245   Chicago Bears (9 play-offs)
191   New York Giants (11 play-offs)

Most Points Scored (one game)

73   Chicago Bears vs Washington, Dec. 8, 1940
59   Detroit vs Cleveland (14), Dec. 29, 1957

Most Points Scored (one game, both teams)

73   Chicago Bears (73) vs Washington (0), Dec. 8, 1940
66   Cleveland (56) vs Detroit (10) Dec. 26, 1954
62   Chicago Bears (41) vs Washington (21), Dec. 25, 1943
58   Cleveland Browns (30) vs Los Angeles (28), Dec. 24, 1950

Most Touchdowns

32   Chicago Bears (9 play-offs)
24   New York Giants (11 play-offs)
23   Cleveland (7 play-offs)

Most Touchdowns (one game)

11   Chicago Bears vs Washington, Dec. 8, 1940
8   Cleveland vs Detroit, Dec. 26, 1954
     Detroit vs Cleveland, Dec. 29, 1957
6   Chicago Bears vs Washington, Dec. 26, 1943

Most Touchdowns Running

21   Chicago Bears (9 play-offs)
13   Cleveland (7 play-offs)

Most Touchdowns Running (one game)

10   Chicago Bears vs Washington, Dec. 8, 1940
5   Cleveland vs Detroit, Dec. 26, 1954
4   Detroit Bears vs New York Giants, Dec. 15, 1935
     Chicago Bears vs New York Giants, Dec. 21, 1941
     Chicago Cardinals vs Philadelphia, Dec. 28, 1947

Most Touchdowns Passing

13   New York Giants (11 play-offs)
11   Chicago Bears (9 play-offs)
10   Cleveland (7 play-offs)

Most Touchdowns Passing (one game)

5   Chicago Bears vs Washington, Dec. 26, 1943
     Detroit vs Cleveland, Dec. 29, 1957
4   Cleveland Browns vs Los Angeles, Dec. 24, 1950

Most Extra Points

26   Chicago Bears (9 play-offs)
22   Cleveland (7 play-offs)
20   New York (11 play-offs)

Most Extra Points (one game)

8   Cleveland vs Detroit, Dec. 26, 1954
     Detroit vs Cleveland, Dec. 29, 1957
7   Chicago Bears vs Washington, Dec. 8, 1940
6   Chicago Bears vs Washington, Dec. 26, 1943

Most Field Goals

9   Chicago Bears (16 attempts in 9 play-offs)
     New York (14 attempts, 11 play-offs)
6   Cleveland (12 attempts in 7 play-offs)

Most Field Goals (one game)

3   Chicago Bears (twice) vs New York Giants, Dec. 17, 1933, and vs New York Giants, Dec. 21, 1941
     Cleveland vs Detroit, Dec. 27, 1953
     New York vs Baltimore (Dec. 27, 1959)

Most Field Goals Attempted

16   Chicago Bears (Made 9 in 9 play-offs)
15   New York (Made 9 in 11 play-offs)
12   Cleveland (Made 6 in 7 play-offs)

Most Field Goals Attempted (one game)

4   Chicago Bears vs New York Giants (thrice): Dec. 17, 1933 (made 3); Dec. 9, 1934 (made 3); Dec. 21, 1941 (made 3)
     Cleveland vs Detroit, Dec. 27, 1953 (made 3)

ALL-TIME TEAM RECORDS

CONSECUTIVE PERFORMANCES

Most Consecutive Victories

18   Chicago Bears (twice) —1933–34 and 1941–42.
13   Washington—1942–43
     Cleveland—1951–52
12   Green Bay—1928–29

Most Consecutive Games Won by Shutouts

7   Detroit Lions—1934

Most Consecutive Games Without Defeat

24   Canton—1922— (won 21, tied 3)
23   Green Bay—1928, 1929, 1930— (won 21, tied 2)

DEFENSE

SEASON

Most Points Allowed

462   Baltimore—1950— (12 games)
432   Washington—1954— (12 games)
427   Dallas—1952— (12 games)
407   Detroit—1948— (12 games)
406   Green Bay—1950— (12 games)

Fewest Points Allowed

20   New York Giants—1927— (13 games)
59   Detroit—1934— (13 games)
75   New York Giants—1944— (10 games)
79   New York Giants—1938— (11 games)

Most Yards Allowed

5,402   Baltimore—1950
5,220   New York Yanks—1950
5,173   New York Yanks—1951
4,858   Boston Yanks—1948

Fewest Yards Allowed

1,578   Chicago Cardinals—1934
1,703   Chicago Bears—1942

Most Yards Allowed Rushing (one season)

2,857   Baltimore—1950— (12 games)
2,610   Green Bay—1956— (12 games)
2,445   New York Yanks—1950— (12 games)
2,391   New York Yanks—1951— (12 games)
2,382   Detroit—1948— (12 games)

Fewest Yards Allowed Rushing

519   Chicago Bears—1942
558   Philadelphia—1944
793   Phil-Pitt—1943

Most Yards Allowed Passing (one season)

2,905   Washington—1954— (12 games)

2,818   Green Bay—1950— (12 games)
2,776   New York Yanks—1951— (12 games)
2,775   New York Yanks—1950— (12 games)
2,668   Washington—1958 (12 games)
2,649   San Francisco—1954— (12 games)

Fewest Yards Allowed Passing

625   Chicago Cardinals—1934
928   Boston Redskins—1934
939   Pittsburgh—1946

GAME

Fewest Yards Allowed

14   Detroit vs Chicago Cardinals, Sept. 15, 1940

Fewest Yards Allowed Rushing

Minus 53   Chicago Cardinals vs Detroit, Oct. 17, 1943
Minus 36   Chicago Bears vs Philadelphia, Nov. 19, 1939
Minus 33   Phil-Pitt vs Brooklyn, Oct. 2, 1943
Minus 29   Washington vs Cleveland, Oct. 11, 1942

Fewest Yards Allowed Passing

Minus 13   Washington vs Pittsburgh, Oct. 18, 1959
Minus 5   Dallas vs Los Angeles, Nov. 9, 1952 (17 passes, 5 completed)
Minus 3   Washington vs New York Giants, Oct. 1, 1939 (6 attempts, 1 complete)
Minus 1   Chicago Bears vs Pittsburgh, Nov. 25, 1945 (20 attempts, 2 com-complete)
0   Several.

FIRST DOWNS

SEASON

Most First Downs (including TDs from scrimmage)

278   Los Angeles—1950— (84 rushing, 111 passing, 24 penalties, 59 TDs)
272   Los Angeles—1951— (92 rushing, 102 passing, 28 penalties, .50 TDs)
263   Chicago Bears—1947— (98 rushing, 94 passing, 18 penalties, 53 TDs)
248   Chicago Bears—1949— (91 rushing, 95 passing, 18 penalties, 44 TDs)

Fewest First Downs

68   Philadelphia—1937
75   Pittsburgh—1941

GAME

Most First Downs (one game)

35 Pittsburgh vs Chicago Cardinals,
Dec. 13, 1958 (11 rushing, 21 passing, 3 penalties, 5 touchdowns)

**34 Los Angeles vs New York Yanks,
Sept. 28, 1951 (8 rushing, 16 passing,
2 penalties, 8 TDs)**

33 Los Angeles vs Green Bay, Dec. 16,
1956 (14 rushing, 10 passing, 2 penalties, 7 TDs)

**32 Los Angeles vs New York Yanks,
Nov. 19, 1950 (7 rushing, 17 pass-
ing, 3 penalties, 5 TDs)
Chicago Cardinals vs New York
Bulldogs, Nov. 13, 1949 (14 rushing,
7 passing, 2 penalties, 9 TDs)
Philadelphia Eagles vs Washington
Redskins, Dec. 2, 1951 (22 rushing,
4 passing, 1 penalty, 5 TDs)**

Fewest First Downs (one team)

0 Hammond vs Canton, Sept. 30, 1923
(lost, 17–0)
Racine vs Chicago Cardinals, Oct. 3,
1926 (lost, 20–0)
New York Giants vs Green Bay,
Oct. 1, 1933 (won, 10–7)
Pittsburgh vs Boston Redskins, Oct.
29, 1933 (won, 16–14)
Philadelphia vs Detroit, Sept. 20,
1935 (lost, 35–0)
New York Giants vs Washington,
Sept. 27, 1942 (won, 14–7)

Most First Downs (both teams)

58 Los Angeles (30), Chicago Bears
(28), Oct. 24, 1954
57 Los Angeles (32), New York Yanks
(25), Nov. 19, 1950
54 New York Giants (31), Pittsburgh
(23), Dec. 5, 1948

Fewest First Downs (both teams)

3 Brooklyn (1), Boston Redskins (2),
Sept. 29, 1935

FORWARD PASSING

SEASON

Most Passes Completed

253 Los Angeles—1950— (attempted 453)
231 Green Bay—1951— (attempted 478)
231 Washington—1947— (attempted 416)
224 Philadelphia—1953—(attempted 438)
223 San Francisco—1958— (attempted
383)
215 Detroit, 1954 (attempted 395)
206 Baltimore—1950— (attempted 438)
202 Washington—1948— (attempted 360)
201 Los Angeles—1948— (attempted 395)
197 Washington—1949— (attempted 378)

Fewest Passes Completed

34 Chicago Cardinals—1934—
(attempted 140)
Detroit Lions—1934— (attempted
144)
39 Boston Redskins—1934— (attempted
138)
Philadelphia—1936— (attempted
170)

Most Passes Attempted

478 Green Bay—1951— (completed 231)
453 Los Angeles—1950— (completed 253)
438 Baltimore—1950— (completed 206)

Fewest Passes Attempted

120 Detroit Lions—1937— (completed
44)
125 New York Giants—1944—
(completed 47)
126 Chicago Cardinals—1935—
(completed 47)

Best Passing Efficiency

Less than 250   64%—Washington,   1945
(146 complete, 228
attempts)
59%—Washington,   1940
(144 complete, 244
attempts)

More than 250   63%—Cleveland,   1953
(191 completions in
303 attempts)
62.6%—San Francisco, 1957
(191 completions in
305 attempts)

Most Passes Had Intercepted

41 Card-Pitt—1944
39 Chicago Cardinals—1943
37 Detroit Lions—1943
Green Bay Packers—1950

Fewest Passes Had Intercepted

5 Cleveland, 1960 (attempted 264)
9 Brooklyn Dodgers—1936 (attempted
141)
New York Giants—1943 (attempted
149)
Cleveland—1953 (attempted 303)
Cleveland—1959 (attempted 276)
10 New York Giants—1950 (attempted
187)

Most Touchdown Passes

33 Philadelphia—1954
32 Baltimore—1959
31 Los Angeles—1950
29 Detroit—1951
Chicago Bears—1947
New York Yanks—1950
Detroit—1951
Philadelphia—1960
28 Green Bay—1942

Chicago Bears—1943
Washington—1947
Los Angeles—1948

Fewest Touchdown Passes

0   Pittsburgh—1945
1   Detroit—1942

GAME

Most Passes Completed

36   New York Giants vs Pittsburgh, Dec. 5, 1948 (attempted 53)

Most Passes Completed (both teams)

55   San Francisco (25) vs Chicago Bears (30), Nov. 1, 1953

Most Passes Attempted

60   Philadelphia vs Washington, Dec. 1, 1940 (completed 33)
59   Chicago Bears vs New York Giants, Oct. 23, 1949 (completed 34)

Fewest Passes Attempted

0   Several

Most Passes Attempted (both teams)

94   Chicago Bears (50), San Francisco (44). (55 completed for 522 yards. San Francisco 278, Chicago Bears 244), Nov. 1. 1953
91   Pittsburgh (48), Los Angeles (43). (47 completed for 602 yards, Los Angeles 358, Pittsburgh 244), Dec. 14, 1952

Most Passes Had Intercepted (one team)

9   Detroit Lions vs Green Bay, Oct. 24, 1943
8   Green Bay vs New York Giants, Nov. 21, 1948
     Chicago Cardinals vs Philadelphia, Sept. 24, 1950
7   Several

Most Passes Had Intercepted (both teams)

11   Several

Most Touchdown Passes (one team)

7   Chicago Bears vs New York Giants, Nov. 14, 1943
6   Several

Most Touchdown Passes (both teams)

10   Chicago Bears (6) vs Chicago Cardinals (4), Dec. 5, 1937
9   Several

FUMBLES

SEASON

Most Fumbles

56   Chicago Bears—1938
54   Philadelphia—1946

Fewest Fumbles

8   Cleveland—1959
11   Green Bay—1944
12   Brooklyn—1934
      Detroit—1943
13   Philadelphia—1938
      Green Bay—1942

Most Fumbles Recovered (opponents' and own)

46   New York Giants—1946
45   Philadelphia—1946
44   Boston Yanks—1948
      Pittsburgh—1948

Fewest Fumbles Recovered (own)

2   Washington—1958 (out of 18)
3   Detroit—1956 (out of 14)
     Cleveland—1959 (out of 8)
4   Green Bay—1944 (out of 11)
     Chicago Cardinals—1949 (out of 20)
5   Green Bay—1942 (out of 13)
     Chicago Cardinals—1948 (out of 21)
6   Chicago Bears—1950 (out of 23)

Most Opponents' Fumbles Recovered

28   Green Bay—1946 (out of 45)
      Cleveland Browns—1951 (out of 34)
27   New York Giants—1950 (out of 43)
      Baltimore—1953 (out of 43)

Fewest Opponents' Fumbles Recovered

4   Philadelphia—1944
6   Brooklyn—1939
     Chicago Bears—1943
     Chicago Bears—1945
     Washington—1945

GAME

Most Fumbles (one team)

10   Phil-Pitt vs New York Giants, Oct. 9, 1943
9   Philadelphia vs Green Bay, Oct. 13, 1946
8   Several

Most Fumbles (both teams)

14   Chicago Bears (7) vs Cleveland Rams (7), Nov. 24, 1940
13   Washington (8) vs Pittsburgh (5), Nov. 4, 1937
      Philadelphia (7) vs Boston (6), Dec. 8, 1946

Most Fumbles Recovered

10   Chicago Bears (7 own, 3 opponents), vs Chicago Cardinals, Sept. 11, 1938
8   Several

Most Opponents' Fumbles Recovered

6   Several

GROUND GAINING

SEASON

Most Yards Gained

5,506	Los Angeles—1951
5,420	Los Angeles—1950
5,187	Los Angeles—1954
5,053	Chicago Bears—1947
4,873	Chicago Bears—1949
4,726	New York Yanks—1950
4,707	Chicago Cardinals—1948
4,679	Washington—1947

Most Yards Gained Rushing

2,885	Detroit—1936
2,835	Chicago Bears—1934
2,763	Detroit—1934
2,607	Philadelphia—1949
2,560	Chicago Cardinals—1948

Most Yards Gained Passing

3,709	Los Angeles--1950
3,336	Washington—1947
3,296	Los Angeles—1951
3,104	Chicago Bears—1954
3,093	Chicago Bears—1947
3,055	Chicago Bears—1949
2,894	New York Yanks—1950
2,861	Washington—1948

Fewest Yards Gained

1,481	Brooklyn—1934
1,506	Boston—1944
1,719	Pittsburgh—1945
1,843	Detroit—1941

Fewest Yards Gained Rushing

298	Philadelphia—1940
471	Boston—1944
472	Detroit—1946

Fewest Yards Gained Passing

577	Brooklyn—1934
652	Pittsburgh—1945

GAME

Most Yards Gained

735   Los Angeles vs New York Yankees, Sept. 28, 1951 (181 rushing, 554 passing)

683   Pittsburgh vs Chicago Cardinals, Dec. 13, 1958 (211 rushing, 472 passing)

682   Chicago Bears vs New York Giants, Nov. 14, 1943 (194 rushing, 488 passing)

636   Los Angeles vs New York Yanks, Nov. 19, 1950 (266 rushing, 370 passing)

625   Washington vs Boston, Oct. 13, 1948 (124 rushing, 501 passing)
      New York Giants vs New York Yanks, Dec. 31, 1950 (377 rushing, 248 passing)

Most Yards Gained Rushing

426   Detroit vs Pittsburgh, Nov. 4, 1934
423   New York Giants vs Baltimore, Nov. 19, 1950

Most Yards Gained Rushing and Passing (both teams)

1,133   Los Angeles (266 rushing, 370 passing) vs New York Yanks (185 rushing, 312 passing), Nov. 19, 1950

Most Yards Gained Passing

554   Los Angeles vs New York Yanks, Sept. 28, 1951 (27 completions, 5 TDs)

501   Washington vs Boston Yanks, Oct. 31, 1948 (22 completions, 4 TDs)

488   Chicago Bears vs New York Giants, Nov. 14, 1943 (22 completions, 7 TDs)

468   Chicago Bears vs Chicago Cardinals, Dec. 11, 1949 (24 completions, 6 TDs)

Most Yards Gained Passing (both teams)

748   Chicago Bears (468), Chicago Cardinals (280), Dec. 11, 1949

Fewest Yards Gained

14   Chicago Cardinals vs Detroit, Sept. 15, 1940

Fewest Yards Gained Rushing

Minus 53   Detroit vs Chicago Cardinals, Oct. 17, 1943

Minus 36   Philadelphia vs Chicago Bears, Nov. 19, 1939

Minus 33   Brooklyn vs Phil-Pitt, Oct. 2, 1943

Fewest Yards Gained Passing

Minus 5   Dallas vs Los Angeles, Nov. 9, 1952 (17 attempts, 5 completed)

Minus 3   New York Giants vs Washington, Oct. 1, 1939 (6 attempts, 1 completed)

Washington vs Pittsburgh, Nov. 27, 1955 (9 attempts, 1 completed)

Minus 1   Pittsburgh vs Chicago Bears, Nov. 25, 1945 (20 attempts, 2 completed)

0   Several

INTERCEPTIONS

SEASON

Best Percentage of Interceptions By

17.3   Green Bay—1943 (opponents attempted 242)

16.3   Detroit—1940 (opponents attempted 177)

15.9   Green Bay—1940 (opponents attempted 252)

Most Passes Intercepted By

42 Green Bay—1943 (opponents attempted 242)
41 New York—1951 (opponents attempted 256)
40 Green Bay—1940 (opponents attempted 252)

Fewest Passes Intercepted

7 Los Angeles—1959 (opponents attempted 287)
8 Pittsburgh—1940 (opponents attempted 192)
10 Brooklyn—1944 (opponents attempted 181)
    Pittsburgh—1955 (opponents attempted 242)

Most Interceptions Returned for Touchdowns

5 Green Bay—1945 (intercepted 24)
   Los Angeles—1958 (intercepted 28)
4 Several

Most Yards Interceptions Returned

712 Los Angeles—1952 (38 interceptions)
663 Detroit—1953 (38 interceptions)
656 Detroit Lions—1949 (32 interceptions)
606 Green Bay—1943 (42 interceptions)

GAME

Most Passes Intercepted By

9 Green Bay vs Detroit, Oct. 24, 1943
8 New York Giants vs Green Bay, Nov. 21, 1948
   Philadelphia vs Chicago Cardinals, Sept. 24, 1950
   New York Giants vs New York Yankees, Dec. 16, 1951

Most Passes Intercepted By (both teams)

11 Several

Most Yards Interceptions Returned

182 Dallas vs Los Angeles, Nov. 2, 1952 (4 interceptions)
161 Chicago Cardinals vs Pittsburgh, Sept. 26, 1955 (5 interceptions)

PENALTIES

SEASON

Most Penalties

122 Washington—1948 (1,100 yards)
     Chicago Bears—1948 (1,066 yards)
121 Chicago Bears—1944 (1,025 yards)
118 Chicago Bears—1951 (1,107 yards)
117 Cleveland Browns—1951 (1,017 yards)
110 Los Angeles—1950 (1,038 yards)
107 Chicago Bears—1947 (1,020 yards)

Fewest Penalties

19 Detroit—1937 (139 yards)
21 Boston—1935 (166 yards)

Most Yards Penalized

1,107 Chicago Bears—1951 (118 penalties)
1,100 Washington—1948 (122 penalties)
1,066 Chicago Bears—1948 (122 penalties)
1,038 Los Angeles—1950 (110 penalties)
1,025 Chicago Bears—1944 (121 penalties)

Fewest Yards Penalized

139 Detroit—1937 (19 penalties)
146 Philadelphia—1937 (25 penalties)
159 Philadelphia—1936 (24 penalties)

GAME

Most Penalties (one team)

22 Brooklyn vs Green Bay, Sept. 17, 1944 (168 yards)
    Chicago Bears vs Philadelphia, Nov. 26, 1944 (170 yards)
21 Cleveland Browns vs Chicago Bears, Nov. 25, 1951 (209 yards)
18 Chicago Bears vs Los Angeles, Nov. 10, 1946 (140 yards)

Most Yards Penalized (one team)

209 Cleveland Browns vs Chicago Bears, Nov. 25, 1951 (21 penalties)
184 Green Bay vs Boston Yanks, Oct. 21, 1945 (17 penalties)
177 New York Giants vs Washington, Oct. 9, 1949 (17 penalties)
175 New York Giants vs Boston Yanks, Oct. 19, 1947 (11 penalties)

Most Yards Penalized (both teams, one game)

374 Cleveland (209), vs Chicago Bears 165, Nov. 25, 1951 (Cleveland 21, Chicago, 16)

PUNTING

SEASON

Most Punts

113 Boston Redskins—1934
     Brooklyn—1934
112 Boston Redskins—1935

Fewest Punts

32 Chicago Bears—1941
33 Washington—1945

GAME

Most Punts (one team)

17 Chicago Bears vs Green Bay, Oct. 22, 1933

16   Chicago Cardinals vs Chicago Bears,
     Nov. 30, 1933
     Chicago Cardinals vs Detroit Lions,
     Sept. 15, 1940

Most Punts (both teams)

31   Chicago Bears (17) vs Green Bay
     (14), Oct. 22, 1933
29   Chicago Cardinals (15) vs Cincin-
     nati (14), Nov. 12, 1933
     Chicago Cardinals (16) vs Chicago
     Bears (13), Nov. 30, 1933

Fewest Punts

0   Several.

SCORING

SEASON

Most Points

466   Los Angeles—1950— (12 games)
396   Chicago Bears—1941— (11 games)
395   Chicago Bears—1948— (12 games)
392   Los Angeles—1951— (12 games)
376   Chicago Bears—1942— (11 games)
      Philadelphia—1948— (12 games)

Most Touchdowns

64   Los Angeles—1950— (12 games)
56   Chicago Bears—1941— (11 games)

Most Touchdowns Rushing

37   Chicago Bears—1941— (11 games)
33   Los Angeles—1950— (12 games)
32   Chicago Bears—1942— (11 games)
32   Green Bay—1960 (12 games)

Most Touchdowns Passing

33   Philadelphia—1954— (12 games)
33   Baltimore—1959— (12 games)
31   Los Angeles—1950— (12 games)
29   Chicago Bears—1947— (12 games)
29   New York Yanks—1950— (12 games)
29   Detroit Lions—1951— (12 games)
29   Philadelphia—1969— (12 games)

Most Points after Touchdown

59   Los Angeles Rams—1950
53   Chicago Cardinals—1948
51   Chicago Bears—1948

Most Field Goals

23   Cleveland Browns—1953—(12 games)
20   New York—1959— (12 games)
19   Cleveland Browns—1952—(12 games)
19   Cleveland Browns—1960— (12 games)
17   Washington—1956— (12 games)
16   Cleveland Browns—1954—(12 games)
     Green Bay—1955— (12 games)

Fewest Points Scored

10   Cincinnati—1934— (8 games)

GAME

Most Points (one team)

70   Los Angeles vs Baltimore, Oct. 22,
     1950
65   Chicago Cardinals vs New York
     Bulldogs, Nov. 13, 1949
     Los Angeles vs Detroit, Oct. 29, 1950
64   Philadelphia vs Cincinnati, Nov. 6,
     1934
63   Chicago Cardinals vs New York
     Giants, Oct. 17, 1948

Most Points (both teams)

98   Chicago Cardinals (63) vs New
     York Giants (35), Oct. 17, 1948
97   Los Angeles (70) vs Baltimore (27),
     Oct. 22, 1950
89   Los Angeles (52) vs New York
     Giants (37), Nov. 14, 1948
     Los Angeles (65) vs Detroit (24),
     Oct. 29, 1950

Most Points (one team, one quarter)

41   Green Bay vs Detroit (2nd qtr),
     Oct. 7, 1945
     Los Angeles vs Detroit (3rd qtr),
     Oct. 29, 1950

Most Touchdowns (one team)

10   Philadelphia vs Cincinnati, Nov. 6,
     1934
     Los Angeles vs Baltimore, Oct. 22,
     1950
9   Several

Most Touchdowns (both teams)

14   Chicago Cardinals (9) vs New York
     Giants (5), Oct. 17, 1948
     Los Angeles (10) vs Baltimore (4),
     Oct. 22, 1950
12   Several

Most Touchdowns Rushing (one team)

7   Chicago Bears vs Detroit, Oct. 19,
    1941
6   Several

Most Touchdowns Passing (one team)

7   Chicago Bears vs New York Giants,
    Nov. 14, 1943
    Philadelphia vs Washington, Oct.
    17, 1954
6   Several

Most Points after Touchdown (one team)

10   Los Angeles vs Baltimore, Oct. 22,
     1950
9   Chicago Cardinals vs New York
    Giants. Oct. 17, 1948
    Pittsburgh vs New York, Nov. 30,
    1952

Most Points after Touchdown (both teams)

14 Chicago Cardinals (9) vs New York Giants (5), Oct. 17, 1948
13 Los Angeles (10) vs Baltimore (3), Oct. 22, 1950

Most Field Goals (one team)

5 Los Angeles Rams vs Detroit Lions, Dec. 9, 1951
Baltimore vs Los Angeles, Dec. 4, 1954
Pittsburgh vs Washington, Nov. 27, 1960
4 Several

LEAGUE STANDINGS

1921

	W	L	T	Pct.
Chicago Bears*	10	1	1	.909
Buffalo	9	1	2	.900
Akron	7	2	1	.778
Green Bay	6	2	2	.750
Canton	4	3	3	.571
Dayton	4	3	1	.571
Rock Island	5	4	1	.556
Chicago Cards	2	3	2	.400
Cleveland	2	6	0	.250
Rochester	2	6	0	.250
Detroit	1	7	1	.125
Columbus	0	6	0	.000
Cincinnati	0	8	0	.000

* Staleys

1922

	W	L	T	Pct.
Canton	10	0	2	1.000
Chicago Bears	9	3	0	.750
Chicago Cards	8	3	0	.727
Toledo	5	2	2	.714
Rock Island	4	2	1	.667
Dayton	4	3	3	.571
Green Bay	4	3	3	.571
Racine	5	4	1	.556
Buffalo	3	4	1	.429
Akron	3	4	2	.429
Milwaukee	2	4	3	.333
Marion	2	6	0	.250
Minneapolis	1	3	0	.250
Evansville	0	2	0	.000
Louisville	0	3	0	.000
Rochester	0	3	1	.000
Hammond	0	4	1	.000
Columbus	0	7	0	.000

1923

	W	L	T	Pct.
Canton	11	0	1	1.000
Chicago Bears	9	2	1	.818
Green Bay	7	2	1	.778
Milwaukee	7	2	3	.778
Cleveland	3	1	3	.750
Chicago Cards	8	4	0	.667
Duluth	4	3	0	.571
Columbus	5	4	1	.556
Buffalo	5	4	3	.556
Racine	4	4	2	.500
Toledo	2	3	2	.400
Rock Island	2	3	3	.400
Minneapolis	2	5	2	.286
St. Louis	1	4	2	.200
Hammond	1	5	1	.167
Dayton	1	6	1	.143
Akron	1	6	0	.143
Marion	1	10	0	.091
Rochester	0	2	0	.000
Louisville	0	3	0	.000

1924

	W	L	T	Pct.
Cleveland	7	1	1	.875
Chicago Bears	6	1	4	.856
Frankford	11	2	1	.846
Duluth	4	1	0	.800
Rock Island	6	2	2	.750
Green Bay	7	4	0	.636
Racine	5	3	2	.625
Buffalo	6	4	4	.600
Chicago Cardinals	5	5	0	.500
Columbus	4	4	1	.500
Hammond	2	2	0	.500
Milwaukee	5	8	0	.385
Dayton	2	6	0	.250
Kansas City	2	7	0	.222
Akron	1	6	0	.143
Kenosha	0	5	1	.000
Minneapolis	0	6	0	.000
Rochester	0	7	0	.000

1925

	W	L	T	Pct.
Chicago Cards	11	2	1	.846
Pottsville	10	2	0	.833
Detroit	8	2	2	.800
New York	8	4	0	.667
Akron	4	2	2	.667
Frankford	13	7	0	.650
Chicago Bears	9	5	3	.643
Rock Island	5	3	3	.625
Green Bay	8	5	0	.615
Providence	6	5	1	.545
Canton	4	4	0	.500
Cleveland	5	8	1	.392
Kansas City	2	5	1	.286
Hammond	1	3	0	.250
Buffalo	1	6	2	.143
Duluth	0	3	0	.000
Rochester	0	6	1	.000
Milwaukee	0	6	0	.000
Dayton	0	7	1	.000
Columbus	0	9	0	.000

1926

	W	L	T	Pct.
Frankford	14	1	1	.933
Chicago Bears	12	1	3	.923
Pottsville	10	2	1	.833
Kansas City	8	3	0	.727
Green Bay	7	3	3	.700
Los Angeles	6	3	1	.667
New York	8	4	0	.667
Duluth	6	5	2	.545
Buffalo	4	4	2	.500
Chicago Cardinals	5	6	1	.455
Providence	5	7	0	.417
Detroit	4	6	2	.400
Hartford	3	7	0	.300
Brooklyn	3	8	0	.272
Milwaukee	2	7	0	.222
Dayton	1	4	1	.200
Akron	1	4	3	.200
Racine	1	4	0	.200
Columbus	1	6	0	.144
Canton	1	9	3	.100
Louisville	0	4	0	.000
Hammond	0	4	0	.000

1927

	W	L	T	Pct.
New York Giants	11	1	1	.917
Green Bay	7	2	1	.778
Chicago Bears	9	3	2	.750
Cleveland	8	4	1	.667
Providence	8	5	1	.615
New York Yankees	7	8	1	.467
Frankford	6	9	3	.400
Pottsville	5	8	0	.385
Chicago Cardinals	3	7	1	.300
Dayton	1	6	1	.143
Duluth	1	8	1	.111
Buffalo	0	5	0	.000

1928

	W	L	T	Pct.
Providence	8	1	2	.888
Frankford	11	3	2	.786
Detroit	7	2	1	.778
Green Bay	6	4	3	.600
Chicago Bears	7	5	1	.583
New York Giants	4	7	2	.364
New York Yankees	4	8	1	.333
Pottsville	2	8	0	.200
Chicago Cardinals	1	5	0	.167
Dayton	0	7	0	.000

1929

	W	L	T	Pct.
Green Bay	12	0	1	1.000
New York	12	1	1	.923
Frankford	9	4	5	.692
Chicago Cardinals	6	6	1	.500
Boston	4	4	0	.500
Stapleton	3	4	3	.429
Orange	3	4	4	.429
Providence	4	6	2	.400
Chicago Bears	4	8	2	.333
Buffalo	1	7	1	.125

	W	L	T	Pct.
Minneapolis	1	9	0	.100
Dayton	0	6	0	.000

1930

	W	L	T	Pct.
Green Bay	11	3	1	.786
New York	13	4	0	.765
Chicago Bears	9	4	1	.692
Brooklyn	7	4	1	.636
Providence	6	4	1	.600
Stapleton	5	5	2	.500
Chicago Cardinals	5	6	2	.455
Portsmouth	5	6	3	.455
Frankford	4	14	1	.222
Minneapolis	1	7	1	.125
Newark	1	10	1	.091

1931

	W	L	T	Pct.
Green Bay	12	2	0	.857
Portsmouth	11	3	0	.786
Chicago Bears	8	4	0	.667
Chicago Cardinals	5	4	0	.556
New York	6	6	1	.500
Providence	4	4	3	.500
Stapleton	4	6	1	.400
Cleveland	2	8	0	.200
Brooklyn	2	12	0	.143
Frankford	1	6	1	.143

1932

	W	L	T	Pct.
Chicago Bears	7	1	6	.875
Green Bay	10	3	1	.767
Portsmouth	6	2	4	.750
Boston	4	4	2	.500
New York	4	6	2	.400
Brooklyn	3	9	0	.250
Chicago Cardinals	2	6	2	.250
Stapleton	2	7	3	.222

1933

WESTERN DIVISION

	W	L	T	Pct.
Chicago Bears	10	2	1	.833
Portsmouth	6	5	0	.554
Green Bay	5	7	1	.418
Cincinnati	3	6	1	.333
Chicago Cardinals	1	9	1	.100

EASTERN DIVISION

	W	L	T	Pct.
New York	11	3	0	.786
Brooklyn	5	4	1	.556
Boston	5	5	2	.500
Philadelphia	3	5	1	.375
Pittsburgh	3	6	2	.333

Chicago Bears 23   New York 21

1934

EASTERN DIVISION

	W	L	T	Pct.
New York	8	5	0	.615
Boston	6	6	0	.500
Brooklyn	4	7	0	.363
Philadelphia	4	7	0	.363
Pittsburgh	2	10	0	.166

WESTERN DIVISION

Chicago Bears	13	0	0	1.000
Detroit	10	3	0	.769
Green Bay	7	6	0	.538
Chicago Cardinals	5	6	0	.454
St. Louis	1	2	0	.333
Cincinnati*	0	8	0	.000

New York 30   Chicago Bears 13

* Franchise transferred to St. Louis, Nov. 5, 1934

1935
WESTERN DIVISION

Detroit	7	3	2	.700
Green Bay	8	4	0	.667
Chicago Cardinals	6	4	2	.600
Chicago Bears	6	4	2	.600

EASTERN DIVISION

New York	9	3	0	.750
Brooklyn	5	6	1	.454
Pittsburgh	4	8	0	.333
Boston*	2	8	1	.200
Philadelphia*	2	9	0	.181

Detroit 26   New York 7

* One game cancelled

1936
WESTERN DIVISION

Green Bay	10	1	1	.909
Chicago Bears	9	3	0	.750
Detroit	8	4	0	.667
Chicago Cardinals	3	8	1	.272

EASTERN DIVISION

Boston	7	5	0	.714
Pittsburgh	6	6	0	.500
New York	5	6	1	.454
Brooklyn	3	8	1	.272
Philadelphia	1	11	0	.084

Green Bay 21   Boston 6

1937
EASTERN DIVISION

Washington	8	3	0	.727
New York	6	3	2	.667
Pittsburgh	4	7	0	.364
Brooklyn	3	7	1	.300
Philadelphia	2	8	1	.200

WESTERN DIVISION

Chicago Bears	9	1	1	.900
Green Bay	7	4	0	.636
Detroit	7	4	0	.636
Chicago Cardinals	5	5	1	.500
Cleveland	1	10	0	.091

Washington 28   Chicago Bears 21

1938
EASTERN DIVISION

New York	8	2	1	.800
Washington	6	3	2	.667
Brooklyn	4	4	3	.500
Philadelphia	5	6	0	.455
Pittsburgh	2	9	0	.182

WESTERN DIVISION

Green Bay	8	3	0	.727
Detroit	7	4	0	.636
Chicago Bears	6	5	0	.545
Cleveland	4	7	0	.364
Chicago Cardinals	2	9	0	.182

New York 23   Green Bay 17

1939
WESTERN DIVISION

Green Bay	9	2	0	.818
Chicago Bears	8	3	0	.727
Detroit	6	5	0	.545
Cleveland	5	5	1	.500
Chicago Cardinals	1	10	0	.091

EASTERN DIVISION

New York	9	1	1	.900
Washington	8	2	1	.800
Brooklyn	4	6	1	.400
Philadelphia	1	9	1	.100
Pittsburgh	1	9	1	.100

Green Bay 27   New York 0

1940
WESTERN DIVISION

Chicago Bears	8	3	0	.727
Green Bay	6	4	1	.600
Detroit	5	5	1	.500
Cleveland	4	6	1	.400
Chicago Cardinals	2	7	2	.222

EASTERN DIVISION

Washington	9	2	0	.818
Brooklyn	8	3	0	.727
New York	6	4	1	.600
Pittsburgh	2	7	2	.222
Philadelphia	1	10	0	.091

Chicago Bears 73   Washington 0

1941
WESTERN DIVISION

Chicago Bears*	10	1	0	.909
Green Bay	10	1	0	.909
Detroit	4	6	1	.400
Chicago Cardinals	3	7	1	.300
Cleveland	2	9	0	.182

EASTERN DIVISION

New York	8	3	0	.727
Brooklyn	7	4	0	.636
Washington	6	5	0	.545

Philadelphia	2	8	1	.200
Pittsburgh	1	9	1	.100

Chicago Bears 37   New York 9

* Bears defeated Green Bay 33–14 in Divisional Play-off

1942
EASTERN DIVISION

Washington	10	1	0	.909
Pittsburgh	7	4	0	.636
New York	5	5	1	.500
Brooklyn	3	8	0	.273
Philadelphia	2	9	0	.182

WESTERN DIVISION

Chicago Bears	11	0	0	1.000
Green Bay	8	2	1	.800
Cleveland	5	6	0	.455
Chicago Cardinals	3	8	0	.273
Detroit	0	11	0	.000

Washington 14   Chicago Bears 6

1943
WESTERN DIVISION

Chicago Bears	8	1	1	.889
Green Bay	7	2	1	.778
Detroit	3	6	1	.333
Chicago Cardinals	0	10	0	.000

EASTERN DIVISION

Washington*	6	3	1	.667
New York	6	3	1	.667
Phil-Pitt	5	4	1	.555
Brooklyn	2	8	0	.200

Chicago Bears 41   Washington 21

* Washington defeated New York 28–0 in Divisional Play-off

1944
WESTERN DIVISION

Green Bay	8	2	0	.800
Chicago Bears	6	3	1	.667
Detroit	6	3	1	.667
Cleveland	4	6	0	.400
Card-Pitt	0	10	0	.000

EASTERN DIVISION

New York	8	1	1	.889
Philadelphia	7	1	2	.875
Washington	6	3	1	.667
Boston	2	8	0	.200
Brooklyn	0	10	0	.000

Green Bay 14   New York 7

1945
WESTERN DIVISION

Cleveland	9	1	0	.900
Detroit	7	3	0	.700
Green Bay	6	4	0	.600
Chicago Bears	3	7	0	.300
Chicago Cardinals	1	9	0	.100

EASTERN DIVISION

Washington	8	2	0	.800
Philadelphia	7	3	0	.700
New York	3	6	1	.333
Boston	3	6	1	.333
Pittsburgh	2	8	0	.200

Cleveland 15   Washington 14

1946
WESTERN DIVISION

Chicago Bears	8	2	1	.800
Los Angeles	6	4	1	.600
Green Bay	6	5	0	.545
Chicago Cardinals	6	5	0	.545
Detroit	1	10	0	.091

EASTERN DIVISION

New York	7	3	1	.700
Philadelphia	6	5	0	.545
Washington	5	5	1	.500
Pittsburgh	5	5	1	.500
Boston	2	8	1	.200

Chicago Bears 24   New York 14

1947
WESTERN DIVISION

Chicago Cardinals	9	3	0	.750
Chicago Bears	8	4	0	.667
Green Bay	6	5	1	.545
Los Angeles	6	6	0	.500
Detroit	3	9	0	.250

EASTERN DIVISION

Philadelphia*	8	4	0	.667
Pittsburgh	8	4	0	.667
Boston	4	7	1	.364
Washington	4	8	0	.333
New York	2	8	2	.200

Chicago Cardinals 28   Philadelphia 21

* Philadelphia defeated Pittsburgh 21–0 in Divisional Play-off

1948
EASTERN DIVISION

Philadelphia	9	2	1	.818
Washington	7	5	0	.583
New York	4	8	0	.333
Pittsburgh	4	8	0	.333
Boston	3	9	0	.250

WESTERN DIVISION

Chicago Cardinals	11	1	0	.917
Chicago Bears	10	2	0	.833

Los Angeles	6	5	1	.545
Green Bay	3	9	0	.250
Detroit	2	10	0	.167

Philadelphia 7   Chicago Cardinals 0

1949
EASTERN DIVISION

Philadelphia	11	1	0	.917
Pittsburgh	6	5	1	.545
New York Giants	6	6	0	.500
Washington	4	7	1	.364
New York Bulldogs	1	10	1	.091

WESTERN DIVISION

Los Angeles	8	2	2	.800
Chicago Bears	9	3	0	.750
Chicago Cardinals	6	5	1	.545
Detroit	4	8	0	.333
Green Bay	2	10	0	.167

Philadelphia 14   Los Angeles 0

1950
AMERICAN CONFERENCE

Cleveland	10	2	0	.833
New York Giants	10	2	0	.833
Philadelphia	6	6	0	.500
Pittsburgh	6	6	0	.500
Chicago Cardinals	5	7	0	.417
Washington	3	9	0	.250

NATIONAL CONFERENCE

Los Angeles	9	3	0	.750
Chicago Bears	9	3	0	.750
New York Yanks	7	5	0	.583
Detroit	6	6	0	.500
Green Bay	3	9	0	.250
San Francisco	3	9	0	.250
Baltimore	1	11	0	.083

Cleveland 30   Los Angeles 28
Cleveland defeated New York Giants, 8–3, in Conference Play-off
Los Angeles defeated Chicago Bears, 24–14, in Conference Play-off

1951
NATIONAL CONFERENCE

Los Angeles	8	4	0	.667
Detroit	7	4	1	.636
San Francisco	7	4	1	.636
Chicago Bears	7	5	0	.583
Green Bay	3	9	0	.250
New York Yanks	1	9	2	.100

AMERICAN CONFERENCE

Cleveland	11	1	1	.917
New York Giants	9	2	1	.818
Washington	5	7	0	.417
Pittsburgh	4	7	1	.364
Philadelphia	4	8	0	.333
Chicago Cardinals	3	9	0	.250

Los Angeles 24   Cleveland 17

1952
NATIONAL CONFERENCE

Detroit	9	3	0	.750
Los Angeles	9	3	0	.750
San Francisco	7	5	0	.583
Green Bay	6	6	0	.500
Chicago Bears	5	7	0	.417
Dallas	1	11	0	.083

Detroit defeated Los Angeles, 31–21, in conference playoff

AMERICAN CONFERENCE

Cleveland	8	4	0	.667
New York	7	5	0	.583
Philadelphia	7	5	0	.583
Pittsburgh	5	7	0	.417
Chicago Cards	4	8	0	.333
Washington	4	8	0	.333

Detroit defeated Cleveland, 17–7

1953
WESTERN CONFERENCE

Detroit	10	2	0	.833
San Francisco	9	3	0	.750
Los Angeles	8	3	1	.727
Chicago Bears	3	8	1	.273
Baltimore	3	9	0	.250
Green Bay	2	9	1	.182

EASTERN CONFERENCE

Cleveland	11	1	0	.917
Philadelphia	7	4	1	.636
Washington	6	5	1	.545
Pittsburgh	6	6	0	.500
New York	3	9	0	.250
Chicago Cardinals	1	10	1	.091

Detroit defeated Cleveland, 17–16

1954
EASTERN CONFERENCE

Cleveland	9	3	0	.750
Philadelphia	7	4	1	.636
New York	7	5	0	.583
Pittsburgh	5	7	0	.417
Washington	3	9	0	.250
Chicago Cardinals	2	10	0	.167

WESTERN CONFERENCE

Detroit	9	2	1	.818
Chicago Bears	8	4	0	.667
San Francisco	7	4	1	.636
Los Angeles	6	5	1	.545
Green Bay	4	8	0	.333
Baltimore	3	9	0	.250

Cleveland defeated Detroit, 56–10

1955
EASTERN CONFERENCE

Cleveland	9	2	1	.818
Washington	8	4	0	.667

New York	6	5	1	.545
Chicago Cards	4	7	1	.364
Philadelphia	4	7	1	.364
Pittsburgh	4	8	0	.333

WESTERN CONFERENCE

Los Angeles	8	3	1	.727
Chicago Bears	8	4	0	.667
Green Bay	6	6	0	.500
Baltimore	5	6	1	.455
San Francisco	4	8	0	.333
Detroit	3	9	0	.250

Cleveland defeated Los Angeles, 38–14

1956
EASTERN CONFERENCE

New York	8	3	1	.727
Chicago Cards	7	5	0	.583
Washington	6	6	0	.500
Cleveland	5	7	0	.417
Pittsburgh	5	7	0	.417
Philadelphia	3	8	1	.273

WESTERN CONFERENCE

Chicago Bears	9	2	1	.818
Detroit	9	3	0	.750
San Francisco	5	6	1	.455
Baltimore	5	7	0	.417
Green Bay	4	8	0	.333
Los Angeles	4	8	0	.333

1957
WESTERN CONFERENCE

Detroit	8	4	0	.667
San Francisco	8	4	0	.667
Baltimore	7	5	0	.583
Los Angeles	6	6	0	.500
Chicago Bears	5	7	0	.417
Green Bay	3	9	0	.250

Detroit defeated San Francisco, 31–27, in
conference playoff

EASTERN CONFERENCE

Cleveland	9	2	1	.818
New York	7	5	0	.583
Pittsburgh	6	6	0	.500
Washington	5	6	1	.455
Philadelphia	4	8	0	.333
Chicago Cardinals	3	9	0	.250

Detroit defeated Cleveland, 59–14

1958
EASTERN CONFERENCE
| New York | 9 | 3 | 0 | .750 |

Cleveland	9	3	0	.750
Pittsburgh	7	4	1	.636
Washington	4	7	1	.364
Philadelphia	2	9	1	.182
Chicago Cards	2	9	1	.182

New York defeated Cleveland, 10–0 in
conference playoff

WESTERN CONFERENCE

Baltimore	9	3	0	.750
Los Angeles	8	4	0	.667
Chicago Bears	8	4	0	.667
San Francisco	6	6	0	.500
Detroit	4	7	1	.364
Green Bay	1	10	1	.091

Baltimore defeated New York, 23–17

1959
EASTERN CONFERENCE

New York	10	2	0	.883
Cleveland	7	5	0	.583
Philadelphia	7	5	0	.583
Pittsburgh	6	5	1	.545
Washington	3	9	0	.250
Chicago Cards	2	10	0	.167

WESTERN CONFERENCE

Baltimore	9	3	0	.750
Chicago Bears	8	4	0	.667
Green Bay	7	5	0	.583
San Francisco	7	5	0	.583
Detroit	3	8	1	.273
Los Angeles	2	10	0	.167

Baltimore defeated New York, 31–16

1960
EASTERN CONFERENCE

Philadelphia	10	2	0	.833
Cleveland	8	3	1	.727
New York Giants	6	4	2	.600
St. Louis	6	5	1	.545
Pittsburgh	5	6	1	.455
Washington	1	9	2	.100

WESTERN CONFERENCE

Green Bay	8	4	0	.667
Detroit	7	5	0	.583
San Francisco	7	5	0	.583
Baltimore	6	6	0	.500
Chicago	5	6	1	.455
L. A. Rams	4	7	1	.364
Dallas Cowboys	0	11	1	.000

Philadelphia defeated Green Bay, 17–13

TEAM GAME RECORDS

BALTIMORE COLTS

1953
COACH—WILBUR EWBANK

BALTIMORE	13	Bears	9
	17	Detroit	27
	16	Bears	14
	14	Green Bay	37
	27	Washington	17
	24	Green Bay	35
	7	Detroit	17
	14	Philadelphia	45
	13	Los Angeles	21
	21	San Francisco	38
	2	Los Angeles	45
	14	San Francisco	45
	——		——
	182		360

Won 3, Lost 9.

1954
COACH—WILBUR EWBANK

BALTIMORE	0	Los Angeles	48
	20	New York	14
	9	Bears	28
	0	Detroit	35
	6	Green Bay	7
	21	Washington	24
	3	Detroit	21
	13	Green Bay	24
	13	Bears	28
	17	San Francisco	13
	22	Los Angeles	21
	7	San Francisco	10
	——		——
	131		273

Won 3, Lost 9.

1955
COACH—WILBUR EWBANK

BALTIMORE	23	Bears	17
	28	Detroit	13
	24	Green Bay	20
	10	Bears	38
	13	Washington	14
	14	Green Bay	10
	14	Detroit	24
	7	New York	17
	17	Los Angeles	17
	26	San Francisco	14
	14	Los Angeles	20
	24	San Francisco	35
	——		——
	214		239

Won 5, Lost 6, Tied 1.

1956
COACH—WILBUR EWBANK

BALTIMORE	28	Bears	21
	14	Detroit	31
	33	Green Bay	38
	27	Bears	58
	28	Green Bay	21
	21	Cleveland	7
	3	Detroit	27
	56	Los Angeles	21
	17	San Francisco	20
	7	Los Angeles	31
	17	San Francisco	30
	19	Washington	17
	——		——
	270		322

Won 5, Lost 7.

1957
COACH—WILBUR EWBANK

BALTIMORE	34	Detroit	14
	21	Bears	10
	45	Green Bay	17
	27	Detroit	31
	21	Green Bay	24
	13	Pittsburgh	19
	21	Washington	17
	29	Bears	14
	27	San Francisco	21
	31	Los Angeles	14
	13	San Francisco	17
	21	Los Angeles	37
	——		——
	303		235

Won 7, Lost 5.

1958
COACH—WILBUR EWBANK

BALTIMORE	28	Detroit	15
	51	Bears	38
	24	Green Bay	17
	40	Detroit	14
	35	Washington	10
	56	Green Bay	0
	21	New York	24
	17	Bears	0
	34	Los Angeles	7
	35	San Francisco	27
	28	Los Angeles	30
	12	San Francisco	21
	——		——
	381		203

Won 9, Lost 3.
Championship Game:
Baltimore 23   New York 17

1959
COACH—WILBUR EWBANK

BALTIMORE	21	Detroit	8
	21	Chi. Bears	26
	31	Detroit	24
	21	Chi. Bears	7
	38	Green Bay	21
	31	Cleveland	38

BALTIMORE	24	Washington	27
	28	Green Bay	24
	45	San Francisco	14
	35	Los Angeles	21
	34	San Francisco	14
	45	Los Angeles	26
	—		—
	374		251

Won 9, Lost 3.

Championship Game:
Baltimore   31   New York   16

1960
COACH—WILBUR EWBANK

BALTIMORE	20	Washington	0
	42	Chicago	7
	21	Green Bay	35
	31	L. A. Rams	17
	17	Detroit	30
	45	Dal. Cowboys	7
	38	Green Bay	24
	24	Chicago	20
	22	San Francisco	30
	15	Detroit	20
	3	L. A. Rams	10
	10	San Francisco	34
	—		—
	288		234

Won 6, Lost 6

CHICAGO BEARS

1920
COACH—GEORGE S. HALAS

CHICAGO BEARS	20	Moline	0
(STALEYS)	27	Kewanee	0
	7	Rock Island	0
	10	Chicago Tigers	0
	29	Rockford	0
	20	Champaign	0
	28	Hammond	0
	0	Rock Island	0
	3	Minneapolis	0
	6	Chicago Tigers	0
	6	Cardinals	7
	10	Cardinals	0
	0	Akron	0
	—		—
	166		7

Won 10, Lost 1, Tied 2.

1921
COACH—GEORGE S. HALAS

CHICAGO BEARS	35	Waukegan	0
	14	Rock Island	0
	16	Rochester	13
	7	Dayton	0
	20	Detroit	9
	3	Rock Island	0
	22	Cleveland	7
	6	Buffalo	7
	20	Green Bay	0

	10	Buffalo	7
	10	Canton	0
	0	Cardinals	0
	—		—
	163		43

Won 10, Lost 1, Tied 1.

1922
COACH—GEORGE S. HALAS

CHICAGO BEARS	6	Racine	0
	10	Rock Island	0
	7	Rochester	0
	7	Buffalo	0
	6	Canton	7
	9	Dayton	0
	33	Marion	6
	3	Rock Island	0
	20	Akron	10
	0	Cardinals	6
	22	Toledo	0
	0	Cardinals	9
	—		—
	123		44

Won 9, Lost 3.

1923
COACH—GEORGE S. HALAS

CHICAGO BEARS	0	Rock Island	3
	3	Racine	0
	3	Green Bay	0
	18	Buffalo	3
	0	Canton	6
	26	Marion	0
	20	Akron	6
	7	Rock Island	3
	14	Hammond	7
	3	Cardinals	0
	0	Milwaukee	0
	29	Rock Island	7
	7	Milwaukee	7
	—		—
	148		45

Won 10, Lost 2, Tied 2.

1924
COACH—GEORGE S. HALAS

CHICAGO BEARS	0	Green Bay	5
	0	Rock Island	0
	14	Cleveland	16
	10	Racine	10
	6	Cardinals	2
	33	Frankford	3
	3	Rock Island	3
	12	Columbus	6
	3	Racine	3
	3	Green Bay	0
	21	Cardinals	0
	31	Milwaukee	14
	23	Cleveland	0
	13	Frankford	10
	6	Rock Island	7
	—		—
	178		79

Won 8, Lost 3, Tied 4.

1925
COACH—GEORGE S. HALAS

CHICAGO BEARS		
0	Rock Island	0
10	Green Bay	14
0	Detroit	0
28	Hammond	7
7	Cleveland	0
0	Cardinals	9
6	Rock Island	0
19	Frankford	0
14	Detroit	0
21	Green Bay	0
0	Cardinals	0
14	Columbus	13
39	St. Louis	6
14	Frankford	7
—		—
172		47

Won 9, Lost 2, Tied 3.

1925—"Post Season Red Grange Tour"

CHICAGO BEARS		
19	New York	7
19	Washington	0
6	Providence	9
0	Pittsburgh	24
0	Detroit	21
0	New York	9
7	Fla. Coll'g'ns	0
26	Tampa	3
19	Jacksonville	6
14	New Orleans	0
17	L.A. Tigers	7
14	Calif. Stars	0
60	Portland	3
34	Northwest	0
—		—
235		89

Won 10, Lost 4.

1926
COACH—GEORGE S. HALAS

CHICAGO BEARS		
10	Milwaukee	7
6	Green Bay	6
10	Detroit	7
7	New York	0
16	Cardinals	0
24	Duluth	6
17	Akron	0
34	Louisville	0
10	Cardinals	0
10	Milwaukee	7
19	Green Bay	13
0	Cardinals	0
35	Canton	0
6	Frankford	7
9	Pottsville	7
3	Green Bay	3
—		—
216		63

Won 12, Lost 1, Tied 3.

1927
COACH—GEORGE S. HALAS

CHICAGO BEARS		
10	Cardinals	0
7	Green Bay	6
12	N.Y. Yanks	0
14	Cleveland	12
14	Dayton	6
0	Providence	0
30	Pottsville	12
14	Green Bay	6
7	N.Y. Giants	13
0	Cardinals	3
0	Frankford	0
9	Frankford	0
27	Duluth	0
—		—
144		58

Won 9, Lost 2, Tied 2.

1928
COACH—GEORGE S. HALAS

CHICAGO BEARS		
15	Cardinals	0
12	Green Bay	12
12	Minneapolis	6
13	N.Y. Giants	0
6	Green Bay	16
6	Detroit	6
27	N.Y. Yanks	0
27	Dayton	0
13	Pottsville	6
34	Cardinals	6
28	Frankford	6
0	Green Bay	6
0	Frankford	19
—		—
153		111

Won 7, Lost 5, Tied 1.

1929
COACH—GEORGE S. HALAS

CHICAGO BEARS		
19	Minneapolis	6
0	Green Bay	23
7	Minneapolis	6
16	Buffalo	0
0	Cardinals	0
27	Minneapolis	0
14	N.Y. Giants	26
0	Green Bay	14
14	Frankford	20
0	N.Y. Giants	34
39	Memphis	19
6	Cardinals	40
0	Frankford	0
0	Green Bay	25
9	N.Y. Giants	14
151		227

Won 5, Lost 8, Tied 2.

1930
COACH—RALPH JONES

CHICAGO BEARS		
0	Brooklyn	0
0	Green Bay	7
20	Milwaukee	0
26	Milwaukee	0
0	New York	12
32	Cardinals	6
6	Portsmouth	7

CHICAGO BEARS	13	Frankford	7
	20	Minneapolis	7
	12	Green Bay	13
	12	New York	0
	6	Cardinals	0
	14	Portsmouth	6
	21	Green Bay	0
	9	Cardinals	7
	——		——
	191		72

Won 10, Lost 4, Tied 1.

	3	Philadelphia	3
	0	New York	3
	17	Portsmouth	14
	22	Cardinals	6
	17	Portsmouth	7
	7	Green Bay	6
	——		——
	165		88

Won 11, Lost 2, Tied 1.
Championship Game:
Chicago Bears 23 New York 21

1931
COACH—RALPH JONES

CHICAGO BEARS	21	Cleveland	0
	0	Green Bay	7
	6	New York	0
	26	Cardinals	13
	12	Frankford	13
	2	Green Bay	6
	9	Portsmouth	6
	12	New York	6
	26	Brooklyn	0
	18	Cardinals	7
	6	New York	25
	7	Green Bay	6
	——		——
	145		89

Won 8, Lost 4.

1934
COACH—GEORGE S. HALAS

CHICAGO BEARS	21	Brooklyn	7
	28	Pittsburgh	0
	20	Cardinals	0
	10	Green Bay	6
	27	Green Bay	14
	27	New York	7
	21	Boston	0
	10	New York	9
	17	Cardinals	6
	19	Detroit	16
	10	Detroit	7
	28	Philadelphia	14
	——		——
	238		86

Won 12.
Championship Game:
Chicago Bears 13 New York 30

1932
COACH—RALPH JONES

CHICAGO BEARS	26	Cleveland	0
	0	Green Bay	0
	0	Stapleton	0
	0	Cardinals	0
	0	Green Bay	2
	13	Brooklyn	0
	27	Stapleton	7
	7	Boston	7
	28	New York	8
	13	Portsmouth	13
	35	St. Louis	0
	20	Brooklyn	0
	34	Cardinals	0
	7	Portsmouth	0
	6	New York	0
	9	Green Bay	0
	9	Portsmouth	0
	——		——
	234		37

Won 12, Lost 1, Tied 5.

1935
COACH—GEORGE S. HALAS

CHICAGO BEARS	0	Green Bay	7
	23	Pittsburgh	7
	39	Philadelphia	0
	24	Brooklyn	14
	14	Green Bay	17
	20	New York	3
	30	Boston	14
	0	New York	3
	20	Detroit	20
	2	Detroit	14
	7	Cardinals	7
	13	Cardinals	0
	——		——
	192		106

Won 6, Lost 4, Tied 2.

1933
COACH—GEORGE S. HALAS

CHICAGO BEARS	14	Green Bay	7
	7	Boston	6
	10	Brooklyn	0
	12	Cardinals	9
	10	Green Bay	7
	14	New York	10
	32	Detroit	0
	0	Boston	10

1936
COACH—GEORGE S. HALAS

CHICAGO BEARS	30	Green Bay	3
	17	Philadelphia	0
	27	Pittsburgh	9
	7	Cardinals	3
	26	Pittsburgh	7
	12	Detroit	10
	10	Green Bay	21
	25	New York	7
	26	Boston	0
	28	Philadelphia	7
	7	Detroit	13

	Cardinals	
7	Cardinals	14

222		94

Won 9, Lost 3.

1937
COACH—GEORGE S. HALAS

CHICAGO BEARS	14	Green Bay	2
	7	Pittsburgh	0
	20	Cleveland	2
	16	Cardinals	7
	28	Detroit	20
	3	New York	3
	14	Green Bay	24
	29	Brooklyn	7
	13	Detroit	0
	15	Cleveland	7
	42	Cardinals	28

201		100

Won 9, Lost 1, Tied 1.
Championship Game:
Chicago Bears 21   Washington 28

1938
COACH—GEORGE S. HALAS

CHICAGO BEARS	16	Cardinals	13
	2	Green Bay	0
	28	Philadelphia	6
	7	Cleveland	14
	34	Cardinals	28
	21	Cleveland	23
	7	Detroit	13
	17	Green Bay	24
	31	Washington	7
	24	Brooklyn	6
	7	Detroit	14

194		148

Won 6, Lost 5.

1939
COACH—GEORGE S. HALAS

CHICAGO BEARS	30	Cleveland	21
	16	Green Bay	21
	32	Pittsburgh	0
	35	Cleveland	21
	44	Cardinals	7
	13	New York	16
	0	Detroit	10
	30	Green Bay	27
	27	Philadelphia	14
	48	Cardinals	7

275		144

Won 7, Lost 3.

1940
COACH—GEORGE S. HALAS

CHICAGO BEARS	41	Green Bay	10
	7	Cardinals	21
	21	Cleveland	14

7	Detroit	0
16	Brooklyn	7
37	New York	21
14	Green Bay	7
14	Detroit	17
3	Washington	7
47	Cleveland	25
31	Cardinals	23

238		150

Won 8, Lost 3.
Championship Game:
Chicago Bears 73   Washington 0

1941
COACH—GEORGE S. HALAS

CHICAGO BEARS	25	Green Bay	17
	48	Cleveland	21
	53	Cardinals	7
	49	Detroit	0
	34	Pittsburgh	7
	14	Green Bay	16
	31	Cleveland	13
	35	Washington	21
	24	Detroit	7
	49	Philadelphia	14
	34	Cardinals	24

396		147

Won 10, Lost 1.
Divisional Play-off:
Chicago Bears 33   Green Bay 14
Championship Game:
Chicago Bears 34   New York 9

1942
COACHES—G. HALAS, L. JOHNSOS,
H. ANDERSON

CHICAGO BEARS	44	Green Bay	28
	21	Cleveland	7
	41	Cardinals	14
	26	New York	7
	45	Philadelphia	14
	16	Detroit	0
	35	Brooklyn	0
	38	Green Bay	7
	42	Detroit	0
	47	Cleveland	7
	21	Cardinals	7

376		91

Won 11.
Championship Game:
Chicago Bears 6   Washington 14

1943
COACHES—HEARTLEY ANDERSON
LUKE JOHNSOS

CHICAGO BEARS	21	Green Bay	21
	27	Detroit	21
	20	Cardinals	0
	48	Philadelphia	21
	33	Brooklyn	21
	35	Detroit	14
	21	Green Bay	7

CHICAGO BEARS	56	New York	7
	7	Washington	21
	35	Cardinals	24
	—		—
	303		157

Won 8, Lost 1, Tied 1.
Championship Game:
Chicago Bears 41   Washington 21

1944
COACHES—HEARTLEY ANDERSON
LUKE JOHNSOS

CHICAGO BEARS	28	Green Bay	42
	28	Washington	0
	7	Cleveland	19
	34	Card-Pitt	7
	21	Detroit	21
	28	Cleveland	21
	21	Green Bay	0
	21	Boston	7
	21	Detroit	41
	28	Philadelphia	7
	49	Card-Pitt	7
	—		—
	286		172

Won 7, Lost 3, Tied 1.

1945
COACHES—HEARTLEY ANDERSON
LUKE JOHNSOS *

CHICAGO BEARS	21	Green Bay	31
	0	Cleveland	17
	7	Cardinals	16
	21	Cleveland	41
	10	Detroit	16
	28	Green Bay	24
	28	Detroit	35
	21	Washington	28
	28	Pittsburgh	7
	28	Cardinals	20
	—		—
	192		225

Won 3, Lost 7.

1946
COACH—GEORGE S. HALAS

CHICAGO BEARS	30	Green Bay	7
	34	Cardinals	17
	28	Los Angeles	28
	21	Philadelphia	14
	0	New York	14
	10	Green Bay	7
	27	Los Angeles	21
	24	Washington	20
	42	Detroit	6
	28	Cardinals	35
	45	Detroit	24
	—		—
	289		193

Won 8, Lost 2, Tied 1.
Championship Game:
Chicago Bears 24   New York 14

1947
COACH—GEORGE S. HALAS

CHICAGO BEARS	20	Green Bay	29
	7	Cardinals	31
	40	Philadelphia	7
	33	Detroit	24
	56	Washington	20
	28	Boston	24
	20	Green Bay	17
	41	Los Angeles	21
	49	Pittsburgh	7
	34	Detroit	14
	14	Los Angeles	17
	21	Cardinals	30
	—		—
	363		240

Won 8, Lost 4.

1948
COACH—GEORGE S. HALAS

CHICAGO BEARS	45	Green Bay	7
	28	Cardinals	17
	42	Los Angeles	21
	28	Detroit	0
	7	Philadelphia	12
	35	New York	14
	21	Los Angeles	6
	7	Green Bay	6
	51	Boston	17
	48	Washington	13
	42	Detroit	14
	21	Cardinals	24
	—		—
	375		151

Won 10, Lost 2.

1949
COACH—GEORGE S. HALAS

CHICAGO BEARS	17	Green Bay	0
	17	Cardinals	7
	16	Los Angeles	31
	38	Philadelphia	21
	28	N.Y. Giants	35
	24	Los Angeles	27
	24	Green Bay	3
	27	Detroit	24
	31	Washington	21
	28	Detroit	7
	30	Pittsburgh	21
	52	Cardinals	21
	—		—
	332		218

Won 9, Lost 3.

1950
COACH—GEORGE S. HALAS

CHICAGO BEARS	24	Los Angeles	10
	32	San Francisco	20
	21	Green Bay	30
	27	Cardinals	6
	28	Green Bay	14
	27	N.Y. Yanks	38
	35	Detroit	21
	28	N.Y. Yanks	20
	17	San Francisco	0
	24	Los Angeles	14

10	Cardinals	20
6	Detroit	3
—		—
279		196

Won 9, Lost 3.
Divisional Play-off:
Chicago Bears 14   Los Angeles 24

1951
COACH—GEORGE S. HALAS

CHICAGO BEARS	31	Green Bay	20
	14	Cardinals	28
	24	N.Y. Yanks	21
	13	San Francisco	7
	28	Detroit	23
	27	Washington	0
	28	Detroit	41
	24	Green Bay	13
	21	Cleveland	42
	17	Los Angeles	42
	45	N.Y. Yanks	21
	14	Cardinals	24
	—		—
	286		282

Won 7, Lost 5.

1952
COACH—GEORGE S. HALAS

CHICAGO BEARS	24	Green Bay	14
	10	Cardinals	21
	38	Dallas	20
	16	San Francisco	40
	7	Los Angeles	31
	20	San Francisco	17
	28	Green Bay	41
	24	Los Angeles	40
	24	Detroit	23
	23	Dallas	27
	21	Detroit	45
	10	Cardinals	7
	—		—
	245		326

Won 5, Lost 7.

1953
COACH—GEORGE S. HALAS

CHICAGO BEARS	9	Baltimore	13
	19	Green Bay	13
	14	Baltimore	16
	28	San Francisco	35
	24	Los Angeles	38
	14	San Francisco	24
	21	Green Bay	21
	27	Washington	24
	16	Detroit	20
	24	Los Angeles	21
	7	Detroit	13
	17	Cardinals	24
	—		—
	220		262

Won 3, Lost 8, Tied 1.

1954
COACH—GEORGE S. HALAS

| CHICAGO BEARS | 23 | Detroit | 48 |

10	Green Bay	3
28	Baltimore	9
24	San Francisco	31
38	Los Angeles	42
31	San Francisco	27
28	Green Bay	23
10	Cleveland	39
28	Baltimore	13
24	Los Angeles	13
29	Cardinals	7
28	Detroit	24
—		—
301		279

Won 8, Lost 4.

1955
COACH—JOHN "PADDY" DRISCOLL

CHICAGO BEARS	17	Baltimore	23
	3	Green Bay	24
	19	San Francisco	20
	38	Baltimore	10
	34	San Francisco	23
	31	Los Angeles	20
	52	Green Bay	31
	24	Los Angeles	3
	24	Detroit	14
	14	Cardinals	53
	21	Detroit	20
	17	Philadelphia	10
	—		—
	294		251

Won 8, Lost 4.

1956
COACH—JOHN "PADDY" DRISCOLL

CHICAGO BEARS	21	Baltimore	28
	37	Green Bay	21
	31	San Francisco	7
	58	Baltimore	27
	38	San Francisco	21
	35	Los Angeles	24
	38	Green Bay	14
	30	Los Angeles	21
	17	New York	17
	10	Detroit	42
	10	Cardinals	3
	38	Detroit	21
	—		—
	363		246

Won 9, Lost 2, Tied 1.
Championship Game:
Chicago Bears 7   New York Giants 47

1957
COACH—GEORGE S. HALAS

CHICAGO BEARS	17	Green Bay	21
	10	Baltimore	21
	17	San Francisco	21
	34	Los Angeles	26
	17	San Francisco	21
	16	Los Angeles	10
	21	Green Bay	14
	14	Baltimore	29
	27	Detroit	7
	3	Washington	14

CHICAGO BEARS	14	Cardinals	6
	13	Detroit	21
	—		—
	203		211

Won 5, Lost 7.

1958
COACH—GEORGE S. HALAS

CHICAGO BEARS	34	Green Bay	20
	38	Baltimore	51
	28	San Francisco	6
	31	Los Angeles	10
	27	San Francisco	14
	35	Los Angeles	41
	24	Green Bay	10
	0	Baltimore	17
	20	Detroit	7
	10	Pittsburgh	24
	30	Cardinals	14
	21	Detroit	16
	—		—
	298		230

Won 8, Lost 4.

1959
COACH—GEORGE S. HALAS

CHICAGO BEARS	6	Green Bay	9
	26	Baltimore	21
	21	Los Angeles	28
	7	Baltimore	21
	17	San Francisco	20
	26	Los Angeles	21
	28	Green Bay	17
	14	San Francisco	3
	24	Detroit	14
	31	Chicago Cards	7
	27	Pittsburgh	21
	25	Detroit	14
	—		—
	252		196

Won 8, Lost 4.

1960
COACH—GEORGE S. HALAS

CHICAGO BEARS	17	Green Bay	14
	7	Baltimore	42
	34	L. A. Rams	27
	27	San Francisco	10
	24	L. A. Rams	24
	7	San Francisco	25
	20	Baltimore	24
	28	Detroit	7
	17	Dal. Cowboys	7
	13	Green Bay	41
	0	Cleveland	42
	0	Detroit	36
	—		—
	194		299

Won 5, Lost 6, Tied 1

CLEVELAND BROWNS
(Formerly AAFC; entered NFL 1950)

1950
COACH—PAUL BROWN

CLEVELAND	35	Philadelphia	10
	31	Baltimore	0
	0	N.Y. Giants	6
	30	Pittsburgh	17
	34	Cardinals	24
	13	N.Y. Giants	17
	45	Pittsburgh	7
	10	Cardinals	7
	34	San Francisco	14
	20	Washington	14
	13	Philadelphia	7
	45	Washington	21
	—		—
	310		144

Won 10, Lost 2.
Divisional Play-off:
Cleveland 8   N.Y. Giants 3
Championship Game:
Cleveland 30   Los Angeles 28

1951
COACH—PAUL BROWN

CLEVELAND	10	San Francisco	24
	38	Los Angeles	23
	45	Washington	0
	17	Pittsburgh	0
	14	N.Y. Giants	13
	34	Chicago Cards	17
	20	Philadelphia	17
	10	N.Y. Giants	0
	42	Chicago Bears	21
	49	Chicago Cards	28
	28	Pittsburgh	0
	24	Philadelphia	9
	—		—
	331		152

Won 11, Lost 1.
Championship Game:
Cleveland 17   Los Angeles 24

1952
COACH—PAUL BROWN

CLEVELAND	37	Los Angeles	7
	21	Pittsburgh	20
	9	New York	17
	49	Philadelphia	7
	19	Washington	15
	6	Detroit	17
	28	Cardinals	13
	29	Pittsburgh	28
	20	Philadelphia	28
	48	Washington	24
	10	Cardinals	0
	34	New York	37
	—		—
	309		213

Won 8, Lost 4.
Championship Game:
Cleveland 7   Detroit 17

1953
COACH—PAUL BROWN

CLEVELAND		
27	Green Bay	0
27	Cardinals	7
37	Philadelphia	13
30	Washington	14
7	New York	0
27	Washington	3
34	Pittsburgh	16
23	San Francisco	21
20	Pittsburgh	16
27	Cardinals	16
62	New York	14
27	Philadelphia	42
—		—
348		162

Won 11, Lost 1.
Championship Game:
Cleveland 16   Detroit 17

1954
COACH—PAUL BROWN

CLEVELAND		
10	Philadelphia	28
31	Cardinals	7
27	Pittsburgh	55
35	Cardinals	3
24	New York	14
62	Washington	3
39	Bears	10
6	Philadelphia	0
16	New York	7
34	Washington	14
42	Pittsburgh	7
10	Detroit	14
—		—
336		162

Won 9, Lost 3.
Championship Game:
Cleveland 56   Detroit 10

1955
COACH—PAUL BROWN

CLEVELAND		
17	Washington	27
38	San Francisco	3
21	Philadelphia	17
24	Washington	14
41	Green Bay	10
26	Cardinals	20
24	New York	14
17	Philadelphia	33
41	Pittsburgh	14
35	New York	35
30	Pittsburgh	7
35	Cardinals	24
—		—
349		218

Won 9, Lost 2, Tied 1.
Championship Game:
Cleveland 38   Los Angeles 14

1956
COACH—PAUL BROWN

CLEVELAND		
7	Cardinals	9
14	Pittsburgh	10
9	New York	21
9	Washington	20
16	Pittsburgh	24
24	Green Bay	7
7	Baltimore	21
16	Philadelphia	0
17	Washington	20
17	Philadelphia	14
24	New York	7
7	Cardinals	24
—		—
167		177

Won 5, Lost 7.

1957
COACH—PAUL BROWN

CLEVELAND		
6	New York	3
23	Pittsburgh	12
24	Philadelphia	7
7	Philadelphia	17
17	Cardinals	7
21	Washington	17
24	Pittsburgh	0
30	Washington	30
45	Los Angeles	31
31	Cardinals	0
7	Detroit	20
34	New York	28
—		—
269		172

Won 9, Lost 2, Tied 1.
Championship Game:
Cleveland 14   Detroit 59

1958
COACH—PAUL BROWN

CLEVELAND		
30	Los Angeles	27
45	Pittsburgh	12
35	Cardinals	28
27	Pittsburgh	10
38	Cardinals	24
17	New York	21
10	Detroit	30
20	Washington	10
28	Philadelphia	14
21	Washington	14
21	Philadelphia	14
10	New York	13
—		—
302		217

Won 9, Lost 3.
Conference Play-off:
New York 10   Cleveland 0

1959
COACH—PAUL BROWN

CLEVELAND		
7	Pittsburgh	17
34	Chicago Cards	7
6	New York	10
17	Chicago Cards	7
34	Washington	7
38	Baltimore	31
28	Philadelphia	7
31	Washington	17
20	Pittsburgh	21
20	San Francisco	21
7	New York	48

CLEVELAND	28	Philadelphia	21
	—		—
	270		214

Won 7, Lost 5

1960
COACH—PAUL BROWN

CLEVELAND	41	Philadelphia	24
	28	Pittsburgh	20
	48	Dal.Cowboys	7
	29	Philadelphia	31
	31	Washington	10
	13	N.Y. Giants	17
	28	St. Louis	27
	10	Pittsburgh	14
	17	St. Louis	17
	27	Washington	16
	42	Chicago	0
	48	N.Y. Giants	34
	—		—
	362		217

Won 8, Lost 3, Tied 1

DALLAS COWBOYS

1960
COACH—THOMAS LANDRY

DALLAS	28	Pittsburgh	35
	25	Philadelphia	27
	14	Washington	26
	7	Cleveland	48
	10	St. Louis	12
	7	Baltimore	45
	13	L. A. Rams	38
	7	Green Bay	41
	14	San Francisco	26
	7	Chicago	17
	31	N.Y. Giants	31
	14	Detroit	23
	—		—
	177		369

Won 0, Lost 11, Tied 1

DETROIT LIONS

1934
COACH—GEORGE "POTSY" CLARK

DETROIT	9	New York	0
	6	Cardinals	0
	3	Green Bay	0
	10	Philadelphia	0
	24	Boston	0
	28	Brooklyn	0
	38	Cin.-St. L.	0
	40	Pittsburgh	7
	17	Cardinals	13
	40	Cin.-St. L.	7
	0	Green Bay	3
	16	Bears	19
	7	Bears	10
	—		—
	238		59

Won 11, Lost 2.

1935
COACH—GEORGE "POTSY" CLARK

DETROIT	35	Philadelphia	0
	10	Cardinals	10
	10	Brooklyn	12
	17	Boston	7
	9	Green Bay	13
	14	Boston	0
	7	Cardinals	6
	7	Green Bay	31
	20	Green Bay	10
	20	Bears	20
	14	Bears	2
	28	Brooklyn	0
	—		—
	191		111

Won 7, Lost 3, Tied 2.
Championship Game:
Detroit 26   New York 7

1936
COACH—GEORGE "POTSY" CLARK

DETROIT	39	Cardinals	0
	23	Philadelphia	0
	14	Brooklyn	7
	18	Green Bay	20
	10	Bears	12
	7	New York	14
	28	Pittsburgh	3
	38	New York	0
	14	Cardinals	7
	13	Bears	7
	17	Green Bay	26
	14	Brooklyn	6
	—		—
	235		102

Won 8, Lost 4.

1937
COACH—EARL "DUTCH" CLARK

DETROIT	28	Cleveland	0
	16	Cardinals	7
	6	Green Bay	26
	7	Pittsburgh	3
	30	Brooklyn	0
	20	Bears	28
	13	Green Bay	14
	27	Cleveland	7
	17	New York	0
	16	Cardinals	7
	0	Bears	13
	—		—
	180		105

Won 7, Lost 4.

1938
COACH—EARL "DUTCH" CLARK

DETROIT	16	Pittsburgh	7
	5	Washington	7
	10	Cardinals	0
	17	Cleveland	21
	17	Green Bay	7
	7	Cardinals	3
	13	Bears	7
	6	Cleveland	0

DETROIT	7	Green Bay	28
	14	Bears	7
	7	Philadelphia	21
	—		—
	119		108

Won 7, Lost 4.

1939
COACH—GUS HENDERSON

DETROIT	21	Cardinals	13
	27	Brooklyn	7
	17	Cardinals	3
	15	Cleveland	7
	7	Green Bay	26
	10	Bears	0
	18	New York	14
	13	Bears	23
	3	Cleveland	14
	7	Washington	31
	7	Green Bay	12
	—		—
	145		150

Won 6, Lost 5.

1940
COACH—GEORGE "POTSY" CLARK

DETROIT	0	Cardinals	0
	7	Pittsburgh	10
	6	Cleveland	0
	43	Cardinals	14
	0	Bears	7
	23	Green Bay	14
	14	Washington	20
	0	Cleveland	24
	17	Bears	14
	21	Philadelphia	0
	7	Green Bay	50
	—		—
	138		153

Won 5, Lost 5, Tied 1.

1941
COACH—WILLIAM EDWARDS

DETROIT	0	Green Bay	23
	7	Brooklyn	14
	14	Cardinals	14
	17	Cleveland	7
	0	Bears	49
	7	Green Bay	24
	14	Cleveland	0
	13	New York	20
	21	Philadelphia	17
	7	Bears	24
	21	Cardinals	3
	—		—
	121		195

Won 4, Lost 6, Tied 1.

1942
COACH—JOHN KARCIS

DETROIT	0	Cardinals	13
	0	Cleveland	14
	7	Brooklyn	28
	7	Green Bay	38
	0	Cardinals	7
	7	Green Bay	28
	0	Bears	16
	7	Pittsburgh	35
	7	Cleveland	27
	0	Bears	42
	3	Washington	15
	—		—
	38		263

Won 0, Lost 11.

1943
COACH—CHARLES E. DORAIS

DETROIT	35	Cardinals	17
	27	Brooklyn	0
	21	Bears	27
	14	Green Bay	35
	7	Cardinals	0
	6	Green Bay	27
	14	Bears	35
	0	New York	0
	20	Washington	42
	34	Phil-Pitt	35
	—		—
	178		218

Won 3, Lost 6, Tied 1.

1944
COACH—CHARLES E. DORAIS

DETROIT	6	Green Bay	27
	19	Brooklyn	14
	17	Cleveland	20
	21	Bears	21
	0	Green Bay	14
	27	Card-Pitt	6
	21	Card-Pitt	7
	41	Bears	21
	26	Cleveland	14
	38	Boston	7
	—		—
	216		151

Won 6, Lost 3, Tied 1.

1945
COACH—CHARLES E. DORAIS

DETROIT	10	Cardinals	0
	21	Green Bay	57
	28	Philadelphia	24
	25	Cardinals	0
	16	Bears	10
	10	Boston	9
	35	Bears	28
	14	New York	35
	21	Cleveland	28
	14	Green Bay	3
	—		—
	195		194

Won 7, Lost 3.

1946
COACH—CHARLES E. DORAIS

DETROIT	14	Cardinals	34
	16	Washington	17
	14	Cardinals	36
	14	Los Angeles	35
	7	Green Bay	10
	20	Los Angeles	41

526   THE ENCYCLOPEDIA OF FOOTBALL

DETROIT	17	Pittsburgh	7
	0	Green Bay	9
	6	Bears	42
	10	Boston	34
	24	Bears	45
	——		——
	142		310

Won 1, Lost 10.

1947
COACH—CHARLES E. DORAIS

DETROIT	10	Pittsburgh	17
	21	Cardinals	45
	21	Boston	7
	13	Los Angeles	27
	24	Bears	33
	17	Green Bay	34
	35	New York	7
	7	Cardinals	17
	38	Washington	21
	17	Los Angeles	28
	14	Bears	34
	14	Green Bay	35
	——		——
	231		305

Won 3, Lost 9.

1948
COACH—ALVIN N. "BO" McMILLIN

DETROIT	7	Los Angeles	44
	21	Green Bay	33
	14	Boston	17
	0	Bears	28
	27	Los Angeles	34
	24	Green Bay	20
	20	Cardinals	56
	21	Washington	46
	17	Pittsburgh	14
	14	Cardinals	28
	14	Bears	42
	21	Philadelphia	45
	——		——
	200		407

Won 2, Lost 10.

1949
COACH—ALVIN N. "BO" McMILLIN

DETROIT	24	Los Angeles	27
	14	Philadelphia	22
	7	Pittsburgh	14
	10	Los Angeles	21
	24	Cardinals	7
	14	Green Bay	16
	19	Cardinals	42
	24	Bears	27
	45	N.Y. Giants	21
	7	Bears	28
	28	N.Y. Bulldogs	27
	21	Green Bay	7
	——		——
	237		259

Won 4, Lost 8.

1950
COACH—ALVIN N. "BO" McMILLIN

DETROIT	45	Green Bay	7
	10	Pittsburgh	7
	21	N.Y. Yanks	44
	24	San Francisco	7
	28	Los Angeles	30
	27	San Francisco	28
	24	Los Angeles	65
	21	Bears	35
	24	Green Bay	21
	49	N.Y. Yanks	14
	45	Baltimore	21
	3	Bears	6
	——		——
	321		285

Won 6, Lost 6.

1951
COACH—RAYMOND PARKER

DETROIT	35	Washington	17
	37	N.Y. Yanks	10
	21	Los Angeles	27
	24	N.Y. Yanks	24
	23	Bears	28
	24	Green Bay	17
	41	Bears	28
	28	Philadelphia	7
	52	Green Bay	35
	10	San Francisco	20
	24	Los Angeles	22
	17	San Francisco	21
	——		——
	336		256

Won 7, Lost 4, Tied 1.

1952
COACH—RAYMOND PARKER

DETROIT	3	San Francisco	17
	17	Los Angeles	14
	0	San Francisco	28
	24	Los Angeles	16
	52	Green Bay	17
	17	Cleveland	6
	31	Pittsburgh	6
	43	Dallas	13
	23	Bears	24
	48	Green Bay	24
	45	Bears	21
	41	Dallas	6
	——		——
	344		187

Won 9, Lost 3.
Conference Play-off:
Detroit 31   Los Angeles 21
Championship Game:
Detroit 17   Cleveland 7

1953
COACH—RAYMOND PARKER

DETROIT	38	Pittsburgh	21
	27	Baltimore	17
	24	San Francisco	21
	19	Los Angeles	31
	14	San Francisco	10
	24	Los Angeles	37
	17	Baltimore	7

14	Green Bay	7
20	Bears	16
34	Green Bay	15
13	Bears	7
27	New York	16
—		—
261		205

Won 10, Lost 2.
Championship Game:
Detroit 17   Cleveland 16

1954
COACH—RAYMOND PARKER

DETROIT	48	Bears	23
	21	Los Angeles	3
	35	Baltimore	0
	31	San Francisco	37
	27	Los Angeles	24
	27	Baltimore	3
	48	San Francisco	7
	21	Green Bay	17
	28	Green Bay	24
	13	Philadelphia	13
	24	Bears	28
	14	Cleveland	10
	—		—
	337		189

Won 9, Lost 2, Tied 1.
Championship Game:
Detroit 10   Cleveland 56

1955
COACH—RAYMOND PARKER

DETROIT	17	Green Bay	20
	13	Baltimore	28
	10	Los Angeles	17
	24	San Francisco	27
	13	Los Angeles	24
	21	San Francisco	38
	24	Baltimore	14
	31	Pittsburgh	28
	14	Bears	24
	24	Green Bay	10
	20	Bears	21
	19	New York	24
	—		—
	230		275

Won 3, Lost 9.

1956
COACH—RAYMOND PARKER

DETROIT	20	Green Bay	16
	31	Baltimore	14
	24	Los Angeles	21
	20	San Francisco	17
	16	Los Angeles	7
	17	San Francisco	13
	17	Washington	18
	27	Baltimore	3
	20	Green Bay	24
	42	Bears	10
	45	Pittsburgh	7
	21	Bears	38
	—		—
	300		188

Won 9, Lost 3.

1957
COACH—GEORGE WILSON

DETROIT	14	Baltimore	34
	24	Green Bay	14
	10	Los Angeles	7
	31	Baltimore	27
	17	Los Angeles	35
	31	San Francisco	35
	27	Philadelphia	16
	31	San Francisco	10
	7	Bears	27
	18	Green Bay	6
	20	Cleveland	7
	21	Bears	13
	—		—
	251		231

Won 8, Lost 4.
Conference Play-off:
Detroit 31   San Francisco 27
Championship Game:
Detroit 59   Cleveland 14

1958
COACH—GEORGE WILSON

DETROIT	15	Baltimore	28
	13	Green Bay	13
	28	Los Angeles	42
	14	Baltimore	40
	41	Los Angeles	24
	21	San Francisco	24
	30	Cleveland	10
	35	San Francisco	21
	7	Bears	20
	24	Green Bay	14
	17	New York	19
	16	Bears	21
	—		—
	261		276

Won 4, Lost 7, Tied 1.

1959
COACH—GEORGE WILSON

DETROIT	9	Baltimore	21
	10	Green Bay	28
	24	Baltimore	31
	13	San Francisco	34
	17	Los Angeles	7
	7	San Francisco	33
	10	Pittsburgh	10
	23	Los Angeles	17
	14	Chicago Bears	24
	17	Green Bay	24
	45	Chi. Cards	21
	14	Chi. Bears	25
	—		—
	203		275

Won 3, Lost 8, Tied 1

1960
COACH—GEORGE WILSON

DETROIT	9	Green Bay	28
	10	San Francisco	14
	10	Philadelphia	28
	30	Baltimore	17
	35	L. A. Rams	48
	24	San Francisco	0

DETROIT	12	L. A. Rams	10
	7	Chicago	28
	23	Green Bay	10
	20	Baltimore	15
	24	Dal. Cowboys	14
	36	Chicago	0
	—		—
	239		212

Won 7, Lost 5

GREEN BAY PACKERS

1920
COACH—EARL LAMBEAU

GREEN BAY	3	Chi. Boosters	3
	56	Kaukauna	0
	3	Stambaugh	0
	25	Marinette	0
	62	DePere	0
	7	Beloit	0
	9	Milwaukee Stars	0
	3	Beloit	14
	19	Menominee	7
	26	Lapham A.C.	0
	14	Stambaugh	0
	—		—
	227		24

Won 9, Lost 1, Tied 1.

1921
COACH—EARL LAMBEAU

GREEN BAY	13	Chi. Boosters	0
	49	Rockford	0
	40	Chi. Cornhuskers	0
	7	Beloit	0
	3	Rock Island	10
	7	Minneapolis	6
	43	Evansville	6
	14	Hammond	7
	3	Cardinals	3
	0	Staleys	20
	3	Racine	3
	—		—
	182		55

Won 7, Lost 2, Tied 2.

1922
COACH—EARL LAMBEAU

GREEN BAY	0	Duluth	6
	3	Cardinals	6
	14	Rock Island	19
	6	Racine	10
	0	Milwaukee	0
	0	Rock Island	0
	3	Columbus	0
	14	Marines	6
	3	Racine	3
	13	Milwaukee	0
	10	Duluth	0
	14	Racine	0
	—		—
	80		50

Won 5, Lost 4, Tied 3.

1923
COACH—EARL LAMBEAU

GREEN BAY	10	Hibbing	0
	12	Marines	0
	0	St. Louis	0
	0	Bears	3
	12	Milwaukee	0
	3	Racine	24
	3	St. Louis	0
	10	Milwaukee	7
	16	Racine	0
	10	Duluth	0
	19	Hammond	0
	—		—
	95		34

Won 8, Lost 2, Tied 1.

1924
COACH—EARL LAMBEAU

GREEN BAY	15	Ironwood	0
	5	Bears	0
	3	Duluth	6
	0	Cardinals	3
	16	Kansas City	0
	17	Milwaukee	0
	19	Marines	0
	6	Racine	3
	13	Duluth	0
	17	Milwaukee	10
	0	Bears	3
	17	Kansas City	6
	0	Racine	7
	—		—
	128		38

Won 9, Lost 4.

1925
COACH—EARL LAMBEAU

GREEN BAY	14	Bears	10
	0	Rock Island	3
	33	Rochester	13
	20	Rock Island	0
	31	Milwaukee	0
	6	Cardinals	9
	7	Dayton	0
	7	Philadelphia	13
	0	Bears	21
	0	Pottsville	31
	14	Providence	10
	—		—
	132		110

Won 6, Lost 5.

1926
COACH—EARL LAMBEAU

GREEN BAY	79	Iron Mountain	0
	21	Detroit	0
	6	Bears	6
	7	Milwaukee	0
	7	Cardinals	13
	0	Duluth	0
	35	Racine	0
	3	Cardinals	0

21	Milwaukee	0
14	Louisville	0
13	Bears	19
14	Yellowjackets	19
7	Detroit	0
3	Bears	3
230		60

Won 8, Lost 3, Tied 3.

1927
COACH—EARL LAMBEAU

GREEN BAY	34	Milwaukee	0
	14	Dayton	0
	12	Cleveland	7
	6	Bears	7
	20	Duluth	0
	13	Cardinals	0
	13	Yankees	0
	22	Milwaukee	7
	6	Cardinals	6
	6	Dayton	0
	6	Bears	14
	17	Frankford	9
	169		50

Won 9, Lost 2, Tied 1.

1928
COACH—EARL LAMBEAU

GREEN BAY	19	Minneapolis	0
	9	Philadelphia	19
	12	Bears	12
	0	New York	6
	20	Cardinals	0
	16	Bears	6
	17	Dayton	0
	26	Pottsville	14
	0	Yankees	0
	7	New York	0
	0	Pottsville	26
	7	Providence	7
	0	Frankford	2
	6	Bears	0
	139		92

Won 7, Lost 4, Tied 3.

1929
COACH—EARL LAMBEAU

GREEN BAY	14	Portsmouth	0
	9	Dayton	2
	23	Bears	0
	9	Cardinals	2
	14	Frankford	2
	24	Minneapolis	0
	7	Cardinals	6
	16	Minneapolis	6
	14	Bears	0
	12	Cardinals	0
	20	New York	6
	0	Frankford	0
	25	Providence	0
	25	Bears	0
	212		24

Won 13, Lost 0, Tied 1.

1930
COACH—EARL LAMBEAU

GREEN BAY	46	Oshkosh	0
	14	Cardinals	0
	7	Bears	0
	14	New York	7
	27	Philadelphia	12
	13	Minneapolis	0
	19	Minneapolis	0
	47	Portsmouth	13
	13	Bears	12
	6	Cardinals	13
	6	New York	13
	25	Philadelphia	7
	37	Stapleton	7
	0	Bears	21
	6	Portsmouth	6
	273		111

Won 10, Lost 3, Tied 1.

1931
COACH—EARL LAMBEAU

GREEN BAY	26	Cleveland	0
	32	Brooklyn	6
	7	Bears	0
	27	New York	7
	26	Cardinals	7
	15	Philadelphia	7
	48	Providence	20
	6	Bears	2
	26	Stapleton	0
	13	Cardinals	21
	14	New York	10
	38	Providence	7
	7	Brooklyn	0
	6	Bears	7
	291		74

Won 12, Lost 2.

1932
COACH—EARL LAMBEAU

GREEN BAY	45	Grand Rapids	0
	15	Cardinals	7
	0	Bears	0
	13	New York	0
	15	Portsmouth	10
	2	Bears	0
	13	Brooklyn	0
	26	Stapleton	0
	19	Cardinals	9
	21	Boston	0
	0	New York	6
	7	Brooklyn	0
	21	Stapleton	3
	0	Portsmouth	19
	0	Bears	9
	197		63

Won 11, Lost 3, Tied 1.

1933
COACH—EARL LAMBEAU

GREEN BAY	7	Boston	7

GREEN BAY	7	Bears	14
	7	New York	10
	17	Portsmouth	0
	47	Pittsburgh	0
	7	Bears	10
	35	Philadelphia	9
	14	Cardinals	6
	0	Portsmouth	7
	7	Boston	20
	6	New York	17
	21	Stapleton	0
	10	Philadelphia	0
	6	Bears	7
	—		—
	191		107

Won 6, Lost 7, Tied 1

1934
COACH—EARL LAMBEAU

GREEN BAY	28	Ft. Atkinson	7
	19	Philadelphia	0
	10	Bears	24
	20	New York	6
	0	Detroit	3
	41	Cincinnati	0
	15	Cardinals	0
	14	Bears	27
	10	Boston	0
	3	New York	17
	0	Cardinals	9
	3	Detroit	0
	0	Cardinals	6
	21	St. Louis	14
	—		—
	184		119

Won 8, Lost 6.

1935
COACH—EARL LAMBEAU

GREEN BAY	49	LaCrosse	0
	6	Cardinals	7
	7	Bears	0
	16	New York	7
	27	Pittsburgh	0
	0	Cardinals	3
	13	Detroit	9
	17	Bears	14
	31	Detroit	7
	10	Detroit	20
	34	Pittsburgh	14
	7	Cardinals	9
	13	Philadelphia	6
	—		—
	230		96

Won 9, Lost 4.

1936
COACH—EARL LAMBEAU

GREEN BAY	10	Cardinals	7
	3	Bears	30
	24	Cardinals	0
	31	Boston	2
	20	Detroit	18
	42	Pittsburgh	10
	21	Bears	10

	7	Boston	3
	38	Brooklyn	7
	26	New York	14
	26	Detroit	17
	0	Cardinals	0
	21	Boston	6
	—		—
	269		124

Won 11, Lost 1, Tied 1.

1937
COACH—EARL LAMBEAU

GREEN BAY	7	Cardinals	14
	2	Bears	14
	26	Detroit	6
	34	Cardinals	13
	35	Cleveland	10
	35	Cleveland	7
	14	Detroit	13
	24	Bears	14
	37	Philadelphia	7
	0	New York	10
	6	Washington	14
	—		—
	220		122

Won 7, Lost 4.

1938
COACH—EARL LAMBEAU

GREEN BAY	26	Cleveland	17
	0	Bears	2
	28	Cardinals	17
	24	Cardinals	22
	7	Detroit	17
	35	Brooklyn	7
	20	Pittsburgh	0
	28	Cleveland	7
	24	Bears	17
	28	Detroit	7
	3	New York	15
	17	New York	23
	—		—
	240		141

Won 8, Lost 4.

1939
COACH—EARL LAMBEAU

GREEN BAY	14	Cardinals	10
	21	Bears	16
	24	Cleveland	27
	26	Detroit	7
	24	Washington	14
	27	Bears	30
	23	Philadelphia	16
	28	Brooklyn	0
	7	Cleveland	6
	12	Detroit	7
	27	New York	0
	—		—
	260		153

Won 9, Lost 2.

1940
COACH—EARL LAMBEAU

GREEN BAY	27	Philadelphia	20
	10	Bears	41
	31	Cardinals	6
	31	Cleveland	14
	14	Detroit	23
	24	Pittsburgh	3
	7	Bears	14
	28	Cardinals	7
	3	New York	7
	50	Detroit	7
	13	Cleveland	13

238   155
Won 6, Lost 4, Tied 1.

1941
COACH—EARL LAMBEAU

GREEN BAY	23	Detroit	0
	24	Cleveland	7
	17	Bears	25
	14	Cardinals	13
	30	Brooklyn	7
	17	Cleveland	14
	24	Detroit	7
	16	Bears	14
	17	Cardinals	9
	54	Pittsburgh	7
	22	Washington	17

258   120
Won 10, Lost 1.
Divisional Play-off:
Green Bay 14   Bears 33

1942
COACH—EARL LAMBEAU

GREEN BAY	28	Bears	44
	17	Cardinals	13
	38	Detroit	7
	45	Cleveland	28
	28	Detroit	7
	55	Cardinals	24
	30	Cleveland	12
	7	Bears	38
	21	New York	21
	7	Philadelphia	0
	24	Pittsburgh	21

300   215
Won 8, Lost 2, Tied 1.

1943
COACH—EARL LAMBEAU

GREEN BAY	21	Bears	21
	28	Cardinals	7
	35	Detroit	14
	7	Washington	33
	27	Detroit	6
	35	New York	21
	7	Bears	21
	35	Cardinals	14
	31	Brooklyn	7

	38	Phil-Pitt	28

264   172
Won 7, Lost 2, Tied 1.

1944
COACH—EARL LAMBEAU

GREEN BAY	17	Brooklyn	7
	42	Bears	28
	27	Detroit	6
	34	Card-Pitt	7
	30	Cleveland	21
	0	Bears	21
	42	Cleveland	7
	0	New York	24
	35	Card-Pitt	20

238   141
Won 7, Lost 2.

1945
COACH—EARL LAMBEAU

GREEN BAY	31	Bears	21
	57	Detroit	21
	14	Cleveland	27
	38	Boston	14
	33	Cardinals	14
	24	Bears	27
	7	Cleveland	20
	28	Boston	0
	23	New York	14
	3	Detroit	14

258   172
Won 6, Lost 4.

1946
COACH—EARL LAMBEAU

GREEN BAY	7	Bears	30
	17	Los Angeles	21
	19	Philadelphia	7
	17	Pittsburgh	7
	10	Detroit	7
	7	Bears	10
	19	Cardinals	7
	9	Detroit	0
	6	Cardinals	24
	20	Washington	7
	17	Los Angeles	38

148   158
Won 6, Lost 5.

1947
COACH—EARL LAMBEAU

GREEN BAY	29	Bears	20
	17	Los Angeles	14
	10	Cardinals	14
	27	Washington	10
	34	Detroit	17
	17	Pittsburgh	18
	17	Bears	20
	20	Cardinals	21
	24	New York	24
	30	Los Angeles	10

GREEN BAY	35	Detroit	14
	14	Philadelphia	28
	—		—
	274		210

Won 6, Lost 5, Tied 1.

1948
COACH—EARL LAMBEAU

GREEN BAY	31	Boston	0
	7	Bears	45
	33	Detroit	21
	7	Cardinals	17
	16	Los Angeles	0
	7	Washington	23
	20	Detroit	24
	7	Pittsburgh	38
	6	Bears	7
	3	New York	49
	10	Los Angeles	24
	7	Cardinals	42
	—		—
	154		290

Won 3, Lost 9.

1949
COACH—EARL LAMBEAU

GREEN BAY	0	Bears	17
	7	Los Angeles	48
	19	N.Y. Bulldogs	0
	17	Cardinals	39
	7	Los Angeles	35
	16	Detroit	14
	3	Bears	24
	10	Giants	30
	7	Pittsburgh	30
	21	Cardinals	41
	0	Washington	30
	7	Detroit	21
	—		—
	114		329

Won 2, Lost 10.

1950
COACH—GENE RONZANI

GREEN BAY	7	Detroit	45
	35	Washington	21
	31	Bears	21
	31	N.Y. Yanks	44
	14	Bears	28
	17	N.Y. Yanks	35
	21	Baltimore	41
	14	Los Angeles	45
	21	Detroit	24
	25	San Francisco	21
	14	Los Angeles	51
	14	San Francisco	30
	—		—
	244		406

Won 3, Lost 9.

1951
COACH—GENE RONZANI

| GREEN BAY | 20 | Chicago Bears | 31 |

	35	Pittsburgh	33
	37	Philadelphia	24
	0	Los Angeles	28
	29	N.Y. Yanks	27
	17	Detroit	24
	7	Pittsburgh	28
	13	Philadelphia	24
	35	Detroit	52
	28	N.Y. Yanks	31
	19	San Francisco	31
	14	Los Angeles	42
	—		—
	254		375

Won 3, Lost 9.

1952
COACH—GENE RONZANI

GREEN BAY	14	Bears	24
	35	Washington	20
	28	Los Angeles	30
	24	Dallas	14
	17	Detroit	52
	12	Philadelphia	10
	41	Bears	28
	17	New York	3
	42	Dallas	14
	24	Detroit	48
	27	Los Angeles	45
	14	San Francisco	24
	—		—
	295		312

Won 6, Lost 6.

1953
COACH—LISLE BLACKBOURN

GREEN BAY	0	Cleveland	27
	13	Bears	17
	20	Los Angeles	38
	37	Baltimore	14
	14	Pittsburgh	31
	35	Baltimore	24
	21	Bears	21
	7	Detroit	14
	7	San Francisco	37
	15	Detroit	34
	14	San Francisco	48
	17	Los Angeles	33
	—		—
	200		338

Won 2, Lost 9, Tied 1.

1954
COACH—LISLE BLACKBOURN

GREEN BAY	21	Pittsburgh	21
	3	Bears	10
	17	San Francisco	23
	35	Los Angeles	17
	7	Baltimore	6
	37	Philadelphia	14
	23	Bears	28
	24	Baltimore	13
	17	Detroit	21
	24	Detroit	28
	0	San Francisco	35

27	Los Angeles	35
—	—
215		251

Won 4, Lost 8.

1955
COACH—LISLE BLACKBOURN

GREEN BAY	20	Detroit	17
	24	Bears	3
	20	Baltimore	24
	30	Los Angeles	28
	10	Cleveland	41
	10	Baltimore	14
	31	Bears	52
	31	Cardinals	14
	27	San Francisco	21
	10	Detroit	24
	28	San Francisco	7
	17	Los Angeles	31
	258		276

Won 6, Lost 6.

1956
COACH—LISLE BLACKBOURN

GREEN BAY	16	Detroit	20
	21	Bears	37
	38	Baltimore	33
	42	Los Angeles	17
	21	Baltimore	28
	7	Cleveland	24
	14	Bears	38
	16	San Francisco	17
	24	Detroit	20
	24	Cardinals	21
	20	San Francisco	38
	21	Los Angeles	49
	264		342

Won 4, Lost 8.

1957
COACH—LISLE BLACKBOURN

GREEN BAY	21	Bears	17
	14	Detroit	24
	17	Baltimore	45
	14	San Francisco	24
	24	Baltimore	21
	17	New York	31
	14	Bears	21
	27	Los Angeles	31
	27	Pittsburgh	10
	6	Detroit	18
	17	Los Angeles	42
	20	San Francisco	27
	218		311

Won 3, Lost 9.

1958
COACH—RAY McLEAN

GREEN BAY	20	Bears	34
	13	Detroit	13
	17	Baltimore	24
	21	Washington	37
	38	Philadelphia	35

0	Baltimore	56
10	Bears	24
7	Los Angeles	20
12	San Francisco	33
14	Detroit	24
21	San Francisco	48
20	Los Angeles	34
193		382

Won 1, Lost 10, Tied 1.

1959
COACH—VINCENT LOMBARDI

GREEN BAY	9	Chi. Bears	6
	28	Detroit	10
	21	San Francisco	20
	6	Los Angeles	45
	21	Baltimore	38
	3	New York	20
	17	Chi. Bears	28
	24	Baltimore	28
	21	Washington	0
	24	Detroit	17
	38	Los Angeles	20
	36	San Francisco	14
	248		246

Won 7, Lost 5.

1960
COACH—VINCENT LOMBARDI

GREEN BAY	14	Chicago	17
	28	Detroit	9
	35	Baltimore	21
	41	San Francisco	14
	19	Pittsburgh	13
	24	Baltimore	38
	41	Dal. Cowboys	7
	31	L. A. Rams	33
	10	Detroit	23
	41	Chicago	13
	13	San Francisco	0
	35	L. A. Rams	21
	332		209

Won 8, Lost 4.
Championship Game:
Green Bay 13 Philadelphia 17

LOS ANGELES RAMS
(formerly Cleveland Rams, 1937–45)

1937
COACH—HUGO BEZDEK

CLEVELAND	0	Detroit	28
	21	Philadelphia	3
	7	Brooklyn	9
	0	Cardinals	6
	2	Bears	20
	10	Green Bay	35
	7	Green Bay	35
	7	Cardinals	13
	7	Detroit	27

CLEVELAND

7	Washington	16
7	Bears	15
—		—
75		207

Won 1, Lost 10, Tied 0.

1938
COACH—HUGO BEZDEK, ARTHUR LEWIS

CLEVELAND

17	Green Bay	26
6	Cardinals	7
13	Washington	37
21	Detroit	17
14	Bears	7
23	Bears	21
7	Green Bay	28
0	Detroit	6
0	New York	28
17	Cardinals	31
13	Pittsburgh	7
—		—
131		215

Won 4, Lost 7, Tied 1.

1939
COACH—EARL CLARK

CLEVELAND

21	Bears	30
12	Brooklyn	23
27	Green Bay	24
21	Bears	35
7	Detroit	15
24	Cardinals	0
14	Pittsburgh	14
14	Cardinals	0
14	Detroit	3
6	Green Bay	7
35	Philadelphia	13
—		—
195		164

Won 5, Lost 5, Tied 1.

1940
COACH—EARL CLARK

CLEVELAND

21	Philadelphia	13
0	Detroit	6
14	Bears	21
14	Green Bay	31
26	Cardinals	14
7	Cardinals	17
24	Detroit	0
13	New York	0
14	Brooklyn	29
25	Bears	47
13	Green Bay	13
—		—
171		191

Won 4, Lost 6, Tied 1.

1941
COACH—EARL CLARK

CLEVELAND

17	Pittsburgh	14
10	Cardinals	6
7	Green Bay	24
21	Bears	48
7	Detroit	17
14	Green Bay	17
13	Washington	17
0	Detroit	14
13	Bears	31
14	New York	49
0	Cardinals	7
—		—
116		244

Won 2, Lost 9, Tied 0.

1942
COACH—EARL CLARK

CLEVELAND

0	Cardinals	7
24	Phil-Pitt	14
14	Detroit	0
7	Bears	21
14	Washington	33
28	Green Bay	45
7	Cardinals	3
17	Brooklyn	0
12	Green Bay	30
27	Detroit	7
0	Bears	47
—		—
150		207

Won 5, Lost 6, Tied 0.

1943 Suspended Operation

1944
COACH—ALDO DONELLI

CLEVELAND

30	Card-Pitt	28
19	Bears	7
20	Detroit	17
21	Green Bay	30
21	Bears	28
10	Washington	14
7	Green Bay	42
33	Card-Pitt	6
14	Detroit	26
13	Philadelphia	26
—		—
188		224

Won 4, Lost 6, Tied 0.

1945
COACH—ADAM WALSH

CLEVELAND

21	Cardinals	0
17	Bears	0
27	Green Bay	14
41	Bears	21
14	Philadelphia	28
21	New York	17
20	Green Bay	7
35	Cardinals	21
28	Detroit	21
20	Boston	7
—		—
244		136

Won 9, Lost 1, Tied 0.

Championship Game:
Cleveland 15   Washington 14

1946
COACH—ADAM WALSH

LOS ANGELES	14	Philadelphia	25
	21	Green Bay	17
	28	Bears	28
	35	Detroit	14
	10	Cardinals	34
	41	Detroit	20
	21	Bears	27
	17	Cardinals	14
	21	Boston	40
	31	New York	21
	38	Green Bay	17
	—		—
	277		257

Won 6, Lost 4, Tied 1.

1947
COACH—ROBERT SNYDER

LOS ANGELES	48	Pittsburgh	7
	14	Green Bay	17
	27	Detroit	13
	27	Cardinals	7
	7	Philadelphia	14
	10	Cardinals	17
	16	Boston	27
	21	Bears	41
	28	Detroit	17
	10	Green Bay	30
	17	Bears	14
	34	New York	10
	—		—
	259		214

Won 6, Lost 6, Tied 0.

1948
COACH—CLARK SHAUGHNESSY

LOS ANGELES	44	Detroit	7
	28	Philadelphia	28
	21	Bears	42
	0	Green Bay	16
	34	Detroit	27
	22	Cardinals	27
	6	Bears	21
	52	New York	37
	24	Cardinals	27
	24	Green Bay	10
	41	Washington	13
	31	Pittsburgh	14
	—		—
	327		269

Won 6, Lost 5, Tied 1.

1949
COACH—CLARK SHAUGHNESSY

LOS ANGELES	27	Detroit	24
	48	Green Bay	7
	31	Bears	16
	21	Detroit	10
	35	Green Bay	7
	27	Bears	24
	14	Philadelphia	38
	7	Pittsburgh	7
	28	Cardinals	28
	42	N.Y. Bulldogs	20

	27	Cardinals	31
	53	Washington	27
	—		—
	360		239

Won 8, Lost 2, Tied 2.
Championship Game:
Los Angeles 0   Philadelphia 14

1950
COACH—JOSEPH STYDAHAR

LOS ANGELES	20	Bears	24
	45	N.Y. Yanks	28
	35	San Francisco	14
	20	Philadelphia	56
	30	Detroit	28
	70	Baltimore	27
	65	Detroit	24
	28	San Francisco	21
	45	Green Bay	14
	43	N.Y. Yanks	35
	14	Bears	24
	51	Green Bay	14
	—		—
	466		309

Won 9, Lost 3, Tied 0.
Championship Game:
Los Angeles 28   Cleveland 30

1951
COACH—JOSEPH STYDAHAR

LOS ANGELES	54	N.Y. Yanks	14
	23	Cleveland	38
	27	Detroit	21
	28	Green Bay	0
	17	San Francisco	44
	23	San Francisco	16
	45	Cardinals	21
	48	N.Y. Yanks	21
	21	Washington	31
	42	Bears	17
	22	Detroit	24
	42	Green Bay	14
	—		—
	392		261

Won 8, Lost 4, Tied 0.
Championship Game:
Los Angeles 24   Cleveland 17

1952
COACH—HAMPTON POOL

LOS ANGELES	7	Cleveland	37
	14	Detroit	17
	30	Green Bay	28
	16	Detroit	24
	31	Bears	7
	42	Dallas	20
	27	Dallas	6
	40	Bears	24
	35	San Francisco	9
	34	San Francisco	21
	45	Green Bay	27
	28	Pittsburgh	14
	—		—
	349		234

LOS ANGELES Won 9, Lost 3.
Conference Play-off:
Los Angeles 21   Detroit 31

1953
COACH—HAMPTON POOL

LOS ANGELES	21	New York	7
	30	San Francisco	31
	38	Green Bay	20
	31	Detroit	19
	38	Bears	24
	37	Detroit	24
	27	San Francisco	31
	24	Cardinals	24
	21	Baltimore	13
	21	Bears	24
	45	Baltimore	2
	33	Green Bay	17
	—		—
	366		236

Won 8, Lost 3, Tied 1.

1954
COACH—SIDNEY GILLMAN

LOS ANGELES	26	Baltimore	0
	24	San Francisco	24
	3	Detroit	21
	17	Green Bay	35
	42	Bears	38
	24	Detroit	27
	42	San Francisco	34
	28	Cardinals	17
	17	New York	16
	13	Bears	24
	21	Baltimore	22
	35	Green Bay	27
	—		—
	292		285

Won 6, Lost 5, Tied 1.

1955
COACH—SIDNEY GILLMAN

LOS ANGELES	23	San Francisco	14
	27	Pittsburgh	26
	17	Detroit	10
	28	Green Bay	30
	24	Detroit	13
	20	Bears	31
	27	San Francisco	14
	3	Bears	24
	17	Baltimore	17
	23	Philadelphia	21
	20	Baltimore	14
	31	Green Bay	17
	—		—
	260		231

Won 8, Lost 3, Tied 1.
Championship Game:
Cleveland 38   Los Angeles 14

1956
COACH—SIDNEY GILLMAN

LOS ANGELES	27	Philadelphia	7
	30	San Francisco	33
	21	Detroit	24
	17	Green Bay	42
	7	Detroit	16
	24	Bears	35
	30	San Francisco	6
	21	Bears	30
	21	Baltimore	56
	13	Pittsburgh	30
	31	Baltimore	7
	49	Green Bay	21
	—		
	291		307

Won 4, Lost 8.

1957
COACH—SIDNEY GILLMAN

LOS ANGELES	17	Philadelphia	13
	20	San Francisco	23
	7	Detroit	10
	26	Bears	34
	35	Detroit	17
	10	Bears	16
	37	San Francisco	24
	31	Green Bay	27
	31	Cleveland	45
	14	Baltimore	31
	42	Green Bay	17
	37	Baltimore	21
	—		—
	307		278

Won 6, Lost 6.

1958
COACH—SIDNEY GILLMAN

LOS ANGELES	27	Cleveland	30
	33	San Francisco	3
	42	Detroit	28
	10	Bears	31
	24	Detroit	41
	41	Bears	35
	56	San Francisco	7
	20	Green Bay	7
	7	Baltimore	34
	20	Cardinals	14
	30	Baltimore	28
	'34	Green Bay	20
	—		—
	344		278

Won 8, Lost 4.

1959
COACH—SIDNEY GILLMAN

LOS ANGELES	21	New York	23
	0	San Francisco	34
	28	Chi. Bears	21
	45	Green Bay	6
	7	Detroit	17
	21	Chi. Bears	26
	16	San Francisco	24
	17	Detroit	23
	20	Philadelphia	23
	21	Baltimore	35
	20	Green Bay	38
	26	Baltimore	45
	—		—
	242		315

Won 2, Lost 10

1960
COACH—ROBERT WATERFIELD
LOS ANGELES

21	St. Louis	43
9	San Francisco	13
27	Chicago	34
17	Baltimore	31
24	Chicago	24
48	Detroit	35
38	Dal. Cowboys	13
10	Detroit	12
33	Green Bay	31
7	San Francisco	23
10	Baltimore	3
21	Green Bay	35
—		—
265		297

Won 4, Lost 7, Tied 1

NEW YORK GIANTS

1925
COACH—ROBERT FOLWELL
N.Y. GIANTS

0	Providence	14
3	Frankford	5
0	Frankford	14
7	Buffalo	0
19	Cleveland	0
19	Columbus	0
13	Rochester	0
13	Providence	12
9	Kansas City	3
23	Dayton	0
7	Chicago Bears	19
9	Chicago Bears	0
—		—
122		67

Won 8, Lost 4, Tied 0.

1926
COACH—JOSEPH ALEXANDER
N.Y. GIANTS

21	Hartford	0
7	Providence	6
0	Chicago Bears	7
0	Frankford	6
0	Frankford	6
13	Kansas City	0
20	Chicago Cards	0
14	Duluth	13
0	Los Angeles	6
21	Providence	0
17	Brooklyn	0
27	Brooklyn	0
—		—
140		44

Won 8, Lost 4, Tied 0.

1927
COACH—EARL POTTEIGER
N.Y. GIANTS

0	Cleveland	0
19	Pottsville	0
0	Cleveland	6
13	Frankford	0
27	Frankford	0
16	Pottsville	0
21	Duluth	0
25	Providence	0
19	Stapleton	0
28	Chicago Cardinals	7
18	Stapleton	0
13	Chicago Bears	7
14	N.Y. Yankees	0
13	N.Y. Yankees	0
—		—
226		20

Won 11, Lost 1, Tied 1. League Champion.

1928
COACH—EARL POTTEIGER
N.Y. GIANTS

7	Orange	0
12	Pottsville	6
6	Green Bay	6
0	Chicago Bears	13
0	Detroit	28
10	N.Y. Yankees	7
0	Frankford	0
19	Detroit	19
0	Green Bay	7
0	Providence	16
0	Stapleton	7
13	N.Y. Yankees	19
6	N.Y. Yankees	7
—		—
73		135

Won 4, Lost 7, Tied 2.

1929
COACH—LEROY ANDREWS
N.Y. GIANTS

0	Orange	0
7	Providence	0
19	Stapleton	9
32	Frankford	0
19	Providence	0
26	Chicago Bears	14
45	Buffalo	6
22	Orange	0
34	Chicago Bears	0
6	Green Bay	20
21	Stapleton	7
24	Chicago Cards	21
12	Frankford	0
31	Frankford	0
—		—
318		77

Won 12, Lost 1, Tied 1.

1930
COACH—LEROY ANDREWS
N.Y. GIANTS

32	Newark	0
27	Providence	7
7	Green Bay	14
12	Chicago Bears	0
25	Chicago Cards	12
53	Frankford	0
25	Providence	0

N.Y. GIANTS	34	Newark	7
	9	Stapleton	7
	19	Portsmouth	6
	13	Chicago Bears	7
	13	Green Bay	6
	0	Chicago Bears	12
	6	Stapleton	7
	6	Brooklyn	7
	14	Frankford	6
	13	Brooklyn	0
	—		—
	308		98

Won 13, Lost 4, Tied 0.

1931
COACH—STEPHEN OWEN

N.Y. GIANTS	14	Providence	6
	6	Portsmouth	14
	7	Green Bay	27
	0	Chicago Bears	6
	7	Stapleton	0
	27	Brooklyn	0
	14	Portsmouth	0
	13	Frankford	0
	6	Chicago Bears	12
	10	Green Bay	14
	6	Stapleton	9
	0	Providence	0
	19	Brooklyn	6
	25	Chicago Bears	6
	—		—
	154		94

Won 6, Lost 6, Tied 1.

1932
COACH—STEPHEN OWEN

N.Y. GIANTS	6	Portsmouth	7
	0	Green Bay	13
	6	Boston	14
	20	Brooklyn	12
	0	Boston	0
	0	Portsmouth	6
	8	Chicago Bears	28
	27	Stapleton	7
	6	Green Bay	0
	13	Stapleton	13
	13	Brooklyn	7
	0	Chicago Bears	6
	—		—
	99		113

Won 4, Lost 6, Tied 2.

1933
COACH—STEPHEN OWEN

N.Y. GIANTS	23	Pittsburgh	2
	20	Boston	21
	10	Green Bay	7
	7	Portsmouth	17
	56	Philadelphia	0
	21	Brooklyn	7
	10	Chicago Bears	14
	13	Portsmouth	10
	7	Boston	0

N.Y. GIANTS	3	Chicago Bears	0
	17	Green Bay	6
	10	Brooklyn	0
	27	Pittsburgh	3
	20	Philadelphia	14
	—		—
	244		101

Won 11, Lost 3, Tied 0.
Championship Game:
N.Y. Giants 21   Chicago Bears 23

1934
COACH—STEPHEN OWEN

N.Y. GIANTS	0	Detroit	9
	6	Green Bay	20
	14	Pittsburgh	12
	16	Boston	13
	14	Brooklyn	0
	17	Philadelphia	0
	17	Philadelphia	7
	7	Chicago Bears	27
	17	Green Bay	3
	9	Chicago Bears	10
	3	Boston	0
	27	Brooklyn	0
	0	Philadelphia	6
	—		—
	147		107

Won 8, Lost 5, Tied 0.
Championship Game:
N.Y. Giants 30   Chicago Bears 13

1935
COACH—STEPHEN OWEN

N.Y. GIANTS	42	Pittsburgh	7
	7	Green Bay	16
	20	Boston	12
	10	Brooklyn	7
	17	Boston	6
	13	Chicago Cards	14
	3	Chicago Bears	20
	3	Chicago Bears	0
	10	Philadelphia	0
	21	Brooklyn	0
	21	Philadelphia	14
	13	Pittsburgh	0
	—		—
	170		96

Won 9, Lost 3, Tied 0.
Championship Game:
N.Y. Giants 7   Detroit Lions 26

1936
COACH—STEPHEN OWEN

N.Y. GIANTS	7	Philadelphia	10
	7	Pittsburgh	10
	7	Boston	0
	10	Brooklyn	10
	14	Chicago Cards	6
	21	Philadelphia	17
	14	Detroit	7
	7	Chicago Bears	25
	0	Detroit	38

N.Y. GIANTS	14	Green Bay	26
	14	Brooklyn	0
	0	Boston	14
	—		—
	115		163

Won 5, Lost 6, Tied 1.

1937
COACH—STEPHEN OWEN

N.Y. GIANTS	3	Washington	13
	10	Pittsburgh	7
	16	Philadelphia	7
	21	Philadelphia	0
	21	Brooklyn	0
	3	Chicago Bears	3
	17	Pittsburgh	0
	0	Detroit	17
	10	Green Bay	0
	13	Brooklyn	13
	14	Washington	49
	—		—
	128		109

Won 6, Lost 3, Tied 2.

1938
COACH—STEPHEN OWEN

N.Y. GIANTS	27	Pittsburgh	14
	10	Philadelphia	14
	10	Pittsburgh	13
	10	Washington	7
	17	Philadelphia	7
	28	Brooklyn	14
	6	Chicago Cards	0
	28	Cleveland	0
	15	Green Bay	3
	7	Brooklyn	7
	36	Washington	0
	—		—
	194		78

Won 8, Lost 2, Tied 1.

Championship Game:
N.Y. Giants 23 Green Bay Packers 17

1939
COACH—STEPHEN OWEN

N.Y. GIANTS	13	Philadelphia	3
	0	Washington	0
	14	Pittsburgh	7
	27	Philadelphia	10
	16	Chicago Bears	13
	7	Brooklyn	6
	14	Detroit	18
	17	Chicago Cards	7
	23	Pittsburgh	7
	28	Brooklyn	7
	9	Washington	7
	—		—
	168		85

Won 9, Lost 1, Tied 1.

Championship Game:
N.Y. Giants 0 Green Bay Packers 27

1940
COACH—STEPHEN OWEN

N.Y. GIANTS	10	Pittsburgh	10
	7	Washington	21
	20	Philadelphia	14
	17	Philadelphia	7
	12	Pittsburgh	0
	21	Chicago Bears	37
	10	Brooklyn	7
	0	Cleveland	13
	7	Green Bay	3
	21	Washington	7
	6	Brooklyn	14
	—		—
	131		133

Won 6, Lost 4, Tied 1.

1941
COACH—STEPHEN OWEN

N.Y. GIANTS	24	Philadelphia	0
	17	Washington	10
	37	Pittsburgh	10
	16	Philadelphia	0
	28	Pittsburgh	7
	13	Brooklyn	16
	7	Chicago Cards	10
	20	Detroit	13
	49	Cleveland	14
	20	Washington	13
	7	Brooklyn	21
	—		—
	238		114

Won 8, Lost 3, Tied 0.
Championship Game:
N.Y. Giants 9 Chicago Bears 37

1942
COACH—STEPHEN OWEN

N.Y. GIANTS	14	Washington	7
	10	Pittsburgh	13
	35	Philadelphia	17
	7	Chicago Bears	26
	7	Brooklyn	17
	9	Pittsburgh	17
	14	Philadelphia	0
	7	Washington	14
	21	Green Bay	21
	21	Chicago Cards	7
	10	Brooklyn	0
	—		—
	155		139

Won 5, Lost 5, Tied 1.

1943
COACH—STEPHEN OWEN

N.Y. GIANTS	14	Phil-Pitt	28
	20	Brooklyn	0
	0	Detroit	0
	31	Washington	7
	42	Phil-Pitt	14
	21	Green Bay	35
	7	Chicago Bears	56
	24	Chicago Cards	13

N.Y. GIANTS	24	Brooklyn	7
	14	Washington	10
	—		—
	197		170

Won 6, Lost 3, Tied 1.
Divisional Play-off:
N.Y. Giants 0   Washington 28

1944
COACH—STEPHEN OWEN

N.Y. GIANTS	22	Boston	10
	14	Brooklyn	7
	23	Card-Pitt	0
	17	Philadelphia	24
	31	Boston	0
	21	Philadelphia	21
	24	Green Bay	0
	7	Brooklyn	0
	16	Washington	13
	31	Washington	0
	—		—
	206		75

Won 8, Lost 1, Tied 1.
Championship Game:
N.Y. Giants 7   Green Bay 14

1945
COACH—STEPHEN OWEN

N.Y. GIANTS	34	Pittsburgh	6
	13	Boston	13
	7	Pittsburgh	21
	14	Washington	24
	17	Cleveland	21
	17	Philadelphia	38
	35	Detroit	14
	14	Green Bay	23
	28	Philadelphia	21
	0	Washington	17
	—		—
	179		197

Won 3, Lost 6, Tied 1.

1946
COACH—STEPHEN OWEN

N.Y. GIANTS	17	Boston	0
	17	Pittsburgh	14
	14	Washington	24
	28	Chicago Cards	24
	14	Chicago Bears	0
	14	Philadelphia	28
	45	Philadelphia	17
	28	Boston	28
	7	Pittsburgh	0
	21	Los Angeles	31
	31	Washington	0
	—		—
	236		166

Won 7, Lost 3, Tied 1.

Championship Game:
N.Y. Giants 14   Chicago Bears 24

1947
COACH—STEPHEN OWEN

N.Y. GIANTS	7	Boston	7
	0	Philadelphia	23
	20	Washington	28
	0	Boston	14
	21	Pittsburgh	38
	7	Detroit	35
	24	Philadelphia	41
	7	Pittsburgh	24
	28	Green Bay	28
	35	Chicago Cards	31
	35	Washington	10
	10	Los Angeles	34
	—		—
	194		313

Won 2, Lost 8, Tied 2.

1948
COACH—STEPHEN OWEN

N.Y. GIANTS	27	Boston	7
	10	Washington	41
	0	Philadelphia	45
	35	Chicago Cards	63
	34	Pittsburgh	27
	14	Chicago Bears	35
	14	Philadelphia	35
	37	Los Angeles	52
	49	Green Bay	3
	28	Boston	14
	28	Pittsburgh	38
	21	Washington	28
	—		—
	287		388

Won 4, Lost 8, Tied 0.

1949
COACH—STEPHEN OWEN

N.Y. GIANTS	7	Pittsburgh	28
	38	N.Y. Bulldogs	14
	45	Washington	35
	17	Pittsburgh	21
	35	Chicago Bears	28
	41	Chicago Cards	38
	24	N.Y. Bulldogs	31
	30	Green Bay	10
	21	Detroit	45
	23	Washington	7
	3	Philadelphia	24
	3	Philadelphia	17
	—		—
	287		298

Won 6, Lost 6, Tied 0.

1950
COACH—STEPHEN OWEN

| N.Y. GIANTS | 18 | Pittsburgh | 7 |
| | 6 | Cleveland | 0 |

21	Washington	17
6	Pittsburgh	17
17	Cleveland	13
3	Chicago Cards	17
24	Washington	21
51	Chicago Cards	21
55	Baltimore	20
7	Philadelphia	3
51	N.Y. Yanks	7
9	Philadelphia	7
268		150

Won 10, Lost 2, Tied 0.
Divisional Play-off:
N.Y. Giants 3   Cleveland Browns 8

1951

COACH—STEPHEN OWEN

N.Y. GIANTS	13	Pittsburgh	13
	35	Washington	14
	28	Chicago Cards	17
	26	Philadelphia	24
	13	Cleveland	14
	37	N.Y. Yanks	31
	28	Washington	14
	0	Cleveland	10
	10	Chicago Cards	0
	14	Pittsburgh	0
	21	Philadelphia	7
	27	N.Y. Yanks	17
	252		161

Won 9, Lost 2, Tied 1.

1952

COACH—STEPHEN OWEN

N.Y. GIANTS	24	Dallas	6
	31	Philadelphia	7
	17	Cleveland	9
	23	Cardinals	24
	10	Philadelphia	14
	28	Cardinals	6
	23	San Francisco	14
	3	Green Bay	17
	14	Washington	10
	7	Pittsburgh	63
	17	Washington	27
	37	Cleveland	34
	234		231

Won 7, Lost 5.

1953

COACH—JIM LEE HOWELL

N.Y. GIANTS	7	Los Angeles	21
	14	Pittsburgh	24
	9	Washington	13
	21	Cardinals	7
	0	Cleveland	7

23	Cardinals	20
7	Philadelphia	30
10	Pittsburgh	14
21	Washington	24
37	Philadelphia	28
14	Cleveland	62
16	Detroit	27
179		277

Won 3, Lost 9.

1954

COACH—JIM LEE HOWELL

N.Y. GIANTS	41	Cardinals	10
	14	Baltimore	20
	51	Washington	21
	31	Cardinals	17
	24	Washington	7
	14	Cleveland	24
	30	Pittsburgh	6
	27	Philadelphia	14
	16	Los Angeles	17
	7	Cleveland	16
	24	Pittsburgh	3
	14	Philadelphia	29
	293		184

Won 7, Lost 5.

1955

COACH—JIM LEE HOWELL

N.Y. GIANTS	17	Philadelphia	27
	17	Cardinals	28
	23	Pittsburgh	30
	10	Cardinals	0
	17	Pittsburgh	19
	35	Washington	7
	14	Cleveland	24
	17	Baltimore	7
	31	Philadelphia	7
	35	Cleveland	35
	27	Washington	20
	24	Detroit	19
	267		223

Won 6, Lost 5, Tied 1.

1956

COACH—JIM LEE HOWELL

N.Y. GIANTS	38	San Francisco	21
	27	Cardinals	35
	21	Cleveland	9
	38	Pittsburgh	10
	20	Philadelphia	3
	17	Pittsburgh	14
	23	Cardinals	10
	7	Washington	33
	17	Bears	17
	28	Washington	14
	7	Cleveland	24
	21	Philadelphia	7
	264		197

Won 8, Lost 3, Tied 1.
Championship Game:
New York 47   Bears 7

1957
COACH—JIM LEE HOWELL

N.Y. GIANTS			
	3	Cleveland	6
	24	Philadelphia	20
	24	Washington	20
	35	Pittsburgh	0
	14	Washington	31
	31	Green Bay	17
	27	Cardinals	14
	13	Philadelphia	0
	28	Cardinals	21
	17	San Francisco	27
	10	Pittsburgh	21
	28	Cleveland	34
	—		—
	254		211

Won 7, Lost 5.

1958
COACH—JIM LEE HOWELL

N.Y. GIANTS			
	37	Cardinals	7
	24	Philadelphia	27
	21	Washington	14
	6	Cardinals	23
	17	Pittsburgh	6
	21	Cleveland	17
	24	Baltimore	21
	10	Pittsburgh	31
	30	Washington	0
	24	Philadelphia	10
	19	Detroit	17
	13	Cleveland	10
	—		—
	246		183

Won 9, Lost 3.
Conference Play-off:
New York 10   Cleveland 0
Championship Game:
Baltimore 23   New York 17

1959
COACH—JIM LEE HOWELL

N.Y. GIANTS			
	23	Los Angeles	21
	21	Philadelphia	49
	10	Cleveland	6
	24	Philadelphia	7
	21	Pittsburgh	16
	20	Green Bay	3
	9	Chi. Cards	3
	9	Pittsburgh	14
	30	Chi. Cards	20
	45	Washington	14
	48	Cleveland	7
	24	Washington	10
	—		—
	284		170

Won 10, Lost 2.
Championship Game:
Baltimore 31   New York 16

1960
COACH—JIM LEE HOWELL

N.Y. GIANTS			
	21	San Francisco	19
	35	St. Louis	14
	19	Pittsburgh	17

	24	Washington	24
	13	St. Louis	20
	17	Cleveland	13
	27	Pittsburgh	24
	10	Philadelphia	17
	23	Philadelphia	31
	31	Dal. Cowboys	31
	17	Washington	3
	34	Cleveland	48
	—		—
	271		261

Won 6, Lost 4, Tied 2.

PHILADELPHIA

1933
COACH—LUDLOW WRAY

PHILADELPHIA			
	0	New York	56
	0	Portsmouth	25
	9	Green Bay	35
	6	Cincinnati	0
	3	Bears	3
	25	Pittsburgh	6
	20	Cincinnati	3
	0	Green Bay	10
	14	New York	20
	—		—
	77		158

Won 3, Lost 5, Tied 1.

1934
COACH—LUDLOW WRAY

PHILADELPHIA			
	6	Green Bay	19
	17	Pittsburgh	0
	7	Pittsburgh	9
	0	Detroit	10
	0	Boston	6
	0	New York	17
	64	Cincinnati	0
	7	Brooklyn	10
	7	Boston	14
	13	Brooklyn	0
	6	New York	0
	—		—
	127		85

Won 4, Lost 7.

1935
COACH—LUDLOW WRAY

PHILADELPHIA			
	7	Pittsburgh	17
	0	Detroit	35
	17	Pittsburgh	6
	0	Bears	39
	6	Brooklyn	17
	7	Boston	6
	0	Brooklyn	3
	3	Cardinals	12
	0	New York	10
	14	New York	21
	6	Green Bay	13
	—		—
	60		179

Won 2, Lost 9.

1936
COACH—LUDLOW WRAY

PHILADELPHIA	7	Brooklyn	13
	10	New York	7
	3	Boston	26
	0	Bears	17
	0	Brooklyn	18
	0	Detroit	23
	0	Pittsburgh	17
	7	Boston	17
	17	New York	21
	0	Pittsburgh	6
	0	Cardinals	13
	7	Bears	28
	51		206

Won 1, Lost 11.

1937
COACH—LUDLOW WRAY

PHILADELPHIA	14	Pittsburgh	27
	7	Brooklyn	13
	3	Cleveland	21
	6	Cardinals	6
	7	New York	16
	14	Washington	0
	0	New York	21
	7	Washington	10
	7	Pittsburgh	16
	14	Brooklyn	10
	7	Green Bay	37
	86		177

Won 2, Lost 8, Tied 1.

1938
COACH—BERT BELL

PHILADELPHIA	23	Washington	26
	27	Pittsburgh	7
	14	New York	10
	6	Bears	28
	7	New York	17
	14	Washington	20
	7	Cardinals	0
	7	Brooklyn	10
	14	Brooklyn	32
	14	Pittsburgh	7
	21	Detroit	7
	154		164

Won 5, Lost 6.

1939
COACH—BERT BELL

PHILADELPHIA	0	Washington	7
	3	New York	13
	0	Brooklyn	0
	10	New York	27
	14	Brooklyn	23
	6	Washington	7
	16	Green Bay	23
	14	Bears	27
	17	Pittsburgh	14

	12	Pittsburgh	24
	13	Cleveland	35
	105		200

Won 1, Lost 9, Tied 1.

1940
COACH—BERT BELL

PHILADELPHIA	20	Green Bay	27
	13	Cleveland	21
	14	New York	20
	17	Brooklyn	30
	7	New York	17
	17	Washington	34
	7	Brooklyn	21
	3	Pittsburgh	7
	0	Detroit	21
	7	Pittsburgh	0
	6	Washington	13
	111		211

Won 1, Lost 10.

1941
COACH—EARLE NEALE

PHILADELPHIA	0	New York	24
	10	Pittsburgh	7
	13	Brooklyn	24
	0	New York	16
	17	Washington	21
	21	Cardinals	14
	6	Brooklyn	15
	7	Pittsburgh	7
	17	Detroit	21
	14	Bears	49
	14	Washington	20
	119		218

Won 2, Lost 8, Tied 1.

1942
COACH—EARLE NEALE

PHILADELPHIA	24	Pittsburgh	14
	14	Cleveland	24
	14	Brooklyn	35
	10	Washington	14
	17	New York	35
	0	Pittsburgh	14
	14	Bears	45
	27	Washington	30
	0	New York	14
	14	Brooklyn	7
	0	Green Bay	7
	134		239

Won 2, Lost 9.

1943
COACHES—EARLE NEALE, W. KIESLING

PHIL-PITT (COMBINE)	17	Brooklyn	0
	28	New York	14
	34	Cardinals	13
	21	Bears	48
	14	New York	42

PHILADELPHIA	14	Washington	14
	7	Brooklyn	13
	35	Detroit	34
	27	Washington	14
	28	Green Bay	38
	——		——
	225		230

Won 5, Lost 4, Tied 1.

1944
COACH—EARLE NEALE

PHILADELPHIA	28	Boston	7
	31	Washington	31
	38	Boston	0
	24	New York	17
	21	Brooklyn	7
	21	New York	21
	37	Washington	7
	7	Bears	28
	34	Brooklyn	0
	26	Cleveland	13
	——		——
	267		131

Won 7, Lost 1, Tied 2.

1945
COACH—EARLE NEALE

PHILADELPHIA	21	Cardinals	6
	24	Detroit	28
	14	Washington	24
	28	Cleveland	14
	45	Pittsburgh	3
	38	New York	17
	30	Pittsburgh	6
	16	Washington	0
	21	New York	28
	35	Boston	7
	——		——
	272		133

Won 7, Lost 3.

1946
COACH—EARLE NEALE

PHILADELPHIA	25	Los Angeles	14
	49	Boston	25
	7	Green Bay	19
	14	Bears	21
	28	Washington	24
	24	New York	14
	17	New York	45
	7	Pittsburgh	10
	10	Washington	27
	10	Pittsburgh	7
	40	Boston	14
	——		——
	231		220

Won 6, Lost 5.

1947
COACH—EARLE NEALE

PHILADELPHIA	45	Washington	42
	23	New York	0
	7	Bears	40
	24	Pittsburgh	35
	14	Los Angeles	7
	38	Washington	14
	41	New York	24
	32	Boston	0
	14	Boston	21
	21	Pittsburgh	0
	21	Cardinals	45
	28	Green Bay	14
	——		——
	308		242

Won 8, Lost 4.
Divisional Play-off:
Philadelphia 21   Pittsburgh 0
Championship Game:
Philadelphia 21   Cardinals 28

1948
COACH—EARLE NEALE

PHILADELPHIA	14	Cardinals	21
	28	Los Angeles	28
	45	New York	0
	45	Washington	0
	12	Bears	7
	34	Pittsburgh	7
	35	New York	14
	45	Boston	0
	42	Washington	21
	17	Pittsburgh	0
	14	Boston	37
	45	Detroit	21
	——		——
	376		156

Won 9, Lost 2, Tied 1.
Championship Game:
Philadelphia 7   Cardinals 0

1949
COACH—EARLE NEALE

PHILADELPHIA	7	N.Y. Bulldogs	0
	22	Detroit	14
	28	Cardinals	3
	21	Bears	38
	49	Washington	14
	38	Pittsburgh	7
	38	Los Angeles	14
	44	Washington	21
	42	N.Y. Bulldogs	0
	34	Pittsburgh	17
	24	N.Y. Giants	3
	17	N.Y. Giants	3
	——		——
	364		134

Won 11, Lost 1.
Championship Game:
Philadelphia 14   Los Angeles 0

1950
COACH—EARLE NEALE

PHILADELPHIA	10	Cleveland	35
	45	Cardinals	7
	56	Los Angeles	20
	24	Baltimore	14
	17	Pittsburgh	10
	35	Washington	3
	7	Pittsburgh	9

33	Washington	0
10	Cardinals	14
3	N.Y. Giants	7
7	Cleveland	13
7	N.Y. Giants	9
——		——
254		141

Won 6, Lost 6.

1951
COACH—ALVIN N. McMILLIN to 10/10/51; WAYNE MILLNER

PHILADELPHIA	17	Chicago Cards	14
	21	San Francisco	14
	24	Green Bay	37
	24	N.Y. Giants	26
	23	Washington	27
	34	Pittsburgh	13
	17	Cleveland	20
	10	Detroit	28
	13	Pittsburgh	17
	35	Washington	21
	7	N.Y. Giants	21
	9	Cleveland	24
	——		——
	234		262

Won 4, Lost 8.

1952
COACH—JAMES TRIMBLE

PHILADELPHIA	31	Pittsburgh	25
	7	New York	31
	26	Pittsburgh	21
	7	Cleveland	49
	14	New York	10
	10	Green Bay	12
	38	Washington	20
	10	Cardinals	7
	28	Cleveland	20
	22	Cardinals	28
	38	Dallas	21
	21	Washington	27
	——		——
	252		271

Won 7, Lost 5.

1953
COACH—JAMES TRIMBLE

PHILADELPHIA	21	San Francisco	31
	21	Washington	21
	13	Cleveland	37
	23	Pittsburgh	7
	56	Cardinals	17
	35	Pittsburgh	7
	30	New York	7
	45	Baltimore	14
	38	Cardinals	0
	28	New York	37
	0	Washington	10
	42	Cleveland	27
	——		——
	352		215

Won 7, Lost 4, Tied 1.

1954
COACH—JAMES TRIMBLE

PHILADELPHIA	28	Cleveland	10
	35	Cardinals	16
	24	Pittsburgh	22
	49	Washington	21
	7	Pittsburgh	17
	14	Green Bay	37
	30	Cardinals	14
	14	New York	27
	0	Cleveland	6
	41	Washington	33
	13	Detroit	13
	29	New York	14
	——		——
	284		230

Won 7, Lost 4, Tied 1.

1955
COACH—JAMES TRIMBLE

PHILADELPHIA	27	New York	17
	30	Washington	31
	17	Cleveland	21
	7	Pittsburgh	13
	24	Cardinals	24
	24	Pittsburgh	0
	21	Washington	34
	33	Cleveland	17
	7	New York	31
	21	Los Angeles	23
	27	Cardinals	3
	10	Bears	17
	——		——
	248		231

Won 4, Lost 7, Tied 1.

1956
COACH—HUGH DEVORE

PHILADELPHIA	7	Los Angeles	27
	13	Washington	9
	35	Pittsburgh	21
	6	Cardinals	20
	3	New York	20
	17	Cardinals	28
	14	Pittsburgh	7
	0	Cleveland	16
	10	San Francisco	10
	14	Cleveland	17
	17	Washington	19
	7	New York	21
	——		——
	143		215

Won 3, Lost 8, Tied 1.

1957
COACH—HUGH DEVORE

PHILADELPHIA	13	Los Angeles	17
	20	New York	24
	7	Cleveland	24
	17	Cleveland	7
	0	Pittsburgh	6
	38	Cardinals	21
	16	Detroit	27
	0	New York	13
	21	Washington	12
	7	Pittsburgh	6

PHILADELPHIA	7	Washington	42
	27	Cardinals	31
	—		—
	173		230

Won 4, Lost 8.

1958
COACH—LAWRENCE SHAW

PHILADELPHIA	14	Washington	24
	27	New York	24
	3	Pittsburgh	24
	24	San Francisco	30
	35	Green Bay	38
	21	Cardinals	21
	24	Pittsburgh	31
	49	Cardinals	21
	14	Cleveland	28
	10	New York	24
	14	Cleveland	21
	0	Washington	20
	—		—
	235		306

Won 2, Lost 9, Tied 1.

1959
COACH—LAWRENCE SHAW

PHILADELPHIA	14	San Francisco	24
	49	New York	21
	28	Pittsburgh	24
	7	New York	24
	28	Chi. Cards	24
	30	Washington	23
	7	Cleveland	28
	27	Chi. Cards	17
	23	Los Angeles	20
	0	Pittsburgh	31
	34	Washington	14
	21	Cleveland	28
	—		—
	268		278

Won 7, Lost 5.

1960
COACH—LAWRENCE SHAW

PHILADELPHIA	24	Cleveland	41
	27	Dal. Cowboys	25
	31	St. Louis	27
	28	Detroit	10
	31	Cleveland	29
	34	Pittsburgh	7
	19	Washington	13
	17	N. Y. Giants	10
	31	N. Y. Giants	23
	20	St. Louis	6
	21	Pittsburgh	27
	38	Washington	28
	—		—
	321		246

Won 10, Lost 2.
Championship Game:
Philadelphia 17   Green Bay 13

PITTSBURGH
1933
COACH—FOREST DOUDS

PITTSBURGH	3	Brooklyn	3
	0	Brooklyn	32
	14	Cardinals	13
	0	Green Bay	47
	2	New York	23
	3	New York	27
	6	Philadelphia	25
	6	Boston	21
	16	Boston	14
	—		—
	50		205

Won 3, Lost 6, Tied 2.

1934
COACH—LUBY DiMELIO

PITTSBURGH	13	Cincinnati	0
	0	Boston	7
	0	Philadelphia	17
	12	New York	14
	9	Philadelphia	7
	0	Bears	28
	0	Boston	39
	7	New York	17
	3	Brooklyn	21
	7	Detroit	40
	0	St. Louis	6
	0	Brooklyn	10
	—		—
	53		206

Won 2, Lost 10.

1935
COACH—JOSEPH BACH

PITTSBURGH	17	Philadelphia	7
	7	New York	42
	7	Bears	23
	0	Green Bay	27
	6	Philadelphia	17
	17	Cardinals	13
	6	Boston	0
	7	Brooklyn	13
	16	Brooklyn	7
	14	Green Bay	34
	3	Boston	13
	0	New York	13
	—		—
	100		209

Won 4, Lost 8.

1936
COACH—JOSEPH BACH

PITTSBURGH	10	Boston	0
	10	Brooklyn	6
	10	New York	7
	9	Bears	27
	17	Philadelphia	0
	7	Bears	26
	10	Green Bay	42
	10	Brooklyn	7
	6	Philadelphia	0
	3	Detroit	28
	6	Cardinals	14
	0	Boston	30
	—		—
	98		187

Won 6, Lost 6.

1937
COACH—JOHN (BLOOD) McNALLY

PITTSBURGH	27	Philadelphia	14
	21	Brooklyn	0
	7	New York	10
	0	Bears	7
	3	Detroit	7
	20	Washington	34
	7	Cardinals	13
	16	Philadelphia	7
	0	New York	17
	21	Washington	13
	0	Brooklyn	23

122   145

Won 4, Lost 7.

1938
COACH—JOHN (BLOOD) McNALLY

PITTSBURGH	7	Detroit	16
	14	New York	27
	7	Philadelphia	27
	17	Brooklyn	3
	13	New York	10
	7	Brooklyn	17
	0	Green Bay	20
	0	Washington	7
	7	Philadelphia	14
	0	Washington	15
	7	Cleveland	13

79   169

Won 2, Lost 9.

1939
COACHES—JOHN McNALLY, WALTER KIESLING

PITTSBURGH	7	Brooklyn	12
	0	Cardinals	10
	0	Bears	32
	7	New York	14
	14	Washington	44
	14	Washington	21
	14	Cleveland	14
	13	Brooklyn	17
	7	New York	23
	14	Philadelphia	17
	24	Philadelphia	12

114   216

Won 1, Lost 9, Tied 1.

1940
COACH—WALTER KIESLING

PITTSBURGH	7	Cardinals	7
	10	New York	10
	10	Detroit	7
	3	Brooklyn	10
	10	Washington	40
	0	Brooklyn	21
	0	New York	12
	3	Green Bay	24
	10	Washington	37
	7	Philadelphia	3

| | 0 | Philadelphia | 7 |

60   178

Won 2, Lost 7, Tied 2.

1941
COACHES—BERT BELL, ALDO DONELLI, WALTER KIESLING

PITTSBURGH	14	Cleveland	17
	7	Philadelphia	10
	10	New York	37
	20	Washington	24
	7	New York	28
	7	Bears	34
	3	Washington	23
	7	Philadelphia	7
	14	Brooklyn	7
	7	Green Bay	54
	7	Brooklyn	35

103   276

Won 1, Lost 9, Tied 1.

1942
COACH—WALTER KIESLING

PITTSBURGH	14	Philadelphia	24
	14	Washington	24
	13	New York	10
	7	Brooklyn	0
	14	Philadelphia	0
	0	Washington	14
	17	New York	9
	35	Detroit	7
	19	Cardinals	3
	13	Brooklyn	0
	21	Green Bay	24

167   115

Won 7, Lost 4.

1943
CO-COACHES—EARLE NEALE, W. KIESLING

PHIL-PITT	17	Brooklyn	0
(STEAGLES)	28	New York	14
	21	Bears	48
	14	New York	42
	34	Cardinals	14
	14	Washington	14
	7	Brooklyn	13
	35	Detroit	34
	27	Washington	14
	28	Green Bay	38

225   230

Won 5, Lost 4, Tied 1.

1944
CO-COACHES—PHIL HANDLER, W. KIESLING

CARD-PITT	28	Cleveland	30
(COMBINE)	7	Green Bay	34
	7	Bears	34
	0	New York	23
	20	Washington	42
	6	Detroit	27

CARD-PITT (COMBINE)	7	Detroit	21
	0	Cleveland	33
	7	Bears	49
	6	Cleveland	33
	20	Green Bay	35
	—		—
	108		328

Won 0, Lost 10.

1945
COACH—JAMES LEONARD

PITTSBURGH	7	Boston	28
	6	New York	34
	0	Washington	14
	21	New York	7
	6	Boston	10
	23	Cardinals	0
	6	Philadelphia	30
	7	Bears	28
	0	Washington	24
	—		—
	79		220

Won 2, Lost 8.

1946
COACH—DR. JOHN B. SUTHERLAND

PITTSBURGH	14	Washington	14
	14	New York	17
	16	Boston	7
	7	Green Bay	17
	33	Boston	7
	14	Washington	7
	7	Detroit	17
	0	New York	7
	7	Philadelphia	10
	14	Cardinals	7
	10	Philadelphia	7
	—		—
	136		117

Won 5, Lost 5.

1947
COACH—DR. JOHN B. SUTHERLAND

PITTSBURGH	17	Detroit	10
	7	Los Angeles	48
	26	Washington	27
	30	Boston	14
	35	Philadelphia	24
	38	New York	21
	18	Green Bay	17
	21	Washington	14
	24	New York	7
	7	Bears	49
	0	Philadelphia	21
	17	Boston	7
	0	Philadelphia	21
	—		—
	240		259

Won 8, Lost 4.

1948
COACH—JOHN P. MICHELOSEN

PITTSBURGH	14	Washington	17
	24	Boston	
	10	Washington	7
	7	Boston	13
	27	New York	34

7	Philadelphia	34
38	Green Bay	7
7	Cardinals	24
14	Detroit	17
0	Philadelphia	17
38	New York	28
14	Los Angeles	31
—		—
200		243

Won 4, Lost 8.

1949
COACH—JOHN P. MICHELOSEN

PITTSBURGH	28	N.Y. Giants	7
	14	Washington	27
	14	Detroit	7
	21	N.Y. Giants	17
	24	N.Y. Bulldogs	13
	7	Philadelphia	38
	14	Washington	27
	7	Los Angeles	7
	30	Green Bay	7
	17	Philadelphia	34
	21	Bears	30
	27	N.Y. Bulldogs	0
	—		—
	224		214

Won 6, Lost 5, Tied 1.

1950
COACH—JOHN P. MICHELOSEN

PITTSBURGH	7	N.Y. Giants	18
	7	Detroit	10
	26	Washington	7
	17	Cleveland	30
	17	N.Y. Giants	6
	10	Philadelphia	17
	7	Cleveland	45
	9	Philadelphia	7
	17	Baltimore	7
	28	Cardinals	17
	7	Washington	24
	28	Cardinals	7
	—		—
	180		195

Won 6, Lost 6.

1951
COACH—JOHN P. MICHELOSEN

PITTSBURGH	13	N.Y. Giants	13
	33	Green Bay	35
	24	San Francisco	28
	0	Cleveland	17
	28	Chicago Cards	14
	13	Philadelphia	34
	28	Green Bay	7
	7	Washington	22
	17	Philadelphia	13
	0	N.Y. Giants	14
	0	Cleveland	28
	20	Washington	10
	—		—
	183		235

Won 4, Lost 7, Tied 1.

1952
COACH—JOSEPH BACH

PITTSBURGH	25	Philadelphia	31
	20	Cleveland	21
	21	Philadelphia	26
	24	Washington	28
	34	Cardinals	28
	24	Washington	23
	6	Detroit	31
	28	Cleveland	29
	17	Cardinals	14
	63	New York	7
	24	San Francisco	7
	14	Los Angeles	28
	——		——
	300		273

Won 5, Lost 7.

1953
COACH—JOSEPH BACH

PITTSBURGH	21	Detroit	38
	24	New York	14
	31	Cardinals	28
	7	Philadelphia	23
	31	Green Bay	14
	7	Philadelphia	35
	16	Cleveland	34
	14	New York	10
	16	Cleveland	20
	9	Washington	17
	21	Cardinals	17
	14	Washington	13
	——		——
	211		263

Won 6, Lost 6.

1954
COACH—WALTER KIESLING

PITTSBURGH	21	Green Bay	20
	37	Washington	7
	22	Philadelphia	24
	55	Cleveland	27
	17	Philadelphia	7
	14	Cardinals	17
	6	New York	30
	14	Washington	17
	3	San Francisco	31
	20	Cardinals	17
	3	New York	24
	7	Cleveland	42
	——		——
	219		263

Won 5, Lost 7.

1955
COACH—WALTER KIESLING

PITTSBURGH	14	Cardinals	7
	26	Los Angeles	27
	30	New York	23
	13	Philadelphia	7
	19	New York	17
	0	Philadelphia	24
	13	Cardinals	27
	28	Detroit	31
	14	Cleveland	41
	14	Washington	23

	7	Cleveland	30
	17	Washington	28
	——		——
	195		285

Won 4, Lost 8.

1956
COACH—WALTER KIESLING

PITTSBURGH	30	Washington	13
	10	Cleveland	14
	21	Philadelphia	35
	10	New York	38
	24	Cleveland	16
	14	New York	17
	7	Philadelphia	14
	14	Cardinals	7
	27	Cardinals	38
	30	Los Angeles	13
	7	Detroit	45
	23	Washington	0
	——		——
	217		250

Won 5, Lost 7.

1957
COACH—RAYMOND PARKER

PITTSBURGH	28	Washington	7
	12	Cleveland	23
	29	Cardinals	20
	0	New York	35
	6	Philadelphia	0
	19	Baltimore	13
	0	Cleveland	24
	10	Green Bay	27
	6	Philadelphia	7
	21	New York	10
	3	Washington	10
	27	Cardinals	2
	——		——
	161		178

Won 6, Lost 6.

1958
COACH—RAYMOND PARKER

PITTSBURGH	20	San Francisco	23
	12	Cleveland	45
	24	Philadelphia	3
	10	Cleveland	27
	6	New York	17
	24	Washington	16
	31	Philadelphia	24
	31	New York	10
	27	Cardinals	20
	24	Bears	10
	14	Washington	14
	38	Cardinals	21
	——		——
	261		230

Won 7, Lost 4, Tied 1.

1959
COACH—RAYMOND PARKER

PITTSBURGH	17	Cleveland	7
	17	Washington	23
	24	Philadelphia	28
	27	Washington	6

PITTSBURGH	16	New York	21
	24	Chi. Cards	45
	10	Detroit	10
	14	New York	9
	21	Cleveland	20
	31	Philadelphia	0
	21	Chi. Bears	27
	35	Chi. Cards	20
	257		216

Won 6, Lost 5, Tied 1.

1960
COACH—RAYMOND PARKER

PITTSBURGH	35	Dal. Cowboys	28
	20	Cleveland	28
	17	N. Y. Giants	19
	27	St. Louis	14
	27	Washington	27
	13	Green Bay	19
	7	Philadelphia	34
	24	N. Y. Giants	27
	14	Cleveland	10
	22	Washington	10
	27	Philadelphia	21
	7	St. Louis	38
	240		275

Won 5, Lost 6, Tied 1.

ST. LOUIS CARDINALS

(Formerly, Chicago Cardinals 1920–59)

1920
COACH—MARSHALL SMITH

CARDINALS	0	Tigers (Chi)	0
	33	Moline	0
	0	Rock Is.	7
	21	Detroit	0
	6	Tigers	3
	20	Cincinnati	0
	7	Staleys	6
	0	Staleys	10
	87		26

Won 5, Lost 2, Tied 1.

1921
COACH—JOHN DRISCOLL

CARDINALS	20	Minneapolis	20
	0	Akron	23
	7	Rock Island	14
	17	Columbus	6
	7	Hammond	0
	3	Green Bay	3
	0	Akron	7
	0	Staleys	0
	54		73

Won 2, Lost 3, Tied 3.

1922
COACH—JOHN DRISCOLL

CARDINALS	3	Milwaukee	0
	16	Green Bay	3
	3	Minneapolis	0
	37	Columbus	6
	9	Buffalo	7
	7	Akron	0
	0	Canton	7
	3	Canton	20
	3	Dayton	7
	6	Bears	0
	9	Bears	0
	96		50

Won 8, Lost 3, Tied 0.

1923
COACH—ARNOLD HORWEEN

CARDINALS	3	Buffalo	0
	60	Rochester	0
	19	Akron	0
	13	Dayton	3
	3	Canton	7
	6	Hammond	0
	10	Duluth	0
	4	Racine	10
	22	Marion	19
	29	Rock Island	7
	0	Bears	3
	169		49

Won 8, Lost 3, Tied 0

1924
COACH—ARNOLD HORWEEN

CARDINALS	17	Milwaukee	7
	13	Minneapolis	0
	0	Bears	6
	3	Hammond	6
	8	Milwaukee	17
	3	Green Bay	0
	23	Dayton	0
	13	Akron	0
	10	Racine	10
	6	Bears	21
	96		67

Won 5, Lost 4, Tied 1.

1925
COACH—NORMAN BARRY

CARDINALS	6	Hammond	10
	34	Milwaukee	0
	19	Columbus	9
	20	Kansas City	7
	9	Bears	0
	10	Duluth	6
	9	Green Bay	6
	23	Buffalo	6
	14	Dayton	0
	0	Bears	0
	7	Rock Island	0
	7	Pottsville	21
	158		65

Won 9, Lost 2, Tied 1.

1926
COACH—NORMAN BARRY

CARDINALS			
	14	Columbus	0
	15	Los Angeles	0
	20	Racine	6
	13	Green Bay	7
	0	Bears	16
	3	Milwaukee	2
	0	Green Bay	3
	0	Frankford	27
	0	New York	20
	0	Bears	0
	2	Kansas City	7
	65		88

Won 5, Lost 5, Tied 1.

1927
COACH—FRED GILLIES

CARDINALS			
	0	Bears	9
	19	Pottsville	7
	7	Dayton	0
	0	Green Bay	13
	6	New York	7
	6	Green Bay	6
	6	N.Y. Yanks	20
	7	N.Y. Giants	28
	3	Bears	0
	7	Cleveland	32
	61		122

Won 4, Lost 6, Tied 1.

1928
COACH—GUY CHAMBERLAIN

CARDINALS			
	0	Bears	15
	7	Dayton	0
	0	Green Bay	20
	0	N.Y. Yanks	19
	0	Bears	34
	7		88

Won 1, Lost 4, Tied 0.

1929
COACH—ERNEST NEVERS

CARDINALS			
	2	Green Bay	9
	7	Minneapolis	14
	0	Bears	0
	6	Green Bay	7
	0	Philadelphia	8
	16	Providence	0
	8	Minneapolis	0
	0	Green Bay	13
	19	Dayton	0
	40	Bears	6
	21	N.Y. Giants	24
	119		81

Won 4, Lost 5, Tied 1.

1930
COACH—ERNEST NEVERS

CARDINALS			
	0	Green Bay	14
	0	Portsmouth	0
	6	Bears	32
	13	Newark	0
	7	Providence	9
	12	New York	25
	13	Green Bay	6
	23	Portsmouth	13
	34	Frankford	7
	7	New York	13
	6	Frankford	0
	23	Portsmouth	0
	144		127

Won 6, Lost 5, Tied 1.

1931
COACH—LEROY ANDREWS
ERNEST NEVERS

CARDINALS			
	3	Portsmouth	13
	7	Green Bay	26
	13	Bears	26
	14	Brooklyn	7
	14	Cleveland	6
	21	Green Bay	13
	20	Portsmouth	19
	7	Bears	18
	21	Cleveland	0
	120		128

Won 5, Lost 4, Tied 0.

1932
COACH—JACK CHEVIGNY

CARDINALS			
	7	Green Bay	15
	7	Portsmouth	7
	0	Bears	0
	9	Boston	0
	27	Brooklyn	7
	9	Green Bay	19
	0	Brooklyn	3
	7	Stapleton	21
	0	Bears	34
	6	Boston	8
	72		114

Won 2, Lost 6, Tied 2.

1933
COACH—PAUL SCHISSLER

CARDINALS			
	13	Pittsburgh	14
	6	Portsmouth	7
	3	Cincinnati	0
	9	Bears	12
	0	Boston	10
	0	Brooklyn	7
	6	Green Bay	14
	9	Cincinnati	12
	0	Brooklyn	3
	6	Bears	22
	0	Boston	0
	52		101

Won 1, Lost 9, Tied 1.

1934
COACH—PAUL SCHISSLER

CARDINALS	9	Cincinnati	0
	0	Detroit	6
	16	Cincinnati	0
	0	Bears	20
	0	Green Bay	15
	0	Boston	9
	21	Brooklyn	0
	13	Detroit	17
	9	Green Bay	0
	6	Bears	17
	6	Green Bay	0
	80		84

Won 5, Lost 6, Tied 0.

1935
COACH—MILAN CREIGHTON

CARDINALS	7	Green Bay	6
	10	Detroit	10
	3	Green Bay	0
	13	Pittsburgh	17
	14	New York	13
	7	Detroit	7
	12	Philadelphia	3
	6	Boston	0
	9	Green Bay	7
	7	Bears	7
	0	Bears	13
	88		83

Won 6, Lost 3, Tied 2.

1936
COACH—MILAN CREIGHTON

CARDINALS	7	Green Bay	10
	0	Detroit	39
	0	Green Bay	24
	3	Bears	7
	6	New York	14
	10	Boston	13
	13	Philadelphia	0
	14	Pittsburgh	6
	7	Detroit	14
	14	Bears	7
	0	Green Bay	0
	74		134

Won 3, Lost 7, Tied 1.

1937
COACH—MILAN CREIGHTON

CARDINALS	14	Green Bay	7
	7	Detroit	16
	21	Washington	14
	6	Philadelphia	6
	6	Cleveland	0
	13	Green Bay	34
	7	Bears	16
	13	Pittsburgh	7
	13	Cleveland	7
	7	Detroit	16

	27	Bears	42
	134		165

Won 5, Lost 5, Tied 1.

1938
COACH—MILAN CREIGHTON

CARDINALS	13	Bears	16
	7	Cleveland	6
	7	Green Bay	28
	22	Green Bay	24
	0	Brooklyn	13
	28	Bears	34
	0	Detroit	10
	0	Philadelphia	7
	0	New York	6
	3	Detroit	7
	31	Cleveland	17
	111		168

Won 2, Lost 9, Tied 0.

1939
COACH—ERNEST NEVERS

CARDINALS	13	Detroit	21
	10	Green Bay	14
	10	Pittsburgh	0
	3	Detroit	17
	20	Green Bay	27
	7	Bears	44
	0	Cleveland	24
	0	Cleveland	14
	7	New York	17
	7	Washington	28
	7	Bears	48
	84		254

Won 1, Lost 10, Tied 0.

1940
COACH—JAMES CONZELMAN

CARDINALS	7	Pittsburgh	7
	0	Detroit	0
	21	Bears	7
	6	Green Bay	31
	14	Detroit	43
	21	Washington	28
	14	Cleveland	26
	17	Cleveland	7
	7	Green Bay	28
	9	Brooklyn	14
	20	Bears	31
	136		222

Won 2, Lost 7, Tied 2.

1941
COACH—JAMES CONZELMAN

CARDINALS	6	Cleveland	10
	14	Detroit	14
	13	Green Bay	14
	7	Bears	53
	20	Brooklyn	6
	14	Philadelphia	21
	10	New York	7
	9	Green Bay	17
	7	Cleveland	0

3	Detroit	21
24	Bears	34
—		—
127		193

Won 3, Lost 7, Tied 1.

1942
COACH—JAMES CONZELMAN

CARDINALS			
	7	Cleveland	0
	13	Detroit	0
	13	Green Bay	17
	14	Bears	44
	7	Detroit	0
	3	Cleveland	7
	24	Green Bay	55
	0	Washington	28
	3	Pittsburgh	19
	7	New York	21
	7	Bears	21
	—		—
	98		209

Won 3, Lost 8, Tied 0.

1943
COACH—PHILIP HANDLER

CARDINALS			
	17	Detroit	35
	7	Green Bay	28
	0	Bears	20
	0	Detroit	7
	7	Washington	13
	13	Phil-Pitt	7
	0	Brooklyn	7
	14	Green Bay	35
	13	New York	24
	24	Bears	35
	—		—
	95		211

Won 1, Lost 9, Tied 0.

1944 (Merged with Pittsburgh)
COACH—PHILIP HANDLER
WALTER KIESLING

CARD-PITT			
	28	Cleveland	30
	7	Green Bay	34
	7	Bears	34
	0	New York	23
	20	Washington	42
	6	Detroit	27
	7	Detroit	21
	6	Cleveland	33
	20	Green Bay	35
	7	Bears	49
	—		—
	108		328

Won 0, Lost 10, Tied 0.

1945
COACH—PHILIP HANDLER

CARDINALS			
	0	Detroit	10
	0	Cleveland	21
	6	Philadelphia	24
	16	Bears	7
	0	Detroit	26
	14	Green Bay	33
	21	Washington	24
	0	Pittsburgh	23

21	Cleveland	35
20	Bears	28
—		—
98		231

Won 1, Lost 9, Tied 0.

1946
COACH—JAMES CONZELMAN

CARDINALS			
	7	Pittsburgh	14
	34	Detroit	14
	17	Bears	34
	36	Detroit	14
	24	New York	28
	34	L.A. Rams	10
	28	Boston	14
	7	Green Bay	19
	14	L.A. Rams	17
	24	Green Bay	6
	35	Bears	28
	—		—
	260		198

Won 6, Lost 5, Tied 0.

1947
COACH—JAMES CONZELMAN

CARDINALS			
	45	Detroit	45
	31	Bears	7
	14	Green Bay	10
	7	L.A. Rams	27
	27	Boston	7
	17	L.A. Rams	10
	17	Detroit	7
	21	Green Bay	20
	21	Washington	45
	31	New York	35
	45	Philadelphia	21
	30	Bears	21
	—		—
	306		231

Won 9, Lost 3, Tied 0.

Championship Game:
Cardinals 28   Philadelphia 21

1948
COACH—JAMES CONZELMAN

CARDINALS			
	21	Philadelphia	14
	17	Bears	28
	17	Green Bay	7
	63	New York	35
	49	Boston	27
	27	L.A. Rams	22
	56	Detroit	20
	24	Pittsburgh	7
	27	L.A. Rams	24
	28	Detroit	14
	42	Green Bay	7
	24	Bears	21
	—		—
	395		226

Won 11, Lost 1, Tied 0.

Championship Game:
Cardinals 0   Philadelphia 7

1949
COACH—PHILIP HANDLER

RAYMOND PARKER

CARDINALS	38	Washington	7
	7	Bears	17
	3	Philadelphia	28
	39	Green Bay	17
	7	Detroit	24
	38	N.Y. Giants	41
	42	Detroit	19
	65	N.Y. Bulldogs	20
	28	L.A. Rams	28
	41	Green Bay	21
	31	L.A. Rams	27
	21	Bears	52
	360		301

Won 6, Lost 5, Tied 1.

1950
COACH—EARL LAMBEAU

CARDINALS	7	Philadelphia	45
	55	Baltimore	13
	6	Bears	27
	24	Cleveland	34
	38	Washington	28
	17	New York	3
	7	Cleveland	10
	21	New York	51
	14	Philadelphia	10
	17	Pittsburgh	28
	20	Bears	10
	7	Pittsburgh	28
	254		266

Won 5, Lost 7, Tied 0.

1951
COACH—EARL LAMBEAU

CARDINALS	14	Philadelphia	17
	28	Bears	14
	17	New York	28
	3	Washington	7
	14	Pittsburgh	28
	17	Cleveland	34
	21	L.A. Rams	45
	27	San Francisco	21
	0	New York	10
	28	Cleveland	49
	17	Washington	20
	24	Bears	14
	206		287

Won 3, Lost 9, Tied 0.

1952
COACH—JOSEPH STYDAHAR

CARDINALS	7	Washington	23
	21	Bears	10
	17	Washington	6
	24	New York	23
	28	Pittsburgh	34
	6	New York	28
	13	Cleveland	28
	7	Philadelphia	10
	14	Pittsburgh	17
	28	Philadelphia	22
	0	Cleveland	10
	7	Bears	10
	176		221

Won 4, Lost 8.

1953
COACH—JOSEPH STYDAHAR

CARDINALS	13	Washington	24
	7	Cleveland	27
	28	Pittsburgh	31
	7	New York	21
	17	Philadelphia	56
	20	New York	23
	17	Washington	28
	24	Los Angeles	24
	0	Philadelphia	38
	16	Cleveland	27
	17	Pittsburgh	21
	24	Bears	17
	190		337

Won 1, Lost 10, Tied 1.

1954
COACH—RAY RICHARDS

CARDINALS	10	New York	41
	16	Philadelphia	35
	7	Cleveland	31
	17	New York	31
	3	Cleveland	35
	17	Pittsburgh	14
	14	Philadelphia	30
	17	Los Angeles	28
	38	Washington	16
	17	Pittsburgh	20
	7	Bears	29
	20	Washington	37
	183		347

Won 2, Lost 10.

1955
COACH—RAY RICHARDS

CARDINALS	7	Pittsburgh	14
	28	New York	17
	24	Washington	10
	0	New York	10
	24	Philadelphia	24
	20	Cleveland	26
	27	Pittsburgh	13
	14	Green Bay	31
	0	Washington	31
	53	Bears	14
	3	Philadelphia	27
	24	Cleveland	35
	224		252

Won 4, Lost 7, Tied 1.

1956
COACH—RAY RICHARDS

CARDINALS	9	Cleveland	7
	35	New York	27

31	Washington	3		14	N. Y. Giants	35
20	Philadelphia	6		27	Philadelphia	31
14	Washington	17		14	Pittsburgh	27
28	Philadelphia	17		12	Dal. Cowboys	10
10	New York	23		20	N. Y. Giants	13
7	Pittsburgh	14		44	Washington	7
38	Pittsburgh	27		27	Cleveland	28
21	Green Bay	24		26	Washington	14
3	Bears	10		17	Cleveland	17
24	Cleveland	7		6	Philadelphia	20
				38	Pittsburgh	7
——		——		——		——
240		182		288		230

Won 7, Lost 5.

Won 6, Lost 5, Tied 1.

1957
COACH—RAY RICHARDS

CARDINALS	20	San Francisco	10
	14	Washington	37
	20	Pittsburgh	29
	44	Washington	14
	7	Cleveland	17
	21	Philadelphia	38
	14	New York	27
	21	New York	28
	0	Cleveland	31
	6	Bears	14
	31	Philadelphia	27
	2	Pittsburgh	27
——	200		299

Won 3, Lost 9.

1958
COACH—FRANK IVY

CARDINALS	7	New York	37
	37	Washington	10
	28	Cleveland	35
	23	New York	6
	24	Cleveland	38
	21	Philadelphia	21
	31	Washington	45
	21	Philadelphia	49
	20	Pittsburgh	27
	14	Los Angeles	20

1959
COACH—FRANK IVY

CARDINALS	49	Washington	21
	7	Cleveland	34
	14	Washington	23
	7	Cleveland	17
	24	Philadelphia	28
	45	Pittsburgh	24
	3	New York	9
	17	Philadelphia	27
	20	New York	30
	7	Chi. Bears	31
	21	Detroit	45
	20	Pittsburgh	35
——	234		324

Won 2, Lost 10.

1960
COACH—FRANK IVY

ST. LOUIS	43	L. A. Rams	21

SAN FRANCISCO
(Formerly AAFC; entered NFL 1950)

1950
COACH—LAWRENCE SHAW

SAN FRANCISCO	20	Bears	32
	14	Cleveland	31
	7	Detroit	24
	21	Green Bay	25
	14	Los Angeles	35
	17	N.Y. Yanks	21
	17	Baltimore	14
	0	Bears	17
	28	Detroit	27
	30	Green Bay	14
	21	Los Angeles	28
	25	N.Y. Yanks	29
——	213		300

Won 3, Lost 9.

1951
COACH—LAWRENCE SHAW

SAN FRANCISCO	24	Cleveland	10
	14	Philadelphia	21
	28	Pittsburgh	24
	7	Chicago Bears	13
	44	Los Angeles	17
	16	Los Angeles	23
	19	N.Y. Yanks	14
	21	Chicago Cards	27
	10	N.Y. Yanks	10
	20	Detroit	10
	31	Green Bay	19
	21	Detroit	17
——	255		205

Won 7, Lost, 4, Tied 1.

1952
COACH—LAWRENCE SHAW

SAN FRANCISCO	17	Detroit	3
	37	Dallas	14
	28	Detroit	0
	40	Bears	16
	48	Dallas	21
	17	Bears	20
	14	New York	23

SAN FRANCISCO	23	Washington	17
	9	Los Angeles	35
	21	Los Angeles	34
	7	Pittsburgh	24
	24	Green Bay	14
	——		——
	285		221

Won 7, Lost 5.

1953
COACH—LAWRENCE SHAW

SAN FRANCISCO	31	Philadelphia	21
	31	Los Angeles	30
	21	Detroit	24
	35	Bears	28
	10	Detroit	14
	24	Bears	14
	31	Los Angeles	27
	21	Cleveland	23
	37	Green Bay	7
	38	Baltimore	21
	49	Green Bay	14
	45	Baltimore	14
	——		——
	373		237

Won 9, Lost 3.

1954
COACH—LAWRENCE SHAW

SAN FRANCISCO	41	Washington	7
	24	Los Angeles	24
	23	Green Bay	17
	31	Bears	24
	37	Detroit	31
	27	Bears	31
	34	Los Angeles	42
	7	Detroit	48
	31	Pittsburgh	3
	13	Baltimore	17
	35	Green Bay	0
	10	Baltimore	7
	——		——
	313		251

Won 7, Lost 4. Tied 1.

1955
COACH—NORMAN STRADER

SAN FRANCISCO	14	Los Angeles	23
	3	Cleveland	38
	20	Bears	19
	27	Detroit	24
	23	Bears	34
	38	Detroit	21
	14	Los Angeles	27
	0	Washington	7
	21	Green Bay	27
	14	Baltimore	26
	7	Green Bay	28
	35	Baltimore	24
	——		——
	216		298

Won 4, Lost 8.

1956
COACH—FRANK ALBERT

SAN FRANCISCO	21	New York	38
	33	Los Angeles	30
	7	Bears	31
	17	Detroit	20
	21	Bears	38
	13	Detroit	17
	6	Los Angeles	30
	17	Green Bay	16
	10	Philadelphia	10
	20	Baltimore	17
	38	Green Bay	20
	30	Baltimore	17
	——		——
	233		284

Won 5, Lost 6, Tied 1.

1957
COACH—FRANK ALBERT

SAN FRANCISCO	10	Cardinals	20
	23	Los Angeles	20
	21	Bears	17
	24	Green Bay	14
	21	Bears	17
	35	Detroit	31
	24	Los Angeles	37
	10	Detroit	31
	21	Baltimore	27
	27	New York	17
	17	Baltimore	13
	27	Green Bay	20
	——		——
	260		264

Won 8, Lost 4.
Conference Playoff:
San Francisco 27   Detroit 31

1958
COACH—FRANK ALBERT

SAN FRANCISCO	23	Pittsburgh	20
	3	Los Angeles	33
	6	Bears	28
	30	Philadelphia	24
	14	Bears	27
	24	Detroit	21
	7	Los Angeles	56
	21	Detroit	35
	33	Green Bay	12
	27	Baltimore	35
	48	Green Bay	21
	21	Baltimore	12
	——		——
	257		324

Won 6, Lost 6.

1959
COACH—HOWARD HICKEY

SAN FRANCISCO	24	Philadelphia	14
	34	Los Angeles	0
	20	Green Bay	21
	34	Detroit	13
	20	Chi. Bears	17
	33	Detroit	7
	24	Los Angeles	16

3	Chi. Bears	14
14	Baltimore	45
21	Cleveland	20
14	Baltimore	34
14	Green Bay	36
—		—
255		237

Won 7, Lost 5.

1960
COACH—HOWARD HICKEY

SAN FRANCISCO	19	N. Y. Giants	21
	13	L. A. Rams	9
	14	Detroit	10
	10	Chicago	27
	14	Green Bay	41
	25	Chicago	7
	0	Detroit	24
	26	Dal. Cowboys	14
	30	Baltimore	22
	23	L. A. Rams	7
	0	Green Bay	13
	34	Baltimore	10
	—		—
	208		205

Won 7, Lost 5.

WASHINGTON REDSKINS
(Formerly Boston Redskins 1932–1936)

1932
COACH—LUDLOW WRAY

BOSTON	0	Brooklyn	14
	7	Bears	7
	0	Cardinals	9
	6	New York	14
	7	Brooklyn	0
	0	Green Bay	21
	0	Pittsburgh	10
	0	Cardinals	9
	0	New York	0
	—		—
	20		84

Won 1, Lost 6, Tied 2.

1933
COACH—WILLIAM DIETZ

BOSTON	7	Green Bay	7
	0	Bears	7
	21	Pittsburgh	6
	21	New York	20
	0	Portsmouth	13
	10	Cardinals	0
	14	Pittsburgh	16
	10	Bears	0
	0	New York	7
	20	Green Bay	7
	0	Brooklyn	14
	0	Cardinals	0
	—		—
	103		97

Won 5, Lost 5, Tied 2.

1934
COACH—WILLIAM DIETZ

BOSTON	7	Pittsburgh	0
	6	Brooklyn	15
	13	New York	16
	39	Pittsburgh	0
	0	Detroit	24
	6	Philadelphia	0
	9	Cardinals	0
	0	Green Bay	10
	0	Bears	21
	14	Philadelphia	7
	0	New York	3
	13	Brooklyn	3
	—		—
	107		99

Won 6, Lost 6, Tied 0.

1935
COACH—EDWARD CASEY

BOSTON	7	Brooklyn	3
	14	Bears	30
	12	New York	20
	0	Cardinals	6
	0	Pittsburgh	6
	7	Detroit	17
	0	Brooklyn	0
	6	New York	17
	6	Philadelphia	7
	13	Pittsburgh	3
	—		—
	65		109

Won 2, Lost 7, Tied 1.

1936
COACH—RAY FLAHERTY

BOSTON	0	Pittsburgh	10
	26	Philadelphia	3
	14	Brooklyn	3
	0	New York	7
	2	Green Bay	31
	17	Philadelphia	7
	13	Cardinals	10
	3	Green Bay	7
	0	Bears	26
	30	Brooklyn	6
	30	Pittsburgh	0
	14	New York	0
	—		—
	149		110

Won 7, Lost 4, Tied 0.

1937
COACH—RAY FLAHERTY

WASHINGTON	13	New York	3
	14	Cardinals	21
	11	Brooklyn	7
	0	Philadelphia	14
	34	Pittsburgh	20
	10	Philadelphia	7
	21	Brooklyn	0
	13	Pittsburgh	21

WASHINGTON	16	Cleveland	7
	14	Green Bay	6
	49	New York	14
	—		—
	195		120

Won 8, Lost 3.
Championship Game:
Washington 28   Bears 21

1938
COACH—RAY FLAHERTY

WASHINGTON	26	Philadelphia	23
	16	Brooklyn	16
	37	Cleveland	13
	7	New York	10
	7	Detroit	5
	20	Philadelphia	14
	6	Brooklyn	6
	7	Pittsburgh	0
	7	Bears	31
	15	Pittsburgh	0
	0	New York	36
	—		—
	148		154

Won 6, Lost 3, Tied 2.

1939
COACH—RAY FLAHERTY

WASHINGTON	7	Philadelphia	0
	0	New York	0
	41	Brooklyn	13
	44	Pittsburgh	14
	21	Pittsburgh	14
	14	Green Bay	24
	7	Philadelphia	6
	42	Brooklyn	0
	28	Cardinals	7
	31	Detroit	7
	7	New York	9
	242		94

Won 8, Lost 2, Tied 1.

1940
COACH—RAY FLAHERTY

WASHINGTON	24	Brooklyn	17
	21	New York	7
	40	Pittsburgh	10
	28	Cardinals	21
	20	Detroit	14
	20	Philadelphia	17
	37	Pittsburgh	10
	14	Brooklyn	16
	7	Bears	3
	7	New York	21
	13	Philadelphia	6
	—		—
	245		142

Won 9, Lost 2.
Championship Game:
Washington 0   Bears 73

1941
COACH—RAY FLAHERTY

| WASHINGTON | 10 | New York | 17 |

	3	Brooklyn	0
	24	Pittsburgh	20
	21	Philadelphia	17
	17	Cleveland	13
	23	Pittsburgh	3
	7	Brooklyn	13
	21	Bears	35
	13	New York	20
	17	Green Bay	22
	20	Philadelphia	14
	—		—
	176		174

Won 6, Lost 5.

1942
COACH—RAY FLAHERTY

WASHINGTON	28	Pittsburgh	14
	7	New York	14
	14	Philadelphia	10
	33	Cleveland	14
	21	Brooklyn	10
	30	Philadelphia	27
	14	Pittsburgh	0
	28	Cardinals	0
	14	New York	7
	23	Brooklyn	3
	15	Detroit	3
	227		102

Won 10, Lost 1.
Championship Game:
Washington 14   Bears 6

1943
COACH—ARTHUR BERGMAN

WASHINGTON	27	Brooklyn	0
	33	Green Bay	7
	13	Cardinals	7
	48	Brooklyn	10
	14	Phil-Pitt	14
	42	Detroit	20
	21	Bears	7
	14	Phil-Pitt	27
	10	New York	14
	7	New York	31
	28	New York	0
	—		—
	257		137

Won 7, Lost 3, Tied 1.
Championship Game:
Washington 21   Bears 41

1944
COACH—DUDLEY DeGROOT

WASHINGTON	31	Philadelphia	31
	21	Boston	14
	17	Brooklyn	14
	42	Card-Pitt	20
	14	Cleveland	10
	10	Brooklyn	0
	7	Philadelphia	37
	14	Boston	7
	13	New York	16

0	New York	31
—		—
169		184

Won 6, Lost 3, Tied 1

1945
COACH—DUDLEY DeGROOT

WASHINGTON	20	Boston	28
	14	Pittsburgh	0
	24	Philadelphia	14
	24	New York	14
	24	Cardinals	21
	34	Boston	7
	28	Bears	21
	0	Philadelphia	16
	24	Pittsburgh	0
	17	New York	0
	—		—
	209		121

Won 8, Lost 2.
Championship Game:
Washington 14   Cleveland 15

1946
COACH—A. GLENN EDWARDS

WASHINGTON	14	Pittsburgh	14
	17	Detroit	16
	24	New York	14
	14	Philadelphia	28
	24	Boston	6
	7	Pittsburgh	14
	17	Boston	14
	20	Bears	24
	27	Philadelphia	10
	7	Green Bay	20
	0	New York	31
	—		—
	171		191

Won 5, Lost 5, Tied 1.

1947
COACH—A. GLENN EDWARDS

WASHINGTON	42	Philadelphia	45
	27	Pittsburgh	26
	28	New York	20
	10	Green Bay	27
	20	Bears	56
	14	Philadelphia	38
	14	Pittsburgh	21
	21	Detroit	38
	45	Cardinals	21
	24	Boston	27
	10	New York	35
	40	Boston	14
	—		—
	295		367

Won 4, Lost 8.

1948
COACH—A. GLENN EDWARDS

WASHINGTON	17	Pittsburgh	14
	41	New York	10
	7	Pittsburgh	10
	0	Philadelphia	45
	23	Green Bay	7
	59	Boston	21
	23	Boston	7
	46	Detroit	21
	21	Philadelphia	42
	13	Bears	48
	13	Los Angeles	41
	28	New York	21
	—		—
	291		287

Won 7, Lost 5.

1949
COACH—JOHN E. WHELCHEL to
11/7/49—HERMAN BALL

WASHINGTON	7	Cardinals	38
	27	Pittsburgh	14
	35	N.Y. Giants	45
	38	N.Y. Bulldogs	14
	14	Philadelphia	49
	14	N.Y. Bulldogs	14
	27	Pittsburgh	14
	21	Philadelphia	44
	21	Bears	31
	7	N.Y. Giants	23
	30	Green Bay	0
	27	Los Angeles	53
	—		—
	268		339

Won 4, Lost 7, Tied 1.

1950
COACH—HERMAN BALL

WASHINGTON	35	Baltimore	14
	21	Green Bay	35
	7	Pittsburgh	26
	17	N.Y. Giants	21
	28	Cardinals	38
	3	Philadelphia	35
	21	N.Y. Giants	24
	0	Philadelphia	33
	14	Cleveland	20
	38	Baltimore	28
	24	Pittsburgh	7
	21	Cleveland	45
	—		—
	229		326

Won 3, Lost 9.

1951
COACH—HERMAN BALL to 10/19/51
RICHARD TODD

WASHINGTON	17	Detroit	35
	14	N.Y. Giants	35
	0	Cleveland	45
	7	Chicago Cards	3
	27	Philadelphia	23
	0	Chicago Bears	27
	14	N.Y. Giants	28
	22	Pittsburgh	7

WASHINGTON	31	Los Angeles	21
	21	Philadelphia	35
	20	Chicago Cards	17
	10	Pittsburgh	20
	183		296

Won 5, Lost 7.

1952
COACH—EARL LAMBEAU

WASHINGTON	23	Cardinals	7
	20	Green Bay	35
	6	Cardinals	17
	28	Washington	24
	15	Cleveland	19
	23	Pittsburgh	24
	20	Philadelphia	38
	17	San Francisco	23
	10	New York	14
	24	Cleveland	48
	27	New York	17
	27	Philadelphia	21
	240		287

Won 4, Lost 8.

1953
COACH—EARL LAMBEAU

WASHINGTON	24	Cardinals	13
	21	Philadelphia	21
	13	New York	9
	14	Cleveland	30
	17	Baltimore	27
	3	Cleveland	27
	28	Cardinals	17
	24	Bears	27
	23	Washington	21
	17	Pittsburgh	9
	10	Philadelphia	0
	13	Pittsburgh	14
	207		215

Won 6, Lost 5, Tied 1.

1954
COACH—JOSEPH KUHARICH

WASHINGTON	7	San Francisco	41
	7	Pittsburgh	37
	21	New York	51
	21	Philadelphia	49
	7	New York	24
	24	Baltimore	21
	3	Cleveland	62
	17	Pittsburgh	14
	16	Cardinals	38
	33	Philadelphia	41
	14	Cleveland	34
	37	Cardinals	20
	207		432

Won 3, Lost 9.

1955
COACH—JOSEPH KUHARICH

WASHINGTON	27	Cleveland	17
	31	Philadelphia	30
	10	Cardinals	24
	14	Cleveland	24
	14	Baltimore	13
	7	New York	35
	34	Philadelphia	21
	7	San Francisco	0
	31	Cardinals	0
	23	Pittsburgh	14
	20	New York	27
	28	Pittsburgh	17
	246		222

Won 8, Lost 4.

1956
COACH—JOSEPH KUHARICH

WASHINGTON	13	Pittsburgh	30
	9	Philadelphia	13
	3	Cardinals	31
	20	Cleveland	9
	17	Cardinals	14
	18	Detroit	17
	33	New York	7
	20	Cleveland	17
	14	New York	28
	19	Philadelphia	17
	0	Pittsburgh	23
	17	Baltimore	19
	183		225

Won 6, Lost 6.

1957
COACH—JOSEPH KUHARICH

WASHINGTON	7	Pittsburgh	28
	37	Cardinals	14
	20	New York	24
	14	Cardinals	44
	31	New York	14
	17	Cleveland	21
	17	Baltimore	21
	30	Cleveland	30
	12	Philadelphia	21
	14	Bears	3
	42	Philadelphia	7
	10	Pittsburgh	3
	251		230

Won 5, Lost 6, Tied 1.

1958
COACH—JOSEPH KUHARICH

WASHINGTON	24	Philadelphia	14
	10	Cardinals	37
	14	New York	21
	37	Green Bay	21
	10	Baltimore	35
	16	Pittsburgh	24
	45	Bears	31
	10	Cleveland	20
	0	New York	30
	14	Cleveland	21
	14	Pittsburgh	14

20 Philadelphia 0
—— ——
214 268
Won 4, Lost 7, Tied 1.

1959
COACH—MICHAEL NIXON

WASHINGTON			
	21	Chi. Cards	49
	23	Pittsburgh	17
	23	Chi. Cards	14
	6	Pittsburgh	27
	7	Cleveland	34
	23	Philadelphia	30
	27	Baltimore	24
	17	Cleveland	31
	0	Green Bay	21
	14	New York	45
	14	Philadelphia	34
	10	New York	24
	——		——

185 350
Won 3, Lost 9.

1960
COACH—MICHAEL NIXON

WASHINGTON	0	Baltimore	20
	26	Dal. Cowboys	14
	24	N. Y. Giants	24
	27	Pittsburgh	27
	10	Cleveland	31
	7	St. Louis	44
	13	Philadelphia	19
	14	St. Louis	26
	10	Pittsburgh	22
	16	Cleveland	27
	3	N. Y. Giants	17
	28	Philadelphia	38
	——		——
	178		309

Won 1, Lost 9, Tied 2.

TEAM vs TEAM RECORDS

CHICAGO BEARS vs
BALTIMORE COLTS

1953	Baltimore	13	Bears	9
	Baltimore	16	Bears	14
1954	Bears	28	Baltimore	9
	Bears	28	Baltimore	13
1955	Baltimore	23	Bears	17
	Bears	38	Baltimore	10
1956	Baltimore	28	Bears	21
	Bears	58	Baltimore	27
1957	Baltimore	21	Bears	10
	Baltimore	29	Bears	14
1958	Baltimore	51	Bears	38
	Baltimore	17	Bears	0
1959	Bears	26	Baltimore	21
	Baltimore	21	Bears	7
1960	Baltimore	42	Bears	7
	Baltimore	24	Bears	20

Baltimore won 11; Bears won 5; Tied 0.
Total points: Baltimore 365, Bears 335.

CHICAGO BEARS vs
DALLAS COWBOYS

1960	Bears	17	Dallas	7

Bears won 1; Dallas won 0; Tied 0.
Total points: Bears 17, Dallas 7.

CHICAGO BEARS vs
DETROIT LIONS

1934	Bears	19	Detroit	16
	Bears	10	Detroit	7
1935	Detroit	20	Bears	20
	Detroit	14	Bears	2
1936	Bears	12	Detroit	10
	Detroit	13	Bears	7
1937	Bears	28	Detroit	20
	Bears	13	Detroit	0
1938	Detroit	13	Bears	7
	Detroit	14	Bears	7
1939	Detroit	10	Bears	0
	Bears	23	Detroit	13
1940	Bears	7	Detroit	0
	Detroit	17	Bears	14
1941	Bears	49	Detroit	0
	Bears	24	Detroit	7
1942	Bears	16	Detroit	0
	Bears	42	Detroit	0
1943	Bears	27	Detroit	21
	Bears	35	Detroit	14
1944	Detroit	21	Bears	21
	Detroit	41	Bears	21
1945	Detroit	16	Bears	10
	Detroit	35	Bears	28
1946	Bears	42	Detroit	6
	Bears	45	Detroit	24
1947	Bears	33	Detroit	24
	Bears	34	Detroit	14
1948	Bears	28	Detroit	0
	Bears	42	Detroit	14
1949	Bears	27	Detroit	24
	Bears	28	Detroit	7
1950	Bears	35	Detroit	21
	Bears	6	Detroit	3
1951	Bears	28	Detroit	23
	Detroit	41	Bears	28
1952	Bears	24	Detroit	23
	Detroit	45	Bears	21
1953	Detroit	20	Bears	16
	Detroit	13	Bears	7
1954	Detroit	48	Bears	23
	Bears	28	Detroit	24
1955	Bears	24	Detroit	14
	Bears	21	Detroit	20

1956	Detroit	42	Bears	10	
	Bears	38	Detroit	21	
1957	Bears	27	Detroit	7	
	Detroit	21	Bears	13	
1958	Bears	20	Detroit	7	
	Bears	21	Detroit	16	
1959	Bears	24	Detroit	14	
	Bears	25	Detroit	14	
1960	Bears	28	Detroit	7	
	Detroit	36	Bears	0	

Bears won 35; Detroit won 17; Tied 2.
Total points: Bears 1,188; Detroit 915.

CHICAGO BEARS vs GREEN BAY PACKERS

1921	Bears	20	Green Bay	0
1923	Bears	3	Green Bay	0
1924	Green Bay	5	Bears	0
	Bears	3	Green Bay	0
1925	Green Bay	14	Bears	10
	Bears	21	Green Bay	0
1926	Green Bay	6	Bears	6
	Bears	19	Green Bay	13
	Green Bay	3	Bears	3
1927	Bears	7	Green Bay	6
	Bears	14	Green Bay	6
1928	Green Bay	12	Bears	12
	Green Bay	16	Bears	6
	Green Bay	6	Bears	0
1929	Green Bay	23	Bears	0
	Green Bay	14	Bears	0
	Green Bay	25	Bears	0
1930	Green Bay	7	Bears	0
	Green Bay	13	Bears	12
	Bears	21	Green Bay	0
1931	Green Bay	7	Bears	0
	Green Bay	6	Bears	2
	Bears	7	Green Bay	6
1932	Green Bay	0	Bears	0
	Green Bay	2	Bears	0
	Bears	9	Green Bay	0
1933	Bears	14	Green Bay	7
	Bears	10	Green Bay	7
	Bears	7	Green Bay	6
1934	Bears	24	Green Bay	10
	Bears	27	Green Bay	14
	†Bears	10	Green Bay	6
1935	Green Bay	7	Bears	0
	Green Bay	17	Bears	14
1936	Bears	30	Green Bay	3
	Green Bay	21	Bears	10
1937	Bears	14	Green Bay	2
	Green Bay	24	Bears	14
1938	Bears	2	Green Bay	0
	Green Bay	24	Bears	17
1939	Green Bay	21	Bears	16
	Bears	30	Green Bay	27
1940	Bears	41	Green Bay	10
	Bears	14	Green Bay	7
1941	Bears	25	Green Bay	17
	Green Bay	16	Bears	14
	*Bears	33	Green Bay	14
1942	Bears	44	Green Bay	28

	Bears	38	Green Bay	7
1943	Green Bay	21	Bears	21
	Bears	21	Green Bay	7
1944	Green Bay	42	Bears	28
	Bears	21	Green Bay	0
1945	Green Bay	31	Bears	21
	Bears	28	Green Bay	24
1946	Bears	30	Green Bay	7
	Bears	10	Green Bay	7
1947	Green Bay	29	Bears	20
	Bears	20	Green Bay	17
1948	Bears	45	Green Bay	7
	Bears	7	Green Bay	6
1949	Bears	17	Green Bay	0
	Bears	24	Green Bay	3
1950	Green Bay	31	Bears	21
	Bears	28	Green Bay	14
1951	Bears	31	Green Bay	20
	Bears	24	Green Bay	13
1952	Bears	24	Green Bay	14
	Green Bay	41	Bears	28
1953	Bears	17	Green Bay	13
	Bears	21	Green Bay	21
1954	Bears	10	Green Bay	3
	Bears	28	Green Bay	23
1955	Green Bay	24	Bears	3
	Bears	52	Green Bay	31
1956	Bears	37	Green Bay	21
	Bears	38	Green Bay	14
1957	Green Bay	21	Bears	17
	Bears	21	Green Bay	14
1958	Bears	34	Green Bay	20
	Bears	24	Green Bay	10
1959	Green Bay	9	Bears	6
	Bears	28	Green Bay	17
1960	Bears	17	Green Bay	14
	Green Bay	41	Bears	13

Bears won 50; Green Bay won 28; Tied 6.
Total points: Bears 1,448; Green Bay 1,109

* Divisional Play-off
† Non-Championship Game

CHICAGO BEARS vs NEW YORK GIANTS

1925	Bears	19	New York	7
	New York	9	Bears	0
1926	Bears	7	New York	0
1927	New York	13	Bears	7
1928	Bears	13	New York	0
1929	New York	26	Bears	14
	New York	14	Bears	9
	New York	34	Bears	0
1930	New York	12	Bears	0
	Bears	12	New York	0
1931	Bears	6	New York	0
	Bears	12	New York	6
	New York	25	Bears	6
1932	Bears	28	New York	8
	Bears	6	New York	0
1933	Bears	14	New York	10
	New York	3	Bears	0

	*Bears	23	New York	21
1934	Bears	27	New York	7
	Bears	10	New York	9
	*New York	30	Bears	13
1935	Bears	20	New York	3
	New York	3	Bears	0
1936	Bears	25	New York	7
1937	New York	3	Bears	3
1939	New York	16	Bears	13
1940	Bears	37	New York	21
1941	*Bears	37	New York	9
1942	Bears	26	New York	7
1943	Bears	56	New York	7
1946	New York	14	Bears	0
	*Bears	24	New York	14
1948	Bears	35	New York	14
1949	New York	35	Bears	28
1956	New York	17	Bears	17
	*New York	47	Bears	7

Bears won 20; New York won 14; Tied 2.

Total points: Bears 547; New York 404.

* Championship Play-off Game

CHICAGO BEARS vs
PHILADELPHIA EAGLES

1933	Philadelphia	3	Bears	3
1935	Bears	39	Philadelphia	0
1936	Bears	17	Philadelphia	0
	Bears	28	Philadelphia	7
1938	Bears	28	Philadelphia	6
1939	Bears	27	Philadelphia	14
1941	Bears	49	Philadelphia	14
1942	Bears	45	Philadelphia	14
1944	Bears	28	Philadelphia	7
1946	Bears	21	Philadelphia	14
1947	Bears	40	Philadelphia	7
1948	Philadelphia	12	Bears	7
1949	Bears	38	Philadelphia	21
1955	Bears	17	Philadelphia	10

Bears won 12; Philadelphia won 1; Tied 1.

Total points: Bears 387; Philadelphia 129.

CHICAGO BEARS vs
PITTSBURGH STEELERS

1934	Bears	28	Pittsburgh	0
1935	Bears	23	Pittsburgh	7
1936	Bears	27	Pittsburgh	9
	Bears	26	Pittsburgh	6
1937	Bears	7	Pittsburgh	0
1939	Bears	32	Pittsburgh	0
1941	Bears	34	Pittsburgh	7
1945	Bears	28	Pittsburgh	7
1947	Bears	49	Pittsburgh	7
1949	Bears	30	Pittsburgh	21
1958	Pittsburgh	24	Bears	10
1959	Bears	27	Pittsburgh	21

Bears won 11; Pittsburgh won 1; Tied 0.
Total points: Bears 321; Pittsburgh 109.

CHICAGO BEARS vs
ST. LOUIS CARDINALS

1920	Cardinals	7	Bears	6
	Bears	10	Cardinals	0
1921	Cardinals	0	Bears	0
1922	Cardinals	6	Bears	0
	Cardinals	9	Bears	0
1923	Bears	3	Cardinals	0
1924	Bears	6	Cardinals	0
	Bears	21	Cardinals	0
1925	Cardinals	9	Bears	0
	Cardinals	0	Bears	0
1926	Bears	16	Cardinals	0
	Bears	0	Cardinals	0
1927	Bears	10	Cardinals	0
	Cardinals	3	Bears	0
1928	Bears	13	Cardinals	0
	Bears	34	Cardinals	0
1929	Cardinals	0	Bears	0
	Cardinals	40	Bears	6
1930	Bears	32	Cardinals	6
	Bears	6	Cardinals	0
	Bears	9	Cardinals	7
1931	Bears	26	Cardinals	13
	Bears	18	Cardinals	7
1932	Bears	0	Cardinals	0
	Bears	34	Cardinals	0
1933	Bears	12	Cardinals	9
	Bears	22	Cardinals	6
1934	Bears	20	Cardinals	0
	Bears	17	Cardinals	6
1935	Bears	7	Cardinals	7
	Bears	13	Cardinals	0
1936	Bears	7	Cardinals	3
	Cardinals	14	Bears	7
1937	Bears	16	Cardinals	7
	Bears	42	Cardinals	28
1938	Bears	16	Cardinals	13
	Bears	34	Cardinals	28
1939	Bears	44	Cardinals	7
	Bears	48	Cardinals	7
1940	Cardinals	21	Bears	7
	Bears	31	Cardinals	23
1941	Bears	53	Cardinals	7
	Bears	34	Cardinals	24
1942	Bears	41	Cardinals	14
	Bears	21	Cardinals	7
1943	Bears	20	Cardinals	0
	Bears	35	Cardinals	24
1944	Cardinals combined with Pittsburgh			
1945	Cardinals	16	Bears	7
	Bears	28	Cardinals	20
1946	Bears	34	Cardinals	17
	Cardinals	35	Bears	28
1947	Cardinals	31	Bears	7
	Cardinals	30	Bears	21
1948	Bears	28	Cardinals	17
	Cardinals	24	Bears	21
1949	Bears	17	Cardinals	7
	Bears	52	Cardinals	21
1950	Bears	27	Cardinals	6
	Cardinals	20	Bears	10
1951	Cardinals	28	Bears	14
	Cardinals	24	Bears	14

1952	Cardinals	21	Bears	10
	Bears	10	Cardinals	7
1953	Cardinals	24	Bears	17
1954	Bears	29	Cardinals	7
1955	Cardinals	53	Bears	14
1956	Bears	10	Cardinals	3
1957	Bears	14	Cardinals	6
1958	Bears	30	Cardinals	14
1959	Bears	31	Cardinals	7

Bears won 45; Cardinals won 19; Tied 6.
Total points: Bears, 1,270; Cardinals 800.

CHICAGO BEARS vs SAN FRANCISCO 49ers

1950	Bears	32	San Francisco	14
	Bears	17	San Francisco	0
1951	Bears	13	San Francisco	7
1952	San Francisco	40	Bears	16
	Bears	20	San Francisco	17
1953	San Francisco	35	Bears	28
	San Francisco	24	Bears	14
1954	San Francisco	31	Bears	24
	Bears	31	San Francisco	27
1955	San Francisco	20	Bears	19
	Bears	34	San Francisco	23
1956	Bears	31	San Francisco	7
	Bears	38	San Francisco	21
1957	San Francisco	21	Bears	17
	San Francisco	21	Bears	17
1958	Bears	28	San Francisco	6
	Bears	27	San Francisco	14
1959	San Francisco	20	Bears	17
	Bears	14	San Francisco	3
1960	Bears	27	San Francisco	10
	San Francisco	25	Bears	7

Bears won 12; San Francisco won 9; Tied 0.
Total points: Bears 471; San Francisco 392.

CHICAGO BEARS vs WASHINGTON REDSKINS

1937	*Washington	28	Bears	21
1938	Bears	31	Washington	7
1940	Washington	7	Bears	3
	*Bears	73	Washington	0
1941	Bears	35	Washington	21
1942	*Washington	14	Bears	6
1943	Washington	21	Bears	7
	*Bears	41	Washington	21
1945	Washington	28	Bears	21
1946	Bears	24	Washington	20
1947	Bears	56	Washington	20
1948	Bears	48	Washington	13
1949	Bears	31	Washington	21
1951	Bears	27	Washington	0
1953	Bears	27	Washington	24
1957	Washington	14	Bears	3

Bears won 10; Washington won 6; Tied 0.
Total points: Bears 454; Washington 259.

* Championship Play-off Game

CLEVELAND BROWNS vs BALTIMORE COLTS

1956	Baltimore	21	Cleveland	7
1959	Cleveland	38	Baltimore	31

Cleveland won 1; Baltimore won 1; Tied 0.
Total points: Cleveland 45; Baltimore 52.

CLEVELAND BROWNS vs CHICAGO BEARS

1951	Cleveland	42	Bears	21
1954	Cleveland	39	Bears	10
1960	Cleveland	42	Bears	0

Cleveland won 3; Bears won 0; Tied 0.
Total points: Cleveland 123; Bears 31.

CLEVELAND BROWNS vs DALLAS COWBOYS

1960	Cleveland	48	Dallas	7

Cleveland won 1; Dallas won 0; Tied 0.
Total points: Cleveland 48; Dallas 7.

CLEVELAND BROWNS vs DETROIT LIONS

1952	Detroit	17	Cleveland	6
	*Detroit	17	Cleveland	7
1953	*Detroit	17	Cleveland	16
1954	Detroit	14	Cleveland	10
	*Cleveland	56	Detroit	10
1957	Detroit	20	Cleveland	7
1958	Detroit	30	Cleveland	10

Cleveland won 1; Detroit won 6; Tied 0.
Total points: Cleveland 112; Detroit 125.

* Championship Play-off Game

CLEVELAND BROWNS vs GREEN BAY PACKERS

1953	Cleveland	27	Green Bay	0
1955	Cleveland	41	Green Bay	10
1956	Cleveland	24	Green Bay	7

Cleveland won 3; Green Bay won 0; Tied 0.

Total points: Cleveland 92; Green Bay 17.

CLEVELAND BROWNS vs SAN FRANCISCO 49ers

1950	Cleveland	34	San Francisco	14
1951	San Francisco	24	Cleveland	10
1953	Cleveland	23	San Francisco	21
1955	Cleveland	38	San Francisco	3
1959	San Francisco	21	Cleveland	20

Cleveland won 3; San Francisco won 2; Tied 0.

Total points: Cleveland 125; San Francisco 83.

DALLAS COWBOYS vs BALTIMORE COLTS

1960   Baltimore   45   Dallas   7

Baltimore won 1; Dallas won 0; Tied 0.
Total points: Dallas 7; Baltimore 45.

DETROIT LIONS vs BALTIMORE COLTS

1953	Detroit	27	Baltimore	17
	Detroit	17	Baltimore	7
1954	Detroit	35	Baltimore	0
	Detroit	27	Baltimore	3
1955	Baltimore	28	Detroit	13
	Detroit	24	Baltimore	14
1956	Detroit	31	Baltimore	14
	Detroit	27	Baltimore	3
1957	Baltimore	34	Detroit	14
	Detroit	31	Baltimore	27
1958	Baltimore	28	Detroit	15
	Detroit	40	Baltimore	14
1959	Baltimore	21	Detroit	9
	Baltimore	31	Detroit	24
1960	Detroit	30	Baltimore	17
	Detroit	20	Baltimore	15

Detroit won 11; Baltimore won 5; Tied 0.
Total points: Detroit 382; Baltimore 273.

DETROIT LIONS vs DALLAS COWBOYS

1960   Detroit   23   Dallas   14

Detroit won 1; Dallas won 0; Tied 0.
Total points: Detroit 23; Dallas 14.

DETROIT LIONS vs GREEN BAY PACKERS

1934	Detroit	3	Green Bay	0
	Green Bay	3	Detroit	0
1935	Green Bay	13	Detroit	9
	Green Bay	31	Detroit	7
	Detroit	20	Green Bay	10
1936	Green Bay	20	Detroit	18
	Green Bay	26	Detroit	17
1937	Green Bay	26	Detroit	6
	Green Bay	14	Detroit	13
1938	Detroit	17	Green Bay	7
	Green Bay	28	Detroit	7
1939	Green Bay	26	Detroit	7
	Green Bay	12	Detroit	7
1940	Detroit	23	Green Bay	14
	Green Bay	50	Detroit	7
1941	Green Bay	23	Detroit	0
	Green Bay	24	Detroit	7
1942	Green Bay	38	Detroit	7
	Green Bay	28	Detroit	7
1943	Green Bay	35	Detroit	14
	Green Bay	27	Detroit	6

1944	Green Bay	27	Detroit	6
	Green Bay	14	Detroit	0
1945	Green Bay	57	Detroit	21
	Detroit	14	Green Bay	3
1946	Green Bay	10	Detroit	7
	Green Bay	9	Detroit	0
1947	Green Bay	34	Detroit	17
	Green Bay	35	Detroit	14
1948	Green Bay	33	Detroit	21
	Detroit	24	Green Bay	20
1949	Green Bay	16	Detroit	14
	Detroit	21	Green Bay	7
1950	Detroit	45	Green Bay	7
	Detroit	24	Green Bay	21
1951	Detroit	24	Green Bay	17
	Detroit	52	Green Bay	35
1952	Detroit	52	Green Bay	17
	Detroit	48	Green Bay	24
1953	Detroit	14	Green Bay	7
	Detroit	34	Green Bay	15
1954	Detroit	21	Green Bay	17
	Detroit	28	Green Bay	24
1955	Green Bay	20	Detroit	17
	Detroit	24	Green Bay	10
1956	Detroit	20	Green Bay	16
	Green Bay	24	Detroit	20
1957	Detroit	24	Green Bay	14
	Detroit	18	Green Bay	6
1958	Detroit	13	Green Bay	13
	Detroit	24	Green Bay	14
1959	Green Bay	28	Detroit	10
	Green Bay	24	Detroit	17
1960	Green Bay	28	Detroit	9
	Detroit	23	Green Bay	10

Detroit won 22; Green Bay won 32; Tied 1.
Total points: Detroit 912; Green Bay 1,121.

DETROIT LIONS vs NEW YORK GIANTS

1934	Detroit	9	New York	0
1935	*Detroit	26	New York	7
1936	New York	14	Detroit	7
	Detroit	38	New York	0
1937	Detroit	17	New York	0
1939	Detroit	18	New York	14
1941	New York	20	Detroit	13
1943	New York	0	Detroit	0
1945	New York	35	Detroit	14
1947	Detroit	35	New York	7
1949	Detroit	45	New York	21
1953	Detroit	27	New York	16
1955	New York	24	Detroit	19
1958	New York	19	Detroit	17

Detroit won 8; New York won 5; Tied 1.
Total points: Detroit 285; New York 177.

* Championship Play-off Game

DETROIT LIONS vs PHILADELPHIA EAGLES

1934   Detroit   10   Philadelphia   0

1935	Detroit	35	Philadelphia	0
1936	Detroit	23	Philadelphia	0
1938	Philadelphia	21	Detroit	7
1940	Detroit	21	Philadelphia	0
1941	Detroit	21	Philadelphia	17
1945	Detroit	28	Philadelphia	24
1948	Philadelphia	45	Detroit	21
1949	Philadelphia	22	Detroit	14
1951	Detroit	28	Philadelphia	7
1954	Detroit	13	Philadelphia	13
1957	Detroit	27	Philadelphia	16
1960	Philadelphia	28	Detroit	10

Detroit won 8; Philadelphia won 4; Tied 1
Total points: Detroit 258; Philadelphia 196.

DETROIT LIONS vs PITTSBURGH STEELERS

1934	Detroit	40	Pittsburgh	7
1936	Detroit	28	Pittsburgh	3
1937	Detroit	7	Pittsburgh	3
1938	Detroit	16	Pittsburgh	7
1940	Pittsburgh	10	Detroit	7
1942	Pittsburgh	35	Detroit	7
1946	Detroit	17	Pittsburgh	7
1947	Pittsburgh	17	Detroit	10
1948	Detroit	17	Pittsburgh	14
1949	Pittsburgh	14	Detroit	7
1950	Detroit	10	Pittsburgh	7
1952	Detroit	31	Pittsburgh	6
1953	Detroit	38	Pittsburgh	21
1955	Detroit	31	Pittsburgh	28
1956	Detroit	45	Pittsburgh	7
1959	Detroit	10	Pittsburgh	10

Detroit won 11; Pittsburgh won 4; Tied 1.
Total points: Detroit 321; Pittsburgh 196.

DETROIT LIONS vs SAN FRANCISCO 49ers

1950	Detroit	24	San Francisco	7
	San Francisco	28	Detroit	27
1951	San Francisco	20	Detroit	10
	San Francisco	21	Detroit	17
1952	San Francisco	17	Detroit	3
	San Francisco	28	Detroit	0
1953	Detroit	24	San Francisco	21
	Detroit	14	San Francisco	10
1954	San Francisco	37	Detroit	31
	Detroit	48	San Francisco	7
1955	San Francisco	27	Detroit	24
	San Francisco	38	Detroit	21
1956	Detroit	20	San Francisco	17
	Detroit	17	San Francisco	13
1957	San Francisco	35	Detroit	31
	Detroit	31	San Francisco	10
1958	San Francisco	24	Detroit	21
	Detroit	35	San Francisco	21
1959	San Francisco	34	Detroit	13
	San Francisco	33	Detroit	7
1960	San Francisco	14	Detroit	10
	Detroit	24	San Francisco	0

Detroit won 9; San Francisco won 13; Tied 0.
Total points: Detroit 452, San Francisco 462.

DETROIT LIONS vs WASHINGTON REDSKINS

1938	Washington	7	Detroit	5
1939	Washington	31	Detroit	7
1940	Washington	20	Detroit	14
1942	Washington	15	Detroit	3
1943	Washington	42	Detroit	20
1946	Washington	17	Detroit	16
1947	Detroit	38	Washington	21
1948	Washington	46	Detroit	21
1951	Detroit	35	Washington	17
1956	Washington	18	Detroit	17

Detroit won 2; Washington won 8; Tied 0.
Total points: Detroit 176; Washington 234.

GREEN BAY PACKERS vs BALTIMORE COLTS

1953	Green Bay	37	Baltimore	14
	Green Bay	35	Baltimore	24
1954	Green Bay	7	Baltimore	6
	Green Bay	24	Baltimore	13
1955	Baltimore	24	Green Bay	20
	Baltimore	14	Green Bay	10
1956	Green Bay	38	Baltimore	33
	Baltimore	28	Green Bay	21
1957	Baltimore	45	Green Bay	17
	Green Bay	24	Baltimore	21
1958	Baltimore	24	Green Bay	17
	Baltimore	56	Green Bay	0
1959	Baltimore	38	Green Bay	21
	Baltimore	28	Green Bay	24
1960	Green Bay	35	Baltimore	21
	Baltimore	38	Green Bay	24

Green Bay won 7; Baltimore won 9; Tied 0.
Total points: Green Bay 354; Baltimore 427.

GREEN BAY PACKERS vs DALLAS COWBOYS

| 1960 | Green Bay | 41 | Dallas | 7 |

Green Bay won 1; Dallas won 0; Tied 0.
Total points: Green Bay 41; Dallas 7.

GREEN BAY PACKERS vs NEW YORK GIANTS

1928	New York	6	Green Bay	0
	Green Bay	7	New York	0
1929	Green Bay	20	New York	6
1930	Green Bay	14	New York	7
	New York	13	Green Bay	6
1931	Green Bay	27	New York	7
	Green Bay	14	New York	10

1932	Green Bay	13	New York	0
	New York	6	Green Bay	0
1933	New York	10	Green Bay	7
	New York	17	Green Bay	6
1934	Green Bay	20	New York	6
	New York	17	Green Bay	3
1935	Green Bay	16	New York	7
1936	Green Bay	26	New York	14
1937	New York	10	Green Bay	0
1938	New York	15	Green Bay	3
	*New York	23	Green Bay	17
1939	Green Bay	27	New York	0
1940	New York	7	Green Bay	3
1942	Green Bay	21	New York	21
1943	Green Bay	35	New York	21
1944	New York	24	Green Bay	0
	*Green Bay	14	New York	7
1945	Green Bay	23	New York	14
1947	Green Bay	24	New York	24
1948	New York	49	Green Bay	3
1949	New York	30	Green Bay	10
1952	Green Bay	17	New York	3
1957	New York	31	Green Bay	17
1959	New York	20	Green Bay	3

Green Bay won 14; New York won 15; Tied 2.
Total points: Green Bay 396; New York 408.

* Championship Play-off Game

GREEN BAY PACKERS vs PHILADELPHIA EAGLES

1933	Green Bay	35	Philadelphia	9
	Green Bay	10	Philadelphia	0
1934	Green Bay	19	Philadelphia	6
1935	Green Bay	13	Philadelphia	6
1937	Green Bay	37	Philadelphia	7
1939	Green Bay	23	Philadelphia	16
1940	Green Bay	27	Philadelphia	20
1942	Green Bay	7	Philadelphia	0
1946	Green Bay	19	Philadelphia	7
1947	Philadelphia	28	Green Bay	14
1951	Green Bay	37	Philadelphia	24
1952	Green Bay	12	Philadelphia	10
1954	Green Bay	37	Philadelphia	14
1958	Green Bay	38	Philadelphia	35

Green Bay won 13; Philadelphia won 1; Tied 0.
Total points: Green Bay 328; Philadelphia 173.

GREEN BAY PACKERS vs PITTSBURGH STEELERS

1933	Green Bay	47	Pittsburgh	0
1935	Green Bay	27	Pittsburgh	0
	Green Bay	34	Pittsburgh	14
1936	Green Bay	42	Pittsburgh	10
1938	Green Bay	20	Pittsburgh	0
1940	Green Bay	24	Pittsburgh	3
1941	Green Bay	54	Pittsburgh	7

1942	Green Bay	24	Pittsburgh	21
1946	Green Bay	17	Pittsburgh	7
1947	Pittsburgh	18	Green Bay	17
1948	Pittsburgh	38	Green Bay	7
1949	Pittsburgh	30	Green Bay	7
1951	Green Bay	35	Pittsburgh	33
	Pittsburgh	28	Green Bay	7
1953	Pittsburgh	31	Green Bay	14
1954	Pittsburgh	21	Green Bay	20
1957	Green Bay	27	Pittsburgh	10
1960	Green Bay	19	Pittsburgh	13

Green Bay won 12; Pittsburgh won 6; Tied 0.
Total points: Green Bay 442; Pittsburgh 284.

GREEN BAY PACKERS vs SAN FRANCISCO 49ers

1950	Green Bay	25	San Francisco	21
	San Francisco	30	Green Bay	14
1951	San Fransico	31	Green Bay	19
1952	San Francisco	24	Green Bay	14
1953	San Francisco	37	Green Bay	7
	San Francisco	48	Green Bay	14
1954	San Francisco	23	Green Bay	17
	San Francisco	35	Green Bay	0
1955	Green Bay	27	San Francisco	21
	Green Bay	28	San Francisco	7
1956	San Francisco	17	Green Bay	16
	San Francisco	38	Green Bay	20
1957	San Francisco	24	Green Bay	14
	San Francisco	27	Green Bay	20
1958	San Francisco	33	Green Bay	12
	San Francisco	48	Green Bay	21
1959	Green Bay	21	San Francisco	20
	Green Bay	36	San Francisco	14
1960	Green Bay	41	San Francisco	14
	Green Bay	13	San Francisco	0

Green Bay won 7; San Francisco won 13; Tied 0.
Total points: Green Bay 379; San Francisco 512.

GREEN BAY PACKERS vs WASHINGTON REDSKINS

1937	Washington	14	Green Bay	6
1939	Green Bay	24	Washington	14
1941	Green Bay	22	Washington	17
1943	Washington	33	Green Bay	7
1946	Green Bay	20	Washington	7
1947	Green Bay	27	Washington	10
1948	Washington	23	Green Bay	7
1949	Washington	30	Green Bay	0
1950	Green Bay	35	Washington	21
1952	Green Bay	35	Washington	20
1958	Washington	37	Green Bay	21
1959	Green Bay	21	Washington	0

Green Bay won 7; Washington won 5; Tied 0.
Total points: Green Bay 225; Washington 226.

LOS ANGELES RAMS vs BALTIMORE COLTS

1953	Los Angeles	21	Baltimore	13
	Los Angeles	45	Baltimore	2
1954	Los Angeles	48	Baltimore	0
	Baltimore	22	Los Angeles	21
1955	Baltimore	17	Los Angeles	17
	Los Angeles	20	Baltimore	14
1956	Baltimore	56	Los Angeles	21
	Los Angeles	31	Baltimore	7
1957	Baltimore	31	Los Angeles	14
	Los Angeles	37	Baltimore	21
1958	Baltimore	34	Los Angeles	7
	Los Angeles	30	Baltimore	28
1959	Baltimore	35	Los Angeles	21
	Baltimore	45	Los Angeles	26
1960	Baltimore	31	Los Angeles	17
	Los Angeles	10	Baltimore	3

Los Angeles won 8; Baltimore won 7; Tied 1.

Total points: Los Angeles 386; Baltimore 359.

LOS ANGELES RAMS vs CHICAGO BEARS

1946	Los Angeles	28	Bears	28
	Bears	27	Los Angeles	21
1947	Bears	41	Los Angeles	21
	Los Angeles	17	Bears	14
1948	Bears	42	Los Angeles	21
	Bears	21	Los Angeles	6
1949	Los Angeles	31	Bears	16
	Los Angeles	27	Bears	24
1950	Bears	24	Los Angeles	20
	Bears	24	Los Angeles	14
	*Los Angeles	24	Bears	14
1951	Los Angeles	42	Bears	17
1952	Los Angeles	31	Bears	7
	Los Angeles	40	Bears	24
1953	Los Angeles	38	Bears	24
	Bears	24	Los Angeles	21
1954	Los Angeles	42	Bears	38
	Bears	24	Los Angeles	13
1955	Bears	31	Los Angeles	20
	Bears	24	Los Angeles	3
1956	Bears	35	Los Angeles	24
	Bears	30	Los Angeles	21
1957	Bears	34	Los Angeles	26
	Bears	16	Los Angeles	10
1958	Bears	31	Los Angeles	10
	Los Angeles	41	Bears	35
1959	Los Angeles	28	Bears	21
	Bears	26	Los Angeles	21
1960	Bears	34	Los Angeles	27
	Bears	24	Los Angeles	24

Los Angeles won 11; Bears won 17; Tied 2. Total points: Los Angeles 689; Bears 774.

* Conference Play-off Game

LOS ANGELES RAMS vs CLEVELAND BROWNS

1950	*Cleveland	30	Los Angeles	28
1951	Cleveland	38	Los Angeles	23
	*Los Angeles	24	Cleveland	17
1952	Cleveland	37	Los Angeles	7
1957	Cleveland	45	Los Angeles	31
1958	Cleveland	30	Los Angeles	27

Los Angeles won 1; Cleveland won 5; Tied 0.

Total points: Los Angeles 140; Cleveland 197.

* Championship Play-off Game

LOS ANGELES RAMS vs DALLAS COWBOYS

1960	Los Angeles	38	Dallas	13

Los Angeles won 1; Dallas won 0; Tied 0. Total points: Los Angeles 38; Dallas 13.

LOS ANGELES RAMS vs DETROIT LIONS

1946	Los Angeles	35	Detroit	14
	Los Angeles	41	Detroit	20
1947	Los Angeles	27	Detroit	13
	Los Angeles	28	Detroit	17
1948	Los Angeles	44	Detroit	7
	Los Angeles	34	Detroit	27
1949	Los Angeles	27	Detroit	24
	Los Angeles	21	Detroit	10
1950	Los Angeles	30	Detroit	28
	Los Angeles	65	Detroit	24
1951	Los Angeles	27	Detroit	21
	Detroit	24	Los Angeles	22
1952	Detroit	17	Los Angeles	14
	Detroit	24	Los Angeles	16
	*Detroit	31	Los Angeles	21
1953	Los Angeles	31	Detroit	19
	Los Angeles	37	Detroit	24
1954	Detroit	21	Los Angeles	3
	Detroit	27	Los Angeles	24
1955	Los Angeles	17	Detroit	10
	Los Angeles	24	Detroit	13
1956	Detroit	24	Los Angeles	21
	Detroit	16	Los Angeles	7
1957	Detroit	10	Los Angeles	7
	Los Angeles	35	Detroit	17
1958	Los Angeles	42	Detroit	28
	Detroit	41	Los Angeles	24
1959	Detroit	17	Los Angeles	7
	Detroit	23	Los Angeles	17
1960	Los Angeles	48	Detroit	35
	Detroit	12	Los Angeles	10

Los Angeles won 18; Detroit won 13; Tied 0.

Total points: Los Angeles 806; Detroit 638.

* Conference Play-off Game

LOS ANGELES RAMS vs GREEN BAY PACKERS

1946	Los Angeles	21	Green Bay	17
	Los Angeles	38	Green Bay	17
1947	Green Bay	17	Los Angeles	14
	Green Bay	30	Los Angeles	10
1948	Green Bay	16	Los Angeles	0
	Los Angeles	24	Green Bay	10
1949	Los Angeles	48	Green Bay	7
	Los Angeles	35	Green Bay	7
1950	Los Angeles	45	Green Bay	14
	Los Angeles	51	Green Bay	14
1951	Los Angeles	28	Green Bay	0
	Los Angeles	42	Green Bay	14
1952	Los Angeles	30	Green Bay	28
	Los Angeles	45	Green Bay	27
1953	Los Angeles	38	Green Bay	20
	Los Angeles	33	Green Bay	17
1954	Green Bay	35	Los Angeles	17
	Los Angeles	35	Green Bay	17
1955	Green Bay	30	Los Angeles	28
	Los Angeles	31	Green Bay	17
1956	Green Bay	42	Los Angeles	17
	Los Angeles	49	Green Bay	21
1957	Los Angeles	31	Green Bay	27
	Los Angeles	42	Green Bay	17
1958	Los Angeles	20	Green Bay	7
	Los Angeles	34	Green Bay	20
1959	Los Angeles	45	Green Bay	6
	Green Bay	38	Los Angeles	20
1960	Los Angeles	33	Green Bay	21
	Green Bay	35	Green Bay	31

Los Angeles won 22; Green Bay won 8, Tied 0.
Total points: Los Angeles 925; Green Bay 598.

LOS ANGELES RAMS vs NEW YORK GIANTS

1946	Los Angeles	31	New York	21
1947	Los Angeles	34	New York	10
1948	Los Angeles	52	New York	37
1953	Los Angeles	21	New York	7
1954	Los Angeles	17	New York	16
1959	New York	23	Los Angeles	21

Los Angeles won 5; New York won 1; Tied 0.
Total points: Los Angeles 176; New York 114.

LOS ANGELES RAMS vs PHILADELPHIA EAGLES

1946	Philadelphia	25	Los Angeles	14
1947	Philadelphia	14	Los Angeles	7
1948	Philadelphia	28	Los Angeles	28
1949	Philadelphia	38	Los Angeles	14
	*Philadelphia	14	Los Angeles	0
1950	Philadelphia	56	Los Angeles	22
1955	Los Angeles	23	Philadelphia	21
1956	Los Angeles	27	Philadelphia	7
1957	Los Angeles	17	Philadelphia	13
1959	Philadelphia	23	Los Angeles	20

Los Angeles won 3; Philadelphia won 6;

Tied 1.
Total points: Los Angeles 170; Philadelphia 239.

* Championship Play-off Game

LOS ANGELES RAMS vs PITTSBURGH STEELERS

1947	Los Angeles	48	Pittsburgh	7
1948	Los Angeles	31	Pittsburgh	14
1949	Los Angeles	7	Pittsburgh	7
1952	Los Angeles	28	Pittsburgh	14
1955	Los Angeles	27	Pittsburgh	26
1956	Pittsburgh	30	Los Angeles	13

Los Angeles won 4; Pittsburgh won 1; Tied 1.
Total points: Los Angeles 154; Pittsburgh 98.

LOS ANGELES RAMS vs ST. LOUIS CARDINALS

1946	Cardinals	34	Los Angeles	10
	Los Angeles	17	Cardinals	14
1947	Los Angeles	27	Cardinals	7
	Cardinals	17	Los Angeles	10
1948	Cardinals	27	Los Angeles	22
	Cardinals	27	Los Angeles	24
1949	Cardinals	28	Los Angeles	28
	Cardinals	31	Los Angeles	27
1951	Los Angeles	45	Cardinals	21
1953	Los Angeles	24	Cardinals	24
1954	Los Angeles	28	Cardinals	17
1958	Los Angeles	20	Cardinals	14
1960	Cardinals	43	Los Angeles	21

Los Angeles won 5; Cardinals won 6; Tied 2.
Total points: Los Angeles 303; Cardinals 304.

LOS ANGELES RAMS vs SAN FRANCISCO 49ers

1950	Los Angeles	35	San Francisco	14
	Los Angeles	28	San Francisco	21
1951	San Francisco	44	Los Angeles	17
	Los Angeles	23	San Francisco	16
1952	Los Angeles	35	San Francisco	9
	Los Angeles	34	San Francisco	21
1953	San Francisco	31	Los Angeles	30
	San Francisco	31	Los Angeles	27
1954	San Francisco	24	Los Angeles	24
	Los Angeles	42	San Francisco	34
1955	Los Angeles	23	San Francisco	14
	Los Angeles	27	San Francisco	14
1956	San Francisco	33	Los Angeles	30
	Los Angeles	30	San Francisco	6
1957	San Francisco	23	Los Angeles	20
	Los Angeles	37	San Francisco	24
1958	Los Angeles	33	San Francisco	3
	Los Angeles	56	San Francisco	7
1959	San Francisco	34	Los Angeles	0
	San Francisco	24	Los Angeles	16

1960	San Francisco	13	Los Angeles	9
	San Francisco	23	Los Angeles	7

Los Angeles won 12; San Francisco won 9; Tied 1.

Total points: Los Angeles 588; San Francisco 458.

LOS ANGELES RAMS vs WASHINGTON REDSKINS

1948	Los Angeles	41	Washington	13
1949	Los Angeles	53	Washington	27
1951	Washington	31	Los Angeles	21

Los Angeles won 2; Washington won 1; Tied 0.

Total points: Los Angeles 115; Washington 71.

NEW YORK GIANTS vs BALTIMORE COLTS

1954	Baltimore	20	New York	14
1955	New York	17	Baltimore	7
1958	New York	24	Baltimore	21
	*Baltimore	23	New York	17
1959	*Baltimore	31	New York	16

New York won 2; Baltimore won 2; Tied 0.

Total points: New York 88; Baltimore 102.

* Championship Game

NEW YORK GIANTS vs CLEVELAND BROWNS

1950	New York	6	Cleveland	0
	New York	17	Cleveland	13
	*Cleveland	8	New York	3
1951	Cleveland	14	New York	13
	Cleveland	10	New York	0
1952	New York	17	Cleveland	9
	New York	37	Cleveland	34
1953	Cleveland	7	New York	0
	Cleveland	62	New York	14
1954	Cleveland	24	New York	14
	Cleveland	16	New York	7
1955	Cleveland	24	New York	14
	Cleveland	35	New York	35
1956	New York	21	Cleveland	9
	Cleveland	24	New York	7
1957	Cleveland	6	New York	3
	Cleveland	34	New York	28
1958	New York	21	Cleveland	17
	New York	13	Cleveland	10
	*New York	10	Cleveland	0
1959	New York	10	Cleveland	6
	New York	48	Cleveland	7
1960	New York	17	Cleveland	13
	Cleveland	48	New York	34

New York won 11; Cleveland won 12; Tied 1.

Total points: New York 389; Cleveland 430.

* Conference Play-off Game

NEW YORK GIANTS vs DALLAS COWBOYS

1960	New York	31	Dallas	31

New York won 0; Dallas won 0; Tied 1.
Total points: New York 31; Dallas 31.

NEW YORK GIANTS vs PHILADELPHIA EAGLES

1933	New York	56	Philadelphia	0
	New York	20	Philadelphia	14
1934	New York	17	Philadelphia	0
	Philadelphia	6	New York	0
1935	New York	10	Philadelphia	0
	New York	21	Philadelphia	14
1936	Philadelphia	10	New York	7
	New York	21	Philadelphia	17
1937	New York	16	Philadelphia	7
	New York	21	Philadelphia	0
1938	Philadelphia	14	New York	10
	New York	17	Philadelphia	7
1939	New York	13	Philadelphia	3
	New York	27	Philadelphia	10
1940	New York	20	Philadelphia	14
	New York	17	Philadelphia	7
1941	New York	24	Philadelphia	0
	New York	16	Philadelphia	0
1942	New York	35	Philadelphia	17
	New York	14	Philadelphia	0
1944	Philadelphia	24	New York	17
	Philadelphia	21	New York	21
1945	Philadelphia	38	New York	17
	New York	28	Philadelphia	21
1946	Philadelphia	24	New York	14
	New York	45	Philadelphia	17
1947	Philadelphia	23	New York	0
	Philadelphia	41	New York	24
1948	Philadelphia	45	New York	0
	Philadelphia	35	New York	14
1949	Philadelphia	24	New York	3
	Philadelphia	17	New York	3
1950	New York	7	Philadelphia	3
	New York	9	Philadelphia	7
1951	New York	26	Philadelphia	24
	New York	23	Philadelphia	7
1952	New York	31	Philadelphia	7
	Philadelphia	14	New York	10
1953	Philadelphia	30	New York	7
	New York	37	Philadelphia	28
1954	New York	27	Philadelphia	14
	Philadelphia	29	New York	14
1955	Philadelphia	27	New York	17
	New York	31	Philadelphia	7
1956	New York	20	Philadelphia	3
	New York	21	Philadelphia	7
1957	New York	24	Philadelphia	20
	New York	13	Philadelphia	0
1958	Philadelphia	27	New York	24
	New York	24	Philadelphia	10
1959	Philadelphia	49	New York	21
	New York	24	Philadelphia	7
1960	Philadelphia	17	New York	10
	Philadelphia	31	New York	23

New York won 33; Philadelphia won 20;

Tied 1.

Total points: New York 1,011; Philadelphia 838.

NEW YORK GIANTS vs PITTSBURGH STEELERS

1933	New York	23	Pittsburgh	2
	New York	27	Pittsburgh	3
1934	New York	14	Pittsburgh	12
	New York	17	Pittsburgh	7
1935	New York	42	Pittsburgh	7
	New York	13	Pittsburgh	0
1936	Pittsburgh	10	New York	7
1937	New York	10	Pittsburgh	7
	New York	17	Pittsburgh	0
1938	New York	27	Pittsburgh	14
	Pittsburgh	13	New York	10
1939	New York	14	Pittsburgh	7
	New York	23	Pittsburgh	7
1940	Pittsburgh	10	New York	10
	New York	12	Pittsburgh	0
1941	New York	37	Pittsburgh	10
	New York	28	Pittsburgh	7
1942	Pittsburgh	13	New York	10
	Pittsburgh	17	New York	9
1945	New York	34	Pittsburgh	6
	Pittsburgh	21	New York	7
1946	New York	17	Pittsburgh	14
	New York	7	Pittsburgh	0
1947	Pittsburgh	38	New York	21
	Pittsburgh	24	New York	7
1948	New York	34	Pittsburgh	27
	Pittsburgh	38	New York	28
1949	Pittsburgh	28	New York	7
	Pittsburgh	21	New York	17
1950	New York	18	Pittsburgh	7
	Pittsburgh	17	New York	6
1951	New York	13	Pittsburgh	13
	New York	14	Pittsburgh	0
1952	Pittsburgh	63	New York	7
1953	Pittsburgh	24	New York	14
	Pittsburgh	14	New York	10
1954	New York	30	Pittsburgh	6
	New York	24	Pittsburgh	3
1955	Pittsburgh	30	New York	23
	Pittsburgh	19	New York	17
1956	New York	38	Pittsburgh	10
	New York	17	Pittsburgh	14
1957	New York	35	Pittsburgh	0
	Pittsburgh	21	New York	10
1958	New York	17	Pittsburgh	6
	Pittsburgh	31	New York	10
1959	New York	21	Pittsburgh	16
	Pittsburgh	14	New York	9
1960	New York	19	Pittsburgh	17
	New York	27	Pittsburgh	24

New York won 29; Pittsburgh won 19; Tied 2.

Total points: New York 929; Pittsburgh 712.

NEW YORK GIANTS vs SAN FRANCISCO 49ers

1952	New York	23	San Francisco	14
1956	New York	38	San Francisco	21
1957	San Francisco	27	New York	17
1960	New York	21	San Francisco	19

New York won 3; San Francisco won 1; Tied 0.

Total points: New York 99; San Francisco 81.

NEW YORK GIANTS vs WASHINGTON REDSKINS

1937	Washington	13	New York	3
	Washington	49	New York	14
1938	New York	10	Washington	7
	New York	36	Washington	0
1939	New York	0	Washington	0
	New York	9	Washington	7
1940	Washington	21	New York	7
	New York	21	Washington	7
1941	New York	17	Washington	7
	New York	20	Washington	13
1942	New York	14	Washington	7
	Washington	14	New York	7
1943	New York	14	Washington	10
	New York	31	Washington	7
*Washington		28	New York	0
1944	New York	16	Washington	13
	New York	31	Washington	0
1945	Washington	24	New York	14
	Washington	17	New York	0
1946	Washington	24	New York	14
	New York	31	Washington	0
1947	Washington	28	New York	20
	New York	35	Washington	10
1948	Washington	41	New York	10
	Washington	28	New York	21
1949	New York	45	Washington	35
	New York	23	Washington	7
1950	New York	21	Washington	17
	New York	24	Washington	21
1951	New York	35	Washington	14
	New York	28	Washington	14
1952	New York	14	Washington	10
	Washington	27	New York	17
1953	Washington	13	New York	9
	Washington	24	New York	21
1954	New York	51	Washington	21
	New York	24	Washington	7
1955	New York	35	Washington	7
	New York	27	Washington	20
1956	Washington	33	New York	7
	New York	28	Washington	14
1957	New York	24	Washington	20
	Washington	31	New York	14
1958	New York	21	Washington	14
	New York	30	Washington	0
1959	New York	45	Washington	14
	New York	24	Washington	10
1960	New York	24	Washington	24
	New York	17	Washington	3

New York won 31; Washington won 16; Tied 2.

Total points: New York 1,003; Washington 727.

PHILADELPHIA EAGLES vs BALTIMORE COLTS

1953   Philadelphia   45   Baltimore   14

Philadelphia won 1; Baltimore won 0; Tied 0.

Total points: Philadelphia 45; Baltimore 14.

PHILADELPHIA EAGLES vs CLEVELAND BROWNS

1950	Cleveland	35	Philadelphia	10
	Cleveland	13	Philadelphia	7
1951	Cleveland	20	Philadelphia	17
	Cleveland	24	Philadelphia	9
1952	Cleveland	49	Philadelphia	7
	Philadelphia	28	Cleveland	20
1953	Cleveland	37	Philadelphia	13
	Philadelphia	42	Cleveland	27
1954	Philadelphia	28	Cleveland	10
	Cleveland	6	Philadelphia	0
1955	Cleveland	21	Philadelphia	17
	Philadelphia	33	Cleveland	17
1956	Cleveland	16	Philadelphia	0
	Cleveland	17	Philadelphia	14
1957	Cleveland	24	Philadelphia	7
	Philadelphia	17	Cleveland	7
1958	Cleveland	28	Philadelphia	14
	Cleveland	21	Philadelphia	14
1959	Cleveland	28	Philadelphia	7
	Cleveland	28	Philadelphia	21

Philadelphia won 5; Cleveland won 13; Tied 0.

Total points: Philadelphia 277; Cleveland 392.

PHILADELPHIA EAGLES vs DALLAS COWBOYS

1960   Philadelphia   27   Dallas   25

Philadelphia won 1; Dallas won 0; Tied 0.
Total points: Philadelphia 27; Dallas 25.

PHILADELPHIA EAGLES vs PITTSBURGH STEELERS

1933	Philadelphia	25	Pittsburgh	6
1934	Philadelphia	17	Pittsburgh	0
	Pittsburgh	9	Philadelphia	7
1935	Pittsburgh	17	Philadelphia	7
	Philadelphia	17	Pittsburgh	6
1936	Pittsburgh	6	Philadelphia	0
	Pittsburgh	17	Philadelphia	0
1937	Pittsburgh	27	Philadelphia	14
	Pittsburgh	16	Philadelphia	7
1938	Philadelphia	27	Pittsburgh	7
	Philadelphia	14	Pittsburgh	7
1939	Philadelphia	17	Pittsburgh	14
	Pittsburgh	24	Philadelphia	12

1940	Pittsburgh	7	Philadelphia	3
	Philadelphia	7	Pittsburgh	0
1941	Philadelphia	10	Pittsburgh	7
	Philadelphia	7	Pittsburgh	7
1942	Philadelphia	24	Pittsburgh	14
	Pittsburgh	14	Philadelphia	0
1945	Philadelphia	45	Pittsburgh	3
	Philadelphia	30	Pittsburgh	6
1946	Pittsburgh	10	Philadelphia	7
	Philadelphia	10	Pittsburgh	7
1947	Pittsburgh	35	Philadelphia	24
	Philadelphia	21	Pittsburgh	0
	*Philadelphia	21	Pittsburgh	0
1948	Philadelphia	34	Pittsburgh	7
	Philadelphia	17	Pittsburgh	0
1949	Philadelphia	38	Pittsburgh	7
	Philadelphia	34	Pittsburgh	17
1950	Philadelphia	17	Pittsburgh	10
	Pittsburgh	9	Philadelphia	7
1951	Philadelphia	34	Pittsburgh	13
	Pittsburgh	17	Philadelphia	13
1952	Philadelphia	31	Pittsburgh	25
	Philadelphia	26	Pittsburgh	21
1953	Philadelphia	23	Pittsburgh	7
	Philadelphia	35	Pittsburgh	7
1954	Philadelphia	24	Pittsburgh	22
	Pittsburgh	17	Philadelphia	7
1955	Pittsburgh	13	Philadelphia	7
	Philadelphia	24	Pittsburgh	0
1956	Philadelphia	35	Pittsburgh	21
	Philadelphia	14	Pittsburgh	7
1957	Pittsburgh	6	Philadelphia	0
	Philadelphia	7	Pittsburgh	6
1958	Pittsburgh	24	Philadelphia	3
	Pittsburgh	31	Philadelphia	24
1959	Philadelphia	28	Pittsburgh	24
	Pittsburgh	31	Philadelphia	0
1960	Philadelphia	34	Pittsburgh	7
	Pittsburgh	21	Philadelphia	27

Philadelphia won 31; Pittsburgh won 20; Tied 1.
Total points: Philadelphia 916; Pittsburgh 636.

* Divisional Play-off Game

PHILADELPHIA EAGLES vs SAN FRANCISCO 49ers

1951	Philadelphia	21	San Francisco	14
1953	San Francisco	31	Philadelphia	7
1956	Philadelphia	10	San Francisco	10
1959	San Francisco	24	Philadelphia	14

Philadelphia won 1; San Francisco won 2; Tied 1.
Total points: Philadelphia 52; San Francisco 79.

PHILADELPHIA EAGLES vs WASHINGTON REDSKINS

1937	Philadelphia	14	Washington	0
	Washington	10	Philadelphia	7
1938	Washington	26	Philadelphia	23
	Washington	20	Philadelphia	14

1939	Washington	7	Philadelphia	0
	Washington	7	Philadelphia	6
1940	Washington	34	Philadelphia	17
	Washington	13	Philadelphia	6
1941	Washington	21	Philadelphia	17
	Washington	20	Philadelphia	14
1942	Washington	14	Philadelphia	10
	Washington	30	Philadelphia	27
1944	Philadelphia	31	Washington	31
	Philadelphia	37	Washington	7
1945	Washington.	24	Philadelphia	14
	Philadelphia	16	Washington	0
1946	Philadelphia	28	Washington	24
	Washington	27	Philadelphia	10
1947	Philadelphia	45	Washington	42
	Philadelphia	38	Washington	14
1948	Philadelphia	45	Washington	0
	Philadelphia	42	Washington	21
1949	Philadelphia	49	Washington	14
	Philadelphia	44	Washington	21
1950	Philadelphia	35	Washington	3
	Philadelphia	33	Washington	0
1951	Washington	27	Philadelphia	23
	Philadelphia	35	Washington	21
1952	Philadelphia	38	Washington	20
	Washington	27	Philadelphia	21
1953	Philadelphia	21	Washington	21
	Washington	10	Philadelphia	0
1954	Philadelphia	49	Washington	21
	Philadelphia	41	Washington	33
1955	Washington	31	Philadelphia	30
	Washington	34	Philadelphia	21
1956	Philadelphia	13	Washington	9
	Washington	19	Philadelphia	17
1957	Philadelphia	21	Washington	12
	Washington	42	Philadelphia	7
1958	Washington	24	Philadelphia	14
	Washington	20	Philadelphia	0
1959	Philadelphia	30	Washington	23
	Philadelphia	34	Washington	14
1960	Philadelphia	19	Washington	13
	Philadelphia	38	Washington	28

Philadelphia won 22; Washington won 22; Tied 2.
Total points: Philadelphia 1,094; Washington 879.

PITTSBURGH STEELERS vs BALTIMORE COLTS

| 1957 | Pittsburgh | 19 | Baltimore | 13 |

Pittsburgh won 1; Baltimore won 0; Tied 0.
Total points: Pittsburgh 19; Baltimore 13.

PITTSBURGH STEELERS vs CLEVELAND BROWNS

1950	Cleveland	30	Pittsburgh	17
	Cleveland	45	Pittsburgh	7
1951	Cleveland	17	Pittsburgh	0
	Cleveland	28	Pittsburgh	0
1952	Cleveland	21	Pittsburgh	20
	Cleveland	29	Pittsburgh	28

1953	Cleveland	34	Pittsburgh	16
	Cleveland	20	Pittsburgh	16
1954	Pittsburgh	55	Cleveland	27
	Cleveland	42	Pittsburgh	7
1955	Cleveland	41	Pittsburgh	14
	Cleveland	30	Pittsburgh	7
1956	Cleveland	14	Pittsburgh	10
	Pittsburgh	24	Cleveland	16
1957	Cleveland	23	Pittsburgh	12
	Cleveland	24	Pittsburgh	0
1958	Cleveland	45	Pittsburgh	12
	Cleveland	27	Pittsburgh	10
1959	Pittsburgh	17	Cleveland	7
	Pittsburgh	21	Cleveland	20
1960	Cleveland	28	Pittsburgh	20
	Pittsburgh	14	Cleveland	10

Pittsburgh won 5; Cleveland won 17; Tied 0.
Total points: Pittsburgh 327; Cleveland 578.

PITTSBURGH STEELERS vs DALLAS COWBOYS

| 1960 | Pittsburgh | 35 | Dallas | 28 |

Pittsburgh won 1; Dallas won 0; Tied 0.
Total points: Pittsburgh 35; Dallas 28.

PITTSBURGH STEELERS vs SAN FRANCISCO 49ers

1951	San Francisco	28	Pittsburgh	24
1952	Pittsburgh	24	San Francisco	7
1954	San Francisco	31	Pittsburgh	3

Pittsburgh won 1; San Francisco won 2; Tied 0.
Total points: Pittsburgh 51; San Francisco 66.

PITTSBURGH STEELERS vs WASHINGTON REDSKINS

1937	Washington	34	Pittsburgh	20
	Pittsburgh	21	Washington	13
1938	Washington	7	Pittsburgh	0
	Washington	15	Pittsburgh	0
1939	Washington	44	Pittsburgh	14
	Washington	21	Pittsburgh	14
1940	Washington	40	Pittsburgh	10
	Washington	37	Pittsburgh	10
1941	Washington	24	Pittsburgh	20
	Washington	23	Pittsburgh	3
1942	Washington	28	Pittsburgh	14
	Washington	14	Pittsburgh	0
1945	Washington	14	Pittsburgh	0
	Washington	24	Pittsburgh	0
1946	Pittsburgh	14	Washington	14
	Pittsburgh	14	Washington	7
1947	Washington	27	Pittsburgh	26
	Pittsburgh	21	Washington	14
1948	Washington	17	Pittsburgh	14
	Pittsburgh	10	Washington	7

1949	Washington	27	Pittsburgh	14
	Washington	27	Pittsburgh	14
1950	Pittsburgh	26	Washington	7
	Washington	24	Pittsburgh	7
1951	Washington	22	Pittsburgh	7
	Pittsburgh	20	Washington	10
1952	Washington	28	Pittsburgh	24
	Pittsburgh	24	Washington	23
1953	Washington	17	Pittsburgh	9
	Pittsburgh	14	Washington	13
1954	Pittsburgh	37	Washington	7
	Washington	17	Pittsburgh	14
1955	Washington	23	Pittsburgh	14
	Washington	28	Pittsburgh	17
1956	Pittsburgh	30	Washington	13
	Pittsburgh	23	Washington	0
1957	Pittsburgh	28	Washington	7
	Washington	10	Pittsburgh	3
1958	Pittsburgh	24	Washington	16
	Pittsburgh	14	Washington	14
1959	Washington	23	Pittsburgh	17
	Pittsburgh	27	Washington	6
1960	Pittsburgh	27	Washington	27
	Pittsburgh	22	Washington	10

Pittsburgh won 15; Washington won 26; Tied 3.
Total points: Pittsburgh 681; Washington 823.

ST. LOUIS CARDINALS vs CLEVELAND BROWNS

1950	Cleveland	34	Cardinals	24
	Cleveland	10	Cardinals	7
1951	Cleveland	34	Cardinals	17
	Cleveland	49	Cardinals	28
1952	Cleveland	28	Cardinals	13
	Cleveland	10	Cardinals	0
1953	Cleveland	27	Cardinals	7
	Cleveland	27	Cardinals	16
1954	Cleveland	31	Cardinals	7
	Cleveland	35	Cardinals	3
1955	Cleveland	26	Cardinals	20
	Cleveland	35	Cardinals	24
1956	Cardinals	9	Cleveland	7
	Cardinals	24	Cleveland	7
1957	Cleveland	17	Cardinals	7
	Cleveland	31	Cardinals	0
1958	Cleveland	35	Cardinals	28
	Cleveland	38	Cardinals	24
1959	Cleveland	34	Cardinals	7
	Cleveland	17	Cardinals	7
1960	Cardinals	27	Cleveland	28
	Cardinals	17	Cleveland	17

Cardinals won 2; Cleveland won 18; Tied 1.
Total points: Cardinals 316; Cleveland 587.

ST. LOUIS CARDINALS vs DALLAS COWBOYS

1960	Cardinals	12	Dallas	10

Cardinals won 1; Dallas won 0; Tied 0.
Total points: Cardinals 12; Dallas 10.

ST. LOUIS CARDINALS vs DETROIT LIONS

1934	Detroit	6	Cardinals	0
	Detroit	17	Cardinals	13
1935	Detroit	10	Cardinals	10
	Detroit	7	Cardinals	6
1936	Detroit	39	Cardinals	0
	Detroit	14	Cardinals	7
1937	Detroit	16	Cardinals	7
	Detroit	16	Cardinals	7
1938	Detroit	10	Cardinals	0
	Detroit	7	Cardinals	3
1939	Detroit	21	Cardinals	13
	Detroit	17	Cardinals	3
1940	Detroit	0	Cardinals	0
	Detroit	43	Cardinals	14
1941	Detroit	14	Cardinals	14
	Detroit	21	Cardinals	3
1942	Cardinals	13	Detroit	0
	Cardinals	7	Detroit	0
1943	Detroit	35	Cardinals	17
	Detroit	7	Cardinals	0
1944	Cardinals combined with Pitts.			
1945	Detroit	10	Cardinals	0
	Detroit	26	Cardinals	0
1946	Cardinals	34	Detroit	14
	Cardinals	36	Detroit	14
1947	Cardinals	45	Detroit	21
	Cardinals	17	Detroit	7
1948	Cardinals	56	Detroit	20
	Cardinals	28	Detroit	14
1949	Detroit	24	Cardinals	7
	Cardinals	42	Detroit	19
1959	Detroit	45	Cardinals	21

Cardinals won 9, Detroit won 19; Tied 3.
Total points: Cardinals 423; Detroit 514.

ST. LOUIS CARDINALS vs GREEN BAY PACKERS

1921	Cardinals	3	Green Bay	3
1922	Cardinals	16	Green Bay	3
1924	Cardinals	3	Green Bay	0
1925	Cardinals	9	Green Bay	6
1926	Cardinals	13	Green Bay	7
	Green Bay	3	Cardinals	0
1927	Green Bay	13	Cardinals	0
	Cardinals	6	Green Bay	6
1928	Green Bay	20	Cardinals	0
1929	Green Bay	9	Cardinals	2
	Green Bay	7	Cardinals	6
	Green Bay	13	Cardinals	0
1930	Green Bay	14	Cardinals	0
	Cardinals	13	Green Bay	6
1931	Green Bay	26	Cardinals	7
	Cardinals	21	Green Bay	13
1932	Green Bay	15	Cardinals	7
	Green Bay	19	Cardinals	9
1933	Green Bay	14	Cardinals	6
1934	Green Bay	15	Cardinals	0
	Cardinals	9	Green Bay	0
	Cardinals	6	Green Bay	0
1935	Cardinals	7	Green Bay	6
	Cardinals	3	Green Bay	0

	Cardinals	9	Green Bay	7
1936	Green Bay	10	Cardinals	7
	Green Bay	24	Cardinals	0
	Green Bay	0	Cardinals	0
1937	Cardinals	14	Green Bay	7
	Green Bay	34	Cardinals	13
1938	Green Bay	28	Cardinals	7
	Green Bay	24	Cardinals	22
1939	Green Bay	14	Cardinals	10
	Green Bay	27	Cardinals	20
1940	Green Bay	31	Cardinals	6
	Green Bay	28	Cardinals	7
1941	Green Bay	14	Cardinals	13
	Green Bay	17	Cardinals	9
1942	Green Bay	17	Cardinals	13
	Green Bay	55	Cardinals	24
1943	Green Bay	28	Cardinals	7
	Green Bay	35	Cardinals	14
1945	Green Bay	33	Cardinals	14
1946	Green Bay	19	Cardinals	7
	Cardinals	24	Green Bay	6
1947	Cardinals	14	Green Bay	10
	Cardinals	21	Green Bay	20
1948	Cardinals	17	Green Bay	7
	Cardinals	42	Green Bay	7
1949	Cardinals	39	Green Bay	17
	Cardinals	41	Green Bay	21
1955	Green Bay	31	Cardinals	14

Cardinals won 19; Green Bay won 30; Tied 3.
Total points: Cardinals 574; Green Bay 789.

ST. LOUIS CARDINALS vs NEW YORK GIANTS

1926	New York	20	Cardinals	0
1927	New York	28	Cardinals	7
1929	New York	24	Cardinals	21
1930	New York	25	Cardinals	12
	New York	13	Cardinals	7
1935	Cardinals	14	New York	13
1936	New York	14	Cardinals	6
1938	New York	6	Cardinals	0
1939	New York	17	Cardinals	7
1941	Cardinals	10	New York	7
1942	New York	21	Cardinals	7
1943	New York	24	Cardinals	13
1946	New York	28	Cardinals	24
1947	New York	35	Cardinals	31
1948	Cardinals	63	New York	35
1949	New York	41	Cardinals	38
1950	Cardinals	17	New York	3
	New York	51	Cardinals	21
1951	New York	28	Cardinals	17
	New York	10	Cardinals	0
1952	Cardinals	24	New York	23
	New York	28	Cardinals	6
1953	New York	21	Cardinals	7
	New York	23	Cardinals	20
1954	New York	41	Cardinals	10
	New York	31	Cardinals	17
1955	Cardinals	28	New York	17
	New York	10	Cardinals	0
1956	Cardinals	35	New York	27
	New York	23	Cardinals	10
1957	New York	27	Cardinals	14
	New York	28	Cardinals	21
1958	New York	37	Cardinals	7
	Cardinals	23	New York	6
1959	New York	9	Cardinals	3
	New York	30	Cardinals	20
1960	New York	35	Cardinals	14
	Cardinals	20	New York	13

Cardinals won 9; New York won 29; Tied 0.
Total points: Cardinals 594; New York 872.

ST. LOUIS CARDINALS vs PHILADELPHIA EAGLES

1935	Cardinals	12	Philadelphia	3
1936	Cardinals	13	Philadelphia	0
1937	Philadelphia	6	Cardinals	6
1938	Philadelphia	7	Cardinals	0
1941	Philadelphia	21	Cardinals	14
1945	Philadelphia	21	Cardinals	6
1947	Cardinals	45	Philadelphia	21
	*Cardinals	28	Philadelphia	21
1948	Cardinals	21	Philadelphia	14
	*Philadelphia	7	Cardinals	0
1949	Philadelphia	28	Cardinals	3
1950	Philadelphia	45	Cardinals	7
	Cardinals	14	Philadelphia	10
1951	Philadelphia	17	Cardinals	14
1952	Philadelphia	10	Cardinals	7
	Cardinals	28	Philadelphia	22
1953	Philadelphia	56	Cardinals	17
	Philadelphia	38	Cardinals	0
1954	Philadelphia	35	Cardinals	16
	Philadelphia	30	Cardinals	14
1955	Philadelphia	24	Cardinals	24
	Philadelphia	27	Cardinals	3
1956	Cardinals	20	Philadelphia	6
	Cardinals	28	Philadelphia	17
1957	Philadelphia	38	Cardinals	21
	Cardinals	31	Philadelphia	27
1958	Cardinals	21	Philadelphia	21
	Philadelphia	49	Cardinals	21
1959	Philadelphia	28	Cardinals	24
	Philadelphia	27	Cardinals	17
1960	Philadelphia	31	Cardinals	27
	Philadelphia	20	Cardinals	6

Cardinals won 10; Philadelphia won 19; Tied 3.
Total points: Cardinals 504; Philadelphia 727.

* Championship Play-off Game

CHICAGO CARDINALS vs PITTSBURGH STEELERS

1933	Pittsburgh	14	Cardinals	13
1935	Pittsburgh	17	Cardinals	13
1936	Cardinals	14	Pittsburgh	6
1937	Cardinals	13	Pittsburgh	7
1939	Cardinals	10	Pittsburgh	0
1940	Cardinals	7	Pittsburgh	7
1942	Pittsburgh	19	Cardinals	3

1945	Pittsburgh	23	Cardinals	0
1946	Pittsburgh	14	Cardinals	7
1948	Cardinals	24	Pittsburgh	7
1950	Pittsburgh	28	Cardinals	17
	Pittsburgh	28	Cardinals	7
1951	Pittsburgh	28	Cardinals	14
1952	Pittsburgh	34	Cardinals	28
	Pittsburgh	17	Cardinals	14
1953	Pittsburgh	31	Cardinals	28
	Pittsburgh	21	Cardinals	17
1954	Cardinals	17	Pittsburgh	14
	Pittsburgh	20	Cardinals	17
1955	Pittsburgh	14	Cardinals	7
	Cardinals	27	Pittsburgh	13
1956	Pittsburgh	14	Cardinals	7
	Cardinals	38	Pittsburgh	27
1957	Pittsburgh	29	Cardinals	20
	Pittsburgh	27	Cardinals	2
1959	Cardinals	45	Pittsburgh	24
	Pittsburgh	35	Cardinals	20
1960	Pittsburgh	27	Cardinals	14
	Cardinals	38	Pittsburgh	7

Cardinals won 9; Pittsburgh won 11; Tied 1.

Total points: Cardinals 522; Pittsburgh 617.

ST. LOUIS CARDINALS vs WASHINGTON REDSKINS

1937	Cardinals	21	Washington	14
1939	Washington	28	Cardinals	7
1940	Washington	28	Cardinals	21
1942	Washington	28	Cardinals	0
1943	Washington	13	Cardinals	7
1945	Washington	24	Cardinals	21
1947	Washington	45	Cardinals	21
1949	Cardinals	38	Washington	7
1950	Cardinals	38	Washington	28
1951	Washington	7	Cardinals	3
	Washington	20	Cardinals	17
1952	Washington	23	Cardinals	7
	Cardinals	17	Washington	6
1953	Washington	24	Cardinals	13
	Washington	28	Cardinals	17
1954	Cardinals	38	Washington	16
	Washington	37	Cardinals	20
1955	Cardinals	24	Washington	10
	Washington	31	Cardinals	0
1956	Cardinals	31	Washington	3
	Washington	17	Cardinals	14
1957	Washington	37	Cardinals	14
	Cardinals	44	Washington	14
1958	Cardinals	37	Washington	10
	Washington	45	Cardinals	31
1959	Cardinals	49	Washington	21
	Washington	23	Cardinals	14
1960	Cardinals	44	Washington	7
	Cardinals	26	Washington	14

Cardinals won 12, Washington won 17; Tied 0.

Total points: Cardinals 634; Washington 608.

SAN FRANCISCO 49ers vs BALTIMORE COLTS

1953	San Francisco	38	Baltimore	21
	San Francisco	45	Baltimore	14
1954	Baltimore	17	San Francisco	13
	San Francisco	10	Baltimore	7
1955	Baltimore	26	San Francisco	14
	San Francisco	35	Baltimore	24
1956	San Francisco	20	Baltimore	17
	San Francisco	30	Baltimore	17
1957	Baltimore	27	San Francisco	21
	San Francisco	17	Baltimore	13
1958	Baltimore	35	San Francisco	21
	San Francisco	21	Baltimore	12
1959	Baltimore	45	San Francisco	14
	Baltimore	34	San Francisco	14
	San Francisco	30	Baltimore	22
	San Francisco	34	Baltimore	10

San Francisco won 16; Baltimore won 6; Tied 0.

Total points: San Francisco 377; Baltimore 341.

SAN FRANCISCO 49ers vs DALLAS COWBOYS

| 1960 | San Francisco | 26 | Dallas | 14 |

San Francisco won 1; Dallas won 0; Tied 0.
Total points: San Francisco 26; Dallas 14.

SAN FRANCISCO 49ers vs ST. LOUIS CARDINALS

| 1951 | Cardinals | 27 | San Francisco | 21 |
| 1957 | Cardinals | 20 | San Francisco | 10 |

San Francisco won 0; Cardinals won 2; Tied 0.
Total points: San Francisco 21; Cardinals 47.

WASHINGTON REDSKINS vs BALTIMORE COLTS

1953	Baltimore	27	Washington	17
1954	Washington	24	Baltimore	21
1955	Washington	14	Baltimore	13
1956	Baltimore	19	Washington	17
1957	Baltimore	21	Washington	17
1958	Baltimore	35	Washington	10
1959	Washington	27	Baltimore	24
1960	Baltimore	20	Washington	0

Washington won 3; Baltimore won 5; Tied 0.
Total points: Washington 126; Baltimore 180.

WASHINGTON REDSKINS vs CLEVELAND BROWNS

1950	Cleveland	20	Washington	14
	Cleveland	45	Washington	21
1951	Cleveland	45	Washington	0
1952	Cleveland	19	Washington	15

	Cleveland	48	Washington	24
1953	Cleveland	30	Washington	14
	Cleveland	27	Washington	3
1954	Cleveland	62	Washington	3
	Cleveland	34	Washington	14
1955	Washington	27	Cleveland	17
	Cleveland	24	Washington	14
1956	Washington	20	Cleveland	9
	Washington	20	Cleveland	17
1957	Cleveland	21	Washington	17
	Cleveland	30	Washington	30
1958	Cleveland	20	Washington	10
	Cleveland	21	Washington	14
1959	Cleveland	34	Washington	7
	Cleveland	31	Washington	17
1960	Cleveland	31	Washington	10
	Cleveland	27	Washington	16

Washington won 3; Cleveland won 17; Tied 1.

Total points: Washington 310; Cleveland 612.

WASHINGTON REDSKINS vs DALLAS COWBOYS

1960	Washington	26	Dallas	14

Washington won 1; Dallas won 0; Tied 0.
Total points: Washington 26; Dallas 14.

WASHINGTON REDSKINS vs SAN FRANCISCO 49ers

1952	San Francisco 23	Washington	17
1954	San Francisco 41	Washington	7
1955	Washington	7	San Francisco	0

Washington won 1; San Francisco won 2; Tied 0.

Total points: Washington 31; San Francisco 64.

TEAM vs TEAM RECORDS (MERGERS)

BROOKLYN vs COMBINES

1943	Brooklyn	13	Phil-Pitt	7
	Phil-Pitt	17	Brooklyn	0

Total points: Combines 24; Brooklyn 13.

CHICAGO BEARS vs COMBINES

1943	Bears	48	Phil-Pitt	21
1944	Bears	34	Card-Pitt	7
	Bears	49	Card-Pitt	7

Bears won 3; Combines won 0; Tied 0.
Total points: Bears 131; Combines 35.

CHICAGO CARDINALS vs COMBINES

1943	Phil-Pitt	34	Cardinals	13

Cardinals won 0; Combines won 1; Tied 0.
Total points: Cardinals 34; Combines 13.

CLEVELAND RAMS vs COMBINES

1944	Cleveland	30	Card-Pitt	28
	Cleveland	33	Card-Pitt	6
1945	Cleveland	20	Yanks	7

Cleveland won 3; Combines won 0; Tied 0.
Total points: Cleveland 83; Combines 41.

DETROIT LIONS vs COMBINES

1943	Phil-Pitt	35	Detroit	34
1944	Detroit	27	Card-Pitt	6
	Detroit	21	Card-Pitt	7
1945	Detroit	10	Yanks	9

Detroit won 3; Combines 1; Tied 0.
Total points: Detroit 92; Combines 57.

GREEN BAY PACKERS vs COMBINES

1943	Green Bay	38	Phil-Pitt	28
1944	Green Bay	34	Card-Pitt	7
	Green Bay	35	Card-Pitt	20
1945	Green Bay	38	Yanks	14
	Green Bay	28	Yanks	0

Green Bay won 5; Combines won 0; Tied 0.
Total points: Green Bay 173; Combines 69.

NEW YORK GIANTS vs COMBINES

1943	Phil-Pitt	28	New York	14
	New York	42	Phil-Pitt	14
1944	New York	23	Card-Pitt	0
1945	New York	13	Yanks	13

New York won 2; Combines won 1; Tied 1.
Total points: New York 92; Combines 55.

PHILADELPHIA EAGLES vs COMBINES

1945	Philadelphia	35	Yanks	7

Philadelphia won 1; Combines won 0; Tied 0.
Total points: Philadelphia 35; Combines 0.

PITTSBURGH STEELERS vs COMBINES

| 1945 | Yanks | 28 | Pittsburgh | 7 |
| | Yanks | 10 | Pittsburgh | 6 |

Pittsburgh won 0; Combines won 2; Tied 0.
Total points: Pittsburgh 13; Combines 38.

WASHINGTON REDSKINS vs COMBINES

| 1943 | Phil-Pitt | 14 | Washington | 14 |

	Phil-Pitt	27	Washington	14
1944	Washington	42	Card-Pitt	20
1945	Yanks	28	Washington	20
	Washington	34	Yanks	7

Washington won 2; Combines won 2; Tied 1.

Total points: Washington 124; Combines 96.

TEAM vs TEAM RECORDS

(Discontinued Series)

BALTIMORE vs CHICAGO CARDINALS

| 1950 | Cardinals | 55 | Baltimore | 13 |

BALTIMORE vs CLEVELAND BROWNS

| 1950 | Cleveland | 31 | Baltimore | 0 |

BALTIMORE vs DETROIT LIONS

| 1950 | Detroit | 45 | Baltimore | 21 |

BALTIMORE vs GREEN BAY PACKERS

| 1950 | Baltimore | 41 | Green Bay | 21 |

BALTIMORE vs LOS ANGELES RAMS

| 1950 | Los Angeles | 70 | Baltimore | 27 |

BALTIMORE vs NEW YORK GIANTS

| 1950 | New York | 55 | Baltimore | 20 |

BALTIMORE vs NEW YORK YANKS

| 1950 | Yanks | 51 | Baltimore | 14 |

BALTIMORE vs PHILADELPHIA EAGLES

| 1950 | Philadelphia | 24 | Baltimore | 14 |

BALTIMORE vs PITTSBURGH STEELERS

| 1950 | Pittsburgh | 17 | Baltimore | 7 |

BALTIMORE vs SAN FRANCISCO 49ers

| 1950 | San Francisco | 17 | Baltimore | 14 |

BALTIMORE vs WASHINGTON REDSKINS

| 1950 | Washington | 38 | Baltimore | 14 |
| | Washington | 38 | Baltimore | 28 |

BOSTON REDSKINS vs BROOKLYN

1932	Brooklyn	14	Boston	0
	Boston	7	Brooklyn	0
1933	Brooklyn	14	Boston	0
1934	Brooklyn	10	Boston	6
	Boston	13	Brooklyn	3
1935	Boston	7	Brooklyn	3
	Boston	0	Brooklyn	0
1936	Boston	14	Brooklyn	3
	Boston	30	Brooklyn	3

Boston won 5; Brooklyn won 3; Tied 1.

Total points: Boston 77; Brooklyn 50.

BOSTON REDSKINS vs CHICAGO BEARS

1932	Boston	7	Bears	7
1933	Bears	7	Boston	0
	Boston	10	Bears	0
1934	Bears	21	Boston	0
1935	Bears	30	Boston	14
1936	Bears	26	Boston	0

Boston won 1; Bears won 4; Tied 1.

Total points: Boston 31; Bears 91.

BOSTON REDSKINS vs CHICAGO CARDINALS

1932	Cardinals	9	Boston	0
	Boston	8	Cardinals	6
1933	Boston	10	Cardinals	0
	Boston	0	Cardinals	0

1934	Boston	9	Cardinals	0
1935	Cardinals	6	Boston	0
1936	Boston	13	Cardinals	10

Boston won 4; Cardinals won 2; Tied 1.

Total points: Boston 40; Cardinals 31.

BOSTON REDSKINS vs DETROIT LIONS

1934	Detroit	24	Boston	0
1935	Detroit	17	Boston	7
	Detroit	14	Boston	0

Boston won 0; Detroit won 3; Tied 0.

Total points: Boston 7; Detroit 55.

BOSTON REDSKINS vs GREEN BAY PACKERS

1932	Green Bay	21	Boston	0
1933	Boston	7	Green Bay	7
	Boston	20	Green Bay	7
1934	Green Bay	10	Boston	0
1936	Green Bay	31	Boston	2
	Green Bay	7	Boston	3
*Green Bay	21	Boston	6

Boston won 1; Green Bay won 5; Tied 1.

Total points: Boston 38; Green Bay 104.

* Championship Play-off Game

BOSTON REDSKINS vs NEW YORK GIANTS

1932	Boston	14	New York	6
	Boston	0	New York	0
1933	Boston	21	New York	20
	New York	7	Boston	0
1934	New York	16	Boston	13
	New York	3	Boston	0
1935	New York	20	Boston	12
	New York	17	Boston	6
1936	New York	7	Boston	0
	Boston	14	New York	0

Boston won 6; New York won 6; Tied 1.

Total points: Boston 80; New York 96.

BOSTON REDSKINS vs PHILADELPHIA EAGLES

1934	Boston	6	Philadelphia	0
	Boston	14	Philadelphia	7
1935	Philadelphia	7	Boston	6
1936	Boston	26	Philadelphia	3
	Boston	17	Philadelphia	7

Boston won 4; Philadelphia won 1; Tied 0.

Total points: Boston 69; Philadelphia 24.

BOSTON REDSKINS vs

PITTSBURGH STEELERS

1933	Boston	21	Pittsburgh	6
	Pittsburgh	16	Boston	14
1934	Boston	7	Pittsburgh	0
	Boston	39	Pittsburgh	0
1935	Pittsburgh	6	Boston	0
	Boston	13	Pittsburgh	3
1936	Pittsburgh	10	Boston	0
	Boston	30	Pittsburgh	0

Boston won 5; Pittsburgh 3; Tied 0.

Total points: Boston 124; Pittsburgh 41.

BOSTON REDSKINS vs PORTSMOUTH SPARTANS

| 1932 | Portsmouth | 10 | Boston | 0 |
| 1933 | Portsmouth | 13 | Boston | 0 |

Boston won 0; Portsmouth won 2; Tied 0.

Total points: Boston 0; Portsmouth 23.

BOSTON YANKS vs BROOKLYN

| 1944 | Boston | 17 | Brooklyn | 14 |
| | Boston | 13 | Brooklyn | 6 |

Boston won 2; Brooklyn won 0; Tied 0.

Total points: Boston 30; Brooklyn 20.

BOSTON YANKS vs CHICAGO BEARS

1944	Bears	21	Boston	7
1947	Bears	27	Boston	7
1948	Bears	51	Boston	17

Boston won 0; Bears won 3; Tied 0.

Total points: Boston 48; Bears 100.

BOSTON YANKS vs CHICAGO CARDINALS

1946	Cardinals	28	Boston	14
1947	Cardinals	27	Boston	7
1948	Cardinals	49	Boston	27

Boston won 0; Cardinals won 3; Tied 0.

Total points: Boston 48; Cardinals 104.

BOSTON YANKS vs DETROIT LIONS

1944	Detroit	38	Boston	7
1945	Detroit	10	Boston	9
1946	Boston	34	Detroit	10

| 1947 | Detroit | 21 | Boston | 7 |
| 1948 | Boston | 17 | Detroit | 14 |

Boston won 2; Detroit won 3; Tied 0.

Total points: Boston 74; Detroit 93.

BOSTON YANKS vs
GREEN BAY PACKERS

| 1945 | Green Bay | 38 | Boston | 14 |
| | Green Bay | 28 | Boston | 0 |

Boston won 0; Green Bay won 2; Tied 0.

Total points: Boston 14; Green Bay 66.

BOSTON YANKS vs
LOS ANGELES RAMS

| 1946 | Boston | 40 | Los Angeles | 21 |
| 1947 | Boston | 27 | Los Angeles | 16 |

Boston won 2; Los Angeles won 0; Tied 0.

Total points: Boston 67; Los Angeles 37.

BOSTON YANKS vs
NEW YORK GIANTS

1944	New York	22	Boston	10
	New York	31	Boston	0
1945	New York	13	Boston	13
1946	New York	17	Boston	0
	New York	28	Boston	28
1947	New York	7	Boston	7
	Boston	14	New York	0
1948	New York	27	Boston	7
	New York	28	Boston	14

Boston won 1; New York won 5; Tied 3.

Total points: Boston 93; New York 173.

BOSTON YANKS vs
PHILADELPHIA EAGLES

1944	Philadelphia	28	Boston	7
	Philadelphia	38	Boston	0
1945	Philadelphia	35	Boston	7
1946	Philadelphia	49	Boston	25
	Philadelphia	40	Boston	14
1947	Philadelphia	32	Boston	0
	Boston	21	Philadelphia	14
1948	Philadelphia	45	Boston	0
	Boston	37	Philadelphia	14

Boston won 2; Philadelphia won 7; Tied 0.

Total points: Boston 111; Philadelphia 295.

BOSTON YANKS vs
PITTSBURGH STEELERS

| 1945 | Boston | 28 | Pittsburgh | 7 |
| | Boston | 10 | Pittsburgh | 6 |

1946	Pittsburgh	16	Boston	7
	Pittsburgh	33	Boston	7
1947	Pittsburgh	30	Boston	14
	Pittsburgh	17	Boston	7
1948	Pittsburgh	24	Boston	14
	Boston	13	Pittsburgh	7

Boston won 3; Pittsburgh won 5; Tied 0.

Total points: Boston 100; Pittsburgh 140.

BOSTON YANKS vs
WASHINGTON

1944	Washington	21	Boston	14
	Washington	14	Boston	7
1945	Boston	28	Washington	20
	Washington	34	Boston	7
1946	Washington	14	Boston	6
	Washington	17	Boston	14
1947	Boston	27	Washington	24
	Washington	40	Boston	13
1948	Washington	59	Boston	21
	Washington	23	Boston	7

Boston won 2; Washington won 8; Tied 0.

Total points: Boston 144; Washington 266.

BROOKLYN vs
CHICAGO BEARS

1931	Bears	26	Brooklyn	0
1932	Bears	13	Brooklyn	0
	Bears	20	Brooklyn	0
1933	Bears	10	Brooklyn	0
1934	Bears	21	Brooklyn	7
1935	Bears	24	Brooklyn	14
1937	Bears	29	Brooklyn	7
1938	Bears	24	Brooklyn	6
1940	Bears	16	Brooklyn	7
1942	Bears	35	Brooklyn	0
1943	Bears	33	Brooklyn	21

Brooklyn won 0; Bears won 11; Tied 0.

Total points: Brooklyn 62; Bears 251.

BROOKLYN vs
CHICAGO CARDINALS

1931	Cardinals	14	Brooklyn	7
1932	Cardinals	27	Brooklyn	7
	Brooklyn	3	Cardinals	0
1933	Brooklyn	7	Cardinals	0
	Brooklyn	3	Cardinals	0
1934	Cardinals	21	Brooklyn	0
1936	Brooklyn	9	Cardinals	0
1938	Brooklyn	13	Cardinals	0
1940	Brooklyn	14	Cardinals	9
1941	Cardinals	20	Brooklyn	6
1943	Brooklyn	7	Cardinals	0

Brooklyn won 7; Cardinals 4; Tied 0.
Total points: Brooklyn 76; Cardinals 91.

BROOKLYN vs
CLEVELAND RAMS

1937	Brooklyn	9	Cleveland	7
1939	Brooklyn	23	Cleveland	12
1940	Brooklyn	29	Cleveland	14
1942	Cleveland	17	Brooklyn	0

Brooklyn won 3; Cleveland 1; Tied 0.

Total points: Brooklyn 61; Cleveland 50.

BROOKLYN vs
DETROIT LIONS

1934	Detroit	28	Brooklyn	0
1935	Brooklyn	12	Detroit	10
	Detroit	28	Brooklyn	0
1936	Detroit	14	Brooklyn	7
	Detroit	14	Brooklyn	6
1937	Detroit	30	Brooklyn	0
1939	Detroit	27	Brooklyn	7
1941	Brooklyn	14	Detroit	7
1942	Brooklyn	28	Detroit	7
1943	Detroit	27	Brooklyn	0
1944	Detroit	19	Brooklyn	14

Brooklyn won 3; Detroit won 8; Tied 0.

Total points: Brooklyn 88; Detroit 211.

BROOKLYN vs
GREEN BAY PACKERS

1931	Green Bay	7	Brooklyn	0
1932	Green Bay	7	Brooklyn	0
1936	Green Bay	38	Brooklyn	7
1938	Green Bay	35	Brooklyn	7
1939	Green Bay	28	Brooklyn	0
1941	Green Bay	30	Brooklyn	7
1943	Green Bay	31	Brooklyn	7
1944	Green Bay	14	Brooklyn	7

Brooklyn won 0; Green Bay won 8; Tied 0.

Total points: Brooklyn 35; Green Bay 190.

BROOKLYN vs
NEW YORK GIANTS

1926	New York	17	Brooklyn	0
	New York	27	Brooklyn	0
1930	Brooklyn	7	New York	6
	New York	13	Brooklyn	0
1931	New York	27	Brooklyn	0
	New York	19	Brooklyn	6
1932	New York	20	Brooklyn	12
	New York	13	Brooklyn	7
1933	New York	21	Brooklyn	7
	New York	10	Brooklyn	0
1934	New York	14	Brooklyn	0
	New York	27	Brooklyn	0
1935	New York	10	Brooklyn	7
	New York	21	Brooklyn	0
1936	Brooklyn	10	New York	10
	New York	14	Brooklyn	0
1937	New York	21	Brooklyn	0
	Brooklyn	13	New York	13
1938	New York	28	Brooklyn	14
	Brooklyn	7	New York	7
1939	New York	7	Brooklyn	6
	New York	28	Brooklyn	7
1940	New York	10	Brooklyn	7
	Brooklyn	14	New York	6
1941	Brooklyn	16	New York	13
	Brooklyn	21	New York	7
1942	Brooklyn	17	New York	7
	New York	10	Brooklyn	0
1943	New York	20	Brooklyn	0
	New York	24	Brooklyn	7
1944	New York	14	Brooklyn	7
	New York	7	Brooklyn	0

Brooklyn won 5; New York won 24; Tied 3.

Total points: Brooklyn 192; New York 49.

BROOKLYN vs
PHILADELPHIA EAGLES

1934	Brooklyn	10	Philadelphia	7
	Philadelphia	13	Brooklyn	0
1935	Brooklyn	17	Philadelphia	6
	Brooklyn	3	Philadelphia	0
1936	Brooklyn	18	Philadelphia	0
	Brooklyn	13	Philadelphia	7
1937	Brooklyn	13	Philadelphia	7
	Philadelphia	14	Brooklyn	10
1938	Brooklyn	10	Philadelphia	7
	Brooklyn	32	Philadelphia	14
1939	Philadelphia	0	Brooklyn	0
	Brooklyn	23	Philadelphia	14
1940	Brooklyn	30	Philadelphia	17
	Brooklyn	21	Philadelphia	7
1941	Brooklyn	24	Philadelphia	13
	Brooklyn	15	Philadelphia	6
1942	Brooklyn	35	Philadelphia	14
	Philadelphia	14	Brooklyn	7
1944	Philadelphia	21	Brooklyn	7
	Philadelphia	34	Brooklyn	0

Brooklyn won 14; Philadelphia won 5; Tied 1.

Total points: Brooklyn 288; Philadelphia 215.

BROOKLYN vs
PITTSBURGH STEELERS

1933	Brooklyn	3	Pittsburgh	3
	Brooklyn	32	Pittsburgh	0
1934	Brooklyn	21	Pittsburgh	3
	Brooklyn	10	Pittsburgh	0
1935	Brooklyn	13	Pittsburgh	7
	Pittsburgh	16	Brooklyn	7
1936	Pittsburgh	10	Brooklyn	6
	Pittsburgh	10	Brooklyn	7
1937	Pittsburgh	21	Brooklyn	0
	Brooklyn	23	Pittsburgh	0
1939	Pittsburgh	17	Brooklyn	3
	Brooklyn	17	Pittsburgh	7

1939	Brooklyn	12	Pittsburgh	7
	Brooklyn	17	Pittsburgh	13
1940	Brooklyn	10	Pittsburgh	3
	Brooklyn	21	Pittsburgh	0
1941	Pittsburgh	14	Brooklyn	7
	Brooklyn	35	Pittsburgh	7
1942	Pittsburgh	7	Brooklyn	0
	Pittsburgh	13	Brooklyn	0

Brooklyn won 11; Pittsburgh won 8; Tied 1.

Total points: Brooklyn 244; Pittsburgh 158.

BROOKLYN vs
PORTSMOUTH SPARTANS

1930	Portsmouth	14	Brooklyn	0
1931	Portsmouth	19	Brooklyn	0
1932	Portsmouth	17	Brooklyn	7

Brooklyn won 0; Portsmouth won 3; Tied 0.

Total points: Brooklyn 7; Portsmouth 50.

BROOKLYN vs
WASHINGTON REDSKINS

1937	Washington	11	Brooklyn	7
	Washington	21	Brooklyn	0
1938	Washington	16	Brooklyn	16
	Washington	6	Brooklyn	6
1939	Washington	41	Brooklyn	13
	Washington	42	Brooklyn	0
1940	Washington	24	Brooklyn	17
	Brooklyn	16	Washington	14
1941	Washington	3	Brooklyn	0
	Brooklyn	13	Washington	7
1942	Washington	21	Brooklyn	10
	Washington	23	Brooklyn	3
1943	Washington	27	Brooklyn	0
	Washington	48	Brooklyn	10
1944	Washington	17	Brooklyn	14
	Washington	10	Brooklyn	0

Brooklyn won 2; Washington 12; Tied 2.

Total points: Brooklyn 125; Washington 331.

CINCINNATI
(Part of 1934 Season)

Pittsburgh	13	Cincinnati	0
Cardinals	9	Cincinnati	0
Cardinals	16	Cincinnati	0
Bears	21	Cincinnati	3
Bears	41	Cincinnati	7
Green Bay	41	Cincinnati	0
Detroit	38	Cincinnati	0
Philadelphia	64	Cincinnati	0

Cincinnati won 0; Opponents won 8; Tied 0.

Total points: Cincinnati 10; Opponents 243.

CLEVELAND RAMS vs
BOSTON YANKS

1945	Cleveland	20	Boston	7

CLEVELAND RAMS vs
CHICAGO BEARS

1937	Bears	20	Cleveland	2
	Bears	15	Cleveland	7
1938	Cleveland	14	Bears	7
	Cleveland	23	Bears	21
1939	Bears	30	Cleveland	21
	Bears	35	Cleveland	21
1940	Bears	21	Cleveland	14
	Bears	47	Cleveland	25
1941	Bears	48	Cleveland	21
	Bears	31	Cleveland	13
1942	Bears	21	Cleveland	7
	Bears	47	Cleveland	0
1944	Cleveland	19	Bears	7
	Bears	28	Cleveland	21
1945	Cleveland	17	Bears	0
	Cleveland	41	Bears	21

Cleveland won 5; Bears won 11; Tied 0.

Total points: Cleveland 266; Bears 399.

CLEVELAND RAMS vs
CHICAGO CARDINALS

1937	Cardinals	6	Cleveland	0
	Cardinals	13	Cleveland	7
1938	Cardinals	7	Cleveland	6
	Cardinals	31	Cleveland	17
1939	Cleveland	24	Cardinals	0
	Cleveland	14	Cardinals	0
1940	Cleveland	26	Cardinals	14
	Cardinals	17	Cleveland	7
1941	Cleveland	10	Cardinals	6
	Cardinals	7	Cleveland	0
1942	Cardinals	7	Cleveland	0
	Cleveland	7	Cardinals	3
1945	Cleveland	21	Cardinals	0
	Cleveland	35	Cardinals	21

Cleveland won 7; Cardinals won 7; Tied 0.

Total points: Cleveland 174; Cardinals 132.

CLEVELAND RAMS vs
DETROIT LIONS

1937	Detroit	28	Cleveland	0
	Detroit	27	Cleveland	7
1938	Cleveland	21	Detroit	17
	Detroit	6	Cleveland	0
1939	Detroit	15	Cleveland	7
	Cleveland	14	Detroit	3
1940	Detroit	6	Cleveland	0
	Cleveland	24	Detroit	0
1941	Detroit	17	Cleveland	7
	Detroit	14	Cleveland	0
1942	Cleveland	14	Detroit	0
	Cleveland	27	Detroit	7
1944	Cleveland	20	Detroit	17
	Detroit	26	Cleveland	14
1945	Cleveland	28	Detroit	21

Cleveland won 7; Detroit won 8; Tied 0.
Total points: Cleveland 183; Detroit 204.

CLEVELAND RAMS vs GREEN BAY PACKERS

1937	Green Bay	35	Cleveland	10
	Green Bay	35	Cleveland	7
1938	Green Bay	26	Cleveland	17
	Green Bay	28	Cleveland	7
1939	Cleveland	27	Green Bay	24
	Green Bay	7	Cleveland	6
1940	Green Bay	31	Cleveland	14
	Green Bay	13	Cleveland	13
1941	Green Bay	24	Cleveland	7
	Green Bay	17	Cleveland	14
1942	Green Bay	45	Cleveland	28
	Green Bay	30	Cleveland	12
1944	Green Bay	30	Cleveland	21
	Green Bay	42	Cleveland	7
1945	Cleveland	27	Green Bay	14
	Cleveland	20	Green Bay	7

Cleveland won 3; Green Bay won 12; Tied 1.

Total points: Cleveland 237; Green Bay 408.

CLEVELAND RAMS vs NEW YORK GIANTS

1938	New York	28	Cleveland	0
1940	Cleveland	13	New York	0
1941	New York	49	Cleveland	14
1945	Cleveland	21	New York	17

Cleveland won 2; New York won 2; Tied 0.

Total points: Cleveland 48; New York 94.

CLEVELAND RAMS vs PHILADELPHIA EAGLES

1937	Cleveland	21	Philadelphia	3
1939	Cleveland	35	Philadelphia	13
1940	Cleveland	21	Philadelphia	13
1942	Cleveland	24	Philadelphia	14
1944	Philadelphia	26	Cleveland	13
1945	Philadelphia	28	Cleveland	14

Cleveland won 4; Philadelphia won 2; Tied 0.

Total points: Cleveland 128; Philadelphia 97.

CLEVELAND RAMS vs PITTSBURGH STEELERS

1938	Cleveland	13	Pittsburgh	7
1939	Cleveland	14	Pittsburgh	14
1941	Cleveland	17	Pittsburgh	14

Cleveland won 2; Pittsburgh won 0; Tied 1.

Total points: Cleveland 44; Pittsburgh 35.

CLEVELAND RAMS vs WASHINGTON REDSKINS

1937	Washington	16	Cleveland	7
1938	Washington	37	Cleveland	13
1941	Washington	17	Cleveland	13
1942	Washington	33	Cleveland	14
1944	Washington	14	Cleveland	10
1945	*Cleveland	15	Washington	14

Cleveland won 1; Washington won 5; Tied 0.

Total points: Cleveland 72; Washington 131.

* Championship Play-off Game

DALLAS TEXANS vs CHICAGO BEARS

1952	Bears	38	Dallas	20
	Dallas	27	Bears	23

Dallas won 1; Bears won 1; Tied 0.

Total points: Dallas 47; Bears 61.

DALLAS TEXANS vs DETROIT LIONS

1952	Detroit	43	Dallas	13
	Detroit	41	Dallas	6

Dallas won 0; Detroit won 2; Tied 0.

Total points: Dallas 19, Detroit 84.

DALLAS TEXANS vs GREEN BAY PACKERS

1952	Green Bay	24	Dallas	14
	Green Bay	42	Dallas	14

Dallas won 0; Green Bay won 2; Tied 0.

Total points: Dallas 28; Green Bay 66.

DALLAS TEXANS vs LOS ANGELES RAMS

1952	Los Angeles	42	Dallas	20
	Los Angeles	27	Dallas	6

Dallas won 0; Los Angeles won 2; Tied 0.

Total points: Dallas 26; Los Angeles 69.

DALLAS TEXANS vs NEW YORK GIANTS

1952	New York	24	Dallas	6

Dallas won 0; New York won 1; Tied 0.

Total points: Dallas 6; New York 24.

DALLAS TEXANS vs PHILADELPHIA EAGLES

1952	Philadelphia	38	Dallas	21

Dallas won 0; Philadelphia won 1; Tied 0.

Total points: Dallas 21; Philadelphia 38.

DALLAS TEXANS vs
SAN FRANCISCO 49ers

1952	San Francisco 37	Dallas	14
	San Francisco 48	Dallas	21

Dallas won 0; San Francisco won 2; Tied 0.

Total points: Dallas 35; San Francisco 85.

NEW YORK BULLDOGS vs
CHICAGO CARDINALS

1949	Cardinals	65	Bulldogs	20

NEW YORK BULLDOGS vs
DETROIT LIONS

1949	Detroit	28	Bulldogs	27

NEW YORK BULLDOGS vs
GREEN BAY PACKERS

1949	Green Bay	19	Bulldogs	0

NEW YORK BULLDOGS vs
LOS ANGELES RAMS

1949	Los Angeles	42	Bulldogs	20

NEW YORK BULLDOGS vs
NEW YORK GIANTS

1949	Giants	38	Bulldogs	14
	Bulldogs	31	Giants	24

NEW YORK BULLDOGS vs
PHILADELPHIA EAGLES

1949	Philadelphia	7	Bulldogs	0
	Philadelphia	42	Bulldogs	0

NEW YORK BULLDOGS vs
PITTSBURGH STEELERS

1949	Pittsburgh	24	Bulldogs	13
	Pittsburgh	27	Bulldogs	0

NEW YORK BULLDOGS vs
WASHINGTON REDSKINS

1949	Washington	38	Bulldogs	14
	Washington	14	Bulldogs	14

NEW YORK YANKS vs
BALTIMORE COLTS

1950	Yanks	51	Colts	14

NEW YORK YANKS vs
CHICAGO BEARS

1950	Yanks	38	Bears	27
	Bears	28	Yanks	20
1951	Bears	24	Yanks	21
	Bears	45	Yanks	21

Yanks won 1; Bears won 3; Tied 0.

Total points: Yanks 100; Bears 124.

NEW YORK YANKS vs
DETROIT LIONS

1950	Yanks	44	Detroit	21
	Detroit	49	Yanks	14
1951	Detroit	37	Yanks	10
	Detroit	24	Yanks	24

Yanks won 1; Detroit won 2; Tied 1.

Total points: Yanks 92; Detroit 131.

NEW YORK YANKS vs
GREEN BAY PACKERS

1950	Yanks	44	Green Bay	31
	Yanks	35	Green Bay	17
1951	Green Bay	29	Yanks	27
	Yanks	31	Green Bay	28

Yanks won 3; Green Bay won 1; Tied 0.

Total points: Yanks 137; Green Bay 105.

NEW YORK YANKS vs
LOS ANGELES RAMS

1950	Los Angeles	45	Yanks	28
	Los Angeles	43	Yanks	35
1951	Los Angeles	54	Yanks	14
	Los Angeles	48	Yanks	21

Yanks won 0; Los Angeles won 4; Tied 0.

Total points: Yanks 98; Los Angeles 190.

NEW YORK YANKS vs
NEW YORK GIANTS

1950	Giants	51	Yanks	7
1951	Giants	37	Yanks	31
	Giants	27	Yanks	17

Yanks won 0; Giants won 3; Tied 0.

Total points: Yanks 55; Giants 115.

NEW YORK YANKS vs
SAN FRANCISCO FORTY NINERS

1950	Yanks	21	San Francisco 17
	Yanks	29	San Francisco 24
1951	San Francisco 19		Yanks	14
	San Francisco 10		Yanks	10

Yanks won 2; S.F. won 1; Tied 1.

Total points: Yanks 74; S.F. 70.

PORTSMOUTH vs
CHICAGO BEARS

1930	Portsmouth	7	Bears	6
	Bears	14	Portsmouth	6
1931	Bears	9	Portsmouth	6
	Portsmouth	3	Bears	0
1932	Portsmouth	13	Bears	13
	Portsmouth	7	Bears	7
	*Bears	9	Portsmouth	0
1933	Bears	17	Portsmouth	14
	Bears	17	Portsmouth	7

Portsmouth won 2; Bears won 5; Tied 2.

Total points: Portsmouth 63; Bears 92.

* Championship Play-off (Played in Chicago Stadium; indoors)

PORTSMOUTH vs
CHICAGO CARDINALS

1930	Portsmouth	0	Cardinals	0
	Cardinals	23	Portsmouth	0
1931	Cardinals	20	Portsmouth	19
1932	Cardinals	7	Portsmouth	7
1933	Portsmouth	7	Cardinals	6

Portsmouth won 1; Cardinals won 2; Tied 2.

Total points: Portsmouth 33; Cardinals 56.

PORTSMOUTH vs
GREEN BAY PACKERS

1930	Green Bay	47	Portsmouth	13
	Green Bay	6	Portsmouth	6
1932	Green Bay	15	Portsmouth	10
	Portsmouth	19	Green Bay	0

| 1933 | Green Bay | 17 | Portsmouth | 0 |
| | Portsmouth | 7 | Green Bay | 0 |

Portsmouth won 2; Green Bay won 3; Tied 1.

Total points: Portsmouth 55; Green Bay 85.

PORTSMOUTH vs
NEW YORK GIANTS

1930	New York	19	Portsmouth	6
1931	Portsmouth	14	New York	6
	New York	14	Portsmouth	0
1932	Portsmouth	7	New York	0
	Portsmouth	6	New York	0
1933	Portsmouth	17	New York	7
	New York	13	Portsmouth	10

Portsmouth won 4; New York won 3; Tied 0.

Total points: Portsmouth 60; New York 59.

PORTSMOUTH vs
PHILADELPHIA EAGLES

| 1933 | Portsmouth | 25 | Philadelphia | 0 |

ST. LOUIS
(Part of 1934 Season)

St. Louis	6	Pittsburgh	0
Detroit	40	St. Louis	7
Green Bay	21	St. Louis	14

St. Louis won 1; Opponents won 2; Tied 0.
Total points: St. Louis 27; Opponents 61.

TEAM DEPARTMENTAL CHAMPIONS

TOTAL YARDS GAINED

1960—Baltimore	4,245
1959—Baltimore	4,458
1958—Baltimore	4,539
1957—Los Angeles	4,143
1956—Chicago Bears	4,537
1955—Chicago Bears	4,316
1954—Los Angeles	5,187
1953—Philadelphia	4,811
1952—Cleveland	4,352
1951—Los Angeles	*5,506
1950—Los Angeles	5,420
1949—Chicago Bears	4,873
1948—Chicago Cards	4,694
1947—Chicago Bears	5,053
1946—Los Angeles	3,763
1945—Washington	3,549
1944—Chicago Bears	3,239
1943—Chicago Bears	4,045
1942—Chicago Bears	3,900
1941—Chicago Bears	4,265
1940—Green Bay	3,400
1939—Chicago Bears	3,988
1938—Green Bay	3,037
1937—Green Bay	3,201
1936—Detroit	3,703
1935—Chicago Bears	3,454
1934—Chicago Bears	3,750
1933—New York	2,970
1932—Chicago Bears	2,755

YARDS RUSHING

1960—St. Louis	2,356
1959—Cleveland	2,149
1958—Cleveland	2,526
1957—Los Angeles	2,142
1956—Chicago Bears	2,468
1955—Chicago Bears	2,388
1954—San Francisco	2,498
1953—San Francisco	2,230
1952—San Francisco	1,905
1951—Chicago Bears	2,408
1950—New York	2,336
1949—Philadelphia	2,607
1948—Chicago Cards	2,560
1947—Los Angeles	2,171

1946—Green Bay	1,765
1945—Cleveland Rams	1,714
1944—Philadelphia	1,663
1943—Phil–Pitt	1,730
1942—Chicago Bears	1,881
1941—Chicago Bears	2,156
1940—Chicago Bears	1,818
1939—Chicago Bears	2,043
1938—Detroit	1,893
1937—Detroit	2,074
1936—Detroit	*2,885
1935—Chicago Bears	2,096
1934—Detroit	2,763
1933—Boston Redskins	2,367
1932—Chicago Bears	1,770

FORWARD PASSING

	Thrown	Completetd	Efficiency %
1960—Cleveland	264	160	60.6
1959—Cleveland	276	159	57.6
1958—San Francisco	383	223	58.2
1957—San Francisco	305	191	62.6
1956—Baltimore	279	158	56.6
1955—Cleveland	234	130	55.6
1954—Cleveland	295	174	59.0
1953—Cleveland	303	191	‡63.0
1952—Green Bay	337	161	47.8
1951—Cleveland	271	151	55.7
1950—Los Angeles	*453	*253	55.8
1949—Los Angeles	366	192	52.5
1948—New York	363	191	52.6
1947—Washington	416	231	55.5
1946—Los Angeles	326	153	46.9
1945—Washington	228	146	†64.0
1944—Washington	299	170	56.8
1943—Washington	254	139	54.7
1942—Washington	257	137	53.3
1941—Green Bay	253	133	52.6
1940—Washington	244	144	59.0
1939—Cleve. Rams	253	127	50.1
1938—Cardinals	240	114	47.5
1937—Washington	222	99	44.5
1936—Green Bay	255	108	42.3
1935—New York	154	69	44.8
1934—New York	154	63	40.9
1933—Brooklyn	169	79	46.7
1932—New York	188	87	46.2
1931—Green Bay	230	93	40.4

*—League record.
†—League record for less than 250 attempts.
‡—League record for more than 250 attempts.

YARDS PASSING

1960—Baltimore	2,956
1959—Baltimore	2,753
1958—Pittsburgh	2,752
1957—Baltimore	2,388
1956—Los Angeles	2,419
1955—Philadelphia	2,472
1954—Chicago Bears	3,104
1953—Philadelphia	3,089
1952—Cleveland Browns	2,566
1951—Los Angeles	3,296
1950—Los Angeles	*3,709
1949—Chicago Bears	3,055
1948—Washington	2,861
1947—Washington	3,336
1946—Los Angeles	2,080
1945—Cleveland Rams	1,857
1944—Washington	2,021
1943—Chicago Bears	2,310
1942—Green Bay	2,407
1941—Chicago Bears	2,002
1940—Washington	1,887
1939—Chicago Bears	1,965
1938—Washington	1,536
1937—Green Bay	1,398
1936—Green Bay	1,629
1935—Green Bay	1,416
1934—Green Bay	1,165
1933—New York Giants	1,335
1932—Chicago Bears	1,013

POINTS SCORED

1960—Baltimore	362
1959—Baltimore (12 games)	374
1958—Baltimore (12 games)	381
1957—Los Angeles (12 games)	307
1956—Chicago Bears (12 games)	363
1955—Cleveland (12 games)	349
1954—Detroit (12 games)	337
1953—San Francisco (12 games)	372
1952—Los Angeles (12 games)	349
1951—Los Angeles (12 games)	392
1950—Los Angeles (12 games)	*466
1949—Philadelphia (12 games)	364
1948—Chicago Cardinals (12 games)	395
1947—Chicago Bears (12 games)	363
1946—Chicago Bears (11 games)	289
1945—Philadelphia (10 games)	272
1944—Philadelphia (10 games)	267
1943—Chicago Bears (10 games)	303
1942—Chicago Bears (11 games)	376
1941—Chicago Bears (11 games)	396
1940—Washington (11 games)	245
1939—Chicago Bears (11 games)	298
1938—Green Bay (11 games)	223
1937—Green Bay (11 games)	220
1936—Green Bay (12 games)	248
1935—Chicago Bears (12 games)	192
1934—Chicago Bears (13 games)	286
1933—New York (14 games)	244
1932—Green Bay (14 games)	152

CHAPTER 6
THE ALL-STAR GAME
THE COLLEGE ALL-STAR FOOTBALL SERIES
By ARCH WARD

Tribune Studio

Figures can be overpowering and we'll begin the story of the glamorous College All-Star series by submitting some. They, more than all the adjectives dear to the heart of a sportswriter, give a picture of the spectacle's tremendous impact on American athletics.

The eighteen games through 1951 were witnessed by 1,537,740 spectators, an average of 85,430 per game. Gross receipts totaled $4,356,689.76. To charities has gone $1,043,478.77.

The eighteenth annual game was witnessed by an estimated fifty million on television screens in a hook-up of forty-eight stations stretching from Jacksonville, Fla., and Birmingham, Ala., in the South, to Minneapolis in the North, from Omaha and Kansas City west to the Pacific coast, and into the major cities in the East. There were five hundred radio outlets and the armed forces sent a word story of the game around the world, wherever our troops were stationed. Requests for the top-priced tickets at $7 exceeded the supply by more than twenty-five thousand. Eight thousand rooters came from Cleveland to watch their Browns beat the Collegians, 33–0.

This is a quick presentation of the game which has thrilled the nation's fans since 1934, when the series was inaugurated. The greatest college players of the last eighteen years and most of the finest professionals have engaged in the intriguing pro versus college gridiron arguments.

This glamorous event in American football was conceived primarily as a means of raising money to help the poor. It has come through war and peace, depression and prosperity, as the top attraction in its field. Invariably it draws one of the largest crowds to see a football game, collegiate or professional, each season. No other event lures so many coaches, newspapermen, and athletic directors. And no other game pulls its audience from so vast an area. Nearly every state in the union is represented—as are many foreign countries—in the stacks of ticket applications.

During World War II, other sports extravaganzas, even including the major league baseball All-Star game, became casualties. But the All-Star football game had its most prosperous years and some of its most exciting contests after the United States entered the conflict. The All-Star game's survival was due, in no small measure, to the co-operation of the Army Air Force and the various collegiate conferences, which permitted use of undergraduates at a time when talent was scarce. In normal times, only athletes whose college eligibility has ended are invited to join the All-Star squad.

From the launching of the game in 1934, until 1942, the net revenue was divided equally among the United Charities, the Catholic Charities and the Jewish Charities of Chicago. In 1943, 1944 and 1945, profits of the enterprise were donated to war charities, such as the Army Air Force Aid Society and the Chicago Servicemen's centers, which made Chicago known as the most hospitable of all cities to the men in uniform.

We are grateful for the support the All-Star game has received, from both professional and collegiate football. A large percentage of football players among graduating seniors sign annually with the twelve National Football League clubs, whose owners relinquish the outstanding ones to the All-Star squad. The game, of course, has great exploitation value for the league.

The All-Star series is sponsored by Chicago Tribune Charities, Inc., which also sponsors the Golden Gloves competition. It, of course, is a non-profit organization.

Each year a staff of a half dozen or more collegiate coaches drill the stars assembled from all over the country. The present training site is Delafield, Wis., eighty miles from Chicago, and the squad is housed in St. John's Military Academy, whose facilities and cool climate are ideal for the rigid three weeks of preparation.

The game is held in August and the team which won the National League title the previous season automatically qualifies to meet the collegians. The All-Star game marks the first appearance of the professional team which comes into the new season as champion.

Invitation to the All-Star squad is the goal of most college players. In this day of commercialism we like to emphasize that it's the honor, not the money, which beckons to the young men. Each player, from the most gifted All-American quarterback to the linemen, receives $150 and expenses. Players prize the All-Star sweaters and blankets and the thrill of playing under the bright lights of Soldier Field. From the start, the $150 payment has been in effect.

Thrills have piled on thrills down the years to create a montage. But, in the blending of mental pictures from the floodlighted field, we still can clearly see the little giant, Eddie LeBaron, of the 1950 All-Star team, dancing away from tacklers, retreating far back—so far it seemed he would be nailed in his own end zone by on-rushing Philadelphia Eagles. Then we see Eddie finally throwing the ball and Charley "Choo Choo" Justice of North Carolina fielding it at about where the line of scrimmage had been and dashing 35 yards to score.

That was the most spectacular play in all the games contested to date. A 31-yard sprint by Justice had started the Collegians on their way to a touchdown in the first quarter against the startled Eagles, who had walloped the All-Stars the year before, 33–0. Later in the game, Justice rambled 47 yards. Sportswriters voted him the most valuable All-Star in the game. But if ever two awards were justified, that was the night, because College of the Pacific's LeBaron, five feet eight inches tall, was a mental giant among physical giants. After the game he joined the Marines and soon afterwards was fighting, and was later wounded, in Korea.

The professionals have won ten of the games, the Collegians six. The other two were ties. That's a respectable showing for the All-Stars against championship units. But never has the game been advanced primarily as a test of skill and strength between rival units. It is presented more as a spectacle, the grand and gala opening of the football season with all its pageantry and excitement. Fans thrill as much to the intermission musical shows as to the action on the field.

And it's the one game of the year when we are as rabid a fan as any in the vast reaches of the gray mass of concrete and steel off the shores of Lake Michigan!

ALL-STAR GAMES, 1934-1960

1934	Chicago Bears	0	All-Stars	0
1935	Chicago Bears	5	All-Stars	0
1936	Detroit Lions	7	All-Stars	7
1937	All-Stars	6	Green Bay Packers	0
1938	All-Stars	28	Washington Redskins	16
1939	New York Giants	9	All-Stars	0
1940	Green Bay Packers	45	All-Stars	28
1941	Chicago Bears	37	All-Stars	13
1942	Chicago Bears	21	All-Stars	0
1943	All-Stars	27	Washington Redskins	7
1944	Chicago Bears	24	All-Stars	21
1945	Green Bay Packers	19	All-Stars	7
1946	All-Stars	16	Los Angeles Rams	0
1947	All-Stars	16	Chicago Bears	0
1948	Chicago Cardinals	28	All-Stars	0
1949	Philadelphia Eagles	38	All-Stars	0
1950	All-Stars	17	Philadelphia Eagles	7
1951	Cleveland Browns	33	All-Stars	0
1952	Los Angeles Rams	10	All-Stars	7
1953	Detroit	24	All-Stars	10
1954	Detroit	31	All-Stars	6
1955	All-Stars	30	Cleveland	27
1956	Cleveland	26	All-Stars	0
1957	New York	22	All-Stars	12
1958	All-Stars	35	Detroit	19
1959	Baltimore	29	All-Stars	0
1960	Baltimore	32	All-Stars	7

1934 CHICAGO ALL-STAR GAME

(Soldier Field, Chicago, Ill., Aug. 31, 1934)

Attendance 79,432

Chicago Bears (0)		College All-Stars (0)
Hewitt	L.E.	Manske (Northwestern)
Lyman	L.T.	Krause (Notre Dame)
Carlson	L.G.	Walton (Pittsburgh)
Miller	C.	Bernard (Michigan)
Zeller	R.G.	Febel (Purdue)
Musso	R.T.	Schwammel (Oregon)
Johnsos	R.E.	Skladany (Pittsburgh)
Brumbaugh	Q.B.	Griffith (Southern California)
Ronzani	L.H.	Feathers (Tennessee)
Corbett	R.H.	Laws (Iowa)
Nagurski	F.B.	Mikulak (Oregon)

Chicago Bears	0	0	0	0—0
College All-Stars	0	0	0	0—0

Coaches—George Halas (Bears), Noble Kizer (Purdue).

SUBSTITUTIONS

Chicago Bears—Ends: Karr, Becker; tackle: Buss; guard: Kopcha, Zizak; center: Kawal; backs: Grange, Manders, Sisk, Westray.

All-Stars—Ends: Smith (Washington), Gillman (Ohio State), Canrinus (St. Mary's); tackles: Crawford (Duke), Mehringer (Kansas), Krueger (Marquette), Rosenquist (Ohio State), Maneikis (Chicago); guards: Jones (Indiana), Hupke (Alabama); centers: Vuchinich (Ohio State), Gorman (Notre Dame); backs: Everhardus (Michigan), Cook (Illinois), Pardonner (Purdue), Sebastian (Pittsburgh), Hecker (Purdue),

Lukats (Notre Dame), Montgomery (Columbia), Sauer (Nebraska), Cramer (Ohio State).

Officials: Referee—James Masker. Umpire—John Schommer. Field judge—Wilfred Smith. Head Linesman—J. J. Lipp.

THE GAME

The spirit and enthusiasm of the first of the brilliant lines of College All-Star squads held the methodical precision of the Chicago Bears, professional football champions, to a scoreless tie.

The Bears, who perhaps did not take their assignment too seriously, twice threatened to score after the All-Stars fumbled on reaching the major leaguers' 13-yard line the first time they had the ball. A 20-yard pass, Corbett to Ronzani, put the ball on the collegians' 10-yard line, late in the first quarter, but Corbett's wild lateral was recovered by the All-Stars' Schwammel.

Late in the third quarter, the All-Stars' Bill Smith missed a field goal from near midfield.

In the fourth period, the Bears reached the All-Stars' 26, aided by Red Grange's 22-yard pass to Johnnie Sisk, but the attack bogged down. Late in the game, Smith tried another field goal, this one from the Bears' 38, but it was low.

1935 CHICAGO ALL-STAR GAME

(Soldier Field, Chicago, Ill., Aug. 29, 1935)

Attendance 77,450

Chicago Bears (5)		College All-Stars (0)
Hewitt	L.E.	Hutson (Alabama)
Buss	L.T.	Blazine (Illinois Wesleyan)
Richards	L.G.	Monahan (Ohio State)
Kawal	C.	Shotwell (Pittsburgh)
Kopcha	R.G.	Bevan (Minnesota)
Musso	R.T.	Barber (San Francisco)
Karr	R.E.	Fuqua (So. Methodist)
Masterson	Q.B.	Munjas (Pittsburgh)
Feathers	L.H.	Shepherd (West. Maryland)
Sisk	R.H.	Nichelini (St. Mary's)
Manders	F.B.	Kostka (Minnesota)

Chicago Bears	3	0	0	2—5
College All-Stars	0	0	0	0—0

Field Goal—Manders. Safety—Shepherd.
Coaches—Frank Thomas (Alabama), George Halas (Chicago Bears).

SUBSTITUTIONS

Chicago Bears—Ends: Johnsos, Becker, Crawford: tackles: Trost, Rosequist; guard: Carlson; center: Miller; backs: Dunlop, Corbett, Pollock, Ronzani, Nagurski.

All-Stars—Ends: Morse (Oregon), Borden (Fordham), Larson (Minnesota), Leeper (Northwestern); tackles: Steen (Syracuse), Lee (Alabama), Bengston (Minnesota); guards: Mucha (Washington), Gundlach (Harvard), Barclay (No. Carolina), Schiarelli (Notre Dame); centers: Siemering (San Francisco), Ford (Michigan), backs: Salatino (Santa Clara), Regeczi (Michigan), Lund (Minnesota), Borries (Navy), Wetzel (Ohio State).

Officials: Referee—James Masker. Umpire—John Schommer. Field Judge—Wilfred Smith. Head Linesman—J. J. Lipp.

THE GAME

Jack Manders' 27-yard field goal from placement late in the first quarter, plus a safety in the fourth period, gave the Chicago Bears a 5 to 0 triumph over the All-Americans before a rain-soaked crowd of 77,450 in Soldier Field.

Thus, after two games in the brilliant series, not a single touchdown had been scored. The Bears were in command most of the time, but in the fifth minute of the final quarter, Alabama's Don Hutson all but got away for a touchdown on a stirring end around play. This threat, sparked by Hutson's 17-yard dash to the Bears' 8, ended after the collegians had reached the 5.

It was after the All-Stars had stemmed a Bear drive on their 3-yard line that Manders, following a 15-yard penalty for holding against the professionals, booted a field goal from the 27.

Beattie Feathers was the top ball-toter for the Bears, with 42 yards on 9 attempts. Bill Shepherd of Western Maryland gained 44 yards in 11 thrusts for the All-Stars.

1936 CHICAGO ALL-STAR GAME

(Soldier Field, Chicago, Ill., Sept. 3, 1936)

Attendance 76,000

Detroit Lions (7)		College All-Stars (7)
Klewicki	L.E.	Millner (Notre Dame)
Johnson	L.T.	Smith, R. (Minnesota)
Knox	L.G.	Tangora (Northwestern)
Randolph	C.	Jones (Ohio)
Emerson	R.G.	Oesch (Minnesota)
Christensen, G.	R.T.	Spain (S.M.U.)
Schneller	R.E.	Topping (Stanford)
Clark	Q.B.	Smith, R. (Alabama)
Christensen, F.	L.H.	Berwanger (Chicago)
Caddel	R.H.	Shakespeare (Notre Dame)
Parker	F.B.	Beise (Minnesota)

Detroit Lions	0	0	0	7—7
College All-Stars	0	7	0	0—7

Touchdowns—Caddel, LeVoir.
Points after touchdown—Clark, Fromhart.
Coaches—George Clark (Detroit), Bernie Bierman (Minnesota).

SUBSTITUTIONS

Detroit Lions—Ends: Ebding, Morse; tackle: Stacy; guards: Hupke, Monahan; center: Ritchart; backs: Presnell, White, Gutowsky, Shepherd, Nori.

All-Stars—Ends: Rees (Ohio State), Loebs (Purdue); tackles: Reynolds (Stanford), Stydahar (W. Virginia), Lutz (California); guards: Fortmann (Colgate), Gryboski (Illinois), Karcher (Ohio State); centers: Lind (Northwestern), Rennebohn (Minnesota); backs: Seidel (Minnesota), Fromhart (Notre Dame), Leemans (George Washington), Cruice (Northwestern), LeVoir (Minnesota), Crayne (Iowa), Maniaci (Fordham), Layden (Notre Dame), Lawrence (T.C.U.), Wilson (S.M.U.), Elser (Notre Dame).

Officials: Referee—Robert Cahn. Umpire—H. G. Hedges. Head Linesman—Ernest Vick. Field Judge—Maurice Meyer.

THE GAME

The College All-Stars marched 61 yards for a touchdown in the second period, and it wasn't until midway in the fourth quarter that the Detroit Lions matched those seven points for the second tie in the series, 7–7. The game was as even as the score indicated. Only five passes were completed, four of them by the collegians.

After a scoreless first quarter, the collegians scored when LeVoir went inside tackle for 17 yards. Fromhart added the point.

The third period was also scoreless; but in the fourth, the Lions recovered Leeman's fumble on their own 29 and drove home for the touchdown. Ernie Caddel going the last 10 yards on a lateral from Frank Christensen. "Dutch" Clark drop-kicked the extra point.

1937 CHICAGO ALL-STAR GAME

(Soldier Field, Chicago, Ill., Sept. 1, 1937)

Attendance 84,560

Green Bay Packers (0)		College All-Stars (6)
Hutson	L.E.	Tinsley (L.S.U.)
Smith	L.T.	Widseth (Minnesota)
Engebretsen	L.G.	Starcevich (Washington)
Svendsen, G.	C.	Svendsen, E. (Minnesota)
Evans	R.G.	Reid (Northwestern)
Gordon	R.T.	Daniell (Pittsburgh)
Gantenbein	R.E.	Wendt (Ohio State)
Bruder	Q.B.	Huffman (Indiana)
Sauer	L.H.	LaRue (Pittsburgh)
Herber	R.H.	Drake (Purdue)
Hinkle	F.B.	Francis (Nebraska)

Green Bay Packers	0	0 0	0—0
College All-Stars	6	0 0	0—6

Touchdowns—Tinsley (L.S.U.).
Coaches—Earl Lambeau (Green Bay), Bernie Bierman (Minnesota).

SUBSTITUTIONS

Green Bay Packers—Ends: Becker, Scherer; tackle: Butler; guards: Seibold, Michalske, Goldenberg, Schwammel, Letlow; center: Lester; back: Schneidman, Miller, Monnett, Laws, Johnson.

College All-Stars—Ends: Antil (Minnesota), Deutsch (St. Benedict's), Galatka (Mississippi State), Stromberg (Army); tackles: Dennerlein (St. Mary's), Bjork (Oregon), Henrion (Carnegie Tech), Kopczak (Notre Dame), Steinkemper (Notre Dame); guards: Lautar (Notre Dame), Bassi (Santa Clara), I. Smith (Ohio State), Dahlgren (Michigan State); centers: Basrak (Duquesne), Wiatrak (Washington); backs: Wilkinson (Minnesota), Baugh (T.C.U.), Agett (Michigan State), Wilke (Notre Dame), Cardwell (Nebraska), Jankowski (Wisconsin), Toth (Northwestern), Danbom (Notre Dame), Glassford (Pittsburgh), Haines (Washington).

Officials: Referee—Robert Cahn. Umpire—John Schommer. Field Judge—Joseph Magidsohn. Head Linesman—Maurice Meyer.

THE GAME

Samuel Adrian Baugh, a name which since became immortal in major league football, scored his first touchdown-pass against the Packers in this defensive thriller. Sixteen years later, Baugh held nearly every passing mark in the records and was still throwing them.

Baugh pitched one to Gaynell Tinsley from the Packer 47 in the first period. Tinsley caught it on the 25 and eluded both Hank Bruder and Joe Laws to score for the All-Stars.

There was no further scoring although both Arnold Herber and Bobby Monnett bombarded the collegians' defense trying to hit Don Hutson, or one of their other great receivers, to retrieve the game. But the defense was solid and Baugh's brilliant punting kept the Packers back on their heels until the final gun.

1938 CHICAGO ALL-STAR GAME

(Soldier Field, Chicago, Ill., Aug. 31, 1938)

Attendance 74,250

Washington Redskins (16)		College All-Stars (28)
Millner	L.E.	Schwartz (California)
Edwards	L.T.	Shirey (Nebraska)
Olsson	L.G.	Routt (Texas A & M)

Carroll	C.	Wolf (Ohio State)
Karcher	R.G.	Monsky (Alabama)
Barber	R.T.	Markov (Washington)
Malone	R.E.	Sweeney (Notre Dame)
Smith, R.	Q.B.	Puplis (Notre Dame)
Baugh	L.H.	Isbell (Purdue)
Pinckert	R.H.	Uram (Minnesota)
Krause	F.B.	Patrick (Pittsburgh)

| Washington Redskins | 7 | 3 | 0 | 6—16 |
| College All-Stars | 3 | 0 | 12 | 13—28 |

Touchdowns—Kovatch, Dougherty, Davis C., Uram, Krause, Karamatic.
Points after touchdown—Patrick, R. Smith.
Field Goals—McDonald, R. Smith.
Coaches—Ray Flaherty (Washington), Alvin N. "Bo" McMillin (All-Stars).

SUBSTITUTIONS

Washington Redskins—Ends: McChesney, Moore; tackles: Wilkin, Bond; guards: Young, Kahn; center: Parks; backs: Tuckey, Justice, Karamatic.
College All-Stars—Ends: Kovatch (Northwestern), P. Smith (Oklahoma), Birr (Indiana), Zachary (Purdue), Benton (Arkansas), Gustitus (St. Ambrose), Wolfe (Texas); tackles: Kinard (Mississippi), Kevorkian (Harvard), Babartsky (Fordham), Ryba (Alabama), Dixon (Boston U.); guards: Zarnas (Ohio State), Kuharich (Notre Dame), Reutz (Notre Dame), Calvano (Northwestern), Hoptowit (Washington State); centers: Nebel (Xavier), McCarty (Notre Dame), Dougherty (Santa Clara), Wegner (North-western), Gallagher (Yale); backs: McDonald (Ohio State), Vanzo (Northwestern), Davis (Indiana), J. White (Princeton), Spadaccini (Minnesota), Gmitro (Minnesota), B. White (Colorado), Rohm (L.S.U.), Heap (Northwestern), Coffis (Stanford), Cal-houn (Loyola, N.O.), Kilgrow (Alabama), Popovich (Montana), Hackney (Duke).
Officials: Referee—Thomas Hughitt. Umpire—E. C. Krieger. Field Judge—Lawrence Conover. Head Linesman—Fred Gardner.

THE GAME

For the first time in the series, offensive power ruled under the lights of Soldier Field as Cecil Isbell of Purdue led the All-Stars to a 28–16 triumph over the Washington Redskins. Baugh, the Redskin star, was handicapped by an ankle injury, but it is doubtful that this was a vital factor.

In the first quarter, Fred Shirey of Nebraska intercepted Baugh's pass and ran to the Redskin 11, where Jim McDonald booted a field goal to put the Collegians ahead. The 'Skins came back 73 yards, Max Krause going over for a touchdown from the four and Riley Smith adding the extra point for 7–3 as the period ended.

Smith kicked a 23-yard field goal in the second period and the Redskins led, 10–3, at the half.

The All-Stars scored two touchdowns in the third. Isbell passed 39 yards to John Kovatch for the first and Phil Dougherty intercepted Karamatic's pass to run 40 yards for the second. Both extra point attempts failed.

Corby Davis crashed over from the Redskin 4 on the first play of the fourth quarter after Baugh's punt had been blocked. Again the point was missed, making it 21–10. Baugh connected with Riley Smith to move to the All-Star one and Karamatic smashed for the touchdown. Andy Uram later scored again for the All-Stars when he intercepted Dick Tuckey's pass and scampered 40 yards.

1939 CHICAGO ALL-STAR GAME

(Soldier Field, Chicago, Ill., Aug. 30, 1939)

Attendance 81,456

| New York Giants (9) | | College All-Stars (0) |
| Poole | L.E. | Wyatt (Tennessee) |

Cope	L.T.	Mihal (Purdue)
Dell Isola	L.G.	Twedell (Minnesota)
Hein	C.	Brock, C. (Nebraska)
Tuttle	R.G.	Heikkinen (Michigan)
Mellus	R.T.	Haak (Indiana)
Howell	R.E.	Brown (Notre Dame)
Danowski	Q.B.	O'Brien (T.C.U.)
Cuff	L.H.	Goldberg (Pittsburgh)
Shaffer	R.H.	McLeod (Dartmouth)
Karcis	F.B.	Weiss (Wisconsin)

New York Giants	3	3	0	3—9
College All-Stars	0	0	0	0—0

Field Goals—Strong 2, Cuff.
Coaches—Steve Owen (New York), Elmer Layden (All-Stars).

SUBSTITUTIONS

New York Giants—Ends: Hanken, Walls; tackles: Widseth, Parry; guards: White, Lunday; center: Johnson; backs: Barnum, Burnett, Leemans, Falaschi, Strong.

College All-Stars—Ends: Jacunski (Fordham), Daddio (Pittsburgh), Young (Oklahoma), Coughlan (Santa Clara), Manders (Drake), Wysocki (Villanova), Wemple (Colgate); tackles: Wolff (Santa Clara), Beinor (Notre Dame), Voigts (Northwestern), Hale (T.C.U.), Schoenbaum (Ohio State); guards: Bock (Ohio State), Hovland (Wisconsin), Bell (Minnesota); centers: Hill (Duke), Kochel (Fordham), Aldrich (T.C.U.), Humphrey (Purdue); backs: Faust (Minnesota), Bottari (California), Osmanski (Holy Cross), Pingel (Michigan State), Patterson (Baylor), Sherman (Chicago), Jefferson (Northwestern), Seidei (Columbia), Buhler (Minnesota), Hofer (Notre Dame), Brunner (Tulane).

Officials: Referee—William Halloran. Umpire—Fred Young. Head Linesman—Lawrence Conover. Field Judge—Jay Wyatt.

THE GAME

The New York Giants, making their debut in the series, played the type of game expected of them—one featuring a rock-ribbed defense, and patience to wait for the breaks. They won the game with three field goals while holding the All-Stars scoreless.

Ward Cuff lofted the first one over from 27 yards out in the first period.

Ken Strong kicked the next, this one from 22 yards in the second quarter.

There was no scoring in the third quarter, and Strong wound up the scoring with a 33-yard shot in the last period.

Bill Osmanski of Holy Cross and Billy Patterson of Baylor were outstanding performers for the collegians.

1940 CHICAGO ALL-STAR GAME

(Soldier Field, Chicago, Ill., Aug. 29, 1940)

Attendance 84,567

Green Bay Packers (45)		College All-Stars (28)
Hutson	L.E.	Fisk (U.S.C.)
Ray	L.T.	Cutlich (Northwestern)
Letlow	L.G.	Logan (Indiana)
Svendsen, E.	C.	Turner (Hardin-Simmons)
Goldenberg	R.G.	Smith, H. (U.S.C.)
Lee	R.T.	Harvey (Notre Dame)
Gantenbein	R.E.	Sarkkinen (Ohio State)
Craig	Q.B.	Schindler (U.S.C.)
Isbell	L.H.	Kinnick (Iowa)
Laws	R.H.	Brock, L. (Purdue)
Hinkle	F.B.	Thesing (Notre Dame)

| Green Bay Packers | 14 | 14 | 7 | 10—45 |
| College All-Stars | 7 | 14 | 0 | 7—28 |

Touchdowns—Hutson 3, Mulleneaux, Uram, Isbell, Schindler 2, Washington, McFadden.

Points after touchdown—E. Smith 4, Engebretsen, Hutson, Kinnard 3, Kellogg.

Field Goal—E. Smith.

Coaches—Earl Lambeau (Green Bay), Dr. Edward Anderson (All-Stars).

SUBSTITUTIONS

Green Bay Packers—Ends: Mulleneaux, Jacunski, Berry, Temple; tackles: E. Smith, Schultz, Kell, Seibold, Kilbourne; guards: P. Tinsley, Zarnas, Engebretsen, Johnson, Midler, Marlin; centers: C. Brock, Greenfield; backs: Uram, Schneidman, Jankowski, Herber, Buhler, Balazs, Lawrence, Weisberger, Gillette, Feathers.

College All-Stars—Ends: Ivy (Oklahoma), Kavanaugh (L.S.U.), Anahu (Santa Clara), Gustafson (Penn), Winslow (U.S.C.), Seeman (Nebraska); tackles: Artoe (Cal), Kolman (Temple), Anderson (Stanford), Pedersen (Minnesota); guards: Brewer (Illinois), Waldorf (Missouri), Method (Northwestern), Riffle (Notre Dame), Morino (Ohio State); centers: Schiechl (Santa Clara), Haman (Northwestern), Kopcha (Chattanooga); backs: Van Every (Minnesota), Emmons (Oregon), Kellogg (Tulane), Hoffman (U.S.C.), Washington (U.C.L.A.), McFadden (Clemson), Heineman (Texas Mines), Sheridan (Notre Dame).

Officials: Referee—Robie Cahn. Umpire—Blake. Head Linesman—Reese. Field Judge—Taylor.

THE GAME

This was a free-scoring thriller with the collegians holding on gamely through the first half, then fading before the power and experience of the devastating Packer squad.

Ambrose Schindler opened the scoring for the All-Stars by smashing over from the one-yard line in the first period. Nile Kinnick kicked the conversion. Cecil Isbell fired a 60-yard pass to Don Hutson who ran 30 more to score for the Packers. Ernie Smith's conversion evened the score at 7-7. Isbell then passed 26 yards to Carl Mulleneaux in the end zone and Smith added the extra point.

Kenny Washington smashed over from a foot away in the second period and Bobby Kellogg's conversion evened the score at 14-14. Arnie Herber passed 18 yards to Andy Uram who scampered 42 more for a touchdown and Tiny Engebretsen converted. Isbell followed with a 35-yard pass to Hutson in the end zone and Smith booted the dividend. Nile Kinnick fired a pass of 38 yards to Banks McFadden who galloped the remaining 28 to touchdown country and Kinnick kicked the conversion to make it 28-21 at the half.

In the third period, Herber passed 29 yards to Hutson in the end zone and Smith converted. The All-Stars were held scoreless in this quarter.

Schindler crashed over from the one in the fourth period and Kinnick again converted. Ernie Smith booted a field goal for the Packers from the 34. Cecil Isbell ran 4 yards on a reverse for a TD and Hutson booted the extra point to make the final score 45-28.

Ambrose Schindler was chosen for the first Chicago *Tribune* award as the most valuable All-Star player.

1941 CHICAGO ALL-STAR GAME

(Soldier Field, Chicago, Ill., Aug. 28, 1941)

Attendance 98,203

Chicago Bears (37)		College All-Stars (13)
Plasman	L.E.	Rankin (Purdue)
Stydahar	L.T.	Pannell (Texas A & M)
Fortmann	L.G.	Lio (Georgetown)

Turner	C.	Mucha (Washington)
Musso	R.G.	O'Boyle (Tulane)
Artoe	R.T.	Drahos (Cornell)
Wilson	R.E.	Rucinski (Indiana)
Luckman	Q.B.	Evashevski (Michigan)
Nolting	L.H.	Harmon (Michigan)
McAfee	R.H.	Franck (Minnesota)
Osmanski, W.	F.B.	Paskvan (Wisconsin)

| Chicago Bears | 6 | 7 | 3 | 21—37 |
| College All-Stars | 6 | 0 | 0 | 7—13 |

Touchdowns—Kavanaugh, Clark 2, McAfee, Nowaskey, Franck, Robinson.
Points after touchdown—Manders 4, Lio.
Field goal—Artoe.
Coaches—George Halas (Chicago), Carl Snavely (All-Stars).

SUBSTITUTIONS

Chicago Bears—Ends: Kavanaugh, Manders, Nowaskey, Pool, Siegel; tackles: Kolman, Mihal, Federovitch; guards: Baisi, Forte, Bray, Lahar; center: Buck; backs: Swisher, Bussey, Clark, Martin, McLean, Lee, Monfort, Famiglietti, Maniaci.

College All-Stars—Ends: Elrod (Miss. State), Severin (N. Carolina), Vosberg (Marquette), Frutig (Michigan), Bodney (Tulane), Darnell (Duke), Uremovich (Indiana), Prochaska (Nebraska); tackles: Hartman (Rice), Routt (Texas A & M), Ruffa (Duke), Pavelec (Detroit); guards: Lokanc (Northwestern), Bucchianeri (Indiana), Sogn (U.S.C.), Alfson (Nebraska), Osa (Bradley), Kerasiotis (St. Andrews); centers: Whitlow (Rice), Hiemenz (Northwestern), Osterman (Notre Dame); backs: Matuszczak (Cornell), Thomson (Texas A & M), Paffrath (Minnesota), Schulte (Rockhurst), Christman (Missouri), McAdams (Washington), Jones (Richmond), O'Rourke (Boston College), Mallouf (S.M.U.), Rohrig (Nebraska), Gallarneau (Stanford), Robinson (U.C.L.A.), Banta (U.S.C.), Eshmont (Fordham), Standlee (Stanford), Piepul (Notre Dame), Davis (Duke), Kracum (Pittsburgh), McGannon (Notre Dame), Allerdice (Princeton).

Officials: Referee—W. H. Friesell. Umpire—John Schommer. Head Linesman—Ernie Vick. Field Judge—Frank Lane.

THE GAME

This All-Star squad was loaded but it was up against the fabulous Bear champions of 1940 who had exploded for the 73–0 annihilation of the Washington Redskins the previous fall. It was a case of a "good little team" facing a "good big team" and the one-sided result was inevitable.

Sid Luckman passed 27 yards to Ken Kavanaugh who ran 7 more for a touchdown to open the scoring in the first period. Jack Mander's try for the extra point was blocked by Ernie Pannell. Tom Harmon passed 22 yards to George Franck in the end zone to put the All-Stars even. This conversion attempt by Tony Ruffa was blocked by Joe Stydahar to end the quarter at 6–6.

Harry Clark plunged over from the 1 to score again for the Bears and Manders conversion was successful to end the half, 13–6.

In the third period Lee Artoe booted a 46-yard field goal for the Bears.

The All-Stars fell apart in the final period, after Charley O'Rourke tossed a touchdown to Jack Robinson who ran an additional 7 yards to score. (This was the same Jackie Robinson who later became the first Negro accepted as such in major league baseball, brilliant second baseman of the Brooklyn Dodgers.) Augie Lio kicked the conversion and the score was 16–13. The Bears opened the throttle then with Harry Clark smashing over from the 1 to set up Manders' conversion for 23–13. Luckman passed to McAfee in the flat and George ran 25 yards for another score with Manders again cashing the extra point. Young Bussey then passed 9 yards to Bob Nowaskey, Manders converted again, and the final score was 37–13.

George Franck of Minnesota was chosen for the Chicago *Tribune* award as the most valuable All-Star player. He later joined the New York Giants.

1942 CHICAGO ALL-STAR GAME

(Soldier Field, Chicago, Ill., Aug. 28, 1942)

Attendance 101,103

Chicago Bears (21)		College All-Stars (0)
Siegal	L.E.	Kutner (Texas)
Kolman	L.T.	Daniell (Ohio State)
Fortmann	L.G.	Jeffries (Missouri)
Turner	C.	Banonis (Detroit)
Bray	R.G.	Crimmins (Notre Dame)
Artoe	R.T.	Blozis (Georgetown)
Pool	R.E.	Ringer (Minnesota)
Luckman	Q.B.	Erdlitz (Northwestern)
Nolting	L.H.	Smith, B. (Minnesota)
Gallarneau	R.H.	Juzwik (Notre Dame)
Osmanski, W.	F.B.	Graf (Ohio State)

Chicago Bears	7	7	7	0 — 21
College All-Stars	0	0	0	0 — 0

Touchdowns—Gallarneau 2, Pool.
Points after touchdown—Stydahar 3.
Coaches—George Halas (Chicago), Robert Zuppke (All-Stars).

SUBSTITUTIONS

Chicago Bears—Ends: Nowaskey, Wilson; tackles: Stydahar, Hoptowit; guards: Drulis, Musso, Akin; center: Matuza; backs: Bussey, O'Rourke, Clark, McLean, Maznicki, Geyer, Famiglietti, Petty, Morris.

College All-Stars—Ends: Fitch (Minnesota), Rast (Alabama), Stanton (Arizona), Elbi (Notre Dame), Ringer (Minnesota), Meyer (Stanford), Kovatch (Notre Dame); tackles: Bauman (Northwestern), Odson (Minnesota), Eason (Oklahoma), Herndon (Nebraska), Lillis (Notre Dame); guards: Frankowski (Washington), Maddock (Notre Dame), Abel (Nebraska), Pukema (Minnesota), Sartori (Fordham); centers: Ingalls (Michigan), Gude (Vanderbilt), Lindskog (Stanford); backs: Cheatham (Auburn), Farris (Wisconsin), Hargrave (Notre Dame), Dudley (Virginia), Jacobs (Oklahoma), Moser (Texas A & M), Kmetovic (Stanford), Robertson (U.S.C.), Westfall (Michigan), Sweiger (Minnesota).

Officials: Referee—Ronald Gibbs. Umpire—E. C. Krieger. Head Linesman—Charles Berry. Field Judge—William Blake.

THE GAME

Although the great Bear team was about to disintegrate because of the demands of World War II, this squad still had enough inherent power to romp at will over the All-Stars. The comparatively small score was a restrained demonstration of the capabilities of the Halas crew.

Hugh Gallarneau plunged 4 yards for a touchdown in the first period and Joe Stydahar kicked the conversion.

In the second quarter, Young Bussey passed 24 yards into the end zone to Hampton Pool and Stydahar converted again to make it 14–0 at the half.

Hugh Gallarneau smashed for 8 yards and another TD in the third period and Stydahar's third conversion ended the scoring to make the final 21–0.

Tragedy was stalking two of the players. Young Bussey of the Bears was to die on the first day of the Lingayen invasion in the Philippines. Al Blozis of the All-Stars, who played for a while with the New York Giants, was to be killed by German machine-gun fire in the Vosges Mountains of France.

Bruce Smith was chosen as winner of the Chicago *Tribune* award as the most valuable All-Star player. He later became a member of the Green Bay Packers.

1943 CHICAGO ALL-STAR GAME
(Dyche Stadium, Evanston, Ill., Aug. 25, 1943)
Attendance 48,437

Washington Redskins (7)		College All-Stars (27)
Masterson	L.E.	Pihos · (Indiana)
Wilkin	L.T.	Wistert (Michigan)
Farman	L.G.	Bucek (Texas A & M)
Smith	C.	Lindskog (Stanford)
Slivinski	R.G.	Ramsey (William and Mary)
Shugart	R.T.	Wildung (Minnesota)
McChesney	R.E.	Huber (Notre Dame)
Hare, C.	Q.B.	Renfro (Washington State)
Baugh	L.H.	Graham (Northwestern)
Moore	R.H.	Steuber (Missouri)
Seymour	F.B.	Harder (Wisconsin)

Washington Redskins	0	7	0	0— 7
College All-Stars	7	7	6	7—27

Touchdowns—Harder 2, Graham, Steuber, Aguirre.
Points after touchdown—Harder 2, Graham, Masterson.
Coaches—Arthur "Dutch" Bergman (Washington), Harry Stuhldreher
(All-Stars).

SUBSTITUTIONS

Washington Redskins—Ends: Aguirre, Haloupek; tackles: Pasqua, Bentz, Zeno; guards: Leon, Florentino; centers: Carroll, Nolander; backs: Jenkins, Zimmerman, Bagarus, Masters, Farkas.
College All-Stars—Ends: Susoeff (Wash. State), Lister (Missouri), Smeja (Michigan), Currivan (Boston College), Sizemore (Furman), Karwales (Michigan); tackles: Kapter (Northwestern), Rhea (Oregon), Werkheiser (Duquesne), Barwegan (Purdue), Ashcom (Oregon), Irish (Arizona); centers: Remington (Wash. State), Ziemba (Notre Dame); backs: Farris (Wisconsin), Zapals (Texas A & M), Kennedy (Wash. State), Youel (Iowa), Trippi (Georgia), Dobbs (Tulsa), Silovich (Minnesota), Dewar (Indiana), Fenton (Mich. State), James (Ohio State), Filipowicz (Fordham), Clatt (Notre Dame), McKay (Texas).
Officials: Referee—E. F. Hughitt. Umpire—Dr. Raymond Huegel. Head Linesman—Charles Berry. Field Judge—Lloyd Larson.

THE GAME

The Redskins, under a new coach, were not even close to ready for this All-Star squad which contained a swarm of the professional stars of the future. Several of the All-Star recruits were to be top players in the NFL for the next decade.

Bob Steuber opened the scoring for the All-Stars when he scampered 50 yards on a punt return for a touchdown and Pat Harder made it 7–0 with the conversion.

Sam Baugh helped tie it up for the Redskins in the second by passing 5 yards to Joe Aguirre in the end zone for a touchdown. Bob Masterson converted. Later in the period Glen Dobbs threw 20 yards to Harder over the goal. Harder booted the extra point and it was 14–7 at the half.

In the third period, Otto Graham intercepted Sam Baugh's pass and ran 97 yards for a TD. Harder's conversion was blocked.

Harder ran 33 yards through tackle for a touchdown in the fourth quarter and Graham's conversion made it 27–7 for the final score.

Marlin "Pat" Harder was chosen for the Chicago *Tribune* award as the most valuable player of the All-Stars. He was to play again as a collegian in the 1946 game and then join the Chicago Cardinals to become, with Charley Trippi, Marshall Goldberg and Paul Christman, the "Dream Backfield" of the 1947 champions coached by Jim Conzelman.

1944 CHICAGO ALL-STAR GAME

(Dyche Stadium, Evanston, Ill., Aug. 30, 1944)

Attendance 49,246

Chicago Bears (24)		College All-Stars (21)
Benton	L.E.	Dugger (Ohio State)
Sigillo	L.T.	Willis (Ohio State)
Gudauskas	L.G.	Barwegan (Purdue)
Turner	C.	Tavener (Indiana)
Zorich	R.G.	Houston (Ohio State)
Hoptowit	R.T.	Zimny (Indiana)
Wilson	R.E.	Yonaker (Notre Dame)
Long	Q.B.	Saban (Indiana)
Nolting	L.H.	Dobbs (Tulsa)
McEnulty	R.H.	Trippi (Georgia)
Famiglietti	F.B.	Miller (Notre Dame)

Chicago Bears	0	14	7	3—24
College All-Stars	14	0	7	0—21

Touchdowns—Benton, Famiglietti, McLean, Miller, Tavener, Saban.
Points after touchdown—Saban 3, Gudauskas 3.
Field goal—Gudauskas.
Coaches—Heartley Anderson and Luke Johnsos (Chicago), Lynn Waldorf (All-Stars).

SUBSTITUTIONS

Chicago Bears—Ends: Berry, Smeja; tackles: Sweeney, Barbartsky; guards: Sprinkle, Musso; center: Mundee; backs: Luckman, Margarita, Mooney, McLean, Masters, Simonich.
College All-Stars—Ends: Huber (Notre Dame), Sizemore (Furman); tackles: McCafferty (Ohio State), Barnes (L.S.U.); guards: Jones (Tulsa), Kolesar (Michigan), Jabbusch (Ohio State), Hecht (Alabama), Gaziano (Holy Cross); center: Appleby (Ohio State); backs: Keuper (Georgia), Hillenbrand (Indiana), Jacoby (Indiana), Ford (Tulsa), Layden (Texas).
Officials: Referee—Ronald Gibbs. Umpire—E. C. Krieger. Head Linesman—John Kelly. Field Judge—H. C. Hedges.

THE GAME

The great Bear teams of the early 1940's were completely wrecked by war at this point in history. Only Luckman, Turner, Wilson and McLean were left to carry on the battle of the gridiron. Coach George Halas was in the Pacific with the Navy and the players were scattered all over the world. The Bears were lucky to squeak out a win on a last-period field goal.

The All-Stars scored first when Glenn Dobbs passed 4 yards to Creighton Miller for a touchdown and Lou Saban booted the conversion. Still in the first period, John Tavener recovered Dobbs' fumble and ran 12 yards for another score which Saban again converted to make it 14-0.

The Bears evened it up in the second quarter. Gary Famiglietti crashed 3 yards for the first score and Sid Luckman passed 12 yards to Jim Benton for another. Pete Gudauskas kicked both extra points and it was 14–14 at the half.

Saban plunged over from one yard away to score again for the All-Stars and kicked the conversion. The Bears pulled even when Ray McLean scampered 19 yards through tackle to score and Gudauskas again added the dividend.

In the last period, Gudauskas booted a field goal from the 13 to give the Bears a 24–21 victory.

Glenn Dobbs of Tulsa was chosen winner of the Chicago *Tribune* award as the most valuable player on the All-Stars. He returned to play in the All-Star game of 1947 before joining the Los Angeles Dons of the All America Football Conference.

1945 CHICAGO ALL-STAR GAME

(Soldier Field, Chicago. Ill., Aug. 30, 1945)

Attendance 92,753

Green Bay Packers (19)		College All-Stars (7)
Hutson	L.E.	Cook (Alabama)
Ray	L.T.	Zimmy (Indiana)
Kuusisto	L.G.	Tassos (Texas A & M)
Brock, C.	C.	Warrington (Auburn)
Goldenberg	R.G.	Burgeis (Tulsa)
Berezney	R.T.	Foster (Oklahoma A & M)
Mason	R.E.	Huber (Notre Dame)
Craig	Q.B.	Mitchell (Tulsa)
Comp	L.H.	Trippi (Georgia)
Brock, L.	R.H.	Greenwood (Illinois)
Fritsch	F.B.	Kennedy (Washington State)

Green Bay Packers	3	9	0	7—19
College All-Stars	0	7	0	0— 7

Touchdowns—McKay, Hutson, Scollard.
Points after touchdown—Hutson 2, Harmon.
Field goal—Hutson.
Safety—Kennedy.
Coaches—Earl Lambeau (Green Bay), Bernie Bierman (All-Stars).

SUBSTITUTIONS

Green Bay Packers—Ends: Goodnight, Jacunski, Luhn, Urban; tackles: Adams, Croft; guards: Tollefson, P. Tinsley; Sorenson, Bucchianeri; center: Flowers; backs: Starret, Akins, Laws, McKay, Rohrig, Perkins.

College All-Stars—Ends: Scollard (St. Joseph), Karmazin (Wake Forest), Sizemore (Furman), Lamb (Oklahoma), Dugger (Ohio State), McCafferty (Ohio State); tackles: Willis (Ohio State), Bentz (Tulane), Bell (Indiana), Crawford (Tennessee), Johnson (Kentucky); guards: Calcagni (Pennsylvania), Colhouer (Oklahoma A & M), Brown (Tennessee), Coffee (Indiana), Enich (Marquette), Jones (Tulsa), Buda (Tulsa); centers: Speegle (Oklahoma), Silovich (Marquette), Appleby (Ohio State); backs: Meek (Tennessee), Long (Tennessee), Stryzkalski (Marquette), Shedlosky (Tulsa), Moss (Tulane), Harmon (Michigan), Bondli (Pittsburgh), Horvath (Ohio State), Yates (Texas A & M), Allen (Pennsylvania), Schlinkman (Texas Tech), Singer (Arizona).

Officials: Referee—Ronald Gibbs. Umpire—E. C. Krieger. Head Linesman—John Kelly. Field Judge—William Blake.

THE GAME

In a hard-fought game, the champion Packers ground out a victory over a hard-fighting All-Star team that made them earn every point and every yard. Because of war, neither the pros nor the All-Stars were of their usual caliber.

The great Don Hutson opened the scoring for Green Bay in the first period with a 12-yard field goal.

The Packers benefited from an unusual safety in the second when Bob Kennedy intercepted Irv Comp's pass, ran forward to his own 2-yard line, then fled back of his own goal and was trapped for a safety. Later in the quarter, Herman Rohrig passed 30 yards to Roy McKay in the end zone and Hutson added the extra point to make it 12-0. Kennedy atoned for his lapse before the period was over when he threw a 28-yard pass to Nick Scollard, who scampered 35 more yards for a touchdown. Tom Harmon added the conversion, to make the score 12-7 at the half.

There was no scoring in the third period. In the fourth, Don Hutson intercepted a pass by Perry Moss and raced 85 yards for a touchdown, then added the extra point himself to end the game at 19-7.

Charley Trippi of Georgia was voted the Chicago *Tribune* award as the most valuable player of the All-Stars. He was soon taken into the Army, then returned to Georgia for another appearance in the All-Star game of 1947 before joining the Chicago Cardinals.

1946 CHICAGO ALL-STAR GAME
(Soldier Field, Chicago, Ill., Aug. 23, 1946)
Attendance 97,380

Los Angeles Rams (0)		College All-Stars (16)
Hickey	L.E.	Russell (Baylor)
Schultz	L.T.	Ruby (Texas A & M)
Matheson	L.G.	Grgich (Santa Clara)
DeLauer	C.	Godwin (Georgia)
Lazetich	R.G.	Ramsey (William and Mary)
Bouley	R.T.	Palmer (T.C.U.)
Pritko	R.E.	Heywood (U.S.C.)
Waterfield	Q.B.	Graham (Northwestern)
Gehrke	L.H.	Hillenbrand (Indiana)
Gillette	R.H.	Jones, W. (Tulane)
West	F.B.	Harder (Wisconsin)

Los Angeles Rams	0	0	0	0— 0
College All-Stars	7	0	7	2—16

Touchdowns—Hirsch 2.
Points after touchdown—Harder 2.
Safety—Against Washington of Los Angeles.
Coaches—Adam Walsh (Los Angeles), Alvin N. "Bo" McMillin (All-Stars).

SUBSTITUTIONS

Los Angeles Rams—Ends: Benton, Shaw, McDowell, Hamilton, Strode, Hightower; tackles: Eason, Johnson, Pasqua; guards: Mergenthal, Levy, Lear, Fawcett; centers: Naumetz, Harding, Scrubbs; backs: Reisz, Hardy, Washington, Farmer, Harmon, Banta, Wilson, Koch, Ruthstrom, Holovak, Sucic, Hoffman.

College All-Stars—Ends: Scollard (St. Joseph), Fitch (Minnesota), Morris (Northwestern), Yonaker (Notre Dame), P. Walker (Yale), Hasse (Amherst); tackles: Blandin (Tulane), Verry (U.S.C.), Stanley (Tulsa), Olenski (Alabama), Mitchell (Minnesota), Mieczkowski (Notre Dame); guards: Jungmichel (Texas), Kapter (Northwestern), Vogds (Wisconsin); centers: Pregulman (Michigan), Blackburn (Rice), Coleman (Notre Dame), Tavener (Indiana); backs: Hoernschemeyer (Indiana), Dekdebrun (Cornell), Dancewicz (Notre Dame), B. Walker (Yale), Hirsch (Wisconsin), Gafford (Auburn), Angsman (Notre Dame), Reynolds (Oklahoma A & M), Hankins (Oklahoma A & M), Doss (Texas), Nussbaumer (Michigan), Griffin (Illinois), Breslin (Michigan State), Saban (Indiana), Johnson (William and Mary).

Officials: Referee—Tom Dowd. Umpire—R. W. Finsterwald. Field Judge—William Blake. Head Linesman—Lloyd Brazil.

THE GAME

The Los Angeles Rams, who had won their championship in the Cleveland Municipal Stadium with the temperature at five degrees below zero, were colder than that when they faced this hopped-up squad of All-Stars. They were held scoreless while the collegians won comfortably, thanks to the sparkling running of Elroy "Crazy Legs" Hirsch of Wisconsin.

In the first period, Hirsch scampered 68 yards around his right for a touchdown and Pat Harder added the conversion. There was no scoring in the second quarter and the half ended 7–0.

Otto Graham fired a 38-yard pass to Hirsch in the second quarter for the second TD, and Harder again converted to put the All-Stars ahead 14–0.

In the fourth period, with the Rams on their own 13, Kenny Washington was smeared behind his own goal by Paul Walker for a safety, and the game ended 16–0.

Elroy Hirsch was chosen for the Chicago *Tribune* award to the most valuable All-Star player and reported immediately to the Chicago Rockets of the All America Football Conference.

1947 CHICAGO ALL-STAR GAME

(Soldier Field, Chicago, Ill., Aug. 22, 1947)

Attendance 80,054

Chicago Bears (0)		College All-Stars (16)
Kavanaugh	L.E.	Skoglund (Notre Dame)
Davis, F.	L.T.	Barwegan (Purdue)
Drulis	L.G.	Haase (Illinois)
Turner	C.	Cannady (Indiana)
Bray	R.G.	Humble (Rice)
Stickel	R.T.	Mastrangelo (Notre Dame)
Sprinkle	R.E.	Tereshinski (Georgia)
Luckman	Q.B.	Ratterman (Notre Dame)
McLean	L.H.	Young (Illinois)
Gallarneau	R.H.	Blanchard (Army)
Osmanski, J.	F.B.	Adamle (Ohio State)

Chicago Bears	0	0	0	0— 0
College All-Stars	13	0	3	0—16

Touchdowns—Mello, Zilly.
Points after touchdown—Case.
Field Goal—Case.
Coaches—George Halas (Chicago), Frank Leahy (All-Stars).

SUBSTITUTIONS

Chicago Bears—Ends: Wilson, F. Johnson, Karwales, Keane; tackles: Kolman, Ecker, Jarmoluk, Hartman; guards: Milner, W. Johnson, Preston; center: Clarkson; backs: Sacrinty, Seiferling, Gulyanics, Geyer, McAfee, Mullen, W. Osmanski, Holovak.
College All-Stars—Ends: Skoglund (Notre Dame), Souders (Ohio State), Poole (Mississippi), Zilly (Notre Dame), Scruggs (Rice), Hayes (Army), Baldwin (U.C.L.A.); tackles: Biles (Army), Moore (Penn State), Niedziela (Iowa), Esser (Wisconsin), Deal (Indiana), Cooper (Tulsa); guards: McBride (Notre Dame), Harris (Miss. State), Alvarez (Dartmouth), Hirsch (Northwestern), Collins (Texas), Clemons (St. Mary's), Knotts (Duke); centers: Cannady (Indiana), Gustafson (George Washington), Kodba (Purdue), Gray (Oregon State), Hellinghausen (Tulsa); backs: Tucker (Army), Cowhig (Notre Dame), Roberts (Chattanooga), Case (U.C.L.A.), Blanchard (Army), Trippi (Georgia), Rykovich (Illinois), Smith (Georgia), Adamle (Ohio State), Raimondi (Indiana), Cody (Purdue).
Officials: Referee—Carl Rebele. Umpire—Rollie Barnum. Head Linesman—Charles Berry. Field Judge—William Blake.

THE GAME

The Chicago Bears were far from their traditional top form for this contest and a series of surprising fumbles and miscues kept them continually back on their heels. The All-Star squad was heavy with talent and took advantage of many breaks to score a spectacular upset.

Jim Mello plowed over from the 6 to score in the first period and the score remained 6–0 when Ernie Case's conversion attempt was blocked. Later in the period, George Ratterman passed 36 yards to John Zilly for a touchdown and this time Case kicked the conversion. There was no scoring in the second period and the All-Stars led by 13–0 at the half.

Ernie Case booted a 21-yard field goal in the third period and that ended the scoring to give the All-Stars a 16–0 victory.

Claude "Buddy" Young of Illinois was chosen to receive the Chicago *Tribune* award as the most valuable All-Star player and reported immediately to the New York Yankees, at that time a member of the All America Football Conference.

1948 CHICAGO ALL-STAR GAME

(Soldier Field, Chicago, Ill., Aug. 20, 1948)

Attendance 101,220

Chicago Cardinals (28)		College All-Stars (0)
Dewell	L.E.	Cleary (Southern California)
Bulger	L.T.	Connor (Notre Dame)
Arms	L.G.	Weinmeister (Washington)
Banonis	C.	Scott (Navy)
Ramsey, G.	R.G.	Brown (Indiana)
Mauldin	R.T.	Czarobski (Notre Dame)
Kutner	R.E.	Ford (Michigan)
Christman	Q.B.	Lujack (Notre Dame)
Trippi	L.H.	Chappuis (Michigan)
Goldberg	R.H.	Conerly (Mississippi)
Harder	F.B.	Elliott (Michigan)

Chicago Cardinals	7 7	0	14—28
College All-Stars	0 0	0	0— 0

Touchdowns—Angsman, Schwall, Banonis, Trippi.
Points after touchdown—Harder 4.
Coaches—James Conzelman (Chicago), Frank Leahy (All-Stars).

SUBSTITUTIONS

Chicago Cardinals—Ends: Dove, Liebel, Ravensberg, Sortal, Doolan, Goldman; tackles: Szot, Coomer, Loepfe, Zimny, Jacobs; guards: Andros, Colhouer, Apolskis, Nichols; centers: Blackburn; backs: Eikenberg, Mallouf, Hanlon, Cochran, Dimancheff, deCorrevont, J. Davis, Schwall, Hollar, Angsman, Yablonski, Clatt.
College All-Stars—Ends: Fears (U.C.L.A.), Swiacki (Columbia), O'Connor (Notre Dame), Mann (Michigan), D. Foldberg (Army), Baumgardner (Texas), North (Vanderbilt), Halliday (S.M.U.), Maloney (Purdue), Owens (Illinois), Edwards (Georgia), Potsklan (Penn State); tackles: Yagiello (Catawba), Pritula (Michigan), Agase (Illinois), Urban (Notre Dame), Sullivan (Notre Dame), R. Davis (Georgia), Carrett (Miss. State), Prchlik (Yale), Smith (N. Carolina), Edwards (T.C.U.), Savitsky (Pennsylvania); guards: Suhey (Penn State), Werder (Georgetown), Wozniak (Alabama), Signaigo (Notre Dame), DiFrancesca (Northwestern), Olsonoski (Minnesota), O'Connor (Notre Dame), Gianelli (Boston College); centers: Nabors (Texas Tech.), Statuto (Notre Dame), Rhodemyre (Kentucky), White (Michigan), Strohmeyer (Notre Dame), Rapacz (Oklahoma); backs: Gray (U.S.C.), Gompers (Notre Dame), Mathews (Georgia Tech.), Sandifer (L.S.U.), Maves (Wisconsin), Wedemeyer (St. Mary's), Cline (Ohio State), Simmons (Notre Dame), Layne (Texas), Luongo (Pennsylvania).
Officials: Referee—William Downes. Umpire—Lylo Clarno. Head Linesman—Dan Tehan. Field Judge—William Blake.

THE GAME

The Chicago Cardinals were out to avenge the humiliating defeat suffered by the Chicago Bears in the previous game and were inspired as only Jim Conzelman could inspire men. They made a shambles of an All-Star team that was loaded with talent but seemed to lack teamwork and cohesion.

Elmer Angsman cracked over from the 2 in the first period and Pat Harder converted to give the Cardinals a 7–0 lead.

In the second quarter, Vic Schwall raced 14 yards through tackle for a touchdown and Harder converted to make it 14–0 at the half.

There was no scoring in the third period, but, early in the fourth, Vince Banonis intercepted Perry Moss's pass and raced 31 yards for the touchdown, Harder again converting. Later, Ray Mallouf passed 13 yards to Charley Trippi in the end zone and Harder's fourth conversion made the final score 28–0.

Jay Rhodemeyre, center from the University of Kentucky, was chosen for the Chicago *Tribune* award as the most valuable All-Star player and reported immediately to the Green Bay Packers.

1949 CHICAGO ALL-STAR GAME

(Soldier Field, Chicago, Ill., Aug. 12, 1949)

Attendance 93,780

Philadelphia Eagles (38)		College All-Stars (0)
Ferrante	L.E.	Poole (Mississippi)
Sears	L.T.	Petrovich (Texas U.)
Patton	L.G.	Wendell (Notre Dame)
Lindskog	C.	Bednarik (Pennsylvania)
Kilroy	R.G.	Fischer (Notre Dame)
Wistert	R.T.	DeRogatis (Duke)
Pihos	R.E.	Sheehan (Missouri)
Thompson	Q.B.	Mitchell (Oklahoma)
Van Buren, S.	L.H.	Taliaferro (Indiana)
Pritchard	R.H.	Williams (Washington State)
Muha	F.B.	Geri (Georgia)

Philadelphia Eagles	0	17	7	14—38
College All-Stars	0	0	0	0— 0

Touchdowns—Van Buren, Craft, Pihos, Doss, Armstrong.
Points after touchdown—Patton 5.
Field goal—Patton.

Coaches—Earl Neale (Eagles), College All-Stars, Charles "Bud" Wilkinson (Oklahoma).

SUBSTITUTIONS

Philadelphia Eagles—Ends: Armstrong, Prescott, Skladany, DiRenzo, Humbert, Green, Laster; tackles: Douglas, Savitsky, MacDowell, Hamberger; guards: Barnes, Maronic, Fusci, Magee, Gianelli; centers: Wojciechowicz, Szymanski, Donley, Yanelli; backs: Mackrides, Craft, Reagen, Ziegler, McHugh, Parmer, Pugh, Doss, Myers, Kish.
College All-Stars—Ends: Wimberly (Louisiana State), Brodnax (Georgia Tech.), O'Brien (Tulane), Cain (Alabama), Canady (Arkansas), Gagne (Minnesota); tackles: O'Reilly (Purdue), Niemi (Wash. State), Szafaryn (N. Carolina), Maddock (Northwestern), Bryant (Army); guards: Burris (Oklahoma), Stautzenberger (Texas A & M), Steffy (Army); centers: Walsh (Notre Dame), Sarkisian (Northwestern), Thompson (William and Mary), McCurry (Mich. State); backs: Tripucka (Notre Dame), Van Brocklin (Oregon), Elliott (Michigan), Di Marco (Iowa), Stuart (Army), Sims (Baylor), Guerro (Mich. State), Sullivan (Dartmouth), Doll (U.S.C.), Davis (Miss. State), Scott (Arkansas), McWilliams (Miss. State), Goode (Texas A & M), Rowan (Army), Jagade (Indiana), Benrick (Wisconsin), Greathouse (Oklahoma).
Officials: Referee—Ronald Gibbs. Umpire—M. G. Volz. Head Linesman—Charles Berry. Field Judge—Lawrence Ely. Alternates—William Downes, E. C. Curtis.

THE GAME

The Philadelphia Eagles were hot and relentless for this one. They piled up the score without pity and the All-Stars, although boasting several future professional stars, were outclassed.

After a scoreless first period, Steve Van Buren went over for the first touchdown from the one-yard line and Cliff Patton cashed the conversion to make it 7–0. Patton then kicked a field goal from the 14. Before the half ended, Russ Craft crashed over from the 4, Patton converted, and it was 17–0 at the rest period.

Tommy Thompson passed into the end zone to Pete Pihos in the third and Patton's conversion made it 24–0.

In the fourth quarter, Noble Doss plunged over from the 4, Patton again obliging with the extra point. Later in the period, Bill Mackrides passed 13 yards to Neill Armstrong and Patton's fifth conversion made the final score 38–0.

Bill Fischer of Notre Dame was chosen winner of the Chicago *Tribune* award as the most valuable All-Star player and reported immediately to the Chicago Cardinals.

1950 CHICAGO ALL-STAR GAME

(Soldier Field, Chicago, Ill., Aug. 11, 1950)

Attendance 88,885

Philadelphia Eagles (7)		College All-Stars (17)
Ferrante	L.E.	Weiner (North Carolina)
Sears	L.T.	Campora (College of the Pacific)
Patton	L.G.	Payne (Georgia)
Lindskog	C.	Tonnemaker (Minnesota)
Kilroy	R.G.	Hughes (William and Mary)
Wistert	R.T.	Manley (Oklahoma)
Pihos	R.E.	Martin (Notre Dame)
Thompson	Q.B.	Tidwell (Auburn)
Van Buren, S.	L.H.	Walker, D. (Southern Methodist)
Scott	R.H.	Haynes (Santa Clara)
Muha	F.B.	Morrison (Ohio State)

Philadelphia Eagles	0	0	0	7— 7
College All-Stars	7	7	0	3—17

Touchdowns—Pasquierello, Justice, Van Buren.
Points after touchdown—Soltau 2, Patton.
Field Goal—Soltau.
Coaches—Earle Neale, Edward Anderson.

SUBSTITUTIONS

Philadelphia Eagles—Ends: Armstrong, Green, Skladany, Hix, Willey, Humbert; tackles: Barnes, MacDowell, Jarmoluk; guards: Magee, Gianelli, Maronic; centers: Bednarik, Wojciechowicz; backs: Panciera, Reagen, Ziegler, Craft, Sutton, Parmer, Pritchard, Myers, Sanders.

All-Stars—Ends: Ison (Baylor), Hart (Notre Dame), Owens (Oklahoma), Soltau (Minnesota), Kersulis (Illinois), Wightkin (Notre Dame), McChesney (Hardin-Simmons), Rowe (Dartmouth); tackles: Nomellini (Minnesota), Sandusky (Villanova), Karras (Purdue), Creekmur (William and Mary), Kiilsgaard (Idaho); guards: Bagdon (Michigan State), Crawford (Mississippi), Winslow (Iowa), West (Oklahoma), Schweder (Pennsylvania); centers: Fuchs (Mississippi), Watson (Rice), Ulinski (Kentucky), Novak (Nebraska); backs: Burk (Baylor), LeBaron (College of the Pacific), Justice (N. Carolina), Chandnois (Michigan State), Chollet (Cornell), Swistowicz (Notre Dame), Hunsinger (Florida), Coutre (Notre Dame), Carpenter (Oregon State), Thomas (Oklahoma), Kempthorn (Michigan), Svoboda (Tulane), Pasquariello (Villanova), Murakowski (Northwestern), Mitchell (Stanford).

Officials: Referee—Emil Heintz. Umpire—John Wilson. Head Linesman—Charles Berry. Field Judge—William Blake. Alternates—William Downes, E. C. Krieger.

THE GAME

Inspired by the brilliant ball-handling of quarterback Eddie LeBaron and the elusive running of Charley "Choo-Choo" Justice, the All-Stars dominated the game throughout, the Eagles appearing sluggish and far off on their timing.

The All-Stars scored in the first period when Ralph Pasquariello smashed over from the 2 and Gordon Soltau converted.

In the second quarter, LeBaron passed to Justice for 35 yards and a touchdown, Soltau again converting to make it 14–0 at the half.

The third period was scoreless and the Eagles finally avoided a shutout in the last quarter when Steve Van Buren plunged over from one yard and Cliff Patton kicked the conversion.

Soltau put the game on ice for the All-Stars with a field goal from the 23 late in the quarter.

Charles Justice was chosen winner of the Chicago *Tribune* trophy as the most valuable All-Star player of the game and reported to the Washington Redskins. Eddie LeBaron, beaten in the ballot by a narrow margin, was also drafted by Washington but reported to the U.S. Marine Corps instead. Before the 1951 game was played, he had been wounded in Korea.

1951 CHICAGO ALL-STAR GAME

(Soldier Field, Chicago, Ill., Aug. 17, 1951)

Attendance 92,180

Cleveland Browns (33)		College All-Stars (0)
Speedie	L.E.	Stonesifer (Northwestern)
Groza	L.T.	Gain (Kentucky)
Gibron	L.G.	McFadin (Texas)
Gatski	C.	Groom (Notre Dame)
Houston	R.G.	Lynch (Illinois)
Rymkus	R.T.	McCormack (Kansas)
Lavelli	R.E.	Wilkinson (U.C.L.A.)
Graham	Q.B.	Williams (Notre Dame)
Bumgardner	L.H.	White (Arizona State)
Jones, W.	R.H.	Rote (S.M.U.)
Motley	F.B.	Dufek (Michigan)

Cleveland Browns	2	10	7 14—33
College All-Stars	0	0	0 0— 0

Touchdowns—Jones 2, Lavelli, Cole.
Points after touchdown—Groza 4.
Field Goal—Groza.
Safety—Williams.
Coaches—Paul Brown (Cleveland), Herman Hickman (Yale).

SUBSTITUTIONS

Cleveland Browns—Ends: Young, Gillom, Ford, Oristaglio; tackles: Kissell, Palmer, Grigg, Sandusky, Donovan; guards: Agase, Michaels, Schroll; centers: Herring, Thompson; backs: Lewis, Shula, Lahr, Carpenter, Loomis, James, Moselle, Adamle, Jagade, Cole.
College All-Stars—Ends: Allis (Michigan), Sherrod (Tennessee), Felker (Marquette), Schroeder (Virginia), Minarik (Michigan State), Pfeifer (Fordham), Wingate (Maryland); tackles: Krouse (Maryland), Joyce (Tulane), Stroud (Tennessee), Wahl (Michigan), Carapella (Miami, Fla.), Jackson (Texas), Tate (Illinois), Yowarsky (Kentucky); guards: Dodrill (Colorado A & M), Lemonick (Pennsylvania), Doyle (Tulane); centers: Moser (College of Pacific), Vohaska (Illinois), Holdash (N. Carolina), Rowden (Maryland); backs: Bagnell (Pennsylvania), Grandelius (Michigan State), Egler (Colgate), Ortmann (Michigan), Nagle (Nebraska), Douglass (Illinois), Hill (Tennessee), Konz (L.S.U.), Volm (Marquette), Gay (Notre Dame), Boydstun (Baylor), Campbell (Wyoming), Dottley (Mississippi).
Officials: Referee—Ronald Gibbs. Umpire—Ernest Vick. Head Linesman—Charles Berry. Field Judge—Jay Berwanger. Alternates—William Downes, Herbert Steiger.

THE GAME

The Cleveland Browns completed their amazing cycle of triumphs with a smashing 33–0 decision over the All-Stars. It followed four straight conference pennants in the All America Football Conference and the 1950 Championship of the National Football League. The game was no-contest although the All-Stars had plenty of talent. Cleveland defense dominated the game and the major leaguers scored almost at will.

In the first period, Kyle Rote's fumble was recovered in the end zone by Bob Williams to give Cleveland the first two points.

"Dub" Jones crashed 2 yards for a touchdown in the second period. Lou Groza kicked the point and later booted a 20-yard field goal for a 12–0 half-time lead.

Jones scored again, this time from the 3, to open the third quarter and Groza again converted.

In the last period, Otto Graham passed 10 yards to Dante Lavelli and 8 yards to Emerson Cole. Groza cashed both extra points.

Lewis "Bud" McFadin of Texas was chosen winner of the Chicago *Tribune* award as the most valuable All-Star player and retired after this game.

1952 CHICAGO ALL-STAR GAME

(Soldier Field, Chicago, Ill., Aug. 15, 1952)

Attendance 90,000 (est)

Los Angeles Rams (10)		College All-Stars (7)
Fears	L.E.	Sugar (Purdue)
Simensen	L.T.	Mitchell (UCLA)
Daugherty	L.G.	Coleman (Michigan)
McLaughlin	C.	Richter (Cal.)
Lange	R.G.	Ward (Maryland)
Dahms	R.T.	Pearman (Tennessee)
Hirsch	R.E.	Howton (Rice)
Waterfield	Q.B.	Parilli (Kentucky)
Towler	L.H.	Janowicz (Ohio State)
Smith, V.	R.H.	McElhenny (Washington)
Myers	F.B.	Boerio (Illinois)

Los Angeles Rams	0 0 0	10—10
College All-Stars	0 7 0	0— 7

Touchdowns—Younger (Los Angeles) ; Janowicz (All-Stars).
Points after touchdowns—Waterfield (Los Angeles) ; Janowicz (All-Stars).
Field Goal—Waterfield (Los Angeles).
Coaches—Joseph Stydahar (Los Angeles), Bobby Dodds (Geo Tech).

SUBSTITUTIONS

Los Angeles—Ends: Lane, Kreuger, Brink, Robustelli, Smith, F., Hacker, N.; tackles: Toogood, Dees, Green, Teeuws, Winkler, Casner; guards: Nanni, Putnam, Fry, Horrell, West; center: Paul; backs: Van Brocklin, Lewis, Quinlan, Williams, Kalmanir, Johnson, Ferguson, Towler, Younger, Reed, Townsend, Rich, English, Hecker, R.
All-Stars—Ends: Brewster (Purdue), Howton (Rice), Gandee (Ohio State), O'Donahue (Wisconsin), Carey (Michigan State), Lemmon (Cal.), Faverty (Wisconsin), McColl (Stanford), Thomas (Oregon State); tackles: Moss (Maryland), Mitchell (UCLA), Pearman (Tennessee), Snyder (Georgia Tech), Johnson (Michigan), Coleman (Michigan), Weatherall (Oklahoma), George (Wake Forest), Campbell (Georgia), Williams (Arkansas), Marchetti (San Francisco), Toneff (Notre Dame) ; guards: Price (Texas Tech), Beck (Georgia Tech), Macrae (Northwestern), Clark (Oregon State), Forester (SMU); centers: Kinson (Missouri), Mosely (Kentucky), Griffin (Arkansas); backs: Dorow (Michigan State), Karras (Illinois), Gifford (S. Cal.), Matson (San Francisco), Flowers (TCU), Wade (Vanderbilt), Crawford (Georgia Tech), Lauricella (Tennessee), Dooley (Miami, Fla.), Rechichar (Tennessee), Petitbon (Notre Dame), Kensler (Maryland), Reichardt (Iowa), Modzelewski (Maryland), Hughes (Michigan State), Toler (San Francisco), Tarasovic (LSU).
Officials: Referee—Ronald Gibbs. Umpire—Don Elser. Head Linesman—Dan Tehan. Field Judge—Dave Noble. Alternates—William Downes (NFL); Lyle Clarno (Bradley).

THE GAME

Rain had drenched the field during the afternoon and continued to fall through most of the game. The All-Stars outplayed the Rams during the scoreless first period, as well as the second when Vic Janowicz (Ohio State) plunged three yards to score the first TD, then placekicked the conversion to give the Stars a 7–0 halftime lead.

The third period was scoreless, but, with time running out, the Rams shifted into high gear for the final fifteen minutes to save the game. An interference penalty called against the Stars on their own seven-yard line on a pass play from Van Brocklin to Volney Quinlan, gave the Rams the break they needed. Van Brocklin quickly pitched to Paul "Tank" Younger for the score and Waterfield converted.

With seven minutes to play, Bob Waterfield kicked a 31-yard field goal to win the game.

Vito Parilli, of Kentucky, was chosen to receive the Chicago *Tribune* award as the most valuable All-Star and reported immediately to the Green Bay Packers.

1953 CHICAGO ALL-STAR GAME

(Soldier Field, Chicago, Ill., Aug. 14, 1953)

Attendance 93,818

Detroit Lions (24)		College All-Stars (10)
Box	L.E.	Flowers (Purdue)
Creekmur	L.T.	Gilbert (Mississippi)
Martin	L.G.	Moomaw (U.C.L.A.)
Banonis	C.	Morris (Georgia Tech)
Stanfel	R.G.	Sewell (Texas)
Cifelli	R.T.	Kimmel (Houston)
Hart	R.E.	Scott (Virginia)
Layne	Q.B.	Scarbath (Maryland)
Walker	L.H.	Bruney (Ohio State)
Hoernschemeyer	R.H.	Sears (U.S.C.)
Harder	F.B.	McPhail (Oklahoma)

Detroit Lions	7	3	7	7—24
All-Stars	0	3	0	7—10

Touchdowns—Detroit: Hoernschemeyer (2), Box. All-Stars: Gib Dawson (Texas).
Point after Touchdown—Detroit: Harder (3). All-Stars: Dale Samuels (Purdue).
Field Goals—Detroit: Walker. All-Stars: Dawson (Texas).

SUBSTITUTIONS

Detroit—Ends: Cain, Earon, Doran, Summerall, Gandee; tackles: Spencer, McGraw, Prchlik, Miller; guards: Flanagan, Bingaman, Schmidt; centers: Ane, Torgeson; backs: Christiansen, Carpenter, Retzlaff, Lary, Doll, Cline, Bailey, Mioduszewski, Smith, Hardy, Scott, Hill.

All-Stars—Ends: Wodziak (Illinois), Bell (Pennsylvania), Alderton (Maryland), Babcock (Georgia), Dekker (Michigan State), Stockert (UCLA), Forester (SMU); tackles: Little (Texas A & M), Modzelewski (Maryland), Matuszak (Tulsa), Hegarty (Villanova), Rimkus (Holy Cross), Miller (Georgia Tech); guards: Pertel (Navy), Michaels (Tennessee), Hager (Purdue), Athey (Baylor), Shalosky (Cincinnati), Barton (Clemson); centers: Brown (Georgia Tech), Cosgrove (Maryland); backs: Rhoden (Rice), Zatkoff (Michigan), Moorhead (Georgia Tech), Walker (SMU), Dawson (Texas), Wilson (Alabama), O'Connell (Illinois), DeCarlo (Georgia), Fullerton (Maryland), Samuels (Purdue), McAuliffe (Michigan State), Kozar (Tennessee), Sears (U.S.C.), Psaltis (U.S.C.), Morris (Georgia Tech), Olszewski (California), Tamburo (Michigan State), Flood (Notre Dame), Lakos (Vanderbilt), Sabol (UCLA).

Officials: Referee—Ronald Gibbs (NFL). Umpire—Don Elser (Notre Dame). Field Judge
—Cleo Diehl (Northwestern). Head Linesman—Sam Wilson (NFL).

THE GAME

The Detroit Lions scored a 24–10 victory over the College All-Stars in the 20th
annual meeting.

Detroit's Bobby Layne furnished most of the spark for the NFL champion Lions
as he established an individual passing record by completing 21 of 31 passes for 323
yards. Lions connected on 24 of 33 aerials for 339 yards (a team record) and accounted
for another team mark by picking up 21 first downs. In addition, Detroit was assessed
a record-breaking penalty total of 112 yards.

Detroit took a lead in the first quarter on an 80-yard march with the key play being
a Layne to Hart pass with a lateral to Walker that gained 47 yards. Hoernschemeyer
scored from the five and Harder converted to give Detroit a 7–0 advantage.

In the second period, after a short All-Star kick, the Lions moved to the collegians'
two-yard line from where Walker kicked a field goal to put Detroit in the lead, 10–0.
Gib Dawson, of Texas, later kicked a 23-yard field goal and the half ended 10–3 in
Detroit's favor.

A Layne to Box pass good for 53 yards set up the Lions' third quarter score and
when Layne again hit Box from eight yards out the Lions led 17–3 going into the final
period. Harder made the extra point attempt.

Each team scored in the fourth quarter. Detroit moved to the All-Stars two-yard line
as Layne passed successfully to Hart, Walker, Box, and Hoernschemeyer during the
drive. Hoernschemeyer drove around left end from the two for the score and Harder
again converted for a 24–3 lead. On an exchange of punts, USC's Jim Sears raced 73
yards to the Lion 17 and Dawson scored on an end sweep Dale Samuels converted, the
final score, 24–10.

1954 CHICAGO ALL-STAR GAME

(Soldier Field, Chicago, Ill., Aug. 13, 1954)

Attendance 93,470

Detroit Lions (31)		College All-Stars (6)
Dibble	L.E.	Massey (Texas)
Creekmur	L.T.	Morgan (Maryland)
Martin	L.G.	Hilgenberg (Iowa)
Torgeson	C.	Beatty (Mississippi)
Sewell	R.G.	Mavraides (Notre Dame)
Ane	R.T.	Jones (Maryland)
Hart	R.E.	Deitrick (Pittsburgh)
Dublinski	Q.B.	Bratkowski (Georgia)
Walker	L.H.	Hanulak (Maryland)
Christiansen	R.H.	Lattner (Notre Dame)
Carpenter	F.B.	Worden (Notre Dame)

Detroit Lions	17	0	7	7—31
All-Stars	0	0	6	0— 6

Touchdowns—Detroit: Walker, Carpenter 2, Doran. All-Stars: Lattner.
Conversions—Detroit:Walker 2, Girard, Martin.
Field Goal—Detroit: Martin.

SUBSTITUTIONS

Detroit—Ends: Candee, Box, Doran, Cain; tackles: McGraw, Miller; guards: Stanfel,
  Schmidt; center: Bingaman; halfbacks: Girard, David, Stits, Karilivacz; fullback:
  Hoernschemeyer.
All-Stars—Ends: Carson (Georgia), Sims (Marquette), Mischak (Army), Meilinger

(Kentucky), Gaskin (Clemson), Fenton (Iowa); tackles: Hunter (Notre Dame), Doud (U.C.L.A.), Whiteaker (Purdue), Chambers (Washington), Gressette (Clemson), Jagielski (Indiana); guards: Hantla (Kansas), Timberlake (U.S.C.), Branch (Texas), Mims (Mississippi), Clem (S.M.U.), Jacoby (Ohio State), Williams (T.C.U.); centers: Schrader (Notre Dame), Tanner (Stanford), McHenry (Washington & Lee); quarterbacks: Dooley (Auburn), Davidson (Baylor), Garrett (Stanford), McHan (Arkansas); halfbacks: Herkommer (Purdue), Cameron (U.C.L.A.), McElroy (Mississippi Southern), Norton (S.M.U.), Filipski (Villanova), Nolan (Maryland), Switzer (Kansas State), Cavazos (Texas Tech); fullbacks: Felton (Maryland), Casares (Florida), Allman (West Virginia).

Officials: Referee—Ron Gibbs (NFL). Umpire—D. A. Daniels (Atlantic Conference). Field Judge—Tatum Gressette (Atlantic Conference). Head Linesman—Dan Tehan (NFL).

THE GAME

The Lions scored a smashing 31–6 victory over the All-Stars and accomplished it without the services of their ace quarterback Bobby Layne. It was the Lions' second straight victory in the August classic. Detroit downed the All-Stars 24–10 in 1953.

Detroit took the lead on a field goal by Martin from the 37-yard line. A few moments later, Christiansen intercepted a Lattner pass at mid-field. From the 5-yard line Walker circled right end for a touchdown and kicked the extra point to give the Lions a 10–0 lead. Carpenter's touchdown gave the Lions a 17–0 lead at the end of the first quarter.

Dublinski, the Lions' quarterback fumbled on his own 4-yard line in the third quarter and the ball was recovered by the All-Stars' Jerry Hilgenberg. Lattner circled left end for the score. The try for the extra point was blocked.

Carpenter bowled over for his second score from the one and Martin converting to give the Lions a 24–6 lead.

Detroit finished up the scoring in the middle of the final period when end Doran grabbed Worden's fumble on the Stars' 34-yard line and sprinted into the end zone. Walker's conversion made the score Lions 31, All-Stars 6.

1955 CHICAGO ALL-STAR GAME

(Soldier Field, Chicago, Ill., Aug. 12, 1955)

Attendance 75,000

College All-Stars (30)		Cleveland Browns (27)
Boydston (Oklahoma)	L.E.	Brewster
Smith (Baylor)	L.T.	Groza
Bullough (Michigan State)	L.G.	Gibron
Szymanski (Notre Dame)	C.	Gatski
Brooks (Arkansas)	R.G.	Bradley
Varrichione (Notre Dame)	R.T.	McCormack
Hair (Georgia Tech)	R.E.	Lavelli
Guglielmi (Notre Dame)	Q.B.	Ratterman
Moegle (Rice)	L.H.	Renfro
Middleton (Auburn)	R.H.	Jones
Ameche (Wisconsin)	F.B.	Bassett

College All-Stars	3	14	3	10—30
Cleveland Browns	7	13	0	7—27

Touchdowns—All-Stars: Eldom, Hair, Triplett. Browns: Ratterman, Renfro 2, Morrison.
Conversions—All-Stars: Weed 2, Leggett. Browns: Groza 3.
Field Goals—All-Stars: Weed 3.

SUBSTITUTIONS

All-Stars—Ends: Hanifan (California), Bernet (Southern Methodist), Temp (Wisconsin),

Dugger (Ohio State); tackles: Lansford (Texas), Fournet (Louisiana State), Jones (Miami, O.), McCord (Tennessee), Boggan (Mississippi), Grier (Penn State); guards: Patera (Oregon), Palumbo (Notre Dame), Lamone (West Virginia), Louderback (San Jose State), Salsbury (U.C.L.A.), Bettis (Purdue), Kraemer (Pittsburgh), Mincevich (South Carolina); centers: Morris (Georgia Tech), Hazeltine (California), Morze (Boston College); quarterbacks: Larson (California), Carey (Notre Dame), Shaw (Oregon), Leggett (Ohio State); halfbacks: Weed (Ohio State), Waller (Maryland), Drzewiecki (Marquette), Weaver (Navy), Heap (Notre Dame), Bernardi (Colorado), Crow (Southern California), Dupre (Baylor), Eidom (Southern Methodist), Watkins (Ohio State); fullbacks: Hammack (Florida), Bielski (Maryland), Triplett (Toledo).

Browns—Ends: Ford, Massey, Hall, Gillom, Dillon; tackles: Gain, Sandusky, Kissell, Colo, Stone; guards: Macerelli, Noll, Forester; center: Weber; halfbacks: Paul, Konz, Dandoy, Lahr, Green, James, Smith, Petitbon, Ford, Robinson; fullbacks: Morrison, Michaels, Motley.

Officials: Referee—Thomas Timlin (NFL). Umpire—George Rennix (Western Conference). Field Judge—Mike Layden (Western Conference). Head Linesman—Dan Tehan (NFL). Back Judge—James Hamer (NFL).

THE GAME

Weed gave the All-Stars a 3–0 lead early in the first period by kicking a 21-yard field goal after Grier recovered a fumble by Bassett on the Browns 33.

Ratterman went over on a quarterback sneak. Groza converted and the Browns led, 7 to 3.

Ron Drzewiecki of Marquette returned the next kickoff 49 yards to the Browns' 43 and the All-Stars were on the way to their first touchdown. They drove to the two-yard line from where Frank Eidom plunged over. Weed's conversion made the score 10–7.

Renfro swept left end for 18 yards and the next touchdown and Groza converting to give the Browns a 14–10 lead.

Guglielmi completed four passes in an 80-yard drive, the last one going to Henry Hair in the end zone. Weed's conversion made it Stars 17, Browns 14.

The Browns came back to take a 20–17 halftime lead on Ratterman's pass to Renfro 18 seconds before the intermission.

The All-Stars lost little time tying the score, taking the second-half kickoff and marching into position for Weed's second field goal from 19 yards out.

The Stars then throttled the Browns' offensive and after an exchange of punts, Bettis intercepted a Ratterman pass and returned 17 yards to Cleveland's 43 to pave the way for another touchdown. Triplett plunged over for the touchdown and Leggett ran around end for the extra point.

A few minutes later Weed clinched the decision with his third field goal from the 41, after which the Browns came back for their only touchdown of the second half, a five-yard plunge by Morrison. Groza converted, making the final score, All-Stars 30, Browns 27.

1956 CHICAGO ALL-STAR GAME

(Soldier Field, Chicago, Ill., Aug. 10, 1956)

Attendance 75,000

Cleveland Browns (26)		College All-Stars (0)
Brewster	L.E.	Beagle (Navy)
Groza	L.T.	D'Agostino (Auburn)
Gibron	L.G.	Pitts (Texas Christian)
Gatski	C.	Pellegrini (Maryland)
Forester	R.G.	Huff (West Virginia)
McCormack	R.T.	Skoronski (Indiana)
Lavelli	R.E.	Holleder (Army)

Ratterman	Q.B.	Morrall (Michigan State)
Morrison	L.H.	Cassady (Ohio State)
Renfro	R.H.	McIlhenny (So. Methodist)
Modzelewski	F.B.	Schaefer (Notre Dame)

| Cleveland Browns | 7 | 6 | 6 | 7—26 |
| College All-Stars | 0 | 0 | 0 | 0— 0 |

Touchdowns—Cleveland Browns: Morrison (13-yard pass-run); Filipski (3-yard run).

Conversions—Cleveland Browns: Groza 2.

Field Goals—Cleveland Browns: Groza 4 (38, 30, 24 and 27 yards).

SUBSTITUTIONS

Cleveland Browns—Ends: Massey, Ford, Gillom, Weber, Gotta, J. Smith, French; tackles: Kissell, Colo, Sandusky, Macerelli; guards: Gain, Bradley, Robinson, Palumbo, Michaels; center: Furey; quarterback: Parilli; halfbacks: Lahr, Konz, Paul, James, Smith, Baldwin, Kinard, Lindo, Filipski, Wren; fullbacks: Bassett, Perini, Fiss.

College All-Stars—Ends: Katcavage (Dayton), Christensen (Richmond), Burnine (Missouri), Paluck (Pittsburgh); tackles: Goss (Southern Methodist), Herchman (Texas Tech), Wolf (Louisville), Krupa (Purdue), Brackett (Auburn); guards: Sardisco (Tulane), Murley (Purdue), Dittrich (Wisconsin), Morris (Oklahoma); centers: Klawitter (South Dakota State), Mence (Notre Dame); quarterbacks: Reichow (Iowa), Welsh (Navy), Haluska (Wisconsin); halfbacks: Glick (Colorado A. & M.), Losch (Miami), Moore (Penn State), Pajackowski (Richmond), Davis (Mississippi State), Vincent (Iowa), Carpenter (Arkansas); fullbacks: Chandler (Florida), Childress (Auburn).

Officials: Referee—Ronald Gibbs (NFL). Umpire—Don Elser (Big Ten). Field Judge—Mike Layden (Big Ten). Head Linesman—Dan Tehan (NFL). Back Judge—James Hamer (NFL).

THE GAME

The Cleveland team had little trouble trouncing this All-Star squad which was loaded with future big league talent but appeared to be badly prepared for the contest.

Ratterman passed 13 yards to Morrison for the first Cleveland score in the opening period. In the second quarter Groza, who had converted the first score, kicked field goals from 45 and 30 yards.

Groza kicked his third from 24 yards in the third period and his fourth in the same quarter from the 27.

In the fourth quarter Filipski smashed three yards for a Cleveland touchdown and Groza added another conversion. The final count was 26–0.

1957 CHICAGO ALL-STAR GAME

(Soldier Field, Chicago, Ill., Aug. 9, 1957)

Attendance 75,000

New York Giants (22)		College All-Stars (12)
Rote	L.E.	Kramer (Michigan)
Brown	L.T.	Vereen (Georgia Tech)
Huth	L.G.	Truax (Tulane)
Wietecha	C.	Amstutz (Indiana)
Stroud	R.G.	Sandusky (Maryland)
Yelvington	R.T.	Leggett (Louisiana State)
McAfee	R.E.	Maenz (Michigan)
Heinrich	Q.B.	Brodie (Stanford)
Gifford	L.H.	Arnett (U.S.C.)
Webster	R.H.	Woodson (Illinois)
Triplett	F.B.	Bosseler (Miami, Fla.)

New York Giants	3	7	7	5—22
College All-Stars	6	3	0	3—12

Touchdowns—New York Giants: McAfee 2 (38-yard pass and run from Conerly, 10-yard pass from Conerly). College All-Stars: Barnes (2-yard run).

Conversions—New York Giants: Agajanian 2.

Field Goals—New York Giants: Agajanian 2 (33 and 45 yards). College All-Stars: Cothren 2 (12 and 25 yards).

Safety—Woodson (tackled by Nolan in end zone).

SUBSTITUTIONS

New York Giants—End: Yowarsky, Schnelker, Bennett, Nery, Robustelli, Topp, Roberts; tackles: Modzelewski, Toogood, Wesley; guards: Huff, Spinks, Mangum, Burnham, Kennard; centers: Svoboda, Hesse, Livingston, Kitzelman; quarterbacks: Tunnell, Conerly, Clatterbuck; halfbacks: Hughes, Filipski, Mendyk, Moore, Patton, Nolan, Chandler, Crawford, Bookman; fullbacks: Epps, Deutschman, Agajanian.

College All-Stars—Ends: Lundy (Purdue), Walton (Pittsburgh), Michael (Ohio State), Shinnick (U.C.L.A.), Bomba (Indiana), Junker (Xavier); tackles: Owens (Mississippi Southern), Wharton (Maryland), Strugar (Washington), Bock (Illinois), Gordy (Tennessee), Jordan (Virginia); guards: Parker (Ohio State), Scorsone (U.C.L.A.), Wiggin (Stanford), DeLuca (U.S.C.), Nisby (College of the Pacific); centers: Tubbs (Oklahoma), Whitmire (Navy), Matsko (Michigan State); quarterbacks: Shofner (Baylor), Hornung (Notre Dame), Dawson (Purdue); halfbacks: Underwood (Arkansas), Barr (Michigan), Brown (Syracuse), Ridlon (Syracuse), McDonald (Oklahoma), Podoley (Central Michigan), Sutton (North Carolina), Harris (Oklahoma); fullbacks: Peaks (Michigan State), Barnes (Wake Forest), Johnson (Miami, Fla.), Cothren (Mississippi).

Officials: Referee—William Downes (NFL). Umpire—Don Elser (Big Ten). Field Judge—Corby Davis (Big Ten). Head Linesman—Dan Tehan (NFL). Back Judge—James Hamer (NFL).

THE GAME

The All-Stars scored first when Bock recovered a Webster fumble and the collegians rolled 55 yards, the final two-yard run by Barnes. The point after was missed.

The Giants struck back with field goal by Agajanian when Toogood recovered Barnes' fumble on the All-Stars' 25. Agajanian kicked from the 33 for three points.

In the second period the Giants scored their first touchdown with a 38-yard pass and run play, Conerly to McAfee. It was now Giants 10, All-Stars 6.

Paige Cothren kicked a 12-yard field goal for the All-Stars and the half ended with the Giants leading 10 to 9.

In the third period the Giants advanced 78 yards on 10 plays to their second touchdown. Conerly found McAfee open in the end zone for the touchdown from 10 yards out.

In the fourth period Conerly's excellent passing set up the last score for the Giants, a booming 45-yard field goal by Agajanian. The All-Stars retaliated when Cothren scored his second three-pointer from the 25. In the closing minutes of the game Nolan trapped Woodson in the end zone and the Giants scored two points to make the final score 22 to 12.

1958 CHICAGO ALL-STAR GAME

(Soldier Field, Chicago, Ill., Aug. 15, 1958)

Attendance 75,000

College All-Stars (35)		Detroit Lions (19)
Krueger (Texas A. & M.)	L.E.	Doran
Michaels (Kentucky)	L.T.	Creekmur
Kramer (Idaho)	L.G.	Sewell
Currie (Michigan State)	C.	Ane
Krisher (Oklahoma)	R.G.	Campbell
Hickerson (Mississippi)	R.T.	Russell
Gibbons (Iowa)	R.E.	Junker

Hill (Rice)	Q.B.	Rote
Pace (Michigan)	L.H.	Gedman
Conrad (Texas A. & M.)	R.H.	Cassady
Kowalczyk (Michigan State)	F.B.	Johnson

| College All-Stars | 0 | 20 | 2 | 13—35 |
| Detroit Lions | 7 | 0 | 6 | 6—19 |

Touchdowns—College All-Stars: Mitchell 2, Howley. Detroit Lions: Doran, Gedman, Pfeiffer.
Conversions—College All-Stars: Conrad 3 (place-kicks). Detroit Lions: Layne (place-kick).
Field Goals—College All-Stars: Conrad 4 (19, 44, 24 and 24 yards).
Safety—College All-Stars: Rote tackled in end zone.

SUBSTITUTIONS

College All-Stars—Ends: Dugan (Dayton), Jewett (Michigan State), Schulte (Eastern Kentucky State), Phillips (Auburn), Preston (Auburn), Cooke (Maryland), Hanson (Illinois); tackles: Jacobs (California), McCusker (Pittsburgh), Youso (Minnesota), Karras (Iowa), Healy (Maryland), Baker (North Carolina College); guards: Mitchell (Florida), Howley (West Virginia), Michaels (Villanova), Nicely (West Virginia), Stremic (Navy), Jobko (Ohio State); centers: Habig (Purdue), Walker (Idaho); backs: Christy (North Carolina State), Thomas (Oklahoma), Lynch (Notre Dame), Ninowski (Michigan State), King (Vanderbilt), Mitchell (Illinois), Taylor (Louisiana State), Forrestal (Navy), Lyles (Louisville), Krutko (West Virginia), Sommer (George Washington), Atkins (Auburn), Brown (Mississippi), Gordon (Tennessee), Jones (Washington), Nitschke (Illinois), Sample (Maryland State), Shofner (Texas Christian).
Detroit Lions—Ends: Mackey, Rychlec, Middleton, McCord; tackles: Glass, Mains, Miller, Perry, Martin; guards: Outten, Cunningham, Koepfer, Cronin; centers: Cunningham, Alderton; backs: Layne, Reichow, Pfeifer, Lewis, Tracy, Barr, Christiansen, David, Karilivacz, Lary, Long, Lowe, Muller, Schmidt, Webb, Zatkoff.
Officials: Referee—Ronald Gibbs (NFL). Umpire—Don Elser (Big Ten). Field Judge—Dr. Robert M. Jones (Big Ten). Head Linesman—Dan Tehan (NFL). Back Judge—Joe Muha (NFL).

COACHES

College All-Stars: Otto Graham. Detroit Lions: George Wilson.

THE GAME

Detroit moved eighty yards in ten plays to score on a 24-yard pass from Tobin Rote to Jim Doran at the 4:25 mark in the first period. Layne converted for a 7–0 bulge.

Another Lions drive later in the quarter was halted after reaching the All-Stars' 40-yard line by two fifteen-yard penalties that forced the Lions back to their own 35.

The collegians took over after a punt on their own 40 and on the second play, King Hill of Rice lobbed a short pass to Jim Pace of Michigan and he scampered 57 yards to the Lion three. Bobby Conrad of Texas A. & M. kicked a 19-yard field goal after the All-Stars were unable to penetrate deeper. Score: Lions 7, All-Stars 3. Time: 13:22.

An interception of a Layne pass in the second period ended another Lions drive on the All-Stars' 17. On the third down, Jim Ninowski, Michigan State, hit Bobby Mitchell of Illinois with a short pass and Mitchell streaked the rest of the way for an 84-yard touchdown play. Conrad converted and the Stars led, 10–7.

Again the Lions stormed back, this time reaching the All-Star eight-yard line, before Layne saw another pass fall into the hands of an All-Star defender, Lou Michaels. The collegians moved 72 yards in five plays, the score coming on an 18-yard toss to Mitchell that gave the Stars a 17–7 edge after Conrad's conversion.

A third Layne interception set up a 39-yard field goal by Conrad with 12 seconds remaining in the half and the collegians held a 20–7 margin at the intermission.

The Stars hiked their lead to 22–7 on the first series of the second half when Tobin Rote was tackled in the end zone on the third play from scrimmage.

Detroit picked up another touchdown in the third period after the Lions had moved from their own 34 to the Stars' 18, where a penalty put the ball on the nine. Gene Gedman bolted over to narrow the margin to 22–13, where it remained when Layne's extra point was blocked. Time: 6:31.

With four seconds gone in the fourth period, Conrad kicked his third field goal from 24 yards to make the score 25–13. The All-Stars took over again in the middle of the period on another key interception and Ninowski's passes moved the club to the 16 where the drive ended and Conrad connected again for a three-pointer from the 24-yard line with 7:57 gone. Fourteen seconds later it became 34–13 as Bobby Layne had his fifth pass intercepted by Chuck Howley and he returned 29 yards for another score. Again Conrad converted to make the score 35–13.

The Lions moved to the Stars' seven-yard line on their next drive but were halted as four straight Layne passes went incomplete. Moments later the Lions scored to cap a 35-yard march when Ralph Pfeiffer carried six straight times from the 13 to score with 28 seconds remaining. Layne's try for point was blocked and the All-Stars had their 35–19 decision over the Lions.

1959 CHICAGO ALL-STAR GAME

(Soldier Field, Chicago, Ill., Aug. 14, 1959)

Attendance 75,000

College All-Stars (0)		Baltimore Colts (29)
Williams (Michigan State)	L.E.	Berry
Karas (Dayton)	L.T.	Parker
Kelly (Michigan State)	L.G.	Spinney
Lewis (Iowa)	C.	Nutter
Guzik (Pittsburg)	R.G.	Sandusky
Beck (Texas A. & M.)	R.T.	Preas
Reifsnyder (Navy)	R.E.	Mutscheller
Ptacek (Michigan)	Q.B.	Unitas
Stacy (Mississippi State)	L.H.	Dupre
Baker (Oklahoma)	R.H.	Moore
Dove (Colorado)	F.B.	Ameche

Baltimore Colts	8	21	0	0–29
College All-Stars	0	0	0	0– 0

Touchdowns—Baltimore Colts: Berry (3-yard pass from Unitas); Mutscheller (29-yard pass-run from Unitas); Dupre (13-yard pass-run from Unitas); Davis (36-yard runback of intercepted pass).

Conversions—Baltimore Colts: Rechichar 3 (place-kicks).
Safety—Baltimore Colts: High pass from center into end zone.

SUBSTITUTIONS

College All-Stars—Ends: Dial (Rice), Sherer (S.M.U.), Kreitling (Illinois), Schleicher (Penn State), Wetosha (Notre Dame); tackles: Selawski (Purdue), O'Brien (Michigan State), Mumley (Purdue), Jacobs (Bradley), Geremia (Notre Dame), McFalls (V.M.I.), Blazer (North Carolina), Raid (Willamette); guards: Cvercko (Northwestern), Wooten (Colorado), Rabold (Indiana), Grottkau (Oregon), Churchwell (Mississippi), Beck (Western Illinois); centers: James (Ohio State); backs: Grosscup (Utah), Brown (Houston), Haley (Pittsburgh), Hickman (Baylor), Newman (Washington State), Dellinger (Texas Tech), Humphrey (Baylor), Austin (Rutgers), Dowler (Colorado), Morrison (Cincinnati), Nick Pietrosante (Notre Dame), Coronado (College of Pacific), Fowler (Northwestern), Jackson (Alabama), Petibon (Tulane).

Baltimore Colts—Ends: Rechichar, Joyce, Marchetti, Richardson, Braase; tackles: Plun-kett, Donovan, Lipscomb, Krouse; guards: Myhra, Smith, Pellington, Sanford, Addison, Matuszak; centers: Szymanski, Shinnick; backs: Brown, Lyles, Call, Pricer, Nelson, Hall, Johnson, Lewis, Carr, Davis, DeCarlo, Taseff, Sample, Simpson, Burkett, Unitas, Dupre, Moore, Ameche.

Officials—Referee: William Downes (NFL); Umpire: Don Elser (Big Ten); Field Judge: Dr. Robert Jones (Big Ten); Head Linesman: Cleo Diehl (NFL); Back Judge: Stanley Jaworowski (NFL).

COACHES

All-Stars: Otto Graham; Baltimore: Wilbur G. Ewbank.

THE GAME

After 12 scoreless minutes, James, center of the All-Stars, lofted the ball over the head of Sherer, back to punt, and it bounced through the end zone for an automatic safety. The Colts started to roll after the ensuing kick and scored their first TD on a 3-yard pass from Unitas to Berry. Myhra missed the extra point and it was 8–0 at the end of the period.

The Colts scored three more touchdowns in the second period. Addison recovered a fumbled punt by Stacy to set up a 29-yard Unitas to Mutscheller pass for a touchdown. Rechichar converted to boost the score to 15–0. Unitas threw a 13-yard pass to Dupre for a TD after marching 81 yards in 11 plays. Rechichar's conversion made it 22–0. Davis intercepted a Humphrey pass, two plays after the kickoff, and dashed 36 yards to paydirt. Rechichar added the extra point. The score at the half was 29–0.

There was no scoring in the second half.

1960 CHICAGO ALL-STAR GAME
(Soldier Field, Chicago, Ill., Aug. 12, 1960)

College All-Stars (7)		Baltimore Colts (32)
Dale (Virginia Tech)	L.E.	Marchetti
Denton (Col. Pacific)	L.T.	Donovan
Janerette (Penn State)	L.G.	Pellington
Lapham (Iowa)	C.	Szymanski
McGee (Duke)	R.G.	Shinnick
Gossage (Northwestern)	R.T.	Lipscomb
McInnis (Miss. Southern)	R.E.	Braase
Izo (Notre Dame)	Q.B.	Nelson
Gautt (Oklahoma)	L.H.	Sample
Moore (Vanderbilt)	R.H.	Davis
Mestnik (Marquette)	F.B.	Brown

Baltimore Colts	7	17	5	3—32
College All-Stars	0	0	0	7— 7

Touchdowns—Baltimore Colts: Moore (4-yard pass from Unitas); Moore (3-yard pass from Unitas); Moore (14-yard pass from Unitas). College All-Stars: Gautt (60-yard pass from Meredith).
Conversions—Baltimore Colts: Myhra 3 (place-kicks). College All-Stars: Khayat 1 (place-kick).
Field Goals—Baltimore Colts: Myhra 3 (38 yards, 27 yards, 26 yards).
Safety—Baltimore Colts: All-Stars' Izo tackled in his end zone.

SUBSTITUTIONS

College All-Stars—Ends: Cogdill (Washington State), Stickles (Notre Dame), Houston

(Ohio State), Cordileone (Clemson), Rochester (Michigan State), Youmans (Syracuse) ; tackles: Butler (North Carolina), Stallings (North Carolina), Brown (Maryland State), Prestel (Idaho), Magac (Missouri), Stynchula (Penn State) ; guards: Khayat (Mississippi), Mesner (Cincinnati), Leclerc (Trinity), Kirk (Mississippi), Leo (Cincinnati), Baughan (Georgia Tech) ; centers: Ellzey (Miss. Southern), Smith (Auburn), Burkett (Auburn), Stalcup (Wisconsin) ; backs: Kovac (Cincinnati), Meredith (S.M.U.), Bass (Col. Pacific), Beach (Central Michigan), Hall (Marquette), Maher (Detroit), Brewer (Mississippi), Britt (Georgia), Ellersick (Washington State), Doelling (Penn), Dean (Wichita), Franklin (Mississippi), Fichtner (Purdue), Acreman (Indiana), Mooty (Arkansas).

Baltimore Colts—Ends: Berry, Mutscheller, Richardson, Cooke, DeCarlo, Aho, Joyce, Colvin; tackles: Parker, Preas, Barnes, Plunkett, Guesman; guards: Spinney, Sandusky, Pyle, Myhra, Kompara, Bansavage; centers: Nutter, Matuszak; backs: Unitas, Sommer, Moore, Ameche, Hawkins, Lewis, Pricer, Boyd, Scudero, Radik, Welch, Taseff, Simpson.

Officials— Referee: William Downes (NFL). Umpire: Tony Skovex (Big Ten). Field Judge: Dr. Robert Jones (Big Ten). Head Linesman: Dan Tehan (NFL). Back Judge: Stanley Jaworoski (NFL).

COACHES

College All-Stars: Otto Graham. Baltimore Colts: Wilbur Ewbank.

THE GAME

The Colts gained possession of the ball early in the opening quarter and Unitas moved the ball 69 yards to the first touchdown. Key maneuvers in the Colt drive were Unitas passes of 41 and 18 yards to Moore and Mutscheller. Myhra converted and the Colts led 7–0 at the end of the quarter.

Marchetti recovered a Meredith fumble and the Colts advanced 95 yards to score on a three-yard Unitas to Moore pass. Myhra converted and later Myhra added a 38-yard field goal to boost the count to 17–0. Pellington intercepted a Meredith pass on the All-Stars 14, and Unitas hurled to Moore for six more points. Myhra's conversion made it 24–0 at the half.

In the third period the Colts picked up a safety when Izo was trapped in his end zone. Minutes later Myhra booted a field goal to increase the margin to 29–0.

The All-Stars avoided a shutout early in the fourth quarter when Meredith and Gautt collaborated on a screen pass for 60 yards and a touchdown. Khayat's conversion made the score 29–7. Boyd's interception and a 24-yard run with Hall's throw put Baltimore in position to close the scoring with a Myhra 26-yard field goal.

CHAPTER 7

THE AMERICAN
FOOTBALL LEAGUE

(Complete roster of AFL teams on pages 427 to 431.)

Born of frustration and nourished by television, the American Football League rushed into action in 1960. It competed head to head with National League teams in four of its eight cities and completed its schedule of games.

Since it was no more than an idea and a hope two years before the gun ended its first season, its owners could be proud of this beginning.

Lamar Hunt of Dallas, a 27-year-old heir to an oil fortune, had been trying to get into professional football for several years. A college player who found his love of the game increasing rather than leveling off, he had made approaches to buy an NFL team or to take over any new franchise that might be open.

After getting little response from the NFL, Hunt discussed in February of 1959, the possibility of forming a new league with C.K. "Bud" Adams, another young oil man who was equally interested in pro football. They went into action and before the summer of 1959 was over there were franchises allotted for Dallas, Houston, New York, Los Angeles, Denver, Buffalo and Boston.

Another was ready for Minneapolis-St. Paul, but the NFL moved in there with a franchise scheduled to begin play in 1961. This left an opening for Oakland to become the eighth AFL team.

Along with Hunt at Dallas and Adams at Houston, the league lined up its owners as follows: New York Titans—Harry Wismer, a veteran of many football activities; Los Angeles—Barron Hilton of the hotel chain family; Oakland—Y. "Chet" Soda and associates; Denver—Robert Howsam, and others; Boston—William H. Sullivan Jr.; and Buffalo—Ralph G. Wilson Jr. as owner.

(At the end of the 1960 season Los Angeles moved its franchise to San Diego.)

In November 1959, Joe Foss, ex-governor of South Dakota, was named Commissioner of the AFL. Foss had been a prominent air hero of World War II, but had had little experience in football.

The National League, remembering that its "war" with the All America Football Conference in 1946 to 1949 had been costly but had ended with unconditional surrender on NFL terms, watched the new league warily. There were some minor skirmishes in courts over rookie players who saw fit to sign contracts with both leagues, and over other players who chose to ignore contract obligations with NFL teams to join the AFL. The AFL won the court suits and retained control of some well-publicized rookies, learning later that some of them had not been worth fighting for.

The American Football League was the third league since 1921 to challenge the NFL. It faced a rush program of organizing, signing coaches and players and arranging coast-to-coast schedules.

The results of the first year were difficult to evaluate. Attendance was disappointing; public interest in the league was not great; the future was not clear. Only television money and the enormous wealth of a few owners and backers kept the league going at a time when the expenses of maintaining and fielding a professional team were astronomical.

Competition in the AFL was well balanced among the eight teams. But, in comparing the league to the short-lived All America Football Conference of 1946–49, the caliber of play was lower. There were no powerhouse teams such as the Cleveland Browns, who left the AAFC to become championship contenders in the NFL; there were no established stars of big league football such as the AAFC had kidnapped from the NFL in

1946. The eight teams were made up of older players who had dropped out of the NFL and of college rookies, whose quality and ability are always in doubt until tested by top professional standards.

The successful teams in the AFL were built around veterans of the NFL, usually quarterbacks, who still could play football, but who no longer had the skill to stay in the older league.

Several high-priced rookies, who had been signed by the AFL in direct competitive bidding against the NFL, proved to be disappointing treasures. The new league learned the hard way what established clubs had known for many years: an All-American rookie is not necessarily able to play big league football. Time would bring the realization that even with a roster of top-flight players it takes many years to mold an effective powerful team.

ROSTER OF COACHES

BOSTON PATRIOTS
Louis Saban

HOUSTON OILERS
Louis Rymkus

BUFFALO BILLS
Garrard Ramsey

LOS ANGELES CHARGERS
Sidney Gillman

DALLAS TEXANS
Henry Stram

NEW YORK TITANS
Samuel Baugh

DENVER BRONCOS
Frank Filchock

OAKLAND RAIDERS
Edward Erdelatz

STATISTICAL CHAMPIONS

BALL CARRYING

1960	Abner Haynes, Dallas			875 yards

SCORING

	TDs	FG	XPTs	Total
Eugene Mingo, Denver	6	18	33	123

FORWARD PASSING

	Atts.	Comp.	Yds.
Jack Kemp, Los Angeles	407	211	3,018

PASS RECEIVING

	Comp.	Yds.
Lionel Taylor, Denver	92	1,235

FIELD GOALS

Eugene Mingo, Denver	18

PUNTING

	Att.	Ave. Yds.
Paul Maguire, Los Angeles	43	40.5

FINAL STANDINGS

EASTERN DIVISION

	W	L	T	Pct.
Houston	10	4	0	.714
N.Y. Titans	7	7	0	.500
Buffalo	5	8	1	.385
Boston	5	9	0	.357

WESTERN DIVISION

	W	L	T	Pct.
L.A. Chargers	10	4	0	.714
Dallas Texans	8	6	0	.571
Oakland	6	8	0	.429
Denver	4	9	1	.308

Championship Game—

Houston   24   L.A. Chargers 16

CHAPTER 8
THE ALL AMERICA
FOOTBALL CONFERENCE

(Complete Roster of AAFC Teams on Pages 431 to 439.)

At the end of World War II, rumors were heard that a new professional football league was being formed. They disturbed the owners of the veteran National Football League who were jubilantly welcoming the return of several hundred players who had been in service—collegians who had gone directly from the campus to uniform as well as other products of the war-time boon in sports.

Out of these rumors, and a few false starts, came the All America Football Conference, organized by the late Arch Ward, sports editor of the Chicago *Tribune,* father of the All-Star football and All-Star baseball games, the man who raised Golden Glove boxing to unprecedented heights through inter-city and international bouts.

National Football League owners, painfully aware of the struggle they had gone through to establish the big league game from the days of 300 fans to crowds of more than 100,000, preferred to ignore both the rumors and the plans. They knew that, in spite of a quarter-century of progress, only four of their franchises could show an over-all profit, while dozens had fallen by the wayside. They said it was financial suicide to try to start another league, basing their opinion on these facts: that they had the best parks in the best cities; that they had the best coaches and the best players; that pro football was not a sound business for investment, particularly for beginners.

Ward's explanation was indicative of his promotional ability: "A man doesn't stand still," he said. "He either goes ahead or slips back. I could see several groups attempting to organize a new league, and, because football has always been the sport closest to my heart, I wanted to see the new group organized properly."

Those were the factors behind the professional football "war" of 1945–1949. It lasted four seasons. It was termed ruinous and catastrophic. It was hailed as the greatest boon the game has ever experienced.

The truth was somewhere between these extremes. It was a boon to the players with salaries forced upward by the law of supply and demand. It was ruinous to several owners who found that fans are fickle and are sure to support only a winner. It attracted to the major league game the most brilliant playing personnel ever assembled in one organization, and they remained after peace came, before the 1950 season. The rumblings, bickering and war-talk between the two leagues accomplished something else, intangible but vitally important to the growth of the game; they focused attention on professional football, created hundreds of thousands of new fans. Before the war it was almost impossible to find the results, even in single agate line, in Monday's papers; now entire pages are devoted to the thrilling stories, games are carried by radio and television from coast to coast. Each year more fans became fanatic devotees of professional contests.

When peace finally came, to start the 1950 season, it was generally recognized that the best college team would have little, if any, chance against an average professional team; that major league football had provided the game's most interesting advances such as the platoon system, the fifth official, the intricate development of the T-formation; that major league football was on a par with major league baseball, and perhaps more evenly balanced than big league baseball.

These facts had not been accepted by the general public previously.

It is doubtful that such developments were foreseen by the six men who met secretly in a St. Louis hotel room on June 4, 1944, to discuss the formation of the new group and to choose its name.

Ward, who had power of attorney for Arthur B. McBride of Cleveland, met with Sam Cordovano of Buffalo, Jack Keeshin of Chicago, Christy Walsh of Los Angeles, Ray Ryan of New York, and A. J. "Tony" Morabito of San Francisco. Cordovano, Walsh and Ryan had departed by the time the first game was played and Keeshin dropped out after the first season, but both McBride and Morabito—whose teams were powerhouses in the AAFC—were still very much in evidence in the NFL after the war ended.

Three months after the original meeting, representatives of the same half-dozen clubs met with "Gene" Tunney, who was interested in starting a club in Baltimore. (He, too, withdrew before the year was out, nearly two years before the first game was played.) Rules and regulations were adopted, player contracts drawn up, and James H. Crowley, formerly one of the "Four Horsemen" of Notre Dame, was elected president and commissioner. Mrs. Lou Gehrig was named secretary, Cordovano treasurer, at a meeting in April, 1945, a year and a half before a game was played. Buffalo, Chicago, Cleveland, Los Angeles, Miami and San Francisco were officially admitted to the AAFC and were followed, six months later, by Brooklyn, headed by William D. Cox.

It was during that April meeting that Paul E. Brown, later to coach the Cleveland Browns, was appointed, along with Jack Keeshin, to try to set up a working agreement with Elmer Layden, then Commissioner of the NFL.

They were unsuccessful, and it was at that time that Layden issued his widely quoted, and even more widely misunderstood statement: "Let them get a football and play a game and then maybe we'll have something to talk about." It is a matter of record that, after Layden was no longer commissioner, and the AAFC had weathered a couple of seasons that were spectacularly successful for a few teams and equally disastrous to others, Layden stated that, in his opinion, the time had come for the NFL to recognize the AAFC.

On October 23, 1945, announcement was made that Christy Walsh had withdrawn from the Los Angeles Dons organization and had been replaced by a syndicate, headed by Don Ameche, and including Ben F. Lindheimer, Louis B. Mayer, Lloyd Wright, Norman W. Church and Daniel F. Rice. This syndicate strengthened the embryo league enormously. Six weeks later another bombshell exploded when Daniel R. Topping stated that he was transferring his NFL club to the new conference because of inability to work out satisfactory dates and territorial agreements with the New York Giants. Topping had been operating in Brooklyn, but now, as part-owner of the Yankee Stadium and the baseball Yankees, he preferred to have his football team paying rent to his own corporation.

This move brought the conference to full strength with eight clubs: Buffalo (James F. Breuil who had replaced Cordovano as principle owner) ; Brooklyn (Cox) ; Chicago (Keeshin) ; Cleveland (McBride) ; Los Angeles (Lindheimer, principal stock-holder) ; Miami (Harvey Hester) ; New York (Topping) ; San Francisco (Morabito) . The roster of coaches was completed with Dudley DeGroot at Los Angeles, Dr. Mal Stevens at Brooklyn, Sam Cordovano at Buffalo, Dick Hanley at Chicago, Paul Brown at Cleveland, Jack Meagher at Miami, Ray Flaherty at New York, and Lawrence Shaw at San Francisco. Only Flaherty had previous major league experience. Cordovano resigned before the first season opened and was replaced by Lowell "Red" Dawson.

The first season, 1946, developed a pattern which was to remain static through the four years of the AAFC's existence. Cleveland dominated the Western Division without serious contention except from the San Francisco 49ers who were never quite good enough; the Eastern Division failed to develop any consistent team; its best was thrashed in four championship games by the Cleveland Browns. More than one hundred former

National Football League players had joined the AAFC, but the Conference failed to shine artistically from lack of experienced major league coaching. Cleveland won four titles, trouncing the New York Yankees in 1946, the same team in 1947, the Buffalo Bills in 1948 and San Francisco in 1949 (when the divisions had been abandoned because only seven teams played the season).

Owners and coaches had appeared and disappeared in the less successful locations. Admiral Jonas Ingram had been named commissioner in 1947 to succeed Crowley, who took over the Chicago Rocket coaching job for a few months. Ingram later gave way to O. O. Kessing in 1949, just before peace was made with the older NFL.

Prodigal intra-league bidding for top college stars was taking its toll in both leagues, and, just after the seasons ended in 1948, committees from the AAFC and NFL met in Philadelphia for "cease-fire" discussion. Nothing definite was decided at this time but the door cracked open wide enough to assure some kind of agreement in the near future. It was a year later that the AAFC was disbanded with Cleveland, San Francisco and Baltimore joining the NFL as complete units and the balance of the other players being put in a pool from which they were later drafted by the thirteen—at that time—clubs of the new NFL.

This consolidation of talent meant depth and balance for major league football. In the first season of the combined operation, the teams were so evenly matched that divisional tie play-offs were necessary in both sections of the NFL before the Cleveland Browns, still following the victory pattern, won the world championship from the Los Angeles Rams, 30–28, in a hair-raising game that was not decided until Lou Groza kicked a field goal for the Browns with eighteen seconds remaining in the game.

Baltimore, unable to develop either an acceptable team or fan support, departed after one disastrous season and the league assumed the more workable pattern of twelve franchises divided into two "Conferences," the "American" and "National."

The war had left countless casualties, particularly financial, but the American football fan had benefited by the development of the most exciting spectacle on the American sporting scene—a true major league schedule of football played at its roughest, most thrilling, best.

ROSTER OF COACHES

BALTIMORE COLTS

1947	Cecil Isbell
1948	Cecil Isbell
1949	Cecil Isbell
	Walter Driskill

BROOKLYN DODGERS

1946	Dr. Malcolm Stevens
	Thomas Scott
	Cliff Battles
1947	Cliff Battles
1948	Carl Voyles
1949	Disbanded

BROOKLYN— NEW YORK YANKEES

1946	Ray Flaherty
1947	Ray Flaherty
1948	Ray Flaherty
	Norman Strader
1949	Norman Strader

BUFFALO BILLS (BISONS)

1946	Lowell Dawson
1947	Lowell Dawson
1948	Lowell Dawson
1949	Lowell Dawson
	Clem Crowe

CHICAGO HORNETS (ROCKETS)

1946	Richard Hanley
	Robert Dove, Ned Mathews, Wilbur Wilkin, Pat Boland
1947	James H. Crowley
	Hampton Pool
1948	Edward McKeever
1949	Ray Flaherty

CLEVELAND BROWNS

1946	Paul E. Brown
1947	Paul E. Brown
1948	Paul E. Brown
1949	Paul E. Brown

LOS ANGELES DONS

1946 Dudley DeGroot
1947 Dudley DeGroot
     Mel Hein, and Ted Shipkey
1948 James M. Phelan
1949 James M. Phelan

SAN FRANCISCO 49ers

1946 Lawrence T. Shaw
1947 Lawrence T. Shaw
1948 Lawrence T. Shaw
1949 Lawrence T. Shaw

MIAMI SEAHAWKS

1946 Jack Meagher
     Hampton Pool

STATISTICAL CHAMPIONS

BALL CARRYING

1949	Fletcher Perry, San Francisco	783 yards
1948	Marion Motley, Cleveland	964 yards
1947	Orban Sanders, New York	1,432 yards
1946	Orban Sanders, New York	709 yards

FIELD GOALS

1949	Howard Johnson, New York	7
1948	Rex Grossman, Baltimore	10
1947	Ben Agajanian, Los Angeles	15
1946	Louis Groza, Cleveland	13

FORWARD PASSING

		Atts.	Comp.	Yds.
1949	Otto Graham, Cleveland	285	161	2,785
1948	Otto Graham, Cleveland	333	173	2,713
1947	Otto Graham, Cleveland	269	163	2,753
1946	*Glenn Dobbs, Brooklyn	269	135	1,886
	*Otto Graham, Cleveland	174	95	1,834

* Co-Champions

PASS RECEIVING

		Comp.	Yds.
1949	Mac Speedie, Cleveland	40	843
1948	Mac Speedie, Cleveland	58	816
1947	Mac Speedie, Cleveland	67	1,146
1946	Dante Lavelli, Cleveland	40	843

PUNTING

		Atts.	Ave. Yds.
1948	Glenn Dobbs, Los Angeles	68	49.1
1947	John Colmer, Brooklyn	56	44.7
1946	Glenn Dobbs	80	47.8

SCORING

		TDs	FG	XPTs	Total
1949	Alyn Beals, San Francisco	12	1	0	73
1948	Chester Mutryn, Buffalo	16	0	0	96
1947	Orban Sanders, New York	19	0	0	114
1946	Lou Groza, Cleveland	0	13	45	84

FINAL STANDINGS

1949

	W	L	T	Pct.
Cleveland	9	1	2	.900
San Francisco	9	3	0	.750
Bklyn-N.Y.	8	4	0	.667
Buffalo	5	5	2	.500
Chicago	4	8	0	.333
Los Angeles	4	8	0	.333
Baltimore	1	11	0	.083

Championship Game—
Cleveland 21, San Francisco 7

1948

WESTERN DIVISION

	W	L	T	Pct.
Cleveland	14	0	0	1.000
San Francisco	12	2	0	.857
Los Angeles	7	7	0	.500
Chicago	1	13	0	.071

EASTERN DIVISION

	W	L	T	Pct.
Buffalo	8*	7	0	.533
Baltimore	7	8*	0	.467
New York	6	8	0	.429
Brooklyn	2	12	0	.143

* Includes divisional play-off

Championship Game—
Cleveland 49, Buffalo 7

1947

WESTERN DIVISION

	W	L	T	Pct.
Cleveland	12	1	1	.923
San Francisco	8	4	2	.667
Los Angeles	7	7	0	.500
Chicago	1	13	0	.071

EASTERN DIVISION

	W	L	T	Pct.
New York	11	2	1	.846
Buffalo	8	4	2	.667
Brooklyn	3	10	1	.231
Baltimore	2	11	1	.154

Championship Game—
Cleveland 14, New York 3

1946

WESTERN DIVISION

	W	L	T	Pct.
Cleveland	12	2	0	.857
San Francisco	9	5	0	.643
Los Angeles	7	5	2	.583
Chicago	5	6	3	.455

EASTERN DIVISION

	W	L	T	Pct.
New York	10	3	1	.769
Brooklyn	3	10	1	.231
Buffalo	3	10	1	.231
Miami	3	11	0	.154

Championship Game—
Cleveland 14, New York 9

SCORING RULES

A Guide to Official Scorers of the National Football League

Official scorers shall be appointed by the Commissioner's office.

Official score sheets shall be compiled by transcribing play-by-play accounts recorded by the official scorer during the progress of the contest.

Official scorers shall retain their play-by-play accounts until the end of the season.

YARDAGE

All yardage shall be computed from the line of scrimmage, except in the case of field goals, which shall be measured from the spot of the kick.

Only net gains shall be computed in final tabulations.

Only yards gained from scrimmage, either by rushing, or by forward passing, shall be included in yards gained.

FIRST DOWNS

Any run or pass for a touchdown during a "Play from Scrimmage" by Team A, no matter what the length of the run or pass, shall now be credited as a first down. A touchdown runback does not count as a first down.

(Approved Ruling—Third down on B's 3, Team A scores a touchdown either by rushing or passing. Ruling: Team A is credited with a first down.)

(Approved Ruling—Second down on B's 15, during a rush Team A fumbles on B's 12 where B1 recovers. B1 fumbles, A1 recovers and runs for a touchdown. Ruling: Team A is not credited with a first down. The play "From Scrimmage" ended when B1 obtained possession. Therefore, the resulting touchdown was not made during a play from scrimmage but during one "Not From Scrimmage.")

FORWARD PASSES

Forward passes ruled complete by interference shall be scored as fouls with the passing team receiving credit only for a first down by penalty. The offending team shall be charged with a penalty and the distance (from the line of scrimmage to the spot of the interference) shall be added to its yards penalized.

(Note—The passer shall not be credited with a pass attempted, a pass completed, nor yards gained and the intended receiver shall not be credited with a pass received on interference plays.)

The forward passer shall be credited with a forward pass attempted when a forward pass is ruled intentionally grounded. Passer is not charged with an attempt if thrown for a loss.

Individual and team forward pass standings are computed on average gain per attempt. Divide the number of attempts into the number of yards gained. To qualify for championship rating a player must throw at least 100 passes during a season.

Separate classification shall be set up in the statistics on yards lost on passing attempts and said yardage shall not be deducted from yards gained passing by the individual passer. However the team statistics should show the net gain passing by subtracting from the total yards gained passing the amount lost by the individual passer or passers.

If a passer is thrown for a loss attempting to run the ball instead of passing, he should be credited with a ball carrying attempt and any loss deducted from his ball carrying yardage.

LATERAL PASSES

The category "Lateral Passes" has been eliminated. In all returns in ball carrying, forward passing, receiving and other classifications when a player makes a pass to another player during the course of a play the player receiving the pass will be credited for his advance. For instance, if a ball carrier advanced 25 yards and lateraled to another player who ran ten additional yards, the first player would be credited with a ball carrying attempt and a gain of 25 yards and the second player would not be credited with an attempt but with a gain of ten yards.

PUNTS

Punts over the goal line (touchbacks) shall be measured from the line of scrimmage to the goal line.

Player of receiving team shall be credited with a punt return when he recovers a blocked punt and advances beyond the spot of recovery. A player making a fair catch is charged with a punt return.

(Approved Ruling—Player of Team B falls on blocked punt. Ruling: No return. Player did not advance ball beyond spot of recovery.)

Blocked punts shall be enumerated on the score sheet under the space marked "Punting" and shall be scored as a punt attempted for the kicker and his team.

(Individual punt standings are computed on average distance. To qualify for cham-

pionship rating a player must punt twenty-four or more times a season.)

(Individual punt return standings are computed on the basis of average return. To qualify for championship rating a player must return twelve or more punts in a season.)

TOUCHDOWNS

Touchdowns shall be scored as "Touchdowns Running" and "Touchdowns Passing."

(Approved Ruling—Team A passes. Team B intercepts, but fumbles during the course of a return and Team A recovers, running the ball over for a touchdown. Ruling: Touchdown running.)

Touchdowns made on fumbles and returns of intercepted passes shall be scored as touchdowns running.

Touchdowns passing include plays that start with a forward pass and result in a touchdown for the offensive team. If the original receiver of the pass tosses the ball to another player on his team and the latter runs the remaining distance for the touchdown it is a touchdown passing. The passer is credited with a pass attempted, completed, a touchdown and with the yardage gained. The first receiver is credited with a pass received and the distance to the point where he passes to a teammate. The last receiver is not credited with a pass received but is credited under receiving with the actual yardage he gained and with a touchdown.

(Approved Ruling—Team B intercepts a forward pass and attempts a lateral pass, which is intercepted by Team A and run over for a touchdown. Ruling: Touchdown running on a fumble.)

Touchdowns scored by recovering a loose ball behind the goal line shall be scored as touchdowns running.

EXTRA POINTS

Players attempting conversions shall not be charged with an extra point missed when a bad pass from center or a fumble by the ball holder precludes an opportunity to kick.

(Note—Attempts at conversion which are blocked shall be scored as extra points missed.)

FIELD GOALS

Field goals shall be measured from the spot of the kick.

Unsuccessful field goal attempts shall not be scored as punts and no credit shall be given a player for returning such kicks.

(Note—Although unsuccessful field goal attempts run out from the end zone are not scored as punt returns, they shall be noted on the back of the official score sheet under remarks.)

(Approved Ruling—Player A, holding ball for field goal attempt, muffs snap or otherwise juggles ball long enough to prevent kicker from making attempt. Ruling: Player A charged with fumble and credited with fumble recovered.)

(Note—Kicker is not charged with attempted field goal if he does not actually kick.)

SAFETIES

Players of the team scored against shall not be credited with scoring safeties.

No individual credit shall be given opponents in the case of deliberate safeties.

Safeties shall be credited in individual scoring statistics to the player who downs an opponent behind the goal line, blocks a kick which results in a safety, causes a forward pass to become incomplete behind the passer's goal line or otherwise causes a safety through an individual effort.

No credit shall be given in individual scoring statistics for automatic safeties, except when automatic safeties are the result of blocked kicks, the breaking up of a forward pass behind the goal line or other individual effort on the part of Team B players.

(Approved Ruling—Center of Team A passes wildly beyond the end line. Ruling: Automatic safety. No safety credited to opponents in individual point table.)

(Approved Ruling—Player, in an attempt to run the ball out from behind his own goal line, slips and remains down, making no effort to continue the attempt. Ruling: Deliberate safety. No safety credited to opponents in individual scoring table.)

(Approved Ruling—Player, back to punt, steps on end line or out of the end zone. Ruling: Automatic safety. No safety credited to opponents in individual scoring table.)

FUMBLES

A fumble is any act, other than a pass or a legal kick, which results in loss of possession.

Loss of possession through an opponent's grabbing or striking the ball from a player's grasp shall be scored as a fumble.

Recovery out of the air by an opponent of a ball being juggled by a player shall be scored as a fumble. (EXCEPTION—Juggling of a forward pass by a receiver and recovery of such a juggled ball by an opponent is not scored as a fumble, but as an interception.)

Fumbles out of bounds shall be scored as fumbles recovered for the team and the player that last had possession of the ball in the field of play.

When a player of the offensive team recovers his own fumble, the play shall be scored as if he had not fumbled, in addition to being entered in the individual fumble table without any credit for an advance or loss.

When a fumble by a player of the offensive team is recovered by a teammate and advanced, the player who recovers shall be given credit in the individual fumble table for a fumble recovered and the yardage he advanced. The player who committed the error shall be charged with a fumble in the individual table.

All gains or losses with recovered opponents' fumbles shall be scored as returns.

(Note—Own fumble recovered designates recovery by the members of the fumbler's team as well as by himself.)

(Note—A back fumbles, recovers ball and advances. He should be charged with fumble and own fumble recovered. No credit is given for yards gained in fumble table but credit as yards gained running as part of original play. On fumble and recovery with loss of yardage, player and team charged with yards lost running and not in fumble table.)

FREE KICKS

Free kicks shall be scored as kick-offs if made from placement and as punts if punted, with the receiver getting credit for either a kick-off or a punt return.

KICK-OFFS

Kick-offs returned from the end zone are

measured from the spot in the end zone where the receiver gains possession of the ball.

(Individual kick-off returns are computed on the basis of average return. To qualify for championship rating a player must return twelve or more kick-offs in a season.)

ROSTER OF OFFICIALS, 1958

No.	Name	College
44	Austin, Robert	St. Ambrose
15	Bauer, Carl	Michigan
17	Beiersdorfer, James	None
31	Berry, Charles F.	Lafayette
23	Brubaker, Harry	Loyola (L. A.)
39	Castree, Gilbert	Virginia
57	Connell, Joseph	Pittsburgh
45	Cooperman, Samuel	Muhlenberg
37	Diehl, Cleo N.	Northwestern
3	Downes, William	Illinois Tech.
53	Evans, Lon	T. C. U.
12	Gardner, Cletus	Villanova
10	Giangreco, Samuel	Manhattan
5	Gibbs, Ronald	St. Thomas
7	Glascott, John A.	Pennsylvania
54	Gonzales, Joseph	U. S. C.
49	Hamer, James E.	Cal. State Teachers
9	Heintz, Emil	Pennsylvania
48	Highberger, John	Carnegie Tech
58	Hutchison, Elvin	U. S. C.
29	Jaworowski, Stanley	Georgetown
38	Kane, James A.	Loyola (Md.)
33	Knight, Warren	Carnegie Tech
16	Lisetski, Michael	Muhlenberg
59	Looney, Don	T. C. U.
35	Mitchell, Orrel	Georgetown
41	Nix, Jack	U. S. C.
43	Muha, Joseph	V. M. I.
55	Pace, John	Illinois
51	Palazzi, Louis	Penn State
40	Pritko, Steve	Villanova
52	Rennix, George	Minnesota
27	Rohrig, Herman	Nebraska
18	Sacco, Tony	St. Ambrose
56	Schachter, Norman	Alfred
20	Sinkovitz, Frank	Duke
44	Smith, George	California
22	Sweeney, Charles	Notre Dame
36	Tehen, Daniel	Xavier (Ohio)
34	Wallace, Yans	None
46	Wiesenbaugh, Henry	Pittsburgh

SEATING DIAGRAMS OF NFL STADIUMS

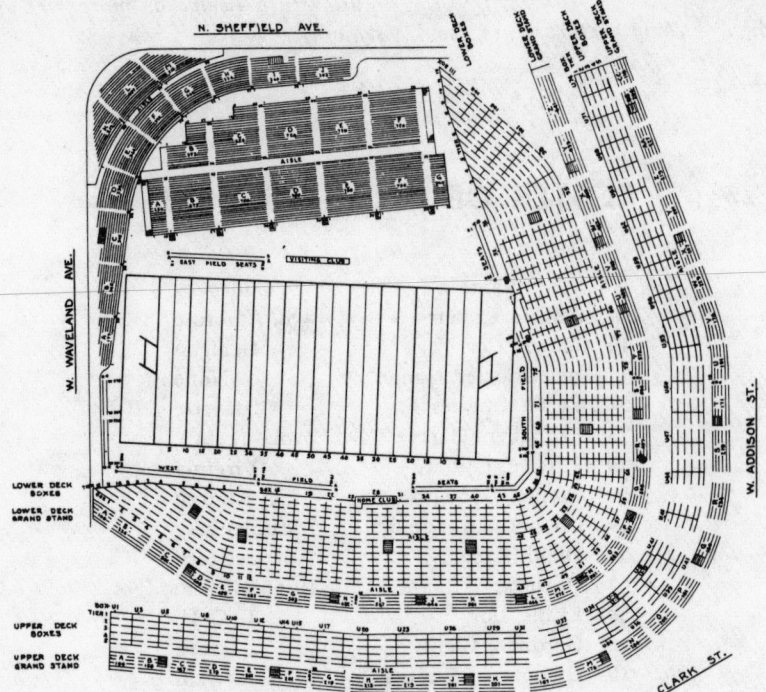

WRIGLEY FIELD, CHICAGO—HOME OF THE BEARS

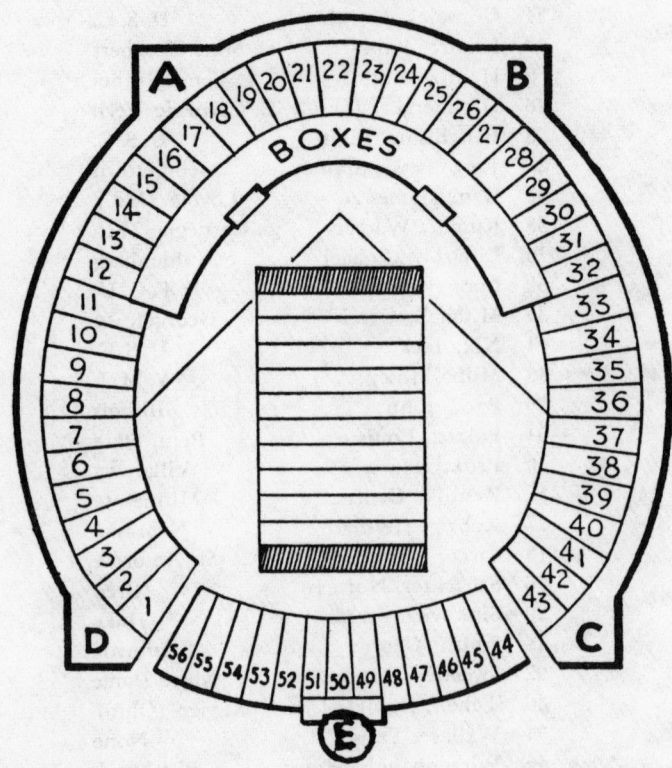

MUNICIPAL STADIUM, CLEVELAND—HOME OF THE BROWNS

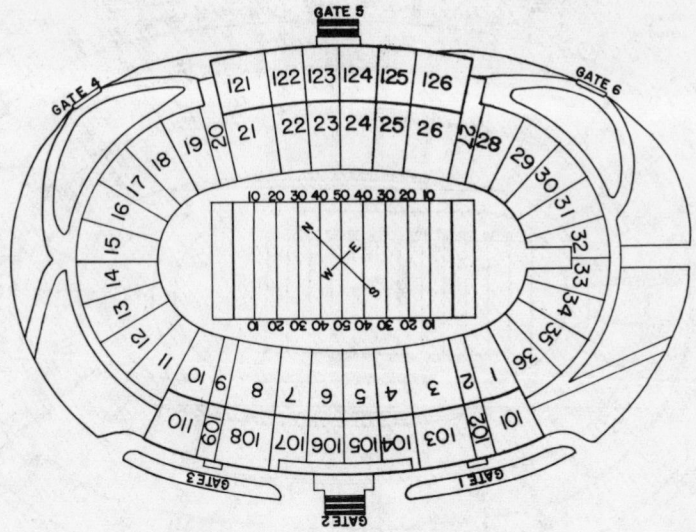

THE COTTON BOWL, DALLAS—HOME OF THE COWBOYS

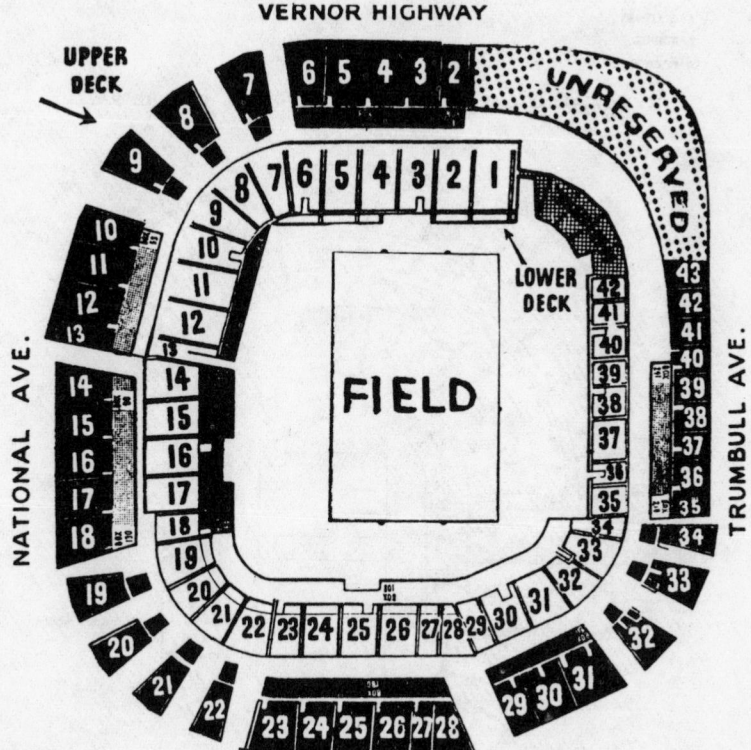

BRIGGS STADIUM, DETROIT—HOME OF THE LIONS

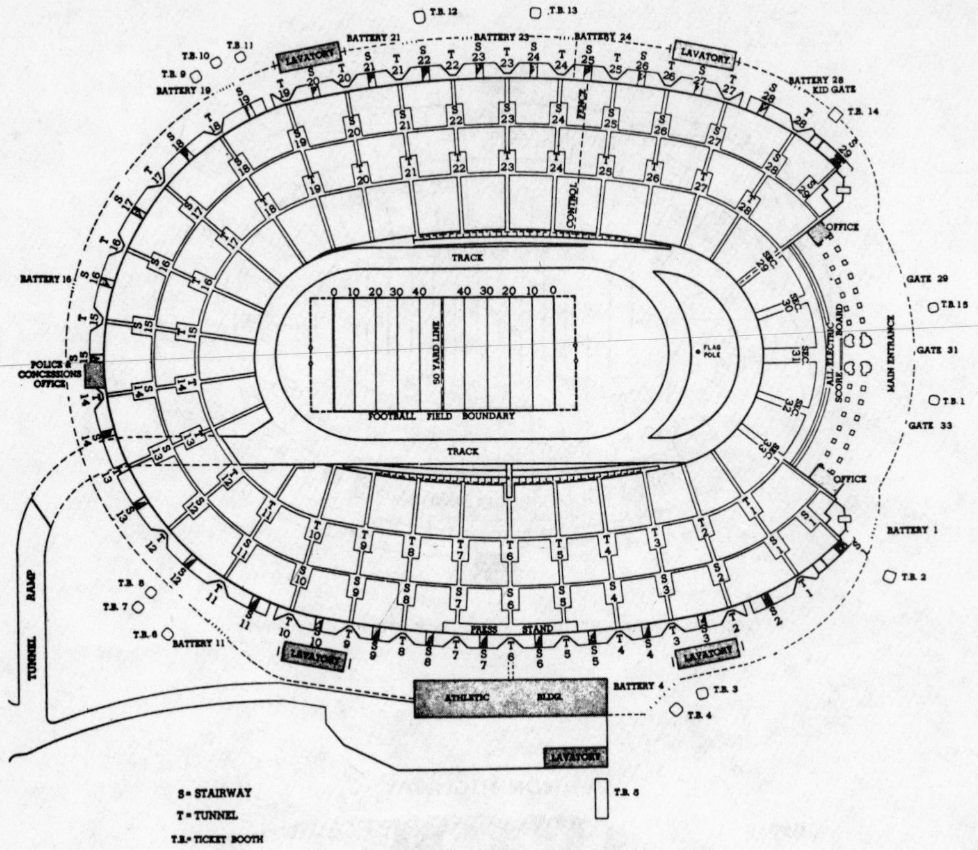

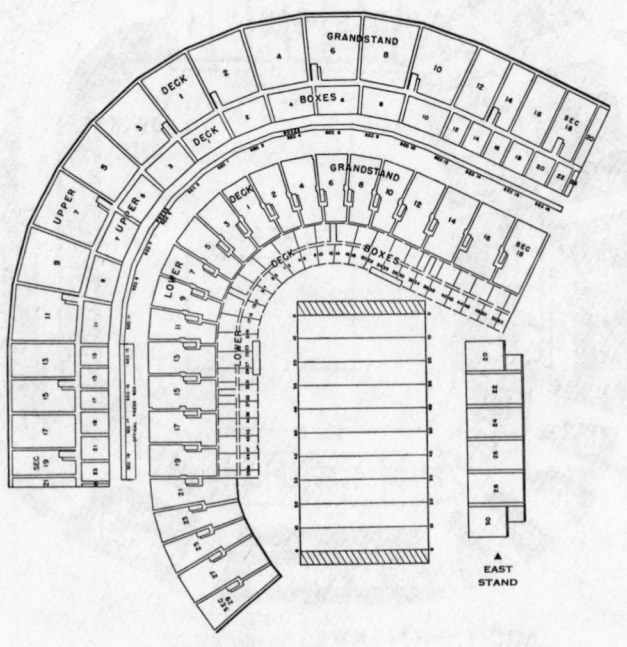

S = STAIRWAY

T = TUNNEL

T.B.= TICKET BOOTH

MEMORIAL COLISEUM, LOS ANGELES—HOME OF THE RAMS

COUNTY STADIUM, MILWAUKEE—HOME OF THE PACKERS

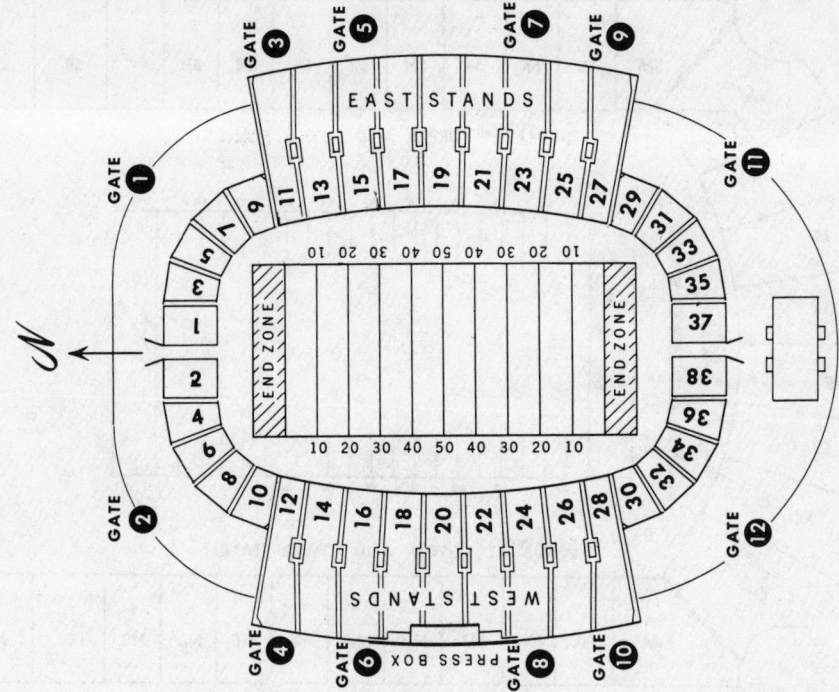

GREEN BAY STADIUM—HOME OF PACKERS

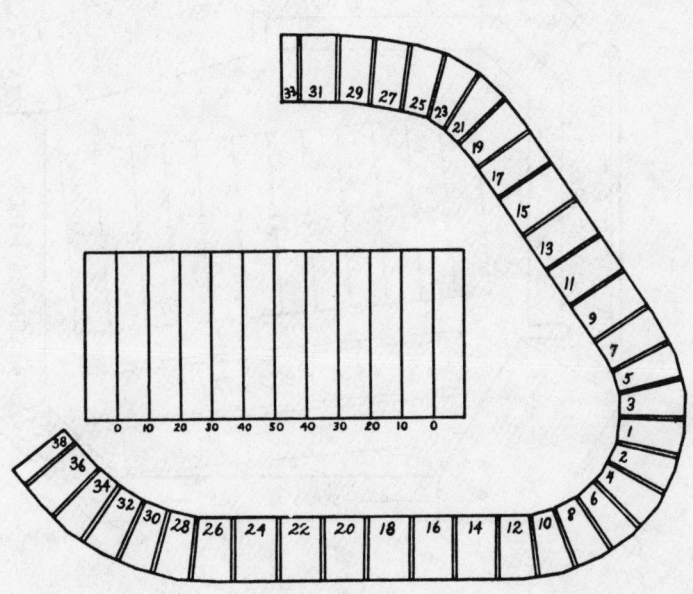

YANKEE STADIUM, NEW YORK CITY—HOME OF THE GIANTS

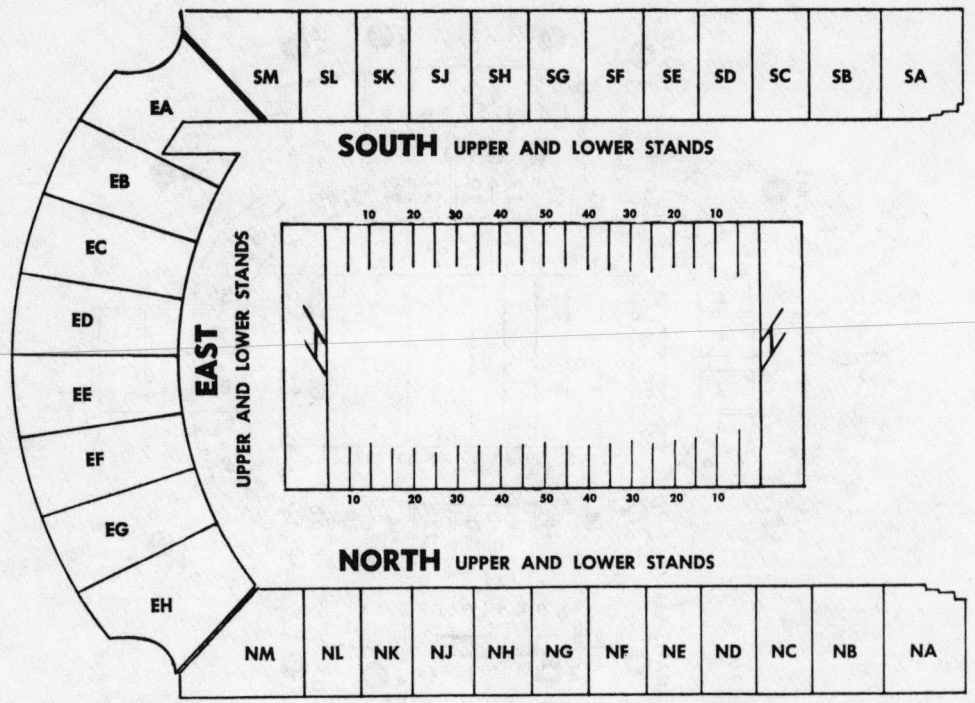

FRANKLIN FIELD, PHILADELPHIA,—HOME OF THE EAGLES

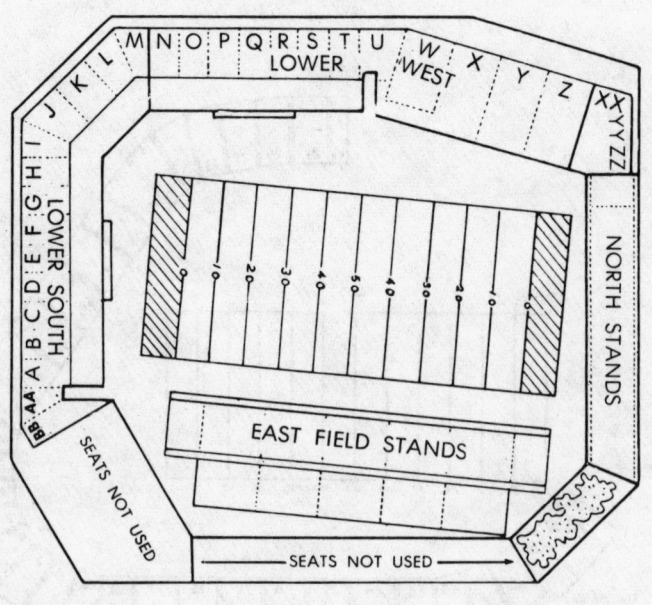

BUSCH STADIUM, ST. LOUIS—HOME OF THE CARDINALS

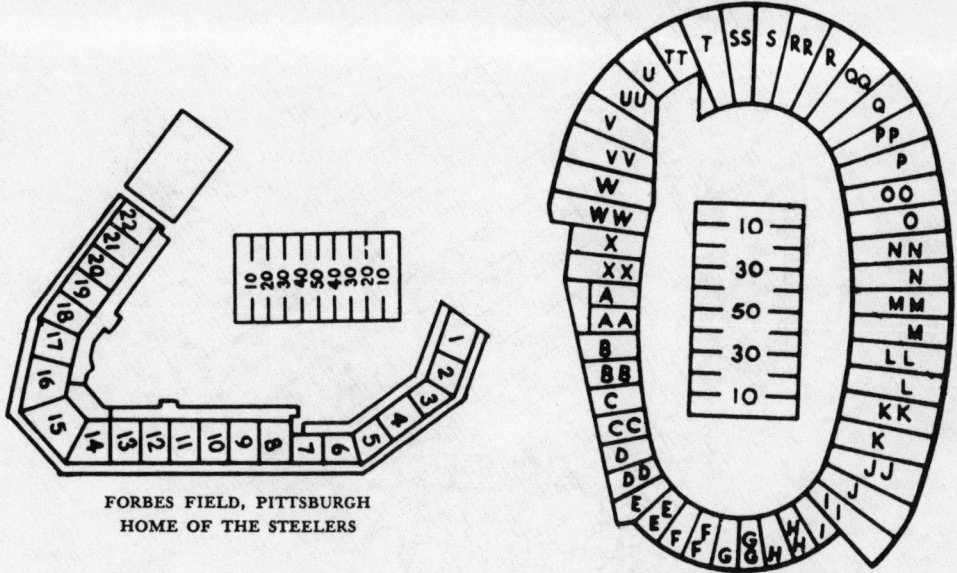

FORBES FIELD, PITTSBURGH
HOME OF THE STEELERS

KEZAR STADIUM, SAN FRANCISCO
HOME OF THE 49ERS

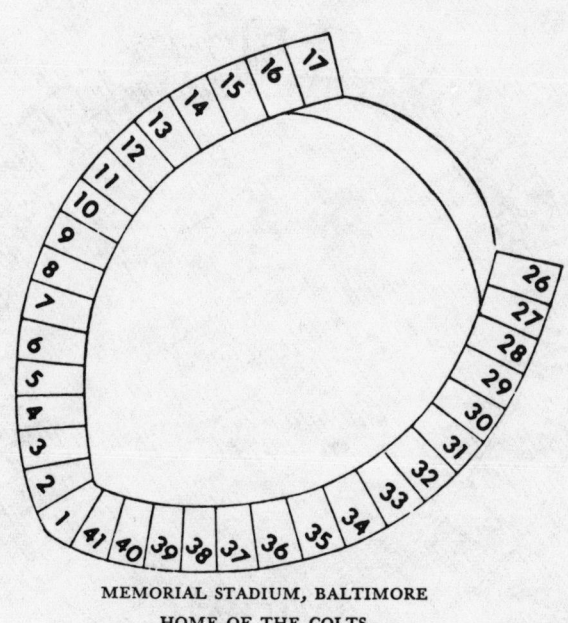

MEMORIAL STADIUM, BALTIMORE
HOME OF THE COLTS

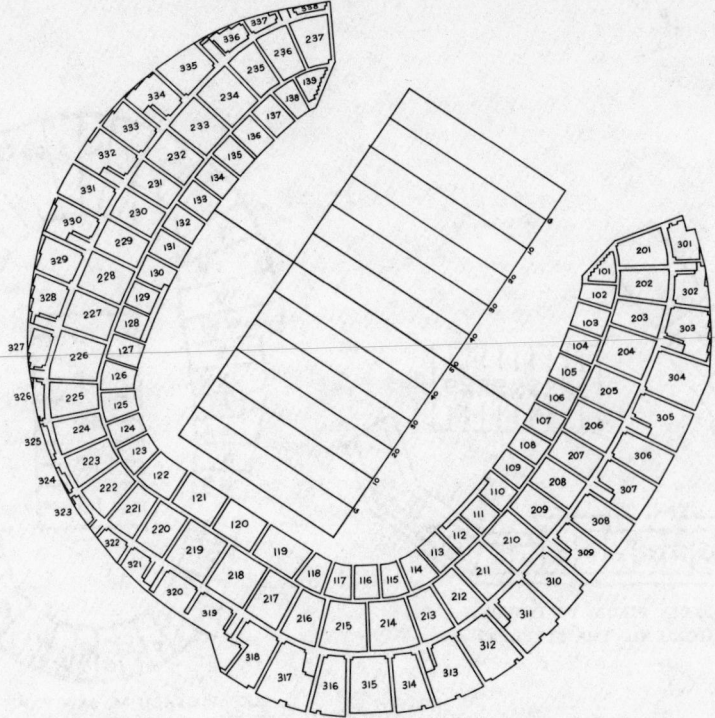

LOWER DECK, WASHINGTON STADIUM—HOME OF THE REDSKINS

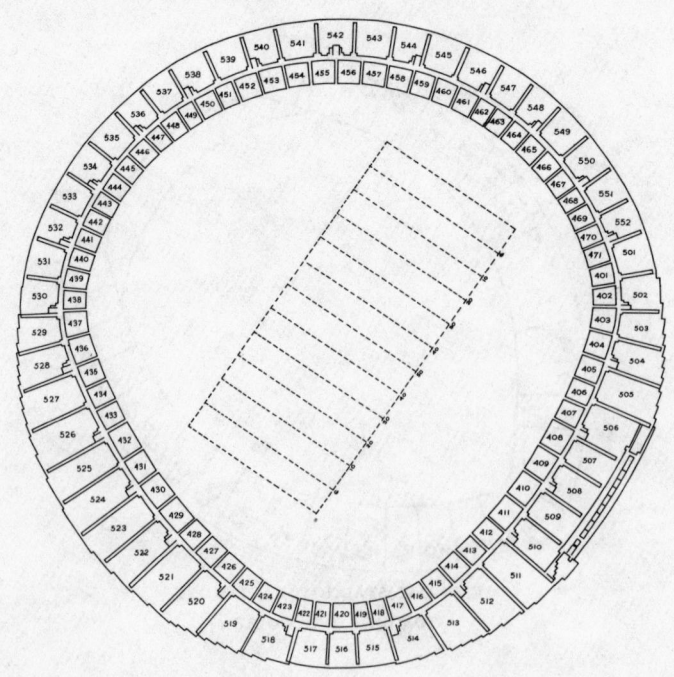

UPPER DECK, WASHINGTON STADIUM